GREAT BOOKS OF THE WESTERN WORLD

O₁

28. GILBERT
GALILEO
HARVEY

29. CERVANTES

30. FRANCIS BACON

31.

32.

33.

34.

35.

36.

37.

38.

39.

40.

41. GIBBON II

42. KANT

43. AMERICAN ST
PAPERS

EN

CHICAGO

The City of God translated by Marcus Dods, and *On Christian Doctrine,*
translated by J. F. Shaw,
are reprinted by arrangement with T. & T. CLARK, Edinburgh

THE UNIVERSITY OF CHICAGO

The Great Books
is published with the editorial advice of the faculties
of The University of Chicago

The Confessions
The City of God
On Christian Doctrine

BY SAINT AUGUSTINE

WILLIAM BENTON, *Publisher*

ENCYCLOPÆDIA BRITANNICA, INC.

CHICAGO · LONDON · TORONTO · GENEVA · SYDNEY · TOKYO

The City of God translated by Marcus Dods, and *On Christian Doctrine*,
translated by J. F. Shaw,
are reprinted by arrangement with T. & T. CLARK, Edinburgh

THE UNIVERSITY OF CHICAGO

The Great Books
is published with the editorial advice of the faculties
of The University of Chicago

Library of Congress Catalog Card Number: 55-10327

BIOGRAPHICAL NOTE

SAINT AUGUSTINE, 354–430

AUGUSTINE was born November 13, 354, at Tagaste, a small town in the Roman province of Numidia, near what is now the eastern borders of Algeria. His father, although not wealthy, was an official in the Roman administration of the village and was then still a pagan. His mother, Monica, was already known as a fervent Christian. Both were probably of Roman stock, although they may have had some Numidian ancestry, and Augustine himself shows an acquaintance with the Punic language.

While still a child, Augustine was enrolled by his mother as a catechumen in the Catholic Church, and although not baptized, he learned something about Christianity from her. At the age of eleven or twelve, he was sent to Madaura, some twenty miles south of Tagaste, to study grammar and literature. He did so well that his father aspired to make a lawyer of him. Augustine spent a year of idleness while his father sought the necessary funds, and it was finally through the generosity of a citizen of Tagaste, who continued for some time as his patron, that in 370 he was able to go to Carthage for the course in rhetoric. Shortly after his arrival he began living with a woman with whom he remained for the next ten years and who bore him a son named Adeodatus. At the schools he had the reputation of being a quiet and studious young man. His reading of Cicero's *Hortensius*, he tells us, made him in love with philosophy. He also fell under the influence of the Manicheans and became an auditor, or beginner, in their sect, which claimed to reconcile philosophy and religion.

On completing his studies in 373, Augustine chose to follow letters rather than law as a career. After a year of teaching grammar at Tagaste, he established himself as a rhetorician at Carthage. In 377 he entered the poetry contest and won the prize with a dramatic poem. Not long afterwards, he wrote his first book, *On the Beautiful and the Fit,* which he later considered not worth preserving. In 383, motivated in part by his ambition as a rhetorician, Augustine went to Rome. His expectations were not realized, and a year later he accepted the municipal chair of rhetoric at Milan.

While at Rome, Augustine had abandoned Manicheism. At Milan he came under the influence of St. Ambrose and also began reading the Neo-Platonists. His ensuing development, recorded in the *Confessions,* culminated in the decision in 386 to become a Christian. That autumn he retired to the estate of a friend at Cassiciacum to prepare for entering the Catholic Church. Accompanying him were his mother, his son, and several friends and pupils—at least eight in all. Under the leadership of Augustine the group spent some time in philosophical discussion. The results were taken down, edited by Augustine, and published as the philosophical dialogues, *Against the Academics, On the Happy Life,* and *On Order.* The following spring he returned to Milan and on Holy Saturday was baptized by St. Ambrose.

Having become a Christian, Augustine decided to return to Africa and to lead a kind of monastic life with a few of his friends and pupils. While waiting for his departure, he worked at several books he had planned, including a series on the liberal arts, of which only one, *On Music,* has survived. The death of his mother, which occurred after they had reached Rome and were at the embarkation port of Ostia, delayed his return. For more than a year he remained in Rome, continued to work on his philosophical dialogues, and furthered his knowledge of Christian doctrine and practice. His first controversial work, *On the Morals of the Catholic Church and of the Manicheans,* was written at this time. It was not until 388 that Augustine with his son and two friends reached Tagaste. He sold his property, gave the proceeds to the poor, and with his few followers set up a kind of monastery devoted to a life of prayer and study. His son, Adeodatus, who was one of the group and whose education had been a particular care of Augustine's, died in 389.

In 391 Augustine's quiet monastic life was brought suddenly to an end. He happened to be on a visit to Hippo and was attending church when the aged bishop was urging his congregation to find a candidate for the priesthood. Augustine, despite his protestations, was immediately chosen, and the bishop ordained him as a priest. Later that year he moved his monastery to Hippo and began his sacerdotal duties. Although it was then customary for preaching to be reserved for the bishop, Augustine even as a priest was assigned that task. He began his sermons on the Scriptures, which, transcribed as they were delivered, constitute his many books of commentary on the Bible. He also began the public disputes with the African heretics which were to engage him for the rest of his life.

In 395 or 396 Augustine was called upon to assume what he called the "burden of the episcopate." For thirty-five years as the Bishop of Hippo nearly all of his energies were given to the defense and promotion of the Catholic Church in northern Africa. He took an influential part in the many councils and conferences called to deal with various heresies and wrote many works against them, in particular against Manicheism, Donatism, and Pelagianism. His diocese was large by African standards and in governing it he also had to preside over the episcopal court which, as was customary at the time, heard civil as well as ecclesiastical cases. The administrative and financial duties of his office made constant demands. Wherever he was, he was called upon to preach, at times for periods of five consecutive days. His fame and position brought requests for advice from Christians and non-Christians alike, which involved him in voluminous correspondence. Augustine also never lost concern for his monastic community. Besides providing a rule for a common life, he made his monastery into something of a theological seminary, and many of its members later became bishops and saints, spreading wherever they went the influence of Augustine's teaching and zeal.

However onerous and varied his duties, Augustine always found time to write. In 397 he wrote the first three books, *On Christian Doctrine;* the final book was not completed until thirty years later. At the same time he also began his *Confessions,* and the completed work seems to have been published by 400. He had no sooner finished that than he began one of his greatest doctrinal treatises, *On the Trinity.* Following the sack of Rome in 410, he was drawn into the controversy regarding the responsibility of Christianity for the fall of the "eternal city," and into a correspondence with two Roman officials on the relation of the Church and the Empire. Out of such reflections he seems to have conceived the *City of God,* which was begun in 413 and appeared serially for thirteen years.

In 426 Augustine arranged for his successor as Bishop of Hippo. Considering it useful "to compile and point out all those things which displease me in my works," he read through all his writings and in his *Retractions* noted down what revisions he would make in their doctrine. In the work as he left it, he comments on two hundred and thirty-two separate titles, not including his letters and sermons, which were to have been considered in a separate account.

While Augustine was engaged in this task, North Africa was becoming involved in what amounted to civil war. Vandals from Spain had been invited to Africa, to help in the fight against the imperial forces, but it was soon evident that they came not to aid but in their own interest. In 430 the imperial forces were defeated and sought refuge in Hippo, where they were besieged by the Vandal army. There, when the siege was in its third month, Augustine died, August 28, 430.

GENERAL CONTENTS

❖❖❖❖❖❖❖❖❖

BIOGRAPHICAL NOTE, Page v

THE CONFESSIONS, Page 1
Translated by EDWARD BOUVERIE PUSEY

THE CITY OF GOD, Page 129
Translated by MARCUS DODS

ON CHRISTIAN DOCTRINE, Page 621
Translated by J. F. SHAW

❖❖❖❖❖❖❖❖❖

CONTENTS: THE CONFESSIONS

BOOK I. *Confessions of the greatness and un-searchableness of God, of God's mercies in infancy and boyhood, and human wilfulness; of his own sins of idleness, abuse of his studies, and of God's gifts up to his fifteenth year.*   1

BOOK II. *Object of these confessions. Further ills of idleness developed in his sixteenth year. Evils of ill society, which betrayed him into theft.*   9

BOOK III. *Augustine's residence at Carthage from his seventeenth to his nineteenth year. Source of his disorders. Love of shows. Advance in studies, and love of wisdom. Distaste for Scripture. Led astray by the Manichæans. Refutation of some of their tenets. Grief of his mother Monica at his heresy, and prayers for his conversion. Her vision from God, and answer through a bishop.*   13

BOOK IV. *Augustine's life from nineteen to eight-and-twenty; himself a Manichæan, and seducing others to the same heresy; partial obedience amidst vanity and sin; consulting astrologers, only partially shaken herein; loss of an early friend, who is converted by being baptized when in a swoon; reflections on grief, on real and unreal friendship, and love of fame; writes on "the fair and fit," yet cannot rightly, though God had given him great talents, since he entertained wrong notions of God; and so even his knowledge he applied ill.*   19

BOOK V. *St. Augustine's twenty-ninth year. Faustus, a snare of Satan to many, made an instrument of deliverance to St. Augustine, by shewing the ignorance of the Manichees on those things wherein they professed to have divine knowledge. Augustine gives up all thought of going further among the Manichees: is guided to Rome and Milan, where he hears St. Ambrose, leaves the Manichees, and becomes again a catechumen in the Church Catholic.*   27

BOOK VI. *Arrival of Monica at Milan; her obedience to St. Ambrose, and his value for her; St. Ambrose's habits; Augustine's gradual abandonment of error; finds that he has blamed the Church Catholic wrongly; desire of absolute certainty, but struck with the contrary analogy of God's natural providence; how shaken in his worldly pursuits; God's guidance of his friend Alypius; Augustine debates with himself and his friends about their mode of life; his inveterate sins, and dread of judgment.*   34

BOOK VII. *Augustine's thirty-first year; gradually extricated from his errors, but still with material conceptions of God; much aided by an argument of Nebridius; sees that the cause of sin lies in free-will, rejects the Manichæan heresy, but cannot altogether embrace the doctrine of the Church; recovered from the belief in astrology, but miserably perplexed about the origin of evil; is led to find in the Platonists the seeds of the doctrine of the divinity of the Word, but not of his humiliation; hence he obtains clearer notions of God's majesty, but, not knowing Christ to be the Mediator, remains estranged from him; all his doubts removed by the study of Holy Scripture, especially St. Paul.*   43

BOOK VIII. *Augustine's thirty-second year. He consults Simplicianus; from him hears the history of the conversion of Victorinus, and longs to devote himself entirely to God, but is mastered by his old habits; is still further roused by the history of St. Anthony, and of the conversion of the two courtiers; during a severe struggle hears a voice from heaven, opens Scripture, and is converted, with his friend Alypius. His mother's visions fulfilled.*   52

BOOK IX. *Augustine determines to devote his life to God, and to abandon his profession of rhetoric, quietly however; retires to the country to prepare himself to receive the grace of baptism, and is baptized with Alypius, and his son Adeodatus. At Ostia, on his way to Africa, his mother Monica dies, in her fifty-sixth year, the thirty-third of Augustine. Her life and character.*   61

BOOK X. *Having in the former books spoken of himself before his receiving the grace of baptism, in this Augustine confesses what he then was. But first, he enquires by what faculty we can know God at all; whence he enlarges on the mysterious character of the memory, wherein God, being made known, dwells, but which could not discover him. Then he examines his own trials under the triple division of temptation, "lust of the flesh, lust of the eyes, and pride"; what Christian continency prescribes as to each. On Christ the only Mediator, Who heals and will heal all infirmities.*   71

BOOK XI. *Augustine breaks off the history of the mode whereby God led him to holy orders, in order to "confess" God's mercies in opening to him the Scripture. Moses is not to be understood but in Christ, not even the first words "In the beginning God created the heaven and the earth." Answer to cavillers who asked, "What did God before He created the heaven and the earth, and whence willed He at length to make them, whereas He did not make them before?" Inquiry into the nature of time.* 89

BOOK XII. *Augustine proceeds to comment on Genesis I, 1 and explains the "heaven" to mean that spiritual and incorporeal creation which* cleaves to God unintermittingly, always beholding his countenance; "earth," the formless matter whereof the corporeal creation was afterwards formed. He does not reject, however, other interpretations, which he adduces, but rather confesses that such is the depth of Holy Scripture, that manifold senses may and ought to be extracted from it, and that whatever truth can be obtained from its words does, in fact, lie concealed in them.* 99

BOOK XIII. *Continuation of the exposition of Genesis I; it contains the mystery of the Trinity, and a type of the formation, extension, and support of the Church.* 110

THE CONFESSIONS

❖❖❖❖❖❖❖❖❖

BOOK I

Confessions of the greatness and unsearchableness of God, of God's mercies in infancy and boyhood, and human wilfulness; of his own sins of idleness, abuse of his studies, and of God's gifts up to his fifteenth year.

[I] 1. Great art Thou, O Lord, and greatly to be praised; great is Thy power, and Thy wisdom infinite.[1] And Thee would man praise; man, but a particle of Thy creation; man, that bears about him his mortality, the witness of his sin, the witness, that "Thou resistest the proud":[2] yet would man praise Thee; he, but a particle of Thy creation. Thou awakest us to delight in Thy praise; for Thou madest us for Thyself, and our heart is restless until it repose in Thee. Grant me, Lord, to know and understand which is first, to call on Thee or to praise Thee? and, again, to know Thee or to call on Thee? For who can call on Thee, not knowing Thee? For he that knoweth Thee not may call on Thee as other than Thou art. Or is it rather that we call on Thee that we may know Thee? " But how shall they call on Him in Whom they have not believed? or how shall they believe without a preacher?"[3] And they that seek the Lord shall praise Him.[4] For they that seek shall find Him,[5] and they that find shall praise Him. I will seek Thee, Lord, by calling on Thee; and will call on Thee, believing in Thee; for to us hast Thou been preached. My faith, Lord, shall call on Thee, which Thou hast given me, wherewith Thou hast inspired me, through the Incarnation of Thy Son, through the ministry of the Preacher.[6]

[II] 2. And how shall I call upon my God, my God and Lord, since, when I call for Him, I shall be calling Him to myself? and what room is there within me, whither my God can come into

[Biblical citations in quotation marks are exact; those not in quotation marks are St. Augustine's paraphrases.]

[1] Ps. 145. 3; 147. 5.   [2] Jas. 4. 6; I Pet. 5. 5.
[3] Rom. 10. 14.   [4] Ps. 22. 26.   [5] Matt. 7. 7.
[6] St. Ambrose.

me? Whither can God come into me, God who made heaven and earth? Is there, indeed, O Lord my God, aught in me that can contain Thee? Do then heaven and earth, which Thou hast made, and wherein Thou hast made me, contain Thee? or, because nothing which exists could exist without Thee, doth therefore whatever exists contain Thee? Since, then, I too exist, why do I seek that Thou shouldest enter into me, who were not, wert Thou not in me? Why? Because I am not gone down in hell, and yet Thou art there also. For "if I go down into hell, Thou art there."[7] I could not be then, O my God, could not be at all, wert Thou not in me; or, rather, unless I were in Thee, of Whom are all things, by whom are all things, in whom are all things?[8] Even so, Lord, even so. Whither do I call Thee, since I am in Thee? or whence canst Thou enter into me? For whither can I go beyond heaven and earth, that thence my God should come into me, Who hath said, "I fill the heaven and the earth?"[9]

[III] 3. Do[10] the heaven and earth then contain Thee, since Thou fillest them? or dost Thou fill them and yet overflow, since they do not contain Thee? And whither, when the heaven and the earth are filled, pourest Thou forth the remainder of Thyself? Or hast Thou no need that aught contain Thee, Who containest all things, since what Thou fillest Thou fillest by containing it? For the vessels which Thou fillest uphold Thee not, since, though they were broken, Thou wert not poured out. And when Thou are poured out[11] on us, Thou art not cast down, but Thou upliftest us; Thou art not dissipated, but Thou gatherest us. But Thou Who fillest all things, fillest Thou them with Thy whole self? or, since all things cannot contain Thee wholly, do they contain part of Thee? and all at once the same part? or each its own part, the greater more, the smaller less? And is, then, one part of Thee greater, another less? or art Thou

[7] Ps. 139. 8.   [8] Rom. 11. 36.   [9] Jer. 23. 24.
[10] Against the Manichees.   [11] Acts, 2. 18.

wholly everywhere, while nothing contains Thee wholly?

[IV] 4. What art Thou then, my God? What, but the Lord God? For who is Lord but the Lord? or who is God save our God?[1] Most highest, most good, most potent, most omnipotent; most merciful, yet most just; most hidden, yet most present; most beautiful, yet most strong; stable, yet incomprehensible; unchangeable, yet all-changing; never new, never old; all-renewing, and bringing age upon the proud, and they know it not; ever working, ever at rest; still gathering, yet nothing lacking; supporting, filling, and over-spreading; creating, nourishing, and maturing; seeking, yet having all things. Thou lovest, without passion; art jealous, without anxiety; repentest, yet grievest not; art angry, yet serene; changest Thy works, Thy purpose unchanged; receivest again what Thou findest, yet didst never lose; never in need, yet rejoicing in gains; never covetous, yet exacting usury. Thou receivest over and above, that Thou mayest owe; and who hath aught that is not Thine? Thou payest debts, owing nothing; remittest debts, losing nothing. And what have I now said, my God, my life, my holy joy? or what saith any man when he speaks of Thee? Yet woe to him that speaketh not, since mute are even the most eloquent.

[V] 5. Oh! that I might repose on Thee! Oh! that Thou wouldest enter into my heart, and inebriate it, that I may forget my ills, and embrace Thee, my sole good? What art Thou to me? In Thy pity, teach me to utter it. Or what am I to Thee that Thou demandest my love, and, if I give it not, are wroth with me, and threatenest me with grievous woes? Is it then a slight woe to love Thee not? Oh! for Thy mercies' sake, tell me, O Lord my God, what Thou art unto me. "Say unto my soul, I am thy salvation."[2] So speak, that I may hear. Behold, Lord, my heart is before Thee; open Thou the ears thereof, and "say unto my soul, I am thy salvation." After this voice let me haste, and take hold on Thee. Hide not Thy face from me. Let me die[3]—lest I die—only let me see Thy face.

6. Narrow is the mansion of my soul; enlarge Thou it, that Thou mayest enter in. It is ruinous! repair Thou it. It has that within which must offend Thine eyes; I confess and know it. But who shall cleanse it? or to whom should I cry, save Thee? Lord, cleanse me from my secret faults, and spare Thy servant from the power of the enemy.[4] I believe, and therefore do I speak.[5] Lord, Thou knowest. Have I not confessed against myself my transgressions unto Thee, and Thou, my God, hast forgiven the iniquity of my heart?[6] I contend not in judgment with Thee,[7] who art the truth; I fear to deceive myself; lest mine iniquity lie unto itself.[8] Therefore I contend not in judgment with Thee; "for if Thou, Lord, shouldest mark iniquities, O Lord, who shall abide it?"[9]

[VI] 7. Yet suffer me to speak unto Thy mercy, me, "dust and ashes."[10] Yet suffer me to speak, since I speak to Thy mercy, and not to scornful man. Thou too, perhaps, despisest me, yet wilt Thou return and have compassion[11] upon me. For what would I say, O Lord my God, but that I know not whence I came into this dying life (shall I call it?) or living death. Then immediately did the comforts of Thy compassion take me up, as I heard (for I remember it not) from the parents of my flesh, out of whose substance Thou didst sometime fashion me. Thus there received me the comforts of woman's milk. For neither my mother nor my nurses stored their own breasts for me; but Thou didst bestow the food of my infancy through them, according to Thine ordinance, whereby Thou distributest Thy riches through the hidden springs of all things. Thou also gavest me to desire no more than Thou gavest; and to my nurses willingly to give me what Thou gavest them. For they, with an heaven-taught affection, willingly gave me what they abounded with from Thee. For this, my good from them, was good for them. Nor, indeed, from them was it, but through them; for from Thee, O God, are all good things, and from my God is all my health.[12] This I since learned, Thou, through these Thy gifts, within me and without, proclaiming Thyself unto me. For then I knew but to suck; to repose in what pleased, and cry at what offended my flesh; nothing more.

8. Afterwards I began to smile; first in sleep, then waking: for so it was told me of myself, and I believed it; for we see the like in other infants, though of myself I remember it not. Thus, little by little, I became conscious where I was; and to have a wish to express my wishes to those who could content them, and I could not; for the wishes were within me, and they without; nor could they by any sense of theirs enter within my spirit. So I flung about at ran-

---

[1]Ps. 18. 31.   [2]Ps. 25. 3.
[3]i.e. Let me see the face of God, though I die (Ex. 33. 20.), since if I see it not, but it be turned away, I must needs die, and that "the second death."

[4]Ps. 19. 12, 13.   [5]Ps. 116. 10.   [6]Ps. 32 5
[7]Job, 9. 3.   [8]Ps. 26. 12.   [9]Ps.130. 3.
[10]Gen. 18. 27.   [11]Jer. 12. 15.   [12]Prov. 21. 31.

dom limbs and voice, making the few signs I could, and such as I could, like, though in truth very little like, what I wished. And when I was not presently obeyed (my wishes being hurtful or unintelligible), then I was indignant with my elders for not submitting to me, with those owing me no service for not serving me, and avenged myself on them by tears. Such have I learnt infants to be from observing them; and that I was myself such, they, all unconscious, have shewn me better than my nurses who knew it.

9. And, lo! my infancy died long since, and I live. But Thou, Lord, Who for ever livest, and in Whom nothing dies; for before the foundation of the worlds, and before all that can be called "before," Thou art, and art God and Lord of all which Thou hast created; in Thee abide, fixed for ever, the first causes of all things unabiding; and of all things changeable, the springs abide in Thee unchangeable: and in Thee live the eternal reasons of all things unreasoning and temporal. Say, Lord, to me, Thy suppliant; say, all-pitying, to me, Thy pitiable one; say, did my infancy succeed another age of mine that died before it? Was it that which I spent within my mother's womb? for of that I have heard somewhat, and have myself seen women with child? and what before that life again, O God my joy, was I anywhere or anybody? For this have I none to tell me, neither father nor mother, nor experience of others, nor mine own memory. Dost Thou mock me for asking this, and bid me praise Thee and acknowledge Thee, for that I do know?

10. I acknowledge Thee, Lord of heaven and earth, and praise Thee for my first rudiments of being, and my infancy, whereof I remember nothing; for Thou hast appointed that man should from others guess much as to himself; and believe much on the strength of weak females. Even then I had being and life, and (at my infancy's close) I could seek for signs whereby to make known to others my sensations. Whence could such a being be, save from Thee, Lord? Shall any be his own artificer? Or can there elsewhere be derived any vein, which may stream essence and life into us, save from Thee, O Lord, in whom essence and life are one? for Thou Thyself art supremely Essence and Life. For "Thou art most high, and art not changed,"[1] neither in Thee doth today come to a close; yet in Thee doth it come to a close; because all such things also are in Thee. For they had no way to pass away, unless Thou upheldest

them. And since "Thy years fail not,"[2] Thy years are one today. How many of ours and our fathers' years have flowed away through Thy "today," and from it received the measure and the mould of such being as they had; and still others shall flow away, and so receive the mould of their degree of being. But "Thou art still the same,"[3] and all things of tomorrow, and all beyond, and all of yesterday, and all behind it, Thou hast done today. What is it to me, though any comprehend not this? Let him also rejoice and say, "What thing is this?"[4] Let him rejoice even thus; and be content rather by not discovering to discover Thee, than by discovering not to discover Thee.

[VII] 11. Hear, O God. Alas, for man's sin! So saith man, and Thou pitiest him; for Thou madest him, but sin in him Thou madest not. Who remindeth me of the sins of my infancy? for in Thy sight none is pure from sin, not even the infant whose life is but a day upon the earth. Who remindeth me? Doth not each little infant, in whom I see what of myself I remember not? What then was my sin? Was it that I hung upon the breast and cried? For should I now so do for food suitable to my age, justly should I be laughed at and reproved. What I then did was worthy reproof; but since I could not understand reproof, custom and reason forbade me to be reproved. For those habits, when grown, we root out and cast away. Now no man, though he prunes, wittingly casts away what is good. Or was it then good, even for a while, to cry for what, if given, would hurt? bitterly to resent that persons free, and its own elders, yea, the very authors of its birth, served it not? that many besides, wiser than it, obeyed not the nod of its good pleasure? to do its best to strike and hurt, because commands were not obeyed, which had been obeyed to its hurt? The weakness then of infant limbs, not its will, is its innocence. Myself have seen and known even a baby envious; it could not speak, yet it turned pale and looked bitterly on its foster-brother. Who knows not this? Mothers and nurses tell you that they allay these things by I know not what remedies. Is that too innocence, when the fountain of milk is flowing in rich abundance, not to endure one to share it, though in extremest need, and whose very life as yet depends thereon? We bear gently with all this, not as being no or slight evils, but because they will disappear as years increase; for, though tolerated now, the very same tempers are utterly intolerable when found in riper years.

[1]Mal. 3. 6.   [2]Ps. 102. 27.   [3]Ibid.   [4]Ex. 16. 15.

12. Thou, then, O Lord my God, Who gavest life to this my infancy, furnishing thus with senses (as we see) the frame Thou gavest, compacting its limbs, ornamenting its proportions, and, for its general good and safety, implanting in it all vital functions, Thou commandest me to praise Thee in these things, "to confess unto Thee, and sing unto Thy name, Thou most Highest."[1] For Thou art God, Almighty and Good, even hadst Thou done nought but only this, which none could do but Thou: whose Unity is the mould of all things; who out of Thy own fairness makest all things fair; and orderest all things by Thy law. This age then, Lord, whereof I have no remembrance, which I take on others' word and guess from other infants that I have passed, true though the guess be, I am yet loth to count in this life of mine which I live in this world. For no less than that which I spent in my mother's womb, is it hid from me in the shadows of forgetfulness. But if "I was shapen in iniquity, and in sin did my mother conceive me,"[2] where, I beseech Thee, O my God, where, Lord, or when, was I Thy servant guiltless? But, lo! that period I pass by; and what have I now to do with that of which I can recall no vestige?

[VIII] 13. Passing hence from infancy, I came to boyhood, or rather it came to me, displacing infancy. Nor did that depart (for whither went it?), and yet it was no more. For I was no longer a speechless infant, but a speaking boy. This I remember; and have since observed how I learned to speak. It was not that my elders taught me words (as, soon after, other learning) in any set method; but I, longing by cries and broken accents and various motions of my limbs to express my thoughts, that so I might have my will, and yet unable to express all I willed or to whom I willed, did myself, by the understanding which Thou, my God, gavest me, practise the sounds in my memory. When they named anything, and as they spoke turned towards it, I saw and remembered that they called what they would point out by the name they uttered. And that they meant this thing, and no other, was plain from the motion of their body, the natural language, as it were, of all nations, expressed by the countenance, glances of the eye, gestures of the limbs, and tones of the voice, indicating the affections of the mind as it pursues, possesses, rejects, or shuns. And thus by constantly hearing words, as they occurred in various sentences, I collected gradually for what they stood; and, having broken in my

mouth to these signs, I thereby gave utterance to my will. Thus I exchanged with those about me these current signs of our wills, and so launched deeper into the stormy intercourse of human life, yet depending on parental authority and the beck of elders.

[IX] 14. O God my God, what miseries and mockeries did I now experience, when obedience to my teachers was proposed to me, as proper in a boy, in order that in this world I might prosper, and excel in tongue-science, which should serve to the "praise of men" and to deceitful riches. Next I was put to school to get learning, in which I (poor wretch) knew not what use there was; and yet, if idle in learning, I was beaten. For this was judged right by our forefathers; and many, passing the same course before us, framed for us weary paths, through which we were fain to pass; multiplying toil and grief upon the sons of Adam. But, Lord, we found that men called upon Thee, and we learnt from them to think of Thee (according to our powers) as of some great One Who, though hidden from our senses, couldst hear and help us. For so I began, as a boy, to pray to Thee, my "aid" and "refuge"; and broke the fetters of my tongue to call on Thee, praying Thee, though small, yet with no small earnestness, that I might not be beaten at school. And when Thou heardest me not (not thereby giving me over to folly[3]), my elders, yea, my very parents, who yet wished me no ill, mocked my stripes, my then great and grievous ill.

15. Is there, Lord, any of soul so great, and cleaving to Thee with so intense affection (for a sort of stupidity will in a way do it); but is there anyone who, from cleaving devoutly to Thee, is endued with so great a spirit that he can think as lightly of the racks and hooks and other torments (against which, throughout all lands, men call on Thee with extreme dread), mocking at those by whom they are feared most bitterly, as our parents mocked the torments which we suffered in boyhood from our masters? For we feared not our torments less; nor prayed we less to Thee to escape them. And yet we sinned, in writing or reading or studying less than was exacted of us. For we wanted not, O Lord, memory or capacity, whereof Thy will gave enough for our age; but our sole delight was play; and for this we were punished by those who yet themselves were doing the like. But elder folks' idleness is called "business"; that of boys, being really the same, is punished by those elders; and none commiserates either

[1]Ps. 92. 1.   [2]Ps. 51. 5.   [3]Ps. 22. 2, Vulg.

boys or men. For will any of sound discretion approve of my being beaten as a boy because, by playing at ball, I made less progress in studies which I was to learn only that, as a man, I might play more unbeseemingly? And what else did he, who beat me? who, if worsted in some trifling discussion with his fellow-tutor, was more embittered and jealous than I, when beaten at ball by a play-fellow?

[X] 16. And yet I sinned herein, O Lord God, the Creator and Disposer of all things in nature, of sin the Disposer only, O Lord my God, I sinned in transgressing the commands of my parents and those my masters. For what they, with whatever motive, would have me learn, I might afterward have put to good use. For I disobeyed, not from a better choice, but from love of play, loving the pride of victory in my contests, and to have my ears tickled with lying fables, that they might itch the more; the same curiosity flashing from my eyes more and more, for the shows and games of my elders. Yet those who give these shows are in such esteem that almost all wish the same for their children, and yet are very willing that they should be beaten if those very games detain them from the studies whereby they would have them attain to be the givers of them. Look with pity, Lord, on these things, and deliver us who call upon Thee now; deliver those too who call not on Thee yet, that they may call on Thee, and Thou mayest deliver them.

[XI] 17. As a boy, then, I had already heard of an eternal life, promised us through the humility of the Lord our God stooping to our pride; and even from the womb of my mother, who greatly hoped in Thee, I was sealed with the mark of His cross and salted with His salt.[1] Thou sawest, Lord, how while yet a boy, being seized on a time with sudden oppression of the stomach, and like near to death—Thou sawest, my God (for Thou wert my keeper), with what eagerness and what faith I sought, from the pious care of my mother and Thy Church, the mother of us all, the baptism of Thy Christ my God and Lord. Whereupon the mother of my flesh, being much troubled (since, with a heart pure in Thy faith, she even more lovingly travailed in birth[2] of my salvation), would in eager haste have provided for my consecration and cleansing by the healthgiving sacraments, confessing Thee, Lord Jesus, for the remission of sins, unless I had suddenly recovered. And so, as if I must needs be again polluted should I live, my cleansing was deferred, because the defilements of sin would, after that washing, bring greater and more perilous guilt. I then already believed; and my mother, and the whole household except my father; yet did not he prevail over the power of my mother's piety in me, that as he did not yet believe, so neither should I. For it was her earnest care that Thou my God, rather than he, shouldest be my father; and in this Thou didst aid her to prevail over her husband, whom she, the better, obeyed, therein also obeying Thee, who hast so commanded.

18. I beseech Thee, my God, I would fain know, if so Thou willest, for what purpose my baptism was then deferred? Was it for my good that the rein was laid loose, as it were, upon me, for me to sin? or was it not laid loose? If not, why does it still echo in our ears on all sides, "Let him alone, let him do as he will, for he is not yet baptized"? But as to bodily health, no one says, "Let him be worse wounded, for he is not yet healed." How much better then, had I been at once healed; and then, by my friends' diligence and my own, my soul's recovered health had been kept safe in Thy keeping who gavest it. Better truly. But how many and great waves of temptation seemed to hang over me after my boyhood! These my mother foresaw; and preferred to expose to them the clay whence I might afterwards be moulded, than the very cast when made.

[XII] 19. In boyhood itself, however (so much less dreaded for me than youth), I loved not study, and hated to be forced to it. Yet I was forced; and this was well done towards me, but I did not well; for, unless forced, I had not learnt. But no one doth well against his will, even though what he doth be well. Yet neither did they well who forced me, but what was well came to me from Thee, my God. For they were regardless how I should employ what they forced me to learn, except to satiate the insatiate desires of a wealthy beggary and a shameful glory. But Thou, by Whom the very hairs of our head are numbered,[3] didst use for my good the error of all who urged me to learn; and my own, who would not learn, Thou didst use for my punishment—a fit penalty for one, so small a boy and so great a sinner. So by those who did not well, Thou didst well for me; and by my own sin Thou didst justly punish me. For Thou hast commanded, and so it is, that every inordinate affection should be its own punishment.

---

[1] A rite in the Western Churches, on admission as a catechumen, previous to Baptism, denoting the purity and uncorruptedness and discretion required of Christians.
[2] Gal. 4. 19.

[3] Matt. 10. 30.

[XIII] 20. But why did I so much hate the Greek, which I studied as a boy? I do not yet fully know. For the Latin I loved; not what my first masters, but what the so-called grammarians taught me. For those first lessons, reading, writing, and arithmetic, I thought as great a burden and penalty as any Greek. And yet whence was this too, but from the sin and vanity of this life, because "I was flesh, and a breath that passeth away and cometh not again?"[1] For those first lessons were better certainly, because more certain; by them I obtained, and still retain, the power of reading what I find written, and myself writing what I will; whereas in the others, I was forced to learn the wanderings of one Æneas, forgetful of my own, and to weep for dead Dido because she killed herself for love; the while, with dry eyes, I endured my miserable self dying among these things, far from Thee, O God my life.

21. For what more miserable than a miserable being who commiserates not himself; weeping the death of Dido for love to Æneas, but weeping not his own death for want of love to Thee, O God? Thou light of my heart, Thou bread of my inmost soul, Thou Power Who givest vigour to my mind, Who quickenest my thoughts, I loved Thee not. I committed fornication against Thee, and all around me thus fornicating there echoed "Well done! well done!" for the friendship of this world is fornication against Thee;[2] and "Well done! well done!" echoes on till one is ashamed not to be thus a man. And all this I wept not, I who wept for Dido slain, and "seeking by the sword a stroke and wound extreme,"[3] myself seeking the while a worse extreme, the extremest and lowest of Thy creatures, having forsaken Thee, earth passing into the earth. And if forbid to read all this, I was grieved that I might not read what grieved me. Madness like this is thought a higher and a richer learning than that by which I learned to read and write.

22. But now, my God, cry Thou aloud in my soul, and let Thy truth tell me, "Not so, not so. Far better was that first study." For, lo, I would readily forget the wanderings of Æneas and all the rest, rather than how to read and write. But over the entrance of the Grammar School is a vail[4] drawn! true; yet is this not so much an emblem of aught recondite as a cloke of error. Let not those whom I no longer fear cry out

against me, while I confess to Thee, my God, whatever my soul will, and acquiesce in the condemnation of my evil ways, that I may love Thy good ways. Let not either buyers or sellers of grammar-learning cry out against me. For if I question them whether it be true that Æneas came on a time to Carthage, as the Poet tells, the less learned will reply that they know not, the more learned that he never did. But should I ask with what letters the name "Æneas" is written, everyone who has learnt this will answer me aright, as to the signs which men have conventionally settled. If, again, I should ask which might be forgotten with least detriment to the concerns of life, reading and writing or these poetic fictions? who does not foresee what all must answer who have not wholly forgotten themselves? I sinned, then, when as a boy I preferred those empty to those more profitable studies, or rather loved the one and hated the other. "One and one, two"; "two and two, four"; this was to me a hateful sing-song: "the wooden horse lined with armed men," and "the burning of Troy," and "Creusa's shade and sad similitude,"[5] were the choice spectacle of my vanity.

[XIV] 23. Why then did I hate the Greek classics, which have the like tales? For Homer also curiously wove the like fictions, and is most sweetly-vain, yet was he bitter to my boyish taste. And so I suppose would Virgil be to Grecian children, when forced to learn him as I was Homer. Difficulty, in truth, the difficulty of a foreign tongue, dashed, as it were, with gall all the sweetness of Grecian fable. For not one word of it did I understand, and to make me understand I was urged vehemently with cruel threats and punishments. Time was also (as an infant) I knew no Latin; but this I learned without fear of suffering, by mere observation, amid the caresses of my nursery and jests of friends, smiling and sportively encouraging me. This I learned without any pressure of punishment to urge me on, for my heart urged me to give birth to its conceptions, which I could only do by learning words not of those who taught, but of those who talked with me; in whose ears also I gave birth to the thoughts, whatever I conceived. No doubt, then, that a free curiosity has more force in our learning these things than a frightful enforcement. Only this enforcement restrains the rovings of that freedom through Thy laws, O my God, Thy laws, from the master's cane to the martyr's trials, being able to temper for us a wholesome bitter, recalling us

---

[1] Ps. 78. 39; Jas, 4. 14.　　[2] Jas. 4. 4.
[3] Aeneid, VI. 457.
[4] An emblem of honour, used in places of worship, and subsequently in courts of law, Emperors' palaces and even private houses.
[5] Aeneid, II. 772.

to Thyself from that deadly pleasure which lures us from Thee.

[XV] 24. Hear, Lord, my prayer; let not my soul faint under Thy discipline, nor let me faint in confessing unto Thee all Thy mercies whereby Thou hast drawn me out of all my most evil ways, that Thou mightest become a delight to me above all the allurements which I once pursued; that I may most entirely love Thee, and clasp Thy hand with all my affections, and Thou mayest yet rescue me from every temptation, even unto the end. For, lo, O Lord, my King and my God, for Thy service be whatever useful thing my childhood learned; for Thy service, that I speak, write, read, reckon. For Thou didst grant me Thy discipline, while I was learning vanities; and my sin of delighting in those vanities Thou hast forgiven. In them, indeed, I learnt many a useful word, but these may as well be learned in things not vain; and that is the safe path for the steps of youth.

[XVI] 25. But woe is thee, thou torrent of human custom! Who shall stand against thee? How long shalt thou not be dried up? How long roll the sons of Eve into that huge and hideous ocean which even they scarcely overpass who climb the cross? Did not I read in thee of Jove the thunderer and the adulterer? Both, doubtless, he could not be; but so the feigned thunder might countenance and pander to real adultery. And now which of our gowned masters lends a sober ear to one who from their own school cries out, "These were Homer's fictions, transferring things human to the gods; would he had brought down things divine to us!" Yet more truly had he said, "These are indeed his fictions; but attributing a divine nature to wicked men, that crimes might be no longer crimes, and whoso commits them might seem to imitate not abandoned men, but the celestial gods."

26. And yet, thou hellish torrent, into thee are cast the sons of men with rich rewards, for compassing such learning; and a great solemnity is made of it when this is going on in the forum, within sight of laws appointing a salary beside the scholar's payments; and thou lashest thy rocks and roarest, "Hence words are learnt; hence eloquence; most necessary to gain your ends, or maintain opinions." As if we should have never known such words as "golden shower," "lap," "beguile," "temples of the heavens," or others in that passage, unless Terence had brought a lewd youth upon the stage, setting up Jupiter as his example of seduction.

Viewing a picture, where the tale was drawn,
Of Jove's descending in a golden shower

To Danaë's lap, a woman to beguile.
And then mark how he excites himself to lust as by celestial authority;

And what God? Great Jove,
Who shakes heav'n's highest temples with his
  thunder,
And I, poor mortal man, not do the same!
I did it, and with all my heart I did it.

Not one whit more easily are the words learnt for all this vileness; but by their means the vileness is committed with less shame. Not that I blame the words, being, as it were, choice and precious vessels; but that wine of error which is drunk to us in them by intoxicated teachers; and if we, too, drink not, we are beaten, and have no sober judge to whom we may appeal. Yet, O my God (in Whose presence I now without hurt may remember this), all this unhappily I learnt willingly with great delight, and for this was pronounced a hopeful boy.

[XVII] 27. Bear with me, my God, while I say somewhat of my wit, Thy gift, and on what dotages I wasted it. For a task was set me, troublesome enough to my soul upon terms of praise or shame and fear of stripes, to speak the words of Juno, as she raged and mourned that she could not.

This Trojan prince from Latium turn.[1]

Which words I had heard that Juno never uttered; but we were forced to go astray in the footsteps of these poetic fictions, and to say in prose much what he expressed in verse. And his speaking was most applauded in whom the passions of rage and grief were most pre-eminent, and clothed in the most fitting language, maintaining the dignity of the character. What is it to me, O my true life, my God, that my declamation was applauded above so many of my own age and class? Is not all this smoke and wind? And was there nothing else whereon to exercise my wit and tongue? Thy praises, Lord, Thy praises might have stayed the yet tender shoot of my heart by the prop of Thy Scriptures; so had it not trailed away amid these empty trifles, a defiled prey for the fowls of the air. For in more ways than one do men sacrifice to the rebellious angels.

[XVIII] 28. But what marvel that I was thus carried away to vanities, and went out from Thy presence, O my God, when men were set before me as models, who, if in relating some action of theirs, in itself not ill, they committed some barbarism or solecism, being censured, were abashed; but when in rich and adorned

[1] *Aeneid*, I. 36–75.

and well-ordered discourse they related their own disordered life, being bepraised, they gloried? These things Thou seest, Lord, and holdest Thy peace; "long-suffering, and plenteous in mercy and truth."[1] Wilt Thou hold Thy peace for ever? And even now Thou drawest out of this horrible gulf the soul that seeketh Thee, that thirsteth for Thy pleasures, "whose heart saith unto Thee," I have sought Thy face; "Thy face, Lord, will I seek."[2] For darkened[3] affections is removal from Thee. For it is not by our feet, or change of place, that men leave Thee, or return unto Thee. Or did that Thy younger son look out for horses or chariots or ships, fly with visible wings, or journey by the motion of his limbs, that he might in a far country waste in riotous living all Thou gavest at his departure? A loving Father when Thou gavest, and more loving unto him when he returned empty.[4] So then in lustful—that is, in darkened—affections, is the true distance from Thy face.

29. Behold, O Lord God, yea, behold patiently as Thou art wont, how carefully the sons of men observe the covenanted rules of letters and syllables received from those who spake before them, neglecting the eternal covenant of everlasting salvation received from Thee. Insomuch that a teacher or learner of the hereditary laws of pronunciation will more offend men by speaking, without the aspirate, of a "'uman being," in despite of the laws of grammar, than if he, a "human being," hate a "human being" in despite of Thine. As if any enemy could be more hurtful than the hatred with which he is incensed against him; or could wound more deeply him whom he persecutes than he wounds his own soul by his enmity. Assuredly no science of letters can be so innate as the record of conscience, "that he is doing to another what from another he would be loth to suffer." How deep are Thy ways, O God, Thou only great, "that sittest" silent "on high"[5] and by an unwearied law dispensing penal blindness to lawless desires. In quest of the fame of eloquence, a man standing before a human judge, surrounded by a human throng, declaiming against his enemy with fiercest hatred, will take heed most watchfully lest, by an error of the tongue, he murder the word "human being"; but takes no heed lest, through the fury of his spirit, he murder the real human being.

30. This was the world at whose gate unhappy I lay in my boyhood; this the stage, where I had feared more to commit a barbarism than,

having committed one, to envy those who had not. These things I speak and confess to Thee, my God; for which I had praise from them whom I then thought it all virtue to please. For I saw not the abyss of vileness wherein I was cast away from Thine eyes.[6] Before them what more foul than I was already, displeasing even such as myself? with innumerable lies deceiving my tutor, my masters, my parents, from love of play, eagerness to see vain shows, and restlessness to imitate them! Thefts also I committed, from my parents' cellar and table, enslaved by greediness, or that I might have to give to boys, who sold me their play, which all the while they liked no less than I. In this play, too, I often sought unfair conquests, conquered myself meanwhile by vain desire of pre-eminence. And what could I so ill endure, or, when I detected it, upbraided I so fiercely, as that I was doing to others? and for which if, detected, I was upbraided, I chose rather to quarrel than to yield. And is this the innocence of boyhood? Not so, Lord, not so; I cry Thy mercy, O my God. For these very sins, as riper years succeed, these very sins are transferred from tutors and masters, from nuts and balls and sparrows, to magistrates and kings, to gold and manors and slaves, just as severer punishments displace the cane. It was the low stature then of childhood which Thou our King didst commend as an emblem of lowliness, when Thou saidst: "Of such is the kingdom of heaven."[7]

31. Yet, Lord, to Thee, the Creator and Governor of the universe, most excellent and most good, thanks were due to Thee our God, even hadst Thou destined for me boyhood only. For even then I was, I lived, and felt; and had an implanted providence over my own well-being— a trace of that mysterious Unity whence I was derived; I guarded by the inward sense the entireness of my senses, and in these minute pursuits, and in my thoughts on things minute, I learnt to delight in truth, I hated to be deceived, had a vigorous memory, was gifted with speech, was soothed by friendship, avoided pain, baseness, ignorance. In so small a creature, what was not wonderful, not admirable? But all are gifts of my God; it was not I who gave them me; and good these are, and these together are myself. Good, then, is He that made me, and He is my good; and before Him will I exult for every good which of a boy I had. For it was my sin that not in Him, but in His creatures—myself and others—I sought for pleasures, sublimities, truths, and so fell headlong into sorrows,

[1]Ps. 86. 15.   [2]Ps. 27. 8.   [3]Rom. 1. 21.
[4]Luke, 15. 11–32.   [5]Isa. 33. 5.   [6]Ps. 31. 22.   [7]Matt. 19. 14.

confusions, errors. Thanks be to Thee, my joy and my glory and my confidence, my God, thanks be to Thee for Thy gifts; but do Thou preserve them to me. For so wilt Thou preserve me, and those things shall be enlarged and perfected which Thou hast given me, and I myself shall be with Thee, since even to be Thou hast given me.

BOOK II. *Object of these Confessions. Further ills of idleness developed in his sixteenth year. Evils of ill society, which betrayed him into theft.*

[I] 1. I will now call to mind my past foulness, and the carnal corruptions of my soul: not because I love them, but that I may love Thee, O my God. For love of Thy love I do it; reviewing my most wicked ways in the very bitterness of my remembrance, that Thou mayest grow sweet unto me (Thou sweetness never failing, Thou blissful and assured sweetness); and gathering me again out of that my dissipation wherein I was torn piecemeal, while, turned from Thee, the One Good, I lost myself among a multiplicity of things. For I even burnt in my youth heretofore, to be satiated in things below; and I dared to grow wild again, with these various and shadowy loves: my beauty consumed away,[1] and I stank in Thine eyes; pleasing myself, and desirous to please in the eyes of men.

[II] 2. And what was it that I delighted in, but to love, and be beloved? but I kept not the measure of love, of mind to mind, friendship's bright boundary; but out of the muddy concupiscence of the flesh, and the bubblings of youth, mists fumed up which beclouded and overcast my heart, that I could not discern the clear brightness of love, from the fog of lustfulness. Both did confusedly boil in me, and hurried my unstayed youth over the precipice of unholy desires, and sunk me in a gulf of flagitiousnesses. Thy wrath had gathered over me, and I knew it not. I was grown deaf by the clanking of the chain of my mortality, the punishment of the pride of my soul, and I strayed further from Thee, and Thou lettest me alone, and I was tossed about, and wasted, and dissipated, and I boiled over in my fornications, and Thou heldest Thy peace, O Thou my tardy joy! Thou then heldest Thy peace, and I wandered further and further from Thee, into more and more fruitless seed-plots of sorrows, with a proud dejectedness and a restless weariness.

3. Oh! that someone had then attempered my disorder, and turned to account the fleeting

[1]Ps. 39. 11.

beauties of these, the extreme points of Thy creation! had put a bound to their pleasurableness, that so the tides of my youth might have cast themselves upon the marriage shore, if they could not be calmed, and kept within the object of a family, as Thy law prescribes, O Lord; who this way formest the offspring of this our death, being able with a gentle hand to blunt the thorns, which were excluded from Thy paradise? For Thy omnipotency is not far from us, even when we be far from Thee. Else ought I more watchfully to have heeded the voice from the clouds; "Nevertheless such shall have trouble in the flesh, but I spare you."[2] And, "It is good for a man not to touch a woman,"[3] And, "He that is unmarried thinketh of the things of the Lord, how he may please the Lord; but he that is married careth for the things of this world, how he may please his wife."[4] To these words I should have listened more attentively and, being severed "for the kingdom of heaven's sake,"[5] had more happily awaited Thy embraces.

4. But I, poor wretch, foamed like a troubled sea, following the rushing of my own tide, forsaking Thee, and exceeded all Thy limits; yet I escaped not Thy scourges. For what mortal can? For Thou wert ever with me mercifully rigorous, and besprinkling with most bitter alloy all my unlawful pleasures, that I might seek pleasures without alloy. But where to find such, I could not discover, save in Thee, O Lord, Who teachest by sorrow,[6] and wounded us, to heal; and killest us, lest we die from Thee. Where was I, and how far was I exiled from the delights of Thy house, in that sixteenth year of the age of my flesh, when the madness of lust (to which human shamelessness giveth free license, though unlicensed by Thy laws) took the rule over me, and I resigned myself wholly to it? My friends meanwhile took no care by marriage to save my fall; their only care was that I should learn to speak excellently and be a persuasive orator.

[III.] 5. For that year were my studies intermitted; whilst after my return from Madaura (a neighbour city, whither I had journeyed to learn grammar and rhetoric), the expenses for a further journey to Carthage were being provided for me; and that, rather by the resolution than the means of my father, who was but a poor freeman of Thagaste. To whom tell I this? not to Thee, my God; but before Thee to mine own kind, even to that small portion of mankind as may light upon these writings of mine. And to what purpose? that whosoever reads this may

[2]I Cor. 7. 28.   [3]I Cor. 7. 1.   [4]I Cor. 7. 32, 33.
[5]Matt. 19. 12.   [6]Ps. 93. 20. Vulg.; Deut. 32. 39.

think out of what depths we are to cry unto Thee.[1] For what is nearer to Thine ears than a confessing heart and a life of faith? Who did not extol my father for that, beyond the ability of his means, he would furnish his son with all necessaries for a far journey for his studies' sake? For many far abler citizens did no such thing for their children. But yet this same father had no concern how I grew towards Thee, or how chaste I were; so that I were but copious in speech, however barren I were to Thy culture, O God, who art the only true and good Lord of Thy field, my heart.

6. But while in that my sixteenth year I lived with my parents, leaving all school for a while (a season of idleness being interposed through the narrowness of my parents' fortunes), the briers of unclean desires grew rank over my head, and there was no hand to root them out. When that my father saw me at the baths, now growing toward manhood, and endued with a restless youthfulness, he, as already hence anticipating his descendants, gladly told it to my mother; rejoicing in that tumult of the senses wherein the world forgetteth Thee its Creator, and becometh enamoured of Thy creature, instead of Thyself, through the fumes of that invisible wine of its self-will, turning aside and bowing down to the very basest things. But in my mother's breast Thou hadst already begun Thy temple, and the foundation of Thy holy habitation, whereas my father was as yet but a catechumen, and that but recently. She then was startled with an holy fear and trembling; and, though I was not as yet baptized, feared for me those crooked ways in which they walk who turn their back to Thee, and not their face.[2]

7. Woe is me! and dare I say that Thou heldest Thy peace, O my God, while I wandered further from Thee? Didst Thou then indeed hold Thy peace to me? And whose but Thine were these words which by my mother, Thy faithful one, Thou sangest in my ears? Nothing whereof sunk into my heart, so as to do it. For she wished, and I remember in private with great anxiety warned me, "not to commit fornication; but especially never to defile another's wife." These seemed to me womanish advices, which I should blush to obey. But they were Thine, and I knew it not: and I thought Thou wert silent, and that it was she who spake; by whom Thou wert not silent unto me; and in her wast despised by me, her son, "the son of Thy handmaid, Thy servant."[3] But I knew it not; and ran headlong with such blindness that amongst my

equals I was ashamed of a less shamelessness, when I heard them boast of their flagitiousness, yea, and the more boasting, the more they were degraded: and I took pleasure, not only in the pleasure of the deed, but in the praise. What is worthy of dispraise but vice? But I made myself worse than I was, that I might not be dispraised; and when in anything I had not sinned as the abandoned ones, I would say that I had done what I had not done, that I might not seem contemptible in proportion as I was innocent; or of less account, the more chaste.

8. Behold with what companions I walked the streets of Babylon, and wallowed in the mire thereof, as if in a bed of spices and precious ointments. And that I might cleave the faster to its very centre, the invisible enemy trod me down, and seduced me, for that I was easy to be seduced. Neither did the mother of my flesh (who had now "fled out of the centre of Babylon,"[4] yet went more slowly in the skirts thereof), as she advised me to chastity, so heed what she had heard of me from her husband, as to restrain within the bounds of conjugal affection (if it could not be pared away to the quick) what she felt to be pestilent at present, and for the future dangerous. She heeded not this, for she feared, lest a wife should prove a clog and hindrance to my hopes. Not those hopes of the world to come, which my mother reposed in Thee; but the hope of learning, which both my parents were too desirous I should attain; my father, because he had next to no thought of Thee, and of me but vain conceits; my mother, because she accounted that those usual courses of learning would not only be no hindrance, but even some furtherance towards attaining Thee. For this I conjecture, recalling, as well as I may, the disposition of my parents. The reins, meantime, were slackened to me, beyond all temper of due severity, to spend my time in sport, yea, even unto dissoluteness in whatsoever I affected. And in all was a mist, intercepting from me, O my God, the brightness of Thy truth; and mine iniquity burst out as from very "fatness."[5]

[IV.] 9. Theft is punished by Thy law, O Lord, and the law written in the hearts of men, which iniquity itself effaces not. For what thief will abide a thief? not even a rich thief, one stealing through want. Yet I lusted to thieve, and did it, compelled by no hunger, nor poverty, but through a cloyedness of well-doing, and a pamperedness of iniquity. For I stole that of which I had enough, and much better. Nor cared I to enjoy what I stole, but joyed in the theft

---

[1]Ps. 130. 1.   [2]Jer. 2. 27.   [3]Ps. 116. 16.   [4]Jer. 51. 6.   [5]Ps. 73. 7.

and sin itself. A pear tree there was near our vineyard, laden with fruit, tempting neither for colour nor taste. To shake and rob this, some lewd young fellows of us went, late one night (having according to our pestilent custom prolonged our sports in the streets till then), and took huge loads, not for our eating, but to fling to the very hogs, having only tasted them. And this, but to do what we liked only because it was misliked. Behold my heart, O God, behold my heart, which Thou hadst pity upon in the bottom of the bottomless pit. Now, behold, let my heart tell Thee what it sought there, that I should be gratuitously evil, having no temptation to ill but the ill itself. It was foul, and I loved it; I loved to perish, I loved mine own fault, not that for which I was faulty, but my fault itself. Foul soul, falling from Thy firmament to utter destruction; not seeking aught through the shame, but the shame itself!

[V.] 10. For there is an attractiveness in beautiful bodies, in gold and silver, and all things; and in bodily touch, sympathy hath much influence, and each other sense hath his proper object answerably tempered. Worldly honour hath also its grace, and the power of overcoming, and of mastery; whence springs also the thirst of revenge. But yet, to obtain all these, we may not depart from Thee, O Lord, nor decline from Thy law. The life also which here we live hath its own enchantment, through a certain proportion of its own, and a correspondence with all things beautiful here below. Human friendship also is endeared with a sweet tie, by reason of the unity formed of many souls. Upon occasion of all these, and the like, is sin committed, while through an immoderate inclination towards these goods of the lowest order, the better and higher are forsaken—Thou, our Lord God, Thy truth, and Thy law. For these lower things have their delights, but not like my God, Who made all things: for in Him doth the righteous delight, and He is the joy of the upright in heart.[1]

11. When, then, we ask why a crime was done, we believe it not, unless it appear that there might have been some desire of obtaining some of those which we called lower goods, or a fear of losing them. For they are beautiful and comely; although, compared with those higher and beatific goods, they are abject and low. A man hath murdered another; why? he loved his wife or his estate; or would rob for his own livelihood; or feared to lose some such thing by him; or, wronged, was on fire to be revenged. Would

[1] Ps. 64. 10.

any commit murder upon no cause, delighted simply in murdering? Who would believe it? For as for that furious and savage man, of whom it is said that he was gratuitously evil and cruel, yet is the cause assigned; "lest," saith he, "through idleness hand or heart should grow inactive." And to what end? That, through that practice of guilt, he might, having taken the city, attain to honours, empire, riches, and be freed from fear of the laws, and his embarrassments from domestic needs, and consciousness of villainies. So then, not even Catiline himself loved his own villainies, but something else, for whose sake he did them.

[VI.] 12. What then did wretched I so love in thee, thou theft of mine, thou deed of darkness, in that sixteenth year of my age? Lovely thou wert not, because thou wert theft. But art thou anything, that thus I speak to thee? Fair were the pears we stole, because they were Thy creation, Thou fairest of all, Creator of all, Thou good God; God, the sovereign good and my true good. Fair were those pears, but not them did my wretched soul desire; for I had store of better, and those I gathered only that I might steal. For, when gathered, I flung them away, my only feast therein being my own sin, which I was pleased to enjoy. For if aught of those pears came within my mouth, what sweetened it was the sin. And now, O Lord my God, I enquire what in that theft delighted me; and behold it hath no loveliness; I mean not such loveliness as in justice and wisdom; nor such as is in the mind and memory, and senses, and animal life of man; nor yet as the stars are glorious and beautiful in their orbs; or the earth, or sea, full of embryo-life, replacing by its birth that which decayeth; nay, nor even that false and shadowy beauty which belongeth to deceiving vices.

13. For so doth pride imitate exaltedness; whereas Thou Alone art God exalted over all. Ambition, what seeks it but honours and glory? whereas Thou Alone art to be honoured above all, and glorious for evermore. The cruelty of the great would fain be feared, but who is to be feared but God alone, out of whose power what can be wrested or withdrawn? when, or where, or whither, or by whom? The tendernesses of the wanton would fain be counted love: yet is nothing more tender than Thy charity; nor is aught loved more healthfully than Thy truth, bright and beautiful above all. Curiosity makes semblance of a desire of knowledge; whereas Thou supremely knowest all. Yea, ignorance and foolishness itself is cloked under the name

of simplicity and uninjuriousness; because both what evils I committed by my own wilfulness, and what by Thy guidance I committed not. What man is he who, weighing his own infirmity, dares to ascribe his purity and innocency to his own strength; that so he should love Thee the less, as if he had less needed Thy mercy, whereby Thou remittest sins to those that turn to Thee? For whosoever, called by Thee, followed Thy voice and avoided those things which he reads me recalling and confessing of myself, let him not scorn me, who being sick, was cured by that Physician, through Whose aid it was that he was not, or rather was less, sick: and for this let him love Thee as much, yea and more; since by Whom he sees me to have been recovered from such deep consumption of sin, by Him he sees himself to have been from the like consumption of sin preserved.

nothing is found more single than Thee: and what less injurious, since they are his own works, which injure the sinner? Yea, sloth would fain be at rest; but what stable rest besides the Lord? Luxury affects to be called plenty and abundance; but Thou art the fulness and neverfailing plenteousness of incorruptible pleasures. Prodigality presents a shadow of liberality: but Thou art the most overflowing Giver of all good. Covetousness would possess many things: and Thou possessest all things. Envy disputes for excellency: what more excellent than Thou? Anger seeks revenge: who revenges more justly than Thou? Fear startles at things unwonted and sudden, which endanger things beloved, and takes forethought for their safety: but to Thee what unwonted or sudden, or who separateth from Thee what Thou lovest? Or where but with Thee is unshaken safety? Grief pines away for things lost, the delight of its desires; because it would have nothing taken from it, as nothing can from Thee.

[VIII] 16. "What fruit had I then" (wretched man!) in those things, of the remembrance whereof I am now ashamed?[3] Especially in that theft which I loved for the theft's sake; and it too was nothing,[4] and therefore the more miserable I, who loved it. Yet alone I had not done it: such was I then, I remember, alone I had never done it. I loved then in it also the company of the accomplices, with whom I did it? I did not then love nothing else but the theft, yea rather I did love nothing else; for that circumstance of the company was also nothing. What is, in truth? who can teach me, save He that enlighteneth my heart and discovereth its dark corners? What is it which hath come into my mind to enquire, and discuss, and consider? For had I then loved the pears I stole, and wished to enjoy them, I might have done it alone, had the bare commission of the theft sufficed to attain my pleasure; nor needed I have inflamed the itching of my desires by the excitement of accomplices. But since my pleasure was not in those pears, it was in the offence itself, which the company of fellow-sinners occasioned.

14. Thus doth the soul commit fornication when she turns from Thee, seeking, without Thee, what she findeth not pure and untainted till she returns to Thee. Thus all pervertedly imitate Thee, who remove far from Thee, and lift themselves up against Thee. But even by thus imitating Thee, they imply Thee to be the Creator of all nature; whence there is no place whither altogether to retire from Thee. What then did I love in that theft? and wherein did I even corruptly and pervertedly imitate my Lord? Did I wish even by stealth to do contrary to Thy law, because by power I could not, so that being a prisoner, I might mimic a maimed liberty by doing with impunity things unpermitted me, a darkened likeness of Thy Omnipotency? Behold Thy servant fleeing from his Lord, and obtaining a shadow. O rottenness, O monstrousness of life, and depth of death! could I like what I might not, only because I might not?

[IX] 17. What then was this feeling? For of a truth it was too foul: and woe was me, who had it. But yet what was it? "Who can understand his errors?"[5] It was the sport, which, as it were, tickled our hearts, that we beguiled, those who little thought what we were doing, and much misliked it. Why then was my delight of such sort, that I did it not alone? Because none doth ordinarily laugh alone? ordinarily no one; yet laughter sometimes masters men alone and singly when no one whatever is with them, if anything very ludicrous presents

[VII] 15. "What shall I render unto the Lord,"[1] that, whilst my memory recalls these things, my soul is not affrighted at them? I will love Thee, O Lord, and thank Thee, and confess unto Thy name;[2] because Thou has forgiven me these so great and heinous deeds of mine. To Thy grace I ascribe it, and to Thy mercy, that Thou hast melted away my sins as it were ice. To Thy grace I ascribe also whatsoever I have not done of evil; for what might I not have done, who even loved a sin for its own sake? Yea, all I confess to have been forgiven me;

---

[1]Ps. 16. 12. [2]Rev. 3. 5.

[3]Rom. 6. 21. [4]See Bk. III. 12; Bk. VII. 18.
[5]Ps. 19. 12.

itself to their senses or mind. Yet I had not done this alone; alone I had never never done it. Behold my God, before Thee, the vivid remembrance of my soul; alone, I had never committed that theft, wherein what I stole pleased me not, but that I stole; nor had it alone liked me to do it, nor had I done it. O friendship too unfriendly! thou incomprehensible inveigler of the soul, thou greediness to do mischief out of mirth and wantonness, thou thirst of others' loss, without lust of my own gain or revenge: but when it is said, "Let's go, let's do it," we are ashamed not to be shameless.

[X] 18. Who can disentangle that twisted and intricate knottiness? Foul is it: I hate to think on it, to look on it. But Thee I long for, O Righteousness and Innocency, beautiful and comely to all pure eyes, and of a satisfaction unsating. With Thee is rest entire, and life imperturbable. Whoso enters into Thee enters into the joy of his Lord:[1] and shall not fear, and shall do excellently in the All-Excellent. I sank away from Thee, and I wandered, O my God, too much astray from Thee my stay, in these days of my youth, and I became to myself a barren land.

BOOK III. *Augustine's residence at Carthage from his seventeenth to his nineteenth year. Source of his disorders. Love of shows. Advance in studies, and love of wisdom. Distaste for Scripture. Led astray to the Manichæans, Refutation of some of their tenets. Grief of his mother Monica at his heresy, and prayers for his conversion. Her vision from God, and answer through a Bishop.*

[I] 1. To Carthage I came, where there sang all around me in my ears a cauldron of unholy loves. I loved not yet, yet I loved to love, and, out of a deep-seated want, I hated myself for wanting not. I sought what I might love, in love with loving, and safety I hated, and a way without snares. For within me was a famine of that inward food, Thyself, my God; yet, through that famine I was not hungered; but was without all longing for incorruptible sustenance, not because filled therewith, but the more empty, the more I loathed it. For this cause my soul was sickly and full of sores, it miserably cast itself forth, desiring to be scraped by the touch of objects of sense. Yet if these had not a soul, they would not be objects of love. To love then, and to be beloved, was sweet to me; but more, when I obtained to enjoy the person I loved. I defiled, therefore, the spring of friendship with

the filth of concupiscence, and I beclouded its brightness with the hell of lustfulness; and thus foul and unseemly, I would fain, through exceeding vanity, be fine and courtly. I fell headlong then into the love wherein I longed to be ensnared. My God, my Mercy, with how much gall didst thou out of thy great goodness besprinkle for me that sweetness? For I was both beloved, and secretly arrived at the bond of enjoying; and was with joy fettered with sorrow-bringing bonds, that I might be scourged with the iron-burning rods of jealousy, and suspicions, and fears, and angers, and quarrels.

[II] 2. Stage-plays also carried me away, full of images of my miseries, and of fuel to my fire. Why is it that man desires to be made sad, beholding doleful and tragical things, which yet himself would by no means suffer? yet he desires as a spectator to feel sorrow at them, and this very sorrow is his pleasure. What is this but a miserable madness? for a man is the more affected with these actions, the less free he is from such affections. Howsoever, when he suffers in his own person, it uses to be styled "misery": when he compassionates others, then it is "mercy." But what sort of compassion is this for feigned and scenical passions? for the auditor is not called on to relieve, but only to grieve: and he applauds the actor of these fictions the more, the more he grieves. And if the calamities of those persons (whether of old times, or mere fiction) be so acted that the spectator is not moved to tears, he goes away disgusted and criticising; but if he be moved to passion, he stays intent, and weeps for joy.

3. Are griefs then too loved? Verily all desire joy. Or, whereas no man likes to be miserable, is he yet pleased to be merciful? which because it cannot be without passion, for this reason alone are passions loved? This also springs from that vein of friendship. But whither goes that vein? whither flows it? wherefore runs it into that torrent of pitch bubbling forth those monstrous tides of foul lustfulness, into which it is wilfully changed and transformed, being of its own will precipitated and corrupted from its heavenly clearness? Shall compassion then be put away? by no means. Be griefs then sometimes loved. But beware of uncleanness, O my soul, under the guardianship of my God, the God of our fathers, who is to be praised and exalted above all for ever,[2] beware of uncleanness. For I have not now ceased to pity; but then in the theatres I rejoiced with lovers, when they wickedly enjoyed one another, although this

[1] Matt. 25. 21.

[2] *Song of the Three Holy Children*, ver. 3.

was imaginary only in the play. And when they lost one another, as if very compassionate, I sorrowed with them, yet had my delight in both. But now I much more pity him that rejoiceth in his wickedness, than him who is thought to suffer hardship by missing some pernicious pleasure and the loss of some miserable felicity. This certainly is the truer mercy, but in it grief delights not. For though he that grieves for the miserable be commended for his office of charity; yet would he, who is genuinely compassionate, rather there were nothing for him to grieve for. For if good will be ill willed (which can never be) then may he who truly and sincerely commiserates wish there might be some miserable that he might commiserate. Some sorrow may then be allowed, none loved. For thus dost Thou, O Lord God, who lovest souls far more purely than we, and hast more incorruptibly pity on them, yet are wounded with no sorrowfulness. "And who is sufficient for these things?" [1]

4. But I, miserable, then loved to grieve, and sought out what to grieve at, when, in another's and that feigned and personated misery, that acting best pleased me, and attracted me the most vehemently, which drew tears from me. What marvel that, an unhappy sheep straying from Thy flock and impatient of Thy keeping, I became infected with a foul disease? And hence the love of griefs; not such as should sink deep into me; for I loved not to suffer what I loved to look on; but such as upon hearing their fictions should lightly scratch the surface; upon which, as on envenomed nails, followed inflamed swelling, impostumes, and a putrefied sore. My life being such, was it life, O my God?

[III] 5. And Thy faithful mercy hovered over me afar. Upon how grievous iniquities consumed I myself, pursuing a sacrilegious curiosity, that, having forsaken Thee, it might bring me to the treacherous abyss, and the beguiling service of devils, to whom I sacrificed my evil actions, and in all these things thou didst scourge me! I dared even, while Thy solemnities were celebrated within the walls of Thy Church, to desire, and to compass a business, deserving death for its fruits, for which Thou scourgedst me with grievous punishments, though nothing to my fault, O Thou my exceeding mercy, my God, my refuge from those terrible destroyers, among whom I wandered with a stiff neck, withdrawing further from Thee, loving mine own ways, and not Thine; loving a vagrant liberty.

6. Those studies also, which were accounted commendable, had a view to excelling in the courts of litigation; the more bepraised, the craftier. Such is men's blindness, glorying even in their blindness. And now I was chief in the rhetoric school, whereat I joyed proudly, and I swelled with arrogancy, though (Lord, Thou knowest) far quieter and altogether removed from the subvertings of those "Subverters"[2](for this ill-omened and devilish name was the very badge of gallantry) among whom I lived, with a shameless shame that I was not even as they. With them I lived, and was sometimes delighted with their friendship, whose doings I ever did abhor, i.e., their "subvertings," wherewith they wantonly persecuted the modesty of strangers, which they disturbed by a gratuitous jeering feeding thereon their malicious mirth. Nothing can be liker the very actions of devils than these. What then could they be more truly called than "subverters"?—themselves subverted and altogether perverted first, the deceiving spirits secretly deriding and seducing them, wherein themselves delight to jeer at, and deceive others.

[IV] 7. Among such as these, in that unsettled age of mine, learned I books of eloquence, wherein I desired to be eminent, out of a damnable and vainglorious end, a joy in human vanity. In the ordinary course of study, I fell upon a certain book of Cicero, whose speech almost all admire, not so his heart. This book of his contains an exhortation to philosophy, and is called *Hortensius*. But this book altered my affections, and turned my prayers to Thyself, O Lord; and made me have other purposes and desires. Every vain hope at once became worthless to me; and I longed with an incredibly burning desire for an immortality of wisdom, and began now to arise, that I might return to Thee. For not to sharpen my tongue (which thing I seemed to be purchasing with my mother's allowances, in that my nineteenth year, my father being dead two years before), not to sharpen my tongue did I employ that book; nor did it infuse into me its style, but its matter.

8. How did I burn then, my God, how did I burn to re-mount from earthly things to Thee, nor knew I what Thou wouldest do with me? For with Thee is wisdom. But the love of wisdom is in Greek called "philosophy," with which that book inflamed me. Some there be that seduce through philosophy, under a great, and smooth, and honourable name colouring and disguising their own errors: and almost all who in that and former ages were such are in that book

[1] II Cor. 2. 16.

[2] *Eversores*. This appears to have been a name which a pestilent and savage set of persons gave themselves, licentious alike in speech and action.

censured and set forth: there also is made plain that wholesome advice of Thy Spirit, by Thy good and devout servant; "Beware lest any man spoil you through philosophy and vain deceit, after the tradition of men, after the rudiments of the world, and not after Christ. For in Him dwelleth all the fulness of the Godhead bodily."[1] And since at that time (Thou, O light of my heart, knowest) Apostolic Scripture was not known to me, I was delighted with that exhortation, so far only that I was thereby strongly roused, and kindled, and inflamed to love, and seek, and obtain, and hold, and embrace not this or that sect, but wisdom itself whatever it were; and this alone checked me thus enkindled, that the name of Christ was not in it. For this name, according to Thy mercy, O Lord, this name of my Saviour Thy Son, had my tender heart, even with my mother's milk, devoutly drunk in, and deeply treasured; and whatsoever was without that name, though never so learnèd, polished, or true, took not entire hold of me.

[V] 9. I resolved then to bend my mind to the holy Scriptures, that I might see what they were. But behold, I see a thing not understood by the proud, nor laid open to children, lowly in access, in its recesses lofty, and veiled with mysteries; and I was not such as could enter into it, or stoop my neck to follow its steps. For not as I now speak did I feel when I turned to those Scriptures; but they seemed to me unworthy to be compared to the stateliness of Tully: for my swelling pride shrunk from their lowliness, nor could my sharp wit pierce the interior thereof. Yet were they such as would grow up in a little one. But I disdained to be a little one; and, swoln with pride, took myself to be a great one.

[VI] 10. Therefore I fell among men proudly doting, exceeding carnal and prating, in whose mouths were the snares of the Devil, lined with the mixture of the syllables of Thy name, and of our Lord Jesus Christ, and of the Holy Ghost, the Paraclete, our Comforter. These names departed not out of their mouth, but so far forth as the sound only and the noise of the tongue, for the heart was void of truth. Yet they cried out "Truth, Truth," and spake much thereof to me, "yet it was not in them":[2] but they spake falsehood, not of Thee only (who truly art Truth), but even of those elements of this world, Thy creatures. And I indeed ought to have passed by even philosophers who spake truth concerning them, for love of Thee, my Father, supremely good, Beauty of all things beautiful. O Truth, Truth, how inwardly did even then the marrow of my soul pant after Thee, when they often and diversely, and in many and huge books, echoed of Thee to me, though it was but an echo? And these were the dishes wherein to me, hungering after Thee, they, instead of Thee, served up the Sun and Moon, beautiful works of Thine, but yet Thy works, not Thyself, no nor Thy first works. For Thy spiritual works are before these corporeal works, celestial though they be, and shining. But I hungered and thirsted not even after those first works of Thine, but after Thee Thyself, the Truth, "in whom is no variableness, neither shadow of turning":[3] yet they still set before me in those dishes, glittering fantasies, than which better were it to love this very sun (which is real to our sight at least), than those fantasies which by our eyes deceive our mind. Yet because I thought them to be Thee, I fed thereon; not eagerly, for Thou didst not in them taste to me as Thou art; for Thou wast not these emptinesses, nor was I nourished by them, but exhausted rather. Food in sleep shews very like our food awake; yet are not those asleep nourished by it, for they are asleep. But those were not even any way like to Thee, as Thou hast now spoken to me; for those were corporeal fantasies, false bodies, than which these true bodies, celestial or terrestrial, which with our fleshly sight we behold, are far more certain: these things the beasts and birds discern as well as we, and they are more certain than when we fancy them. And again, we do with more certainty fancy them, than by them conjecture other vaster and infinite bodies which have no being. Such empty husks was I then fed on; and was not fed. But Thou, my soul's Love, in looking for whom I fail,[4] that I may become strong, art neither those bodies which we see, though in heaven; nor those which we see not there; for Thou hast created them, nor dost Thou account them among the chiefest of Thy works. How far then art Thou from those fantasies of mine, fantasies of bodies which altogether are not, than which the images of those bodies which are, are far more certain; and more certain still the bodies themselves, which yet Thou art not; no, nor yet the soul, which is the life of the bodies. So then, better and more certain is the life of the bodies than the bodies. But Thou art the life of souls, the life of lives, having life in Thyself; and changest not, life of my soul.

11. Where then wert Thou then to me, and how far from me? Far verily was I straying from Thee, barred from the very husks of the

[1]Col. 2. 8, 9.   [2]I John, 2. 4.   [3]James, 1. 17.   [4]Ps. 69. 3.

swine, whom with husks I fed. For how much
better are the fables of poets and grammarians,
than these snares? For verses, and poems, and
"Medea flying," are more profitable, truly, than
these men's five elements, variously disguised,
answering to five dens of darkness, which have
no being, yet slay the believer. For verses and
poems I can turn to true food, and "Medea flying," though I did sing, I maintained not;
though I heard it sung, I believed not: but those
things I did believe. Woe, woe, by what steps
was I brought down "to the depths of hell!" [1]
toiling and turmoiling through want of Truth,
since I sought after Thee, my God (to Thee I
confess it, who hadst mercy on me, not as yet
confessing), not according to the understanding of the mind, wherein Thou willedst that I
should excel the beasts, but according to the
sense of the flesh. But Thou wert more inward
to me than my most inward part; and higher
than my highest. I lighted upon that bold woman, "simple and knoweth nothing," [2] shadowed
out in Solomon, "sitting at the door, and saying,
Eat ye bread of secrecies willingly, and drink ye
stolen waters which are sweet":[3] she seduced
me, because she found my soul dwelling abroad
in the eye of my flesh, and ruminating on such
food as through it I had devoured.

[VII] 12. For, other than this, that which
really is I knew not; and was, as it were through
sharpness of wit, persuaded to assent to foolish
deceivers, when they asked me, "Whence is
evil?" "Is God bounded by a bodily shape, and
has hairs and nails?" "Are they to be esteemed
righteous who had many wives at once, and did
kill men, and sacrificed living creatures?" [4] At
which I, in my ignorance, was much troubled,
and, departing from the truth, seemed to myself to be making towards it; because as yet I
knew not that evil was nothing but a privation
of good, until at last a thing ceases altogether
to be; which how should I see, the sight of
whose eyes reached only to bodies, and of my
mind to a phantasm? And I knew not God to be
a Spirit,[5] not One who hath parts extended in
length and breadth, or whose being was bulk;
for every bulk is less in a part than in the whole:
and if it be infinite, it must be less in such part
as is defined by a certain space, than in its in-
finitude; and so is not wholly everywhere, as
Spirit, as God. And what that should be in us by
which we were like to God, and might in Scripture be rightly said to be "after the Image of
God," [6] I was altogether ignorant.

13. Nor knew I that true inward righteousness
which judgeth not according to custom, but out
of the most rightful law of God Almighty,
whereby the ways of places and times were disposed according to those times and places; itself meantime being the same always and everywhere, not one thing in one place, and another
in another; according to which Abraham, and
Isaac, and Jacob, and Moses, and David, were
righteous, and all those commended by the
mouth of God; but were judged unrighteous by
silly men, judging out of man's judgment,[7] and
measuring by their own petty habits, the moral
habits of the whole human race. As if in an ar-
mory, one ignorant what were adapted to each
part should cover his head with greaves, or seek
to be shod with a helmet, and complain that
they fitted not: or as if, on a day when business
is publicly stopped in the afternoon, one were
angered at not being allowed to keep open shop,
because he had been in the forenoon; or when
in one house he observeth some servant take a
thing in his hand which the butler is not suffered
to meddle with; or something permitted out of
doors which is forbidden in the dining-room;
and should be angry that in one house, and one
family, the same thing is not allotted everywhere, and to all. Even such are they who are
fretted to hear something to have been lawful
for righteous men formerly, which now is not;
or that God, for certain temporal respects, commanded them one thing, and these another,
obeying both the same righteousness: whereas
they see, in one man, and one day, and one
house, different things to be fit for different
members, and a thing formerly lawful, after a
certain time not so; in one corner permitted or
commanded, but in another rightly forbidden
and punished. Is justice therefore various or
mutable? No, but the times over which it presides flow not evenly, because they are times.
But men, whose days are few upon the earth,[8]
for that by their senses they cannot harmonize
the causes of things in former ages and other nations which they had no experience of, with
these which they have experience of, whereas in
one and the same body, day, or family, they
easily see what is fitting for each member, and
season, part, and person; to the one they take
exceptions, to the other they submit.

14. These things I then knew not, nor observed; they struck my sight on all sides, and I
saw them not. I indited verses, in which I might
not place every foot everywhere, but differently
in different metres; nor even in any one metre

---

[1]Prov. 9. 18.   [2]*Ibid.*, 9. 13.   [3]*Ibid.*, 9. 14, 17.
[4]I Kings, 18. 40.   [5]John, 4. 24.   [6]Gen. 1. 27.

[7]I Cor. 7. 3.   [8]Job, 14. 1.

the self-same foot in all places. Yet the art itself, by which I indited, had not different principles for these different cases, but comprised all in one. Still I saw not how that righteousness, which good and holy men obeyed, did far more excellently and sublimely contain in one all those things which God commanded, and in no part varied; although in varying times it prescribed not everything at once, but apportioned and enjoined what was fit for each. And I, in my blindness, censured the holy Fathers, not only wherein they made use of things present as God commanded and inspired them, but also wherein they were foretelling things to come, as God was revealing in them.[1]

[VIII] 15. Can it at any time or place be unjust to love God with all his heart, with all his soul, and with all his mind; and his neighbour as himself?[2] Therefore are those foul offences which be against nature to be everywhere and at all times detested and punished; such as were those of the men of Sodom: which should all nations commit, they should all stand guilty of the same crime, by the law of God, which hath not so made men that they should so abuse one another. For even that intercourse which should be between God and us is violated when that same nature, of which He is Author, is polluted by the perversity of lust. But those actions which are offences against the customs of men are to be avoided according to the customs severally prevailing; so that a thing agreed upon, and confirmed, by custom or law of any city or nation may not be violated at the lawless pleasure of any, whether native or foreigner. For any part which harmonizeth not with its whole is offensive. But when God commands a thing to be done against the customs or compact of any people, though it were never by them done heretofore, it is to be done; and if intermitted, it is to be restored; and if never ordained, is now to be ordained. For lawful if it be for a king, in the state which he reigns over, to command that which no one before him, nor he himself heretofore, had commanded, and to obey him cannot be against the common weal of the state; (nay, it were against it if he were not obeyed, for to obey princes is a general compact of human society); how much more unhesitatingly ought we to obey God, in all which He commands, the Ruler of all His creatures! For, as among the powers in man's society the greater authority is obeyed in preference to the lesser, so must God above all.

16. So in acts of violence, where there is a wish to hurt, whether by reproach or injury; and these either for revenge, as one enemy against another; or for some profit belonging to another, as the robber to the traveller; or to avoid some evil, as towards one who is feared; or through envy, as one less fortunate to one more so; or one well thriven in anything, to him whose being on a par with himself he fears, or grieves at; or for the mere pleasure at another's pain, as spectators of gladiators, or deriders and mockers of others. These be the heads of iniquity which spring from the lust of the flesh, of the eye, or of rule, either singly, or two combined, or all together; and so do men live ill against the three, and seven, that psaltery "of ten strings,"[3] Thy Ten Commandments, O God, most high, and most sweet. But what foul offences can there be against Thee, Who canst not be defiled? or what acts of violence against Thee, Who canst not be harmed? But Thou avengest what men commit against themselves, seeing also when they sin against Thee, they do wickedly against their own souls, and iniquity gives itself the lie,[4] by corrupting and perverting their nature, which Thou hast created and ordained, or by an immoderate use of things allowed, or in "burning" in things unallowed, to that use which is against nature;[5] or are found guilty, raging with heart and tongue against Thee, kicking against the pricks;[6] or when, bursting the pale of human society, they boldly joy in self-willed combinations or divisions, according as they have any object to gain or subject of offence. And these things are done when Thou art forsaken, O Fountain of Life, Who art the only and true Creator and Governor of the Universe, and by a self-willed pride, any one false thing is selected therefrom and loved. So then by a humble devoutness we return to Thee; and Thou cleanest us from our evil habits, and art merciful to their sins who confess, and "hearest the groaning of the prisoner,"[7] and loosest us from the chains which we made for ourselves, if we lift not up against Thee the horns of an unreal liberty, suffering the loss of all through covetousness of more, by loving more our own private good than Thee, the Good of all.

[IX] 17. Amidst these offences of foulness and violence, and so many iniquities, are sins of men, who are on the whole making proficiency; which by those that judge rightly are, after the rule of perfection, discommended, yet the per-

---

[1] As in typical actions of the Patriarchs.
[2] Deut. 6. 5; Matt. 22. 37–9.

[3] Ps. 144. 9. [4] Ps. 27. 12, Vulg. [5] Rom. 1. 24–9.
[6] Acts, 9. 15. [7] Ps. 102. 20.

sons commended, upon hope of future fruit, as in the green blade of growing corn. And there are some, resembling offences of foulness or violence, which yet are no sins; because they offend neither Thee, our Lord God, nor human society; when, namely, things fitting for a given period are obtained for the service of life, and we know not whether out of a lust of having; or when things are, for the sake of correction, by constituted authority punished, and we know not whether out of a lust of hurting. Many an action then which in men's sight is disapproved is by Thy testimony approved; and many, by men praised, are (Thou being witness) condemned: because the shew of the action, and the mind of the doer, and the unknown exigency of the period, severally vary. But when Thou on a sudden commandest an unwonted and unthought-of thing, yea, although Thou hast sometime forbidden it, and still for the time hidest the reason of Thy command, and it be against the ordinance of some society of men, who doubts but it is to be done,[1] seeing that society of men is just which serves Thee? But blessed are they who know Thy commands! For all things were done by Thy servants;[2] either to shew forth something needful for the present, or to foreshew things to come.

[X] 18. These things I being ignorant of, scoffed at those Thy holy servants and prophets. And what gained I by scoffing at them, but to be scoffed at by Thee, being insensibly and step by step drawn on to those follies, as to believe that a fig-tree wept when it was plucked, and the tree, its mother, shed milky tears? Which fig notwithstanding (plucked by some other's, not his own, guilt) had some (Manichæan) "saint" eaten, and mingled with his bowels, he should breathe out of its angels, yea, there shall burst forth particles of divinity, at every moan or groan in his prayer, which particles of the most high and true God had remained bound in that fig, unless they had been set at liberty by the teeth or belly of some "Elect saint"! And I, miserable, believed that more mercy was to be shewn to the fruits of the earth, than men, for whom they were created. For if anyone being hungry and not being a Manichæan, should ask for any, that morsel would seem as it were condemned to capital punishment, which should be given him.

[XI] 19. And Thou sentest Thine hand from above,[3] and drewest my soul out of that profound darkness, my mother, Thy faithful one, weeping to Thee for me, more than mothers weep the bodily deaths of their children. For she, by that faith and spirit which she had from Thee, discerned the death wherein I lay, and Thou heardest her, O Lord; Thou heardest her, and despisedst not her tears when, streaming down, they watered the ground under her eyes in every place where she prayed; yea Thou heardest her. For whence was that dream whereby Thou comfortedst her; so that she allowed me to live with her, and to eat at the same table in the house, which she had begun to shrink from, abhorring and detesting the blasphemies of my error? For she saw herself standing on a certain wooden rule, and a shining youth coming towards her, cheerful and smiling upon her, herself grieving, and overwhelmed with grief. But he having (in order to instruct, as is their wont, not to be instructed) enquired of her the causes of her grief and daily tears, and she answering that she was bewailing my perdition, he bade her rest contented, and told her to look and observe, "That where she was, there was I also." And when she looked, she saw me standing by her in the same rule. Whence was this, but that Thine ears were towards her heart? O Thou Good omnipotent, Who so carest for every one of us as if Thou caredst for him only; and so for all, as if they were but one!

20. Whence was this also, that when she had told me this vision, and I would fain bend it to mean, "That she rather should not despair of being one day what I was"; she presently, without any hesitation, replies, "No; for it was not told me that, 'where he, there thou also'; but 'where thou, there he also'"? I confess to Thee, O Lord, that, to the best of my remembrance (and I have oft spoken of this), Thy answer, through my waking mother—that she was not perplexed by the plausibility of my false interpretation, and so quickly saw what was to be seen, and which I certainly had not perceived, before she spake—even then moved me more than the dream itself, by which a joy to the holy woman, to be fulfilled so long after, was, for the consolation of her present anguish, so long before foresignified. For almost nine years passed, in which I wallowed in the mire of that deep pit, and the darkness of falsehood, often assaying to rise, but dashed down the more grievously. All which time that chaste, godly, and sober widow (such as Thou lovest), now more cheered with hope, yet no whit relaxing in her weeping and mourning, ceased not at all hours of her devotions to bewail my case unto Thee. And her prayers entered into Thy pres-

---

[1]*City of God*, BK. I. 26.   [2]The Patriarchs.
[3]Ps. 144. 7.

ence;[1] and yet Thou sufferest me to be yet involved and reinvolved in that darkness.

[XII] 21. Thou gavest her meantime another answer, which I call to mind; for much I pass by, hasting to those things which more press me to confess unto Thee, and much I do not remember. Thou gavest her then another answer, by a priest of Thine, a certain Bishop brought up in Thy Church, and well studied in Thy books. Whom when this woman had entreated to vouchsafe to converse with me, refute my errors, unteach me ill things, and teach me good things (for this he was wont to do, when he found persons fitted to receive it), he refused, wisely, as I afterwards perceived. For he answered that I was yet unteachable, being puffed up with the novelty of that heresy, and had already perplexed divers unskilful persons with captious questions, as she had told him. "But let him alone a while," saith he; "only pray God for him, he will of himself by reading find what that error is, and how great its impiety." At the same time he told her how himself, when a little one, had by his seduced mother been consigned over to the Manichees, and had not only read, but frequently copied out almost all, their books, and had (without any argument or proof from anyone) seen how much that sect was to be avoided; and had avoided it. Which when he had said, and she would not be satisfied, but urged him more, with entreaties and many tears, that he would see me and discourse with me, he, a little displeased at her importunity, saith, "Go thy ways, and God bless Thee, for it is not possible that the son of these tears should perish." Which answer she took (as she often mentioned in her conversations with me) as if it had sounded from heaven.

BOOK IV. *Augustine's life from nineteen to eight and twenty; himself a Manichæan, and seducing others to the same heresy; partial obedience amidst vanity and sin, consulting astrologers; only partially shaken herein; loss of an early friend, who is converted by being baptized when in a swoon; reflections on grief, on real and unreal friendship, and love of fame; writes on "the fair and fit," yet cannot rightly, though God had given him great talents, since he entertained wrong notions of God; and so even his knowledge he applied ill.*

[I] 1. For this space of nine years then (from my nineteenth year to my eight-and-twentieth) we lived seduced and seducing, deceived and deceiving, in divers lusts; openly, by sciences which they call "liberal"; secretly, with a false-named religion; here proud, there superstitious, everywhere vain! Here, hunting after the emptiness of popular praise, down even to theatrical applauses, and poetic prizes, and strifes for grassy garlands, and the follies of shows, and the intemperance of desires. There, desiring to be cleansed from these defilements, by carrying food to those who were called "elect" and "holy," out of which, in the workhouse of their stomachs, they should forge for us Angels and Gods, by whom we might be cleansed. These things did I follow, and practise with my friends, deceived by me and with me. Let the arrogant mock me, and such as have not been, to their soul's health, stricken and cast down by Thee, O my God; but I would still confess to Thee mine own shame in Thy praise. Suffer me, I beseech Thee, and give me grace to go over in my present remembrance the wanderings of my forepassed time, and to "offer unto Thee the sacrifice of thanksgiving."[2] For what am I to myself without Thee but a guide to mine own downfall? or what am I even at the best, but an infant sucking the milk Thou givest, and feeding upon Thee, the food that perisheth not?[3] But what sort of man is any man, seeing he is but a man? Let now the strong and the mighty laugh at us, but let us "poor and needy"[4] confess unto Thee.

[II] 2. In those years I taught rhetoric and, overcome by cupidity, made sale of a loquacity to overcome by. Yet I preferred (Lord, Thou knowest) honest scholars (as they are accounted), and these I, without artifice, taught artifices, not to be practised against the life of the guiltless, though sometimes for the life of the guilty. And Thou, O God, from afar perceivedst me stumbling in that slippery course, and amid much smoke sending out some sparks of faithfulness, which I shewed in that my guidance of such as loved vanity, and sought after leasing,[5] myself their companion. In those years I had one—not in that which is called lawful marriage, but whom I had found out in a wayward passion, void of understanding; yet but one, remaining faithful even to her; in whom I in my own case experienced what difference there is betwixt the self-restraint of the marriage-covenant, for the sake of issue, and the bargain of a lustful love, where children are born against their parents' will, although, once born, they constrain love.

3. I remember also, that when I had settled to enter the lists for a theatrical prize, some wiz-

[1] Ps. 88. 1.
[2] Ps. 116. 17.   [3] John, 6. 27.   [4] Ps. 74. 21.
[5] Ps. 4. 2.

ard asked me what I would give him to win: but I, detesting and abhorring such foul mysteries, answered, "Though the garland were of imperishable gold, I would not suffer a fly to be killed to gain me it." For he was to kill some living creatures in his sacrifices, and by those honours to invite the devils to favour me. But this ill also I rejected, not out of a pure love[1] for Thee, O God of my heart; for I knew not how to love Thee, who knew not how to conceive aught beyond a material brightness. And doth not a soul, sighing after such fictions, commit fornication against Thee, trust in things unreal, and feed the wind?[2] Still I would not forsooth have sacrifices offered to devils for me, to whom I was sacrificing myself by that superstition. For what else is it to feed the wind but to feed them, that is, by going astray to become their pleasure and derision?

[III] 4. Those impostors then, whom they style mathematicians, I consulted without scruple; because they seemed to use no sacrifice, nor to pray to any spirit for their divinations: which art, however, Christian and true piety consistently rejects and condemns. For it is a good thing to confess unto Thee, and to say, "Have mercy upon me, heal my soul, for I have sinned against Thee";[3] and not to abuse Thy mercy for a license to sin, but to remember the Lord's words, "Behold, thou art made whole, sin no more, lest a worse thing come unto thee."[4] All which wholesome advice they labour to destroy, saying, "The cause of thy sin is inevitably determined in heaven;" and "This did Venus, or Saturn, or Mars": that man, forsooth, flesh and blood, and proud corruption, might be blameless; while the Creator and Ordainer of heaven and the stars is to bear the blame. And who is He but our God? the very sweetness and well-spring of righteousness, Who renderest "to every man according to his works":[5] and "a broken and contrite heart" wilt Thou not despise.[6]

5. There was in those days a wise man,[7] very skilful in physic, and renowned therein, who had with his own proconsular hand put the Agonistic garland upon my distempered head, but not as a physician: for this disease Thou only curest, who resistest the proud, and givest grace to the humble.[8] But didst Thou fail me even by that old man, or forbear to heal my soul? For having become more acquainted with him, and hanging assiduously and fixedly on his speech (for though in simple terms, it was vivid, lively, and earnest), when he had gathered by my discourse that I was given to the books of nativity-casters, he kindly and fatherly advised me to cast them away, and not fruitlessly bestow a care and diligence, necessary for useful things, upon these vanities; saying that he had in his earliest years studied that art, so as to make it the profession whereby he should live, and that, understanding Hippocrates, he could soon have understood such a study as this; and yet he had given it over, and taken to physic, for no other reason but that he found it utterly false; and he, a grave man, would not get his living by deluding people. "But thou," saith he, "hast rhetoric to maintain thyself by, so that thou followest this of free choice, not of necessity: the more then oughtest Thou to give me credit herein, who laboured to acquire it so perfectly as to get my living by it alone." Of whom when I had demanded, how then could many true things be foretold by it, he answered me (as he could), "that the force of chance, diffused throughout the whole order of things, brought this about. For if when a man by hap-hazard opens the pages of some poet, who sang and thought of something wholly different, a verse oftentimes fell out, wondrously agreeable to the present business: it were not to be wondered at if, out of the soul of man, unconscious what takes place in it, by some higher instinct an answer should be given, by hap, not by art, corresponding to the business and actions of the demander."

6. And thus much, either from or through him, Thou conveyedst to me, and tracedst in my memory, what I might hereafter examine for myself. But at that time neither he, nor my dearest Nebridius, a youth singularly good and of a holy fear, who derided the whole body of divination, could persuade me to cast it aside, the authority of the authors swaying me yet more, and as yet I had found no certain proof (such as I sought) whereby it might without all doubt appear that what had been truly foretold by those consulted was the result of hap-hazard, not of the art of the star-gazers.

[IV] 7. In those years when I first began to teach rhetoric in my native town, I had made one my friend, but too dear to me from a community of pursuits, of mine own age, and, as myself, in the first opening flower of youth. He had grown up of a child with me, and we had been both school-fellows and play-fellows. But he was not yet my friend as afterwards, nor even then as true friendship is; for true it cannot be, unless in such as Thou cementest to-

[1]Cf. *City of God*, Bk. XIV. 9. [2]Hosea, 12. 1.
[3]Ps. 41. 4. [4]John, 5. 14. [5]Rom. 2. 6; Matt. 16. 27.
[6]Ps. 51. 17. [7]Vindicianus. [8]I Pet. 5. 5; James, 4. 6.

gether, cleaving unto Thee, by that love which is shed abroad in our hearts by the Holy Ghost, which is given unto us.[1] Yet was it but too sweet, ripened by the warmth of kindred studies: for, from the true faith (which he as a youth had not soundly and thoroughly imbibed), I had warped him also to those superstitious and pernicious fables for which my mother bewailed me. With me he now erred in mind, nor could my soul be without him. But behold Thou wert close on the steps of Thy fugitives, at once God of vengeance[2] and Fountain of mercies, turning us to Thyself by wonderful means; Thou tookest that man out of this life, when he had scarce filled up one whole year of my friendship, sweet to me above all sweetness of that my life.

8. "Who can recount all Thy praises,"[3] which he hath felt in his one self? What diddest Thou then, my God, and how unsearchable is the abyss of Thy judgments?[4] For long, sore sick of a fever, he lay senseless in a death-sweat; and, his recovery being despaired of, he was baptized, unknowing; myself meanwhile little regarding, and presuming that his soul would retain rather what it had received of me, not what was wrought on his unconscious body. But it proved far otherwise: for he was refreshed, and restored. Forthwith, as soon as I could speak with him (and I could, so soon as he was able, for I never left him, and we hung but too much upon each other), I essayed to jest with him, as though he would jest with me at that baptism which he had received when utterly absent in mind and feeling, but had now understood that he had received. But he so shrunk from me, as from an enemy; and with a wonderful and sudden freedom bade me, as I would continue his friend, forbear such language to him. I, all astonished and amazed, suppressed all my emotions till he should grow well, and his health were strong enough for me to deal with him as I would. But he was taken away from my phrensy, that with Thee he might be preserved for my comfort; a few days after, in my absence, he was attacked again by the fever, and so departed.

9. At this grief my heart was utterly darkened; and whatever I beheld was death. My native country was a torment to me, and my father's house a strange unhappiness; and whatever I had shared with him, wanting him, became a distracting torture. Mine eyes sought him everywhere, but he was not granted them; and I hated all places, for that they had not him; nor could they now tell me, "he is com-ing," as when he was alive and absent. I became a great riddle to myself, and I asked my soul, why she was so sad, and why she disquieted me sorely:[5] but she knew not what to answer me. And if I said, "Trust in God," [6] she very rightly obeyed me not; because that most dear friend, whom she had lost, was, being man, both truer and better than that phantasm she was bid to trust in. Only tears were sweet to me, for they succeeded my friend in the dearest of my affections.

[V] 10. And now, Lord, these things are passed by, and time hath assuaged my wound. May I learn from Thee, Who art Truth, and approach the ear of my heart unto Thy mouth, that Thou mayest tell me why weeping is sweet to the miserable? Hast Thou, although present everywhere, cast away our misery far from Thee? And Thou abidest in Thyself, but we are tossed about in divers trials. And yet, unless we mourned in Thine ears, we should have no hope left. Whence then is sweet fruit gathered from the bitterness of life, from groaning, tears, sighs, and complaints? Doth this sweeten it, that we hope Thou hearest? This is true of prayer, for therein is a longing to approach unto Thee. But is it also in grief for a thing lost, and the sorrow wherewith I was then overwhelmed? For I neither hoped he should return to life, nor did I desire this with my tears; but I wept only and grieved. For I was miserable, and had lost my joy. Or is weeping indeed a bitter thing, and for very loathing of the things which we before enjoyed, does it then, when we shrink from them, please us?

[VI] 11. But what speak I of these things? for now is no time to question, but to confess unto Thee. Wretched I was; and wretched is every soul bound by the friendship of perishable things; he is torn asunder when he loses them, and then he feels the wretchedness which he had ere yet he lost them. So was it then with me; I wept most bitterly, and found my repose in bitterness. Thus was I wretched, and that wretched life I held dearer than my friend. For though I would willingly have changed it, yet was I more unwilling to part with it than with him; yea, I know not whether I would have parted with it even for him, as is related (if not feigned) of Pylades and Orestes, that they would gladly have died for each other or together, not to live together being to them worse than death. But in me there had arisen some unexplained feeling, too contrary to this, for at once I loathed exceedingly to live, and feared to die. I suppose,

[1]Rom. 5.5.   [2]Ps. 94. 1.   [3]Ps. 106. 2.
[4]Ps. 36. 6; Rom. 11. 33.

[5]Ps. 42. 5.   [6]Ibid.

the more I loved him, the more did I hate, and fear (as a most cruel enemy) death, which had bereaved me of him: and I imagined it would speedily make an end of all men, since it had power over him. Thus was it with me, I remember. Behold my heart, O my God, behold and see into me; for well I remember it, O my Hope, who cleansest me from the impurity of such affections, directing mine eyes towards Thee, and plucking my feet out of the snare.[1] For I wondered at others, subject to death, did live, since he whom I loved, as if he should never die, was dead: and I wondered yet more that myself, who was to him a second self, could live, he being dead. Well said one of his friend, "Thou half of my soul": for I felt that my soul and his soul were "one soul in two bodies": and therefore was my life a horror to me, because I would not live halved. And therefore perchance I feared to die, lest he whom I had much loved should die wholly.

[VII] 12. O madness, which knowest not how to love men, like men! O foolish man that I then was, enduring impatiently the lot of man! I fretted then, sighed, wept, was distracted; had neither rest nor counsel. For I bore about a shattered and bleeding soul, impatient of being borne by me, yet where to repose it I found not. Not in calm groves, not in games and music, nor in fragrant spots, nor in curious banquettings, nor in the pleasures of the bed and the couch; nor (finally) in books or poesy, found in repose. All things looked ghastly, yea, the very light; whatsoever was not what he was, was revolting and hateful, except groaning and tears. For in those alone found I a little refreshment. But when my soul was withdrawn from them, a huge load of misery weighed me down. To Thee, O Lord, it ought to have been raised, for Thee to lighten; I knew it; but neither could nor would; the more since, when I thought of Thee, Thou wert not to me any solid or substantial thing. For Thou wert not Thyself, but a mere phantom, and my error was my God. If I offered to discharge my load thereon, that it might rest, it glided through the void, and came rushing down again on me; and I had remained to myself a hapless spot, where I could neither be, nor be from thence. For whither should my heart flee from my heart? Whither should I flee from myself? Whither not follow myself? And yet I fled out of my country; for so should mine eyes less look for him, where they were not wont to see him. And thus from Thagaste I came to Carthage.

[VIII] 13. Times lose no time; nor do they roll idly by; through our senses they work strange operations on the mind. Behold, they went and came day by day, and by coming and going introduced into my mind other imaginations and other remembrances; and little by little patched me up again with my old kind of delights, unto which that my sorrow gave way. And yet there succeeded, not indeed other griefs, yet the causes of other griefs. For whence had that former grief so easily reached my very inmost soul, but that I had poured out my soul upon the dust, in loving one that must die, as if he would never die? For what restored and refreshed me chiefly was the solaces of other friends, with whom I did love what instead of Thee I loved: and this was a great fable, and protracted lie, by whose adulterous stimulus our soul, which lay itching in our ears, was being defiled. But that fable would not die to me, so oft as any of my friends died. There were other things which in them did more take my mind; to talk and jest together, to do kind offices by turns; to read together honied books; to play the fool or be earnest together; to dissent at times without discontent, as a man might with his own self; and even with the seldomness of these dissentings, to season our more frequent consentings; sometimes to teach, and sometimes learn; long for the absent with impatience; and welcome the coming with joy. These and the like expressions, proceeding out of the hearts of those that loved and were loved again, by the countenance, the tongue, the eyes, and a thousand pleasing gestures, were so much fuel to melt our souls together, and out of many make but one.

[IX] 14. This is it that is loved in friends; and so loved that a man's conscience condemns itself if he love not him that loves him again, or love not again him that loves him, looking for nothing from his person but indications of his love. Hence that mourning, if one die, and darkenings of sorrows, that steeping of the heart in tears, all sweetness turned to bitterness; and upon the loss of life of the dying, the death of the living. Blessed whoso loveth Thee, and his friend in Thee, and his enemy for Thee. For he alone loses none dear to him, to whom all are dear in Him Who cannot be lost. And who is this but our God, the God that made heaven and earth,[2] and filleth them,[3] because by filling them He created them?[4] Thee none loseth, but who leaveth. And who leaveth Thee, whither goeth or whither fleeth he, but from Thee well-pleased, to Thee

---

[1] Ps. 25. 15.

[2] Gen. 1. 1.   [3] Jer. 23. 24.   [4] See bk. 1. 2, 3.

displeased? For where doth he not find Thy law in his own punishment? "And Thy law is truth,"[1] and truth Thou.[2]

[X] 15. "Turn us, O God of Hosts, shew us Thy countenance, and we shall be whole."[3] For whithersoever the soul of man turns itself, unless towards Thee, it is rivetted upon sorrows,[4] yea though it is rivetted on things beautiful. And yet they, out of Thee, and out of the soul, were not, unless they were from Thee. They rise, and set; and by rising, they begin as it were to be; they grow, that they may be perfected; and perfected, they wax old and wither; and all grow not old, but all wither. So then when they rise and tend to be, the more quickly they grow that they may be, so much the more they haste not to be. This is the law of them. Thus much hast Thou allotted them, because they are portions of things, which exist not all at once, but by passing away and succeeding they together complete that universe whereof they are portions. And even thus is our speech completed by signs giving forth a sound: but this again is not perfected unless one word pass away when it hath sounded its part, that another may succeed. Out of all these things let my soul praise Thee, O God, Creator of all; yet let not my soul be rivetted unto these things with the glue of love, through the senses of the body. For they go whither they were to go, that they might not be; and they rend her with pestilent longings, because she longs to be, yet loves to repose in what she loves. But in these things is no place of repose; they abide not, they flee; and who can follow them with the senses of the flesh? yea, who can grasp them, when they are hard by? For the sense of the flesh is slow, because it is the sense of the flesh; and thereby is it bounded. It sufficeth for that it was made for; but it sufficeth not to stay things running their course from their appointed starting place to the end appointed. For in Thy Word, by which they are created, they hear their decree, "hence and hitherto."

[XI] 16. Be not foolish, O my soul, nor become deaf in the ear of thine heart with the tumult of thy folly. Hearken thou too. The Word Itself calleth thee to return: and there is the place of rest imperturbable, where love is not forsaken, if itself forsaketh not. Behold, these things pass away, that others may replace them, and so this lower universe be completed by all his parts. But do I depart any whither? saith the Word of God. There fix thy dwelling, trust there

whatsoever thou hast thence, O my soul, at least now thou art tired out with vanities. Entrust Truth, whatsoever thou hast from the Truth, and thou shalt lose nothing; and thy decay shall bloom again, and all thy diseases be healed,[5] and thy mortal parts be re-formed and renewed, and bound around thee: nor shall they lay thee whither themselves descend; but they shall stand fast with thee, and abide for ever before God, Who abideth and standeth fast for ever.[6]

17. Why then be perverted and follow thy flesh? Be it converted and follow thee. Whatever by her thou hast sense of is in part; and the whole, whereof these are parts, thou knowest not; and yet they delight thee. But had the sense of thy flesh a capacity for comprehending the whole, and not itself also, for thy punishment, been justly restricted to a part of the whole, thou wouldest that whatsoever existeth at this present should pass away, that so the whole might better please thee.[7] For what we speak also, by the same sense of the flesh thou hearest; yet wouldest not thou have the syllables stay, but fly away, that others may come, and thou hear the whole. And so ever, when any one thing is made up of many, all of which do not exist together, all collectively would please more than they do severally, could all be perceived collectively. But far better than these is He who made all; and He is our God, nor doth He pass away, for neither doth aught succeed Him.

[XII] 18. If bodies please thee, praise God on occasion of them, and turn back thy love upon their Maker; lest in these things which please thee, thou displease. If souls please thee, be they loved in God: for they too are mutable, but in Him are they firmly stablished; else would they pass, and pass away. In Him then be they beloved; and carry unto Him along with thee what souls thou canst, and say to them, "Him let us love, Him let us love: He made these, nor is He far off. For He did not make them, and so depart, but they are of Him, and in Him. See there He is, where truth is loved. He is within the very heart, yet hath the heart strayed from Him. Go back into your heart, ye transgressors,[8] and cleave fast to Him that made you. Stand with Him, and ye shall stand fast. Rest in Him, and ye shall be at rest. Whither go ye in rough ways? Whither go ye? The good that you love is from Him; but it is good and pleasant[9] through reference to Him, and justly shall it be embittered, because unjustly is anything loved

[1]Ps. 119. 142; John, 17. 17.   [2]John, 14. 6.
[3]Ps. 80. 19   [4]See Bk. IV. 13.

[5]Ps. 103. 3.   [6]I Pet. I. 23.   [7]See Bk. XIII. 22 below.
[8]Isa. 66. 8.   [9]Cf. *City of God*, Bk. XI. 8.

which is from Him, if He be forsaken for it. To what end then would ye still and still walk these difficult and toilsome ways? There is no rest where ye seek it. Seek what ye seek; but it is not there where ye seek. Ye seek a blessed life in the land of death; it is not there. For how should there be a blessed life, where life itself is not?"

19. But our true Life came down hither, and bore our death, and slew him, out of the abundance of His own life: and He thundered, calling aloud to us to return hence to Him into that secret place whence He came forth to us, first into the Virgin's womb, wherein He espoused the human creation, our mortal flesh, that it might not be for ever mortal, and thence "like a bridegroom coming out of his chamber, rejoicing as a giant to run his course."[1] For He lingered not, but ran, calling aloud by words, deeds, death, life, descent, ascension; crying aloud to us to return unto Him. And He departed from our eyes, that we might return into our heart, and there find Him. For He departed, and lo, He is here. He would not be long with us, yet left us not; for He departed thither, whence He never parted, "because the world was made by Him."[2] And in this world He was, and into this world He came to save sinners,[3] unto Whom my soul confesseth, and He healeth it, for it hath sinned against Him.[4] O ye sons of men, how long so slow of heart?[5] Even now, after the descent of Life to you, will ye not ascend and live? But whither ascend ye, when ye are on high, and set your mouth against the heavens?[6] Descend, that ye may ascend,[7] and ascend to God. For ye have fallen, by "ascending against Him."[8] Tell them this, that they may weep in the valley of tears, and so carry them up with thee unto God; because out of His Spirit thou speakest thus unto them, if thou speakest, burning with the fire of charity.

[XIII] 20. These things I then knew not, and I loved these lower beauties, and I was sinking to the very depths, and to my friends I said, "Do we love anything but the beautiful? What then is the beautiful? And what is beauty? What is it that attracts and wins us to the things we love? For unless there were in them a grace and beauty, they could by no means draw us unto them." And I marked and perceived that in bodies themselves there was a beauty, from their forming a sort of whole, and again, another from apt and mutual correspondence, as of a part of the body with its whole, or a shoe with a foot, and the like. And this consideration sprang up in my mind, out of my inmost heart, and I wrote "on the fair and fit," I think, two or three books. Thou knowest, O Lord, for it is gone from me; for I have them not, but they are strayed from me, I know not how.

[XIV] 21. But what moved me, O Lord my God, to dedicate these books unto Hierius, an orator of Rome, whom I knew not by face, but loved for the fame of his learning which was eminent in him, and some words of his I had heard, which pleased me? But more did he please me, for that he pleased others, who highly extolled him, amazed that out of a Syrian, first instructed in Greek eloquence, should afterwards be formed a wonderful Latin orator, and one most learned in things pertaining unto philosophy. One is commended, and, unseen, he is loved: doth this love enter the heart of the hearer from the mouth of the commender? Not so. But by one who loveth is another kindled. For hence he is loved, who is commended, when the commender is believed to extol him with an unfeigned heart; that is, when one that loves him praises him.

22. For so did I then love men upon the judgment of men, not thine, O my God, in Whom no man is deceived. But yet why not for qualities like those of a famous charioteer, or fighter with beasts in the theatre,[9] known far and wide by a vulgar popularity, but far otherwise, and earnestly, and so as I would be myself commended? For I would not be commended or loved, as actors are (though I myself did commend and love them), but had rather be unknown than so known; and even hated than so loved. Where now are the impulses to such various and divers kinds of loves laid up in one soul? Why, since we are equally men, do I love in another what, if I did not hate, I should not spurn and cast from myself? For it holds not that, as a good horse is loved by him who would not, though he might, be that horse, therefore the same may be said of an actor, who shares our nature. Do I then love in a man what I hate to be, who am a man? Man himself is a great deep, whose very hairs Thou numberest, O Lord, and they fall not to the ground without Thee.[10] And yet are the hairs of his head easier to be numbered than are his feelings, and the beatings of his heart.

23. But that orator was of that sort whom I loved, as wishing to be myself such; and I erred through a swelling pride, and was "tossed about

[1] Ps. 19. 5. [2] John, 1. 10. [3] I Tim. 1. 15.
[4] Ps. 41. 4. [5] Luke, 24. 25. [6] Ps. 72. 9.
[7] Cf. *City of God*, bk. XIV. 13. [8] Ps. 84. 6.

[9] See bk. VI. 13, below. [10] Matt. 10. 29, 30.

with every wind," [1] but yet was steered by Thee, though very secretly. And whence do I know, and whence do I confidently confess unto Thee, that I had loved him more for the love of his commenders than for the very things for which he was commended? Because, had he been unpraised, and these self-same men had dispraised him, and with dispraise and contempt told the very same things of him, I had never been so kindled and excited to love him. And yet the things had not been other, nor he himself other; but only the feelings of the relators. See where the impotent soul lies along, that is not yet stayed up by the solidity of truth! Just as the gales of tongues blow from the breast of the opinionative, so is it carried this way and that, driven forward and backward, and the light is overclouded to it, and the truth unseen. And lo, it is before us. And it was to me a great matter that my discourse and labours should be known to that man: which should he approve, I were the more kindled; but if he disapproved, my empty heart, void of Thy solidity, had been wounded. And yet the "fair and fit," whereon I wrote to him, I dwelt on with pleasure, and surveyed it, and admired it, though none joined therein.

[XV] 24. But I saw not yet, whereon this weighty matter turned in Thy wisdom, O Thou Omnipotent, "Who only doest wonders"; [2] and my mind ranged through corporeal forms; and "fair" I defined and distinguished what is so in itself, and "fit" whose beauty is in correspondence to some other thing: and this I supported by corporeal examples. And I turned to the nature of the mind, but the false notion which I had of spiritual things let me not see the truth. Yet the force of truth did of itself flash into mine eyes, and I turned away my panting soul from incorporeal substance to lineaments, and colours, and bulky magnitudes. And, not being able to see these in the mind, I thought I could not see my mind. And whereas in virtue I loved peace, and in viciousness I abhorred discord; in the first I observed an unity, but in the other, a sort of division. And in that unity, I conceived the rational soul, and the nature of truth and of the chief good to consist: but in this division I miserably imagined there to be some unknown substance of irrational life, and the nature of the chief evil, which should not only be a substance, but real life also, and yet not derived from Thee, O my God, of whom are all things. And yet that first I called a Monad, as it had been a soul without sex; [3] but the latter a Duad: anger in deeds

of violence, and in flagitiousness, lust; not knowing whereof I spake. For I had not known or learned that neither was evil a substance, nor our soul that chief and unchangeable good.

25. For as deeds of violence arise, if that emotion of the soul be corrupted whence vehement action springs, stirring itself insolently and unrulily, and lusts, when that affection of the soul is ungoverned, whereby carnal pleasures are drunk in, so do errors and false opinions defile the conversation, if the reasonable soul itself be corrupted; as it was then in me, who knew not that it must be enlightened by another light, that it may be partaker of truth, seeing itself is not that nature of truth. "For Thou shalt light my candle, O Lord my God, Thou shalt enlighten my darkness": [4] and "of Thy fulness have we all received," [5] for "Thou art the true light that lighteth every man that cometh into the world"; [6] for in Thee there is no variableness, neither shadow of change." [7]

26. But I pressed towards Thee, and was thrust from Thee, that I might taste of death: for thou "resistest the proud." [8] But what prouder than for me with a strange madness to maintain myself to be that by nature which Thou art? For whereas I was subject to change (so much being manifest to me, my very desire to become wise, being the wish, of worse to become better); yet chose I rather to imagine Thee subject to change, than myself not to be that which Thou art. Therefore I was repelled by Thee, and Thou resistedst my vain stiff-neckedness, and I imagined corporeal forms, and, myself flesh, I accused flesh; and, "a wind that passeth away," I returned not [9] to Thee, but I passed on and on to things which have no being, neither in Thee, nor in me, nor in the body. Neither were they created for me by Thy truth, but by my vanity devised out of things corporeal. And I was wont to ask Thy faithful little ones, my fellow-citizens (from whom, unknown to myself, I stood exiled)—I was wont, prating and foolishly, to ask them, "Why then doth the soul err which God created?" But I would not be asked, "Why then doth God err?" And I maintained that Thy unchangeable substance did err upon constraint, rather than confess that my changeable substance had gone astray voluntarily, and now, in punishment, lay in error.

27. I was then some six or seven and twenty years old when I wrote those volumes; revolving within me corporeal fictions, buzzing in the ears of my heart, which I turned, O sweet truth,

---

[1] Eph. 4. 14.   [2] Ps. 136. 4.   [3] Or "an unintelligent soul."

[4] Ps. 18. 28.   [5] John, 1. 16.   [6] John, 1. 9.
[7] James, 1. 17.   [8] *Ibid.*, 4. 6; I Pet. 5. 5.   [9] Ps. 78. 39.

to thy inward melody, meditating on the "fair and fit," and longing to stand and hearken to Thee, and to rejoice greatly at the Bridegroom's voice,[1] but could not; for by the voices of mine own errors I was hurried abroad, and through the weight of my own pride I was sinking into the lowest pit. For Thou didst not "make me to hear joy and gladness," nor did the bones exult which were not yet humbled.[2]

[XVI] 28. And what did it profit me that, scarce twenty years old, a book of Aristotle, which they call *The Ten Predicaments,* falling into my hands (on whose very name I hung, as on something great and divine, so often as my rhetoric master of Carthage, and others, accounted learned, mouthed it with cheeks bursting with pride), I read and understood it unaided? And on my conferring with others, who said that they scarcely understood it with very able tutors, not only orally explaining it, but drawing many things in sand, they could tell me no more of it than I had learned, reading it by myself. And the book appeared to me to speak very clearly of substances, such as "man," and of their qualities, as the figure of a man, of what sort it is; and stature, how many feet high; and his relationship, whose brother he is; or where placed; or when born; or whether he stands or sits; or be shod or armed; or does or suffers anything; and all the innumerable things which might be ranged under these nine Predicaments, of which I have given some specimens, or under that chief Predicament of Substance.

29. What did all this further me, seeing it even hindered me? when, imagining whatever was, was comprehended under those ten Predicaments, I essayed in such wise to understand, O my God, Thy wonderful and unchangeable Unity also, as if Thou also hadst been subjected to Thine own greatness or beauty; so that (as in bodies) they should exist in Thee, as their subject: whereas Thou Thyself art Thy greatness and beauty; but a body is not great or fair in that it is a body, seeing that, though it were less great or fair, it should notwithstanding be a body. But it was falsehood which of Thee I conceived, not truth; fictions of my misery, not the realities of Thy Blessedness. For Thou hadst commanded, and it was done in me, that the earth should bring forth briars and thorns to me,[3] and that in the sweat of my brows I should eat my bread.[4]

30. And what did it profit me that all the books I could procure of the so-called liberal

arts, I, the vile slave of vile affections, read by myself, and understood? And I delighted in them, but knew not whence came all that therein was true or certain. For I had my back to the light, and my face to the things enlightened; whence my face, with which I discerned the things enlightened, itself was not enlightened. Whatever was written, either on rhetoric, or logic, geometry, music, and arithmetic, by myself without much difficulty or any instructor, I understood, Thou knowest, O Lord my God; because both quickness of understanding, and acuteness in discerning, is Thy gift: yet did I not thence sacrifice to Thee. So then it served not to my use, but rather to my perdition, since I went about to get so good a portion of my substance[5] into my own keeping; and I kept not my strength for Thee,[6] but wandered from Thee into a far country, to spend it upon harlotries.[7] For what profited me good abilities, not employed to good uses? For I felt not that those arts were attained with great difficulty, even by the studious and talented, until I attempted to explain them to such; when he most excelled in them, who followed me not altogether slowly.

31. But what did this further me, imagining that Thou, O Lord God, the Truth, wert a vast and bright body,[8] and I a fragment of that body? Perverseness too great! But such was I. Nor do I blush, O my God, to confess to Thee Thy mercies towards me, and to call upon Thee, who blushed not then to profess to men my blasphemies, and to bark against Thee. What profited me then my nimble wit in those sciences and all those most knotty volumes, unravelled by me without aid from human instruction; seeing I erred so foully, and with such sacrilegious shamefulness, in the doctrine of piety? Or what hindrance was a far slower wit to Thy little ones, since they departed not far from Thee, that in the nest of Thy Church they might securely be fledged, and nourish the wings of charity, by the food of a sound faith. O Lord our God, under the shadow of Thy wings let us hope;[9] protect us, and carry us. Thou wilt carry us both when little, and even to hoar hairs wilt Thou carry us;[10] for our firmness, when it is Thou, then is it firmness; but when our own, it is infirmity. Our good ever lives with Thee; from which when we turn away, we are turned aside. Let us now, O Lord, return, that we may not be overturned, because with Thee our good lives without any decay, which good art Thou; nor need we fear,

---

[1]John, 3. 29.   [2]Ps. 51. 8, Vulg.   [3]Isa. 32. 13.
[4]Gen. 3. 19.

[5]Luke, 15. 12.   [6]Ps. 59. 5, Vulg.   [7]Luke, 15. 13.
[8]See Bk. III. 12; Bk. IV. 3, 12; Bk. V. 19.
[9]Ps. 36. 7.   [10]Isa. 46. 4.

lest there be no place whither to return, because we fell from it: for through our absence, our mansion fell not—Thy eternity.

BOOK V. *Augustine's twenty-ninth year. Faustus, a snare of Satan to many, made an instrument of deliverance to Augustine, by shewing the ignorance of the Manichees on those things wherein they professed to have divine knowledge. Augustine gives up all thought of going further among the Manichees: is guided to Rome and Milan, where he hears St. Ambrose, leaves the Manichees, and becomes again a catechumen in the Church Catholic.*

[I] 1. Accept the sacrifice of my confessions from the ministry of my tongue, which Thou hast formed and stirred up to confess unto Thy name. Heal Thou all my bones, and let them say, "O Lord, who is like unto Thee?"[1] For he who confesses to Thee doth not teach Thee what takes place within him; seeing a closed heart closes not out Thy eye, nor can man's hardheartedness thrust back Thy hand: for Thou dissolvest it at Thy will in pity or in vengeance, "and nothing can hide itself from Thy heat."[2] But let my soul praise Thee, that it may love Thee; and let it confess Thy own mercies to Thee, that it may praise Thee. Thy whole creation ceaseth not, nor is silent in Thy praises; neither the spirit of man with voice directed unto Thee, nor creation animate or inanimate, by the voice of those who meditate thereon: that so our souls may from their weariness arise towards Thee, leaning on those things which Thou hast created, and passing on to Thyself, who madest them wonderfully; and there is refreshment and true strength.

2. Let the restless, the godless, depart and flee from Thee; yet Thou seest them, and dividest the darkness. And behold, the universe with them is fair, though they are foul.[3] And how have they injured Thee?[4] or how have they disgraced Thy government which, from the heaven to this lowest earth, is just and perfect? For whither fled they, when they fled from Thy presence?[5] Or where dost not Thou find them? But they fled, that they might not see Thee seeing them, and, blinded, might stumble against Thee[6] (because Thou forsakest nothing Thou hast made);[7] that the unjust, I say, might stumble upon Thee, and justly be hurt; withdrawing themselves from Thy gentleness, and stumbling at Thy uprightness, and falling upon their own

ruggedness. Ignorant, in truth, that Thou art everywhere, Whom no place encompasseth! and Thou alone art near, even to those that remove far from Thee.[8] Let them then be turned, and seek Thee; because not as they have forsaken their Creator, hast Thou forsaken Thy creation. Let them be turned and seek Thee; and behold, Thou art there in their heart, in the heart of those that confess to Thee, and cast themselves upon Thee, and weep in Thy bosom, after all their rugged ways. Then dost Thou gently wipe away their tears, and they weep the more, and joy in weeping; even for that Thou, Lord—not man of flesh and blood, but Thou, Lord, who madest them—re-makest and comfortest them. But where was I, when I was seeking Thee? And Thou wert before me, but I had gone away from Thee; nor did I find myself, how much less Thee!

[III] 3. I would lay open before my God that nine-and-twentieth year of mine age. There had then come to Carthage a certain Bishop of the Manichees, Faustus by name, a great snare of the Devil, and many were entangled by him through that lure of his smooth language: which though I did commend, yet could I separate from the truth of the things which I was earnest to learn: nor did I so much regard the service of oratory, as the science which this Faustus, so praised among them, set before me to feed upon. Fame had before bespoken him most knowing in all valuable learning, and exquisitely skilled in the liberal sciences. And since I had read and well remembered much of the philosophers, I compared some things of theirs with those long fables of the Manichees, and found the former the more probable; even although they could only prevail so far as to make judgment of this lower world, the Lord of it they could by no means find out.[9] For Thou art great, O Lord, and hast "respect unto the humble, but the proud Thou beholdest afar off."[10] Nor dost thou draw near but to the contrite in heart,[11] nor art found by the proud, no, not though by curious skill they could number the stars and the sand, and measure the starry heavens, and track the courses of the planets.

4. For with their understanding and wit, which Thou bestowedst on them, they search out these things; and much have they found out; and foretold, many years before, eclipses of those luminaries, the sun and moon—what day and hour, and how many digits; nor did their calculation fail; and it came to pass as they

---

[1] Ps. 35. 10.   [2] *Ibid.*, 19. 6.   [3] *City of God*, BK. XI. 23.
[4] *Ibid.*, BK. XII. 3.   [5] Ps. 139. 7.   [6] Gen. 16. 13, 14.
[7] Wisd. 2. 26. old version.

[8] Ps. 73. 27.   [9] Wisd. 13. 9.   [10] Ps. 138. 6.
[11] Ps. 34. 18; 145. 18.

foretold; and they wrote down the rules they had found out, and these are read at this day, and out of them do others foretell in what year, and month of the year, and what day of the month, and what hour of the day, and what part of its light, moon or sun is to be eclipsed, and so it shall be, as it is foreshewed. At these things men that know not this art marvel and are astonished, and they that know it exult and are puffed up; and by an ungodly pride departing from Thee, and failing of Thy light, they foresee a failure of the sun's light, which shall be, so long before, but see not their own, which is. For they search not religiously whence they have the wit, wherewith they search out this. And finding that Thou madest them, they give not themselves up to Thee, to preserve what Thou madest, nor sacrifice to Thee what they have made themselves; nor slay their own soaring imaginations, as fowls of the air,[1] nor their own diving curiosities (wherewith, like the fishes of the sea, they wander over the unknown paths of the abyss), nor their own luxuriousness, as "beasts of the field,"[2] that Thou, Lord, "a consuming fire,"[3] mayest burn up those dead cares of theirs, and re-create themselves immortally.

5. But they knew not the way, Thy Word, by Whom Thou madest these things which they number, and themselves who number, and the sense whereby they perceive what they number, and the understanding out of which they number; or that of Thy wisdom there is no number.[4] But the Only Begotten is Himself "made unto us wisdom, and righteousness, and sanctification,"[5] and was numbered among us, and paid tribute unto Cæsar.[6] They knew not this Way whereby to descend to Him from themselves, and by Him ascend unto Him. They knew not this way, and deemed themselves exalted amongst the stars[7] and shining; and behold, they fell upon the earth,[8] and "their foolish heart was darkened."[9] They discourse many things truly concerning the creature; but Truth, Artificer of the creature, they seek not piously, and therefore find Him not; or if they find Him, knowing Him to be God, they glorify Him not as God, neither are thankful,[10] but become vain in their imaginations, and profess themselves to be wise,[11] attributing to themselves what is Thine; and thereby with most perverse blindness, study to impute to Thee what is their own, forging lies of Thee Who are the Truth, and changing the glory of

the uncorruptible God into an image made like corruptible man, and to birds, and four-footed beasts, and creeping things,[12] changing Thy truth into a lie, and worshipping and serving the creature more than the Creator.[13]

6. Yet many truths concerning the creature retained I from these men, and saw the reason thereof from calculations, the succession of times, and the visible testimonies of the stars; and compared them with the saying of Manichæus, which in his phrenzy he had written most largely on these subjects; but discovered not any account of the solstices, or equinoxes, or the eclipses of the greater lights, nor whatever of this sort I had learned in the books of secular philosophy. But I was commanded to believe; and yet it corresponded not with what had been established by calculations and my own sight, but was quite contrary.

[IV] 7. Doth then, O Lord God of truth, whoso knoweth these things therefore please Thee? Surely unhappy is he who knoweth all these, and knoweth not Thee: but happy whoso knoweth Thee, though he know not these. And whoso knoweth both Thee and them is not the happier for them, but for Thee only, if, knowing Thee, he glorifies Thee as God, and is thankful, and becomes not vain in his imaginations.[14] For as he is better off who knows how to possess a tree, and returns thanks to Thee for the use thereof, although he know not how many cubits high it is, or how wide it spreads, than he that can measure it and count all its boughs, and neither owns it nor knows or loves its Creator: so a believer, whose all this world of wealth is,[15] and who having nothing yet possesseth all things,[16] by cleaving unto Thee, whom all things serve, though he know not even the circles of the Great Bear, yet is it folly to doubt but he is in a better state than one who can measure the heavens, and number the stars, and poise the elements, yet neglecteth Thee "who hast made all things in number, weight, and measure."[17]

[V] 8. But yet who bade that Manichæus write on these things also, skill in which was no element of piety? For Thou hast said to man, Behold, piety and wisdom;[18] of which he might be ignorant, though he had perfect knowledge of these things; but these things, since, knowing not, he most impudently dared to teach, he plainly could have no knowledge of piety. For it is vanity to make profession of these worldly things even when known; but confession to

[1]See above. bk. iii. 16, below bk. x. 41.
[2]Ps. 8. 7, 8.   [3]Deut. 4. 24.   [4]Ps. 147. 5, Vulg.
[5]I Cor. 1. 30.   [6]Matt. 17. 27.   [7]Isa. 14. 13.
[8]Rev. 12. 4.   [9]Rom. 1. 21.   [10]Ibid.   [11]Ibid., 22.

[12]Ibid., 23.   [13]Ibid., 25.   [14]Rom. 1. 21.
[15]Prov. 17. 6, in the LXX.   [16]II Cor. 6. 10.
[17]Wisd. 2. 20.   [18]Cf. Job, 28. 28, in the LXX.

Thee is piety. Wherefore this wanderer to this end spake much of these things, that, convicted by those who had truly learned them, it might be manifest what understanding he had in the other abstruser things. For he would not have himself meanly thought of, but went about to persuade men, "That the Holy Ghost, the Comforter and Enricher of Thy faithful ones, was with plenary authority personally within him." When then he was found out to have taught falsely of the heaven and stars, and of the motions of the sun and moon (although these things pertain not to the doctrine of religion), yet his sacrilegious presumption would become evident enough, seeing he delivered things which not only he knew not, but which were falsified, with so mad a vanity of pride that he sought to ascribe them to himself, as to a divine person.

9. For when I hear any Christian brother ignorant of these things, and mistaken on them, I can patiently behold such a man holding his opinion; nor do I see that any ignorance as to the position or character of the corporeal creation can injure him, so long as he doth not believe anything unworthy of Thee, O Lord, the Creator of all. But it doth injure him if he imagine it to pertain to the form of the doctrine of piety, and will yet affirm that too stiffly whereof he is ignorant. And yet is even such an infirmity, in the infancy of faith, borne by our mother Charity, till the new-born may grow up "unto a perfect man," so as not to be "carried about with every wind of doctrine."[1] But in him who in such wise presumed to be the teacher, source, guide, chief of all whom he could so persuade, that whoso followed him thought that he followed not a mere man, but Thy Holy Spirit; who would not judge that so great madness, when once convicted of having taught anything false, were to be detested and utterly rejected? But I had not as yet clearly ascertained whether the vicissitudes of longer and shorter days and nights, and of day and night itself, with the eclipses of the greater lights, and whatever else of the kind I had read of in other books, might be explained consistently with his sayings; so that, if they by any means might, it should still remain a question to me whether it were so or no; but I might, on account of his reputed sanctity, rest my credence upon his authority.

[VI] 10. And for almost all those nine years, wherein with unsettled mind I had been their disciple, I had longed but too intensely for the coming of this Faustus. For the rest of the sect, whom by chance I had lighted upon when unable to solve my objections about these things, still held out to me the coming of this Faustus, by conference with whom these and greater difficulties, if I had them, were to be most readily and abundantly cleared. When then he came, I found him a man of pleasing discourse, and who could speak fluently and in better terms, yet still but the self-same things which they were wont to say. But what availed the utmost neatness of the cup-bearer to my thirst for a more precious draught? Mine ears were already cloyed with the like, nor did they seem to me therefore better, because better said; nor therefore true, because eloquent; nor the soul therefore wise, because the face was comely and the language graceful. But they who held him out to me were no good judges of things; and therefore to them he appeared understanding and wise, because in words pleasing. I felt however that another sort of people were suspicious even of truth, and refused to assent to it, if delivered in a smooth and copious discourse. But Thou, O my God, hadst already taught me by wonderful and secret ways, and therefore I believe that Thou taughtest me, because it is truth, nor is there besides Thee any teacher of truth, where or whencesoever it may shine upon us.[2] Of Thyself therefore had I now learned, that neither ought anything to seem to be spoken truly, because eloquently; nor therefore falsely, because the utterance of the lips is inharmonious; nor, again, therefore true, because rudely delivered; nor therefore false, because the language is rich; but that wisdom and folly are as wholesome and unwholesome food; and adorned or unadorned phrases, as courtly or country vessels; either kind of meats may be served up in either kind of dishes.

11. That greediness then, wherewith I had of so long time expected that man, was delighted verily with his action and feeling when disputing, and his choice and readiness of words to clothe his ideas. I was then delighted, and, with many others and more than they, did I praise and extol him. It troubled me, however, that in the assembly of his auditors I was not allowed to put in, and communicate those questions that troubled me, in familiar converse with him. Which when I might, and with my friends began to engage his ears at such times as it was not unbecoming for him to discuss with me, and had brought forward such things as moved me, I found him first utterly ignorant of liberal sciences, save grammar, and that but in an ordinary way. But because he had read some of Tully's *Orations*, a very few books of Seneca,

[1] Eph. 4. 13, 14.

[2] See below, BK. VII. 15.

some things of the poets, and such few volumes of his own sect as were written in Latin and neatly, and was daily practised in speaking, he acquired a certain eloquence, which proved the more pleasing and seductive because under the guidance of a good wit and with a kind of natural gracefulness. Is it not thus, as I recall it, O Lord my God, Thou Judge of my conscience? Before Thee is my heart, and my remembrance, Who didst at that time direct me by the hidden mystery of Thy providence, and didst set those shameful errors of mine before my face, that I might see and hate them.

[VII] 12. For after it was clear that he was ignorant of those arts in which I thought he excelled, I began to despair of his opening and solving the difficulties which perplexed me (of which indeed however ignorant, he might have held the truths of piety, had he not been a Manichee). For their books are fraught with prolix fables, of the heaven, and stars, sun, and moon, and I now no longer thought him able satisfactorily to decide what I much desired, whether, on comparison of these things with the calculations I had elsewhere read, the account given in the books of Manichæus were preferable, or at least as good. Which when I proposed to be considered and discussed, he, so far modestly, shrunk from the burthen. For he knew that he knew not these things, and was not ashamed to confess it. For he was not one of those talking persons, many of whom I had endured, who undertook to teach me these things, and said nothing. But this man had a heart, though not right towards Thee, yet neither altogether treacherous to himself. For he was not altogether ignorant of his own ignorance, nor would he rashly be entangled in a dispute whence he could neither retreat, nor extricate himself fairly. Even for this I liked him the better. For fairer is the modesty of a candid mind than the knowledge of those things which I desired; and such I found him, in all the more difficult and subtile questions.

13. My zeal for the writings of Manichæus being thus blunted, and despairing yet more of their other teachers, seeing that, in divers things which perplexed me, he, so renowned among them, had so turned out; I began to engage with him in the study of that literature on which he also was much set (and which as rhetoric-reader I was at that time teaching young students at Carthage), and to read with him either what himself desired to hear, or such as I judged fit for his genius. But all my efforts whereby I had purposed to advance in that sect, upon knowledge of that man, came utterly to an end; not that I detached myself from them altogether, but as one finding nothing better, I had settled to be content meanwhile with what I had in whatever way fallen upon, unless by chance something more eligible should dawn upon me. Thus that Faustus, to so many a snare of death, had now, neither willing nor witting it, begun to loosen that wherein I was taken. For Thy hands, O my God, in the secret purpose of Thy providence, did not forsake my soul; and out of my mother's heart's blood, through her tears night and day poured out, was a sacrifice offered for me unto Thee; and Thou didst deal with me by wondrous ways.[1] Thou didst it, O my God: for the steps of a man are ordered by the Lord, and He shall dispose his way.[2] Or how shall we obtain salvation, but from Thy hand, re-making what It made?

[VIII] 14. Thou didst deal with me, that I should be persuaded to go to Rome, and to teach there rather what I was teaching at Carthage. And how I was persuaded to this, I will not neglect to confess to Thee: because herein also the deepest recesses of Thy wisdom, and Thy most present mercy to us, must be considered and confessed. I did not wish therefore to go to Rome, because higher gains and higher dignities were warranted me by my friends who persuaded me to this (though even these things had at that time an influence over my mind), but my chief and almost only reason was that I heard that young men studied there more peacefully, and were kept quiet under a restraint of more regular discipline; so that they did not, at their pleasure, petulantly rush into the school of one whose pupils they were not, nor were even admitted without his permission. Whereas at Carthage there reigns among the scholars a most disgraceful and unruly license. They burst in audaciously, and with gestures almost frantic disturb all order which anyone hath established for the good of his scholars. Divers outrages they commit, with a wonderful stolidity, punishable by law, did not custom uphold them; that custom evincing them to be the more miserable, in that they now do as lawful what by Thy eternal law shall never be lawful; and they think they do it unpunished, whereas they are punished with the very blindness whereby they do it, and suffer incomparably worse than what they do. The manners then which, when a student, I would not make my own,[3] I was fain, as a teacher, to endure in others: and so I was well pleased to go where all that knew it assured me that the

[1]Joel, 2. 26.   [2]Ps. 37. 23.   [3]See above, Bk. III. 6.

like was not done. But Thou, "my refuge and my portion in the land of the living,"[1] that I might change my earthly dwelling for the salvation of my soul, at Carthage didst goad me, that I might thereby be torn from it; and at Rome didst proffer me allurements, whereby I might be drawn thither by men in love with a dying life, the one doing frantic, the other promising vain, things; and, to correct my steps, didst secretly use their and my own perverseness. For both they who disturbed my quiet were blinded with a disgraceful phrenzy, and they who invited me elsewhere savoured of earth. And I, who here detested real misery, was there seeking unreal happiness.

15. But why I went hence, and went thither, Thou knewest, O God, yet shewedst it neither to me nor to my mother, who grievously bewailed my journey, and followed me as far as the sea. But I deceived her, holding me by force, that either she might keep me back, or go with me, and I feigned that I had a friend whom I could not leave till he had a fair wind to sail. And I lied to my mother, and such a mother, and escaped: for this also hast Thou mercifully forgiven me, preserving me, thus full of execrable defilements, from the waters of the sea, for the water[2] of Thy Grace; whereby when I was cleansed, the streams of my mother's eyes should be dried, with which for me she daily watered the ground under her face. And yet refusing to return without me, I scarcely persuaded her to stay that night in a place hard by our ship, where was an Oratory in memory of the blessed Cyprian. That night I privily departed, but she was not behind in weeping and prayer. And what, O Lord, was she with so many tears asking of Thee, but that Thou wouldest not suffer me to sail? But Thou, in the depth of Thy counsels and hearing the main point of her desire, regardest not what she then asked, that Thou mightest make me what she ever asked. The wind blew and swelled our sails, and withdrew the shore from our sight; and she on the morrow was there, frantic with sorrow, and with complaints and groans filled Thine ears, who didst then disregard them; whilst, through my desires, Thou wert hurrying me to end all desire, and the earthly part of her affection to me was chastened by the allotted scourge of sorrows. For she loved my being with her, as mothers do, but much more than many; and she knew not how great joy Thou wert about to work for her out of my absence. She knew not; therefore did she weep and wail, and by this agony there appeared in her the inheritance of Eve, with sorrow seeking what in sorrow she had brought forth. And yet, after accusing my treachery and hardheartedness, she betook herself again to intercede to Thee for me, went to her wonted place, and I to Rome.

[IX] 16. And lo, there was I received by the scourge of bodily sickness, and I was going down to hell, carrying all the sins which I had committed, both against Thee and myself, and others, many and grievous, over and above that bond of original sin whereby we all die in Adam.[3] For Thou hadst not forgiven me any of these things in Christ, nor had He "abolished" by His cross "the enmity" which by my sins I had incurred with Thee. For how should He, by the crucifixion of a phantasm, which I believed Him to be? So true, then, was the death of my soul, as that of His flesh seemed to me false; and how true the death of His body, so false was the life of my soul, which did not believe it. And now the fever heightening, I was parting and departing for ever. For had I then parted hence, whither had I departed, but into fire and torments, such as my misdeeds deserved in the truth of Thy appointment? And this she knew not, yet in absence prayed for me. But Thou, everywhere present, heardst her where she was, and, where I was, hadst compassion upon me; that I should recover the health of my body, though phrenzied as yet in my sacrilegious heart. For I did not in all that danger desire Thy baptism; and I was better as a boy, when I begged it of my mother's piety, as I have before recited and confessed.[4] But I had grown up to my own shame, and I madly scoffed at the prescripts of Thy medicine, who wouldest not suffer me, being such, to die a double death. With which wound had my mother's heart been pierced, it could never be healed. For I cannot express the affection she bare to me, and with how much more vehement anguish she was now in labour of me in the spirit than at her childbearing in the flesh.

17. I see not then how she should have been healed, had such a death of mine stricken through the bowels of her love. And where would have been those her so strong and unceasing prayers, unintermitting to Thee alone? But wouldest Thou, God of mercies, despise the "contrite and humbled heart"[5] of that chaste and sober widow, so frequent in almsdeeds, so full of duty and service to Thy saints, no day intermitting the oblation at Thine altar, twice a day, morning and evening, without any intermission, coming to Thy church, not for idle tat-

---

[1] Ps. 142. 5.   [2] The waters of Baptism.

[3] I Cor. 15. 22.   [4] See above, BK. I. 10.   [5] Ps. 51. 19.

tlings and old wives' "fables";[1] but that she might hear Thee in Thy discourses, and Thou her in her prayers. Couldest Thou despise and reject from Thy aid the tears of such an one, wherewith she begged of Thee not gold or silver, nor any mutable or passing good, but the salvation of her son's soul? Thou, by whose gift she was such? Never, Lord. Yea, Thou wert at hand, and wert hearing and doing, in that order wherein Thou hadst determined before that it should be done. Far be it that Thou shouldest deceive her in Thy visions and answers, some whereof I have,[2] some I have not[3] mentioned, which she laid up in her faithful heart, and ever praying, urged upon Thee, as Thine own handwriting. For Thou, because Thy mercy endureth for ever,[4] vouchsafest to those to whom Thou forgivest all their debts, to become also a debtor by Thy promises.

[X] 18. Thou recoveredst me then of that sickness, and healedst the son of Thy handmaid, for the time in body, that he might live, for Thee to bestow upon him a better and more abiding health. And even then, at Rome, I joined myself to those deceiving and deceived "holy ones"; not with their disciples only (of which number was he in whose house I had fallen sick and recovered); but also with those whom they call "The Elect." For I still thought "that it was not we that sin, but that I know not what other nature sinned in us"; and it delighted my pride to be free from blame; and when I had done any evil, not to confess I had done any, "that Thou mightest heal my soul because it had sinned against Thee":[5] but I loved to excuse it, and to accuse I know not what other thing, which was with me, but which I was not. But in truth it was wholly I, and mine impiety had divided me against myself: and that sin was the more incurable whereby I did not judge myself a sinner; and execrable iniquity it was, that I had rather have Thee, Thee, O God Almighty, to be overcome in me to my destruction, than myself of Thee to salvation. Not as yet then hadst Thou set a watch before my mouth, and a door of safe keeping around my lips, that my heart might not turn aside to wicked speeches, to make excuses of sins, with men that work iniquity:[6] and, therefore, was I still united with their "Elect."

19. But now despairing to make proficiency in that false doctrine, even those things (with which if I should find no better, I had resolved to rest contented) I now held more laxly and

carelessly. For there half arose a thought in me, that those philosophers whom they call "Academics" were wiser than the rest, for that they held, men ought to doubt everything, and laid down that no truth can be comprehended by man: for so, not then understanding even their meaning, I also was clearly convinced that they thought, as they are commonly reported. Yet did I freely and openly discourage that host of mine from that over-confidence which I perceived him to have in those fables which the books of Manichæus are full of. Yet I lived in more familiar friendship with them than with others who were not of this heresy. Nor did I maintain it with my ancient eagerness; still my intimacy with that sect (Rome secretly harbouring many of them) made me slower to seek any other way: especially since I despaired of finding the truth, from which they had turned me aside, in Thy Church, O Lord of heaven and earth, Creator of all things visible and invisible: and it seemed to me very unseemly to believe Thee to have the shape of human flesh, and to be bounded by the bodily lineaments of our members. And because, when I wished to think on my God, I knew not what to think of, but a mass of bodies (for what was not such, did not seem to me to be any thing), this was the greatest and almost only cause of my inevitable error.

20. For hence I believed Evil also to be some such kind of substance, and to have its own foul and hideous bulk; whether gross, which they called earth, or thin and subtile (like the body of the air), which they imagine to be some malignant mind, creeping through that earth. And because a piety, such as it was, constrained me to believe, that the good God never created any evil nature, I conceived two masses, contrary to one another, both unbounded, but the evil narrower, the good more expansive. And from this pestilent beginning, the other sacrilegious conceits followed on me. For when my mind endeavoured to recur to the Catholic faith, I was driven back, since that was not the Catholic faith, which I thought to be so. And I seemed to myself more reverential, if I believed of Thee, my God (to whom Thy mercies confess out of my mouth), as unbounded, at least on other sides, although on that one where the mass of evil was opposed to Thee, I was constrained to confess Thee bounded; than if on all sides I should imagine Thee to be bounded by the form of a human body. And it seemed to me better to believe Thee to have created no evil (which to me ignorant seemed not some only, but a bodily, substance, because I could not conceive of mind

---

[1]I Tim. 5. 10.   [2]See above, Bk. III. 19, 20, 21.
[3]Ibid., 21.   [4]Ps. 118. 1.   [5]Ps. 41. 4.
[6]Ps. 141. 3, 4, old version.

unless as a subtile body, and that diffused in definite spaces) than to believe the nature of evil, such as I conceived it, could come from Thee. Yea, and our Saviour Himself, Thy Only Begotten, I believed to have been reached forth (as it were) for our salvation, out of the mass of Thy most lucid substance, so as to believe nothing of Him but what I could imagine in my vanity. His Nature then, being such, I thought could not be born of the Virgin Mary, without being mingled with the flesh: and how that which I had so figured to myself, could be mingled, and not defiled, I saw not. I feared therefore to believe Him born in the flesh, lest I should be forced to believe Him defiled by the flesh. Now will Thy spiritual ones mildly and lovingly smile upon me if they shall read these my confessions. Yet such was I.

[XI] 21. Furthermore, what the Manichees had criticised[1] in Thy Scriptures, I thought could not be defended; yet at times verily I had a wish to confer upon these several points with someone very well skilled in those books, and to make trial what he thought thereon: for the words of one Helpidius, as he spoke and disputed face to face against the said Manichees, had begun to stir me even at Carthage: in that he had produced things out of the Scriptures not easily withstood, the Manichees' answer whereto seemed to me weak. And this answer they liked not to give publicly, but only to us in private. It was that the Scriptures of the New Testament had been corrupted by I know not whom, who wished to ingraft the law of the Jews upon the Christian faith: yet themselves produced not any uncorrupted copies. But I, conceiving of things corporeal only, was mainly held down, vehemently oppressed and in a manner suffocated by those "masses";[2] panting under which after the breath of Thy truth, I could not breathe it pure and untainted.

[XII] 22. I began then diligently to practise that for which I came to Rome, to teach rhetoric; and first, to gather some to my house to whom, and through whom, I had begun to be known; when lo, I found other offences committed in Rome, to which I was not exposed in Africa. True, those "subvertings"[3] by profligate young men were not here practised, as was told me: but on a sudden, said they, to avoid paying their master's stipend, a number of youths plot together, and remove to another; breakers of faith, who for love of money hold justice cheap. These also my heart "hated," though not with

a "perfect hatred":[4] for perchance I hated them more because I was to suffer by them, than because they did things utterly unlawful. Of a truth such are base persons, and they go a-whoring from Thee, loving these fleeting mockeries of things temporal, and filthy lucre which fouls the hand that grasps it; hugging the fleeting world, and despising Thee, Who abidest, and recallest, and forgivest the adulteress soul of man, when she returns to Thee. And now I hate such depraved and crooked persons, though I love them if corrigible, so as to prefer to money the learning which they acquire, and to learning, Thee, O God, the truth and fulness of assured good, and most pure peace. But then I rather for my own sake misliked them evil, than liked and wished them good for Thine.

[XIII] 23. When therefore they of Milan had sent to Rome to the prefect of the city, to furnish them with a rhetoric reader for their city, and send him at the public expense, I made application (through those very persons, intoxicated with Manichæan vanities, to be freed wherefrom I was to go, neither of us however knowing it) that Symmachus, then prefect of the city, would try me by setting me some subject, and so send me. To Milan I came, to Ambrose the Bishop, known to the whole world as among the best of men, Thy devout servant; whose eloquent discourse did then plentifully dispense unto Thy people the flour of Thy wheat, the "gladness" of Thy "oil," and the sober inebriation of Thy "wine."[5] To him was I unknowing led by Thee, that by him I might knowingly be led to Thee. That man of God received me as a father, and shewed me an episcopal kindness on my coming. Thenceforth I began to love him, at first indeed not as a teacher of the truth (which I utterly despaired of in Thy Church), but as a person kind towards myself. And I listened diligently to him preaching to the people, not with that intent I ought, but, as it were, trying his eloquence, whether it answered the fame thereof, or flowed fuller or lower than was reported; and I hung on his words attentively; but of the matter I was as a careless and scornful looker-on; and I was delighted with the sweetness of his discourse, more recondite, yet in manner less winning and harmonious than that of Faustus. Of the matter, however, there was no comparison; for the one was wandering amid Manichæan delusions, the other teaching salvation most soundly. But "salvation is far from sinners,"[6] such as I then stood before

---

[1]See above, BK. III. 14.   [2]See above, BK. V. 19.
[3]See BK. III. 6.

[4]Ps. 139. 22.   [5]Ps. 4. 7; 104. 15.
[6]Ps. 119. 155.

him; and yet was I drawing nearer by little and little, and unconsciously.

[XIV] 24. For though I took no pains to learn what he spake, but only to hear how he spake (for that empty care alone was left me, despairing of a way open for man to Thee); yet, together with the words which I would choose, came also into my mind the things which I would refuse; for I could not separate them. And while I opened my heart to admit "how eloquently he spake," there also entered "how truly he spake"; but this by degrees. For first, these things also had now begun to appear to me capable of defence; and the Catholic faith, for which I had thought nothing could be said against the Manichees' objections, I now thought might be maintained without shamelessness; especially after I had heard one or two places of the Old Testament resolved, and oft-times "in a figure," which when I understood literally, I was "slain" spiritually.[1] Very many places then of those books having been explained, I now blamed my despair in believing that no answer could be given to such as hated and scoffed at the Law and the Prophets. Yet did I not therefore then see that the Catholic way was to be held because it also could find learned maintainers, who could at large and with some shew of reason answer objections; nor that what I held was therefore to be condemned because both sides could be maintained. For the Catholic cause seemed to me in such sort not vanquished, as still not as yet to be victorious.

25. Hereupon I earnestly bent my mind, to see if in any way I could by any certain proof convict the Manichees of falsehood. Could I once have conceived a spiritual substance, all their strong holds had been beaten down, and cast utterly out of my mind; but I could not. Notwithstanding, concerning the frame of this world, and the whole of nature, which the senses of the flesh can reach to, as I more and more considered and compared things, I judged the tenets of most of the philosophers to have been much more probable. So then after the manner of the Academics (as they are supposed[2]) doubting of everything, and wavering between all, I settled so far, that the Manichees were to be abandoned; judging that, even while doubting, I might not continue in that sect, to which I already preferred some of the philosophers; to which philosophers notwithstanding, for that they were without the saving Name of Christ, I utterly refused to commit the cure of my sick soul. I determined therefore so long to be a cate-

chumen in the Catholic Church, to which I had been commended by my parents, till something certain should dawn upon me, whither I might steer my course.

BOOK VI. *Arrival of Monica at Milan; her obedience to St. Ambrose, and his value for her; St. Ambrose's habits; Augustine's gradual abandonment of error; finds that he has blamed the Church Catholic wrongly; desire of absolute certainty, but struck with the contrary analogy of God's natural Providence; how shaken in his worldly pursuits; God's guidance of his friend Alypius; Augustine debates with himself and his friends about their mode of life; his inveterate sins, and dread of judgment.*

[I] 1. O Thou, my hope from my youth,[3] where wert Thou to me, and wither wert Thou gone? Hadst not Thou created me, and separated me from the beasts of the field, and fowls of the air? Thou hadst made me wiser, yet did I walk in darkness, and in slippery places, and sought Thee abroad[4] out of myself, and found not the God of my heart; and had come into the depths of the sea, and distrusted and despaired of ever finding truth. My mother had now come to me, resolute through piety, following me over sea and land, in all perils confiding in Thee. For in perils of the sea, she comforted the very mariners (by whom passengers unacquainted with the deep use rather to be comforted when troubled), assuring them of a safe arrival, because Thou hadst by a vision assured her thereof. She found me in grievous peril, through despair of ever finding truth. But when I had discovered to her that I was now no longer a Manichee, though not yet a Catholic Christian, she was not overjoyed as at something unexpected; although she was now assured concerning that part of my misery for which she bewailed me as one dead, though to be reawakened by Thee, carrying me forth upon the bier of her thoughts, that Thou mightest say to the son of the widow, "Young man, I say unto thee, Arise"; and he should revive, and begin to speak, and thou shouldest deliver him to his mother.[5] Her heart then was shaken with no tumultuous exultation, when she heard that what she daily with tears desired of Thee was already in so great part realized; in that, though I had not yet attained the truth, I was rescued from falsehood; but, as being assured that Thou, Who hadst promised the whole, wouldest one day give the rest, most

[1] I Cor. 113. 12; II Cor. 3. 6. [2] See above, BK. V. 19.

[3] Ps. 71. 5. [4] See below, BK. VII. 11, 16.
[5] Luke, 7. 12. 15.

calmly, and with an heart full of confidence, she replied to me, "She believed in Christ, that before she departed this life, she should see me a Catholic believer."[1] Thus much to me. But to Thee, Fountain of mercies, poured she forth more copious prayers and tears, that Thou wouldest hasten Thy help, and enlighten my darkness; and she hastened the more eagerly to the church, and hung upon the lips of Ambrose, praying for the fountain of that water, which springeth up into life everlasting.[2] But that man she loved as an angel of God, because she knew that by him I had been brought for the present to that doubtful state of faith I now was in, through which she anticipated most confidently that I should pass from sickness unto health, after the access, as it were, of a sharper fit, which physicians call "the crisis."

[II] 2. When then my mother had once, as she was wont in Africa, brought to the churches built in memory of the Saints[3] certain cakes, and bread and wine, and was forbidden by the door-keeper; so soon as she knew that the Bishop had forbidden this, she so piously and obediently embraced his wishes that I myself wondered how readily she censured her own practice rather than discuss his prohibition. For wine-bibbing did not lay siege to her spirit, nor did love of wine provoke her to hatred of the truth, as it doth too many (both men and women), who revolt at a lesson of sobriety, as men well-drunk at a draught mingled with water. But she, when she had brought her basket with the accustomed festival-food, to be but tasted by herself and then given away, never joined therewith more than one small cup of wine, diluted according to her own abstemious habits, which for courtesy she would taste. And if there were many churches of the departed saints, that were to be honoured in that manner, she still carried round that same one cup, to be used everywhere; and this, though not only made very watery, but unpleasantly heated with carrying about, she would distribute to those about her by small sips; for she sought their devotion, not pleasure. So soon, then, as she found this custom to be forbidden by that famous preacher and most pious prelate, even to those that would use it soberly, lest so an occasion of excess might be given to the drunken; and for that these, as it were, anniversary funeral solemnities did much resemble the superstition of the Gentiles, she most willingly forbore it: and for a basket filled

with fruits of the earth, she had learned to bring to the churches of the martyrs a breast filled with more purified petitions, and to give what she could to the poor; that so the communication of the Lord's Body might be there rightly celebrated where, after the example of His Passion, the martyrs had been sacrificed and crowned. But yet it seems to me, O Lord my God, and thus thinks my heart of it in Thy sight, that perhaps she would not so readily have yielded to the cutting off of this custom, had it been forbidden by another, whom she loved not as Ambrose, whom, for my salvation, she loved most entirely; and he her again, for her most religious conversation, whereby in good works, so "fervent in spirit,"[4] she was constant at church; so that, when he saw me, he often burst forth into her praises; congratulating me that I had such a mother; not knowing what a son she had in me, who doubted of all these things, and imagined the way to life could not be found out.

[III] 3. Nor did I yet groan in my prayers that Thou wouldest help me; but my spirit was wholly intent on learning, and restless to dispute. And Ambrose himself, as the world counts happy, I esteemed a happy man, whom personages so great held in such honour; only his celibacy seemed to me a painful course. But what hope he bore within him, what struggles he had against the temptations which beset his very excellencies, or what comfort in adversities, and what sweet joys Thy Bread had for the hidden mouth of his spirit when chewing the cud thereof, I neither could conjecture, nor had experienced. Nor did he know the tides of my feelings, or the abyss of my danger. For I could not ask of him what I would as I would, being shut out both from his ear and speech by multitudes of busy people, whose weaknesses he served. With whom when he was not taken up (which was but a little time), he was either refreshing his body with the sustenance absolutely necessary, or his mind with reading. But when he was reading, his eye glided over the pages, and his heart searched out the sense, but his voice and tongue were at rest. Oft-times when we had come (for no man was forbidden to enter, nor was it his wont that any who came should be announced to him), we saw him thus reading to himself, and never otherwise; and having long sat silent (for who durst intrude on one so intent?), we were fain to depart, conjecturing that in the small interval which he obtained, free from the din of others' business, for the recruiting of his mind, he was loath to be taken off; and perchance he dreaded

---

[1]*Fidelem Catholicum*, one baptized into the Catholic faith.

[2]John, 4. 14.   [3]Cf. *City of God*, Bk. VIII. 27.   [4]Rom. 12. 11.

lest, if the author he read should deliver anything obscurely, some attentive or perplexed
hearer should desire him to expound it, or to discuss some of the harder questions; so that his
time being thus spent, he could not turn over so
many volumes as he desired; although the preserving of his voice (which a very little speaking
would weaken) might be the truer reason for his
reading to himself. But with what intent soever
he did it, certainly in such a man it was good.

4. I however certainly had no opportunity of
enquiring what I wished of that so holy oracle
of Thine, his breast, unless the thing might be
answered briefly. But those tides in me, to be
poured out to him, required his full leisure, and
never found it. I heard him indeed, every Lord's
day, "rightly expounding the Word of Truth"[1]
among the people; and I was more and more
convinced that all the knots of those crafty calumnies, which those our deceivers had knit
against the Divine Books, could be unravelled.
But when I understood withal that "man, created by Thee, after Thine own image"[2] was not
so understood by Thy spiritual sons, whom of
the Catholic Mother Thou hast born again
through grace, as though they believed and conceived of Thee as bounded by human shape (although what a spiritual substance should be I
had not even a faint or shadowy notion); yet
with joy I blushed at having so many years
barked not against the Catholic faith, but against
the fictions of carnal imaginations. For so rash
and impious had I been that what I ought by enquiring to have learned, I had pronounced on,
condemning. For Thou, Most High, and most
near; most secret, and most present; Who hast
not limbs some larger, some smaller, but art
wholly everywhere and nowhere in space, art not
of such corporeal shape, yet hast Thou made
man after Thine own image; and behold, from
head to foot is he contained in space.

[IV] 5. Ignorant then how this Thy image
should subsist, I should have knocked and proposed the doubt, how it was to be believed, not
insultingly opposed it, as if believed. Doubt,
then, what to hold for certain the more sharply
gnawed my heart, the more ashamed I was that,
so long deluded and deceived by the promise of
certainties, I had with childish error and vehemence prated of so many uncertainties. For that
they were falsehoods became clear to me later.
However I was certain that they were uncertain,
and that I had formerly accounted them certain,
when with a blind contentiousness I accused
Thy Catholic Church, whom I now discovered,

not indeed as yet to teach truly, but at least not
to teach that for which I had grievously censured her. So I was confounded, and converted:
and I joyed, O my God, that the One Only
Church, the body of Thine Only Son (wherein
the name of Christ had been put upon me as an
infant), had no taste for infantine conceits;
nor, in her sound doctrine, maintained any tenet
which should confine Thee, the Creator of all, in
space, however great and large, yet bounded everywhere by the limits of a human form.

6. I joyed also that the old Scriptures of the
Law and the Prophets were laid before me, not
now to be perused with that eye to which before
they seemed absurd, when I reviled Thy holy
ones for so thinking, whereas indeed they
thought not so: and with joy I heard Ambrose
in his sermons to the people oftentimes most
diligently recommend this text for a rule, "The
letter killeth, but the Spirit giveth life";[3] whilst
he drew aside the mystic veil, laying open spiritually what according to the "letter" seemed to
teach something unsound; teaching herein nothing that offended me, though he taught what I
knew not as yet whether it were true. For I kept
my heart from assenting to anything, fearing to
fall headlong; but by hanging in suspense I was
the worse killed. For I wished to be as assured
of the things I saw not as I was that seven and
three are ten. For I was not so mad as to think
that even this could not be comprehended; but
I desired to have other things as clear as this,
whether things corporeal, which were not present to my senses, or spiritual, whereof I knew
not how to conceive, except corporeally. And by
believing might I have been cured, that so the
eyesight of my soul, being cleared, might in
some way be directed to Thy truth, which abideth always, and in no part faileth. But as it happens that one who has tried a bad physician
fears to trust himself with a good one, so was it
with the health of my soul, which could not be
healed but by believing, and, lest it should believe falsehoods, refused to be cured; resisting
Thy hands, Who hast prepared the medicines of
faith, and hast applied them to the diseases of
the whole world. and given unto them so great
authority.

[V] 7. Being led, however, from this to prefer
the Catholic doctrine, I felt that her proceeding
was more unassuming and honest, in that she required to be believed things not demonstrated
(whether it was that they could in themselves
be demonstrated but not to certain persons, or
could not at all be), whereas among the Mani-

---

[1] II Tim. 2. 15.   [2] Col. 13. 10; Gen. 1. 26, 27.   [3] II Cor. 3. 6.

chees our credulity was mocked by a promise of certain knowledge, and then so many most fabulous and absurd things were imposed to be believed, because they could not be demonstrated. Then Thou, O Lord, little by little with most tender and most merciful hand touching and composing my heart, didst persuade me—considering what innumerable things I believed, which I saw not, nor was present while they were done, as so many things in secular history, so many reports of places and of cities which I had not seen; so many of friends, so many of physicians, so many continually of other men, which unless we should believe, we should do nothing at all in this life; lastly, with how unshaken an assurance I believed of what parents I was born, which I could not know had I not believed upon hearsay—considering all this, Thou didst persuade me, that not they who believed Thy Books (which Thou hast established in so great authority among almost all nations), but they who believed them not, were to be blamed; and that they were not to be heard, who should say to me, "How knowest thou those Scriptures to have been imparted unto mankind by the Spirit of the one true and most true God?" For this very thing was of all most to be believed, since no contentiousness of blasphemous questionings, of all that multitude which I had read in the self-contradicting philosophers, could wring this belief from me, "That Thou art" whatsoever Thou wert (what I knew not), and "That the government of human things belongs to Thee."

8. This I believed, sometimes more strongly, more weakly other-whiles; yet I ever believed both that Thou wert and hadst a care of us; though I was ignorant, both what was to be thought of Thy substance and what way led or led back to Thee. Since then we were too weak by abstract reasonings to find out truth, and for this very cause needed the authority of Holy Writ, I had now begun to believe that Thou wouldest never have given such excellency of authority to that Writ in all lands, hadst Thou not willed thereby to be believed in, thereby sought. For now what things sounding strangely in the Scripture were wont to offend me, having heard divers of them expounded satisfactorily, I referred to the depth of the mysteries, and its authority appeared to me the more venerable, and more worthy of religious credence, in that, while it lay open to all to read, it reserved the majesty of its mysteries within its profounder meaning, stooping to all in the great plainness of its words and lowliness of its style, yet calling

forth the intensest application of such as are not light of heart; that so it might receive all in its open bosom, and through narrow passages waft over towards Thee some few, yet many more than if it stood not aloft on such a height of authority, nor drew multitudes within its bosom by its holy lowliness. These things I thought on, and Thou wert with me; I sighed, and Thou heardest me; I wavered, and Thou didst guide me; I wandered through the broad way[1] of the world, and Thou didst not forsake me.

[VI] 9. I panted after honours, gains, marriage; and Thou deridedst me. In these desires I underwent most bitter crosses, Thou being the more gracious, the less Thou sufferedst aught to grow sweet to me, which was not Thou. Behold my heart, O Lord, who wouldest I should remember all this, and confess to Thee. Let my soul cleave unto Thee, now that Thou hast freed it from that fast-holding birdlime of death. How wretched was it! and Thou didst irritate the feeling of its wound, that, forsaking all else, it might be converted unto Thee, Who art above all and without Whom all things would be nothing; be converted, and be healed. How miserable was I then, and how didst Thou deal with me, to make me feel my misery on that day when I was preparing to recite a panegyric of the Emperor wherein I was to utter many a lie, and, lying, was to be applauded by those who knew I lied; and my heart was panting with these anxieties, and boiling with the feverishness of consuming thoughts. For, passing through one of the streets of Milan, I observed a poor beggar, then, I suppose, with a full belly, joking and joyous; and I sighed, and spoke to the friends around me of the many sorrows of our phrenzies; for that by all such efforts of ours, as those wherein I then toiled, dragging along, under the goading of desire, the burthen of my own wretchedness, and, by dragging, augmenting it, we yet looked to arrive only at that very joyousness whither that beggar-man had arrived before us, who should never perchance attain it. For what he had obtained by means of a few begged pence, the same was I plotting for by many a toilsome turning and winding: the joy of a temporary felicity. For he verily had not the true joy; but yet I with those my ambitious designs was seeking one much less true. And certainly he was joyous, I anxious; he void of care, I full of fears. But should any ask me, had I rather be merry or fearful? I would answer, merry. Again, if he asked had I rather be such as he was, or what I then was? I should choose to be myself,

[1] Matt. 7. 13.

though worn with cares and fears; but out of wrong judgment; for was it the truth? For I ought not to prefer myself to him, because more learned than he, seeing I had no joy therein, but sought to please men by it; and that not to instruct, but simply to please. Wherefore also Thou didst break my bones with the staff of Thy correction.[1]

10. Away with those then from my soul, who say to her, "It makes a difference whence a man's joy is. That beggar-man joyed in drunkenness; thou desiredst to joy in glory." What glory, Lord? That which is not in Thee. For even as his was no true joy, so was that no true glory: and it overthrew my soul more. He that very night should digest his drunkenness; but I had slept and risen again with mine, and was to sleep again, and again to rise with it, how many days, Thou, God, knowest. But "it doth make a difference whence a man's joy is." I know it, and the joy of a faithful hope lieth incomparably beyond such vanity. Yea, and so was he then beyond me: for he verily was the happier; not only for that he was thoroughly drenched in mirth, I disembowelled with cares: but he, by fair wishes, had gotten wine; I, by lying, was seeking for empty, swelling praise. Much to this purpose said I then to my friends; and I often marked in them how it fared with me; and I found it went ill with me, and grieved, and doubled that very ill; and if any prosperity smiled on me, I was loath to catch at it, for, almost before I could grasp it, it flew away.

[VII] 11. These things we, who were living as friends together, bemoaned together, but chiefly and most familiarly did I speak thereof with Alypius and Nebridius, of whom Alypius was born in the same town with me, of persons of chief rank there, but younger than I. For he had studied under me, both when I first lectured in our town, and afterwards at Carthage, and he loved me much, because I seemed to him kind and learned; and I him, for his great towardliness to virtue, which was eminent enough in one of no greater years. Yet the whirlpool of Carthaginian habits (amongst whom those idle spectacles are hotly followed) had drawn him into the madness of the Circus. But while he was miserably tossed therein, and I, professing rhetoric there, had a public school, as yet he used not my teaching, by reason of some unkindness risen betwixt his father and me. I had found then how deadly he doted upon the Circus, and was deeply grieved that he seemed likely, nay, or had thrown away so great promise:

yet had I no means of advising or with a sort of constraint reclaiming him, either by the kindness of a friend or the authority of a master. For I supposed that he thought of me as did his father; but he was not such; laying aside then his father's mind in that matter, he began to greet me, come sometimes into my lecture-room, hear a little, and be gone.

12. I however had forgotten to deal with him, that he should not, through a blind and headlong desire of vain pastimes, undo so good a wit. But Thou, O Lord, Who guidest the course of all Thou hast created, hadst not forgotten him, who was one day to be among Thy children, Priest and Dispenser of Thy Sacrament; and that his amendment might plainly be attributed to Thyself, Thou effectedst it through me, but unknowingly. For as one day I sat in my accustomed place, with my scholars before me, he entered, greeted me, sat down, and applied his mind to what I then handled. I had by chance a passage in hand, which while I was explaining, a likeness from the Circensian races occurred to me, as likely to make what I would convey pleasanter and plainer, seasoned with biting mockery of those whom that madness had enthralled; God, Thou knowest that I then thought not of curing Alypius of that infection. But he took it wholly to himself, and thought that I said it simply for his sake. And whence another would have taken occasion of offence with me, that right-minded youth took as a ground of being offended at himself, and loving me more fervently. For Thou hadst said it long ago, and put it into Thy book, "Rebuke a wise man and he will love thee."[2] But I had not rebuked him, but Thou, Who employest all, knowing or not knowing, in that order which Thyself knowest (and that order is just), didst of my heart and tongue make burning coals, by which to set on fire the hopeful mind, thus languishing, and so cure it. Let him be silent in Thy praises, who considers not Thy mercies, which confess unto Thee out of my inmost soul. For he, upon that speech, burst out of that pit so deep, wherein he was wilfully plunged, and was blinded with its wretched pastimes; and he shook his mind with a strong self-command; whereupon all the filths of the Circensian pastimes flew off from him, nor came he again thither. Upon this, he prevailed with his unwilling father, that he might be my scholar. He gave way, and gave in. And Alypius, beginning to be my hearer again, was involved in the same superstition with me, loving in the Manichees that show of continency which he sup-

---

[1] Prov. 22. 15.

[2] Prov. 9. 8.

posed true and unfeigned. Whereas it was a senseless and seducing continency, ensnaring precious souls, unable as yet to reach the depth of virtue, yet readily beguiled with the surface of what was but a shadowy and counterfeit virtue.

[VIII] 13. He, not forsaking that secular course which his parents had charmed him to pursue, had gone before me to Rome, to study law, and there he was carried away incredibly with an incredible eagerness after the shows of gladiators. For being utterly averse to and detesting such spectacles, he was one day by chance met by divers of his acquaintance and fellow-students coming from dinner, and they with a familiar violence haled him, vehemently refusing and resisting, into the Amphitheatre, during these cruel and deadly shows, he thus protesting; "Though you hale my body to that place, and there set me, can you force me also to turn my mind or my eyes to those shows? I shall then be absent while present, and so shall overcome both you and them." They, hearing this, led him on nevertheless, desirous perchance to try that very thing, whether he could do as he said. When they were come thither, and had taken their places as they could, the whole place kindled with that savage pastime. But he, closing the passages of his eyes, forbade his mind to range abroad after such evils; and would he had stopped his ears also! For in the fight, when one fell, a mighty cry of the whole people striking him strongly, overcome by curiosity and as if prepared to despise and be superior to it whatsoever it were, even when seen, he opened his eyes, and was stricken with a deeper wound in his soul than the other, whom he desired to behold, was in his body; and he fell more miserably than he upon whose fall that mighty noise was raised, which entered through his ears and unlocked his eyes, to make way for the striking and beating down of a soul, bold rather than resolute, and the weaker in that it had presumed on itself, which ought to have relied on Thee. For so soon as he saw that blood, he therewith drunk down savageness; nor turned away, but fixed his eye, drinking in phrenzy, unawares, and was delighted with that guilty fight, and intoxicated with the bloody pastime. Nor was he now the man he came, but one of the throng he came unto, yea, a true associate of theirs that brought him thither. Why say more? He beheld, shouted, kindled, carried thence with him the madness which should goad him to return not only with them who first drew him thither, but also before them, yea and to draw in others. Yet thence

didst Thou with a most strong and most merciful hand pluck him, and taughtest him to have confidence not in himself, but in Thee. But this was after.

[IX] 14. But this was already being laid up in his memory to be a medicine hereafter. So was that also that, when he was yet studying under me at Carthage, and was thinking over at midday in the market-place what he was to say by heart (as scholars use to practise), Thou sufferedst him to be apprehended by the officers of the market-place for a thief. For no other cause, I deem, didst Thou, our God, suffer it, but that he, who was hereafter to prove so great a man, should already begin to learn that, in judging of causes, man was not readily to be condemned by man out of a rash credulity. For as he was walking up and down by himself before the judgment-seat, with his note-book and pen, lo, a young man, a lawyer, the real thief, privily bringing a hatchet, got in, unperceived by Alypius, as far as the leaden gratings which fence in the silversmiths' shops, and began to cut away the lead. But the noise of the hatchet being heard, the silversmiths beneath began to make a stir, and sent to apprehend whomever they should find. But he, hearing their voices, ran away, leaving his hatchet, fearing to be taken with it. Alypius now, who had not seen him enter, was aware of his going, and saw with what speed he made away. And, being desirous to know the matter, entered the place; where, finding the hatchet, he was standing, wondering and considering it, when behold, those that had been sent, find him alone with the hatchet in his hand, the noise whereof had startled and brought them thither. They seize him, hale him away, and gathering the dwellers in the market-place together, boast of having taken a notorious thief, and so he was being led away to be taken before the judge.

15. But thus far was Alypius to be instructed. For forthwith, O Lord, Thou succouredst his innocency, whereof Thou alone wert witness. For as he was being led either to prison or to punishment, a certain architect met them, who had the chief charge of the public buildings. Glad they were to meet him especially, by whom they were wont to be suspected of stealing the goods lost out of the market-place, as though to shew him at last by whom these thefts were committed. He, however, had divers times seen Alypius at a certain Senator's house, to whom he often went to pay his respects; and, recognizing him immediately, took him aside by the hand, and enquiring the occasion of so great a calamity,

heard the whole matter, and bade all present, amid much uproar and threats, to go with him. So they came to the house of the young man who had done the deed. There, before the door, was a boy so young as to be likely, not apprehending any harm to his master, to disclose the whole. For he had attended his master to the market-place. Whom so soon as Alypius remembered, he told the architect: and he shewing the hatchet to the boy, asked him "Whose that was?" "Ours," quoth he presently: and, being further questioned, he discovered everything. Thus the crime being transferred to that house, and the multitude ashamed, which had begun to insult over Alypius, he who was to be a dispenser of Thy Word, and an examiner of many causes in Thy Church, went away better experienced and instructed.

[X] 16. Him then I had found at Rome, and he clave to me by a most strong tie, and went with me to Milan, both that he might not leave me, and might practise something of the law he had studied, more to please his parents than himself. There he had thrice sat as assessor with an uncorruptness much wondered at by others, he wondering at others, rather, who could prefer gold to honesty. His character was tried besides, not only with the bait of covetousness, but with the goad of fear. At Rome he was assessor to the Count of the Italian Treasury. There was at that time a very powerful senator, to whose favours many stood indebted, many much feared. He would needs, by his usual power, have a thing allowed him which by the laws was unallowed. Alypius resisted it; a bribe was promised; with all his heart he scorned it; threats were held out; he trampled upon them: all wondering at so unwonted a spirit, which neither desired the friendship nor feared the enmity of one so great and so mightily renowned for innumerable means of doing good or evil. And the very judge whose councillor Alypius was, although also unwilling it should be, yet did not openly refuse, but put the matter off upon Alypius, alleging that he would not allow him to do it; for in truth had the judge done it, Alypius would have decided otherwise. With this one thing in the way of learning was he well-nigh seduced, that he might have books copied for him at Prætorian prices,[1] but, consulting justice, he altered his deliberation for the better; esteeming equity whereby he was hindered more gainful than the power whereby he were allowed. These are slight things, but "he that is faithful in little

is faithful also in much."[2] Nor can that anyhow be void which proceeded out of the mouth of Thy Truth; "If ye have not been faithful in the unrighteous Mammon, who will commit to your trust true riches? And if ye have not been faithful in that which is another man's, who shall give you that which is your own?"[3] He, being such, did at that time cleave to me, and with me wavered in purpose, what course of life was to be taken.

17. Nebridius also, having left his native country near Carthage, yea, and Carthage itself, where he had much lived, leaving his excellent family-estate and house and a mother behind, who was not to follow him, had come to Milan, for no other reason but that with me he might live in a most ardent search after truth and wisdom. Like me he sighed, like me he wavered, an ardent searcher after true life, and a most acute examiner of the most difficult questions. Thus were there the mouths of three indigent persons, sighing out their wants one to another, and waiting upon Thee that Thou mightest give them their meat in due season.[4] And in all the bitterness which by Thy mercy followed our worldly affairs, as we looked towards the end, why we should suffer all this, darkness met us; and we turned away groaning, and saying, "How long shall these things be?" This too we often said; and so saying forsook them not, for as yet there dawned nothing certain, which, these forsaken, we might embrace.

[XI] 18. And I, viewing and reviewing things, most wondered at the length of time from that my nineteenth year, wherein I had begun to kindle with the desire of wisdom, settling, when I had found her, to abandon all the empty hopes and lying phrenzies of vain desires. And lo, I was now in my thirtieth year, sticking in the same mire, greedy of enjoying things present, which passed away and wasted my soul; while I said to myself, "Tomorrow I shall find it; it will appear manifestly, and I shall grasp it; lo, Faustus the Manichee will come, and clear everything! O you great men, ye Academicians, it is true, then, that no certainty can be attained for the ordering of life! Nay, let us search the more diligently, and despair not. Lo, things in the ecclesiastical books are not absurd to us now, which sometimes seemed absurd, and may be otherwise taken, and in a good sense. I will take my stand where, as a child, my parents placed me, until the clear truth be found out. But where shall it be sought or when? Ambrose has no leisure; we have no leisure to read; where

---

[1] *Pretiis Prætorianis, Pretium regium,* is the privilege of a king or lord to purchase things at a fixed price.

[2] Luke, 16. 10.   [3] *Ibid.,* 11, 12.   [4] Ps. 145. 15.

shall we find even the books? Whence, or when, procure them? from whom borrow them? Let set times be appointed, and certain hours be ordered for the health of our soul. Great hope has dawned; the Catholic Faith teaches not what we thought, and vainly accused it of; her instructed members hold it profane, to believe God to be bounded by the figure of a human body; and do we doubt to 'knock,' that the rest 'may be opened?' [1] The forenoons our scholars take up; what do we during the rest? Why not this? But when then pay we court to our great friends, whose favour we need? When compose what we may sell to scholars? When refresh ourselves, unbending our minds from this intenseness of care?"

19. "Perish everything, dismiss we these empty vanities, and betake ourselves to the one search for truth! Life is vain, death uncertain; if it steals upon us on a sudden, in what state shall we depart hence? and where shall we learn what here we have neglected? and shall we not rather suffer the punishment of this negligence? What, if death itself cut off and end all care and feeling? Then must this be ascertained. But God forbid this! It is no vain and empty thing that the excellent dignity of the authority of the Christian Faith hath overspread the whole world. Never would such and so great things be by God wrought for us, if with the death of the body the life of the soul came to an end. Wherefore delay then to abandon worldly hopes, and give ourselves wholly to seek after God and the blessed life? But wait! Even those things are pleasant; they have some, and no small sweetness. We must not lightly abandon them, for it were a shame to return again to them. See, it is no great matter now to obtain some station, and then what should we more wish for? We have store of powerful friends; if nothing else offer, and we be in much haste, at least a presidentship may be given us: and a wife with some money, that she increase not our charges: and this shall be the bound of desire. Many great men, and most worthy of imitation, have given themselves to the study of wisdom in the state of marriage."

20. While I went over these things, and these winds shifted and drove my heart this way and that, time passed on, but I delayed to turn to the Lord; and from day to day deferred to live in Thee, and deferred not daily to die in myself. Loving a happy life, I feared it in its own abode, and sought it, by fleeing from it. I thought I should be too miserable, unless folded in female

arms; and of the medicine of Thy mercy to cure that infirmity I thought not, not having tried it. As for continency, I suppose it to be in our own power (though in myself I did not find that power), being so foolish as not to know what is written, None can be continent unless Thou give it; [2] and that Thou wouldest give it, if with inward groanings I did knock at Thine ears, and with a settled faith did cast my care on Thee.

[XII] 21. Alypius indeed kept me from marrying; alleging that so could we by no means with undistracted leisure live together in the love of wisdom, as we had long desired. For himself was even then most pure in this point, so that it was wonderful; and that the more, since in the outset of his youth he had entered into that course, but had not stuck fast therein; rather had he felt remorse and revolting at it, living thenceforth until now most continently. But I opposed him with the examples of those who as married men had cherished wisdom, and served God acceptably, and retained their friends, and loved them faithfully. Of whose greatness of spirit I was far short; and bound with the disease of the flesh, and its deadly sweetness, drew along my chain, dreading to be loosed, and, as if my wound had been fretted, put back his good persuasions, as it were the hand of one that would unchain me. Moreover, by me did the serpent speak unto Alypius himself, by my tongue weaving and laying in his path pleasurable snares, wherein his virtuous and free feet might be entangled.

22. For when he wondered that I, whom he esteemed not slightly, should stick so fast in the birdlime of that pleasure as to protest (so oft as we discussed it) that I could never lead a single life; and urged in my defence, when I saw him wonder, that there was great difference between his momentary and scarce-remembered knowledge of that life, which so he might easily despise, and my continued acquaintance whereto, if but the honourable name of marriage were added, he ought not to wonder why I could not contemn that course; he began also to desire to be married; not as overcome with desire of such pleasure, but out of curiosity. For he would fain know, he said, what that should be, without which my life, to him so pleasing, would to me seem not life but a punishment. For his mind, free from that chain, was amazed at my thraldom; and through that amazement was going on to a desire of trying it, thence to the trial itself, and thence perhaps to sink into that bondage whereat he wondered, seeing he was willing to

[1] Matt. 7. 7.   [2] Wisd. 8. 2, Vulg.

make "a covenant with death";[1] and he that loves danger, shall fall into it.[2] For whatever honour there be in the office of well-ordering a married life, and a family, moved us but slightly. But me for the most part the habit of satisfying an insatiable appetite tormented, while it held me captive; him, an admiring wonder was leading captive. So were we, until Thou, O Most High, not forsaking our dust, commiserating us miserable, didst come to our help by wondrous and secret ways.

[XIII] 23. Continual effort was made to have me married. I wooed, I was promised, chiefly through my mother's pains, that so once married, the health-giving baptism might cleanse me, towards which she rejoiced that I was being daily fitted, and observed that her prayers, and Thy promises, were being fulfilled in my faith. At which time verily, both at my request and her own longing, with strong cries of heart she daily begged of Thee that Thou wouldest by a vision discover unto her something concerning my future marriage; Thou never wouldest. She saw indeed certain vain and phantastic things, such as the energy of the human spirit, busied thereon, brought together; and these she told me of, not with that confidence she was wont, when Thou shewedst her anything, but slighting them. For she could, she said, through a certain feeling, which in words she could not express, discern betwixt Thy revelations and the dreams of her own soul. Yet the matter was pressed on, and a maiden asked in marriage, two years under the fit age; and, as pleasing, was waited for.

[XIV] 24. And many of us friends, conferring about and detesting the turbulent turmoils of human life, had debated and now almost resolved on living apart from business and the bustle of men; and this was to be thus obtained: we were to bring whatever we might severally procure, and make one household of all; so that through the truth of our friendship nothing should belong especially to any; but the whole, thus derived from all, should as a whole belong to each, and all to all. We thought there might be some ten persons in this society; some of whom were very rich, especially Romanianus our townsman, from childhood a very familiar friend of mine, whom the grievous perplexities of his affairs had brought up to court; who was the most earnest for this project; and therein was his voice of great weight, because his ample estate far exceeded any of the rest. We had settled also that two annual officers, as it were,

should provide all things necessary, the rest being undisturbed. But when we began to consider whether the wives, which some of us already had, others hoped to have, would allow this, all that plan, which was being so well moulded, fell to pieces in our hands, was utterly dashed and cast aside. Thence we betook us to sighs, and groans, and our steps to follow the broad and beaten ways[3] of the world; for many thoughts were in our heart, but Thy counsel standeth for ever.[4] Out of which counsel Thou didst deride ours, and preparedst Thine own; purposing to give us meat in due season, and to open Thy hand, and to fill our souls with blessing.[5]

[XV] 25. Meanwhile my sins were being multiplied, and my concubine being torn from my side as a hindrance to my marriage, my heart which clave unto her was torn and wounded and bleeding. And she returned to Africa, vowing unto Thee never to know any other man, leaving with me my son by her. But unhappy I, who could not imitate a very woman, impatient of delay, inasmuch as not till after two years was I to obtain her I sought, not being so much a lover of marriage as a slave to lust, procured another, though no wife, that so, by the servitude of an enduring custom, the disease of my soul might be kept up and carried on in its vigor, or even augmented, into the dominion of marriage. Nor was that my wound cured, which had been made by the cutting away of the former, but after inflammation and most acute pain, it mortified, and my pains became less acute, but more desperate.

[XVI] 26. To Thee be praise, glory to Thee, Fountain of mercies. I was becoming more miserable, and Thou nearer. Thy right hand was continually ready to pluck me out of the mire, and to wash me thoroughly, and I knew it not; nor did anything call me back from a yet deeper gulf of carnal pleasures, but the fear of death and of Thy judgment to come, which amid all my changes never departed from my breast. And in my disputes with my friends Alypius and Nebridius, of the nature of good and evil, I held that Epicurus had in my mind won the palm, had I not believed that after death there remained a life for the soul, and places of requital according to men's deserts, which Epicurus would not believe. And I asked, "Were we immortal, and to live in perpetual bodily pleasure without fear of losing it, why should we not be happy, or what else should we seek?" not knowing that great misery was involved in this very thing, that, being thus sunk and blinded, I could

[1]Isa. 28. 15.   [2]Ecclus. 3. 27.   [3]Matt. 7. 13.   [4]Ps. 33. 11.   [5]Ps. 114. 15, 16.

not discern that light of excellence and beauty, to be embraced for its own sake, which the eye of flesh cannot see, and is seen by the inner man. Nor did I, unhappy, consider from what source it sprung that even on these things, foul as they were, I with pleasure discoursed with my friends; nor could I, even according to the notions I then had of happiness, be happy without friends, amid what abundance soever of carnal pleasures. And yet these friends I loved for themselves only, and I felt that I was beloved of them again for myself only.

O crooked paths! Woe to the audacious soul which hoped, by forsaking Thee, to gain some better thing! Turned it hath, and turned again, upon back, sides, and belly, yet all was painful, and Thou alone rest. And behold, Thou art at hand, and deliverest us from our wretched wanderings, and placest us in Thy way, and dost comfort us, and say, "Run; I will carry you; yea I will bring you through; there also will I carry you."

BOOK VII. *Augustine's thirty-first year; gradually extricated from his errors, but still with material conceptions of God; much aided by an argument of Nebridius; sees that the cause of sin lies in free-will, rejects the Manichæan heresy, but cannot altogether embrace the doctrine of the Church; recovered from the belief in Astrology, but miserably perplexed about the origin of evil; is led to find in the Platonists the seeds of the doctrine of the Divinity of the WORD, but not of His humiliation; hence he obtains clearer notions of God's majesty, but, not knowing Christ to be the Mediator, remains estranged from Him; all his doubts removed by the study of Holy Scripture, especially St. Paul.*

[I] 1. Deceased was now that my evil and abominable youth, and I was passing into early manhood; the more defiled by vain things as I grew in years, who could not imagine any substance but such as is wont to be seen with these eyes. I thought not of Thee, O God, under the figure of an human body; since I began to hear aught of wisdom, I always avoided this; and rejoiced to have found the same in the faith of our spiritual mother, Thy Catholic Church. But what else to conceive Thee I knew not. And I, a man, and such a man, sought to conceive of Thee the sovereign, only, true God; and I did in my inmost soul believe that Thou wert incorruptible, and uninjurable, and unchangeable; because, though not knowing whence or how, yet I saw plainly and was sure that that which may be corrupted must be inferior to that which cannot; what could not be injured I preferred unhesitatingly to what could receive injury; the unchangeable to things subject to change. My heart passionately cried out against all my phantoms, and with this one blow I sought to beat away from the eye of my mind all that unclean troop which buzzed around it.[1] And lo, being scarce put off, in the twinkling of an eye they gathered again thick about me, flew against my face and beclouded it; so that, though not under the form of the human body, yet was I constrained to conceive of Thee (that incorruptible, uninjurable, and unchangeable, which I preferred before the corruptible, and injurable, and changeable) as being in space, whether infused into the world, or diffused infinitely without it. Because whatsoever I conceived, deprived of this space, seemed to me nothing, yea altogether nothing, not even a void, as if a body were taken out of its place, and the place should remain empty of any body at all, of earth and water, air and heaven, yet would it remain a void place, as it were a spacious nothing.

2. I then being thus gross-hearted, nor clear even to myself, whatsoever was not extended over certain spaces, nor diffused, nor condensed, nor swelled out, or did not or could not receive some of these dimensions, I thought to be altogether nothing. For over such forms as my eyes are wont to range, did my heart then range: nor yet did I see that this same notion of the mind, whereby I formed those very images, was not of this sort, and yet it could not have formed them, had not itself been some great thing. So also did I endeavour to conceive of Thee, Life of my life, as vast, through infinite spaces, on every side penetrating the whole mass of the universe, and beyond it, every way, through unmeasurable boundless spaces; so that the earth should have Thee, the heaven have Thee, all things have Thee, and they be bounded in Thee, and Thou bounded nowhere. For that as the body of this air which is above the earth hindereth not the light of the sun from passing through it, penetrating it, not by bursting or by cutting, but by filling it wholly: so I thought the body not of heaven, air, and sea only, but of the earth too, pervious to Thee, so that in all its parts, the greatest as the smallest, it should admit Thy presence, by a secret inspiration, within and without, directing all things which Thou hast created. So I guessed, only as unable to conceive aught else, for it was false. For thus should a greater part of the earth contain a greater por-

[1]See BK. III. 12; BK. IV. 3, 12; BK. V. 19, above.

tion of Thee, and a less, a lesser: and all things should in such sort be full of Thee that the body of an elephant should contain more of Thee than that of a sparrow, by how much larger it is, and takes up more room; and thus shouldest Thou make the several portions of Thyself present unto the several portions of the world, in fragments, large to the large, petty to the petty. But such art not Thou. But not as yet hadst Thou enlightened my darkness.

[II] 3. It was enough for me, Lord, to oppose to those deceived deceivers and dumb praters, since Thy word sounded not out of them; that was enough which long ago, while we were yet at Carthage, Nebridius used to propound, at which all we that heard it were staggered: "That said nation of darkness, which the Manichees are wont to set as an opposing mass over against Thee, what could it have done unto Thee, hadst Thou refused to fight with it? For, if they answered, 'it would have done Thee some hurt,' then shouldest Thou be subject to injury and corruption: but if 'it could do Thee no hurt,' then was no reason brought for Thy fighting with it; and fighting in such wise, as that a certain portion or member of Thee, or offspring of Thy very Substance, should be mingled with opposed powers, and natures not created by Thee, and be by them so far corrupted and changed to the worse, as to be turned from happiness into misery, and need assistance, whereby it might be extricated and purified; and that this offspring of Thy Substance was the soul, which being enthralled, defiled, corrupted, Thy Word, free, pure, and whole, might relieve; that Word Itself being still corruptible, because It was of one and the same Substance. So then, should they affirm Thee, whatsoever Thou art, that is, Thy Substance whereby Thou art, to be incorruptible, then were all these sayings false and execrable; but if corruptible, the very statement shewed it to be false and revolting." This argument then of Nebridius sufficed against those who deserved wholly to be vomited out of the overcharged stomach; for they had no escape, without horrible blasphemy of heart and tongue, thus thinking and speaking of Thee.

[III] 4. But I also as yet, although I held and was firmly persuaded that Thou our Lord the true God, Who madest not only our souls, but our bodies, and not only our souls and bodies, but all beings, and all things, wert undefilable and unalterable, and in no degree mutable; yet understood I not, clearly and without difficulty, the cause of evil. And yet, whatever it were, I perceived it was in such wise to be sought out

as should not constrain me to believe the immutable God to be mutable, lest I should become that evil I was seeking out. I sought it out then, thus far free from anxiety, certain of the untruth of what these held from whom I shrunk with my whole heart: for I saw that, through enquiring the origin of evil, they were filled with evil, in that they preferred to think that Thy substance did suffer ill than their own did commit it.

5. And I strained to perceive what I now heard, that free-will was the cause of our doing ill, and Thy just judgment, of our suffering ill. But I was not able clearly to discern it. So then, endeavouring to draw my soul's vision out of that deep pit, I was again plunged therein, and, endeavouring often, I was plunged back as often. But this raised me a little into Thy light, that I knew as well that I had a will as that I lived: when then I did will or nill anything, I was most sure that no other than myself did will and nill: and I all but saw that there was the cause of my sin. But what I did against my will, I saw that I suffered rather than did, and I judged not to be my fault, but my punishment; whereby, however, holding thee to be just, I speedily confessed myself to be not unjustly punished. But again I said, "Who made me? Did not my God, Who is not only good, but goodness itself? Whence then came I to will evil and nill good, so that I am thus justly punished? who set this in me, and ingrafted into me this plant of bitterness, seeing I was wholly formed by my most sweet God? If the devil were the author, whence is that same devil? And if he also, by his own perverse will, of a good angel became a devil, whence, again, came in him that evil will whereby he became a devil, seeing the whole nature of angels was made by that most good Creator?" By these thoughts I was again sunk down and choked; yet not brought down to that hell of error (where no man confesseth unto Thee),[1] to think rather that Thou dost suffer ill than that man doth it.

[IV] 6. For I was in such wise striving to find out the rest, as one who had already found that the incorruptible must needs be better than the corruptible; and Thee therefore, whatsoever Thou wert, I confessed to be incorruptible. For never soul was, nor shall be, able to conceive anything which may be better than Thou, Who art the sovereign and the best good. But since, most truly and certainly, the incorruptible is preferable to the corruptible (as I did now prefer it), then, wert Thou not incorruptible, I

[1] Ps. 6. 5.

could in thought have arrived at something better than my God. Where then I saw the incorruptible to be preferable to the corruptible, there ought I to seek for Thee, and there observe "wherein evil itself was"; that is, whence corruption comes, by which Thy substance can by no means be impaired. For corruption does no ways impair our God; by no will, by no necessity, by no unlooked-for chance: because He is God, and what He wills is good, and Himself is that good; but to be corrupted is not good. Nor art Thou against Thy will constrained to anything, since Thy will is not greater than Thy power. But greater should it be, were Thyself greater than Thyself. For the will and power of God is God Himself. And what can be unlooked-for by Thee, Who knowest all things? Nor is there any nature in things, but Thou knowest it. And what should we more say, "why that substance which God is should not be corruptible," seeing if it were so, it should not be God?

[V] 7. And I sought "whence is evil," and sought in an evil way; and saw not the evil in my very search. I set now before the sight of my spirit the whole creation, whatsoever we can see therein (as sea, earth, air, stars, trees, mortal creatures); yea, and whatever in it we do not see, as the firmament of heaven, all angels moreover, and all the spiritual inhabitants thereof. But these very beings, as though they were bodies, did my fancy dispose in place, and I made one great mass of Thy creation, distinguished as to the kinds of bodies; some, real bodies, some, what myself had feigned for spirits. And this mass I made huge, not as it was (which I could not know), but as I thought convenient, yet every way finite. But Thee, O Lord, I imagined on every part environing and penetrating it, though every way infinite: as if there were a sea, everywhere and on every side, through unmeasured space, one only boundless sea, and it contained within it some sponge, huge, but bounded; that sponge must needs, in all its parts, be filled from that unmeasurable sea: so conceived I Thy creation, itself finite, full of Thee, the Infinite; and I said, Behold God, and behold what God hath created; and God is good, yea, most mightily and incomparably better than all these: but yet He, the Good, created them good; and see how He environeth and fulfils them. Where is evil then, and whence, and how crept it in hither? What is its root, and what its seed? Or hath it no being? Why then fear we and avoid what is not? Or, if we fear it idly, then is that very fear evil, whereby the soul is thus idly goaded and racked. Yea and so

much a greater evil, as we have nothing to fear, and yet do fear. Therefore either is that evil which we fear, or else evil is, that we fear. Whence is it then? seeing God, the Good, hath created all these things good. He indeed, the greater and chiefest Good, hath created these lesser goods; still both Creator and created, all are good. Whence is evil? Or, was there some evil matter of which He made, and formed, and ordered it, yet left something in it which He did not convert into good? Why so then? Had He no might to turn and change the whole, so that no evil should remain in it, seeing He is Almighty? Lastly, why would He make anything at all of it, and not rather by the same Almightiness cause it not to be at all? Or could it then be against His will? Or, if it were from eternity, why suffered He it so to be for infinite spaces of times past, and was pleased so long after to make something out of it? Or if He were suddenly pleased now to effect somewhat, this rather should the Almighty have effected, that this evil matter should not be, and He alone be, the whole, true, sovereign, and infinite Good. Or if it was not good that He who was good should not also frame and create something that were good, then, that evil matter being taken away and brought to nothing, He might form good matter, whereof to create all things. For He should not be Almighty if He might not create something good without the aid of that matter which Himself had not created. These thoughts I revolved in my miserable heart, overcharged with most gnawing cares, lest I should die ere I had found the truth; yet was the faith of Thy Christ our Lord and Saviour, professed in the Church Catholic, firmly fixed in my heart, in many points, indeed, as yet unformed, and fluctuating from the rule of doctrine; yet did not my mind utterly leave it, but rather daily took in more and more of it.

8. By this time also had I rejected the lying divinations and impious dotages of the astrologers. Let Thine own mercies, out of my very inmost soul, confess unto Thee[1] for this also, O my God. For Thou, Thou altogether (for who else calls us back from the death of all errors, save the Life which cannot die, and the Wisdom which needing no light enlightens the minds that need it, whereby the universe is directed, down to the whirling leaves of trees?)—Thou madest provision for my obstinacy wherewith I struggled against Vindicianus,[2] an acute old man, and Nebridius, a young man of admirable talents; the first vehemently affirming, and the latter of-

[1] Ps. 107. 8, Vulg.   [2] See Bk. IV. 5.

ten (though with some doubtfulness) saying, "That there was no such art whereby to foresee things to come, but that men's conjectures were a sort of lottery, and that out of many things, which they said should come to pass, some actually did, unawares to them who spake it, who stumbled upon it through their oft speaking." Thou providedst then a friend for me, no negligent consulter of the astrologers; nor yet well skilled in those arts, but (as I said) a curious consulter with them, and yet knowing something which he said he had heard of his father, which how far it went to overthrow the estimation of that art, he knew not. This man then, Firminus by name, having had a liberal education and well taught in Rhetoric, consulted me, as one very dear to him, what, according to his so-called constellations, I thought on certain affairs of his, wherein his worldly hopes had risen; and I, who had herein now begun to incline towards Nebridius' opinion, did not altogether refuse to conjecture, and tell him what came into my unresolved mind; but added that I was now almost persuaded that these were but empty and ridiculous follies. Thereupon he told me that his father had been very curious in such books, and had a friend as earnest in them as himself, who with joint study and conference fanned the flame of their affections to these toys, so that they would observe the moments whereat the very dumb animals, which bred about their houses, gave birth, and then observed the relative position of the heavens, thereby to make fresh experiments in this so-called art. He said then that he had heard of his father that, what time his mother was about to give birth to him, Firminus, a woman-servant of that friend of his father's was also with child, which could not escape her master, who took care with most exact diligence to know the births of his very puppies. And so it was that (the one for his wife, and the other for his servant, with the most careful observation, reckoning days, hours, nay, the lesser divisions of the hours) both were delivered at the same instant; so that both were constrained to allow the same constellations, even to the minutest points, the one for his son, the other for his new-born slave. For so soon as the women began to be in labour, they each gave notice to the other what was fallen out in their houses, and had messengers ready to send to one another, so soon as they had notice of the actual birth, of which they had easily provided, each in his own province, to give instant intelligence. Thus then the messengers of the respective parties met, he averred, at such an equal distance from either house that neither of them could make out any difference in the position of the stars, or any other minutest points; and yet Firminus, born in a high estate in his parents' house, ran his course through the gilded paths of life, was increased in riches, raised to honours; whereas that slave continued to serve his masters, without any relaxation of his yoke, as Firminus, who knew him, told me.

9. Upon hearing and believing these things, told by one of such credibility, all that my resistance gave way; and first I endeavoured to reclaim Firminus himself from that curiosity by telling him that, upon inspecting his constellations, I ought, if I were to predict truly, to have seen in them, parents eminent among their neighbours, a noble family in its own city, high birth, good education, liberal learning. But if that servant had consulted me upon the same constellations, since they were his also, I ought again (to tell him too truly) to see in them a lineage the most abject, a slavish condition, and everything else utterly at variance with the former. Whence then, if I spake the truth, I should, from the same constellations, speak diversely, or if I spake the same, speak falsely: thence it followed most certainly that whatever, upon consideration of the constellations, was spoken truly, was spoken not out of art, but chance; and whatever spoken falsely was not out of ignorance in the art, but the failure of the chance.

10. An opening thus made, ruminating with myself on the like things, that no one of those dotards (who lived by such a trade, and whom I longed to attack, and with derision to confute) might urge against me, that Firminus had informed me falsely, or his father him; I bent my thoughts on those that are born twins, who for the most part come out of the womb so near one to other that the small interval (how much force soever in the nature of things folk may pretend it to have) cannot be noted by human observation, or be at all expressed in those figures which the astrologer is to inspect, that he may pronounce truly. Yet they cannot be true: for looking into the same figures, he must have predicted the same of Esau and Jacob,[1] whereas the same happened not to them. Therefore he must speak falsely; or if truly, then, looking into the same figures, he must not give the same answer. Not by art, then, but by chance, would he speak truly. For Thou, O Lord, most righteous Ruler of the Universe, while consulters and consulted know it not, dost by Thy hidden inspiration effect that the consulter should hear what, accord-

[1] See also, *On Christian Doctrine*, BK. II. ch. 22.

ing to the hidden deservings of souls, he ought to hear, out of the unsearchable depth of Thy just judgment, to Whom let no man say, "What is this?" "Why that?" Let him not so say, for he is man.

[VII] 11. Now then, O my Helper, hadst Thou loosed me from those fetters; and I sought "whence is evil," and found no way. But Thou sufferedst me not by any fluctuations of thought to be carried away from the Faith whereby I believed Thee both to be, and Thy substance to be unchangeable, and that Thou hast a care of, and wouldest judge men, and that in Christ, Thy Son, our Lord, and the holy Scriptures, which the authority of Thy Catholic Church pressed upon me, Thou hadst set the way of man's salvation, to that life which is to be after this death. These things being safe and immoveably settled in my mind, I sought anxiously "whence was evil?" What were the pangs of my teeming heart, what groans, O my God! yet even there were Thine ears open, and I knew it not: and when in silence I vehemently sought, those silent contritions of my soul were strong cries unto Thy mercy. Thou knewest what I suffered, and no man. For what was that which was thence through my tongue distilled into the ears of my most familiar friends? Did the whole tumult of my soul, for which neither time nor utterance sufficed, reach them? Yet went up the whole to Thy hearing, all which I roared out from the groanings of my heart; and my desire was before Thee, and the light of mine eyes was not with me:[1] for that was within, I without: nor was that confined to place, but I was intent on things contained in place, but there found I no resting-place, nor did they so receive me, that I could say, "It is enough," "it is well": nor did they yet suffer me to turn back, where it might be well enough with me. For to these things was I superior, but inferior to Thee; and Thou art my true joy when subjected to Thee, and Thou hadst subjected to me what Thou createdst below me. And this was the true temperament, and middle region of my safety, to remain in Thy Image, and by serving Thee rule the body. But when I rose proudly against Thee, and "ran against the Lord with my neck, with the thick bosses" of my buckler,[2] even these inferior things were set above me, and pressed me down, and nowhere was there respite or space of breathing. They met my sight on all sides by heaps and troops, and in thought the images thereof presented themselves unsought, as I would return to Thee, as if they would say unto

me, "Whither goest thou, unworthy and defiled?" And these things had grown out of my wound; for Thou "humbledst the proud like one that is wounded," and through my own swelling was I separated from Thee; yea, my pride-swollen face closed up mine eyes.

[VIII] 12. "But Thou, Lord, abidest for ever,"[3] yet not for ever art Thou angry with us; because Thou pitiest our dust and ashes, and it was pleasing in Thy sight to reform my deformities; and by inward goads didst Thou rouse me, that I should be ill at ease until Thou wert manifested to my inward sight. Thus, by the secret hand of Thy medicining, was my swelling abated, and the troubled and bedimmed eyesight of my mind, by the smarting anointings of healthful sorrows, was from day to day healed.

[IX] 13. And Thou, willing first to shew me how Thou "resistest the proud, but givest grace unto the humble,"[4] and by how great an act of Thy mercy Thou hadst traced out to men the way of humility, in that Thy "WORD was made flesh," and dwelt among men—Thou procuredst for me, by means of one puffed up with most unnatural pride, certain books of the Platonists, translated from Greek into Latin. And therein I read, not indeed in the very words, but to the very same purpose, enforced by many and divers reasons, that "In the beginning was the Word, was with God, and the Word was God: the Same was in the beginning with God: all things were made by Him, and without Him was nothing made: that which was made by Him is 'life', and the life was the light of men, and the light shineth in the darkness, and the darkness comprehended it not."[5] And that the soul of man,[6] though it "bears witness to the light,[7] yet itself is not that light; but the Word of God, being God, "is that true light that lighteth every man that cometh into the world."[8] And that "He was in the world, and the world was made by Him, and the world knew Him not."[9] But that "He came unto His own, and His own received Him not;[10] but as many as received Him, to them gave He power to become the sons of God, as many as believed in His name";[11] this I read not there.

14. Again I read there, that God the Word was born not of flesh nor of blood, nor of the will of man, nor of the will of the flesh, but of God. But that "the Word was made flesh, and dwelt among us,"[12] I read not there. For I traced in

[1]Ps. 37. 9–11, Vulg.   [2]Job, 15. 26.

[3]Ps. 102. 12.   [4]James, 4. 6; I Pet. 5. 5.
[5]John, 1. 1–5.   [6]See also, *City of God*, BK. X. 2.
[7]John, 1. 7, 8.   [8]*Ibid.*, 1. 9.   [9]*Ibid.*, 1. 10.
[10]*Ibid.*, 1. 11.   [11]John, 1. 12.   [12]*Ibid.*, 1. 14.

those books that it was many and divers ways said that the Son was in the form of the Father, and "thought it not robbery to be equal with God," for that naturally He was the Same Substance. But that He emptied himself, "taking the form of a servant, being made in the likeness of men, and found in fashion as a man, humbled Himself, and became obedient unto death, and that the death of the cross: wherefore God exalted Him" from the dead, "and gave Him a name above every name, that at the name of Jesus every knee should bow, of things in heaven, and things in earth, and things under the earth; and that every tongue should confess that the Lord Jesus Christ is in the glory of God the Father";[1] those books have not. For that before all times and above all times Thy Only-Begotten Son remaineth unchangeably co-eternal with Thee, and that of "His fulness" souls receive[2] that they may be blessed; and that by participation of wisdom abiding in them, they are renewed, so as to be wise, is there. But that "in due time He died for the ungodly";[3] and that Thou sparedst not Thine Only Son, but deliveredst Him for us all[4] is not there. "For Thou hiddest these things from the wise, and revealedst them to babes";[5] that they "that labour and are heavy laden might "come" unto Him, and He refresh them, because "He is meek and lowly in heart";[6] and "the meek He directeth in judgment, and the gentle He teacheth His ways,"[7] beholding our lowliness and trouble, and forgiving all our sins.[8] But such as are lifted up in the lofty walk of some would-be sublimer learning, hear not Him, saying, "Learn of Me, for I am meek and lowly in heart, and ye shall find rest to your souls."[9] "Although they knew God, yet they glorify Him not as God, nor are thankful, but wax vain in their thoughts; and their foolish heart is darkened; professing that they were wise, they became fools."[10]

15. And therefore did I read there also that they had changed the glory of Thy incorruptible nature into idols and divers shapes, "into the likeness of the image of corruptible man, and birds, and beasts, and creeping things";[11] namely into that Egyptian food, for which Esau lost his birthright, for that Thy first-born people worshipped the head of a four-footed beast instead of Thee; turning in heart back towards Egypt, and bowing Thy image, their own soul, before the image of "a calf that eateth hay."[12]

These things found I here, but I fed not on them. For it pleased Thee, O Lord, to take away the reproach of diminution from Jacob, that the elder should serve the younger;[13] and Thou calledst the Gentiles into Thine inheritance. And I had come to Thee from among the Gentiles; and I set my mind upon the gold which Thou willedst Thy people to take from Egypt, seeing Thine it was, whersoever it were. And to the Athenians Thou saidst by Thy Apostle that in Thee "we live, move, and have our being," as one of their own poets had said.[14] And verily these books came from thence. But I set not my mind on the idols of Egypt, whom they served with Thy gold,[15] "who changed the truth of God into a lie, and worshipped and served the creature more than the Creator."[16]

[X] 16. And being thence admonished to return to myself, I entered even into my inward self, Thou being my Guide: and able I was, for Thou wert become my Helper. And I entered and beheld with the eye of my soul (such as it was), above the same eye of my soul, above my mind, the Light Unchangeable. Not this ordinary light, which all flesh may look upon,[17] nor as it were a greater of the same kind, as though the brightness of this should be manifold brighter, and with its greatness take up all space. Not such was this light, but other, yea, far other from all these. Nor was it above my soul, as oil is above water, nor yet as heaven above earth: but above to my soul, because It made me; and I below It, because I was made by It. He that knows the Truth knows what that Light is; and he that knows It knows eternity. Love knoweth it. O Truth Who art Eternity! and Love Who art Truth! and Eternity Who art Love![18] Thou art my God, to Thee do I sigh night and day. Thee when I first knew, Thou liftedst me up, that I might see there was what I might see, and that I was not yet such as to see. And Thou didst beat back the weakness of my sight, streaming forth Thy beams of light upon me most strongly, and I trembled with love and awe; and I perceived myself to be far off from Thee, in the region of unlikeness, as if I heard this Thy voice from on high: "I am the food of grown men; grow, and thou shalt feed upon Me; nor shalt thou convert Me, like the food of thy flesh, into thee, but thou shalt be converted into Me." And I learned that Thou for iniquity chastenest man, and Thou madest

[1]Phil. 2. 6–11.   [2]John, 1. 16.   [3]Rom. 5. 6.
[4]Ibid., 8. 32.   [5]Matt. 11. 25.   [6]Ibid., 11. 28, 29.
[7]Ps. 25. 9.   [8]Ibid., ver. 18.   [9]Matt. 11. 29.
[10]Rom. 1. 21, 22.   [11]Ibid., 1. 23.
[12]Ps. 106. 20; Ex. 32. 1–6.

[13]Rom. 9. 12.   [14]Acts, 17. 28.   [15]Hosea, 2. 8.
[16]On Christian Doctrine, Bk. II. ch. 18, 40; Rom. 1. 25.
[17]See above, Bk. III. 10, 12; Bk. IV. 3; Bk. VII. 2.
[18]See also, City of God, Bk. XI. 28.

my soul to consume away like a spider.[1] And I said, "Is Truth therefore nothing because it is not diffused through space finite or infinite?" And Thou criedst to me from afar; "Yea verily, 'I AM that I AM'."[2] And I heard as the heart heareth, nor had I room to doubt, and I should sooner doubt that I live than that Truth is not, which is "clearly seen being understood by those things which are made."[3]

[XI] 17. And I beheld the other things below Thee, and I perceived that they neither altogether are, nor altogether are not, for they are, since they are from Thee, but are not, because they are not what Thou art. For that truly is which remains unchangeably. It is good then for me to hold fast unto God;[4] for if I remain not in Him, I cannot in myself; but He remaining in himself, reneweth all things.[5] And Thou art the Lord my God, since Thou standest not in need of my goodness.[6]

[XII] 18. And it was manifested unto me that those things be good which yet are corrupted; which neither were they sovereignly good, nor, unless they were good, could be corrupted; for if sovereignly good, they were incorruptible, if not good at all, there were nothing in them to be corrupted. For corruption injures, but unless it diminished goodness, it could not injure. Either then corruption injures not, which cannot be; or, which is most certain, all which is corrupted is deprived of good. But if they be deprived of all good, they shall cease to be. For if they shall be, and can now no longer be corrupted, they shall be better than before, because they shall abide incorruptibly. And what more monstrous than to affirm things to become better by losing all their good? Therefore, if they shall be deprived of all good, they shall no longer be. So long therefore as they are, they are good: therefore whatsoever is, is good. That evil then, which I sought whence it is, is not any substance: for were it a substance, it should be good. For either it should be an incorruptible substance, and so a chief good; or a corruptible substance, which, unless it were good, could not be corrupted. I perceived therefore, and it was manifested to me, that Thou madest all things good, nor is there any substance at all which Thou madest not; and for that Thou madest not all things equal, therefore are all[7] things; because each is good, and altogether very good, because our God made all things very good.[8]

[1]Ps. 39. 11, Vulg.   [2]Ex. 3. 14.   [3]Rom. 1. 20.
[4]Ps. 73. 28.   [5]Wisd. 7. 27.   [6]Ps. 17. 2.
[7]See also, *City of God*, BK. II. 22.
[8]Gen. 1. 31; Ecclus. 39. 21.

[XIII] 19. And to Thee is nothing whatsoever evil: yea, not only to Thee, but also to Thy creation as a whole, because there is nothing without, which may break in and corrupt that order which Thou hast appointed. But in the parts thereof some things, because unharmonizing with other some, are accounted evil; whereas those very things harmonize[9] with others, and are good; and in themselves are good. And all these things which harmonize not together do yet with the inferior part, which we call Earth, having its own cloudy and windy sky harmonizing with it. Far be it then that I should say, "These things should not be": for should I see nought but these, I should indeed long for the better; but still must even for these alone praise Thee; for that Thou art to be praised, do shew from the "earth, dragons, and all deeps, fire, hail, snow, ice, and stormy wind, which fulfil Thy word; mountains, and all hills, fruitful trees, and all cedars; beasts, and all cattle, creeping things, and flying fowls; kings of the earth, and all people, princes, and all judges of the earth; young men and maidens, old men and young," praise Thy Name. But when, from heaven, these praise Thee, praise Thee, our God, "in the heights," all Thy "angels," all Thy "hosts," "sun and moon," all the stars and light, "the Heaven of heavens," and "the waters that be above the heavens," praise Thy Name;[10] I did not now long for things better, because I conceived of all: and with a sounder judgment I apprehended that the things above were better than these below, but all together better than those above by themselves.

[XIV] 20. There is no soundness in them whom aught of Thy creation displeaseth: as neither in me, when much which Thou hast made displeased me. And because my soul durst not be displeased at my God, it would fain not account that Thine which displeased it. Hence it had gone into the opinion of two substances, and had no rest, but talked idly. And returning thence, it had made to itself a God, through infinite measures of all space; and thought it to be Thee, and placed it in its heart; and had again become the temple of its own idol, to Thee abominable. But after Thou hadst soothed my head, unknown to me, and closed mine eyes that they should not "behold vanity,"[11] I ceased somewhat of my former self, and my phrenzy was lulled to sleep; and I awoke in Thee, and saw Thee infinite, but in another way, and this sight was not derived from the flesh.

[XV] 21. And I looked back on other things;

[9]See above, BK. V. 1.   [10]Ps. 148. 1–12.   [11]Ps. 119. 37.

and I saw that they owed their being to Thee, and were all bounded in Thee, but in a different way: not as being in space, but because Thou containest all things in Thine hand in Thy Truth; and all things are true so far as they be; nor is there any falsehood, unless when that is thought to be which is not. And I saw that all things did harmonize, not with their places only, but with their seasons. And that Thou, Who only art Eternal, didst not begin to work after innumerable spaces of times spent; for that all spaces of times, both which have passed and which shall pass, neither go nor come, but through Thee, working, and abiding.[1]

[XVI] 22. And I perceived and found it nothing strange that bread which is pleasant to a healthy palate is loathsome to one distempered: and to sore eyes light is offensive, which to the sound is delightful. And Thy righteousness displeaseth the wicked; much more the viper and reptiles, which Thou hast created good, fitting in with the inferior portions of Thy Creation, with which the very wicked also fit in; and that the more, by how much they be unlike Thee; but with the superior creatures, by how much they become more like to Thee. And I enquired what iniquity was, and found it to be no substance, but the perversion of the will, turned aside from Thee, O God, the Supreme, towards these lower things, and casting out its bowels,[2] and puffed up outwardly.

[XVII] 23. And I wondered that I now loved Thee, and no phantasm for Thee. And yet did I not press on to enjoy my God; but was borne up to Thee by Thy beauty, and soon borne down from Thee by mine own weight, sinking with sorrow into these inferior things. This weight was carnal custom. Yet dwelt there with me a remembrance of Thee; nor did I any way doubt that there was One to Whom I might cleave, but that I was not yet such as to cleave to Thee: for that the body which is corrupted presseth down the soul, and the earthly tabernacle weigheth down the mind that museth upon many things.[3] And most certain I was that Thy "invisible works from the creation of the world are clearly seen, being understood by the things that are made, even Thy eternal power and Godhead."[4] For examining whence it was that I admired the beauty of bodies celestial or terrestrial, and what aided me in judging soundly on things mutable and pronouncing, "This ought to be thus, this not"; examining, I say, whence it was that I so judged, seeing I did so judge, I had found the unchange-

able and true Eternity of Truth, above my changeable mind. And thus by degrees, I passed from bodies to the soul, which through the bodily senses perceives; and thence to its inward[5] faculty, to which the bodily senses represent things external, whitherto reach the faculties of beasts; and thence again to the reasoning faculty, to which what is received from the senses of the body is referred to be judged. Which, finding itself also to be in me a thing variable, raised itself up to its own understanding, and drew away my thoughts from the power of habit, withdrawing itself from those troops of contradictory phantasms; that so it might find what that light was, whereby it was bedewed, when, without all doubting, it cried out, "That the unchangeable was to be preferred to the changeable"; whence also it knew That Unchangeable, which unless it had in some way known, it had had no sure ground to prefer it to the changeable. And thus with the flash of one trembling glance it arrived at THAT WHICH IS. And then I saw Thy invisible things understood by the things which are made.[6] But I could not fix my gaze thereon; and my infirmity being struck back, I was thrown again on my wonted habits, carrying along with me only a loving memory thereof, and a longing for what I had, as it were, perceived the odour of, but was not yet able to feed on.

[XVIII] 24. Then I sought a way of obtaining strength, sufficient to enjoy Thee; and found it not until I embraced that "Mediator betwixt God and men, the Man Christ Jesus,"[7] "who is over all, God blessed for evermore,"[8] calling unto me, and saying, "I am the way, the truth, and the life,"[9] and mingling that food which I was unable to receive, with our flesh. For "the Word was made flesh,"[10] that Thy wisdom, whereby Thou createdst all things, might provide milk for our infant state. For I did not hold to my Lord Jesus Christ, I humbled to the humble; nor knew I yet whereto His infirmity would guide us. For Thy Word, the Eternal Truth, far above the higher parts of Thy Creation, raises up the subdued unto Itself: but in this lower world built for Itself a lowly habitation of our clay, whereby to abase from themselves such as would be subdued, and bring them over to Himself; allaying their swelling, and fomenting their love; to the end they might go on no further in self-confidence, but rather consent to become weak, seeing before their feet the Divinity weak

---

[1]See below, BK. XI. 15, 16, 26.   [2]Ecclus. 10. 9.
[3]Wisd. 9. 15.   [4]Rom. 1. 20.

[5]See above, BK. VII. 16.   [6]Rom. 1. 20.
[7]I Tim. 2. 5.   [8]Rom. 9. 5.   [9]John, 14. 6.
[10]Ibid., 1. 14.

by taking our "coats of skin";[1] and, wearied, might cast themselves down upon It, and It, rising, might lift them up.

[XIX] 25. But I thought otherwise; conceiving only of my Lord Christ, as of a man of excellent wisdom, whom no one could be equalled unto; especially, for that being wonderfully born of a Virgin, He seemed, in conformity therewith, through the Divine care for us, to have attained that great eminence of authority, for an ensample of despising things temporal for the obtaining of immortality. But what mystery there lay in "The Word was made flesh,"[2] I could not even imagine. Only I had learnt out of what is delivered to us in writing of Him, that He did eat, and drink, sleep, walk, rejoiced in spirit, was sorrowful, discoursed; that flesh did not cleave by itself unto Thy Word, but with the human soul and mind. All know this, who know the unchangeableness of Thy Word, which I now knew, as far as I could, nor did I at all doubt thereof. For, now to move the limbs of the body by will, now not; now to be moved by some affection, now not; now to deliver wise sayings through human signs, now to keep silence—belong to soul and mind subject to variation. And should these things be falsely written of Him, all the rest also would risk the charge, nor would there remain in those books any saving faith for mankind. Since then they were written truly, I acknowledged a perfect man to be in Christ; not the body of a man only, nor, with the body, a sensitive soul without a rational, but very man; whom, not only as being a form of Truth, but for a certain great excellency of human nature and a more perfect participation of wisdom, I judged to be preferred before others. But Alypius imagined the Catholics to believe God to be so clothed with flesh that, besides God and flesh, there was no soul at all in Christ, and did not think that a human mind was ascribed to Him. And because he was well persuaded that the actions recorded of Him could only be performed by a vital and a rational creature, he moved the more slowly towards the Christian Faith. But understanding afterwards that this was the error of the Apollinarian heretics, he joyed in and was conformed to the Catholic Faith. But somewhat later, I confess, did I learn how in that saying, "The Word was made flesh," the Catholic Truth is distinguished from the falsehood of Photinus. For the rejection of heretics makes the tenets of Thy Church and sound doctrine to stand out more clearly. For there must also be heresies, that the ap-

proved may be made manifest among the weak.[3]

[XX] 26. But having then read those books of the Platonists, and thence been taught to search for incorporeal truth, I saw Thy invisible things, understood by those things which are made;[4] and though cast back, I perceived what that was, which through the darkness of my mind I was hindered from contemplating, being assured, "That Thou wert, and wert infinite, and yet not diffused in space, finite or infinite; and that Thou truly art who art the same ever,[5] in no part nor motion, varying; and that all other things are from Thee, on this most sure ground alone, that they are." Of these things I was assured, yet too unsure to enjoy Thee. I prated as one well skilled; but had I not sought Thy way in Christ our Saviour, I had proved to be, not skilled, but killed. For now I had begun to wish to seem wise, being filled with mine own punishment, yet I did not mourn, but rather scorn, puffed up with knowledge.[6] For where was that charity building upon the "foundation" of humility, "which is Christ Jesus"?[7] or when should these books teach me it? Upon these, I believe, Thou therefore willedst that I should fall, before I studied Thy Scriptures, that it might be imprinted on my memory, how I was affected by them; and that afterwards when my spirits were tamed through Thy books, and my wounds touched by Thy healing fingers, I might discern and distinguish between presumption and confession; between those who saw whither they were to go, yet saw not the way,[8] and the way that leadeth not to behold only but to dwell in the beatific country. For had I first been formed in Thy Holy Scriptures, and hadst Thou, in the familiar use of them, grown sweet unto me, and had I then fallen upon those other volumes, they might perhaps have withdrawn me from the solid ground of piety; or, had I continued in that healthful frame which I had thence imbibed, I might have thought that it might have been obtained by the study of those books alone.

[XXI] 27. Most eagerly then did I seize that venerable writing of Thy Spirit; and chiefly the Apostle Paul. Whereupon those difficulties vanished away, wherein he once seemed to me to contradict himself, and the text of his discourse not to agree with the testimonies of the Law and the Prophets. And the face of that pure word appeared to me one and the same; and I learned to "rejoice with trembling."[9] So I began; and

---

[1]Gen. 3. 21.   [2]John, 1. 14.

[3]I Cor. 11. 19.   [4]Rom. 1. 20.
[5]See above, Bk. VII. 17.   [6]I Cor. 8. 1.   [7]Ibid., 3. 11.
[8]See also, City of God, Bk. XI. 2.   [9]Ps. 2. 11.

whatsoever truth I had read in those other books, I found here amid the praise of Thy Grace; that whoso sees may not so glory as if he had not received,[1] not only what he sees, but also that he sees (for what hath he, which he hath not received?), and that he may be not only admonished to behold Thee, Who art ever the same, but also healed, to hold Thee; and that he who cannot see afar off may yet walk on the way, whereby he may arrive, and behold, and hold Thee. For, though a man be "delighted with the law of God after the inner man,"[2] what shall he do with that other law in his members which warreth against the law of his mind, and bringeth him into captivity to the law of sin which is in his members?[3] For Thou art righteous, O Lord, but we have sinned and committed iniquity, and have done wickedly,[4] and Thy hand is grown heavy upon us, and we are justly delivered over unto that ancient sinner, the king of death; because he persuaded our will to be like his will, whereby he abode not in Thy truth. What shall "wretched man" do? "Who shall deliver him from the body of this death," but only Thy Grace, "through Jesus Christ our Lord,"[5] whom Thou hast begotten co-eternal, and formedst in the beginning of Thy ways,[6] in whom the prince of this world found nothing worthy of death,[7] yet killed he Him;[8] and the handwriting, which was contrary to us, was blotted out?[9] This those writings contain not. Those pages present not the image of this piety, the tears of confession. Thy sacrifice, a troubled spirit, "a broken and a contrite heart,"[10] the salvation of the people, the Bridal City,[11] the earnest of the Holy Ghost,[12] the Cup of our Redemption.[13] No man sings there, Shall not my soul be submitted unto God? for of Him cometh my salvation. For he is my God and my salvation, my guardian, I shall no more be moved.[14] No one there hears Him call, "Come unto Me all ye that labour." They scorn to learn of Him, because He is meek and lowly in heart;[15] for these things "hast Thou hid from the wise and prudent, and hast revealed them unto babes.[16] For it is one thing, from the mountain's shaggy top to see the land of peace,[17] and to find no way thither; and in vain to essay through ways unpassable, opposed and beset by fugitives and deserters, under their captain the "lion"[18] and the "dragon":[19] and another to keep on the way that leads thither, guarded by the host of the heavenly General; where they spoil not who have deserted the heavenly army; for they avoid it, as very torment. These things did wonderfully sink into my bowels, when I read that "least of Thy Apostles,"[20] and had meditated upon Thy works, and trembled exceedingly.

BOOK VIII. *Augustine's thirty-second year. He consults Simplicianus, from him hears the history of the conversion of Victorinus, and longs to devote himself entirely to God, but is mastered by his old habits; is still further roused by the history of St. Anthony, and the conversion of two courtiers; during a severe struggle, hears a voice from heaven, opens Scripture, and is converted, with his friend Alypius. His mother's vision fulfilled.*

[I] 1. O my God, let me with thanksgiving remember, and confess unto Thee, Thy mercies on me. Let my bones be bedewed with Thy love, and let them say unto Thee, "Who is like unto Thee, O Lord?"[21] Thou hast broken my bonds in sunder, I will offer unto Thee the sacrifice of thanksgiving."[22] And how Thou hast broken them, I will declare; and all who worship Thee, when they hear this, shall say, "Blessed be the Lord, in heaven and in earth, great and wonderful is His name." Thy words had stuck fast in my heart, and I was hedged round about on all sides by Thee.[23] Of Thy eternal life I was now certain, though I saw it in a figure and as "through a glass."[24] Yet I had ceased to doubt that there was an incorruptible substance, whence was all other substance; nor did I now desire to be more certain of Thee, but more steadfast in Thee. But for my temporal life, all was wavering, and my heart had to be purged from the old leaven.[25] The "Way,"[26] the Saviour Himself, well pleased me, but as yet I shrunk from going through its straitness. And Thou didst put into my mind, and it seemed good in my eyes, to go to Simplicianus, who seemed to me a good servant of Thine; and Thy grace shone in him. I had heard also that from his very youth he had lived most devoted unto Thee. Now he was grown into years; and by reason of so great age spent in such zealous following of Thy ways, he seemed to me likely to have learned much experience; and so he had. Out of which store, I wished that he would tell me (setting before him my anxie-

---

[1] I Cor. 4. 7.   [2] Rom. 7. 22.   [3] *Ibid.*, ver. 23.
[4] *Song of the Three Holy Children*, 4 sq.
[5] Rom. 8. 24, 25.
[6] See also, *On Christian Doctrine*, Bk. I, ch. 34.
[7] John, 18. 38.   [8] See below, Bk. IX. 36.   [9] Col. 2. 14.
[10] Ps. 51. 17.   [11] Rev. 22. 2.   [12] II Cor. 5. 2.
[13] Ps. 116, 13.   [14] *Ibid.*, 62. 1, 2.   [15] Matt. 11. 28, 29.
[16] *Ibid.*, ver. 25.   [17] Deut. 32. 49.

[18] I Pet. 5. 8.   [19] Rev. 12. 3.   [20] I Cor. 15. 9.
[21] Ps. 35. 10.   [22] Ps. 116. 16, 17.   [23] Job, 1. 10.
[24] I Cor. 13. 12.   [25] *Ibid.*, 5. 7.   [26] John, 14. 6.

ties) which were the fittest way for one in my case to walk in Thy paths.

2. For I saw the church full; and one went this way, and another that way. But I was displeased that I led a secular life; yea, now that my desires no longer inflamed me, as of old, with hopes of honour and profit, a very grievous burden it was to undergo so heavy a bondage. For, in comparison of Thy sweetness, and the beauty of Thy house which I loved,[1] those things delighted me no longer. But still I was enthralled with the love of woman; nor did the Apostle forbid me to marry, although he advised me to something better, chiefly wishing that all men were as himself was.[2] But I, being weak, chose the more indulgent place; and because of this alone was tossed up and down in all beside, faint and wasted with withering cares, because in other matters I was constrained against my will to conform myself to a married life, to which I was given up and enthralled. I had heard from the mouth of the Truth that "there were some eunuchs, which had made themselves eunuchs for the kingdom of heaven's sake": but, saith He, "let him who can receive it receive it."[3] Surely vain are all men who are ignorant of God, and could not out of the good things which are seen, find out Him who is good.[4] But I was no longer in that vanity; I had surmounted it; and, by the common witness of all Thy creatures, had found Thee our Creator,[5] and Thy Word, God with Thee, and together with Thee one God, by whom Thou createdst all things. There is yet another kind of ungodly, who "knowing God, glorified Him not as God, neither were thankful."[6] Into this also had I fallen, but Thy right hand upheld me,[7] and took me thence, and Thou placedst me where I might recover. For Thou hadst said unto man, "Behold, the fear of the Lord is wisdom,"[8] and desire not to seem wise;[9] because they "who affirmed themselves to be wise became fools."[10] But I had now found the goodly pearl, which, selling all that I had, I ought to have bought,[11] and I hesitated.

[II] 3. To Simplicianus then I went, the father of Ambrose (a Bishop now) in receiving Thy grace, and whom Ambrose truly loved as a father. To him I related the mazes of my wanderings. But when I mentioned that I had read certain books of the Platonists, which Victorinus, sometime Rhetoric Professor of Rome (who had died a Christian, as I had heard), had

translated into Latin, he testified his joy that I had not fallen upon the writings of other philosophers, full of fallacies and deceits, "after the rudiments of this world,"[12] whereas the Platonists[13] many ways led to the belief in God, and His Word. Then to exhort me to the humility of Christ,[14] hidden from the wise, and revealed to little ones,[15] he spoke of Victorinus himself whom while at Rome he had most intimately known: and of him he related what I will not conceal. For it contains great praise of Thy grace, to be confessed unto Thee, how that aged man, most learned and skilled in the liberal sciences, and who had read and weighed so many works of the philosophers; the instructor of so many noble Senators, who also, as a monument of his excellent discharge of his office, had (which men of this world esteem a high honour) both deserved and obtained a statue in the Roman Forum; he, to that age a worshipper of idols, and a partaker of the sacrilegious rites, to which almost all the nobility of Rome were given up, and had inspired the people with the love of

Anubis, barking Deity, and all
The monster Gods of every kind, who fought
'Gainst Neptune, Venus, and Minerva:[16]

whom Rome once conquered, now adored, all which the aged Victorinus had with thundering eloquence so many years defended—he now blushed not to be the child of Thy Christ, and the new-born babe of Thy fountain; submitting his neck to the yoke of humility, and subduing his forehead to the reproach of the Cross.

4. O Lord, Lord, which hast bowed the heavens and come down, touched the mountains and they did smoke,[17] by what means didst Thou convey Thyself into that breast? He used to read (as Simplicianus said) the Holy Scripture, most studiously sought and searched into all the Christian writings, and said to Simplicianus (not openly, but privately and as a friend), "Understand that I am already a Christian." Whereto he answered, "I will not believe it, nor will I rank you among Christians, unless I see you in the Church of Christ." The other, in banter, replied. "Do walls then make Christians?" And this he often said, that he was already a Christian; and Simplicianus as often made the same answer, and the conceit of the "walls" was by the other as often renewed. For he feared to offend his friends, proud dæmon-worshippers,

[1]Ps. 26. 8. [2]I Cor. 7. 7. [3]Matt. 19. 12. [4]Wisd. 13. 1. [5]See above, Bk. IV. 18. [6]Rom. 1. 21. [7]Ps. 18. 35. [8]Job, 28. 28. [9]Prov. 3. 7. [10]Rom. 1. 22. [11]Matt. 13. 46. [12]Col. 2. 8. [13]Cf. *City of God*, Bk. X. 29. [14]See above, Bk. IV. 19. [15]Matt. 11. 25. [16]*Æneid*, VIII. 698–700. [17]Ps. 144. 5.

from the height of whose Babylonian dignity, as from cedars of Libanus, which the Lord had not yet broken down,[1] he supposed the weight of enmity would fall upon him. But after that by reading and earnest thought he had gathered firmness, and feared to be denied by Christ before the holy angels, should he now be afraid to confess him before men,[2] and appeared to himself guilty of a heavy offence, in being ashamed of the Sacraments of the humility of Thy Word, and not being ashamed of the sacrilegious rites of those proud dæmons, whose pride he had imitated and their rites adopted, he became boldfaced against vanity, and shame-faced towards the truth, and suddenly and unexpectedly said to Simplicianus (as himself told me), "Go we to the Church; I wish to be made a Christian." But he, not containing himself for joy, went with him. And having been admitted to the first Sacrament and become a catechumen, not long after he further gave in his name that he might be regenerated by baptism, Rome wondering, the Church rejoicing. The proud saw, and were wroth; they gnashed with their teeth, and melted away.[3] But the Lord God was the hope of Thy servant, and he regarded not vanities and lying madness.[4]

5. To conclude, when the hour was come for making profession of his faith (which at Rome they who are about to approach to Thy grace deliver, from an elevated place, in the sight of all the faithful, in a set form of words[5] committed to memory), the presbyters, he said, offered Victorinus (as was done to such as seemed likely through bashfulness to be alarmed) to make his profession more privately; but he chose rather to profess his salvation in the presence of the holy multitude. "For it was not salvation that he taught in rhetoric, and yet that he had publicly professed. How much less then ought he, when pronouncing Thy word, to dread Thy meek flock, who, when delivering his own words, had not feared a mad multitude!" When, then, he went up to make his profession, all, as they knew him, whispered his name one to another with the voice of congratulation. And who there knew him not? and there ran a low murmur through all the mouths of the rejoicing multitude, "Victorinus! Victorinus!" Sudden was the burst of rapture, that they saw him; suddenly were they hushed that they might hear him. He pronounced the true faith with an excellent boldness, and all wished to draw him into their very heart: yea, by their love and joy they drew him thither; such were the hands wherewith they drew him.

[III] 6. Good God! what takes place in man, that he should more rejoice at the salvation of a soul despaired of, and freed from greater peril, than if there had always been hope of him, or the danger had been less? For so Thou also, merciful Father, dost "more rejoice over one penitent, than over ninety-nine just persons that need no repentance." And with much joyfulness do we hear, so often as we hear with what joy the sheep which had strayed, is brought back upon the shepherd's shoulder, and the groat is restored to Thy treasury, the neighbours rejoicing with the woman who found it;[6] and the joy of the solemn service of Thy house forceth to tears, when in Thy house it is read of Thy younger son, that he "was dead, and lived again; had been lost, and is found."[7] For Thou rejoicest in us, and in Thy holy angels, holy through holy charity. For Thou art ever the same; for all things which abide not the same nor for ever, Thou for ever knowest in the same way.

7. What then takes place in the soul, when it is more delighted at finding or recovering the things it loves than if it had ever had them? yea, and other things witness hereunto; and all things are full of witnesses, crying out, "so is it." The conquering commander triumpheth; yet had he not conquered, unless he had fought; and the more peril there was in the battle, so much the more joy is there in the triumph. The storm tosses the sailors, threatens shipwreck; all wax pale at approaching death; sky and sea are calmed, and they are exceeding joyed, as having been exceeding afraid. A friend is sick, and his pulse threatens danger; all who long for his recovery are sick in mind with him. He is restored, though as yet he walks not with his former strength; yet there is such joy as was not when before he walked sound and strong. Yea, the very pleasures of human life men acquire by difficulties, not those only which fall upon us unlooked for, and against our wills, but even by self-chosen and pleasure-seeking trouble. Eating and drinking have no pleasure, unless there precede the pinching of hunger and thirst. Men, given to drink, eat certain salt meats, to procure a troublesome heat, which, the drink allaying, causes pleasure. It is also ordered that the affianced bride should not at once be given, lest as a husband he should hold cheap whom, as betrothed, he sighed not after.

8. This law holds in foul and accursed joy; this, in permitted and lawful joy; this, in the

---

[1]Ps. 29. 5. [2]Luke, 9. 26. [3]Ps. 112. 10.
[4]Ibid., 31. 6, 14, 18. [5]The Apostles' Creed. [6]Luke 15. 4-10. [7]Ibid., ver. 32.

very purest perfection of friendship; this, in him who was dead, and lived again, had been lost, and was found.[1] Everywhere the greater joy is ushered in by the greater pain. What means this, O Lord my God, whereas Thou art everlastingly joy to Thyself, and some things around Thee evermore rejoice in Thee?[2] What means this, that this portion of things thus ebbs and flows alternately displeased and reconciled? Is this their allotted measure? Is this all Thou hast assigned to them, whereas from the highest heavens to the lowest earth, from the beginning of the world to the end of ages, from the angel to the worm, from the first motion to the last, Thou settest each in its place, and realizest each in their season, everything good after its kind? Woe is me! how high art Thou in the highest, and how deep in the deepest! and Thou never departest, and we scarcely return to Thee.

9. Up, Lord, and do; stir us up, and recall us; kindle and draw us; inflame, grow sweet unto us; let us now love, "let us run."[3] Do not many, out of a deeper hell of blindness than Victorinus, return to Thee, approach, and are enlightened, receiving that Light which they who receive, receive power from Thee to become Thy sons?[4] But if they be less known to the nations, even they that know them joy less for them. For when many joy together, each also has more exuberant joy; for that they are kindled and inflamed one by the other. Again, because those known to many influence the more towards salvation, and lead the way with many to follow. And therefore do they also who preceded them much rejoice in them, because they rejoice not in them alone. For far be it that in Thy tabernacle the persons of the rich should be accepted before the poor, or the noble before the ignoble; seeing rather "Thou hast chosen the weak things of the world, to confound the strong; and the base things of this world, and the things despised hast Thou chosen, and those things which are not, that Thou mightest bring to nought things that are.[5] And yet even that "least of Thy apostles," [6] by whose tongue Thou soundedst forth these words, when through his warfare Paulus the Proconsul,[7] his pride conquered, was made to pass under the easy yoke[8] of Thy Christ, and became a provincial of the great King; he also, for his former name Saul, was pleased to be called Paul, in testimony of so great a victory. For the enemy is more overcome in one of whom he hath more hold; by whom he

hath hold of more. But the proud he hath more hold of, through their nobility; and by them, of more through their authority. By how much the more welcome then the heart of Victorinus was esteemed, which the devil had held as an impregnable possession; the tongue of Victorinus, with which mighty and keen weapon he had slain many; so much the more abundantly ought Thy sons to rejoice, for that our King hath bound the strong man,[9] and they saw his vessels taken from him and cleansed,[10] and made meet for Thy honour, and become serviceable for the Lord, unto every good work.[11]

[V] 10. But when that man of Thine, Simplicianus, related to me this of Victorinus, I was on fire to imitate him; for for this very end had he related it. But when he had subjoined also how, in the days of the Emperor Julian, a law was made whereby Christians were forbidden to teach the liberal sciences or oratory; and how he, obeying this law, chose rather to give over the wordy school, than Thy Word, by which Thou makest eloquent the tongues of the dumb;[12] he seemed to me not more resolute than blessed, in having thus found opportunity to wait on Thee only. Which thing I was sighing for, bound as I was, not with another's irons, but by my own iron will. My will the enemy held, and thence had made a chain for me, and bound me. For of a froward will was a lust made; and a lust served became custom; and custom not resisted became necessity. By which links, as it were, joined together (whence I called it a "chain"), a hard bondage held me enthralled. But that new will which had begun to be in me, freely to serve Thee, and to wish to enjoy Thee, O God, the only assured pleasantness, was not yet able to overcome my former wilfulness, strengthened by age. Thus did my two wills, one new, and the other old, one carnal, the other spiritual, struggle within me; and by their discord, undid my soul.

11. Thus I understood, by my own experience, what I had read, how "the flesh lusteth against the spirit and the spirit against the flesh." [13] Myself verily either way; yet more myself, in that which I approved in myself, than in that which in myself I disapproved. For in this last, it was now for the more part not myself, because in much I rather endured against my will, than acted willingly. And yet it was through me that custom had obtained this power of warring against me, because I had come willingly, whither I willed not. And who has any right to speak

---

[1]Luke, 15. 32.   [2]See below, Bk. XII. 12; Bk. XIII. 11.
[3]Cant. 1. 4.   [4]John, 1. 12.   [5]I Cor. 1. 27, 28.
[6]Ibid., 15. 9.   [7]Acts, 13. 12.   [8]Matt. 11. 30.

[9]Ibid., 12. 29.   [10]Luke, 11. 22, 25.   [11]II Tim. 2. 21.
[12]Wisd. 10. 21.   [13]Gal. 5. 17.

against it, if just punishment follow the sinner? Nor had I now any longer my former plea, that I therefore as yet hesitated to be above the world and serve Thee, for that the truth was not altogether ascertained to me; for now it too was. But I, still under service to the earth, refused to fight under Thy banner, and feared as much to be freed of all incumbrances, as we should fear to be encumbered with it. Thus with the baggage of this present world was I held down pleasantly, as in sleep: and the thoughts wherein I meditated on Thee were like the efforts of such as would awake, who yet, overcome with a heavy drowsiness, are again drenched therein. And as no one would sleep for ever, and in all men's sober judgment, waking is better, yet a man for the most part, feeling a heavy lethargy in all his limbs, defers to shake off sleep, and, though half displeased, yet, even after it is time to rise, with pleasure yields to it, so was I assured that much better were it for me to give myself up to thy charity, than to give myself over to mine own cupidity; but though the former course satisfied me and gained the mastery, the latter pleased me and held me mastered. Nor had I anything to answer Thee calling to me, "Awake, thou that sleepest, and arise from the dead, and Christ shall give thee light."[1] And when Thou didst on all sides shew me that what Thou saidst was true, I, convicted by the truth, had nothing at all to answer, but only those dull and drowsy words, "Anon, anon," "presently," "leave me but a little." But "presently, presently," had no present, and my "little while" went on for a long while; in vain I "delighted in Thy law according to the inner man," when "another law in my members rebelled against the law of my mind, and led me captive under the law of sin which was in my members." For the law of sin is the violence of custom, whereby the mind is drawn and holden, even against its will; but deservedly, for that it willingly fell into it. "Who then should deliver me thus wretched from the body of this death," but Thy grace only, through Jesus Christ our Lord?[2]

[VI] 13. And how Thou didst deliver me out of the bonds of desire, wherewith I was bound most straitly to carnal concupiscence, and out of the drudgery of worldly things, I will now declare, and confess unto Thy name, "O Lord, my helper and my redeemer."[3] Amid increasing anxiety, I was doing my wonted business, and daily sighing unto Thee. I attended Thy Church, whenever free from the business under the burden of which I groaned. Alypius was with me,

now after the third sitting released from his law business, and awaiting to whom to sell his counsel, as I sold the skill of speaking, if indeed teaching can impart it. Nebridius had now, in consideration of our friendship, consented to teach under Verecundus, a citizen and a grammarian of Milan, and a very intimate friend of us all; who urgently desired, and by the right of friendship challenged from our company, such faithful aid as he greatly needed. Nebridius then was not drawn to this by any desire of advantage (for he might have made much more of his learning had he so willed) but, as a most kind and gentle friend, he would not be wanting to a good office, and slight our request. But he acted herein very discreetly, shunning to become known to personages great according to this world, avoiding the distraction of mind thence ensuing, and desiring to have it free and at leisure, as many hours as might be, to seek, or read, or hear something concerning wisdom.

14. Upon a day then, Nebridius being absent (I recollect not why), lo, there came to see me and Alypius one Pontitianus, our countryman so far as being an African, in high office in the Emperor's court. What he would with us, I know not, but we sat down to converse, and it happened that upon a table for some game before us, he observed a book, took, opened it, and contrary to his expectation, found it the Apostle Paul; for he had thought it some of those books which I was wearing myself in teaching. Whereat smiling, and looking at me, he expressed his joy and wonder that he had on a sudden found this book, and this only before my eyes. For he was a Christian, and baptized, and often bowed himself before Thee our God in the Church, in frequent and continued prayers. When then I had told him that I bestowed very great pains upon those Scriptures, a conversation arose (suggested by his account) on Anthony[4] the Egyptian monk, whose name was in high reputation among Thy servants, though to that hour unknown to us. Which when he discovered, he dwelt the more upon that subject, informing and wondering at our ignorance of one so eminent. But we stood amazed, hearing Thy wonderful works most fully attested, in times so recent, and almost in our own, wrought in the true Faith and Church Catholic. We all wondered; we, that they were so great, and he, that they had not reached us.

15. Thence his discourse turned to the flocks in the monasteries, and their holy ways, a sweet-

---

[1] Eph. 5. 14.   [2] Rom. 7. 22–24.   [3] Ps. 19. 14.   [4] See also, *On Christian Doctrine*, Pref. 4.

smelling savour unto Thee, and the fruitful deserts of the wilderness, whereof we knew nothing.
And there was a monastery at Milan, full of
good brethren, without the city walls, under the
fostering care of Ambrose, and we knew it not.
He went on with his discourse, and we listened
in intent silence. He told us then how one afternoon at Trier, when the Emperor was taken up
with the Circensian games, he and three others,
his companions, went out to walk in gardens
near the city walls, and there as they happened
to walk in pairs, one went apart with him, and
the other two wandered by themselves; and
these, in their wanderings, lighted upon a certain
cottage, inhabited by certain of thy servants,
"poor in spirit, of whom is the kingdom of heav-
en,"[1] and there they found a little book, containing the life of Anthony. This one of them began to read, admire, and kindle at it; and, as he
read, to meditate on taking up such a life, and
giving over his secular service to serve Thee.
And these two were of those whom they style
"Agents for the Public Affairs. "[2] Then suddenly, filled with an holy love and a sober shame, in
anger with himself he cast his eyes upon his
friend, saying, "Tell me, I pray thee, what would
we attain by all these labours of ours? what aim
we at? what serve we for? Can our hopes in
court rise higher than to be the Emperor's fa-
vourites? and in this, what is there not brittle,
and full of perils? and by how many perils arrive we at a greater peril? And when arrive we
thither? But a friend of God, if I wish it, I become now at once." So spake he. And in pain
with the travail of a new life, he turned his eyes
again upon the book, and read on, and was
changed inwardly, where Thou sawest, and his
mind was stripped of the world, as soon appeared. For as he read, and rolled up and down
the waves of his heart, he stormed at himself a
while, then discerned and determined on a better course; and now being Thine, said to his
friend, "Now have I broken loose from those
our hopes, and am resolved to serve God; and
this, from this hour, in this place, I begin upon.
If thou likest not to imitate me, oppose not."
The other answered, he would cleave to him, to
partake so glorious a reward, so glorious a service. Thus both, being now Thine, were building
the tower at the necessary cost, the forsaking all
that they had, and following Thee.[3] Then Pontitianus and the other with him, that had walked
in other parts of the garden, came in search of
them to the same place; and finding them, reminded them to return, for the day was now far

spent. But they, relating their resolution and
purpose, and how that will was begun and settled in them, begged them, if they would not
join, not to molest them. But the others, though
nothing altered from their former selves, did yet
bewail themselves (as he affirmed) and piously
congratulated them, recommending themselves
to their prayers; and so, with hearts lingering on
the earth, went away to the palace. But the other
two, fixing their heart on heaven, remained in
the cottage. And both had affianced brides, who,
when they heard hereof, also dedicated their virginity unto God.

[VII] 16. Such was the story of Pontitianus;
but Thou, O Lord, while he was speaking, didst
turn me round towards myself, taking me from
behind my back, where I had placed me, unwilling to observe myself; and setting me before my
face, that I might see how foul I was, how
crooked and defiled, bespotted and ulcerous.
And I beheld and stood aghast; and whither to
flee from myself I found not. And if I sought to
turn mine eye from off myself, he went on with
his relation, and Thou again didst set me over
against myself, and thrustedst me before my
eyes, that I might find out mine iniquity, and
hate it.[4] I had known it, but made as though I
saw it not, winked at it, and forgot it.

17. But now, the more ardently I loved those
whose healthful affections I heard of, that they
had resigned themselves wholly to Thee to be
cured, the more did I abhor myself, when compared with them. For many of my years (some
twelve) had now run out with me since my nineteenth, when, upon the reading of Cicero's *Hortensius*,[5] I was stirred to an earnest love of wisdom; and still I was deferring to reject mere
earthly felicity, and give myself to search out
that whereof not the finding only, but the very
search, was to be preferred to the treasures and
kingdoms of the world, though already found,
and to the pleasures of the body, though spread
around me at my will. But I wretched, most
wretched, in the very commencement of my
early youth, had begged chastity of Thee, and
said, "Give me chastity and continency, only not
yet." For I feared lest Thou shouldest hear me
soon, and soon cure me of the disease of concupiscence, which I wished to have satisfied, rather
than extinguished. And I had wandered through
crooked ways in a sacrilegious superstition, not
indeed assured thereof, but as preferring it to
the others which I did not seek religiously, but
opposed maliciously.

18. And I had thought that I therefore de-

[1]Matt. 5. 3.   [2]*Agentes in rebus.*   [3]Luke, 14. 26–35.   [4]Ps. 36. 2.   [5]See above, BK. III. 7.

ferred from day to day to reject the hopes of this world, and follow Thee only, because there did not appear aught certain, whither to direct my course. And now was the day come wherein I was to be laid bare to myself, and my conscience was to upbraid me. "Where art thou now, my tongue? Thou saidst that for an uncertain truth thou likedst not to cast off the baggage of vanity; now, it is certain, and yet that burthen still oppresseth thee, while they who neither have so worn themselves out with seeking it, nor for ten years and more have been thinking thereon, have had their shoulders lightened, and received wings to fly away." Thus was I gnawed within, and exceedingly confounded with an horrible shame, while Pontitianus was so speaking. And he, having brought to a close his tale and the business he came for, went his way; and I into myself. What said I not against myself? with what scourges of condemnation lashed I not my soul, that it might follow me, striving to go after Thee! Yet it drew back; refused, but excused not itself. All arguments were spent and confuted; there remained a mute shrinking; and she feared, as she would death, to be restrained from the flux of that custom, whereby she was wasting to death.

[VIII] 19. Then in this great contention of my inward dwelling, which I had strongly raised against my soul, in the chamber of my heart,[1] troubled in mind and countenance, I turned upon Alypius. "What ails us?" I exclaim. "What is it? what heardest thou? The unlearned start up and 'take' heaven by force,[2] and we with our learning, and without heart, lo, where we wallow in flesh and blood! Are we ashamed to follow, because others are gone before, and not ashamed not even to follow?" Some such words I uttered, and my fever of mind tore me away from him, while he, gazing on me in astonishment, kept silence. For it was not my wonted tone; and my forehead, cheeks, eyes, colour, tone of voice, spake my mind more than the words I uttered. A little garden there was to our lodging, which we had the use of, as of the whole house; for the master of the house, our host, was not living there. Thither had the tumult of my breast hurried me, where no man might hinder the hot contention wherein I had engaged with myself, until it should end as Thou knewest, I knew not. Only I was healthfully distracted and dying, to live; knowing what evil thing I was, and not knowing what good thing I was shortly to become. I retired then into the garden, and Alypius on my steps. For his presence did not lessen my

privacy; or how could he forsake me so disturbed? We sat down as far removed as might be from the house. I was troubled in spirit, most vehemently indignant that I entered not into Thy will and covenant, O my God, which all my bones cried out unto me to enter, and praised it to the skies. And therein we enter not by ships, or chariots, or feet, no, move not so far as I had come from the house to that place where we were sitting. For not to go only, but to go in thither, was nothing else but to will to go, but to will resolutely and thoroughly; not to turn and toss, this way and that, a maimed and half-divided will, struggling, with one part sinking as another rose.

20. Lastly, in the very fever of my irresoluteness, I made with my body many such motions as men sometimes would, but cannot, if either they have not the limbs, or these be bound with bands, weakened with infirmity, or any other way hindered. Thus, if I tore my hair, beat my forehead, if locking my fingers I clasped my knee, I willed, I did it. But I might have willed, and not done it, if the power of motion in my limbs had not obeyed. So many things then I did, when "to will" was not in itself "to be able"; and I did not what both I longed incomparably more to do, and which soon after, when I should will, I should be able to do; because soon after, when I should will, I should will thoroughly. For in these things the ability was one with the will, and to will was to do; and yet was it not done: and more easily did my body obey the weakest willing of my soul, in moving its limbs at its nod, than the soul obeyed itself to accomplish in the will alone this its momentous will.

[IX] 21. Whence is this monstrousness? and to what end? Let Thy mercy gleam that I may ask, if so be the secret penalties of men, and those darkest pangs of the sons of Adam, may perhaps answer me. Whence is this monstrousness? and to what end? The mind commands the body, and it obeys instantly; the mind commands itself, and is resisted. The mind commands the hand to be moved; and such readiness is there that command is scarce distinct from obedience. Yet the mind is mind, the hand is body. The mind commands the mind, its own self, to will, and yet it doth not. Whence this monstrousness? and to what end? It commands itself, I say, to will, and would not command, unless it willed, and what it commands is not done. But it willeth not entirely: therefore doth it not command entirely. For so far forth it commandeth, as it willeth: and, so far forth is the

[1]Isa. 26. 20; Matt. 6. 6.   [2]Matt. 11. 12.

thing commanded, not done, as it willeth not. For the will commandeth that there be a will; not another, but itself. But it doth not command entirely, therefore what it commandeth is not. For were the will entire, it would not even command it to be, because it would already be. It is therefore no monstrousness partly to will, partly to nill, but a disease of the mind, that it doth not wholly rise, by truth up-borne, borne down by custom. And therefore are there two wills, for that one of them is not entire: and what the one lacketh, the other hath.

[X] 22. Let them perish from Thy presence,[1] O God, as perish vain talkers, and seducers[2] of the soul: who, observing that in deliberating there were two wills, affirm that there are two minds in us of two kinds, one good, the other evil. Themselves are truly evil, when they hold these evil things; and themselves shall become good, when they hold the truth, and assent unto the truth, that Thy Apostle may say to them, "Ye were sometimes darkness, but now light in the Lord."[3] But they, wishing to be light, not "in the Lord," but in themselves, imagining the nature of the soul to be that which God is,[4] are made more gross darkness through a dreadful arrogancy; for that they went back farther from Thee, "the true Light that enlighteneth every man that cometh into the world."[5] Take heed what you say, and blush for shame: draw near unto Him and be "enlightened," and your faces shall not be "ashamed."[6] Myself when I was deliberating upon serving the Lord my God now, as I had long purposed, it was I who willed, I who nilled, I, I myself. I neither willed entirely, nor nilled entirely. Therefore was I at strife with myself, and rent asunder by myself. And this rent befel me against my will, and yet indicated, not the presence of another mind, but the punishment of my own. "Therefore it was no more I that wrought it, but sin that dwelt in me";[7] the punishment of a sin more freely committed, in that I was a son of Adam.

23. For if there be so many contrary natures, as there be conflicting wills; there shall now be not two only, but many. If a man deliberate whether he should go to their conventicle or to the theatre, these Manichees cry out, "Behold, here are two natures: one good, draws this way; another bad, draws back that way. For whence else is this hesitation between conflicting wills?" But I say that both be bad: that which draws to them, as that which draws back to the theatre.

But they believe not that will to be other than good, which draws to them. What then if one of us should deliberate, and amid the strife of his two wills be in a strait, whether he should go to the theatre, or to our church? would not these Manichees also be in a strait what to answer? For either they must confess (which they fain would not) that the will which leads to our church is good, as well as theirs, who have received and are held by the mysteries of theirs: or they must suppose two evil natures, and two evil souls conflicting in one man, and it will not be true, which they say, that there is one good and another bad; or they must be converted to the truth, and no more deny, that where one deliberates, one soul fluctuates between contrary wills.

24. Let them no more say then, when they perceive two conflicting wills in one man, that the conflict is between two contrary souls, of two contrary substances, from two contrary principles, one good, and the other bad. For Thou, O true God, dost disprove, check, and convict them; as when, both wills being bad, one deliberates whether he should kill a man by poison or by the sword; whether he should seize this or that estate of another's, when he cannot both; whether he should purchase pleasure by luxury, or keep his money by covetousness; whether he go to the circus, or the theatre, if both be open on one day; or, thirdly, to rob another's house, if he have the opportunity; or, fourthly, to commit adultery, if at the same time he have the means thereof also; all these meeting together in the same juncture of time, and all being equally desired, which cannot at one time be acted: for they rend the mind amid four, or even (amid the vast variety of things desired) more, conflicting wills, nor do they yet allege that there are so many divers substances. So also in wills which are good. For I ask them, is it good to take pleasure in reading the Apostle?[8] or good to take pleasure in a sober Psalm? or good to discourse on the Gospel? They will answer to each, "It is good." What then if all give equal pleasure, and all at once? Do not divers wills distract the mind, while he deliberates which he should rather choose? yet are they all good, and are at variance till one be chosen, whither the one entire will may be borne, which before was divided into many. Thus also, when, above, eternity delights us, and the pleasure of temporal good holds us down below, it is the same soul which willeth not this or that with an entire will, and therefore is rent asunder with

[1]Ps. 68. 2.   [2]Titus, 1. 10.   [3]Eph. 5.8.
[4]See above, BK. IV. 26.   [5]John, 1. 9.
[6]Ps. 4. 5.   [7]Rom. 7. 17.

[8]St. Paul.

grievous perplexities; while out of truth it sets this first, but out of habit sets not that aside.

[XI] 25. Thus soul-sick was I, and tormented, accusing myself much more severely than my wont, rolling and turning me in my chain, till that were wholly broken, whereby I now was but just, but still was, held. And Thou, O Lord, pressedst upon me in my inward parts by a severe mercy, re-doubling the lashes of fear and shame, lest I should again give way, and not bursting that same slight remaining tie, it should recover strength, and bind me the faster. For I said within myself, "Be it done now, be it done now." And as I spake, I all but enacted it. I all but did it, and did it not: yet sunk not back to my former state, but kept my stand hard by, and took breath. And I essayed again, and wanted somewhat less of it, and somewhat less, and all but touched and laid hold of it; and yet came not at it, nor touched, nor laid hold of it: hesitating to die to death and to live to life: and the worse whereto I was inured prevailed more with me than the better, whereto I was unused: and the very moment wherein I was to become other than I was, the nearer it approached me, the greater horror did it strike into me; yet did it not strike me back, nor turned me away, but held me in suspense.

26. The very toys of toys, and vanities of vanities, my ancient mistresses, still held me; they plucked my fleshly garment, and whispered softly, "Dost thou cast us off? and from that moment shall we no more be with thee for ever? and from that moment shall not this or that be lawful for thee for ever?" And what was it which they suggested in that I said, "this or that," what did they suggest, O my God? Let Thy mercy turn it away from the soul of Thy servant. What defilements did they suggest! what shame! And now I much less than half heard them, and not openly shewing themselves and contradicting me, but muttering as it were behind my back, and privily plucking me, as I was departing, but to look back on them. Yet they did retard me, so that I hesitated to burst and shake myself free from them, and to spring over whither I was called; a violent habit saying to me, "Thinkest thou, thou canst live without them?"

27. But now it spake very faintly. For on that side whither I had set my face, and whither I trembled to go, there appeared unto me the chaste dignity of Continency, serene, yet not relaxedly gay, honestly alluring me to come and doubt not; and stretching forth to receive and embrace me, her holy hands full of multitudes of good examples. There were so many young men and maidens here, a multitude of youth and every age, grave widows and aged virgins; and Continence herself in all, not barren, but a fruitful mother of children of joys, by Thee her Husband, O Lord. And she smiled on me with a persuasive mockery, as would she say, "Canst not thou what these youths, what these maidens can? or can they either in themselves, and not rather in the Lord their God? The Lord their God gave me unto them. Why standest thou in thyself, and so standest not? Cast thyself upon Him, fear not He will not withdraw Himself that thou shouldest fall; cast thyself fearlessly upon Him, He will receive, and will heal thee." And I blushed exceedingly, for that I yet heard the muttering of those toys, and hung in suspense. And she again seemed to say, "Stop thine ears against those thy unclean members on the earth, that they may be mortified.[1] They tell thee of delights, but not as doth the law of the Lord thy God." [2] This controversy in my heart was self against self only. But Alypius, sitting close by my side, in silence waited the issue of my unwonted emotion.

[XII] 28. But when a deep consideration had from the secret bottom of my soul drawn together and heaped up all my misery in the sight of my heart, there arose a mighty storm, bringing a mighty shower of tears. Which that I might pour forth wholly, in its natural expressions, I rose from Alypius: solitude was suggested to me as fitter for the business of weeping; so I retired so far that even his presence could not be a burthen to me. Thus was it then with me, and he perceived something of it; for something I suppose I had spoken, wherein the tones of my voice appeared choked with weeping, and so had risen up. He then remained where we were sitting, most extremely astonished. I cast myself down I know not how, under a certain fig-tree, giving full vent to my tears; and the floods of mine eyes gushed out, an acceptable sacrifice to Thee.[3] And, not indeed in these words, yet to this purpose, spake I much unto Thee: "And Thou, O Lord, how long?"[4] "How long, Lord, wilt Thou be angry, for ever? Remember not our former iniquities,"[5] for I felt that I was held by them. I sent up these sorrowful words: "How long? how long? Tomorrow, and tomorrow? Why not now? why not is there this hour an end to my uncleanness?"

29. So was I speaking, and weeping in the most bitter contrition of my heart, when, lo! I

[1]Col. 3. 5.   [2]Ps. 119. 85, old version.
[3]I Pet. 2. 5.   [4]Ps. 6. 3.   [5]Ps. 79. 5, 8.

heard from a neighbouring house a voice, as of boy or girl, I know not, chanting, and oft repeating, "Take up and read; take up and read." Instantly, my countenance altered, I began to think most intently, whether children were wont in any kind of play to sing such words; nor could I remember ever to have heard the like. So checking the torrent of my tears, I arose; interpreting it to be no other than a command from God, to open the book, and read the first chapter I should find. For I had heard of Anthony that, coming in during the reading of the Gospel, he received the admonition, as if what was being read, was spoken to him; "Go, sell all that thou hast, and give to the poor, and thou shalt have treasure in heaven, and come and follow me."[1] And by such oracle he was forthwith converted unto Thee. Eagerly then I returned to the place where Alypius was sitting; for there had I laid the volume of the Apostle, when I arose thence. I seized, opened, and in silence read that section, on which my eyes first fell: "Not in rioting and drunkenness, not in chambering and wantonness, not in strife and envying: but put ye on the Lord Jesus Christ, and make not provision for the flesh,"[2] in concupiscence. No further would I read; nor needed I: for instantly at the end of this sentence, by a light as it were of serenity infused into my heart, all the darkness of doubt vanished away.

30. Then putting my finger between, or some other mark, I shut the volume, and with a calmed countenance made it known to Alypius. And what was wrought in him, which I knew not, he thus shewed me. He asked to see what I had read: I shewed him; and he looked even further than I had read, and I knew not what followed. This followed, "Him that is weak in the faith, receive";[3] which he applied to himself, and disclosed to me. And by this admonition was he strengthened; and by a good resolution and purpose, and most corresponding to his character, wherein he did always very far differ from me for the better, without any turbulent delay he joined me. Thence we go into my mother; we tell her; she rejoiceth: we relate in order how it took place; she leaps for joy, and triumpheth, and blesseth Thee, "Who art able to do above that which we ask or think";[4] for she perceived that Thou hadst given her more for me than she was wont to beg by her pitiful and most sorrowful groanings. For Thou convertedst me unto Thyself, so that I sought neither wife, nor any hope of this world, standing in that rule of faith[5]

where Thou hadst shewed me unto her in a vision, so many years before. And Thou didst convert her mourning into joy,[6] much more plentiful than she had desired, and in a much more precious and purer way than she erst required, by having grandchildren of my body.

BOOK IX. *Augustine determines to devote his life to God, and to abandon his profession of Rhetoric, quietly however; retires to the country to prepare himself to receive the grace of baptism, and is baptized with Alypius, and his son Adeodatus. At Ostia, on his way to Africa, his mother Monica dies, in her fifty-sixth year, the thirty-third of Augustine. Her life and character.*

[I] 1. "O Lord, I am Thy servant; I am Thy servant, and the son of Thy handmaid: Thou hast broken my bonds in sunder. I will offer to Thee the sacrifice of praise."[7] Let my heart and my tongue praise Thee; yea let all my bones say, "O Lord, who is like unto Thee?"[8] Let them say, and answer Thou me, and "say unto my soul, I am thy salvation."[9] Who am I, and what am I? What evil have not been either my deeds, or if not my deeds, my words, or if not my words, my will? But Thou, O Lord, art good and merciful, and Thy right hand had respect unto the depth of my death, and from the bottom of my heart emptied that abyss of corruption. And this Thy whole gift was, to nill what I willed, and to will what Thou willedst. But where through all those years, and out of what low and deep recess was my free-will called forth in a moment, whereby to submit my neck to Thy "easy yoke," and my shoulders unto Thy "light burthen,"[10] O Christ Jesus, "my Helper and my Redeemer?"[11] How sweet did it at once become to me to want the sweetnesses of those joys! and what I feared to be parted from was now a joy to part with. For Thou didst cast them forth from me, Thou true and highest sweetness. Thou castest them forth, and for them enteredst in Thyself, sweeter than all pleasure, though not to flesh and blood; brighter than all light, but more hidden than all depths; higher than all honour, but not to the high in their own conceits. Now was my soul free from the biting cares of canvassing and getting, and weltering in filth, and scratching off the itch of lust. And my infant tongue spake freely to Thee, my brightness, and my riches, and my health, the Lord my God.

[II] 2. And I resolved in Thy sight, not tu-

---

[1]Matt. 19. 21.   [2]Rom. 13. 13, 14.   [3]Rom. 14. 1.
[4]Eph. 3. 20.   [5]See above, Bk. III. 19.

[6]Ps. 30. 11.   [7]Ps. 116. 16, 17.   [8]*Ibid.*, 35. 10.
[9]*Ibid.*, ver. 3.   [10]Matt. 11. 30.   [11]Ps. 19. 14.

multuously to tear, but gently to withdraw, the service of my tongue from the marts of lip-labour: that the young, no students in Thy law, nor in Thy peace, but in lying dotages and law-skirmishes, should no longer buy at my mouth arms for their madness. And very seasonably, it now wanted but very few days unto the[1] Vacation of the Vintage, and I resolved to endure them, then in a regular way to take my leave, and, having been purchased by Thee, no more to return for sale. Our purpose then was known to Thee; but to men, other than our own friends, was it not known. For we had agreed among ourselves not to let it out abroad to any: although to us, now ascending from the valley of tears,[2] and singing that song of degrees, Thou hadst given "sharp arrows," and destroying coals against the "subtile tongue"[3] which, as though advising for us, would thwart, and would out of love devour us, as it doth its meat.

3. Thou hadst pierced our hearts with Thy charity, and we carried Thy words as it were fixed in our entrails; and the examples of Thy servants, whom for black Thou hadst made bright, and for dead, alive, being piled together in the receptacle of our thoughts, kindled and burned up that our heavy torpor, that we should not sink down to the abyss; and they fired us so vehemently, that all the blasts of subtile tongues from gainsayers might only inflame us the more fiercely, not extinguish us. Nevertheless, because for Thy Name's sake which Thou hast hallowed throughout the earth, this our vow and purpose might also find some to commend it, it seemed like ostentation not to wait for the vacation now so near, but to quit beforehand a public profession, which was before the eyes of all; so that all looking on this act of mine, and observing how near was the time of vintage which I wished to anticipate, would talk much of me, as if I had desired to appear some great one. And what end had it served me, that people should repute and dispute upon my purpose, and that our good should be evil spoken of?[4]

4. Moreover, it had at first troubled me that in this very summer my lungs began to give way, amid too great literary labour, and to breathe deeply with difficulty, and by the pain in my chest to shew that they were injured, and to refuse any full or lengthened speaking; this had troubled me, for it almost constrained me of necessity to lay down that burthen of teaching, or, if I could be cured and recover, at least to intermit it. But when the full wish for leisure, that

I might see how that Thou art the Lord,[5] arose, and was fixed, in me; my God, Thou knowest, I began even to rejoice that I had this secondary, and that no feigned, excuse, which might something moderate the offence taken by those who, for their sons' sake, wished me never to have the freedom of Thy sons. Full then of such joy, I endured till that interval of time were run; it may have been some twenty days, yet they were endured manfully; endured, for the covetousness which aforetime bore a part of this heavy business, had left me, and I remained alone, and had been overwhelmed had not patience taken its place. Perchance some of Thy servants, my brethren, may say that I sinned in this, that with a heart fully set on Thy service, I suffered myself to sit even one hour in the chair of lies. Nor would I be contentious. But hast not Thou, O most merciful Lord, pardoned and remitted this sin also, with my other most horrible and deadly sins, in the holy water?

[III] 5. Verecundus was worn down with care about this our blessedness, for that being held back by bonds, whereby he was most straitly bound, he saw that he should be severed from us. For himself was not yet a Christian, his wife one of the faithful; and yet hereby, more rigidly than by any other chain, was he let and hindered from the journey which we had now essayed. For he would not, he said, be a Christian on any other terms than on those he could not. However, he offered us courteously to remain at his country-house, so long as we should stay there. Thou, O Lord, shalt reward him "in the resurrection of the just," [6] seeing thou hast already given him "the lot of the righteous." [7] For although, in our absence, being now at Rome, he was seized with bodily sickness, and therein being made a Christian and one of the faithful, he departed this life, yet hadst Thou mercy not on him only, but on us also:[8] lest remembering the exceeding kindness of our friend towards us, yet unable to number him among Thy flock, we should be agonized with intolerable sorrow. Thanks unto Thee, our God, we are Thine: Thy suggestions and consolations tell us, Faithful in promises, Thou now requitest Verecundus for his country-house of Cassiacum, where from the fever of the world we reposed in Thee, with the eternal freshness of Thy Paradise: for that Thou hast forgiven him his sins upon earth, in that rich mountain, that mountain which yieldeth milk, Thine own mountain.[9]

---

[1]In harvest and vintage-time the lawyers had their vacation. [2]Ps. 84. 6. [3]*Ibid.*, 120. 3, 4, old version. [4]Rom. 14. 16.

[5]Ps. 41. 10. [6]Luke, 14. 14. [7]Ps. 125. 2. [8]Phil. 2. 27.

[9]Ps. 68. 16, old version. See also, Augustine, *Epist.*

6. He then had at that time sorrow, but Nebridius joy. For although he also, not being yet a Christian, had fallen into the pit of that most pernicious error, believing the flesh of Thy Son to be a phantom, yet emerging thence, he believed as we did; not as yet indued with any Sacraments of Thy Church, but a most ardent searcher out of truth. Whom, not long after our conversion and regeneration by Thy baptism, being also a faithful member of the Church Catholic, and serving Thee in perfect chastity and continence amongst his people in Africa, his whole house having through him first been made Christian, didst Thou release from the flesh; and now he lives in Abraham's bosom.[1] Whatever that be which is signified by that bosom, there lives my Nebridius, my sweet friend, and Thy child, O Lord, adopted of a freed man; there he liveth. For what other place is there for such a soul? There he liveth, whereof he asked much of me, a poor inexperienced man. Now lays he not his ear to my mouth, but his spiritual mouth unto Thy fountain, and drinketh as much as he can receive, wisdom in proportion to his thirst, endlessly happy. Nor do I think that he is so inebriated therewith as to forget me; seeing Thou, Lord, Whom he drinketh, art mindful of us. So were we then, comforting Verecundus, who sorrowed, as far as friendship permitted, that our conversion was of such sort; and exhorting him to become faithful, according to his measure, namely, of a married estate; and awaiting Nebridius to follow us, which, being so near, he was all but doing: and so, lo! those days rolled by at length; for long and many they seemed, for the love I bare to the easeful liberty, that I might sing to Thee from my inmost marrow, My heart hath said unto Thee, I have sought Thy face: "Thy face, Lord, will I seek."[2]

[IV] 7. Now was the day come wherein I was in deed to be freed of my Rhetoric Professorship, whereof in thought I was already freed. And it was done. Thou didst rescue my tongue, whence Thou hadst before rescued my heart. And I blessed Thee, rejoicing; retiring with all mine to the villa. What I there did in writing, which was now enlisted in Thy service, though still, in this breathing-time it were, panting from the school of pride, my books may witness,[3] as well what I debated with others, as what with myself alone,[4] before Thee: what

with Nebridius, who was absent, my epistles bear witness. And when shall I have time to rehearse all Thy great benefits towards us at that time, especially when hasting on to yet greater mercies? For my remembrance recalls me, and pleasant is it to me, O Lord, to confess to Thee by what inward goads Thou tamedst me; and how Thou hast evened me, lowering the mountains and hills of my high imaginations, straightening my crookedness, and smoothing my rough ways;[5] and how Thou also subduedst the brother of my heart, Alypius, unto the Name of Thy Only Begotten, our Lord and Saviour Jesus Christ, which he would not at first vouchsafe to have inserted in our writings. For rather would he have them savour of the lofty "cedars" of the Schools, which the Lord hath now broken down,[6] than of the wholesome herbs of the Church, the antidote against serpents.

8. Oh, in what accents spake I unto Thee, my God, when I read the Psalms of David, those faithful songs and sounds of devotion, which allow of no swelling spirit, as yet a catechumen, and a novice in Thy real love, resting in that villa, with Alypius, a catechumen, my mother cleaving to us, in female garb with masculine faith, with the tranquillity of age, motherly love, Christian piety. Oh, what accents did I utter unto Thee in those Psalms, and how was I by them kindled towards Thee, and on fire to rehearse them, if possible, through the whole world, against the pride of mankind. And yet they are sung through the whole world, nor can any hide himself from Thy heat.[7] With what vehement and bitter sorrow was I angered at the Manichees! and again I pitied them, for that they knew not those Sacraments, those medicines, and were made against the antidote, which might have recovered them of their madness. How I would they had then been somewhere near me, and, without my knowing that they were there, could have beheld my countenance, and heard my words, when I read the fourth Psalm in that time of my rest, and how that Psalm wrought upon me, when I called, the God of my righteousness heard me; in tribulation Thou enlargedst me. Have mercy upon me, O Lord, and hear my prayer.[8] Would that what I uttered on these words, they could hear, without my knowing whether they heard, lest they should think I spake it for their sakes! Because in truth neither should I speak the same things, nor in the same way, if I perceived that they heard and saw me; nor if I spake them would they so receive them, as when I spake by and for

---

[1]See *City of God*, Bk. XIII. 19.   [2]Ps. 27. 8.
[3]These are the three disputations against the Academics. His book *De Vita Beata*, and the two books, *De Ordine*.
[4]His *Soliloquies*, two books, in which, "being alone, he held a dialogue with himself, he and his reason, as though they were two."

[5]Luke, 3. 5.   [6]Ps. 29. 5.   [7]Ps. 19. 6.   [8]*Ibid.*, 4. 1.

myself before Thee, out of the natural feelings of my soul.

9. I trembled for fear, and again kindled with hope, and with rejoicing in Thy mercy, O Father; and all issued forth both by mine eyes and voice, when Thy good Spirit, turning unto us, said, O ye sons of men, how long slow of heart?" why do ye love vanity, and seek after leasing?"[1] For I had loved vanity, and sought after leasing. And Thou, O Lord, hadst already magnified Thy Holy One, raising Him from the dead, and setting Him at Thy right hand,[2] whence from on high He should send His promise,[3] the Comforter, "the Spirit of truth."[4] And He had already sent Him,[5] but I knew it not; He had sent Him, because He was now magnified, rising again from the dead, and ascending into heaven. For till then, "the Spirit was not yet given, because Jesus was not yet glorified."[6] And the prophet cries out, How long, slow of heart? why do ye love vanity, and seek after leasing? Know this, that the Lord hath magnified his Holy One. He cries out, "How long?" He cries out, "Know this": and I so long, not knowing, "loved vanity, and sought after leasing"; and therefore I heard and trembled, because it was spoken unto such as I remembered myself to have been. For in those phantoms which I had held for truths was there "vanity" and "leasing"; and I spake aloud many things earnestly and forcibly, in the bitterness of my remembrance. Which would they had heard, who yet "love vanity and seek after leasing"! They would perchance have been troubled, and have vomited it up; and Thou wouldest hear them when they cried unto Thee;[7] for by a true death in the flesh did He die for us, Who now intercedeth unto Thee for us.[8]

10. I further read, "Be angry, and sin not."[9] And how was I moved, O my God, who had now learned to "be angry" at myself for things past, that I might not sin in time to come! Yea, to be justly angry; for that it was not another nature of a people of darkness which sinned for me, as they say who are not angry at themselves, and treasure up wrath against the day of wrath, and of the revelation of Thy just judgment.[10] Nor were my good things[11] now without, nor sought with the eyes of flesh in that earthly sun; for they that would have joy from without soon become vain, and waste themselves on the things seen, and temporal, and in their famished thoughts do lick their very shadows. Oh that

they were wearied out with their famine, and said, "Who will shew us good things?"[12] And we would say, and they hear, The light of Thy countenance is sealed upon us.[13] For we are not that light which enlighteneth every man,[14] but we are enlightened by Thee; that having been sometimes darkness, we may be light in Thee.[15] Oh that they could see the eternal Internal, which having tasted, I was grieved that I could not shew It them, so long as they brought me their heart in their eyes, roving abroad from Thee, while they said, "Who will shew us good things?" For there, where I was angry within myself in my chamber, where I was inwardly pricked, where I had sacrificed, slaying my old man and commencing the purpose of a new life, putting my trust in Thee[16]—there hadst Thou begun to grow sweet unto me, and "hadst put gladness in my heart."[17] And I cried out, as I read this outwardly, finding it inwardly. Nor would I be multiplied with worldly goods; wasting away time, and wasted by time; whereas I had in thy eternal Simple Essence other corn, and wine, and oil.[18]

11. And with a loud cry of my heart I cried out in the next verse, "Oh in peace," O for "The Self-Same!"[19] Oh what said he, "I will lay me down and sleep,"[20] for who shall hinder us, when "cometh to pass that saying which is written, Death is swallowed up in victory"?[21] And Thou surpassingly art "the Self-same," Who art not changed; and in Thee is rest which forgetteth all toil, for there is none other with Thee, nor are we to seek those many other things, which are not what Thou art; but Thou Lord, alone hast made me dwell in hope.[22] I read, and kindled; nor found I what to do to those deaf and dead, of whom myself had been, a pestilent person, a bitter and a blind bawler against those writings which are honied with the honey of heaven, and lightsome with Thine own light: and I was consumed with zeal at the enemies of this Scripture.

12. When shall I recall all which passed in those holy-days? Yet neither have I forgotten nor will I pass over the severity of Thy scourge, and the wonderful swiftness of Thy mercy. Thou didst then torment me with pain in my teeth; which when it had come to such height that I could not speak, it came into my heart to desire all my friends present to pray for me to Thee, the God of all manner of health. And this I wrote on wax, and gave it them to read. Pres-

[1]*Ibid.*, ver. 23.   [2]Eph. 1. 20.   [3]Luke, 24. 49.
[4]John, 14. 16, 17.   [5]Acts, 2. 1–4.   [6]John, 7. 39.
[7]Ps. 4. 1.   [8]Rom. 8. 34.   [9]Eph. 4. 26.
[10]Rom. 2. 5.   [11]Ps. 4. 6.

[12]Ps. 4. 6.   [13]*Ibid.*   [14]John, 1. 9.   [15]Eph. 5. 8.
[16]Ps. 4. 5.   [17]*Ibid.*, ver. 7.   [18]Ps. 4. 7.
[19]*Ibid.*, ver. 8, Vulg.   [20]Ps. 4. 8.
[21]I Cor. 15. 54.   [22]Ps. 9. 9, Vulg.

ently, so soon as with humble devotion we had bowed our knees, that pain went away. But what pain? or how went it away? I was affrighted, O my Lord, my God; for from infancy I had never experienced the like. And the power of Thy Nod was deeply conveyed to me, and rejoicing in faith, I praised Thy Name. And that faith suffered me not to be at ease about my past sins, which were not yet forgiven me by Thy baptism.

[V] 13. The Vintage Vacation ended, I gave notice to the Milanese to provide their scholars with another master to sell words to them; for that I had both made choice to serve Thee, and through my difficulty of breathing and pain in my chest was not equal to the professorship. And by letters I signified to Thy Prelate, the holy man Ambrose, my former errors and present desires, begging his advice what of Thy Scriptures I had best read, to become readier and fitter for receiving so great grace. He recommended Isaiah[1] the Prophet: I believe because he above the rest is a more clear foreshewer of the Gospel and of the calling of the Gentiles. But I, not understanding the first lesson in him, and imagining the whole to be like it, laid it by, to be resumed when better practised in our Lord's own words.

[VI] 14. Thence, when the time was come, wherein I was to give in my name, we left the country and returned to Milan. It pleased Alypius also to be with me born again in Thee, being already clothed with the humility befitting Thy Sacraments; and a most valiant tamer of the body, so as, with unwonted venture, to wear the frozen ground of Italy with his bare feet. We joined with us the boy Adeodatus, born after the flesh of my sin. Excellently hadst Thou made him. He was not quite fifteen, and in wit surpassed many grave and learned men. I confess unto Thee Thy gifts, O Lord my God, Creator of all, and abundantly able to reform our deformities: for I had no part in that boy, but the sin. For that we brought him up in Thy discipline, it was Thou, none else, had inspired us with it. I confess unto Thee Thy gifts. There is a book of ours entitled *The Master;*[2] it is a dialogue between him and me. Thou knowest that all there ascribed to the person conversing with me were his ideas, in his sixteenth year. Much besides, and yet more admirable, I found in him. That talent struck awe into me. And Who but Thou could be the workmaster of such wonders? Soon didst Thou take his life from the earth: and I now remember him without anxiety, fearing nothing for his childhood or youth, or his whole

self. Him we joined with us, our contemporary in grace, to be brought up in Thy discipline; and we were baptized, and anxiety for our past life vanished from us. Nor was I sated in those days with the wondrous sweetness of considering the depth of Thy counsels concerning the salvation of mankind. How did I weep, in Thy Hymns and Canticles, touched to the quick by the voices of Thy sweet-attuned Church! The voices flowed into mine ears, and the Truth distilled into my heart, whence the affections of my devotion overflowed, and tears ran down, and happy was I therein.

[VII] 15. Not long had the Church of Milan begun to use this kind of consolation and exhortation, the brethren zealously joining with harmony of voice and hearts. For it was a year, or not much more, that Justina, mother to the Emperor Valentinian, a child, persecuted Thy servant Ambrose, in favour of her heresy, to which she was seduced by the Arians. The devout people kept watch in the church ready to die with their Bishop Thy servant. There my mother Thy handmaid, bearing a chief part of those anxieties and watchings, lived for prayer. We, yet unwarmed by the heat of Thy Spirit, still were stirred up by the sight of the amazed and disquieted city. Then it was first instituted that, after the manner of the Eastern churches, Hymns and Psalms should be sung, lest the people should wax faint through the tediousness of sorrow: and from that day to this the custom is retained, divers, yea, almost all Thy congregations, throughout other parts of the world, following herein.

16. Then didst Thou by a vision discover to Thy forenamed Bishop where the bodies of Gervasius and Protasius the martyrs lay hid (whom Thou hadst in Thy secret treasury stored uncorrupted so many years), whence Thou mightest seasonably produce them to repress the fury of a woman, but an Empress. For when they were discovered and dug up, and with due honour translated to the Ambrosian Basilica, not only they who were vexed with unclean spirits (the devils confessing themselves) were cured, but a certain man who had for many years been blind,[3] a citizen and well known to the city, asking and hearing the reason of the people's confused joy, sprang forth, desiring his guide to lead him thither. Led thither, he begged to be allowed to touch with his handkerchief the bier of Thy saints, whose death is precious in Thy sight.[4] Which when he had done, and put to his eyes, they were forthwith opened. Thence did

---

[1]Cf. *City of God*, bk. xviii. 29.   [2]*De Magistro.*   [3]Cf. *City of God*, bk. xxii. 8.   [4]Ps. 116. 15.

the fame spread, thence Thy praises glowed, shone; thence the mind of that enemy, though not turned to the soundness of believing, was yet turned back from her fury of persecuting. Thanks to Thee, O my God. Whence and whither hast Thou thus led my remembrance, that I should confess these things also unto Thee? which, great though they be, I had passed by in forgetfulness. And yet then, when the "odour" of Thy "ointments" was so fragrant, did we not "run after Thee." [1] Therefore did I more weep among the singing of Thy Hymns, formerly sighing after Thee, and at length breathing in Thee, as far as the breath may enter into this our house of grass.

[VIII] 17. Thou that makest men to dwell of one mind in one house[2] didst join with us Euodius also, a young man of our own city. Who, being an officer of Court, was before us converted to Thee and baptized: and quitting his secular warfare, girded himself to Thine. We were together, about to dwell together in our devout purpose. We sought where we might serve Thee most usefully, and were together returning to Africa: whitherward being as far as Ostia, my mother departed this life. Much I omit, as hastening much. Receive my confessions and thanksgivings, O my God, for innumerable things whereof I am silent. But I will not omit whatsoever my soul would bring forth concerning that Thy handmaid, who brought me forth, both in the flesh, that I might be born to this temporal light, and in heart, that I might be born to Light eternal. Not her gifts, but Thine in her, would I speak of; for neither did she make nor educate herself. Thou createdst her; nor did her father and mother know what a one should come from them. And the sceptre of Thy Christ, the discipline of Thine only Son, in a Christian house, a good member of Thy Church, educated her in Thy fear. Yet for her good discipline was she wont to commend not so much her mother's diligence, as that of a certain decrepit maid-servant, who had carried her father when a child, as little ones used to be carried at the backs of elder girls. For which reason, and for her great age, and excellent conversation, was she, in that Christian family, well respected by its heads. Whence also the charge of her master's daughters was entrusted to her, to which she gave diligent heed, restraining them earnestly, when necessary, with a holy severity, and teaching them with a grave discretion. For, except at those hours wherein they were most temperately fed at their parents' table, she would not suffer them, though parched with thirst, to drink even water; preventing an evil custom, and adding this wholesome advice; 'Ye drink water now, because you have not wine in your power; but when you come to be married, and be made mistresses of cellars and cupboards, you will scorn water, but the custom of drinking will abide." By this method of instruction, and the authority she had, she refrained the greediness of childhood, and moulded their very thirst to such an excellent moderation, that what they should not, that they would not.

18. And yet (as Thy handmaid told me her son) there had crept upon her a love of wine. For when (as the manner was) she, as though a sober maiden, was bidden by her parents to draw wine out of the hogshead, holding the vessel under the opening, before she poured the wine into the flagon she sipped a little with the tip of her lips; for more her instinctive feelings refused. For this she did, not out of any desire of drink, but out of the exuberance of youth, whereby it boils over in mirthful freaks, which in youthful spirits are wont to be kept under by the gravity of their elders. And thus by adding to that little, daily littles (for whoso despiseth little things shall fall by little and little"),[3] she had fallen into such a habit as greedily to drink off her little cup brimfull almost of wine. Where was then that discreet old woman, and that her earnest countermanding? Would aught avail against a secret disease if Thy healing hand, O Lord, watched not over us? Father, mother, and governors absent, Thou present, Who createdst, Who callest, Who also by those set over us workest something towards the salvation of our souls, what didst Thou then, O my God? how didst Thou cure her? how heal her? didst Thou not out of another soul bring forth a hard and a sharp taunt, like a lancet out of Thy secret store, and with one touch remove all that foul stuff? For a maid-servant with whom she used to go to the cellar, falling to words (as it happens) with her little mistress, when alone with her, taunted her with this fault, with most bitter insult, calling her "wine-bibber." With which taunt she, stung to the quick, saw the foulness of her fault, and instantly condemned and forsook it. As flattering friends pervert, so reproachful enemies mostly correct. Yet not what by them Thou doest, but what themselves purposed, dost Thou repay them. For she in her anger sought to vex her young mistress, not to amend her; and did it in private, either for that the time and place of the quarrel so found them, or lest her-

---

[1] Cant. 1. 3. 4.　　[2] Ps. 69. 6.　　[3] Ecclus. 19. 1.

self also should have anger, for discovering it thus late. But Thou, Lord, Governor of all in heaven and earth, Who turnest to Thy purposes the deepest currents, and the ruled turbulence of the tide of times,[1] didst by the very unhealthiness of one soul heal another; lest any, when he observes this, should ascribe it to his own power, even when another, whom he wished to be reformed is reformed through words of his.

[IX] 19. Brought up thus modestly and soberly, and made subject rather by Thee to her parents than by her parents to Thee, so soon as she was of marriageable age being bestowed upon a husband, she served him as her lord; and did her diligence to win him unto Thee, preaching Thee unto him by her conversation; by which Thou ornamentedst her, making her reverently amiable, and admirable unto her husband. And she so endured the wronging of her bed, as never to have any quarrel with her husband thereon. For she looked for Thy mercy upon him, that, believing in Thee, he might be made chaste. But besides this, he was fervid, as in his affections, so in anger: but she had learnt not to resist an angry husband, not in deed only, but not even in word. Only when he was smoothed and tranquil, and in a temper to receive it, she would give an account of her actions, if haply he had overhastily taken offence. In a word, while many matrons, who had milder husbands, yet bore even in their faces marks of shame, would in familiar talk blame their husbands' lives, she would blame their tongues, giving them, as in jest, earnest advice: "That from the time they heard the marriage writings read to them, they should account them as indentures, whereby they were made servants; and so, remembering their condition, ought not to set themselves up against their lords." And when they, knowing what a choleric husband she endured, marvelled, that it had never been heard, nor by any token perceived, that Patricius had beaten his wife, or that there had been any domestic difference between them, even for one day, and confidentially asking the reason, she taught them her practice above mentioned. Those wives who observed it found the good, and returned thanks; those who observed it not, found no relief, and suffered.

20. Her mother-in-law also, at first by whisperings of evil servants incensed against her, she so overcame by observance and persevering endurance and meekness, that she of her own accord discovered to her son the meddling tongues whereby the domestic peace betwixt her and her daughter-in-law had been disturbed, asking him to correct them. Then, when in compliance with his mother and for the well-ordering of the family and the harmony of its members, he had with stripes corrected those discovered, at her will who had discovered them, she promised the like reward to any who, to please her, should speak ill of her daughter-in-law to her; and, none now venturing, they lived together with a remarkable sweetness of mutual kindness.

21. This great gift also Thou bestowedst, O my God, my mercy, upon that good handmaid of Thine, in whose womb Thou createdst me, that between any disagreeing and discordant parties, where she was able, she shewed herself such a peacemaker that, hearing on both sides most bitter things, such as swelling and indigested choler uses to break out into when the crudities of enmities are breathed out in sour discourses to a present friend against an absent enemy, she never would disclose aught of the one unto the other, but what might tend to their reconcilement. A small good this might appear to me, did I not to my grief know numberless persons who, through some horrible and widespreading contagion of sin, not only disclose to persons mutually angered things said in anger, but add withal things never spoken; whereas to humane humanity, it ought to seem a light thing not to foment or increase ill will by ill words, unless one study withal by good words to quench it. Such was she, Thyself, her most inward Instructor, teaching her in the school of the heart.

22. Finally, her own husband, towards the very end of his earthly life, did she gain unto Thee; nor had she to complain of that in him as a believer which before he was a believer she had borne from him. She was also the servant of thy servants; whosoever of them knew her did in her much praise and honour and love Thee; for that through the witness of the fruits of a holy conversation they perceived Thy presence in her heart. For she had "been the wife of one man," had requited her parents, had governed her house piously, was "well reported of for good works," had "brought up children," [2] so often travailing in birth of them[3] as she saw them swerving from Thee. Lastly, of all of us Thy servants, O Lord (whom on occasion of Thy own gift Thou sufferest to speak)—us, who before her sleeping in Thee[4] lived united together, having received the grace of Thy baptism, did she so take care of, as though she had been mother of us all; so served us, as though she had been child to us all.

[1] Cf. *City of God*, BK. XXII. 2.

[2] I Tim. 5. 4, 9, 10, 14.   [3] Gal. 4. 19.   [4] I Thess. 4. 14.

[X] 23. The day now approaching whereon she was to depart this life (which day Thou well knewest, we knew not), it came to pass, Thyself, as I believe, by Thy secret ways so ordering it that she and I stood alone, leaning in a certain window, which looked into the garden of the house where we now lay, at Ostia; where, removed from the din of men, we were recruiting from the fatigues of a long journey, for the voyage. We were discoursing then together, alone, very sweetly; and "forgetting those things which are behind, and reaching forth unto those things which are before,"[1] we were enquiring between ourselves in the presence of the Truth, which Thou art, of what sort the eternal life of the saints was to be, which eye hath not seen, nor ear heard, nor hath it entered into the heart of man.[2] But yet we gasped with the mouth of our heart after those heavenly streams of Thy fountain, "the fountain of life," which is "with Thee";[3] that, being bedewed thence according to our capacity, we might in some sort meditate upon so high a mystery.

24. And when our discourse was brought to that point, that the very highest delight of the earthly senses, in the very purest material light, was, in respect of the sweetness of that life, not only not worthy of comparison, but not even of mention; we, raising up ourselves with a more glowing affection towards the "Self-same,"[4] did by degrees pass through all things bodily, even the very heaven, whence sun and moon and stars shine upon the earth; yea, we were soaring higher yet, by inward musing, and discourse, and admiring of Thy works; and we came to our own minds, and went beyond them, that we might arrive at that region of never-failing plenty, where Thou feedest Israel[5] for ever with the food of truth, and where life is the Wisdom by whom all these things are made, and what have been, and what shall be, and she is not made, but is, as she hath been, and so shall be ever; yea rather, to "have been," and "hereafter to be," are not in her, but only "to be," seeing she is eternal. For to "have been," and to "be hereafter," are not eternal. And while we were discoursing and panting after her, we slightly touched on her with the whole effort of our heart; and we sighed, and there we leave bound "the first fruits of the Spirit";[6] and returned to vocal expressions of our mouth, where the word spoken has beginning and end. And what is like unto Thy Word, our Lord, Who endureth in Himself without becoming old, and "maketh all things new"?[7]

25. We were saying then: If to any the tumult of the flesh were hushed, hushed the images of earth, and waters, and air, hushed also the poles of heaven, yea, the very soul be hushed to herself, and by not thinking on self surmount self, hushed all dreams and imaginary revelations, every tongue and every sign, and whatsoever exists only in transition; since, if any could hear, all these say, "We made not ourselves, but He made us that abideth for ever"; if then, having uttered this, they too should be hushed, having roused only our ears to Him Who made them, and He alone speak, not by them, but by Himself, that we may hear His Word, not through any tongue of flesh, nor Angel's voice, nor sound of thunder, nor in the dark riddle of a similitude, but might hear Whom in these things we love, might hear His Very Self without these (as we two now strained ourselves, and in swift thought touched on that Eternal Wisdom, which abideth over all)—could this be continued on, and other visions of kind far unlike be withdrawn, and this one ravish, and absorb, and wrap up its beholder amid these inward joys, so that life might be for ever like that one moment of understanding which now we sighed after; were not this, "Enter into thy Master's joy"?[8] And when shall that be? When we shall all rise again, though we shall not all be changed?[9]

26. Such things was I speaking, and even if not in this very manner and these same words, yet, Lord, Thou knewest that in that day when we were speaking of these things, and this world with all its delights became, as we spake, contemptible to us, my mother said: "Son, for mine own part I have no further delight in anything in this life. What I do here any longer, and to what end I am here, I know not, now that my hopes in this world are accomplished. One thing there was, for which I desired to linger for a while in this life, that I might see thee a Catholic Christian before I died. My God hath done this for me more abundantly, that I should now see thee withall, despising earthly happiness, become His servant: what do I here?"

[XI] 27. What answer I made her unto these things, I remember not. For scarce five days after, or not much more, she fell sick of a fever; and in that sickness one day she fell into a swoon, and was for a while withdrawn from these visible things. We hastened round her; but she was soon brought back to her senses; and, looking on me and my brother standing by her, said to us enquiringly, "Where was I?" And

[1]Phil. 3. 13.   [2]I Cor. 2. 9; Isa. 64. 4.   [3]Ps. 36. 9.
[4]See above 11. and Ps. 4. 8, Vulg.
[5]Ps. 80. 5.   [6]Rom. 8. 23.

[7]Wisd. 7. 27.   [8]Matt. 25. 21.   [9]I Cor. 15. 51.

then looking fixedly on us, with grief amazed: "Here," saith she, "shall you bury your mother." I held my peace and refrained weeping; but my brother spake something, wishing for her, as the happier lot, that she might die, not in a strange place, but in her own land. Whereat, she with anxious look, checking him with her eyes, for that he still savoured such things, and then looking upon me: "Behold," saith she, "what he saith." And soon after to us both: "Lay," she saith, "this body anywhere; let not the care for that any way disquiet you: this only I request, that you would remember me at the Lord's altar, wherever you be." And, having delivered this sentiment in what words she could, she held her peace, being exercised by her growing sickness.

28. But I, considering Thy gifts, Thou unseen God, which Thou instillest into the hearts of Thy faithful ones, whence wondrous fruits do spring, did rejoice and give thanks to Thee, recalling what I before knew, how careful and anxious she had ever been as to her place of burial, which she had provided and prepared for herself by the body of her husband. For, because they had lived in great harmony together, she also wished (so little can the human mind embrace things divine) to have this addition to that happiness, and to have it remembered among men that, after her pilgrimage beyond the seas, what was earthly of this united pair had been permitted to be united beneath the same earth. But when this emptiness had through the fulness of Thy goodness begun to cease in her heart, I knew not, and rejoiced admiring what she had so disclosed to me; though indeed in that our discourse also in the window, when she said, "What do I here any longer?" there appeared no desire of dying in her own country. I heard afterwards also that, when we were now at Ostia, she with a mother's confidence, when I was absent, one day discoursed with certain of my friends about the contempt of this life and the blessing of death; and when they were amazed at such courage which Thou hadst given to a woman, and asked, "Whether she were not afraid to leave her body so far from her own city?" she replied, "Nothing is far to God; nor was it to be feared lest, at the end of the world, He should not recognize whence He were to raise me up." On the ninth day then of her sickness, and the fifty-sixth year of her age, and the three-and-thirtieth of mine, was that religious and holy soul freed from the body.

[XII] 29. I closed her eyes; and there flowed withal a mighty sorrow into my heart, which was overflowing into tears; mine eyes at the same time, by the violent command of my mind, drank up their fountain wholly dry; and woe was me in such a strife! But when she breathed her last, the boy Adeodatus burst out into a loud lament; then, checked by us all, held his peace. In like manner also a childish feeling in me, which was, through my heart's youthful voice, finding its vent in weeping, was checked and silenced. For we thought it not fitting to solemnize that funeral with tearful lament and groanings: for thereby do they for the most part express grief for the departed, as though unhappy, or altogether dead; whereas she was neither unhappy in her death, nor altogether dead. Of this, we were assured on good grounds, the testimony of her good conversation and her "faith unfeigned."[1]

30. What then was it which did grievously pain me within, but a fresh wound wrought through the sudden wrench of that most sweet and dear custom of living together? I joyed indeed in her testimony, when, in that her last sickness, mingling her endearments with my acts of duty, she called me "dutiful," and mentioned, with great affection of love, that she never had heard any harsh or reproachful sound uttered by my mouth against her. But yet, O my God, Who madest us, what comparison is there betwixt that honour that I paid to her, and her slavery for me? Being then forsaken of so great comfort in her, my soul was wounded, and that life rent asunder as it were, which, of hers and mine together, had been made but one.

31. The boy then being stilled from weeping, Euodius took up the Psalter, and began to sing, our whole house answering him, the Psalm, "I will sing of mercy and judgment to Thee, O Lord."[2] But hearing what we were doing, many brethren and religious women came together; and whilst they (whose office it was) made ready for the burial, as the manner is, I (in a part of the house where I might properly), together with those who thought not fit to leave me, discoursed upon something fitting the time; and by this balm of truth assuaged that torment known to Thee, they unknowing and listening intently, and conceiving me to be without all sense of sorrow. But in Thy ears, where none of them heard, I blamed the weakness of my feelings, and refrained my flood of grief, which gave way a little unto me; but again came, as with a tide, yet not so as to burst out into tears, nor to a change of countenance; still I knew what I was keeping down in my heart. And being very much

[1] I Tim. i. 5.   [2] Ps. ci. i.

displeased that these human things had such power over me, which in the due order and appointment of our natural condition must needs come to pass, with a new grief I grieved for my grief, and was thus worn by a double sorrow.

32. And behold, the corpse was carried to the burial; we went and returned without tears. For neither in those prayers which we poured forth unto Thee, when the sacrifice of our ransom[1] was offered for her, when now the corpse was by the grave's side, as the manner there is, previous to its being laid therein, did I weep even during those prayers; yet was I the whole day in secret heavily sad, and with troubled mind prayed Thee, as I could, to heal my sorrow, yet Thou didst not; impressing, I believe, upon my memory by this one instance how strong is the bond of all habit, even upon a soul, which now feeds upon no deceiving Word. It seemed also good to me to go and bathe, having heard that the bath had its name (*balneum*) from the Greek βαλαν-εῖον, for that it drives sadness from the mind. And this also I confess unto Thy mercy, "Father of the fatherless,"[2] that I bathed, and was the same as before I bathed. For the bitterness of sorrow could not exude out of my heart. Then I slept, and woke up again, and found my grief not a little softened; and as I was alone in my bed, I remembered those true verses of Thy Ambrose. For Thou art the

> Maker of all, the Lord,
> And Ruler of the height,
> Who, robing day in light, hast poured
> Soft slumbers o'er the night,
>
> That to our limbs the power
> Of toil may be renew'd,
> And hearts be rais'd that sink and cower,
> And sorrows be subdu'd.

33. And then by little and little I recovered my former thoughts of Thy handmaid, her holy conversation towards Thee, her holy tenderness and observance towards us, whereof I was suddenly deprived: and I was minded to weep in Thy sight, for her and for myself, in her behalf and in my own. And I gave way to the tears which I before restrained, to overflow as much as they desired; reposing my heart upon them; and it found rest in them, for it was in Thy ears, not in those of man, who would have scornfully interpreted my weeping. And now, Lord, in writing I confess it unto Thee. Read it who will, and

interpret it how he will; and if he finds sin therein, that I wept my mother for a small portion of an hour (the mother who for the time was dead to mine eyes, who had for many years wept for me, that I might live in Thine eyes), let him not deride me; but rather, if he be one of large charity, let him weep himself for my sins unto Thee, the Father of all the brethren of Thy Christ.

[XIII] 34. But now, with a heart cured of that wound, wherein it might seem blameworthy for an earthly feeling,[3] I pour out unto Thee, our God, in behalf of that Thy handmaid, a far different kind of tears, flowing from a spirit shaken by the thoughts of the dangers of every soul that dieth in Adam. And although she, having been "quickened" in Christ,[4] even before her release from the flesh, had lived to the praise of Thy name for her faith and conversation, yet dare I not say that, from what time Thou regeneratedst her by baptism, no word issued from her mouth against Thy Commandment. Thy Son, the Truth, hath said, "Whosoever shall say unto his brother, Thou fool, shall be in danger of hell fire."[5] And woe be even unto the commendable life of men if, laying aside mercy, Thou shouldest examine it. But, because Thou art not extreme in enquiring after sins, we confidently hope to find some place with Thee. But whosoever reckons up his real merits to Thee, what reckons he up to Thee but[6] Thine own gifts? O that men would know themselves to be men; and that "he that glorieth" would "glory in the Lord."[7]

35. I therefore, O my Praise and my Life, God of my heart, laying aside for a while her good deeds, for which I give thanks to Thee with joy, do now beseech Thee for the sins of my mother. Hearken unto me, I entreat Thee, by the Medicine of our wounds Who hung upon the tree, and now sitting at Thy right hand "maketh intercession to Thee for us."[8] I know that she dealt mercifully, and from her heart[9] forgave her debtors their debts; do Thou also forgive her debts,[10] whatever she may have contracted in so many years, since the water of salvation. Forgive her, Lord, forgive, I beseech Thee; "enter not into judgment" with her.[11] Let Thy mercy be exalted above Thy justice,[12] since Thy words are true, and Thou hast promised mercy unto "the merciful";[13] which Thou gavest them to be, Who wilt "have mercy" on whom Thou wilt have mercy;

---

[1] The sacrifice of the Mass offered for the dead.
[2] Ps. 68. 5.

[3] Rom. 8. 7.　[4] I Cor. 15. 22.　[5] Matt. 12. 36.
[6] See above 17, and below BK. XIII. 1.　[7] II Cor. 10. 17.
[8] Rom. 8. 34.　[9] Matt. 18. 35.　[10] *Ibid.*, 6. 12.
[11] Ps. 143. 2.　[12] James, 2. 13.　[13] Matt. 5. 7.

and wilt "have compassion" on whom Thou hast had compassion.[1]

36. And I believe Thou hast already done what I ask; but "accept, O Lord, the free-will offerings of my mouth."[2] For she, the day of her dissolution now at hand, took no thought to have her body sumptuously wound up, or embalmed with spices; nor desired she a choice monument, or to be buried in her own land. These things she enjoined us not; but desired only to have her name commemorated at Thy Altar, which she had served without intermission of one day; whence she knew that holy sacrifice to be dispensed by which the hand-writing that was against us is blotted out;[3] through which the enemy was triumphed over, who, summing up our offences and seeking what to lay to our charge, found nothing in Him[4] in Whom we conquer. Who shall restore to Him the innocent blood? Who repay Him the price wherewith He bought us, and so take us from Him? Unto the Sacrament of which our ransom, Thy handmaid bound her soul by the bond of faith. Let none sever her from Thy protection; let neither the "lion" nor the "dragon"[5] interpose himself by force or fraud. For she will not answer that she owes nothing, lest she be convicted and seized by the crafty accuser; but she will answer that her "sins are forgiven"[6] her by Him, to Whom none can repay that price, which He Who owed nothing paid for us.

37. May she rest then in peace with the husband before and after whom she had never any; whom she obeyed, with patience bringing forth fruit[7] unto Thee, that she might win him also unto Thee. And inspire, O Lord my God, inspire Thy servants my brethren, Thy sons my masters, whom with voice, and heart, and pen I serve, that so many as shall read these Confessions may at Thy Altar remember Monica Thy handmaid, with Patricius, her sometime husband, by whose bodies Thou broughtest me into this life, how I know not. May they with devout affection remember my parents in this transitory light, my brethren under Thee our Father in our Catholic Mother, and my fellow-citizens in that eternal Jerusalem, which Thy pilgrim people sigh after from their Exodus, even unto their return thither. That so, my mother's last request of me may, through my confessions more than through my prayers, be, through the prayers of many, more abundantly fulfilled to her.

BOOK X. *Having in the former books spoken of himself before his receiving the grace of Baptism, in this Augustine confesses what he then was. But first, he enquires by what faculty we can know God at all, whence he enlarges on the mysterious character of the memory, wherein God, being made known, dwells, but which could not discover Him. Then he examines his own trials under the triple division of temptation, "lust of the flesh, lust of the eyes, and pride"; what Christian continency prescribes as to each. On Christ the Only Mediator, who heals and will heal all infirmities.*

[I] 1. Let me know Thee, O Lord, Who knowest me: let me know Thee, as I am known.[8] Power of my soul, enter into it, and fit it for Thee, that Thou mayest have and hold it without "spot or wrinkle."[9] This is my hope, "therefore do I speak";[10] and in this hope do I rejoice, when I rejoice healthfully. Other things of this life are the less to be sorrowed for, the more they are sorrowed for; and the more to be sorrowed for, the less men sorrow for them. For behold, "Thou lovest the truth,"[11] and he that doth it "cometh to the light."[12] This would I do in my heart before Thee in confession: and in my writing, before many witnesses.

[II] 2. And from Thee, O Lord, unto Whose eyes the abyss of man's conscience is naked,[13] what could be hidden in me though I would not confess it? For I should hide Thee from me, not me from Thee. But now, for that my groaning is witness, that I am displeased with myself, Thou shinest out, and art pleasing, and beloved, and longed for; that I may be ashamed of myself, and renounce myself, and choose Thee, and neither please Thee, nor myself, but in Thee. To Thee therefore, O Lord, am I open, whatever I am; and with what fruit I confess unto Thee, I have said. Nor do I it with words and sounds of the flesh, but with the words of my soul, and the cry of the thought which Thy ear knoweth. For when I am evil, then to confess to Thee is nothing else than to be displeased with myself; but, when holy, nothing else than not to ascribe it to myself: because Thou, O Lord, "blessest the godly,"[14] but first Thou justifieth him when "ungodly."[15] My confession then, O my God, in Thy sight, is made silently, and not silently. For in sound, it is silent; in affection, it cries aloud. For neither do I utter anything right unto men, which Thou hast not before heard from me; nor

---

[1]Rom. 9. 15.   [2]Ps. 119. 108.   [3]Col. 2. 14.
[4]John, 14. 30.   [5]Ps. 91. 13.   [7]Luke, 8. 15.
[6]Matt. 9. 2.

[8]I Cor. 13. 12.   [9]Eph. 5. 27.   [10]Ps. 116. 10.
[11]*Ibid.*, 51. 6.   [12]John, 3. 20.   [13]Heb. 4. 13.
[14]Ps. 5. 12.   [15]Rom. 4. 5.

dost Thou hear any such thing from me, which Thou hast not first said unto me.

[III] 3. What then have I to do with men, that they should hear my confessions; as if they could heal all my infirmities? [1] A race curious to know the lives of others, slothful to amend their own. Why seek they to hear from me what I am, who will not hear from Thee what themselves are? And how know they, when from myself they hear of myself, whether I say true; seeing no man knows what is in man, "but the spirit of man which is in him"? [2] But if they hear from Thee of themselves, they cannot say, "The Lord lieth." For what is it to hear from Thee of themselves, but to know themselves? And who knoweth and saith, "It is false," unless himself lieth? But because "charity" believeth all things[3] (that is, among those whom knitting unto itself it maketh one), I also, O Lord, will in such wise confess unto Thee; that men may hear, to whom I cannot demonstrate whether I confess truly; yet they believe me, whose ears charity openeth unto me.

4. But do Thou, my inmost Physician, make plain unto me what fruit I may reap by doing it. For the confessions of my past sins, which Thou hast "forgiven" and "covered," [4] that Thou mightest bless me in Thee, changing my soul by Faith and Thy Sacrament, when read and heard stirs up the heart, that it sleep not in despair and say, "I cannot," but awake in the love of Thy mercy and the sweetness of Thy grace, whereby whoso is weak is strong,[5] when by it he became conscious of his own weakness. And the good delight to hear of the past evils of such as are now freed from them, not because they are evils, but because they have been and are not. With what fruit then, O Lord my God, to Whom my conscience daily confesseth, trusting more in the hope of Thy mercy than in their own innocency, with what fruit, I pray, do I by this book confess to men, also in Thy presence, what I now am, not what I have been? For that other fruit I have seen and spoken of. But what I now am, at the very time of making these confessions, divers desire to know, who have or have not known me, who have heard from me or of me; but their ear is not at my heart, where I am, whatever I am. They wish then to hear me confess what I am within; whither neither their eye, nor ear, nor understanding, can reach; they wish it, as ready to believe—but will they know? For charity, whereby they are good, telleth them that in my confessions I lie not; and she in them believeth me.

[IV] 5. But for what fruit would they hear this? do they desire to joy with me, when they hear how near, by Thy gift, I approach unto Thee? and to pray for me, when they shall hear how much I am held back by my own weight? To such will I discover myself. For it is no mean fruit, O Lord my God, that by many thanks should be given to Thee on our behalf,[6] and Thou be by many intreated for us. Let the brotherly mind love in me what Thou teachest is to be loved, and lament in me what Thou teachest is to be lamented. Let a brotherly, not a stranger, mind—not that "of the strange children, whose mouth talketh of vanity, and their right hand is a right hand of iniquity,"[7]—but that brotherly mind which, when it approveth, rejoiceth for me, and when it disapproveth me, is sorry for me; because whether it approveth or disapproveth, it loveth me. To such will I discover myself; they will breathe freely at my good deeds, sigh for my ill. My good deeds are Thine appointments, and Thy gifts; my evil ones are my offences, and Thy judgments. Let them breathe freely at the one, sigh at the other; and let hymns and weeping go up into Thy sight, out of the hearts of my brethren, Thy censers.[8] And do Thou, O Lord, be pleased with the incense of Thy holy temple, have mercy upon me according to Thy great mercy[9] "for Thine own name's sake";[10] and no ways forsaking what Thou hast begun, perfect my imperfections.

6. This is the fruit of my confessions of what I am, not of what I have been, to confess this, not before Thee only, in a secret exultation with trembling,[11] and a secret sorrow with hope; but in the ears also of the believing sons of men, sharers of my joy and partners in my mortality, my fellow-citizens, and fellow-pilgrims, who are gone before, or are to follow on, companions of my way. These are Thy servants, my brethren, whom Thou willest to be Thy sons; my masters whom Thou commandest me to serve, if I would live with Thee, of Thee. But this Thy Word were little did it only command by speaking, and not go before in performing. This then I do in deed and word, this I do under Thy wings; in over-great peril, were not my soul subdued unto Thee under Thy wings, and my infirmity known unto Thee. I am a little one, but my Father ever liveth, and my Guardian is "sufficient" for me.[12] For He is the same who begat me, and defends me; and Thou Thyself art all my good; Thou, Almighty, Who art with me, yea, before I am

---

[1]Ps. 113. 3.   [2]I Cor. 2. 11.   [3]Ibid., 13. 7.
[4]Ps. 32. 1.   [5]II Cor. 12. 10.

[6]II Cor. 1. 11.   [7]Ps. 114. 11.   [8]Rev. 8. 3.
[9]Ps. 51. 1.   [10]Ps. 25. 11.   [11]Ps. 2. 11.
[12]II Cor. 12. 9.

with Thee. To such then whom Thou command-est me to serve will I discover, not what I have been, but what I now am, and what I yet am. But neither do I judge myself.[1] Thus therefore I would be heard.

[V] 7. For Thou, Lord, dost judge me;[2] be-cause, although no "man knoweth the things of a man, but the spirit of a man which is in him,"[3] yet is there something of man which neither "the spirit of man that is in him" itself knoweth. But Thou, Lord, knowest all of him, Who hast made him. Yet I, though in Thy sight I despise myself and account "myself dust and ashes,"[4] yet know I something of Thee, which I know not of myself. And truly, "now we see through a glass darkly," not "face to face"[5] as yet. So long therefore as I be "absent" from Thee, I am more "present" with myself than with Thee;[6] and yet know I Thee that Thou are in no ways passible;[7] but I, what temptations I can resist, what I cannot, I know not. And there is hope, because Thou art faithful, Who wilt not suffer us to be tempted above that we are able; but wilt with the temptation also make a way to es-cape, that we may be able to bear it.[8] I will con-fess then what I know of myself, I will confess also what I know not of myself. And that be-cause what I do know of myself, I know by Thy shining upon me; and what I know not of my-self, so long know I not it, until my "darkness be made as the noon-day"[9] in Thy countenance.

[VI] 8. Not with doubting, but with assured consciousness, do I love Thee, Lord. Thou hast stricken my heart with Thy word, and I loved Thee. Yea, also heaven, and earth, and all that therein is, behold, on every side they bid me love Thee; nor cease to say so unto all, "that they may be without excuse."[10] But more deeply wilt Thou have mercy on whom Thou wilt have mercy, and wilt have compassion on whom Thou hast had compassion:[11] else in deaf ears do the heaven and the earth speak Thy praises. But what do I love when I love Thee? Not beauty of bodies, nor the fair harmony of time, nor the brightness of the light, so gladsome to our eyes, nor sweet melodies of varied songs, nor the fra-grant smell of flowers, and ointments, and spices, not manna and honey, not limbs acceptable to embracements of flesh. None of these I love, when I love my God; and yet I love a kind of light, and melody, and fragrance, and meat, and embracement, when I love my God, the light,

melody, fragrance, meat, embracement of my inner man: where there shineth unto my soul what space cannot contain, and there sound-eth what time beareth not away, and there smell-eth what breathing disperseth not, and there tasteth what eating diminisheth not, and there clingeth what satiety divorceth not. This is it which I love, when I love my God.

9. And what is this? I asked the earth, and it answered me, "I am not He"; and whatsoever are in it confessed the same. I asked the sea, and the deeps, and the living creeping things, and they answered, "We are not thy God, seek above us." I asked the moving air; and the whole air with his inhabitants answered, "Anaximenes was deceived, I am not God." I asked the heav-ens, sun, moon, stars, "Nor [say they] are we the God Whom thou seekest." And I replied un-to all the things which encompass the door of my flesh; "Ye have told me of my God, that ye are not He; tell me something of Him." And they cried out with a loud voice, "He made us." My questioning them was my thoughts on them: and their form of beauty gave the answer. And I turned myself unto myself, and said to myself, "Who art thou?" And I answered, "A man." And behold, in me there present themselves to me soul and body, one without, the other within. By which of these ought I to seek my God? I had sought Him in the body from earth to heav-en, so far as I could send messengers, the beams of mine eyes. But the better is the inner, for to it as presiding and judging, all the bodily mes-sengers reported the answers of heaven and earth, and all things therein, who said, "We are not God, but He made us." These things did my inner man know by the ministry of the outer: I, the inner, knew them; I, the mind, through the senses of my body. I asked the whole frame of the world about my God; and it answered me, "I am not He, but He made me."

10. Is not this corporeal figure apparent to all whose senses are perfect? Why then speaks it not the same to all? Animals small and great see it, but they cannot ask it, because no reason is set over their senses to judge on what they re-port. But men can ask, so that "the invisible things of God are clearly seen, being understood by the things that are made";[12] but by love of them, they are made subject unto them: and subjects cannot judge. Nor yet do the creatures answer such as ask, unless they can judge: nor yet do they change their voice (i.e., their ap-pearance) if one man only sees, another seeing asks, so as to appear one way to this man, an-

[1] I Cor. 4. 3.   [2] *Ibid.*, ver. 4.   [3] *Ibid.*, 2. 11.
[4] Gen. 18. 27.   [5] I Cor. 13. 12.   [6] II Cor. 5. 6.
[7] See above Bk. VII. 3.   [8] I Cor. 10. 13.
[9] Isa. 58. 10.   [10] Rom. 1. 20.   [11] Rom. 9. 15.

[12] Rom. 1. 20.

other way to that; but appearing the same way to both, it is dumb to this, speaks to that; yea, rather it speaks to all; but they only understand, who compare its voice received from without with the truth within. For truth saith unto me, "Neither heaven, nor earth, nor any other body is thy God." This their very nature saith to him that seeth them; "They are a mass; a mass is less in a part thereof, than in the whole." Now to thee I speak, O my soul, thou art my better part; for thou quickenest the mass of my body, giving it life, which no body can give to a body: but thy God is even unto thee the Life of thy life.

[VII] 11. What then do I love, when I love my God? Who is He above the head of my soul? By my very soul will I ascend to Him. I will pass beyond that power whereby I am united to my body, and fill its whole frame with life. Nor can I by that power find my God; for so horse and mule "that have no understanding"[1] might find Him, seeing it is the same power whereby even their bodies live. But another power there is, not that only whereby I animate, but that too whereby I imbue with sense my flesh, which the Lord hath framed for me; commanding the eye not to hear, and the ear not to see; but the eye, that through it I should see, and the ear, that through it I should hear; and to the other senses severally, what is to each their own peculiar seats and offices; which, being divers, I the one mind do through them enact. I will pass beyond this power of mine also; for this also have the horse and mule, for they also perceive through the body.

[VIII] 12. I will pass then beyond this power of my nature also, rising by degrees unto Him Who made me. And I come to the fields and spacious palaces of my memory, where are the treasures of innumerable images, brought into it from things of all sorts perceived by the senses. There is stored up whatsoever besides we think, either by enlarging or diminishing, or any other way varying those things which the sense hath come to; and whatever else hath been committed and laid up, which forgetfulness hath not yet swallowed up and buried. When I enter there, I require what I will to be brought forth, and something instantly comes; others must be longer sought after, which are fetched, as it were, out of some inner receptacle; others rush out in troops, and while one thing is desired and required, they start forth, as who should say, "Is it perchance I?" These I drive away with the hand of my heart, from the face of my remem-

[1]Ps. 31. 9.

brance; until what I wished for be unveiled, and appear in sight, out of its secret place. Other things come up readily, in unbroken order, as they are called for; those in front making way for the following; and, as they make way, they are hidden from sight, ready to come when I will. All which takes place when I repeat a thing by heart.

13. There are all things preserved distinctly and under general heads, each having entered by its own avenue: as light, and all colours and forms of bodies, by the eyes; by the ears all sorts of sounds; all smells by the avenue of the nostrils; all tastes by the mouth; and by the sensation of the whole body, what is hard or soft; hot or cold; smooth or rugged; heavy or light; either outwardly or inwardly to the body. All these doth that great harbour of the memory receive in her numberless secret and inexpressible windings, to be forthcoming and brought out at need; each entering in by his own gate, and there laid up. Nor yet do the things themselves enter in; only the images of the things perceived are there in readiness, for thought to recall. Which images, how they are formed, who can tell, though it doth plainly appear by which sense each hath been brought in and stored up? For even while I dwell in darkness and silence, in my memory I can produce colours if I will, and discern betwixt black and white, and what others I will; nor yet do sounds break in and disturb the image drawn in by my eyes, which I am reviewing, though they also are there, lying dormant, and laid up, as it were, apart. For these too I call for, and forthwith they appear. And though my tongue be still, and my throat mute, so can I sing as much as I will; nor do those images of colours, which notwithstanding be there, intrude themselves and interrupt, when another store is called for, which flowed in by the ears. So the other things, piled in and up by the other senses, I recall at my pleasure. Yea, I discern the breath of lilies from violets, though smelling nothing; and I prefer honey to sweet wine, smooth before rugged, at the time neither tasting nor handling, but remembering only.

14. These things do I within, in that vast court of my memory. For there are present with me heaven, earth, sea, and whatever I could think of therein, besides what I have forgotten. There also meet I with myself, and recall myself, and when, where, and what I have done, and under what feelings. There be all which I remember, either on my own experience, or others' credit. Out of the same store do I myself with the past continually combine fresh and

fresh likenesses of things which I have experienced, or, from what I have experienced, have believed; and thence again infer future actions, events and hopes, and all these again I reflect on, as present. "I will do this or that," say I to myself, in that great receptacle of my mind, stored with the images of things so many and so great, "and this or that will follow." "O that this or that might be!" "God avert this or that!" So speak I to myself; and when I speak, the images of all I speak of are present, out of the same treasury of memory; nor would I speak of any thereof, were the images wanting.

15. Great is this force of memory, excessive great, O my God; a large and boundless chamber! Who ever sounded the bottom thereof? Yet is this a power of mine, and belongs unto my nature; nor do I myself comprehend all that I am. Therefore is the mind too strait to contain itself. And where should that be, which it containeth not of itself? Is it without it, and not within? how then doth it not comprehend itself? A wonderful admiration surprises me, amazement seizes me upon this. And men go abroad to admire the heights of mountains, the mighty billows of the sea, the broad tides of rivers, the compass of the ocean, and the circuits of the stars, and pass themselves by; nor wonder that, when I spake of all these things, I did not see them with mine eyes, yet could not have spoken of them unless I then actually saw the mountains, billows, rivers, stars, which I had seen, and that ocean which I believe to be, inwardly in my memory, and that, with the same vast spaces between, as if I saw them abroad. Yet did not I by seeing draw them into myself, when with mine eyes I beheld them; nor are they themselves with me, but their images only. And I know by what sense of the body each was impressed upon me.

[IX] 16. Yet not these alone does the unmeasurable capacity of my memory retain. Here also is all learnt of the liberal sciences and as yet unforgotten; removed as it were to some inner place, which is yet no place: nor are they the images thereof, but the things themselves. For what is literature, what the art of disputing, how many kinds of questions there be, whatsoever of these I know, in such manner exists in my memory as that I have not taken in the image and left out the thing, or that it should have sounded and passed away like a voice fixed on the ear by that impress, whereby it might be recalled, as if it sounded when it no longer sounded; or as a smell while it passes, and evaporates into air, affects the sense of smell, whence it

conveys into the memory an image of itself, which remembering we renew, or as meat, which verily in the belly hath now no taste, and yet in the memory still in a manner tasteth; or as anything which the body by touch perceiveth, and which, when removed from us, the memory still conceives. For those things are not transmitted into the memory, but their images only are with an admirable swiftness caught up, and stored as it were in wondrous cabinets, and thence wonderfully, by the act of remembering, brought forth.

[X] 17. But now when I hear that there be three kinds of questions: "Whether the thing be? what it is? of what kind it is?" I do indeed hold the images of the sounds, of which those words be composed, and that those sounds, with a noise passed through the air, and now are not. But the things themselves which are signified by those sounds, I never reached with any sense of my body, nor ever discerned them otherwise than in my mind; yet in my memory have I laid up not their images, but themselves. Which how they entered into me, let them say if they can; for I have gone over all the avenues of my flesh, but cannot find by which they entered. For the eyes say, "If those images were coloured, we reported of them." The ears say, "If they sound, we gave knowledge of them." The nostrils says, "If they smell, they passed by us." The taste says, "Unless they have a savour, ask me not." The touch says, "If it have not size, I handled it not; if I handled it not, I gave no notice of it." Whence and how entered these things into my memory? I know not how. For when I learned them, I gave not credit to another man's mind, but recognized them in mine; and, approving them for true, I commended them to it, laying them up as it were, whence I might bring them forth when I willed. In my heart then they were, even before I learned them, but in my memory they were not. Where then? or wherefore, when they were spoken, did I acknowledge them, and said, "So is it, it is true," unless that they were already in the memory, but so thrown back and buried as it were in deeper recesses, that, had not the suggestion of another drawn them forth, I had perchance been unable to conceive of them?

[XI] 18. Wherefore we find that to learn these things whereof we imbibe not the images by our senses, but perceive within by themselves, without images, as they are, is nothing else but by conception to receive, and by making to take heed that those things which the memory did before contain at random and unarranged, be laid up at hand as it were in that same memory, where before they lay unknown, scattered and neglected, and so readily occur to the mind familiarized to them. And how many things of this kind does my memory bear which have been already found out and, as I said, placed as it were at hand, which we are said to have learned and come to know; which were I for some short space of time to cease to call to mind, they are again so buried, and glide back, as it were, into the deeper recesses, that they must again, as if new, be thought out thence, for other abode they have none; but they must be drawn together again, that they may be known; that is to say, they must as it were be collected together from their dispersion; whence the word "cogitation" is derived. For *cogo* (collect) and *cogito* (re-collect) have the same relation to each other as *ago* and *agito*, *facio* and *factito*. But the mind hath appropriated to itself this word (cogitation), so that, not what is "collected" anyhow, but what is "recollected"—i.e., brought together in the mind—is properly said to be cogitated, or thought upon.

[XII] 19. The memory containeth also reasons and laws innumerable of numbers and dimensions, none of which hath any bodily sense impressed; seeing they have neither colour, nor sound, nor taste, nor smell, nor touch. I have heard the sound of the words whereby when discussed they are denoted; but the sounds are other than the things. For the sounds are other in Greek than in Latin; but the things are neither Greek, nor Latin, nor any other language. I have seen the lines of architects, the very finest like a spider's thread; but those are still different, they are not the images of those lines which the eye of flesh shewed me; he knoweth them, whosoever without any conception whatsoever of a body recognizes them within himself. I have perceived also the numbers of the things with which we number all the senses of my body; but those numbers wherewith we number are different, nor are they the images of these, and therefore they indeed are. Let him who seeth them not deride me for saying these things, and I will pity him while he derides me.

[XIII] 20. All these things I remember, and how I learnt them I remember. Many things also most falsely objected against them have I heard, and remember; which though they be false, yet is it not false that I remember them; and I remember also that I have discerned betwixt those truths and these falsehoods objected to them. And I perceive that the present discerning of these things is different from remembering that I oftentimes discerned them when I often thought upon them. I both remember then to have often understood these things; and what I now discern and understand, I lay up in my memory, that hereafter I may remember that I understood it now. So then I remember also to have remembered; as, if hereafter I shall call to remembrance that I have now been able to remember these things, by the force of memory shall I call it to remembrance.

[XIV] 21. The same memory contains also the affections of my mind, not in the same manner that my mind itself contains them when it feels them; but far otherwise, according to a power of its own. For without rejoicing I remember myself to have joyed; and without sorrow do I recollect my past sorrow. And that I once feared, I review without fear; and without desire call to mind a past desire. Sometimes, on the contrary, with joy do I remember my forepast sorrow, and with sorrow, joy. Which is not wonderful, as to the body; for mind is one thing, body another. If I therefore with joy remember some past pain of body, it is not so wonderful. But now seeing this very memory itself is mind (for when we give a thing in charge, to be kept in memory, we say, "See that you keep it in mind"; and when we forget, we say, "It did not come to my mind," and, "It slipped out of my mind," calling the memory itself the mind)— this being so, how is it that, when with joy I remember my past sorrow, the mind hath joy, the memory hath sorrow; the mind upon the joyfulness which is in it, is joyful, yet the memory upon the sadness which is in it, is not sad? Does the memory perchance not belong to the mind? Who will say so? The memory then is, as it were, the belly of the mind, and joy and sadness, like sweet and bitter food; which, when committed to the memory, are as it were passed into the belly, where they may be stowed, but cannot taste. Ridiculous it is to imagine these to be alike; and yet are they not utterly unlike.

22. But behold, out of my memory I bring it, when I say there be four perturbations of the mind: desire, joy, fear, sorrow; and whatsoever I can dispute thereon, by dividing each into its subordinate species, and by defining it, in my memory find I what to say, and thence do I bring it; yet am I not disturbed by any of these perturbations, when by calling them to mind I remember them; yea, and before I recalled and brought them back, they were there; and therefore could they, by recollection, thence be brought. Perchance, then, as meat is by chewing the cud brought up out of the belly, so by recol-

lection these out of the memory. Why then does not the disputer, thus recollecting, taste in the mouth of his musing the sweetness of joy, or the bitterness of sorrow? Is the comparison unlike in this, because not in all repects like? For who would willingly speak thereof if, so oft as we name grief or fear, we should be compelled to be sad or fearful? And yet could we not speak of them, did we not find in our memory not only the sounds of the names according to the images impressed by the senses of the body, but notions of the very things themselves which we never received by any avenue of the body, but which the mind itself perceiving by the experience of its own passions, committed to the memory, or the memory of itself retained, without being committed unto it.

[XV] 23. But whether by images or no, who can readily say? Thus, I name a stone, I name the sun, the things themselves not being present to my senses, but their images to my memory. I name a bodily pain, yet it is not present with me, when nothing aches; yet, unless its image were present to my memory, I should not know what to say thereof, nor in discoursing discern pain from pleasure. I name bodily health; being sound in body, the thing itself is present with me; yet, unless its image also were present in my memory, I could by no means recall what the sound of this name should signify. Nor would the sick, when health were named, recognize what were spoken, unless the same image were by the force of memory retained, although the thing itself were absent from the body. I name numbers whereby we number; and not their images, but themselves are present in my memory. I name the image of the sun, and that image is present in my memory. For I recall not the image of its image, but the image itself is present to me, calling it to mind. I name memory, and I recognize what I name. And where do I recognize it, but in the memory itself? Is it also present to itself by its image, and not by itself?

[XVI] 24. What, when I name forgetfulness, and withal recognize what I name? whence should I recognize it, did I not remember it? I speak not of the sound of the name, but of the thing which it signifies: which if I had forgotten, I could not recognize what that sound signifies. When then I remember memory, memory itself is, through itself, present with itself; but when I remember forgetfulness, there are present both memory and forgetfulness; memory whereby I remember, forgetfulness which I remember. But what is forgetfulness but the privation of memory? How then is it present that I re-

member it, since when present I cannot remember? But if what we remember we hold it in memory, yet, unless we did remember forgetfulness, we could never at the hearing of the name recognize the thing thereby signified, then forgetfulness is retained by memory. Present then it is, that we forget not, and being so, we forget. It is to be understood from this that forgetfulness, when we remember it, is not present to the memory by itself, but by its image: because if it were present by itself, it would not cause us to remember, but to forget. Who now shall search out this? who shall comprehend how it is?

25. Lord, I truly toil therein, yea, and toil in myself; I am become a heavy soil requiring over-much sweat of the brow. For we are not now searching out the regions of heaven, or measuring the distances of the stars, or enquiring the balancings of the earth. It is I myself who remember, I the mind. It is not so wonderful, if what I myself am not be far from me. But what is nearer to me than myself? And lo, the force of mine own memory is not understood by me; though I cannot so much as name myself without it. For what shall I say when it is clear to me that I remember forgetfulness? Shall I say that that is not in my memory, which I remember? or shall I say that forgetfulness is for this purpose in my memory, that I might not forget? Both were most absurd. What third way is there? How can I say that the image of forgetfulness is retained by my memory, not forgetfulness itself, when I remember it? How could I say this either, seeing that when the image of any thing is impressed on the memory, the thing itself must needs be first present, whence that image may be impressed? For thus do I remember Carthage, thus all places where I have been, thus men's faces whom I have seen, and things reported by the other senses; thus the health or sickness of the body. For when these things were present, my memory received from them images which, being present with me, I might look on and bring back in my mind, when I remembered them in their absence. If then this forgetfulness is retained in the memory through its image, not through itself, then plainly, itself was once present, that its image might be taken. But when it was present, how did it write its image in the memory, seeing that forgetfulness by its presence effaces even what it finds already noted? And yet, in whatever way, although that way be past conceiving and explaining, yet certain am I that I remember forgetfulness itself also, whereby what we remember is effaced.

[XVII] 26. Great is the power of memory, a fearful thing, O my God, a deep and boundless manifoldness; and this thing is the mind, and this am I myself. What am I then, O my God? What nature am I? A life various and manifold, and exceeding immense. Behold in the plains, and caves, and caverns of my memory, innumerable and innumerably full of innumerable kinds of things, either through images, as all bodies; or by actual presence, as the arts; or by certain notions or impressions, as the affections of the mind, which, even when the mind doth not feel, the memory retaineth, while yet whatsoever is in the memory is also in the mind— over all these do I run, I fly; I dive on this side and on that, as far as I can, and there is no end. So great is the force of memory, so great the force of life, even in the mortal life of man. What shall I do then, O Thou my true life, my God? I will pass even beyond this power of mine which is called memory; yea, I will pass beyond it, that I may approach unto Thee, O sweet Light. What sayest Thou to me? See, I am mounting up through my mind towards Thee who abidest above me. Yea, I now will pass beyond this power of mine which is called memory, desirous to arrive at Thee, whence Thou mayest be arrived at; and to cleave unto Thee, whence one may cleave unto Thee. For even beasts and birds have memory; else could they not return to their dens and nests, nor many other things they are used unto; nor indeed could they be used to anything, but by memory. I will pass then beyond memory also, that I may arrive at Him Who hath separated me from the four-footed beasts and made me wiser than the fowls of the air, I will pass beyond memory also, and where shall I find Thee, Thou truly good and certain sweetness? And where shall I find Thee? If I find Thee without my memory, then do I not retain Thee in my memory. And how shall I find Thee, if I remember Thee not?

[XVIII] 27. For the woman that had lost her groat, and sought it with a light;[1] unless she had remembered it, she had never found it. For when it was found, whence should she know whether it were the same, unless she remembered it? I remember to have sought and found many a thing; and this I thereby know, that when I was seeking any of them, and was asked, "Is this it?" "Is that it?" so long said I "No," until that were offered me which I sought. Which had I not remembered (whatever it were) though it were offered me, yet should I not find it, because I could not recognize it. And so it ever is, when we seek and find any lost thing. Notwithstanding, when anything is by chance lost from the sight, not from the memory (as any visible body), yet its image is still retained within, and it is sought until it be restored to sight; and when it is found, it is recognized by the image which is within: nor do we say that we have found what was lost, unless we recognize it; nor can we recognize it, unless we remember it. But this was lost to the eyes, but retained in the memory.

[XIX] 28. But what when the memory itself loses anything, as falls out when we forget and seek that we may recollect? Where in the end do we search, but in the memory itself? And there, if one thing be perchance offered instead of another, we reject it, until what we seek meets us; and when it doth, we say, "This is it"; which we should not unless we recognized it, nor recognize it unless we remembered it. Certainly then we had forgotten it. Or, had not the whole escaped us, but by the part whereof we had hold was the lost part sought for; in that the memory felt that it did not carry on together all which it was wont, and maimed, as it were, by the curtailment of its ancient habit, demanded the restoration of what it missed? For instance, if we see or think of someone known to us and, having forgotten his name, try to recover it; whatever else occurs connects itself not therewith; because it was not wont to be thought upon together with him, and therefore is rejected, until that present itself whereon the knowledge reposes equally as its wonted object. And whence does that present itself, but out of the memory itself? For even when we recognize it, on being reminded by another, it is thence it comes. For we do not believe it as something new, but, upon recollection, allow what was named to be right. But were it utterly blotted out of the mind, we should not remember it, even when reminded. For we have not as yet utterly forgotten that which we remember ourselves to have forgotten. What then we have utterly forgotten, though lost, we cannot even seek after.

[XX] 29. How then do I seek Thee, O Lord? For when I seek Thee, my God, I seek a happy life. I will seek Thee, that my soul may live.[2] For my body liveth by my soul; and my soul by Thee. How then do I seek a happy life, seeing I have it not, until I can say, where I ought to say it, "It is enough?" How seek I it? By remembrance, as though I had forgotten it, remembering that I had forgotten it? Or, desiring to learn it as a thing unknown, either never having known, or so forgotten it as not even to remem-

[1] Luke, 15. 8.

[2] Amos, 5. 4.

ber that I had forgotten it? Is not a happy life what all will, and no one altogether wills it not? Where have they known it, that they so will it? where seen it, that they so love it? Truly we have it, how, I know not. Yea, there is another way, wherein when one hath it, then is he happy; and there are, who are blessed, in hope. These have it in a lower kind than they who have it in very deed; yet are they better off than such as are happy neither in deed nor in hope. Yet even these, had they it not in some sort, would not so will to be happy, which that they do will is most certain. They have known it then, I know not how, and so have it by some sort of knowledge; what, I know not, and am perplexed whether it be in the memory, which if it be, then we have been happy once; whether all severally, or in that man who first sinned, in whom also we all died,[1] and from whom we are all born with misery, I now enquire not; but only, whether the happy life be in the memory? For neither should we love it, did we not know it. We hear the name, and we all confess that we desire the thing; for we are not delighted with the mere sound. For when a Greek hears it in Latin, he is not delighted, not knowing what is spoken; but we Latins are delighted, as would he too if he heard it in Greek; because the thing itself is neither Greek nor Latin, which Greeks and Latins, and men of all other tongues, long for so earnestly. Known therefore it is to all, for could they with one voice be asked, "Would they be happy?" they would answer without doubt, "They would." And this could not be, unless the thing itself whereof it is the name were retained in their memory.

[XXI] 30. But is it so, as one remembers Carthage who hath seen it? No. For a happy life is not seen with the eye, because it is not a body. As we remember numbers then? No. For these, he that hath in his knowledge seeks not further to attain unto; but a happy life we have in our knowledge, and therefore love it, and yet still desire to attain it, that we may be happy. As we remember eloquence then? No. For although upon hearing this name also, some call to mind the thing, who still are not yet eloquent, and many who desire to be so, whence it appears that it is in their knowledge; yet these have by their bodily senses observed others to be eloquent, and been delighted, and desire to be the like (though indeed they would not be delighted but for some inward knowledge thereof, nor wish to be the like, unless they were thus delighted); whereas a happy life, we do by no bodily sense

experience in others. As then we remember joy? Perchance; for my joy I remember, even when sad, as a happy life, when unhappy; nor did I ever with bodily sense see, hear, smell, taste, or touch my joy; but I experienced it in my mind, when I rejoiced; and the knowledge of it clave to my memory, so that I can recall it with disgust sometimes, at others with longing, according to the nature of the things wherein I remember myself to have joyed. For even from foul things have I been immersed in a sort of joy; which, now recalling, I detest and execrate; otherwhiles in good and honest things, which I recall with longing, although perchance no longer present; and therefore with sadness I recall former joy.

31. Where then, and when, did I experience my happy life, that I should remember, and love, and long for it? Nor is it I alone, or some few besides, but we all would fain be happy; which, unless by some certain knowledge we know, we should not with so certain a will desire. But how is this, that if two men be asked whether they would go to the wars, one perchance would answer that he would, the other, that he would not; but if they were asked whether they would be happy, both would instantly without any doubting say they would; and for no other reason would the one go to the wars, and the other not, but to be happy. Is it perchance that, as one looks for his joy in this thing, another in that, all agree in their desire of being happy, as they would (if they were asked) that they wished to have joy, and this joy they call a happy life? Although then one obtains this joy by one means, another by another, all have one end which they strive to attain, namely, joy. Which being a thing which all must say they have experienced, it is therefore found in the memory, and recognized whenever the name of a happy life is mentioned.

[XXII] 32. Far be it, Lord, far be it from the heart of Thy servant who here confesseth unto Thee, far be it that, be the joy what it may, I should therefore think myself happy. For there is a joy which is not given to the ungodly,[2] but to those who love Thee for Thine own sake, whose joy Thou Thyself art. And this is the happy life, to rejoice to Thee, of Thee, for Thee; this is it, and there is no other.[3] For they who think there is another pursue some other and not the true joy. Yet is not their will turned away from some semblance of joy.

[XXIII] 33. It is not certain then that all wish to be happy, inasmuch as they who wish

[1] I Cor. 15. 22.

[2] Isa. 48. 22.   [3] Cf. *City of God*, BK. VIII. 9.

not to joy in Thee, which is the only happy life, do not truly desire the happy life. Or do all men desire this, but, because "the flesh lusteth against the Spirit, and the Spirit against the flesh," that they "cannot do what they would," [1] they fall upon that which they can, and are content therewith; because what they are not able to do, they do not will so strongly, as would suffice to make them able? [2] For I ask anyone, had he rather joy in truth, or in falsehood? They will as little hesitate to say, "in the truth," as to say, "that they desire to be happy"; for a happy life is joy in the truth: for this a joying in Thee, Who art "the Truth,"[3] O God "my light,"[4] the "health of my countenance, my God."[5] This is the happy life which all desire; this life which alone is happy, all desire; to joy in the truth all desire.[6] I have met with many that would deceive; who would be deceived, no one. Where then did they know this happy life, save where they knew the truth also? For they love it also, since they would not be deceived. And when they love a happy life, which is no other than joying in the truth, then also do they love the truth; which yet they would not love, were there not some notice of it in their memory. Why then joy they not in it? Why are they not happy? Because they are more strongly taken up with other things which have more power to make them miserable, than that which they so faintly remember to make them happy. For there is yet a little light in men; let them walk, let them "walk," that the "darkness" overtake them not.[7]

34. But why doth "truth generate hatred," [8] and the man of thine,[9] preaching the truth, become an enemy to them? whereas a happy life is loved, which is nothing else but joying in the truth; unless that truth is in that kind loved, that they who love anything else would gladly have that which they love to be the truth; and, because they would not be deceived, would not be convinced that they are so? Therefore do they hate the truth, for that thing's sake which they love instead of the truth. They love truth when she enlightens, they hate her when she reproves. For since they would not be deceived, and would deceive, they love her when she discovers herself unto them, and hate her when she discovers them. Whence she shall so repay them, that they who would not be made manifest by her, she both against their will makes manifest,

and herself becometh not manifest unto them. Thus, thus, yea, thus doth the mind of man, thus blind and sick, foul and ill-favoured, wish to be hidden; but that aught should be hidden from it, it wills not. But the contrary is requited it, that itself should not be hidden from the Truth; but the Truth is hid from it. Yet even thus miserable, it had rather joy in truths than in falsehoods. Happy then will it be when, no distraction interposing, it shall joy in that only Truth by Whom all things are true.

[XXIV] 35. See what a space I have gone over in my memory seeking Thee, O Lord; and I have not found Thee, without it. Nor have I found anything concerning Thee, but what I have kept in memory, ever since I learnt Thee. For since I learnt Thee, I have not forgotten Thee. For where I found Truth, there found I my God, the Truth Itself;[10] which since I learnt, I have not forgotten. Since then I learned Thee, Thou residest in my memory; and there do I find Thee, when I call Thee to remembrance, and delight in Thee. These be my holy delights, which Thou hast given me in Thy mercy, having regard to my poverty.

[XXV] 36. But where in my memory residest Thou, O Lord, where residest Thou there? What manner of lodging hast Thou framed for Thee? What manner of sanctuary hast Thou builded for Thee? Thou hast given this honour to my memory, to reside in it; but in what quarter of it Thou residest, that am I considering. For in thinking on Thee, I passed[11] beyond such parts of it as the beasts also have, for I found Thee not there among the images of corporeal things; and I came to those parts to which I committed the affections of my mind, nor found Thee there. And I entered into the very seat of my mind (which it hath in my memory, inasmuch as the mind remembers itself also), neither wert Thou there; for as Thou art not a corporeal image, nor the affection of a living being (as when we rejoice, condole, desire, fear, remember, forget, or the like); so neither art Thou the mind itself; because Thou art the Lord God of the mind; and all these are changed, but Thou remainest unchangeable over all, and yet hast vouchsafed to dwell in my memory, since I learnt Thee. And why seek I now, in what place thereof Thou dwellest, as if there were places therein? Sure I am that in it Thou dwellest, since I have remembered Thee, ever since I learnt Thee, and there I find Thee when I call Thee to remembrance.

[1]Gal. 5. 17. [2]See above, BK. VIII. 10, 11, 20.
[3]John, 14. 6. [4]Ps. 27. 1. [5]Ps. 42. 11.
[6]See above, 29. [7]John, 12. 35.
[8]Terence, *Andria*, 1. 40. [9]John, 8. 40.

[10]See above, BK. IV. 18, 19; BK. VII. 16.
[11]See above, 26.

[XXVI] 37. Where then did I find Thee, that I might learn Thee? For in my memory Thou wert not, before I learned Thee. Where then did I find Thee, that I might learn Thee, but in Thee above me? Place there is none; we go "backward" and "forward,"[1] and there is no place. Everywhere, O Truth, dost Thou give audience to all who ask counsel of Thee, and at once answerest all, though on manifold matters they ask Thy counsel. Clearly dost Thou answer, though all do not clearly hear. All consult Thee on what they will, though they hear not always what they will. He is thy best servant who looks not so much to hear that from Thee which himself willeth; as rather to will that which from Thee he heareth.

[XXVII] 38. Too late loved I Thee, O Thou Beauty of ancient days, yet ever new! too late I loved Thee! And behold, Thou wert within, and I abroad, and there I searched for Thee; deformed I, plunging amid those fair forms which Thou hadst made. Thou wert with me, but I was not with Thee. Things held me far from Thee, which, unless they were in Thee, were not at all. Thou calledst, and shoutedst, and burstest my deafness. Thou flashedst, shonest, and scatteredst my blindness. Thou breathedst odours, and I drew in breath and pant for Thee. I tasted, and hunger and thirst. Thou touchedst me, and I burned for Thy peace.

[XXVIII] 39. When I shall with my whole self cleave to Thee, I shall nowhere have sorrow, or labour; and my life shall wholly live, as wholly full of Thee. But now, since whom Thou fillest Thou liftest up, because I am not full of Thee I am a burthen to myself. Lamentable joys strive with joyous sorrows; and on which side is the victory, I know not. Woe is me! Lord, have pity on me. My evil sorrows strive with my good joys; and on which side is the victory, I know not. Woe is me! Lord, have pity on me. Woe is me! lo! I hide not my wounds; Thou art the Physician, I the sick; Thou merciful, I miserable. Is not the life of man upon earth all trial?[2] Who wishes for troubles and difficulties? Thou commandest them to be endured, not to be loved. No man loves what he endures, though he love to endure. For though he rejoices that he endures, he had rather there were nothing for him to endure. In adversity I long for prosperity, in prosperity I fear adversity. What middle place is there betwixt these two, where the life of man is not all trial? Woe to the prosperities of the world, once and again, through fear of adversity, and corruption of joy! Woe to the

adversities of the world, once and again, and the third time, from the longing for prosperity, and because adversity itself is a hard thing, and lest it shatter endurance. Is not the life of man upon earth all trial, without any interval?

[XXIX] 40. And all my hope is nowhere but in Thy exceeding great mercy. Give what Thou enjoinest, and enjoin what Thou wilt. Thou enjoinest us continency; and, "When I knew [saith one] that no man can be continent unless God give it, this also was a part of wisdom to know whose gift she is."[3] By continency, verily, are we bound up and brought back into One, whence we were dissipated into many. For too little doth he love Thee who loves anything with Thee, which he loveth not for Thee. O love, who ever burnest and never consumest! O charity, my God! kindle me. Thou enjoinest continency: give me what Thou enjoinest, and enjoin what Thou wilt.

[XXX] 41. Verily Thou enjoinest me continency from the "lust of the flesh, the lust of the eyes, and the ambition of the world."[4] Thou enjoinest continency from concubinage; and for wedlock itself, Thou has counselled something better than what Thou hast permitted And since Thou gavest it, it was done, even before I became a dispenser of Thy Sacrament. But there yet live in my memory (whereof I have much spoken) the images of such things as my ill custom there fixed; which haunt me, strengthless when I am awake; but in sleep, not only so as to give pleasure, but even to obtain assent, and what is very like reality. Yea, so far prevails the illusion of the image, in my soul and in my flesh, that, when asleep, false visions persuade to that which, when waking, the true cannot. Am I not then myself, O Lord my God? And yet there is so much difference betwixt myself and myself, within that moment wherein I pass from waking to sleeping, or return from sleeping to waking! Where is reason then, which, awake, resisteth such suggestions? And should the things themselves be urged on it, it remaineth unshaken. Is it clasped up with the eyes? is it lulled asleep with the senses of the body? And whence is it that often even in sleep we resist, and mindful of our purpose, and abiding most chastely in it, yield no assent to such enticements? And yet so much difference there is that, when it happeneth otherwise, upon waking we return to peace of conscience: and by this very difference discover that we did not what yet we be sorry that in some way it was done in us.

[1] Job, 23. 8.   [2] Job, 7. 1.   [3] Wisd. 8. 21.   [4] I John, 2. 16.

42. Art Thou not mighty, God Almighty, so as to heal all the diseases of my soul,[1] and by Thy more abundant grace to quench even the impure motions of my sleep? Thou wilt increase, Lord, Thy gifts more and more in me, that my soul may follow me to Thee, disentangled from the bird-lime of concupiscence; that it rebel not against itself, and even in dreams not only not, through images of sense, commit those debasing corruptions, even to pollution of the flesh, but not even to consent unto them. For that nothing of this sort should have, over the pure affections even of a sleeper, the very least influence, not even such as a thought would restrain—to work this, not only during life, but even at my present age, is not hard for the Almighty, Who art "able to do above all that we ask or think."[2] But what I yet am in this kind of my evil, have I confessed unto my good Lord; rejoicing with trembling,[3] in that which Thou hast given me, and bemoaning that wherein I am still imperfect; hoping that Thou wilt perfect Thy mercies in me, even to perfect peace, which my outward and inward man shall have with Thee, when death shall be swallowed up in victory.[4]

[XXXI] 43. There is another evil of the day, which I would were "sufficient" for it.[5] For by eating and drinking we repair the daily decays of our body, until Thou destroy both belly and meat, when Thou shalt slay my emptiness with a wonderful fulness, and clothe this incorruptible with an eternal incorruption.[6] But now the necessity is sweet unto me, against which sweetness I fight, that I be not taken captive; and carry on a daily war by fastings, often "bringing my body into subjection";[7] and my pains are removed by pleasure. For hunger and thirst are in a manner pains: they burn and kill like a fever, unless the medicine of nourishments come to our aid. Which since it is at hand through the consolations of Thy gifts, with which land, and water, and air serve our weakness, our calamity is termed gratification.

44. This hast Thou taught me, that I should set myself to take food as physic. But while I am passing from the discomfort of emptiness to the content of replenishing, in the very passage the snare of concupiscence besets me. For that passing is pleasure, nor is there any other way to pass thither, whither we needs must pass. And health being the cause of eating and drinking, there joineth itself as an attendant a dangerous pleasure, which mostly endeavours to go before

it, so that I may for her sake do what I say I do, or wish to do, for health's sake. Nor has each the same measure; for what is enough for health is too little for pleasure. And oft it is uncertain whether it be the necessary care of the body which is yet asking for sustenance, or whether a voluptuous deceivableness of greediness is proffering its services. In this uncertainty the unhappy soul rejoiceth, and therein prepares an excuse to shield itself, glad that it appeareth not what sufficeth for the moderation of health, that under the cloak of health it may disguise the matter of gratification. These temptations I daily endeavour to resist, and I call on Thy right hand, and to Thee do I refer my perplexities; because I have as yet no settled counsel herein.

45. I hear the voice of my God commanding, Let not "your hearts be overcharged with surfeiting and drunkenness."[8] "Drunkenness" is far from me; Thou wilt have mercy that it come not near me. But full-feeding sometimes creepeth upon Thy servant; Thou wilt have mercy that it may be far from me. For no one can be continent unless Thou give it.[9] Many things Thou givest us, praying for them; and what good soever we have received before we prayed, from Thee we received it; yea, to the end we might afterwards know this, did we before receive it. Drunkard was I never, but drunkards have I known made sober by Thee. From Thee then it was that they who never were such should not so be, as from Thee it was that they who have been should not ever so be; and from Thee it was that both might know from Whom it was. I heard another voice of Thine, "Go not after thy lusts, and from thy pleasure turn away."[10] Yea, by Thy favour have I heard that which I have much loved; "neither if we eat, shall we abound; neither if we eat not, shall we lack";[11] which is to say, neither shall the one make me plenteous, nor the other miserable. I heard also another, "For I have learned in whatsoever state I am, therewith to be content; I know how to abound, and how to suffer need. I can do all things through Christ that strengtheneth me." [12] Behold a soldier of the heavenly camp, not the dust which we are. But remember, Lord, "that we are dust,"[13] and that of dust thou hast made man;[14] and he "was lost and is found." [15] Nor could he of himself do this, because he whom I so loved, saying this through the in-breathing of Thy inspiration, was of

---

[1]Ps. 103. 3.   [2]Eph. 13. 20.
[3]Ps. 2. 11.   [4]I Cor. 15. 54.   [5]Matt. 6. 34.
[6]I Cor. 15. 54.   [7]I Cor. 9. 27.

[8]Luke, 21. 34.   [9]Wisd. 8. 21.   [10]Ecclus. 18. 30.
[11]I Cor. 8. 8.   [12]Phil. 4. 11-14.   [13]Ps. 103. 14.
[14]Gen. 3. 19.   [15]Luke, 15. 32.

the same dust. "I can do all things," saith he, "through Him that strengtheneth me."[1] Strengthen me, that I can. Give what Thou enjoinest, and enjoin what Thou wilt. He confesses to have received, and, when he glorieth, in the Lord he glorieth.[2] Another have I heard begging that he might receive, "Take from me," saith he, "the desires of the belly";[3] whence it appeareth, O my holy God, that Thou givest, when that is done which Thou commandest to be done.

46. Thou hast taught me, good Father, that "to the pure, all things are pure";[4] but that "it is evil unto the man that eateth with offence";[5] and that "every creature of Thine is good, and nothing to be refused, which is received with thanksgiving";[6] and that "meat commendeth us not to God";[7] and that "no man should judge us in meat or drink";[8] and that he which eateth, let him not despise him that eateth not; and let not him that eateth not, judge him that eateth.[9] These things have I learned, thanks be to Thee, praise to Thee, my God, my Master, knocking at my ears, enlightening my heart; deliver me out of all temptation. I fear not uncleanness of meat, but the uncleanness of lusting. I know that Noah was permitted to eat all kind of flesh[10] that was good for food;[11] that Elijah was fed with flesh;[12] that John, endued with an admirable abstinence, was not polluted by feeding on living creatures, locusts.[13] I know also that Esau was deceived by lusting for lentils;[14] and that David blamed himself for desiring a draught of water;[15] and that our King was tempted, not concerning flesh, but bread.[16] And therefore the people in the wilderness also deserved to be reproved, not for desiring flesh, but because, in the desire of food, they murmured against the Lord.[17]

47. Placed then amid these temptations, I strive daily against concupiscence in eating and drinking. For it is not of such nature that I can settle on cutting it off once for all, and never touching it afterward, as I could of concubinage. The bridle of the throat then is to be held attempered between slackness and stiffness. And who is he, O Lord, who is not somewhit transported beyond the limits of necessity? Whoever he is, he is a great one; let him make Thy Name

great. But I am not such, "for I am a sinful man."[18] Yet do I too magnify Thy name; and He maketh intercession to Thee[19] for my sins, Who hath "overcome the world,"[20] numbering me among the "weak members" of His body;[21] because thine eyes have seen that of Him which is imperfect, and in Thy book shall all be written.[22]

[XXXII] 48. With the allurements of smells, I am not much concerned. When absent, I do not miss them; when present, I do not refuse them; yet ever ready to be without them. So I seem to myself; perchance I am deceived. For that also is a mournful darkness, whereby my abilities within me are hidden from me; so that my mind, making enquiry into herself of her own powers, ventures not readily to believe herself; because even what is in it is mostly hidden, unless experience reveal it. And no one ought to be secure in that life, the whole whereof is called a trial,[23] that he, who hath been capable of worse to be made better may not likewise of better be made worse. Our only hope, only confidence, only assured promise, is Thy mercy.

[XXXIII] 49. The delights of the ear had more firmly entangled and subdued me; but Thou didst loosen and free me. Now, in those melodies which Thy words breathe soul into, when sung with a sweet and attuned voice, I do a little repose; yet not so as to be held thereby, but that I can disengage myself when I will. But with the words which are their life and whereby they find admission into me, themselves seek in my affections a place of some estimation, and I can scarcely assign them one suitable. For at one time I seem to myself to give them more honour than is seemly, feeling our minds to be more holily and fervently raised unto a flame of devotion by the holy words themselves when thus sung, than when not; and that the several affections of our spirit, by a sweet variety, have their own proper measures in the voice and singing, by some hidden correspondence wherewith they are stirred up. But this contentment of the flesh, to which the soul must not be given over to be enervated, doth oft beguile me, the sense not so waiting upon reason as patiently to follow her; but, having been admitted merely for her sake, it strives even to run before her, and lead her. Thus in these things I unawares sin, but afterwards am aware of it.

50. At other times, shunning over-anxiously this very deception, I err in too great strictness;

[1]Phil. 4. 13.   [2]I Cor. 1. 31.   [3]Ecclus. 23. 6.
[4]Titus, 1. 15.   [5]Rom. 14. 20.   [6]I Tim. 4. 4.
[7]I Cor. 8. 8.   [8]Col. 2. 16.   [9]Rom. 13. 23.
[10]Against the Manichees who forbad to eat flesh.
[11]Gen. 9. 13.   [12]I Kings, 17. 6.
[13]According to the Manichees the most impure food of all, as being insects. Matt. 13. 4.   [14]Gen. 25. 34.
[15]II Sam. 23. 15–17.   [16]Matt. 4. 3.   [17]Num. 1.

[18]Luke, 5. 8.   [19]Rom. 8. 34.   [20]John, 16. 33.
[21]I Cor. 12. 22.   [22]Ps. 139. 16.
[23]Job, 7. 1, old version.

and sometimes to that degree as to wish the whole melody of sweet music which is used to David's Psalter banished from my ears, and the Church's too; and that mode seems to me safer, which I remember to have been often told me of Athanasius Bishop of Alexandria, who made the reader of the psalm utter it with so slight inflection of voice that it was nearer speaking than singing. Yet again, when I remember the tears I shed at the Psalmody of Thy Church, in the beginning of my recovered faith; and how at this time I am moved, not with the singing, but with the things sung, when they are sung with a clear voice and modulation most suitable, I acknowledge the great use of this institution. Thus I fluctuate between peril of pleasure, and approved wholesomeness; inclined the rather (though not as pronouncing an irrevocable opinion) to approve of the usage of singing in the church; that so, by the delight of the ears, the weaker minds may rise to the feeling of devotion. Yet when it befalls me to be more moved with the voice than the words sung, I confess to have sinned penally, and then had rather not hear music. See now my state; weep with me, and weep for me, ye who so regulate your feelings within as that good action ensues. For you who do not act, these things touch not you. But Thou, O Lord my God, hearken; behold, and see, and have mercy, and heal me,[1] Thou, in Whose presence I have become a problem to myself; and "that is my infirmity."[2]

[XXXIV] 51. There remains the pleasure of these eyes of my flesh, on which to make my confessions in the hearing of the ears of Thy temple, those brotherly and devout ears; and so to conclude the temptations of "the lust of the flesh,"[3] which yet assail me, groaning earnestly, and desiring to be clothed upon with my house from heaven.[4] The eyes love fair and varied forms, and bright and soft colours. Let not these occupy my soul; let God rather occupy it, Who made these things, "very good"[5] indeed, yet is He my good, not they. And these affect me, waking the whole day, nor is any rest given me from them, as there is from music, sometimes in silence, from all voices. For this queen of colours, the light, bathing all which we behold, wherever I am through the day, gliding by me in varied forms, soothes me when engaged on other things and not observing it. And so strongly doth it entwine itself that, if it be suddenly withdrawn, it is with longing sought for, and, if absent long, saddeneth the mind.

52. O Thou Light, which Tobias saw[6] when, these eyes closed, he taught his son the way of life; and himself went before with the feet of charity, never swerving. Or which Isaac saw, when his fleshy "eyes being heavy"[7] and closed by old age, it was vouchsafed him, not knowingly to bless his sons, but by blessing to know them. Or which Jacob saw, when he also, blind through great age, with illumined heart, in the persons of his sons shed light on the different races of the future people, in them foresignified; and laid his hands, mystically crossed, upon his grandchildren by Joseph, not as their father by his outward eye corrected them, but as himself inwardly discerned.[8] This is the light, it is one, and all are one, who see and love it. But that corporeal light whereof I spake, it seasoneth the life of this world for her blind lovers, with an enticing and dangerous sweetness. But they who know how to praise Thee for it, O "Maker of all, the Lord,"[9] take it up in Thy hymns, and are not taken up with it in their sleep. Such would I be. These seductions of the eyes I resist, lest my feet wherewith I walk upon Thy way be ensnared; and I lift up mine invisible eyes to Thee, that Thou wouldest "pluck my feet out of the snare."[10] Thou dost ever and anon pluck them out, for they are ensnared. Thou ceasest not to pluck them out, while I often entangle myself in the snares on all sides laid; because Thou "that keepest Israel shalt neither slumber nor sleep."[11]

53. What innumerable toys, made by divers arts and manufactures, in our apparel, shoes, utensils and all sorts of works, in pictures also and divers images, and these far exceeding all necessary and moderate use and all pious meaning, have men added to tempt their own eyes withal; outwardly following what themselves make, inwardly forsaking Him by Whom themselves were made, and destroying that which themselves have been made! But I, my God and my Glory, do hence also sing a hymn to Thee, and do consecrate praise to Him Who consecrateth me, because those beautiful patterns, which through men's souls, are conveyed into their cunning hands,[12] come from that Beauty Which is above our souls, Which my soul day and night sigheth after. But the framers and followers of the outward beauties derive thence the rule of judging of them, but not of using them. And He is there, though they perceive Him not, that so they might not wander, but

[1] Ps. 6. 2. [2] Ps. 77. 10. [3] I John, 2. 16.
[4] II Cor. 5. 2. [5] Gen. 1. 31.

[6] Tobit, 4. [7] Gen. 27. 1. [8] Ibid., 48. 13–19.
[9] See BK. IX. 32. [10] Ps. 25. 15.
[11] Ps. 121. 4. [12] See below, BK. XI. 7.

keep their strength for Thee,[1] and not scatter it abroad upon pleasurable wearinesses. And I, though I speak and see this, entangle my steps with these outward beauties; but Thou pluckest me out, O Lord, Thou pluckest me out; "because Thy loving-kindness is before my eyes."[2] For I am taken miserably, and Thou pluckest me out mercifully; sometimes not perceiving it, when I had but lightly lighted upon them; otherwhiles with pain, because I had stuck fast in them.

[XXXV] 54. To this is added another form of temptation more manifoldly dangerous. For, besides that concupiscence of the flesh which consisteth in the delight of all senses and pleasures, wherein its slaves, who "go far from Thee," waste and "perish,"[3] the soul hath, through the same senses of the body, a certain vain and curious desire, veiled under the title of knowledge and learning, not of delighting in the flesh, but of making experiments through the flesh. The seat whereof being in the appetite of knowledge, and sight being the sense chiefly used for attaining knowledge, it is in Divine language called "the lust of the eyes."[4] For to see belongeth properly to the eyes; yet we use this word of the other senses also, when we employ them in seeking knowledge. For we do not say, hark how it flashes, or smell how it glows, or taste how it shines, or feel how it gleams; for all these are said to be seen. And yet we say not only, see how it shineth, which the eyes alone can perceive; but also, see how it soundeth, see how it smelleth, see how it tasteth, see how hard it is. And so the general experience of the senses, as was said, is called "the lust of the eyes," because the office of seeing, wherein the eyes hold the prerogative, the other senses by way of similitude take to themselves when they make search after any knowledge.

55. But by this may more evidently be discerned wherein pleasure and wherein curiosity is the object of the senses; for pleasure seeketh objects beautiful, melodious, fragrant, savoury, soft; but curiosity, for trial's sake, the contrary as well, not for the sake of suffering annoyance, but out of the lust of making trial and knowing them. For what pleasure hath it to see, in a mangled carcase, what will make you shudder? And yet if it be lying near, they flock thither, to be made sad, and to turn pale. Even in sleep they are afraid to see it. As if when awake, anyone forced them to see it, or any report of its beauty drew them thither! Thus also

in the other senses, which it were long to go through. From this disease of curiosity are all those strange sights exhibited in the theatre. Hence men go on to search out the hidden powers of nature (which is beside our end), which to know profits not, and wherein men desire nothing but to know. Hence also, if with that same end of perverted knowledge magical arts be enquired by. Hence also in religion itself is God tempted, when signs and wonders are demanded of Him, not desired for any good end, but merely to make trial of.

56. In this so vast wilderness, full of snares and dangers, behold many of them I have cut off, and thrust out of my heart, as Thou hast given me, O God of my salvation. And yet when dare I say, since so many things of this kind buzz on all sides about our daily life—when dare I say that nothing of this sort engages my attention, or causes in me an idle interest? True, the theatres do not now carry me away, nor care I to know the courses of the stars, nor did my soul ever consult ghosts departed; all sacrilegious mysteries I detest. From Thee, O Lord my God, to whom I owe humble and single-hearted service, by what artifices and suggestions doth the enemy deal with me to desire some sign! But I beseech thee by our King, and by our pure and holy country, Jerusalem, that, as any consenting thereto is far from me, so may it ever be further and further. But when I pray Thee for the salvation of any, my end and intention is far different. Thou givest and wilt give me to "follow Thee" willingly, doing what Thou wilt.[5]

57. Notwithstanding, in how many most petty and contemptible things is our curiosity daily tempted, and how often we give way, who can recount? How often do we begin, as if we were tolerating people telling vain stories, lest we offend the weak; then by degrees we take interest therein! I go not now to the circus to see a dog coursing a hare; but in the field, if passing, that coursing peradventure will distract me even from some weighty thought, and draw me after it; not that I turn aside the body of my beast, yet still incline my mind thither. And unless Thou, having made me see my infirmity, didst speedily admonish me either through the sight itself, by some contemplation to rise towards Thee, or altogether to despise and pass it by, I dully stand fixed therein. What, when sitting at home, a lizard catching flies, or a spider entangling them rushing into her nets, oft-times takes my attention? Is the thing different because they are but small creatures? I go on from them to praise

---

[1] Ps. 58. 10, Vulg.   [2] Ps. 26. 3.
[3] Ps. 63. 27.   [4] I John, 2. 16.
[5] John, 21. 22.

Thee the wonderful Creator and Orderer of all, but this does not first draw my attention. It is one thing to rise quickly, another not to fall. And of such things is my life full; and my one hope is Thy wonderful great mercy. For when our heart becomes the receptacle of such things, and is over-charged with throngs of this abundant vanity, then are our prayers also thereby often interrupted and distracted, and whilst in Thy presence we direct the voice of our heart to Thine ears, this so great concern is broken off by the rushing in of I know not what idle thoughts. Shall we then account this also among things of slight concernment, or shall aught bring us back to hope, save Thy complete mercy, since Thou hast begun to change us?

[XXXVI] 58. And Thou knowest how far Thou hast already changed me, Who first healedst me of the lust of vindicating myself, that so Thou mightest forgive all the rest of my "iniquities," and heal all my "infirmities," and redeem my life from corruption, and crown me with "mercy and pity," and satisfy my desire with "good things";[1] Who didst curb my pride with Thy fear, and tame my neck to Thy "yoke." And now I bear it and it is "light"[2] unto me, because so hast Thou promised, and hast made it; and verily so it was, and I knew it not, when I feared to take it.

59. But, O Lord, Thou alone Lord without pride, because Thou art the only true Lord, Who hast no lord, hath this third kind of temptation also ceased from me, or can it cease through this whole life? To wish, namely, to be feared and loved of men, for no other end but that we may have a joy therein which is no joy? A miserable life this, and a foul boastfulness! Hence especially it comes that men do neither purely love nor fear Thee. And therefore dost Thou resist the proud, and givest grace to the humble;[3] yea, Thou thunderest down upon the ambitions of the world, and "the foundations of the mountains" tremble.[4] Because now certain offices of human society make it necessary to be loved and feared of men, the adversary of our true blessedness layeth hard at us, everywhere spreading his snares of "well-done, well-done"; that, greedily catching at them, we may be taken unawares, and sever our joy from Thy truth, and set it in the deceivingness of men; and be pleased at being loved and feared, not for Thy sake, but in Thy stead: and thus having been made like him, he may have them for his own, not in the bands of charity, but in the bonds of

punishment; who purposed to set his throne in the north,[5] that dark and chilled they might serve him, pervertedly and crookedly imitating Thee. But we, O Lord, behold we are Thy "little flock";[6] possess us as Thine, stretch Thy wings over us, and let us fly under them. Be Thou our glory; let us be loved for Thee, and Thy word feared in us. Who would be praised of men, when Thou blamest, will not be defended of men, when Thou judgest; nor delivered, when Thou condemnest. But when not the sinner is praised in the desires of his soul, nor he blessed who doth ungodlily,[7] but a man is praised for some gift which Thou hast given him, and he rejoices more at the praise for himself than that he hath the gift for which he is praised, he also is praised, while Thou dispraisest; and better is he who praised than he who is praised. For the one took pleasure in the gift of God in man; the other was better pleased with the gift of man than of God.

[XXXVII] 60. By these temptations we are assailed daily, O Lord; without ceasing are we assailed. Our daily "furnace"[8] is the tongue of men. And in this way also Thou commandest us continence. Give what Thou enjoinest, and enjoin what Thou wilt. Thou knowest on this matter the groans of my heart, and the floods[9] of mine eyes. For I cannot learn how far I am more cleansed from this plague, and I much fear my "secret sins,"[10] which Thine eyes know, mine do not. For in other kinds of temptations I have some sort of means of examining myself; in this, scarce any. For, in refraining my mind from the pleasures of the flesh, and idle curiosity, I see how much I have attained to when I do without them; foregoing or not having them. For then I ask myself how much more or less troublesome it is to me not to have them? Then riches, which are desired that they may serve to some one or two or all of the three concupiscences,[11] if the soul cannot discern whether, when it hath them, it despiseth them, they may be cast aside, that so it may prove itself. But to be without praise, and therein essay our powers, must we live ill, yea, so abandonedly and atrociously that no one should know without detesting us? What greater madness can be said, or thought of? But if praise useth and ought to accompany a good life and good works, we ought as little to forgo its company as good life itself. Yet I know not whether I can well or ill be without anything, unless it be absent.

[1]Ps. 103. 3–5. [2]Matt. 2. 30.
[3]James. 4. 6. [4]Ps. 18. 7.

[5]Isa. 14. 13, 14. [6]Luke, 13. 32.
[7]Ps. 10. 3., Vulg. and LXX. [8]Isa. 48. 10; Prov. 27. 21.
[9]Lam. 3. 48. [10]Ps. 19. 12. [11]I John, 2. 16, see 41 above.

61. What then do I confess unto Thee in this kind of temptation, O Lord? What, but that I am delighted with praise, but with truth itself more than with praise? For were it proposed to me whether I would, being phrenzied in error on all things, be praised by all men, or being consistent and most settled in the truth be blamed by all, I see which I should choose. Yet fain would I that the approbation of another should not even increase my joy for any good in me. Yet I own, it doth increase it, and not so only, but dispraise doth diminish it. And when I am troubled at this my misery, an excuse occurs to me, which of what value it is, Thou God knowest, for it leaves me uncertain. For since Thou hast commanded us not continency alone, that is, from what things to refrain our love, but righteousness also, that is, whereon to bestow it, and hast willed us to love not Thee only, but our neighbour[1] also; often, when pleased with intelligent praise, I seem to myself to be pleased with the proficiency or towardliness of my neighbour, or to be grieved for evil in him, when I hear him dispraise either what he understands not, or is good. For sometimes I am grieved at my own praise, either when those things be praised in me in which I mislike myself, or even lesser and slight goods are more esteemed than they ought. But again, how know I whether I am therefore thus affected because I would not have him who praiseth me differ from me about myself; not as being influenced by concern for him, but because those same good things which please me in myself please me more when they please another also? For somehow I am not praised when my judgment of myself is not praised; forasmuch as either those things are praised which displease me; or those more, which please me less. Am I then doubtful of myself in this matter?

62. Behold, in Thee, O Truth, I see that I ought not to be moved at my own praises for my own sake, but for the good of my neighbour. And whether it be so with me, I know not. For herein I know less of myself than of Thee.[2] I beseech now, O my God, discover to me myself also, that I may confess unto my brethren, who are to pray for me, wherein I find myself maimed. Let me examine myself again more diligently. If in my praise I am moved with the good of my neighbour, why am I less moved if another be unjustly dispraised than if it be myself? Why am I more stung by reproach cast upon myself than at that cast upon another, with the same injustice, before me? Know I not this

also? or is it at last that I deceive myself,[3] and do not the "truth" before Thee in my heart and tongue? This madness put far from me, O Lord, lest mine own mouth be to me the sinner's oil to make fat my head.[4] "I am poor and needy";[5] yet best, while in hidden groanings I displease myself, and seek Thy mercy, until what is lacking in my defective state be renewed and perfected, on to that peace which the eye of the proud knoweth not.

[XXXVIII] 63. Yet the word which cometh out of the mouth, and deeds known to men, bring with them a most dangerous temptation through the love of praise: which, to establish a certain excellency of our own, solicits and collects men's suffrages. It tempts, even when it is reproved by myself in myself, on the very ground that it is reproved; and often glories more vainly of the very contempt of vain-glory; and so it is no longer contempt of vain-glory whereof it glories, for it doth not contemn when it glorieth.

[XXXIX] 64. Within also, within is another evil, arising out of a like temptation; whereby men become vain, pleasing themselves in themselves, though they please not, or displease, or care not to please others. But, pleasing themselves, they much displease Thee, not only taking pleasure in things not good, as if good, but in Thy good things, as though their own;[6] or even if as Thine, yet as though for their own merits; or even if as though from Thy grace, yet not with brotherly rejoicing, but envying that grace to others. In all these and the like perils and travails, Thou seest the trembling of my heart; and I rather feel my wounds to be cured by Thee than not inflicted by me.

[XL] 65. Where hast Thou not walked with me, O Truth, teaching me what to beware, and what to desire, when I referred to Thee what I could discover here below, and consulted Thee? With my outward senses, as I might, I surveyed the world, and observed the life which my body hath from me, and these my senses. Thence entered I the recesses of my memory, those manifold and spacious chambers, wonderfully furnished with innumerable stores; and I considered, and stood aghast; being able to discern nothing of these things without Thee, and finding none of them to be Thee. Nor was I myself, who found out these things, who went over them all, and laboured to distinguish and to value everything according to its dignity, taking some things upon the report of my senses, question-

---

[1]Lev. 19. 18. See below, XII. 35, 41.   [2]See above, 7.

[3]Gal. 6. 3.   [4]Ps. 141. 5, *Vulg.* and LXX.
[5]Ps. 109. 22.   [6]Cf. *City of God*, BK. V. 20.

ing about others which I felt to be mingled with myself, numbering and distinguishing the reporters themselves, and in the large treasure-house of my memory revolving some things, storing up others, drawing out others. Nor yet was I myself when I did this, i.e., that my power whereby I did it, neither was it Thou, for Thou art the abiding light, which I consulted concerning all these, whether they were, what they were, and how to be valued; and I heard Thee directing and commanding me; and this I often do, this delights me, and, as far as I may be freed from necessary duties, unto this pleasure have I recourse. Nor in all these which I run over consulting Thee, can I find any safe place for my soul, but in Thee; whither my scattered[1] members may be gathered, and nothing of me depart from Thee. And sometimes Thou admittest me to an affection, very unusual, in my inmost soul; rising to a strange sweetness, which if it were perfected in me, I know not what in it would not belong to the life to come. But through my miserable encumbrances[2] I sink down again into these lower things, and am swept back by former custom, and am held, and greatly weep, but am greatly held. So much doth the burthen of a bad custom weigh us down. Here I can stay, but would not; there I would, but cannot; both ways, miserable.

[XLI] 66. Thus then have I considered the sicknesses of my sins in that threefold concupiscence,[3] and have called Thy right hand to my help. For with a wounded heart have I beheld Thy brightness, and stricken back I said, "Who can attain thither?" "I am cast away from the sight of Thine eyes."[4] Thou art the Truth Who presidest over all, but I through my covetousness would not indeed forgo Thee, but would with Thee possess a lie; as no man would in such wise speak falsely, as himself to be ignorant of the truth. So then I lost Thee, because Thou vouchsafest not to be possessed with a lie.

[XLII] 67. Whom could I find to reconcile me to Thee? was I to have recourse to Angels? by what prayers? by what sacraments? Many endeavouring to return unto Thee, and of themselves unable, have, as I hear, tried this, and fallen into the desire of curious visions, and been accounted worthy to be deluded. For they, being high minded, sought Thee by the pride of learning, swelling out rather, than smiting upon, their breasts, and so by the agreement of their heart drew unto themselves the princes of the air,[5] the fellow-conspirators of their pride, by whom,

through magical influences, they were deceived, seeking a mediator by whom they might be purged, and there was none. For the Devil it was, transforming himself into an Angel of light.[6] And it much enticed proud flesh, that he had no body of flesh. For they were mortal, and sinners; but Thou, Lord, to Whom they proudly sought to be reconciled, art immortal and without sin. But a mediator between God and man must have something like to God, something like to men: lest being in both like to man, he should be far from God; or if in both like God, too unlike man; and so not be a mediator. That deceitful mediator then, by whom in Thy secret judgments pride deserved to be deluded, hath one thing in common with man, that is, sin; another, he would seem to have in common with God; and, not being clothed with the mortality of flesh,[7] would vaunt himself to be immortal. But since "the wages of sin is death,"[8] this hath he in common with men, that with them he should be condemned to death.

[XLIII] 68. But the true Mediator, Whom in Thy secret mercy Thou hast shewed to the humble, and sentest that by His example also they might learn that same humility, that "Mediator between God and man, the Man Christ Jesus,"[9] appeared betwixt mortal sinners and the immortal Just One; mortal with men, just with God: that because the wages of righteousness is life and peace, He might, by a righteousness conjoined with God, make void that death of sinners, now made righteous, which He willed to have in common with them. Hence He was shewed forth to holy men of old; that so they, through faith in His Passion to come, as we through faith of it passed, might be saved. For as Man, He was a Mediator; but as the Word, not in the middle between God and man, because equal to God, and God with God, and together one God.

69. How hast Thou loved us, good Father, who sparedst not Thine only Son, but deliveredst Him up for us ungodly![10] How hast Thou loved us, for whom He that thought it no robbery to be equal with Thee," was made subject even to the death of the cross,"[11] He alone "free among the dead,"[12] having power to lay down His life, and power to take it again:[13] for us to Thee both Victor and Victim, and therefore Victor because the Victim; for us to Thee Priest and Sacrifice, and therefore Priest because the Sacrifice; making us to Thee, of servants, sons,

---

[1]See above, Bk. IX. 10; below, Bk. XI. 39.   [2]Heb. 12. 1.
[3]See above, 41.   [4]Ps. 31. 24.   [5]Eph. 2. 2.

[6]II Cor. 11. 13.   [7]Cf. *City of God*, Bk. X. 24.
[8]Rom. 6. 23.   [9]I Tim. 2. 5.   [10]Rom. 8. 34.
[11]Phil. 2. 6, 8.   [12]Ps. 88. 5.   [13]John, 10. 18.

by being born of Thee, and serving us. Well then is my hope strong in Him, that Thou wilt heal all my infirmities,[1] by Him Who sitteth at Thy right hand and maketh intercession for us;[2] else should I despair. For many and great are my infirmities, many they are and great; but Thy medicine is mightier. We might imagine that Thy Word was far from any union with man, and despair of ourselves, unless He had been "made flesh and dwelt among us."[3]

70. Affrighted with my sins and the burthen of my misery, I had cast in my heart, and had purposed to flee to the wilderness:[4] but Thou forbadest me and strengthenedst me, saying, therefore Christ "died for all, that they which live may now no longer live unto themselves, but unto Him that died for them."[5] See, Lord, I cast my care upon Thee,[6] that I may live, and "consider wondrous things out of Thy law."[7] Thou knowest my unskilfulness and my infirmities; teach me, and heal me. He Thine only Son, "in Whom are hid all the treasures of wisdom and knowledge,"[8] hath redeemed me with His blood. Let not the proud speak evil of me[9]; because I meditate on my ransom, and eat and drink, and communicate it; and poor, desired to be satisfied from Him, amongst those that eat and are satisfied, and they shall praise the Lord who seek Him.[10]

BOOK XI. *Augustine breaks off the history of the mode whereby God led him to Holy Orders, in order to "confess" God's mercies in opening to him the Scripture. Moses is not to be understood but in Christ, not even the first words "In the beginning God created the heaven and the earth." Answer to cavillers who asked what did God before He created the heaven and the earth, and whence willed He at length to make them, whereas He did not make them before. Inquiry into the nature of Time.*

[I] 1. Lord, since eternity is Thine, art Thou ignorant of what I say to Thee? or dost Thou see in time what passeth in time? Why then do I lay in order before Thee so many relations? Not, of a truth, that Thou mightest learn them through me, but to stir up mine own and my readers' devotions towards Thee, that we may all say, "Great is the Lord, and greatly to be praised."[11] I have said already, and again will say, for love of Thy love do I this. For we pray

also, and yet Truth hath said, "Your Father knoweth what you have need of, before you ask."[12] It is then our affections which we lay open unto Thee, confessing our own miseries, and Thy mercies upon us, that Thou mayest free us wholly, since Thou hast begun, that we may cease to be wretched in ourselves, and be blessed in Thee; seeing Thou hast called us to become poor in spirit, and meek, and mourners, and hungering and athirst after righteousness, and merciful, and pure in heart, and peace-makers.[13] See, I have told Thee many things, as I could and as I would, because Thou first wouldest that I should confess unto Thee, my Lord God. For Thou art good, for Thy "mercy endureth for ever."[14]

[II] 2. But how shall I suffice with the tongue of my pen to utter all Thy exhortations, and all Thy terrors, and comforts, and guidances, whereby Thou broughtest me to preach Thy Word, and dispense Thy Sacrament to Thy people? And if I suffice to utter them in order, the drops of time are precious with me; and long have I burned to meditate in Thy law, and therein to confess to Thee my skill and unskilfulness, the day-break of Thy enlightening, and the remnants of my darkness, until infirmity be swallowed up by strength. And I would not have aught besides steal away those hours which I find free from the necessities of refreshing my body and the powers of my mind, and of the service which we owe to men,[15] or which though we owe not, we yet pay.

3. O Lord my God, give ear unto my prayer, and let Thy mercy hearken unto my desire; because it is anxious not for myself alone, but would serve brotherly charity; and Thou seest my heart, that so it is. I would sacrifice to Thee the service of my thought and tongue; do Thou give me what I may offer Thee. For "I am poor and needy,"[16] Thou rich to all that call upon Thee;[17] Who, inaccessible to care, carest for us. Circumcise from all rashness and all lying both my inward and outward lips;[18] let Thy Scriptures be my pure delights; let me not be deceived in them, nor deceive out of them. Lord, hearken and pity, O Lord my God, Light of the blind and Strength of the weak; yea also, Light of those that see and Strength of the strong; hearken unto my soul, and hear it crying "out of the depths."[19] For if thine ears be not with us in the depths also, whither shall we go? whither cry? "The day is Thine, and the night is

---

[1]Ps. 103. 3.   [2]Rom. 8. 34.   [3]John, 1. 14.
[4]Ps. 55. 7.   [5]II Cor. 5. 15.   [6]Ps. 55. 22.
[7]Ps. 119. 18.   [8]Col. 2. 3.   [9]Ps. 119. 122, old version.
[10]Ps. 22. 26.   [11]Ps. 96. 4.

[12]Matt. 6. 8.   [13]Matt. 5. 3–9.   [14]Ps. 98. 1.
[15]See above, bk. VI. 3.   [16]Ps. 96. 1.   [17]Rom. 10. 12.
[18]Ex. 6. 12.   [19]Ps. 130. 1.

Thine"[1]; at Thy beck the moments flee by. Grant thereof a space for our meditations in the hidden things of Thy law, and close it not against us who knock. For not in vain wouldest Thou have the darksome secrets of so many pages written; nor are those forests without their harts[2] which retire therein and range and walk; feed, lie down, and ruminate.[3] Perfect me, O Lord, and reveal them unto me. Behold, Thy voice is my joy; Thy voice exceedeth the abundance of pleasures. Give what I love; for I do love; and this hast Thou given; forsake not Thy own gifts, nor despise Thy green herb that thirsteth. Let me confess unto Thee whatsoever I shall find in Thy books, and hear the voice of praise, and drink-in Thee, and meditate on the wonderful things out of Thy law;[4] even from the beginning, wherein Thou madest the heaven and the earth, unto the everlasting reigning of Thy holy city with Thee.

4. Lord, have mercy on me, and hear my desire. For it is not, I deem, of the earth, not of gold and silver and precious stones, or gorgeous apparel, or honours and offices, or the pleasures of the flesh, or necessaries for the body and for this life of our pilgrimage: all which shall be added unto those that seek Thy kingdom and Thy righteousness.[5] Behold, O Lord my God, wherein is my desire. The wicked have told me of delights, but not such as Thy law, O Lord.[6] Behold, wherein is my desire. Behold, Father, behold, and see and approve; and be it pleasing in the sight of Thy mercy, that I may find grace before Thee, that the inward parts of Thy words be opened to me knocking. I beseech by our Lord Jesus Christ Thy Son, "the Man of Thy right hand, the Son of man, Whom Thou hast established for Thyself," [7] as Thy Mediator and ours, through Whom Thou soughtest us, not seeking Thee, but soughtest us, that we might seek Thee —Thy Word, through Whom Thou madest all things,[8] and among them, me also—Thy Only-Begotten, through Whom Thou calledst to adoption the believing people, and therein me also; I beseech Thee by Him Who sitteth at Thy right hand, and "intercedeth with Thee for us,[9] "in Whom are hidden all the treasures of wisdom and knowledge."[10] These do I seek in Thy books. Of Him did Moses write;[11] this saith Himself; this saith the Truth.

[III] 5. I would hear and understand how in the beginning Thou madest the heaven and earth.[12] Moses wrote this, wrote and departed, passed hence from Thee to Thee; nor is he now before me. For, if he were, I would hold him and ask him and beseech him by Thee to open these things unto me, and would lay the ears of my body to the sounds bursting out of his mouth. And should he speak Hebrew, in vain will it strike on my senses, nor would aught of it touch my mind; but if Latin, I should know what he said. But whence should I know whether he spake truth? Yea, and if I knew this also, should I know it from him? Truly within me, within, in the chamber of my thoughts, Truth, neither Hebrew, nor Greek, nor Latin, nor barbarian, without organs of voice or tongue, or sound of syllables, would say, "It is truth," and I forthwith should say confidently to that man of Thine, "Thou sayest truly." Whereas then I cannot enquire of him, Thee, Thee I beseech, O Truth, full of Whom he spake truth, Thee, my God, I beseech, forgive my sins; and Thou, who gavest him Thy servant to speak these things, give to me also to understand them.

[IV] 6. Behold, the heavens and the earth are; they proclaim that they were created; for they change and vary.[13] Whereas whatsoever hath not been made, and yet is, hath nothing in it which before it had not; and that it is, to change and vary. They proclaim also, that they made not themselves; "therefore we are, because we have been made; we were not therefor, before we were, so as to make ourselves." Now the evidence of the thing is the voice of the speakers. Thou, therefore, Lord, madest them; Who art beautiful, for they are beautiful; Who art good, for they are good; Who Art, for they are; yet are they not beautiful nor good nor are they, as Thou their Creator art; compared with Whom they are neither beautiful, nor good, nor are. This we know, thanks be to Thee. And our knowledge, compared with Thy knowledge, is ignorance.

[V] 7. But how didst Thou make the heaven and the earth? And what the engine of Thy so mighty fabric? For it was not as a human artificer, forming one body from another according to the discretion of his mind, which can in some way invest with such a form as it seeth in itself by its inward eye.[14] And whence should he be able to do this, unless Thou hadst made that mind? And he invests with a form what already existeth and hath a being, as clay, or stone, or wood, or gold, or the like. And whence should they be, hadst not Thou appointed them? Thou

---

[1]Ps. 74. 16. [2]Ps. 79. 9. [3]See Bk. VI. 3.
[4]Ps. 26. 7. [5]Matt. 6. 33. [6]Ps. 119. 35.
[7]Ps. 80. 17. [8]John, 1. 3. [9]Rom. 8. 34.
[10]Col. 2. 3. [11]John, 5. 4–6.

[12]Gen. 1. 1. [13]See above, bk. VII. 17.
[14]See Bk. X. 53.

madest the artificer his body, Thou the mind commanding the limbs, Thou the matter whereof he makes any thing; Thou the apprehension whereby to take in his art, and see within what he doth without; Thou the sense of his body, whereby, as by an interpreter, he may from mind to matter convey that which he doth, and report to his mind what is done; that it within may consult the truth, which presideth over itself, whether it be well done or no. All these praise Thee, the Creator of all. But how dost Thou make them? How, O God, didst Thou make heaven and earth? Verily, neither in the heaven, nor in the earth, didst Thou make heaven and earth; nor in the air, or waters, seeing these also belong to the heaven and the earth; nor in the whole world didst Thou make the whole world; because there was no place where to make it, before it was made, that it might be. Nor didst Thou hold anything in Thy hand, whereof to make heaven and earth. For whence shouldest Thou have this, which Thou hadst not made, thereof to make anything? For what is, but because Thou art? Therefore Thou spakest, and they were made,[1] and in Thy Word Thou madest them.[2]

[VI] 8. But how didst Thou speak? In the way that the voice came out of the cloud, saying, "This is my beloved Son"?[3] For that voice passed by and passed away, began and ended; the syllables sounded and passed away, the second after the first, the third after the second, and so forth in order, until the last after the rest, and silence after the last. Whence it is abundantly clear and plain that the motion of a creature expressed it, itself temporal, serving Thy eternal will. And these Thy words, created for a time, the outward ear reported to the intelligent soul, whose inward ear lay listening to Thy Eternal Word. But she compared these words sounding in time, with that Thy Eternal Word in silence, and said, "It is different, far different. These words are far beneath me, nor are they, because they flee and pass away; but the Word of my Lord abideth above me for ever." If then in sounding and passing words Thou saidst that heaven and earth should be made, and so madest heaven and earth, there was a corporeal creature before heaven and earth, by whose motions in time that voice might take his course in time. But there was naught corporeal before heaven and earth; or, if there were, surely thou hadst, without such a passing voice, created that, whereof to make this passing voice, by which to say, Let the

heaven and the earth be made. For whatsoever that were, whereof such a voice were made, unless by Thee it were made it could not be at all. By what Word then didst Thou speak, that a body might be made, whereby these words again might be made?

[VII] 9. Thou callest us then to understand the Word, God, with Thee God,[4] Which is spoken eternally, and by It are all things spoken eternally. For what was spoken and was not spoken successively, one thing concluded that the next might be spoken, but all things together and eternally. Else have we time and change; and not a true eternity nor true immortality. This I know, O my God, and give thanks. I know, I confess to Thee, O Lord, and with me there knows and blesses Thee whoso is not unthankful to assured Truth. We know, Lord, we know; since inasmuch as anything is not which was, and is, what was not, so far forth it dieth and ariseth. Nothing then of Thy Word doth give place or replace, because It is truly immortal and eternal. And therefore unto the Word coeternal with Thee Thou dost at once and eternally say all that Thou dost say; and whatever Thou sayest shall be made is made; nor dost Thou make, otherwise than by saying; and yet are not all things made together, or everlasting, which Thou makest by saying.

[VIII] 10. Why, I beseech Thee, O Lord my God? I see it in a way; but how to express it, I know not, unless it be that whatsoever begins to be, and leaves off to be, begins then, and leaves off then, when in Thy eternal Reason it is known that it ought to begin or leave off; in which Reason nothing beginneth or leaveth off. This is Thy Word, which is also "the Beginning," because also It speaketh unto us.[5] Thus in the Gospel He speaketh through the flesh; and this sounded outwardly in the ears of men, that it might be believed and sought inwardly, and found in the eternal Verity; where the good and only Master teacheth all His disciples. There, Lord, hear I Thy voice speaking unto me; because He speaketh unto us, who teacheth us; but He that teacheth us not, though He speaketh, to us He speaketh not. Who now teacheth us, but the unchangeable Truth? For, even when we are admonished through a changeable creature, we are but led to the unchangeable Truth; where we learn truly, while we stand and hear Him, and rejoice greatly "because of the Bridegroom's voice,"[6] restoring us to Him, from Whom we are. And therefore the Beginning, because unless It abided, there should not, when

---

[1] Ps. 33. 9. [2] Ibid., ver. 6. [3] Matt. 17. 5.   [4] John, 1. 1. [5] John, 8. 25, old version. [6] John, 3. 29.

we went astray, be whither to return. But when we return from error, it is through knowing that we return; and that we may know, He teacheth us, because He is the Beginning, and speaking unto us.

[IX] 11. In this Beginning, O God, hast Thou made heaven and earth, in Thy Word, in Thy Son, in Thy Power, in Thy Wisdom, in Thy Truth; wondrously speaking, and wondrously making. Who shall comprehend? Who declare it? What is that which gleams through me, and strikes my heart without hurting it; and I shudder and kindle? I shudder, inasmuch as I am unlike it; I kindle, inasmuch as I am like it. It is Wisdom, Wisdom's self which gleameth through me; severing my cloudiness which yet again mantles over me, fainting from it, through the darkness which for my punishment gathers upon me. For my strength is brought down in need,[1] so that I cannot support my blessings, till Thou, Lord, Who hast been gracious to all mine iniquities, shalt heal all my infirmities. For Thou shalt also redeem my life from corruption, and crown me with loving kindness and tender mercies, and shalt satisfy my desire with good things, because my youth shall be renewed like an eagle's.[2] For in hope we are saved, wherefore we through patience wait for Thy promises.[3] Let him that is able hear Thee inwardly discoursing out of Thy oracle: I will boldly cry out, How wonderful are Thy works, O Lord, in Wisdom hast Thou made them all[4]; and this Wisdom is the Beginning, and in that Beginning didst Thou make heaven and earth.

[X] 12. Lo, are they not full of their old leaven who say to us, "What was God doing before He made heaven and earth?" "For if (say they) He were unemployed and wrought not, why does He not also henceforth, and for ever, as He did heretofore? For did any new motion arise in God, and a new will to make a creature which He had never before made, how then would that be a true eternity, where there ariseth a will which was not? For the will of God is not a creature, but before the creature; seeing nothing could be created, unless the will of the Creator had preceded. The will of God then belongeth to His very Substance. And if aught have arisen in God's Substance which before was not, that Substance cannot be truly called eternal. But if the will of God has been from eternity that the creature should be, why was not the creature also from eternity?"

[XI] 13. Who speak thus, do not yet understand Thee, O Wisdom of God, Light of souls, understand not yet how the things be made, which by Thee and in Thee are made; yet they strive to comprehend things eternal, whilst their heart fluttereth between the motions of things past and to come, and is still unstable. Who shall hold it, and fix it, that it be settled awhile, and awhile catch the glory of that ever-fixed Eternity, and compare it with the times which are never fixed, and see that it cannot be compared; and that a long time cannot become long, but out of many motions passing by, which cannot be prolonged altogether; but that in the Eternal nothing passeth, but the whole is present; whereas no time is all at once present; and that all time past is driven on by time to come, and all to come followeth upon the past; and all past and to come is created, and flows out of that which is ever present? Who shall hold the heart of man, that it may stand still, and see how eternity, ever still-standing, neither past nor to come, uttereth the times past and to come? Can my hand do this, or the hand of my mouth by speech bring about a thing so great?

[XII] 14. See, I answer him that asketh, "What did God before He made heaven and earth?" I answer not as one is said to have done merrily (eluding the pressure of the question): "He was preparing hell (saith he) for pryers into mysteries." It is one thing to answer enquiries, another to make sport of enquirers. So I answer not; for rather had I answer, "I know not" what I know not, than so as to raise a laugh at him who asketh deep things and gain praise for one who answereth false things. But I say that Thou, our God, art the Creator of every creature; and, if by the name "heaven and earth" every creature be understood, I boldly say, "that before God made heaven and earth, He did not make anything. For if He made, what did He make but a creature?" And would I knew whatsoever I desire to know to my profit, as I know that no creature was made before there was made any creature.

[XIII] 15. But if any excursive brain rove over the images of forepassed times, and wonder that Thou the God Almighty and All-creating and All-supporting, Maker of heaven and earth, didst for innumerable ages forbear from so great a work, before Thou wouldest make it; let him awake and consider that he wonders at false conceits. For whence could innumerable ages pass by, which Thou madest not, Thou the Author and Creator of all ages? or what times should there be, which were not made by Thee?[5]

[1] Ps. 31. 10. [2] Ps. 103. 3-5. [3] Rom. 8. 24, 25.
[4] Ps. 104. 24.

[5] See above, BK. VII. 21.

or how should they pass by, if they never were? Seeing then Thou are the Creator of all times, if any time was before Thou madest heaven and earth, why say they that Thou didst forego working? For that very time didst Thou make, nor could times pass by before thou madest those times. But if before heaven and earth there was no time, why is it demanded what Thou then didst? For there was no "then," when there was no time.

16. Nor dost Thou by time precede time; else shouldest Thou not precede all times. But Thou precedest all things past, by the sublimity of an ever-present eternity; and surpassest all future because they are future, and when they come, they shall be past; but "Thou art the Same, and Thy years fail not." [1] Thy years neither come nor go; whereas ours both come and go, that they all may come. Thy years stand together, because they do stand; nor are departing thrust out by coming years, for they pass not away; but ours shall all be, when they shall no more be. Thy years are one day; and Thy day is not daily, but Today, seeing Thy Today gives not place unto tomorrow, for neither doth it replace yesterday. Thy Today is Eternity; therefore didst Thou beget the Coeternal, to whom Thou saidst, "This day have I begotten Thee." [2] Thou hast made all things; and before all times Thou art; neither in any time was time not.

[XIV] 17. At no time, then, hadst Thou not made anything, because time itself Thou madest. And no times are coeternal with Thee, because Thou abidest; but if they abode, they should not be times. For what is time? Who can readily and briefly explain this? Who can even in thought comprehend it, so as to utter a word about it? But what in discourse do we mention more familiarly and knowingly than time? And we understand, when we speak of it; we understand also when we hear it spoken of by another. What then is time? If no one asks me, I know; if I wish to explain it to one that asketh, I know not; yet I say boldly that I know that, if nothing passed away, time past were not; and if nothing were coming, a time to come were not; and if nothing were, time present were not. Those two times then, past and to come, how are they, seeing the past now is not, and that to come is not yet? But the present, should it always be present and never pass into time past, verily it should not be time, but eternity. If time present (if it is to be time) only cometh into existence because it passeth into time past, how can we say that either this is, whose cause

[1] Ps. 102. 27.   [2] Ps. 2. 7; Heb. 5. 5.

of being is that it shall not be; so, namely, that we cannot truly say that time is, but because it is tending not to be?

[XV] 18. And yet we say, "a long time" and "a short time"; still, only of time past or to come. A long time past (for example) we call an hundred years since; and a long time to come, an hundred years hence. But a short time past, we call (suppose) ten days since; and a short time to come, ten days hence. But in what sense is that long or short, which is not? For the past is not now; and the future is not yet. Let us not then say, "It is long"; but of the past, "It hath been long"; and of the future, "It will be long." O my Lord, my Light, shall not here also Thy Truth mock at man? For that past time which was long, was it long when it was now past, or when it was yet present? For then might it be long, when there was what could be long; but when past, it was no longer; wherefore neither could that be long, which was not at all. Let us not then say, "Time past hath been long"; for we shall not find what hath been long, seeing that since it was past it is no more; but let us say, "That present time was long"; because, when it was present, it was long. For it had not yet passed away, so as not to be; and therefore there was what could be long; but after it was past, that ceased also to be long, which ceased to be.

19. Let us see then, thou soul of man, whether present time can be long; for to thee it is given to feel and to measure length of time. What wilt thou answer me? Are an hundred years, when present, a long time? See first, whether an hundred years can be present. For if the first of these years be now current, it is present, but the other ninety and nine are to come, and therefore are not yet; but if the second year be current, one is now past, another present, the rest to come. And so if we assume any middle year of this hundred to be present, all before it are past; all after it, to come; wherefore an hundred years cannot be present. But see at least whether that one which is now current, itself is present; for if the current month be its first, the rest are to come; if the second, the first is already past, and the rest are not yet. Therefore, neither is the year now current present; and, if not present as a whole, then is not the year present. For twelve months are a year; of which whatever be the current month is present; the rest past, or to come. Although neither is that current month present; but one day only; the rest being to come, if it be the first; past, if the last; if any of the middle, then amid past and to come.

20. See how the present time, which alone we found could be called long, is abridged to the length scarce of one day. But let us examine that also; because neither is one day present as a whole. For it is made up of four and twenty hours of night and day: of which the first hath the rest to come; the last hath them past; and any of the middle hath those before it past, those behind it to come. Yea, that one hour passeth away in flying particles. Whatsoever of it hath flown away is past; whatsoever remaineth is to come. If an instant of time be conceived which cannot be divided into the smallest particles of moments, that alone is it, which may be called present. Which yet flies with such speed from future to past, as not to be lengthened out with the least stay. For if it be, it is divided into past and future. The present hath no space. Where then is the time, which we may call long? Is it to come? Of it we do not say, "It is long"; because it is not yet, so as to be long; but we say, "It will be long." When therefore will it be? For if even then, when it is yet to come, it shall not be long (because what can be long as yet is not) and so it shall then be long when, from future which as yet is not, it shall begin now to be, and have become present, that so there should exist what may be long; then does time present cry out in the words above, that it cannot be long.

[XVI] 21. And yet, Lord, we perceive intervals of times, and compare them, and say, some are shorter, and others longer. We measure also, how much longer or shorter this time is than that; and we answer, "This is double, or treble; and that, but once, or only just so much as that." But we measure times as they are passing, by perceiving them; but past, which now are not, or the future, which are not yet, who can measure? unless a man shall presume to say, that can be measured which is not. When then time is passing, it may be perceived and measured; but when it is past, it cannot, because it is not.

[XVII] 22. I ask, Father, I affirm not. O my God, rule and guide me. "Who will tell me that there are not three times (as we learned when boys, and taught boys): past, present, and future; but present only, because those two are not? Or are they also; and when from future it becometh present, doth it come out of some secret place; and so, when retiring, from present it becometh past? For where did they who foretold things to come see them, if as yet they be not? For that which is not cannot be seen. And they who relate things past could not relate them, if in mind they did not discern them; and if they were not, they could no way be discerned. Things then past and to come are."

[XVIII] 23. Permit me, Lord, to seek further. O my hope, let not my purpose be confounded. For if times past and to come be, I would know where they be. Which yet if I cannot, yet I know that, wherever they be, they are not there as future, or past, but present. For if there also they be future, they are not yet there; if there also they be past, they are no longer there. Wheresoever then is whatsoever is, it is only as present. Although when past facts are related, there are drawn out of the memory, not the things themselves which are past, but words which, conceived by the images of the things, they, in passing, have through the senses left as traces in the mind. Thus my childhood, which now is not, is in time past, which now is not; but now when I recall its image, and tell of it, I behold it in the present, because it is still in my memory. Whether there be a like cause of foretelling things to come also; that of things which as yet are not, the images may be perceived before, already existing—I confess, O my God, I know not. This indeed I know, that we generally think before on our future actions, and that that fore-thinking is present, but the action whereof we forethink is not yet, because it is to come. Which, when we have set upon, and have begun to do what we were forethinking, then shall that action be; because then it is no longer future, but present.

24. Which way soever then this secret fore-perceiving of things to come be, that only can be seen which is. But what now is, is not future, but present. When then things to come are said to be seen, it is not themselves which as yet are not (that is, which are to be), but their causes perchance or signs are seen, which already are. Therefore they are not future but present to those who now see that, from which the future, being fore-conceived in the mind, is foretold. Which fore-conceptions again now are; and those who foretell those things do behold the conceptions present before them. Let now the numerous variety of things furnish me some example. I behold the day-break, I foreshew that the sun is about to rise. What I behold is present; what I fore-signify, to come: not the sun, which already is; but the sun-rising, which is not yet. And yet did I not in my mind imagine the sun-rising itself (as now while I speak of it), I could not foretell it. But neither is that day-break which I discern in the sky the sun-rising, although it goes before it; nor that imagination

of my mind; which two are seen now present, that the other which is to be may be foretold. Future things then are not yet; and if they be not yet, they are not: and if they are not, they cannot be seen; yet foretold they may be from things present, which are already, and are seen.

[XIX] 25. Thou then, Ruler of Thy creation, by what way dost Thou teach souls things to come? For Thou didst teach Thy Prophets. By what way dost Thou, to Whom nothing is to come, teach things to come; or rather of the future, dost teach things present? For what is not, neither can it be taught. Too far is this way out of my ken: it is too mighty for me, I cannot attain unto it[1]; but from Thee I can, when Thou shalt vouchsafe it, O sweet light of my hidden eyes.

[XX] 26. What now is clear and plain is that neither things to come nor past are. Nor is it properly said, "There be three times: past, present, and to come"; yet perchance it might be properly said: "There be three times: a present of things past, a present of things present, and a present of things future." For these three do exist in some sort, in the soul, but otherwhere do I not see them: present of things past, memory; present of things present, sight; present of things future, expectation. If thus we be permitted to speak, I see three times, and I confess there are three. Let it be said too, "There be three times, past, present, and to come"; in our incorrect way. See, I object not, nor gainsay, nor find fault, if what is so said be but understood, that neither what is to be now is, nor what is past. For but few things are there, which we speak properly, most things improperly; still the things intended are understood.

[XXI] 27. I said then even now, we measure times as they pass, in order to be able to say, this time is twice so much as that one; or, this is just so much as that; and so of any other parts of time which be measurable. Wherefore, as I said, we measure times as they pass. And if any should ask me, "How knowest thou?" I might answer, "I know that we do measure, nor can we measure, things that are not; and things past and to come are not." But time present how do we measure, seeing it hath no space? It is measured while passing; but when it shall have passed, it is not measured; for there will be nothing to be measured. But whence, by what way, and whither passes it while it is a measuring? Whence, but from the future? Which way, but through the present? whither, but into the past? From that, therefore, which is not yet,

through that which hath no space, into that which now is not. Yet what do we measure, if not time in some space? For we do not say, single, and double, and triple, and equal, or any other like way that we speak of time, except of spaces of times. In what space then do we measure time passing? In the future, whence it passeth through? But what is not yet, we measure not. Or in the present, by which it passes? But no space, we do not measure. Or in the past, to which it passes? But neither do we measure that which now is not.

[XXII] 28. My soul is on fire to know this most intricate enigma. Shut it not up, O Lord my God, good Father; through Christ I beseech Thee, do not shut up these usual, yet hidden, things from my desire, that it be hindered from piercing into them; but let them dawn through Thy enlightening mercy, O Lord. Whom shall I enquire of concerning these things? And to whom shall I more fruitfully confess my ignorance than to Thee, to Whom these my studies, so vehemently kindled toward Thy Scriptures, are not troublesome? Give what I love; for I do love, and this hast Thou given me. Give, Father, Who truly knowest to give good gifts unto Thy children.[2] Give, because I have taken upon me to know, and trouble is before me until Thou openest it.[3] By Christ I beseech Thee, in His Name, Holy of holies, let no man disturb me. For I believed, and therefore do I speak.[4] This is my hope, for this do I live, that I may contemplate the delights of the Lord.[5] Behold, Thou hast made my days old,[6] and they pass away, and how, I know not. And we talk of time, and time, and times, and times: "How long time is it since he said this?" "How long time since he did this?" And "How long time since I saw that?" And "This syllable hath double time to that single short syllable." These words we speak, and these we hear, and are understood, and understand. Most manifest and ordinary they are, and the self-same things again are but too deeply hidden, and the discovery of them were new.

[XXIII] 29. I heard once from a learned man that the motions of the sun, moon, and stars constituted time, and I assented not. For why should not the motions of all bodies rather be times? Or, if the lights of heaven should cease, and a potter's wheel run round, should there be no time by which we might measure those whirlings, and say that either it moved with equal pauses, or if it turned sometimes slower, other-

[1] Ps. 139. 6.

[2] Matt. 7. 11.   [3] Ps. 73. 16.   [4] Ps. 116. 10.
[5] Ps. 27. 4.   [6] Ps. 39. 5.

whiles quicker, that some rounds were longer, other shorter? Or, while we were saying this, should we not also be speaking in time? Or should there in our words be some syllables short, others long, but because those sounded in a shorter time, these in a longer? God, grant to men to see in a small thing notices common to things great and small. The stars and lights of heaven are also "for signs, and for seasons, and for years, and for days";[1] they are; yet neither should I say that the going round of that wooden wheel was a day, nor yet he, that it was therefore no time.

30. I desire to know the force and nature of time, by which we measure the motions of bodies, and say (for example) this motion is twice as long as that. For I ask: seeing "day" denotes not the stay only of the sun upon the earth (according to which day is one thing, night another), but also its whole circuit from east to east again; according to which we say, "There passed so many days," the night being included when we say, "so many days," and the nights not reckoned apart; seeing then a day is completed by the motion of the sun and by his circuit from east to east again, I ask, does the motion alone make the day, or the stay in which that motion is completed, or both? For if the first be the day, then should we have a day, although the sun should finish that course in so small a space of time as one hour comes to. If the second, then should not that make a day, if between one sun-rise and another there were but so short a stay as one hour comes to; but the sun must go four and twenty times about to complete one day. If both, then neither could that be called a day, if the sun should run his whole round in the space of one hour; nor that, if, while the sun stood still, so much time should overpass as the sun usually makes his whole course in, from morning to morning. I will not therefore now ask what that is which is called day; but what time is, whereby we, measuring the circuit of the sun, should say that it was finished in half the time it was wont, if so be it was finished in so small a space as twelve hours; and, comparing both times, should call this a single time, that a double time; even supposing the sun to run his round from east to east sometimes in that single, sometimes in that double time. Let no man then tell me that the motions of the heavenly bodies constitute times, because, when at the prayer of one, the sun had stood still, till he could achieve his victorious battle, the sun stood still, but time went on. For in its own al-

lotted space of time was that battle waged and ended.[2] I perceive time then to be a certain extension. But do I perceive it, or seem to perceive it? Thou, Light and Truth, wilt shew me.

[XXIV] 31. Dost Thou bid me assent, if any define time to be "motion of a body"? Thou dost not bid me. For that no body is moved, but in time, I hear; this Thou sayest; but that the motion of a body is time, I hear not; Thou sayest it not. For when a body is moved, I by time measure how long it moveth, from the time it began to move until it left off. And if I did not see whence it began; and it continue to move so that I see not when it ends, I cannot measure save perchance from the time I began until I cease to see. And if I look long, I can only pronounce it to be a long time, but not how long; because when we say "how long," we do it by comparison; as, "This is as long as that," or "twice so long as that," or the like. But when we can mark the distances of the places whence and whither goeth the body moved, or his parts, if it moved as in a lathe, then can we say precisely in how much time the motion of that body or his part, from this place unto that, was finished. Seeing therefore the motion of a body is one thing, that by which we measure how long it is, another; who sees not which of the two is rather to be called time? For and if a body be sometimes moved, sometimes stands still, then we measure not his motion only, but his standing still too by time; and we say, "It stood still, as much as it moved"; or "It stood still twice or thrice so long as it moved"; or any other space which our measuring hath either ascertained or guessed; more or less, as we use to say. Time then is not the motion of a body.

[XXV] 32. And I confess to Thee, O Lord, that I yet know not what time is, and again I confess unto Thee, O Lord, that I know that I speak this in time, and that having long spoken of time, that very "long" is not long, but by the pause of time. How then know I this, seeing I know not what time is? Or is it perchance that I know not how to express what I know? Woe is me that do not even know what I know not. Behold, O my God, before Thee I lie not; but as I speak, so is my heart. Thou shalt light my candle; Thou, O Lord my God, wilt enlighten my darkness.[3]

[XXVI] 33. Does not my soul most truly confess unto Thee that I do measure times? Do I then measure, O my God, and know not what I measure? I measure the motion of a body in time; and the time itself do I not measure? Or

[1]Gen. I. 14.　　　　[2]Josh. 10. 12-14.　[3]Ps. 118. 28.

could I indeed measure the motion of a body how long it were, and in how long space it could come from this place to that, without measuring the time in which it is moved? This same time then, how do I measure? Do we by a shorter time measure a longer, as by the space of a cubit, the space of a rood? For so indeed we seem by the space of a short syllable to measure the space of a long syllable, and to say that this is double the other. Thus measure we the spaces of stanzas, by the spaces of the verses; and the spaces of the verses, by the spaces of the feet; and the spaces of the feet, by the spaces of the syllables; and the spaces of long, by the spaces of short syllables; not measuring by pages (for then we measure spaces, not times), but when we utter the words and they pass by, and we say, "It is a long stanza, because composed of so many verses; long verses, because consisting of so many feet; long feet, because prolonged by so many syllables; a long syllable because double to a short one." But neither do we this way obtain any certain measure of time; because it may be that a shorter verse, pronounced more fully, may take up more time than a longer, pronounced hurriedly. And so for a verse, a foot, a syllable. Whence it seemed to me that time is nothing else than protraction; but of what, I know not; and I marvel if it be not of the mind itself? For what, I beseech Thee, O my God, do I measure, when I say, either indefinitely, "This is a longer time than that," or definitely, "This is double that"? That I measure time, I know; and yet I measure not time to come, for it is not yet; nor present, because it is not protracted by any space; nor past, because it now is not. What then do I measure? Times passing, not past? for so I said.

[XXVII] 34. Courage, my mind, and press on mightily. God is our helper, He made us, and not we ourselves.[1] Press on where truth begins to dawn. Suppose, now, the voice of a body begins to sound, and does sound, and sounds on, and now, it ceases; it is silence now, and that voice is past, and is no more a voice. Before it sounded, it was to come, and could not be measured, because as yet it was not, and now it cannot, because it is no longer. Then therefore while it sounded, it might; because there then was what might be measured. But yet even then it was not at a stay; for it was passing on, and passing away. Could it be measured the rather, for that? For while passing, it was being extended into some space of time, so that it might be measured, since the present hath no space. If there-

[1] Ps. 100. 3.

fore then it might, then, lo, suppose another voice hath begun to sound, and still soundeth in one continued tenor without any interruption; let us measure it while it sounds; seeing, when it hath left sounding, it will then be past, and nothing left to be measured; let us measure it verily, and tell how much it is. But it sounds still, nor can it be measured but from the instant it began in, unto the end it left in. For the very space between is the thing we measure, namely, from some beginning unto some end. Wherefore, a voice that is not yet ended, cannot be measured, so that it may be said how long, or short it is; nor can it be called equal to another, or double to a single, or the like. But when ended, it no longer is. How may it then be measured? And yet we measure times; but yet neither those which are not yet, nor those which no longer are, nor those which are not lengthened out by some pause, nor those which have no bounds. We measure neither times to come, nor past, nor present, nor passing; and yet we do measure times.

35. *"Deus Creator omnium"*—this verse of eight syllables alternates between short and long syllables. The four short then: the first, third, fifth, and seventh, are but single, in respect of the four long: the second, fourth, sixth, and eighth. Every one of these, to every one of those, hath a double time: I pronounce them, report on them, and find it so, as one's plain sense perceives. By plain sense, then, I measure a long syllable by a short, and I sensibly find it to have twice so much; but when one sounds after the other, if the former be short, the latter long, how shall I detain the short one, and how, measuring, shall I apply it to the long, that I may find this to have twice so much; seeing the long does not begin to sound, unless the short leaves sounding? And that very long one do I measure as present, seeing I measure it not till it be ended? Now his ending is his passing away. What then is it I measure? Where is the short syllable by which I measure? Where the long which I measure? Both have sounded, have flown, passed away, are no more; and yet I measure, and confidently answer (so far as is presumed on a practised sense) that as to space of time this syllable is but single, that double. And yet I could not do this, unless they were already past and ended. It is not them themselves, which now are not, that I measure, but something in my memory, which there remains fixed.

36. It is in thee, my mind, that I measure times. Interrupt me not, that is, interrupt not thyself with the tumults of thy impressions. In

thee I measure times; the impression, which things as they pass by cause in thee, remains even when they are gone; this it is which, still present, I measure, not the things which pass by to make this impression. This I measure, when I measure times. Either then this is time, or I do not measure times. What when we measure silence, and say that this silence hath held as long time as did that voice? Do we not stretch out our thought to the measure of a voice, as if it sounded, that so we may be able to report of the intervals of silence in a given space of time? For though both voice and tongue be still, yet in thought we go over poems, and verses, and any other discourse, or dimensions of motions, and report as to the spaces of times, how much this is in respect of that, no otherwise than if vocally we did pronounce them. If a man would utter a lengthened sound, and had settled in thought how long it should be, he hath in silence already gone through a space of time and, committing it to memory, begins to utter that speech, which sounds on until it be brought unto the end proposed. Yea it hath sounded, and will sound; for so much of it as is finished hath sounded already, and the rest will sound. And thus passeth it on, until the present intent conveys over the future into the past; the past increasing by the diminution of the future, until, by the consumption of the future, all is past.

[XXVIII] 37. But how is that future diminished or consumed, which as yet is not? Or how that past increased, which is now no longer, save that in the mind which enacteth this there be three things done? For it expects, it considers, it remembers; that so that which it expecteth, through that which it considereth, passeth into that which it remembereth. Who therefore denieth that things to come are not as yet? and yet there is in the mind an expectation of things to come. And who denies past things to be now no longer? and yet is there still in the mind a memory of things past. And who denieth that the present time hath no space, because it passeth away in a moment? and yet our consideration continueth, through which that which shall be present proceedeth to become absent. It is not then future time that is long, for as yet it is not; but a "long future" is "a long expectation of the future"; nor is it time past, which now is not, that is long; but a long past is "a long memory of the past."

38. I am about to repeat a Psalm that I know. Before I begin, my expectation is extended over the whole; but when I have begun, how much soever of it I shall separate off into the past is

extended along my memory; thus the life of this action of mine is divided between my memory as to what I have repeated, and expectation as to what I am about to repeat; but "consideration" is present with me, that through it what was future may be conveyed over, so as to become past. Which the more it is done again and again, so much the more the expectation being shortened, is the memory enlarged; till the whole expectation be at length exhausted, when that whole action, being ended, shall have passed into memory. And this which takes place in the whole Psalm, the same takes place in each several portion of it, and each several syllable; the same holds in that longer action, whereof this Psalm may be a part; the same holds in the whole life of man, whereof all the actions of man are parts; the same holds through the whole age of the sons of men, whereof all the lives of men are parts.

[XXIX] 39. But "because Thy loving kindness is better than all lives,"[1] behold, my life is but a distraction, and Thy right hand upheld me,[2] in my Lord the Son of man, the Mediator betwixt Thee,[3] The One, and us many, many also through our manifold distractions amid many things, that by Him I may apprehend in Whom I have been apprehended, and may be recollected from my old conversation, to follow The One, forgetting what is behind, and not distended but extended, not to things which shall be and shall pass away, but to those things which are before,[4] not distractedly but intently, I follow on for the prize of my heavenly calling,[5] where I may hear the voice of Thy praise, and contemplate Thy delights,[6] neither to come, nor to pass away. But now are my years spent in mourning.[7] And Thou, O Lord, art my comfort, my Father everlasting, but I have been severed amid times whose order I know not; and my thoughts, even the inmost bowels of my soul, are rent and mangled with tumultuous varieties, until I flow together into Thee, purified and molten by the fire of Thy love.[8]

[XXX] 40. And now will I stand, and become firm in Thee, in my mould, Thy truth; nor will I endure the questions of men, who by a penal disease thirst for more than they can contain, and say, "What did God before He made heaven and earth?" Or, How came it into His mind to make anything, having never before made anything?" Give them, O Lord, well to bethink themselves what they say, and to find that "never" cannot be predicated, when "time" is

[1]Ps. 63. 3.   [2]Ibid., 8.   [3]I Tim. 2. 5.   [4]Phil. 3. 13.
[5]Ibid., 14.   [6]Ps. 26. 7.   [7]Ps. 27. 4.   [8]Ps. 31. 10.

not. This then that He is said "never to have made," what else is it to say than "in 'no time' to have made"? Let them see, therefore, that time cannot be without created being,[1] and cease to speak that vanity. May they also be extended towards those things which are before;[2] and understand Thee before all times, the eternal Creator of all times, and that no times be coeternal with Thee, nor any creature, even if there be any creature before all times.

[XXXI] 41. O Lord my God, what a depth is that recess of Thy mysteries, and how far from it have the consequences of my transgressions cast me! Heal mine eyes, that I may share the joy of Thy light. Certainly, if there be a mind gifted with such vast knowledge and foreknowledge as to know all things past and to come, as I know one well-known Psalm, truly that mind is passing wonderful, and fearfully amazing; in that nothing past, nothing to come in after-ages, is any more hidden from him than, when I sung that Psalm, was hidden from me what and how much of it passed away from the beginning, what and how much there remained unto the end. But far be it that Thou the Creator of the Universe, the Creator of souls and bodies, far be it that Thou shouldest in such wise know all things past and to come. Far, far more wonderfully, and far more mysteriously, dost thou know them. For not as the feelings of one who singeth what he knoweth, or heareth some well-known song, are through expectation of the words to come, and the remembering of those that are past, varied, and his senses divided— not so doth anything happen unto Thee, unchangeably eternal, that is, the eternal Creator of minds. Like then as Thou in the Beginning knewest the heaven and the earth, without any variety of Thy knowledge, so madest Thou in the Beginning heaven and earth, without any distraction of Thy action. Whoso understandeth let him confess unto Thee; and whoso understandeth not, let him confess unto Thee. Oh how high art Thou, and yet the humble in heart are Thy dwelling-place; for Thou raisest up those that are bowed down,[3] and they fall not, whose elevation Thou art.

BOOK XII. *Augustine proceeds to comment on Genesis, I. I, and explains the "heaven" to mean that spiritual and incorporeal creation, which cleaves to God unintermittingly, always beholding His countenance; "earth," the formless matter whereof the corporeal crea-*

tion was afterwards formed. He does not reject, however, other interpretations, which he adduces, but rather confesses that such is the depth of Holy Scripture, that manifold senses may and ought to be extracted from it, and that whatever truth can be obtained from its words, does, in fact, lie concealed in them.*

[I] 1. My heart, O Lord, touched with the words of Thy Holy Scripture is much busied amid this poverty of my life. And therefore most-times is the poverty of human understanding copious in words, because enquiring hath more to say than discovering, and demanding is longer than obtaining, and our hand that knocks hath more work to do than our hand that receives. We hold the promise, who shall make it null? "If God be for us, who can be against us?"[4] Ask, and ye shall have; seek, and ye shall find; knock, and it shall be opened unto you. For everyone that asketh, receiveth; and he that seeketh, findeth; and to him that knocketh, shall it be opened."[5] These be Thine own promises; and who need fear to be deceived, when the Truth promiseth?

[II] 2. The lowliness of my tongue confesseth unto Thy Highness that Thou madest heaven and earth; this heaven which I see, and this earth that I tread upon, whence is this earth that I bear about me; Thou madest it. But where is that heaven of heavens, O Lord, which we hear of in the words of the Psalm, The heaven of heavens are the Lord's; but the earth hath He given to the children of men?[6] Where is that heaven which we see not, to which all this which we see is earth? For this corporeal whole, not being wholly everywhere, hath in such wise received its portion of beauty in these lower parts, whereof the lowest is this our earth; but to that heaven of heavens, even the heaven of our earth is but earth; yea, both these great bodies may not absurdly be called earth, to that unknown heaven, which is the Lord's, not the sons' of men.

[III] 3. And now this earth was invisible and without form,[7] and there was I know not what depth of abyss, upon which there was no light, because it had no shape. Therefore didst Thou command it to be written, that darkness was upon the face of the deep; what else than the absence of light? For had there been light, where should it have been but by being over all, aloft, and enlightening? Where then light was not, what was the presence of darkness, but the ab-

[1]Cf. *City of God*, BK. XI. 6; see BK. XII. 44.
[2]Phil. 3.13.   [3]Ps. 146.8.
[4]Rom. 8.31.   [5]Matt. 7.7, 8.
[6]Ps. 115. 16, in LXX, Vulgate, and Syriac.
[7]Gen. I.2, LXX.

sence of light?[1] Darkness therefore was upon it, because light was not upon it; as where sound is not, there is silence. And what is it to have silence there, but to have no sound there? Hast not Thou, O Lord, taught this soul, which confesseth unto Thee? Hast not Thou taught me, Lord, that before Thou formedst and diversifiedst this formless matter, there was nothing, neither colour, nor figure, nor body, nor spirit? and yet not altogether nothing; for there was a certain formlessness, without any beauty.

[IV] 4. How then should it be called, that it might be in some measure conveyed to those of duller mind, but by some ordinary word? And what, among all parts of the world can be found nearer to an absolute formlessness than earth and deep? For, occupying the lowest stage, they are less beautiful than the other higher parts are, transparent all and shining. Wherefore then may I not conceive the formlessness of matter (which Thou hadst created without beauty, whereof to make this beautiful world) to be suitably intimated unto men by the name of earth invisible and without form?

[V] 5. So that when thought seeketh what the sense may conceive under this, and saith to itself, "It is no intellectual form, as life, or justice; because it is the matter of bodies; nor object of sense, because being invisible, and without form, there was in it no object of sight or sense"—while man's thought thus saith to itself, it may endeavour either to know it, by being ignorant of it; or to be ignorant, by knowing it.

[VI] 6. But I, Lord, if I would, by my tongue and my pen, confess unto Thee the whole, whatever Thyself hath taught me of that matter—the name whereof hearing before, and not understanding, when they who understood it not told me of it, so I conceived[2] of it as having innumerable forms and diverse, and therefore did not conceive it at all, my mind tossed up and down foul and horrible "forms" out of all order, but yet "forms"; and I called it "without form" not that it wanted all form, but because it had such as my mind would, if presented to it, turn from, as unwonted and jarring, and human frailness would be troubled at. And still that which I conceived was without form, not as being deprived of all form, but in comparison of more beautiful forms; and true reason did persuade me that I must utterly uncase it of all remnants of form whatsoever, if I would conceive matter absolutely without form; and I could not; for sooner could I imagine that not to

be at all, which should be deprived of all form, than conceive a thing betwixt form and nothing, neither formed, nor nothing, a formless almost nothing. So my mind gave over to question thereupon with my spirit, it being filled with the images of formed bodies, and changing and varying them, as it willed; and I bent myself to the bodies themselves, and looked more deeply into their changeableness, by which they cease to be what they have been, and begin to be what they were not; and this same shifting from form to form, I suspected to be through a certain formless state,[3] not through a mere nothing; yet this I longed to know, not to suspect only. If then my voice and pen would confess unto Thee the whole, whatsoever knots Thou didst open for me in this question, what reader would hold out to take in the whole? Nor shall my heart for all this cease to give Thee honour, and a song of praise, for those things which it is not able to express. For the changeableness of changeable things is itself capable of all those forms into which these changeable things are changed. And this changeableness, what is it? Is it soul? Is it body? Is it that which constituteth soul or body? Might one say, "a nothing something," an "is, is not," I would say, this were it: and yet in some way was it even then, as being capable of receiving these visible and compound figures.

[VII] 7. But whence had it this degree of being, but from Thee, from Whom are all things, so far forth as they are? But so much the further from Thee, as the unliker Thee; for it is not farness of place. Thou therefore, Lord, Who are not one in one place, and otherwise in another, but the Self-same,[4] and the Self-same, and the Self-same, Holy, Holy, Holy, Lord God Almighty, didst in the Beginning, which is of Thee, in Thy Wisdom, which was born of Thine own Substance, create something, and that out of nothing. For thou createdst heaven and earth; not out of Thyself;[5] for so should they have been equal to Thine Only Begotten Son, and thereby to Thee also; whereas no way were it right that aught should be equal to Thee, whis was not of Thee. And aught else besides Thee was there not, whereof Thou mightest create them, O God, One Trinity, and Trine Unity; and therefore out of nothing didst Thou create heaven and earth; a great thing, and a small thing; for Thou art Almighty and Good, to make all things good, even the great heaven, and the petty earth. Thou wert, and nothing was there

---

[1]Cf. *City of God*, BK. XI. 9, 10.
[2]See above, BK. III. 11.

[3]See below, 8, end.   [4]See above, BK. IX. 11.
[5]See above, BK. III. 10; BK. IV. 26.

doth in no place and at no time put forth its natural mutability; and, Thyself being ever present with it, unto Whom with its whole affection it keeps itself, having neither future to expect, nor conveying[1] into the past what it remembereth, is neither altered by any change, nor distracted into any times. O blessed creature, if such there be, for cleaving unto Thy Blessedness; blest in Thee, its eternal Inhabitant and its Enlightener! Nor do I find by what name I may the rather call the heaven of heavens which is the Lord's, than Thine house, which contemplateth Thy delights without any defection of going forth to another; one pure mind, most harmoniously one, by that settled estate of peace of holy spirits,[2] the citizens of Thy city in "heavenly places" far above those heavenly places that we see.[3]

13. By this may the soul whose pilgrimage is made long and far away, by this may she understand, if she now thirsts for Thee, if her tears be now become her bread, while they daily say unto her, "Where is thy God"?[4] if she now seeks of Thee one thing, and desireth it, that she may dwell in Thy house all the days of her life[5] (and what is her life, but Thou? and what Thy days, but Thy eternity, as Thy years which fail not, because Thou art ever the same?); by this then may the soul that is able, understand how far Thou art, above all times, eternal; seeing Thy house which at no time went into a far country, although it be not coeternal with Thee, yet by continually and unfailingly cleaving unto Thee suffers no changeableness of times. This is in Thy sight clear unto me, and let it be more and more cleared unto me, I beseech Thee, and in the manifestation thereof, let me with sobriety abide under Thy wings.

14. There is, behold, I know not what formlessness in those changes of these last and lowest creatures; and who shall tell me (unless such a one as through the emptiness of his own heart wanders and tosses himself up and down amid his own fancies), who but such a one would tell me that, if all figure be so wasted and consumed away, there should only remain that formlessness through which the thing was changed and turned from one figure to another, that that could exhibit the vicissitudes of times? For plainly it could not, because, without the variety of motions, there are no times; and no variety, where there is no figure.

[XII] 15. These things considered, as much as Thou givest, O my God, as much as Thou

stirrest me up to "knock," and as much as Thou openest to me knocking,[6] two things I find that Thou hast made, not within the compass of time, neither of which is coeternal with Thee. One which is so formed that, without any ceasing of contemplation, without any interval of change, though changeable, yet not changed, it may thoroughly enjoy Thy eternity and unchangeableness; the other which was so formless that it had not that which could be changed from one form into another, whether of motion, or of repose, so as to become subject unto time. But this Thou didst not leave thus formless, because before all days Thou in the Beginning didst create Heaven and Earth; the two things that I spake of. But the Earth was invisible and without form, and darkness was upon the deep.[7] In which words is the formlessness conveyed unto us (that such capacities may hereby be drawn on by degrees, as are not able to conceive an utter privation of all form, without yet coming to nothing) out of which another Heaven might be created, together with a visible and well-formed earth: and the waters diversly ordered, and whatsoever further is in the formation of the world, recorded to have been, not without days, created; and that, as being of such nature, the successive changes of times may take place in them, as being subject to appointed alterations of motions and of forms.[8]

[XIII] 16. This then is what I conceive, O my God, when I hear Thy Scripture saying, In the beginning God made Heaven and Earth: and the Earth was invisible and without form, and darkness was upon the deep, and not mentioning what day Thou createdst them; this is what I conceive, that, because of the Heaven of heavens—that intellectual Heaven whose Intelligences know all at once, not "in part," not "darkly," not "through a glass,"[9] but as a whole, in manifestation, "face to face"; not this thing now, and that thing anon; but (as I said) know all at once, without any succession of times—and because of the earth invisible and without form, without any succession of times, which succession presents "this thing now, that thing anon"; because where is no form there is no distinction of things—it is, then, on account of these two, a primitive formed, and a primitive formless; the one, heaven but the Heaven of heaven, the other earth but the earth invisible and without form—because of these two, do I conceive, did Thy Scripture say without mention of days, "In the Beginning God created

[1]Above, Bk. XI. 38; below, 18. [2]See below, Bk. XIII. 50.
[3]Eph. 1.20, etc. [4]Ps. 42.2, 3, 10. [5]Ps. 27.4.
[6]Matt. 7.7. [7]Gen. 1.2.
[8]See below, 40, end. [9]I Cor. 13.12.

besides, out of which Thou createdst heaven and earth; things of two sorts: one near Thee, the other near to nothing; one, to which Thou alone shouldest be superior; the other, to which nothing should be inferior.

[VIII] 8. But that heaven of heavens was for Thyself, O Lord; but the earth which Thou gavest to the sons of men,[1] to be seen and felt, was not such as we now see and feel. For it was invisible, "without form,"[2] and there was a deep, upon which there was no light; or darkness was above the deep, that is, more than in the deep. Because this deep of waters, visible now, hath even in his depths a light proper for its nature; perceivable in whatever degree unto the fishes and creeping things in the bottom of it. But that whole deep was almost nothing, because hitherto it was altogether without form; yet there was already that which could be formed. For Thou, Lord, madest the world of a matter without form, which, out of nothing, Thou madest next to nothing, thereof to make those great things which we sons of men wonder at. For very wonderful is this corporeal heaven; of which firmament between water and water, the second day, after the creation of light, Thou saidst, Let it be made, and it was made.[3] Which firmament Thou calledst heaven; the heaven, that is, to this earth and sea, which Thou madest the third day, by giving a visible figure to the formless matter, which Thou madest before all days. For already hadst Thou made both an heaven, before all days; but that was the heaven of this heaven; because In the beginning Thou hadst made heaven and earth. But this same earth which Thou madest was formless matter, because it was invisible and without form, and darkness was upon the deep, of which invisible earth and without form, of which formlessness, of which almost nothing, Thou mightest make all these things of which this changeable world consists, but subsists not; whose very changeableness appears therein, that times can be observed and numbered in it. For times are made by the alterations of things, while the figures, the matter whereof is the invisible earth aforesaid, are varied and turned.

[IX] 9. And therefore the Spirit, the Teacher of Thy servant,[4] when It recounts Thee to have in the Beginning created heaven and earth, speaks nothing of times, nothing of days. For verily that heaven of heavens which Thou createdst in the Beginning is some intellectual creature, which although no ways coeternal unto Thee, the Trinity, yet partaketh of Thy eternity,

and doth through the sweetness of that most happy contemplation of Thyself strongly restrain its own changeableness; and without any fall since its first creation, cleaving close unto Thee, is placed beyond all the rolling vicissitude of times. Yea, neither is this very formlessness of the earth invisible, and without form, numbered among the days. For where no figure nor order is, there does nothing come or go; and where this is not, there plainly are no days, nor any vicissitude of spaces of times.

[X] 10. O let the Light, the Truth, the Light of my heart, not mine own darkness, speak unto me. I fell off into that, and became darkened; but even thence, even thence I loved Thee. I went astray, and remembered Thee. I heard Thy voice behind me, calling to me to return, and scarcely heard it, through the tumultuousness of the enemies of peace. And now, behold, I return in distress and panting after Thy fountain. Let no man forbid me! of this will I drink, and so live. Let me not be mine own life; from myself I lived ill, death was I to myself; and I revive in Thee. Do Thou speak unto me, do Thou discourse unto me. I have believed Thy Books and their words be most full of mystery.

[XI] 11. Already Thou hast told me with a strong voice, O Lord, in my inner ear, that Thou art eternal, Who only hast immortality[5]: since Thou canst not be changed as to figure or motion, nor is Thy will altered by times; seeing no will which varies is immortal. This is in Thy sight clear to me, and let it be more and more cleared to me, I beseech Thee; and in the manifestation thereof, let me with sobriety abide under Thy wings. Thou hast told me also with a strong voice, O Lord, in my inner ear, that Thou hast made all natures and substances, which are not what Thyself is, and yet are; and that only is not from Thee, which is not, and the motion of the will from Thee Who Art unto that which in a less degree is, because such motion is transgression and sin[6]; and that no man's sin doth either hurt Thee or disturb the order of Thy government, first or last.[7] This is in Thy sight clear unto me, and let it be more and more cleared to me, I beseech Thee: and in the manifestation thereof, let me with sobriety abide under Thy wings.

12. Thou hast told me also with a strong voice, in my inner ear, that neither is that creature coeternal unto Thyself, whose happiness Thou only art, and which with a most persevering purity, drawing its nourishment from Thee,

---

[1]Ps. 115.16.   [2]Gen. 1.2.   [3]Gen. 1.6–8.   [4]Moses.

[5]I Tim. 6.16.

[6]See above, BK. VII. 22.   [7]See above, BK. V. 2.

Heaven and Earth." For forthwith it subjoined what earth it spake of; and also, in that the Firmament is recorded to be created the second day, and called Heaven, it conveys to us of which Heaven He before spake, without mention of days.

[XIV] 17. Wondrous depth of Thy words! whose surface, behold! is before us, inviting to little ones; yet are they a wondrous depth, O my God, a wondrous depth! It is awful to look therein; an awfulness of honour, and a trembling of love. The enemies thereof I hate vehemently;[1] oh, that Thou wouldest slay them with Thy two-edged sword,[2] that they might no longer be enemies unto it; for so do I love to have them slain unto themselves, that they may live unto Thee. But behold others not faultfinders, but extollers of the Book of Genesis. "The Spirit of God," say they, "Who by His servant Moses wrote these things, would not have those words thus understood; He would not have it understood, as thou sayest, but otherwise, as we say." Unto Whom Thyself, O Thou God of us all, being Judge, do I thus answer.

[XV]) 18. "Will you affirm that to be false, which with a strong voice Truth tells me in my inner ear, concerning the Eternity of the Creator, that His substance is no ways changed by time, nor His will separate from His substance? Wherefore He willeth not one thing now, another anon, but once, and at once, and always, He willeth all things that He willeth; not again and again, nor now this, now that; nor willeth afterwards what before He willed not, nor willeth not what before He willed; because such a will is mutable; and no mutable thing is eternal; but our God is eternal. Again, what He tells me in my inner ear, the expectation of things to come becomes sight when they are come, and this same sight becomes memory when they be past. Now all thought which thus varies is mutable; and no mutable is eternal: but our God is eternal." These things I infer, and put together, and find that my God, the eternal God, hath not upon any new will made any creature, nor doth His knowledge admit of anything transitory.

"What will ye say then, O ye gainsayers? Are these things false?" "No," they say. "What then? Is it false that every nature already formed, or matter capable of form, is not, but from Him Who is supremely good, because He is supremely?" "Neither do we deny this," say they. "What then? do you deny this, that there is a certain sublime creature, with so chaste a

love cleaving unto the true and truly eternal God that, although not coeternal with Him, yet is it not detached from Him, nor dissolved into the variety and vicissitude of times, but reposeth in the most true contemplation of Him only?" Because Thou, O God, unto him that loveth Thee so much as Thou commandest, dost shew Thyself, and sufficest him; and therefore doth he not decline from Thee, nor toward himself. This is the house of God, not of earthly mould, nor of any celestial bulk corporeal, but spiritual, and partaker of Thy eternity, because without defection for ever. For Thou hast made it fast for ever and ever, Thou hast given it a law which it shall not pass.[3] Nor yet is it coeternal with Thee, O God, because not without beginning; for it was made.

20. For although we find no time before it, for wisdom was created before all things;[4] not that Wisdom which is altogether equal and coeternal unto Thee, our God, His Father, and by Whom all things were created, and in Whom, as the Beginning, Thou createdst heaven and earth; but that wisdom which is created, that is, the intellectual nature which, by contemplating the light, is light. For this, though created, is also called wisdom. But what difference there is betwixt the Light which enlighteneth, and which is enlightened, so much is there betwixt the Wisdom that createth, and that created, as betwixt the Righteousness which justifieth, and the righteousness which is made by justification. For we also are called Thy righteousness: for so saith a certain servant of Thine, "That we might be made the righteousness of God in Him."[5] Therefore since a certain created wisdom was created before all things, the rational and intellectual mind of that chaste city of Thine, our mother which is above, and is free[6] and "eternal in the heavens"[7] (in what heavens, if not in those that praise Thee, the "Heaven of heavens"? Because this is also the "Heaven of heavens"[8] for the Lord); though we find no time before it (because that which hath been created before all things, precedeth also the creature of time), yet is the Eternity of the Creator Himself before it, from Whom, being created it took the beginning, not indeed of time (for time itself was not yet), but of its creation.

21. Hence it is so of Thee, our God, as to be altogether other than Thou, and not the Selfsame; because though we find time neither before it, nor even in it (it being meet ever to behold Thy face, nor is ever drawn away from it,

---

[1]Ps. 139.21. [2]Ps. 149.6.

[3]Ps. 148.6. [4]Ecclus. 1.4. [5]II Cor. 5.21.
[6]Gal. 4.26. [7]II Cor. 5.1. [8]Ps. 148.4.

wherefore it is not varied by any change), yet is there in it a liability to change, whence it would wax dark, and chill, but that by a strong affection cleaving unto Thee, like perpetual noon, it shineth and gloweth from Thee. O house most lightsome and delightsome! I have loved thy beauty, and the place of the habitation of the glory of my Lord,[1] thy builder and possessor. Let my wayfaring sigh after thee; and I say to Him that made thee, let Him take possession of me also in thee, seeing He hath made me likewise. "I have gone astray like a lost sheep";[2] yet upon the shoulders of my Shepherd,[3] thy builder, hope I to be brought back to thee.

22. "What say ye to me, O ye gainsayers that I was speaking unto, who yet believe Moses to have been the holy servant of God, and his books the oracles of the Holy Ghost? Is not this house of God not coeternal indeed with God, yet, after its measure, eternal in the heavens,[4] when you seek for changes of times in vain, because you will not find them? For that, to which it is ever good to cleave fast to God,[5] surpasses all extension, and all revolving periods of time." "It is," say they. "What then of all that which my heart loudly uttered unto my God, when inwardly it heard the voice of His praise, what part thereof do you affirm to be false? Is it that the matter was without form, in which because there was no form, there was no order. But where no order was, there could be no vicissitude of times; and yet this 'almost nothing,' inasmuch as it was not altogether nothing, was from Him certainly, from Whom is whatsoever is, in what degree soever it is." "This also," say they, "do we not deny."

[XVI] 23. With these would I now parley a little in Thy presence, O my God, who grant all these things to be true, which Thy Truth whispers unto my soul. For those who deny these things, let them bark and deafen themselves as much as they please; I will essay to persuade them to quiet, and to open in them a way for Thy word. But if they refuse and repel me, I beseech, O my God, "be not Thou silent to me."[6] Speak Thou truly in my heart; for only Thou so speakest: and I will let them alone blowing upon the dust without, and raising it up into their own eyes; and myself will enter my chamber,[7] and sing there a song of loves unto Thee; groaning with groanings unutterable,[8] in my wayfaring, and remembering Jerusalem, with heart lifted up towards it, Jerusalem my country, Jerusalem my mother, and Thyself that rulest over it, the Enlightener, Father, Guardian, Husband, the pure and strong delight, and solid joy, and all good things unspeakable, yea, all at once, because the One Sovereign and true Good. Nor will I be turned away until Thou gather all that I am, from this dispersed[9] and disordered estate, into the peace of that our most dear mother, where the first-fruits of my spirit[10] be already (whence I am ascertained of these things), and Thou conform and confirm it for ever, O my God, my Mercy. But those who do not affirm all these truths to be false, who honour Thy holy Scripture, set forth by holy Moses, placing it, as we, on the summit of authority to be followed, and do yet contradict me in something, I answer thus; Be Thyself Judge, O our God, between my Confessions and these men's contradictions.

[XVII] 24. For they say: "Though these things be true, yet did not Moses intend those two, when, by revelation of the Spirit, he said, 'In the beginning God created heaven and earth.'[11] He did not under the name of heaven signify that spiritual or intellectual creature which always beholds the face of God; nor under the name of earth, that formless matter." "What then?" "That man of God," say they, "meant as we say, this declared he by those words." "What?" "By the name of heaven and earth would he first signify," say they, "universally and compendiously, all this visible world; so as afterwards by the enumeration of the several days, to arrange in detail, and, as it were, piece by piece, all those things which it pleased the Holy Ghost thus to enounce. For such were that rude and carnal people to which he spake, that he thought them fit to be entrusted with the knowledge of such works of God only as were visible." They agree, however, that under the words "earth invisible and without form," and that darksome "deep" (out of which it is subsequently shewn that all these visible things which we all know were made and arranged during those "days") may, not incongruously, be understood of this formless (first) matter.

25. What now if another should say, "That this same formlessness and confusedness of matter was for this reason first conveyed under the name of heaven and earth, because out of it was this visible world with all those natures which most manifestly appear in it, which is oft-times called by the name of heaven and earth, created and perfected"? What again if another say,

---

[1]Ps. 26.8.   [2]Ps. 119.176.   [3]Luke, 15.5   [4]II Cor. 5.1.
[5]Ps. 73.28.   [6]Ps. 28.1.   [7]Isa. 26.20.   [8]Rom. 8.26.
[9]See above, Bk. II. I; Bk. IX. 10.
[10]See above, Bk. IX. 24, end; see below, Bk. XIII. 14.
[11]Gen. I.1.

"That invisible and visible nature is not indeed inappropriately called heaven and earth; and so, that the universal creation, which God made in His Wisdom, that is, 'in the Beginning,' was comprehended under those two words? Notwithstanding, since all things be made not of the substance of God, but out of nothing (because they are not the same that God is, and there is a mutable nature in them all, whether they abide, as doth the eternal house of God, or be changed, as the soul and body of man are); therefore the common matter of all things visible and invisible (as yet unformed though capable of form) out of which was to be created both heaven and earth (i.e., the invisible and visible creature when formed) was entitled by the same names given to the earth invisible and without form and the darkness upon the deep, but with this distinction, that by the earth invisible and without form is understood corporeal matter, antecedent to its being qualified by any form; and by the darkness upon the deep, spiritual matter, before it underwent any restraint of its unlimited fluidness, or received any light from Wisdom"?

26. It yet remains for a man to say, if he will, "That the already perfected and formed natures, visible and invisible, are not signified under the name of heaven and earth, when we read, 'In the beginning God made heaven and earth,' but that the yet unformed commencement of things, the stuff apt to receive form and making, was called by these names, because therein were confusedly contained, not as yet distinguished by their qualities and forms, all those things which, being now digested into order, are called Heaven and Earth, the one being the spiritual, the other the corporeal, creation."

[XVIII] 27. All which things being heard and well considered, I will not strive about words; for that is profitable to nothing, but the subversion of the hearers.[1] But the law is good to edify, if a man use it lawfully;[2] for that the end of it "is charity, out of a pure heart and good conscience, and faith unfeigned."[3] And well did our Master know, upon which two commandments He hung all the Law and the Prophets.[4] And what doth it prejudice me, O my God, Thou light of my eyes in secret, zealously confessing these things, since divers things may be understood under these words which yet are all true— what, I say, doth it prejudice me, if I think otherwise than another thinketh the writer thought? All we readers verily strive to trace out and to understand his meaning whom we read; and seeing we believe him to speak truly, we dare not imagine him to have said anything which ourselves either know or think to be false. While every man endeavours then to understand in the holy Scriptures the same as the writer understood, what hurt is it, if a man understand what Thou, the light of all true-speaking minds, dost shew him to be true, although he whom he reads understood not this, seeing he also understood a Truth, though not this truth?

[XIX] 28. For true it is, O Lord, that Thou madest heaven and earth; and it is true, too, that the Beginning is Thy Wisdom, in Which Thou createdst all[5]; and true again, that this visible world hath for its greater parts the heaven and the earth, which briefly comprise all made and created natures. And true, too, that whatsoever is mutable gives us to understand a certain want of form, whereby it receiveth a form, or is changed, or turned. It is true that that is subject to no times, which so cleaveth to the unchangeable Form as, though subject to change, never to be changed. It is true that that formlessness which is almost nothing cannot be subject to the alteration of times. It is true that that whereof a thing is made may, by a certain mode of speech, be called by the name of the thing made of it; whence that formlessness, whereof heaven and earth were made, might be called "heaven and earth." It is true that, of things having form, there is not any nearer to having no form than the earth and the deep. It is true that not only every created and formed thing, but whatsoever is capable of being created and formed, Thou madest, "of whom are all things."[6] It is true that whatsoever is formed out of that which had no form was unformed before it was formed.

[XX] 29. Out of these truths, of which they doubt not whose inward eye Thou hast enabled to see such things, and who unshakenly believe Thy servant Moses to have spoken in the Spirit of truth; of all these then, he taketh one, who saith, "In the Beginning God made the heaven and the earth," that is, "In His word coeternal with Himself, God made the intelligible and the sensible, or the spiritual and the corporeal creature." He another, that saith, "In the Beginning God made heaven and earth"; that is, "in His Word coeternal with Himself, did God make the universal bulk of this corporeal world, together with all those apparent and known creatures, which it containeth." He another, that saith, "In the Beginning God made heaven and earth"; that is, "In His Word coeternal with Himself,

[1]II. Tim. 2.14   [2]I Tim. 1.8.
[3]Ibid., ver. 5.   [4]Matt. 22.40.
[5]Ps. 104.24.   [6]I. Cor. 8.6.

did God make the formless matter of creatures spiritual and corporeal." He another, that saith, "In the Beginning God created heaven and earth"; that is, "In His Word coeternal with Himself, did God create the formless matter of the creature corporeal, wherein heaven and earth lay as yet confused, which, being now distinguished and formed, we at this day see in the bulk of this world." He another, who saith, "In the Beginning God made heaven and earth," that is, "In the very beginning of creating and working, did God make that formless matter, confusedly containing in itself both heaven and earth; out of which, being formed, do they now stand out, and are apparent, with all that is in them."

[XXI] 30. And, with regard to the understanding of the words following out of all those truths, he chooses one to himself, who saith, "But the earth was invisible, and without form, and darkness was upon the deep"; that is, "That corporeal thing that God made was as yet a formless matter of corporeal things, without order, without light." Another he who says, "The earth was invisible and without form, and darkness was upon the deep"; that is, "This all, which is called heaven and earth, was still a formless and darksome matter, of which the corporeal heaven and the corporeal earth were to be made, with all things in them, which are known to our corporeal senses." Another he who says, "The earth was invisible and without form, and darkness was upon the deep"; that is, "This all, which is called heaven and earth, was still a formless and a darksome matter; out of which was to be made both that intelligible heaven, otherwhere called the Heaven of heavens, and the earth, that is, the whole corporeal nature, under which name is comprised this corporeal heaven also; in a word, out of which every visible and invisible creature was to be created." Another he who says, "The earth was invisible and without form, and darkness was upon the deep," "The Scripture did not call that formlessness by the name of heaven and earth; but that formlessness, saith he, already was, which he called the earth invisible without form, and darkness upon the deep; of which he had before said that God had made heaven and earth, namely, the spiritual and corporeal creature." Another he who says, "The earth was invisible and without form, and darkness was upon the deep"; that is, "There already was a certain formless matter, of which the Scripture said before, that God made heaven and earth; namely, the whole corporeal bulk of the world, divided into two great parts, upper and lower, with all the common and known creatures in them."

[XXII] 31. For should any attempt to dispute against these two last opinions, thus, "If you will not allow that this formlessness of matter seems to be called by the name of heaven and earth; ergo, there was something which God had not made, out of which to make heaven and earth; for neither hath Scripture told us that God made this matter, unless we understand it to be signified by the name of heaven and earth, or of earth alone, when it is said, 'In the Beginning God made the heaven and earth'; that so in what follows, and the earth was invisible and without form (although it pleased Him so to call the formless matter), we are to understand no other matter, but that which God made, whereof is written above, 'God made heaven and earth.'" The maintainers of either of those two latter opinions will, upon hearing this, return for answer, "We do not deny this formless matter to be indeed created by God, that God of Whom are all things, very good; for as we affirm that to be a greater good which is created and formed, so we confess that to be a lesser good which is made capable of creation and form, yet still good. We say however that Scripture hath not set down that God made this formlessness, as also it hath not many others; as the 'Cherubim,' and 'Seraphim,'[1] and those which the Apostle distinctly speaks of, 'Thrones,' 'Dominions,' 'Principalities,' 'Powers.'[2] All which that God made is most apparent. Or if in that which is said, 'He made heaven and earth,' all things be comprehended, what shall we say of the waters upon which the Spirit of God moved? For if they be comprised in this word earth, how then can formless matter be meant in that name of earth, when we see the waters so beautiful? Or if it be so taken, why then is it written that out of the same formlessness the firmament was made, and called heaven; and that the waters were made is not written? For the waters remain not formless and invisible, seeing we behold them flowing in so comely a manner. But if they then received that beauty, when God said, 'Let the water which is under the firmament be gathered together,' that so the gathering together be itself the forming of them; what will be answered as to those waters which be above the firmament? Seeing neither if formless would they have been worthy of so honourable a seat, nor is it written by what word they were formed. If then Genesis is silent as to God's making of any thing, which yet that God did make neither

¹Isa. 6.2; 37.16.   ²Col. 1.16.

sound faith nor well-grounded understanding doubteth, nor again will any sober teaching dare to affirm these waters to be coeternal with God, on the ground that we find them to be mentioned in the Book of Genesis, but when they were created we do not find; why (seeing truth teaches us) should we not understand that formless matter (which this Scripture calls the earth invisible and without form, and darksome deep) to have been created of God out of nothing, and therefore not to be coeternal to Him; notwithstanding this history hath omitted to shew when it was created?"

[XXIII] 32. These things then being heard and perceived, according to the weakness of my capacity (which I confess unto Thee, O Lord, that knowest it), two sorts of disagreements I see may arise, when a thing is in words related by true reporters: one, concerning the truth of the things, the other, concerning the meaning of the relater. For we enquire one way about the making of the creature, what is true; another way, what Moses, that excellent minister of Thy Faith, would have his reader and hearer understand by those words. For the first sort, away with all those who imagine themselves to know as a truth what is false; and for this other, away with all them too, which imagine Moses to have written things that be false. But let me be united in Thee, O Lord, with those, and delight myself in Thee, with them that feed on Thy truth, in the largeness of charity, and let us approach together unto the words of Thy book, and seek in them for Thy meaning, through the meaning of Thy servant, by whose pen Thou hast dispensed them.

[XXIV] 33. But which of us shall, among those so many truths which occur to enquirers in those words, as they are differently understood, so discover that one meaning, as to affirm, "This Moses thought," and "This would he have understood in that history"; with the same confidence as he would, "This is true," whether Moses thought this or that? For behold, O my God, I Thy servant, who have in this book vowed a sacrifice of confession unto Thee, and pray that by Thy mercy I may pay my vows unto Thee,[1] can I, with the same confidence wherewith I affirm that in Thy incommutable world Thou createdst all things visible and invisible, affirm also that Moses meant no other than this when he wrote, "In the Beginning God made heaven and earth"? No. Because I see not in his mind that he thought of this when he wrote these things, as I do see it in Thy truth to be

certain. For he might have his thoughts upon God's commencement of creating, when he said "In the beginning"; and by "heaven and earth," in this place he might intend no formed and perfected nature whether spiritual or corporeal, but both of them inchoate and as yet formless. For I perceive that whichsoever of the two had been said, it might have been truly said; but which of the two he thought of in these words, I do not so perceive. Although, whether it were either of these, or any sense beside (that I have not here mentioned), which this so great man saw in his mind when he uttered these words, I doubt not but that he saw it truly, and expressed it aptly.

[XXV] 34. Let no man harass me then, by saying, "Moses thought not as you say, but as I say"; for if he should ask me, "How know you that Moses thought that which you infer out of his words?" I ought to take it in good part, and would answer perchance as I have above, or something more at large, if he were unyielding. But when he saith, "Moses meant not what you say, but what I say," yet denieth not that what each of us say may both be true, O my God, life of the poor, in Whose bosom is no contradiction, pour down a softening dew into my heart, that I may patiently bear with such as say this to me, not because they have a divine Spirit, and have seen in the heart of Thy servant what they speak, but because they be proud; not knowing Moses' opinion, but loving their own, not because it is truth but because it is theirs. Otherwise they would equally love another true opinion, as I love what they say when they say true: not because it is theirs, but because it is true; and on that very ground not theirs because it is true. But if they therefore love it because it is true, then is it both theirs and mine; as being in common to all lovers of truth. But whereas they contend that Moses did not mean what I say, but what they say, this I like not, love not; for though it were so, yet that their rashness belongs not to knowledge, but to overboldness, and not insight but vanity was its parent. And therefore, O Lord, are Thy judgments terrible; seeing Thy truth is neither mine, nor his, nor another's; but belonging to us all, whom Thou callest publicly to partake of it, warning us terribly not to account it private to ourselves, lest we be deprived of it. For whosoever challenges that as proper to himself, which Thou propoundest to all to enjoy, and would have that his own which belongs to all, is driven from what is in common to his own; that is, from truth, to a lie. For he that "speaketh a lie, speaketh it of his own."[2]

[1]Ps. 22.25. [2]John, 8.44.

35. Hearken, O God, Thou best Judge; Truth Itself, hearken to what I shall say to this gain-sayer, hearken, for before Thee do I speak, and before my brethren, who employ Thy law law-fully, to the end of charity;[1] hearken and behold, if it please Thee, what I shall say to him. For this brotherly and peaceful word do I return un-to Him: "If we both see that to be true that Thou sayest, and both see that to be true that I say, where, I pray Thee, do we see it? Neither I in thee, nor thou in me; but both in the un-changeable Truth itself, which is above our souls." Seeing then we strive not about the very light of the Lord our God, why strive we about the thoughts of our neighbour which we cannot so see, as the unchangeable Truth is seen; for that, if Moses himself had appeared to us and said, "This I meant"; neither so should we see it, but should believe it. Let us not then "be puffed up for one against another,"[2] above that which is written: "Let us love the Lord our God with all our heart, with all our soul, and with all our mind; and our neighbour as ourself."[3] With a view to which two precepts of charity, unless we believe that Moses meant, whatsoever in those books he did mean, we shall make God a liar, imagining otherwise of our fellow servant's mind than He hath taught us. Behold now how foolish it is, in such abundance of most true meanings, as may be extracted out of those words, rashly to affirm which of them Moses principally meant; and with pernicious conten-tions to offend charity itself, for whose sake he spake everything, whose words we go about to expound.

[XXVI] 36. And yet I, O my God, Thou lifter up of my humility, and rest of my labour, Who hearest my confessions, and forgivest my sins; seeing Thou commandest me to love my neighbour as myself, I cannot believe that Thou gavest a less gift unto Moses Thy faithful ser-vant, than I would wish or desire Thee to have given me, had I been born in the time he was, and hadst Thou set me in that office, that by the service of my heart and tongue those books might be dispensed which for so long after were to profit all nations, and through the whole world, from such an eminence of authority, were to surmount all sayings of false and proud teachings. I should have desired verily, had I then been Moses (for we all come from the same lump, and what is man, saving that Thou art mindful of him?[4]), I would then, had I been then what he was, and been enjoined by Thee

to write the book of Genesis, have desired such a power of expression and such style to be giv-en me, that neither they who cannot yet under-stand how God created might reject the sayings as beyond their capacity; and they who had at-tained thereto might find what true opinion so-ever they had by thought arrived at, not passed over in those few words of that Thy servant; and should another man by the light of truth have discovered another, neither should that fail of being discoverable in those same words.

[XXVII] 37. For as a fountain within a nar-row compass is more plentiful, and supplies a tide for more streams over larger spaces, than any one of those streams which, after a wide in-terval, is derived from the same fountain; so the relation of that dispenser of Thine, which was to benefit many who were to discourse thereon, does out of a narrow scantling of lan-guage overflow into streams of clearest truth, whence every man may draw out for himself such truth as he can upon these subjects, one, one truth, another, another, by larger circumlocu-tions of discourse. For some, when they read or hear these words, conceive that God like a man or some mass endued with unbounded power, by some new and sudden resolution did, exterior to itself, as it were at a certain distance, create heaven and earth, two great bodies above and below, wherein all things were to be contained. And when they hear, "God said, Let it be made, and it was made," they conceive of words begun and ended, sounding in time, and passing away; after whose departure, that came into being which was commanded so to do; and whatever of the like sort, men's acquaintance with the material world would suggest. In whom, being yet little ones and carnal, while their weakness is by this humble kind of speech carried on, as in a mother's bosom, their faith is wholesomely built up, whereby they hold assured that God made all natures, which in admirable variety their eye beholdeth around. Which words, if any despising as too simple, with a proud weakness, shall stretch himself beyond the guardian nest, he will, alas, fall miserably. Have pity, O Lord God, lest they who go by the way trample on the unfledged bird, and send Thine angel to re-place it into the nest, that it may live, till it can fly.

[XXVIII] 38. But others, unto whom these words are no longer a nest, but deep shady fruit-bowers, see the fruits concealed therein, fly joy-ously around, and with cheerful notes seek out and pluck them. For, reading or hearing these words, they see that all times past and to come

[1]I Tim. 1.8.   [2]I Cor. 4.6.   [3]Mark, 12.30, 31.
[4]Ps. 8.8.

are surpassed by Thy eternal and stable abiding; and yet that there is no creature formed in time, not of Thy making. Whose will, because it is the same that Thou art, Thou madest all things, not by any change of will, nor by a will which before was not, and that these things were not out of Thyself, in Thine own likeness, which is the form of all things, but out of nothing, a formless unlikeness, which should be formed by Thy likeness (recurring to Thy Unity, according to their appointed capacity, so far as is given to each thing in his kind), and might all be made very good; whether they abide around Thee, or, being in gradation removed in time and place, make or undergo the beautiful variations of the Universe. These things they see, and rejoice, in the little degree they here may, in the light of Thy truth.

39. Another bends his mind on that which is said, "In the Beginning God made heaven and earth"; and beholdeth therein Wisdom, the Beginning because It also speaketh unto us.[1] Another likewise bends his mind on the same words, and by "Beginning" understands the commencement of things created; In the beginning He made, as if it were said, He at first made. And among them that understand "In the Beginning" to mean, "In Thy Wisdom Thou createdst heaven and earth," one believes the matter out of which the heaven and earth were to be created, to be there called "heaven and earth"; another, natures already formed and distinguished; another, one formed nature, and that a spiritual, under the name Heaven, the other formless, of corporeal matter, under the name Earth. They again who, by the names "heaven and earth," understand matter as yet formless, out of which heaven and earth were to be formed, neither do they understand it in one way; but the one, that matter out of which both the intelligible and the sensible creature were to be perfected; another, that only out of which this sensible corporeal mass was to be made, containing in its vast bosom these visible and ordinary natures. Neither do they who believe the creatures already ordered and arranged, to be in this place called heaven and earth, understand the same; but the one, both the invisible and visible, the other, the visible only, in which we behold this lightsome heaven and darksome earth, with the things in them contained.

[XXIX] 40. But he that no otherwise understands "In the Beginning He made," than if it were said, "At first He made," can only truly understand heaven and earth of the matter of

[1]John, 8.23.

heaven and earth, that is, of the universal intelligible and corporeal creation. For if he would understand thereby the universe, as already formed, it may be rightly demanded of him, "If God made this first, what made He afterwards?" And after the universe, he will find nothing; whereupon must he against his will hear another question; "How this first, if nothing after?" But when he says, God made matter first formless, then formed, there is no absurdity, if he be but qualified to discern what precedes by eternity, what by time, what by choice, and what in original. By eternity, as God is before all things; by time, as the flower before the fruit; by choice, as the fruit before the flower; by original, as the sound before the tune. Of these four, the first and last mentioned are with extreme difficulty understood, the two middle, easily. For a rare and too lofty a vision is it, to behold Thy Eternity, O Lord, unchangeably making things changeable; and thereby before them. And who, again, is of so sharp-sighted understanding as to be able without great pains to discern how the sound is therefore before the tune; because a tune is a formed sound; and a thing not formed may exist; whereas that which existeth not cannot be formed. Thus is the matter before the thing made; not because it maketh it, seeing itself is rather made; nor is it before by interval of time; for we do not first in time utter formless sounds without singing, and subsequently adapt or fashion them into the form of a chant, as wood or silver whereof a chest or vessel is fashioned. For such materials do by time also precede the forms of the things made of them, but in singing it is not so; for when it is sung, its sound is heard; for there is not first a formless sound, which is afterwards formed into a chant. For each sound, so soon as made, passeth away, nor canst thou find ought to recall and by art to compose. So then the chant is concentrated in its sound, which sound of his is his matter. And this indeed is formed, that it may be a tune; and therefore (as I said) the matter of the sound is before the form of the tune; not before, through any power it hath to make it a tune; for a sound is no way the workmaster of the tune; but is something corporeal, subjected to the soul which singeth, whereof to make a tune. Nor is it first in time, for it is given forth together with the tune; nor first in choice, for a sound is not better than a tune, a tune being not only a sound, but a beautiful sound. But it is first in original, because a tune receives not form to become a sound, but a sound receives a form to become a tune. By this example, let him that is able, understand how the matter of things was first made, and called heaven and earth, because heaven and earth were made out of it. Yet was it not made first in time; because the forms of things give rise to time; but that was without form; but now is, in time, an object of sense together with its form. And yet nothing can be related of that matter, but as though prior in time, whereas in value it is last (because things formed are superior to things without form) and is preceded by the Eternity of the Creator: that so there might be out of nothing, whereof somewhat might be created.

[XXX] 41. In this diversity of the true opinions, let Truth herself produce concord. And our God have mercy upon us, that we may use the law lawfully,[1] the end of the commandment, pure charity. By this if a man demands of me, "which of these was the meaning of Thy servant Moses"; this were not the language of my *Confessions* should I not confess unto Thee, "I know not"; and yet I know that those senses are true, those carnal ones excepted, of which I have spoken what seemed necessary. And even those hopeful little ones who so think the words of Thy Book affright them not, delivering high things lowlily, and with few words a copious meaning. And all we who, I confess, see and express the truth delivered in those words, let us love one another, and jointly love Thee our God, the fountain of truth, if we are athirst for it, and not for vanities; yea, let us so honor this Thy servant, the dispenser of this Scripture, full of Thy Spirit, as to believe that, when by Thy revelation he wrote these things, he intended that which among them chiefly excels both for light of truth, and fruitfulness of profit.

[XXXI] 42. So when one says, "Moses meant as I do"; and another, "Nay, but as I do"; I suppose that I speak more reverently: "Why not rather as both, if both be true?" And if there be a third, or a fourth, yea, if any other seeth any other truth in those words, why may not he be believed to have seen all these, through whom the One God hath tempered the holy Scriptures to the senses of many, who should see therein things true but divers? For I certainly (and fearlessly I speak it from my heart) that were I to indite anything to have supreme authority, I should prefer so to write that whatever truth any could apprehend on those matters might be conveyed in my words, rather than set down my own meaning so clearly as to exclude the rest, which, not being false, could not offend me. I will not therefore, O my God, be so rash as not

to believe that Thou vouchsafedst as much to that great man. He without doubt, when he wrote those words, perceived and thought on what truth soever we have been able to find, yea, and whatsoever we have not been able, nor yet are, but which may be found in them.

[XXXII] 43. Lastly, O Lord, Who are God and not flesh and blood, if man did see less, could anything be concealed from "Thy good Spirit" (who shall "lead me into the land of uprightness")[2] which Thou Thyself by those words wert about to reveal to readers in times to come, though he through whom they were spoken, perhaps among many true meanings, thought on some one? which if so it be, let that which he thought on be of all the highest. But to us, O Lord, do Thou either reveal that same, or any other true one which Thou pleasest; that so, whether Thou discoverest the same to us as to that Thy servant, or some other by occasion of those words, yet Thou mayest feed us, not error deceive us. Behold, O Lord my God, how much we have written upon a few words, how much I beseech Thee! What strength of ours, yea, what ages would suffice for all Thy books in this manner? Permit me then in these more briefly to confess unto Thee, and to choose some one true, certain, and good sense that Thou shalt inspire me, although many should occur, where many may occur; this being the law of my confession, that if I should say that which Thy minister intended, that is right and best; for this should I endeavour, which if I should not attain, yet I should say that, which Thy Truth willed by his words to tell me, which revealed also unto him, what It willed.

BOOK XIII. *Continuation of the exposition of Genesis, 1; it contains the mystery of the Trinity, and a type of the formation, extension, and support of the Church.*

[I] 1. I call upon Thee, O my God, my mercy, Who createdst me, and forgottest not me, forgetting Thee. I call Thee into[3] my soul, which, by the longing Thyself inspirest into her, Thou preparest for Thee. Forsake me not now calling upon Thee, whom Thou preventedst before I called, and urgedst me with much variety of repeated calls that I would hear Thee from afar, and be converted, and call upon Thee, that calledst after me; for Thou, Lord, blottedst out all my evil deservings, so as not to repay into my hands wherewith I fell from Thee; and Thou hast prevented all my well deservings, so as to repay the work of Thy hands wherewith Thou

[1] I Tim. 1.18.   [2] Ps. 143.10.   [3] See Bk. I.2.

madest me; because before I was, Thou wert; nor was I anything, to which Thou mightest grant to be; and yet behold, I am, out of Thy goodness, preventing all this which Thou hast made me, and whereof Thou has made me. For neither hadst Thou need of me, nor am I any such good as to be helpful unto Thee, my Lord and God; not in serving Thee, as though Thou wouldest tire in working; or lest Thy power might be less, if lacking my service: nor cultivating Thy service, as a land that must remain uncultivated unless I cultivated Thee: but serving and worshipping Thee, that I might receive a well-being from Thee, from whom it comes that I have a being capable of well-being.

[II] 2. For of the fulness of Thy goodness doth Thy creature subsist, that so a good, which could no ways profit Thee, nor was of Thee (lest so it should be equal to Thee), might yet be since it could be made of Thee. For what did heaven and earth, which Thou madest in the Beginning, deserve of Thee? Let those spiritual and corporeal natures which Thou madest in Thy Wisdom say wherein they deserved of Thee, to depend thereon (even in that their several inchoate and formless state, whether spiritual or corporeal, ready to fall away into an immoderate liberty and far-distant unlikeliness unto Thee; the spiritual, though without form, superior to the corporeal though formed, and the corporeal though without form, better than were it altogether nothing), and so to depend upon Thy Word, as formless, unless by the same Word they were brought back to Thy Unity, indued with form, and from Thee the One Sovereign Good were made all very good. How did they deserve of Thee to be even without form, since they had not been even this, but from Thee?

3. How did corporeal matter deserve of Thee to be even invisible and without form?[1] seeing it were not even this, but that Thou madest it, and therefore, because it was not, could not deserve of Thee to be made. Or how could the inchoate spiritual creature deserve of Thee, even to ebb and flow darksomely like the deep, unlike Thee, unless it had been by the same Word turned to that by Whom it was created, and by Him so enlightened, become light; though not equally, yet conformably to that Form which is equal unto Thee? For as in a body, to be is not one with being beautiful, else could it not be deformed; so likewise, to a created spirit, to live is not one with living wisely; else should it be wise unchangeably. But good it is[2] for it always to hold fast to Thee[3]; lest what light it hath obtained by turning to Thee, it lose by turning from Thee, and relapse into life resembling the darksome deep. For we ourselves also, who as to the soul are a spiritual creature, turned away from Thee our light, were in that life "sometimes darkness"; and still labour amidst the relics of our darkness, until in Thy Only One we become Thy righteousness, like the mountains of God. For we have been Thy judgments, which are like the great deep.[4]

[III] 4. That which Thou saidst in the beginning of the creation, "Let there be light, and there was light"[5]; I do, not unsuitably, understand of the spiritual creature: because there was already a sort of life, which Thou mightest illuminate. But as it had no claim on Thee for a life, which could be enlightened, so neither now that it was, had it any, to be enlightened. For neither could its formless estate be pleasing unto Thee, unless it became light, and that not by existing simply, but by beholding the illuminating light, and cleaving to it; so that, that it lived, and lived happily,[6] it owes to nothing but Thy grace, being turned by a better change unto That which cannot be changed into worse or better; which Thou alone art, because Thou alone simply art; unto Thee it being not one thing to live, another to live blessedly, seeing Thyself art Thine own Blessedness.[7]

[IV] 5. What then could be wanting unto Thy good, which Thou Thyself art, although these things had either never been, or remained without form; which thou madest, not out of any want, but out of the fulness of Thy goodness, restraining them and converting them to form, not as though Thy joy were fulfilled by them? For to Thee, being perfect, is their imperfection displeasing, and hence were they perfected by Thee, and please Thee, not as wert Thou imperfect, and by their perfecting wert also to be perfected. For Thy good Spirit indeed was borne over the waters,[8] not borne up by them, as if He rested upon them. For those on whom Thy good Spirit is said to rest,[9] He causes to rest in Himself. But Thy incorruptible and unchangeable will, in itself all-sufficient for itself, was borne upon that life which Thou hadst created; to which, living is not one with happy living, seeing it liveth also, ebbing and flowing in its own darkness; for which it remaineth to be converted unto Him by Whom it was made, and to live more and more by "the fountain of life," and in His light to "see light,"[10] and to be perfected, and enlightened, and beautified.

[4]Ps. 36. 6.   [5]Gen. 1.3.   [6]Cf. *City of God*, Bk. XI. 24.
[7]*Ibid.*, Bk. XII. 1.   [8]*Gen.* 1. 2.   [9]Num. 11.25.   [10]Ps. 36. 9.

[1]Gen. 1.2.   [2]Ps. 73.28.   [3]Cf. *City of God*, Bk. XII. 1.

[V] 6. Lo, now the Trinity appears unto me in a glass darkly, which is Thou my God, because Thou, O Father, in Him Who is the Beginning of our wisdom, Which is Thy Wisdom, born of Thyself, equal unto Thee and coeternal, that is, in Thy Son, createdst heaven and earth. Much now have we said of the Heaven of heavens, and of the earth invisible and without form, and of the darksome deep, in reference to the wandering instability of its spiritual deformity, unless it had been converted unto Him from Whom it had its then degree of life, and by His enlightening became a beauteous life, and the heaven of that heaven, which was afterwards set between water and water. And under the name of God, I now held the Father, Who made these things, and under the name of Beginning, the Son, in Whom He made these things; and believing, as I did, my God as the Trinity, I searched further in His holy words, and lo, Thy Spirit moved upon the waters. Behold the Trinity, my God: Father, and Son, and Holy Ghost, Creator of all creation.

[VI] 7. But what was the cause, O true-speaking Light? Unto Thee lift I up my heart, let it not teach me vanities, dispel its darkness; and tell me, I beseech Thee, by our mother charity, tell me the reason, I beseech Thee, why after the mention of heaven, and of the earth invisible and without form, and darkness upon the deep, Thy Scripture should then at length mention Thy Spirit? Was it because it was meet that the knowledge of Him should be conveyed, as being "borne above"; and this could not be said unless that were first mentioned, "over" which Thy Spirit may be understood to have been "borne." For neither was He "borne above" the Father, nor the Son, nor could He rightly be said to be "borne above," if He were "borne over" nothing. First then was that to be spoken of, "over" which He might be "borne"; and then He, whom it was meet not otherwise to be spoken of than as being "borne." But wherefore was it not meet that the knowledge of Him should be conveyed otherwise than as being "borne above"?

[VII] 8. Hence let him that is able follow with his understanding Thy Apostle, where he thus speaks, Because Thy "love is shed abroad in our hearts by the Holy Ghost which is given unto us"[1]; and where "concerning spiritual gifts" he teacheth and sheweth unto us a more excellent way of charity[2]; and where he bows his knee, unto Thee for us, that we may know the super-eminent knowledge of the love of Christ.[3] And therefore from the beginning was He "borne" super-eminent "above the waters." To whom shall I speak this? How speak of the weight of evil desires, downwards to the steep abyss; and how charity raises up again by Thy Spirit which was "borne above the waters"? to whom shall I speak it? how speak it? For it is not in space that we are merged and emerge. What can be more, and yet what less like? They be affections, they be loves; the uncleanness of our spirit flowing away downwards with the love of cares, and the holiness of Thine raising us upward by love of unanxious repose; that we may lift our hearts unto Thee, where Thy Spirit is "borne above the waters"; and come to that super-eminent repose, when our soul shall have passed through the waters which yield no support.

[VIII] 9. Angels fell away, man's soul fell away, and thereby pointed out the abyss in that dark depth, ready for the whole spiritual creation, hadst not Thou said from the beginning, "Let there be light," and there had been light, and every obedient intelligence of Thy heavenly City had cleaved to Thee, and rested in Thy Spirit, Which is "borne" unchangeably "over" everything changeable. Otherwise, had even the heaven of heavens been in itself a darksome deep; but now it is light in the Lord. For even in that miserable restlessness of the spirits, who fell away and discovered their own darkness when bared of the clothing of Thy light, dost Thou sufficiently reveal how noble Thou madest the reasonable creature; to which nothing will suffice to yield a happy rest, less than Thee[4]; and so not even herself. For Thou, O our God, shalt lighten our darkness[5]; from Thee riseth our garment of light[6]; and then shall our darkness be as the noon day.[7] Give Thyself unto me, O my God, restore Thyself unto me; behold I love, and if it be too little, I would love more strongly. I cannot measure so as to know how much love there yet lacketh to me, ere my life may run into Thy embracements, nor turn away, until it be hidden in the hidden place of Thy Presence.[8] This only I know, that woe is me except in Thee; not only without but within myself also; and all abundance, which is not my God, is emptiness to me.

[IX] 10. But was not either the Father, or the Son, "borne above the water"? If this means, in space, like a body, then neither was the Holy Spirit; but, if the unchangeable super-eminence

[1] Rom. 5. 5.   [2] II Cor. 12. 1, 31.

[3] Eph. 3. 14-19.   [4] Cf. City of God, BK. XXII. 1.
[5] Ps. 18. 28.   [6] Ps. 104. 2.   [7] Ps. 139. 12.
[8] Ps. 31. 20.

of Divinity above all things changeable, then were both Father, and Son, and Holy Ghost borne "upon the waters." Why then is this said of Thy Spirit only, why is it said only of Him? As if He had been in place, Who is not in place, of Whom only it is written, that He is Thy gift? In Thy Gift we rest; there we enjoy Thee. Our rest is our place. Love lifts us up thither, and Thy good Spirit lifts up our lowliness from the gates of death.[1] In Thy good pleasure is our peace.[2] The body by its own weight strives towards its own place. Weight makes not downward only, but to his own place. Fire tends upward, a stone downward. They are urged by their own weight, they seek their own places. Oil poured below water is raised above the water; water poured upon oil sinks below the oil. They are urged by their own weights to seek their own places. When out of their order, they are restless; restored to order, they are at rest. My weight is my love[3]; thereby am I borne whithersoever I am borne. We are inflamed, by Thy Gift we are kindled, and are carried upwards; we glow inwardly, and go forwards. We ascend Thy ways that be in our heart,[4] and sing a song of degrees; we glow inwardly with Thy fire, with Thy good fire, and we go; because we go upwards to the peace of Jerusalem: for gladdened was I in those who said unto me, "We will go up to the house of the Lord."[5] There hath Thy good pleasure placed us, that we may desire nothing else but to abide there for ever.

[X] 11. Blessed creature which, being itself other than Thou, has known no other condition that that, so soon as it was made, it was, without any interval, by Thy Gift. Which is borne above everything changeable, borne aloft by that calling whereby Thou saidst, "Let there be light, and there was light." Whereas in us this took place at different times, in that we were darkness, and are made light[6]: but of that is only said, what it would have been, had it not been enlightened. And this is so spoken, as if it had been unsettled and darksome before; that so the cause whereby it was made otherwise might appear, namely, that being turned to the Light unfailing it became light. Whoso can, let him understand this; let him ask of Thee. Why should he trouble me, as if I could enlighten "any man that cometh into this world"?[7]

[XI] 12. Which of us comprehendeth the Almighty Trinity? and yet which speaks not of It, if indeed it be It? Rare is the soul which, while

it speaks of It, knows what it speaks of. And they contend and strive, yet, without peace, no man sees that vision. I would that men would consider these three, that are in themselves.[8] These three be indeed far other than the Trinity; I do but tell where they may practise themselves, and there prove and feel how far they be. Now the three I spake of are, to Be, to Know, and to Will. For I Am, and Know, and Will: I Am Knowing and Willing: and I Know myself to Be, and to Will: and I Will to Be, and to Know. In these three, then, let him discern that can, how inseparable a life there is, yea, one life, one mind, and one essence; yea, lastly how inseparable a distinction there is, and yet a distinction. Surely a man hath it before him; let him look into himself, and see, and tell me. But when he discovers and can say anything of these, let him not therefore think that he has found that which is above these Unchangeable, which Is unchangeably, and Knows unchangeably, and Wills unchangeably; and whether because of these three, there is in God also a Trinity, or whether all three be in Each, so that the three belong to Each; or whether both ways at once, wondrously, simply and yet manifoldly, Itself a bound unto Itself within Itself, yet unbounded; whereby It is, and is Known unto Itself, and sufficeth to Itself, unchangeably the Self-same, by the abundant greatness of its Unity—who can readily conceive this? who could any way express it? who would, any way, pronounce thereon rashly?

[XII] 13. Proceed in thy confession, say to the Lord thy God, O my faith, Holy, Holy, Holy, O Lord my God, in Thy Name have we been baptized, Father, Son, and Holy Ghost; in Thy Name do we baptize, Father, Son, and Holy Ghost,[9] because among us also, in His Christ did God make heaven and earth, namely, the spiritual and carnal people of His Church. Yea, and our earth, before it received the "form of doctrine,"[10] was invisible and without form; and we were covered with the darkness of ignorance. For Thou chastenedst man for iniquity,[11] and "Thy judgments were like the great deep" unto him.[12] But because Thy "Spirit was borne above the waters,"[13] Thy mercy forsook not our misery, and Thou saidst, "Let there be light," "Repent ye, for the kingdom of heaven is at hand."[14] Repent ye, let there be light.[15] And because our

---

[1]Ps. 9. 13.   [2]Luke, 2. 14, Vulg.
[3]Cf. *City of God*, Bk. XI. 28.   [4]Ps. 84. 5.
[5]Ps. 122. 1.   [6]Eph. 5. 8.   [7]John, 1. 9.

[8]See also *City of God*, bk. XI. 24, 26, 27.
[9]Matt. 28. 19.   [10]Rom. 6, 17.   [11]Ps. 39. 11.
[12]Ps. 36. 6.   [13]Gen. 1. 3.   [14]Matt. 3. 2.
[15]Baptism was anciently called illumination, as Heb. 6. 4; Ps. 42.2.

soul was troubled within us,[1] we remembered Thee, O Lord, from the land of Jordan, and that mountain[2] equal unto Thyself, but little for our sakes; and our darkness displeased us, we turned unto Thee "and there was light." And, behold, we were sometimes darkness, but now light in the Lord.[3]

[XIII] 14. But as yet "by faith and not by sight,"[4] for "by hope we are saved"; but hope that is seen, is not hope."[5] As yet doth deep call unto deep, but now "in the voice of Thy waterspouts."[6] As yet doth he that saith, "I could not speak unto you as unto spiritual, but as unto carnal,"[7] even he as yet doth not think himself to have apprehended, and forgetteth those things which are behind, and reacheth forth to those which are before,[8] and groaneth being burthened,[9] and his soul thirsteth after the Living God, as the hart after the water-brooks, and saith, "When shall I come?" [10] "desiring to be clothed upon with his house which is from heaven," [11] and calleth upon this lower deep, saying, "And be not conformed to this world; but be ye transformed by the renewing of your mind." [12] And "Be not children in understanding, but in malice, be ye children," that in "understanding ye may be perfect"[13]; and "O foolish Galatians, who hath bewitched you?" [14] But now no longer in his own voice; but in Thine who sentest Thy Spirit from above[15]; through Him "who ascended up on high," [16] and set open the flood-gates of His gifts,[17] that the force of His streams might make glad the city of God.[18] Him doth this "friend of the bridegroom" [19] sigh after, having now the first-fruits of the Spirit laid up with Him, yet still groaning within himself, waiting for the adoption, to wit, the redemption of his body[20]; to Him he sighs, a member of the Bride; for Him he is jealous, as being a friend of the Bridegroom[19]; for Him he is jealous, not for himself; because in the voice of Thy "waterspouts," not in his own voice, doth he call to that other depth, over whom being jealous he feareth, lest as the serpent beguiled Eve through his subtilty, so their minds should be corrupted from the purity that is in our Bridegroom Thy only Son.[21] O what a light of beauty will that be, when we shall "see Him as He is,"[22] and those

tears be passed away, which "have been my meat day and night, whilst they daily say unto me, 'Where is now Thy God?' "[23]

[XIV] 15. Behold, I too say, O my God, Where art Thou? see, where Thou art! in Thee I breathe a little, when I pour out my soul by myself in the voice of joy and praise, the sound of him that keeps holy-day.[24] And yet again "it is sad," because it relapseth, and becomes a deep, or rather perceives itself still to be a deep. Unto it speaks my faith which Thou hast kindled to enlighten my feet in the night, "Why art thou sad, O my soul, and why dost thou trouble me? Hope in the Lord"[25]; His "word is a lamp unto thy feet"[26]: hope and endure, until the night, the mother of the wicked, until the wrath of the Lord, be overpast,[27] whereof we also were once children, who were sometimes darkness,[28] relics whereof we bear about us in our body, dead because of sin[29]; "until the day break, and the shadows fly away." [30] "Hope thou in the Lord"; in the morning I shall stand in Thy presence, and contemplate Thee[31]; I shall for ever confess unto Thee.[32] In the morning I shall stand in Thy presence, and shall see "the health of my countenance,"[33] my God, Who also shall quicken our mortal bodies, by the Spirit that dwelleth in us,[34] because He hath in mercy been borne over our inner darksome and floating deep; from Whom we have in this pilgrimage received "an earnest," [35] that we should now be light; whilst we "are saved by hope," [36] and are the children of light, and the children of the day, not the children of the night, nor of the darkness, which yet sometimes we were.[37] Betwixt whom and us, in this uncertainty of human knowledge, Thou only dividest; Thou, Who provest our hearts,[38] and callest the light, day, and the darkness, night.[39] For who discerneth us, but Thou? And what have we, that we have not received of Thee? [40] out of the same lump vessels unto honour, whereof others also are made unto dishonour.[41]

[XV] 16. Or who, except Thou, our God, made for us that firmament[42] of authority over us in Thy Divine Scripture? As it is said, for heaven shall be folded up like a scroll[43]; and now is it stretched over us like a skin.[44] For Thy Divine Scripture is of more eminent authority,

---

[1]Ps. 42. 6.　　[2]Christ.　　[3]Eph. 5. 8.　　[4]II Cor. 5. 7.
[5]Rom. 8. 24.　　[6]Ps. 42. 7.　　[7]I Cor. 3. 1.
[8]Phil. 3. 13.　　[9]II Cor. 5. 2, 4.　　[10]Ps. 42. 20.
[11]II Cor. 5. 2.　　[12]Rom. 12. 2.
[13]I Cor. 14. 20 (margin).　　[14]Gal. 3. 1.　　[15]Acts, 2. 19.
[16]Eph. 4. 8.　　[17]Mal. 3. 10.　　[18]Ps. 46. 4.
[19]John, 3. 29.　　[20]Rom. 8. 23.
[21]II Cor. 11. 3; I John, 3. 3.　　[22]Ibid., ver. 2.

[23]Ps. 42. 3.　　[24]Ibid., ver. 4.　　[25]Ibid., ver. 5.
[26]Ps. 119. 105.　　[27]Job, 14. 13.　　[28]Eph. 2. 3, 8.
[29]Rom. 8. 10.　　[30]Cant. 2, 17.　　[31]Ps. 10. 3.
[32]Ps. 30. 12.　　[33]Ps. 43. 5.　　[34]Rom. 8. 11.
[35]II Cor. 1. 22.　　[36]Rom. 8. 24.
[37]Eph. 5. 8; I Thess. 5. 5.　　[38]Ps. 7. 9.
[39]Gen. 1. 5.　　[40]I Cor. 4. 7.　　[41]Rom. 9. 21.
[42]Gen. 1. 6.　　[43]Isa. 34. 4; Rev. 6. 14.
[44]Ps. 104. 2.

since those mortals by whom Thou dispensest it unto us underwent mortality. And Thou knowest, Lord, Thou knowest, how Thou with skins didst clothe men,[1] when they by sin became mortal. Whence Thou hast like a skin stretched out the firmament of Thy book, that is, Thy harmonizing words, which by the ministry of mortal men Thou spreadest over us. For by their very death was that solid firmament of authority, in Thy discourses set forth by them, more eminently extended over all that be under it; which, whilst they lived here, was not so eminently extended. Thou hadst not as yet spread abroad the heaven like a skin; Thou hadst not as yet enlarged in all directions the glory of their deaths.

17. Let us look, O Lord, "upon the heavens, the work of Thy fingers"[2]; clear from our eyes that cloud which Thou hast spread under them. There is Thy testimony, which giveth wisdom unto the little ones[3]; perfect, O my God, Thy praise out of the mouth of babes and sucklings.[4] For we know no other books which so destroy pride, which so destroy the enemy and the defender,[5] who resisteth Thy reconciliation by defending his own sins. I know not, Lord, I know not any other such "pure"[6] words, which so persuade me to confess, and make my neck pliant to Thy yoke, and invite me to serve Thee for nought. Let me understand them, good Father; grant this to me, who am placed under them; because for those placed under them, hast Thou established them.

18. Other "waters" there be "above" this "firmament," I believe immortal, and separated from earthly corruption. Let them praise Thy Name, let them praise Thee, the super-celestial people, Thine angels, who have no need to gaze up at this firmament, or by reading to know of Thy Word. For they always behold Thy face,[7] and there read without any syllables in time what willeth Thy eternal will; they read, they choose, they love. They are ever reading; and that never passes away which they read; for by choosing, and by loving, they read the very unchangeableness of Thy counsel. Their book is never closed, nor their scroll folded up;[8] seeing Thou Thyself art this to them, and art eternally; because Thou hast ordained them above this firmament, which Thou hast firmly settled over the infirmity of the lower people, where they might gaze up and learn Thy mercy, announcing in time Thee Who madest times. "For Thy mer-

cy, O Lord, is in the heavens, and Thy truth reacheth unto the clouds."[9] The clouds pass away, but the heaven abideth. The preachers of Thy word pass out of this life into another; but Thy Scripture is spread abroad over the people, even unto the end of the world. Yet heaven and earth also shall pass away, but Thy words shall not pass away.[10] Because the scroll shall be rolled together; and the grass over which it was spread shall with the goodliness of it pass away; but Thy Word remaineth for ever,[11] which now appeareth unto us under the dark image of the clouds, and through the glass of the heavens, not as it is[12]; because we also, though the well-beloved of Thy Son, yet it hath not yet appeared what we shall be.[13] He looketh through the lattice[14] of our flesh, and He spake us tenderly, and kindled us, and we ran after His odours.[15] But "when He shall appear, then shall we be like Him, for we shall see Him as He is." As He is, Lord, will our sight be.

[XVI] 19. For altogether, as Thou art, Thou only knowest; Who art unchangeably, and knowest unchangeably, and willest unchangeably. And Thy Essence Knoweth and Willeth unchangeably; and Thy Knowledge Is and Willeth unchangeably; and Thy Will Is and Knoweth unchangeably. Nor seemeth it right in Thine eyes that, as the Unchangeable Light knoweth Itself, so should it be known by the thing enlightened, and changeable. Therefore is my soul like a "land where no water is,"[16] because as it cannot of itself enlighten itself, so can it not of itself satisfy itself. For so is the fountain of life with Thee, like as in Thy light we shall see light.[17]

[XVII] 20. Who gathered the embittered together into one society? For they have all one end, a temporal and earthly felicity, for attaining whereof they do all things, though they waver up and down with an innumerable variety of cares. Who, Lord, but Thou, saidst, "Let the waters be gathered together into one place, and let the dry land appear,"[18] which thirsteth after Thee?[19] For the sea also is Thine, and Thou hast made it, and Thy hands prepared the dry land.[20] Nor is the bitterness of men's wills, but the gathering together of the waters, called sea; for Thou restrainest the wicked desires of men's souls, and settest them their bounds, how far they may be allowed to pass,[21] that their waves

---

[1]Gen. 3. 21.   [2]Ps. 8. 3.   [3]Ps. 19. 7.
[4]Ps. 8. 2.   [5]See above, bk. IV. 26.
[6]Ps. 19. 8.   [7]Matt. 18. 10.   [8]Isa. 24. 4.

[9]Ps. 36. 5.   [10]Matt. 24. 35.   [11]Isa. 40. 6–8.
[12]I Cor. 13. 12.   [13]I John, 3. 2.   [14]Cant. 2. 9.
[15]Cant. 1. 3.   [16]Ps. 63. 1.   [17]Ps. 36. 9.
[18]Gen. 1. 9.   [19]Ps. 143. 6; 63. 1.   [20]Ps. 95. 5.
[21]Ps. 104. 9; Job, 38. 11, 12.

may break one against another; and thus makest Thou it a sea, by the order of Thy dominion over all things.

21. But the souls that thirst after Thee, and that appear before Thee (being by other bounds divided from the society of the sea), Thou waterest by a sweet spring, that the earth may bring forth her fruit, and Thou, Lord God, so commanding, our soul may bud forth works of mercy according to their kind, loving our neighbour in the relief of his bodily necessities, having seed in itself according to its likeness[1]; when, from feeling of our infirmity, we compassionate so as to relieve the needy; helping them as we would be helped if we were in like need; not only in things easy, as in "herb yielding seed," but also in the protection of our assistance, with our best strength, like the tree yielding fruit: that is, well-doing in rescuing him that suffers wrong, from the hand of the powerful, and giving him the shelter of protection, by the mighty strength of just judgment.

[XVIII] 22. So, Lord, so, I beseech Thee, let there spring up, as Thou doest, as Thou givest cheerfulness and ability, let "truth spring out of the earth, and righteousness look down from heaven,"[2] and let there be "lights in the firmament."[3] Let us break our bread to the hungry, and bring the houseless poor to our house. Let us clothe the naked, and despise not those of our own flesh.[4] Which fruits having sprung out of the earth, see it is good[5]; and let our temporary light break forth[6]; and ourselves, from this lower fruitfulness of action, arriving at the delightfulness of contemplation, obtaining the Word of Life above, appear like lights in the world,[7] cleaving to the firmament of Thy Scripture. For there Thou instructest us, to divide between the things intellectual and things of sense, as betwixt the day and the night; or between souls, given either to things intellectual or things of sense, so that now not Thou only in the secret of Thy judgment, as before the firmament was made, dividest between the light and the darkness, but Thy spiritual children also set and ranked in the same firmament (now that Thy grace is laid open throughout the world) may give light upon the earth, and divide betwixt the day and the night, and be for signs of times, that "old things are passed away," and, "behold, all things are become new";[8] and "that our salvation is nearer than when we believed":[9] and "that the night is far spent, and the day is

at hand":[9] and that Thou wilt crown Thy year with blessing,[10] sending the labourers of Thy goodness into Thy harvest,[11] in sowing whereof others have laboured, sending also into another field, whose harvest shall be in the end.[12] Thus grantest Thou the prayers of him that asketh, and blessest the years of the just;[13] but Thou art the same, and in Thy years which fail not,[14] Thou preparest a garner for our passing years. For Thou by an eternal counsel dost in their proper seasons bestow heavenly blessings upon the earth.

23. For to one is given by the Spirit the word of wisdom, as it were the greater light, for their sakes who are delighted with the light of perspicuous truth, as it were for the rule of the day. To another the word of knowledge by the same Spirit, as it were the lesser light; to another faith; to another the gift of healing; to another the working of miracles; to another prophecy; to another discerning of spirits; to another divers kinds of tongues. And all these as it were stars. For all these worketh the one and self-same spirit, dividing to every man his own as He will;[15] and causing stars to appear manifestly, to profit withal.[16] But the word of knowledge, wherein are contained all Sacraments,[17] which are varied in their seasons as it were the moon, and those other notices of gifts, which are reckoned up in order, as it were stars, inasmuch as they come short of that brightness of wisdom, which gladdens the forementioned day, are only for the rule of the night. For they are necessary to such, as that Thy most prudent servant could not speak unto as unto spiritual, but as unto carnal;[18] even he, who speaketh wisdom among those that are perfect.[19] But the natural man, as it were a babe in Christ and fed on milk, until he be strengthened for solid meat[20] and his eye be enabled to behold the Sun, let him not dwell in a night forsaken of all light, but be content with the light of the moon and the stars. So dost Thou speak to us, our All-wise God, in Thy Book, Thy firmament; that we may discern all things, in an admirable contemplation; though as yet in signs, and in times, and in days, and in years.

[XIX] 24. But first, "wash you, make you clean"; put away evil from your souls, and from before mine eyes, that the dry land may appear. Learn to do good, "judge the fatherless, plead for the widow,"[21] that the earth may bring forth

[1]Gen. 1. 12.   [2]Ps. 85. 11.   [3]Gen. 1. 14.
[4]Isa. 58. 7.   [5]Gen. 1. 12.   [6]Isa. 58. 8.
[7]Phil. 2. 15.   [8]II Cor. 5. 17.   [9]Rom. 13. 11, 12.

[10]Ps. 65. 11.   [11]Matt. 9. 38.   [12]Matt. 13. 30.
[13]Prov. 10. 6.   [14]Ps. 102. 27.   [15]I Cor. 12. 8–11.
[16]Ibid., ver. 7.   [17]I Cor. 13. 2.   [18]I Cor. 3. 1.
[19]I Cor. 2. 6.   [20]I Cor. 3. 2; Heb. 5. 12.
[21]Isa. 1. 16, 17.

the green herb for meat, and the tree bearing fruit;[1] and come, let us reason together, saith the Lord,[2] that there may be lights in the firmament of the heaven, and they may shine upon the earth.[3] That rich man asked of the good Master, what he should do to attain eternal life.[4] Let the good Master tell him (whom he thought no more than man; but He is "good" because He is God), let Him tell him, if he would "enter into life," he must "keep the commandments":[5] let him put away from him the bitterness of malice and wickedness;[6] not kill, not commit adultery, not steal, not bear false witness; that the dry land may appear, and bring forth the honouring of father and mother, and the love of our neighbour.[7] All these, saith he, have I kept.[8] Whence then so many thorns, if the earth be fruitful? Go, root up the spreading thickets of covetousness; sell that thou hast, and be filled with fruit, by giving to the poor, and thou shalt have treasure in heaven; and follow the Lord "if thou wilt be perfect," [9] associated with them, among whom He speaketh wisdom, Who knoweth what to distribute to the day and to the night, that thou also mayest know it, and for thee there may be lights in the firmament of heaven; which will not be, unless thy heart be there:[10] nor will that either be, unless there thy treasure be; as thou hast heard of the good Master. But that barren earth was grieved;[11] and the thorns choked the word.[12]

25. But you, "chosen generation,"[13] you weak things of the world, who have forsaken all that ye may "follow the Lord"; go after Him, and "confound the mighty";[14] go after Him, ye beautiful feet,[15] and shine ye in the firmament,[16] that the heavens may declare His glory, dividing between the light of the perfect, though not as the angels, and the darkness of the little ones, though not despised. Shine over the earth; and let the day, lightened by the sun, utter unto day, speech of wisdom; and night, shining with the moon, shew unto night the word of knowledge.[17] The moon and stars shine for the night; yet doth not the night obscure them, seeing they give it light in its degree. For behold God saying, as it were, "Let there be lights in the firmament of heaven"; there came suddenly a sound from heaven, as it had been the rushing of a mighty wind, and there appeared cloven tongues like as of fire, and it sat upon each of them.[18] And there

were made lights in the firmament of heaven, having the word of life.[19] Run ye to and fro everywhere, ye holy fires, ye beauteous fires; for ye are the light of the world, nor are ye put under a bushel;[20] He whom you cleave unto is exalted, and hath exalted you. Run ye to and fro, and be known unto all nations.

[XX] 26. Let the sea also conceive and bring forth your works; and let the waters bring forth the moving creature that hath life.[21] For ye, "separating the precious from the vile," [22] are made the mouth of God, by whom He saith, "Let the waters bring forth," not the living creature which the earth brings forth, but the moving creature having life, and the fowls that fly above the earth. For Thy Sacraments, O God, by the ministry of Thy holy ones, have moved amid the waves of temptations of the world, to hallow the Gentiles in Thy Name, in Thy Baptism. And amid these things, many great wonders were wrought, as it were great whales; and the voices of Thy messengers flying above the earth, in the open firmament of Thy Book; that being set over them, as their authority under which they were to fly, whithersoever they went. For "there is no speech nor language, where their voice is not heard"; seeing their sound [23] "is gone through all the earth, and their words to the end of the world," because Thou, Lord, multipliedst them by blessing.[24]

27. Speak I untruly, or do I mingle and confound, and not distinguish between the lucid knowledge of these things in the firmament of heaven, and the material works in the wavy sea, and under the firmament of heaven? For of those things whereof the knowledge is substantial and defined, without any increase by generation, as it were lights of wisdom and knowledge, yet even of them, the material operations are many and divers; and, one thing growing out of another, they are multiplied by Thy blessing, O God, who hast refreshed the fastidiousness of mortal senses; that so one thing in the understanding of our mind may, by the motions of the body, be many ways set out and expressed. These Sacraments have the waters brought forth, but in Thy word. The necessities of the people estranged from the eternity of Thy truth have brought them forth, but in Thy Gospel; because the waters themselves cast them forth, the diseased bitterness whereof was the cause, why they were sent forth in Thy Word.

28. Now are all things fair that Thou hast made; but behold, Thyself art unutterably

---

[1]Gen. 1. 11, 30.   [2]Isa. 1. 18.   [3]Gen. 1. 15.
[4]Matt. 19. 16.   [5]Ibid., ver. 17.   [6]I Cor. 5. 8.
[7]Matt. 19. 16–19.   [8]Ibid., ver. 20.   [9]Ibid., ver. 21.
[10]Matt. 6. 21.   [11]Matt. 19. 22.   [12]Matt. 13. 7, 22.
[13]I Pet. 2. 9.   [14]I Cor. 1. 27.   [15]Isa. 52. 7.
[16]Dan. 12. 3.   [17]Ps. 19.   [18]Acts, 2. 3.

[19]I John, 1. 1.   [20]Matt. 5. 14.   [21]Gen. 1. 20.
[22]Jer. 15. 19.   [23]Ps. 19. 3, 4.   [24]Gen. 1. 4.

fairer, That madest all; from whom had not Adam fallen, the brackishness of the sea had never flowed out of him, that is, the human race so profoundly curious, and tempestuously swelling, and restlessly tumbling up and down; and then had there been no need of Thy dispensers to work in many waters, after a corporeal and sensible manner, mysterious doings and sayings. For such those moving and flying creatures now seem to me to mean, whereby people being initiated and consecrated by corporeal Sacraments should not further profit, unless their soul had a spiritual life, and unless after the word of admission it looked forwards to perfection.

[XXI] 29. And hereby, in Thy Word, not the deepness of the sea, but the earth separated from the bitterness of the waters, brings forth, 1.ot the moving creature that hath life,[1] but the living soul.[2] For now hath it no more need of baptism, as the heathen have, and as itself had, when it was covered with the waters (for no other entrance is there into the kingdom of heaven,[3] since Thou hast appointed that this should be the entrance); nor does it seek after wonderfulness of miracles to work belief; for it is not such that, unless it sees signs and wonders, it will not believe,[4] now that the faithful earth is separated from the waters that were bitter with infidelity; and "tongues are for a sign, not to them that believe, but to them that believe not."[5] Neither then does that earth which Thou hast founded upon the waters need that flying kind, which at Thy word the waters brought forth. Send Thou Thy word into it by Thy messengers: for we speak of their working, yet it is Thou that workest in them that they may work out a living soul in it. The earth brings it forth, because the earth is the cause that they work this in the soul; as the sea was the cause that they wrought upon the moving creatures that have life, and the fowls that fly under the firmament of heaven, of whom the earth hath no need; although it feeds upon that fish which was taken out of the deep, upon that table which Thou hast prepared in the presence of them that believe.[6] For therefore was He taken out of the deep, that He might feed the dry land; and the fowl, though bred in the sea, is yet multiplied upon the earth. For of the first preachings of the Evangelists, man's infidelity was the cause; yet are the faithful also exhorted and blessed by them manifoldly, from day to day. But the living soul takes his beginning from the earth; for it profits only those already among the Faithful,

to contain themselves from the love of this world, that so their soul may live unto Thee, which was dead while it lived in pleasures;[7] in death-bringing pleasures, Lord, for Thou, Lord, art the life-giving delight of the pure heart.

30. Now then let Thy ministers work upon the earth, not as upon the waters of infidelity, by preaching and speaking by miracles, and Sacraments, and mystic words; wherein ignorance, the mother of admiration, might be intent upon them, out of a reverence towards those secret signs. For such is the entrance unto the Faith for the sons of Adam forgetful of Thee, while they hide themselves from Thy face,[8] and become a darksome deep. But let Thy ministers work now as on the dry land, separated from the whirlpools of the great deep; and let them be a pattern unto the Faithful, by living before them, and stirring them up to imitation. For thus do men hear, so as not to hear only, but to do so also. Seek the Lord, and your soul shall live,[9] that the earth may bring forth the living soul. "Be not conformed to the world."[10] Contain yourselves from it; the soul lives by avoiding what it dies by affecting. Contain yourselves from the ungoverned wilderness of pride, the sluggish voluptuousness of luxury, and the false name of knowledge:[11] that so the wild beasts may be tamed, the cattle broken to the yoke, the serpents, harmless. For these be the motions of our mind under an allegory; that is to say, the haughtiness of pride, the delight of lust, and the poison of curiosity are the motions of a dead soul; for the soul dies not so as to lose all motion; because it dies by forsaking the fountain of life,[12] and so is taken up by this transitory world, and is conformed unto it.

31. But Thy word, O God, is the fountain of life eternal; and passeth not away; wherefore this departure of the soul is restrained by Thy word, when it is said unto us, "Be not conformed unto this world";[13] that so the earth may in the fountain of life bring forth a living soul; that is, a soul made continent in Thy Word, by Thy Evangelists, by following the followers of Thy Christ.[14] For this is after his kind; because a man is wont to imitate his friend. "Be ye," saith he, "as I am, for I also am as you are."[15] Thus in this living soul shall there be good beasts, in meekness of action (for Thou hast commanded, Go on with thy business in meekness, so shalt thou be beloved by all men);[16] and good cattle, which neither if they eat, shall they

---

[1]Gen. 1. 20.   [2]Gen. 2. 7.   [3]John, 3. 5.
[4]John, 4. 48.   [5]I Cor. 14. 22.   [6]Ps. 23. 5.

[7]I Tim. 5. 6.   [8]Gen. 3. 8.   [9]Ps. 69. 32.   [10]Rom. 12. 2.
[11]I Tim. 6. 20.   [12]Jer. 2. 13.   [13]Rom. 12. 2.
[14]I Cor. 11. 1.   [15]Gal. 4. 12.   [16]Ecclus. 3. 17, etc.

over-abound, nor, if they eat not, have any lack;[1] and good serpents, not dangerous to do hurt, but "wise"[2] to take heed; and only making so much search into this temporal nature as may suffice that eternity be clearly seen, being understood by the things that are made."[3] For these creatures are obedient unto reason, when, being restrained from deadly prevailing upon us, they live, and are good.

32. For behold, O Lord, our God, our Creator, when our affections have been restrained from the love of the world, by which we died through evil-living; and begun to be a "living soul," through good living; and Thy word which Thou spakest by Thy apostle is made good in us, "Be not conformed to this world"; there follows that also, which Thou presently subjoinedst, saying, "But be ye transformed by the renewing of your mind";[4] not now after your kind, as though following your neighbour who went before you, nor as living after the example of some better man (for Thou saidst not, "Let man be made after his kind." but, Let us make man after our own image and similitude)[5] that we might prove what Thy will is. For to this purpose said that dispenser of Thine (who begat children by the Gospel)[6] that he might not for ever have them "babes," whom he must be fain to feed with milk, and cherish as a nurse;[7] "be ye transformed," saith he "by the renewing of your mind, that ye may prove what is that good and acceptable and perfect will of God."[8] Wherefore Thou sayest not, "Let man be made," but "Let us make man." Nor saidst Thou, "according to his kind," but "after our image and likeness." For man, being renewed in his mind, and beholding and understanding Thy truth, needs not man as his director,[9] so as to follow after his kind; but by Thy direction proveth what is that good, that acceptable, and perfect will of Thine; yea, Thou teachest him, now made capable, to discern the Trinity of the Unity, and the Unity of the Trinity. Wherefore to that said in the plural, "Let us make man," is yet subjoined in the singular, "And God made man"; and to that said in the plural, "After our likeness," is subjoined in the singular, "After the image of God."[10] Thus is man renewed in the knowledge of God, after the image of Him that created him;[11] and being made spiritual, he judgeth all things (all things which are to be judged), "yet himself is judged of no man."[12]

[XXIII] 33. But that he judgeth all things, this answers to his having dominion over the fish of the sea, and over the fowls of the air, and over all cattle and wild beasts, and over all the earth, and over every creeping thing that creepeth upon the earth. For this he doth by the understanding of his mind, whereby he perceiveth the things "of the Spirit of God";[13] whereas otherwise, man being placed in honour, had no understanding, and is compared unto the brute beasts, and is become like unto them.[14] In Thy Church therefore, O our God, according to Thy grace which Thou hast bestowed upon it (for we are Thy workmanship created unto good works),[15] not those only who are spiritually set over, but they also who spiritually are subject to those that are set over them, for in this way didst Thou make man male and female,[10] in Thy grace spiritual, where, according to the sex of body, there is neither male nor female, because neither Jew nor Grecian, neither bond nor free.[16] —Spiritual persons (whether such as are set over, or such as obey) do judge spiritually; not of that spiritual knowledge which shines in the firmament (for they ought not to judge as to so supreme authority), nor may they judge of Thy Book itself, even though something there shineth not clearly; for we submit our understanding unto it, and hold for certain that even what is closed to our sight is yet rightly and truly spoken.[17] For so man, though now spiritual and renewed in the knowledge of God after His image that created him, ought to be "a doer of the law, not a judge."[18] Neither doth he judge of that distinction of spiritual and carnal men, who are known unto Thine eyes, O our God, and have not as yet discovered themselves unto us by works, that by their fruits we might know them;[19] but Thou, Lord, dost even now know them, and hast divided and called them in secret, or ever the firmament was made. Nor doth he, though spiritual, judge the unquiet people of this world; for what hath he to do, to judge them are without,[20] knowing not which of them shall hereafter come into the sweetness of Thy grace, and which continue in the perpetual bitterness of ungodliness?

34. Man therefore, whom Thou hast made after Thine own image, received not dominion over the lights of heaven, nor over that hidden heaven itself, nor over the day and the night, which Thou calledst before the foundation of the heaven, nor over the gathering together of

---

[1]I Cor. 8. 8.   [2]Matt. 10. 16.   [3]Rom. 1. 20.
[4]Rom. 12. 2.   [5]Gen. 1. 26.   [6]I Cor. 4. 15.
[7]I Thess. 2. 7.   [8]Rom. 12. 2.   [9]Jer. 31. 34.
[10]Gen. 1. 27.   [11]Col. 3. 10.   [12]I Cor. 2. 15.

[13]I Cor. 2. 14.   [14]Ps. 49. 20.   [15]Eph. 2. 10.
[16]Gal. 3. 28.   [17]See *City of God*, BK. XI. 3.
[18]Ias. 4. 2.   [19]Matt. 8. 20.   [20]I Cor. 5. 12.

the waters, which is the sea; but He received
dominion over the fishes of the sea, and the
fowls of the air, and over all cattle, and over all
the earth, and over all creeping things which
creep upon the earth. For He judgeth and approveth what He findeth right, and He disal-
loweth what He findeth amiss, whether in the
celebration of those Sacraments by which such
are initiated, as Thy mercy searches out in
many waters; or in that in which that Fish is
set forth which, taken out of the deep, the devout earth feedeth upon; or in the expressions
and signs of words, subject to the authority of
Thy Book—such signs as proceed out of the
mouth, and sound forth, flying as it were under
the firmament, by interpreting, expounding, discoursing, disputing, consecrating, or praying unto Thee, so that the people may answer,
"Amen." The vocal pronouncing of all which
words is occasioned by the deep of this world,
and the blindness of the flesh, which cannot see
thoughts; so that there is need to speak aloud
into the ears; so that, although flying fowls be
multiplied upon the earth, yet they derive their
beginning from the waters. The spiritual man
judgeth also by allowing of what is right, and
disallowing what he finds amiss in the works
and lives of the faithful; their alms, as it were
"the earth bringing forth fruit," and of the "living soul," living by the taming of the affections,
in chastity, in fasting, in holy meditations; and
of those things which are perceived by the senses
of the body. Upon all these is he now said to
judge, wherein he hath also power of correction.

35. But what is this, and what kind of mystery? Behold, Thou blessest mankind, O Lord,
that they may "increase and multiply, and replenish the earth"[1]; dost Thou not thereby give
us a hint to understand something? Why didst
Thou not as well bless the light, which Thou
calledst day; nor the firmament of heaven, nor
the lights, nor the stars, nor the earth, nor the
sea? I might say that Thou, O God, Who created
us after Thine Image, I might say that it had
been Thy good pleasure to bestow this blessing
peculiarly upon man, hadst Thou not in like
manner blessed the fishes and the whales, that
they should increase and multiply, and replenish the waters of the sea, and that the fowls
should be multiplied upon the earth. I might say
likewise that this blessing pertained properly unto such creatures as are bred of their own kind,
had I found it given to the fruit-trees, and
plants, and beasts of the earth. But now neither
unto the herbs, nor the trees, nor the beasts, nor

[1]Gen. i. 28.

serpents is it said, "Increase and multiply"; notwithstanding all these, as well as the fishes,
fowls, or men, do by generation increase and
continue their kind.

36. What then shall I say, O Truth my Light?
"That it was idly said, and without meaning?"
Not so, O Father of piety, far be it from a minister of Thy word to say so. And if I understand
not what Thou meanest by that phrase, let my
betters, that is, those of more understanding
than myself, make better use of it, according as
Thou, my God, hast given to each man to understand. But let my confession also be pleasing
in Thine eyes, wherein I confess unto Thee that
I believe, O Lord, that Thou spakest not so in
vain; nor will I suppress what this lesson suggests to me. For it is true, nor do I see what
should hinder me from thus understanding the
figurative sayings of Thy Bible. For I know a
thing to be manifoldly signified by corporeal expressions, which is understood one way by the
mind; and that understood many ways in the
mind, which is signified one way by corporeal
expression. Behold, the single love of God and
our neighbour, by what manifold sacraments,
and innumerable languages, and in each several
language, in how innumerable modes of speaking, it is corporeally expressed. Thus do the offspring of the waters increase and multiply. Observe again, whosoever readest this; behold, what
Scripture delivers, and the voice pronounces
one only way, "In the Beginning God created
heaven and earth"; is it not understood manifoldly, not through any deceit of error, but by
various kinds of true senses? Thus do man's offspring "increase" and "multiply."

37. If therefore we conceive of the natures of
the things themselves, not allegorically, but
properly, then does the phrase "increase and
multiply" agree unto all things that come of
seed. But if we treat of the words as figuratively
spoken (which I rather suppose to be the purpose of the Scripture, which doth not, surely,
superfluously ascribe this benediction to the offspring of aquatic animals and man only), then
do we find "multitude" to belong to creatures
spiritual as well as corporeal, as in heaven and
earth, and to souls both righteous and unrighteous, as in light and darkness; and to holy authors who have been the ministers of the Law
unto us, as in the firmament which is settled betwixt the waters and the waters; and to the society of people yet in the bitterness of infidelity,
as in the sea; and to the zeal of holy souls, as in
the dry land; and to works of mercy belonging
to this present life, as in the herbs bearing seed,

and in trees bearing fruit; and to spiritual gifts set forth for edification, as in the lights of heaven; and to affections formed unto temperance, as in the living soul. In all these instances we meet with multitudes, abundance, and increase; but what shall in such wise "increase and multiply" that one thing may be expressed many ways, and one expression understood many ways, we find not, except in signs corporeally expressed, and in things mentally conceived. By signs corporeally pronounced we understand the generations of the waters, necessarily occasioned by the depth of the flesh; by things mentally conceived, human generations, on account of the fruitfulness of reason. And for this end do we believe Thee, Lord, to have said to these kinds, "Increase and multiply." For in this blessing I conceive Thee to have granted us a power and a faculty, both to express several ways what we understand but one, and to understand several ways what we read to be obscurely delivered but in one. Thus are the waters of the sea replenished, which are not moved but by several significations; thus with human increase is the earth also replenished, whose dryness appeareth in its longing,[1] and reason ruleth over it.

[XXV] 38. I would also say, O Lord my God, what the following Scripture minds me of; yea, I will say, and not fear. For I will say the truth, Thyself inspiring me with what Thou willedst me to deliver out of those words. But by no other inspiration than Thine do I believe myself to speak truth, seeing Thou art the Truth, and every man a liar.[2] He therefore "that speaketh a lie speaketh of his own";[3] that therefore I may speak truth, I will speak of Thine. Behold, Thou hast given unto us for food "every herb bearing seed" which is upon all the earth, "and every tree, in which is the fruit of a tree yielding seed."[4] And not to us alone, but also to all the fowls of the air, and to the beasts of the earth, and to all creeping things;[5] but unto the fishes and to the great whales, hast Thou not given them. Now we said that by these fruits of the earth were signified, and figured in an allegory, the works of mercy which are provided for the necessities of this life out of the fruitful earth. Such an earth was the devout Onesiphorus, unto whose house Thou gavest mercy, because he often refreshed Thy Paul, and was not ashamed of his chain.[6] Thus did also the brethren, and such fruit did they bear, who out of Macedonia, supplied what was lacking to

him.[7] But how grieved he for some trees, which did not afford him the fruit due unto him, where he saith, "At my first answer no man stood by me, but all men forsook me. I pray God that it may not be laid to their charge."[8] For these fruits are due to such as minister the spiritual doctrine unto us out of their understanding of the divine mysteries; and they are due to them, as men; yea, and due to them also as the living soul, which giveth itself as an example, in all continency; and due unto them also as flying creatures, for their blessings which are multiplied upon the earth, because their sound went out into all lands.[9]

[XXVI] 39. But they are fed by these fruits, that are delighted with them; nor are they delighted with them "whose God is their belly."[10] For neither in them that yield them are the things yielded the fruit, but with what mind they yield them. He therefore that served God, and not his own belly,[11] I plainly see why he rejoiced; I see it, and I rejoice with him. For he had received from the Philippians what they had sent by Epaphroditus[12] unto him: and yet I perceive why he rejoiced. For whereat he rejoiced upon that he fed; for, speaking in truth, "I rejoiced," saith he "greatly in the Lord, that now at the last your care of me hath flourished again, wherein ye were also careful,"[13] but it had become wearisome unto you. These Philippians then had now dried up with a long weariness, and withered as it were as to bearing this fruit of a good work; and he rejoiceth for them, that they flourished again, not for himself, that they supplied his wants. Therefore subjoins he, "not that I speak in respect of want, for I have learned in whatsoever state I am, therewith to be content. I know both how to be abased, and I know how to abound; everywhere and in all things I am instructed both to be full, and to be hungry; both to abound, and to suffer need. I can do all things through Him Which strengtheneth me."[14]

40. Whereat then rejoicest thou, O great Paul? whereat rejoicest thou? whereon feedest thou, O man, renewed in the knowledge of God, after the image of Him that created thee, thou living soul, of so much continency, thou tongue like flying fowls, speaking mysteries? (For to such creatures is this food due.) What is it that feeds thee? Joy. Hear we what follows: "notwithstanding, ye have well done, that ye did communicate with my affliction.[15] Hearat he re-

---

[1]See above, 21.   [2]Rom. 3. 4; Ps. 116. 11.
[3]John, 8. 44.   [4]Gen. 1. 29.
[5]Ibid., ver. 30.   [6]II Tim. 1. 16.

[7]II Cor. 2. 9.   [8]II Tim. 4. 16.   [9]Ps. 19. 4.
[10]Phil. 3. 19.   [11]Rom. 16. 18.   [12]Phil. 4. 18.
[13]Ibid., ver. 10.   [14]Phil. 4. 11-13.   [15]Ibid., ver. 14.

joiceth, hereon feedeth; because they had well done, not because his strait was eased who saith unto Thee, "Thou hast enlarged me when I was in distress";[1] for that he knew "to abound, and to suffer want," in Thee Who strengthenest him. "For ye Philippians also know," saith he, "that in the beginning of the Gospel, when I departed from Macedonia, no Church communicated with me as concerning giving and receiving, but ye only. For even in Thessalonica ye sent once and again unto my necessity."[2] Unto these good works, he now rejoiceth that they are returned, and is gladdened that they flourished again, as when a fruitful field resumes its green.

41. Was it for his own necessities, because he said, "Ye sent unto my necessity"? Rejoiceth he for that? Verily not for that. But how know we this? Because himself says immediately, "not because I desire a gift, but I desire fruit."[3] I have learned of Thee, my God, to distinguish betwixt a "gift" and "fruit." A "gift" is the thing itself which he gives, that imparts these necessaries unto us, as money, meat, drink, clothing, shelter, help; but the "fruit" is the good and right will of the giver. For the Good Master said not only, "He that receiveth a prophet," but added, "in the name of a prophet": nor did He only say, "He that receiveth a righteous man," but added, "in the name of a righteous man." So verily shall the one receive the reward of a prophet, the other, the reward of a righteous man: nor saith He only, "Whosoever shall give to drink unto one of these little ones a cup of cold water"; but added, "in the name of a disciple": and so concludeth, "Verily I say unto you, he shall in no wise lose his reward."[4] The gift is, to receive a prophet, to receive a righteous man, to give a cup of cold water to a disciple: but the fruit, to do this in the name of a prophet, in the name of a righteous man, in the name of a disciple. With fruit was Elijah fed by the widow that knew she fed a man of God, and therefore fed him: but by the raven was he fed with a gift. Nor was the inner man[5] of Elijah so fed, but the outer only, which might also for want of that food have perished.

[XXVII] 42. I will then speak what is true in Thy sight, O Lord, that when carnal men and infidels (for the gaining and initiating whom, the initiatory Sacraments and the mighty workings of miracles are necessary,[6] which we suppose to be signified by the name of "fishes" and "whales") undertake the bodily refreshment, or otherwise succour Thy servant with something useful for this present life; whereas they be ignorant, why this is to be done, and to what end; neither do they feed these, nor are these fed by them; because neither do the one do it out of an holy and right intent; nor do the other rejoice at their gifts, whose fruit they as yet behold not. For upon that is the mind fed, of which it is glad. And therefore do not the fishes and whales feed upon such meats as the earth brings not forth until after it was separated and divided from the bitterness of the waves of the sea.

[XXVIII] 43. And Thou, O God, sawest every thing that Thou hadst made, and, behold, it was very good.[7] Yea, we also see the same, and behold, all things are very good. Of the several kinds of Thy works, when Thou hadst said "Let them be," and they were, Thou sawest each that it was good. Seven times have I counted it to be written that Thou sawest that that which Thou madest was "good," and this is the eighth, that Thou sawest every thing that Thou hadst made, and, behold, it was not only good, but also "very good," as being now altogether. For severally, they were only good; but altogether, both good, and very good. All beautiful bodies express the same; by reason that a body consisting of members all beautiful is far more beautiful than the same members by themselves are, by whose well-ordered blending the whole is perfected; notwithstanding that the members severally be also beautiful.

[XXIX] 44. And I looked narrowly to find whether seven or eight times Thou sawest that Thy works were good, when they pleased Thee; but in Thy seeing I found no times, whereby I might understand that Thou sawest so often, what Thou madest. And I said, "Lord, is not this Thy Scripture true, since Thou art true, and being Truth, hast set it forth? why then dost Thou say unto me, 'that in Thy seeing there be no times'; whereas this Thy Scripture tells me that what Thou madest each day, Thou sawest that it was good; and when I counted them, I found how often." Unto this Thou answerest me, for Thou art my God, and with a strong voice tellest Thy servant in his inner ear, breaking through my deafness and crying, "O man, that which My Scripture saith, I say; and yet doth that speak in time; but time has no relation to My Word; because My Word exists in equal eternity with Myself. So the things which ye see through My Spirit, I see; like as what ye speak by My Spirit, I speak. And so when ye see those things in time, I see them not in time; as when ye speak in time, I speak them not in time."

---

[1]Ps. 4. 1.　　[2]Phil. 4. 15, 16.　　[3]Ibid., ver. 17.
[4]Matt. 10. 41, 42.　　[5]I Kings, 17.
[6]See City of God, bk. XXII, 8.　　　　　[7]Gen. 1. 31.

[XXX] 45. And I heard, O Lord my God, and drank up a drop of sweetness out of Thy truth, and understood that certain men there be who mislike Thy works; and say, that many of them Thou madest, compelled by necessity; such as the fabric of the heavens, and harmony of the stars; and that Thou madest them not of what was Thine, but that they were otherwhere and from other sources created, for Thee to bring together and compact and combine, when out of Thy conquered enemies Thou raisedst up the walls of the universe; that they, bound down by the structure, might not again be able to rebel against Thee. For other things, they say Thou neither madest them, nor even compactedst them, such as all flesh and all very minute creatures and whatsoever hath its root in the earth; but that a mind at enmity with Thee, and another nature not created by Thee, and contrary unto Thee, did, in these lower stages of the world, beget and frame these things. Phrenzied are they who say thus, because they see not Thy works by Thy Spirit, nor recognize Thee in them.

[XXXI] 46. But they who by Thy Spirit see these things, Thou seest in them. Therefore when they see that these things are good, Thou seest that they are good; and whatsoever things for Thy sake please, Thou pleasest in them, and what through Thy Spirit please us, they please Thee in us. "For what man knoweth the things of a man, save the spirit of a man, which is in him? even so the things of God knoweth no one, but the Spirit of God. Now we," saith he, "have received, not the spirit of this world, but the Spirit which is of God, that we might know the things that are freely given to us of God."[1] And I am admonished, "Truly, 'the things of God knoweth no one, but the Spirit of God'; how then do we also know 'what things are given us of God'?" Answer is made me: "Because the things which we know by His Spirit, even these 'no one knoweth, but the Spirit of God.' For as it is rightly said unto those that were to speak by the Spirit of God, 'it is not ye that speak';[2] so is it rightly said to them that know through the Spirit of God, 'It is not ye that know.' And no less then is it rightly said to those that see through the Spirit of God, 'It is not ye that see'; so whatsoever through the Spirit of God they see to be good, it is not they, but God that 'sees that it is good.' " It is one thing then for a man to think that to be ill which is good, as the fore-named do; another, that that which is good, a man should see that it is good (as Thy creatures be pleasing unto many, because they be good, whom yet Thou pleasest not in them, when they prefer to enjoy them, to Thee); and another, that when a man sees a thing that it is good, God should in him see that it is good, so, namely, that He should be loved in that which He made, Who cannot be loved but by the Holy Ghost Which He hath given. "Because the love of God is shed abroad in our hearts by the Holy Ghost, Which is given unto us";[3] by Whom we see that whatsoever in any degree is, is good. For from Him it is, who Himself Is not in degree, but what He Is, Is.

[XXXII] 47. Thanks to Thee, O Lord. We behold the heaven and earth, whether the corporeal part, superior and inferior, or the spiritual and corporeal creature; and in the adorning of these parts whereof the universal pile of the world, or rather the universal creation, doth consist, we see light made, and divided from the darkness. We see the firmament of heaven, whether that primary body of the world between the spiritual upper waters and the inferior corporeal waters, or (since this also is called heaven) this space of air through which wander the fowls of heaven, betwixt those waters which are in vapours borne above them, and in clear nights distil down in dew; and those heavier waters which flow along the earth. We behold a face of waters gathered together in the fields of the sea; and the dry land both void and formed so as to be visible and harmonized, yea, and the matter of herbs and trees. We behold the lights shining from above, the sun to suffice for the day, the moon and the stars to cheer the night; and that, by all these, times should be marked and signified. We behold on all sides a moist element, replenished with fishes, beasts, and birds; because the grossness of the air, which bears up the flights of birds, thickeneth itself by the exhalation of the waters. We behold the face of the earth decked out with earthly creatures, and man, created after Thy image and likeness, even through that Thy very image and likeness (that is the power of reason and understanding), set over all irrational creatures. And as in his soul there is one power which has dominion by directing, another made subject, that it might obey; so was there for the man, corporeally also, made a woman, who in the mind of her reasonable understanding should have a parity of nature, but in the sex of her body should be in like manner subject to the sex of her husband, as the appetite of doing is fain to conceive the skill of right-doing, from the reason of the mind. These

[1] I Cor. 2. 12.   [2] Matt. 10. 20.   [3] Rom. 5. 5.

things we behold, and they are severally good, and altogether very good.

[XXXIII] 48. Let Thy works praise Thee, that we may love Thee; and let us love Thee, that Thy works may praise Thee, which from time have beginning and ending, rising and setting, growth and decay, form and privation. They have then their succession of morning and evening, part secretly, part apparently; for they were made of nothing, by Thee, not of Thee; not of any matter not Thine, or that was before, but of matter concreated (that is, at the same time created by Thee), because, to its state without form, Thou without any interval of time didst give form. For seeing the matter of heaven and earth is one thing, and the form another, Thou madest the matter of merely nothing, but the form of the world out of the matter without form; yet both together, so that the form should follow the matter without any interval of delay.

[XXXIV] 49. We have also examined what Thou willedst to be shadowed forth, whether by the creation, or the relation of things in such an order. And we have seen that things singly are good, and together very good,[1] in Thy Word, in Thy Only-Begotten, both heaven and earth, the Head and the body of the Church, in Thy predestination before all times, without morning and evening. But when Thou begannest to execute in time the things predestinated, to the end Thou mightest reveal hidden things, and rectify our disorders; for our sins hung over us, and we had sunk into the dark deep, and Thy good Spirit was borne over us, to help us in due season; and Thou didst justify the ungodly,[2] and dividest them from the wicked; and Thou madest the firmament of authority of Thy Book between those placed above, who were to be docile unto Thee, and those under, who were to be subject to them: and Thou gatheredst together the society of unbelievers into one conspiracy, that the zeal of the faithful might appear, and they might bring forth works of mercy, even distributing to the poor their earthly riches, to obtain heavenly. And after this didst Thou kindle certain lights in the firmament, Thy Holy ones, having the word of life; and shining with an eminent authority set on high through spiritual gifts; after that again, for the initiation of the unbelieving Gentiles, didst Thou out of corporeal matter produce the Sacraments, and visible miracles, and forms of words according to the firmament of Thy Book, by which the faithful should be blessed and multiplied. Next didst

Thou form the living soul of the faithful, through affections well ordered by the vigour of continency; and after that, the mind subjected to Thee alone and needing to imitate no human authority, hast Thou renewed after Thy image and likeness; and didst subject its rational actions to the excellency of the understanding, as the woman to the man; and to all Offices of Thy Ministry, necessary for the perfecting of the faithful in this life, Thou willedst that for their temporal uses, good things, fruitful to themselves in time to come, be given by the same faithful.[3] All these we see, and they are very good, because Thou seest them in us, Who hast given unto us Thy Spirit, by which we might see them, and in them love Thee.

[XXXV] 50. O Lord God, give peace unto us, for Thou hast given us all things: the peace of rest, the peace of the Sabbath, which hath no evening. For all this most goodly array of things "very good," having finished their courses, is to pass away, for in them there was morning and evening.

[XXXVI] 51. But the seventh day hath no evening, nor hath it setting; because Thou hast sanctified it to an everlasting continuance; that that which Thou didst after Thy works which were very good, resting the seventh day, although Thou madest them in unbroken rest, that may the voice of Thy Book announce beforehand unto us, that we also after our works (therefore very good, because Thou hast given them us) shall rest in Thee also in the Sabbath of eternal life.

[XXXVII] 52. For then shalt Thou so rest in us, as now Thou workest in us; and so shall that be Thy rest through us, as these are Thy works through us. But Thou, Lord, ever workest, and art ever at rest. Nor dost Thou see in time, nor art moved in time, nor restest in a time; and yet Thou makest things seen in time, yea, the times themselves, and the rest which results from time.

[XXXVIII] 53. We therefore see these things which Thou madest, because they are; but they are, because Thou seest them. And we see without, that they are, and within, that they are good, but Thou sawest them there, when made, where Thou sawest them, yet to be made. And we were at a later time moved to do well, after our hearts had conceived of Thy Spirit; but in the former time we were moved to do evil, forsaking Thee; but Thou, the One, the Good God, didst never cease doing good. And we also have some good works, of Thy gift, but

[1]Gen. I. 31.   [2]Rom. 4. 5.   [3]Cf. *City of God*, Bk. IX. 17.

not eternal; after them we trust to rest in Thy great hallowing. But Thou, being the Good which needeth no good, art ever at rest, because Thy rest is Thou Thyself. And what man can teach man to understand this? or what Angel, an Angel? or what Angel, a man? Let it be asked of Thee, sought in Thee, knocked for at Thee; so, so shall it be received, so shall it be found, so shall it be opened.[1] *Amen.*

[1]Matt. 7. 7.

GRATIAS TIBI DOMINE

BOOK I. *Augustine censures the pagans, who attributed the calamities of the world, and especially the recent sack of Rome by the Goths, to the Christian religion, and its prohibition of the worship of the gods. He speaks of the blessings and ills of life, which then, as always, happened to good and bad men alike. Finally, he rebukes the shamelessness of those who cast up to the Christians that their women had been violated by the soldiers.* 129

BOOK II. *In this book Augustine reviews those calamities which the Romans suffered before the time of Christ, and while the worship of the false gods was universally practised; and demonstrates that, far from being preserved from misfortune by the gods, the Romans have been by them overwhelmed with the only, or at least the greatest, of all calamities—the corruption of manners, and the vices of the soul.* 150

BOOK III. *As in the foregoing book Augustine has proved regarding moral and spiritual calamities, so in this book he proves regarding external and bodily disasters, that since the foundation of the city the Romans have been continually subject to them; and that even when the false gods were worshipped without a rival, before the advent of Christ, they afforded no relief from such calamities.* 169

BOOK IV. *In this book it is proved that the extent and long duration of the Roman Empire is to be ascribed, not to Jove or the gods of the heathen, to whom individually scarce even single things and the very basest functions were believed to be entrusted, but to the one true God, the author of felicity, by whose power and judgment earthly kingdoms are founded and maintained.* 188

BOOK V. *Augustine first discusses the doctrine of fate, for the sake of confuting those who are disposed to refer to fate the power and increase of the Roman Empire, which could not be attributed to false gods, as has been shown in the preceding book. After that, he proves that there is no contradiction between God's prescience and our free-will. He then speaks of the manners of the ancient Romans, and shows in what sense it was due to the virtue of the Romans themselves, and in how far to the counsel of God, that He in-* creased their dominion, though they did not worship Him. Finally, he explains what is to be accounted the true happiness of the Christian emperors. 207

BOOK VI. *Hitherto the argument has been conducted against those who believe that the gods are to be worshipped for the sake of temporal advantages. Now it is directed against those who believe that they are to be worshipped for the sake of eternal life. Augustine devotes the five following books to the confutation of this latter belief, and first of all shows how mean an opinion of the gods was held by Varro himself, the most esteemed writer on heathen theology. Of this theology Augustine adopts Varro's division into three kinds, mythical, natural, and civil; and at once demonstrates that neither the mythical nor the civil can contribute anything to the happiness of the future life.* 230

BOOK VII. *In this Book it is shown that eternal life is not obtained by the worship of Janus, Jupiter, Saturn, and the other "select gods" of the civil theology.* 243

BOOK VIII. *Augustine comes now to the third kind of theology, that is, the natural, and takes up the question whether the worship of the gods of the natural theology is of any avail towards securing blessedness in the life to come. This question he prefers to discuss with the Platonists, because the Platonic system is* facile princeps *among philosophies and makes the nearest approximation to Christian truth. In pursuing this argument, he first refutes Apuleius, and all who maintain that the demons should be worshipped as messengers and mediators between gods and men; demonstrating that by no possibility can men be reconciled to good gods by demons, who are the slaves of vice, and who delight in and patronize what good and wise men abhor and condemn—the blasphemous fictions of poets, theatrical exhibitions, and magical arts.* 264

BOOK IX. *Having in the preceding book shown that the worship of demons must be abjured, since they in a thousand ways proclaim themselves to be wicked spirits, Augustine in this book meets those who allege a distinction among demons, some being evil, while others are good; and, having exploded this distinction, he proves*

that to no demon, but to Christ alone, belongs
the office of providing men with eternal blessedness.   285

BOOK X. *In this book Augustine teaches that the
good angels wish God alone, whom they themselves serve, to receive that divine honour which
is rendered by sacrifice, and which is called* latreia. *He then goes on to dispute against Porphyry about the principle and way of the soul's
cleansing and deliverance.*   298

BOOK XI. *Here begins the second part of this
work, which treats of the origin, history, and
destinies of the Two Cities, the earthly and the
heavenly. In the first place, Augustine shows in
this book how the Two Cities were formed originally, by the separation of the good and bad
angels; and takes occasion to treat of the creation
of the World, as it is described in Holy Scripture
in the beginning of the Book of Genesis.*   322

BOOK XII. *Augustine first institutes two inquiries regarding the angels: namely, whence is
there in some a good and in others an evil will?
and, what is the reason of the blessedness of the
good and the misery of the evil? Afterwards he
treats of the creation of man, and teaches that he
is not from eternity, but was created, and by
none other than God.*   342

BOOK XIII. *In this book it is taught that death
is penal and had its origin in Adam's sin.*   360

BOOK XIV. *Augustine again treats of the sin of
the first man and teaches that it is the cause of
the carnal life and vicious affections of man.
Especially he proves that the shame which accompanies lust is the just punishment of that
disobedience, and inquires how man, if he had
not sinned, would have been able without lust to
propagate his kind.*   376

BOOK XV. *Having treated in the four preceding
books of the origin of the Two Cities, the earthly and the heavenly, Augustine explains their
growth and progress in the four books which follow; and, in order to do so, he explains the chief
passages of the sacred history which bear upon
this subject. In this fifteenth book he opens this
part of his work by explaining the events recorded in Genesis from the time of Cain and
Abel to the Deluge.*   397

BOOK XVI. *In the former part of this book, from
the first to the twelfth chapter, the progress of
the Two Cities, the earthly and the heavenly,
from Noah to Abraham, is exhibited from Holy
Scripture: in the latter part, the progress of the
heavenly alone, from Abraham to the Kings of
Israel, is the subject.*   422

BOOK XVII. *In this Book the history of the City
of God is traced during the period of the kings
and prophets from Samuel to David, even to
Christ; and the prophecies which are recorded
in the Books of Kings, Psalms, and those of
Solomon, are interpreted of Christ and the
Church.*   449

BOOK XVIII. *Augustine traces the parallel courses
of the earthly and heavenly cities from the time
of Abraham to the end of the world; and alludes
to the oracles regarding Christ, both those uttered
by the sibyls, and those of the sacred prophets
who wrote after the foundation of Rome, Hosea,
Amos, Isaiah, Micah, and their successors.*   472

BOOK XIX. *In this book the end of the Two
Cities, the earthly and the heavenly, is discussed.
Augustine reviews the opinions of the philosophers regarding the supreme good, and their vain
efforts to make for themselves a happiness in this
life; and, while he refutes these, he takes occasion to show what the peace and happiness belonging to the heavenly city, or the people of
Christ, are both now and hereafter.*   507

BOOK XX. *Concerning the Last Judgment, and
the declarations regarding it in the Old and New
Testaments.*   530

BOOK XXI. *Of the end reserved for the city of the
Devil, namely, the eternal punishment of the
damned; and of the arguments which unbelief
brings against it.*   560

BOOK XXII. *This book treats of the end of the City
of God, that is to say, of the eternal happiness of
the saints; the faith of the resurrection of the
body is established and explained; and the
work concludes by showing how the saints,
clothed in immortal and spiritual bodies, shall be
employed.*   586

THE CITY OF GOD

❖❖❖❖❖❖❖❖❖❖

BOOK I

ARGUMENT. AUGUSTINE CENSURES THE PAGANS, WHO ATTRIBUTED THE CALAM-
ITIES OF THE WORLD, AND ESPECIALLY THE RECENT SACK OF ROME BY THE GOTHS,
TO THE CHRISTIAN RELIGION, AND ITS PROHIBITION OF THE WORSHIP OF THE GODS.
HE SPEAKS OF THE BLESSINGS AND ILLS OF LIFE, WHICH THEN, AS ALWAYS, HAP-
PENED TO GOOD AND BAD MEN ALIKE. FINALLY, HE REBUKES THE SHAMELESSNESS
OF THOSE WHO CAST UP TO THE CHRISTIANS THAT THEIR WOMEN HAD BEEN VIO-
LATED BY THE SOLDIERS.

PREFACE

Explaining his design in undertaking this work

THE glorious city of God is my theme in this work, which you, my dearest son Marcellinus,[1] suggested, and which is due to you by my promise. I have undertaken its defence against those who prefer their own gods to the Founder of this city,—a city surpassingly glorious, whether we view it as it still lives by faith in this fleeting course of time, and sojourns as a stranger in the midst of the ungodly, or as it shall dwell in the fixed stability of its eternal seat, which it now with patience waits for, expecting until "right-eousness shall return unto judgement,"[2] and it obtain, by virtue of its excellence, final victory and perfect peace. A great work this, and an ar-duous; but God is my helper. For I am aware what ability is requisite to persuade the proud how great is the virtue of humility, which raises us, not by a quite human arrogance, but by a divine grace, above all earthly dignities that tot-ter on this shifting scene. For the King and Founder of this city of which we speak has in Scripture uttered to His people a dictum of the divine law in these words: "God resisteth the proud, but giveth grace unto the humble."[3] But

[1] Marcellinus was a friend of Augustine, and urged him to write this work. He was commissioned by the Emperor Honorius to convene a conference of Catholic and schis-matic Donatist bishops in the summer of 411, and con-ceded the victory to the Catholics; but on account of his rigor in executing the laws against the Donatists, he fell a victim to their revenge, and was honored by a place among the martyrs.

[2] Ps. 94. 15. In the Revised Vers.: "Judgment shall re-turn unto righteousness."

[3] Jas. 4. 6 and 1 Pet. 5. 5.

this, which is God's prerogative, the inflated am-bition of a proud spirit also affects, and dearly loves that this be numbered among its attri-butes, to

> *Show pity to the humbled soul,*
> *And crush the sons of pride.*[4]

And therefore, as the plan of this work we have undertaken requires, and as occasion offers, we must speak also of the earthly city, which, though it be mistress of the nations, is itself ruled by its lust of rule.

CHAP. I. *Of the adversaries of the name of Christ, whom the barbarians for Christ's sake spared when they stormed the city*

For to this earthly city belong the enemies against whom I have to defend the city of God. Many of them, indeed, being reclaimed from their ungodly error, have become sufficiently creditable citizens of this city; but many are so inflamed with hatred against it, and are so un-grateful to its Redeemer for His signal benefits, as to forget that they would now be unable to utter a single word to its prejudice, had they not found in its sacred places, as they fled from the enemy's steel, that life in which they now boast themselves.[5] Are not those very Romans, who were spared by the barbarians through their re-spect for Christ, become enemies to the name of Christ? The reliquaries of the martyrs and the churches of the apostles bear witness to this;

[4] Virgil, *Æneid*, BK. VI. 854.
[5] Augustine refers to the sacking of the city of Rome by the West-Gothic King Alaric, 410. He spared the Catholic Christians. See Gibbon's *Decline and Fall.*

for in the sack of the city they were open sanctuary for all who fled to them, whether Christian or Pagan. To their very threshold the blood-thirsty enemy raged; there his murderous fury owned a limit. Thither did such of the enemy as had any pity convey those to whom they had given quarter, lest any less mercifully disposed might fall upon them. And, indeed, when even those murderers who everywhere else showed themselves pitiless came to those spots where that was forbidden which the licence of war permitted in every other place, their furious rage for slaughter was bridled, and their eagerness to take prisoners was quenched. Thus escaped multitudes who now reproach the Christian religion, and impute to Christ the ills that have befallen their city; but the preservation of their own life—a boon which they owe to the respect entertained for Christ by the barbarians—they attribute not to our Christ, but to their own good luck. They ought rather, had they any right perceptions, to attribute the severities and hardships inflicted by their enemies to that divine providence which is wont to reform the depraved manners of men by chastisement, and which exercises with similar afflictions the righteous and praiseworthy—either translating them, when they have passed through the trial, to a better world, or detaining them still on earth for ulterior purposes. And they ought to attribute it to the spirit of these Christian times that, contrary to the custom of war, these blood-thirsty barbarians spared them, and spared them for Christ's sake, whether this mercy was actually shown in promiscuous places, or in those places specially dedicated to Christ's name, and of which the very largest were selected as sanctuaries, that full scope might thus be given to the expansive compassion which desired that a large multitude might find shelter there. Therefore ought they to give God thanks, and with sincere confession flee for refuge to His name, that so they may escape the punishment of eternal fire —they who with lying lips took upon them this name, that they might escape the punishment of present destruction. For of those whom you see insolently and shamelessly insulting the servants of Christ, there are numbers who would not have escaped that destruction and slaughter had they not pretended that they themselves were Christ's servants. Yet now, in ungrateful pride and most impious madness, and at the risk of being punished in everlasting darkness, they perversely oppose that name under which they fraudulently protected themselves for the sake of enjoying the light of this brief life.

CHAP. 2. *That it is quite contrary to the usage of war, that the victors should spare the vanquished for the sake of their gods*

There are histories of numberless wars, both before the building of Rome and since its rise and the extension of its dominion; let these be read, and let one instance be cited in which, when a city had been taken by foreigners, the victors spared those who were found to have fled for sanctuary to the temples of their gods; or one instance in which a barbarian general gave orders that none should be put to the sword who had been found in this or that temple. Did not Æneas see

Dying Priam at the shrine,
Staining the hearth he made divine?[1]

Did not Diomede and Ulysses

Drag with red hands, the sentry slain,
Her fateful image from your fane,
Her chaste locks touch, and stain with gore
The virgin coronal she wore?[2]

Neither is that true which follows, that

Thenceforth the tide of fortune changed,
And Greece grew weak.[3]

For after this they conquered and destroyed Troy with fire and sword; after this they beheaded Priam as he fled to the altars. Neither did Troy perish because it lost Minerva. For what had Minerva herself first lost, that she should perish? Her guards perhaps? No doubt; just her guards. For as soon as they were slain, she could be stolen. It was not, in fact, the men who were preserved by the image, but the image by the men. How, then, was she invoked to defend the city and the citizens, she who could not defend her own defenders?

CHAP. 3. *That the Romans did not show their usual sagacity when they trusted that they would be benefited by the gods who had been unable to defend Troy*

And these be the gods to whose protecting care the Romans were delighted to entrust their city! O too, too piteous mistake! And they are enraged at us when we speak thus about their gods, though, so far from being enraged at their own writers, they part with money to learn what they say; and, indeed, the very teachers of these authors are reckoned worthy of a salary from the public purse, and of other honours. There is

[1] Virgil, *Æneid*, BK. II. 501–2. The renderings of Virgil are from Conington.
[2] *Ibid.*, BK. II. 166. [3] *Ibid.*

Virgil, who is read by boys, in order that this great poet, this most famous and approved of all poets, may impregnate their virgin minds, and may not readily be forgotten by them, according to that saying of Horace,

The fresh cask long keeps its first tang.

Well, in this Virgil, I say, Juno is introduced as hostile to the Trojans, and stirring up Æolus, the king of the winds, against them in the words,

A race I hate now ploughs the sea,
Transporting Troy to Italy,
And home-gods conquered[1] ...

And ought prudent men to have entrusted the defence of Rome to these conquered gods? But it will be said, this was only the saying of Juno, who, like an angry woman, did not know what she was saying. What, then, says Æneas himself —Æneas who is so often designated "pious"? Does he not say,

Lo! Panthus, 'scaped from death by flight,
Priest of Apollo on the height,
His conquered gods with trembling hands
He bears, and shelter swift demands?[2]

Is it not clear that the gods (whom he does not scruple to call "conquered") were rather entrusted to Æneas than he to them, when it is said to him,

The gods of her domestic shrines
Your country to your care consigns?[3]

If, then, Virgil says that the gods were such as these, and were conquered, and that when conquered they could not escape except under the protection of a man, what a madness is it to suppose that Rome had been wisely entrusted to these guardians, and could not have been taken unless it had lost them! Indeed, to worship conquered gods as protectors and champions, what is this but to worship, not good divinities, but evil omens?[4] Would it not be wiser to believe, not that Rome would never have fallen into so great a calamity had not they first perished, but rather that they would have perished long since had not Rome preserved them as long as she could? For who does not see, when he thinks of it, what a foolish assumption it is that they could not be vanquished under vanquished defenders, and that they only perished because they had lost their guardian gods, when, indeed, the only cause of their perishing was that they chose for their protectors gods condemned to perish? The

poets, therefore, when they composed and sang these things about the conquered gods, had no intention to invent falsehoods, but uttered, as honest men, what the truth extorted from them. This, however, will be carefully and copiously discussed in another and more fitting place. Meanwhile I will briefly, and to the best of my ability, explain what I meant to say about these ungrateful men who blasphemously impute to Christ the calamities which they deservedly suffer in consequence of their own wicked ways, while that which is for Christ's sake spared them in spite of their wickedness they do not even take the trouble to notice; and in their mad and blasphemous insolence, they use against His name those very lips wherewith they falsely claimed that same name that their lives might be spared. In the places consecrated to Christ, where for His sake no enemy would injure them, they restrained their tongues that they might be safe and protected; but no sooner do they emerge from these sanctuaries, than they unbridle these tongues to hurl against Him curses full of hate.

CHAP. 4. *Of the asylum of Juno in Troy, which saved no one from the Greeks; and of the churches of the apostles, which protected from the barbarians all who fled to them*

Troy itself, the mother of the Roman people, was not able, as I have said, to protect its own citizens in the sacred places of their gods from the fire and sword of the Greeks, though the Greeks worshipped the same gods. Not only so, but

Phoenix and Ulysses fell
In the void courts by Juno's cell
Were set the spoils to keep;
Snatched from the burning shrines away,
There Ilium's mighty treasure lay,
Rich altars, bowls of massy gold,
And captive raiment, rudely rolled
In one promiscuous heap;
While boys and matrons, wild with fear,
In long array were standing near.[5]

In other words, the place consecrated to so great a goddess was chosen, not that from it none might be led out a captive, but that in it all the captives might be immured. Compare now this "asylum"—the asylum not of an ordinary god, not of one of the rank and file of gods, but of Jove's own sister and wife, the queen of all the gods—with the churches built in memory of the apostles. Into it were collected the spoils rescued from the blazing temples and snatched from the gods, not that they might be restored to the van-

---

[1] Virgil, *Æneid*, BK. I. 71.   [3]*Ibid.*, 293.
[2]*Ibid.*, BK. II. 319.   [4]*Non numina bona, sed omina mala.*

[5]Virgil, *Æneid*, BK. II. 761.

quished, but divided among the victors; while into these was carried back, with the most religious observance and respect, everything which belonged to them, even though found elsewhere. There liberty was lost; here preserved. There bondage was strict; here strictly excluded. Into that temple men were driven to become the chattels of their enemies, now lording it over them; into these churches men were led by their relenting foes, that they might be at liberty. In fine, the gentle Greeks appropriated that temple of Juno to the purposes of their own avarice and pride; while these churches of Christ were chosen even by the savage barbarians as the fit scenes for humility and mercy. But perhaps, after all, the Greeks did in that victory of theirs spare the temples of those gods whom they worshipped in common with the Trojans, and did not dare to put to the sword or make captive the wretched and vanquished Trojans who fled thither; and perhaps Virgil, in the manner of poets, has depicted what never really happened? But there is no question that he depicted the usual custom of an enemy when sacking a city.

CHAP. 5. *Cæsar's statement regarding the universal custom of an enemy when sacking a city*

Even Cæsar himself gives us positive testimony regarding this custom; for, in his deliverance in the senate about the conspirators, he says (as Sallust, a historian of distinguished veracity, writes) "that virgins and boys are violated, children torn from the embrace of their parents, matrons subjected to whatever should be the pleasure of the conquerors, temples and houses plundered, slaughter and burning rife; in fine, all things filled with arms, corpses, blood, and wailing." If he had not mentioned temples here, we might suppose that enemies were in the habit of sparing the dwellings of the gods. And the Roman temples were in danger of these disasters, not from foreign foes, but from Catiline and his associates, the most noble senators and citizens of Rome. But these, it may be said, were abandoned men, and the parricides of their fatherland.

CHAP. 6. *That not even the Romans, when they took cities, spared the conquered in their temples*

Why, then, need our argument take note of the many nations who have waged wars with one another, and have nowhere spared the conquered in the temples of their gods? Let us look at the practice of the Romans themselves: let us, I say, recall and review the Romans, whose chief praise it has been "to spare the vanquished and subdue the proud," and that they preferred "rather to forgive than to revenge an injury"; and among so many and great cities which they have stormed, taken, and overthrown for the extension of their dominion, let us be told what temples they were accustomed to exempt, so that whoever took refuge in them was free. Or have they really done this, and has the fact been suppressed by the historians of these events? Is it to be believed that men who sought out with the greatest eagerness points they could praise, would omit those which, in their own estimation, are the most signal proofs of piety? Marcus Marcellus, a distinguished Roman, who took Syracuse, a most splendidly adorned city, is reported to have bewailed its coming ruin, and to have shed his own tears over it before he spilt its blood. He took steps also to preserve the chastity even of his enemy. For before he gave orders for the storming of the city, he issued an edict forbidding the violation of any free person. Yet the city was sacked according to the custom of war; nor do we anywhere read that even by so chaste and gentle a commander orders were given that no one should be injured who had fled to this or that temple. And this certainly would by no means have been omitted, when neither his weeping nor his edict preservative of chastity could be passed in silence. Fabius, the conqueror of the city of Tarentum, is praised for abstaining from making booty of the images. For when his secretary proposed the question to him, what he wished done with the statues of the gods, which had been taken in large numbers, he veiled his moderation under a joke. For he asked of what sort they were; and when they reported to him that there were not only many large images, but some of them armed, "Oh," says he, "let us leave with the Tarentines their angry gods." Seeing, then, that the writers of Roman history could not pass in silence, neither the weeping of the one general nor the laughing of the other, neither the chaste pity of the one nor the facetious moderation of the other, on what occasion would it be omitted, if, for the honour of any of their enemy's gods, they had shown this particular form of leniency, that in any temple slaughter or captivity was prohibited?

CHAP. 7. *That the cruelties which occurred in the sack of Rome were in accordance with the custom of war, whereas the acts of clemency resulted from the influence of Christ's name*

All the spoiling, then, which Rome was exposed to in the recent calamity—all the slaughter, plundering, burning, and misery—was the result of the custom of war. But what was novel was that savage barbarians showed themselves in so gentle a guise, that the largest churches were chosen and set apart for the purpose of being filled with the people to whom quarter was given, and that in them none were slain, from them none forcibly dragged; that into them many were led by their relenting enemies to be set at liberty, and that from them none were led into slavery by merciless foes. Whoever does not see that this is to be attributed to the name of Christ, and to the Christian temper, is blind; whoever sees this, and gives no praise, is ungrateful; whoever hinders any one from praising it, is mad. Far be it from any prudent man to impute this clemency to the barbarians. Their fierce and bloody minds were awed, and bridled, and marvellously tempered by Him who so long before said by His prophet, "I will visit their transgression with the rod, and their iniquities with stripes; nevertheless my loving-kindness will I not utterly take from them."[1]

CHAP. 8. *Of the advantages and disadvantages which often indiscriminately accrue to good and wicked men*

Will some one say, Why, then, was this divine compassion extended even to the ungodly and ungrateful? Why, but because it was the mercy of Him who daily "maketh His sun to rise on the evil and on the good, and sendeth rain on the just and on the unjust."[2] For though some of these men, taking thought of this, repent of their wickedness and reform, some, as the apostle says, "despising the riches of His goodness and long-suffering, after their hardness and impenitent heart, treasure up unto themselves wrath against the day of wrath and revelation of the righteous judgment of God, who will render to every man according to his deeds":[3] nevertheless does the patience of God still invite the wicked to repentance, even as the scourge of God educates the good to patience. And so, too, does the mercy of God embrace the good that it may cherish them, as the severity of God arrests the wicked to punish them. To the divine providence it has seemed good to prepare in the world to come for the righteous good things, which the unrighteous shall not enjoy; and for the wicked evil things, by which the good shall not be tormented. But as for the good things of this life, and its ills, God has willed that these should be common to both; that we might not too eagerly covet the things which wicked men

[1] Ps. 89. 32. [2] Matt. 5. 45. [3] Rom. 2. 4.

are seen equally to enjoy, nor shrink with an unseemly fear from the ills which even good men often suffer.

There is, too, a very great difference in the purpose served both by those events which we call adverse and those called prosperous. For the good man is neither uplifted with the good things of time, nor broken by its ills; but the wicked man, because he is corrupted by this world's happiness, feels himself punished by its unhappiness. Yet often, even in the present distribution of temporal things, does God plainly evince His own interference. For if every sin were now visited with manifest punishment, nothing would seem to be reserved for the final judgement; on the other hand, if no sin received now a plainly divine punishment, it would be concluded that there is no divine providence at all. And so of the good things of this life: if God did not by a very visible liberality confer these on some of those persons who ask for them, we should say that these good things were not at His disposal; and if He gave them to all who sought them, we should suppose that such were the only rewards of His service; and such a service would make us not godly, but greedy rather, and covetous. Wherefore, though good and bad men suffer alike, we must not suppose that there is no difference between the men themselves, because there is no difference in what they both suffer. For even in the likeness of the sufferings, there remains an unlikeness in the sufferers; and though exposed to the same anguish, virtue and vice are not the same thing. For as the same fire causes gold to glow brightly, and chaff to smoke; and under the same flail the straw is beaten small, while the grain is cleansed; and as the lees are not mixed with the oil, though squeezed out of the vat by the same pressure, so the same violence of affliction proves, purges, clarifies the good, but damns, ruins, exterminates the wicked. And thus it is that in the same affliction the wicked detest God and blaspheme, while the good pray and praise. So material a difference does it make, not what ills are suffered, but what kind of man suffers them. For, stirred up with the same movement, mud exhales a horrible stench, and ointment emits a fragrant odour.

CHAP. 9. *Of the reasons for administering correction to bad and good together*

What, then, have the Christians suffered in that calamitous period, which would not profit every one who duly and faithfully considered the following circumstances? First of all, they must humbly consider those very sins which have provoked God to fill the world with such terrible disasters; for although they be far from the excesses of wicked, immoral, and ungodly men, yet they do not judge themselves so clean removed from all faults as to be too good to suffer for these even temporal ills. For every man, however laudably he lives, yet yields in some points to the lust of the flesh. Though he do not fall into gross enormity of wickedness, and abandoned viciousness, and abominable profanity, yet he slips into some sins, either rarely or so much the more frequently as the sins seem of less account. But not to mention this, where can we readily find a man who holds in fit and just estimation those persons on account of whose revolting pride, luxury, and avarice, and cursed iniquities and impiety, God now smites the earth as His predictions threatened? Where is the man who lives with them in the style in which it becomes us to live with them? For often we wickedly blind ourselves to the occasions of teaching and admonishing them, sometimes even of reprimanding and chiding them, either because we shrink from the labour or are ashamed to offend them, or because we fear to lose good friendships, lest this should stand in the way of our advancement, or injure us in some worldly matter, which either our covetous disposition desires to obtain, or our weakness shrinks from losing. So that, although the conduct of wicked men is distasteful to the good, and therefore they do not fall with them into that damnation which in the next life awaits such persons, yet, because they spare their damnable sins through fear, therefore, even though their own sins be slight and venial, they are justly scourged with the wicked in this world, though in eternity they quite escape punishment. Justly, when God afflicts them in common with the wicked, do they find this life bitter, through love of whose sweetness they declined to be bitter to these sinners.

If any one forbears to reprove and find fault with those who are doing wrong, because he seeks a more seasonable opportunity, or because he fears they may be made worse by his rebuke, or that other weak persons may be disheartened from endeavouring to lead a good and pious life, and may be driven from the faith; this man's omission seems to be occasioned not by covetousness, but by a charitable consideration. But what is blameworthy is, that they who themselves revolt from the conduct of the wicked, and live in quite another fashion, yet spare those faults in other men which they ought to reprehend and wean them from; and spare them be-

cause they fear to give offence, lest they should injure their interests in those things which good men may innocently and legitimately use—though they use them more greedily than becomes persons who are strangers in this world, and profess the hope of a heavenly country. For not only the weaker brethren who enjoy married life, and have children (or desire to have them), and own houses and establishments, whom the apostle addresses in the churches, warning and instructing them how they should live, both the wives with their husbands, and the husbands with their wives, the children with their parents, and parents with their children, and servants with their masters, and masters with their servants—not only do these weaker brethren gladly obtain and grudgingly lose many earthly and temporal things on account of which they dare not offend men whose polluted and wicked life greatly displeases them; but those also who live at a higher level, who are not entangled in the meshes of married life, but use meagre food and raiment, do often take thought of their own safety and good name, and abstain from finding fault with the wicked, because they fear their wiles and violence. And although they do not fear them to such an extent as to be drawn to the commission of like iniquities, nay, not by any threats or violence soever; yet those very deeds which they refuse to share in the commission of, they often decline to find fault with, when possibly they might by finding fault prevent their commission. They abstain from interference, because they fear that, if it fail of good effect, their own safety or reputation may be damaged or destroyed; not because they see that their preservation and good name are needful, that they may be able to influence those who need their instruction, but rather because they weakly relish the flattery and respect of men, and fear the judgments of the people, and the pain or death of the body; that is to say, their non-intervention is the result of selfishness and not of love.

Accordingly this seems to me to be one principal reason why the good are chastised along with the wicked, when God is pleased to visit with temporal punishments the profligate manners of a community. They are punished together, not because they have spent an equally corrupt life, but because the good as well as the wicked, though not equally with them, love this present life; while they ought to hold it cheap, that the wicked, being admonished and reformed by their example, might lay hold of life eternal. And if they will not be the companions of the good in seeking life everlasting, they should be loved as enemies and be dealt with patiently. For so long as they live, it remains uncertain whether they may not come to a better mind. These selfish persons have more cause to fear than those to whom it was said through the prophet, "He is taken away in his iniquity, but his blood will I require at the watchman's hand."[1] For watchmen or overseers of the people are appointed in churches that they may unsparingly rebuke sin. Nor is that man guiltless of the sin we speak of, who, though he be not a watchman, yet sees in the conduct of those with whom the relationships of this life bring him into contact, many things that should be blamed, and yet overlooks them, fearing to give offence, and lose such worldly blessings as may legitimately be desired, but which he too eagerly grasps. Then, lastly, there is another reason why the good are afflicted with temporal calamities—the reason which Job's case exemplifies: that the human spirit may be proved, and that it may be manifested with what fortitude of pious trust, and with how unmercenary a love, it cleaves to God.

CHAP. 10. *That the saints lose nothing in losing temporal goods*

These are the considerations which one must keep in view, that he may answer the question whether any evil happens to the faithful and godly which cannot be turned to profit. Or shall we say that the question is needless, and that the apostle is vapouring when he says, "We know that all things work together for good to them that love God?"[2]

They lost all they had. Their faith? Their godliness? The possessions of the hidden man of the heart, which in the sight of God are of great price?[3] Did they lose these? For these are the wealth of Christians, to whom the wealthy apostle said, "Godliness with contentment is great gain. For we brought nothing into this world, and it is certain we can carry nothing out. And having food and raiment, let us be therewith content. But they that will be rich fall into temptation and a snare, and into many foolish and hurtful lusts, which drown men in destruction and perdition. For the love of money is the root of all evil; which, while some coveted after, they have erred from the faith, and pierced themselves through with many sorrows."[4]

They, then, who lost their worldly all in the sack of Rome, if they owned their possessions as they had been taught by the apostle, who himself was poor without, but rich within—that is to say, if they used the world as not using it—could say in the words of Job, heavily tried but not overcome: "Naked came I out of my mother's womb, and naked shall I return thither: the Lord gave, and the Lord hath taken away; as it pleased the Lord, so has it come to pass: blessed be the name of the Lord."[5] Like a good servant, Job counted the will of his Lord his great possession, by obedience to which his soul was enriched; nor did it grieve him to lose, while yet living, those goods which he must shortly leave at his death. But as to those feebler spirits who, though they cannot be said to prefer earthly possessions to Christ, do yet cleave to them with a somewhat immoderate attachment, they have discovered by the pain of losing these things how much they were sinning in loving them. For their grief is of their own making; in the words of the apostle quoted above, "they have pierced themselves through with many sorrows." For it was well that they who had so long despised these verbal admonitions should receive the teaching of experience. For when the apostle says, "They that will be rich fall into temptation," and so on, what he blames in riches is not the possession of them, but the desire of them. For elsewhere he says, "Charge them that are rich in this world, that they be not high-minded, nor trust in uncertain riches, but in the living God, who giveth us richly all things to enjoy; that they do good, that they be rich in good works, ready to distribute, willing to communicate; laying up in store for themselves a good foundation against the time to come, that they may lay hold on eternal life."[6] They who were making such a use of their property have been consoled for light losses by great gains, and have had more pleasure in those possessions which they have securely laid past, by freely giving them away, than grief in those which they entirely lost by an anxious and selfish hoarding of them. For nothing could perish on earth save what they would be ashamed to carry away from earth. Our Lord's injunction runs, "Lay not up for yourselves treasures upon earth, where moth and rust doth corrupt, and where thieves break through and steal; but lay up for yourselves treasures in heaven, where neither moth nor rust doth corrupt, and where thieves do not break through nor steal: for where your treasure is, there will your heart be also."[7] And

---

[1]Ezek. 33. 6.   [3]I Pet. 3, 4.
[2]Rom. 8. 28.   [4]I Tim. 6. 6–10.

[5]Job, I. 21.   [6]I Tim. 6. 17–19.   [7]Matt. 6. 19–21.

they who have listened to this injunction have proved in the time of tribulation how well they were advised in not despising this most trustworthy teacher, and most faithful and mighty guardian of their treasure. For if many were glad that their treasure was stored in places which the enemy chanced not to light upon, how much better founded was the joy of those who, by the counsel of their God, had fled with their treasure to a citadel which no enemy can possibly reach! Thus our Paulinus, bishop of Nola, who voluntarily abandoned vast wealth and became quite poor, though abundantly rich in holiness, when the barbarians sacked Nola, and took him prisoner, used silently to pray, as he afterwards told me, "O Lord, let me not be troubled for gold and silver, for where all my treasure is Thou knowest." For all his treasure was where he had been taught to hide and store it by Him who had also foretold that these calamities would happen in the world. Consequently those persons who obeyed their Lord when He warned them where and how to lay up treasure, did not lose even their earthly possessions in the invasion of the barbarians; while those who are now repenting that they did not obey Him have learnt the right use of earthly goods, if not by the wisdom which would have prevented their loss, at least by the experience which follows it.

But some good and Christian men have been put to the torture, that they might be forced to deliver up their goods to the enemy. They could indeed neither deliver nor lose that good which made themselves good. If, however, they preferred torture to the surrender of the mammon of iniquity, then I say they were not good men. Rather they should have been reminded that, if they suffered so severely for the sake of money, they should endure all torment, if need be, for Christ's sake; that they might be taught to love Him rather who enriches with eternal felicity all who suffer for Him, and not silver and gold, for which it was pitiable to suffer, whether they preserved it by telling a lie or lost it by telling the truth. For under these tortures no one lost Christ by confessing Him, no one preserved wealth save by denying its existence. So that possibly the torture which taught them that they should set their affections on a possession they could not lose was more useful than those possessions which, without any useful fruit at all, disquieted and tormented their anxious owners. But then we are reminded that some were tortured who had no wealth to surrender, but who were not believed

when they said so. These too, however, had perhaps some craving for wealth, and were not willingly poor with a holy resignation; and to such it had to be made plain, that not the actual possession alone, but also the desire of wealth, deserved such excruciating pains. And even if they were destitute of any hidden stores of gold and silver, because they were living in hopes of a better life—I know not indeed if any such person was tortured on the supposition that he had wealth; but if so, then certainly in confessing, when put to the question, a holy poverty, he confessed Christ. And though it was scarcely to be expected that the barbarians should believe him, yet no confessor of a holy poverty could be tortured without receiving a heavenly reward.

Again, they say that the long famine laid many a Christian low. But this, too, the faithful turned to good uses by a pious endurance of it. For those whom famine killed outright it rescued from the ills of this life, as a kindly disease would have done; and those who were only hunger-bitten were taught to live more sparingly, and inured to longer fasts.

CHAP. 11. *Of the end of this life, whether it is material that it be long delayed*

But, it is added, many Christians were slaughtered, and were put to death in a hideous variety of cruel ways. Well, if this be hard to bear, it is assuredly the common lot of all who are born into this life. Of this at least I am certain, that no one has ever died who was not destined to die some time. Now the end of life puts the longest life on a par with the shortest. For of two things which have alike ceased to be, the one is not better, the other worse—the one greater, the other less. And of what consequence is it what kind of death puts an end to life, since he who has died once is not forced to go through the same ordeal a second time? And as in the daily casualties of life every man is, as it were, threatened with numberless deaths, so long as it remains uncertain which of them is his fate, I would ask whether it is not better to suffer one and die, than to live in fear of all? I am not unaware of the poor-spirited fear which prompts us to choose rather to live long in fear of so many deaths, than to die once and so escape them all; but the weak and cowardly shrinking of the flesh is one thing, and the well-considered and reasonable persuasion of the soul quite another. That death is not to be judged an evil which is the end of a good life; for death becomes evil only by the retribution which follows it. They, then, who are destined to die, need not be careful to inquire what death they are to die, but into what place death will usher them. And since Christians are well aware that the death of the godly pauper whose sores the dogs licked was far better than of the wicked rich man who lay in purple and fine linen, what harm could these terrific deaths do to the dead who had lived well?

CHAP. 12. *Of the burial of the dead: that the denial of it to Christians does them no injury*

Further still, we are reminded that in such a carnage as then occurred, the bodies could not even be buried. But godly confidence is not appalled by so ill-omened a circumstance; for the faithful bear in mind that assurance has been given that not a hair of their head shall perish, and that, therefore, though they even be devoured by beasts, their blessed resurrection will not hereby be hindered. The Truth would nowise have said, "Fear not them which kill the body, but are not able to kill the soul,"[1] if anything whatever that an enemy could do to the body of the slain could be detrimental to the future life. Or will some one perhaps take so absurd a position as to contend that those who kill the body are not to be feared before death, and lest they kill the body, but after death, lest they deprive it of burial? If this be so, then that is false which Christ says, "Be not afraid of them that kill the body, and after that have no more that they can do";[2] for it seems they can do great injury to the dead body. Far be it from us to suppose that the Truth can be thus false. They who kill the body are said "to do something," because the deathblow is felt, the body still having sensation; but after that, they have no more that they can do, for in the slain body there is no sensation. And so there are indeed many bodies of Christians lying unburied; but no one has separated them from heaven, nor from that earth which is all filled with the presence of Him who knows whence He will raise again what He created. It is said, indeed, in the Psalm: "The dead bodies of Thy servants have they given to be meat unto the fowls of the heaven, the flesh of Thy saints unto the beasts of the earth. Their blood have they shed like water round about Jerusalem; and there was none to bury them."[3] But this was said rather to exhibit the cruelty of those who did these things, than the misery of those who suffered them. To the eyes of men this appears a harsh

and doleful lot, yet "precious in the sight of the Lord is the death of His saints."[4] Wherefore all these last offices and ceremonies that concern the dead, the careful funeral arrangements, and the equipment of the tomb, and the pomp of obsequies, are rather the solace of the living than the comfort of the dead. If a costly burial does any good to a wicked man, a squalid burial, or none at all, may harm the godly. His crowd of domestics furnished the purple-clad Dives with a funeral gorgeous in the eye of man; but in the sight of God that was a more sumptuous funeral which the ulcerous pauper received at the hands of the angels, who did not carry him out to a marble tomb, but bore him aloft to Abraham's bosom.

The men against whom I have undertaken to defend the city of God laugh at all this. But even their own philosophers[5] have despised a careful burial; and often whole armies have fought and fallen for their earthly country without caring to inquire whether they would be left exposed on the field of battle, or become the food of wild beasts. Of this noble disregard of sepulture poetry has well said: "He who has no tomb has the sky for his vault." How much less ought they to insult over the unburied bodies of Christians, to whom it has been promised that the flesh itself shall be restored, and the body formed anew, all the members of it being gathered not only from the earth, but from the most secret recesses of any other of the elements in which the dead bodies of men have lain hid!

CHAP. 13. *Reasons for burying the bodies of the saints*

Nevertheless the bodies of the dead are not on this account to be despised and left unburied; least of all the bodies of the righteous and faithful, which have been used by the Holy Spirit as His organs and instruments for all good works. For if the dress of a father, or his ring, or anything he wore, be precious to his children, in proportion to the love they bore him, with how much more reason ought we to care for the bodies of those we love, which they wore far more closely and intimately than any clothing! For the body is not an extraneous ornament or aid, but a part of man's very nature. And therefore to the righteous of ancient times the last offices were piously rendered, and sepulchres provided for them, and obsequies celebrated;[6] and they themselves, while yet alive, gave commandment to their sons about the burial, and,

[1] Matt. 10. 28.   [2] Luke, 12. 4.   [3] Ps. 79. 2, 3.

[4] Ps. 116. 15.   [5] Diogenes especially, and his followers.
[6] Gen. 25. 9; 35. 29, etc.

on occasion, even about the removal of their bodies to some favorite place.[1] And Tobit, according to the angel's testimony, is commended, and is said to have pleased God by burying the dead.[2] Our Lord Himself, too, though He was to rise again the third day, applauds, and commends to our applause, the good work of the religious woman who poured precious ointment over His limbs, and did it against His burial.[3] And the Gospel speaks with commendation of those who were careful to take down His body from the cross, and wrap it lovingly in costly cerements, and see to its burial.[4] These instances certainly do not prove that corpses have any feeling; but they show that God's providence extends even to the bodies of the dead, and that such pious offices are pleasing to Him, as cherishing faith in the resurrection. And we may also draw from them this wholesome lesson, that if God does not forget even any kind office which loving care pays to the unconscious dead, much more does He reward the charity we exercise towards the living. Other things, indeed, which the holy patriarchs said of the burial and removal of their bodies, they meant to be taken in a prophetic sense; but of these we need not here speak at large, what we have already said being sufficient. But if the want of those things which are necessary for the support of the living, as food and clothing, though painful and trying, does not break down the fortitude and virtuous endurance of good men, nor eradicate piety from their souls, but rather renders it more fruitful, how much less can the absence of the funeral, and of the other customary attentions paid to the dead, render those wretched who are already reposing in the hidden abodes of the blessed! Consequently, though in the sack of Rome and of other towns the dead bodies of the Christians were deprived of these last offices, this is neither the fault of the living, for they could not render them; nor an infliction to the dead, for they cannot feel the loss.

CHAP. 14. *Of the captivity of the saints, and that divine consolation never failed them therein*

But, say they, many Christians were even led away captive. This indeed were a most pitiable fate, if they could be led away to any place where they could not find their God. But for this calamity also sacred Scripture affords great consolation. The three youths[5] were captives; Daniel was a captive; so were other prophets: and

God, the comforter, did not fail them. And in like manner He has not failed His own people in the power of a nation which, though barbarous, is yet human—He who did not abandon the prophet in the belly of a monster. These things, indeed, are turned to ridicule rather than credited by those with whom we are debating; though they believe what they read in their own books, that Arion of Methymna, the famous lyrist, when he was thrown overboard, was received on a dolphin's back and carried to land.[6] But that story of ours about the prophet Jonah is far more incredible—more incredible because more marvellous, and more marvellous because a greater exhibition of power.

CHAP. 15. *Of Regulus, in whom we have an example of the voluntary endurance of captivity for the sake of religion; which yet did not profit him, though he was a worshipper of the gods*

But among their own famous men they have a very noble example of the voluntary endurance of captivity in obedience to a religious scruple. Marcus Attilius Regulus, a Roman general, was a prisoner in the hands of the Carthaginians. But they, being more anxious to exchange their prisoners with the Romans than to keep them, sent Regulus as a special envoy with their own ambassadors to negotiate this exchange, but bound him first with an oath, that if he failed to accomplish their wish, he would return to Carthage. He went and persuaded the senate to the opposite course, because he believed it was not for the advantage of the Roman republic to make an exchange of prisoners. After he had thus exerted his influence, the Romans did not compel him to return to the enemy; but what he had sworn he voluntarily performed. But the Carthaginians put him to death with refined, elaborate, and horrible tortures. They shut him up in a narrow box, in which he was compelled to stand, and in which finely sharpened nails were fixed all round about him, so that he could not lean upon any part of it without intense pain; and so they killed him by depriving him of sleep. With justice, indeed, do they applaud the virtue which rose superior to so frightful a fate. However, the gods he swore by were those who are now supposed to avenge the prohibition of their worship, by inflicting these present calamities on the human race. But if these gods, who were worshipped specially in this behalf, that they might confer happiness in this life, either willed or permitted these pun-

---

[1]Gen. 47. 29; 50. 24. [2]Tob. 12. 12.
[3]Matt. 26. 10-13. [4]John, 19. 38. [5]Dan. 3.

[6]Herodotus, *History*, BK. I. 23, 24.

ishments to be inflicted on one who kept his oath to them, what more cruel punishment could they in their anger have inflicted on a perjured person? But why may I not draw from my reasoning a double inference? Regulus certainly had such reverence for the gods that for his oath's sake he would neither remain in his own land nor go elsewhere, but without hesitation returned to his bitterest enemies. If he thought that this course would be advantageous with respect to this present life, he was certainly much deceived, for it brought his life to a frightful termination. By his own example, in fact, he taught that the gods do not secure the temporal happiness of their worshippers; since he himself, who was devoted to their worship, as both conquered in battle and taken prisoner, and then, because he refused to act in violation of the oath he had sworn by them, was tortured and put to death by a new, and hitherto unheard of, and all too horrible kind of punishment. And on the supposition that the worshippers of the gods are rewarded by felicity in the life to come, why, then, do they calumniate the influence of Christianity? why do they assert that this disaster has overtaken the city because it has ceased to worship its gods, since, worship them as assiduously as it may, it may yet be as unfortunate as Regulus was? Or will some one carry so wonderful a blindness to the extent of wildly attempting, in the face of the evident truth, to contend that though one man might be unfortunate, though a worshipper of the gods, yet a whole city could not be so? That is to say, the power of their gods is better adapted to preserve multitudes than individuals—as if a multitude were not composed of individuals.

But if they say that M. Regulus, even while a prisoner and enduring these bodily torments, might yet enjoy the blessedness of a virtuous soul, then let them recognize that true virtue by which a city also may be blessed. For the blessedness of a community and of an individual flow from the same source; for a community is nothing else than a harmonious collection of individuals. So that I am not concerned meantime to discuss what kind of virtue Regulus possessed; enough that by his very noble example they are forced to own that the gods are to be worshipped not for the sake of bodily comforts or external advantages; for he preferred to lose all such things rather than offend the gods by whom he had sworn. But what can we make of men who glory in having such a citizen, but dread having a city like him? If they do not dread this, then let them acknowledge that some such calamity as befell Regulus may also befall a community, though they be worshipping their gods as diligently as he; and let them no longer throw the blame of their misfortunes on Christianity. But as our present concern is with those Christians who were taken prisoners, let those who take occasion from this calamity to revile our most wholesome religion in a fashion not less imprudent than impudent, consider this and hold their peace; for if it was no reproach to their gods that a most punctilious worshipper of theirs should, for the sake of keeping his oath to them, be deprived of his native land without hope of finding another, and fall into the hands of his enemies, and be put to death by a long-drawn and exquisite torture, much less ought the Christian name to be charged with the captivity of those who believe in its power, since they, in confident expectation of a heavenly country, know that they are pilgrims even in their own homes.

CHAP. 16. *Of the violation of the consecrated and other Christian virgins, to which they were subjected in captivity, and to which their own will gave no consent; and whether this contaminated their souls*

But they fancy they bring a conclusive charge against Christianity, when they aggravate the horror of captivity by adding that not only wives and unmarried maidens, but even consecrated virgins, were violated. But truly, with respect to this, it is not Christian faith, nor piety, nor even the virtue of chastity, which is hemmed into any difficulty; the only difficulty is so to treat the subject as to satisfy at once modesty and reason. And in discussing it we shall not be so careful to reply to our accusers as to comfort our friends. Let this, therefore, in the first place, be laid down as an unassailable position, that the virtue which makes the life good has its throne in the soul, and thence rules the members of the body, which becomes holy in virtue of the holiness of the will; and that while the will remains firm and unshaken, nothing that another person does with the body, or upon the body, is any fault of the person who suffers it, so long as he cannot escape it without sin. But as not only pain may be inflicted, but lust gratified on the body of another, whenever anything of this latter kind takes place, shame invades even a thoroughly pure spirit from which modesty has not departed—shame, lest that act which could not be suffered without some sensual pleasure, should be believed to have been committed also with some assent of the will.

Chap. 17. Of suicide committed through fear of punishment or dishonour

And consequently, even if some of these virgins killed themselves to avoid such disgrace, who that has any human feeling would refuse to forgive them? And as for those who would not put an end to their lives, lest they might seem to escape the crime of another by a sin of their own, he who lays this to their charge as a great wickedness is himself not guiltless of the fault of folly. For if it is not lawful to take the law into our own hands and slay even a guilty person, whose death no public sentence has warranted, then certainly he who kills himself is a homicide, and so much the guiltier of his own death as he was more innocent of that offence for which he doomed himself to die. Do we justly execrate the deed of Judas, and does truth itself pronounce that by hanging himself he rather aggravated than expiated the guilt of that most iniquitous betrayal, since, by despairing of God's mercy in his sorrow that wrought death, he left to himself no place for a healing penitence? How much more ought he to abstain from laying violent hands on himself who has done nothing worthy of such a punishment! For Judas, when he killed himself, killed a wicked man; but he passed from this life chargeable not only with the death of Christ, but with his own: for though he killed himself on account of his crime, his killing himself was another crime. Why, then, should a man who has done no ill do ill to himself, and by killing himself kill the innocent to escape another's guilty act, and perpetrate upon himself a sin of his own, that the sin of another may not be perpetrated on him?

Chap. 18. Of the violence which may be done to the body by another's lust while the mind remains inviolate

But is there a fear that even another's lust may pollute the violated? It will not pollute, if it be another's: if it pollute, it is not another's, but is shared also by the polluted. But since purity is a virtue of the soul, and has for its companion virtue, the fortitude which will rather endure all ills than consent to evil; and since no one, however magnanimous and pure, has always the disposal of his own body, but can control only the consent and refusal of his will, what sane man can suppose that, if his body be seized and forcibly made use of to satisfy the lust of another, he thereby loses his purity? For if purity can be thus destroyed, then assuredly purity is no virtue of the soul; nor can it be numbered among those good things by which the life is made good, but among the good things of the body, in the same category as strength, beauty, sound and unbroken health, and, in short, all such good things as may be diminished without at all diminishing the goodness and rectitude of our life. But if purity be nothing better than these, why should the body be perilled that it may be preserved? If, on the other hand, it belongs to the soul, then not even when the body is violated is it lost. Nay more, the virtue of holy continence, when it resists the uncleanness of carnal lust, sanctifies even the body, and therefore when this continence remains unsubdued, even the sanctity of the body is preserved, because the will to use it holily remains, and, so far as lies in the body itself, the power also.

For the sanctity of the body does not consist in the integrity of its members, nor in their exemption from all touch; for they are exposed to various accidents which do violence to and wound them, and the surgeons who administer relief often perform operations that sicken the spectator. A midwife, suppose, has (whether maliciously or accidentally, or through unskilfulness) destroyed the virginity of some girl, while endeavouring to ascertain it: I suppose no one is so foolish as to believe that, by this destruction of the integrity of one organ, the virgin has lost anything even of her bodily sanctity. And thus, so long as the soul keeps this firmness of purpose which sanctifies even the body, the violence done by another's lust makes no impression on this bodily sanctity, which is preserved intact by one's own persistent continence. Suppose a virgin violates the oath she has sworn to God, and goes to meet her seducer with the intention of yielding to him, shall we say that as she goes she is possessed even of bodily sanctity, when already she has lost and destroyed that sanctity of soul which sanctifies the body? Far be it from us to so misapply words. Let us rather draw this conclusion, that while the sanctity of the soul remains even when the body is violated, the sanctity of the body is not lost; and that, in like manner, the sanctity of the body is lost when the sanctity of the soul is violated, though the body itself remains intact. And therefore a woman who has been violated by the sin of another, and without any consent of her own, has no cause to put herself to death; much less has she cause to commit suicide in order to avoid such violation, for in that case she commits certain homicide to prevent a crime which is uncertain as yet, and not her own.

CHAP. 19. *Of Lucretia, who put an end to her life because of the outrage done her.*

This, then, is our position, and it seems sufficiently lucid. We maintain that when a woman is violated while her soul admits no consent to the iniquity, but remains inviolably chaste, the sin is not hers, but his who violates her. But do they against whom we have to defend not only the souls, but the sacred bodies too of these outraged Christian captives—do they, perhaps, dare to dispute our position? But all know how loudly they extol the purity of Lucretia, that noble matron of ancient Rome. When King Tarquin's son had violated her body, she made known the wickedness of this young profligate to her husband Collatinus, and to Brutus her kinsman, men of high rank and full of courage, and bound them by an oath to avenge it. Then, heart-sick, and unable to bear the shame, she put an end to her life. What shall we call her? An adulteress, or chaste? There is no question which she was. Not more happily than truly did a declaimer say of this sad occurrence: "Here was a marvel: there were two, and only one committed adultery." Most forcibly and truly spoken. For this declaimer, seeing in the union of the two bodies the foul lust of the one, and the chaste will of the other, and giving heed not to the contact of the bodily members, but to the wide diversity of their souls, says: "There were two, but the adultery was committed only by one."

But how is it, that she who was no partner to the crime bears the heavier punishment of the two? For the adulterer was only banished along with his father; she suffered the extreme penalty. If that was not impurity by which she was unwillingly ravished, then this is not justice by which she, being chaste, is punished. To you I appeal, ye laws and judges of Rome. Even after the perpetration of great enormities, you do not suffer the criminal to be slain untried. If, then, one were to bring to your bar this case, and were to prove to you that a woman not only untried, but chaste and innocent, had been killed, would you not visit the murderer with punishment proportionally severe? This crime was committed by Lucretia; that Lucretia so celebrated and lauded slew the innocent, chaste, outraged Lucretia. Pronounce sentence. But if you cannot, because there does not appear any one whom you can punish, why do you extol with such unmeasured laudation her who slew an innocent and chaste woman? Assuredly you will find it impossible to defend her before the judges of the realms below, if they be such as

your poets are fond of representing them; for she is among those:

Who guiltless sent themselves to doom,
And all for loathing of the day,
In madness threw their lives away.

And if she with the others wishes to return,

Fate bars the way: around their keep
The slow unlovely waters creep,
And bind with ninefold chain.[1]

Or perhaps she is not there, because she slew herself conscious of guilt, not of innocence? She herself alone knows her reason; but what if she was betrayed by the pleasure of the act, and gave some consent to Sextus, though so violently abusing her, and then was so affected with remorse, that she thought death alone could expiate her sin? Even though this were the case, she ought still to have held her hand from suicide, if she could with her false gods have accomplished a fruitful repentance. However, if such were the state of the case, and if it were false that there were two, but one only committed adultery; if the truth were that both were involved in it, one by open assault, the other by secret consent, then she did not kill an innocent woman; and therefore her erudite defenders may maintain that she is not among that class of the dwellers below "who guiltless sent themselves to doom." But this case of Lucretia is in such a dilemma that if you extenuate the homicide, you confirm the adultery; if you acquit her of adultery, you make the charge of homicide heavier; and there is no way out of the dilemma, when one asks: If she was adulterous, why praise her? if chaste, why slay her?

Nevertheless, for our purpose of refuting those who are unable to comprehend what true sanctity is, and who therefore insult over our outraged Christian women, it is enough that in the instance of this noble Roman matron it was said in her praise, "There were two, but the adultery was the crime of only one." For Lucretia was confidently believed to be superior to the contamination of any consenting thought to the adultery. And accordingly, since she killed herself for being subjected to an outrage in which she had no guilty part, it is obvious that this act of hers was prompted not by the love of purity, but by the overwhelming burden of her shame. She was ashamed that so foul a crime had been perpetrated upon her, though without her abetting; and this matron, with the Roman love of glory in her veins, was seized with a proud dread that, if she continued to live, it would be sup-

[1]Virgil, *Æneid*, BK. VI. 434.

posed she willingly did not resent the wrong that had been done her. She could not exhibit to men her conscience, but she judged that her self-inflicted punishment would testify her state of mind; and she burned with shame at the thought that her patient endurance of the foul affront that another had done her, should be construed into complicity with him. Not such was the decision of the Christian women who suffered as she did and yet survive. They declined to avenge upon themselves the guilt of others and so add crimes of their own to those crimes in which they had no share. For this they would have done had their shame driven them to homicide, as the lust of their enemies had driven them to adultery. Within their own souls, in the witness of their own conscience, they enjoy the glory of chastity. In the sight of God, too, they are esteemed pure, and this contents them; they ask no more; it suffices them to have opportunity of doing good, and they decline to evade the distress of human suspicion, lest they thereby deviate from the divine law.

CHAP. 20. *That Christians have no authority for committing suicide in any circumstances whatever*

It is not without significance, that in no passage of the holy canonical books there can be found either divine precept or permission to take away our own life, whether for the sake of entering on the enjoyment of immortality, or of shunning, or ridding ourselves of anything whatever. Nay, the law, rightly interpreted, even prohibits suicide, where it says, "Thou shalt not kill." This is proved especially by the omission of the words "thy neighbour," which are inserted when false witness is forbidden: "Thou shalt not bear false witness against thy neighbour." Nor yet should any one on this account suppose he has not broken this commandment if he has borne false witness only against himself. For the love of our neighbour is regulated by the love of ourselves, as it is written, "Thou shalt love thy neighbour as thyself." If, then, he who makes false statements about himself is not less guilty of bearing false witness than if he had made them to the injury of his neighbour; although in the commandment prohibiting false witness only his neighbour is mentioned, and persons taking no pains to understand it might suppose that a man was allowed to be a false witness to his own hurt; how much greater reason have we to understand that a man may not kill himself, since in the commandment, "Thou shalt not kill," there is no limita-

tion added nor any exception made in favour of any one, and least of all in favour of him on whom the command is laid! And so some attempt to extend this command even to beasts and cattle, as if it forbade us to take life from any creature. But if so, why not extend it also to the plants, and all that is rooted in and nourished by the earth? For though this class of creatures have no sensation, yet they also are said to live, and consequently they can die; and therefore, if violence be done them, can be killed. So, too, the apostle, when speaking of the seeds of such things as these, says, "That which thou sowest is not quickened except it die"; and in the Psalm it is said, "He killed their vines with hail." Must we therefore reckon it a breaking of this commandment, "Thou shalt not kill," to pull a flower? Are we thus insanely to countenance the foolish error of the Manichæans? Putting aside, then, these ravings, if, when we say, Thou shalt not kill, we do not understand this of the plants, since they have no sensation, nor of the irrational animals that fly, swim, walk, or creep, since they are dissociated from us by their want of reason, and are therefore by the just appointment of the Creator subjected to us to kill or keep alive for our own uses; if so, then it remains that we understand that commandment simply of man. The commandment is, "Thou shalt not kill man"; therefore neither another nor yourself, for he who kills himself still kills nothing else than man.

CHAP. 21. *Of the cases in which we may put men to death without incurring the guilt of murder*

However, there are some exceptions made by the divine authority to its own law that men may not be put to death. These exceptions are of two kinds, being justified either by a general law, or by a special commission granted for a time to some individual. And in this latter case, he to whom authority is delegated, and who is but the sword in the hand of him who uses it, is not himself responsible for the death he deals. And, accordingly, they who have waged war in obedience to the divine command, or in conformity with His laws, have represented in their persons the public justice or the wisdom of government, and in this capacity have put to death wicked men; such persons have by no means violated the commandment, "Thou shalt not kill." Abraham indeed was not merely deemed guiltless of cruelty, but was even applauded for his piety, because he was ready to slay his son in obedience to God, not to his own passion.

And it is reasonably enough made a question, whether we are to esteem it to have been in compliance with a command of God that Jephthah killed his daughter, because she met him when he had vowed that he would sacrifice to God whatever first met him as he returned victorious from battle. Samson, too, who drew down the house on himself and his foes together, is justified only on this ground, that the Spirit who wrought wonders by him had given him secret instructions to do this. With the exception, then, of these two classes of cases, which are justified either by a just law that applies generally, or by a special intimation from God Himself, the fountain of all justice, whoever kills a man, either himself or another, is implicated in the guilt of murder.

CHAP. 22. *That suicide can never be prompted by magnanimity*

But they who have laid violent hands on themselves are perhaps to be admired for their greatness of soul, though they cannot be applauded for the soundness of their judgment. However, if you look at the matter more closely, you will scarcely call it greatness of soul, which prompts a man to kill himself rather than to bear up against some hardships of fortune, or sins in which he is not implicated. Is it not rather proof of a feeble mind, to be unable to bear either the pains of bodily servitude or the foolish opinion of the vulgar? And is not that to be pronounced the greater mind, which rather faces than flees the ills of life, and which, in comparison of the light and purity of conscience, holds in small esteem the judgment of men, and specially of the vulgar, which is frequently involved in a mist of error? And, therefore, if suicide is to be esteemed a magnanimous act, none can take higher rank for magnanimity than that Cleombrotus, who (as the story goes), when he had read Plato's book in which he treats of the immortality of the soul, threw himself from a wall, and so passed from this life to that which he believed to be better. For he was not hard pressed by calamity, nor by any accusation, false or true, which he could not very well have lived down; there was, in short, no motive but only magnanimity urging him to seek death, and break away from the sweet detention of this life. And yet that this was a magnanimous rather than a justifiable action, Plato himself, whom he had read, would have told him; for he would certainly have been forward to commit, or at least to recommend suicide, had not the same bright intellect which saw that the soul was immortal,

discerned also that to seek immortality by suicide was to be prohibited rather than encouraged.

Again, it is said many have killed themselves to prevent an enemy doing so. But we are not inquiring whether it has been done, but whether it ought to have been done. Sound judgment is to be preferred even to examples, and indeed examples harmonize with the voice of reason; but not all examples, but those only which are distinguished by their piety, and are proportionately worthy of imitation. For suicide we cannot cite the example of patriarchs, prophets, or apostles; though our Lord Jesus Christ, when He admonished them to flee from city to city if they were persecuted, might very well have taken that occasion to advise them to lay violent hands on themselves, and so escape their persecutors. But seeing He did not do this, nor proposed this mode of departing this life, though He were addressing His own friends for whom He had promised to prepare everlasting mansions, it is obvious that such examples as are produced from the "nations that forget God," give no warrant of imitation to the worshippers of the one true God.

CHAP. 23. *What we are to think of the example of Cato, who slew himself because unable to endure Cæsar's victory*

Beside Lucretia, of whom enough has already been said, our advocates of suicide have some difficulty in finding any other prescriptive example, unless it be that of Cato, who killed himself at Utica. His example is appealed to, not because he was the only man who did so, but because he was so esteemed as a learned and excellent man, that it could plausibly be maintained that what he did was and is a good thing to do. But of this action of his, what can I say but that his own friends, enlightened men as he, prudently dissuaded him, and therefore judged his act to be that of a feeble rather than a strong spirit, and dictated not by honourable feeling forestalling shame, but by weakness shrinking from hardships? Indeed, Cato condemns himself by the advice he gave to his dearly loved son. For if it was a disgrace to live under Cæsar's rule, why did the father urge the son to this disgrace, by encouraging him to trust absolutely to Cæsar's generosity? Why did he not persuade him to die along with himself? If Torquatus was applauded for putting his son to death, when contrary to orders he had engaged, and engaged successfully, with the enemy, why did conquered Cato spare his conquered son, though he did not spare himself? Was it more disgraceful to be a victor contrary to orders, than to submit to a victor contrary to the received ideas of honour? Cato, then, cannot have deemed it to be shameful to live under Cæsar's rule; for had he done so, the father's sword would have delivered his son from this disgrace. The truth is that his son, whom he both hoped and desired would be spared by Cæsar, was not more loved by him than Cæsar was envied the glory of pardoning him (as indeed Cæsar himself is reported to have said[1]); or if envy is too strong a word, let us say he was *ashamed* that this glory should be his.

CHAP. 24. *That in that virtue in which Regulus excels Cato, Christians are pre-eminently distinguished*

Our opponents are offended at our preferring to Cato the saintly Job, who endured dreadful evils in his body rather than deliver himself from all torment by self-inflicted death; or other saints, of whom it is recorded in our authoritative and trustworthy books that they bore captivity and the oppression of their enemies rather than commit suicide. But their own books authorize us to prefer to Marcus Cato, Marcus Regulus. For Cato had never conquered Cæsar; and when conquered by him, disdained to submit himself to him, and that he might escape this submission put himself to death. Regulus, on the contrary, had formerly conquered the Carthaginians, and in command of the army of Rome had won for the Roman republic a victory which no citizen could bewail, and which the enemy himself was constrained to admire; yet afterwards, when he in his turn was defeated by them, he preferred to be their captive rather than to put himself beyond their reach by suicide. Patient under the domination of the Carthaginians, and constant in his love of the Romans, he neither deprived the one of his conquered body, nor the other of his unconquered spirit. Neither was it love of life that prevented him from killing himself. This was plainly enough indicated by his unhesitatingly returning, on account of his promise and oath, to the same enemies whom he had more grievously provoked by his words in the senate than even by his arms in battle. Having such a contempt of life, and preferring to end it by whatever torments excited enemies might contrive, rather than terminate it by his own hand, he could not more distinctly have declared how great a crime he judged suicide to be. Among all their famous

[1]Plutarch, *Cato, the Younger.*

and remarkable citizens, the Romans have no better man to boast of than this, who was neither corrupted by prosperity, for he remained a very poor man after winning such victories; nor broken by adversity, for he returned intrepidly to the most miserable end. But if the bravest and most renowned heroes, who had but an earthly country to defend, and who, though they had but false gods, yet rendered them a true worship, and carefully kept their oath to them; if these men, who by the custom and right of war put conquered enemies to the sword, yet shrank from putting an end to their own lives even when conquered by their enemies; if, though they had no fear at all of death, they would yet rather suffer slavery than commit suicide, how much rather must Christians, the worshippers of the true God, the aspirants to a heavenly citizenship, shrink from this act, if in God's providence they have been for a season delivered into the hands of their enemies to prove or to correct them! And certainly, Christians subjected to this humiliating condition will not be deserted by the Most High, who for their sakes humbled Himself. Neither should they forget that they are bound by no laws of war, nor military orders, to put even a conquered enemy to the sword; and if a man may not put to death the enemy who has sinned, or may yet sin against him, who is so infatuated as to maintain that he may kill himself because an enemy has sinned, or is going to sin, against him?

CHAP. 25. *That we should not endeavour by sin to obviate sin*

But, we are told, there is ground to fear that, when the body is subjected to the enemy's lust, the insidious pleasure of sense may entice the soul to consent to the sin, and steps must be taken to prevent so disastrous a result. And is not suicide the proper mode of preventing not only the enemy's sin, but the sin of the Christian so allured? Now, in the first place, the soul which is led by God and His wisdom, rather than by bodily concupiscence, will certainly never consent to the desire aroused in its own flesh by another's lust. And, at all events, if it be true, as the truth plainly declares, that suicide is a detestable and damnable wickedness, who is such a fool as to say, "Let us sin now, that we may obviate a possible future sin; let us now commit murder, lest we perhaps afterwards should commit adultery"? If we are so controlled by iniquity that innocence is out of the question, and we can at best but make a choice of sins, is not a future and uncertain adultery preferable to a present and certain murder? Is it not better to commit a wickedness which penitence may heal, than a crime which leaves no place for healing contrition? I say this for the sake of those men or women who fear they may be enticed into consenting to their violator's lust, and think they should lay violent hands on themselves, and so prevent, not another's sin, but their own. But far be it from the mind of a Christian confiding in God, and resting in the hope of His aid; far be it, I say, from such a mind to yield a shameful consent to pleasures of the flesh, howsoever presented. And if that lustful disobedience, which still dwells in our mortal members, follows its own law irrespective of our will, surely its motions in the body of one who rebels against them are as blameless as its motions in the body of one who sleeps.

Chap. 26. That in certain peculiar cases the examples of the saints are not to be followed

But, they say, in the time of persecution some holy women escaped those who menaced them with outrage, by casting themselves into rivers which they knew would drown them; and having died in this manner, they are venerated in the Church Catholic as martyrs. Of such persons I do not presume to speak rashly. I cannot tell whether there may not have been vouchsafed to the Church some divine authority, proved by trustworthy evidences, for so honouring their memory: it may be that it is so. It may be they were not deceived by human judgment, but prompted by divine wisdom, to their act of self-destruction. We know that this was the case with Samson. And when God enjoins any act, and intimates by plain evidence that He has enjoined it, who will call obedience criminal? Who will accuse so religious a submission? But then every man is not justified in sacrificing his son to God, because Abraham was commendable in so doing. The soldier who has slain a man in obedience to the authority under which he is lawfully commissioned, is not accused of murder by any law of his state; nay, if he has not slain him, it is then he is accused of treason to the state and of depising the law. But if he has been acting on his own authority, and at his own impulse, he has in this case incurred the crime of shedding human blood. And thus he is punished for doing without orders the very thing he is punished for neglecting to do when he has been ordered. If the commands of a general make so great a difference, shall the commands of God make none? He, then, who knows it is unlawful to kill himself, may nevertheless do so if he is ordered by Him whose commands we may not neglect. Only let him be very sure that the divine command has been signified. As for us, we can become privy to the secrets of conscience only in so far as these are disclosed to us, and so far only do we judge: "No one knoweth the things of a man, save the spirit of man which is in him."[1] But this we affirm, this we maintain, this we every way pronounce to be right, that no man ought to inflict on himself voluntary death, for this is to escape the ills of time by plunging into those of eternity; that no man ought to do so on account of another man's sins, for this were to escape a guilt which could not pollute him, by incurring great guilt of his own; that no man ought to do so on account of his own past sins, for he has all the more need of this life that these sins may be healed by repentance; that no man should put an end to this life to obtain that better life we look for after death, for those who die by their own hand have no better life after death.

Chap. 27. Whether voluntary death should be sought in order to avoid sin

There remains one reason for suicide which I mentioned before, and which is thought a sound one—namely, to prevent one's falling into sin either through the blandishments of pleasure or the violence of pain. If this reason were a good one, then we should be impelled to exhort men at once to destroy themselves, as soon as they have been washed in the laver of regeneration and have received the forgiveness of all sin. Then is the time to escape all future sin, when all past sin is blotted out. And if this escape be lawfully secured by suicide, why not then specially? Why does any baptized person hold his hand from taking his own life? Why does any person who is freed from the hazards of this life again expose himself to them, when he has power so easily to rid himself of them all, and when it is written, "He who loveth danger shall fall into it?"[2] Why does he love, or at least face, so many serious dangers, by remaining in this life from which he may legitimately depart? But is any one so blinded and twisted in his moral nature, and so far astray from the truth, as to think that, though a man ought to make away with himself for fear of being led into sin by the oppression of one man, his master, he ought yet to live, and so expose himself to the hourly temptations of this world, both to all those evils which the oppression of one master involves, and to numberless other miseries in which this life inevitably implicates us? What reason, then,

[1] I Cor. 2. 11.   [2] Ecclus. 3. 27.

is there for our consuming time in those exhortations by which we seek to animate the baptized, either to virginal chastity, or vidual continence, or matrimonial fidelity, when we have so much more simple and compendious a method of deliverance from sin, by persuading those who are fresh from baptism to put an end to their lives, and so pass to their Lord pure and well-conditioned? If any one thinks that such persuasion should be attempted, I say not he is foolish, but mad. With what face, then, can he say to any man, "Kill yourself, lest to your small sins you add a heinous sin, while you live under an unchaste master, whose conduct is that of a barbarian"? How can he say this, if he cannot without wickedness say, "Kill yourself, now that you are washed from all your sins, lest you fall again into similar or even aggravated sins, while you live in a world which has such power to allure by its unclean pleasures, to torment by its horrible cruelties, to overcome by its errors and terrors"? It is wicked to say this; it is therefore wicked to kill oneself. For if there could be any just cause of suicide, this were so. And since not even this is so, there is none.

CHAP. 28. *By what judgment of God the enemy was permitted to indulge his lust on the bodies of continent Christians*

Let not your life, then, be a burden to you, ye faithful servants of Christ, though your chastity was made the sport of your enemies. You have a grand and true consolation, if you maintain a good conscience, and know that you did not consent to the sins of those who were permitted to commit sinful outrage upon you. And if you should ask why this permission was granted, indeed it is a deep providence of the Creator and Governor of the world; and "unsearchable are His judgments and His ways past finding out."[1] Nevertheless, faithfully interrogate your own souls, whether ye have not been unduly puffed up by your integrity, and continence, and chastity; and whether ye have not been so desirous of the human praise that is accorded to these virtues, that ye have envied some who possessed them. I, for my part, do not know your hearts, and therefore I make no accusation; I do not even hear what your hearts answer when you question them. And yet, if they answer that it is as I have supposed it might be, do not marvel that you have lost that by which you can win men's praise, and retain that which cannot be exhibited to men. If you did not consent to sin, it was because God added His aid to His grace

[1] Rom. 11. 33.

that it might not be lost, and because shame before men succeeded to human glory that it might not be loved. But in both respects even the faint-hearted among you have a consolation, approved by the one experience, chastened by the other; justified by the one, corrected by the other. As to those whose hearts, when interrogated, reply that they have never been proud of the virtue of virginity, widowhood, or matrimonial chastity, but, condescending to those of low estate, rejoiced with trembling in these gifts of God, and that they have never envied any one the like excellences of sanctity and purity, but rose superior to human applause, which is wont to be abundant in proportion to the rarity of the virtue applauded, and rather desired that their own number be increased, than that by the smallness of their numbers each of them should be conspicuous; even such faithful women, I say, must not complain that permission was given to the barbarians so grossly to outrage them; nor must they allow themselves to believe that God overlooked their character when He permitted acts which no one with impunity commits. For some most flagrant and wicked desires are allowed free play at present by the secret judgment of God, and are reserved to the public and final judgment. Moreover, it is possible that those Christian women, who are unconscious of any undue pride on account of their virtuous chastity, whereby they sinlessly suffered the violence of their captors, had yet some lurking infirmity which might have betrayed them into a proud and contemptuous bearing, had they not been subjected to the humiliation that befell them in the taking of the city. As, therefore, some men were removed by death that no wickedness might change their disposition, so these women were outraged lest prosperity should corrupt their modesty. Neither those women, then, who were already puffed up by the circumstance that they were still virgins, nor those who might have been so puffed up had they not been exposed to the violence of the enemy, lost their chastity, but rather gained humility; the former were saved from pride already cherished, the latter from pride that would shortly have grown upon them.

We must further notice that some of those sufferers may have conceived that continence is a bodily good, and abides so long as the body is inviolate, and did not understand that the purity both of the body and the soul rests on the steadfastness of the will strengthened by God's grace, and cannot be forcibly taken from an unwilling person. From this error they are probably now delivered. For when they reflect how conscientiously they served God, and when they settle again to the firm persuasion that He can in nowise desert those who so serve Him, and so invoke His aid; and when they consider, what they cannot doubt, how pleasing to Him is chastity, they are shut up to the conclusion that He could never have permitted these disasters to befall His saints, if by them that saintliness could be destroyed which He Himself had bestowed upon them, and delights to see in them.

CHAP. 29. *What the servants of Christ should say in reply to the unbelievers who cast in their teeth that Christ did not rescue them from the fury of their enemies*

The whole family of God, most high and most true, has therefore a consolation of its own—a consolation which cannot deceive, and which has in it a surer hope than the tottering and falling affairs of earth can afford. They will not refuse the discipline of this temporal life, in which they are schooled for life eternal; nor will they lament their experience of it, for the good things of earth they use as pilgrims who are not detained by them, and its ills either prove or improve them. As for those who insult over them in their trials, and when ills befall them say, "Where is thy God?"[1] we may ask them where their gods are when they suffer the very calamities for the sake of avoiding which they worship their gods, or maintain they ought to be worshipped; for the family of Christ is furnished with its reply: our God is everywhere present, wholly everywhere; not confined to any place. He can be present unperceived, and be absent without moving; when He exposes us to adversities, it is either to prove our perfections or correct our imperfections; and in return for our patient endurance of the sufferings of time, He reserves for us an everlasting reward. But who are you, that we should deign to speak with you even about your own gods, much less about our God, who is "to be feared above all gods? For all the gods of the nations are idols; but the Lord made the heavens."[2]

CHAP. 30. *That those who complain of Christianity really desire to live without restraint in shameful luxury*

If the famous Scipio Nasica were now alive, who was once your pontiff and was unanimously chosen by the senate, when, in the panic created by the Punic war, they sought for the best citizen to entertain the Phrygian goddess, he

[1] Ps. 42. 10.   [2] Ps. 96. 4, 5.

would curb this shamelessness of yours, though you would perhaps scarcely dare to look upon the countenance of such a man. For why in your calamities do you complain of Christianity, unless because you desire to enjoy your luxurious licence unrestrained and to lead an abandoned and profligate life without the interruption of any uneasiness or disaster? For certainly your desire for peace, and prosperity, and plenty is not prompted by any purpose of using these blessings honestly, that is to say, with moderation, sobriety, temperance, and piety; for your purpose rather is to run riot in an endless variety of sottish pleasures, and thus to generate from your prosperity a moral pestilence which will prove a thousandfold more disastrous than the fiercest enemies. It was such a calamity as this that Scipio, your chief pontiff, your best man in the judgment of the whole senate, feared when he refused to agree to the destruction of Carthage, Rome's rival, and opposed Cato, who advised its destruction. He feared security, that enemy of weak minds, and he perceived that a wholesome fear would be a fit guardian for the citizens. And he was not mistaken; the event proved how wisely he had spoken. For when Carthage was destroyed, and the Roman republic delivered from its great cause of anxiety, a crowd of disastrous evils forthwith resulted from the prosperous condition of things. First concord was weakened, and destroyed by fierce and bloody seditions; then followed, by a concatenation of baleful causes, civil wars, which brought in their train such massacres, such bloodshed, such lawless and cruel proscription and plunder, that those Romans who, in the days of their virtue, had expected injury only at the hands of their enemies, now that their virtue was lost, suffered greater cruelties at the hands of their fellow-citizens. The lust of rule, which with other vices existed among the Romans in more unmitigated intensity than among any other people, after it had taken possession of the more powerful few, subdued under its yoke the rest, worn and wearied.

CHAP. 31. *By what steps the passion for governing increased among the Romans*

For at what stage would that passion rest when once it has lodged in a proud spirit, until by a succession of advances it has reached even the throne. And to obtain such advances nothing avails but unscrupulous ambition. But unscrupulous ambition has nothing to work upon, save in a nation corrupted by avarice and luxury. Moreover, a people becomes avaricious and luxurious by prosperity; and it was this which that very prudent man Nasica was endeavouring to avoid when he opposed the destruction of the greatest, strongest, wealthiest city of Rome's enemy. He thought that thus fear would act as a curb on lust, and that lust being curbed would not run riot in luxury, and that luxury being prevented avarice would be at an end; and that these vices being banished, virtue would flourish and increase the great profit of the state; and liberty, the first companion of virtue, would abide unfettered. For similar reasons, and animated by the same considerate patriotism, that same chief pontiff of yours—I still refer to him who was adjudged Rome's best man without one dissentient voice—threw cold water on the proposal of the senate to build a circle of seats round the theatre, and in a very weighty speech warned them against allowing the luxurious manners of Greece to sap the Roman manliness, and persuaded them not to yield to the enervating and emasculating influence of foreign licentiousness. So authoritative and forcible were his words that the senate was moved to prohibit the use even of those benches which hitherto had been customarily brought to the theatre for the temporary use of the citizens. How eagerly would such a man as this have banished from Rome the scenic exhibitions themselves, had he dared to oppose the authority of those whom he supposed to be gods! For he did not know that they were malicious devils; or if he did, he supposed they should rather be propitiated than despised. For there had not yet been revealed to the Gentiles the heavenly doctrine which should purify their hearts by faith, and transform their natural disposition by humble godliness, and turn them from the service of proud devils to seek the things that are in heaven, or even above the heavens.

CHAP. 32. *Of the establishment of scenic entertainments*

Know then, ye who are ignorant of this, and ye who feign ignorance be reminded, while you murmur against Him who has freed you from such rulers, that the scenic games, exhibitions of shameless folly and licence, were established at Rome, not by men's vicious cravings, but by the appointment of your gods. Much more pardonably might you have rendered divine honours to Scipio than to such gods as these. The gods were not so moral as their pontiff. But give me now your attention, if your mind, inebriated by its deep potations of error, can take in any sober truth. The gods enjoined that games be ex-

hibited in their honour to stay a physical pestilence; their pontiff prohibited the theatre from being constructed, to prevent a moral pestilence. If, then, there remains in you sufficient mental enlightenment to prefer the soul to the body, choose whom you will worship. Besides, though the pestilence was stayed, this was not because the voluptuous madness of stage-plays had taken possession of a warlike people hitherto accustomed only to the games of the circus; but these astute and wicked spirits, foreseeing that in due course the pestilence would shortly cease, took occasion to infect, not the bodies, but the morals of their worshippers, with a far more serious disease. And in this pestilence these gods find great enjoyment, because it benighted the minds of men with so gross a darkness, and dishonoured them with so foul a deformity, that even quite recently (will posterity be able to credit it?) some of those who fled from the sack of Rome and found refuge in Carthage, were so infected with this disease, that day after day they seemed to contend with one another who should most madly run after the actors in the theatres.

CHAP. 33. *That the overthrow of Rome has not corrected the vices of the Romans*

Oh infatuated men, what is this blindness, or rather madness, which possesses you? How is it that while, as we hear, even the eastern nations are bewailing your ruin, and while powerful states in the most remote parts of the earth are mourning your fall as a public calamity, ye yourselves should be crowding to the theatres, should be pouring into them and filling them; and, in short, be playing a madder part now than ever before? This was the foul plague-spot, this the wreck of virtue and honour that Scipio sought to preserve you from when he prohibited the construction of theatres; this was his reason for desiring that you might still have an enemy to fear, seeing as he did how easily prosperity would corrupt and destroy you. He did not consider that republic flourishing whose walls stand, but whose morals are in ruins. But the seductions of evil-minded devils had more influence with you than the precautions of prudent men. Hence the injuries you do you will not permit to be imputed to you: but the injuries you suffer you impute to Christianity. Depraved by good fortune, and not chastened by adversity, what you desire in the restoration of a peaceful and secure state is not the tranquillity of the commonwealth, but the impunity of your own vicious luxury. Scipio wished you to be hard pressed by an enemy, that you might not abandon yourselves to luxurious manners; but so abandoned are you that not even when crushed by the enemy is your luxury repressed. You have missed the profit of your calamity; you have been made most wretched, and have remained most profligate.

CHAP. 34. Of God's clemency in moderating the ruin of the city

And that you are yet alive is due to God, Who spares you that you may be admonished to repent and reform your lives. It is He Who has permitted you, ungrateful as you are, to escape the sword of the enemy, by calling yourselves His servants, or by finding asylum in the sacred places of the martyrs.

It is said that Romulus and Remus, in order to increase the population of the city they founded, opened a sanctuary in which every man might find asylum and absolution of all crime, —a remarkable foreshadowing of what has recently occurred in honour of Christ. The destroyers of Rome followed the example of its founders. But it was not greatly to their credit that the latter, for the sake of increasing the number of their citizens, did that which the former have done, lest the number of their enemies should be diminished.

CHAP. 35. Of the sons of the Church who are hidden among the wicked, and of false Christians within the Church

Let these and similar answers (if any fuller and fitter answers can be found) be given to their enemies by the redeemed family of the Lord Christ, and by the pilgrim city of King Christ. But let this city bear in mind that among her enemies lie hid those who are destined to be fellow-citizens, that she may not think it a fruitless labour to bear what they inflict as enemies until they become confessors of the faith. So, too, as long as she is a stranger in the world, the city of God has in her communion, and bound to her by the sacraments, some who shall not eternally dwell in the lot of the saints. Of these, some are not now recognized; others declare themselves, and do not hesitate to make common cause with our enemies in murmuring against God, whose sacramental badge they wear. These men you may to-day see thronging the churches with us, to-morrow crowding the theatres with the godless. But we have the less reason to despair of the reclama-

tion even of such persons, if among our most declared enemies there are now some, unknown to themselves, who are destined to become our friends. In truth, these two cities are entangled together in this world, and intermixed until the last judgment effects their separation. I now proceed to speak, as God shall help me, of the rise, progress, and end of these two cities; and what I write, I write for the glory of the city of God, that, being placed in comparison with the other, it may shine with a brighter lustre.

CHAP. 36. What subjects are to be handled in the following discourse

But I have still some things to say in confutation of those who refer the disasters of the Roman republic to our religion, because it prohibits the offering of sacrifices to the gods. For this end I must recount all, or as many as may seem sufficient, of the disasters which befell that city and its subject provinces, before these sacrifices were prohibited; for all these disasters they would doubtless have attributed to us, if at that time our religion had shed its light upon them, and had prohibited their sacrifices. I must then go on to show what social well-being the true God, in Whose hand are all kingdoms, vouchsafed to grant to them that their empire might increase. I must show why He did so, and how their false gods, instead of at all aiding them, greatly injured them by guile and deceit. And, lastly, I must meet those who, when on this point convinced and confuted by irrefragable proofs, endeavour to maintain that they worship the gods, not hoping for the present advantages of this life, but for those which are to be enjoyed after death. And this, if I am not mistaken, will be the most difficult part of my task, and will be worthy of the loftiest arguments; for we must then enter the lists with the philosophers, not the mere common herd of philosophers, but the most renowned, who in many points agree with ourselves, as regarding the immortality of the soul, and that the true God created the world, and by His providence rules all He has created. But as they differ from us on other points, we must not shrink from the task of exposing their errors, that, having refuted the gainsaying of the wicked with such ability as God may vouchsafe, we may assert the city of God, and true piety, and the worship of God, to which alone the promise of true and everlasting felicity is attached. Here, then, let us conclude, that we may enter on these subjects in a fresh book.

BOOK II

ARGUMENT. IN THIS BOOK AUGUSTINE REVIEWS THOSE CALAMITIES WHICH THE ROMANS SUFFERED BEFORE THE TIME OF CHRIST, AND WHILE THE WORSHIP OF THE FALSE GODS WAS UNIVERSALLY PRACTISED; AND DEMONSTRATES THAT, FAR FROM BEING PRESERVED FROM MISFORTUNE BY THE GODS, THE ROMANS HAVE BEEN BY THEM OVERWHELMED WITH THE ONLY, OR AT LEAST THE GREATEST, OF ALL CALAMITIES— THE CORRUPTION OF MANNERS, AND THE VICES OF THE SOUL.

CHAP. 1. *Of the limits which must be put to the necessity of replying to an adversary*

IF the feeble mind of man did not presume to resist the clear evidence of truth, but yielded its infirmity to wholesome doctrines, as to a health-giving medicine, until it obtained from God, by its faith and piety, the grace needed to heal it, they who have just ideas, and express them in suitable language, would need to use no long discourse to refute the errors of empty conjecture. But this mental infirmity is now more prevalent and hurtful than ever, to such an extent that even after the truth has been as fully demonstrated as man can prove it to man, they hold for the very truth their own unreasonable fancies, either on account of their great blindness, which prevents them from seeing what is plainly set before them, or on account of their opiniona-tive obstinacy, which prevents them from acknowledging the force of what they do see. There therefore frequently arises a necessity of speaking more fully on those points which are already clear, that we may, as it were, present them not to the eye, but even to the touch, so that they may be felt even by those who close their eyes against them. And yet to what end shall we ever bring our discussions, or what bounds can be set to our discourse, if we proceed on the principle that we must always reply to those who reply to us? For those who are either unable to understand our arguments, or are so hardened by the habit of contradiction, that though they understand they cannot yield to them, reply to us, and, as it is written, "speak hard things,"[1] and are incorrigibly vain. Now, if we were to propose to confute their objections as often as they with brazen face chose to disregard our arguments, and so often as they could by any means contradict our statements, you see how endless, and fruitless, and painful a task we should be undertaking. And therefore I do not wish my writings to be judged even by you, my son Marcellinus, nor by any of those others at whose service this work of mine is freely and

in all Christian charity put, if at least you intend always to require a reply to every exception which you hear taken to what you read in it; for so you would become like those silly women of whom the apostle says that they are "always learning, and never able to come to the knowledge of the truth."[2]

CHAP. 2. *Recapitulation of the contents of the first book*

In the foregoing book, having begun to speak of the city of God, to which I have resolved, Heaven helping me, to consecrate the whole of this work, it was my first endeavour to reply to those who attribute the wars by which the world is being devastated, and especially the recent sack of Rome by the barbarians, to the religion of Christ, which prohibits the offering of abominable sacrifices to devils. I have shown that they ought rather to attribute it to Christ, that for His name's sake the barbarians, in contravention of all custom and law of war, threw open as sanctuaries the largest churches, and in many instances showed such reverence to Christ that not only His genuine servants, but even those who in their terror feigned themselves to be so, were exempted from all those hardships which by the custom of war may lawfully be inflicted. Then out of this there arose the question why wicked and ungrateful men were permitted to share in these benefits; and why, too, the hardships and calamities of war were inflicted on the godly as well as on the ungodly. And in giving a suitably full answer to this large question, I occupied some considerable space, partly that I might relieve the anxieties which disturb many when they observe that the blessings of God, and the common and daily human casualties, fall to the lot of bad men and good without distinction; but mainly that I might minister some consolation to those holy and chaste women who were outraged by the enemy, in such a way as to shock their modesty, though not to sully their purity, and that I might preserve them from being ashamed of life, though they have no guilt

[1] Ps. 94. 4.

[2] II Tim. 3. 7.

to be ashamed of. And then I briefly spoke against those who with a most shameless wantonness insult over those poor Christians who were subjected to those calamities, and especially over those broken-hearted and humiliated, though chaste and holy women; these fellows themselves being most depraved and unmanly profligates, quite degenerate from the genuine Romans, whose famous deeds are abundantly recorded in history and everywhere celebrated, but who have found in their descendants the greatest enemies of their glory. In truth, Rome, which was founded and increased by the labours of these ancient heroes, was more shamefully ruined by their descendants, while its walls were still standing, than it is now by the razing of them. For in this ruin there fell stones and timbers; but in the ruin those profligates effected, there fell, not the mural, but the moral bulwarks and ornaments of the city, and their hearts burned with passions more destructive than the flames which consumed their houses. Thus I brought my first book to a close. And now I go on to speak of those calamities which that city itself, or its subject provinces, have suffered since its foundation; all of which they would equally have attributed to the Christian religion, if at that early period the doctrine of the gospel against their false and deceiving gods had been as largely and freely proclaimed as now.

CHAP. 3. *That we need only to read history in order to see what calamities the Romans suffered before the religion of Christ began to compete with the worship of the gods*

But remember that, in recounting these things, I have still to address myself to ignorant men; so ignorant, indeed, as to give birth to the common saying, "Drought and Christianity go hand in hand." There are indeed some among them who are thoroughly well-educated men, and have a taste for history, in which the things I speak of are open to their observation; but in order to irritate the uneducated masses against us, they feign ignorance of these events and do what they can to make the vulgar believe that those disasters, which in certain places and at certain times uniformly befall mankind, are the result of Christianity, which is being everywhere diffused, and is possessed of a renown and brilliancy which quite eclipse their own gods. Let them then, along with us, call to mind with what various and repeated disasters the prosperity of Rome was blighted, before ever Christ had come in the flesh, and before His name had been blazoned among the nations with that glory which

they vainly grudge. Let them, if they can, defend their gods in this article, since they maintain that they worship them in order to be preserved from these disasters, which they now impute to us if they suffer in the least degree. For why did these gods permit the disasters I am to speak of to fall on their worshippers before the preaching of Christ's name offended them, and put an end to their sacrifices?

CHAP. 4. *That the worshippers of the gods never received from them any healthy moral precepts, and that in celebrating their worship all sorts of impurities were practiced*

First of all, we would ask why their gods took no steps to improve the morals of their worshippers. That the true God should neglect those who did not seek His help, that was but justice; but why did those gods, from whose worship ungrateful men are now complaining that they are prohibited, issue no laws which might have guided their devotees to a virtuous life? Surely it was but just that such care as men showed to the worship of the gods, the gods on their part should have to the conduct of men. But, it is replied, it is by his own will a man goes astray. Who denies it? But none the less was it incumbent on these gods, who were men's guardians, to publish in plain terms the laws of a good life, and not to conceal them from their worshippers. It was their part to send prophets to reach and convict such as broke these laws, and publicly to proclaim the punishments which await evil-doers, and the rewards which may be looked for by those that do well. Did ever the walls of any of their temples echo to any such warning voice? I myself, when I was a young man, used sometimes to go to the sacrilegious entertainments and spectacles; I saw the priests raving in religious excitement and heard the choristers; I took pleasure in the shameful games which were celebrated in honour of gods and goddesses, of the virgin Cœlestis, and Berecynthia,[1] the mother of all the gods. And on the holy day consecrated to her purification, there were sung before her couch productions so obscene and filthy for the ear—I do not say of the mother of the gods, but of the mother of any senator or honest man—nay, so impure, that not even the mother of the foul-mouthed players themselves could have formed one of the audience. For natural reverence for parents is a bond which the most abandoned cannot ignore. And, accordingly, the lewd actions and filthy

[1]Berecynthia is one of the many names of Rhea or Cybele.

words with which these players honoured the mother of the gods, in presence of a vast assemblage and audience of both sexes, they could not for very shame have rehearsed at home in presence of their own mothers. And the crowds that were gathered from all quarters by curiosity, offended modesty must, I should suppose, have scattered in the confusion of shame. If these are sacred rites, what is sacrilege? If this is purification, what is pollution? This festivity was called the Tables, as if a banquet were being given at which unclean devils might find suitable refreshment. For it is not difficult to see what kind of spirits they must be who are delighted with such obscenities, unless, indeed, a man be blinded by these evil spirits passing themselves off under the name of gods, and either disbelieves in their existence, or leads such a life as prompts him rather to propitiate and fear them than the true God.

CHAP. 5. *Of the obscenities practiced in honour of the mother of the gods*

In this matter I would prefer to have as my assessors in judgment, not those men who rather take pleasure in these infamous customs than take pains to put an end to them, but that same Scipio Nasica who was chosen by the senate as the citizen most worthy to receive in his hands the image of that demon Cybele, and convey it into the city. He would tell us whether he would be proud to see his own mother so highly esteemed by the state as to have divine honours adjudged to her; as the Greeks and Romans and other nations have decreed divine honours to men who had been of material service to them, and have believed that their mortal benefactors were thus made immortal, and enrolled among the gods. Surely he would desire that his mother should enjoy such felicity were it possible. But if we proceeded to ask him whether, among the honours paid to her, he would wish such shameful rites as these to be celebrated, would he not at once exclaim that he would rather his mother lay stone-dead, than survive as a goddess to lend her ear to these obscenities? Is it possible that he who was of so severe a morality that he used his influence as a Roman senator to prevent the building of a theatre, in that city dedicated to the manly virtues, would wish his mother to be propitiated as a goddess with words which would have brought the blush to her cheek when a Roman matron? Could he possibly believe that the modesty of an estimable woman would be so transformed by her promotion to divinity that she would suffer herself to be invoked and celebrated in terms so gross and immodest, that if she had heard the like while alive upon earth, and had listened without stopping her ears and hurrying from the spot, her relatives, her husband, and her children would have blushed for her? Therefore, the mother of the gods being such a character as the most profligate man would be ashamed to have for his mother, and meaning to enthral the minds of the Romans, demanded for her service their best citizen, not to ripen him still more in virtue by her helpful counsel, but to entangle him by her deceit, like her of whom it is written, "The adulteress will hunt for the precious soul." [1] Her intent was to puff up this high-souled man by an apparently divine testimony to his excellence, in order that he might rely upon his own eminence in virtue, and make no further efforts after true piety and religion, without which natural genius, however brilliant, vapours into pride and comes to nothing. For what but a guileful purpose could that goddess demand the best man, seeing that in her own sacred festivals she requires such obscenities as the best men would be covered with shame to hear at their own tables?

CHAP. 6. *That the gods of the pagans never inculcated holiness of life*

This is the reason why those divinities quite neglected the lives and morals of the cities and nations who worshipped them, and threw no dreadful prohibition in their way to hinder them from becoming utterly corrupt, and to preserve them from those terrible and detestable evils which visit not harvests and vintages, not house and possessions, not the body which is subject to the soul, but the soul itself, the spirit that rules the whole man. If there was any such prohibition, let it be produced, let it be proved. They will tell us that purity and probity were inculcated upon those who were initiated in the mysteries of religion, and that secret incitements to virtue were whispered in the ear of the élite; but this is an idle boast. Let them show or name to us the places which were at any time consecrated to assemblages in which, instead of the obscene songs and licentious acting of players, instead of the celebration of those most filthy and shameless Fugalia (well called *Fugalia*, since they banish modesty and right feeling), the people were commanded in the name of the gods to restrain avarice, bridle impurity, and conquer ambition; where, in short, they might learn in that school which Persius vehemently lashes them to, when he says: "Be taught, ye

[1] Prov. 6. 26.

abandoned creatures, and ascertain the causes of things; what we are, and for what end we are born; what is the law of our success in life; and by what art we may turn the goal without making shipwreck; what limit we should put to our wealth, what we may lawfully desire, and what uses filthy lucre serves; how much we should bestow upon our country and our family; learn, in short, what God meant thee to be, and what place He has ordered you to fill." Let them name to us the places where such instructions were wont to be communicated from the gods, and where the people who worshipped them were accustomed to resort to hear them, as we can point to our churches built for this purpose in every land where the Christian religion is received.

CHAP. 7. *That the suggestions of philosophers are precluded from having any moral effect, because they have not the authority which belongs to divine instruction, and because man's natural bias to evil induces him rather to follow the examples of the gods than to obey the precepts of men*

But will they perhaps remind us of the schools of the philosophers, and their disputations? In the first place, these belong not to Rome, but to Greece; and even if we yield to them that they are now Roman, because Greece itself has become a Roman province, still the teachings of the philosophers are not the commandments of the gods, but the discoveries of men, who, at the prompting of their own speculative ability, made efforts to discover the hidden laws of nature and the right and wrong in ethics, and in dialectic what was consequent according to the rules of logic and what was inconsequent and erroneous. And some of them, by God's help, made great discoveries; but when left to themselves they were betrayed by human infirmity, and fell into mistakes. And this was ordered by divine providence, that their pride might be restrained, and that by their example it might be pointed out that it is humility which has access to the highest regions. But of this we shall have more to say, if the Lord God of truth permit, in its own place.[1] However, if the philosophers have made any discoveries which are sufficient to guide men to virtue and blessedness, would it not have been greater justice to vote divine honours to them? Were it not more accordant with every virtuous sentiment to read Plato's writings in a "Temple of Plato," than to be present in the temples of devils to witness the priests of Cy-

[1] See below, Books VIII–XII.

bele mutilating themselves, the effeminate being consecrated, the raving fanatics cutting themselves, and whatever other cruel or shameful, or shamefully cruel or cruelly shameful, ceremony is enjoined by the ritual of such gods as these? Were it not a more suitable education, and more likely to prompt the youth to virtue, if they heard public recitals of the laws of the gods, instead of the vain laudation of the customs and laws of their ancestors? Certainly all the worshippers of the Roman gods, when once they are possessed by what Persius calls "the burning poison of lust," prefer to witness the deeds of Jupiter rather than to hear what Plato taught or Cato censured. Hence the young profligate in Terence, when he sees on the wall a fresco representing the fabled descent of Jupiter into the lap of Danaë in the form of a golden shower, accepts this as authoritative precedent for his own licentiousness, and boasts that he is an imitator of God. "And what God?" he says. "He who with His thunder shakes the loftiest temples. And was I, a poor creature compared to Him, to make bones of it? No; I did it, and with all my heart."

CHAP. 8. *That the theatrical exhibitions publishing the shameful actions of the gods, propitiated rather than offended them*

But, some one will interpose, these are the fables of poets, not the deliverances of the gods themselves. Well, I have no mind to arbitrate between the lewdness of theatrical entertainments and of mystic rites; only this I say, and history bears me out in making the assertion, that those same entertainments, in which the fictions of poets are the main attraction, were not introduced in the festivals of the gods by the ignorant devotion of the Romans, but that the gods themselves gave the most urgent commands to this effect, and indeed extorted from the Romans these solemnities and celebrations in their honour. I touched on this in the preceding book, and mentioned that dramatic entertainments were first inaugurated at Rome on occasion of a pestilence and by authority of the pontiff. And what man is there who is not more likely to adopt, for the regulation of his own life, the examples that are represented in plays which have a divine sanction, rather than the precepts written and promulgated with no more than human authority? If the poets gave a false representation of Jove in describing him as adulterous, then it were to be expected that the chaste gods should in anger avenge so wicked a fiction, in place of encouraging the games which circulated it. Of these plays, the most inoffensive are comedies and tragedies, that is to say, the dramas which poets write for the stage, and which, though they often handle impure subjects, yet do so without the filthiness of language which characterizes many other performances; and it is these dramas which boys are obliged by their seniors to read and learn as a part of what is called a liberal and gentlemanly education.

CHAP. 9. *That the poetical licence which the Greeks, in obedience to their gods, allowed, was restrained by the ancient Romans*

The opinion of the ancient Romans on this matter is attested by Cicero in his work *De Republica,* in which Scipio, one of the interlocutors, says, "The lewdness of comedy could never have been suffered by audiences, unless the customs of society had previously sanctioned the same lewdness." And in the earlier days the Greeks preserved a certain reasonableness in their licence, and made it a law, that whatever comedy wished to say of any one, it must say it of him by name. And so in the same work of Cicero's, Scipio says, "Whom has it not aspersed? Nay, whom has it not worried? Whom has it spared? Allow that it may assail demagogues and factions, men injurious to the commonwealth—a Cleon, a Cleophon, a Hyperbolus. That is tolerable, though it had been more seemly for the public censor to brand such men, than for a poet to lampoon them; but to blacken the fame of Pericles with scurrilous verse, after he had with the utmost dignity presided over their state alike in war and in peace, was as unworthy of a poet, as if our own Plautus or Nævius were to bring Publius and Cneius Scipio on the comic stage, or as if Cæcilius were to caricature Cato." And then a little after he goes on: "Though our Twelve Tables attached the penalty of death only to a very few offences, yet among these few this was one: if any man should have sung a pasquinade, or have composed a satire calculated to bring infamy or disgrace on another person. Wisely decreed. For it is by the decisions of magistrates, and by a well-informed justice, that our lives ought to be judged, and not by the flighty fancies of poets; neither ought we to be exposed to her calumnies, save where we have the liberty of replying, and defending ourselves before an adequate tribunal." This much I have judged it advisable to quote from the fourth book of Cicero's *De Republica;* and I have made the quotation word for word, with the exception of some words omitted, and some slight-

ly transposed, for the sake of giving the sense more readily. And certainly the extract is pertinent to the matter I am endeavouring to explain. Cicero makes some further remarks, and concludes the passage by showing that the ancient Romans did not permit any living man to be either praised or blamed on the stage. But the Greeks, as I said, though not so moral, were more logical in allowing this licence which the Romans forbade; for they saw that their gods approved and enjoyed the scurrilous language of low comedy when directed not only against men, but even against themselves; and this, whether the infamous actions imputed to them were the fictions of poets, or were their actual iniquities commemorated and acted in the theatres. And would that the spectators had judged them worthy only of laughter, and not of imitation! Manifestly it had been a stretch of pride to spare the good name of the leading men and the common citizens, when the very deities did not grudge that their own reputation should be blemished.

CHAP. 10. *That the devils, in suffering either false or true crimes to be laid to their charge, meant to do men a mischief*

It is alleged, in excuse of this practice, that the stories told of the gods are not true, but false, and mere inventions; but this only makes matters worse, if we form our estimate by the morality our religion teaches; and if we consider the malice of the devils, what more wily and astute artifice could they practise upon men? When a slander is uttered against a leading statesman of upright and useful life, is it not reprehensible in proportion to its untruth and groundlessness? What punishment, then, shall be sufficient when the gods are the objects of so wicked and outrageous an injustice? But the devils, whom these men repute gods, are content that even iniquities they are guiltless of should be ascribed to them, so long as they may entangle men's minds in the meshes of these opinions, and draw them on along with themselves to their predestinated punishment: whether such things were actually committed by the men whom these devils, delighting in human infatuation, cause to be worshipped as gods, and in whose stead they, by a thousand malign and deceitful artifices, substitute themselves, and so receive worship; or whether, though they were really the crimes of men, these wicked spirits gladly allowed them to be attributed to higher beings, that there might seem to be conveyed from heaven itself a sufficient sanction for the perpetration of shameful wickedness. The Greeks, therefore, seeing the character of the gods they served, thought that the poets should certainly not refrain from showing up human vices on the stage, either because they desired to be like their gods in this, or because they were afraid that, if they required for themselves a more unblemished reputation than they asserted for the gods, they might provoke them to anger.

CHAP. 11. *That the Greeks admitted players to offices of state on the ground that men who pleased the gods should not be contemptuously treated by their fellows*

It was a part of this same reasonableness of the Greeks which induced them to bestow upon the actors of these same plays no inconsiderable civic honours. In the above-mentioned book of the *De Republica*, it is mentioned that Æschines, a very eloquent Athenian, who had been a tragic actor in his youth, became a statesman, and that the Athenians again and again sent another tragedian, Aristodemus, as their plenipotentiary to Philip. For they judged it unbecoming to condemn and treat as infamous persons those who were the chief actors in the scenic entertainments which they saw to be so pleasing to the gods. No doubt this was immoral of the Greeks, but there can be as little doubt they acted in conformity with the character of their gods; for how could they have presumed to protect the conduct of the citizens from being cut to pieces by the tongues of poets and players, who were allowed, and even enjoined by the gods, to tear their divine reputation to tatters? And how could they hold in contempt the men who acted in the theatres those dramas which, as they had ascertained, gave pleasure to the gods whom they worshipped? Nay, how could they but grant to them the highest civic honours? On what plea could they honour the priests who offered for them acceptable sacrifices to the gods, if they branded with infamy the actors who in behalf of the people gave to the gods that pleasure or honour which they demanded, and which, according to the account of the priests, they were angry at not receiving. Labeo,[1] whose learning makes him an authority on such points, is of opinion that the distinction between good and evil deities should find expression in a difference of worship; that the evil should be propitiated by bloody sacrifices and doleful rites, but the good with a joyful and pleasant observance, as, e.g. (as he says himself), with plays, festivals, and banquets. All

[1] A jurist of the time of Augustus.

this we shall, with God's help, hereafter discuss. At present, and speaking to the subject on hand, whether all kinds of offerings are made indiscriminately to all the gods, as if all were good (and it is an unseemly thing to conceive that there are evil gods; but these gods of the pagans are all evil, because they are not gods, but evil spirits), or whether, as Labeo thinks, a distinction is made between the offerings presented to the different gods the Greeks are equally justified in honouring alike the priests by whom the sacrifices are offered, and the players by whom the dramas are acted, that they may not be open to the charge of doing an injury to all their gods, if the plays are pleasing to all of them, or (which were still worse) to their good gods, if the plays are relished only by them.

CHAP. 12. *That the Romans, by refusing to the poets the same licence in respect of men which they allowed them in the case of the gods, showed a more delicate sensitiveness regarding themselves than regarding the gods*

The Romans, however, as Scipio boasts in that same discussion, declined having their conduct and good name subjected to the assaults and slanders of the poets, and went so far as to make it a capital crime if any one should dare to compose such verses. This was a very honourable course to pursue, so far as they themselves were concerned, but in respect of the gods it was proud and irreligious: for they knew that the gods not only tolerated, but relished, being lashed by the injurious expressions of the poets, and yet they themselves would not suffer this same handling; and what their ritual prescribed as acceptable to the gods, their law prohibited as injurious to themselves. How then, Scipio, do you praise the Romans for refusing this licence to the poets, so that no citizen could be calumniated, while you know that the gods were not included under this protection? Do you count your senate-house worthy of so much higher a regard than the Capitol? Is the one city of Rome more valuable in your eyes than the whole heaven of gods, that you prohibit your poets from uttering any injurious words against a citizen, though they may with impunity cast what imputations they please upon the gods, without the interference of senator, censor, prince, or pontiff? It was, forsooth, intolerable that Plautus or Nævius should attack Publius and Cneius Scipio, insufferable that Cæcilius should lampoon Cato; but quite proper that your Terence should encourage youthful lust by the wicked example of supreme Jove.

CHAP. 13. *That the Romans should have understood that gods who desired to be worshipped in licentious entertainments were unworthy of divine honour*

But Scipio, were he alive, would possibly reply: "How could we attach a penalty to that which the gods themselves have consecrated? For the theatrical entertainments in which such things are said, and acted, and performed, were introduced into Roman society by the gods, who ordered that they should be dedicated and exhibited in their honour." But was not this, then, the plainest proof that they were no true gods, nor in any respect worthy of receiving divine honours from the republic? Suppose they had required that in their honour the citizens of Rome should be held up to ridicule, every Roman would have resented the hateful proposal. How then, I would ask, can they be esteemed worthy of worship, when they propose that their own crimes be used as material for celebrating their praises? Does not this artifice expose them, and prove that they are detestable devils? Thus the Romans, though they were superstitious enough to serve as gods those who made no secret of their desire to be worshipped in licentious plays, yet had sufficient regard to their hereditary dignity and virtue, to prompt them to refuse to players any such rewards as the Greeks accorded them. On this point we have this testimony of Scipio, recorded in Cicero: "They considered comedy and all theatrical performances as disgraceful, and therefore not only debarred players from offices and honours open to ordinary citizens, but also decreed that their names should be branded by the censor, and erased from the roll of their tribe." An excellent decree, and another testimony to the sagacity of Rome; but I could wish their prudence had been more thoroughgoing and consistent. For when I hear that if any Roman citizen chose the stage as his profession, he not only closed to himself every laudable career, but even became an outcast from his own tribe, I cannot but exclaim: This is the true Roman spirit, this is worthy of a state jealous of its reputation. But then some one interrupts my rapture, by inquiring with what consistency players are debarred from all honours, while plays are counted among the honours due to the gods? For a long while the virtue of Rome was uncontaminated by theatrical exhibitions; and if they had been adopted for the sake of gratifying the taste of the citizens, they would have been introduced hand in hand with the relaxation of manners. But the fact is that it was the gods who demanded that they should be exhibited to gratify them. With what justice, then, is the player excommunicated by whom God is worshipped? On what pretext can you at once adore him who exacts and brand him who acts these plays? This, then, is the controversy in which the Greeks and Romans are engaged. The Greeks think they justly honour players, because they worship the gods who demand plays; the Romans, on the other hand, do not suffer an actor to disgrace by his name his own plebeian tribe, far less the senatorial order. And the whole of this discussion may be summed up in the following syllogism. The Greeks give us the major premise: If such gods are to be worshipped, then certainly such men may be honoured. The Romans add the minor: But such men must by no means be honoured. The Christians draw the conclusion: Therefore such gods must by no means be worshipped.

CHAP. 14. *That Plato, who excluded poets from a well-ordered city, was better than these gods who desire to be honoured by theatrical plays*

We have still to inquire why the poets who write the plays, and who by the law of the Twelve Tables are prohibited from injuring the good name of the citizens, are reckoned more estimable than the actors, though they so shamefully asperse the character of the gods? Is it right that the actors of these poetical and God-dishonouring effusions be branded, while their authors are honoured? Must we not here award the palm to a Greek, Plato, who, in framing his ideal republic,[1] conceived that poets should be banished from the city as enemies of the state? He could not brook that the gods be brought into disrepute, nor that the minds of the citizens be depraved and besotted, by the fictions of the poets. Compare now human nature as you see it in Plato, expelling poets from the city that the citizens be uninjured, with the divine nature as you see it in these gods exacting plays in their own honour. Plato strove, though unsuccessfully, to persuade the light-minded and lascivious Greeks to abstain from so much as writing such plays; the gods used their authority to extort the acting of the same from the dignified and sober-minded Romans. And not content with having them acted, they had them dedicated to themselves, consecrated to themselves, solemnly celebrated in their own honour. To which, then, would it be more becoming in a state to decree divine honours—to Plato, who prohibited these wicked and licen-

[1] See the *Republic*, BK. III.

tious plays, or to the demons who delighted in blinding men to the truth of what Plato unsuccessfully sought to inculcate?

This philosopher, Plato, has been elevated by Labeo to the rank of a demigod, and set thus upon a level with such as Hercules and Romulus. Labeo ranks demigods higher than heroes, but both he counts among the deities. But I have no doubt that he thinks this man whom he reckons a demigod worthy of greater respect not only than the heroes, but also than the gods themselves. The laws of the Romans and the speculations of Plato have this resemblance, that the latter pronounce a wholesale condemnation of poetical fictions, while the former restrain the licence of satire, at least so far as men are the objects of it. Plato will not suffer poets even to dwell in his city: the laws of Rome prohibit actors from being enrolled as citizens; and if they had not feared to offend the gods who had asked the services of the players, they would in all likelihood have banished them altogether. It is obvious, therefore, that the Romans could not receive, nor reasonably expect to receive, laws for the regulation of their conduct from their gods, since the laws they themselves enacted far surpassed and put to shame the morality of the gods. The gods demand stageplays in their own honour; the Romans exclude the players from all civic honours; the former commanded that they should be celebrated by the scenic representation of their own disgrace; the latter commanded that no poet should dare to blemish the reputation of any citizen. But that demigod Plato resisted the lust of such gods as these and showed the Romans what their genius had left incomplete; for he absolutely excluded poets from his ideal state, whether they composed fictions with no regard to truth or set the worst possible examples before wretched men under the guise of divine actions. We for our part, indeed, reckon Plato neither a god nor a demigod; we would not even compare him to any of God's holy angels; nor to the truth-speaking prophets, nor to any of the apostles or martyrs of Christ, nay, not to any faithful Christian man. The reason of this opinion of ours we will, God prospering us, render in its own place. Nevertheless, since they wish him to be considered a demigod, we think he certainly is more entitled to that rank, and is every way superior, if not to Hercules and Romulus (though no historian could ever narrate nor any poet sing of him that he had killed his brother, or committed any crime), yet certainly to Priapus, or a Cynocephalus, or the Fever—divinities whom the Romans have partly received from foreigners, and partly consecrated by home-grown rites. How, then, could gods such as these be expected to promulgate good and wholesome laws, either for the prevention of moral and social evils, or for their eradication where they had already sprung up?—gods who used their influence even to sow and cherish profligacy, by appointing that deeds truly or falsely ascribed to them should be published to the people by means of theatrical exhibitions, and by thus gratuitously fanning the flame of human lust with the breath of a seemingly divine approbation. In vain does Cicero, speaking of poets, exclaim against this state of things in these words: "When the plaudits and acclamation of the people, who sit as infallible judges, are won by the poets, what darkness benights the mind, what fears invade, what passions inflame it!"

CHAP. 15. *That it was vanity, not reason, which created some of the Roman gods*

But is it not manifest that vanity rather than reason regulated the choice of some of their false gods? This Plato, whom they reckon a demigod, and who used all his eloquence to preserve men from the most dangerous spiritual calamities, has yet not been counted worthy even of a little shrine; but Romulus, because they can call him their own, they have esteemed more highly than many gods, though their secret doctrine can allow him the rank only of a demigod. To him they allotted a flamen, that is to say, a priest of a class so highly esteemed in their religion (distinguished, too, by their conical mitres), that for only three of their gods were flamens appointed, —the Flamen Dialis for Jupiter, Martialis for Mars, and Quirinalis for Romulus (for when the ardour of his fellow-citizens had given Romulus a seat among the gods, they gave him this new name Quirinus). And thus by this honour Romulus has been preferred to Neptune and Pluto, Jupiter's brothers, and to Saturn himself, their father. They have assigned the same priesthood to serve him as to serve Jove; and in giving Mars (the reputed father of Romulus) the same honour, is this not rather for Romulus' sake than to honour Mars?

CHAP. 16. *That if the gods had really possessed any regard for righteousness, the Romans should have received good laws from them, instead of having to borrow them from other nations*

Moreover, if the Romans had been able to receive a rule of life from their gods, they would not have borrowed Solon's laws from the Athenians, as they did some years after Rome was founded; and yet they did not keep them as they received them, but endeavoured to improve and amend them. Although Lycurgus pretended that he was authorized by Apollo to give laws to the Lacedemonians, the sensible Romans did not choose to believe this and were not induced to borrow laws from Sparta. Numa Pompilius, who succeeded Romulus in the kingdom, is said to have framed some laws, which, however, were not sufficient for the regulation of civic affairs. Among these regulations were many pertaining to religious observances, and yet he is not reported to have received even these from the gods. With respect, then, to moral evils, evils of life and conduct—evils which are so mighty, that, according to the wisest pagans, by them states are ruined while their cities stand uninjured—their gods made not the smallest provision for preserving their worshippers from these evils, but, on the contrary, took special pains to increase them, as we have previously endeavoured to prove.

CHAP. 17. *Of the rape of the Sabine women, and other iniquities perpetrated in Rome*

But possibly we are to find the reason for this neglect of the Romans by their gods, in the saying of Sallust, that "equity and virtue prevailed among the Romans not more by force of laws than of nature." I presume it is to this inborn equity and goodness of disposition we are to ascribe the rape of the Sabine women. What, indeed, could be more equitable and virtuous, than to carry off by force, as each man was fit, and without their parents' consent, girls who were strangers and guests, and who had been decoyed and entrapped by the pretence of a spectacle! If the Sabines were wrong to deny their daughters when the Romans asked for them, was it not a greater wrong in the Romans to carry them off after that denial? The Romans might more justly have waged war against the neighbouring nation for having refused their daughters in marriage when they first sought them, than for having demanded them back when they had stolen them. War should have been proclaimed at first; it was then that Mars should have helped his warlike son, that he might by force of arms avenge the injury done him by the refusal of marriage, and might also thus win the women he desired. There might have been some appearance of "right of war" in a victor carrying off, in

virtue of this right, the virgins who had been without any show of right denied him; whereas there was no "right of peace" entitling him to carry off those who were not given to him, and to wage an unjust war with their justly enraged parents. One happy circumstance was indeed connected with this act of violence, viz., that though it was commemorated by the games of the circus, yet even this did not constitute it a precedent in the city or realm of Rome. If one would find fault with the results of this act, it must rather be on the ground that the Romans made Romulus a god in spite of his perpetrating this iniquity; for one cannot reproach them with making this deed any kind of precedent for the rape of women.

Again, I presume it was due to this natural equity and virtue, that after the expulsion of King Tarquin, whose son had violated Lucretia, Junius Brutus the consul forced Lucius Tarquinius Collatinus, Lucretia's husband and his own colleague, a good and innocent man, to resign his office and go into banishment, on the one sole charge that he was of the name and blood of the Tarquins. This injustice was perpetrated with the approval, or at least connivance, of the people, who had themselves raised to the consular office both Collatinus and Brutus. Another instance of this equity and virtue is found in their treatment of Marcus Camillus. This eminent man, after he had rapidly conquered the Veians, at that time the most formidable of Rome's enemies, and who had maintained a ten years' war, in which the Roman army had suffered the usual calamities attendant on bad generalship, after he had restored security to Rome, which had begun to tremble for its safety, and after he had taken the wealthiest city of the enemy, had charges brought against him by the malice of those that envied his success, and by the insolence of the tribunes of the people; and seeing that the city bore him no gratitude for preserving it, and that he would certainly be condemned, he went into exile, and even in his absence was fined 10,000 asses. Shortly after, however, his ungrateful country had again to seek his protection from the Gauls. But I cannot now mention all the shameful and iniquitous acts with which Rome was agitated, when the aristocracy attempted to subject the people, and the people resented their encroachments, and the advocates of either party were actuated rather by the love of victory than by any equitable or virtuous consideration.

CHAP. 18. *What the history of Sallust reveals regarding the life of the Romans, either when straitened by anxiety or relaxed in security*

I will therefore pause, and adduce the testimony of Sallust himself, whose words in praise of the Romans (that "equity and virtue prevailed among them not more by force of laws than of nature") have given occasion to this discussion. He was referring to that period immediately after the expulsion of the kings, in which the city became great in an incredibly short space of time. And yet this same writer acknowledges in the first book of his history, in the very exordium of his work, that even at that time, when a very brief interval had elapsed after the government had passed from kings to consuls, the more powerful men began to act unjustly, and occasioned the defection of the people from the patricians, and other disorders in the city. For after Sallust had stated that the Romans enjoyed greater harmony and a purer state of society between the second and third Punic wars than at any other time, and that the cause of this was not their love of good order, but their fear lest the peace they had with Carthage might be broken (this also, as we mentioned, Nasica contemplated when he opposed the destruction of Carthage, for he supposed that fear would tend to repress wickedness, and to preserve wholesome ways of living), he then goes on to say: "Yet, after the destruction of Carthage, discord, avarice, ambition, and the other vices which are commonly generated by prosperity, more than ever increased." If they "increased," and that "more than ever," then already they had appeared, and had been increasing. And so Sallust adds this reason for what he said. "For," he says, "the oppressive measures of the powerful, and the consequent secessions of the plebs from the patricians, and other civil dissensions, had existed from the first, and affairs were administered with equity and well-tempered justice for no longer a period than the short time after the expulsion of the kings, while the city was occupied with the serious Tuscan war and Tarquin's vengeance." You see how, even in that brief period after the expulsion of the kings, fear, he acknowledges, was the cause of the interval of equity and good order. They were afraid, in fact, of the war which Tarquin waged against them, after he had been driven from the throne and the city, and had allied himself with the Tuscans. But observe what he adds: "After that, the patricians treated the people as their slaves, ordering them to be scourged or beheaded just as the kings had done, driving them from their holdings, and harshly tyrannizing over those who had no property to lose. The people, overwhelmed by these oppressive measures, and most of all by exorbitant usury, and obliged to contribute both money and personal service to the constant wars, at length took arms, and seceded to Mount Aventine and Mount Sacer, and thus obtained for themselves tribunes and protective laws. But it was only the second Punic war that put an end on both sides to discord and strife." You see what kind of men the Romans were, even so early as a few years after the expulsion of the kings; and it is of these men he says, that "equity and virtue prevailed among them not more by force of law than of nature."

Now, if these were the days in which the Roman republic shows fairest and best, what are we to say or think of the succeeding age, when, to use the words of the same historian, "changing little by little from the fair and virtuous city it was, it became utterly wicked and dissolute?" This was, as he mentions, after the destruction of Carthage. Sallust's brief sum and sketch of this period may be read in his own history, in which he shows how the profligate manners which were propagated by prosperity resulted at last even in civil wars. He says: "And from this time the primitive manners, instead of undergoing an insensible alteration as hitherto they had done, were swept away as by a torrent: the young men were so depraved by luxury and avarice that it may justly be said that no father had a son who could either preserve his own patrimony, or keep his hands off other men's." Sallust adds a number of particulars about the vices of Sulla, and the debased condition of the republic in general; and other writers make similar observations, though in much less striking language.

However, I suppose you now see, or at least any one who gives his attention has the means of seeing, in what a sink of iniquity that city was plunged before the advent of our heavenly King. For these things happened not only before Christ had begun to teach, but before He was even born of the Virgin. If, then, they dare not impute to their gods the grievous evils of those former times, more tolerable before the destruction of Carthage, but intolerable and dreadful after it, although it was the gods who by their malign craft instilled into the minds of men the conceptions from which such dreadful vices branched out on all sides, why do they impute these present calamities to Christ, Who teaches life-giving truth, and forbids us to worship false and deceitful gods, and Who, abominating and condemning with His divine authority those wicked and hurtful lusts of men, gradually withdraws His own people from a world that is corrupted by these vices, and is falling into ruins, to make of them an eternal city, whose glory rests not on the acclamations of vanity, but on the judgment of truth?

CHAP. 19. *Of the corruption which had grown upon the Roman republic before Christ abolished the worship of the gods*

Here, then, is this Roman republic, "which has changed little by little from the fair and virtuous city it was, and has become utterly wicked and dissolute." It is not I who am the first to say this, but their own authors, from whom we learned it for a fee, and who wrote it long before the coming of Christ. You see how, before the coming of Christ, and after the destruction of Carthage, "the primitive manners, instead of undergoing insensible alteration, as hitherto they had done, were swept away as by a torrent; and how depraved by luxury and avarice the youth were." Let them now, on their part, read to us any laws given by their gods to the Roman people, and directed against luxury and avarice. And would that they had only been silent on the subjects of chastity and modesty, and had not demanded from the people indecent and shameful practices, to which they lent a pernicious patronage by their so-called divinity. Let them read our commandments in the Prophets, Gospels, Acts of the Apostles or Epistles; let them peruse the large number of precepts against avarice and luxury which are everywhere read to the congregations that meet for this purpose, and which strike the ear, not with the uncertain sound of a philosophical discussion, but with the thunder of God's own oracle pealing from the clouds. And yet they do not impute to their gods the luxury and avarice, the cruel and dissolute manners, that had rendered the republic utterly wicked and corrupt. even before the coming of Christ; but whatever affliction their pride and effeminacy have exposed them to in these latter days, they furiously impute to our religion. If the kings of the earth and all their subjects, if all princes and judges of the earth, if young men and maidens, old and young, every age, and both sexes; if they whom the Baptist addressed, the publicans and the soldiers, were all together to hearken to and observe the precepts of the Christian religion regarding a just and virtuous

life, then should the republic adorn the whole earth with its own felicity, and attain in life everlasting to the pinnacle of kingly glory. But because this man listens, and that man scoffs, and most are enamoured of the blandishments of vice rather than the wholesome severity of virtue, the people of Christ, whatever be their condition—whether they be kings, princes, judges, soldiers, or provincials, rich or poor, bond or free, male or female—are enjoined to endure this earthly republic, wicked and dissolute as it is, that so they may by this endurance win for themselves an eminent place in that most holy and august assembly of angels and republic of heaven, in which the will of God is the law.

CHAP. 20. *Of the kind of happiness and life truly delighted in by those who inveigh against the Christian religion*

But the worshippers and admirers of these gods delight in imitating their scandalous iniquities, and are nowise concerned that the republic be less depraved and licentious. Only let it remain undefeated, they say, only let it flourish and abound in resources; let it be glorious by its victories, or still better, secure in peace; and what matters it to us? This is our concern, that every man be able to increase his wealth so as to supply his daily prodigalities, and so that the powerful may subject the weak for their own purposes. Let the poor court the rich for a living, and that under their protection they may enjoy a sluggish tranquillity; and let the rich abuse the poor as their dependants, to minister to their pride. Let the people applaud not those who protect their interests, but those who provide them with pleasure. Let no severe duty be commanded, no impurity forbidden. Let kings estimate their prosperity, not by the righteousness, but by the servility of their subjects. Let the provinces stand loyal to the kings, not as moral guides, but as lords of their possessions and purveyors of their pleasures; not with a hearty reverence, but a crooked and servile fear. Let the laws take cognizance rather of the injury done to another man's property, than of that done to one's own person. If a man be a nuisance to his neighbour, or injure his property, family, or person, let him be actionable; but in his own affairs let every one with impunity do what he will in company with his own family, and with those who willingly join him. Let there be a plentiful supply of public prostitutes for every one who wishes to use them, but specially for those who are too poor to keep one for their private use.

Let there be erected houses of the largest and most ornate description: in these let there be provided the most sumptuous banquets, where every one who pleases may, by day or night, play, drink, vomit, dissipate. Let there be everywhere heard the rustling of dancers, the loud, immodest laughter of the theatre; let a succession of the most cruel and the most voluptuous pleasures maintain a perpetual excitement. If such happiness is distasteful to any, let him be branded as a public enemy; and if any attempt to modify or put an end to it let him be silenced, banished, put an end to. Let these be reckoned the true gods, who procure for the people this condition of things, and preserve it when once possessed. Let them be worshipped as they wish; let them demand whatever games they please, from or with their own worshippers; only let them secure that such felicity be not imperilled by foe, plague, or disaster of any kind. What sane man would compare a republic such as this, I will not say to the Roman empire, but to the palace of Sardanapalus, the ancient king who was so abandoned to pleasures that he caused it to be inscribed on his tomb that, now that he was dead, he possessed only those things which he had swallowed and consumed by his appetites while alive? If these men had such a king as this, who, while self-indulgent, should lay no severe restraint on them, they would more enthusiastically consecrate to him a temple and a flamen than the ancient Romans did to Romulus.

CHAP. 21. *Cicero's opinion of the Roman republic*

But if our adversaries do not care how foully and disgracefully the Roman republic be stained by corrupt practices, so long only as it holds together and continues in being, and if they therefore pooh-pooh the testimony of Sallust to its "utterly wicked and profligate" condition, what will they make of Cicero's statement that even in his time it had become entirely extinct and that there remained extant no Roman republic at all? He introduces Scipio (the Scipio who had destroyed Carthage) discussing the republic, at a time when already there were presentiments of its speedy ruin by that corruption which Sallust describes. In fact, at the time when the discussion took place, one of the Gracchi, who, according to Sallust, was the first great instigator of seditions, had already been put to death. His death, indeed, is mentioned in the same book. Now Scipio, at the end of the second book, says: "As among the different sounds which proceed from lyres, flutes, and the human voice, there must be maintained a certain harmony which a cultivated ear cannot endure to hear disturbed or jarring, but which may be elicited in full and absolute concord by the modulation even of voices very unlike one another; so, where reason is allowed to modulate the diverse elements of the state, there is obtained a perfect concord from the upper, lower, and middle classes as from various sounds; and what musicians call harmony in singing, is concord in matters of state, which is the strictest bond and best security of any republic, and which by no ingenuity can be retained where justice has become extinct." Then, when he had expatiated somewhat more fully, and had more copiously illustrated the benefits of its presence and the ruinous effects of its absence upon a state, Pilus, one of the company present at the discussion, struck in and demanded that the question should be more thoroughly sifted, and that the subject of justice should be freely discussed for the sake of ascertaining what truth there was in the maxim which was then becoming daily more current, that "the republic cannot be governed without injustice." Scipio expressed his willingness to have this maxim discussed and sifted, and gave it as his opinion that it was baseless, and that no progress could be made in discussing the republic unless it was established not only that this maxim, that "the republic cannot be governed without injustice," was false, but also that the truth is that it cannot be governed without the most absolute justice. And the discussion of this question, being deferred till the next day, is carried on in the third book with great animation. For Pilus himself undertook to defend the position that the republic cannot be governed without injustice, at the same time being at special pains to clear himself of any real participation in that opinion. He advocated with great keenness the cause of injustice against justice, and endeavoured by plausible reasons and examples to demonstrate that the former is beneficial, the latter useless, to the republic. Then, at the request of the company, Lælius attempted to defend justice, and strained every nerve to prove that nothing is so hurtful to a state as injustice; and that without justice a republic can neither be governed nor even continue to exist.

When this question has been handled to the satisfaction of the company, Scipio reverts to the original thread of discourse, and repeats with commendation his own brief definition of a republic, that it is the weal of the people. "The people" he defines as being not every assemblage or mob, but an assemblage associated by a common acknowledgment of law, and by a community of interests. Then he shows the use of definition in debate; and from these definitions of his own he gathers that a republic, or "weal of the people," then exists only when it is well and justly governed, whether by a monarch, or an aristocracy, or by the whole people. But when the monarch is unjust, or, as the Greeks say, a tyrant; or the aristocrats are unjust, and form a faction; or the people themselves are unjust, and become, as Scipio for want of a better name calls them, themselves the tyrant, then the republic is not only blemished (as had been proved the day before), but, by legitimate deduction from those definitions, it altogether ceases to be. For it could not be the people's weal when a tyrant factiously lorded it over the state; neither would the people be any longer a people if it were unjust, since it would no longer answer the definition of a people—"an assemblage associated by a common acknowledgment of law, and by a community of interests."

When, therefore, the Roman republic was such as Sallust described it, it was not "utterly wicked and profligate," as he says, but had altogether ceased to exist, if we are to admit the reasoning of that debate maintained on the subject of the republic by its best representatives. Tully himself, too, speaking not in the person of Scipio or any one else, but uttering his own sentiments, uses the following language in the beginning of the fifth book, after quoting a line from the poet Ennius, in which he said, "Rome's severe morality and her citizens are her safeguard." "This verse," says Cicero, "seems to me to have all the sententious truthfulness of an oracle. For neither would the citizens have availed without the morality of the community, nor would the morality of the commons without outstanding men have availed either to establish or so long to maintain in vigour so grand a republic with so wide and just an empire. Accordingly, before our day, the hereditary usages formed our foremost men, and they on their part retained the usages and institutions of their fathers. But our age, receiving the republic as a chef-d'œuvre of another age which has already begun to grow old, has not merely neglected to restore the colours of the original, but has not even been at the pains to preserve so much as the general outline and most outstanding features. For what survives of that primitive morality which the poet called Rome's safeguard? It is so obsolete and forgotten, that, far from practising it, one does not even know it. And of the citizens what shall I say? Morality has perished through poverty of great men; a poverty for which we must not only assign a reason, but for the guilt of which we must answer as criminals charged with a capital crime. For it is through our vices, and not by any mishap, that we retain only the name of a republic, and have long since lost the reality."

This is the confession of Cicero, long indeed after the death of Africanus, whom he introduced as an interlocutor in his work De Republica, but still before the coming of Christ. Yet, if the disasters he bewails had been lamented after the Christian religion had been diffused and had begun to prevail, is there a man of our adversaries who would not have thought that they were to be imputed to the Christians? Why, then, did their gods not take steps then to prevent the decay and extinction of that republic, over the loss of which Cicero, long before Christ had come in the flesh, sings so lugubrious a dirge? Its admirers have need to inquire whether, even in the days of primitive men and morals, true justice flourished in it; or was it not perhaps even then, to use the casual expression of Cicero, rather a coloured painting than the living reality? But, if God will, we shall consider this elsewhere. For I mean in its own place to show that—according to the definitions in which Cicero himself, using Scipio as his mouthpiece, briefly propounded what a republic is, and what a people is, and according to many testimonies, both of his own lips and of those who took part in that same debate—Rome never was a republic, because true justice had never a place in it. But accepting the more feasible definitions of a republic, I grant there was a republic of a certain kind, and certainly much better administered by the more ancient Romans than by their modern representatives. But the fact is, true justice has no existence save in that republic whose founder and ruler is Christ, if at least any choose to call this a republic; and indeed we cannot deny that it is the people's weal. But if perchance this name, which has become familiar in other connections, be considered alien to our common parlance, we may at all events say that in this city is true justice; the city of which Holy Scripture says, "Glorious things are said of thee, O city of God."

CHAP. 22. That the Roman gods never took any steps to prevent the republic from being ruined by immorality

But what is relevant to the present question is this, that, however admirable our adversaries say the republic was or is, it is certain that by the testimony of their own most learned writers it had become, long before the coming of Christ, utterly wicked and dissolute, and indeed had no existence, but had been destroyed by profligacy. To prevent this, surely these guardian gods ought to have given precepts of morals and a rule of life to the people by whom they were worshipped in so many temples, with so great a variety of priests and sacrifices, with such numberless and diverse rites, so many festal solemnities, so many celebrations of magnificent games. But in all this the demons only looked after their own interest, and cared not at all how their worshippers lived, or rather were at pains to induce them to lead an abandoned life, so long as they paid these tributes to their honour, and regarded them with fear. If any one denies this, let him produce, let him point to, let him read the laws which the gods had given against sedition, and which the Gracchi transgressed when they threw everything into confusion; or those Marius, and Cinna, and Carbo broke when they involved their country in civil wars, most iniquitous and unjustifiable in their causes, cruelly conducted, and yet more cruelly terminated; or those which Sulla scorned, whose life, character, and deeds, as described by Sallust and other historians, are the abhorrence of all mankind. Who will deny that at that time the republic had become extinct?

Possibly they will be bold enough to suggest in defence of the gods, that they abandoned the city on account of the profligacy of the citizens, according to the lines of Virgil:

> Gone from each fane, each sacred shrine,
> Are those who made this realm divine.[1]

But, firstly, if it be so, then they cannot complain against the Christian religion, as if it were that which gave offence to the gods and caused them to abandon Rome, since the Roman immorality had long ago driven from the altars of the city a cloud of little gods, like as many flies. And yet where was this host of divinities, when, long before the corruption of the primitive morality, Rome was taken and burnt by the Gauls? Perhaps they were present, but asleep? For at that time the whole city fell into the hands of the enemy, with the single exception of the Capitoline Hill; and this too would have been taken, had not the watchful geese aroused the sleeping gods! And this gave occasion to the festival of the goose, in which Rome sank nearly to the superstition of the Egyptians, who worship beasts

[1] *Æneid*, BK. II. 351-2.

and birds. But of these adventitious evils which are inflicted by hostile armies or by some disaster, and which attach rather to the body than the soul, I am not meanwhile disputing. At present I speak of the decay of morality, which at first almost imperceptibly lost its brilliant hue, but afterwards was wholly obliterated, was swept away as by a torrent, and involved the republic in such disastrous ruin, that though the houses and walls remained standing the leading writers do not scruple to say that the republic was destroyed. Now, the departure of the gods "from each fane, each sacred shrine," and their abandonment of the city to destruction, was an act of justice, if their laws inculcating justice and a moral life had been held in contempt by that city. But what kind of gods were these, pray, who declined to live with a people who worshipped them, and whose corrupt life they had done nothing to reform?

CHAP. 23. *That the vicissitudes of this life are dependent not on the favour or hostility of demons, but on the will of the true God*

But, further, is it not obvious that the gods have abetted the fulfilment of men's desires, instead of authoritatively bridling them? For Marius, a low-born and self-made man, who ruthlessly provoked and conducted civil wars, was so effectually aided by them that he was seven times consul, and died full of years in his seventh consulship, escaping the hands of Sulla, who immediately afterwards came into power. Why, then, did they not also aid him, so as to restrain him from so many enormities? For if it is said that the gods had no hand in his success, this is no trivial admission that a man can attain the dearly coveted felicity of this life even though his own gods be not propitious; that men can be loaded with the gifts of fortune as Marius was, can enjoy health, power, wealth, honours, dignity, length of days, though the gods be hostile to him; and that, on the other hand, men can be tormented as Regulus was, with captivity, bondage, destitution, watchings, pain, and cruel death, though the gods be his friends. To concede this is to make a compendious confession that the gods are useless, and their worship superfluous. If the gods have taught the people rather what goes clean counter to the virtues of the soul, and that integrity of life which meets a reward after death; if even in respect of temporal and transitory blessings they neither hurt those whom they hate nor profit whom they love, why are they worshipped, why are they invoked with such eager homage? Why do men murmur in difficult and sad emergencies, as if the gods had retired in anger? and why, on their account, is the Christian religion injured by the most unworthy calumnies? If in temporal matters they have power either for good or for evil, why did they stand by Marius, the worst of Rome's citizens, and abandon Regulus, the best? Does this not prove themselves to be most unjust and wicked? And even if it be supposed that for this very reason they are the rather to be feared and worshipped, this is a mistake; for we do not read that Regulus worshipped them less assiduously than Marius. Neither is it apparent that a wicked life is to be chosen, on the ground that the gods are supposed to have favoured Marius more than Regulus. For Metellus, the most highly esteemed of all the Romans, who had five sons in the consulship, was prosperous even in this life; and Catiline, the worst of men, reduced to poverty and defeated in the war his own guilt had aroused, lived and perished miserably. Real and secure felicity is the peculiar possession of those who worship that God by whom alone it can be conferred.

It is thus apparent that, when the republic was being destroyed by profligate manners, its gods did nothing to hinder its destruction by the direction or correction of its manners, but rather accelerated its destruction by increasing the demoralization and corruption that already existed. They need not pretend that their goodness was shocked by the iniquity of the city, and that they withdrew in anger. For they were there, sure enough; they are detected, convicted: they were equally unable to break silence so as to guide others, and to keep silence so as to conceal themselves. I do not dwell on the fact that the inhabitants of Minturnæ took pity on Marius, and commended him to the goddess Marica in her grove, that she might give him success in all things, and that from the abyss of despair in which he then lay he forthwith returned unhurt to Rome, and entered the city the ruthless leader of a ruthless army; and they who wish to know how bloody was his victory, how unlike a citizen and how much more relentlessly than any foreign foe he acted, let them read the histories. But this, as I said, I do not dwell upon; nor do I attribute the bloody bliss of Marius to I know not what Minturnian goddess, but rather to the secret providence of God, that the mouths of our adversaries might be shut, and that they who are not led by passion, but by prudent consideration of events, might be delivered from error. And even if the demons have any power in these matters, they have only that power

which the secret decree of the Almighty allots to them, in order that we may not set too great store by earthly prosperity, seeing it is oftentimes vouchsafed even to wicked men like Marius; and that we may not, on the other hand, regard it as an evil, since we see that many good and pious worshippers of the one true God are, in spite of the demons, pre-eminently successful; and, finally, that we may not suppose that these unclean spirits are either to be propitiated or feared for the sake of earthly blessings or calamities: for as wicked men on earth cannot do all they would, so neither can these demons, but only in so far as they are permitted by the decree of Him whose judgments are fully comprehensible, justly reprehensible by none.

CHAP. 24. *Of the deeds of Sulla, in which the demons boasted that he had their help*

It is certain that Sulla—whose rule was so cruel that, in comparison with it, the preceding state of things which he came to avenge was regretted—when first he advanced towards Rome to give battle to Marius, found the auspices so favourable when he sacrificed that, according to Livy's account, the augur Postumius expressed his willingness to lose his head if Sulla did not, with the help of the gods, accomplish what he designed. The gods, you see, had not departed from "every fane and sacred shrine," since they were still predicting the issue of these affairs, and yet were taking no steps to correct Sulla himself. Their presages promised him great prosperity, but no threatenings of theirs subdued his evil passions. And then, when he was in Asia conducting the war against Mithridates, a message from Jupiter was delivered to him by Lucius Titius, to the effect that he would conquer Mithridates; and so it came to pass. And afterwards, when he was meditating a return to Rome for the purpose of avenging in the blood of the citizens injuries done to himself and his friends, a second message from Jupiter was delivered to him by a soldier of the sixth legion, to the effect that it was he who had predicted the victory over Mithridates, and that now he promised to give him power to recover the republic from his enemies, though with great bloodshed. Sulla at once inquired of the soldier what form had appeared to him; and, on his reply, recognized that it was the same as Jupiter had formerly employed to convey to him the assurance regarding the victory over Mithridates. How, then, can the gods be justified in this matter for the care they took to predict these shadowy successes, and for their negligence in correcting

Sulla and restraining him from stirring up a civil war so lamentable and atrocious that it not merely disfigured, but extinguished, the republic? The truth is, as I have often said, and as Scripture informs us, and as the facts themselves sufficiently indicate, the demons are found to look after their own ends only, that they may be regarded and worshipped as gods, and that men may be induced to offer to them a worship which associates them with their crimes, and involves them in one common wickedness and judgment of God.

Afterwards, when Sulla had come to Tarentum and had sacrificed there, he saw on the head of the victim's liver the likeness of a golden crown. Thereupon the same soothsayer Postumius interpreted this to signify a signal victory and ordered that he only should eat of the entrails. A little afterwards, the slave of a certain Lucius Pontius cried out, "I am Bellona's messenger; the victory is yours, Sulla!" Then he added that the Capitol should be burned. As soon as he had uttered this prediction he left the camp, but returned the following day more excited than ever, and shouted, "The Capitol is fired!" And fired indeed it was. This it was easy for a demon both to foresee and quickly to announce. But observe, as relevant to our subject, what kind of gods they are under whom these men desire to live, who blaspheme the Saviour that delivers the wills of the faithful from the dominion of devils. The man cried out in prophetic rapture, "The victory is yours, Sulla!" And to certify that he spoke by a divine spirit, he predicted also an event which was shortly to happen, and which indeed did fall out, in a place from which he in whom this spirit was speaking was far distant. But he never cried, "Forbear thy villanies, Sulla!"—the villanies which were committed at Rome by that victor to whom a golden crown on the calf's liver had been shown as the divine evidence of his victory. If such signs as this were customarily sent by just gods, and not by wicked demons, then certainly the entrails he consulted should rather have given Sulla intimation of the cruel disasters that were to befall the city and himself. For that victory was not so conducive to his exaltation to power as it was fatal to his ambition; for by it he became so insatiable in his desires, and was rendered so arrogant and reckless by prosperity, that he may be said rather to have inflicted a moral destruction on himself than corporal destruction on his enemies. But these truly woeful and deplorable calamities the gods gave him no previous hint of, neither by entrails, augury,

dream, nor prediction. For they feared his amendment more than his defeat. Yea, they took good care that this glorious conqueror of his own fellow-citizens should be conquered and led captive by his own infamous vices, and should thus be the more submissive slave of the demons themselves.

CHAP. 25. *How powerfully the evil spirits incite men to wicked actions, by giving them the quasi-divine authority of their example*

Now, who does not hereby comprehend—unless he has preferred to imitate such gods rather than by divine grace to withdraw himself from their fellowship—who does not see how eagerly these evil spirits strive by their example to lend, as it were, divine authority to crime? Is not this proved by the fact that they were seen in a wide plain in Campania rehearsing among themselves the battle which shortly after took place there with great bloodshed between the armies of Rome? For at first there were heard loud crashing noises, and afterwards many reported that they had seen for some days together two armies engaged. And when this battle ceased, they found the ground all indented with just such footprints of men and horses as a great conflict would leave. If, then, the deities were veritably fighting with one another, the civil wars of men are sufficiently justified; yet, by the way, let it be observed that such pugnacious gods must be very wicked or very wretched. If, however, it was but a sham-fight, what did they intend by this, but that the civil wars of the Romans should seem no wickedness, but an imitation of the gods? For already the civil wars had begun; and before this, some lamentable battles and execrable massacres had occurred. Already many had been moved by the story of the soldier, who, on stripping the spoils of his slain foe, recognized in the stripped corpse his own brother, and, with deep curses on civil wars, slew himself there and then on his brother's body. To disguise the bitterness of such tragedies, and kindle increasing ardour in this monstrous warfare, these malign demons, who were reputed and worshipped as gods, fell upon this plan of revealing themselves in a state of civil war, that no compunction for fellow-citizens might cause the Romans to shrink from such battles, but that the human criminality might be justified by the divine example. By a like craft, too, did these evil spirits command that scenic entertainments, of which I have already spoken, should be instituted and dedicated to them. And in these entertainments the poetical compositions and actions of the drama ascribed such iniquities to the gods that every one might safely imitate them, whether he believed the gods had actually done such things, or, not believing this, yet perceived that they most eagerly desired to be represented as having done them. And that no one might suppose, that in representing the gods as fighting with one another, the poets had slandered them, and imputed to them unworthy actions, the gods themselves, to complete the deception, confirmed the compositions of the poets by exhibiting their own battles to the eyes of men, not only through actions in the theatres, but in their own persons on the actual field.

We have been forced to bring forward these facts, because their authors have not scrupled to say and to write that the Roman republic had already been ruined by the depraved moral habits of the citizens, and had ceased to exist before the advent of our Lord Jesus Christ. Now this ruin they do not impute to their own gods, though they impute to our Christ the evils of this life, which cannot ruin good men, be they alive or dead. And this they do, though our Christ has issued so many precepts inculcating virtue and restraining vice; while their own gods have done nothing whatever to preserve that republic that served them, and to restrain it from ruin by such precepts, but have rather hastened its destruction, by corrupting its morality through their pestilent example. No one, I fancy, will now be bold enough to say that the republic was then ruined because of the departure of the gods "from each fane, each sacred shrine," as if they were the friends of virtue and were offended by the vices of men. No, there are too many presages from entrails, auguries, soothsayings, whereby they boastingly proclaimed themselves prescient of future events and controllers of the fortune of war— all which prove them to have been present. And had they been indeed absent, the Romans would never in these civil wars have been so far transported by their own passions as they were by the instigations of these gods.

CHAP. 26. *That the demons gave in secret certain obscure instructions in morals, while in public their own solemnities inculcated all wickedness*

Seeing that this is so—seeing that the filthy and cruel deeds, the disgraceful and criminal actions of the gods, whether real or feigned, were at their own request published, and were consecrated, and dedicated in their honour as sacred and stated solemnities; seeing they vowed vengeance on those who refused to exhibit them to the eyes of all, that they might be proposed as deeds worthy of imitation, why is it that these same demons, who, by taking pleasure in such obscenities, acknowledge themselves to be unclean spirits, and by delighting in their own villanies and iniquities, real or imaginary, and by requesting from the immodest, and extorting from the modest, the celebration of these licentious acts, proclaim themselves instigators to a criminal and lewd life—why, I ask, are they represented as giving some good moral precepts to a few of their own elect, initiated in the secrecy of their shrines? If it be so, this very thing only serves further to demonstrate the malicious craft of these pestilent spirits. For so great is the influence of probity and chastity that all men, or almost all men, are moved by the praise of these virtues; nor is any man so depraved by vice, but he hath some feeling of honour left in him. So that, unless the devil sometimes transformed himself, as Scripture says, into an angel of light,[1] he could not compass his deceitful purpose. Accordingly, in public, a bold impurity fills the ear of the people with noisy clamour; in private, a feigned chastity speaks in scarce audible whispers to a few: an open stage is provided for shameful things, but on the praiseworthy the curtain falls: grace hides, disgrace flaunts: a wicked deed draws an overflowing house, a virtuous speech finds scarce a hearer, as though purity were to be blushed at, impurity boasted of. Where else can such confusion reign, but in devils' temples? Where, but in the haunts of deceit? For the secret precepts are given as a sop to the virtuous, who are few in number; the wicked examples are exhibited to encourage the vicious, who are countless.

Where and when those initiated in the mysteries of Cœlestis received any good instructions, we know not. What we do know is, that before her shrine, in which her image is set, and amidst a vast crowd gathering from all quarters and standing closely packed together, we were intensely interested spectators of the games which were going on, and saw, as we pleased to turn the eye, on this side a grand display of harlots, on the other the virgin goddess; we saw this virgin worshipped with prayer and with obscene rites. There we saw no shame-faced mimes, no actress overburdened with modesty; all that the obscene rites demanded was fully complied with. We were plainly shown what was pleasing to the virgin deity, and the matron who

[1] II Cor. 11. 14.

witnessed the spectacle returned home from the temple a wiser woman. Some, indeed, of the more prudent women turned their faces from the immodest movements of the players, and learned the art of wickedness by a furtive regard. For they were restrained, by the modest demeanour due to men, from looking boldly at the immodest gestures; but much more were they restrained from condemning with chaste heart the sacred rites of her whom they adored. And yet this licentiousness—which, if practised in one's home, could only be done there in secret—was practised as a public lesson in the temple; and if any modesty remained in men, it was occupied in marvelling that wickedness which men could not unrestrainedly commit should be part of the religious teaching of the gods, and that to omit its exhibition should incur the anger of the gods. What spirit can that be, which by a hidden inspiration stirs men's corruption, and goads them to adultery, and feeds on the full-fledged iniquity, unless it be the same that finds pleasure in such religious ceremonies, sets in the temples images of devils, and loves to see in play the images of vices; that whispers in secret some righteous sayings to deceive the few who are good, and scatters in public invitations to profligacy, to gain possession of the millions who are wicked?

CHAP. 27. *That the obscenities of those plays which the Romans consecrated in order to propitiate their gods, contributed largely to the overthrow of public order.*

Cicero, a weighty man, and a philosopher in his way, when about to be made edile, wished the citizens to understand that, among the other duties of his magistracy, he must propitiate Flora by the celebration of games. And these games are reckoned devout in proportion to their lewdness. In another place, and when he was now consul, and the state in great peril, he says that games had been celebrated for ten days together, and that nothing had been omitted which could pacify the gods: as if it had not been more satisfactory to irritate the gods by temperance than to pacify them by debauchery, and to provoke their hate by honest living than soothe it by such unseemly grossness. For no matter how cruel was the ferocity of those men who were threatening the state, and on whose account the gods were being propitiated, it could not have been more hurtful than the alliance of gods who were won with the foulest vices. To avert the danger which threatened men's bodies, the gods were conciliated in a fashion that drove

virtue from their spirits; and the gods did not enrol themselves as defenders of the battlements against the besiegers, until they had first stormed and sacked the morality of the citizens. This propitiation of such divinities—a propitiation so wanton, so impure, so immodest, so wicked, so filthy, whose actors the innate and praiseworthy virtue of the Romans disabled from civic honours, erased from their tribe, recognized as polluted and made infamous—this propitiation, I say, so foul, so detestable, and alien from every religious feeling, these fabulous and ensnaring accounts of the criminal actions of the gods, these scandalous actions which they either shamefully and wickedly committed, or more shamefully and wickedly feigned, all this the whole city learned in public both by the words and gestures of the actors. They saw that the gods delighted in the commission of these things and therefore believed that they wished them not only to be exhibited to them, but to be imitated by themselves. But as for that good and honest instruction which they speak of, it was given in such secrecy, and to so few (if indeed given at all), that they seemed rather to fear it might be divulged, than that it might not be practised.

CHAP. 28. *That the Christian religion is healthgiving*

They, then, are but abandoned and ungrateful wretches, in deep and fast bondage to that malign spirit, who complain and murmur that men are rescued by the name of Christ from the hellish thraldom of these unclean spirits, and from a participation in their punishment, and are brought out of the night of pestilential ungodliness into the light of most healthful piety. Only such men could murmur that the masses flock to the churches and their chaste acts of worship, where a seemly separation of the sexes is observed; where they learn how they may so spend this earthly life, as to merit a blessed eternity hereafter; where Holy Scripture and instruction in righteousness are proclaimed from a raised platform in presence of all, that both they who do the word may hear to their salvation and they who do it not may hear to judgment. And though some enter who scoff at such precepts, all their petulance is either quenched by a sudden change, or is restrained through fear or shame. For no filthy and wicked action is there set forth to be gazed at or to be imitated; but either the precepts of the true God are recommended, His miracles narrated, His gifts praised, or His benefits implored.

CHAP. 29. *An exhortation to the Romans to re-nounce paganism*

This, rather, is the religion worthy of your desires, O admirable Roman race—the progeny of your Scævolas and Scipios, of Regulus, and of Fabricius. This rather covet, this distinguish from that foul vanity and crafty malice of the devils. If there is in your nature any eminent virtue, only by true piety is it purged and perfected, while by impiety it is wrecked and punished. Choose now what you will pursue, that your praise may be not in yourself, but in the true God, in Whom is no error. For of popular glory you have had your share; but by the secret providence of God, the true religion was not offered to your choice. Awake, it is now day; as you have already awaked in the persons of some in whose perfect virtue and sufferings for the true faith we glory: for they, contending on all sides with hostile powers, and conquering them all by bravely dying, have purchased for us this country of ours with their blood; to which country we invite you, and exhort you to add yourselves to the number of the citizens of this city, which also has a sanctuary of its own in the true remission of sins. Do not listen to those degenerate sons of thine who slander Christ and Christians, and impute to them these disastrous times, though they desire times in which they may enjoy rather impunity for their wickedness than a peaceful life. Such has never been Rome's ambition even in regard to her earthly country. Lay hold now on the celestial country, which is easily won, and in which you will reign truly and for ever. For there shalt thou find no vestal fire, no Capitoline stone, but the one true God.

No date, no goal will here ordain:
But grant an endless, boundless reign.[1]

No longer, then, follow after false and deceitful gods; abjure them rather, and despise them, bursting forth into true liberty. Gods they are not, but malignant spirits, to whom your eternal happiness will be a sore punishment. Juno, from whom you deduce your origin according to the flesh, did not so bitterly grudge Rome's citadels to the Trojans as these devils whom yet ye repute gods grudge an everlasting seat to the race of mankind. And thou thyself hast in no waver-

[1]Virgil, *Æneid*, BK. I. 278.

ing voice passed judgment on them, when thou didst pacify them with games, and yet didst account as infamous the men by whom the plays were acted. Suffer us, then, to assert thy freedom against the unclean spirits who had imposed on thy neck the yoke of celebrating their own shame and filthiness. The actors of these divine crimes thou hast removed from offices of honour; supplicate the true God, that He may remove from thee those gods who delight in their crimes—a most disgraceful thing if the crimes are really theirs, and a most malicious invention if the crimes are feigned. Well done, in that thou hast spontaneously banished from the number of your citizens all actors and players. Awake more fully: the majesty of God cannot be propitiated by that which defiles the dignity of man. How, then, can you believe that gods who take pleasure in such lewd plays, belong to the number of the holy powers of heaven, when the men by whom these plays are acted are by yourselves refused admission into the number of Roman citizens even of the lowest grade? Incomparably more glorious than Rome is that heavenly city in which for victory you have truth; for dignity, holiness; for peace, felicity; for life, eternity. Much less does it admit into its society such gods, if thou dost blush to admit into thine such men. Wherefore, if thou wouldst attain to the blessed city, shun the society of devils. They who are propitiated by deeds of shame, are unworthy of the worship of right-hearted men. Let these, then, be obliterated from your worship by the cleansing of the Christian religion, as those men were blotted from your citizenship by the censor's mark.

But, so far as regards carnal benefits, which are the only blessings the wicked desire to enjoy, and carnal miseries, which alone they shrink from enduring, we will show in the following book that the demons have not the power they are supposed to have; and although they had it, we ought rather on that account to despise these blessings, than for the sake of them to worship those gods and by worshipping them to miss the attainment of these blessings they grudge us. But that they have not even this power which is ascribed to them by those who worship them for the sake of temporal advantages, this, I say, I will prove in the following book; so let us here close the present argument.

BOOK III

ARGUMENT. AS IN THE FOREGOING BOOK AUGUSTINE HAS PROVED REGARDING MORAL AND SPIRITUAL CALAMITIES, SO IN THIS BOOK HE PROVES REGARDING EXTERNAL AND BODILY DISASTERS, THAT SINCE THE FOUNDATION OF THE CITY THE ROMANS HAVE BEEN CONTINUALLY SUBJECT TO THEM; AND THAT EVEN WHEN THE FALSE GODS WERE WORSHIPPED WITHOUT A RIVAL, BEFORE THE ADVENT OF CHRIST, THEY AFFORDED NO RELIEF FROM SUCH CALAMITIES.

CHAP. 1. *Of the ills which alone the wicked fear, and which the world continually suffered, even when the gods were worshipped*

OF moral and spiritual evils, which are above all others to be deprecated, I think enough has already been said to show that the false gods took no steps to prevent the people who worshipped them from being overwhelmed by such calamities, but rather aggravated the ruin. I see I must now speak of those evils which alone are dreaded by the heathen—famine, pestilence, war, pillage, captivity, massacre, and the like calamities, already enumerated in the first book. For evil men account those things alone evil which do not make men evil; neither do they blush to praise good things, and yet to remain evil among the good things they praise. It grieves them more to own a bad house than a bad life, as if it were man's greatest good to have everything good but himself. But not even such evils as were alone dreaded by the heathen were warded off by their gods, even when they were most unrestrictedly worshipped. For in various times and places before the advent of our Redeemer, the human race was crushed with numberless and sometimes incredible calamities; and at that time what gods but those did the world worship, if you except the one nation of the Hebrews, and, beyond them, such individuals as the most secret and most just judgment of God counted worthy of divine grace? But that I may not be prolix, I will be silent regarding the heavy calamities that have been suffered by any other nations, and will speak only of what happened to Rome and the Roman empire, by which I mean Rome properly so called, and those lands which already, before the coming of Christ, had by alliance or conquest become, as it were, members of the body of the state.

CHAP. 2. *Whether the gods, whom the Greeks and Romans worshipped in common, were justified in permitting the destruction of Ilium*

First, then, why was Troy or Ilium, the cradle of the Roman people (for I must not overlook nor disguise what I touched upon in the first book[1]), conquered, taken and destroyed by the Greeks, though it esteemed and worshipped the same gods as they? Priam, some answer, paid the penalty of the perjury of his father Laomedon.[2] Then it is true that Laomedon hired Apollo and Neptune as his workmen. For the story goes that he promised them wages and then broke his bargain. I wonder that famous diviner Apollo toiled at so huge a work, and never suspected Laomedon was going to cheat him of his pay. And Neptune too, his uncle, brother of Jupiter, king of the sea, it really was not seemly that he should be ignorant of what was to happen. For he is introduced by Homer[3] (who lived and wrote before the building of Rome) as predicting something great of the posterity of Æneas, who in fact founded Rome. And as Homer says, Neptune also rescued Æneas in a cloud from the wrath of Achilles, though (according to Virgil)

> All his will was to destroy
> His own creation, perjured Troy.[4]

Gods, then, so great as Apollo and Neptune, in ignorance of the cheat that was to defraud them of their wages, built the walls of Troy for nothing but thanks and thankless people. There may be some doubt whether it is not a worse crime to believe such persons to be gods, than to cheat such gods. Even Homer himself did not give full credence to the story; for while he represents Neptune, indeed, as hostile to the Trojans, he introduces Apollo as their champion, though the story implies that both were offended by that fraud. If, therefore, they believe their fables, let them blush to worship such gods; if they discredit the fables, let no more be said of the "Trojan perjury"; or let them explain how the gods hated Trojan, but loved Roman perjury. For how did the conspiracy of Catiline, even in so large and corrupt a city, find so abundant a supply of men whose hands and tongues found them a living by perjury and civic broils? What

[1]Chap. 4.　　[2]Virgil, *Georgics*, BK. I. 502.
[3]*Iliad*, BK. XX. 293, *et seq.*　　[4]*Æneid*, BK. V. 810, 811.

else but perjury corrupted the judgments pronounced by so many of the senators? What else corrupted the people's votes and decisions of all causes tried before them? For it seems that the ancient practice of taking oaths has been preserved even in the midst of the greatest corruption, not for the sake of restraining wickedness by religious fear, but to complete the tale of crimes by adding that of perjury.

CHAP. 3. *That the gods could not be offended by the adultery of Paris, this crime being so common among themselves*

There is no ground, then, for representing the gods (by whom, as they say, that empire stood, though they are proved to have been conquered by the Greeks) as being enraged at the Trojan perjury. Neither, as others again plead in their defence, was it indignation at the adultery of Paris that caused them to withdraw their protection from Troy. For their habit is to be instigators and instructors in vice, not its avengers. "The city of Rome," says Sallust, "was first built and inhabited, as I have heard, by the Trojans, who, flying their country, under the conduct of Æneas, wandered about without making any settlement." If, then, the gods were of opinion that the adultery of Paris should be punished, it was chiefly the Romans, or at least the Romans also, who should have suffered; for the adultery was brought about by Æneas' mother. But how could they hate in Paris a crime which they made no objection to in their own sister Venus, who (not to mention any other instance) committed adultery with Anchises, and so became the mother of Æneas? Is it because in the one case Menelaus was aggrieved, while in the other Vulcan connived at the crime? For the gods, I fancy, are so little jealous of their wives that they make no scruple of sharing them with men. But perhaps I may be suspected of turning the myths into ridicule, and not handling so weighty a subject with sufficient gravity. Well, then, let us say that Æneas is not the son of Venus. I am willing to admit it; but is Romulus any more the son of Mars? For why not the one as well as the other? Or is it lawful for gods to have intercourse with women, unlawful for men to have intercourse with goddesses? A hard, or rather an incredible, condition that what was allowed to Mars by the law of Venus, should not be allowed to Venus herself by her own law. However, both cases have the authority of Rome; for Cæsar in modern times believed no less that he was descended from Venus, than the ancient Romulus believed himself the son of Mars.

CHAP. 4. *Of Varro's opinion, that it is useful for men to feign themselves the offspring of the gods*

Some one will say, But do you believe all this? Not I indeed. For even Varro, a very learned heathen, all but admits that these stories are false, though he does not boldly and confidently say so. But he maintains it is useful for states that brave men believe, though falsely, that they are descended from the gods; for that thus the human spirit, cherishing the belief of its divine descent, will both more boldly venture into great enterprises, and will carry them out more energetically, and will therefore by its very confidence secure more abundant success. You see how wide a field is opened to falsehood by this opinion of Varro's, which I have expressed as well as I could in my own words; and how comprehensible it is that many of the religions and sacred legends should be feigned in a community in which it was judged profitable for the citizens that lies should be told even about the gods themselves.

CHAP. 5. *That it is not credible that the gods should have punished the adultery of Paris, seeing they showed no indignation at the adultery of the mother of Romulus*

But whether Venus could bear Æneas to a human father Anchises, or Mars beget Romulus of the daughter of Numitor, we leave as unsettled questions. For our own Scriptures suggest the very similar question, whether the fallen angels had sexual intercourse with the daughters of men, by which the earth was at that time filled with giants, that is, with enormously large and strong men. At present, then, I will limit my discussion to this dilemma: If that which their books relate about the mother of Æneas and the father of Romulus be true, how can the gods be displeased with men for adulteries which, when committed by themselves, excite no displeasure? If it is false, not even in this case can the gods be angry that men should really commit adulteries, which, even when falsely attributed to the gods, they delight in. Moreover, if the adultery of Mars be discredited, that Venus also may be freed from the imputation, then the mother of Romulus is left unshielded by the pretext of a divine seduction. For Sylvia was a vestal priestess, and the gods ought to avenge this sacrilege on the Romans with greater severity than Paris' adultery on the Trojans. For even the Romans themselves in primitive times used to go so far as to bury alive any vestal who was detected in adultery, while women unconsecrated, though they were punished, were never punished with death for that crime; and thus they more earnestly vindicated the purity of shrines they esteemed divine, than of the human bed.

Chap. 6. *That the gods exacted no penalty for the fratricidal act of Romulus*

I add another instance: If the sins of men so greatly incensed those divinities that they abandoned Troy to fire and sword to punish the crime of Paris, the murder of Romulus' brother ought to have incensed them more against the Romans than the cajoling of a Greek husband moved them against the Trojans: fratricide in a newly-born city should have provoked them more than adultery in a city already flourishing. It makes no difference to the question we now discuss whether Romulus ordered his brother to be slain, or slew him with his own hand; it is a crime which many shamelessly deny, many through shame doubt, many in grief disguise. And we shall not pause to examine and weigh the testimonies of historical writers on the subject. All agree that the brother of Romulus was slain, not by enemies, not by strangers. If it was Romulus who either commanded or perpetrated this crime; Romulus was more truly the head of the Romans than Paris of the Trojans; why then did he who carried off another man's wife bring down the anger of the gods on the Trojans, while he who took his brother's life obtained the guardianship of those same gods? If, on the other hand, that crime was not wrought either by the hand or will of Romulus, then the whole city is chargeable with it, because it did not see to its punishment, and thus committed, not fratricide, but parricide, which is worse. For both brothers were the founders of that city, of which the one was by villainy prevented from being a ruler. So far as I see, then, no evil can be ascribed to Troy which warranted the gods in abandoning it to destruction, nor any good to Rome which accounts for the gods visiting it with prosperity; unless the truth be, that they fled from Troy because they were vanquished, and betook themselves to Rome to practise their characteristic deceptions there. Nevertheless they kept a footing for themselves in Troy, that they might deceive future inhabitants who repeopled these lands; while at Rome, by a wider exercise of their malignant arts, they exulted in more abundant honours.

Chap. 7. *Of the destruction of Ilium by Fimbria, a lieutenant of Marius*

And surely we may ask what wrong poor Ilium had done, that, in the first heat of the civil wars of Rome, it should suffer at the hand of Fimbria, the veriest villain among Marius' partisans, a more fierce and cruel destruction than the Grecian sack. For when the Greeks took it many escaped, and many who did not escape were suffered to live, though in captivity. But Fimbria from the first gave orders that not a life should be spared, and burnt up together the city and all its inhabitants. Thus was Ilium requited, not by the Greeks, whom she had provoked by wrong-doing; but by the Romans, who had been built out of her ruins; while the gods, adored alike of both sides, did simply nothing, or, to speak more correctly, could do nothing. Is it then true, that at this time also, after Troy had repaired the damage done by the Grecian fire, all the gods by whose help the kingdom stood, "forsook each fane, each sacred shrine"?

But if so, I ask the reason; for in my judgment, the conduct of the gods was as much to be reprobated as that of the townsmen to be applauded. For these closed their gates against Fimbria, that they might preserve the city for Sulla, and were therefore burnt and consumed by the enraged general. Now, up to this time, Sulla's cause was the more worthy of the two; for till now he used arms to restore the republic, and as yet his good intentions had met with no reverses. What better thing, then, could the Trojans have done? What more honourable, what more faithful to Rome, or more worthy of her relationship, than to preserve their city for the better part of the Romans, and to shut their gates against a parricide of his country? It is for the defenders of the gods to consider the ruin which this conduct brought on Troy. The gods deserted an adulterous people, and abandoned Troy to the fires of the Greeks, that out of her ashes a chaster Rome might arise. But why did they a second time abandon this same town, allied now to Rome, and not making war upon her noble daughter, but preserving a most steadfast and pious fidelity to Rome's most justifiable faction? Why did they give her up to be destroyed, not by the Greek heroes, but by the basest of the Romans? Or, if the gods did not favor Sulla's cause, for which the unhappy Trojans maintained their city, why did they themselves predict and promise Sulla such successes? Must we call them flatterers of the fortunate, rather than helpers of the wretched? Troy was not destroyed, then, because the gods deserted it. For the demons, always watchful to deceive, did what they could. For, when all the statues were overthrown and burnt together with the town, Livy tells us that only the image of Minerva is said to have been found standing uninjured amidst the ruins of her temple; not that it might be said in their praise, "The gods who made this realm divine," but that it might not be said in their defence, They are "gone from each fane, each sacred shrine": for that marvel was permitted to them, not that they might be proved to be powerful, but that they might be convicted of being present.

Chap. 8. *Whether Rome ought to have been entrusted to the Trojan gods*

Where, then, was the wisdom of entrusting Rome to the Trojan gods, who had demonstrated their weakness in the loss of Troy? Will some one say that, when Fimbria stormed Troy, the gods were already resident in Rome? How, then, did the image of Minerva remain standing? Besides, if they were at Rome when Fimbria destroyed Troy, perhaps they were at Troy when Rome itself was taken and set on fire by the Gauls. But as they are very acute in hearing, and very swift in their movements, they came quickly at the cackling of the goose to defend at least the Capitol, though to defend the rest of the city they were too long in being warned.

Chap. 9. *Whether it is credible that the peace during the reign of Numa was brought about by the gods*

It is also believed that it was by the help of the gods that the successor of Romulus, Numa Pompilius, enjoyed peace during his entire reign, and shut the gates of Janus, which are customarily kept open during war. And it is supposed he was thus requited for appointing many religious observances among the Romans. Certainly that king would have commanded our congratulations for so rare a leisure, had he been wise enough to spend it on wholesome pursuits, and, subduing a pernicious curiosity, had sought out the true God with true piety. But as it was, the gods were not the authors of his leisure; but possibly they would have deceived him less had they found him busier. For the more disengaged they found him, the more they themselves occupied his attention. Varro informs us of all his efforts and of the arts he employed to associate

these gods with himself and the city; and in its own place, if God will, I shall discuss these matters. Meanwhile, as we are speaking of the benefits conferred by the gods, I readily admit that peace is a great benefit; but it is a benefit of the true God, which, like the sun, the rain, and other supports of life, is frequently conferred on the ungrateful and wicked. But if this great boon was conferred on Rome and Pompilius by their gods, why did they never afterwards grant it to the Roman empire during even more meritorious periods? Were the sacred rites more efficient at their first institution than during their subsequent celebration? But they had no existence in Numa's time, until he added them to the ritual; whereas afterwards they had already been celebrated and preserved, that benefit might arise from them. How, then, is it that those forty-three, or as others prefer it, thirty-nine years of Numa's reign, were passed in unbroken peace, and yet that afterwards, when the worship was established, and the gods themselves, who were invoked by it, were the recognized guardians and patrons of the city, we can with difficulty find during the whole period, from the building of the city to the reign of Augustus, one year— that, viz., which followed the close of the first Punic war—in which, for a marvel, the Romans were able to shut the gates of war?

Chap. 10. *Whether it was desirable that the Roman empire should be increased by such a furious succession of wars, when it might have been quiet and safe by following in the peaceful ways of Numa*

Do they reply that the Roman empire could never have been so widely extended, nor so glorious, save by constant and unintermitting wars? A fit argument, truly! Why must a kingdom be distracted in order to be great? In this little world of man's body, is it not better to have a moderate stature, and health with it, than to attain the huge dimensions of a giant by unnatural torments, and when you attain it to find no rest, but to be pained the more in proportion to the size of your members? What evil would have resulted, or rather what good would not have resulted, had those times continued which Sallust sketched, when he says, "At first the kings (for that was the first title of empire in the world) were divided in their sentiments: part cultivated the mind, others the body: at that time the life of men was led without covetousness; every one was sufficiently satisfied with his own"! Was it requisite, then, for

Rome's prosperity, that the state of things which Virgil reprobates should succeed:

> At length stole on a baser age
> And war's indomitable rage,
> And greedy lust of gain.[1]

But obviously the Romans have a plausible defence for undertaking and carrying on such disastrous wars—to wit, that the pressure of their enemies forced them to resist, so that they were compelled to fight, not by any greed of human applause, but by the necessity of protecting life and liberty. Well, let that pass. Here is Sallust's account of the matter: "For when their state, enriched with laws, institutions, territory, seemed abundantly prosperous and sufficiently powerful, according to the ordinary law of human nature, opulence gave birth to envy. Accordingly, the neighbouring kings and states took arms and assaulted them. A few allies lent assistance; the rest, struck with fear, kept aloof from dangers. But the Romans, watchful at home and in war, were active, made preparations, encouraged one another, marched to meet their enemies, protected by arms their liberty, country, parents. Afterwards, when they had repelled the dangers by their bravery, they carried help to their allies and friends, and procured alliances more by conferring than by receiving favours." This was to build up Rome's greatness by honourable means. But, in Numa's reign, I would know whether the long peace was maintained in spite of the incursions of wicked neighbours, of if these incursions were discontinued that the peace might be maintained? For if even then Rome was harassed by wars, and yet did not meet force with force, the same means she then used to quiet her enemies without conquering them in war, or terrifying them with the onset of battle, she might have used always, and have reigned in peace with the gates of Janus shut. And if this was not in her power, then Rome enjoyed peace not at the will of her gods, but at the will of her neighbours round about, and only so long as they cared to provoke her with no war, unless perhaps these pitiful gods will dare to sell to one man as their favour what lies not in their power to bestow, but in the will of another man. These demons, indeed, in so far as they are permitted, can terrify or incite the minds of wicked men by their own peculiar wickedness. But if they always had this power, and if no action were taken against their efforts by a more secret and higher power, they would be supreme to give peace or the victories of war, which almost always fall out through some human emotion, and frequently in opposition to the will of the gods, as is proved not only by lying legends, which scarcely hint or signify any grain of truth, but even by Roman history itself.

CHAP. 11. *Of the statue of Apollo at Cumæ, whose tears are supposed to have portended disaster to the Greeks, whom the god was unable to succour*

And it is still this weakness of the gods which is confessed in the story of the Cumæan Apollo, who is said to have wept for four days during the war with the Achæans and King Aristonicus. And when the augurs were alarmed at the portent, and had determined to cast the statue into the sea, the old men of Cumæ interposed, and related that a similar prodigy had occurred to the same image during the wars against Antiochus and against Perseus, and that by a decree of the senate, gifts had been presented to Apollo, because the event had proved favourable to the Romans. Then soothsayers were summoned who were supposed to have greater professional skill, and they pronounced that the weeping of Apollo's image was propitious to the Romans, because Cumæ was a Greek colony, and that Apollo was bewailing (and thereby presaging) the grief and calamity that was about to light upon his own land of Greece, from which he had been brought. Shortly afterwards it was reported that King Aristonicus was defeated and made prisoner, a defeat certainly opposed to the will of Apollo; and this he indicated by even shedding tears from his marble image. And this shows us that, though the verses of the poets are mythical, they are not altogether devoid of truth, but describe the manners of the demons in a sufficiently fit style. For in Virgil, Diana mourned for Camilla,[2] and Hercules wept for Pallas doomed to die.[3] This is perhaps the reason why Numa Pompilius, too, when, enjoying prolonged peace, but without knowing or inquiring from whom he received it, he began in his leisure to consider to what gods he should entrust the safe keeping and conduct of Rome, and not dreaming that the true, almighty, and most high God cares for earthly affairs, but recollecting only that the Trojan gods which Æneas had brought to Italy had been able to preserve neither the Trojan nor Lavinian kingdom founded by Æneas himself, concluded that he must provide other gods as guardians of fugitives and helpers of the weak, and add them to those earlier divinities who had

[1] *Æneid*, BK. VIII. 326-7.
[2] *Æneid*, BK. XI. 532.
[3] *Ibid*, BK. X. 464.

either come over to Rome with Romulus, or when Alba was destroyed.

CHAP. 12. *That the Romans added a vast number of gods to those introduced by Numa, and that their numbers helped them not at all*

But though Pompilius introduced so ample a ritual, yet did not Rome see fit to be content with it. For as yet Jupiter himself had not his chief temple, it being King Tarquin who built the Capitol. And Æsculapius left Epidaurus for Rome, that in this foremost city he might have a finer field for the exercise of his great medical skill. The mother of the gods, too, came I know not whence from Pessinuns; it being unseemly that, while her son presided on the Capitoline Hill, she herself should lie hid in obscurity. But if she is the mother of all the gods, she not only followed some of her children to Rome, but left others to follow her. I wonder, indeed, if she were the mother of Cynocephalus, who a long while afterwards came from Egypt. Whether also the goddess Fever was her offspring, is a matter for her grandson Æsculapius to decide. But of whatever breed she be, the foreign gods will not presume, I trust, to call a goddess baseborn who is a Roman citizen. Who can number the deities to whom the guardianship of Rome was entrusted? Indigenous and imported, both of heaven, earth, hell, seas, fountains, rivers; and, as Varro says, gods certain and uncertain, male and female: for, as among animals, so among all kinds of gods are there these distinctions. Rome, then, enjoying the protection of such a cloud of deities, might surely have been preserved from some of those great and horrible calamities, of which I can mention but a few. For by the great smoke of her altars she summoned to her protection, as by a beacon-fire, a host of gods, for whom she appointed and maintained temples, altars, sacrifices, priests, and thus offended the true and most high God, to whom alone all this ceremonial is lawfully due. And, indeed, she was more prosperous when she had fewer gods; but the greater she became, the more gods she thought she should have, as the larger ship needs to be manned by a larger crew. I suppose she despaired of the smaller number under whose protection she had spent comparatively happy days, being able to defend her greatness. For even under the kings (with the exception of Numa Pompilius, of whom I have already spoken), how wicked a contentiousness must have existed to occasion the death of Romulus' brother!

CHAP. 13. *By what right or agreement the Romans obtained their first wives*

How is it that neither Juno, who with her husband Jupiter even then cherished

Rome's sons, the nation of the gown,[1]

nor Venus herself, could assist the children of the loved Æneas to find wives by some right and equitable means? For the lack of this entailed upon the Romans the lamentable necessity of stealing their wives, and then waging war with their fathers-in-law; so that the wretched women, before they had recovered from the wrong done them by their husbands, were dowried with the blood of their fathers. "But the Romans conquered their neighbours." Yes, but with what wounds on both sides, and with what sad slaughter of relatives and neighbours! The war of Cæsar and Pompey was the contest of only one father-in-law with one son-in-law; and before it began, the daughter of Cæsar, Pompey's wife, was already dead. But with how keen and just an accent of grief does Lucan exclaim: "I sing that worse than civil war waged in the plains of Emathia, and in which the crime was justified by the victory!"

The Romans, then, conquered that they might, with hands stained in the blood of their fathers-in-law, wrench the miserable girls from their embrace—girls who dared not weep for their slain parents, for fear of offending their victorious husbands, and while yet the battle was raging, stood with their prayers on their lips, and knew not for whom to utter them. Such nuptials were certainly prepared for the Roman people not by Venus, but Bellona; or possibly that infernal fury Alecto had more liberty to injure them now that Juno was aiding them, than when the prayers of that goddess had excited her against Æneas. Andromache in captivity was happier than these Roman brides. For though she was a slave, yet, after she had become the wife of Pyrrhus, no more Trojans fell by his hand; but the Romans slew in battle the very fathers of the brides they fondled. Andromache, the victor's captive, could only mourn, not fear, the death of her people. The Sabine women, related to men still combatants, feared the death of their fathers when their husbands went out to battle, and mourned their death as they returned, while neither their grief nor their fear could be freely expressed. For the victories of their husbands, involving the destruction of fellow-townsmen, relatives, brothers, fathers, caused either pious agony or cruel exultation.

[1] *Ibid*, BK. I. 286

Moreover, as the fortune of war is capricious, some of them lost their husbands by the sword of their parents, while others lost husband and father together in mutual destruction. For the Romans by no means escaped with impunity, but they were driven back within their walls and defended themselves behind closed gates; and when the gates were opened by guile, and the enemy admitted into the town, the Forum itself was the field of a hateful and fierce engagement of fathers-in-law and sons-in-law. The ravishers were indeed quite defeated, and, flying on all sides to their houses, sullied with new shame their original shameful and lamentable triumph. It was at this juncture that Romulus, hoping no more from the valour of his citizens, prayed Jupiter that they might stand their ground; and from this occasion the god gained the name of Stator. But not even thus would the mischief have been finished, had not the ravished women themselves flashed out with dishevelled hair, and cast themselves before their parents, and thus disarmed their just rage, not with the arms of victory, but with the supplications of filial affection. Then Romulus, who could not brook his own brother as a colleague, was compelled to accept Titus Tatius, king of the Sabines, as his partner on the throne. But how long would he who misliked the fellowship of his own twin-brother endure a stranger? So, Tatius being slain, Romulus remained sole king, that he might be the greater god. See what rights of marriage these were that fomented unnatural wars. These were the Roman leagues of kindred, relationship, alliance, religion. This was the life of the city so abundantly protected by the gods. You see how many severe things might be said on this theme; but our purpose carries us past them, and requires our discourse for other matters.

CHAP. 14. *Of the wickedness of the war waged by the Romans against the Albans, and of the victories won by the lust of power*

But what happened after Numa's reign, and under the other kings, when the Albans were provoked into war, with sad results not to themselves alone, but also to the Romans? The long peace of Numa had become tedious; and with what endless slaughter and detriment of both states did the Roman and Alban armies bring it to an end! For Alba, which had been founded by Ascanius, son of Æneas, and which was more properly the mother of Rome than Troy herself, was provoked to battle by Tullus Hostilius, king of Rome, and in the conflict both inflicted and received such damage, that at length both par-

ties wearied of the struggle. It was then devised that the war should be decided by the combat of three twin-brothers from each army: from the Romans the three Horatii stood forward, from the Albans the three Curiatii. Two of the Horatii were overcome and disposed of by the Curiatii; but by the remaining Horatius the three Curiatii were slain. Thus Rome remained victorious, but with such a sacrifice that only one survivor returned to his home. Whose was the loss on both sides? Whose the grief, but of the offspring of Æneas, the descendants of Ascanius, the progeny of Venus, the grandsons of Jupiter? For this, too, was a "worse than civil" war, in which the belligerent states were mother and daughter. And to this combat of the three twin-brothers there was added another atrocious and horrible catastrophe. For as the two nations had formerly been friendly (being related and neighbours), the sister of the Horatii had been betrothed to one of the Curiatii; and she, when she saw her brother wearing the spoils of her betrothed, burst into tears, and was slain by her own brother in his anger. To me, this one girl seems to have been more humane than the whole Roman people. I cannot think her to blame for lamenting the man to whom already she had plighted her troth, or, as perhaps she was doing, for grieving that her brother should have slain him to whom he had promised his sister. For why do we praise the grief of Æneas (in Virgil[1]) over the enemy cut down even by his own hand? Why did Marcellus shed tears over the city of Syracuse, when he recollected, just before he destroyed, its magnificence and meridian glory, and thought upon the common lot of all things? I demand, in the name of humanity, that if men are praised for tears shed over enemies conquered by themselves, a weak girl should not be counted criminal for bewailing her lover slaughtered by the hand of her brother. While, then, that maiden was weeping for the death of her betrothed inflicted by her brother's hand, Rome was rejoicing that such devastation had been wrought on her mother state and that she had purchased a victory with such an expenditure of the common blood of herself and the Albans.

Why allege to me the mere names and words of "glory" and "victory"? Tear off the disguise of wild delusion, and look at the naked deeds: weigh them naked, judge them naked. Let the

---

[1]*Ibid*, BK. X. 821, of Lausus:

> *But when Anchises' son surveyed*
> *The fair, fair face so ghastly made,*
> *He groaned, by tenderness unmanned,*
> *And stretched the sympathizing hand,* etc.

charge be brought against Alba, as Troy was charged with adultery. There is no such charge, none like it found: the war was kindled only in order that there

> Might sound in languid ears the cry
> Of Tullus and of victory.[1]

This vice of restless ambition was the sole motive to that social and parricidal war—a vice which Sallust brands in passing; for when he has spoken with brief but hearty commendation of those primitive times in which life was spent without covetousness, and every one was sufficiently satisfied with what he had, he goes on: "But after Cyrus in Asia, and the Lacedemonians and Athenians in Greece, began to subdue cities and nations, and to account the lust of sovereignty a sufficient ground for war, and to reckon that the greatest glory consisted in the greatest empire"; and so on, as I need not now quote. This lust of sovereignty disturbs and consumes the human race with frightful ills. By this lust Rome was overcome when she triumphed over Alba and, praising her own crime, called it glory. For, as our Scriptures say, "the wicked boasteth of his heart's desire, and blesseth the covetous, whom the Lord abhorreth." [2] Away, then, with these deceitful masks, these deluding whitewashes, that things may be truthfully seen and scrutinized. Let no man tell me that this and the other was a "great" man, because he fought and conquered so and so. Gladiators fight and conquer, and this barbarism has its meed of praise; but I think it were better to take the consequences of any sloth, than to seek the glory won by such arms. And if two gladiators entered the arena to fight, one being father, the other his son, who would endure such a spectacle? who would not be revolted by it? How, then, could that be a glorious war which a daughter-state waged against its mother? Or did it constitute a difference, that the battlefield was not an arena, and that the wide plains were filled with the carcasses not of two gladiators, but of many of the flower of two nations; and that those contests were viewed not by the amphitheatre, but by the whole world, and furnished a profane spectacle both to those alive at the time, and to their posterity, so long as the fame of it is handed down?

Yet those gods, guardians of the Roman empire, and, as it were, theatric spectators of such contests as these, were not satisfied until the sister of the Horatii was added by her brother's sword as a third victim from the Roman side, so that Rome herself, though she won the day,

should have as many deaths to mourn. Afterwards, as a fruit of the victory, Alba was destroyed, though it was there the Trojan gods had formed a third asylum after Ilium had been sacked by the Greeks, and after they had left Lavinium, where Æneas had founded a kingdom in a land of banishment. But probably Alba was destroyed because from it too the gods had migrated, in their usual fashion, as Virgil says:

> Gone from each fane, each sacred shrine,
> Are those who made this realm divine.[3]

Gone, indeed, and from now their third asylum, that Rome might seem all the wiser in committing herself to them after they had deserted three other cities. Alba, whose king Amulius had banished his brother, displeased them; Rome, whose king Romulus had slain his brother, pleased them. But before Alba was destroyed, its population, they say, was amalgamated with the inhabitants of Rome, so that the two cities were one. Well, admitting it was so, yet the fact remains that the city of Ascanius, the third retreat of the Trojan gods, was destroyed by the daughter-city. Besides, to effect this pitiful conglomerate of the war's leavings, much blood was spilt on both sides. And how shall I speak in detail of the same wars, so often renewed in subsequent reigns, though they seemed to have been finished by great victories; and of wars that time after time were brought to an end by great slaughters, and which yet time after time were renewed by the posterity of those who had made peace and struck treaties? Of this calamitous history we have no small proof, in the fact that no subsequent king closed the gates of war; and therefore, with all their tutelar gods, no one of them reigned in peace.

CHAP. 15. *What manner of life and death the Roman kings had*

And what was the end of the kings themselves? Of Romulus, a flattering legend tells us that he was assumed into heaven. But certain Roman historians relate that he was torn in pieces by the senate for his ferocity, and that a man, Julius Proculus, was suborned to give out that Romulus had appeared to him, and through him commanded the Roman people to worship him as a god; and that in this way the people, who were beginning to resent the action of the senate, were quieted and pacified. For an eclipse of the sun had also happened; and this was attributed to the divine power of Romulus by the ignorant multitude, who did not know that it was brought about by the fixed laws of the sun's

[1] *Ibid.* BK. VI. 813.　[2] Ps. 10. 3.

[3] *Æneid.* BK. II. 351-2.

course: though this grief of the sun might rather have been considered proof that Romulus had been slain, and that the crime was indicated by this deprivation of the sun's light; as, in truth, was the case when the Lord was crucified through the cruelty and impiety of the Jews. For it is sufficiently demonstrated that this latter obscuration of the sun did not occur by the natural laws of the heavenly bodies, because it was then the Jewish Passover, which is held only at full moon, whereas natural eclipses of the sun happen only at the last quarter of the moon. Cicero, too, shows plainly enough that the apotheosis of Romulus was imaginary rather than real, when, even while he is praising him in one of Scipio's remarks in the *De Republica,* he says: "Such a reputation had he acquired, that when he suddenly disappeared during an eclipse of the sun, he was supposed to have been assumed into the number of the gods, which could be supposed of no mortal who had not the highest reputation for virtue." By these words, "he suddenly disappeared," we are to understand that he was mysteriously made away with by the violence either of the tempest or of a murderous assault. For their other writers speak not only of an eclipse, but of a sudden storm also, which certainly either afforded opportunity for the crime, or itself made an end of Romulus. And of Tullus Hostilius, who was the third king of Rome, and who was himself destroyed by lightning, Cicero in the same book says, that "he was not supposed to have been deified by this death, possibly because the Romans were unwilling to vulgarize the promotion they were assured or persuaded of in the case of Romulus, lest they should bring it into contempt by gratuitously assigning it to all and sundry." In one of his invectives, too, he says, in round terms, "The founder of this city, Romulus, we have raised to immortality and divinity by kindly celebrating his services"; implying that his deification was not real, but reputed, and called so by courtesy on account of his virtues. In the dialogue *Hortensius,* too, while speaking of the regular eclipses of the sun, he says that they "produce the same darkness as covered the death of Romulus, which happened during an eclipse of the sun." Here you see he does not at all shrink from speaking of his "death," for Cicero was more of a reasoner than an eulogist.

The other kings of Rome, too, with the exception of Numa Pompilius and Ancus Marcius, who died natural deaths, what horrible ends they had! Tullus Hostilius, the conqueror and destroyer of Alba, was, as I said, himself and all his house consumed by lightning. Priscus Tarquinius was slain by his predecessor's sons. Servius Tullius was foully murdered by his son-in-law Tarquinius Superbus, who succeeded him on the throne. Nor did so flagrant a parricide committed against Rome's best king drive from their altars and shrines those gods who were said to have been moved by Paris' adultery to treat poor Troy in this style, and abandon it to the fire and sword of the Greeks. Nay, the very Tarquin who had murdered, was allowed to succeed his father-in-law. And this infamous parricide, during the reign he had secured by murder, was allowed to triumph in many victorious wars, and to build the Capitol from their spoils; the gods meanwhile not departing, but abiding, and abetting, and suffering their king Jupiter to preside and reign over them in that very spendid Capitol, the work of a parricide. For he did not build the Capitol in the days of his innocence, and then suffer banishment for subsequent crimes; but to that reign during which he built the Capitol, he won his way by unnatural crime. And when he was afterwards banished by the Romans, and forbidden the city, it was not for his own but his son's wickedness in the affair of Lucretia—a crime perpetrated not only without his cognizance, but in his absence. For at that time he was besieging Ardea, and fighting Rome's battles; and we cannot say what he would have done had he been aware of his son's crime. Notwithstanding, though his opinion was neither inquired into nor ascertained, the people stripped him of royalty; and when he returned to Rome with his army, it was admitted, but he was excluded, abandoned by his troops, and the gates shut in his face. And yet, after he had appealed to the neighbouring states, and tormented the Romans with calamitous but unsuccessful wars, and when he was deserted by the ally on whom he most depended, despairing of regaining the kingdom, he lived a retired and quiet life for fourteen years, as it is reported, in Tusculum, a Roman town, where he grew old in his wife's company, and at last terminated his days in a much more desirable fashion than his father-in-law, who had perished by the hand of his son-in-law; his own daughter abetting, if report be true. And this Tarquin the Romans called, not the Cruel, nor the Infamous, but the Proud; their own pride perhaps resenting his tyrannical airs. So little did they make of his murdering their best king, his own father-in-law, that they elected him their own king. I wonder if it was not even more criminal in them to reward so bountifully so great a criminal. And yet there was no word of the gods abandoning the altars; unless, perhaps, some one will say in defence of the gods, that they remained at Rome for the purpose of punishing the Romans, rather than of aiding and profiting them, seducing them by empty victories, and wearing them out by severe wars. Such was the life of the Romans under the kings during the much-praised epoch of the state which extends to the expulsion of Tarquinius Superbus in the 243d year, during which all those victories which were bought with so much blood and such disasters, hardly pushed Rome's dominion twenty miles from the city; a territory which would by no means bear comparison with that of any petty Gætulian state.

CHAP. 16. *Of the first Roman consuls, the one of whom drove the other from the country, and shortly after perished at Rome by the hand of a wounded enemy, and so ended a career of unnatural murders*

To this epoch let us add also that of which Sallust says, that it was ordered with justice and moderation, while the fear of Tarquin and of a war with Etruria was impending. For so long as the Etrurians aided the efforts of Tarquin to regain the throne, Rome was convulsed with distressing war. And therefore he says that the state was ordered with justice and moderation, through the pressure of fear, not through the influence of equity. And in this very brief period, how calamitous a year was that in which consuls were first created, when the kingly power was abolished! They did not fulfill their term of office. For Junius Brutus deprived his colleague Lucius Tarquinius Collatinus, and banished him from the city; and shortly after he himself fell in battle, at once slaying and slain, having formerly put to death his own sons and his brothers-in-law, because he had discovered that they were conspiring to restore Tarquin. It is this deed that Virgil shudders to record, even while he seems to praise it; for when he says:

> An call his own rebellious seed
> For menaced liberty to bleed,

he immediately exclaims,

> Unhappy father! howsoe'er
> The deed be judged by after days;

that is to say, let posterity judge the deed as they please, let them praise and extol the father who slew his sons, he is unhappy. And then he adds, as if to console so unhappy a man:

> His country's love shall all o'erbear,
> And unextinguished thirst of praise.[1]

[1]Ibid., BK. VI. 820, etc.

In the tragic end of Brutus, who slew his own sons, and though he slew his enemy, Tarquin's son, yet could not survive him, but was survived by Tarquin the elder, does not the innocence of his colleague Collatinus seem to be vindicated, who, though a good citizen, suffered the same punishment as Tarquin himself, when that tyrant was banished? For Brutus himself is said to have been a relative of Tarquin. But Collatinus had the misfortune to bear not only the blood but the name of Tarquin. To change his name, then, not his country, would have been his fit penalty: to abridge his name by this word, and be called simply L. Collatinus. But he was not compelled to lose what he could lose without detriment, but was stripped of the honour of the first consulship, and was banished from the land he loved. Is this, then, the glory of Brutus—this injustice, alike detestable and profitless to the republic? Was it to this he was driven by "his country's love, and unextinguished thirst of praise?"

When Tarquin the tyrant was expelled, L. Tarquinius Collatinus, the husband of Lucretia, was created consul along with Brutus. How justly the people acted, in looking more to the character than the name of a citizen! How unjustly Brutus acted, in depriving of honour and country his colleague in that new office, whom he might have deprived of his name, if it were so offensive to him! Such were the ills, such the disasters, which fell out when the government was "ordered with justice and moderation." Lucretius, too, who succeeded Brutus, was carried off by disease before the end of that same year. So P. Valerius, who succeeded Collatinus, and M. Horatius, who filled the vacancy occasioned by the death of Lucretius, completed that disastrous and funereal year, which had five consuls. Such was the year in which the Roman republic inaugurated the new honour and office of the consulship.

CHAP. 17. *Of the disasters which vexed the Roman republic after the inauguration of the consulship, and of the non-intervention of the gods of Rome.*

After this, when their fears were gradually diminished—not because the wars ceased, but because they were not so furious—that period in which things were "ordered with justice and moderation" drew to an end, and there followed that state of matters which Sallust thus briefly sketches: "Then began the patricians to oppress the people as slaves, to condemn them to death or scourging, as the kings had done, to drive them from their holdings, and to tyrannize over those who had no property to lose. The people, overwhelmed by these oppressive measures, and most of all by usury, and obliged to contribute both money and personal service to the constant wars, at length took arms and seceded to Mount Aventine and Mount Sacer, and thus secured for themselves tribunes and protective laws. But it was only the second Punic war that put an end on both sides to discord and strife." But why should I spend time in writing such things, or make others spend it in reading them? Let the terse summary of Sallust suffice to intimate the misery of the republic through all that long period till the second Punic war, how it was distracted from without by unceasing wars, and torn with civil broils and dissensions. So that those victories they boast were not the substantial joys of the happy, but the empty comforts of wretched men, and seductive incitements to turbulent men to concoct disasters upon disasters. And let not the good and prudent Romans be angry at our saying this; and indeed we need neither deprecate nor denounce their anger, for we know they will harbour none. For we speak no more severely than their own authors, and much less elaborately and strikingly; yet they diligently read these authors, and compel their children to learn them. But they who are angry, what would they do to me were I to say what Sallust says? "Frequent mobs, seditions, and at last civil wars, became common, while a few leading men on whom the masses were dependent, affected supreme power under the seemly pretence of seeking the good of senate and people; citizens were judged good or bad without reference to their loyalty to the republic (for all were equally corrupt); but the wealthy and dangerously powerful were esteemed good citizens, because they maintained the existing state of things." Now, if those historians judged that an honourable freedom of speech required that they should not be silent regarding the blemishes of their own state, which they have in many places loudly applauded in their ignorance of that other and true city in which citizenship is an everlasting dignity; what does it become us to do, whose liberty ought to be so much greater, as our hope in God is better and more assured, when they impute to our Christ the calamities of this age, in order that men of the less instructed and weaker sort may be alienated from that city in which alone eternal and blessed life can be enjoyed? Nor do we utter against their gods anything more horrible than their own authors do, whom they read

and circulate. For, indeed, all that we have said we have derived from them, and there is much more to say of a worse kind which we are unable to say.

Where, then, were those gods who are supposed to be justly worshipped for the slender and delusive prosperity of this world, when the Romans, who were seduced to their service by lying wiles, were harassed by such calamities? Where were they when Valerius the consul was killed while defending the Capitol, that had been fired by exiles and slaves? He was himself better able to defend the temple of Jupiter, than that crowd of divinities with their most high and mighty king, whose temple he came to the rescue of, were able to defend him. Where were they when the city, worn out with unceasing seditions, was waiting in some kind of calm for the return of the ambassadors who had been sent to Athens to borrow laws, and was desolated by dreadful famine and pestilence? Where were they when the people, again distressed with famine, created for the first time a prefect of the market; and when Spurius Melius, who, as the famine increased, distributed corn to the famishing masses, was accused of aspiring to royalty, and at the instance of this same prefect, and on the authority of the superannuated dictator L. Quintius, was put to death by Quintus Servilius, master of the horse—an event which occasioned a serious and dangerous riot? Where were they when that very severe pestilence visited Rome, on account of which the people, after long and wearisome and useless supplications of the helpless gods, conceived the idea of celebrating *Lectisternia*, which had never been done before; that is to say, they set couches in honour of the gods, which accounts for the name of this sacred rite, or rather sacrilege? Where were they when, during ten successive years of reverses, the Roman army suffered frequent and great losses among the Veians, and would have been destroyed but for the succour of Furius Camillus, who was afterwards banished by an ungrateful country? Where were they when the Gauls took, sacked, burned, and desolated Rome? Where were they when that memorable pestilence wrought such destruction, in which Furius Camillus too perished, who first defended the ungrateful republic from the Veians, and afterwards saved it from the Gauls? Nay, during this plague, they introduced a new pestilence of scenic entertainments, which spread its more fatal contagion, not to the bodies, but the morals of the Romans. Where were they when another frightful pestilence visited the city—I mean the poisonings imputed to an incredible number of noble Roman matrons, whose characters were infected with a disease more fatal than any plague? Or when both consuls at the head of the army were beset by the Samnites in the Caudine Forks, and forced to strike a shameful treaty, 600 Roman knights being kept as hostages; while the troops, having laid down their arms, and being stripped of everything, were made to pass under the yoke with one garment each? Or when, in the midst of a serious pestilence, lightning struck the Roman camp and killed many? Or when Rome was driven, by the violence of another intolerable plague, to send to Epidaurus for Æsculapius as a god of medicine; since the frequent adulteries of Jupiter in his youth had not perhaps left this king of all who so long reigned in the Capitol, any leisure for the study of medicine? Or when, at one time, the Lucanians, Brutians, Samnites, Tuscans, and Senonian Gauls conspired against Rome, and first slew her ambassadors, then overthrew an army under the prætor, putting to the sword 13,000 men, besides the commander and seven tribunes? Or when the people, after the serious and long-continued disturbances at Rome, at last plundered the city and withdrew to Janiculus; a danger so grave, that Hortensius was created dictator, an office which they had recourse to only in extreme emergencies; and he, having brought back the people, died while yet he retained his office, an event without precedent in the case of any dictator, and which was a shame to those gods who had now Æsculapius among them?

At that time, indeed, so many wars were everywhere engaged in, that through scarcity of soldiers they enrolled for military service the *proletarii,* who received this name, because, being too poor to equip for military service, they had leisure to beget offspring.[1] Pyrrhus, king of Greece, and at that time of wide-spread renown, was invited by the Tarentines to enlist himself against Rome. It was to him that Apollo, when consulted regarding the issue of his enterprise, uttered with some pleasantry so ambiguous an oracle, that whichever alternative happened, the god himself should be counted divine. For he so worded the oracle that whether Pyrrhus was conquered by the Romans, or the Romans by Pyrrhus, the soothsaying god would securely await the issue. And then what frightful massacres of both armies ensued! Yet Pyrrhus remained conqueror, and would have been able now to proclaim Apollo a true diviner, as he understood the oracle, had not the Romans been

[1] *Proletarius,* from *proles,* offspring.

the conquerors in the next engagement. And while such disastrous wars were being waged, a terrible disease broke out among the women. For the pregnant women died before delivery. And Æsculapius, I fancy, excused himself in this matter on the ground that he professed to be arch-physician, not midwife. Cattle, too, similarly perished; so that it was believed that the whole race of animals was destined to become extinct. Then what shall I say of that memorable winter in which the weather was so incredibly severe, that in the Forum frightfully deep snow lay for forty days together, and the Tiber was frozen? Had such things happened in our time, what accusations we should have heard from our enemies! And that other great pestilence, which raged so long and carried off so many; what shall I say of it? Spite of all the drugs of Æsculapius, it only grew worse in its second year, till at last recourse was had to the Sibylline books—a kind of oracle which, as Cicero says in his *De Divinatione,* owes significance to its interpreters, who make doubtful conjectures as they can or as they wish. In this instance, the cause of the plague was said to be that so many temples had been used as private residences. And thus Æsculapius for the present escaped the charge of either ignominious negligence or want of skill. But why were so many allowed to occupy sacred tenements without interference, unless because supplication had long been addressed in vain to such a crowd of gods, and so by degrees the sacred places were deserted of worshippers, and being thus vacant, could without offence be put at least to some human uses? And the temples, which were at that time laboriously recognized and restored that the plague might be stayed, fell afterwards into disuse, and were again devoted to the same human uses. Had they not thus lapsed into obscurity, it could not have been pointed to as proof of Varro's great erudition that in his work on sacred places he cites so many that were unknown. Meanwhile, the restoration of the temples procured no cure of the plague, but only a fine excuse for the gods.

CHAP. 18. *The disasters suffered by the Romans in the Punic wars, which were not mitigated by the protection of the gods*

In the Punic wars, again, when victory hung so long in the balance between the two kingdoms, when two powerful nations were straining every nerve and using all their resources against one another, how many smaller kingdoms were crushed, how many large and flourishing cities were demolished, how many states were overwhelmed and ruined, how many districts and lands far and near were desolated! How often were the victors on either side vanquished! What multitudes of men, both of those actually in arms and of others, were destroyed! What huge navies, too, were crippled in engagements, or were sunk by every kind of marine disaster! Were we to attempt to recount or mention these calamities, we should become writers of history. At that period Rome was mightily perturbed, and resorted to vain and ludicrous expedients. On the authority of the Sibylline books, the secular games were re-appointed, which had been inaugurated a century before but had faded into oblivion in happier times. The games consecrated to the infernal gods were also renewed by the pontiffs; for they, too, had sunk into disuse in the better times. And no wonder; for when they were renewed, the great abundance of dying men made all hell rejoice at its riches, and give itself up to sport: for certainly the ferocious wars, and disastrous quarrels, and bloody victories—now on one side, and now on the other—though most calamitous to men, afforded great sport and a rich banquet to the devils. But in the first Punic war there was no more disastrous event than the Roman defeat in which Regulus was taken. We made mention of him in the two former books as an incontestably great man, who had before conquered and subdued the Carthaginians, and who would have put an end to the first Punic war, had not an inordinate appetite for praise and glory prompted him to impose on the worn-out Carthagians harder conditions than they could bear. If the unlooked-for captivity and unseemly bondage of this man, his fidelity to his oath, and his surpassingly cruel death, do not bring a blush to the face of the gods, it is true that they are brazen and bloodless.

Nor were there wanting at that time very heavy disasters within the city itself. For the Tiber was extraordinarily flooded, and destroyed almost all the lower parts of the city; some buildings being carried away by the violence of the torrent, while others were soaked to rottenness by the water that stood round them even after the flood was gone. This visitation was followed by a fire which was still more destructive, for it consumed some of the loftier buildings round the Forum, and spared not even its own proper temple, that of Vesta, in which virgins chosen for this honour, or rather for this punishment, had been employed in conferring, as it were, everlasting life on fire, by ceaselessly feed-

ing it with fresh fuel. But at the time we speak of, the fire in the temple was not content with being kept alive: it raged. And when the virgins, scared by its vehemence, were unable to save those fatal images which had already brought destruction on three cities[1] in which they had been received, Metellus the priest, forgetful of his own safety, rushed in and rescued the sacred things, though he was half roasted in doing so. For either the fire did not recognize even him, or else the goddess of fire was there—a goddess who would not have fled from the fire supposing she had been there. But here you see how a man could be of greater service to Vesta than she could be to him. Now if these gods could not avert the fire from themselves, what help against flames or flood could they bring to the state of which they were the reputed guardians? Facts have shown that they were useless. These objections of ours would be idle if our adversaries maintained that their idols are consecrated rather as symbols of things eternal, than to secure the blessings of time; and that thus, though the symbols, like all material and visible things, might perish, no damage thereby resulted to the things for the sake of which they had been consecrated, while, as for the images themselves, they could be renewed again for the same purposes they had formerly served. But with lamentable blindness, they suppose that, through the intervention of perishable gods, the earthly well-being and temporal prosperity of the state can be preserved from perishing. And so, when they are reminded that even when the gods remained among them this well-being and prosperity were blighted, they blush to change the opinion they are unable to defend.

CHAP. 19. *Of the calamity of the second Punic war, which consumed the strength of both parties*

As to the second Punic war, it were tedious to recount the disasters it brought on both the nations engaged in so protracted and shifting a war that (by the acknowledgment even of those writers who have made it their object not so much to narrate the wars as to eulogize the dominion of Rome) the people who remained victorious were less like conquerors than conquered. For, when Hannibal poured out of Spain over the Pyrenees, and overran Gaul, and burst through the Alps, and during his whole course gathered strength by plundering and subduing as he went, and inundated Italy like a torrent, how bloody were the wars, and how continuous

[1]Troy, Lavinia, Alba.

the engagements, that were fought! How often were the Romans vanquished! How many towns went over to the enemy, and how many were taken and subdued! What fearful battles there were, and how often did the defeat of the Romans shed lustre on the arms of Hannibal! And what shall I say of the wonderfully crushing defeat at Cannæ, where even Hannibal, cruel as he was, was yet sated with the blood of his bitterest enemies, and gave orders that they be spared? From this field of battle he sent to Carthage three bushels of gold rings, signifying that so much of the rank of Rome had that day fallen, that it was easier to give an idea of it by measure than by numbers and that the frightful slaughter of the common rank and file whose bodies lay undistinguished by the ring, and who were numerous in proportion to their meanness, was rather to be conjectured than accurately reported. In fact, such was the scarcity of soldiers after this, that the Romans impressed their criminals on the promise of impunity, and their slaves by the bribe of liberty, and out of these infamous classes did not so much recruit as create an army. But these slaves, or, to give them all their titles, these freedmen who were enlisted to do battle for the republic of Rome, lacked arms. And so they took arms from the temples, as if the Romans were saying to their gods: Lay down those arms you have held so long in vain, if by chance our slaves may be able to use to purpose what you, our gods, have been impotent to use. At that time, too, the public treasury was too low to pay the soldiers, and private resources were used for public purposes; and so generously did individuals contribute of their property, that, saving the gold ring and bulla which each wore, the pitiful mark of his rank, no senator, and much less any of the other orders and tribes, reserved any gold for his own use. But if in our day they were reduced to this poverty, who would be able to endure their reproaches, barely endurable as they are now, when more money is spent on actors for the sake of a superfluous gratification, than was then disbursed to the legions?

CHAP. 20. *Of the destruction of the Saguntines, who received no help from the Roman gods, though perishing on account of their fidelity to Rome*

But among all the disasters of the second Punic war, there occurred none more lamentable, or calculated to excite deeper complaint, than the fate of the Saguntines. This city of Spain, eminently friendly to Rome, was destroyed by its fidelity to the Roman people. For when Hannibal had broken treaty with the Romans, he sought occasion for provoking them to war and accordingly made a fierce assault upon Saguntum. When this was reported at Rome, ambassadors were sent to Hannibal, urging him to raise the siege; and when this remonstrance was neglected, they proceeded to Carthage, lodged complaint against the breaking of the treaty, and returned to Rome without accomplishing their object. Meanwhile the siege went on; and in the eighth or ninth month, this opulent but ill-fated city, dear as it was to its own state and to Rome, was taken, and subjected to treatment which one cannot read, much less narrate, without horror. And yet, because it bears directly on the matter in hand, I will briefly touch upon it. First, then, famine wasted the Saguntines, so that even human corpses were eaten by some: so at least it is recorded. Subsequently, when thoroughly worn out, that they might at least escape the ignominy of falling into the hands of Hannibal, they publicly erected a huge funeral pile, and cast themselves into its flames, while at the same time they slew their children and themselves with the sword. Could these gods, these debauchees and gourmands, whose mouths water for fat sacrifices, and whose lips utter lying divinations, could they not do anything in a case like this? Could they not interfere for the preservation of a city closely allied to the Roman people, or prevent it perishing for its fidelity to that alliance of which they themselves had been the mediators? Saguntum, faithfully keeping the treaty it had entered into before these gods, and to which it had firmly bound itself by an oath, was besieged, taken, and destroyed by a perjured person. If afterwards, when Hannibal was close to the walls of Rome, it was the gods who terrified him with lightning and tempest, and drove him to a distance, why, I ask, did they not thus interfere before? For I make bold to say, that this demonstration with the tempest would have been more honourably made in defence of the allies of Rome—who were in danger on account of their reluctance to break faith with the Romans, and had no resources of their own—than in defence of the Romans themselves, who were fighting in their own cause, and had abundant resources to oppose Hannibal. If, then, they had been the guardians of Roman prosperity and glory, they would have preserved that glory from the stain of this Saguntine disaster; and how silly it is to believe that Rome was preserved from destruction at the hands of Hannibal by the guardian care of those gods who were unable to rescue the city of Saguntum from perishing through its fidelity to the alliance of Rome. If the population of Saguntum had been Christian, and had suffered as it did for the Christian faith (though, of course, Christians would not have used fire and sword against their own persons), they would have suffered with that hope which springs from faith in Christ—the hope not of a brief temporal reward, but of unending and eternal bliss. What then, will the advocates and apologists of these gods say in their defence, when charged with the blood of these Saguntines; for they are professedly worshipped and invoked for this very purpose of securing prosperity in this fleeting and transitory life? Can anything be said but what was alleged in the case of Regulus' death? For though there is a difference between the two cases, the one being an individual, the other a whole community, yet the cause of destruction was in both cases the keeping of their plighted troth. For it was this which made Regulus willing to return to his enemies, and this which made the Saguntines unwilling to revolt to their enemies. Does, then, the keeping of faith provoke the gods to anger? Or is it possible that not only individuals, but even entire communities, perish while the gods are propitious to them? Let our adversaries choose which alternative they will. If, on the one hand, those gods are enraged at the keeping of faith, let them enlist perjured persons as their worshippers. If, on the other hand, men and states can suffer great and terrible calamities, and at last perish while favoured by the gods, then does their worship not produce happiness as its fruit. Let those, therefore, who suppose that they have fallen into distress because their religious worship has been abolished, lay aside their anger; for it were quite possible that did the gods not only remain with them, but regard them with favour, they might yet be left to mourn an unhappy lot, or might, even like Regulus and the Saguntines, be horribly tormented, and at last perish miserably.

CHAP. 21. *Of the ingratitude of Rome to Scipio, its deliverer, and of its manners during the period which Sallust describes as the best*

Omitting many things, that I may not exceed the limits of the work I have proposed to myself, I come to the epoch between the second and last Punic wars, during which, according to Sallust, the Romans lived with the greatest virtue and concord. Now, in this period of virtue and harmony, the great Scipio, the liberator of Rome and Italy, who had with surprising ability

brought to a close the second Punic war—that horrible, destructive, dangerous contest—who had defeated Hannibal and subdued Carthage, and whose whole life is said to have been dedicated to the gods and cherished in their temples, this Scipio, after such a triumph, was obliged to yield to the accusations of his enemies and to leave his country, which his valour had saved and liberated, to spend the remainder of his days in the town of Liternum, so indifferent to a recall from exile, that he is said to have given orders that not even his remains should lie in his ungrateful country. It was at that time also that the pro-consul Cn. Manlius, after subduing the Galatians, introduced into Rome the luxury of Asia, more destructive than all hostile armies. It was then that iron bedsteads and expensive carpets were first used; then, too, that female singers were admitted to banquets, and other licentious abominations were introduced. But at present I meant to speak not of the evils men voluntarily practise, but of those they suffer in spite of themselves. So that the case of Scipio, who succumbed to his enemies and died in exile from the country he had rescued, was mentioned by me as being pertinent to the present discussion; for this was the reward he received from those Roman gods whose temples he saved from Hannibal, and who are worshipped only for the sake of securing temporal happiness. But since Sallust, as we have seen, declares that the manners of Rome were never better than at that time, I therefore judged it right to mention the Asiatic luxury then introduced, that it might be seen that what he says is true, only when that period is compared with the others, during which the morals were certainly worse and the factions more violent. For at that time—I mean between the second and third Punic war—that notorious Lex Voconia was passed, which prohibited a man from making a woman, even an only daughter, his heir; than which law I am at a loss to conceive what could be more unjust. It is true that in the interval between these two Punic wars the misery of Rome was somewhat less. Abroad, indeed, their forces were consumed by wars, yet also consoled by victories; while at home there were not such disturbances as at other times. But when the last Punic war had terminated in the utter destruction of Rome's rival, which quickly succumbed to the other Scipio, who thus earned for himself the surname of Africanus, then the Roman republic was overwhelmed with such a host of ills, which sprang from the corrupt manners induced by prosperity and security, that the sudden overthrow of Carthage is seen to have injured Rome more seriously than her long-continued hostility. During the whole subsequent period down to the time of Cæsar Augustus, who seems to have entirely deprived the Romans of liberty— a liberty, indeed, which in their own judgment was no longer glorious, but full of broils and dangers, and which now was quite enervated and languishing—and who submitted all things again to the will of a monarch, and infused as it were a new life into the sickly old age of the republic, and inaugurated a fresh *régime;* during this whole period, I say, many military disasters were sustained on a variety of occasions, all of which I here pass by. There was specially the treaty of Numantia, blotted as it was with extreme disgrace; for the sacred chickens, they say, flew out of the coop, and thus augured disaster to Mancinus the consul; just as if, during all these years in which that little city of Numantia had withstood the besieging army of Rome, and had become a terror to the republic, the other generals had all marched against it under unfavourable auspices.

CHAP. 22. *Of the edict of Mithridates, commanding that all Roman citizens found in Asia should be slain*

These things, I say, I pass in silence; but I can by no means be silent regarding the order given by Mithridates, king of Asia, that on one day all Roman citizens residing anywhere in Asia (where great numbers of them were following their private business) should be put to death: and this order was executed. How miserable a spectacle was then presented, when each man was suddenly and treacherously murdered wherever he happened to be, in the field or on the road, in the town, in his own home, or in the street, in market or temple, in bed or at table! Think of the groans of the dying, the tears of the spectators, and even of the executioners themselves. For how cruel a necessity was it that compelled the hosts of these victims, not only to see these abominable butcheries in their own houses, but even to perpetrate them: to change their countenance suddenly from the bland kindliness of friendship, and in the midst of peace set about the business of war; and, shall I say, give and receive wounds, the slain being pierced in body, the slayer in spirit! Had all these murdered persons, then, despised auguries? Had they neither public nor household gods to consult when they left their homes and set out on that fatal journey? If they had not, our adversaries have no reason to complain of

these Christian times in this particular, since long ago the Romans despised auguries as idle. If, on the other hand, they did consult omens, let them tell us what good they got thereby, even when such things were not prohibited, but authorized, by human, if not by divine law.

CHAP. 23. *Of the internal disasters which vexed the Roman republic, and followed a portentous madness which seized all the domestic animals*

But let us now mention, as succinctly as possible, those disasters which were still more vexing, because nearer home; I mean those discords which are erroneously called civil, since they destroy civil interests. The seditions had now become urban wars, in which blood was freely shed and in which parties raged against one another, not with wrangling and verbal contention, but with physical force and arms. What a sea of Roman blood was shed, what desolations and devastations were occasioned in Italy by wars social, wars servile, wars civil! Before the Latins began the social war against Rome, all the animals used in the service of man—dogs, horses, asses, oxen, and all the rest that are subject to man—suddenly grew wild, and forgot their domesticated tameness, forsook their stalls and wandered at large, and could not be closely approached either by strangers or their own masters without danger. If this was a portent, how serious a calamity must have been portended by a plague which, whether portent or no, was in itself a serious calamity! Had it happened in our day, the heathen would have been more rabid against us than their animals were against them.

CHAP. 24. *Of the civil dissension occasioned by the sedition of the Gracchi*

The civil wars originated in the seditions which the Gracchi excited regarding the agrarian laws; for they were minded to divide among the people the lands which were wrongfully possessed by the nobility. But to reform an abuse of so long standing was an enterprise full of peril, or rather, as the event proved, of destruction. For what disasters accompanied the death of the elder Gracchus! what slaughter ensued when, shortly after, the younger brother met the same fate! For noble and ignoble were indiscriminately massacred; and this not by legal authority and procedure, but by mobs and armed rioters. After the death of the younger Gracchus, the consul Lucius Opimius, who had given battle to him within the city, and had defeated and put to the sword both himself and his confederates, and had massacred many of the citizens, instituted a judicial examination of others, and is reported to have put to death as many as 3000 men. From this it may be gathered how many fell in the riotous encounters, when the result even of a judicial investigation was so bloody. The assassin of Gracchus himself sold his head to the consul for its weight in gold, such being the previous agreement. In this massacre, too, Marcus Fulvius, a man of consular rank, with all his children, was put to death.

Chap. 25. Of the temple of Concord, which was erected by a decree of the senate on the scene of these seditions and massacres

A pretty decree of the senate it was, truly, by which the temple of Concord was built on the spot where that disastrous rising had taken place, and where so many citizens of every rank had fallen. I suppose it was that the monument of the Gracchi's punishment might strike the eye and affect the memory of the pleaders. But what was this but to deride the gods, by building a temple to that goddess who, had she been in the city, would not have suffered herself to be torn by such dissensions? Or was it that Concord was chargeable with that bloodshed because she had deserted the minds of the citizens and was therefore incarcerated in that temple? For if they had any regard to consistency, why did they not rather erect on that site a temple of Discord? Or is there a reason for Concord being a goddess while Discord is none? Does the distinction of Labeo hold here, who would have made the one a good, the other an evil deity?—a distinction which seems to have been suggested to him by the mere fact of his observing at Rome a temple to Fever as well as one to Health. But, on the same ground, Discord as well as Concord ought to be deified. A hazardous venture the Romans made in provoking so wicked a goddess, and in forgetting that the destruction of Troy had been occasioned by her taking offence. For, being indignant that she was not invited with the other gods, she created dissension among the three goddesses by sending in the golden apple, which occasioned strife in heaven, victory to Venus, the rape of Helen, and the destruction of Troy. Wherefore, if she was perhaps offended that the Romans had not thought her worthy of a temple among the other gods in their city, and therefore disturbed the state with such tumults, to how much fiercer passion would she be roused when she saw the temple of her adversary erected on the scene of that massacre, or, in other words, on the scene of her own handiwork! Those wise and learned men are enraged at our laughing at these follies; and yet, being worshippers of good and bad divinities alike, they cannot escape this dilemma about Concord and Discord: either they have neglected the worship of these goddesses, and preferred Fever and War, to whom there are shrines erected of great antiquity, or they have worshipped them, and after all Concord has abandoned them, and Discord has tempestuously hurled them into civil wars.

Chap. 26. Of the various kinds of wars which followed the building of the temple of Concord

But they supposed that, in erecting the temple of Concord within the view of the orators, as a memorial of the punishment and death of the Gracchi, they were raising an effectual obstacle to sedition. How much effect it had is indicated by the still more deplorable wars that followed. For after this the orators endeavoured not to avoid the example of the Gracchi, but to surpass their projects; as did Lucius Saturninus, a tribune of the people, and Caius Servilius the prætor, and, some time after, Marcus Drusus, all of whom stirred seditions which first of all occasioned bloodshed, and then the social wars by which Italy was grievously injured, and reduced to a piteously desolate and wasted condition. Then followed the servile war and the civil wars; and in them what battles were fought, and what blood was shed, so that almost all the peoples of Italy, which formed the main strength of the Roman empire, were conquered as if they were barbarians! Then even historians themselves find it difficult to explain how the servile war was begun by a very few, certainly less than seventy gladiators, what numbers of fierce and cruel men attached themselves to these, how many of the Roman generals this band defeated, and how it laid waste many districts and cities. And that was not the only servile war: the province of Macedonia, and subsequently Sicily and the sea-coast, were also depopulated by bands of slaves. And who can adequately describe either the horrible atrocities which the pirates first committed, or the wars they afterwards maintained against Rome?

Chap. 27. Of the civil war between Marius and Sulla

But when Marius, stained with the blood of his fellow-citizens, whom the rage of party had sacrificed, was in his turn vanquished and driven from the city, it had scarcely time to breathe freely, when, to use the words of Cicero, "Cinna and Marius together returned and took possession of it. Then, indeed, the foremost men in the state were put to death, its lights quenched. Sulla afterwards avenged this cruel victory; but we need not say with what loss of life, and with what ruin to the republic." For of this vengeance, which was more destructive than if the crimes which it punished had been committed with impunity, Lucan says: "The cure was excessive and too closely resembled the disease. The guilty perished, but when none but the guilty survived: and then private hatred and anger, unbridled by law, were allowed free indulgence." In that war between Marius and Sulla, besides those who fell in the field of battle, the city, too, was filled with corpses in its streets, squares, markets, theatres, and temples; so that it is not easy to reckon whether the victors slew more before or after victory, that they might be, or because they were, victors. As soon as Marius triumphed, and returned from exile, besides the butcheries everywhere perpetrated, the head of the consul Octavius was exposed on the rostrum; Cæsar and Fimbria were assassinated in their own houses; the two Crassi, father and son, were murdered in one another's sight; Bebius and Numitorius were disembowelled by being dragged with hooks; Catulus escaped the hands of his enemies by drinking poison; Merula, the flamen of Jupiter, cut his veins and made a libation of his own blood to his god. Moreover, every one whose salutation Marius did not answer by giving his hand, was at once cut down before his face.

Chap. 28. Of the victory of Sulla, the avenger of the cruelties of Marius

Then followed the victory of Sulla, the so-called avenger of the cruelties of Marius. But not only was his victory purchased with great bloodshed; but when hostilities were finished, hostility survived, and the subsequent peace was bloody as the war. To the former and still recent massacres of the elder Marius, the younger Marius and Carbo, who belonged to the same party, added greater atrocities. For when Sulla approached, and they despaired not only of victory but of life itself, they made a promiscuous massacre of friends and foes. And, not satisfied with staining every corner of Rome with blood, they besieged the senate and led forth the senators to death from the Curia as from a prison. Mucius Scævola the pontiff was slain at the altar of Vesta, which he had clung to because no spot in Rome was more sacred than her temple; and

his blood well-nigh extinguished the fire which was kept alive by the constant care of the virgins. Then Sulla entered the city victorious, after having slaughtered in the Villa Publica, not by combat, but by an order, 7000 men who had surrendered, and were therefore unarmed; so fierce was the rage of peace itself, even after the rage of war was extinct. Moreover, throughout the whole city every partisan of Sulla slew whom he pleased, so that the number of deaths went beyond computation, till it was suggested to Sulla that he should allow some to survive that the victors might not be destitute of subjects. Then this furious and promiscuous licence to murder was checked, and much relief was expressed at the publication of the proscription list, containing though it did the death-warrant of two thousand men of the highest ranks, the senatorial and equestrian. The large number was indeed saddening, but it was consolatory that a limit was fixed; nor was the grief at the numbers slain so great as the joy that the rest were secure. But this very security, hard-hearted as it was, could not but bemoan the exquisite torture applied to some of those who had been doomed to die. For one was torn to pieces by the unarmed hands of the executioners; men treating a living man more savagely than wild beasts are used to tear an abandoned corpse. Another had his eyes dug out, and his limbs cut away bit by bit, and was forced to live a long while, or rather to die a long while, in such torture. Some celebrated cities were put up to auction, like farms; and one was collectively condemned to slaughter, just as an individual criminal would be condemned to death. These things were done in peace when the war was over, not that victory might be more speedily obtained, but that, after being obtained, it might not be thought lightly of. Peace vied with war in cruelty, and surpassed it: for while war overthrew armed hosts, peace slew the defenceless. War gave liberty to him who was attacked, to strike if he could; peace granted to the survivors not life but an unresisting death.

Chap. 29. A comparison of the disasters which Rome experienced during the Gothic and Gallic invasions, with those occasioned by the authors of the civil wars

What fury of foreign nations, what barbarian ferocity, can compare with this victory of citizens over citizens? Which was more disastrous, more hideous, more bitter to Rome: the recent Gothic and the old Gallic invasion, or the cruelty displayed by Marius and Sulla and their partisans against men who were members of the same body as themselves? The Gauls, indeed, massacred all the senators they found in any part of the city except the Capitol, which alone was defended; but they at least sold life to those who were in the Capitol, though they might have starved them out if they could not have stormed it. The Goths, again, spared so many senators that it is the more surprising that they killed any. But Sulla, while Marius was still living, established himself as conqueror in the Capitol, which the Gauls had not violated, and thence issued his death-warrants; and when Marius had escaped by flight, though destined to return more fierce and bloodthirsty than ever, Sulla issued from the Capitol even decrees of the senate for the slaughter and confiscation of the property of many citizens. Then, when Sulla left, what did the Marian faction hold sacred or spare, when they gave no quarter even to Mucius, a citizen, a senator, a pontiff, and though clasping in piteous embrace the very altar in which, they say, reside the destinies of Rome? And that final proscription list of Sulla's, not to mention countless other massacres, despatched more senators than the Goths could even plunder.

CHAP. 30. *Of the connection of the wars which with great severity and frequency followed one another before the advent of Christ*

With what effrontery, then, with what assurance, with what impudence, with what folly or rather insanity, do they refuse to impute these disasters to their own gods, and impute the present to our Christ! These bloody civil wars, more distressing, by the avowal of their own historians than any foreign wars, and which were pronounced to be not merely calamitous, but absolutely ruinous to the republic, began long before the coming of Christ and gave birth to one another; so that a concatenation of unjustifiable causes led from the wars of Marius and Sulla to those of Sertorius and Catiline, of whom the one was proscribed, the other brought up by Sulla; from this to the war of Lepidus and Catulus, of whom the one wished to rescind, the other to defend the acts of Sulla; from this to the war of Pompey and Cæsar, of whom Pompey had been a partisan of Sulla, whose power he equalled or even surpassed, while Cæsar condemned Pompey's power because it was not his own, and yet exceeded it when Pompey was defeated and slain. From him the chain of civil wars extended to the second Cæsar, afterwards called Augustus, and in whose reign Christ was

born. For even Augustus himself waged many civil wars; and in these wars many of the foremost men perished, among them that skilful manipulator of the republic, Cicero. Caius Cæsar, when he had conquered Pompey, though he used his victory with clemency, and granted to men of the opposite faction both life and honours, was suspected of aiming at royalty, and was assassinated in the Curia by a party of noble senators, who had conspired to defend the liberty of the republic. His power was then coveted by Antony, a man of very different character, polluted and debased by every kind of vice, who was strenuously resisted by Cicero on the same plea of defending the liberty of the republic. At this juncture that other Cæsar, the adopted son of Caius, and afterwards, as I said, known by the name of Augustus, had made his *début* as a young man of remarkable genius. This youthful Cæsar was favoured by Cicero, in order that his influence might counteract that of Antony; for he hoped that Cæsar would overthrow and blast the power of Antony, and establish a free state—so blind and unaware of the future was he: for that very young man, whose advancement and influence he was fostering, allowed Cicero to be killed as the seal of an alliance with Antony, and subjected to his own rule the very liberty of the republic in defence of which he had made so many orations.

CHAP. 31. *That it is effrontery to impute the present troubles to Christ and the prohibition of polytheistic worship, since even when the gods were worshipped such calamities befell the people*

Let those who have no gratitude to Christ for His great benefits, blame their own gods for these heavy disasters. For certainly when these occurred the altars of the gods were kept blazing, and there rose the mingled fragrance of "Sabæan incense and fresh garlands";[1] the priests were clothed with honour, the shrines were maintained in splendour; sacrifices, games, sacred ecstasies, were common in the temples; while the blood of the citizens was being so freely shed, not only in remote places, but among the very altars of the gods. Cicero did not choose to seek sanctuary in a temple, because Mucius had sought it there in vain. But they who most unpardonably calumniate this Christian era, are the very men who either themselves fled for asylum to the places specially dedicated to Christ, or were led there by the barbarians that they might be safe. In short, not to recapit-

[1]Virgil, *Æneid*, BK. I. 417.

ulate the many instances I have cited, and not to add to their number others which it were tedious to enumerate, this one thing I am persuaded of, and this every impartial judgment will readily acknowledge, that if the human race had received Christianity before the Punic wars, and if the same desolating calamities which these wars brought upon Europe and Africa had followed the introduction of Christianity, there is no one of those who now accuse us who would not have attributed them to our religion. How intolerable would their accusations have been, at least so far as the Romans are concerned, if the Christian religion had been received and diffused prior to the invasion of the Gauls, or to the ruinous floods and fires which desolated Rome, or to those most calamitous of all events, the civil wars! And those other disasters, which were of so strange a nature that they were reckoned prodigies, had they happened since the Christian era, to whom but to the Christians would they have imputed these as crimes? I do not speak of those things which were rather surprising than hurtful—oxen speaking, unborn infants articulating some words in their mothers' wombs, serpents flying, hens and women being changed into the other sex; and other similar prodigies which, whether true or false, are recorded not in their imaginative, but in their historical works, and which do not injure, but only astonish men. But when it rained earth, when it rained chalk, when it rained stones—not hailstones, but real stones—this certainly was calculated to do serious damage. We have read in their books that the fires of Etna, pouring down from the top of the mountain to the neighbouring shore, caused the sea to boil, so that rocks were burnt up, and the pitch of ships began to run—a phenomenon incredibly surprising, but at the same time no less hurtful. By the same violent heat, they relate that on another occasion Sicily was filled with cinders, so that the houses of the city Catina were destroyed and buried under them—a calamity which moved the Romans to pity them, and remit their tribute for that year. One may also read that Africa, which had by that time become a province of Rome, was visited by a prodigious multitude of locusts, which, after consuming the fruit and foliage of the trees, were driven into the sea in one vast and measureless cloud; so that when they were drowned and cast upon the shore the air was polluted, and so serious a pestilence produced that in the kingdom of Masinissa alone they say there perished 800,000 persons, besides a much greater number in the neighbouring districts. At Utica they assure us that, of 30,000 soldiers then garrisoning it, there survived only ten. Yet which of these disasters, suppose they happened now, would not be attributed to the Christian religion by those who thus thoughtlessly accuse us, and whom we are compelled to answer? And yet to their own gods they attribute none of these things, though they worship them for the sake of escaping lesser calamities of the same kind, and do not reflect that they who formerly worshipped them were not preserved from these serious disasters.

BOOK IV

ARGUMENT. IN THIS BOOK IT IS PROVED THAT THE EXTENT AND LONG DURATION OF THE ROMAN EMPIRE IS TO BE ASCRIBED, NOT TO JOVE OR THE GODS OF THE HEATHEN, TO WHOM INDIVIDUALLY SCARCE EVEN SINGLE THINGS AND THE VERY BASEST FUNCTIONS WERE BELIEVED TO BE ENTRUSTED, BUT TO THE ONE TRUE GOD, THE AUTHOR OF FELICITY, BY WHOSE POWER AND JUDGMENT EARTHLY KINGDOMS ARE FOUNDED AND MAINTAINED.

CHAP. I. *Of the things which have been discussed in the first book*

HAVING begun to speak of the city of God, I have thought it necessary first of all to reply to its enemies, who, eagerly pursuing earthly joys and gaping after transitory things, throw the blame of all the sorrow they suffer in them—rather through the compassion of God in admonishing than His severity in punishing—on the Christian religion, which is the one salutary and true religion. And since there is among them also an unlearned rabble, they are stirred up as by the authority of the learned to hate us more bitterly, thinking in their inexperience that things which have happened unwontedly in their days were not wont to happen in other times gone by; and whereas this opinion of theirs is confirmed even by those who know that it is false, and yet dissemble their knowledge in order that they may seem to have just cause for murmuring against us, it was necessary, from books in which their authors recorded and published the history of bygone times that it might be known, to demonstrate that it is far otherwise than they think; and at the same time to teach that the false gods, whom they openly worshipped, or still worship in secret, are most unclean spirits, and most malignant and deceitful demons, even to such a pitch that they take delight in crimes which, whether real or only fictitious, are yet their own, which it has been their will to have celebrated in honour of them at their own festivals; so that human infirmity cannot be called back from the perpetration of damnable deeds, so long as authority is furnished for imitating them that seems even divine. These things we have proved, not from our own conjectures, but partly from recent memory, because we ourselves have seen such things celebrated, and to such deities, partly from the writings of those who have left these things on record to posterity, not as if in reproach but as in honour of their own gods. Thus Varro, a most learned man among them, and of the weightiest authority, when he made separate books concerning things human and things divine, distributing some among the human, others among the divine, according to the special dignity of each, placed the scenic plays not at all among things human, but among things divine; though, certainly, if only there were good and honest men in the state, the scenic plays ought not to be allowed even among things human. And this he did not on his own authority, but because, being born and educated at Rome, he found them among the divine things. Now as we briefly stated in the end of the first book what we intended afterwards to discuss, and as we have disposed of a part of this in the next two books, we see what our readers will expect us now to take up.

CHAP. 2. *Of those things which are contained in books second and third*

We had promised, then, that we would say something against those who attribute the calamities of the Roman republic to our religion, and that we would recount the evils, as many and great as we could remember or might deem sufficient, which that city, or the provinces belonging to its empire, had suffered before their sacrifices were prohibited, all of which would beyond doubt have been attributed to us, if our religion had either already shone on them or had thus prohibited their sacrilegious rites. These things we have, as we think, fully disposed of in the second and third books, treating in the second of evils in morals, which alone or chiefly are

to be accounted evils; and in the third, of those which only fools dread to undergo—namely, those of the body or of outward things—which for the most part the good also suffer. But those evils by which they themselves become evil, they take, I do not say patiently, but with pleasure. And how few evils have I related concerning that one city and its empire! Not even all down to the time of Cæsar Augustus. What if I had chosen to recount and enlarge on those evils, not which men have inflicted on each other, such as the devastations and destructions of war, but which happen in earthly things, from the elements of the world itself. Of such evils Apuleius speaks briefly in one passage of that book which he wrote, *De Mundo,* saying that all earthly things are subject to change, overthrow, and destruction. For, to use his own words, by excessive earthquakes the ground has burst asunder, and cities with their inhabitants have been clean destroyed: by sudden rains whole regions have been washed away; those also which formerly had been continents, have been insulated by strange and new-come waves, and others, by the subsiding of the sea, have been made passable by the foot of man: by winds and storms cities have been overthrown; fires have flashed forth from the clouds, by which regions in the East being burnt up have perished; and on the western coasts the like destructions have been caused by the bursting forth of waters and floods. So, formerly, from the lofty craters of Etna, rivers of fire kindled by God have flowed like a torrent down the steeps. If I had wished to collect from history wherever I could, these and similar instances, where should I have finished what happened even in those times before the name of Christ had put down those of their idols, so vain and hurtful to true salvation? I promised that I should also point out which of their customs, and for what cause, the true God, in whose power all kingdoms are, had deigned to favour to the enlargement of their empire; and how those whom they think gods can have profited them nothing, but much rather hurt them by deceiving and beguiling them; so that it seems to me I must now speak of these things, and chiefly of the increase of the Roman empire. For I have already said not a little, especially in the second book, about the many evils introduced into their manners by the hurtful deceits of the demons whom they worshipped as gods. But throughout all the three books already completed, where it appeared suitable, we have set forth how much succour God, through the name of Christ, to Whom the barbarians beyond the custom of war paid so much honour, has bestowed on the good and bad, according as it is written, "Who maketh His sun to rise on the good and the evil, and giveth rain to the just and the unjust."[1]

CHAP. 3. *Whether the great extent of the empire, which has been acquired only by wars, is to be reckoned among the good things either of the wise or the happy*

Now, therefore, let us see how it is that they dare to ascribe the very great extent and duration of the Roman empire to those gods whom they contend that they worship honourably, even by the obsequies of vile games and the ministry of vile men: although I should like first to inquire for a little what reason, what prudence, there is in wishing to glory in the greatness and extent of the empire, when you cannot point out the happiness of men who are always rolling, with dark fear and cruel lust, in warlike slaughters and in blood, which, whether shed in civil or foreign war, is still human blood; so that their joy may be compared to glass in its fragile splendour, of which one is horribly afraid lest it should be suddenly broken in pieces. That this may be more easily discerned, let us not come to nought by being carried away with empty boasting, or blunt the edge of our attention by loud-sounding names of things, when we hear of peoples, kingdoms, provinces. But let us suppose a case of two men; for each individual man, like one letter in a language, is as it were the element of a city or kingdom, however far-spreading in its occupation of the earth. Of these two men let us suppose that one is poor, or rather of middling circumstances; the other very rich. But the rich man is anxious with fears, pining with discontent, burning with covetousness, never secure, always uneasy, panting from the perpetual strife of his enemies, adding to his patrimony indeed by these miseries to an immense degree, and by these additions also heaping up most bitter cares. But that other man of moderate wealth is contented with a small and compact estate, most dear to his own family, enjoying the sweetest peace with his kindred neighbours and friends, in piety religious, benignant in mind, healthy in body, in life frugal, in manners chaste, in conscience secure. I know not whether any one can be such a fool, that he dare hesitate which to prefer. As, therefore, in the case of these two men, so in two families, in two nations, in two kingdoms, this test of tranquillity holds good; and if we apply it vigilantly

and without prejudice, we shall quite easily see where the mere show of happiness dwells, and where real felicity. Wherefore if the true God is worshipped, and if He is served with genuine rites and true virtue, it is advantageous that good men should long reign both far and wide. Nor is this advantageous so much to themselves as to those over whom they reign. For, so far as concerns themselves, their piety and probity, which are great gifts of God, suffice to give them true felicity, enabling them to live well the life that now is, and afterwards to receive that which is eternal. In this world, therefore, the dominion of good men is profitable, not so much for themselves as for human affairs. But the dominion of bad men is hurtful chiefly to themselves who rule, for they destroy their own souls by greater licence in wickedness; while those who are put under them in service are not hurt except by their own iniquity. For to the just all the evils imposed on them by unjust rulers are not the punishment of crime, but the test of virtue. Therefore the good man, although he is a slave, is free; but the bad man, even if he reigns, is a slave, and that not of one man, but, what is far more grievous, of as many masters as he has vices; of which vices when the divine Scripture treats, it says, "For of whom any man is overcome, to the same he is also the bond-slave."[2]

CHAP. 4. *How like kingdoms without justice are to robberies*

Justice being taken away, then, what are kingdoms but great robberies? For what are robberies themselves, but little kingdoms? The band itself is made up of men; it is ruled by the authority of a prince, it is knit together by the pact of the confederacy; the booty is divided by the law agreed on. If, by the admittance of abandoned men, this evil increases to such a degree that it holds places, fixes abodes, takes possession of cities, and subdues peoples, it assumes the more plainly the name of a kingdom, because the reality is now manifestly conferred on it, not by the removal of covetousness, but by the addition of impunity. Indeed, that was an apt and true reply which was given to Alexander the Great by a pirate who had been seized. For when that king had asked the man what he meant by keeping hostile possession of the sea, he answered with bold pride, "What thou meanest by seizing the whole earth; but because I do it with a petty ship, I am called a robber, whilst thou who dost it with a great fleet art styled emperor."

[1]Matt. 5. 45.

[2]II Pet. 2. 19.

CHAP. 5. *Of the runaway gladiators whose power became like that of royal dignity*

I shall not therefore stay to inquire what sort of men Romulus gathered together, seeing he deliberated much about them—how, being assumed out of that life they led into the fellowship of his city, they might cease to think of the punishment they deserved, the fear of which had driven them to greater villainies; so that henceforth they might be made more peaceable members of society. But this I say, that the Roman empire, which by subduing many nations had already grown great and an object of universal dread, was itself greatly alarmed, and only with much difficulty avoided a disastrous overthrow, because a mere handful of gladiators in Campania, escaping from the games, had recruited a great army, appointed three generals, and most widely and cruelly devastated Italy. Let them say what god aided these men, so that from a small and contemptible band of robbers they attained to a kingdom, feared even by the Romans, who had such great forces and fortresses. Or will they deny that they were divinely aided because they did not last long? As if, indeed, the life of any man whatever lasted long. In that case, too, the gods aid no one to reign, since all individuals quickly die; nor is sovereign power to be reckoned a benefit, because in a little time in every man, and thus in all of them one by one, it vanishes like a vapour. For what does it matter to those who worshipped the gods under Romulus, and are long since dead, that after their death the Roman empire has grown so great, while they plead their causes before the powers beneath? Whether those causes are good or bad, it matters not to the question before us. And this is to be understood of all those who carry with them the heavy burden of their actions, having in the few days of their life swiftly and hurriedly passed over the stage of the imperial office, although the office itself has lasted through long spaces of time, being filled by a constant succession of dying men. If, however, even those benefits which last only for the shortest time are to be ascribed to the aid of the gods, these gladiators were not a little aided, who broke the bonds of their servile condition, fled, escaped, raised a great and most powerful army, obedient to the will and orders of their chiefs and much feared by the Roman majesty, and remaining unsubdued by several Roman generals, seized many places, and, having won very many victories, enjoyed whatever pleasures they wished, and did what their lust suggested,

and, until at last they were conquered, which was done with the utmost difficulty, lived sublime and dominant. But let us come to greater matters.

CHAP. 6. *Concerning the covetousness of Ninus, who was the first who made war on his neighbours, that he might rule more widely*

Justinus, who wrote Greek or rather foreign history in Latin, and briefly, like Trogus Pompeius whom he followed, begins his work thus: "In the beginning of the affairs of peoples and nations the government was in the hands of kings, who were raised to the height of this majesty not by courting the people, but by the knowledge good men had of their moderation. The people were held bound by no laws; the decisions of the princes were instead of laws. It was the custom to guard rather than to extend the boundaries of the empire; and kingdoms were kept within the bounds of each ruler's native land. Ninus king of the Assyrians first of all, through new lust of empire, changed the old and, as it were, ancestral custom of nations. He first made war on his neighbours, and wholly subdued as far as to the frontiers of Libya the nations as yet untrained to resist." And a little after he says: "Ninus established by constant possession the greatness of the authority he had gained. Having mastered his nearest neighbours, he went on to others, strengthened by the accession of forces, and by making each fresh victory the instrument of that which followed, subdued the nations of the whole East." Now, with whatever fidelity to fact either he or Trogus may in general have written—for that they sometimes told lies is shown by other more trustworthy writers —yet it is agreed among other authors that the kingdom of the Assyrians was extended far and wide by King Ninus. And it lasted so long that the Roman empire has not yet attained the same age; for, as those write who have treated of chronological history, this kingdom endured for twelve hundred and forty years from the first year in which Ninus began to reign, until it was transferred to the Medes. But to make war on your neighbours, and thence to proceed to others, and through mere lust of dominion to crush and subdue people who do you no harm, what else is this to be called than great robbery?

CHAP. 7. *Whether earthly kingdoms in their rise and fall have been either aided or deserted by the help of the gods*

If this kingdom was so great and lasting without the aid of the gods, why is the ample territory and long duration of the Roman empire to be ascribed to the Roman gods? For whatever is the cause in it, the same is in the other also. But if they contend that the prosperity of the other also is to be attributed to the aid of the gods, I ask of which? For the other nations whom Ninus overcame, did not then worship other gods. Or if the Assyrians had gods of their own, who, so to speak, were more skilful workmen in the construction and preservation of the empire, whether are they dead, since they themselves have also lost the empire; or, having been defrauded of their pay, or promised a greater, have they chosen rather to go over to the Medes, and from them again to the Persians, because Cyrus invited them, and promised them something still more advantageous? This nation, indeed, since the time of the kingdom of Alexander the Macedonian, which was as brief in duration as it was great in extent, has preserved its own empire, and at this day occupies no small territories in the East. If this is so, then either the gods are unfaithful, who desert their own and go over to their enemies, which Camillus, who was but a man, did not do, when, being victor and subduer of a most hostile state, although he had felt that Rome, for whom he had done so much, was ungrateful, yet afterwards, forgetting the injury and remembering his native land, he freed her again from the Gauls; or they are not so strong as gods ought to be, since they can be overcome by human skill or strength. Or if, when they carry on war among themselves, the gods are not overcome by men, but some gods who are peculiar to certain cities are perchance overcome by other gods, it follows that they have quarrels among themselves which they uphold, each for his own part. Therefore a city ought not to worship its own gods, but rather others who aid their own worshippers. Finally, whatever may have been the case as to this change of sides, or flight, or migration, or failure in battle on the part of the gods, the name of Christ had not yet been proclaimed in those parts of the earth when these kingdoms were lost and transferred through great destructions in war. For if, after more than twelve hundred years, when the kingdom was taken away from the Assyrians, the Christian religion had there already preached another eternal kingdom and put a stop to the sacrilegious worship of false gods, what else would the foolish men of that nation have said, but that the kingdom which had been so long preserved could be lost for no other cause than the desertion of their own religions and the reception of Christianity? In which foolish speech that might have been uttered, let those we speak of observe their own likeness, and blush, if there is any sense of shame in them, because they have uttered similar complaints; although the Roman empire is afflicted rather than changed—a thing which has befallen it in other times also, before the name of Christ was heard, and it has been restored after such affliction—a thing which even in these times is not to be despaired of. For who knows the will of God concerning this matter?

CHAP. 8. *Which of the gods can the Romans suppose presided over the increase and preservation of their empire, when they have believed that even the care of single things could scarcely be committed to single gods?*

Next let us ask, if they please, out of so great a crowd of gods which the Romans worship, whom in especial, or what gods they believe to have extended and preserved that empire. Now, surely of this work, which is so excellent and so very full of the highest dignity, they dare not ascribe any part to the goddess Cloacina; or to Volupia, who has her appelation from voluptuousness; or to Libentina, who has her name from lust; or to Vaticanus, who presides over the screaming of infants; or to Cunina, who rules over their cradles. But how is it possible to recount in one part of this book all the names of gods or goddesses, which they could scarcely comprise in great volumes, distributing among these divinities their peculiar offices about single things? They have not even thought that the charge of their lands should be committed to any one god: but they have entrusted their farms to Rusina; the ridges of the mountains to Jugatinus; over the downs they have set the goddess Collatina; over the valleys, Vallonia. Nor could they even find one Segetia so competent, that they could commend to her care all their corn crops at once; but so long as their seed-corn was still under the ground, they would have the goddess Seia set over it; then, whenever it was above ground and formed straw, they set over it the goddess Segetia; and when the grain was collected and stored, they set over it the goddess Tutilina, that it might be kept safe. Who would not have thought that goddess Segetia sufficient to take care of the standing corn until it had passed from the first green blades to the dry ears? Yet she was not enough for men, who loved a multitude of gods, that the miserable soul, despising the chaste embrace of the one true God, should be prostituted to a crowd of demons. Therefore they set Proserpina over the germinating seeds; over the joints and knots of the stems, the god Nodotus; over the sheaths enfolding the ears, the goddess Voluntina; when the sheaths opened that the spike might shoot forth, it was ascribed to the goddess Patelana; when the stems stood all equal with new ears, because the ancients described this equalizing by the term *hostire*, it was ascribed to the goddess Hostilina; when the grain was in flower, it was dedicated to the goddess Flora; when full of milk, to the god Lacturnus; when maturing, to the goddess Matuta; when the crop was runcated—that is, removed from the soil— to the goddess Runcina. Nor do I yet recount them all, for I am sick of all this, though it gives them no shame. Only, I have said these very few things, in order that it may be understood they dare by no means say that the Roman empire has been established, increased, and preserved by their deities, who had all their own functions assigned to them in such a way that no general oversight was entrusted to any one of them. When, therefore, could Segetia take care of the empire, who was not allowed to take care of the corn and the trees? When could Cunina take thought about war, whose oversight was not allowed to go beyond the cradles of the babies? When could Nodotus give help in battle, who had nothing to do even with the sheath of the ear, but only with the knots of the joints? Every one sets a porter at the door of his house, and, because he is a man, he is quite sufficient; but these people have set three gods, Forculus to the doors, Cardea to the hinge, Limentinus to the threshold. Thus Forculus could not at the same time take care also of the hinge and the threshold.

CHAP. 9. *Whether the great extent and long duration of the Roman empire should be ascribed to Jove, whom his worshippers believe to be the chief god*

Therefore omitting, or passing by for a little, that crowd of petty gods, we ought to inquire into the part performed by the great gods, whereby Rome has been made so great as to reign so long over so many nations. Doubtless, therefore, this is the work of Jove. For they will have it that he is the king of all the gods and goddesses, as is shown by his sceptre and by the Capitol on the lofty hill. Concerning that god they publish a saying which, although that of a poet, is most apt, "All things are full of Jove."[1] Varro believes that this god is worshipped, although called by another name, even by those

who worship one God alone without any image. But if this is so, why has he been so badly used at Rome (and indeed by other nations too) that an image of him should be made?—a thing which was so displeasing to Varro himself that although he was overborne by the perverse custom of so great a city he had not the least hesitation in both saying and writing that those who have appointed images for the people have both taken away fear and added error.

CHAP. 10. *What opinions those have followed who have set divers gods over divers parts of the world*

Why, also, is Juno united to him as his wife, who is called at once "sister and yoke-fellow"?[2] Because, say they, we have Jove in the ether, Juno in the air; and these two elements are united, the one being superior, the other inferior. It is not he, then, of whom it is said, "All things are full of Jove," if Juno also fills some part. Does each fill either, and are both of this couple in both of these elements, and in each of them at the same time? Why, then, is the ether given to Jove, the air to Juno? Besides, these two should have been enough. Why is it that the sea is assigned to Neptune, the earth to Pluto? And that these also might not be left without mates, Salacia is joined to Neptune, Proserpine to Pluto. For they say that as Juno possesses the lower part of the heavens—that is, the air—so Salacia possesses the lower part of the sea, and Proserpine the lower part of the earth. They seek how they may patch up these fables, but they find no way. For if these things were so, their ancient sages would have maintained that there are three chief elements of the world, not four, in order that each of the elements might have a pair of gods. Now, they have positively affirmed that the ether is one thing, the air another. But water, whether higher or lower, is surely water. Suppose it ever so unlike, can it ever be so much so as no longer to be water? And the lower earth, by whatever divinity it may be distinguished, what else can it be than earth? Lo, then, since the whole physical world is complete in these four or three elements, where shall Minerva be? What should she possess, what should she fill? For she is placed in the Capitol along with these two, although she is not the offspring of their marriage. Or if they say that she possesses the higher part of the ether—and on that account the poets have feigned that she sprang from the head of Jove—why then is she not rather reckoned queen of the gods, because she

[1]Virgil *Eclogues*, BK. III. 60.

[2]Virgil, *Æneid*, BK. I. 47.

is superior to Jove? Is it because it would be improper to set the daughter before the father? Why, then, is not that rule of justice observed concerning Jove himself toward Saturn? Is it because he was conquered? Have they fought then? By no means, say they; that is an old wife's fable. Lo, we are not to believe fables, and must hold more worthy opinions concerning the gods! Why, then, do they not assign to the father of Jove a seat, if not of higher, at least of equal honour? Because Saturn, say they, is length of time. Therefore they who worship Saturn worship Time; and it is insinuated that Jupiter, the king of the gods, was born of Time. For is anything unworthy said when Jupiter and Juno are said to have been sprung from Time, if he is the heaven and she is the earth, since both heaven and earth have been made, and are therefore not eternal? For their learned and wise men have this also in their books. Nor is that saying taken by Virgil out of poetic figments, but out of the books of philosophers.

Then Ether, the Father Almighty, in copious showers descended
Into his spouse's glad bosom, making it fertile.[1]

—that is, into the bosom of Tellus, or the earth. Although here, also, they will have it that there are some differences, and think that in the earth herself Terra is one thing, Tellus another, and Tellumo another. And they have all these as gods, called by their own names, distinguished by their own offices, and venerated with their own altars and rites. This same earth also they call the mother of the gods, so that even the fictions of the poets are more tolerable, if, according not to their poetical but sacred books, Juno is not only the sister and wife, but also the mother of Jove. The same earth they worship as Ceres, and also as Vesta; while yet they more frequently affirm that Vesta is nothing else than fire, pertaining to the hearths, without which the city cannot exist; and therefore virgins are wont to serve her, because as nothing is born of a virgin, so nothing is born of fire; but all this nonsense ought to be completely abolished and extinguished by Him who is born of a virgin. For who can bear that, while they ascribe to the fire so much honour, and, as it were, chastity, they do not blush sometimes even to call Vesta Venus, so that honoured virginity may vanish in her hand-maidens? For if Vesta is Venus, how can virgins rightly serve her by abstaining from venery? Are there two Venuses, the one a virgin, the other not a maid? Or rather, are there

three, one the goddess of virgins, who is also called Vesta, another the goddess of wives, and another of harlots? To her also the Phœnicians offered a gift by prostituting their daughters before they united them to husbands. Which of these is the wife of Vulcan? Certainly not the virgin, since she has a husband. Far be it from us to say it is the harlot, lest we should seem to wrong the son of Juno and fellow-worker of Minerva. Therefore it is to be understood that she belongs to the married people; but we would not wish them to imitate her in what she did with Mars. "Again," say they, "you return to fables." What sort of justice is that, to be angry with us because we say such things of their gods, and not to be angry with themselves, who in their theatres most willingly behold the crimes of their gods? And—a thing incredible, if it were not thoroughly well proved—these very theatric representations of the crimes of their gods have been instituted in honour of these same gods.

CHAP. 11. *Concerning the many gods whom the pagan doctors defend as being one and the same Jove*

Let them therefore assert as many things as ever they please in physical reasonings and disputations. One while let Jupiter be the soul of this corporeal world, who fills and moves that whole mass, constructed and compacted out of four, or as many elements as they please; another while, let him yield to his sister and brothers their parts of it: now let him be the ether, that from above he may embrace Juno, the air spread out beneath; again, let him be the whole heaven along with the air, and impregnate with fertilizing showers and seeds the earth, as his wife, and, at the same time, his mother (for this is not vile in divine beings); and yet again (that it may not be necessary to run through them all), let him, the one god, of whom many think it has been said by a most noble poet,

For God pervadeth all things,
All lands, and the tracts of the sea, and the depth of the heavens.[2]

Let it be him who in the ether is Jupiter; in the air, Juno; in the sea, Neptune; in the lower parts of the sea, Salacia; in the earth, Pluto; in the lower part of the earth, Proserpine; on the domestic hearths, Vesta; in the furnace of the workmen, Vulcan; among the stars, Sol and Luna, and the Stars; in divination, Apollo; in merchandise, Mercury; in Janus, the initiator; in Terminus, the terminator; Saturn, in time;

[1]Virgil, *Georgics*, BK. II, 325, 326.

[2]*Ibid.*, BK. IV. 221, 222.

Mars and Bellona, in war; Liber, in vineyards; Ceres, in cornfields; Diana, in forests; Minerva, in learning. Finally, let it be him who is in that crowd, as it were, of plebeian gods: let him preside under the name of Liber over the seed of men, and under that of Libera over that of women: let him be Diespiter, who brings forth the birth to the light of day: let him be the goddess Mena, whom they set over the menstruation of women: let him be Lucina, who is invoked by women in childbirth: let him bring help to those who are being born, by taking them up from the bosom of the earth, and let him be called Opis: let him open the mouth in the crying babe, and be called the god Vaticanus: let him lift it from the earth, and be called the goddess Levana; let him watch over cradles, and be called the goddess Cunina: let it be no other than he who is in those goddesses, who sing the fates of the new born, and are called Carmentes: let him preside over fortuitous events, and be called Fortuna: in the goddess Rumina, let him milk out the breast to the little one, because the ancients termed the breast *ruma:* in the goddess Potina, let him administer drink: in the goddess Educa, let him supply food: from the terror of infants, let him be styled Paventia: from the hope which comes, Venilia: from voluptuousness, Volupia: from action, Agenor: from the stimulants by which man is spurred on to much action, let him be named the goddess Stimula: let him be the goddess Strenia, for making strenuous; Numeria, who teaches to number; Camœna, who teaches to sing: let him be both the god Consus for granting counsel, and the goddess Sentia for inspiring sentences: let him be the goddess Juventas, who, after the robe of boyhood is laid aside, takes charge of the beginning of the youthful age: let him be Fortuna Barbata, who endues adults with a beard, whom they have not chosen to honour; so that this divinity, whatever it may be, should at least be a male god, named either Barbatus, from *barba,* like Nodotus, from *nodus;* or, certainly, not Fortuna, but because he has beards, Fortunius: let him, in the god Jugatinus, yoke couples in marriage; and when the girdle of the virgin wife is loosed, let him be invoked as the goddess Virginiensis: let him be Mutunus or Tuternus, who, among the Greeks, is called Priapus. If they are not ashamed of it, let all these which I have named, and whatever others I have not named (for I have not thought fit to name all), let all these gods and goddesses be that one Jupiter, whether, as some will have it, all these are parts of him, or are his powers, as those

think who are pleased to consider him the soul of the world, which is the opinion of most of their doctors, and these the greatest. If these things are so (how evil they may be I do not yet meanwhile inquire), what would they lose, if they, by a more prudent abridgment, should worship one god? For what part of him could be contemned if he himself should be worshipped? But if they are afraid lest parts of him should be angry at being passed by or neglected, then it is not the case, as they will have it, that this whole is as the life of one living being, which contains all the gods together, as if they were its virtues, or members, or parts; but each part has its own life separate from the rest, if it is so that one can be angered, appeased, or stirred up more than another. But if it is said that all together—that is, the whole Jove himself—would be offended if his parts were not also worshipped singly and minutely, it is foolishly spoken. Surely none of them could be passed by if he who singly possesses them all should be worshipped. For, to omit other things which are innumerable, when they say that all the stars are parts of Jove, and are all alive, and have rational souls, and therefore without controversy are gods, can they not see how many they do not worship, to how many they do not build temples or set up altars, and to how very few, in fact, of the stars they have thought of setting them up and offering sacrifice? If, therefore, those are displeased who are not severally worshipped, do they not fear to live with only a few appeased, while all heaven is displeased? But if they worship all the stars because they are part of Jove whom they worship, by the same compendious method they could supplicate them all in him alone. For in this way no one would be displeased, since in him alone all would be supplicated. No one would be contemned, instead of there being just cause of displeasure given to the much greater number who are passed by in the worship offered to some; especially when Priapus, stretched out in vile nakedness, is preferred to those who shine from their supernal abode.

CHAP. 12. *Concerning the opinion of those who have thought that God is the soul of the world, and the world is the body of God*

Ought not men of intelligence, and indeed men of every kind, to be stirred up to examine the nature of this opinion? For there is no need of excellent capacity for this task, that putting away the desire of contention, they may observe that if God is the soul of the world, and the world is as a body to Him, who is the soul, He must be one living being consisting of soul and body, and that this same God is a kind of womb of nature containing all things in Himself, so that the lives and souls of all living things are taken, according to the manner of each one's birth, out of His soul which vivifies that whole mass, and therefore nothing at all remains which is not a part of God. And if this is so, who cannot see what impious and irreligious consequences follow such as that whatever one may trample, he must trample a part of God, and in slaying any living creature, a part of God must be slaughtered? But I am unwilling to utter all that may occur to those who think of it, yet cannot be spoken without irreverence.

CHAP. 13. *Concerning those who assert that only rational animals are parts of the one God*

But if they contend that only rational animals, such as men, are parts of God, I do not really see how, if the whole world is God, they can separate beasts from being parts of Him. But what need is there of striving about that? Concerning the rational animal himself—that is, man—what more unhappy belief can be entertained than that a part of God is whipped when a boy is whipped? And who, unless he is quite mad, could bear the thought that parts of God can become lascivious, iniquitous, impious, and altogether damnable? In brief, why is God angry at those who do not worship Him, since these offenders are parts of Himself? It remains, therefore, that they must say that all the gods have their own lives; that each one lives for himself, and none of them is a part of any one; but that all are to be worshipped—at least as many as can be known and worshipped; for they are so many it is impossible that all can be so. And of all these, I believe that Jupiter, because he presides as king, is thought by them to have both established and extended the Roman empire. For if he has not done it, what other god do they believe could have attempted so great a work, when they must all be occupied with their own offices and works, nor can one intrude on that of another? Could the kingdom of men then be propagated and increased by the king of the gods?

CHAP. 14. *The enlargement of kingdoms is unsuitably ascribed to Jove; for if, as they will have it, Victoria is a goddess, she alone would suffice for this business.*

Here, first of all, I ask, why even the kingdom itself is not some god. For why should not it also be so, if Victory is a goddess? Or what need is there of Jove himself in this affair, if victory favours and is propitious, and always goes to those whom she wishes to be victorious? With this goddess favourable and propitious, even if Jove was idle and did nothing, what nations could remain unsubdued, what kingdom would not yield? But perhaps it is displeasing to good men to fight with most wicked unrighteousness, and provoke with voluntary war neighbours who are peaceable and do no wrong, in order to enlarge a kingdom? If they feel thus, I entirely approve and praise them.

CHAP. 15. *Whether it is suitable for good men to wish to rule more widely*

Let them ask, then, whether it is quite fitting for good men to rejoice in extended empire. For the iniquity of those with whom just wars are carried on favours the growth of a kingdom, which would certainly have been small if the peace and justice of neighbours had not by any wrong provoked the carrying on of war against them; and human affairs being thus more happy, all kingdoms would have been small, rejoicing in neighbourly concord; and thus there would have been very many kingdoms of nations in the world, as there are very many houses of citizens in a city. Therefore, to carry on war and extend a kingdom over wholly subdued nations seems to bad men to be felicity, to good men necessity. But because it would be worse that the injurious should rule over those who are more righteous, therefore even that is not unsuitably called felicity. But beyond doubt it is greater felicity to have a good neighbour at peace, than to conquer a bad one by making war. Your wishes are bad, when you desire that one whom you hate or fear should be in such a condition that you can conquer him. If, therefore, by carrying on wars that were just, not impious or unrighteous, the Romans could have acquired so great an empire, ought they not to worship as a goddess even the injustice of foreigners? For we see that this has co-operated much in extending the empire, by making foreigners so unjust that they became people with whom just wars might be carried on and the empire increased. And why may not injustice, at least that of foreign nations, also be a goddess, if Fear and Dread and Ague have deserved to be Roman gods? By these two, therefore—that is, by foreign injustice, and the goddess Victoria, for injustice stirs up causes of wars, and Victoria brings these same wars to a happy termination—the empire has increased, even although Jove has been idle.

For what part could Jove have here, when those things which might be thought to be his benefits are held to be gods, called gods, worshipped as gods, and are themselves invoked for their own parts? He also might have some part here, if he himself might be called Empire, just as she is called Victory. Or if empire is the gift of Jove, why may not victory also be held to be his gift? And it certainly would have been held to be so, had he been recognized and worshipped, not as a stone in the Capitol, but as the true King of kings and Lord of lords.

CHAP. 16. *What was the reason that the Romans in detailing separate gods for all things and all movements of the mind, chose to have the Temple of Quiet outside the gates*

But I wonder very much, that while they assigned to separate gods single things, and (well nigh) all movements of the mind; that while they invoked the goddess Agenoria, who should excite to action; the goddess Stimula, who should stimulate to unusual action; the goddess Murcia, who should not move men beyond measure, but make them, as Pomponius says, *murcid*—that is, too slothful and inactive; the goddess Strenua, who should make them strenuous; and that while they offered to all these gods and goddesses solemn and public worship, they should yet have been unwilling to give public acknowledgment to her whom they name Quies because she makes men quiet, but built her temple outside the Colline gate. Whether was this a symptom of an unquiet mind, or rather was it thus intimated that he who should persevere in worshipping that crowd, not, to be sure, of gods, but of demons, could not dwell with quiet; to which the true Physician calls, saying, "Learn of me, for I am meek and lowly in heart, and ye shall find rest unto your souls"?

CHAP. 17. *Whether, if the highest power belongs to Jove, Victoria also ought to be worshipped*

Or do they say, perhaps, that Jupiter sends the goddess Victoria, and that she, as it were, acting in obedience to the king of the gods, comes to those to whom he may have despatched her, and takes up her quarters on their side? This is truly said, not of Jove, whom they, according to their own imagination, feign to be king of the gods, but of Him who is the true eternal King, because he sends, not Victory, who is no person, but His angel, and causes whom He pleases to conquer; whose counsel may be hidden, but cannot be unjust. For if Victory is a goddess, why is not Triumph also a god,

and joined to Victory either as husband, or brother, or son? Indeed, they have imagined such things concerning the gods that if the poets had feigned the like, and they should have been discussed by us, they would have replied that they were laughable figments of the poets not to be attributed to true deities. And yet they themselves did not laugh when they were, not reading in the poets, but worshipping in the temples such doting follies. Therefore they should entreat Jove alone for all things, and supplicate him only. For if Victory is a goddess, and is under him as her king, wherever he might have sent her, she could not dare to resist and do her own will rather than his.

CHAP. 18. *With what reason they who think Felicity and Fortune goddesses have distinguished them*

What shall we say, besides, of the idea that Felicity also is a goddess? She has received a temple; she has merited an altar; suitable rites of worship are paid to her. She alone, then, should be worshipped. For where she is present, what good thing can be absent? But what does a man wish that he thinks Fortune also a goddess and worships her? Is felicity one thing, fortune another? Fortune, indeed, may be bad as well as good; but felicity, if it could be bad, would not be felicity. Certainly we ought to think all the gods of either sex (if they also have sex) are only good. This says Plato; this say other philosophers; this say all estimable rulers of the republic and the nations. How is it, then, that the goddess Fortune is sometimes good, sometimes bad? Is it perhaps the case that when she is bad she is not a goddess, but is suddenly changed into a malignant demon? How many Fortunes are there then? Just as many as there are men who are fortunate, that is, of good fortune. But since there must also be very many others who at the very same time are men of bad fortune, could she, being one and the same Fortune, be at the same time both bad and good—the one to these, the other to those? She who is the goddess, is she always good? Then she herself is felicity. Why, then, are two names given her? Yet this is tolerable; for it is customary that one thing should be called by two names. But why different temples, different altars, different rituals? There is a reason, say they, because Felicity is she whom the good have by previous merit; but fortune, which is termed good without any trial of merit, befalls both good and bad men fortuitously, whence also she is named Fortune. How, therefore, is she good, who without any discernment comes both to the good and to the bad? Why is she worshipped, who is thus blind, running at random on any one whatever, so that for the most part she passes by her worshippers and cleaves to those who despise her? Or if her worshippers profit somewhat, so that they are seen by her and loved, then she follows merit and does not come fortuitously. What, then, becomes of that definition of fortune? What becomes of the opinion that she has received her very name from fortuitous events? For it profits one nothing to worship her if she is truly *fortune*. But if she distinguishes her worshippers, so that she may benefit them, she is not fortune. Or does Jupiter send her too, whither he pleases? Then let him alone be worshipped; because Fortune is not able to resist him when he commands her, and sends her where he pleases. Or, at least, let the bad worship her, who do not choose to have merit by which the goddess Felicity might be invited.

CHAP. 19. *Concerning Fortuna Muliebris*

To this supposed deity, whom they call Fortuna, they ascribe so much, indeed, that they have a tradition that the image of her, which was dedicated by the Roman matrons, and called *Fortuna Muliebris*, has spoken, and has said, once and again, that the matrons pleased her by their homage; which, indeed, if it is true, ought not to excite our wonder. For it is not so difficult for malignant demons to deceive, and they ought the rather to advert to their wits and wiles, because it is that goddess who comes by haphazard who has spoken, and not she who comes to reward merit. For Fortuna was loquacious, and Felicitas mute; and for what other reason but that men might not care to live rightly, having made Fortuna their friend, who could make them fortunate without any good desert? And truly, if Fortuna speaks, she should at least speak, not with a womanly, but with a manly voice; lest they themselves who have dedicated the image should think so great a miracle has been wrought by feminine loquacity.

CHAP. 20. *Concerning Virtue and Faith, which the pagans have honoured with temples and sacred rites, passing by other good qualities which ought likewise to have been worshipped, if deity was rightly attributed to these*

They have made Virtue also a goddess, which, indeed, if it could be a goddess, had been preferable to many. And now, because it is not a goddess, but a gift of God, let *it* be obtained by prayer from Him, by whom alone it can be given, and the whole crowd of false gods vanishes. But why is Faith believed to be a goddess, and why does she herself receive temple and altar? For whoever prudently acknowledges her makes his own self an abode for her. But how do they know what faith is, of which it is the prime and greatest function that the true God may be believed in? But why had not virtue sufficed? Does it not include faith also? Forasmuch as they have thought proper to distribute virtue into four divisions—prudence, justice, fortitude, and temperance—and as each of these divisions has its own virtues, faith is among the parts of justice, and has the chief place with as many of us as know what that saying means, "The just shall live by faith."[1] But if Faith is a goddess, I wonder why these keen lovers of a multitude of gods have wronged so many other goddesses, by passing them by, when they could have dedicated temples and altars to them likewise. Why has temperance not deserved to be a goddess, when some Roman princes have obtained no small glory on account of her? Why, in fine, is fortitude not a goddess, who aided Mucius when he thrust his right hand into the flames; who aided Curtius, when for the sake of his country he threw himself headlong into the yawning earth; who aided Decius the sire, and Decius the son, when they devoted themselves for the army? though we might question whether these men had *true* fortitude, if this concerned our present discussion. Why have prudence and wisdom merited no place among the gods? Is it because they are all worshipped under the general name of Virtue itself? Then they could thus worship the true God also, of whom all the other gods are thought to be parts. But in that one name of virtue is comprehended both faith and chastity, which yet have obtained separate altars in temples of their own.

CHAP. 21. *That although not understanding them to be the gifts of God, they ought at least to have been content with virtue and felicity*

These, not verity but vanity has made goddesses. For these are gifts of the true God, not themselves goddesses. However, where virtue and felicity are, what else is sought for? What can suffice the man whom virtue and felicity do not suffice? For surely virtue comprehends all things we need do, felicity all things we need wish for. If Jupiter, then, was worshipped in order that he might give these two things—be-

[1]Hab. 2. 4.

cause, if extent and duration of empire is something good, it pertains to this same felicity—why is it not understood that they are not goddesses, but the gifts of God? But if they are judged to be goddesses, then at least that other great crowd of gods should not be sought after. For, having considered all the offices which their fancy has distributed among the various gods and goddesses, let them find out, if they can, anything which could be bestowed by any god whatever on a man possessing virtue, possessing felicity. What instruction could be sought either from Mercury or Minerva, when Virtue already possessed all in herself? Virtue, indeed, is defined by the ancients as itself the art of living well and rightly. Hence, because virtue is called in Greek ἀρετη, it has been thought the Latins have derived from it the term *art*. But if Virtue cannot come except to the clever, what need was there of the god Father Catius, who should make men cautious, that is, acute, when Felicity could confer this? Because, to be born clever belongs to felicity. Whence, although goddess Felicity could not be worshipped by one not yet born, in order that, being made his friend, she might bestow this on him, yet she might confer this favour on parents who were her worshippers, that clever children should be born to them. What need had women in childbirth to invoke Lucina, when, if Felicity should be present, they would have, not only a good delivery, but good children too? What need was there to commend the children to the goddess Ops when they were being born; to the god Vaticanus in their birthcry; to the goddess Cunina when lying cradled; to the goddess Rumina when sucking; to the god Statilinus when standing; to the goddess Adeona when coming; to Abeona when going away; to the goddess Mens that they might have a good mind; to the god Volumnus, and the goddess Volumna, that they might wish for good things; to the nuptial gods, that they might make good matches; to the rural gods, and chiefly to the goddess Fructesca herself, that they might receive the most abundant fruits; to Mars and Bellona, that they might carry on war well; to the goddess Victoria, that they might be victorious; to the god Honor, that they might be honoured; to the goddess Pecunia, that they might have plenty of money; to the god Aesculanus, and his son Argentinus, that they might have brass and silver coin? For they set down Aesculanus as the father of Argentinus for this reason, that brass coin began to be used before silver. But I wonder Argentinus has not begotten Aurinus, since gold coin also has followed.

Could they have him for a god, they would prefer Aurinus both to his father Argentinus and his grandfather Aesculanus, just as they set Jove before Saturn. Therefore, what necessity was there on account of these gifts, either of soul, or body, or outward estate, to worship and invoke so great a crowd of gods, all of whom I have not mentioned, nor have they themselves been able to provide for all human benefits, minutely and singly methodized, minute and single gods, when the one goddess Felicity was able, with the greatest ease, compendiously to bestow the whole of them? nor should any other be sought after, either for the bestowing of good things, or for the averting of evil. For why should they invoke the goddess Fessonia for the weary; for driving away enemies, the goddess Pellonia; for the sick, as a physician, either Apollo or Æsculapius, or both together if there should be great danger? Neither should the god Spiniensis be entreated that he might root out the thorns from the fields; nor the goddess Rubigo that the mildew might not come—Felicitas alone being present and guarding, either no evils would have arisen, or they would have been quite easily driven away. Finally, since we treat of these two goddesses, Virtue and Felicity, if felicity is the reward of virtue, she is not a goddess, but a gift of God. But if she is a goddess, why may she not be said to confer virtue itself, inasmuch as it is a great felicity to attain virtue?

CHAP. 22. *Concerning the knowledge of the worship due to the gods, which Varro glories in having himself conferred on the Romans*

What is it, then, that Varro boasts he has bestowed as a very great benefit on his fellow-citizens, because he not only recounts the gods who ought to be worshipped by the Romans, but also tells what pertains to each of them? "Just as it is of no advantage," he says, "to know the name and appearance of any man who is a physician, and not know that he is a physician, so," he says, "it is of no advantage to know well that Æsculapius is a god, if you are not aware that he can bestow the gift of health, and consequently do not know why you ought to supplicate him." He also affirms this by another comparison, saying, "No one is able, not only to live well, but even to live at all, if he does not know who is a smith, who a baker, who a weaver, from whom he can seek any utensil, whom he may take for a helper, whom for a leader, whom for a teacher"; asserting, "that in this way it can be doubtful to no one, that thus the knowledge of the gods is useful, if one can know what force, and faculty, or power any god may have in any thing. For from this we may be able," he says, "to know what god we ought to call to, and invoke for any cause; lest we should do as too many are wont to do, and desire water from Liber, and wine from Lymphs." Very useful, forsooth! Who would not give this man thanks if he could show true things, and if he could teach that the one true God, from whom all good things are, is to be worshipped by men?

CHAP. 23. *Concerning Felicity, whom the Romans, who venerate many gods, for a long time did not worship with divine honour, though she alone would have sufficed instead of all*

But how does it happen, if their books and rituals are true, and Felicity is a goddess, that she herself is not appointed as the only one to be worshipped, since she could confer all things, and all at once make men happy? For who wishes anything for any other reason than that he may become happy? Why was it left to Lucullus to dedicate a temple to so great a goddess at so late a date, and after so many Roman rulers? Why did Romulus himself, ambitious as he was of founding a fortunate city, not erect a temple to this goddess before all others? Why did he supplicate the other gods for anything, since he would have lacked nothing had she been with him? For even he himself would neither have been first a king, then afterwards, as they think, a god, if this goddess had not been propitious to him. Why, therefore, did he appoint as gods for the Romans, Janus, Jove, Mars, Picus, Faunus, Tibernus, Hercules, and others, if there were more of them? Why did Titus Tatius add Saturn, Ops, Sun, Moon, Vulcan, Light, and whatever others he added, among whom was even the goddess Cloacina, while Felicity was neglected? Why did Numa appoint so many gods and so many goddesses without this one? Was it perhaps because he could not see her among so great a crowd? Certainly king Hostilius would not have introduced the new gods Fear and Dread to be propitiated, if he could have known or might have worshipped this goddess. For, in presence of Felicity, Fear and Dread would have disappeared— I do not say propitiated, but put to flight. Next, I ask, how is it that the Roman empire had already immensely increased before any one worshipped Felicity? Was the empire, therefore, more great than happy? For how could true felicity be there, where there was not true piety? For piety is the genuine worship of the true God,

and not the worship of as many demons as there are false gods. Yet even afterwards, when Felicity had already been taken into the number of the gods, the great infelicity of the civil wars ensued. Was Felicity perhaps justly indignant, both because she was invited so late, and was invited not to honour, but rather to reproach, because along with her were worshipped Priapus, and Cloacina, and Fear and Dread, and Ague, and others which were not gods to be worshipped, but the crimes of the worshippers? Last of all, if it seemed good to worship so great a goddess along with a most unworthy crowd, why at least was she not worshipped in a more honourable way than the rest? For is it not intolerable that Felicity is placed neither among the gods *Consentes*, whom they allege to be admitted into the council of Jupiter, nor among the gods whom they term *Select*? Some temple might be made for her which might be pre-eminent, both in loftiness of site and dignity of style. Why, indeed, not something better than is made for Jupiter himself? For who gave the kingdom even to Jupiter but Felicity? I am supposing that when he reigned he was happy. Felicity, however, is certainly more valuable than a kingdom. For no one doubts that a man might easily be found who may fear to be made a king; but no one is found who is unwilling to be happy. Therefore, if it is thought they can be consulted by augury, or in any other way, the gods themselves should be consulted about this thing, whether they may wish to give place to Felicity. If, perchance, the place should already be occupied by the temples and altars of others, where a greater and more lofty temple might be built to Felicity, even Jupiter himself might give way, so that Felicity might rather obtain the very pinnacle of the Capitoline Hill. For there is not any one who would resist Felicity, except, which is impossible, one who might wish to be unhappy. Certainly, if he should be consulted, Jupiter would in no case do what those three gods, Mars, Terminus, and Juventas, did, who positively refused to give place to their superior and king. For, as their books record, when king Tarquin wished to construct the Capitol, and perceived that the place which seemed to him to be the most worthy and suitable was preoccupied by other gods, not daring to do anything contrary to their pleasure, and believing that they would willingly give place to a god who was so great, and was their own master, because there were many of them there when the Capitol was founded, he inquired by augury whether they chose to give place to Jupiter, and they were all

willing to remove thence except those whom I
have named, Mars, Terminus, and Juventas;
and therefore the Capitol was built in such a
way that these three also might be within it, yet
with such obscure signs that even the most
learned men could scarcely know this. Surely,
then, Jupiter himself would by no means despise
Felicity, as he was himself despised by Terminus, Mars, and Juventas. But even they themselves who had not given place to Jupiter, would
certainly give place to Felicity, who had made
Jupiter king over them. Or if they should not
give place, they would act thus not out of contempt of her, but because they chose rather to
be obscure in the house of Felicity, than to be
eminent without her in their own places.

Thus the goddess Felicity being established in
the largest and loftiest place, the citizens should
learn whence the furtherance of every good desire should be sought. And so, by the persuasion
of nature herself, the superfluous multitude of
other gods being abandoned, Felicity alone
would be worshipped, prayer would be made to
her alone, her temple alone would be frequented
by the citizens who wished to be happy, which
no one of them would not wish; and thus felicity, who was sought for from all the gods,
would be sought for only from her own self. For
who wishes to receive from any god anything
else than felicity, or what he supposes to tend to
felicity? Wherefore, if Felicity has it in her power to be with what man she pleases (and she has
it if she is a goddess), what folly is it, after all,
to seek from any other god her whom you can
obtain by request from her own self! Therefore
they ought to honour this goddess above other
gods, even by dignity of place. For, as we read
in their own authors, the ancient Romans paid
greater honours to I know not what Summanus,
to whom they attributed nocturnal thunderbolts, than to Jupiter, to whom diurnal thunderbolts were held to pertain. But, after a famous
and conspicuous temple had been built to Jupiter, owing to the dignity of the building, the
multitude resorted to him in so great numbers
that scarce one can be found who remembers
even to have read the name of Summanus,
which now he cannot once hear named. But if
Felicity is not a goddess, because, as is true, it is
a gift of God, that god must be sought who has
power to give it, and that hurtful multitude of
false gods must be abandoned which the vain
multitude of foolish men follows after, making
gods to itself of the gifts of God, and offending
Himself Whose gifts they are by the stubborn-
ness of a proud will. For he cannot be free from

infelicity who worships Felicity as a goddess,
and forsakes God, the giver of felicity; just as
he cannot be free from hunger who licks a painted loaf of bread, and does not buy it of the man
who has a real one.

CHAP. 24. *The reasons by which the pagans attempt to defend their worshipping among the
gods the divine gifts themselves*

We may, however, consider their reasons. Is
it to be believed, say they, that our forefathers
were besotted even to such a degree as not to
know that these things are divine gifts, and not
gods? But as they knew that such things are
granted to no one, except by some god freely bestowing them, they called the gods whose names
they did not find out by the names of those
things which they deemed to be given by them;
sometimes slightly altering the name for that
purpose, as, for example, from war they have
named Bellona, not *bellum;* from cradles, Cunina, not *cunæ;* from standing corn, Segetia, not
seges; from apples, Pomona, not *pomum;* from
oxen, Bubona, not *bos.* Sometimes, again, with
no alteration of the word, just as the things
themselves are named, so that the goddess who
gives money is called Pecunia, and money is not
thought to be itself a goddess: so of Virtus, who
gives virtue; Honor, who gives honour; Con-
cordia, who gives concord; Victoria, who gives
victory. So, they say, when Felicitas is called a
goddess, what is meant is not the thing itself
which is given, but that deity by whom felicity
is given.

CHAP. 25. *Concerning the one God only to be
worshipped, who, although his name is unknown, is yet deemed to be the giver of felicity*

Having had that reason rendered to us, we
shall perhaps much more easily persuade, as we
wish, those whose heart has not become too
much hardened. For if now human infirmity has
perceived that felicity cannot be given except
by some god; if this was perceived by those who
worshipped so many gods, at whose head they
set Jupiter himself; if, in their ignorance of the
name of Him by whom felicity was given, they
agreed to call Him by the name of that very
thing which they believed He gave; then it follows that they thought that felicity could not be
given even by Jupiter himself, whom they already worshipped, but certainly by him whom
they thought fit to worship under the name of
Felicity itself. I thoroughly affirm the statement
that they believed felicity to be given by a certain God whom they knew not: let Him there-

fore be sought after, let Him be worshipped, and it is enough. Let the train of innumerable demons be repudiated, and let this God suffice every man whom his gift suffices. For him, I say, God the giver of felicity will not be enough to worship, for whom felicity itself is not enough to receive. But let him for whom it suffices (and man has nothing more he ought to wish for) serve the one God, the giver of felicity. This God is not he whom they call Jupiter. For if they acknowledged him to be the giver of felicity, they would not seek, under the name of Felicity itself, for another god or goddess by whom felicity might be given; nor could they tolerate that Jupiter himself should be worshipped with such infamous attributes. For he is said to be the debaucher of the wives of others; he is the shameless lover and ravisher of a beautiful boy.

Chap. 26. *Of the scenic plays, the celebration of which the gods have exacted from their worshippers*

"But," says Cicero, "Homer invented these things, and transferred things human to the gods: I would rather transfer things divine to us." The poet, by ascribing such crimes to the gods, has justly displeased the grave man. Why, then, are the scenic plays, where these crimes are habitually spoken of, acted, exhibited, in honour of the gods, reckoned among things divine by the most learned men? Cicero should exclaim, not against the inventions of the poets, but against the customs of the ancients. Would not they have exclaimed in reply, What have we done? The gods themselves have loudly demanded that these plays should be exhibited in their honour, have fiercely exacted them, have menaced destruction unless this was performed, have avenged its neglect with great severity, and have manifested pleasure at the reparation of such neglect. Among their virtuous and wonderful deeds the following is related. It was announced in a dream to Titus Latinius, a Roman rustic, that he should go to the senate and tell them to recommence the games of Rome, because on the first day of their celebration a condemned criminal had been led to punishment in sight of the people, an incident so sad as to disturb the gods who were seeking amusement from the games. And when the peasant who had received this intimation was afraid on the following day to deliver it to the senate, it was renewed next night in a severer form: he lost his son, because of his neglect. On the third night he was warned that a yet graver punishment was

impending, if he should still refuse obedience. When even thus he did not dare to obey, he fell into a virulent and horrible disease. But then, on the advice of his friends, he gave information to the magistrates, and was carried in a litter into the senate, and having, on declaring his dream, immediately recovered strength, went away on his own feet whole. The senate, amazed at so great a miracle, decreed that the games should be renewed at fourfold cost. What sensible man does not see that men, being put upon by malignant demons, from whose domination nothing save the grace of God through Jesus Christ our Lord sets free, have been compelled by force to exhibit to such gods as these, plays which, if well advised, they should condemn as shameful? Certain it is that in these plays the poetic crimes of the gods are celebrated, yet they are plays which were re-established by decree of the senate, under compulsion of the gods. In these plays the most shameless actors celebrated Jupiter as the corrupter of chastity, and thus gave him pleasure. If that was a fiction, he would have been moved to anger; but if he was delighted with the representation of his crimes, even although fabulous, then, when he happened to be worshipped, who but the devil could be served? Is it so that he could found, extend, and preserve the Roman empire, who was more vile than any Roman man whatever, to whom such things were displeasing? Could he give felicity who was so infelicitously worshipped, and who, unless he should be thus worshipped, was yet more infelicitously provoked to anger?

Chap. 27. *Concerning the three kinds of gods about which the pontiff Scævola has discoursed*

It is recorded that the very learned pontiff Scævola had distinguished about three kinds of gods—one introduced by the poets, another by the philosophers, another by the statesmen. The first kind he declares to be trifling, because many unworthy things have been invented by the poets concerning the gods; the second does not suit states, because it contains some things that are superfluous, and some, too, which it would be prejudicial for the people to know. It is no great matter about the superfluous things, for it is a common saying of skillful lawyers, "Superfluous things do no harm." But what are those things which do harm when brought before the multitude? "These," he says, "that Hercules, Æsculapius, Castor and Pollux, are not gods; for it is declared by learned men that these were but men, and yielded to the common lot of mortals." What else? "That states have not the true images of the gods; because the true God has neither sex, nor age, nor definite corporeal members." The pontiff is not willing that the people should know these things; for he does not think they are false. He thinks it expedient, therefore, that states should be deceived in matters of religion; which Varro himself does not even hesitate to say in his books about things divine. Excellent religion! to which the weak, who requires to be delivered, may flee for succour; and when he seeks for the truth by which he may be delivered, it is believed to be expedient for him that he be deceived. And, truly, in these same books, Scævola is not silent as to his reason for rejecting the poetic sort of gods, to wit, "because they so disfigure the gods that they could not bear comparison even with good men, when they make one to commit theft, another adultery; or, again, to say or do something else basely and foolishly; as that three goddesses contested (with each other) the prize of beauty, and the two vanquished by Venus destroyed Troy; that Jupiter turned himself into a bull or swan that he might copulate with some one; that a goddess married a man, and Saturn devoured his children; that, in fine, there is nothing that could be imagined, either of the miraculous or vicious, which may not be found there, and yet is far removed from the nature of the gods." O chief pontiff Scævola, take away the plays if thou art able; instruct the people that they may not offer such honours to the immortal gods, in which, if they like, they may admire the crimes of the gods, and, so far as it is possible, may, if they please, imitate them. But if the people shall have answered thee, "You, O pontiff, have brought these things in among us," then ask the gods themselves at whose instigation you have ordered these things, that they may not order such things to be offered to them. For if they are bad, and therefore in no way to be believed concerning the majority of the gods, the greater is the wrong done the gods about whom they are feigned with impunity. But they do not hear thee, they are demons, they teach wicked things, they rejoice in vile things; not only do they not count it a wrong if these things are feigned about them, but it is a wrong they are quite unable to bear if they are not acted at their stated festivals. But now, if thou wouldst call on Jupiter against them, chiefly for that reason that more of his crimes are wont to be acted in the scenic plays, is it not the case that, although you call him god Jupiter, by whom this whole world is ruled and administered, it is he to whom the greatest wrong is done by you, because you have thought he ought to be worshipped along with them, and have styled him their king?

CHAP. 28. *Whether the worship of the gods has been of service to the Romans in obtaining and extending the empire*

Therefore such gods, who are propitiated by such honours, or rather are impeached by them (for it is a greater crime to delight in having such things said of them falsely than even if they could be said truly), could never by any means have been able to increase and preserve the Roman empire. For if they could have done it, they would rather have bestowed so grand a gift on the Greeks, who, in this kind of divine things—that is, in scenic plays—have worshipped them more honourably and worthily, although they have not exempted themselves from those slanders of the poets, by whom they saw the gods torn in pieces, giving them licence to ill-use any man they pleased, and have not deemed the scenic players themselves to be base, but have held them worthy even of distinguished honour. But just as the Romans were able to have gold money, although they did not worship a god Aurinus, so also they could have silver and brass coin, and yet worship neither Argentinus nor his father Æsculanus; and so of all the rest, which it would be irksome for me to detail. It follows, therefore, both that they could not by any means attain such dominion if the true God was unwilling; and that if these gods, false and many, were unknown or contemned, and He alone was known and worshipped with sincere faith and virtue, they would both have a better kingdom here, whatever might be its extent, and, whether they might have one here or not, would afterwards receive an eternal kingdom.

CHAP. 29. *Of the falsity of the augury by which the strength and stability of the Roman empire was considered to be indicated*

For what kind of augury is that which they have declared to be most beautiful, and to which I referred a little ago, that Mars, and Terminus, and Juventas would not give place even to Jove, the king of the gods? For thus, they say, it was signified that the nation dedicated to Mars—that is, the Roman—should yield to none the place it once occupied; likewise, that on account of the god Terminus, no one would be able to disturb the Roman frontiers; and also that the Roman youth, because of the goddess Juventas, should yield to no one. Let them see, therefore, how they can hold him to be the king of their gods, and the giver of their own kingdom, if these auguries set him down for an adversary, to whom it would have been honourable not to yield. However, if these things are true, they need not be at all afraid. For they are not going to confess that the gods who would not yield to Jove have yielded to Christ. For, without altering the boundaries of the empire, Jesus Christ has proved Himself able to drive them, not only from their temples, but from the hearts of their worshippers. But, before Christ came in the flesh, and, indeed, before these things which we have quoted from their books could have been written, but yet after that auspice was made under king Tarquin, the Roman army has been divers times scattered or put to flight, and has shown the falseness of the auspice, which they derived from the fact that the goddess Juventas had not given place to Jove; and the nation dedicated to Mars was trodden down in the city itself by the invading and triumphant Gauls; and the boundaries of the empire, through the falling away of many cities to Hannibal, had been hemmed into a narrow space. Thus the beauty of the auspices is made void, and there has remained only the contumacy against Jove, not of gods, but of demons. For it is one thing not to have yielded, and another to have returned whither you have yielded. Besides, even afterwards, in the oriental regions, the boundaries of the Roman empire were changed by the will of Hadrian; for he yielded up to the Persian empire those three noble provinces, Armenia, Mesopotamia, and Assyria. Thus that god Terminus, who according to these books was the guardian of the Roman frontiers, and by that most beautiful auspice had not given place to Jove, would seem to have been more afraid of Hadrian, a king of men, than of the king of the gods. The aforesaid provinces having also been taken back again, almost within our own recollection the frontier fell back, when Julian, given up to the oracles of their gods, with immoderate daring ordered the victualling ships to be set on fire. The army being thus left destitute of provisions, and he himself also being presently killed by the enemy, and the legions being hard pressed, while dismayed by the loss of their commander, they were reduced to such extremities that no one could have escaped, unless by articles of peace the boundaries of the empire had then been established where they still remain; not, indeed, with so great a loss as was suffered by the concession of Hadrian, but still at a considerable sacrifice. It was a vain augury, then, that the god Terminus did not yield to

Jove, since he yielded to the will of Hadrian, and yielded also to the rashness of Julian, and the necessity of Jovian. The more intelligent and grave Romans have seen these things, but have had little power against the custom of the state, which was bound to observe the rites of the demons; because even they themselves, although they perceived that these things were vain, yet thought that the religious worship which is due to God should be paid to the nature of things which is established under the rule and government of the one true God, "serving," as saith the apostle, "the creature more than the Creator, who is blessed for evermore."[1] The help of this true God was necessary to send holy and truly pious men, who would die for the true religion that they might remove the false from among the living.

CHAP. 30. *What kind of things even their worshippers have owned they have thought about the gods of the nations*

Cicero the augur laughs at auguries, and reproves men for regulating the purposes of life by the cries of crows and jackdaws. But it will be said that an academic philosopher, who argues that all things are uncertain, is unworthy to have any authority in these matters. In the second book of his *De Natura Deorum,* he introduces Lucilius Balbus, who, after showing that superstitions have their origin in physical and philosophical truths, expresses his indignation at the setting up of images and fabulous notions, speaking thus: "Do you not therefore see that from true and useful physical discoveries the reason may be drawn away to fabulous and imaginary gods? This gives birth to false opinions, and turbulent errors, and superstitions well-nigh old-wifeish. For both the forms of the gods, and their ages, and clothing, and ornaments, are made familiar to us; their genealogies, too, their marriages, kinships, and all things about them, are debased to the likeness of human weakness. They are even introduced as having perturbed minds; for we have accounts of the lusts, cares, and angers of the gods. Nor, indeed, as the fables go, have the gods been without their wars and battles. And that not only when, as in Homer, some gods on either side have defended two opposing armies, but they have even carried on wars on their own account, as with the Titans or with the Giants. Such things it is quite absurd either to say or to believe: they are utterly frivolous and groundless." Behold, now, what is confessed by those

[1] Rom. i. 25.

who defend the gods of the nations. Afterwards he goes on to say that some things belong to superstition, but others to religion, which he thinks good to teach according to the Stoics. "For not only the philosophers," he says, "but also our forefathers, have made a distinction between superstition and religion. For those," he says, "who spent whole days in prayer, and offered sacrifice, that their children might outlive them, are called superstitious." Who does not see that he is trying, while he fears the public prejudice, to praise the religion of the ancients, and that he wishes to disjoin it from superstition, but cannot find out how to do so? For if those who prayed and sacrificed all day were called superstitious by the ancients, were those also called so who instituted (what he blames) the images of the gods of diverse age and distinct clothing, and invented the genealogies of gods, their marriages, and kinships? When, therefore, these things are found fault with as superstitious, he implicates in that fault the ancients who instituted and worshipped such images. Nay, he implicates himself, who, with whatever eloquence he may strive to extricate himself and be free, was yet under the necessity of venerating these images; nor dared he so much as whisper in a discourse to the people what in this disputation he plainly sounds forth. Let us Christians, therefore, give thinks to the Lord our God—not to heaven and earth, as that author argues, but to Him who has made heaven and earth; because these superstitions, which that Balbus, like a babbler,[1] scarcely reprehends, He, by the most deep lowliness of Christ, by the preaching of the apostles, by the faith of the martyrs dying for the truth and living with the truth, has overthrown, not only in the hearts of the religious, but even in the temples of the superstitious, by their own free service.

CHAP. 31. *Concerning the opinions of Varro, who, while reprobating the popular belief, thought that their worship should be confined to one god, though he was unable to discover the true God.*

What says Varro himself, whom we grieve to have found, although not by his own judgment, placing the scenic plays among things divine? When in many passages he is exhorting, like a religious man, to the worship of the gods, does he not in doing so admit that he does not in his own judgment believe those things which he relates that the Roman state has instituted; so that he does not hesitate to affirm that if he were found-

ing a new state, he could enumerate the gods and their names better by the rule of nature? But being born into a nation already ancient, he says that he finds himself bound to accept the traditional names and surnames of the gods and the histories connected with them, and that his purpose in investigating and publishing these details is to incline the people to worship the gods and not to despise them. By which words this most acute man sufficiently indicates that he does not publish all things, because they would not only have been contemptible to himself, but would have seemed despicable even to the rabble, unless they had been passed over in silence. I should be thought to conjecture these things, unless he himself, in another passage, had openly said, in speaking of religious rites, that, many things are true which it is not only not useful for the common people to know, but that it is expedient that the people should think otherwise, even though falsely, and therefore the Greeks have shut up the religious ceremonies and mysteries in silence and within walls. In this he no doubt expresses the policy of the so-called wise men by whom states and peoples are ruled. Yet by this crafty device the malign demons are wonderfully delighted, who possess alike the deceivers and the deceived, and from whose tyranny nothing sets free save the grace of God through Jesus Christ our Lord.

The same most acute and learned author also says, that those alone seem to him to have perceived what God is, who have believed Him to be the soul of the world, governing it by design and reason. And by this, it appears, that although he did not attain to the truth—for the true God is not a soul, but the maker and author of the soul—yet if he could have been free to go against the prejudices of custom, he could have confessed and counselled others that the one God ought to be worshipped, who governs the world by design and reason; so that on this subject only this point would remain to be debated with him, that he had called Him a soul, and not rather the creator of the soul. He says, also, that the ancient Romans, for more than a hundred and seventy years, worshipped the gods without an image.[2] "And if this custom," he says, "could have remained till now, the gods would have been more purely worshipped." In favour of this opinion, he cites as a witness among others the Jewish nation; nor does he hesitate to conclude that passage by saying of those who first consecrated images for the people that they have both taken away religious

---

[1]Balbus, from *balbutiens*, stammering, babbling.

[2]Plutarch, *Numa*.

fear from their fellow-citizens and increased error, wisely thinking that the gods easily fall into contempt when exhibited under the stolidity of images. But as he does not say they have transmitted error, but that they have increased it, he therefore wishes it to be understood that there was error already when there were no images. Wherefore, when he says they alone have perceived what God is who have believed Him to be the governing soul of the world, and thinks that the rites of religion would have been more purely observed without images, who fails to see how near he has come to the truth? For if he had been able to do anything against so inveterate an error, he would certainly have given it as his opinion both that the one God should be worshipped, and that He should be worshipped without an image; and having so nearly discovered the truth, perhaps he might easily have been put in mind of the mutability of the soul and might thus have perceived that the true God is that immutable nature which made the soul itself. Since these things are so, whatever ridicule such men have poured in their writings against the plurality of the gods, they have done so rather as compelled by the secret will of God to confess them than as trying to persuade others. If, therefore, any testimonies are adduced by us from these writings, they are adduced for the confutation of those who are unwilling to consider from how great and malignant a power of the demons the singular sacrifice of the shedding of the most holy blood, and the gift of the imparted Spirit, can set us free.

CHAP. 32. *In what interest the princes of the nations wished false religions to continue among the people subject to them*

Varro says also, concerning the generations of the gods, that the people have inclined to the poets rather than to the natural philosophers; and that therefore their forefathers—that is, the ancient Romans—believed both in the sex and the generations of the gods, and settled their marriages; which certainly seems to have been done for no other cause except that it was the business of such men as were prudent and wise to deceive the people in matters of religion, and in that very thing not only to worship, but also to imitate the demons, whose greatest lust is to deceive. For just as the demons cannot possess any but those whom they have deceived with guile, so also men in princely office, not indeed being just, but like demons, have persuaded the people in the name of religion to receive as true those things which they themselves knew to be false; in this way, as it were binding them up more firmly in civil society, so that they might in like manner possess them as subjects. But who that was weak and unlearned could escape the deceits of both the princes of the state and the demons?

CHAP. 33. *That the times of all kings and kingdoms are ordained by the judgment and power of the true God*

Therefore that God, the author and giver of felicity, because He alone is the true God, Himself gives earthly kingdoms both to good and bad. Neither does He do this rashly, and, as it were, fortuitously—because He is God not fortune—but according to the order of things and times, which is hidden from us, but thoroughly known to Himself; which same order of times, however, He does not serve as subject to it, but Himself rules as lord and appoints as governor. Felicity He gives only to the good. Whether a man be a subject or a king makes no difference; he may equally either possess or not possess it. And it shall be full in that life where kings and subjects exist no longer. And therefore earthly kingdoms are given by Him both to the good and the bad; lest His worshippers, still under the conduct of a very weak mind, should covet these gifts from Him as some great things. And this is the mystery of the Old Testament, in which the New was hidden, that there even earthly gifts are promised: those who were spiritual understanding even then, although not yet openly declaring, both the eternity which was symbolized by these earthly things, and in what gifts of God true felicity could be found.

CHAP. 34. *Concerning the kingdom of the Jews, which was founded by the one and true God, and preserved by Him as long as they remained in the true religion*

Therefore, that it might be known that these earthly good things, after which those pant who cannot imagine better things, remain in the power of the one God Himself, not of the many false gods whom the Romans have formerly believed worthy of worship, He multiplied His people in Egypt from being very few and delivered them out of it by wonderful signs. Nor did their women invoke Lucina when their offspring was being incredibly multiplied; and that nation having increased incredibly, He Himself delivered, He Himself saved them from the hands of the Egyptians, who persecuted them and wished to kill all their infants. Without the goddess Rumina they sucked; without Cunina they were cradled, without Educa and Potina they took food and drink; without all those puerile gods they were educated; without the nuptial gods they were married; without the worship of Priapus they had conjugal intercourse; without invocation of Neptune the divided sea opened up a way for them to pass over, and overwhelmed with its returning waves their enemies who pursued them. Neither did they consecrate any goddess Mannia when they received manna from heaven; nor, when the smitten rock poured forth water to them when they thirsted, did they worship Nymphs and Lymphs. Without the mad rites of Mars and Bellona they carried on war; and while, indeed, they did not conquer without victory, yet they did not hold it to be a goddess, but the gift of their God. Without Segetia they had harvests; without Bubona, oxen; honey without Mellona; apples without Pomona: and, in a word, everything for which the Romans

thought they must supplicate so great a crowd of false gods, they received much more happily from the one true God. And if they had not sinned against Him with impious curiosity, which seduced them like magic arts, and drew them to strange gods and idols, and at last led them to kill Christ, their kingdom would have remained to them and would have been, if not more spacious, yet more happy than that of Rome. And now that they are dispersed through almost all lands and nations, it is through the providence of that one true God; that whereas the images, altars, groves, and temples of the false gods are everywhere overthrown, and their sacrifices prohibited, it may be shown from their books how this has been foretold by their prophets so long before; lest, perhaps, when they should be read in ours, they might seem to be invented by us. But now, reserving what is to follow for the following book, we must here set a bound to the prolixity of this one.

BOOK V[1]

ARGUMENT. Augustine first discusses the doctrine of fate, for the sake of confuting those who are disposed to refer to fate the power and increase of the Roman empire, which could not be attributed to false gods, as has been shown in the preceding book. After that, he proves that there is no contradiction between God's prescience and our free will. He then speaks of the manners of the ancient Romans, and shows in what sense it was due to the virtue of the Romans themselves, and in how far to the counsel of God, that he increased their dominion, though they did not worship him. Finally, he explains what is to be accounted the true happiness of the Christian emperors.

PREFACE

Since, then, it is established that the complete attainment of all we desire is that which constitutes felicity, which is no goddess, but a gift of God, and that therefore men can worship no god save Him who is able to make them happy—and were Felicity herself a goddess, she would with reason be the only object of worship —since, I say, this is established, let us now go on to consider why God, who is able to give with all other things those good gifts which can be possessed by men who are not good, and consequently not happy, has seen fit to grant such extended and long-continued dominion to the Roman empire; for that this was not effected by that multitude of false gods which they worshipped, we have both already adduced, and shall, as occasion offers, yet adduce considerable proof.

[1]Written in 415.

CHAP. I. *That the cause of the Roman empire, and of all kingdoms, is neither fortuitous nor consists in the position of the stars*

The cause, then, of the greatness of the Roman empire is neither fortuitous nor fatal, according to the judgment or opinion of those who call those things *fortuitous* which either have no causes, or such causes as do not proceed from some intelligible order, and those things *fatal* which happen independently of the will of God and man, by the necessity of a certain *order*. In a word, human kingdoms are established by divine providence. And if any one attributes their existence to fate, because he calls the will or the power of God itself by the name of fate, let him keep his opinion, but correct his language. For why does he not say at first what he will say afterwards, when some one shall put the question to him, What he means by *fate?* For when men hear that word, according to the ordinary use of the language, they simply understand by it the virtue of that particular position of the stars which may exist at the time when any one is born or conceived, which some separate altogether from the will of God, whilst others affirm that this also is dependent on that will. But those who are of opinion that, apart from the will of God, the stars determine what we shall do, or what good things we shall possess, or what evils we shall suffer, must be refused a hearing by all, not only by those who hold the true religion, but by those who wish to be the worshippers of any gods whatsoever, even false gods. For what does this opinion really amount to but this, that no god whatever is to be worshipped or prayed to? Against these, however, our present disputation is not intended to be directed, but against those who, in defence of those whom they think to be gods, oppose the Christian religion. They, however, who make the position of the stars depend on the divine will, and in a manner decree what character each man shall have, and what good or evil shall happen to him, if they think that these same stars have that power conferred upon them by the supreme power of God, in order that they may determine these things according to their will, do a great injury to the celestial sphere, in whose most brilliant senate, and most splendid senate-house, as it were, they suppose that wicked deeds are decreed to be done—such deeds as that, if any terrestrial state should decree them, it would be condemned to overthrow by the decree of the whole human race. What judgment, then, is left to God concerning the deeds of men, who is Lord both of the stars and of men, when to these deeds a celestial necessity is attributed? Or, if they do not say that the stars, though they have indeed received a certain power from God, who is supreme, determine those things according to their own discretion, but simply that His commands are fulfilled by them instrumentally in the application and enforcing of such necessities, are we thus to think concerning God even what it seemed unworthy that we should think concerning the will of the stars? But, if the stars are said rather to signify these things than to effect them, so that that *position of the stars* is, as it were, a kind of speech predicting, not causing future things—for this has been the opinion of men of no ordinary learning—certainly the mathematicians are not wont so to speak, saying, for example, Mars in such or such a position *signifies* a homicide, but *makes* a homicide. But, nevertheless, though we grant that they do not speak as they ought, and that we ought to ac-

cept as the proper form of speech that employed by the philosophers in predicting those things which they think they discover in the position of the stars, how comes it that they have never been able to assign any cause why, in the life of twins, in their actions, in the events which befall them, in their professions, arts, honours, and other things pertaining to human life, also in their very death, there is often so great a difference that, as far as these things are concerned, many entire strangers are more like them than they are like each other, though separated at birth by the smallest interval of time, but at conception generated by the same act of copulation, and at the same moment?

CHAP. 2. *On the difference in the health of twins*

Cicero says that the famous physician Hippocrates has left in writing that he had suspected that a certain pair of brothers were twins, from the fact that they both took ill at once, and their disease advanced to its crisis and subsided in the same time in each of them. Posidonius the Stoic, who was much given to astrology, used to explain the fact by supposing that they had been born and conceived under the same constellation. In this question the conjecture of the physician is by far more worthy to be accepted, and approaches much nearer to credibility, since, according as the parents were affected in body at the time of copulation, so might the first elements of the fœtuses have been affected, so that all that was necessary for their growth and development up till birth having been supplied from the body of the same mother, they might be born with like constitutions. Thereafter, nourished in the same house, on the same kinds of food, where they would have also the same kinds of air, the same locality, the same quality of water—which, according to the testimony of medical science, have a very great influence, good or bad, on the condition of bodily health—and where they would also be accustomed to the same kinds of exercise, they would have bodily constitutions so similar that they would be similarly affected with sickness at the same time and by the same causes. But, to wish to adduce that particular position of the stars which existed at the time when they were born or conceived as the cause of their being simultaneously affected with sickness, manifests the greatest arrogance, when so many beings of most diverse kinds, in the most diverse conditions, and subject to the most diverse events, may have been conceived and born at the same time, and in the same district, lying under the same sky. But we know that twins do not only act differently, and travel to very different places, but that they also suffer from different kinds of sickness; for which Hippocrates would give what is in my opinion the simplest reason, namely, that, through diversity of food and exercise, which arises not from the constitution of the body, but from the inclination of the mind, they may have come to be different from each other in respect of health. Moreover, Posidonius, or any other asserter of the fatal influence of the stars, will have enough to do to find anything to say to this, if he be unwilling to impose upon the minds of the uninstructed in things of which they are ignorant. But, as to what they attempt to make out from that very small interval of time elapsing between the births of twins, on account of that point in the heavens where the mark of the natal hour is placed, and which they call the "horoscope," it is either disproportionately small to the diversity which is found in the dispositions, actions, habits, and fortunes of twins, or it is disproportionately great when compared with the estate of twins, whether low or high, which is the same for both of them, the cause for whose greatest difference they place, in every case, in the hour on which one is born; and, for this reason, if the one is born so immediately after the other that there is no change in the horoscope, I demand an entire similarity in all that respects them both, which can never be found in the case of any twins. But if the slowness of the birth of the second give time for a change in the horoscope, I demand different parents, which twins can never have.

CHAP. 3. *Concerning the arguments which Nigidius the mathematician drew from the potter's wheel, in the question about the birth of twins*

It is to no purpose, therefore, that that famous fiction about the potter's wheel is brought forward, which tells of the answer which Nigidius is said to have given when he was perplexed with this question, and on account of which he was called *Figulus*.[1] For, having whirled round the potter's wheel with all his strength he marked it with ink, striking it twice with the utmost rapidity, so that the strokes seemed to fall on the very same part of it. Then, when the rotation had ceased, the marks which he had made were found upon the rim of the wheel at no small distance apart. Thus, said he, considering the great rapidity with which the celestial sphere revolves, even though twins were born with as

[1] i. e. the potter.

short an interval between their births as there was between the strokes which I gave this wheel, that brief interval of time is equivalent to a very great distance in the celestial sphere. Hence, said he, come whatever dissimilitudes may be remarked in the habits and fortunes of twins. This argument is more fragile than the vessels which are fashioned by the rotation of that wheel. For if there is so much significance in the heavens which cannot be comprehended by observation of the constellations, that, in the case of twins, an inheritance may fall to the one and not to the other, why, in the case of others who are not twins, do they dare, having examined their constellations, to declare such things as pertain to that secret which no one can comprehend, and to attribute them to the precise moment of the birth of each individual? Now, if such predictions in connection with the natal hours of others who are not twins are to be vindicated on the ground that they are founded on the observation of more extended spaces in the heavens, whilst those very small moments of time which separated the births of twins, and correspond to minute portions of celestial space, are to be connected with trifling things about which the mathematicians are not wont to be consulted—for who would consult them as to when he is to sit, when to walk abroad, when and on what he is to dine?—how can we be justified in so speaking, when we can point out such manifold diversity both in the habits, doings, and destinies of twins?

CHAP. 4. *Concerning the twins Esau and Jacob, who were very unlike each other both in their character and actions*

In the time of the ancient fathers, to speak concerning illustrious persons, there were born two twin brothers, the one so immediately after the other, that the first took hold of the heel of the second. So great a difference existed in their lives and manners, so great a dissimilarity in their actions, so great a difference in their parents' love for them respectively, that the very contrast between them produced even a mutual hostile antipathy. Do we mean, when we say that they were so unlike each other, that when the one was walking the other was sitting, when the one was sleeping the other was waking—which differences are such as are attributed to those minute portions of space which cannot be appreciated by those who note down the position of the stars which exists at the moment of one's birth, in order that the mathematicians may be consulted concerning it? One of these twins was for a long time a hired servant; the other never served. One of them was beloved by his mother; the other was not so. One of them lost that honour which was so much valued among their people; the other obtained it. And what shall we say of their wives, their children, and their possessions? How different they were in respect to all these! If, therefore, such things as these are connected with those minute intervals of time which elapse between the births of twins, and are not to be attributed to the constellations, wherefore are they predicted in the case of others from the examination of their constellations? And if, on the other hand, these things are said to be predicted, because they are connected, not with minute and inappreciable moments, but with intervals of time which can be observed and noted down, what purpose is that potter's wheel to serve in this matter, except it be to whirl round men who have hearts of clay, in order that they may be prevented from detecting the emptiness of the talk of the mathematicians?

CHAP. 5. *In what manner the mathematicians are convicted of professing a vain science*

Do not those very persons whom the medical sagacity of Hippocrates led him to suspect to be twins, because their disease was observed by him to develop to its crisis and to subside again in the same time in each of them—do not these, I say, serve as a sufficient refutation of those who wish to attribute to the influence of the stars that which was owing to a similarity of bodily constitution? For wherefore were they both sick of the same disease, and at the same time, and not the one after the other in the order of their birth? (for certainly they could not both be born at the same time). Or, if the fact of their having been born at different times by no means necessarily implies that they must be sick at different times, why do they contend that the difference in the time of their births was the cause of their difference in other things? Why could they travel in foreign parts at different times, marry at different times, beget children at different times, and do many other things at different times, by reason of their having been born at different times, and yet could not, for the same reason, also be sick at different times? For if a difference in the moment of birth changed the horoscope, and occasioned dissimilarity in all other things, why has that simultaneousness which belonged to their conception remained in their attacks of sickness? Or, if the destinies of health are involved in the time of

conception, but those of other things be said to be attached to the time of birth, they ought not to predict anything concerning health from examination of the constellations of birth, when the hour of conception is not also given, that its constellations may be inspected. But if they say that they predict attacks of sickness without examining the horoscope of conception, because these are indicated by the moments of birth, how could they inform either of these twins when he would be sick, from the horoscope of his birth, when the other also, who had not the same horoscope of birth, must of necessity fall sick at the same time? Again, I ask, if the distance of time between the births of twins is so great as to occasion a difference of their constellations on account of the difference of their horoscopes, and therefore of all the cardinal points to which so much influence is attributed, that even from such change there comes a difference of destiny, how is it possible that this should be so, since they cannot have been conceived at different times? Or, if two conceived at the same moment of time could have different destinies with respect to their births, why may not also two born at the same moment of time have different destinies for life and for death? For if the one moment in which both were conceived did not hinder that the one should be born before the other, why, if two are born at the same moment, should anything hinder them from dying at the same moment? If a simultaneous conception allows of twins being differently affected in the *womb,* why should not simultaneousness of birth allow of any two individuals having different fortunes in the *world?* and thus would all the fictions of this art, or rather delusion, be swept away. What strange circumstance is this, that two children conceived at the same time, nay, at the same moment, under the same position of the stars, have different fates which bring them to different hours of birth, whilst two children, born of two different mothers, at the same moment of time, under one and the same position of the stars, cannot have different fates which shall conduct them by necessity to diverse manners of life and of death? Are they at conception as yet without destinies, because they can only have them if they be born? What, therefore, do they mean when they say that, if the hour of the conception be found, many things can be predicted by these astrologers? from which also arose that story which is reiterated by some, that a certain sage chose an hour in which to lie with his wife, in order to secure his begetting an illustrious son. From this opinion also came that answer of Posidonius, the great astrologer and also philosopher, concerning those twins who were attacked with sickness at the same time, namely, "That this had happened to them because they were conceived at the same time and born at the same time." For certainly he added "conception," lest it should be said to him that they could not both be *born* at the same time, knowing that at any rate they must both have been conceived at the same time; wishing thus to show that he did not attribute the fact of their being similarly and simultaneously affected with sickness to the similarity of their bodily constitutions as its proximate cause, but that he held that even in respect of the similarity of their health they were bound together by a sidereal connection. If, therefore, the time of conception has so much to do with the similarity of destinies, these same destinies ought not to be changed by the circumstances of birth; or, if the destinies of twins be said to be changed because they are born at different times, why should we not rather understand that they had been already changed in order that they might be born at different times? Does not, then, the will of men living in the world change the destinies of birth, when the order of birth can change the destinies they had at conception?

CHAP. 6. *Concerning twins of different sexes*

But even in the very conception of twins, which certainly occurs at the same moment in the case of both, it often happens that the one is conceived a male, and the other a female. I know two of different sexes who are twins. Both of them are alive, and in the flower of their age; and though they resemble each other in body, as far as difference of sex will permit, still they are very different in the whole scope and purpose of their lives (consideration being had of those differences which necessarily exist between the lives of males and females), the one holding the office of a count, and being almost constantly away from home with the army in foreign service, the other never leaving her country's soil or her native district. Still more—and this is more incredible, if the destinies of the stars are to be believed in, though it is not wonderful if we consider the wills of men and the free gifts of God—he is married, she is a sacred virgin: he has begotten a numerous offspring, she has never even married. But is not the virtue of the horoscope very great? I think I have said enough to show the absurdity of that. But, say those astrologers, whatever be the virtue of the

horoscope in other respects, it is certainly of significance with respect to birth. But why not also with respect to conception, which takes place undoubtedly with one act of copulation? And, indeed, so great is the force of nature that after a woman has once conceived, she ceases to be liable to conception. Or were they, perhaps, changed at birth, either he into a male, or she into a female, because of the difference in their horoscopes? But, whilst it is not altogether absurd to say that certain sidereal influences have some power to cause differences in bodies alone—as, for instance, we see that the seasons of the year come round by the approaching and receding of the sun, and that certain kinds of things are increased in size or diminished by the waxings and wanings of the moon, such as sea-urchins, oysters, and the wonderful tides of the ocean—it does not follow that the *wills of men* are to be made subject to the position of the stars. The astrologers, however, when they wish to bind our actions also to the constellations, only set us on investigating whether, even in these bodies, the changes may not be attributable to some other than a sidereal cause. For what is there which more intimately concerns a body than its sex? And yet, under the same position of the stars, twins of different sexes may be conceived. Wherefore, what greater absurdity can be affirmed or believed than that the position of the stars, which was the same for both of them at the time of conception, could not cause that the one child should not have been of a different sex from her brother, with whom she had a common constellation, whilst the position of the stars which existed at the hour of their birth could cause that she should be separated from him by the great distance between marriage and holy virginity?

CHAP. 7. *Concerning the choosing of a day for marriage, or for planting, or sowing*

Now, will any one bring forward this, that in choosing certain particular days for particular actions, men bring about certain new destinies for their actions? That man, for instance, according to this doctrine, was not born to have an illustrious son, but rather a contemptible one, and therefore, being a man of learning, he chose an hour in which to lie with his wife. He made, therefore, a destiny which he did not have before, and from that destiny of his own making something began to be fatal which was not contained in the destiny of his natal hour. Oh, singular stupidity! A day is chosen on which to marry; and for this reason, I believe, that unless a day be chosen, the marriage may fall on an unlucky day, and turn out an unhappy one. What then becomes of what the stars have already decreed at the hour of birth? Can a man be said to change by an act of choice that which has already been determined for him, whilst that which he himself has determined in the choosing of a day cannot be changed by another power? Thus, if men alone, and not all things under heaven, are subject to the influence of the stars, why do they choose some days as suitable for planting vines or trees, or for sowing grain, other days as suitable for taming beasts on, or for putting the males to the females, that the cows and mares may be impregnated, and for such-like things? If it be said that certain chosen days have an influence on these things, because the constellations rule over all terrestrial bodies, animate and inanimate, according to differences in moments of time, let it be considered what innumerable multitudes of beings are born or arise, or take their origin at the very same instant of time, which come to ends so different, that they may persuade any little boy that these observations about days are ridiculous. For who is so mad as to dare affirm that all trees, all herbs, all beasts, serpents, birds, fishes, worms, have each separately their own moments of birth or commencement? Nevertheless, men are wont, in order to try the skill of the mathematicians, to bring before them the constellations of dumb animals, the constellations of whose birth they diligently observe at home with a view to this discovery; and they prefer those mathematicians to all others, who say from the inspection of the constellations that they indicate the birth of a beast and not of a man. They also dare tell what kind of beast it is, whether it is a wool-bearing beast, or a beast suited for carrying burthens, or one fit for the plough, or for watching a house; for the astrologers are also tried with respect to the fates of dogs, and their answers concerning these are followed by shouts of admiration on the part of those who consult them. They so deceive men as to make them think that during the birth of a man the births of all other beings are suspended, so that not even a fly comes to life at the same time that he is being born, under the same region of the heavens. And if this be admitted with respect to the fly, the reasoning cannot stop there, but must ascend from flies till it lead them up to camels and elephants. Nor are they willing to attend to this that, when a day has been chosen whereon to sow a field, so many grains fall into the ground simultaneously, germinate simultaneously, spring up, come to perfection, and ripen simultaneously; and yet, of all the ears which are coeval, and, so to speak, *congerminal*, some are destroyed by mildew, some are devoured by the birds, and some are pulled by men. How can they say that all these had their different constellations, which they see coming to so different ends? Will they confess that it is folly to choose days for such things, and to affirm that they do not come within the sphere of the celestial decree, whilst they subject men alone to the stars, on whom alone in the world God has bestowed free wills? All these things being considered, we have good reason to believe that, when the astrologers give very many wonderful answers, it is to be attributed to the occult inspiration of spirits not of the best kind, whose care it is to insinuate into the minds of men, and to confirm in them, those false and noxious opinions concerning the fatal influence of the stars, and not to their marking and inspecting of horoscopes, according to some kind of art which in reality has no existence.

CHAP. 8. *Concerning those who call by the name of fate, not the position of the stars, but the connexion of causes which depends on the will of God*

But, as to those who call by the name of fate, not the disposition of the stars as it may exist when any creature is conceived, or born, or commences its existence, but the whole connexion and train of causes which makes everything become what it does become, there is no need that I should labour and strive with them in a merely verbal controversy, since they attribute the so-called order and connexion of causes to the will and power of God most high, who is most rightly and most truly believed to know all things before they come to pass, and to leave nothing unordained; from whom are all powers, although the wills of all are not from Him. Now, that it is chiefly the will of God most high, whose power extends itself irresistibly through all things which they call fate, is proved by the following verses, of which, if I mistake not, Annæus Seneca is the author:—

Father supreme, Thou ruler of the lofty heavens,
Lead me where'er it is Thy pleasure; I will give
A prompt obedience, making no delay,
Lo! here I am. Promptly I come to do Thy sovereign will;
If Thy command shall thwart my inclination, I will still
Follow Thee groaning, and the work assigned,
With all the suffering of a mind repugnant,

Will perform, being evil; which, had I been good,
I should have undertaken and performed, though
*   hard,*
With virtuous cheerfulness.
The Fates do lead the man that follows willing;
But the man that is unwilling, him they drag.

Most evidently, in this last verse, he calls that "fate" which he had before called "the will of the Father supreme," whom, he says, he is ready to obey that he may be led, being willing, not dragged, being unwilling, since "the Fates do lead the man that follows willing, but the man that is unwilling, him they drag."

The following Homeric lines, which Cicero translates into Latin, also favour this opinion:—

Such are the minds of men, as is the light
Which Father Jove himself doth pour
Illustrious o'er the fruitful earth.[1]

Not that Cicero wishes that a poetical sentiment should have any weight in a question like this; for when he says that the Stoics when asserting the power of fate, were in the habit of using these verses from Homer, he is not treating concerning the opinion of that poet, but concerning that of those philosophers, since by these verses, which they quote in connexion with the controversy which they hold about fate, is most distinctly manifested what it is which they reckon fate, since they call by the name of Jupiter him whom they reckon the supreme god, from whom, they say, hangs the whole chain of fates.

CHAP. 9. *Concerning the foreknowledge of God and the free will of man, in opposition to the definition of Cicero*

The manner in which Cicero addresses himself to the task of refuting the Stoics, shows that he did not think he could effect anything against them in argument unless he had first demolished divination. And this he attempts to accomplish by denying that there is any knowledge of future things, and maintains with all his might that there is no such knowledge either in God or man, and that there is no prediction of events. Thus he both denies the foreknowledge of God and attempts by vain arguments, and by opposing to himself certain oracles very easy to be refuted, to overthrow all prophecy, even such as is clearer than the light (though even these oracles are not refuted by him).

But, in refuting these conjectures of the mathematicians, his argument is triumphant, because truly these are such as destroy and re-

fute themselves. Nevertheless, they are far more tolerable who assert the fatal influence of the stars than they who deny the foreknowledge of future events. For, to confess that God exists, and at the same time to deny that He has foreknowledge of future things, is the most manifest folly. This Cicero himself saw and therefore attempted to assert the doctrine embodied in the words of Scripture, "The fool hath said in his heart, There is no God."[2] That, however, he did not do in his own person, for he saw how odious and offensive such an opinion would be; and therefore, in his book on the nature of the gods, he makes Cotta dispute concerning this against the Stoics, and preferred to give his own opinion in favour of Lucilius Balbus, to whom he assigned the defence of the Stoical position, rather than in favour of Cotta, who maintained that no divinity exists. However, in his book on divination, he in his own person most openly opposes the doctrine of the prescience of future things. But all this he seems to do in order that he may not grant the doctrine of fate and by so doing destroy free will. For he thinks that, the knowledge of future things being once conceded, fate follows as so necessary a consequence that it cannot be denied.

But, let these perplexing debatings and disputations of the philosophers go on as they may, we, in order that we may confess the most high and true God Himself, do confess His will, supreme power, and prescience. Neither let us be afraid lest, after all, we do not do by will that which we do by will, because He, Whose foreknowledge is infallible, foreknew that we would do it. It was this which Cicero was afraid of, and therefore opposed foreknowledge. The Stoics also maintained that all things do not come to pass by necessity, although they contended that all things happen according to destiny. What is it, then, that Cicero feared in the prescience of future things? Doubtless it was this —that if all future things have been foreknown, they will happen in the order in which they have been foreknown; and if they come to pass in this order, there is a certain order of things foreknown by God; and if a certain order of things, then a certain order of causes, for nothing can happen which is not preceded by some efficient cause. But if there is a certain order of causes according to which everything happens which does happen, then by fate, says he, all things happen which do happen. But if this be so, then is there nothing in our own power, and there is no such thing as freedom of will; and if we

[1] *Odyssey*, BK. XVIII. 136, 137.

[2] Ps. 15. 1.

grant that, says he, the whole economy of human life is subverted. In vain are laws enacted. In vain are reproaches, praises, chidings, exhortations had recourse to; and there is no justice whatever in the appointment of rewards for the good, and punishments for the wicked. And that consequences so disgraceful, and absurd, and pernicious to humanity may not follow, Cicero chooses to reject the foreknowledge of future things, and shuts up the religious mind to this alternative, to make choice between two things, either that something is in our own power, or that there is foreknowledge, both of which cannot be true; but if the one is affirmed, the other is thereby denied. He therefore, like a truly great and wise man, and one who consulted very much and very skilfully for the good of humanity, of those two chose the freedom of the will, to confirm which he denied the foreknowledge of future things; and thus, wishing to make men free, he makes them sacrilegious. But the religious mind chooses both, confesses both, and maintains both by the faith of piety. But how so? says Cicero; for the knowledge of future things being granted, there follows a chain of consequences which ends in this, that there can be nothing depending on our own free wills. And further, if there is anything depending on our wills, we must go backwards by the same steps of reasoning till we arrive at the conclusion that there is no foreknowledge of future things. For we go backwards through all the steps in the following order: If there is free will, all things do not happen according to fate; if all things do not happen according to fate, there is not a certain order of causes; and if there is not a certain order of causes, neither is there a certain order of things foreknown by God—for things cannot come to pass except they are preceded by efficient causes—but, if there is no fixed and certain order of causes foreknown by God, all things cannot be said to happen according as He foreknew that they would happen. And further, if it is not true that all things happen just as they have been foreknown by Him, there is not, says he, in God any foreknowledge of future events.

Now, against the sacrilegious and impious darings of reason, we assert both that God knows all things before they come to pass and that we do by our free will whatsoever we know and feel to be done by us only because we will it. But that all things come to pass by fate, we do not say; nay we affirm that nothing comes to pass by fate; for we demonstrate that the name of fate, as it is wont to be used by those who

speak of fate, meaning thereby the position of the stars at the time of each one's conception or birth, is an unmeaning word, for astrology itself is a delusion. But an order of causes in which the highest efficiency is attributed to the will of God, we neither deny nor do we designate it by the name of fate, unless, perhaps, we may understand fate to mean that which is spoken, deriving it from *fari*, to speak; for we cannot deny that it is written in the sacred Scriptures, "God hath spoken once; these two things have I heard, that power belongeth unto God. Also unto Thee, O God, belongeth mercy: for Thou wilt render unto every man according to his works."[1] Now the expression, "Once hath He spoken," is to be understood as meaning *"immovably,"* that is, unchangeably hath He spoken, inasmuch as He knows unchangeably all things which shall be and all things which He will do. We might, then, use the word fate in the sense it bears when derived from *fari*, to speak, had it not already come to be understood in another sense, into which I am unwilling that the hearts of men should unconsciously slide. But it does not follow that, though there is for God a certain order of all causes, there must therefore be nothing depending on the free exercise of our own wills, for our wills themselves are included in that order of causes which is certain to God and is embraced by His foreknowledge, for human wills are also causes of human actions; and He Who foreknew all the causes of things would certainly among those causes not have been ignorant of our wills. For even that very concession which Cicero himself makes is enough to refute him in this argument. For what does it help him to say that nothing takes place without a cause, but that every cause is not fatal, there being a fortuitous cause, a natural cause, and a voluntary cause? It is sufficient that he confesses that whatever happens must be preceded by a cause. For we say that those causes which are called fortuitous are not a mere name for the absence of causes, but are only latent, and we attribute them either to the will of the true God, or to that of spirits of some kind or other. And as to natural causes, we by no means separate them from the will of Him who is the author and framer of all nature. But now as to voluntary causes. They are referable either to God, or to angels, or to men, or to animals of whatever description, if indeed those instinctive movements of animals devoid of reason, by which, in accordance with their own nature, they seek or shun various things, are to be

[1] Ps. 62. 11, 12.

called wills. And when I speak of the wills of angels, I mean either the wills of good angels, whom we call the angels of God, or of the wicked angels, whom we call the angels of the devil, or demons. Also by the wills of men I mean the wills either of the good or of the wicked. And from this we conclude that there are no efficient causes of all things which come to pass unless voluntary causes, that is, such as belong to that nature which is the spirit of life. For the air or wind is called spirit, but, inasmuch as it is a body, it is not the spirit of life. The spirit of life, therefore, which quickens all things, and is the creator of every body and of every created spirit, is God Himself, the uncreated spirit. In His supreme will resides the power which acts on the wills of all created spirits, helping the good, judging the evil, controlling all, granting power to some, not granting it to others. For, as He is the creator of all natures, so also is He the bestower of all powers, not of all wills; for wicked wills are not from Him, being contrary to nature, which is from Him. As to bodies, they are more subject to wills: some to our wills, by which I mean the wills of all living mortal creatures, but more to the wills of men than of beasts. But all of them are most of all subject to the will of God, to Whom all wills also are subject, since they have no power except what He has bestowed upon them. The cause of things, therefore, which makes but is not made, is God; but all other causes both make and are made. Such are all created spirits, and especially the rational. Material causes, therefore, which may rather be said to be made than to make, are not to be reckoned among efficient causes, because they can only do what the wills of spirits do by them. How, then, does an order of causes which is certain to the foreknowledge of God necessitate that there should be nothing which is dependent on our wills, when our wills themselves have a very important place in the order of causes? Cicero, then, contends with those who call this order of causes fatal, or rather designate this order itself by the name of fate; to which we have an abhorrence, especially on account of the word, which men have become accustomed to understand as meaning what is not true. But, whereas he denies that the order of all causes is most certain and perfectly clear to the prescience of God, we detest his opinion more than the Stoics do. For he either denies that God exists—which, indeed, in an assumed personage, he has laboured to do, in his book *De Natura Deorum*—or if he confesses that He exists, but denies that He is prescient of future

things, what is that but just "the fool saying in his heart there is no God"? For one who is not prescient of all future things is not God. Wherefore our wills also have just so much power as God willed and foreknew that they should have; and therefore whatever power they have, they have it within most certain limits; and whatever they are to do, they are most assuredly to do, for He whose foreknowledge is infallible foreknew that they would have the power to do it and would do it. Wherefore, if I should choose to apply the name of fate to anything at all, I should rather say that fate belongs to the weaker of two parties, will to the stronger, who has the other in his power, than that the freedom of our will is excluded by that order of causes, which, by an unusual application of the word peculiar to themselves, the Stoics call *Fate*.

CHAP. 10. *Whether our wills are ruled by necessity*

Wherefore, neither is that necessity to be feared, for dread of which the Stoics laboured to make such distinctions among the causes of things as should enable them to rescue certain things from the dominion of necessity, and to subject others to it. Among those things which they wished not to be subject to necessity they placed our wills, knowing that they would not be free if subjected to necessity. For if that is to be called *our necessity* which is not in our power, but even though we be unwilling effects what it can effect—as, for instance, the necessity of death—it is manifest that our wills by which we live uprightly or wickedly are not under such a necessity; for we do many things which, if we were not willing, we should certainly not do. This is primarily true of the act of willing itself —for if we will, it *is*; if we will not, it *is* not— for we should not will if we were unwilling. But if we define necessity to be that according to which we say that it is necessary that anything be of such or such a nature, or be done in such and such a manner, I know not why we should have any dread of that necessity taking away the freedom of our will. For we do not put the life of God or the foreknowledge of God under necessity if we should say that it is necessary that God should live forever, and foreknow all things; as neither is His power diminished when we say that He cannot die or fall into error, for this is in such a way impossible to Him, that if it were possible for Him, He would be of less power. But assuredly He is rightly called omnipotent, though He can neither die nor fall into error. For He is called omnipotent on account of His doing what He wills, not on account of His suffering what He wills not; for if that should befall Him, He would by no means be omnipotent. Wherefore, He cannot do some things for the very reason that He is omnipotent. So also, when we say that it is necessary that, when we will, we will by free choice, in so saying we both affirm what is true beyond doubt and do not still subject our wills thereby to a necessity which destroys liberty. Our wills, therefore, *exist* as *wills* and do themselves whatever we do by willing, and which would not be done if we were unwilling. But when any one suffers anything, being unwilling, by the will of another, even in that case will retains its essential validity—we do not mean the will of the party who inflicts the suffering, for we resolve it into the power of God. For if a will should simply exist, but not be able to do what it wills, it would be overborne by a more powerful will. Nor would this be the case unless there had existed will, and that not the will of the other party, but the will of him who willed, but was not able to accomplish what he willed. Therefore, whatsoever a man suffers contrary to his own will, he ought not to attribute to the will of men, or of angels, or of any created spirit, but rather to His will who gives power to wills. It is not the case, therefore, that because God foreknew what would be in the power of our wills, there is for that reason nothing in the power of our wills. For He Who foreknew this did not foreknow nothing. Moreover, if He Who foreknew what would be in the power of our wills did not foreknow nothing, but something, assuredly, even though He did foreknow, there is something in the power of our wills. Therefore we are by no means compelled, either, retaining the prescience of God, to take away the freedom of the will, or, retaining the freedom of the will, to deny that He is prescient of future things, which is impious. But we embrace both. We faithfully and sincerely confess both. The former, that we may believe well; the latter, that we may live well. For he lives ill who does not believe well concerning God. Wherefore, be it far from us, in order to maintain our freedom, to deny the prescience of Him by Whose help we are or shall be free. Consequently, it is not in vain that laws are enacted, and that reproaches, exhortations, praises, and vituperations are had recourse to; for these also He foreknew, and they are of great avail, even as great as He foreknew that they would be of. Prayers, also, are of avail to procure those things which He foreknew that He would grant to those who offered them; and with

justice have rewards been appointed for good deeds and punishments for sins. For a man does not therefore sin because God foreknew that he would sin. Nay, it cannot be doubted but that it is the man himself who sins when he does sin, because He, Whose foreknowledge is infallible, foreknew not that fate, or fortune, or something else would sin, but that the man himself would sin, who, if he wills not, sins not. But if he shall not will to sin, even this did God foreknow.

CHAP. 11. *Concerning the universal providence of God in the laws of which all things are comprehended*

Therefore God supreme and true, with His Word and Holy Spirit (which three are one), one God omnipotent, creator and maker of every soul and of every body; by Whose gift all are happy who are happy through verity and not through vanity; Who made man a rational animal consisting of soul and body, Who, when he sinned, neither permitted him to go unpunished, nor left him without mercy; Who has given to the good and to the evil, being in common with stones, vegetable life in common with trees, sensuous life in common with brutes, intellectual life in common with angels alone; from Whom is every mode, every species, every order; from Whom are measure, number, weight; from Whom is everything which has an existence in nature, of whatever kind it be and of whatever value; from Whom are the seeds of forms and the forms of seeds, and the motion of seeds and of forms; Who gave also to flesh its origin, beauty, health, reproductive fecundity, disposition of members, and the salutary concord of its parts; Who also to the irrational soul has given memory, sense, appetite, but to the rational soul, in addition to these, has given intelligence and will; Who has not left, not to speak of heaven and earth, angels and men, but not even the entrails of the smallest and most contemptible animal, or the feather of a bird, or the little flower of a plant, or the leaf of a tree, without an harmony, and, as it were, a mutual peace among all its parts—that God can never be believed to have left the kingdoms of men, their dominations and servitudes, outside of the laws of His providence.

CHAP. 12. *By what virtues the ancient Romans merited that the true God, although they did not worship him, should enlarge their empire*

Wherefore let us go on to consider what virtues of the Romans they were which the true God, in Whose power are also the kingdoms of the earth, condescended to help in order to raise the empire, and also for what reason He did so. And, in order to discuss this question on clearer ground, we have written the former books, to show that the power of those gods, who, they thought, were to be worshipped with such trifling and silly rites, had nothing to do in this matter; and also what we have already accomplished of the present volume, to refute the doctrine of fate, lest any one who might have been already persuaded that the Roman empire was not extended and preserved by the worship of these gods, might still be attributing its extension and preservation to some kind of fate, rather than to the most powerful will of God most high. The ancient and primitive Romans, therefore, though their history shows us that, like all the other nations, with the sole exception of the Hebrews, they worshipped false gods, and sacrificed victims, not to God, but to demons, have nevertheless this commendation bestowed on them by their historian, that they were "greedy of praise, prodigal of wealth, desirous of great glory, and content with a moderate fortune." Glory they most ardently loved: for it they wished to live, for it they did not hesitate to die. Every other desire was repressed by the strength of their passion for that one thing. At length their country itself, because it seemed inglorious to serve but glorious to rule and to command, they first earnestly desired to be free, and then to be mistress. Hence it was that, not enduring the domination of kings, they put the government into the hands of two chiefs, holding office for a year, who were called consuls, not kings or lords.[1] But royal pomp seemed inconsistent with the administration of a ruler (*regentis*), or the benevolence of one who consults (that is, for the public good) (*consulentis*), but rather with the haughtiness of a lord (*dominantis*). King Tarquin, therefore, having been banished, and the consular government having been instituted, it followed, as the same author already alluded to says in his praises of the Romans, that "the state grew with amazing rapidity after it had obtained liberty, so great a desire of glory had taken possession of it." That eagerness for praise and desire of glory, then, was that which accomplished those many wonderful things, laudable, doubtless, and glorious according to human judgment. The same Sallust praises the great men of his own time, Marcus Cato and Caius Cæsar, saying that for a

long time the republic had no one great in virtue, but that within his memory there had been these two men of eminent virtue, and very different pursuits. Now, among the praises which he pronounces on Cæsar he put this, that he wished for a great empire, an army, and a new war, that he might have a sphere where his genius and virtue might shine forth. Thus it was ever the prayer of men of heroic character that Bellona would excite miserable nations to war and lash them into agitation with her bloody scourge, so that there might be occasion for the display of their valour. This, forsooth, is what that desire of praise and thirst for glory did. Wherefore, by the love of liberty in the first place, afterwards also by that of domination and through the desire of praise and glory, they achieved many great things; and their most eminent poet testifies to their having been prompted by all these motives:

> Porsenna there, with pride elate,
> Bids Rome to Tarquin ope her gate;
> With arms he hems the city in,
> Æneas' sons stand firm to win.[2]

At that time it was their greatest ambition either to die bravely or to live free; but when liberty was obtained, so great a desire of glory took possession of them, that liberty alone was not enough unless domination also should be sought, their great ambition being that which the same poet puts into the mouth of Jupiter:

> Nay, Juno's self, whose wild alarms
> Set ocean, earth, and heaven in arms,
> Shall change for smiles her moody frown,
> And vie with me in zeal to crown
> Rome's sons, the nation of the gown.
> So stands my will. There comes a day,
> While Rome's great ages hold their way,
> When old Assaracus's sons
> Shall quit them on the myrmidons,
> O'er Phthia and Mycenæ reign,
> And humble Argos to their chain.[3]

Which things, indeed, Virgil makes Jupiter predict as future, whilst, in reality, he was only himself passing in review in his own mind things which were already done and which were beheld by him as present realities. But I have mentioned them with the intention of showing that, next to liberty, the Romans so highly esteemed domination, that it received a place among those things on which they bestowed the greatest praise. Hence also it is that that poet, preferring to the arts of other nations those arts which peculiarly belong to the Romans, namely, the arts of ruling and commanding, and of subju-

[1]Augustine notes that the name consul is derived from *consulere*, and thus signifies a more benign rule than that of a *rex* (from *regere*), or *dominus* (from *dominari*).

[2]Virgil, *Æneid*, BK. VIII. 646.   [3]*Ibid.*, BK. I. 279.

gating and vanquishing nations, says,

> Others, belike, with happier grace,
> From bronze or stone shall call the face,
> Plead doubtful causes, map the skies,
> And tell when planets set or rise;
> But Roman thou, do thou control
>   The nations far and wide;
> Be this thy genius, to impose
> The rule of peace on vanquished foes,
> Show pity to the humble soul,
>   And crush the sons of pride.[1]

These arts they exercised with the more skill the less they gave themselves up to pleasures, and to enervation of body and mind in coveting and amassing riches, and through these corrupting morals, by extorting them from the miserable citizens and lavishing them on base stage-players. Hence these men of base character, who abounded when Sallust wrote and Virgil sang these things, did not seek after honours and glory by these arts, but by treachery and deceit. Wherefore the same says, "But at first it was rather ambition than avarice that stirred the minds of men, which vice, however, is nearer to virtue. For glory, honour, and power are desired alike by the good man and by the ignoble; but the former," he says, "strives onward to them by the true way, whilst the other, knowing nothing of the good arts, seeks them by fraud and deceit." And what is meant by seeking the attainment of glory, honour, and power by good arts, is to seek them by virtue, and not by deceitful intrigue; for the good and the ignoble man alike desire these things, but the good man strives to overtake them by the true way. The way is virtue, along which he presses as to the goal of possession—namely, to glory, honour, and power. Now that this was a sentiment engrained in the Roman mind, is indicated even by the temples of their gods; for they built in very close proximity the temples of Virtue and Honor, worshipping as gods the gifts of God. Hence we can understand what they who were good thought to be the end of virtue, and to what they ultimately referred it, namely, to honour; for, as to the bad, they had no virtue though they desired honour, and strove to possess it by fraud and deceit. Praise of a higher kind is bestowed upon Cato, for he says of him, "The less he sought glory, the more it followed him." We say praise of a higher kind; for the glory with the desire of which the Romans burned is the judgment of men thinking well of men. And therefore virtue is better, which is content with no human judgment save that of

one's own conscience. Whence the apostle says, "For this is our glory, the testimony of our conscience." [2] And in another place he says, "But let every one prove his own work, and then he shall have glory in himself and not in another."[3] That glory, honour, and power, therefore, which they desired for themselves, and to which the good sought to attain by good arts, should not be sought after by virtue, but virtue by them. For there is no true virtue except that which is directed towards that end in which is the highest and ultimate good of man. Wherefore even the honours which Cato sought he ought not to have sought, but the state ought to have conferred them on him unsolicited, on account of his virtues.

But, of the two great Romans of that time, Cato was he whose virtue was by far the nearest to the true idea of virtue. Wherefore, let us refer to the opinion of Cato himself, to discover what was the judgment he had formed concerning the condition of the state both then and in former times. "I do not think," he says, "that it was by arms that our ancestors made the republic great from being small. Had that been the case, the republic of our day would have been by far more flourishing than that of their times, for the number of our allies and citizens is far greater; and, besides, we possess a far greater abundance of armour and of horses than they did. But it was other things than these that made them great, and we have none of them: industry at home, just government without, a mind free in deliberation, addicted neither to crime nor to lust. Instead of these, we have luxury and avarice, poverty in the state, opulence among citizens; we laud riches, we follow laziness; there is no difference made between the good and the bad; all the rewards of virtue are got possession of by intrigue. And no wonder, when every individual consults only for his own good, when ye are the slaves of pleasure at home, and, in public affairs, of money and favour, no wonder that an onslaught is made upon the unprotected republic."

He who hears these words of Cato or of Sallust probably thinks that such praise bestowed on the ancient Romans was applicable to all of them, or, at least, to very many of them. It is not so; otherwise the things which Cato himself writes, and which I have quoted in the second book of this work, would not be true. In that passage he says that even from the very beginning of the state wrongs were committed by the more powerful, which led to the separation of

---

[1]Ibid., BK. VI. 847.   [2]II Cor. I. 12.   [3]Gal. 6. 4.

the people from the fathers, besides which there were other internal dissensions; and the only time at which there existed a just and moderate administration was after the banishment of the kings, and that no longer than whilst they had cause to be afraid of Tarquin and were carrying on the grievous war which had been undertaken on his account against Etruria; but afterwards the fathers oppressed the people as slaves, flogged them as the kings had done, drove them from their land, and, to the exclusion of all others, held the government in their own hands alone. And to these discords, whilst the fathers were wishing to rule, and the people were unwilling to serve, the second Punic war put an end; for again great fear began to press upon their disquieted minds, holding them back from those distractions by another and greater anxiety, and bringing them back to civil concord. But the great things which were then achieved were accomplished through the administration of a few men, who were good in their own way. And by the wisdom and forethought of these few good men, which first enabled the republic to endure these evils and mitigated them, it waxed greater and greater. And this the same historian affirms, when he says that, reading and hearing of the many illustrious achievements of the Roman people in peace and in war, by land and by sea, he wished to understand what it was by which these great things were specially sustained. For he knew that very often the Romans had with a small company contended with great legions of the enemy; and he knew also that with small resources they had carried on wars with opulent kings. And he says that, after having given the matter much consideration, it seemed evident to him that the pre-eminent virtue of a few citizens had achieved the whole, and that that explained how poverty overcame wealth, and small numbers great multitudes. But, he adds, after that the state had been corrupted by luxury and indolence, again the republic, by its own greatness, was able to bear the vices of its magistrates and generals. Wherefore even the praises of Cato are only applicable to a few; for only a few were possessed of that virtue which leads men to pursue after glory, honour, and power by the true way—that is, by virtue itself. This industry at home, of which Cato speaks, was the consequence of a desire to enrich the public treasury, even though the result should be poverty at home; and therefore, when he speaks of the evil arising out of the corruption of morals, he reverses the expression, and says, "Poverty n the state, riches at home."

CHAP. 13. *Concerning the love of praise, which, though it is a vice, is reckoned a virtue, because by it greater vice is restrained*

Wherefore, when the kingdoms of the East had been illustrious for a long time, it pleased God that there should also arise a Western empire, which, though later in time, should be more illustrious in extent and greatness. And, in order that it might overcome the grievous evils which existed among other nations, He purposely granted it to such men as, for the sake of honour, and praise, and glory, consulted well for their country, in whose glory they sought their own, and whose safety they did not hesitate to prefer to their own, suppressing the desire of wealth and many other vices for this one vice, namely, the love of praise. For he has the soundest perception who recognizes that even the love of praise is a vice; nor has this escaped the perception of the poet Horace, who says,

> *You're bloated by ambition? take advice:*
> *Yon book will ease you if you read it thrice.*

And the same poet, in a lyric song, hath thus spoken with the desire of repressing the passion for domination:

> *Rule an ambitious spirit, and thou hast*
> *A wider kingdom than if thou shouldst join*
> *To distant Gades Lybia, and thus*
> *Shouldst hold in service either Carthaginian.*

Nevertheless, they who restrain baser lusts, not by the power of the Holy Spirit obtained by the faith of piety, or by the love of intelligible beauty, but by desire of human praise, or, at all events, restrain them better by the love of such praise, are not indeed yet holy, but only less base. Even Tully was not able to conceal this fact: for, in the same books which he wrote, *De Republica,* when speaking concerning the education of a chief of the state, who ought, he says, to be nourished on glory, goes on to say that their ancestors did many wonderful and illustrious things through desire of glory. So far, therefore, from resisting this vice, they even thought that it ought to be excited and kindled up, supposing that that would be beneficial to the republic. But not even in his books on philosophy does Tully dissimulate this poisonous opinion, for he there avows it more clearly than day. For when he is speaking of those studies which are to be pursued with a view to the *true good,* and not with the vainglorious desire of human praise, he introduces the following universal and general statement:

Honour nourishes the arts, and all are stimulated to the prosecution of studies by glory; and those pursuits are always neglected which are generally discredited.

CHAP. 14. *Concerning the eradication of the love of human praise, because all the glory of the righteous is in God*

It is, therefore, doubtless far better to resist this desire than to yield to it, for the purer one is from this defilement, the liker is he to God; and, though this vice be not thoroughly eradicated from his heart—for it does not cease to tempt even the minds of those who are making good progress in virtue—at any rate, let the desire of glory be surpassed by the love of righteousness, so that, if there be seen anywhere "lying neglected things which are generally discredited," if they are good, if they are right, even the love of human praise may blush and yield to the love of truth. For so hostile is this vice to pious faith, if the love of glory be greater in the heart than the fear or love of God, that the Lord said, "How can ye believe, who look for glory from one another, and do not seek the glory which is from God alone?"[1] Also, concerning some who had believed on Him, but were afraid to confess Him openly, the evangelist says, "They loved the praise of men more than the praise of God";[2] which did not the holy apostles, who, when they proclaimed the name of Christ in those places where it was not only discredited, and therefore neglected—according as Cicero says, "Those things are always neglected which are generally discredited"—but was even held in the utmost detestation, holding to what they had heard from the Good Master, who was also the physician of minds, "If any one shall deny me before men, him will I also deny before my Father Who is in heaven, and before the angels of God,"[3] amidst maledictions and reproaches, and most grievous persecutions and cruel punishments, were not deterred from the preaching of human salvation by the noise of human indignation. And when, as they did and spake divine things, and lived divine lives, conquering, as it were, hard hearts, and introducing into them the peace of righteousness, great glory followed them in the church of Christ, they did not rest in that as in the end of their virtue, but, referring that glory itself to the glory of God, by whose grace they were what they were, they sought to kindle, also by that same flame, the minds of those for whose good they consulted, to the love of Him, by Whom they could be made to be what they themselves were. For their Master had taught them not to seek to be good for the sake of human glory, saying, "Take heed that ye do not your righteousness before men to be seen of them, or otherwise ye shall not have a reward from your Father Who is in heaven."[4] But again, lest, understanding this wrongly, they should, through fear of pleasing men, be less useful through concealing their goodness, showing for what end they ought to make it known, He says, "Let your works shine before men, that they may see your good deeds, and glorify your Father Who is in heaven."[5] Not, observe, "that ye may be seen by them, that is, in order that their eyes may be directed upon you"—for of yourselves ye are nothing—but "that they may glorify your Father Who is in heaven," by fixing their regards on whom they may become such as ye are. These the martyrs followed, who surpassed the Scævolas, and the Curtiuses, and the Deciuses, both in true virtue, because in true piety, and also in the greatness of their number. But since those Romans were in an earthly city and had before them, as the end of all the offices undertaken in its behalf, its safety, and a kingdom, not in heaven, but in earth—not in the sphere of eternal life, but in the sphere of demise and succession, where the dead are succeeded by the dying—what else but glory should they love, by which they wished even after death to live in the mouths of their admirers?

CHAP. 15. *Concerning the temporal reward which God granted to the virtues of the Romans*

Now, therefore, with regard to those to whom God did not purpose to give eternal life with His holy angels in His own celestial city, to the society of which that true piety which does not render the service of religion, which the Greeks call λατρεία, to any save the true God conducts, if He had also withheld from them the terrestrial glory of that most excellent empire, a reward would not have been rendered to their good arts—that is, their virtues—by which they sought to attain so great glory. For as to those who seem to do some good that they may receive glory from men, the Lord also says, "Verily I say unto you, they have received their reward."[6] So also these despised their own private affairs for the sake of the republic, and for its treasury resisted avarice, consulted for the good of their country with a spirit of freedom, addicted neither to what their laws pronounced to be crime nor to lust. By all these acts, as by the

---

[1]John, 5. 44.   [2]John, 12. 43.   [3]Matt. 10. 33.   [4]Matt. 6. 1.   [5]Matt. 5. 10.   [6]Matt. 6. 2.

true way, they pressed forward to honours, power, and glory; they were honoured among almost all nations; they imposed the laws of their empire upon many nations; and at this day, both in literature and history, they are glorious among almost all nations. There is no reason why they should complain against the justice of the supreme and true God—"they have received their reward."

CHAP. 16. *Concerning the reward of the holy citizens of the celestial city, to whom the example of the virtues of the Romans are useful*

But the reward of the saints is far different, who even here endured reproaches for that city of God which is hateful to the lovers of this world. That city is eternal. There none are born, for none die. There is true and full felicity—not a goddess, but a gift of God. Thence we receive the pledge of faith, whilst on our pilgrimage we sigh for its beauty. There rises not the sun on the good and the evil, but the Sun of Righteousness protects the good alone. There no great industry shall be expended to enrich the public treasury by suffering privations at home, for there is the common treasury of truth. And, therefore, it was not only for the sake of recompensing the citizens of Rome that her empire and glory had been so signally extended, but also that the citizens of that eternal city, during their pilgrimage here, might diligently and soberly contemplate these examples and see what a love they owe to the supernal country on account of life eternal, if the terrestrial country was so much beloved by its citizens on account of human glory.

CHAP. 17. *To what profit the Romans carried on wars, and how much they contributed to the well-being of those whom they conquered*

For, as far as this life of mortals is concerned, which is spent and ended in a few days, what does it matter under whose government a dying man lives, if they who govern do not force him to impiety and iniquity? Did the Romans at all harm those nations, on whom, when subjugated, they imposed their laws, except in as far as that was accomplished with great slaughter in war? Now, had it been done with consent of the nations, it would have been done with greater success, but there would have been no glory of conquest, for neither did the Romans themselves live exempt from those laws which they imposed on others. Had this been done without Mars and Bellona, so that there should have been no place for victory, no one conquering where no one had

fought, would not the condition of the Romans and of the other nations have been one and the same, especially if that had been done at once which afterwards was done most humanely and most acceptably, namely, the admission of all to the rights of Roman citizens who belonged to the Roman empire, and if that had been made the privilege of all which was formerly the privilege of a few, with this one condition, that the humbler class who had no lands of their own should live at the public expense—an alimentary impost, which would have been paid with a much better grace by them into the hands of good administrators of the republic, of which they were members, by their own hearty consent, than it would have been paid with had it to be extorted from them as conquered men? For I do not see what it makes for the safety, good morals, and certainly not for the dignity, of men, that some have conquered and others have been conquered, except that it yields them that most insane pomp of human glory, in which "they have received their reward" who burned with excessive desire of it and carried on most eager wars. For do not their lands pay tribute? Have they any privilege of learning what the others are not privileged to learn? Are there not many senators in the other countries who do not even know Rome by sight? Take away outward show, and what are all men after all but men? But even though the perversity of the age should permit that all the better men should be more highly honoured than others, neither thus should human honour be held at a great price, for it is smoke which has no weight. But let us avail ourselves even in these things of the kindness of God. Let us consider how great things they despised, how great things they endured, what lusts they subdued for the sake of human glory, who merited that glory, as it were, in reward for such virtues; and let this be useful to us even in suppressing pride, so that, as that city in which it has been promised us to reign as far surpasses this one as heaven is distant from the earth, as eternal life surpasses temporal joy, solid glory empty praise, or the society of angels the society of mortals, or the glory of Him Who made the sun and moon the light of the sun and moon, the citizens of so great a country may not seem to themselves to have done anything very great, if, in order to obtain it, they have done some good works or endured some evils, when those men for this terrestrial country already obtained, did such great things, suffered such great things. And especially are all these things to be considered because the remission of sins which collects citizens to the celestial country has something in it to which a shadowy resemblance is found in the asylum of Romulus, whither escape from the punishment of all manner of crimes congregated that multitude with which the state was to be founded.

CHAP. 18. *How far Christians ought to be from boasting, if they have done anything for the love of the eternal country, when the Romans did such great things for human glory and a terrestrial city*

What great thing, therefore, is it for that eternal and celestial city to despise all the charms of this world, however pleasant, if for the sake of this terrestrial city Brutus could even put to death his son—a sacrifice which the heavenly city compels no one to make? But certainly it is more difficult to put to death one's sons than to do what is required to be done for the heavenly country, even to distribute to the poor those things which were looked upon as things to be amassed and laid up for one's children, or to let them go, if there arise any temptation which compels us to do so, for the sake of faith and righteousness. For it is not earthly riches which make us or our sons happy; for they must either be lost by us in our lifetime, or be possessed when we are dead, by whom we know not, or perhaps by whom we would not. But it is God Who makes us happy, Who is the true riches of minds. But of Brutus, even the poet who celebrates his praises testifies that it was the occasion of unhappiness to him that he slew his son, for he says,

> And call his own rebellious seed
> For menaced liberty to bleed.
> Unhappy father! howsoe'er
> The deed be judged by after days.[1]

But in the following verse he consoles him in his unhappiness, saying,

> His country's love shall all o'erbear.

There are those two things, namely, liberty and the desire of human praise, which compelled the Romans to admirable deeds. If, therefore, for the liberty of dying men and for the desire of human praise which is sought after by mortals, sons could be put to death by a father, what great thing is it, if, for the true liberty which has made us free from the dominion of sin, and death, and the devil—not through the desire of human praise, but through the earnest desire of freeing men, not from King Tarquin, but from demons and the prince of the demons—we should, I do not say put to death our sons, but

[1] Virgil, *Æneid*, BK. VI. 820.

reckon among our sons Christ's poor ones? If, also, another Roman chief, surnamed Torquatus, slew his son, not because he fought against his country, but because, being challenged by an enemy, he through youthful impetuosity fought, though for his country, yet contrary to orders which he his father had given as general; and this he did, notwithstanding that his son was victorious, lest there should be more evil in the example of authority despised than good in the glory of slaying an enemy; if, I say, Torquatus acted thus, wherefore should they boast themselves, who, for the laws of a celestial country, despise all earthly good things, which are loved far less than sons? If Furius Camillus, who was condemned by those who envied him, notwithstanding that he had thrown off from the necks of his countrymen the yoke of their most bitter enemies, the Veientes, again delivered his ungrateful country from the Gauls, because he had no other in which he could have better opportunities for living a life of glory; if Camillus did thus, why should he be extolled as having done some great thing, who, having, it may be, suffered in the Church at the hands of carnal enemies most grievous and dishonouring injury, has not betaken himself to heretical enemies, or himself raised some heresy against her, but has rather defended her, as far as he was able, from the most pernicious perversity of heretics, since there is not another church, I say not in which one can live a life of glory, but in which eternal life can be obtained? If Mucius, in order that peace might be made with King Porsenna, who was pressing the Romans with a most grievous war, when he did not succeed in slaying Porsenna, but slew another by mistake for him, reached forth his right hand and laid it on a red-hot altar, saying that many such as he saw him to be had conspired for his destruction, so that Porsenna, terrified at his daring, and at the thought of a conspiracy of such as he, without any delay recalled all his warlike purposes, and made peace; if, I say, Mucius did this, who shall speak of his meritorious claims to the kingdom of heaven, if for it he may have given to the flames not one hand, but even his whole body, and that not by his own spontaneous act, but because he was persecuted by another? If Curtius, spurring on his steed, threw himself all armed into a precipitous gulf, obeying the oracles of their gods, which had commanded that the Romans should throw into that gulf the best thing which they possessed, and they could only understand thereby that, since they excelled in men and arms, the gods had commanded that an armed man should be cast headlong into that destruction; if he did this, shall we say that that man has done a great thing for the eternal city who may have died by a like death, not, however, precipitating himself spontaneously into a gulf, but having suffered this death at the hands of some enemy of his faith, more especially when he has received from his Lord, who is also King of his country, a more certain oracle, "Fear not them who kill the body, but cannot kill the soul?" [1] If the Decii dedicated themselves to death, consecrating themselves in a form of words, as it were, that falling, and pacifying by their blood the wrath of the gods, they might be the means of delivering the Roman army; if they did this, let not the holy martyrs carry themselves proudly, as though they had done some meritorious thing for a share in that country where are eternal life and felicity, if even to the shedding of their blood, loving not only the brethren for whom it was shed, but, according as had been commanded them, even their enemies by whom it was being shed, they have vied with one another in faith of love and love of faith. If Marcus Pulvillus, when engaged in dedicating a temple to Jupiter, Juno, and Minerva, received with such indifference the false intelligence which was brought to him of the death of his son, with the intention of so agitating him that he should go away, and thus the glory of dedicating the temple should fall to his colleague; if he received that intelligence with such indifference that he even ordered that his son should be cast out unburied, the love of glory having overcome in his heart the grief of bereavement, how shall any one affirm that he had done a great thing for the preaching of the gospel, by which the citizens of the heavenly city are delivered from divers errors and gathered together from divers wanderings, to whom his Lord has said, when anxious about the burial of his father, "Follow me, and let the dead bury their dead"? [2] Regulus, in order not to break his oath, even with his most cruel enemies, returned to them from Rome itself, because (as he is said to have replied to the Romans when they wished to retain him) he could not have the dignity of an honourable citizen at Rome after having been a slave to the Africans, and the Carthaginians put him to death with the utmost tortures, because he had spoken against them in the senate. If Regulus acted thus, what tortures are not to be despised for the sake of good faith toward that country to whose beatitude faith itself leads? Or what will a man have rendered to the Lord for all He has bestowed upon him, if, for the faithfulness he owes to Him, he shall have suffered such things as Regulus suffered at the hands of his most ruthless enemies for the good faith which he owed to them? And how shall a Christian dare vaunt himself of his voluntary poverty, which he has chosen in order that during the pilgrimage of this life he may walk the more disencumbered on the way which leads to the country where the true riches are, even God Himself; how, I say, shall he vaunt himself for this, when he hears or reads that Lucius Valerius, who died when he was holding the office of consul, was so poor that his funeral expenses were paid with money collected by the people? —or when he hears that Quintius Cincinnatus, who, possessing only four acres of land, and cultivating them with his own hands, was taken from the plough to be made dictator—an office more honourable even than that of consul—and that, after having won great glory by conquering the enemy, he preferred notwithstanding to continue in his poverty? Or how shall he boast of having done a great thing, who has not been prevailed upon by the offer of any reward of this world to renounce his connexion with that heavenly and eternal country, when he hears that Fabricius could not be prevailed on to forsake the Roman city by the great gifts offered to him by Pyrrhus king of the Epirots, who promised him the fourth part of his kingdom, but preferred to abide there in his poverty as a private individual? For if, when their republic— that is, the interest of the people, the interest of the country, the common interest—was most prosperous and wealthy, they themselves were so poor in their own houses that one of them, who had already been twice a consul, was expelled from that senate of poor men by the censor, because he was discovered to possess ten pounds weight of silver-plate—since, I say, those very men by whose triumphs the public treasury was enriched were so poor, ought not all Christians, who make common property of their riches with a far nobler purpose, even that (according to what is written in the Acts of the Apostles) they may distribute to each one according to his need, and that no one may say that anything is his own, but that all things may be their common possession [3]—ought they not to understand that they should not vaunt themselves, because they do that to obtain the society of angels, when those men did well-nigh the same thing to preserve the glory of the Romans?

How could these, and whatever like things

[1]Matt. 10. 28.   [2]Matt. 8. 22.   [3]Acts, 2. 45.

are found in the Roman history, have become so widely known, and have been proclaimed by so great a fame, had not the Roman empire, extending far and wide, been raised to its greatness by magnificent successes? Wherefore, through that empire, so extensive and of so long continuance, so illustrious and glorious also through the virtues of such great men, the reward which they sought was rendered to their earnest aspirations, and also examples are set before us, containing necessary admonition, in order that we may be stung with shame if we shall see that we have not held fast those virtues for the sake of the most glorious city of God, which are, in whatever way, resembled by those virtues which they held fast for the sake of the glory of a terrestrial city, and that, too, if we shall feel conscious that we have held them fast, we may not be lifted up with pride, because, as the apostle says, "The sufferings of the present time are not worthy to be compared to the glory which shall be revealed in us."[1] But so far as regards human and temporal glory, the lives of these ancient Romans were reckoned sufficiently worthy. Therefore, also, we see, in the light of that truth which, veiled in the Old Testament, is revealed in the New, namely, that it is not in view of terrestrial and temporal benefits, which divine providence grants promiscuously to good and evil, that God is to be worshipped, but in view of eternal life, everlasting gifts, and of the society of the heavenly city itself; in the light of this truth we see that the Jews were most righteously given as a trophy to the glory of the Romans; for we see that these Romans, who rested on earthly glory, and sought to obtain it by virtues, such as they were, conquered those who, in their great depravity, slew and rejected the giver of true glory, and of the eternal city.

CHAP. 19. *Concerning the difference between true glory and the desire of domination*

There is assuredly a difference between the desire of human glory and the desire of domination; for, though he who has an overweening delight in human glory will be also very prone to aspire earnestly after domination, nevertheless they who desire the true glory even of human praise strive not to displease those who judge well of them. For there are many good moral qualities, of which many are competent judges, although they are not possessed by many; and by those good moral qualities those men press on to glory, honour and domination,

[1] Rom. 8. 18.

of whom Sallust says, "But they press on by the true way."

But whosoever, without possessing that desire of glory which makes one fear to displease those who judge his conduct, desires domination and power, very often seeks to obtain what he loves by most open crimes. Therefore he who desires glory presses on to obtain it either by the true way, or certainly by deceit and artifice, wishing to appear good when he is not. Therefore to him who possesses virtues it is a great virtue to despise glory; for contempt of it is seen by God, but is not manifest to human judgment. For whatever any one does before the eyes of men in order to show himself to be a despiser of glory, if they suspect that he is doing it in order to get greater praise—that is, greater glory—he has no means of demonstrating to the perceptions of those who suspect him that the case is really otherwise than they suspect it to be. But he who despises the judgment of praisers, despises also the rashness of suspectors. Their salvation, indeed, he does not despise, if he is truly good; for so great is the righteousness of that man who receives his virtues from the Spirit of God that he loves his very enemies, and so loves them that he desires that his haters and detractors may be turned to righteousness and become his associates, and that not in an earthly but in a heavenly country. But with respect to his praisers, though he sets little value on their praise, he does not set little value on their love; neither does he elude their praise, lest he should forfeit their love. And, therefore, he strives earnestly to have their praises directed to Him from Whom every one receives whatever in him is truly praiseworthy. But he who is a despiser of glory, but is greedy of domination, exceeds the beasts in the vices of cruelty and luxuriousness. Such, indeed, were certain of the Romans, who, wanting the love of esteem, wanted not the thirst for domination; and that there were many such, history testifies. But it was Nero Cæsar who was the first to reach the summit and, as it were, the citadel of this vice; for so great was his luxuriousness that one would have thought there was nothing manly to be dreaded in him, and such his cruelty that, had not the contrary been known, no one would have thought there was anything effeminate in his character. Nevertheless power and domination are not given even to such men save by the providence of the most high God, when He judges that the state of human affairs is worthy of such lords. The divine utterance is clear on this matter; for the Wisdom of God thus speaks: "By me kings reign, and tyrants possess the land." [1] But, that it may not be thought that by "tyrants" is meant, not wicked and impious kings, but brave men, in accordance with the ancient use of the word, as when Virgil says,

For know that treaty may not stand
Where king greets king and joins not hand,[2]

in another place it is most unambiguously said of God that He "maketh the man who is an hypocrite to reign on account of the perversity of the people."[3] Wherefore, though I have, according to my ability, shown for what reason God, who alone is true and just, helped forward the Romans, who were good according to a certain standard of an earthly state, to the acquirement of the glory of so great an empire, there may be, nevertheless, a more hidden cause, known better to God than to us, depending on the diversity of the merits of the human race. Among all who are truly pious, it is at all events agreed that no one without true piety—that is, true worship of the true God—can have true virtue; and that it is not true virtue which is the slave of human praise. Though, nevertheless, they who are not citizens of the eternal city, which is called the city of God in the sacred Scriptures, are more useful to the earthly city when they possess even that virtue than if they had not even that. But there could be nothing more fortunate for human affairs than that, by the mercy of God, they who are endowed with true piety of life, if they have the skill for ruling people, should also have the power. But such men, however great virtues they may possess in this life, attribute it solely to the grace of God that He has bestowed it on them—willing, believing, seeking. And, at the same time, they understand how far they are short of that perfection of righteousness which exists in the society of those holy angels for which they are striving to fit themselves. But however much that virtue may be praised and cried up, which without true piety is the slave of human glory, it is not at all to be compared even to the feeble beginnings of the virtue of the saints, whose hope is placed in the grace and mercy of the true God.

CHAP. 20. *That it is as shameful for the virtues to serve human glory as bodily pleasure*

Philosophers—who place the end of human good in virtue itself, in order to put to shame certain other philosophers, who indeed approve of the virtues, but measure them all with reference to the end of bodily pleasure and think that this pleasure is to be sought for its own sake, but

[1] Prov. 8. 15.   [2] *Æneid*, BK. VII. 266.   [3] Job, 34. 30.

the virtues on account of pleasure—are wont to paint a kind of word-picture, in which Pleasure sits like a luxurious queen on a royal seat and all the virtues are subjected to her as slaves, watching her nod that they may do whatever she shall command. She commands Prudence to be ever on the watch to discover how Pleasure may rule, and be safe. Justice she orders to grant what benefits she can, in order to secure those friendships which are necessary for bodily pleasure; to do wrong to no one, lest, on account of the breaking of the laws, Pleasure be not able to live in security. Fortitude she orders to keep her mistress, that is, Pleasure, bravely in her mind, if any affliction befall her body which does not occasion death, in order that by remembrance of former delights she may mitigate the poignancy of present pain. Temperance she commands to take only a certain quantity even of the most favourite food, lest, through immoderate use, anything prove hurtful by disturbing the health of the body, and thus Pleasure, which the Epicureans make to consist chiefly in the health of the body, be grievously offended. Thus the virtues, with the whole dignity of their glory, will be the slaves of Pleasure, as of some imperious and disreputable woman.

There is nothing, say our philosophers, more disgraceful and monstrous than this picture, and which the eyes of good men can less endure. And they say the truth. But I do not think that the picture would be sufficiently becoming, even if it were made so that the virtues should be represented as the slaves of human glory; for, though that glory be not a luxurious woman, it is nevertheless puffed up, and has much vanity in it. Wherefore it is unworthy of the solidity and firmness of the virtues to represent them as serving this glory, so that Prudence shall provide nothing, Justice distribute nothing, Temperance moderate nothing, except to the end that men may be pleased and vain glory served. Nor will they be able to defend themselves from the charge of such baseness, whilst they, by way of being despisers of glory, disregard the judgment of other men, seem to themselves wise, and please themselves. For their virtue—if, indeed, it is virtue at all—is only in another way subjected to human praise; for he who seeks to please himself seeks still to please man. But he who, with true piety towards God, whom he loves, believes, and hopes in, fixes his attention more on those things in which he displeases himself than on those things, if there are any such, which please himself, or rather, not himself, but the truth, does not attribute that by which he can now please the truth to anything but to the mercy of Him Whom he has feared to displease, giving thanks for what in him is healed, and pouring out prayers for the healing of that which is yet unhealed.

CHAP. 21. *That the Roman dominion was granted by Him from Whom is all power, and by Whose providence all things are ruled*

These things being so, we do not attribute the power of giving kingdoms and empires to any save to the true God, Who gives happiness in the kingdom of heaven to the pious alone, but gives kingly power on earth both to the pious and the impious, as it may please Him, Whose good pleasure is always just. For though we have said something about the principles which guide His administration, in so far as it has seemed good to Him to explain it, nevertheless it is too much for us, and far surpasses our strength, to discuss the hidden things of men's hearts and by a clear examination to determine the merits of various kingdoms. He, therefore, Who is the one true God, Who never leaves the human race without just judgment and help, gave a kingdom to the Romans when He would, and as great as He would, as He did also to the Assyrians, and even the Persians, by whom, as their own books testify, only two gods are worshipped, the one good and the other evil—to say nothing concerning the Hebrew people, of whom I have already spoken as much as seemed necessary, who, as long as they were a kingdom, worshipped none save the true God. The same, therefore, Who gave to the Persians harvests, though they did not worship the goddess Segetia, Who gave the other blessings of the earth, though they did not worship the many gods which the Romans supposed to preside, each one over some particular thing, or even many of them over each several thing, He, I say, gave the Persians dominion, though they worshipped none of those gods to whom the Romans believed themselves indebted for the empire. And the same is true in respect of men as well as nations. He Who gave power to Marius gave it also to Caius Cæsar; He Who gave it to Augustus gave it also to Nero; He also Who gave it to the most benignant emperors, the Vespasians, father and son, gave it also to the cruel Domitian; and, finally, to avoid the necessity of going over them all, He Who gave it to the Christian Constantine gave it also to the apostate Julian, whose gifted mind was deceived by a sacrilegious and detestable curiosity, stimulated by the love of power. And it was because he was addicted through curiosity to

vain oracles that, confident of victory, he burned the ships which were laden with the provisions necessary for his army, and therefore, engaging with hot zeal in rashly audacious enterprises, he was soon slain, as the just consequence of his recklessness, and left his army unprovisioned in an enemy's country, and in such a predicament that it never could have escaped, save by altering the boundaries of the Roman empire, in violation of that omen of the god Terminus of which I spoke in the preceding book; for the god Terminus yielded to necessity, though he had not yielded to Jupiter. Manifestly these things are ruled and governed by the one God according as He pleases; and if His motives are hid, are they therefore unjust?

CHAP. 22. *The durations and issues of war depend on the will of God*

Thus also the durations of wars are determined by Him as He may see meet, according to His righteous will, and pleasure, and mercy, to afflict or to console the human race, so that they are sometimes of longer, sometimes of shorter duration. The war of the Pirates and the third Punic war were terminated with incredible celerity. Also the war of the fugitive gladiators, though in it many Roman generals and the consuls were defeated, and Italy was terribly wasted and ravaged, was nevertheless ended in the third year, having itself been, during its continuance, the end of much. The Picentes, the Marsi, and the Peligni, not distant but Italian nations, after a long and most loyal servitude under the Roman yoke, attempted to raise their heads into liberty, though many nations had now been subjected to the Roman power, and Carthage had been overthrown. In this Italian war the Romans were very often defeated, and two consuls perished, besides other noble senators; nevertheless this calamity was not protracted over a long space of time, for the fifth year put an end to it. But the second Punic war, lasting for the space of eighteen years, and occasioning the greatest disasters and calamities to the republic, wore out and well-nigh consumed the strength of the Romans; for in two battles[1] about seventy thousand Romans fell. The first Punic war was terminated after having been waged for three-and-twenty years. The Mithridatic war was waged for forty years. And that no one may think that in the early and much belauded times of the Romans they were far braver and more able to bring wars to a speedy termination, the Samnite war was pro-

[1] Of the Thrasymene Lake and Cannæ.

tracted for nearly fifty years; and in this war the Romans were so beaten that they were even put under the yoke. But because they did not love glory for the sake of justice, but seemed rather to have loved justice for the sake of glory, they broke the peace and the treaty which had been concluded. These things I mention, because many, ignorant of past things, and some also dissimulating what they know, if in Christian times they see any war protracted a little longer than they expected, straightway make a fierce and insolent attack on our religion, exclaiming that, but for it, the deities would have been supplicated still, according to ancient rites; and then, by that bravery of the Romans, which, with the help of Mars and Bellona, speedily brought to an end such great wars, this war also would be speedily terminated. Let them, therefore, who have read history recollect what long-continued wars, having various issues and entailing woeful slaughter, were waged by the ancient Romans, in accordance with the general truth that the earth, like the tempestuous deep, is subject to agitations from tempests—tempests of such evils, in various degrees—and let them sometimes confess what they do not like to own, and not, by madly speaking against God, destroy themselves and deceive the ignorant.

CHAP. 23. *Concerning the war in which Radagaisus, king of the Goths, a worshipper of demons, was conquered in one day, with all his mighty forces*

Nevertheless they do not mention with thanksgiving what God has very recently, and within our own memory, wonderfully and mercifully done, but as far as in them lies they attempt, if possible, to bury it in universal oblivion. But should we be silent about these things, we should be in like manner ungrateful. When Radagaisus, king of the Goths, having taken up his position very near to the city, with a vast and savage army, was already close upon the Romans, he was in one day so speedily and so thoroughly beaten that, whilst not even one Roman was wounded much less slain, far more than a hundred thousand of his army were prostrated, and he himself and his sons, having been captured, were forthwith put to death, suffering the punishment they deserved. For had so impious a man, with so great and so impious a host, entered the city, whom would he have spared? what tombs of the martyrs would he have respected? in his treatment of what person would he have manifested the fear of God? whose blood would he have refrained from shedding?

whose chastity would he have wished to preserve inviolate? But how loud would they not have been in the praises of their gods! How insultingly they would have boasted, saying that Radagaisus had conquered, that he had been able to achieve such great things, because he propitiated and won over the gods by daily sacrifices—a thing which the Christian religion did not allow the Romans to do! For when he was approaching to those places where he was overwhelmed at the nod of the Supreme Majesty, as his fame was everywhere increasing, it was being told us at Carthage that the pagans were believing, publishing, and boasting, that he, on account of the help and protection of the gods friendly to him, because of the sacrifices which he was said to be daily offering to them, would certainly not be conquered by those who were not performing such sacrifices to the Roman gods, and did not even permit that they should be offered by any one. And now these wretched men do not give thanks to God for His great mercy, Who, having determined to chastise the corruption of men, which was worthy of far heavier chastisement than the corruption of the barbarians, tempered His indignation with such mildness as, in the first instance, to cause that the king of the Goths should be conquered in a wonderful manner, lest glory should accrue to demons, whom he was known to be supplicating, and thus the minds of the weak should be overthrown; and then, afterwards, to cause that, when Rome was to be taken, it should be taken by those barbarians who, contrary to any custom of all former wars, protected, through reverence for the Christian religion, those who fled for refuge to the sacred places and who so opposed the demons themselves, and the rites of impious sacrifices, that they seemed to be carrying on a far more terrible war with them than with men. Thus did the true Lord and Governor of things both scourge the Romans mercifully and, by the marvellous defeat of the worshippers of demons, show that those sacrifices were not necessary even for the safety of present things; so that, by those who do not obstinately hold out, but prudently consider the matter, true religion may not be deserted on account of the urgencies of the present time, but may be more clung to in most confident expectation of eternal life.

CHAP. 24. *What was the happiness of the Christian emperors, and how far it was true happiness*

For neither do we say that certain Christian emperors were therefore happy because they ruled a long time, or, dying a peaceful death, left their sons to succeed them in the empire, or subdued the enemies of the republic, or were able both to guard against and to suppress the attempt of hostile citizens rising against them. These and other gifts or comforts of this sorrowful life even certain worshippers of demons have merited to receive, who do not belong to the kingdom of God to which these belong; and this is to be traced to the mercy of God, Who would not have those who believe in Him desire such things as the highest good. But we say that they are happy if they rule justly; if they are not lifted up amid the praises of those who pay them sublime honours and the obsequiousness of those who salute them with an excessive humility, but remember that they are men; if they make their power the handmaid of His majesty by using it for the greatest possible extension of His worship; if they fear, love, worship God; if more than their own they love that kingdom in which they are not afraid to have partners; if they are slow to punish, ready to pardon; if they apply that punishment as necessary to government and defence of the republic, and not in order to gratify their own enmity; if they grant pardon, not that iniquity may go unpunished, but with the hope that the transgressor may amend his ways; if they compensate with the lenity of mercy and the liberality of benevolence for whatever severity they may be compelled to decree; if their luxury is as much restrained as it might have been unrestrained; if they prefer to govern depraved desires rather than any nation whatever; and if they do all these things, not through ardent desire of empty glory, but through love of eternal felicity, not neglecting to offer to the true God, who is their God, for their sins, the sacrifices of humility, contrition, and prayer. Such Christian emperors, we say, are happy in the present time by hope, and are destined to be so in the enjoyment of the reality itself, when that which we wait for shall have arrived.

CHAP. 25. *Concerning the prosperity which God granted to the Christian Emperor Constantine*

For the good God, lest men, who believe that He is to be worshipped with a view to eternal life, should think that no one could attain to all this high estate, and to this terrestrial dominion, unless he should be a worshipper of the demons —supposing that these spirits have great power with respect to such things—for this reason He gave to the Emperor Constantine, who was not a worshipper of demons, but of the true God

Himself, such fullness of earthly gifts as no one would even dare wish for. To him also He granted the honour of founding a city,[1] a companion to the Roman empire, the daughter, as it were, of Rome itself, but without any temple or image of the demons. He reigned for a long period as sole emperor and unaided held and defended the whole Roman world. In conducting and carrying on wars he was most victorious; in overthrowing tyrants he was most successful. He died at a great age, of sickness and old age, and left his sons to succeed him in the empire.[2] But again, lest any emperor should become a Christian in order to merit the happiness of Constantine, when every one should be a Christian for the sake of eternal life, God took away Jovian far sooner than Julian, and permitted that Gratian should be slain by the sword of a tyrant. But in his case there was far more mitigation of the calamity than in the case of the great Pompey, for he could not be avenged by Cato, whom he had left, as it were, heir to the civil war. But Gratian, though pious minds require not such consolations, was avenged by Theodosius, whom he had associated with himself in the empire, though he had a little brother of his own, being more desirous of a faithful alliance than of extensive power.

CHAP. 26. *On the faith and piety of Theodosius Augustus*

And on this account, Theodosius not only preserved during the lifetime of Gratian that fidelity which was due to him, but also, after his death, he, like a true Christian, took his little brother Valentinianus under his protection, as joint emperor, after he had been expelled by Maximus, the murderer of his father. He guarded him with paternal affection, though he might without any difficulty have got rid of him, being entirely destitute of all resources, had he been animated with the desire of extensive empire and not with the ambition of being a benefactor. It was therefore a far greater pleasure to him, when he had adopted the boy and preserved to him his imperial dignity, to console him by his very humanity and kindness. Afterwards, when that success was rendering Maximus terrible, Theodosius, in the midst of his perplexing anxieties, was not drawn away to follow the suggestions of a sacrilegious and unlawful curiosity, but sent to John, whose abode was in the desert of Egypt—for he had learned that this servant

---

[1]Constantinople.
[2]Constantius, Constantine, and Constans.

of God (whose fame was spreading abroad) was endowed with the gift of prophecy—and from him he received assurance of victory. Immediately the slayer of the tyrant Maximus, with the deepest feelings of compassion and respect, restored the boy Valentinianus to his share in the empire from which he had been driven. Valentinianus being soon after slain by secret assassination, or by some other plot or accident, Theodosius, having again received a response from the prophet, and placing entire confidence in it, marched against the tyrant Eugenius, who had been unlawfully elected to succeed that emperor, and defeated his very powerful army, more by prayer than by the sword. Some soldiers who were at the battle reported to me that all the missiles they were throwing were snatched from their hands by a vehement wind, which blew from the direction of Theodosius' army upon the enemy; nor did it only drive with greater velocity the darts which were hurled against them, but also turned back upon their own bodies the darts which they themselves were throwing. And therefore the poet Claudian, although an alien from the name of Christ, nevertheless says in his praises of him, "O prince, too much beloved by God, for thee Æolus pours armed tempests from their caves; for thee the air fights, and the winds with one accord obey thy bugles." But the victor, as he had believed and predicted, overthrew the statues of Jupiter, which had been, as it were, consecrated by I know not what kind of rites against him and set up in the Alps. And the thunderbolts of these statues, which were made of gold, he mirthfully and graciously presented to his couriers, who (as the joy of the occasion permitted) were jocularly saying that they would be most happy to be struck by such thunderbolts. The sons of his own enemies, whose fathers had been slain not so much by his orders as by the vehemence of war, having fled for refuge to a church, though they were not yet Christians, he was anxious, taking advantage of the occasion, to bring over to Christianity, and treated them with Christian love. Nor did he deprive them of their property, but, besides allowing them to retain it, bestowed on them additional honours. He did not permit private animosities to affect the treatment of any man after the war. He was not like Cinna, and Marius, and Sulla, and other such men, who wished not to finish civil wars even when they were finished, but rather grieved that they had arisen at all, than wished that when they were finished they should harm any one. Amid all these events, from the very commencement of his reign, he

did not cease to help the troubled Church against the impious by most just and merciful laws, which the heretical Valens, favouring the Arians, had vehemently afflicted. Indeed, he rejoiced more to be a member of this Church than he did to be a king upon the earth. The idols of the Gentiles he everywhere ordered to be overthrown, understanding well that not even terrestrial gifts are placed in the power of demons, but in that of the true God. And what could be more admirable than his religious humility, when, compelled by the urgency of certain of his intimates, he avenged the grievous crime of the Thessalonians, which at the prayer of the bishops he had promised to pardon, and, being laid hold of by the discipline of the Church, did penance in such a way that the sight of his imperial loftiness prostrated made the people who were interceding for him weep more than the consciousness of offence had made them fear it when enraged? These and other similar good works, which it would be long to tell, he carried with him from this world of time, where the greatest human nobility and loftiness are but vapour. Of these works the reward is eternal happiness, of which God is the giver, though only to those who are sincerely pious. But all other blessings and privileges of this life, as the world itself, light, air, earth, water, fruits, and the soul of man himself, his body, senses, mind, life, He lavishes on good and bad alike. And among these blessings is also to be reckoned the possession of an empire, whose extent He regulates according to the requirements of His providential government at various times. Whence, I see we must now answer those who, being confuted and convicted by the most manifest proofs, by which it is shown that for obtaining these terrestrial things, which are all the foolish desire to have, that multitude of false gods is of no use, attempt to assert that the gods are to be worshipped with a view to the interest, not of the present life, but of that which is to come after death. For as to those who, for the sake of the friendship of this world, are willing to worship vanities and do not grieve that they are left to their puerile understandings, I think they have been sufficiently answered in these five books; of which books, when I had published the first three, and they had begun to come into the hands of many, I heard that certain persons were preparing against them an answer of some kind or other in writing. Then it was told me that they had already written their answer, but were waiting a time when they could publish it without danger. Such persons I would advise not to desire what cannot be of any advantage to them; for it is very easy for a man to seem to himself to have answered arguments, when he has only been unwilling to be silent. For what is more loquacious than vanity? And though it be able, if it like, to shout more loudly than the truth, it is not, for all that, more powerful than the truth. But let men consider diligently all the things that we have said, and if, perchance, judging without party spirit, they shall clearly perceive that they are such things as may rather be shaken than torn up by their most impudent garrulity, and, as it were, satirical and mimic levity, let them restrain their absurdities, and let them choose rather to be corrected by the wise than to be lauded by the foolish. For if they are waiting an opportunity, not for liberty to speak the truth, but for licence to revile, may not that befall them which Tully says concerning some one, "Oh, wretched man! who was at liberty to sin"? Wherefore, whoever he be who deems himself happy because of licence to revile, he would be far happier if that were not allowed him at all; for he might all the while, laying aside empty boast, be contradicting those to whose views he is opposed by way of free consultation with them and be listening, as it becomes him, honourably, gravely, candidly, to all that can be adduced by those whom he consults by friendly disputation.

BOOK VI

ARGUMENT. HITHERTO THE ARGUMENT HAS BEEN CONDUCTED AGAINST THOSE WHO BELIEVE THAT THE GODS ARE TO BE WORSHIPPED FOR THE SAKE OF TEMPORAL ADVANTAGES; NOW IT IS DIRECTED AGAINST THOSE WHO BELIEVE THAT THEY ARE TO BE WORSHIPPED FOR THE SAKE OF ETERNAL LIFE. AUGUSTINE DEVOTES THE FIVE FOLLOWING BOOKS TO THE CONFUTATION OF THIS LATTER BELIEF, AND FIRST OF ALL SHOWS HOW MEAN AN OPINION OF THE GODS WAS HELD BY VARRO HIMSELF, THE MOST ESTEEMED WRITER ON HEATHEN THEOLOGY. OF THIS THEOLOGY AUGUSTINE ADOPTS VARRO'S DIVISION INTO THREE KINDS, MYTHICAL, NATURAL, AND CIVIL; AND AT ONCE DEMONSTRATES THAT NEITHER THE MYTHICAL NOR THE CIVIL CAN CONTRIBUTE ANYTHING TO THE HAPPINESS OF THE FUTURE LIFE.

PREFACE

IN the five former books, I think I have sufficiently disputed against those who believe that the many false gods, which the Christian truth shows to be useless images, or unclean spirits and pernicious demons, or certainly creatures, not the Creator, are to be worshipped for the advantage of this mortal life, and of terrestrial affairs, with that rite and service which the Greeks call λατρεία, and which is due to the one true God. And who does not know that, in the face of excessive stupidity and obstinacy, neither these five nor any other number of books whatsoever could be enough, when it is esteemed the glory of vanity to yield to no amount of strength on the side of truth—certainly to his destruction over whom so heinous a vice tyrannizes? For, notwithstanding all the assiduity of the physician who attempts to effect a cure, the disease remains unconquered, not through any fault of his, but because of the incurableness of the sick man. But those who thoroughly weigh the things which they read, having understood and considered them, without any, or with no great and excessive degree of that obstinacy which belongs to a long-cherished error, will more readily judge that, in the five books already finished, we have done more than the necessity of the question demanded, than that we have given it less discussion than it required. And they cannot have doubted but that all the hatred which the ignorant attempt to bring upon the Christian religion on account of the disasters of this life, and the destruction and change which befall terrestrial things, whilst the learned do not merely dissimulate, but encourage that hatred, contrary to their own consciences, being possessed by a mad impiety; they cannot have doubted, I say, but that this hatred is devoid of right reflection and reason, and full of most light temerity, and most pernicious animosity.

CHAP. I. *Of those who maintain that they worship the gods not for the sake of temporal but eternal advantages*

Now, as, in the next place (as the promised order demands), those are to be refuted and taught who contend that the gods of the nations, which the Christian truth destroys, are to be worshipped not on account of this life, but on account of that which is to be after death, I shall do well to commence my disputation with the truthful oracle of the holy psalm, "Blessed is the man whose hope is the Lord God, and who respecteth not vanities and lying follies."[1] Nevertheless, in all vanities and lying follies the philosophers are to be listened to with far more toleration, who have repudiated those opinions and errors of the people; for the people set up images to the deities, and either feigned concerning those whom they call immortal gods many false and unworthy things, or believed them, already feigned, and, when believed, mixed them up with their worship and sacred rites.

With those men who, though not by free avowal of their convictions, do still testify that they disapprove of those things by their muttering disapprobation during disputations on the subject, it may not be very far amiss to discuss the following question: Whether, for the sake of the life which is to be after death, we ought to worship, not the one God, Who made all creatures spiritual and corporeal, but those many gods who, as some of these philosophers hold, were made by that one God, and placed by Him in their respective sublime spheres, and are therefore considered more excellent and more noble than all the others?[2] But who will assert that it must be affirmed and contended that those gods, certain of whom I have mentioned in the fourth book,[3] to whom are distributed, each to each, the charges of minute things, do bestow eternal life? But will those most skilled and most acute men, who glory in having written for the great benefit of men, to teach on what account each god is to be worshipped, and what is to be sought from each, lest with most disgraceful absurdity, such as a mimic is wont for the sake of merriment to exhibit, water should be sought from Liber, wine from the Lymphs—will those men indeed affirm to any man supplicating the immortal gods, that when he shall have asked wine from the Lymphs, and they shall have answered him, "We have water, seek wine from Liber," he may rightly say, "If ye have not wine, at least give me eternal life"? What more monstrous than this absurdity? Will not these Lymphs—for they are wont to be very easily made laugh[4]—laughing loudly (if they do not attempt to deceive like demons), answer the suppliant, "O man, dost thou think that we have life (*vitam*) in our power, who thou hearest have not even the vine (*vitem*)?" It is therefore

most impudent folly to seek and hope for eternal life from such gods as are asserted so to preside over the separate minute concernments of this most sorrowful and short life, and whatever is useful for supporting and propping it, as that if anything which is under the care and power of one be sought from another, it is so incongruous and absurd that it appears very like to mimic drollery—which, when it is done by mimics knowing what they are doing, is deservedly laughed at in the theatre, but when it is done by foolish persons, who do not know better, is more deservedly ridiculed in the world. Wherefore, as concerns those gods which the states have established, it has been cleverly invented and handed down to memory by learned men, what god or goddess is to be supplicated in relation to every particular thing—what, for instance, is to be sought from Liber, what from the Lymphs, what from Vulcan, and so of all the rest, some of whom I have mentioned in the fourth book, and some I have thought right to omit. Further, if it is an error to seek wine from Ceres, bread from Liber, water from Vulcan, fire from the Lymphs, how much greater absurdity ought it to be thought, if supplication be made to any one of these for eternal life?

Wherefore, if, when we were inquiring what gods or goddesses are to be believed to be able to confer earthly kingdoms upon men, all things having been discussed, it was shown to be very far from the truth to think that even terrestrial kingdoms are established by any of those many false deities, is it not most insane impiety to believe that eternal life, which is, without any doubt or comparison, to be preferred to all terrestrial kingdoms, can be given to any one by any of these gods? For the reason why such gods seemed to us not to be able to give even an earthly kingdom, was not because they are very great and exalted, whilst that is something small and abject, which they, in their so great sublimity, would not condescend to care for, but because, however deservedly any one may, in consideration of human frailty, despise the falling pinnacles of an earthly kingdom, these gods have presented such an appearance as to seem most unworthy to have the granting and preserving of even those entrusted to them; and consequently, if (as we have taught in the two last books of our work, where this matter is treated of) no god out of all that crowd, either belonging to, as it were, the plebeian or to the noble gods, is fit to give mortal kingdoms to mortals, how much less is he able to make immortals of mortals?

[1]Ps. 40. 4.   [2]Plato, in the *Timæus*.
[3]Chaps. 11 and 21.   [4]See Virgil, *Eclogues*, III. 9.

And more than this, if, according to the opinion of those with whom we are now arguing, the gods are to be worshipped, not on account of the present life, but of that which is to be after death, then, certainly, they are not to be worshipped on account of those particular things which are distributed and portioned out (not by any law of rational truth, but by mere vain conjecture) to the power of such gods, as they believe they ought to be worshipped, who contend that their worship is necessary for all the desirable things of this mortal life, against whom I have disputed sufficiently, as far I was able, in the five preceding books. These things being so, if the age itself of those who worshipped the goddess Juventas should be characterized by remarkable vigour, whilst her despisers should either die within the years of youth, or should, during that period, grow cold as with the torpor of old age; if bearded Fortuna should cover the cheeks of her worshippers more handsomely and more gracefully than all others, whilst we should see those by whom she was despised either altogether beardless or ill-bearded; even then we should most rightly say that thus far these several gods had power, limited in some way by their functions, and that, consequently, neither ought eternal life to be sought from Juventas, who could not give a beard, nor ought any good thing after this life to be expected from Fortuna Barbata, who has no power even in this life to give the age itself at which the beard grows. But now, when their worship is necessary not even on account of those very things which they think are subjected to their power—for many worshippers of the goddess Juventas have not been at all vigorous at that age, and many who do not worship her rejoice in youthful strength; and also many suppliants of Fortuna Barbata have either not been able to attain to any beard at all, not even an ugly one, although they who adore her in order to obtain a beard are ridiculed by her bearded despisers—is the human heart really so foolish as to believe that that worship of the gods, which it acknowledges to be vain and ridiculous with respect to those very temporal and swiftly passing gifts, over each of which one of these gods is said to preside, is fruitful in results with respect to eternal life? And that they are able to give eternal life has not been affirmed even by those who, that they might be worshipped by the silly populace, distributed in minute division among them these temporal occupations, that none of them might sit idle; for they had supposed the existence of an exceedingly great number.

CHAP. 2. *What we are to believe that Varro thought concerning the gods of the nations, whose various kinds and sacred rites he has shown to be such that he would have acted more reverently towards them had he been altogether silent concerning them*

Who has investigated those things more carefully than Marcus Varro? Who has discovered them more learnedly? Who has considered them more attentively? Who has distinguished them more acutely? Who has written about them more diligently and more fully?—who, though he is less pleasing in his eloquence, is nevertheless so full of instruction and wisdom, that in all the erudition which we call secular, but they liberal, he will teach the student of things as much as Cicero delights the student of words. And even Tully himself renders him such testimony, as to say in his Academic books that he had held that disputation which is there carried on with Marcus Varro, "a man," he adds, "unquestionably the acutest of all men, and, without any doubt, the most learned." He does not say the most eloquent or the most fluent, for in reality he was very deficient in this faculty, but he says, "of all men the most acute." And in those books—that is, the Academic—where he contends that all things are to be doubted, he adds of him, "without any doubt the most learned." In truth, he was so certain concerning this thing, that he laid aside that doubt which he is wont to have recourse to in all things, as if, when about to dispute in favour of the doubt of the Academics, he had, with respect to this one thing, forgotten that he was an Academic. But in the first book, when he extols the literary works of the same Varro, he says, "Us straying and wandering in our own city like strangers, thy books, as it were, brought home that at length we might come to know of who we were and where we were. Thou has opened up to us the age of the country, the distribution of seasons, the laws of sacred things, and of the priests; thou hast opened up to us domestic and public discipline; thou hast pointed out to us the proper places for religious ceremonies, and hast informed us concerning sacred places. Thou hast shown us the names, kinds, offices, causes of all divine and human things."

This man, then, of so distinguished and excellent acquirements, and, as Terentian briefly says of him in a most elegant verse,

Varro, a man universally informed

who read so much that we wonder when he had

time to write, wrote so much that we can scarcely believe any one could have read it all—this man, I say, so great in talent, so great in learning, had he been an opposer and destroyer of the so-called divine things of which he wrote and had he said that they pertained to superstition rather than to religion, might perhaps, even in that case, not have written so many things which are ridiculous, contemptible, detestable. But when he so worshipped these same gods and so vindicated their worship as to say, in that same literary work of his, that he was afraid lest they should perish, not by an assault by enemies, but by the negligence of the citizens, and that from this ignominy they are being delivered by him, and are being laid up and preserved in the memory of the good by means of such books, with a zeal far more beneficial than that through which Metellus is declared to have rescued the sacred things of Vesta from the flames, and Æneas to have rescued the Penates from the burning of Troy; and when he, nevertheless, gives forth such things to be read by succeeding ages as are deservedly judged by wise and unwise to be unfit to be read and to be most hostile to the truth of religion, what ought we to think but that a most acute and learned man—not, however, made free by the Holy Spirit—was overpowered by the custom and laws of his state and, not being able to be silent about those things by which he was influenced, spoke of them under pretence of commending religion?

CHAP. 3. *Varro's distribution of his book which he composed concerning the antiquities of human and divine things*

He wrote forty-one books of antiquities. These he divided into human and divine things. Twenty-five he devoted to human things, sixteen to divine things; following this plan in that division—namely, to give six books to each of the four divisions of human things. For he directs his attention to these considerations: who perform, where they perform, when they perform, what they perform. Therefore in the first six books he wrote concerning men; in the second six, concerning places; in the third six, concerning times; in the fourth and last six, concerning things. Four times six, however, make only twenty-four. But he placed at the head of them one separate work, which spoke of all these things conjointly.

In divine things, the same order he preserved throughout, as far as concerns those things which are performed to the gods. For sacred things are performed by men in places and times. These four things I have mentioned he embraced in twelve books, allotting three to each. For he wrote the first three concerning men, the following three concerning places, the third three concerning times, and the fourth three concerning sacred rites—showing who should perform, where they should perform, when they should perform, what they should perform, with most subtle distinction. But because it was necessary to say—and that especially was expected—to whom they should perform sacred rites, he wrote concerning the gods themselves the last three books; and these five times three made fifteen. But they are in all, as we have said, sixteen. For he put also at the beginning of these one distinct book, speaking by way of introduction of all which follows; which being finished, he proceeded to subdivide the first three in that five-fold distribution which pertain to men, making the first concerning high priests, the second concerning augurs, the third concerning the fifteen men presiding over the sacred ceremonies. The second three he made concerning places, speaking in one of them concerning their chapels, in the second concerning their temples, and in the third concerning religious places. The next three which follow these and pertain to times—that is, to festival days—he distributed so as to make one concerning holidays, the other concerning the circus games, and the third concerning scenic plays. Of the fourth three, pertaining to sacred things, he devoted one to consecrations, another to private, the last to public, sacred rites. In the three which remain, the gods themselves follow this pompous train, as it were, for whom all this culture has been expended. In the first book are the certain gods, in the second the uncertain, in the third, and last of all, the chief and select gods.

CHAP. 4. *That from the disputation of Varro, it follows that the worshippers of the gods regard human things as more ancient than divine things*

In this whole series of most beautiful and most subtle distributions and distinctions, it will most easily appear evident from the things we have said already and from what is to be said hereafter, to any man who is not, in the obstinacy of his heart, an enemy to himself, that it is vain to seek and to hope for and even most impudent to wish for eternal life. For these institutions are either the work of men or of demons —not of those whom they call good demons, but, to speak more plainly, of unclean, and, without controversy, malign spirits, who with wonderful slyness and secretness suggest to the thoughts of the impious, and sometimes openly present to their understandings, noxious opinions, by which the human mind grows more and more foolish, and becomes unable to adapt itself to and abide in the immutable and eternal truth, and seek to confirm these opinions by every kind of fallacious attestation in their power. This very same Varro testifies that he wrote first concerning human things, but afterwards concerning divine things, because the states existed first, and afterward these things were instituted by them. But the true religion was not instituted by any earthly state, but plainly it established the celestial city. It, however, is inspired and taught by the true God, the giver of eternal life to His true worshippers.

The following is the reason Varro gives when he confesses that he had written first concerning human things and afterwards of divine things, because these divine things were instituted by men: "As the painter is before the painted tablet, the mason before the edifice, so states are before those things which are instituted by states." But he says that he would have written first concerning the gods, afterwards concerning men, if he had been writing concerning the whole nature of the gods—as if he were really writing concerning some portion of, and not all, the nature of the gods; or as if, indeed, some portion of, though not all, the nature of the gods ought not to be put before that of men. How, then, comes it that in those three last books, when he is diligently explaining the certain, uncertain and select gods, he seems to pass over no portion of the nature of the gods? Why, then, does he say, "If we had been writing on the whole nature of the gods, we would first have finished the divine things before we touched the human"? For he either writes concerning the whole nature of the gods, or concerning some portion of it, or concerning no part of it at all. If concerning it all, it is certainly to be put before human things; if concerning some part of it, why should it not, from the very nature of the case, precede human things? Is not even some part of the gods to be preferred to the whole of humanity? But if it is too much to prefer a part of the divine to all human things, that part is certainly worthy to be preferred to the Romans at least. For he writes the books concerning human things, not with reference to the whole world, but only to Rome; which books he says he had properly placed, in the order of writing, before the books on divine things, like a painter before the painted tablet, or a mason

before the building, most openly confessing that, as a picture or a structure, even these divine things were instituted by men. There remains only the third supposition, that he is to be understood to have written concerning no divine nature, but that he did not wish to say this openly, but left it to the intelligent to infer; for when one says "not all," usage understands that to mean "some," but it *may* be understood as meaning *none,* because that which is *none* is neither all nor some. In fact, as he himself says, if he had been writing concerning all the nature of the gods, its due place would have been before human things in the order of writing. But, as the truth declares, even though Varro is silent, the divine nature should have taken precedence of Roman things, though it were not *all,* but only some. But it is properly put after, therefore it is *none.* His arrangement, therefore, was due, not to a desire to give human things priority to divine things, but to his unwillingness to prefer false things to true. For in what he wrote on human things, he followed the history of affairs; but in what he wrote concerning those things which they call divine, what else did he follow but mere conjectures about vain things? This, doubtless, is what, in a subtle manner, he wished to signify; not only writing concerning divine things after the human, but even giving a reason why he did so; for if he had suppressed this, some, perchance, would have defended his doing so in one way, and some in another. But in that very reason he has rendered, he has left nothing for men to conjecture at will, and has sufficiently proved that he preferred men to the institutions of men, not the nature of men to the nature of the gods. Thus he confessed that, in writing the books concerning divine things, he did not write concerning the truth which belongs to nature, but the falseness which belongs to error; which he has elsewhere expressed more openly (as I have mentioned in the fourth book),[1] saying that, had he been founding a new city himself, he would have written according to the order of nature; but as he had only found an old one, he could not but follow its custom.

CHAP. 5. *Concerning the three kinds of theology according to Varro, namely, one fabulous, the other natural, the third civil*

Now what are we to say of this proposition of his, namely, that there are three kinds of theology, that is, of the account which is given of the gods; and of these, the one is called myth-

[1]Chap. 31.

ical, the other physical, and the third civil? Did the Latin usage permit, we should call the kind which he has placed first in order *fabular,* but let us call it *fabulous,* for mythical is derived from the Greek μῦθος, a fable; but that the second should be called *natural,* the usage of speech now admits; the third he himself has designated in Latin, calling it *civil.* Then he says, "they call that kind *mythical* which the poets chiefly use; *physical,* that which the philosophers use; *civil,* that which the people use. As to the first I have mentioned," says he, "in it are many fictions, which are contrary to the dignity and nature of the immortals. For we find in it that one god has been born from the head, another from the thigh, another from drops of blood; also, in this we find that gods have stolen, committed adultery, served men; in a word, in this all manner of things are attributed to the gods, such as may befall, not merely any man, but even the most contemptible man." He certainly, where he could, where he dared, where he thought he could do it with impunity, has manifested, without any of the haziness of ambiguity, how great injury was done to the nature of the gods by lying fables; for he was speaking, not concerning natural theology, not concerning civil, but concerning fabulous theology, which he thought he could freely find fault with.

Let us see, now, what he says concerning the second kind. "The second kind which I have explained," he says, "is that concerning which philosophers have left many books, in which they treat such questions as these: what gods there are, where they are, of what kind and character they are, since what time they have existed, or if they have existed from eternity; whether they are of fire, as Heraclitus believes; or of number, as Pythagoras; or of atoms, as Epicurus says; and other such things, which men's ears can more easily hear inside the walls of a school than outside in the Forum." He finds fault with nothing in this kind of theology which they call *physical,* and which belongs to philosophers, except that he has related their controversies among themselves, through which there has arisen a multitude of dissentient sects. Nevertheless he has removed this kind from the Forum, that is, from the populace, but he has shut it up in schools. But that first kind, most false and most base, he has not removed from the citizens. Oh, the religious ears of the people, and among them even those of the Romans, that are not able to bear what the philosophers dispute concerning the gods! But when the poets sing and stage-

players act such things as are derogatory to the dignity and the nature of the immortals, such as may befall not a man merely, but the most contemptible man, they not only bear, but willingly listen to. Nor is this all, but they even consider that these things please the gods, and that they are propitiated by them.

But some one may say, "Let us distinguish these two kinds of theology, the mythical and the physical—that is, the fabulous and the natural—from this civil kind about which we are now speaking." Anticipating this, he himself has distinguished them. Let us see now how he explains the civil theology itself. I see, indeed, why it should be distinguished as fabulous, even because it is false, because it is base, because it is unworthy. But to wish to distinguish the natural from the civil, what else is that but to confess that the civil itself is false? For if that be natural, what fault has it that it should be excluded? And if this which is called civil be not natural, what merit has it that it should be admitted? This, in truth, is the cause why he wrote first concerning human things, and afterwards concerning divine things; since in divine things he did not follow nature, but the institution of men. Let us look at this civil theology of his. "The third kind," says he, "is that which citizens in cities, and especially the priests, ought to know and to administer. From it is to be known what god each one may suitably worship, what sacred rites and sacrifices each one may suitably perform." Let us still attend to what follows. "The first theology," he says, "is especially adapted to the theatre, the second to the world, the third to the city." Who does not see to which he gives the palm? Certainly to the second, which he said above is that of the philosophers. For he testifies that this pertains to the world, than which they think there is nothing better. But those two theologies, the first and the third—to wit, those of the theatre and of the city—has he distinguished them or united them? For although we see that the city is in the world, we do not see that it follows that any things belonging to the city pertain to the world. For it is possible that such things may be worshipped and believed in the city, according to false opinions, as have no existence either in the world or out of it. But where is the theatre but in the city? Who instituted the theatre but the state? For what purpose did it constitute it but for scenic plays? And to what class of things do scenic plays belong but to those divine things concerning which these books of Varro's are written with so much ability?

CHAP. 6. *Concerning the mythic, that is, the fabulous, theology, and the civil, against Varro*

O Marcus Varro! thou art the most acute, and without doubt the most learned, but still a man, not God—now lifted up by the Spirit of God to see and to announce divine things, thou seest, indeed, that divine things are to be separated from human trifles and lies, but thou fearest to offend those most corrupt opinions of the populace and their customs in public superstitions, which thou thyself, when thou considerest them on all sides, perceivest, and all your literature loudly pronounces to be abhorrent from the nature of the gods, even of such gods as the frailty of the human mind supposes to exist in the elements of this world. What can the most excellent human talent do here? What can human learning, though manifold, avail thee in this perplexity? Thou desirest to worship the natural gods; thou art compelled to worship the civil. Thou hast found some of the gods to be fabulous, on whom thou vomitest forth very freely what thou thinkest, and, whether thou willest or not, thou wettest therewith even the civil gods. Thou sayest, forsooth, that the fabulous are adapted to the theatre, the natural to the world, and the civil to the city; though the world is a divine work, but cities and theatres are the works of men, and though the gods who are laughed at in the theatre are not other than those who are adored in the temples; and ye do not exhibit games in honour of other gods than those to whom ye immolate victims. How much more freely and more subtly wouldst thou have decided these hadst thou said that some gods are natural, others established by men; and concerning those who have been so established, the literature of the poets gives one account, and that of the priests another—both of which are, nevertheless, so friendly the one to the other, through fellowship in falsehood, that they are both pleasing to the demons, to whom the doctrine of the truth is hostile.

That theology, therefore, which they call natural, being put aside for a moment, as it is afterwards to be discussed, we ask if any one is really content to seek a hope for eternal life from poetical, theatrical, scenic gods? Perish the thought! The true God avert so wild and sacrilegious a madness! What, is eternal life to be asked from those gods whom these things pleased and whom these things propitiate, in which their own crimes are represented? No one, as I think, has arrived at such a pitch of headlong and furious impiety. So then, neither by the fabulous nor by the civil theology does any one obtain eternal life. For the one sows base things concerning the gods by feigning them, the other reaps by cherishing them; the one scatters lies, the other gathers them together; the one pursues divine things with false crimes, the other incorporates among divine things the plays which are made up of these crimes; the one sounds abroad in human songs impious fictions concerning the gods, the other consecrates these for the festivities of the gods themselves; the one sings the misdeeds and crimes of the gods, the other loves them; the one gives forth or feigns, the other either attests the true or delights in the false. Both are base; both are damnable. But the one which is theatrical teaches public abomination, and that one which is of the city adorns itself with that abomination. Shall eternal life be hoped for from these, by which this short and temporal life is polluted? Does the society of wicked men pollute our life if they insinuate themselves into our affections and win our assent? and does not the society of demons pollute the life, who are worshipped with their own crimes?—if with true crimes, how wicked the demons! if with false, how wicked the worship!

When we say these things, it may perchance seem to some one who is very ignorant of these matters that only those things concerning the gods which are sung in the songs of the poets and acted on the stage are unworthy of the divine majesty, and ridiculous, and too detestable to be celebrated, whilst those sacred things which not stage-players but priests perform are pure and free from all unseemliness. Had this been so, never would any one have thought that these theatrical abominations should be celebrated in their honour, never would the gods themselves have ordered them to be performed to them. But men are in nowise ashamed to perform these things in the theatres, because similar things are carried on in the temples. In short, when the fore-mentioned author attempted to distinguish the civil theology from the fabulous and natural, as a sort of third and distinct kind, he wished it to be understood to be rather tempered by both than separated from either. For he says that those things which the poets write are less than the people ought to follow, whilst what the philosophers say is more than it is expedient for the people to pry into. "Which," says he, "differ in such a way, that nevertheless not a few things from both of them have been taken to the account of the civil theology; wherefore we will indicate what the civil theology has in common with that of the poet, though it ought to be more closely connected with the theology of philosophers." Civil theology is therefore not quite disconnected from that of the poets. Nevertheless, in another place, concerning the generations of the gods, he says that the people are more inclined toward the poets than toward the physical theologists. For in this place he said what ought to be done; in that other place, what was really done. He said that the latter had written for the sake of utility, but the poets for the sake of amusement. And hence the things from the poets' writings, which the people ought not to follow, are the crimes of the gods; which, nevertheless, amuse both the people and the gods. For, for amusement's sake, he says, the poets write, and not for that of utility; nevertheless they write such things as the gods will desire, and the people perform.

CHAP. 7. *Concerning the likeness and agreement of the fabulous and civil theologies*

That theology, therefore, which is fabulous, theatrical, scenic, and full of all baseness and unseemliness, is taken up into the civil theology; and part of that theology, which in its totality is deservedly judged to be worthy of reprobation and rejection, is pronounced worthy to be cultivated and observed—not at all an incongruous part, as I have undertaken to show, and one which, being alien to the whole body, was unsuitably attached to and suspended from it, but a part entirely congruous with, and most harmoniously fitted to the rest, as a member of the same body. For what else do those images, forms, ages, sexes, characteristics of the gods show? If the poets have Jupiter with a beard, and Mercury beardless, have not the priests the same? Is the Priapus of the priests less obscene than the Priapus of the players? Does he receive the adoration of worshippers in a different form from that in which he moves about the stage for the amusement of spectators? Is not Saturn old and Apollo young in the shrines where their images stand, as well as when represented by actors' masks? Why are Forculus, who presides over doors, and Limentinus, who presides over thresholds and lintels, male gods, and Cardea between them feminine, who presides over hinges? Are not those things found in books on divine things, which grave poets have deemed unworthy of their verses? Does the Diana of the theatre carry arms, whilst the Diana of the city is simply a virgin? Is the stage Apollo a lyrist, but the Delphic Apollo ignorant of this art? But these things are decent compared with the more shameful things. What was thought of Jupiter himself by those who placed his wet nurse in the Capitol? Did they not bear witness to Euhemerus, who, not with the garrulity of a fable-teller, but with the gravity of an historian who had diligently investigated the matter, wrote that all such gods had been men and mortals? And they who appointed the Epulones as parasites at the table of Jupiter, what else did they wish for but mimic sacred rites? For if any mimic had said that parasites of Jupiter were made use of at his table, he would assuredly have appeared to be seeking to call forth laughter. Varro said it —not when he was mocking, but when he was commending the gods did he say it. His books on divine, not on human, things testify that he wrote this—not where he set forth the scenic games, but where he explained the Capitoline laws. In a word, he is conquered, and confesses that, as they made the gods with a human form, so they believed that they are delighted with human pleasures.

For also malign spirits were not so wanting to their own business as not to confirm noxious opinions in the minds of men by converting them into sport. Whence also is that story about the sacristan of Hercules, which says that, having nothing to do, he took to playing at dice as a pastime, throwing them alternately with the one hand for Hercules, with the other for himself, with this understanding, that if he should win, he should from the funds of the temple prepare himself a supper, and hire a mistress; but if Hercules should win the game, he himself should, at his own expense, provide the same for the pleasure of Hercules. Then, when he had been beaten by himself, as though by Hercules, he gave to the god Hercules the supper he owed him, and also the most noble harlot Larentina. But she, having fallen asleep in the temple, dreamed that Hercules had had intercourse with her, and had said to her that she would find her payment with the youth whom she should first meet on leaving the temple, and that she was to believe this to be paid to her by Hercules. And so the first youth that met her on going out was the wealthy Tarutius, who kept her a long time, and when he died left her his heir. She, having obtained a most ample fortune, that she should not seem ungrateful for the divine hire, in her turn made the Roman people her heir, which she thought to be most acceptable to the deities; and, having disappeared, the will was found. By which meritorious conduct they say that she gained divine honours.

Now had these things been feigned by the poets and acted by the mimics, they would without any doubt have been said to pertain to the fabulous theology and would have been judged worthy to be separated from the dignity of the civil theology. But when these shameful things —not of the poets, but of the people; not of the mimics, but of the sacred things; not of the theatres, but of the temples, that is, not of the fabulous, but of the civil theology—are reported by so great an author, not in vain do the actors represent with theatrical art the baseness of the gods, which is so great; but surely in vain do the priests attempt, by rites called sacred, to represent their nobleness of character, which has no existence. There are sacred rites of Juno; and these are celebrated in her beloved island, Samos, where she was given in marriage to Jupiter. There are sacred rites of Ceres, in which Proserpine is sought for, having been carried off by Pluto. There are sacred rites of Venus, in which, her beloved Adonis being slain by a boar's tooth, the lovely youth is lamented. There are sacred rites of the mother of the gods, in which the beautiful youth Atys, loved by her, and castrated by her through a woman's jealousy, is deplored by men who have suffered the like calamity, whom they call Galli. Since, then, these things are more unseemly than all scenic abomination, why is it that they strive to separate, as it were, the fabulous fictions of the poet concerning the gods, as, forsooth, pertaining to the theatre, from the civil theology which they wish to belong to the city, as though they were separating from noble and worthy things, things unworthy and base? Wherefore there is more reason to thank the stage-actors, who have spared the eyes of men and have not laid bare by theatrical exhibition all the things which are hid by the walls of the temples. What good is to be thought of their sacred rites which are concealed in darkness, when those which are brought forth into the light are so detestable? And certainly they themselves have seen what they transact in secret through the agency of mutilated and effeminate men. Yet they have *not* been able to hide those same men miserably and vilely enervated and corrupted. Let them persuade whom they can that they transact anything holy through such men, who, they cannot deny, are numbered, and live among their sacred things. We know not what they transact, but we know through whom they transact; for we know what things are transacted on the stage, where never, even in a chorus of harlots, hath one who is mutilated or an effeminate appeared. And, nevertheless, even these things are acted by vile and infamous characters; for, indeed,

they ought not to be acted by men of good character. What, then, are those sacred rites, for the performance of which holiness has chosen such men as not even the obscenity of the stage has admitted?

CHAP. 8. *Concerning the interpretations, consisting of natural explanations, which the pagan teachers attempt to show for their gods*

But all these things, they say, have certain physical, that is, natural interpretations, showing their natural meaning; as though in this disputation we were seeking physics and not theology, which is the account, not of nature, but of God. For although He Who is the true God is God, not by opinion, but by nature, nevertheless all nature is not God; for there is certainly a nature of man, of a beast, of a tree, of a stone— none of which is God. For if, when the question is concerning the mother of the gods, that from which the whole system of interpretation starts certainly is that the mother of the gods is the earth, why do we make further inquiry? why do we carry our investigation through all the rest of it? What can more manifestly favour them who say that all those gods were men? For they are earth-born in the sense that the earth is their mother. But in the true theology the earth is the work, not the mother, of God. But in whatever way their sacred rites may be interpreted, and whatever reference they may have to the nature of things, it is not according to nature, but contrary to nature, that men should be effeminates. This disease, this crime, this abomination, has a recognized place among those sacred things, though even depraved men will scarcely be compelled by torments to confess they are guilty of it. Again, if these sacred rites, which are proved to be fouler than scenic abominations, are excused and justified on the ground that they have their own interpretations, by which they are shown to symbolize the nature of things, why are not the poetical things in like manner excused and justified? For many have interpreted even these in like fashion, to such a degree that even that which they say is the most monstrous and most horrible—namely, that Saturn devoured his own children—has been interpreted by some of them to mean that length of time, which is signified by the name of Saturn, consumes whatever it begets; or that, as the same Varro thinks, Saturn belongs to seeds which fall back again into the earth from whence they spring. And so one interprets it in one way, and one in another. And the same is to be said of all the rest of this theology.

And, nevertheless, it is called the fabulous theology, and is censured, cast off, rejected, together with all such interpretations belonging to it. And not only by the natural theology, which is that of the philosophers, but also by this civil theology, concerning which we are speaking, which is asserted to pertain to cities and peoples, it is judged worthy of repudiation, because it has invented unworthy things concerning the gods. Of which, I wot, this is the secret: that those most acute and learned men, by whom those things were written, understood that both theologies ought to be rejected—to wit, both that fabulous and this civil one—but the former they dared to reject, the latter they dared not; the former they set forth to be censured, the latter they showed to be very like it; not that it might be chosen to be held in preference to the other, but that it might be understood to be worthy of being rejected together with it. And thus, without danger to those who feared to censure the civil theology, both of them being brought into contempt, that theology which they call natural might find a place in better disposed minds; for the civil and the fabulous are both fabulous and both civil. He who shall wisely inspect the vanities and obscenities of both will find that they are both fabulous; and he who shall direct his attention to the scenic plays pertaining to the fabulous theology in the festivals of the civil gods, and in the divine rites of the cities, will find they are both civil. How, then, can the power of giving eternal life be attributed to any of those gods whose own images and sacred rites convict them of being most like to the fabulous gods, which are most openly reprobated, in forms, ages, sex, characteristics, marriages, generations, rites; in all which things they are understood either to have been men, and to have had their sacred rites and solemnities instituted in their honour according to the life or death of each of them, the demons suggesting and confirming this error, or certainly most foul spirits, who, taking advantage of some occasion or other, have stolen into the minds of men to deceive them?

Chap. 9. Concerning the special offices of the gods

And as to those very offices of the gods, so meanly and so minutely portioned out, so that they say that they ought to be supplicated, each one according to his special function—about which we have spoken much already, though not all that is to be said concerning it—are they not more consistent with mimic buffoonery than divine majesty? If any one should use two nurses for his infant, one of whom should give nothing but food, the other nothing but drink, as these make use of two goddesses for this purpose, Educa and Potina, he should certainly seem to be foolish, and to do in his house a thing worthy of a mimic. They would have Liber to have been named from "liberation," because through him males at the time of copulation are liberated by the emission of the seed. They also say that Libera (the same in their opinion as Venus) exercises the same function in the case of women, because they say that they also emit seed; and they also say that on this account the same part of the male and of the female is placed in the temple, that of the male to Liber, and that of the female to Libera. To these things they add the women assigned to Liber, and the wine for exciting lust. Thus the Bacchanalia are celebrated with the utmost insanity, with respect to which Varro himself confesses that such things would not be done by the Bacchanals except their minds were highly excited. These things, however, afterwards displeased a saner senate, and it ordered them to be discontinued. Here, at length, they perhaps perceived how much power unclean spirits, when held to be gods, exercise over the minds of men. These things, certainly, were not to be done in the theatres; for there they play, not rave, although to have gods who are delighted with such plays is very like raving.

But what kind of distinction is this which he makes between the religious and the superstitious man, saying that the gods are feared by the superstitious man, but are reverenced as parents by the religious man, not feared as enemies; and that they are all so good that they will more readily spare those who are impious than hurt one who is innocent? And yet he tells us that three gods are assigned as guardians to a woman after she has been delivered, lest the god Silvanus come in and molest her; and that in order to signify the presence of these protectors, three men go round the house during the night, and first strike the threshold with a hatchet, next with a pestle, and the third time sweep it with a brush, in order that these symbols of agriculture having been exhibited, the god Silvanus might be hindered from entering, because neither are trees cut down or pruned without a hatchet, neither is grain ground without a pestle, nor corn heaped up without a besom. Now from these three things three gods have been named: Intercidona, from the cut[1] made by the hatchet; Pilumnus, from the pestle; Diverra, from the

[1] *Intercido*, I cut or cleave.

besom; by which guardian gods the woman who has been delivered is preserved against the power of the god Silvanus. Thus the guardianship of kindly-disposed gods would not avail against the malice of a mischievous god, unless they were three to one, and fought against him, as it were, with the opposing emblems of cultivation, who, being an inhabitant of the woods, is rough, horrible, and uncultivated. Is this the innocence of the gods? Is this their concord? Are these the health-giving deities of the cities, more ridiculous than the things which are laughed at in the theatres?

When a male and a female are united, the god Jugatinus presides. Well, let this be borne with. But the married woman must be brought home: the god Domiducus also is invoked. That she may be in the house, the god Domitius is introduced. That she may remain with her husband, the goddess Manturnæ is used. What more is required? Let human modesty be spared. Let the lust of flesh and blood go on with the rest, the secret of shame being respected. Why is the bed-chamber filled with a crowd of deities, when even the groomsmen have departed? And, moreover, it is so filled, not that in consideration of their presence more regard may be paid to chastity, but that by their help the woman, naturally of the weaker sex, and trembling with the novelty of her situation, may the more readily yield her virginity. For there are the goddess Virginiensis, and the god-father Subigus, and the goddess-mother Prema, and the goddess Pertunda, and Venus, and Priapus. What is this? If it was absolutely necessary that a man labouring at this work, should be helped by the gods, might not some one god or goddess have been sufficient? Was Venus not sufficient alone, who is even said to be named from this, that without her power a woman does not cease to be a virgin? If there is any shame in men, which is not in the deities, is it not the case that, when the married couple believe that so many gods of either sex are present, and busy at this work, they are so much affected with shame, that the man is less moved, and the woman more reluctant? And certainly, if the goddess Virginiensis is present to loose the virgin's zone, if the god Subigus is present that the virgin may be got under the man, if the goddess Prema is present that, having been got under him, she may be kept down, and may not move herself, what has the goddess Pertunda to do there? Let her blush; let her go forth. Let the husband himself do something. It is disgraceful that any one but himself should do that from which she gets her

name. But perhaps she is tolerated because she is said to be a goddess, and not a god. For if she were believed to be a male, and were called Pertundus, the husband would demand more help against him for the chastity of his wife than the newly-delivered woman against Silvanus. But why am I saying this, when Priapus, too, is there, a male to excess, upon whose immense and most unsightly member the newly-married bride is commanded to sit, according to the most honourable and most religious custom of matrons?

Let them go on, and let them attempt with all the subtlety they can to distinguish the civil theology from the fabulous, the cities from the theatres, the temples from the stages, the sacred things of the priests from the songs of the poets, as honourable things from base things, truthful things from fallacious, grave from light, serious from ludicrous, desirable things from things to be rejected, we understand what they do. They are aware that that theatrical and fabulous theology hangs by the civil, and is reflected back upon it from the songs of the poets as from a mirror; and thus, that theology having been exposed to view which they do not dare to condemn, they more freely assail and censure that picture of it, in order that those who perceive what they mean may detest this very face itself of which that is the picture—which, however, the gods themselves, as though seeing themselves in the same mirror, love so much that it is better seen in both of them who and what they are. Whence, also, they have compelled their worshippers, with terrible commands, to dedicate to them the uncleanness of the fabulous theology, to put them among their solemnities, and reckon them among divine things; and thus they have both shown themselves more manifestly to be most impure spirits, and have made that rejected and reprobated theatrical theology a member and a part of this, as it were, chosen and approved theology of the city, so that, though the whole is disgraceful and false, and contains in it fictitious gods, one part of it is in the literature of the priests, the other in the songs of the poets. Whether it may have other parts is another question. At present, I think, I have sufficiently shown, on account of the division of Varro, that the theology of the city and that of the theatre belong to one civil theology. Wherefore, because they are both equally disgraceful, absurd, shameful, false, far be it from religious men to hope for eternal life from either the one or the other.

In fine, even Varro himself, in his account and

enumeration of the gods, starts from the moment of a man's conception. He commences the series of those gods who take charge of man with Janus, carries it on to the death of the man decrepit with age, and terminates it with the goddess Nænia, who is sung at the funerals of the aged. After that, he begins to give an account of the other gods, whose province is not man himself, but man's belongings, as food, clothing, and all that is necessary for this life; and, in the case of all these, he explains what is the special office of each, and for what each ought to be supplicated. But with all this scrupulous and comprehensive diligence, he has neither proved the existence, nor so much as mentioned the name, of any god from whom eternal life is to be sought —the one object for which we are Christians. Who, then, is so stupid as not to perceive that this man, by setting forth and opening up so diligently the civil theology, and by exhibiting its likeness to that fabulous, shameful, and disgraceful theology, and also by teaching that that fabulous sort is also a part of this other, was labouring to obtain a place in the minds of men for none but that natural theology, which he says pertains to philosophers, with such subtlety that he censures the fabulous, and, not daring openly to censure the civil, shows its censurable character by simply exhibiting it; and thus, both being reprobated by the judgment of men of right understanding, the natural alone remains to be chosen? But concerning this in its own place, by the help of the true God, we have to discuss more diligently.

CHAP. 10. *Concerning the liberty of Seneca, who more vehemently censured the civil theology than Varro did the fabulous*

That liberty, in truth, which this man wanted, so that he did not dare to censure that theology of the city, which is very similar to the theatrical, so openly as he did the theatrical itself, was, though not fully, yet in part possessed by Annæus Seneca, whom we have some evidence to show to have flourished in the times of our apostles. It was in part possessed by him, I say, for he possessed it in writing, but not in living. For in that book which he wrote against superstition, he more copiously and vehemently censured that civil and urban theology than Varro the theatrical and fabulous. For, when speaking concerning images, he says, "They dedicate images of the sacred and inviolable immortals in most worthless and motionless matter. They give them the appearance of man, beasts, and fishes, and some make them of mixed sex, and

heterogeneous bodies. They call them deities, when they are such that if they should get breath and should suddenly meet them, they would be held to be monsters." Then, a while afterwards, when extolling the natural theology, he had expounded the sentiments of certain philosophers, he opposes to himself a question, and says, "Here some one says, Shall I believe that the heavens and the earth are gods, and that some are above the moon and some below it? Shall I bring forward either Plato or the peripatetic Strato, one of whom made God to be without a body, the other without a mind?" In answer to which he says, "And, really, what truer do the dreams of Titus Tatius, or Romulus, or Tullus Hostilius appear to thee? Tatius declared the divinity of the goddess Cloacina; Romulus that of Picus and Tiberinus; Tullus Hostilius that of Pavor and Pallor, the most disagreeable affections of men, the one of which is the agitation of the mind under fright, the other that of the body, not a disease, indeed, but a change of colour." Wilt thou rather believe that these are deities, and receive them into heaven? But with what freedom he has written concerning the rites themselves, cruel and shameful! "One," he says, "castrates himself, another cuts his arms. Where will they find room for the fear of these gods when angry, who use such means of gaining their favour when propitious? But gods who wish to be worshipped in this fashion should be worshipped in none. So great is the frenzy of the mind when perturbed and driven from its seat that the gods are propitiated by men in a manner in which not even men of the greatest ferocity and fable-renowned cruelty vent their rage. Tyrants have lacerated the limbs of some; they never ordered any one to lacerate his own. For the gratification of royal lust, some have been castrated; but no one ever, by the command of his lord, laid violent hands on himself to emasculate himself. They kill themselves in the temples. They supplicate with their wounds and with their blood. If any one has time to see the things they do and the things they suffer, he will find so many things unseemly for men of respectability, so unworthy of freemen, so unlike the doings of sane men, that no one would doubt that they are mad, had they been mad with the minority; but now the multitude of the insane is the defence of their sanity."

He next relates those things which are wont to be done in the Capitol, and with the utmost intrepidity insists that they are such things as one could only believe to be done by men making sport, or by madmen. For, having spoken with derision of this, that in the Egyptian sacred rites Osiris, being lost, is lamented for, but straightway, when found is the occasion of great joy by his reappearance, because both the losing and the finding of him are feigned; and yet that grief and that joy which are elicited thereby from those who have lost nothing and found nothing are real; having I say, so spoken of this, he says, "Still there is a fixed time for this frenzy. It is tolerable to go mad once in the year. Go into the Capitol. One is suggesting divine commands[1] to a god; another is telling the hours to Jupiter; one is a lictor; another is an anointer, who with the mere movement of his arms imitates one anointing. There are women who arrange the hair of Juno and Minerva, standing far away not only from her image, but even from her temple. These move their fingers in the manner of hairdressers. There are some women who hold a mirror. There are some who are calling the gods to assist them in court. There are some who are holding up documents to them and are explaining to them their cases. A learned and distinguished comedian, now old and decrepit, was daily playing the mimic in the Capitol, as though the gods would gladly be spectators of that which men had ceased to care about. Every kind of artificers working for the immortal gods is dwelling there in idleness." And a little after he says, "Nevertheless these, though they give themselves up to the gods for purposes superfluous enough, do not do so for any abominable or infamous purpose. There sit certain women in the Capitol who think they are beloved by Jupiter; nor are they frightened even by the look of the, if you will believe the poets, most wrathful Juno."

This liberty Varro did not enjoy. It was only the poetical theology he seemed to censure. The civil, which this man cuts to pieces, he was not bold enough to impugn. But if we attend to the truth, the temples where these things are performed are far worse than the theatres where they are represented. Whence, with respect to these sacred rites of the civil theology, Seneca preferred, as the best course to be followed by a wise man, to feign respect for them in act, but to have no real regard for them at heart. "All which things," he says, "a wise man will observe as being commanded by the laws, but not as being pleasing to the gods." And a little after he says, "And what of this, that we unite the gods

in marriage, and that not even naturally, for we join brothers and sisters? We marry Bellona to Mars, Venus to Vulcan, Salacia to Neptune. Some of them we leave unmarried, as though there were no match for them, which is surely needless, especially when there are certain unmarried goddesses, as Populonia, or Fulgora, or the goddess Rumina, for whom I am not astonished that suitors have been awanting. All this ignoble crowd of gods, which the superstition of ages has amassed, we ought," he says, "to adore in such a way as to remember all the while that its worship belongs rather to custom than to reality." Wherefore, neither those laws nor customs instituted in the civil theology that which was pleasing to the gods, or which pertained to reality. But this man, whom philosophy had made, as it were, free, nevertheless, because he was an illustrious senator of the Roman people, worshipped what he censured, did what he condemned, adored what he reproached, because, forsooth, philosophy had taught him something great—namely, not to be superstitious in the world, but, on account of the laws of cities and the customs of men, to be an actor, not on the stage, but in the temples—conduct the more to be condemned, that those things which he was deceitfully acting he so acted that the people thought he was acting sincerely. But a stageactor would rather delight people by acting plays than take them in by false pretences.

CHAP. 11. *What Seneca thought concerning the Jews*

Seneca, among the other superstitions of civil theology, also found fault with the sacred things of the Jews, and especially the sabbaths, affirming that they act uselessly in keeping those seventh days, whereby they lose through idleness about the seventh part of their life, and also many things which demand immediate attention are damaged. The Christians, however, who were already most hostile to the Jews, he did not dare to mention, either for praise or blame, lest, if he praised them, he should do so against the ancient custom of his country, or, perhaps, if he should blame them, he should do so against his own will.

When he was speaking concerning those Jews, he said, "When, meanwhile, the customs of that most accursed nation have gained such strength that they have been now received in all lands, the conquered have given laws to the conquerors." By these words he expresses his astonishment; and, not knowing what the providence of God was leading him to say, subjoins in plain

---

[1]*Numina.* Another reading is *nomina:* and with either reading another translation is admissible: "One is announcing to a god the names (or gods) who salute him."

words an opinion by which he showed what he thought about the meaning of those sacred institutions: "For," he says, "those, however, know the cause of their rites, whilst the greater part of the people know not why they perform theirs." But concerning the solemnities of the Jews, either why or how far they were instituted by divine authority, and afterwards, in due time, by the same authority taken away from the people of God, to whom the mystery of eternal life was revealed, we have both spoken elsewhere, especially when we were treating against the Manichæans, and also intend to speak in this work in a more suitable place.

CHAP. 12. *That when once the vanity of the gods of the nations has been exposed, it cannot be doubted that they are unable to bestow eternal life on any one, when they cannot afford help even with respect to the things of this temporal life*

Now, since there are three theologies, which the Greeks call respectively mythical, physical, and political, and which may be called in Latin fabulous, natural, and civil; and since neither from the fabulous, which even the worshippers of many and false gods have themselves most freely censured, nor from the civil, of which that is convicted of being a part, or even worse than it, can eternal life be hoped for from any of these theologies—if any one thinks that what has been said in this book is not enough for him, let him also add to it the many and various dissertations concerning God as the giver of felicity, contained in the former books, especially the fourth one.

For to what but to felicity should men consecrate themselves, were felicity a goddess? However, as it is not a goddess, but a gift of God, to what God but the giver of happiness ought we to consecrate ourselves, who piously love eternal life, in which there is true and full felicity? But I think, from what has been said, no one ought to doubt that none of those gods is the giver of happiness, who are worshipped with such shame, and who, if they are not so worshipped, are more shamefully enraged, and thus confess that they are most foul spirits. Moreover, how can he give eternal life who cannot give happiness? For we mean by eternal life that life where there is endless happiness. For if the soul live in eternal punishments, by which also those unclean spirits shall be tormented, that is rather eternal death than eternal life. For there is no greater or worse death than when death never dies. But because the soul from its very nature, being created immortal, cannot be without some kind of life, its utmost death is alienation from the life of God in an eternity of punishment. So, then, He only Who gives true happiness gives eternal life, that is, an endlessly happy life. And since those gods whom this civil theology worships have been proved to be unable to give this happiness, they ought not to be worshipped on account of those temporal and terrestrial things, as we showed in the five former books, much less on account of eternal life, which is to be after death; as we have sought to show in this one book especially, whilst the other books also lend it their co-operation. But since the strength of inveterate habit has its roots very deep, if any one thinks that I have not disputed sufficiently to show that this civil theology ought to be rejected and shunned, let him attend to another book which, with God's help, is to be joined to this one.

BOOK VII

ARGUMENT. IN THIS BOOK IT IS SHOWN THAT ETERNAL LIFE IS NOT OBTAINED BY THE WORSHIP OF JANUS, JUPITER, SATURN, AND THE OTHER "SELECT GODS" OF THE CIVIL THEOLOGY.

PREFACE

IT will be the duty of those who are endowed with quicker and better understandings, in whose case the former books are sufficient and more than sufficient to effect their intended object, to bear with me with patience and equanimity whilst I attempt with more than ordinary diligence to tear up and eradicate depraved and ancient opinions hostile to the truth of piety, which the long-continued error of the human race has fixed very deeply in unenlightened minds; co-operating also in this, according to my little measure, with the grace of Him Who, being the true God, is able to accomplish it, and on Whose help I depend in my work; and, for the sake of others, such should not deem superfluous what they feel to be no longer necessary for themselves. A very great matter is at stake when the true and truly holy divinity is commended to men as that which they ought to seek after and to worship; not, however, on account of the transitory vapour of mortal life, but on account of life eternal, which alone is blessed, although the help necessary for this frail life we are now living is also afforded us by it.

CHAP. 1. *Whether, since it is evident that deity is not to be found in the civil theology, we are to believe that it is to be found in the select gods*

If there is any one whom the sixth book, which I have last finished, has not persuaded that this divinity, or, so to speak, deity—for this word also our authors do not hesitate to use, in order to translate more accurately that which the Greeks call θεότης—if there is any one, I say, whom the sixth book has not persuaded that this divinity or deity is not to be found in that theology which they call civil, and which Marcus Varro has explained in sixteen books— that is, that the happiness of eternal life is not attainable through the worship of gods such as states have established to be worshipped, and that in such a form—perhaps, when he has read this book, he will not have anything further to desire in order to the clearing up of this question. For it is possible that some one may think that at least the select and chief gods, whom Varro comprised in his last book, and of whom we have not spoken sufficiently, are to be worshipped on account of the blessed life, which is none other than eternal. In respect to which matter I do not say what Tertullian said, perhaps more wittily than truly, "If gods are selected like onions, certainly the rest are rejected as bad." I do not say this, for I see that even from among the select, some are selected for some greater and more excellent office: as in warfare, when recruits have been elected, there are some again elected from among those for the performance of some greater military service; and in the Church, when persons are elected to be overseers, certainly the rest are not rejected, since all good Christians are deservedly called elect; in the erection of a building corner-stones are elected, though the other stones, which are destined for other parts of the structure, are not rejected; grapes are elected for eating, whilst the others, which we leave for drinking, are not rejected. There is no need of adducing many illustrations, since the thing is evident. Wherefore the selection of certain gods from among

many affords no proper reason why either he who wrote on this subject, or the worshippers of the gods, or the gods themselves, should be spurned. We ought rather to seek to know what gods these are, and for what purpose they may appear to have been selected.

CHAP. 2. *Who are the select gods, and whether they are held to be exempt from the offices of the commoner gods*

The following gods, certainly, Varro signalizes as select, devoting one book to this subject: Janus, Jupiter, Saturn, Genius, Mercury, Apollo, Mars, Vulcan, Neptune, Sol, Orcus, father Liber, Tellus, Ceres, Juno, Luna, Diana, Minerva, Venus, Vesta; of which twenty gods, twelve are males and eight females. Whether are these deities called select, because of their higher spheres of administration in the world, or because they have become better known to the people, and more worship has been expended on them? If it be on account of the greater works which are performed by them in the world, we ought not to have found them among that, as it were, plebeian crowd of deities, which has assigned to it the charge of minute and trifling things. For, first of all, at the conception of a fœtus, from which point all the works commence which have been distributed in minute detail to many deities, Janus himself opens the way for the reception of the seed; there also is Saturn, on account of the seed itself; there is Liber, who liberates the male by the effusion of the seed; there is Libera, whom they also would have to be Venus, who confers this same benefit on the woman, namely, that she also be liberated by the emission of the seed; all these are of the number of those who are called select. But there is also the goddess Mena, who presides over the menses; though the daughter of Jupiter, ignoble nevertheless. And this province of the menses the same author, in his book on the select gods, assigns to Juno herself, who is even queen among the select gods; and here, as Juno Lucina, along with the same Mena, her step-daughter, she presides over the same blood. There also are two gods, exceedingly obscure, Vitumnus and Sentinus—the one of whom imparts life to the fœtus, and the other sensation; and, of a truth, they bestow, most ignoble though they be, far more than all those noble and select gods bestow. For, surely, without life and sensation, what is the whole fœtus which a woman carries in her womb, but a most vile and worthless thing, no better than slime and dust?

CHAP. 3. *How there is no reason which can be shown for the selection of certain gods, when the administration of more exalted offices is assigned to many inferior gods*

What is the cause, therefore, which has driven so many select gods to these very small works, in which they are excelled by Vitumnus and Sentinus, though little known and sunk in obscurity, inasmuch as they confer the munificent gifts of life and sensation? For the select Janus bestows an entrance, and, as it were, a door for the seed; the select Saturn bestows the seed itself; the select Liber bestows on men the emission of the same seed; Libera, who is Ceres or Venus, confers the same on women; the select Juno confers (not alone, but together with Mena, the daughter of Jupiter) the menses, for the growth of that which has been conceived; and the obscure and ignoble Vitumnus confers life, whilst the obscure and ignoble Sentinus confers sensation—which two last things are as much more excellent than the others as they themselves are excelled by reason and intellect. For as those things which reason and understand are preferable to those which, without intellect and reason, as in the case of cattle, live and feel; so also those things which have been endowed with life and sensation are deservedly preferred to those things which neither live nor feel. Therefore Vitumnus the life-giver, and Sentinus the sense-giver, ought to have been reckoned among the select gods, rather than Janus the admitter of seed, and Saturn the giver or sower of seed, and Liber and Libera the movers and liberators of seed; which seed is not worth a thought, unless it attain to life and sensation. Yet these select gifts are not given by select gods, but by certain unknown and, considering their dignity, neglected gods. But if it be replied that Janus has dominion over all beginnings, and therefore the opening of the way for conception is not without reason assigned to him; and that Saturn has dominion over all seeds, and therefore the sowing of the seed whereby a human being is generated cannot be excluded from his operation; that Liber and Libera have power over the emission of all seeds, and therefore preside over those seeds which pertain to the procreation of men; that Juno presides over all purgations and births, and therefore she has also charge of the purgations of women and the births of human beings; if they give this reply, let them find an answer to the question concerning Vitumnus and Sentinus, whether they are willing that these likewise should have dominion over all things

which live and feel. If they grant this, let them observe in how sublime a position they are about to place them. For to spring from seeds is in the earth and of the earth, but to live and feel are supposed to be properties even of the sidereal gods. But if they say that only such things as come to life in flesh and are supported by senses are assigned to Sentinus, why does not that God who made all things live and feel bestow on flesh also life and sensation, in the universality of His operation conferring also on fœtuses this gift? And what, then, is the use of Vitumnus and Sentinus? But if these, as it were, extreme and lowest things have been committed by Him who presides universally over life and sense to these gods as to servants, are these select gods then so destitute of servants that they could not find any to whom even they might commit those things, but with all their dignity, for which they are, it seems, deemed worthy to be selected, were compelled to perform their work along with ignoble ones? Juno is select queen of the gods, and the sister and wife of Jupiter; nevertheless she is Iterduca, the conductor to boys, and performs this work along with a most ignoble pair—the goddesses Abeona and Adeona. There they have also placed the goddess Mena, who gives to boys a good mind, and she is not placed among the select gods; as if anything greater could be bestowed on a man than a good mind. But Juno is placed among the select because she is Iterduca and Domiduca (she who conducts one on a journey, and who conducts him home again); as if it is of any advantage for one to make a journey and to be conducted home again, if his mind is not good. And yet the goddess who bestows that gift has not been placed by the selectors among the select gods, though she ought indeed to have been preferred even to Minerva, to whom, in this minute distribution of work, they have allotted the memory of boys. For who will doubt that it is a far better thing to have a good mind than ever so great a memory? For no one is bad who has a good mind; but some who are very bad are possessed of an admirable memory, and are so much the worse, the less they are able to forget the bad things which they think. And yet Minerva is among the select gods, whilst the goddess Mena is hidden by a worthless crowd. What shall I say concerning Virtus? What concerning Felicitas?—concerning whom I have already spoken much in the fourth book;[1] to whom, though they held them to be goddesses, they have not thought fit to assign a place among the

[1] Chaps. 21, 23.

select gods, among whom they have given a place to Mars and Orcus, the one the causer of death, the other the receiver of the dead.

Since, therefore, we see that even the select gods themselves work together with the others, like a senate with the people, in all those minute works which have been minutely portioned out among many gods; and since we find that far greater and better things are administered by certain gods who have not been reckoned worthy to be selected than by those who are called select, it remains that we suppose that they were called select and chief, not on account of their holding more exalted offices in the world, but because it happened to them to become better known to the people. And even Varro himself says that in that way obscurity had fallen to the lot of some father gods and mother goddesses as it falls to the lot of man. If, therefore, Felicity ought not perhaps to have been put among the select gods, because they did not attain to that noble position by merit, but by chance, Fortune at least should have been placed among them, or rather before them; for they say that that goddess distributes to every one the gifts she receives, not according to any rational arrangement, but according as chance may determine. She ought to have held the uppermost place among the select gods, for among them chiefly it is that she shows what power she has. For we see that they have been selected not on account of some eminent virtue or rational happiness, but by that random power of Fortune which the worshippers of these gods think that she exerts. For that most eloquent man Sallust also may perhaps have the gods themselves in view when he says: "But, in truth, fortune rules in everything; it renders all things famous or obscure, according to caprice rather than according to truth." For they cannot discover a reason why Venus should have been made famous, whilst Virtus has been made obscure, when the divinity of both of them has been solemnly recognized by them, and their merits are not to be compared. Again, if she has deserved a noble position on account of the fact that she is much sought after—for there are more who seek after Venus than after Virtus—why has Minerva been celebrated whilst Pecunia has been left in obscurity, although throughout the whole human race avarice allures a far greater number than skill? And even among those who are skilled in the arts, you will rarely find a man who does not practise his own art for the purpose of pecuniary gain; and that for the sake of which anything is made is always valued more than that which is made for the sake of something else. If, then, this selection of gods has been made by the judgment of the foolish multitude, why has not the goddess Pecunia been preferred to Minerva, since there are many artificers for the sake of money? But if this distinction has been made by the few wise, why has Virtus been preferred to Venus, when reason by far prefers the former? At all events, as I have already said, Fortune herself—who, according to those who attribute most influence to her, renders all things famous or obscure according to caprice rather than according to the truth—since she has been able to exercise so much power even over the gods as, according to her capricious judgment, to render those of them famous whom she would and those obscure whom she would; Fortune herself ought to occupy the place of pre-eminence among the select gods, since over them also she has such pre-eminent power. Or must we suppose that the reason why she is not among the select is simply this, that even Fortune herself has had an adverse fortune? She was adverse, then, to herself, since, whilst ennobling others, she herself has remained obscure.

Chap. 4. *The inferior gods, whose names are not associated with infamy, have been better dealt with than the select gods, whose infamies are celebrated*

However, any one who eagerly seeks for celebrity and renown, might congratulate those select gods, and call them fortunate, were it not that he saw that they have been selected more to their injury than to their honour. For that low crowd of gods have been protected by their very meanness and obscurity from being overwhelmed with infamy. We laugh, indeed, when we see them distributed by the mere fiction of human opinions, according to the special works assigned to them, like those who farm small portions of the public revenue, or like workmen in the street of the silversmiths, where one vessel, in order that it may go out perfect, passes through the hands of many, when it might have been finished by one perfect workman. But the only reason why the combined skill of many workmen was thought necessary, was, that it is better that each part of an art should be learned by a special workman, which can be done speedily and easily, than that they should all be compelled to be perfect in one art throughout all its parts, which they could only attain slowly and with difficulty. Nevertheless there is scarcely to be found one of the non-select gods who has brought infamy on himself by any crime, whilst there is scarce any one of the select gods who has not received upon himself the brand of notable infamy. These latter have descended to the humble works of the others, whilst the others have not come up to their sublime crimes. Concerning Janus, there does not readily occur to my recollection anything infamous; and perhaps he was such an one as lived more innocently than the rest and further removed from misdeeds and crimes. He kindly received and entertained Saturn when he was fleeing; he divided his kingdom with his guest, so that each of them had a city for himself,[1] the one Janiculum, and the other Saturnia. But those seekers after every kind of unseemliness in the worship of the gods have disgraced him, whose life they found to be less disgraceful than that of the other gods, with an image of monstrous deformity, making it sometimes with two faces, and sometimes, as it were, double, with four faces. Did they wish that, as the most of the select gods had lost shame through the perpetration of shameful crimes, his greater innocence should be marked by a greater number of faces?

CHAP. 5. *Concerning the more secret doctrine of the pagans, and concerning the physical interpretations*

But let us hear their own physical interpretations by which they attempt to colour, as with the appearance of profounder doctrine, the baseness of most miserable error. Varro, in the first place, commends these interpretations so strongly as to say that the ancients invented the images, badges, and adornments of the gods, in order that when those who went to the mysteries should see them with their bodily eyes, they might with the eyes of their mind see the soul of the world, and its parts, that is, the true gods; and also that the meaning which was intended by those who made their images with the human form, seemed to be this—namely, that the mind of mortals, which is in a human body, is very like to the immortal mind, just as vessels might be placed to represent the gods, as, for instance, a wine-vessel might be placed in the temple of Liber, to signify wine, that which is contained being signified by that which contains. Thus by an image which had the human form the rational soul was signified, because the human form is the vessel, as it were, in which that nature is

[1] Virgil, *Æneid*, BK. VIII. 357, 358.

wont to be contained which they attribute to God, or to the gods. These are the mysteries of doctrine to which that most learned man penetrated in order that he might bring them forth to the light. But, O thou most acute man, hast thou lost among those mysteries that prudence which led thee to form the sober opinion, that those who first established those images for the people took away fear from the citizens and added error, and that the ancient Romans honoured the gods more chastely without images? For it was through consideration of them that thou wast emboldened to speak these things against the later Romans. For if those most ancient Romans also had worshipped images, perhaps thou wouldst have suppressed by the silence of fear all those sentiments (true sentiments, nevertheless) concerning the folly of setting up images, and wouldst have extolled more loftily, and more loquaciously, those mysterious doctrines consisting of these vain and pernicious fictions. Thy soul, so learned and so clever (and for this I grieve much for thee), could never through these mysteries have reached its God; that is, the God by Whom, not with Whom, it has made, of Whom it is not a part, but a work; that God Who is not the soul of all things, but Who made every soul, and in Whose light alone every soul is blessed, if it be not ungrateful for His grace.

But the things which follow in this book will show what is the nature of these mysteries, and what value is to be set upon them. Meanwhile, this most learned man confesses as his opinion that the soul of the world and its parts are the true gods, from which we perceive that his theology (to wit, that same natural theology to which he pays great regard) has been able, in its completeness, to extend itself even to the nature of the rational soul. For in this book (concerning the select gods) he says a very few things by anticipation concerning the natural theology; and we shall see whether he has been able in that book, by means of physical interpretations, to refer to this natural theology that civil theology, concerning which he wrote last when treating of the select gods. Now, if he has been able to do this, the whole is natural; and in that case, what need was there for distinguishing so carefully the civil from the natural? But if it has been distinguished by a veritable distinction, then, since not even this natural theology with which he is so much pleased is true (for though it has reached as far as the soul, it has not reached to the true God Who made the soul), how much more contemptible and false is that civil theology which is chiefly occupied about what is corporeal, as will be shown by its very interpretations, which they have with such diligence sought out and enucleated, some of which I must necessarily mention!

CHAP. 6. *Concerning the opinion of Varro, that God is the soul of the world, which nevertheless, in its various parts, has many souls whose nature is divine*

The same Varro, then, still speaking by anticipation, says that he thinks that God is the soul of the world (which the Greeks call κόσμος) and that this world itself is God; but as a wise man, though he consists of body and mind, is nevertheless called wise on account of his mind, so the world is called God on account of mind, although it consists of mind and body. Here he seems, in some fashion at least, to acknowledge one God; but that he may introduce more, he adds that the world is divided into two parts, heaven and earth, which are again divided each into two parts, heaven into ether and air, earth into water and land, of all which the ether is the highest, the air second, the water third, and the earth the lowest. All these four parts, he says, are full of souls; those which are in the ether and air being immortal, and those which are in the water and on the earth mortal. From the highest part of the heavens to the orbit of the moon there are souls, namely, the stars and planets; and these are not only understood to be gods, but are seen to be such. And between the orbit of the moon and the commencement of the region of clouds and winds there are aerial souls; but these are seen with the mind, not with the eyes, and are called Heroes, and Lares, and Genii. This is the natural theology which is briefly set forth in these anticipatory statements, and which satisfied not Varro only, but many philosophers besides. This I must discuss more carefully, when, with the help of God, I shall have completed what I have yet to say concerning the civil theology, as far as it concerns the select gods.

CHAP. 7. *Whether it is reasonable to separate Janus and Terminus as two distinct deities*

Who, then, is Janus, with whom Varro commences? He is the world. Certainly a very brief and unambiguous reply. Why, then, do they say that the beginnings of things pertain to him, but the ends to another whom they call Terminus? For they say that two months have been dedicated to these two gods, with reference to beginnings and ends—January to Janus, and February to Terminus—over and above those ten months which commence with March and end with December. And they say that that is the reason why the Terminalia are celebrated in the month of February, the same month in which the sacred purification is made which they call Februum, and from which the month derives its name.[1] Do the beginnings of things, therefore, pertain to the world, which is Janus, and not also the ends, since another god has been placed over them? Do they not own that all things which they say begin in this world also come to an end in this world? What folly it is to give him only half power in work, when in his image they give him two faces! Would it not be a far more elegant way of interpreting the two-faced image to say that Janus and Terminus are the same and that the one face has reference to beginnings, the other to ends? For one who works ought to have respect to both. For he who in every forthputting of activity does not look back on the beginning, does not look forward to the end. Wherefore it is necessary that prospective intention be connected with retrospective memory. For how shall one find how to finish anything, if he has forgotten what it was which he had begun? But if they thought that the blessed life is begun in this world, and perfected beyond the world, and for that reason attributed to Janus, that is, to the world, only the power of beginnings, they should certainly have preferred Terminus to him, and should not have shut him out from the number of the select gods. Yet even now, when the beginnings and ends of temporal things are represented by these two gods, more honour ought to have been given to Terminus. For the greater joy is that which is felt when anything is finished; but things begun are always cause of much anxiety until they are brought to an end, which end he who begins anything very greatly longs for, fixes his mind on, expects, desires; nor does any one ever rejoice over anything he has begun, unless it be brought to an end.

CHAP. 8. *For what reason the worshippers of Janus have made his image with two faces, when they would sometimes have it be seen with four*

But now let the interpretation of the two-faced image be produced. For they say that it has two faces, one before and one behind, because our gaping mouths seem to resemble the world: whence the Greeks call the palate οὐρανός and some Latin poets, he says, have

[1] Cf. Plutarch, *Numa*.

called the heavens *palatum;* and from the gaping mouth, they say, there is a way out in the direction of the teeth, and a way in in the direction of the gullet. See what the world has been brought to on account of a Greek or a poetical word for our palate! Let this god be worshipped only on account of saliva, which has two open doorways under the heavens of the palate—one through which part of it may be spitten out, the other through which part of it may be swallowed down. Besides, what is more absurd than not to find in the world itself two doorways opposite to each other, through which it may either receive anything into itself, or cast it out from itself; and to seek of our throat and gullet, to which the world has no resemblance, to make up an image of the world in Janus, because the world is said to resemble the *palate,* to which Janus bears no likeness? But when they make him four-faced, and call him double Janus, they interpret this as having reference to the four quarters of the world, as though the world looked out on anything, like Janus through his four faces. Again, if Janus is the world, and the world consists of four quarters, then the image of the two-faced Janus is false. Or if it is true, because the whole world is sometimes understood by the expression east and west, will any one call the world double when north and south also are mentioned, as they call Janus double when he has four faces? They have no way at all of interpreting, in relation to the world, four doorways by which to go in and to come out as they did in the case of the two-faced Janus, where they found, at any rate in the human mouth, something which answered to what they said about him; unless perhaps Neptune come to their aid and hand them a fish, which, besides the mouth and gullet, has also the openings of the gills, one on each side. Nevertheless, with all the doors, no soul escapes this vanity but that one which hears the truth saying, "I am the door." [1]

CHAP. 9. *Concerning the power of Jupiter, and a comparison of Jupiter with Janus*

But they also show whom they would have Jove (who is also called Jupiter) understood to be. He is the god, say they, who has the power of the causes by which anything comes to be in the world. And how great a thing this is that most noble verse of Virgil testifies:

Happy is he who has learned the causes of things. [2]

But why is Janus preferred to him? Let that most acute and most learned man answer us this question. "Because," says he, "Janus has dominion over first things, Jupiter over highest[3] things. Therefore Jupiter is deservedly held to be the king of all things; for highest things are better than first things: for although first things precede in time, highest things excel by dignity."

Now this would have been rightly said had the first parts of things which are done been distinguished from the highest parts; as, for instance, it is the beginning of a thing done to set out, the highest part to arrive. The commencing to learn is the first part of a thing begun, the acquirement of knowledge is the highest part. And so of all things: the beginnings are first, the ends highest. This matter, however, has been already discussed in connection with Janus and Terminus. But the causes which are attributed to Jupiter are things effecting, not things effected; and it is impossible for them to be prevented in time by things which are made or done, or by the beginnings of such things; for the thing which makes is always prior to the thing which is made. Therefore, though the beginnings of things which are made or done pertain to Janus, they are nevertheless not prior to the efficient causes which they attribute to Jupiter. For as nothing takes place without being preceded by an efficient cause, so without an efficient cause nothing begins to take place. Verily, if the people call this god Jupiter, in whose power are all the causes of all natures which have been made and of all natural things, and worship him with such insults and infamous criminations, they are guilty of more shocking sacrilege than if they should totally deny the existence of any god. It would therefore be better for them to call some other god by the name of Jupiter—some one worthy of base and criminal honours; substituting instead of Jupiter some vain fiction (as Saturn is said to have had a stone given to him to devour instead of his son), which they might make the subject of their blasphemies, rather than speak of *that* god as both thundering and committing adultery—ruling the whole world, and laying himself out for the commission of so many licentious acts—having in his power nature and the highest causes of all natural things, but not having his own causes good.

Next, I ask what place they find any longer for this Jupiter among the gods, if Janus is the world; for Varro defined the true gods to be the soul of the world, and the parts of it. And therefore whatever falls not within this definition, is certainly not a true god, according to them.

[1] John, 10. 9. [2] *Georgics,* BK. II. 470.

[3] *Summa,* which also includes the meaning *last.*

Will they then say that Jupiter is the soul of the world and Janus the body—that is, this visible world? If they say this, it will not be possible for them to affirm that Janus is a god. For even, according to them, the body of the world is not a god, but the soul of the world and its parts. Wherefore Varro, seeing this, says that he thinks God is the soul of the world, and that this world itself is God; but that as a wise man, though he consists of soul and body, is nevertheless called wise from the soul, so the world is called God from the soul, though it consists of soul and body. Therefore the body of the world alone is not God, but either the soul of it alone, or the soul and the body together, yet so as that it is God not by virtue of the body, but by virtue of the soul. If, therefore, Janus is the world and Janus is a god, will they say, in order that Jupiter may be a god, that he is some part of Janus? For they are wont rather to attribute universal existence to Jupiter; whence the saying, "All things are full of Jupiter."[1] Therefore they must think Jupiter also, in order that he may be a god, and especially king of the gods, to be the world, that he may rule over the other gods— according to them, his parts. To this effect, also, the same Varro expounds certain verses of Valerius Soranus in that book which he wrote apart from the others concerning the worship of the gods. These are the verses:

Almighty Jove, progenitor of kings, and things, and gods,
And eke the mother of the gods, god one and all.

But in the same book he expounds these verses by saying that as the male emits seed and the female receives it, so Jupiter, whom they believed to be the world, both emits all seeds from himself and receives them into himself. For which reason, he says, Soranus wrote, "Jove, progenitor and mother"; and with no less reason said that one and all were the same. For the world is one, and in that one are all things.

CHAP. 10. *Whether the distinction between Janus and Jupiter is a proper one*

Since, therefore, Janus is the world, and Jupiter is the world, wherefore are Janus and Jupiter two gods, while the world is but one? Why do they have separate temples, separate altars, different rites, dissimilar images? If it be because the nature of beginnings is one, and the nature of causes another, and the one has received the name of Janus, the other of Jupiter;

[1] Virgil, *Eclogues*, BK. III. 60.

is it then the case, that if one man has two distinct offices of authority, or two arts, two judges or two artificers are spoken of, because the nature of the offices or the arts is different? So also with respect to one god: if he have the power of beginnings and of causes, must he therefore be thought to be two gods, because beginnings and causes are two things? But if they think that this is right, let them also affirm that Jupiter is as many gods as they have given him surnames, on account of many powers; for the things from which these surnames are applied to him are many and diverse. I shall mention a few of them.

CHAP. 11. *Concerning the surnames of Jupiter, which are referred not to many gods, but to one and the same god*

They have called him "Victor," "Invictus," "Opitulus," "Impulsor," "Stator," "Centumpeda," "Supinalis," "Tigillus," "Almus," "Ruminus," and other names which it were long to enumerate. But these surnames they have given to one god on account of diverse causes and powers, but yet have not compelled him to be, on account of so many things, as many gods. They gave him these surnames because he conquered all things; because he was conquered by none; because he brought help to the needy; because he had the power of impelling, stopping, establishing, throwing on the back; because as a beam[2] he held together and sustained the world; because he nourished all things; because, like the pap,[3] he nourished animals. Here, we perceive, are some great things and some small things; and yet it is one who is said to perform them all. I think that the causes and the beginnings of things, on account of which they have thought that the one world is two gods, Jupiter and Janus, are nearer to each other than the holding together of the world and the giving of the pap to animals; and yet, on account of these two works so far apart from each other, both in nature and dignity, there has not been any necessity for the existence of two gods; but one Jupiter has been called, on account of the one Tigillus, on account of the other Ruminus. I am unwilling to say that the giving of the pap to sucking animals might have become Juno rather than Jupiter, especially when there was the goddess Rumina to help and to serve her in this work; for I think it may be replied that Juno herself is nothing else than Jupiter, according to those verses of Valerius Soranus, where it has been said:

[2] *Tigillus.* [3] *Ruma.*

Almighty Jove, progenitor of kings, and things, and gods,
And eke the mother of the gods, etc.

Why, then, was he called Ruminus, when they who may perchance inquire more diligently may find that he is also that goddess Rumina?

If, then, it was rightly thought unworthy of the majesty of the gods that in one ear of corn one god should have the care of the joint, another that of the husk, how much more unworthy of that majesty is it that one thing, and that of the lowest kind, even the giving of the pap to animals that they may be nourished, should be under the care of two gods, one of whom is Jupiter himself, the very king of all things, who does this not along with his own wife, but with some ignoble Rumina (unless perhaps he himself is Rumina, being Ruminus for males and Rumina for females)! I should certainly have said that they had been unwilling to apply to Jupiter a feminine name, had he not been styled in these verses "progenitor and mother," and had I not read among other surnames of his that of Pecunia, which we found as a goddess among those petty deities, as I have already mentioned in the fourth book. But since both males and females have money, why has he not been called both Pecunius and Pecunia? That is their concern.

CHAP. 12. *That Jupiter is also called Pecunia*

How elegantly they have accounted for this name! "He is also called Pecunia," say they, "because all things belong to him." Oh how grand an explanation of the name of a deity! Yes; he to whom all things belong is most meanly and most contumeliously called Pecunia. In comparison of all things which are contained by heaven and earth, what are all things together which are possessed by men under the name of money? And this name, forsooth, hath avarice given to Jupiter, that whoever was a lover of money might seem to himself to love not an ordinary god, but the very king of all things himself. But it would be a far different thing if he had been called Riches. For riches are one thing, money another. For we call rich the wise, the just, the good, who have either no money or very little. For they are more truly rich in possessing virtue, since by it, even as respects things necessary for the body, they are content with what they have. But we call the greedy poor, who are always craving and always wanting. For they may possess ever so great an amount of money; but whatever be the abundance of that, they are not able but to want.

And we properly call God Himself rich; not, however, in money, but in omnipotence. Therefore they who have abundance of money are called rich, but inwardly needy if they are greedy. So also, those who have no money are called poor, but inwardly rich if they are wise.

What, then, ought the wise man to think of this theology, in which the king of the gods receives the name of that thing "which no wise man has desired"? For had there been anything wholesomely taught by this philosophy concerning eternal life, how much more appropriately would that god who is the ruler of the world have been called by them, not money, but wisdom, the love of which purges from the filth of avarice, that is, of the love of money!

CHAP. 13. *That when it is expounded what Saturn is, what Genius is, it comes to this, that both of them are shown to be Jupiter*

But why speak more of this Jupiter, with whom perchance all the rest are to be identified; so that, he being all, the opinion as to the existence of many gods may remain as a mere opinion, empty of all truth? And they are all to be referred to him, if his various parts and powers are thought of as so many gods, or if the principle of mind which they think to be diffused through all things has received the names of many gods from the various parts which the mass of this visible world combines in itself, and from the manifold administration of nature. For what is Saturn also? "One of the principal gods," he says, "who has dominion over all sowings." Does not the exposition of the verses of Valerius Soranus teach that Jupiter is the world, and that he emits all seeds from himself, and receives them into himself?

It is he, then, with whom is the dominion of all sowings. What is Genius? "He is the god who is set over, and has the power of begetting, all things." Who else than the world do they believe to have this power, to which it has been said:

Almighty Jove, progenitor and mother?

And when in another place he says that Genius is the rational soul of every one and therefore exists separately in each individual, but that the corresponding soul of the world is God, he just comes back to this same thing—namely, that the soul of the world itself is to be held to be, as it were, the universal genius. This, therefore, is what he calls Jupiter. For if every genius is a god, and the soul of every man a genius, it follows that the soul of every man is a god. But if very absurdity compels even these theologists themselves to shrink from this, it remains that they call that genius god by special and pre-eminent distinction, whom they call the soul of the world, and therefore Jupiter.

CHAP. 14. *Concerning the offices of Mercury and Mars*

But they have not found how to refer Mercury and Mars to any parts of the world, and to the works of God which are in the elements; and therefore they have set them at least over human works, making them assistants in speaking and in carrying on wars. Now Mercury, if he has also the power of the speech of the gods, rules also over the king of the gods himself, if Jupiter, as he receives from him the faculty of speech, also speaks according as it is his pleasure to permit him—which surely is absurd; but if it is only the power over human speech which is held to be attributed to him, then we say it is incredible that Jupiter should have condescended to give the pap not only to children, but also to beasts—from which he has been surnamed Ruminus—and yet should have been unwilling that the care of our speech, by which we excel the beasts, should pertain to him. And thus speech itself both belongs to Jupiter and is Mercury. But if speech itself is said to be Mercury, as those things which are said concerning him by way of interpretation show it to be; for he is said to have been called Mercury, that is, he who runs between, because speech runs between men: they say also that the Greeks call him Ἑρμῆς, because speech, or interpretation, which certainly belongs to speech, is called by them ἑρμηνεία: also he is said to preside over payments, because speech passes between sellers and buyers: the wings, too, which he has on his head and on his feet, they say mean that speech passes winged through the air: he is also said to have been called the messenger,[1] because by means of speech all our thoughts are expressed;[2] if, therefore, speech itself is Mercury, then, even by their own confession, he is not a god. But when they make to themselves gods of such as are not even demons, by praying to unclean spirits, they are possessed by such as are not gods, but demons. In like manner, because they have not been able to find for Mars any element or part of the world in which he might perform some works of nature of whatever kind, they have said that he is the god of war, which is a work of men, and that not one which is considered desirable by them. If, therefore, Felicitas should give perpetual peace, Mars

[1] *Nuncius.*   [2] *Enunciantur.*

would have nothing to do. But if war itself is Mars, as speech is Mercury, I wish it were as true that there were no war to be falsely called a god, as it is true that it is not a god.

CHAP. 15. *Concerning certain stars which the pagans have called by the names of their gods*

But possibly these stars which have been called by their names are these gods. For they call a certain star Mercury, and likewise a certain other star Mars. But among those stars which are called by the names of gods is that one which they call Jupiter, and yet with them Jupiter is the world. There also is that one they call Saturn, and yet they give to him no small property besides—namely, all seeds. There also is that brightest of them all which is called by them Venus, and yet they will have this same Venus to be also the moon: not to mention how Venus and Juno are said by them to contend about that most brilliant star, as though about another golden apple. For some say that Lucifer belongs to Venus, and some to Juno. But, as usual, Venus conquers. For by far the greatest number assign that star to Venus, so much so that there is scarcely found one of them who thinks otherwise. But since they call Jupiter the king of all, who will not laugh to see his star so far surpassed in brilliancy by the star of Venus? For it ought to have been as much more brilliant than the rest as he himself is more powerful. They answer that it only appears so because it is higher up, and very much farther away from the earth. If, therefore, its greater dignity has deserved a higher place, why is Saturn higher in the heavens than Jupiter? Was the vanity of the fable which made Jupiter king not able to reach the stars? And has Saturn been permitted to obtain at least in the heavens, what he could not obtain in his own kingdom nor in the Capitol?

But why has Janus received no star? If it is because he is the world, and they are all in him, the world is also Jupiter's, and yet he has one. Did Janus compromise his case as best he could, and instead of the one star which he does not have among the heavenly bodies, accept so many faces on earth? Again, if they think that on account of the stars alone Mercury and Mars are parts of the world, in order that they may be able to have them for gods, since speech and war are not parts of the world, but acts of men, how is it that they have made no altars, established no rites, built no temples for Aries, and Taurus, and Cancer, and Scorpio, and the rest which they number as the celestial signs, and which consist not of single stars, but each of them of many stars, which also they say are situated above those already mentioned in the highest part of the heavens, where a more constant motion causes the stars to follow an undeviating course? And why have they not reckoned them as gods, I do not say among those select gods, but not even among those, as it were, plebeian gods?

CHAP. 16. *Concerning Apollo and Diana, and the other select gods whom they would have to be parts of the world*

Although they would have Apollo to be a diviner and physician, they have nevertheless given him a place as some part of the world. They have said that he is also the sun; and likewise they have said that Diana, his sister, is the moon, and the guardian of roads. Whence also they will have her be a virgin, because a road brings forth nothing. They also make both of them have arrows, because those two planets send their rays from the heavens to the earth. They make Vulcan to be the fire of the world; Neptune the waters of the world; Father Dis, that is, Orcus, the earthy and lowest part of the world. Liber and Ceres they set over seeds—the former over the seeds of males, the latter over the seeds of females; or the one over the fluid part of seed, but the other over the dry part. And all this together is referred to the world, that is, to Jupiter, who is called "progenitor and mother," because he emitted all seeds from himself, and received them into himself. For they also make this same Ceres to be the Great Mother, who they say is none other than the earth, and call her also Juno. And therefore they assign to her the second causes of things, notwithstanding that it has been said to Jupiter, "progenitor and mother of the gods"; because, according to them, the whole world itself is Jupiter's. Minerva, also, because they set her over human arts, and did not find even a star in which to place her, has been said by them to be either the highest ether, or even the moon. Also Vesta herself they have thought to be the highest of the goddesses, because she is the earth; although they have thought that the milder fire of the world, which is used for the ordinary purposes of human life, not the more violent fire, such as belongs to Vulcan, is to be assigned to her. And thus they will have all those select gods to be the world and its parts—some of them the whole world, others of them its parts; the whole of it Jupiter—its parts, Genius, Mater Magna, Sol and Luna, or rather Apollo and Diana, and so on. And sometimes they make one god many

things; sometimes one thing many gods. Many things are one god in the case of Jupiter; for both the whole world is Jupiter, and the sky alone is Jupiter, and the star alone is said and held to be Jupiter. Juno also is mistress of second causes—Juno is the air, Juno is the earth; and had she won it over Venus, Juno would have been the star. Likewise Minerva is the highest ether, and Minerva is likewise the moon, which they suppose to be in the lowest limit of the ether. And also they make one thing many gods in this way. The world is both Janus and Jupiter; also the earth is Juno, and Mater Magna, and Ceres.

CHAP. 17. *That even Varro himself pronounced his own opinions regarding the gods ambiguous*

And the same is true with respect to all the rest, as is true with respect to those things which I have mentioned for the sake of example. They do not explain them, but rather involve them. They rush hither and thither, to this side or to that, according as they are driven by the impulse of erratic opinion; so that even Varro himself has chosen rather to doubt concerning all things than to affirm anything. For, having written the first of the three last books concerning the certain gods, and having commenced in the second of these to speak of the uncertain gods, he says: "I ought not to be censured for having stated in this book the doubtful opinions concerning the gods. For he who, when he has read them, shall think that they both ought to be, and can be, conclusively judged of, will do so himself. For my own part, I can be more easily led to doubt the things which I have written in the first book, than to attempt to reduce all the things I shall write in this one to any orderly system." Thus he makes uncertain not only that book concerning the uncertain gods, but also that other concerning the certain gods. Moreover, in that third book concerning the select gods, after having exhibited by anticipation as much of the natural theology as he deemed necessary, and when about to commence to speak of the vanities and lying insanities of the civil theology, where he was not only without the guidance of the truth of things, but was also pressed by the authority of tradition, he says: "I will write in this book concerning the public gods of the Roman people, to whom they have dedicated temples, and whom they have conspicuously distinguished by many adornments; but, as Xenophon of Colophon writes, I will state what I think, not what I am prepared to maintain: it is for man to think those things, for God to know them."

It is not, then, an account of things comprehended and most certainly believed which he promised, when about to write those things which were instituted by men. He only timidly promises an account of things which are but the subject of doubtful opinion. Nor, indeed, was it possible for him to affirm with the same certainty that Janus was the world, and such like things; or to discover with the same certainty such things as how Jupiter was the Son of Saturn, while Saturn was made subject to him as king: he could, I say, neither affirm nor discover such things with the same certainty with which he knew such things as that the world existed, that the heavens and earth existed, the heavens bright with stars, and the earth fertile through seeds; or with the same perfect conviction with which he believed that this universal mass of nature is governed and administered by a certain invisible and mighty force.

CHAP. 18. *A more credible cause of the rise of pagan error*

A far more credible account of these gods is given, when it is said that they were men, and that to each one of them sacred rites and solemnities were instituted, according to his particular genius, manners, actions, circumstances; which rites and solemnities, by gradually creeping through the souls of men, which are like demons, and eager for things which yield them sport, were spread far and wide; the poets adorning them with lies, and false spirits seducing men to receive them. For it is far more likely that some youth, either impious himself, or afraid of being slain by an impious father, being desirous to reign, dethroned his father, than that (according to Varro's interpretation) Saturn was overthrown by his son Jupiter; for cause, which belongs to Jupiter, is before seed, which belongs to Saturn. For had this been so, Saturn would never have been before Jupiter, nor would he have been the father of Jupiter. For cause always precedes seed, and is never generated from seed. But when they seek to honour by natural interpretation most vain fables or deeds of men, even the acutest men are so perplexed that we are compelled to grieve for their folly also.

CHAP. 19. *Concerning the interpretations which compose the reason of the worship of Saturn*

"They said," says Varro, "that Saturn was wont to devour all that sprang from him, because seeds returned to the earth from whence they sprang. And when it is said that a lump of earth was put before Saturn to be devoured instead of Jupiter, it is signified," he says, "that before the art of ploughing was discovered, seeds were buried in the earth by the hands of men." The earth itself, then, and not seeds, should have been called Saturn, because it in a manner devours what it has brought forth, when the seeds which have sprung from it return again into it. And what has Saturn's receiving of a lump of earth instead of Jupiter to do with this, that the seeds were covered in the soil by the hands of men? Was the seed kept from being devoured, like other things, by being covered with the soil? For what they say would imply that he who put on the soil took away the seed, as Jupiter is said to have been taken away when the lump of soil was offered to Saturn instead of him, and not rather that the soil, by covering the seed, only caused it to be devoured the more eagerly. Then, in that way, Jupiter is the seed and not the cause of the seed, as was said a little before.

But what shall men do who cannot find anything wise to say, because they are interpreting foolish things? Saturn has a pruning-knife. "That," says Varro, "is on account of agriculture." Certainly in Saturn's reign there as yet existed no agriculture, and therefore the former times of Saturn are spoken of, because, as the same Varro interprets the fables, the primeval men lived on those seeds which the earth produced spontaneously. Perhaps he received a pruning-knife when he had lost his sceptre; that he who had been a king, and lived at ease during the first part of his time, should become a laborious workman whilst his son occupied the throne. Then he says that boys were wont to be immolated to him by certain peoples, the Carthaginians for instance; and also that adults were immolated by some nations, for example the Gauls—because, of all seeds, the human race is the best. What need we say more concerning this most cruel vanity. Let us rather attend to and hold by this, that these interpretations are not carried up to the true God—a living, incorporeal, unchangeable nature, from whom a blessed life enduring for ever may be obtained—but that they end in things which are corporeal, temporal, mutable, and mortal. And whereas it is said in the fables that Saturn castrated his father Cœlus, this signifies, says Varro, that the divine seed belongs to Saturn, and not to Cœlus; for this reason, as far as a reason can be discovered, namely, that in heaven nothing is born from seed. But, lo! Saturn, if he is the son of Cœlus, is the son of Jupiter. For they affirm times without number, and that emphatically, that the heavens are Jupiter. Thus those things which come not of the truth, do very often, without being impelled by any one, themselves overthrow one another. He says that Saturn was called Κρονος, which in the Greek tongue signifies a space of time, because, without that, seed cannot be productive. These and many other things are said concerning Saturn, and they are all referred to seed. But Saturn surely, with all that great power, might have sufficed for seed. Why are other gods demanded for it, especially Liber and Libera, that is, Ceres?—concerning whom again, as far as seed is concerned, he says as many things as if he had said nothing concerning Saturn.

Chap. 20. Concerning the rites of Eleusinian Ceres

Now among the rites of Ceres, those Eleusinian rites are much famed which were in the highest repute among the Athenians, of which Varro offers no interpretation except with respect to corn, which Ceres discovered, and with respect to Proserpine, whom Ceres lost, Orcus having carried her away. And this Proserpine herself, he says, signifies the fecundity of seeds. But as this fecundity departed at a certain season, whilst the earth wore an aspect of sorrow through the consequent sterility, there arose an opinion that the daughter of Ceres, that is, fecundity itself, who was called Proserpine, from *proserpere* (to creep forth, to spring), had been carried away by Orcus and detained among the inhabitants of the nether world; which circumstance was celebrated with public mourning. But since the same fecundity again returned, there arose joy because Proserpine had been given back by Orcus, and thus these rites were instituted. Then Varro adds that many things are taught in the mysteries of Ceres which only refer to the discovery of fruits.

Chap. 21. Concerning the shamefulness of the rites which are celebrated in honour of Liber

Now as to the rites of Liber, whom they have set over liquid seeds, and therefore not only over the liquors of fruits, among which wine holds, so to speak, the primacy, but also over the seeds of animals: as to these rites, I am unwilling to undertake to show to what excess of turpitude they had reached, because that would entail a lengthened discourse, though I am not unwilling to do so as a demonstration of the proud stupidity of those who practise them. Among other rites which I am compelled from the greatness of their number to omit, Varro says that in

Italy, at the places where roads crossed each other, the rites of Liber were celebrated with such unrestrained turpitude that the private parts of a man were worshipped in his honour. Nor was this abomination transacted in secret, that some regard at least might be paid to modesty, but was openly and wantonly displayed. For during the festival of Liber, this obscene member, placed on a car, was carried with great honour, first over the crossroads in the country, and then into the city. But in the town of Lavinium a whole month was devoted to Liber alone, during the days of which all the people gave themselves up to the most dissolute conversation, until that member had been carried through the Forum and brought to rest in its own place; on which unseemly member it was necessary that the most honourable matron should place a wreath in the presence of all the people. Thus, forsooth, was the god Liber to be appeased in order to the growth of seeds. Thus was enchantment to be driven away from fields, even by a matron's being compelled to do in public what not even a harlot ought to be permitted to do in a theatre, if there were matrons among the spectators. For these reasons, then, Saturn alone was not believed to be sufficient for seeds—namely, that the impure mind might find occasions for multiplying the gods; and that, being righteously abandoned to uncleanness by the one true God, and being prostituted to the worship of many false gods, through an avidity for ever greater and greater uncleanness, it should call these sacrilegious rites sacred things, and should abandon itself to be violated and polluted by crowds of foul demons.

Chap. 22. Concerning Neptune, and Salacia and Venilia

Now Neptune had Salacia to wife, who they say is the nether waters of the sea. Wherefore was Venilia also joined to him? Was it not simply through the lust of the soul desiring a greater number of demons to whom to prostitute itself, and not because this goddess was necessary to the perfection of their sacred rites? But let the interpretation of this illustrious theology be brought forward to restrain us from this censuring by rendering a satisfactory reason. Venilia, says this theology, is the wave which comes to the shore, Salacia the wave which returns into the sea. Why, then, are there two goddesses, when it is one wave which comes and returns? Certainly it is mad lust itself, which in its eagerness for many deities resembles the waves which break on the shore. For though the water which goes is not different from that which returns, still the soul which goes and returns not is defiled by two demons, whom it has taken occasion by this false pretext to invite. I ask thee, O Varro, and you who have read such works of learned men and think ye have learned something great—I ask you to interpret this, I do not say in a manner consistent with the eternal and unchangeable nature which alone is God, but only in a manner consistent with the doctrine concerning the soul of the world and its parts, which ye think to be the true gods. It is a somewhat more tolerable thing that ye have made that part of the soul of the world which pervades the sea your god Neptune. Is the wave, then, which comes to the shore and returns to the main, two parts of the world, or two parts of the soul of the world? Who of you is so silly as to think so? Why, then, have they made to you two goddesses? The only reason seems to be that your wise ancestors have provided, not that many gods should rule you, but that many of such demons as are delighted with those vanities and falsehoods should possess you. But why has that Salacia, according to this interpretation, lost the lower part of the sea, seeing that she was represented as subject to her husband? For in saying that she is the receding wave, ye have put her on the surface. Was she enraged at her husband for taking Venilia as a concubine and thus drove him from the upper part of the sea?

CHAP. 23. *Concerning the earth, which Varro affirms to be a goddess, because that soul of the world which he thinks to be god pervades also this lowest part of his body, and imparts to it a divine force*

Surely the earth, which we see full of its own living creatures, is one; but for all that, it is but a mighty mass among the elements, and the lowest part of the world. Why, then, would they have it to be a goddess? Is it because it is fruitful? Why, then, are not men rather held to be gods, who render it fruitful by cultivating it; but though they plough it, do not adore it? But, say they, the part of the soul of the world which pervades it makes it a goddess. As if it were not a far more evident thing, nay, a thing which is not called in question, that there is a soul in man. And yet men are not held to be gods, but (a thing to be sadly lamented), with wonderful and pitiful delusion, are subjected to those who are not gods and than whom they themselves are better, as the objects of deserved worship and adoration. And certainly the same Varro, in the book concerning the select gods, affirms that

there are three grades of soul in universal nature. One which pervades all the living parts of the body, and has not sensation, but only the power of life, that principle which penetrates into the bones, nails and hair. By this principle in the world trees are nourished and grow without being possessed of sensation, and live in a manner peculiar to themselves. The second grade of soul is that in which there is sensation. This principle penetrates into the eyes, ears, nostrils, mouth, and the organs of sensation. The third grade of soul is the highest, and is called mind, where intelligence has its throne. This grade of soul no mortal creatures except man are possessed of. "Now this part of the soul of the world," Varro says, "is called 'God,' and in us is called 'Genius.' And the stones and earth in the world, which we see, and which are not pervaded by the power of sensation, are, as it were, the bones and nails of God. Again, the sun, moon, and stars, which we perceive, and by which He perceives, are His organs of perception. Moreover, the ether is His mind; and by the virtue which is in it, which penetrates into the stars, it also makes them gods; and because it penetrates through them into the earth, it makes it the goddess Tellus, whence again it enters and permeates the sea and ocean, making them the god Neptune."

Let him return from this, which he thinks to be natural theology, back to that from which he went out, in order to rest from the fatigue occasioned by the many turnings and windings of his path. Let him return, I say, let him return to the civil theology. I wish to detain him there a while. I have somewhat to say which has to do with that theology. I am not yet saying that, if the earth and stones are similar to our bones and nails, they are in like manner devoid of intelligence, as they are devoid of sensation. Nor am I saying that, if our bones and nails are said to have intelligence, because they are in a man who has intelligence, he who says that the things analogous to these in the world are gods is as stupid as he is who says that our bones and nails are men. We shall perhaps have occasion to dispute these things with the philosophers. At present, however, I wish to deal with Varro as a political theologian. For it is possible that, though he may seem to have wished to lift up his head, as it were, into the liberty of natural theology, the consciousness that the book with which he was occupied was one concerning a subject belonging to civil theology, may have caused him to relapse into the point of view of that theology and to say this in order that the ancestors of his nation and other states might not be believed to have bestowed on Neptune an irrational worship. What I am to say is this: Since the earth is one, why has not that part of the soul of the world which permeates the earth made it that one goddess which he calls Tellus? But had it done so, what then had become of Orcus, the brother of Jupiter and Neptune, whom they call Father Dis?[1] And where, in that case, had been his wife Proserpine, who, according to another opinion given in the same book, is called, not the fecundity of the earth, but its lower part? But if they say that part of the soul of the world, when it permeates the upper part of the earth, makes the god Father Dis, but when it pervades the nether part of the same the goddess Proserpine; what, in that case, will that Tellus be? For all that which she was has been divided into these two parts and these two gods; so that it is impossible to find what to make or where to place her as a third goddess, except it be said that those divinities Orcus and Proserpine are the one goddess Tellus, and that they are not three gods, but one or two, whilst notwithstanding they are called three, held to be three, worshipped as three, having their own several altars, their own shrines, rites, images, priests, whilst their own false demons also through these things defile the prostituted soul. Let this further question be answered: "What part of the earth does a part of the soul of the world permeate in order to make the god Tellumo?" "No," says he; "but the earth being one and the same, has a double life—the masculine, which produces seed, and the feminine, which receives and nourishes the seed. Hence it has been called Tellus from the feminine principle, and Tellumo from the masculine." Why, then, do the priests, as he indicates, perform divine service to four gods, two others being added—namely, to Tellus, Tellumo, Altor, and Rusor? We have already spoken concerning Tellus and Tellumo. But why do they worship Altor?[2] "Because," says he, "all that springs of the earth is nourished by the earth." Wherefore do they worship Rusor?[3] "Because all things return back again to the place whence they proceeded."

CHAP. 24. *Concerning the surnames of Tellus and their significations, which, although they indicate many properties, ought not to have established the opinion that there is a corresponding number of gods*

The one earth, then, on account of this fourfold virtue, ought to have had four surnames,

[1]See Chap. 16.   [2]*Nourisher.*   [3]*Returner.*

but not to have been considered as four gods—as Jupiter and Juno, though they have so many surnames, are for all that only single deities—for by all these surnames it is signified that a manifold virtue belongs to one god or to one goddess; but the multitude of surnames does not imply a multitude of gods. But as sometimes even the vilest women themselves grow tired of those crowds which they have sought after under the impulse of wicked passion, so also the soul, become vile and prostituted to impure spirits, sometimes begins to loathe to multiply to itself gods to whom to surrender itself to be polluted by them, as much as it once delighted in so doing. For Varro himself, as if ashamed of that crowd of gods, would make Tellus to be one goddess. "They say," says he, "that whereas the one great mother has a tympanum, it is signified that she is the orb of the earth; whereas she has towers on her head, towns are signified; and whereas seats are fixed round about her, it is signified that whilst all things move, she moves not. And their having made the Galli to serve this goddess, signifies that they who are in need of seed ought to follow the earth, for in it all seeds are found. By their throwing themselves down before her, it is taught," he says, "that they who cultivate the earth should not sit idle, for there is always something for them to do. The sound of the cymbals signifies the noise made by the throwing of iron utensils, and by men's hands, and all other noises connected with agricultural operations; and these cymbals are of brass, because the ancients used brazen utensils in their agriculture before iron was discovered. They place beside the goddess an unbound and tame lion, to show that there is no kind of land so wild and so excessively barren as that it would be profitless to attempt to bring it in and cultivate it." Then he adds that, because they gave many names and surnames to mother Tellus, it came to be thought that these signified many gods. "They think," says he, "that Tellus is Ops, because the earth is improved by labour; Mother, because it brings forth much; Great, because it brings forth seed; Proserpine, because fruits creep forth from it; Vesta, because it is invested with herbs. And thus," says he, "they not at all absurdly identify other goddesses with the earth." If, then, it is one goddess (though, if the truth were consulted it is not even that), why do they nevertheless separate it into many? Let there be many names of one goddess, and let there not be as many goddesses as there are names.

But the authority of the erring ancients

weighs heavily on Varro, and compels him, after having expressed this opinion, to show signs of uneasiness; for he immediately adds, "With which things the opinion of the ancients, who thought that there were really many goddesses, does not conflict." How does it not conflict, when it is entirely a different thing to say that one goddess has many names and to say that there are many goddesses? "But it is possible," he says, "that the same thing may both be one, and yet have in it a plurality of things." I grant that there are many things in one man; are there therefore in him many men? In like manner, in one goddess there are many things; are there therefore also many goddesses? But let them divide, unite, multiply, reduplicate, and implicate as they like.

These are the famous mysteries of Tellus and the Great Mother, all of which are shown to have reference to mortal seeds and to agriculture. Do these things, then—namely, the tympanum, the towers, the Galli, the tossing to and fro of limbs, the noise of cymbals, the images of lions—do these things, having this reference and this end, promise eternal life? Do the mutilated Galli, then, serve this Great Mother in order to signify that they who are in need of seed should follow the earth, as though it were not rather the case that this very service caused them to want seed? For whether do they, by following this goddess, acquire seed, being in want of it, or, by following her, lose seed when they have it? Is this to interpret or to deprecate? Nor is it considered to what a degree malign demons have gained the upper hand, inasmuch as they have been able to exact such cruel rites without having dared to promise any great things in return for them. Had the earth not been a goddess, men would have, by labouring, laid their hands on *it* in order to obtain seed through it, and would not have laid violent hands on themselves in order to lose seed on account of it. Had it not been a goddess, it would have become so fertile by the hands of others that it would not have compelled a man to be rendered barren by his own hands; nor that in the festival of Liber an honourable matron put a wreath on the private parts of a man in the sight of the multitude, where perhaps her husband was standing by blushing and perspiring, if there is any shame left in men; and that in the celebration of marriages the newly-married bride was ordered to sit upon Priapus. These things are bad enough, but they are small and contemptible in comparison with that most cruel abomination, or most abominable cruelty, by which either set is

so deluded that neither perishes of its wound. There the enchantment of fields is feared; here the amputation of members is not feared. There the modesty of the bride is outraged, but in such a manner as that neither her fruitfulness nor even her virginity is taken away; here a man is so mutilated that he is neither changed into a woman nor remains a man.

CHAP. 25. *The interpretation of the mutilation of Atys which the doctrine of the Greek sages set forth*

Varro has not spoken of that Atys, nor sought out any interpretation for him, in memory of whose being loved by Ceres the Gallus is mutilated. But the learned and wise Greeks have by no means been silent about an interpretation so holy and so illustrious. The celebrated philosopher Porphyry has said that Atys signifies the flowers of spring, which is the most beautiful season, and therefore was mutilated because the flower falls before the fruit appears. They have not, then, compared the man himself, or rather that semblance of a man they called Atys, to the flower, but his male organs—these, indeed, fell whilst he was living. Did I say fell? nay, truly they did not fall, nor were they plucked off, but torn away. Nor when that flower was lost did any fruit follow, but rather sterility. What, then, do they say is signified by the castrated Atys himself, and whatever remained to him after his castration? To what do they refer that? What interpretation does that give rise to? Do they, after vain endeavours to discover an interpretation, seek to persuade men that that is rather to be believed which report has made public, and which has also been written concerning his having been a mutilated man? Our Varro has very properly opposed this and has been unwilling to state it; for it certainly was not unknown to that most learned man.

CHAP. 26. *Concerning the abomination of the sacred rites of the Great Mother*

Concerning the effeminates consecrated to the same Great Mother, in defiance of all the modesty which belongs to men and women, Varro has not wished to say anything, nor do I remember to have read anywhere aught concerning them. These effeminates, no later than yesterday, were going through the streets and places of Carthage with anointed hair, whitened faces, relaxed bodies, and feminine gait, exacting from the people the means of maintaining their ignominious lives. Nothing has been said concerning them. Interpretation failed, reason blushed, speech was silent. The Great Mother has surpassed all her sons, not in greatness of deity, but of crime. To this monster not even the monstrosity of Janus is to be compared. His deformity was only in his image; hers was the deformity of cruelty in her sacred rites. He has a redundancy of members in stone images; she inflicts the loss of members on men. This abomination is not surpassed by the licentious deeds of Jupiter, so many and so great. He, with all his seductions of women, only disgraced heaven with one Ganymede; she, with so many avowed and public effeminates, has both defiled the earth and outraged heaven. Perhaps we may either compare Saturn to this Magna Mater, or even set him before her in this kind of abominable cruelty, for he mutilated his father. But at the festivals of Saturn, men could rather be slain by the hands of others than mutilated by their own. He devoured his sons, as the poets say, and the natural theologists interpret this as they list. History says he slew them. But the Romans never received, like the Carthaginians, the custom of sacrificing their sons to him. This Great Mother of the gods, however, has brought mutilated men into Roman temples, and has preserved that cruel custom, being believed to promote the strength of the Romans by emasculating their men. Compared with this evil, what are the thefts of Mercury, the wantonness of Venus, and the base and flagitious deeds of the rest of them, which we might bring forward from books, were it not that they are daily sung and danced in the theatres? But what are these things to so great an evil—an evil whose magnitude was only proportioned to the greatness of the Great Mother—especially as these are said to have been invented by the poets? as if the poets had also invented this, that they are acceptable to the gods. Let it be imputed, then, to the audacity and impudence of the poets that these things have been sung and written of. But that they have been incorporated into the body of divine rites and honours, the deities themselves demanding and extorting that incorporation, what is that but the crime of the gods? nay more, the confession of demons and the deception of wretched men? But as to this, that the Great Mother is considered to be worshipped in the appropriate form when she is worshipped by the consecration of mutilated men, this is not an invention of the poets, nay, they have rather shrunk from it with horror than sung of it. Ought any one, then, to be consecrated to these select gods, that he may live blessedly after death, consecrated to whom he could not live de-

cently before death, being subjected to such foul superstitions, and bound over to unclean demons? "But all these things," says Varro, "are to be referred to the world."[1] Let him consider if it be not rather to the unclean.[2] But why not refer that to the world which is demonstrated to be in the world? We, however, seek for a mind which, trusting to true religion, does not adore the world as its god, but for the sake of God praises the world as a work of God, and, purified from mundane defilements, comes pure[3] to God Himself Who founded the world.[4]

CHAP. 27. *Concerning the figments of the physical theologists, who neither worship the true divinity, nor perform the worship wherewith the true divinity should be served*

We see that these select gods have, indeed, become more famous than the rest; not, however, that their merits may be brought to light, but that their opprobrious deeds may not be hid. Whence it is more credible that they were men, as not only poetic but also historical literature has handed down. For this which Virgil says,

> Then from Olympus' heights came down
> Good Saturn, exiled from his throne
> By Jove, his mightier heir;[5]

and what follows with reference to this affair is fully related by the historian Euhemerus and has been translated into Latin by Ennius. And as they who have written before us in the Greek or in the Latin tongue against such errors as these have said much concerning this matter, I have thought it unnecessary to dwell upon it. When I consider those physical reasons, then, by which learned and acute men attempt to turn human things into divine things, all I see is that they have been able to refer these things only to temporal works and to that which has a corporeal nature, and even though invisible still mutable; and this is by no means the true God. But if this worship had been performed as the symbolism of ideas at least congruous with religion, though it would indeed have been cause of grief that the true God was not announced and proclaimed by its symbolism, nevertheless it could have been in some degree borne with, when it did not occasion and command the performance of such foul and abominable things. But since it is impiety to worship the body or the soul for the true God, by whose indwelling alone the soul is happy, how much more impious is it to wor-

[1]*Mundum.* [2]*Immundum.* [3]*Mundus.* [4]*Mundum.*
[5]Virgil, *Æneid*, BK. VIII. 319-20.

ship those things through which neither soul nor body can obtain either salvation or human honour? Wherefore if with temple, priest, and sacrifice, which are due to the true God, any element of the world be worshipped, or any created spirit, even though not impure and evil, that worship is still evil, not because the things are evil by which the worship is performed, but because those things ought only to be used in the worship of Him to Whom alone such worship and service are due. But if any one insist that he worships the one true God—that is, the Creator of every soul and of every body—with stupid and monstrous idols, with human victims, with putting a wreath on the male organ, with the wages of unchastity, with the cutting of limbs, with emasculation, with the consecration of effeminates, with impure and obscene plays, such a one does not sin because he worships One Who ought not to be worshipped, but because he worships Him Who ought to be worshipped in a way in which He ought not to be worshipped. But he who worships with such things—that is, foul and obscene things—and that not the true God, namely, the Maker of soul and body, but a creature, even though not a wicked creature, whether it be soul or body, or soul and body together, twice sins against God, because he both worships for God what is not God, and also worships with such things as neither God nor what is not God ought to be worshipped with. It is, indeed, manifest how these pagans worship—that is, how shamefully and criminally they worship; but what or whom they worship would have been left in obscurity, had not their history testified that those same confessedly base and foul rites were rendered in obedience to the demands of the gods, who exacted them with terrible severity. Wherefore it is evident beyond doubt that this whole civil theology is occupied in inventing means for attracting wicked and most impure spirits, inviting them to visit senseless images and through these to take possession of stupid hearts.

CHAP. 28. *That the doctrine of Varro concerning theology is in no part consistent with itself.*

To what purpose, then, is it that this most learned and most acute man Varro attempts as it were, with subtle disputation to reduce and refer all these gods to heaven and earth? He cannot do it. They go out of his hands like water; they shrink back; they slip down and fall. For when about to speak of the females, that is, the goddesses, he says, "Since, as I observed in the first book concerning places, heaven and earth are the two origins of the gods, on which account they are called celestials and terrestrials, and as I began in the former books with heaven, speaking of Janus, whom some have said to be heaven, and others the earth, so I now commence with Tellus in speaking concerning the goddesses." I can understand what embarrassment so great a mind was experiencing. For he is influenced by the perception of a certain plausible resemblance, when he says that the heaven is that which does, and the earth that which suffers, and therefore attributes the masculine principle to the one, and the feminine to the other, not considering that it is rather He Who made both heaven and earth Who is the maker of both activity and passivity. On this principle he interprets the celebrated mysteries of the Samothracians, and promises, with an air of great devoutness, that he will by writing expound these mysteries, which have not been so much as known to his countrymen, and will send them his exposition. Then he says that he had from many proofs gathered that, in those mysteries, among the images one signifies heaven, another the earth, another the patterns of things, which Plato calls ideas. He makes Jupiter to signify heaven, Juno the earth, Minerva the ideas. Heaven, by which anything is made; the earth, from which it is made; and the pattern, according to which it is made. But, with respect to the last, I am forgetting to say that Plato attributed so great an importance to these ideas as to say, not that anything was made by heaven according to them, but that according to them heaven itself was made.[1] To return, however, it is to be observed that Varro has, in the book on the select gods, lost that theory of these gods, in whom he has, as it were, embraced all things. For he assigns the male gods to heaven, the females to earth; among which latter he has placed Minerva, whom he had before placed above heaven itself. Then the male god Neptune is in the sea, which pertains rather to earth than to heaven. Last of all, Father Dis, who is called in Greek Πλούτων, another male god, brother of both (Jupiter and Neptune), is also held to be a god of the earth, holding the upper region of the earth himself, and allotting the nether region to his wife Proserpine. How, then, do they attempt to refer the gods to heaven and the goddesses to earth? What solidity, what consistency, what sobriety has this disputation? But that Tellus is the origin of the goddesses, the great mother, to wit, beside whom there is continually the noise of the mad and abominable revelry of effeminates and

[1] In the *Timœus*.

mutilated men, and men who cut themselves and indulge in frantic gesticulations; how is it, then, that Janus is called the head of the gods, and Tellus the head of the goddesses? In the one case error does not make one head, and in the other frenzy does not make a sane one. Why do they vainly attempt to refer these to the world? Even if they could do so, no pious person worships the world for the true God. Nevertheless, plain truth makes it evident that they are not able even to do this. Let them rather identify them with dead men and most wicked demons, and no further question will remain.

CHAP. 29. *That all things which the physical theologists have referred to the world and its parts, they ought to have referred to the one true God*

For all those things which, according to the account given of those gods, are referred to the world by so-called physical interpretation, may, without any religious scruple, be rather assigned to the true God, Who made heaven and earth and created every soul and every body; and the following is the manner in which we see that this may be done. We worship God—not heaven and earth, of which two parts this world consists, nor the soul or souls diffused through all living things—but God Who made heaven and earth and all things which are in them; who made every soul, whatever be the nature of its life, whether it have life without sensation and reason, or life with sensation, or life with both sensation and reason.

CHAP. 30. *How piety distinguishes the Creator from the creatures, so that, instead of one God, there are not worshipped as many gods as there are works of the one Author*

And now, to begin to go over those works of the one true God, on account of which these have made to themselves many and false gods, whilst they attempt to give an honourable interpretation to their many most abominable and most infamous mysteries—we worship that God Who has appointed to the natures created by Him both the beginnings and the end of their existing and moving: Who holds, knows, and disposes the causes of things; Who hath created the virtue of seeds; Who hath given to what creatures He would a rational soul, which is called mind; Who hath bestowed the faculty and use of speech; Who hath imparted the gift of foretelling future things to whatever spirits it seemed to Him good; Who also Himself predicts future things through whom He pleases, and

through whom He will remove diseases; Who, when the human race is to be corrected and chastised by wars, regulates also the beginnings, progress, and ends of these wars; Who hath created and governs the most vehement and most violent fire of this world, in due relation and proportion to the other elements of immense nature; Who is the governor of all the waters; Who hath made the sun brightest of all material lights, and hath given him suitable power and motion; Who hath not withdrawn, even from the inhabitants of the nether world, His dominion and power; Who hath appointed to mortal natures their suitable seed and nourishment, dry or liquid; Who establishes and makes fruitful the earth; Who bountifully bestows its fruits on animals and on men; Who knows and ordains, not only principal causes, but also subsequent causes; Who hath determined for the moon her motion; Who affords ways in heaven and on earth for passage from one place to another; Who hath granted also to human minds, which He hath created, the knowledge of the various arts for the help of life and nature; Who hath appointed the union of male and female for the propagation of offspring; Who hath favoured the societies of men with the gift of terrestrial fire for the simplest and most familiar purposes, to burn on the hearth and to give light. These are, then, the things which that most acute and most learned man Varro has laboured to distribute among the select gods, by I know not what physical interpretation, which he has got from other sources and also conjectured for himself. But these things the one true God makes and does, but as *the same* God—that is, as He who is wholly everywhere, included in no space, bound by no chains, mutable in no part of His being, filling heaven and earth with omnipresent power, not with a needy nature. Therefore He governs all things in such a manner as to allow them to perform and exercise their own proper movements. For although they can be nothing without Him, they are not what He is. He does also many things through angels; but only from Himself does He beatify angels. So also, though He send angels to men for certain purposes, He does not for all that beatify men by the good inherent in the angels, but by Himself, as He does the angels themselves.

CHAP. 31. *What benefits God gives to the followers of the truth to enjoy over and above his general bounty*

For, besides such benefits as, according to this administration of nature of which we have made some mention, He lavishes on good and bad alike, we have from Him a great manifestation of great love, which belongs only to the good. For although we can never sufficiently give thanks to Him, that we are, that we live, that we behold heaven and earth, that we have mind and reason by which to seek after Him who made all these things, nevertheless, what hearts, what number of tongues, shall affirm that they are sufficient to render thanks to Him for this, that He hath not wholly departed from us, laden and overwhelmed with sins, averse to the contemplation of His light and blinded by the love of darkness, that is, of iniquity, but hath sent to us His own Word, who is His only Son, that by His birth and suffering for us in the flesh, which He assumed, we might know how much God valued man, and that by that unique sacrifice we might be purified from all our sins, and that, love being shed abroad in our hearts by His Spirit, we might, having surmounted all difficulties, come into eternal rest, and the ineffable sweetness of the contemplation of Himself?

CHAP. 32. *That at no time in the past was the mystery of Christ's redemption awanting, but was at all times declared, though in various forms*

This mystery of eternal life, even from the beginning of the human race, was by certain signs and sacraments suitable to the times, announced through angels to those to whom it was meet. Then the Hebrew people was congregated into one republic, as it were, to perform this mystery; and in that republic was foretold, sometimes through men who understood what they spake and sometimes through men who understood not, all that had transpired since the advent of Christ until now and all that will transpire. This same nation, too, was afterwards dispersed through the nations, in order to testify to the scriptures in which eternal salvation in Christ had been declared. For not only the prophecies which are contained in words, nor only the precepts for the right conduct of life, which teach morals and piety, and are contained in the sacred writings—not only these, but also the rites, priesthood, tabernacle or temple, altars, sacrifices, ceremonies, and whatever else belongs to that service which is due to God and which in Greek is properly called λατρεία—all these signified and fore-announced those things which we who believe in Jesus Christ unto eternal life believe to have been fulfilled, or behold in process of fulfillment, or confidently believe shall yet be fulfilled.

CHAP. 33. *That only through the Christian religion could the deceit of malign spirits, who rejoice in the errors of men, have been manifested*

This, the only true religion, has alone been able to manifest that the gods of the nations are most impure demons, who desire to be thought gods, availing themselves of the names of certain defunct souls, or the appearance of mundane creatures, and with proud impurity rejoicing in things most base and infamous, as though in divine honours, and envying human souls their conversion to the true God. From whose most cruel and most impious dominion a man is liberated when he believes on Him who has afforded an example of humility, following which men may rise as great as was that pride by which they fell. Hence are not only those gods, concerning whom we have already spoken much, and many others belonging to different nations and lands, but also those of whom we are now treating, who have been selected as it were into the senate of the gods—selected, however, on account of the notoriousness of their crimes, not on account of the dignity of their virtues— whose sacred things Varro attempts to refer to certain natural reasons, seeking to make base things honourable, but cannot find how to square and agree with these reasons, because these are not the causes of those rites, which he thinks, or rather wishes to be thought to be so. For had not only these, but also all others of this kind, been real causes, even though they had nothing to do with the true God and eternal life, which is to be sought in religion, they would, by affording some sort of reason drawn from the nature of things, have mitigated in some degree that offence which was occasioned by some turpitude or absurdity in the sacred rites, which was not understood. This he attempted to do in respect to certain fables of the theatres, or mysteries of the shrines; but he did not acquit the theatres of likeness to the shrines, but rather condemned the shrines for likeness to the theatres. However, he in some way made the attempt to soothe the feelings shocked by horrible things, by rendering what he would have to be natural interpretations.

CHAP. 34. *Concerning the books of Numa Pompilius, which the senate ordered to be burned, in order that the causes of sacred rites therein assigned should not become known*

But, on the other hand, we find, as the same most learned man has related, that the causes of the sacred rites which were given from the books of Numa Pompilius could by no means be tolerated and were considered unworthy, not only to become known to the religious by being read, but even to lie written in the darkness in which they had been concealed. For now let me say what I promised in the third book of this work to say in its proper place. For, as we read in the same Varro's book on the worship of the gods, "A certain one Terentius had a field at the Janiculum, and once, when his ploughman was passing the plough near to the tomb of Numa Pompilius, he turned up from the ground the books of Numa, in which were written the causes of the sacred institutions; which books he carried to the prætor, who, having read the beginnings of them, referred to the senate what seemed to be a matter of so much importance. And when the chief senators had read certain of the causes why this or that rite was instituted, the senate assented to the dead Numa, and the conscript fathers, as though concerned for the interests of religion, ordered the prætor to burn the books."[1] Let each one believe what he thinks; nay, let every champion of such impiety say whatever mad contention may suggest. For my part, let it suffice to suggest that the causes of those sacred things which were written down by King Numa Pompilius, the institutor of the Roman rites, ought never to have become known to people or senate, or even to the priests themselves; and also that Numa himself attained to these secrets of demons by an illicit curiosity, in order that he might write them down, so as to be able, by reading, to be reminded of them. However, though he was king and had no cause to be afraid of any one, he neither dared to teach them to any one, nor to destroy them by obliteration, or any other form of destruction. Therefore, because he was unwilling that any one should know them, lest men should be taught infamous things, and because he was afraid to violate them, lest he should enrage the demons against himself, he buried them in what he thought a safe place, believing that a plough could not approach his sepulchre. But the senate, fearing to condemn the religious solemnities of their ancestors, and therefore compelled to assent to Numa, were nevertheless so convinced that those books were pernicious that they did not order them to be buried again, knowing that human curiosity would thereby be excited to seek with far greater eagerness after the matter already divulged, but ordered the scandalous relics to be destroyed with fire; be-

[1]Plutarch, *Numa.*

cause, as they thought it was now a necessity to perform those sacred rites, they judged that the error arising from ignorance of their causes was more tolerable than the disturbance which the knowledge of them would occasion the state.

CHAP. 35. *Concerning the hydromancy through which Numa was befooled by certain images of demons seen in the water*

For Numa himself also, to whom no prophet of God, no holy angel was sent, was driven to have recourse to hydromancy, that he might see the images of the gods in the water (or, rather, appearances whereby the demons made sport of him) and might learn from them what he ought to ordain and observe in the sacred rites. "This kind of divination," says Varro, "was introduced from the Persians, and was used by Numa himself, and at an after time by the philosopher Pythagoras. In this divination," he says, "they also inquire at the inhabitants of the nether world, and make use of blood; and this the Greeks called νεκρομαντίαν." But whether it be called necromancy or hydromancy it is the same thing, for in either case the dead are supposed to foretell future things. But by what artifices these things are done, let themselves consider; for I am unwilling to say that these artifices were wont to be prohibited by the laws, and to be very severely punished even in the Gentile states, before the advent of our Saviour. I am unwilling, I say, to affirm this, for perhaps even such things were then allowed. However, it was by these arts that Pompilius learned those sacred rites which he gave forth as facts, whilst he concealed their causes; for even he himself was afraid of that which he had learned. The senate also caused the books in which those causes were recorded to be burned. What is it, then, to me, that Varro attempts to adduce all sorts of fanciful physical interpretations, which if these books had contained, they would certainly not have been burned? For otherwise the conscript fathers would also have burned those books which Varro published and dedicated to the high priest Cæsar. Now Numa is said to have married the nymph Egeria, because (as Varro explains it in the forementioned book) he carried forth water wherewith to perform his hydromancy. Thus facts are wont to be converted into fables through false colourings. It was by that hydromancy, then, that that over-curious Roman king learned both the sacred rites which were to be written in the books of the priests, and also the causes of those rites, which latter, however, he was unwilling that any one besides himself should know. Wherefore he made these causes, as it were, to die along with himself, taking care to have them written by themselves and removed from the knowledge of men by being buried in the earth. Wherefore the things which are written in those books were either abominations of demons, so foul and noxious as to render that whole civil theology execrable even in the eyes of such men as those senators, who had accepted so many shameful things in the sacred rites themselves, or they were nothing else than the accounts of dead men, whom, through the lapse of ages, almost all the Gentile nations had come to believe to be immortal gods; whilst those same demons were delighted even with such rites, having presented themselves to receive worship under pretence of being those very dead men whom they had caused to be thought immortal gods by certain fallacious miracles, performed in order to establish that belief. But, by the hidden providence of the true God, these demons were permitted to confess these things to their friend Numa, having been gained by those arts through which necromancy could be performed, and yet were not constrained to admonish him rather at his death

to burn than to bury the books in which they were written. But, in order that these books might be unknown, the demons could not resist the plough by which they were thrown up, or the pen of Varro, through which the things which were done in reference to this matter have come down even to our knowledge. For they are not able to effect anything which they are not allowed; but they are permitted to influence those whom God, in His deep and just judgment, according to their deserts, gives over either to be simply afflicted by them, or to be also subdued and deceived. But how pernicious these writings were judged to be, or how alien from the worship of the true Divinity, may be understood from the fact that the senate preferred to burn what Pompilius had hid, rather than to fear what he feared, so that he could not dare to do that. Wherefore let him who does not desire to live a pious life even now seek eternal life by means of such rites. But let him who does not wish to have fellowship with malign demons have no fear for the noxious superstition wherewith they are worshipped, but let him recognize the true religion by which they are unmasked and vanquished.

BOOK VIII

ARGUMENT. AUGUSTINE COMES NOW TO THE THIRD KIND OF THEOLOGY, THAT IS, THE NATURAL, AND TAKES UP THE QUESTION WHETHER THE WORSHIP OF THE GODS OF THE NATURAL THEOLOGY IS OF ANY AVAIL TOWARDS SECURING BLESSEDNESS IN THE LIFE TO COME. THIS QUESTION HE PREFERS TO DISCUSS WITH THE PLATONISTS, BECAUSE THE PLATONIC SYSTEM IS "FACILE PRINCEPS" AMONG PHILOSOPHIES, AND MAKES THE NEAREST APPROXIMATION TO CHRISTIAN TRUTH. IN PURSUING THIS ARGUMENT, HE FIRST REFUTES APULEIUS, AND ALL WHO MAINTAIN THAT THE DEMONS SHOULD BE WORSHIPPED AS MESSENGERS AND MEDIATORS BETWEEN GODS AND MEN; DEMONSTRATING THAT BY NO POSSIBILITY CAN MEN BE RECONCILED TO GOOD GODS BY DEMONS, WHO ARE THE SLAVES OF VICE, AND WHO DELIGHT IN AND PATRONIZE WHAT GOOD AND WISE MEN ABHOR AND CONDEMN—THE BLASPHEMOUS FICTIONS OF POETS, THEATRICAL EXHIBITIONS, AND MAGICAL ARTS.

CHAP. I. *That the question of natural theology is to be discussed with those philosophers who sought a more excellent wisdom*

WE shall require to apply our mind with far greater intensity to the present question than was requisite in the solution and unfolding of the questions handled in the preceding books; for it is not with ordinary men, but with philosophers that we must confer concerning the theology which they call natural. For it is not like the fabulous, that is, the theatrical; nor the civil, that is, the urban theology: the one of

which displays the crimes of the gods, whilst the other manifests their criminal desires, which demonstrate them to be rather malign demons than gods. It is, we say, with philosophers we have to confer with respect to this theology— men whose very name, if rendered into Latin, signifies those who profess the love of wisdom. Now, if wisdom is God, who made all things, as is attested by the divine authority and truth,[1] then the philosopher is a lover of God. But since the thing itself, which is called by this name, exists not in all who glory in the name—for it

[1]Wisd. 7. 24-27.

does not follow, of course, that all who are called philosophers are lovers of true wisdom—we must needs select from the number of those with whose opinions we have been able to acquaint ourselves by reading, some with whom we may not unworthily engage in the treatment of this question. For I have not in this work undertaken to refute all the vain opinions of the philosophers, but only such as pertain to theology, which Greek word we understand to mean an account or explanation of the divine nature. Nor, again, have I undertaken to refute all the vain theological opinions of all the philosophers, but only of such of them as, agreeing in the belief that there is a divine nature, and that this divine nature is concerned about human affairs, do nevertheless deny that the worship of the one unchangeable God is sufficient for the obtaining of a blessed life after death, as well as at the present time; and hold that, in order to obtain that life, many gods, created, indeed, and appointed to their several spheres by that one God, are to be worshipped. These approach nearer to the truth than even Varro; for, whilst he saw no difficulty in extending natural theology in its entirety even to the world and the soul of the world, these acknowledge God as existing above all that is of the nature of soul, and as the Creator not only of this visible world, which is often called heaven and earth, but also of every soul whatsoever, and as Him Who gives blessedness to the rational soul—of which kind is the human soul—by participation in His own unchangeable and incorporeal light. There is no one, who has even a slender knowledge of these things, who does not know of the Platonic philosophers, who derive their name from their master Plato. Concerning this Plato, then, I will briefly state such things as I deem necessary to the present question, mentioning beforehand those who preceded him in time in the same department of literature.

CHAP. 2. *Concerning the two schools of philosophers, that is, the Italic and Ionic, and their founders*

As far as concerns the literature of the Greeks, whose language holds a more illustrious place than any of the languages of the other nations, history mentions two schools of philosophers, the one called the Italic school, originating in that part of Italy which was formerly called Magna Græcia; the other called the Ionic school, having its origin in those regions which are still called by the name of Greece. The Italic school had for its founder Pythagoras of Samos, to whom also the term "philosophy" is said to owe its origin. For whereas formerly those who seemed to excel others by the laudable manner in which they regulated their lives were called sages, Pythagoras, on being asked what he professed, replied that he was a philosopher, that is, a student or lover of wisdom; for it seemed to him to be the height of arrogance to profess oneself a sage. The founder of the Ionic school, again, was Thales of Miletus, one of those seven who were styled the "seven sages," of whom six were distinguished by the kind of life they lived, and by certain maxims which they gave forth for the proper conduct of life. Thales was distinguished as an investigator into the nature of things; and, in order that he might have successors in his school, he committed his dissertations to writing. That, however, which especially rendered him eminent was his ability, by means of astronomical calculations, even to predict eclipses of the sun and moon. He thought, however, that water was the first principle of things and that of it all the elements of the world, the world itself and all things which are generated in it, ultimately consist. Over all this work, however, which, when we consider the world, appears so admirable, he set nothing of the nature of divine mind. To him succeeded Anaximander, his pupil, who held a different opinion concerning the nature of things; for he did not hold that all things spring from one principle, as Thales did, who held that principle to be water, but thought that each thing springs from its own proper principle. These principles of things he believed to be infinite in number and thought that they generated innumerable worlds and all the things which arise in them. He thought, also, that these worlds are subject to a perpetual process of alternate dissolution and regeneration, each one continuing for a longer or shorter period of time, according to the nature of the case; nor did he any more than Thales, attribute anything to a divine mind in the production of all this activity of things. Anaximander left as his successor his disciple Anaximenes, who attributed all the causes of things to an infinite air. He neither denied nor ignored the existence of gods, but, so far from believing that the air was made by them, he held, on the contrary, that they sprang from the air. Anaxagoras, however, who was his pupil, perceived that a divine mind was the productive cause of all things which we see, and said that all the various kinds of things, according to their several modes and species, were produced out of an infinite matter consisting of homogeneous particles, but by the efficiency of a divine mind. Diogenes, also, another pupil of Anaximenes, said that a certain air was the original substance of things out of which all things were produced, but that it was possessed of a divine reason, without which nothing could be produced from it. Anaxagoras was succeeded by his disciple Archelaus, who also thought that all things consisted of homogeneous particles, of which each particular thing was made, but that those particles were pervaded by a divine mind, which perpetually energized all the eternal bodies, namely, those particles, so that they are alternately united and separated. Socrates, the master of Plato, is said to have been the disciple of Archelaus; and on Plato's account it is that I have given this brief historical sketch of the whole history of these schools.

CHAP. 3. *Of the Socratic philosophy*

Socrates is said to have been the first who directed the entire effort of philosophy to the correction and regulation of manners, all who went before him having expended their greatest efforts in the investigation of physical, that is, natural phenomena. However, it seems to me that it cannot be certainly discovered whether Socrates did this because he was wearied of obscure and uncertain things, and so wished to direct his mind to the discovery of something manifest and certain, which was necessary in order to the obtaining of a blessed life—that one great object toward which the labour, vigilance, and industry of all philosophers seem to have been directed—or whether (as some yet more favourable to him suppose) he did it because he was unwilling that minds defiled with earthly desires should essay to raise themselves upward to divine things. For he saw that the causes of things were sought for by them—which causes he believed to be ultimately reducible to nothing else than the will of the one true and supreme God—and on this account he thought they could only be comprehended by a purified mind; and therefore that all diligence ought to be given to the purification of the life by good morals, in order that the mind, delivered from the depressing weight of lusts, might raise itself upward by its native vigour to eternal things and might, with purified understanding, contemplate that nature which is incorporeal and unchangeable light, where live the causes of all created natures. It is evident, however, that he hunted out and pursued, with a wonderful pleasantness of style and argument and with a most pointed and insinuating urbanity, the foolishness of ignorant men, who thought that they knew this or that, sometimes confessing his own ignorance and sometimes dissimulating his knowledge, even in those very moral questions to which he seems to have directed the whole force of his mind. And hence there arose hostility against him, which ended in his being calumniously impeached, and condemned to death. Afterwards, however, that very city of the Athenians, which had publicly condemned him, did publicly bewail him, the popular indignation having turned with such vehemence on his accusers that one of them perished by the violence of the multitude, whilst the other only escaped a like punishment by voluntary and perpetual exile.

Illustrious, therefore, both in his life and in his death, Socrates left very many disciples of his philosophy, who vied with one another in desire for proficiency in handling those moral questions which concern the chief good (*summum bonum*), the possession of which can make a man blessed; and because, in the disputations of Socrates, where he raises all manner of questions, makes assertions, and then demolishes them, it did not evidently appear what he held to be the chief good, every one took from these disputations what pleased him best, and every one placed the final good in whatever it appeared to himself to consist. Now, that which is called the final good is that at which, when one has arrived, he is blessed. But so diverse were the opinions held by those followers of Socrates concerning this final good that (a thing scarcely to be credited with respect to the followers of one master) some placed the chief good in pleasure, as Aristippus, others in virtue, as Antisthenes. Indeed, it were tedious to recount the various opinions of various disciples.

CHAP. 4. *Concerning Plato, the chief among the disciples of Socrates, and his threefold division of philosophy*

But, among the disciples of Socrates, Plato was the one who shone with a glory which far excelled that of the others and who not unjustly eclipsed them all. By birth an Athenian of honourable parentage, he far surpassed his fellow-disciples in natural endowments, of which he was possessed in a wonderful degree. Yet, deeming himself and the Socratic discipline far from sufficient for bringing philosophy to perfection, he travelled as extensively as he was able, going to every place famed for the cultivation of any science of which he could make himself master. Thus he learned from the Egyptians whatever they held and taught as important; and from

Egypt, passing into those parts of Italy which were filled with the fame of the Pythagoreans, he mastered, with the greatest facility, and under the most eminent teachers, all the Italic philosophy which was then in vogue. And, as he had a peculiar love for his master Socrates, he made him the speaker in all his dialogues, putting into his mouth whatever he had learned, either from others, or from the efforts of his own powerful intellect, tempering even his moral disputations with the grace and politeness of the Socratic style. And, as the study of wisdom consists in action and contemplation, so that one part of it may be called active, and the other contemplative—the active part having reference to the conduct of life, that is, to the regulation of morals, and the contemplative part to the investigation into the causes of nature and into pure truth—Socrates is said to have excelled in the active part of that study, while Pythagoras gave more attention to its contemplative part, on which he brought to bear all the force of his great intellect. To Plato is given the praise of having perfected philosophy by combining both parts into one. He then divides it into three parts—the first moral, which is chiefly occupied with action; the second natural, of which the object is contemplation; and the third rational, which discriminates between the true and the false. And though this last is necessary both to action and contemplation, it is contemplation, nevertheless, which lays peculiar claim to the office of investigating the nature of truth. Thus this tripartite division is not contrary to that which made the study of wisdom to consist in action and contemplation. Now, as to what Plato thought with respect to each of these parts—that is, what he believed to be the end of all actions, the cause of all natures, and the light of all intelligences—it would be a question too long to discuss, and about which we ought not to make any rash affirmation. For, as Plato liked and constantly affected the well-known method of his master Socrates, namely, that of dissimulating his knowledge or his opinions, it is not easy to discover clearly what he himself thought on various matters, any more than it is to discover what were the real opinions of Socrates. We must, nevertheless, insert into our work certain of those opinions which he expresses in his writings, whether he himself uttered them, or narrates them as expressed by others, and seems himself to approve of—opinions sometimes favourable to the true religion, which our faith takes up and defends, and sometimes contrary to it, as, for example, in the questions concern-ing the existence of one God or of many, as it relates to the truly blessed life which is to be after death. For those who are praised as having most closely followed Plato, who is justly preferred to all the other philosophers of the Gentiles, and who are said to have manifested the greatest acuteness in understanding him, do perhaps entertain such an idea of God as to admit that in Him are to be found the cause of existence, the ultimate reason for the understanding, and the end in reference to which the whole life is to be regulated. Of which three things, the first is understood to pertain to the natural, the second to the rational, and the third to the moral part of philosophy. For if man has been so created as to attain, through that which is most excellent in him, to that which excels all things—that is, to the one true and absolutely good God, without Whom no nature exists, no doctrine instructs, no exercise profits—let Him be sought in Whom all things are secure to us, let Him be discovered in Whom all truth becomes certain to us, let Him be loved in Whom all becomes right to us.

CHAP. 5. *That it is especially with the Platonists that we must carry on our disputations on matters of theology, their opinions being preferable to those of all other philosophers*

If, then, Plato defined the wise man as one who imitates, knows, loves this God, and who is rendered blessed through fellowship with Him in His own blessedness, why discuss with the other philosophers? It is evident that none come nearer to us than the Platonists. To them, therefore, let that fabulous theology give place which delights the minds of men with the crimes of the gods; and that civil theology also, in which impure demons, under the name of gods, have seduced the peoples of the earth given up to earthly pleasures, desiring to be honoured by the errors of men, and by filling the minds of their worshippers with impure desires, exciting them to make the representation of their crimes one of the rites of their worship, whilst they themselves found in the spectators of these exhibitions a most pleasing spectacle—a theology in which, whatever was honourable in the temple, was defiled by its mixture with the obscenity of the theatre, and whatever was base in the theatre was vindicated by the abominations of the temples. To these philosophers also the interpretations of Varro must give place, in which he explains the sacred rites as having reference to heaven and earth, and to the seeds and operations of perishable things; for, in the first place, those rites have not the signification which he would have men believe is attached to them, and therefore truth does not follow him in his attempt so to interpret them; and even if they had this signification, still those things ought not to be worshipped by the rational soul as its god which are placed below it in the scale of nature, nor ought the soul to prefer to itself as gods things to which the true God has given it the preference. The same must be said of those writings pertaining to the sacred rites, which Numa Pompilius took care to conceal by causing them to be buried along with himself, and which, when they were afterwards turned up by the plough, were burned by order of the senate. And, to treat Numa with all honour, let us mention as belonging to the same rank as these writings that which Alexander of Macedon wrote to his mother as communicated to him by Leo, an Egyptian high priest. In this letter not only Picus and Faunus, and Æneas and Romulus or even Hercules, and Æsculapius and Liber, born of Semele, and the twin sons of Tyndareus, or any other mortals who have been deified, but even the principal gods themselves to whom Cicero, in his Tusculan questions, alludes without mentioning their names, Jupiter, Juno, Saturn, Vulcan, Vesta, and many others whom Varro attempts to identify with the parts or the elements of the world, are shown to have been men. There is, as we have said, a similarity between this case and that of Numa; for the priest being afraid because he had revealed a mystery, earnestly begged of Alexander to command his mother to burn the letter which conveyed these communications to her. Let these two theologies, then, the fabulous and the civil, give place to the Platonic philosophers, who have recognized the true God as the author of all things, the source of the light of truth, and the bountiful bestower of all blessedness. And not these only, but to these great acknowledgers of so great a God, those philosophers must yield who, having their mind enslaved to their body, supposed the principles of all things to be material; as Thales, who held that the first principle of all things was water; Anaximenes, that it was air; the Stoics, that it was fire; Epicurus, who affirmed that it consisted of atoms, that is to say, of minute corpuscles; and many others whom it is needless to enumerate, but who believed that bodies, simple or compound, animate or inanimate, but nevertheless bodies, were the cause and principle of all things. For some of them— as, for instance, the Epicureans—believed that living things could originate from things without life; others held that all things living or without life spring from a living principle, but that, nevertheless, all things, being material, spring from a material principle. For the Stoics thought that fire, that is, one of the four material elements of which this visible world is composed, was both living and intelligent, the maker of the world and of all things contained in it—that it was in fact God. These and others like them have only been able to suppose that which their hearts enslaved to sense have vainly suggested to them. And yet they have within themselves something which they could not see: they represented to themselves inwardly things which they had seen without, even when they were not seeing them, but only thinking of them. But this representation in thought is no longer a body, but only the similitude of a body; and that faculty of the mind by which this similitude of a body is seen is neither a body nor the similitude of a body; and the faculty which judges whether the representation is beautiful or ugly is without doubt superior to the object judged of. This principle is the understanding of man, the rational soul; and it is certainly not a body, since that similitude of a body which it beholds and judges of is itself not a body. The soul is neither earth, nor water, nor air, nor fire, of which four bodies, called the four elements, we see that this world is composed. And if the soul is not a body, how should God, its Creator, be a body? Let all those philosophers, then, give place, as we have said, to the Platonists, and those also who have been ashamed to say that God is a body, but yet have thought that our souls are of the same nature as God. They have not been staggered by the great changeableness of the soul—an attribute which it would be impious to ascribe to the divine nature—but they say it is the body which changes the soul, for in itself it is unchangeable. As well might they say, "Flesh is wounded by some body, for in itself it is invulnerable." In a word, that which is unchangeable can be changed by nothing, so that that which can be changed by the body cannot properly be said to be immutable.

CHAP. 6. *Concerning the meaning of the Platonists in that part of philosophy called physical*

These philosophers, then, whom we see not undeservedly exalted above the rest in fame and glory, have seen that no material body is God, and therefore they have transcended all bodies in seeking for God. They have seen that whatever is changeable is not the most high God, and therefore they have transcended every soul and all changeable spirits in seeking the supreme. They have seen also that, in every changeable thing, the form which makes it that which it is, whatever be its mode or nature, can only *be* through Him who truly *is*, because He is unchangeable. And therefore, whether we consider the whole body of the world, its figure, qualities, and orderly movement, and also all the bodies which are in it; or whether we consider all life, either that which nourishes and maintains, as the life of trees, or that which, besides this, has also sensation, as the life of beasts; or that which adds to all these intelligence, as the life of man; or that which does not need the support of nutriment, but only maintains, feels, understands, as the life of angels— all can only *be* through Him who absolutely *is*. For to Him it is not one thing to *be,* and another to live, as though He could *be*, not living; nor is it to Him one thing to live, and another thing to understand, as though He could live, not understanding; nor is it to Him one thing to understand, another thing to be blessed, as though He could understand and not be blessed. But to Him to live, to understand, to be blessed, are to *be*. They have understood, from this unchangeableness and this simplicity, that all things must have been made by Him, and that He could Himself have been made by none. For they have considered that whatever *is* is either body or life, and that life is something better than body, and that the nature of body is sensible, and that of life intelligible. Therefore they have preferred the intelligible nature to the sensible. We mean by sensible things such things as can be perceived by the sight and touch of the body; by intelligible things, such as can be understood by the sight of the mind. For there is no corporeal beauty, whether in the condition of a body, as figure, or in its movement, as in music, of which it is not the mind that judges. But this could never have been had there not existed in the mind itself a superior form of these things, without bulk, without noise of voice, without space and time. But even in respect of these things, had the mind not been mutable, it would not have been possible for one to judge better than another with regard to sensible forms. He who is clever, judges better than he who is slow, he who is skilled than he who is unskillful, he who is practised than he who is unpractised; and the same person judges better after he has gained experience than he did before. But that which is capable of more and less is mutable; whence able men, who have thought deeply on these things, have gathered that the first form is not to be found in those things whose form is changeable. Since, therefore, they saw that body and mind might be more or less beautiful in form, and that, if they wanted form, they could have no existence, they saw that there is some existence in which is the first form, unchangeable, and therefore not admitting of degrees of comparison, and in that they most rightly believed was the first principle of things which was not made, and by which all things were made. Therefore that which is known of God He manifested to them when His invisible things were seen by them, being understood by those things which have been made; also His eternal power and Godhead by whom all visible and temporal things have been created.[1] We have said enough upon that part of theology which they call physical, that is, natural.

CHAP. 7. *How much the Platonists are to be held as excelling other philosophers in logic, i.e. rational philosophy*

Then, again, as far as regards the doctrine which treats of that which they call logic, that is, rational philosophy, far be it from us to compare them with those who attributed to the bodily senses the faculty of discriminating truth, and thought, that all we learn is to be measured by their untrustworthy and fallacious rules. Such were the Epicureans, and all of the same school. Such also were the Stoics, who ascribed to the bodily senses that expertness in disputation which they so ardently love, called by them dialectic, asserting that from the senses the mind conceives the notions ἔννοιαι of those things which they explicate by definition. And hence is developed the whole plan and connection of their learning and teaching. I often wonder, with respect to this, how they can say that none are beautiful but the wise; for by what bodily sense have they perceived that beauty, by what eyes of the flesh have they seen wisdom's comeliness of form? Those, however, whom we justly rank before all others, have distinguished those things which are conceived by the mind from those which are perceived by the senses, neither taking away from the senses anything to which they are competent, nor attributing to them anything beyond their competency. And the light of our understandings, by which all things are learned by us, they have affirmed to be that selfsame God by Whom all things were made.

[1] Rom. i. 19, 20.

CHAP. 8. *That the Platonists hold the first rank in moral philosophy also*

The remaining part of philosophy is morals, or what is called by the Greeks ἠθική, in which is discussed the question concerning the chief good—that which will leave us nothing further to seek in order to be blessed, if only we make all our actions refer to it, and seek it not for the sake of something else, but for its own sake. Therefore it is called the end, because we wish other things on account of it, but itself only for its own sake. This beatific good, therefore, according to some, comes to a man from the body, according to others, from the mind, and, according to others, from both together. For they saw that man himself consists of soul and body; and therefore they believed that from either of these two, or from both together, their well-being must proceed, consisting in a certain final good, which could render them blessed, and to which they might refer all their actions, not requiring anything ulterior to which to refer that good itself. This is why those who have added a third kind of good things, which they call extrinsic—as honour, glory, wealth, and the like—have not regarded them as part of the final good, that is, to be sought after for their own sake, but as things which are to be sought for the sake of something else, affirming that this kind of good is good to the good, and evil to the evil. Wherefore, whether they have sought the good of man from the mind or from the body, or from both together, it is still only from man they have supposed that it must be sought. But they who have sought it from the body have sought it from the inferior part of man; they who have sought it from the mind, from the superior part; and they who have sought it from both, from the whole man. Whether, therefore, they have sought it from any part or from the whole man, still they have only sought it from man; nor have these differences, being three, given rise only to three dissentient sects of philosophers, but to many. For diverse philosophers have held diverse opinions, both concerning the good of the body, and the good of the mind, and the good of both together. Let, therefore, all these give place to those philosophers who have not affirmed that a man is blessed by the enjoyment of the body, or by the enjoyment of the mind, but by the enjoyment of God—enjoying Him, however, not as the mind does the body or itself, or as one friend enjoys another, but as the eye enjoys light, if, indeed, we may draw any comparison between these things. But what the nature of this comparison is, will, if God help me, be shown in another place, to the best of my ability. At present, it is sufficient to mention that Plato determined the final good to be to live according to virtue, and affirmed that he only can attain to virtue who knows and imitates God—which knowledge and imitation are the only cause of blessedness. Therefore he did not doubt that to philosophize is to love God, whose nature is incorporeal. Whence it certainly follows that the student of wisdom, that is, the philosopher, will then become blessed when he shall have begun to enjoy God. For though he is not necessarily blessed who enjoys that which he loves (for many are miserable by loving that which ought not to be loved and still more miserable when they enjoy it), nevertheless no one is blessed who does not enjoy that which he loves. For even they who love things which ought not to be loved do not count themselves blessed by loving merely, but by enjoying them. Who, then, but the most miserable will deny that he is blessed, who enjoys that which he loves and loves the true and highest good? But the true and highest good, according to Plato, is God, and therefore he would call him a philosopher who loves God; for philosophy is directed to the obtaining of the blessed life, and he who loves God is blessed in the enjoyment of God.

CHAP. 9. *Concerning that philosophy which has come nearest to the Christian faith*

Whatever philosophers, therefore, thought concerning the supreme God, that He is both the maker of all created things, the light by which things are known, and the good in reference to which things are to be done; that we have in Him the first principle of nature, the truth of doctrine, and the happiness of life—whether these philosophers may be more suitably called Platonists, or whether they may give some other name to their sect; whether we say that only the chief men of the Ionic school, such as Plato himself and they who have well understood him, have thought thus; or whether we also include the Italic school, on account of Pythagoras and the Pythagoreans and all who may have held like opinions; and, lastly, whether also we include all who have been held wise men and philosophers among all nations who are discovered to have seen and taught this, be they Atlantics, Libyans, Egyptians, Indians, Persians, Chaldeans, Scythians, Gauls, Spaniards, or of other nations—we prefer these to all other philosophers, and confess that they approach nearest to us.

CHAP. 10. *That the excellency of the Christian religion is above all the science of philosophers*

For although a Christian man instructed only in ecclesiastical literature may perhaps be ignorant of the very name of Platonists and may not even know that there have existed two schools of philosophers speaking the Greek tongue, to wit, the Ionic and Italic, he is nevertheless not so deaf with respect to human affairs as not to know that philosophers profess the study, and even the possession, of wisdom. He is on his guard, however, with respect to those who philosophize according to the elements of this world, not according to God, by Whom the world itself was made; for he is warned by the precept of the apostle, and faithfully hears what has been said, "Beware that no one deceive you through philosophy and vain deceit, according to the elements of the world."[1] Then, that he may not suppose that all philosophers are such as do this, he hears the same apostle say concerning certain of them, "Because that which is known of God is manifest among them, for God has manifested it to them. For His invisible things from the creation of the world are clearly seen, being understood by the things which are made, also His eternal power and Godhead."[2] And, when speaking to the Athenians, after having spoken a mighty thing concerning God, which few are able to understand, "In Him we live, and move, and have our being,"[3] he goes on to say, "As certain also of your own have said." He knows well, too, to be on his guard against even these philosophers in their errors. For where it has been said by him, "that God has manifested to them by those things which are made His invisible things, that they might be seen by the understanding," there it has also been said that they did not rightly worship God Himself, because they paid divine honours, which are due to Him alone, to other things also to which they ought not to have paid them— "because, knowing God, they glorified Him not as God; neither were thankful, but became vain in their imaginations, and their foolish heart was darkened. Professing themselves to be wise, they became fools, and changed the glory of the incorruptible God into the likeness of the image of corruptible man, and of birds, and of fourfooted

beasts, and creeping things"[4]—where the apostle would have us understand him as meaning the Romans, and Greeks, and Egyptians, who gloried in the name of wisdom; but concerning this we will dispute with them afterwards. With respect, however, to that wherein they agree with us we prefer them to all others, namely, concerning the one God, the author of this universe, Who is not only above every body, being incorporeal, but also above all souls, being incorruptible—our principle, our light, our good. And though the Christian man, being ignorant of their writings, does not use in disputation words which he has not learned—not calling that part of philosophy natural (which is the Latin term), or physical (which is the Greek one), which treats of the investigation of nature; or that part rational, or logical, which deals with the question how truth may be discovered; or that part moral, or ethical, which concerns morals, and shows how good is to be sought, and evil to be shunned—he is not, therefore, ignorant that it is from the one true and supremely good God that we have that nature in which we are made in the image of God, and that doctrine by which we know Him and ourselves, and that grace through which, by cleaving to Him, we are blessed. This, therefore, is the cause why we prefer these to all the others, because, whilst other philosophers have worn out their minds and powers in seeking the causes of things and endeavouring to discover the right mode of learning and of living, these, by knowing God, have found where resides the cause by which the universe has been constituted, and the light by which truth is to be discovered, and the fountain at which felicity is to be drunk. All philosophers, then, who have had these thoughts concerning God, whether Platonists or others, agree with us. But we have thought it better to plead our cause with the Platonists, because their writings are better known. For the Greeks, whose tongue holds the highest place among the languages of the Gentiles, are loud in their praises of these writings; and the Latins, taken with their excellence, or their renown, have studied them more heartily than other writings and, by translating them into our tongue, have given them greater celebrity and notoriety.

CHAP. 11. *How Plato has been able to approach so nearly to Christian knowledge*

Certain partakers with us in the grace of Christ wonder when they hear and read that

[1]Col. 2. 8.   [2]Rom. 1. 19, 20.   [3]Acts, 17. 28.   [4]Rom. 1. 21–23.

Plato had conceptions concerning God, in which they recognize considerable agreement with the truth of our religion. Some have concluded from this that when he went to Egypt he had heard the prophet Jeremiah, or, whilst travelling in the same country, had read the prophetic scriptures, which opinion I myself have expressed in certain of my writings.[1] But a careful calculation of dates, contained in chronological history, shows that Plato was born about a hundred years after the time in which Jeremiah prophesied, and, as he lived eighty-one years, there are found to have been about seventy years from his death to that time when Ptolemy, king of Egypt, requested the prophetic scriptures of the Hebrew people to be sent to him from Judea, and committed them to seventy Hebrews, who also knew the Greek tongue, to be translated and kept. Therefore, on that voyage of his, Plato could neither have seen Jeremiah, who was dead so long before, nor have read those same scriptures which had not yet been translated into the Greek language, of which he was a master, unless, indeed, we say that, as he was most earnest in the pursuit of knowledge, he also studied those writings through an interpreter, as he did those of the Egyptians—not, indeed, writing a translation of them (the facilities for doing which were only gained even by Ptolemy in return for munificent acts of kindness, though fear of his kingly authority might have seemed a sufficient motive), but learning as much as he possibly could concerning their contents by means of conversation. What warrants this supposition are the opening verses of Genesis: "In the beginning God made the heaven and earth. And the earth was invisible, and without order; and darkness was over the abyss: and the Spirit of God moved over the waters."[2] For in the *Timæus*, when writing on the formation of the world, he says that God first united earth and fire; from which it is evident that he assigns to fire a place in heaven. This opinion bears a certain resemblance to the statement, "In the beginning God made heaven and earth." Plato next speaks of those two intermediary elements, water and air, by which the other two extremes, namely, earth and fire, were mutually united; from which circumstance he is thought to have so understood the words, "The Spirit of God moved over the waters." For, not paying sufficient attention to the designations given by those scriptures to the Spirit of God, he may have thought that the four elements are spoken of in that place, because the air also is called

spirit.[3] Then, as to Plato's saying that the philosopher is a lover of God, nothing shines forth more conspicuously in those sacred writings. But the most striking thing in this connexion, and that which most of all inclines me almost to assent to the opinion that Plato was not ignorant of those writings, is the answer which was given to the question elicited from the holy Moses when the words of God were conveyed to him by the angel; for, when he asked what was the name of that God who was commanding him to go and deliver the Hebrew people out of Egypt, this answer was given: "I am who am; and thou shalt say to the children of Israel, He who *is* sent me unto you";[4] as though compared with Him that truly *is*, because He is unchangeable, those things which have been created mutable *are* not—a truth which Plato zealously held, and most diligently commended. And I know not whether this sentiment is anywhere to be found in the books of those who were before Plato, unless in that book where it is said, "I am who am; and thou shalt say to the children of Israel, *who is* sent me unto you."

CHAP. 12. *That even the Platonists, though they say these things concerning the one true God, nevertheless thought that sacred rites were to be performed in honour of many gods*

But we need not determine from what source he learned these things—whether it was from the books of the ancients who preceded him, or, as is more likely, from the words of the apostle: "Because that which is known of God, has been manifested among them, for God hath manifested it to them. For His invisible things from the creation of the world are clearly seen, being understood by those things which have been made, also His eternal power and Godhead."[5] From whatever source he may have derived this knowledge, then, I think I have made it sufficiently plain that I have not chosen the Platonic philosophers undeservedly as the parties with whom to discuss; because the question we have just taken up concerns the natural theology—the question, namely, whether sacred rites are to be performed to one God, or to many, for the sake of the happiness which is to be after death. I have specially chosen them because their juster thoughts concerning the one God Who made heaven and earth have made them illustrious among philosophers. This has given them such superiority to all others in the judgment of posterity that, though Aristotle, the disciple of

[1] *On Christian Doctrine*, BK. II. ch. 28. [2] Gen. I. I, 2.   [3] *Spiritus*.   [4] Ex. 3. 14.   [5] Rom. I. 20.

Plato, a man of eminent abilities, inferior in eloquence to Plato, yet far superior to many in that respect, had founded the Peripatetic sect—so called because they were in the habit of walking about during their disputations—and though he had, through the greatness of his fame, gathered very many disciples into his school, even during the life of his master; and though Plato at his death was succeeded in his school, which was called the Academy, by Speusippus, his sister's son, and Xenocrates, his beloved disciple, who, together with their successors, were called from this name of the school, Academics; nevertheless the most illustrious recent philosophers, who have chosen to follow Plato, have been unwilling to be called Peripatetics, or Academics, but have preferred the name of Platonists. Among these were the renowned Plotinus, Iamblichus, and Porphyry, who were Greeks, and the African Apuleius, who was learned both in the Greek and Latin tongues. All these, however, and the rest who were of the same school, and also Plato himself, thought that sacred rites ought to be performed in honour of many gods.

CHAP. 13. *Concerning the opinion of Plato, according to which he defined the gods as beings entirely good and the friends of virtue*

Therefore, although in many other important respects they differ from us, nevertheless with respect to this particular point of difference, which I have just stated, as it is one of great moment, and the question on hand concerns it, I will first ask them to what gods they think that sacred rites are to be performed—to the good or to the bad, or to both the good and the bad? But we have the opinion of Plato affirming that all the gods are good, and that there is not one of the gods bad. It follows, therefore, that these are to be performed to the good, for then they are performed to gods; for if they are not good, neither are they gods. Now, if this be the case (for what else ought we to believe concerning the gods?), certainly it explodes the opinion that the bad gods are to be propitiated by sacred rites in order that they may not harm us, but the good gods are to be invoked in order that they may assist us. For there are no bad gods, and it is to the good that, as they say, the due honour of such rites is to be paid. Of what character, then, are those gods who love scenic displays, even demanding that a place be given them among divine things, and that they be exhibited in their honour? The power of these gods proves that they exist, but their liking such things proves that they are bad. For it is well-

known what Plato's opinion was concerning scenic plays. He thinks that the poets themselves, because they have composed songs so unworthy of the majesty and goodness of the gods, ought to be banished from the state. Of what character, therefore, are those gods who contend with Plato himself about those scenic plays? He does not suffer the gods to be defamed by false crimes; the gods command those same crimes to be celebrated in their own honour.

In fine, when they ordered these plays to be inaugurated, they not only demanded base things, but also did cruel things, taking from Titus Latinius his son, and sending a disease upon him because he had refused to obey them, which they removed when he had fulfilled their commands. Plato, however, bad though they were, did not think they were to be feared; but, holding to his opinion with the utmost firmness and constancy, does not hesitate to remove from a well-ordered state all the sacrilegious follies of the poets, with which these gods are delighted because they themselves are impure. But Labeo places this same Plato (as I have mentioned already in the second book)[1] among the demigods. Now Labeo thinks that the bad deities are to be propitiated with bloody victims, and by fasts accompanied with the same, but the good deities with plays, and all other things which are associated with joyfulness. How comes it, then, that the demi-god Plato so persistently dares to take away those pleasures, because he deems them base, not from the demi-gods but from the gods, and these the good gods? And, moreover, those very gods themselves do certainly refute the opinion of Labeo, for they showed themselves in the case of Latinius to be not only wanton and sportive, but also cruel and terrible. Let the Platonists, therefore, explain these things to us, since, following the opinion of their master, they think that all the gods are good and honourable, and friendly to the virtues of the wise, holding it unlawful to think otherwise concerning any of the gods. We will explain it, say they. Let us then attentively listen to them.

CHAP. 14. *Of the opinion of those who have said that rational souls are of three kinds, to wit, those of the celestial gods, those of the aerial demons, and those of terrestrial men*

There is, say they, a threefold division of all animals endowed with a rational soul, namely, into gods, men, and demons. The gods occupy the loftiest region, men the lowest, the demons the middle region. For the abode of the gods is

[1]Chap. 14.

heaven, that of men the earth, that of the demons the air. As the dignity of their regions is diverse, so also is that of their natures; therefore the gods are better than men and demons. Men have been placed below the gods and demons, both in respect of the order of the regions they inhabit, and the difference of their merits. The demons, therefore, who hold the middle place, as they are inferior to the gods, than whom they inhabit a lower region, so they are superior to men, than whom they inhabit a loftier one. For they have immortality of body in common with the gods, but passions of the mind in common with men. On which account, say they, it is not wonderful that they are delighted with the obscenities of the theatre, and the fictions of the poets, since they are also subject to human passions, from which the gods are far removed, and to which they are altogether strangers. Whence we conclude that it was not the gods, who are all good and highly exalted, that Plato deprived of the pleasure of theatric plays, by reprobating and prohibiting the fictions of the poets, but the demons.

Of these things many have written: among others Apuleius, the Platonist of Madaura, who composed a whole work on the subject, entitled, *Concerning the God of Socrates*. He there discusses and explains of what kind that deity was who attended on Socrates, a sort of familiar, by whom it is said he was admonished to desist from any action which would not turn out to his advantage. He asserts most distinctly, and proves at great length, that it was not a god but a demon; and he discusses with great diligence the opinion of Plato concerning the lofty estate of the gods, the lowly estate of men, and the middle estate of demons. These things being so, how did Plato dare to take away, if not from the gods, whom he removed from all human contagion, certainly from the demons, all the pleasures of the theatre, by expelling the poets from the state? Evidently in this way he wished to admonish the human soul, although still confined in these moribund members, to despise the shameful commands of the demons, and to detest their impurity, and to choose rather the splendour of virtue. But if Plato showed himself virtuous in answering and prohibiting these things, then certainly it was shameful of the demons to command them. Therefore either Apuleius is wrong, and Socrates' familiar did not belong to this class of deities, or Plato held contradictory opinions, now honouring the demons, now removing from the well-regulated state the things in which they delighted, or Socrates is

not to be congratulated on the friendship of the demon, of which Apuleius was so ashamed that he entitled his book *On the God of Socrates*, whilst according to the tenor of his discussion, wherein he so diligently and at such length distinguishes gods from demons, he ought not to have entitled it, *Concerning the God*, but *Concerning the Demon of Socrates*. But he preferred to put this into the discussion itself rather than into the title of his book. For, through the sound doctrine which has illuminated human society, all, or almost all men have such a horror at the name of demons that every one who before reading the dissertation of Apuleius, which sets forth the dignity of demons, should have read the title of the book, *On the Demon of Socrates*, would certainly have thought that the author was not a sane man. But what did even Apuleius find to praise in the demons, except subtlety and strength of body and a higher place of habitation? For when he spoke generally concerning their manners, he said nothing that was good, but very much that was bad. Finally, no one, when he has read that book, wonders that they desired to have even the obscenity of the stage among divine things, or that, wishing to be thought gods, they should be delighted with the crimes of the gods, or that all those sacred solemnities, whose obscenity occasions laughter, and whose shameful cruelty causes horror, should be in agreement with their passions.

CHAP. 15. *That the demons are not better than men because of their aerial bodies, or on account of their superior place of abode*

Wherefore let not the mind truly religious, and submitted to the true God, suppose that demons are better than men, because they have better bodies. Otherwise it must put many beasts before itself which are superior to us both in acuteness of the senses, in ease and quickness of movement, in strength and in long-continued vigour of body. What man can equal the eagle or the vulture in strength of vision? Who can equal the dog in acuteness of smell? Who can equal the hare, the stag, and all the birds in swiftness? Who can equal in strength the lion or the elephant? Who can equal in length of life the serpents, which are affirmed to put off old age along with their skin and to return to youth again? But as we are better than all these by the possession of reason and understanding, so we ought also to be better than the demons by living good and virtuous lives. For divine providence gave to them bodies of a better quality than ours, that that in which we excel them might in this way be commended to us as deserving to be far more cared for than the body, and that we should learn to despise the bodily excellence of the demons compared with goodness of life, in respect of which we are better than they, knowing that we too shall have immortality of body—not an immortality tortured by eternal punishment, but that which is consequent on purity of soul.

But now, as regards loftiness of place, it is altogether ridiculous to be so influenced by the fact that the demons inhabit the air and we the earth as to think that on that account they are to be put before us; for in this way we put all the birds before ourselves. But the birds, when they are weary with flying, or require to repair their bodies with food, come back to the earth to rest or to feed, which the demons, they say, do not. Are they, therefore, inclined to say that the birds are superior to us and the demons superior to the birds? But if it be madness to think so, there is no reason why we should think that, on account of their inhabiting a loftier element, the demons have a claim to our religious submission. But as it is really the case that the birds of the air are not only not put before us who dwell on the earth, but are even subjected to us on account of the dignity of the rational soul which is in us, so also it is the case that the demons, though they are aerial, are not better than we who are terrestrial because the air is higher than the earth, but, on the contrary, men are to be put before demons because their despair is not to be compared to the hope of pious men. Even that law of Plato's, according to which he mutually orders and arranges the four elements, inserting between the two extreme elements—namely, fire, which is in the highest degree mobile, and the immovable earth—the two middle ones, air and water, that by how much the air is higher up than the water, and the fire than the air, by so much also are the waters higher than the earth—this law, I say, sufficiently admonishes us not to estimate the merits of animated creatures according to the grades of the elements. And Apuleius himself says that man is a terrestrial animal in common with the rest, who is nevertheless to be put far before aquatic animals, though Plato puts the waters themselves before the land. By this he would have us understand that the same order is not to be observed when the question concerns the merits of animals, though it seems to be the true one in the gradation of bodies; for it appears to be possible that a soul of a higher order

may inhabit a body of a lower, and a soul of a lower order a body of a higher.

Chap. 16. *What Apuleius the Platonist thought concerning the manners and actions of demons*

The same Apuleius, when speaking concerning the manners of demons, said that they are agitated with the same perturbations of mind as men; that they are provoked by injuries, propitiated by services and by gifts, rejoice in honours, are delighted with a variety of sacred rites, and are annoyed if any of them be neglected. Among other things, he also says that on them depend the divinations of augurs, soothsayers, and prophets, and the revelations of dreams, and that from them also are the miracles of the magicians. But, when giving a brief definition of them, he says, "Demons are of an animal nature, passive in soul, rational in mind, aerial in body, eternal in time." "Of which five things, the three first are common to them and us, the fourth peculiar to themselves, and the fifth common to them with the gods." But I see that they have in common with the gods two of the first things, which they have in common with us. For he says that the gods also are animals; and when he is assigning to every order of beings its own element, he places us among the other terrestrial animals which live and feel upon the earth. Wherefore, if the demons are animals as to genus, this is common to them, not only with men, but also with the gods and with beasts; if they are rational as to their mind, this is common to them with the gods and with men; if they are eternal in time, this is common to them with the gods only; if they are passive as to their soul, this is common to them with men only; if they are aerial in body, in this they are alone. Therefore it is no great thing for them to be of an animal nature, for so also are the beasts; in being rational as to mind, they are not above ourselves, for so are we also; and as to their being eternal as to time, what is the advantage of that if they are not blessed? for better is temporal happiness than eternal misery. Again, as to their being passive in soul, how are they in this respect above us, since we also are so, but would not have been so had we not been miserable? Also, as to their being aerial in body, how much value is to be set on that, since a soul of any kind whatsoever is to be set above everybody? and therefore religious worship, which ought to be rendered from the soul, is by no means due to that thing which is inferior to the soul. Moreover, if he had, among those things which he says belong to demons, enumerated virtue, wisdom, happiness, and affirmed that they have those things in common with the gods, and, like them, eternally, he would assuredly have attributed to them something greatly to be desired, and much to be prized. And even in that case it would not have been our duty to worship them like God on account of these things, but rather to worship Him from Whom we know they had received them. But how much less are they really worthy of divine honour—those aerial animals who are only rational that they may be capable of misery, passive that they may be actually miserable, and eternal that it may be impossible for them to end their misery!

CHAP. 17. *Whether it is proper that men should worship those spirits from whose vices it is necessary that they be freed*

Wherefore, to omit other things, and confine our attention to that which he says is common to the demons with us, let us ask this question: If all the four elements are full of their own animals, the fire and the air of immortal, and the water and the earth of mortal ones, why are the souls of demons agitated by the whirlwinds and tempests of passions?—for the Greek word πάθος means perturbation, when he chose to call the demons "passive in soul," because the word passion, which is derived from πάθος, signified a commotion of the mind contrary to reason. Why, then, are these things in the minds of demons which are not in beasts? For if anything of this kind appears in beasts, it is not perturbation, because it is not contrary to reason, of which they are devoid. Now it is foolishness or misery which is the cause of these perturbations in the case of men, for we are not yet blessed in the possession of that perfection of wisdom which is promised to us at last, when we shall be set free from our present mortality. But the gods, they say, are free from these perturbations, because they are not only eternal, but also blessed; for they also have the same kind of rational souls, but most pure from all spot and plague. Wherefore, if the gods are free from perturbation because they are blessed, not miserable animals, and the beasts are free from them because they are animals which are capable neither of blessedness nor misery, it remains that the demons, like men, are subject to perturbations because they are not blessed but miserable animals. What folly, therefore, or rather what madness, to submit ourselves through any sentiment of religion to demons, when it belongs to the true religion to deliver us from that

depravity which makes us like to them! For Apuleius himself, although he is very sparing toward them, and thinks they are worthy of divine honours, is nevertheless compelled to confess that they are subject to anger; and the true religion commands us not to be moved with anger, but rather to resist it. The demons are won over by gifts; and the true religion commands us to favour no one on account of gifts received. The demons are flattered by honours; but the true religion commands us by no means to be moved by such things. The demons are haters of some men and lovers of others, not in consequence of a prudent and calm judgment, but because of what he calls their "passive soul"; whereas the true religion commands us to love even our enemies. Lastly, the true religion commands us to put away all disquietude of heart, and agitation of mind, and also all commotions and tempests of the soul, which Apuleius asserts to be continually swelling and surging in the souls of demons. Why, therefore, except through foolishness and miserable error, shouldst thou humble thyself to worship a being to whom thou desirest to be unlike in thy life? And why shouldst thou pay religious homage to him whom thou are unwilling to imitate, when it is the highest duty of religion to imitate Him Whom thou worshippest?

CHAP. 18. *What kind of religion that is which teaches that men ought to employ the advocacy of demons in order to be recommended to the favour of the good gods*

In vain, therefore, have Apuleius and they who think with him conferred on the demons the honour of placing them in the air, between the ethereal heavens and the earth, that they may carry to the gods the prayers of men, to men the answers of the gods: for Plato held, they say, that no god has intercourse with man. They who believe these things have thought it unbecoming that men should have intercourse with the gods and the gods with men, but a befitting thing that the demons should have intercourse with both gods and men, presenting to the gods the petitions of men, and conveying to men what the gods have granted; so that a chaste man, and one who is a stranger to the crimes of the magic arts, must use as patrons, through whom the gods may be induced to hear him, demons who love these crimes, although the very fact of his not loving them ought to have recommended him to them as one who deserved to be listened to with greater readiness and willingness on their part. They love the abominations of the stage, which chastity does not love. They love, in the sorceries of the magicians, *"a thousand arts of inflicting harm,"*[1] which innocence does not love. Yet both chastity and innocence, if they wish to obtain anything from the gods, will not be able to do so by their own merits, except their enemies act as mediators on their behalf. Apuleius need not attempt to justify the fictions of the poets, and the mockeries of the stage. If human modesty can act so faithlessly towards itself as not only to love shameful things, but even to think that they are pleasing to the divinity, we can cite on the other side their own highest authority and teacher, Plato.

CHAP. 19. *Of the impiety of the magic art, which is dependent on the assistance of malign spirits*

Moreover, against those magic arts, concerning which some men, exceedingly wretched and exceedingly impious, delight to boast, may not public opinion itself be brought forward as a witness? For why are those arts so severely punished by the laws, if they are the works of deities who ought to be worshipped? Shall it be said that the Christians have ordained those laws by which magic arts are punished? With what other meaning, except that these sorceries are without doubt pernicious to the human race, did the most illustrious poet say,

> By heaven, I swear, and your dear life,
> Unwillingly these arms I wield,
> And take, to meet the coming strife,
> Enchantment's sword and shield.[2]

And that also which he says in another place concerning magic arts,

> I've seen him to another place
> transport the standing corn.[3]

has reference to the fact that the fruits of one field are said to be transferred to another by these arts which this pestiferous and accursed doctrine teaches. Does not Cicero inform us that, among the laws of the Twelve Tables, that is, the most ancient laws of the Romans, there was a law written which appointed a punishment to be inflicted on him who should do this? Lastly, was it before Christian judges that Apuleius himself was accused of magic arts? Had he known these arts to be divine and pious, and congruous with the works of divine power, he ought not only to have confessed, but also to have professed them, rather blaming the laws by

which these things were prohibited and pronounced worthy of condemnation, while they ought to have been held worthy of admiration and respect. For by so doing, either he would have persuaded the judges to adopt his own opinion, or, if they had shown their partiality for unjust laws and condemned him to death notwithstanding his praising and commending such things, the demons would have bestowed on his soul such rewards as he deserved, who, in order to proclaim and set forth their divine works, had not feared the loss of his human life. As our martyrs, when that religion was charged on them as a crime, by which they knew they were made safe and most glorious throughout eternity, did not choose, by denying it, to escape temporal punishments, but rather by confessing, professing, and proclaiming it, by enduring all things for it with fidelity and fortitude, and by dying for it with pious calmness, put to shame the law by which that religion was prohibited, and caused its revocation. But there is extant a most copious and eloquent oration of this Platonic philosopher, in which he defends himself against the charge of practising these arts, affirming that he is wholly a stranger to them, and only wishing to show his innocence by denying such things as cannot be innocently committed. But all the miracles of the magicians, who he thinks are justly deserving of condemnation, are performed according to the teaching and by the power of demons. Why, then, does he think that they ought to be honoured? For he asserts that they are necessary, in order to present our prayers to the gods, and yet their works are such as we must shun if we wish our prayers to reach the true God. Again, I ask, what kind of prayers of men does he suppose are presented to the good gods by the demons? If magical prayers, they will have none such; if lawful prayers, they will not receive them through such beings. But if a sinner who is penitent pour out prayers, especially if he has committed any crime of sorcery, does he receive pardon through the intercession of those demons by whose instigation and help he has fallen into the sin he mourns? or do the demons themselves, in order that they may merit pardon for the penitent, first become penitents because they have deceived them? This no one ever said concerning the demons; for had this been the case, they would never have dared to seek for themselves divine honours. For how should they do so who desired by penitence to obtain the grace of pardon, seeing that such detestable pride could not exist along with a humility worthy of pardon?

[1]Virgil, *Æneid*, BK. VII, 338.   [2]*Ibid.*, BK. IV. 492, 493.
[3]Virgil, *Eclogues*, BK. VIII. 99.

CHAP. 20. *Whether we are to believe that the good gods are more willing to have intercourse with demons than with men*

But does any urgent and most pressing cause compel the demons to mediate between the gods and men, that they may offer the prayers of men, and bring back the answers from the gods? and if so, what, pray, is that cause, what is that so great necessity? Because, say they, no god has intercourse with man. Most admirable holiness of God, which has no intercourse with a supplicating man, and yet has intercourse with an arrogant demon! which has no intercourse with a penitent man, and yet has intercourse with a deceiving demon! which has no intercourse with a man fleeing for refuge to the divine nature, and yet has intercourse with a demon feigning divinity! which has no intercourse with a man seeking pardon, and yet has intercourse with a demon persuading to wickedness! which has no intercourse with a man expelling the poets by means of philosophical writings from a well-regulated state, and yet has intercourse with a demon requesting from the princes and priests of a state the theatrical performance of the mockeries of the poets! which has no intercourse with the man who prohibits the ascribing of crime to the gods, and yet has intercourse with a demon who takes delight in the fictitious representation of their crimes! which has no intercourse with a man punishing the crimes of the magicians by just laws, and yet has intercourse with a demon teaching and practising magical arts! which has no intercourse with a man shunning the imitation of a demon, and yet has intercourse with a demon lying in wait for the deception of a man!

CHAP. 21. *Whether the gods use the demons as messengers and interpreters, and whether they are deceived by them willingly, or without their own knowledge*

But herein, no doubt, lies the great necessity for this absurdity, so unworthy of the gods, that the ethereal gods, who are concerned about human affairs, would not know what terrestrial men were doing unless the aerial demons should bring them intelligence, because the ether is suspended far away from the earth and far above it, but the air is contiguous both to the ether and to the earth. O admirable wisdom! what else do these men think concerning the gods who, they say, are all in the highest degree good, but that they are concerned about human affairs, lest they should seem unworthy of worship, whilst, on the other hand, from the distance between the elements, they are ignorant of terrestrial things? It is on this account that they have supposed the demons to be necessary as agents, through whom the gods may inform themselves with respect to human affairs, and through whom, when necessary, they may succour men; and it is on account of this office that the demons themselves have been held as deserving of worship. If this be the case, then a demon is better known by these good gods through nearness of body than a man is by goodness of mind. O mournful necessity, or shall I not rather say detestable and vain error, that I may not impute vanity to the divine nature! For if the gods can, with their minds free from the hindrance of bodies, see our mind, they do not need the demons as messengers from our mind to them; but if the ethereal gods, by means of their bodies, perceive the corporeal indices of minds, as the countenance, speech, motion, and thence understand what the demons tell them, then it is also possible that they may be deceived by the falsehoods of demons. Moreover, if the divinity of the gods cannot be deceived by the demons, neither can it be ignorant of our actions. But I would they would tell me whether the demons have informed the gods that the fictions of the poets concerning the crimes of the gods displease Plato, concealing the pleasure which they themselves take in them; or whether they have concealed both, and have preferred that the gods should be ignorant with respect to this whole matter, or have told both, as well the pious prudence of Plato with respect to the gods as their own lust, which is injurious to the gods; or whether they have concealed Plato's opinion, according to which he was unwilling that the gods should be defamed with falsely alleged crimes through the impious licence of the poets, whilst they have not been ashamed nor afraid to make known their own wickedness, which make them love theatrical plays, in which the infamous deeds of the gods are celebrated. Let them choose which they will of these four alternatives, and let them consider how much evil any one of them would require them to think of the gods. For if they choose the first, they must then confess that it was not possible for the good gods to dwell with the good Plato, though he sought to prohibit things injurious to them, whilst they dwelt with evil demons, who exulted in their injuries; and this because they suppose that the good gods can only know a good man, placed at so great a distance from them, through the mediation of evil demons, whom they could know on account of their nearness to themselves.[1] If they shall choose the second, and shall say that both these things are concealed by the demons, so that the gods are wholly ignorant both of Plato's most religious law and the sacrilegious pleasure of the demons, what, in that case, can the gods know to any profit with respect to human affairs through these mediating demons, when they do not know those things which are decreed, through the piety of good men, for the honour of the good gods against the lust of evil demons? But if they shall choose the third and reply that these intermediary demons have communicated, not only the opinion of Plato, which prohibited wrongs to be done to the gods, but also their own delight in these wrongs, I would ask if such a communication is not rather an insult? Now the gods, hearing both and knowing both, not only permit the approach of those malign demons, who desire and do things contrary to the dignity of the gods and the religion of Plato, but also, through these wicked demons, who are near to them, send good things to the good Plato, who is far away from them; for they inhabit such a place in the concatenated series of the elements, that they can come into contact with those by whom they are accused, but not with him by whom they are defended—knowing the truth on both sides, but not being able to change the weight of the air and the earth. There remains the fourth supposition; but it is worse than the rest. For who will suffer it to be said that the demons have made known the calumnious fictions of the poets concerning the immortal gods, and also the disgraceful mockeries of the theatres, and their own most ardent lust after and most sweet pleasure in these things, whilst they have concealed from them that Plato, with the gravity of a philosopher, gave it as his opinion that all these things ought to be removed from a well-regulated republic; so that the good gods are now compelled, through such messengers, to know the evil doings of the most wicked beings, that is to say, of the messengers themselves, and are not allowed to know the good deeds of the philosophers, though the former are for the injury, but these latter for the honour of the gods themselves?

CHAP. 22. *That we must, notwithstanding the opinion of Apuleius, reject the worship of demons*

None of these four alternatives, then, is to be chosen; for we dare not suppose such unbecom-

[1]Another reading: "whom they could not know, though near to themselves."

ing things concerning the gods as the adoption of any one of them would lead us to think. It remains, therefore, that no credence whatever is to be given to the opinion of Apuleius and the other philosophers of the same school, namely, that the demons act as messengers and interpreters between the gods and men to carry our petitions from us to the gods, and to bring back to us the help of the gods. On the contrary, we must believe them to be spirits most eager to inflict harm, utterly alien from righteousness, swollen with pride, pale with envy, subtle in deceit; who dwell indeed in this air as in a prison, in keeping with their own character, because, cast down from the height of the higher heaven, they have been condemned to dwell in this element as the just reward of irretrievable transgression. But, though the air is situated above the earth and the waters, they are not on that account superior in merit to men, who, though they do not surpass them as far as their earthly bodies are concerned, do nevertheless far excel them through piety of mind—they having made choice of the true God as their helper. Over many, however, who are manifestly unworthy of participation in the true religion, they tyrannize as over captives whom they have subdued—the greatest part of whom they have persuaded of their divinity by wonderful and lying signs, consisting either of deeds or of predictions. Some, nevertheless, who have more attentively and diligently considered their vices, they have not been able to persuade that they are gods and so have feigned themselves to be messengers between the gods and men. Some, indeed, have thought that not even this latter honour ought to be acknowledged as belonging to them, not believing that they were gods, because they saw that they were wicked, whereas the gods, according to their view, are all good. Nevertheless they dared not say that they were wholly unworthy of all divine honour, for fear of offending the multitude, by whom, through inveterate superstition, the demons were served by the performance of many rites and the erection of many temples.

CHAP. 23. *What Hermes Trismegistus thought concerning idolatry, and from what source he knew that the superstitions of Egypt were to be abolished*

The Egyptian Hermes, whom they call Trismegistus, had a different opinion concerning those demons. Apuleius, indeed, denies that they are gods; but when he says that they hold a middle place between the gods and men, so that they seem to be necessary for men as mediators between them and the gods, he does not distinguish between the worship due to them and the religious homage due to the supernal gods. This Egyptian, however, says that there are some gods made by the supreme God and some made by men. Any one who hears this, as I have stated it, no doubt supposes that it has reference to images, because they are the works of the hands of men; but he asserts that visible and tangible images are, as it were, only the bodies of the gods, and that there dwell in them certain spirits, which have been invited to come into them, and which have power to inflict harm, or to fulfil the desires of those by whom divine honours and services are rendered to them. To unite, therefore, by a certain art, those invisible spirits to visible and material things, so as to make, as it were, animated bodies, dedicated and given up to those spirits who inhabit them—this, he says, is to make gods, adding that men have received this great and wonderful power. I will give the words of this Egyptian as they have been translated into our tongue: "And, since we have undertaken to discourse concerning the relationship and fellowship between men and the gods, know, O Æsculapius, the power and strength of man. As the Lord and Father, or that which is highest, even God, is the maker of the celestial gods, so man is the maker of the gods who are in the temples, content to dwell near to men." And a little after he says, "Thus humanity, always mindful of its nature and origin, perseveres in the imitation of divinity; and as the Lord and Father made eternal gods, that they should be like Himself, so humanity fashioned its own gods according to the likeness of its own countenance." When this Æsculapius, to whom especially he was speaking, had answered him, and had said, "Dost thou mean the statues, O Trismegistus?"—"Yes, the statues," replied he, "however unbelieving thou art, O Æsculapius—the statues, animated, and full of sensation and spirit, and who do such great and wonderful things, the statues, prescient of future things, and foretelling them by lot, by prophet, by dreams, and many other things, who bring diseases on men and cure them again, giving them joy or sorrow according to their merits. Dost thou not know, O Æsculapius, that Egypt is an image of heaven, or, more truly, a translation and descent of all things which are ordered and transacted there, that it is, in truth, if we may say so, to be the temple of the whole world? And yet, as it becomes the prudent man to know all things beforehand, ye ought not to be ignorant of this, that there is a time coming when it shall appear that the Egyptians have all in vain, with pious mind, and with most scrupulous diligence, waited on the divinity, and when all their holy worship shall come to nought, and be found to be in vain."

Hermes then follows out at great length the statements of this passage, in which he seems to predict the present time, in which the Christian religion is overthrowing all lying figments with a vehemence and liberty proportioned to its superior truth and holiness, in order that the grace of the true Saviour may deliver men from those gods which man has made, and subject them to that God by Whom man was made. But when Hermes predicts these things, he speaks as one who is a friend to these same mockeries of demons and does not clearly express the name of Christ. On the contrary, he deplores, as if it had already taken place, the future abolition of those things by the observance of which there was maintained in Egypt a resemblance of heaven; he bears witness to Christianity by a kind of mournful prophecy. Now it was with reference to such that the apostle said, that "knowing God, they glorified Him not as God, neither were thankful, but became vain in their imaginations, and their foolish heart was darkened; professing themselves to be wise, they became fools, and changed the glory of the incorruptible God into the likeness of the image of corruptible man,"[1] and so on, for the whole passage is too long to quote. For Hermes makes many such statements agreeable to the truth concerning the one true God Who fashioned this world. And I know not how he has become so bewildered by that "darkening of the heart" as to stumble into the expression of a desire that men should always continue in subjection to those gods which he confesses to be made by men and to bewail their future removal; as if there could be anything more wretched than mankind tyrannized over by the work of his own hands, since man, by worshipping the works of his own hands, may more easily cease to be man, than the works of his hands can, through his worship of them, become gods. For it can sooner happen that man, who has received an honourable position, may, through lack of understanding, become comparable to the beasts, than that the works of man may become preferable to the work of God, made in His own image, that is, to man himself. Wherefore deservedly is man left to fall away from Him Who made Him, when he prefers to himself that which he himself has made.

[1] Rom. i. 21.

For these vain, deceitful, pernicious, sacrilegious things did the Egyptian Hermes sorrow, because he knew that the time was coming when they should be removed. But his sorrow was as impudently expressed as his knowledge was imprudently obtained; for it was not the Holy Spirit Who revealed these things to him, as He had done to the holy prophets, who, foreseeing these things, said with exultation, "If a man shall make gods, lo, they are no gods";[1] and in another place, "And it shall come to pass in that day, saith the Lord, that I will cut off the names of the idols out of the land, and they shall no more be remembered."[2] But the holy Isaiah prophesies expressly concerning Egypt in reference to this matter, saying, "And the idols of Egypt shall be moved at His presence, and their heart shall be overcome in them,"[3] and other things to the same effect. And with the prophet are to be classed those who rejoiced that that which they knew was to come had actually come —as Simeon, or Anna, who immediately recognized Jesus when He was born, or Elisabeth, who in the Spirit recognized Him when He was conceived, or Peter, who said by the revelation of the Father, "Thou art Christ, the Son of the living God."[4] But to this Egyptian those spirits indicated the time of their own destruction, who also, when the Lord was present in the flesh, said with trembling, "Art Thou come hither to destroy us before the time?"[5] meaning by destruction before the time, either that very destruction which they expected to come, but which they did not think would come so suddenly as it appeared to have done, or only that destruction which consisted in their being brought into contempt by being made known. And, indeed, this was a destruction before the time, that is, before the time of judgment, when they are to be punished with eternal damnation, together with all men who are implicated in their wickedness, as the true religion declares, which neither errs nor leads into error; for it is not like him who, blown hither and thither by every wind of doctrine, and mixing true things with things which are false, bewails as about to perish a religion which he afterwards confesses to be error.

CHAP. 24. *How Hermes openly confessed the error of his forefathers, the coming destruction of which he nevertheless bewailed*

After a long interval, Hermes again comes back to the subject of the gods which men have made, saying as follows: "But enough on this subject. Let us return to man and to reason, that divine gift on account of which man has been called a rational animal. For the things which have been said concerning man, wonderful though they are, are less wonderful than those which have been said concerning reason. For man to discover the divine nature, and to make it, surpasses the wonder of all other wonderful things. Because, therefore, our forefathers erred very far with respect to the knowledge of the gods, through incredulity and through want of attention to their worship and service, they invented this art of making gods; and this art once invented, they associated with it a suitable virtue borrowed from universal nature and, being incapable of making souls, they evoked those of demons or of angels and united them with these holy images and divine mysteries, in order that through these souls the images might have power to do good or harm to men." I know not whether the demons themselves could have been made, even by adjuration, to confess as he has confessed in these words: "Because our forefathers erred very far with respect to the knowledge of the gods, through incredulity and through want of attention to their worship and service, they invented the art of making gods." Does he say that it was a moderate degree of error which resulted in their discovery of the art of making gods, or was he content to say "they erred?" No; he must needs add "very far," and say, *"They erred very far."* It was this great error and incredulity, then, of their forefathers who did not attend to the worship and service of the gods, which was the origin of the art of making gods. And yet this wise man grieves over the ruin of this art at some future time, as if it were a divine religion. Is he not verily compelled by divine influence, on the one hand, to reveal the past error of his forefathers, and by a diabolical influence, on the other hand, to bewail the future punishment of demons? For if their forefathers, by erring very far with respect to the knowledge of the gods, through incredulity and aversion of mind from their worship and service, invented the art of making gods, what wonder is it that all that is done by this detestable art, which is opposed to the divine religion, should be taken away by that religion when truth corrects error, faith refutes incredulity, and conversion rectifies aversion?

For if he had only said, without mentioning the cause, that his forefathers had discovered the art of making gods, it would have been our duty, if we paid any regard to what is right and

[1]Jer. 16. 20.　[2]Zech. 13. 2.　[3]Isa. 19. 1.
[4]Matt. 16. 16.　[5]Matt. 8. 29.

pious, to consider and to see that they could never have attained to this art if they had not erred from the truth, if they had believed those things which are worthy of God, if they had attended to divine worship and service. However, if we alone should say that the causes of this art were to be found in the great error and incredulity of men, and aversion of the mind erring from and unfaithful to divine religion, the impudence of those who resist the truth were in some way to be borne with; but when he who admires in man, above all other things, this power which it has been granted him to practise, and sorrows because a time is coming when all those figments of gods invented by men shall even be commanded by the laws to be taken away—when even this man confesses nevertheless and explains the causes which led to the discovery of this art, saying that their ancestors, through great error and incredulity, and through not attending to the worship and service of the gods, invented this art of making gods—what ought we to say, or rather to do, but to give to the Lord our God all the thanks we are able, because He has taken away those things by causes the contrary of those which led to their institution? For that which the prevalence of error instituted, the way of truth took away; that which incredulity instituted, faith took away; that which aversion from divine worship and service instituted, conversion to the one true and holy God took away. Nor was this the case only in Egypt, for which country alone the spirit of the demons lamented in Hermes, but in all the earth, which sings to the Lord a new song,[1] as the truly holy and truly prophetic Scriptures have predicted, in which it is written, "Sing unto the Lord a new song; sing unto the Lord, all the earth." For the title of this psalm is, "When the house was built after the captivity." For a house is being built to the Lord in all the earth, even the city of God, which is the holy Church, after that captivity in which demons held captive those men who, through faith in God, became living stones in the house. For although man made gods, it did not follow that he who made them was not held captive by them, when, by worshipping them, he was drawn into fellowship with them—into the fellowship not of stolid idols, but of cunning demons; for what are idols but what they are represented to be in the same Scriptures, "They have eyes, but they do not see,"[2] and, though artistically fashioned, are still without life and sensation? But unclean spirits, associated through that wicked art with these same idols,

have miserably taken captive the souls of their worshippers, by bringing them down into fellowship with themselves. Whence the apostle says, "We know that an idol is nothing, but those things which the Gentiles sacrifice they sacrifice to demons, and not to God; and I would not ye should have fellowship with demons."[3] After this captivity, therefore, in which men were held by malign demons, the house of God is being built in all the earth; whence the title of that psalm in which it is said, "Sing unto the Lord a new song; sing unto the Lord, all the earth. Sing unto the Lord, bless His name; declare well His salvation from day to day. Declare His glory among the nations, among all people His wonderful things. For great is the Lord, and much to be praised: He is terrible above all gods. For all the gods of the nations are demons: but the Lord made the heavens."[4]

Wherefore he who sorrowed because a time was coming when the worship of idols should be abolished, and the domination of the demons over those who worshipped them, wished, under the influence of a demon, that that captivity should always continue, at the cessation of which that psalm celebrates the building of the house of the Lord in all the earth. Hermes foretold these things with grief, the prophet with joyfulness; and because the Spirit is victorious Who sang these things through the ancient prophets, even Hermes himself was compelled in a wonderful manner to confess that those very things which he wished not to be removed, and at the prospect of whose removal he was sorrowful, had been instituted, not by prudent, faithful, and religious, but by erring and unbelieving men, averse to the worship and service of the gods. And although he calls them gods, nevertheless, when he says that they were made by such men as we certainly ought not to be, he shows, whether he will or not, that they are not to be worshipped by those who do not resemble these image-makers, that is, by prudent, faithful, and religious men, at the same time also making it manifest that the very men who made them involved themselves in the worship of those as gods who were not gods. For true is the saying of the prophet, "If a man *make* gods, lo, they are no gods."[5] Such gods, therefore, acknowledged by such worshippers and made by such men, did Hermes call "gods made by men," that is to say, demons, through some art of I know not what description, bound by the chains of their own lusts to images. But, nevertheless, he did not agree with that opinion of the Platonic Apuleius, of which we have already shown the incongruity and absurdity, namely, that they were interpreters and intercessors between the gods whom God made, and men whom the same God made, bringing to God the prayers of men, and from God the gifts given in answer to these prayers. For it is exceedingly stupid to believe that gods whom men have made have more influence with gods whom God has made than men themselves have, whom the very same God has made. And consider, too, that it is a demon which, bound by a man to an image by means of an impious art, has been made a god, but a god to such a man only, not to every man. What kind of god, therefore, is that which no man would make but one erring, incredulous, and averse to the true God? Moreover, if the demons which are worshipped in the temples, being introduced by some kind of strange art into images, that is, into visible representations of themselves, by those men who by this art made gods when they were straying away from, and were averse to the worship and service of the gods—if, I say, those demons are neither mediators nor interpreters between men and the gods, both on account of their own most wicked and base manners, and because men, though erring, incredulous, and averse from the worship and service of the gods, are nevertheless beyond doubt better than the demons whom they themselves have evoked, then it remains to be affirmed that what power they possess they possess as demons, doing harm by bestowing pretended benefits—harm all the greater for the deception—or else openly and undisguisedly doing evil to men. They cannot, however, do anything of this kind unless where they are permitted by the deep and secret providence of God and then only so far as they are permitted. When, however, they are permitted, it is not because they, being midway between men and the gods, have through the friendship of the gods great power over men; for these demons cannot possibly be friends to the good gods who dwell in the holy and heavenly habitation, by whom we mean holy angels and rational creatures, whether thrones, or dominations, or principalities, or powers, from whom they are as far separated in disposition and character as vice is distant from virtue, wickedness from goodness.

Chap. 25. Concerning those things which may be common to the holy angels and to men

Wherefore we must by no means seek, through the supposed mediation of demons, to avail ourselves of the benevolence or benefi- cence of the gods, or rather of the good angels, but through resembling them in the possession of a good will, through which we are with them, and live with them, and worship with them the same God, although we cannot see them with the eyes of our flesh. But it is not in locality we are distant from them, but in merit of life, caused by our miserable unlikeness to them in will, and by the weakness of our character; for the mere fact of our dwelling on earth under the conditions of life in the flesh does not prevent our fellowship with them. It is only prevented when we, in the impurity of our hearts, mind earthly things. But in this present time, while we are being healed that we may eventually be as they are, we are brought near to them by faith, if by their assistance we believe that He Who is their blessedness is also ours.

Chap. 26. That all the religion of the pagans has reference to dead men

It is certainly a remarkable thing how this Egyptian, when expressing his grief that a time was coming when those things would be taken away from Egypt, which he confesses to have been invented by men erring, incredulous, and averse to the service of divine religion, says, among other things, "Then shall that land, the most holy place of shrines and temples, be full of sepulchres and dead men," as if, in sooth, if these things were not taken away, men would not die! as if dead bodies could be buried elsewhere than in the ground! as if, as time advanced, the number of sepulchres must not necessarily increase in proportion to the increase of the number of the dead! But they who are of a perverse mind, and opposed to us, suppose that what he grieves for is that the memorials of our martyrs were to succeed to their temples and shrines, in order, forsooth, that they may have grounds for thinking that gods were worshipped by the pagans in temples, but that dead men are worshipped by us in sepulchres. For with such blindness do impious men, as it were, stumble over mountains, and will not see the things which strike their own eyes, that they do not attend to the fact that in all the literature of the pagans there are not found any, or scarcely any gods, who have not been men, to whom, when dead, divine honours have been paid. I will not enlarge on the fact that Varro says that all dead men are thought by them to be gods—Manes— and proves it by those sacred rites which are performed in honour of almost all the dead, among which he mentions funeral games, considering this the very highest proof of divinity, because games are only wont to be celebrated in honour of divinities. Hermes himself, of whom we are now treating, in that same book in which, as if foretelling future things, he says with sorrow "Then shall that land, the most holy place of shrines and temples, be full of sepulchres and dead men," testifies that the gods of Egypt were dead men. For, having said that their forefathers, erring very far with respect to the knowledge of the gods, incredulous and inattentive to the divine worship and service, invented the art of making gods, with which art, when invented, they associated the appropriate virtue which is inherent in universal nature, and by mixing up that virtue with this art, they called forth the souls of demons or of angels (for they could not make souls) and caused them to take possession of, or associate themselves with holy images and divine mysteries, in order that through these souls the images might have power to do good or harm to men; having said this, he goes on, as it were, to prove it by illustrations, saying, "Thy grandsire, O Æsculapius, the first discoverer of medicine, to whom a temple was consecrated in a mountain of Libya, near to the shore of the crocodiles, in which temple lies his earthly man, that is, his body—for the better part of him, or rather the whole of him, if the whole man is in the intelligent life, went back to heaven—affords even now by his divinity all those helps to infirm men, which formerly he was wont to afford to them by the art of medicine." He says, therefore, that a dead man was worshipped as a god in that place where he had his sepulchre. He deceives men by a falsehood, for the man "went back to heaven." Then he adds, "Does not Hermes, who was my grandsire, and whose name I bear, abiding in the country which is called by his name, help and preserve all mortals who come to him from every quarter?" For this elder Hermes, that is, Mercury, who, he says, was his grandsire, is said to be buried in Hermopolis, that is, in the city called by his name; so here are two gods whom he affirms to have been men, Æsculapius and Mercury. Now concerning Æsculapius, both the Greeks and the Latins think the same thing; but as to Mercury, there are many who do not think that he was formerly a mortal, though Hermes testifies that he was his grandsire. But are these two different individuals who were called by the same name? I will not dispute much whether they are different individuals or not. It is sufficient to know that this Mercury of whom Hermes speaks is, as well as Æsculapius, a god who once was a man, according to the testimony of this same Trisme-

gistus, esteemed so great by his countrymen, and also the grandson of Mercury himself.

Hermes goes on to say, "But do we know how many good things Isis, the wife of Osiris, bestows when she is propitious, and what great opposition she can offer when enraged?" Then, in order to show that there were gods made by men through this art, he goes on to say, "For it is easy for earthly and mundane gods to be angry, being made and composed by men out of either nature"; thus giving us to understand that he believed that demons were formerly the souls of dead men, which, as he says, by means of a certain art invented by men very far in error, incredulous, and irreligious, were caused to take possession of images, because they who made such gods were not able to make souls. When, therefore, he says "either nature," he means soul and body—the demon being the soul, and the image the body. What, then, becomes of that mournful complaint that the land of Egypt, the most holy place of shrines and temples, was to be full of sepulchres and dead men? Verily, the fallacious spirit, by whose inspiration Hermes spoke these things, was compelled to confess through him that even already that land was full of sepulchres and of dead men, whom they were worshipping as gods. But it was the grief of the demons which was expressing itself through his mouth, who were sorrowing on account of the punishments which were about to fall upon them at the tombs of the martyrs. For in many such places they are tortured and compelled to confess, and are cast out of the bodies of men, of which they had taken possession.

CHAP. 27. Concerning the nature of the honour which the Christians pay to their martyrs

But, nevertheless, we do not build temples, and ordain priests, rites, and sacrifices for these same martyrs; for they are not our gods, but their God is our God. Certainly we honour their reliquaries, as the memorials of holy men of God who strove for the truth even to the death of their bodies, that the true religion might be made known, and false and fictitious religions exposed. For if there were some before them who thought that these religions were really false and fictitious, they were afraid to give expression to their convictions. But who ever heard a priest of the faithful, standing at an altar built for the honour and worship of God over the holy body of some martyr, say in the prayers, I offer to thee a sacrifice, O Peter, or O Paul, or O Cyprian? for it is to God that sacrifices are offered at their tombs—the God Who made them both men and martyrs, and associated them with holy angels in celestial honour; and the reason that we pay such honours to their memory is that by so doing we may both give thanks to the true God for their victories, and, by recalling them afresh to remembrance, may stir ourselves up to imitate them by seeking to obtain like crowns and palms, calling to our help that same God on whom they called. Therefore, whatever honours the religious may pay in the places of the martyrs, they are but honours rendered to their memory, not sacred rites or sacrifices offered to dead men as to gods. And even such as bring thither food—which, indeed, is not done by the better Christians, and in most places of the world is not done at all—do so in order that it may be sanctified to them through the merits of the martyrs, in the name of the Lord of the martyrs, first presenting the food and offering prayer, and thereafter taking it away to be eaten, or to be in part bestowed upon the needy.[1] But he who knows the one sacrifice of Christians, which is the sacrifice offered in those places, also knows that these are not sacrifices offered to the martyrs. It is, then, neither with divine honours nor with human crimes, by which they worship their gods, that we honour our martyrs; neither do we offer sacrifices to them, or convert the crimes of the gods into their sacred rites. For let those who will and can read the letter of Alexander to his mother Olympias, in which he tells the things which were revealed to him by the priest Leon, and let those who have read it recall to memory what it contains, that they may see what great abominations have been handed down to memory, not by poets, but by the mystic writings of the Egyptians, concerning the goddess Isis, the wife of Osiris, and

[1] Cf. *The Confessions*, BK. VI. 2.

the parents of both, all of whom, according to these writings, were royal personages. Isis, when sacrificing to her parents, is said to have discovered a crop of barley, of which she brought some ears to the king her husband and his councillor Mercurius, and hence they identify her with Ceres. Those who read the letter may there see what was the character of those people to whom when dead sacred rites were instituted as to gods, and what those deeds of theirs were which furnished the occasion for these rites. Let them not once dare to compare in any respect those people, though they hold them to be gods, to our holy martyrs, though we do not hold them to be gods. For we do not ordain priests and offer sacrifices to our martyrs, as they do to their dead men, for that would be incongruous, undue, and unlawful, such being due only to God; and thus we do not delight them with their own crimes, or with such shameful plays as those in which the crimes of the gods are celebrated, which are either real crimes committed by them at a time when they were men, or else, if they never were men, fictitious crimes invented for the pleasure of noxious demons. The god of Socrates, if he had a god, cannot have belonged to this class of demons. But perhaps they who wished to excel in this art of making gods, imposed a god of this sort on a man who was a stranger to, and innocent of any connexion with that art. What need we say more? No one who is even moderately wise imagines that demons are to be worshipped on account of the blessed life which is to be after death. But perhaps they will say that all the gods are good, but that of the demons some are bad and some good, and that it is the good who are to be worshipped, in order that through them we may attain to the eternally blessed life. To the examination of this opinion we will devote the following book.

BOOK IX

ARGUMENT. HAVING IN THE PRECEDING BOOK SHOWN THAT THE WORSHIP OF DE-MONS MUST BE ABJURED, SINCE THEY IN A THOUSAND WAYS PROCLAIM THEMSELVES TO BE WICKED SPIRITS, AUGUSTINE IN THIS BOOK MEETS THOSE WHO ALLEGE A DIS-TINCTION AMONG DEMONS, SOME BEING EVIL, WHILE OTHERS ARE GOOD; AND, HAVING EXPLODED THIS DISTINCTION, HE PROVES THAT TO NO DEMON, BUT TO CHRIST ALONE, BELONGS THE OFFICE OF PROVIDING MEN WITH ETERNAL BLESSEDNESS.

CHAP. 1. *The point at which the discussion has arrived, and what remains to be handled*

SOME have advanced the opinion that there are both good and bad gods; but some, thinking more respectfully of the gods, have attributed to them so much honour and praise as to preclude the supposition of any god being wicked. But those who have maintained that there are wicked gods as well as good ones have included the demons under the name "gods," and sometimes, though more rarely, have called the gods demons; so that they admit that Jupiter, whom they make the king and head of all the rest, is called a demon by Homer. Those, on the other hand, who maintain that the gods are all good, and far more excellent than the men who are justly called good, are moved by the actions of the demons, which they can neither deny nor impute to the gods whose goodness they affirm, to distinguish between gods and demons; so that, whenever they find anything offensive in the deeds or sentiments by which unseen spirits manifest their power, they believe this to proceed not from the gods, but from the demons. At the same time they believe that, as no god can hold direct intercourse with men, these demons hold the position of mediators, ascending with prayers and returning with gifts. This is the opinion of the Platonists, the ablest and most esteemed of their philosophers, with whom we therefore chose to debate this question—whether the worship of a number of gods is of any service towards obtaining blessedness in the future life. And this is the reason why, in the preceding book, we have inquired how the demons, who take pleasure in such things as good and wise men loathe and execrate, in the sacrilegious and immoral fictions which the poets have written not of men, but of the gods themselves, and in the wicked and criminal violence of magical arts, can be regarded as more nearly related and more friendly to the gods than men are, and can mediate between good men and the good gods; and it has been demonstrated that this is absolutely impossible.

CHAP. 2. *Whether among the demons, inferior to the gods, there are any good spirits under whose guardianship the human soul might reach true blessedness*

This book, then, ought, according to the promise made in the end of the preceding one, to contain a discussion, not of the difference which exists among the gods, who, according to the Platonists, are all good, nor of the difference between gods and demons, the former of whom they separate by a wide interval from men, while the latter are placed intermediately between the gods and men, but of the difference, since they make one, among the demons themselves. This we shall discuss so far as it bears on our theme. It has been the common and usual belief that some of the demons are bad, others good; and this opinion, whether it be that of the Platonists or any other sect, must by no means

be passed over in silence, lest some one suppose he ought to cultivate the good demons in order that by their mediation he may be accepted by the gods, all of whom he believes to be good, and that he may live with them after death; whereas he would thus be ensnared in the toils of wicked spirits, and would wander far from the true God, with Whom alone, and in Whom alone, the human soul, that is to say, the soul that is rational and intellectual, is blessed.

CHAP. 3. *What Apuleius attributes to the demons, to whom, though he does not deny them reason, he does not ascribe virtue*

What, then, is the difference between good and evil demons? For the Platonist Apuleius, in a treatise on this whole subject, while he says a great deal about their aerial bodies, has not a word to say of the spiritual virtues with which, if they were good, they must have been endowed. Not a word has he said, then, of that which could give them happiness; but proof of their misery he has given, acknowledging that their mind, by which they rank as reasonable beings, is not only not imbued and fortified with virtue so as to resist all unreasonable passions, but that it is somehow agitated with tempestuous emotions and is thus on a level with the mind of foolish men. His own words are: "It is this class of demons the poets refer to, when, without serious error, they feign that the gods hate and love individuals among men, prospering and ennobling some, and opposing and distressing others. Therefore pity, indignation, grief, joy, every human emotion is experienced by the demons, with the same mental disturbance, and the same tide of feeling and thought. These turmoils and tempests banish them far from the tranquility of the celestial gods." Can there be any doubt that in these words it is not some inferior part of their spiritual nature, but the very mind by which the demons hold their rank as rational beings, which he says is tossed with passion like a stormy sea? They cannot, then, be compared even to wise men, who with undisturbed mind resist these perturbations to which they are exposed in this life, and from which human infirmity is never exempt, and who do not yield themselves to approve of or perpetrate anything which might deflect them from the path of wisdom and law of rectitude. They resemble in character, though not in bodily appearance, wicked and foolish men. I might indeed say they are worse, inasmuch as they have grown old in iniquity, and incorrigible by punishment. Their mind, as Apuleius says, is a sea tossed with tempest, having no rallying point of truth or virtue in their soul from which they can resist their turbulent and depraved emotions.

CHAP. 4. *The opinion of the Peripatetics and Stoics about mental emotions*

Among the philosophers there are two opinions about these mental emotions, which the Greeks call παθη, while some of our own writers, as Cicero, call them perturbations, some affections, and some, to render the Greek word more accurately, passions. Some say that even the wise man is subject to these perturbations, though moderated and controlled by reason, which imposes laws upon them, and so restrains them within necessary bounds. This is the opinion of the Platonists and Aristotelians; for Aristotle was Plato's disciple, and the founder of the Peripatetic school. But others, as the Stoics, are of opinion that the wise man is not subject to these perturbations. But Cicero, in his book *De Finibus,* shows that the Stoics are here at variance with the Platonists and Peripatetics rather in words than in reality; for the Stoics decline to apply the term "goods" to external and bodily advantages, because they reckon that the only good is virtue, the art of living well, and this exists only in the mind. The other philosophers, again, use the simple and customary phraseology, and do not scruple to call these things goods, though in comparison of virtue, which guides our life, they are little and of small esteem. And thus it is obvious that, whether these outward things are called goods or advantages, they are held in the same estimation by both parties and that in this matter the Stoics are pleasing themselves merely with a novel phraseology. It seems, then, to me that in this question, whether the wise man is subject to mental passions, or wholly free from them, the controversy is one of words rather than of things; for I think that, if the reality and not the mere sound of the words is considered, the Stoics hold precisely the same opinion as the Platonists and Peripatetics. For, omitting for brevity's sake other proofs which I might adduce in support of this opinion, I will state but one which I consider conclusive. Aulus Gellius, a man of extensive erudition, and gifted with an eloquent and graceful style, relates, in his work entitled *Noctes Atticæ* that he once made a voyage with an eminent Stoic philosopher; and he goes on to relate fully and with gusto what I shall barely state, that when the ship was tossed and in danger from a violent storm, the philosopher grew pale with terror. This was noticed by those on board, who, though themselves threatened with death, were curious to see whether a philosopher would be agitated like other men. When the tempest had passed over, and as soon as their security gave them freedom to resume their talk, one of the passengers, a rich and luxurious Asiatic, begins to banter the philosopher, and rally him because he had even become pale with fear, while he himself had been unmoved by the impending destruction. But the philosopher availed himself of the reply of Aristippus the Socratic, who, on finding himself similarly bantered by a man of the same character, answered, "You had no cause for anxiety for the soul of a profligate debauchee, but I had reason to be alarmed for the soul of Aristippus." The rich man being thus disposed of, Aulus Gellius asked the philosopher, in the interests of science and not to annoy him, what was the reason of his fear? And he willing to instruct a man so zealous in the pursuit of knowledge, at once took from his wallet a book of Epictetus the Stoic, in which doctrines were advanced which precisely harmonized with those of Zeno and Chrysippus, the founders of the Stoical school. Aulus Gellius says that he read in this book that the Stoics maintain that there are certain impressions made on the soul by external objects which they call *phantasiæ*, and that it is not in the power of the soul to determine whether or when it shall be invaded by these. When these impressions are made by alarming and formidable objects, it must needs be that they move the soul even of the wise man, so that for a little he trembles with fear, or is depressed by sadness, these impressions anticipating the work of reason and self-control; but this does not imply that the mind accepts these evil impressions, or approves or consents to them. For this consent is, they think, in a man's power; there being this difference between the mind of the wise man and that of the fool, that the fool's mind yields to these passions and consents to them, while that of the wise man, though it cannot help being invaded by them, yet retains with unshaken firmness a true and steady persuasion of those things which it ought rationally to desire or avoid. This account of what Aulus Gellius relates that he read in the book of Epictetus about the sentiments and doctrines of the Stoics I have given as well as I could, not, perhaps, with his choice language, but with greater brevity, and, I think, with greater clearness. And if this be true, then there is no difference, or next to none, between the opinion of the Stoics and that of the other philosophers regarding mental passions and per-turbations, for both parties agree in maintaining that the mind and reason of the wise man are not subject to these. And perhaps what the Sto-ics mean by asserting this is that the wisdom which characterizes the wise man is clouded by no error and sullied by no taint, but, with this reservation that his wisdom remains undis-turbed, he is exposed to the impressions which the goods and ills of this life (or, as they prefer to call them, the advantages or disadvantages) make upon them. For we need not say that if that philosopher had thought nothing of those things which he thought he was forthwith to lose, life and bodily safety, he would not have been so terrified by his danger as to betray his fear by the pallor of his cheek. Nevertheless, he might suffer this mental disturbance, and yet maintain the fixed persuasion that life and bod-ily safety, which the violence of the tempest threatened to destroy, are not those good things which make their possessors good, as the pos-session of righteousness does. But in so far as they persist that we must call them not goods but advantages, they quarrel about words and neglect things. For what difference does it make whether goods or advantages be the better name, while the Stoic no less than the Peripatetic is alarmed at the prospect of losing them, and while, though they name them differently, they hold them in like esteem? Both parties assure us that, if urged to the commission of some im-morality or crime by the threatened loss of these goods or advantages, they would prefer to lose such things as preserve bodily comfort and se-curity rather than commit such things as violate righteousness. And thus the mind in which this resolution is well grounded suffers no pertur-bations to prevail with it in opposition to rea-son, even though they assail the weaker parts of the soul; and not only so, but it rules over them, and, while it refuses its consent and re-sists them, administers a reign of virtue. Such a character is ascribed to Æneas by Virgil when he says,

> He stands immovable by tears,
> Nor tenderest words with pity hears.[1]

CHAP. 5. *That the passions which assail the souls of Christians do not seduce them to vice, but exercise their virtue*

We need not at present give a careful and co-pious exposition of the doctrine of Scripture, the sum of Christian knowledge, regarding these passions. It subjects the mind itself to God, that

[1]*Æneid*, BK. IV. 449.

He may rule and aid it, and the passions, again, to the mind, to moderate and bridle them, and turn them to righteous uses. In our ethics, we do not so much inquire whether a pious soul is an-gry, as why he is angry; not whether he is sad, but what is the cause of his sadness; not wheth-er he fears, but what he fears. For I am not aware that any right thinking person would find fault with anger at a wrongdoer which seeks his amendment, or with sadness which intends relief to the suffering, or with fear lest one in danger be destroyed. The Stoics, indeed, are accus-tomed to condemn compassion. But how much more honourable had it been in that Stoic we have been telling of had he been disturbed by compassion prompting him to relieve a fellow-creature than to be disturbed by the fear of shipwreck! Far better, and more humane, and more consonant with pious sentiments, are the words of Cicero in praise of Cæsar, when he says, "Among your virtues none is more admir-able and agreeable than your compassion." And what is compassion but a fellow-feeling for an-other's misery, which prompts us to help him if we can? And this emotion is obedient to reason, when compassion is shown without violating right, as when the poor are relieved, or the peni-tent forgiven. Cicero, who knew how to use lan-guage, did not hesitate to call this a virtue, which the Stoics are not ashamed to reckon among the vices, although, as the book of the eminent Stoic, Epictetus, quoting the opinions of Zeno and Chrysippus, the founders of the school, has taught us, they admit that passions of this kind invade the soul of the wise man, whom they would have to be free from all vice. Whence it follows that these very passions are not judged by them to be vices, since they assail the wise man without forcing him to act against reason and virtue; and that, therefore, the opin-ion of the Peripatetics or Platonists and of the Stoics is one and the same. But, as Cicero says, mere logomachy is the bane of these pitiful Greeks, who thirst for contention rather than for truth. However, it may justly be asked, whether our subjection to these affections, even while we follow virtue, is a part of the infirmity of this life? For the holy angels feel no anger while they punish those whom the eternal law of God consigns to punishment, no fellow-feel-ing with misery while they relieve the miserable, no fear while they aid those who are in danger; and yet ordinary language ascribes to them also these mental emotions, because, though they have none of our weakness, their acts resemble the actions to which these emotions move us;

and thus even God Himself is said in Scripture to be angry, and yet without any perturbation. For this word is used of the effect of His vengeance, not of the disturbing mental affection.

CHAP. 6. *Of the passions which, according to Apuleius, agitate the demons who are supposed by him to mediate between gods and men*

Deferring for the present the question about the holy angels, let us examine the opinion of the Platonists that the demons who mediate between gods and men are agitated by passions. For if their mind, though exposed to their incursion, still remained free and superior to them, Apuleius could not have said that their hearts are tossed with passions as the sea by stormy winds. Their mind, then—that superior part of their soul whereby they are rational beings, and which, if it actually exists in them, should rule and bridle the turbulent passions of the inferior parts of the soul—this mind of theirs, I say, is, according to the Platonist referred to, tossed with a hurricane of passions. The mind of the demons, therefore, is subject to the emotions of fear, anger, lust, and all similar affections. What part of them, then, is free, and endued with wisdom, so that they are pleasing to the gods, and the fit guides of men into purity of life, since their very highest part, being the slave of passion and subject to vice, only makes them more intent on deceiving and seducing, in proportion to the mental force and energy of desire they possess?

CHAP. 7. *That the Platonists maintain that the poets wrong the gods by representing them as distracted by party feeling, to which the demons and not the gods are subject*

But if any one says that it is not of all the demons, but only of the wicked, that the poets, not without truth, say that they violently love or hate certain men—for it was of them Apuleius said that they were driven about by strong currents of emotion—how can we accept this interpretation, when Apuleius, in the very same connexion, represents all the demons, and not only the wicked, as intermediate between gods and men by their aerial bodies? The fiction of the poets, according to him, consists in their making gods of demons, and giving them the names of gods, and assigning them as allies or enemies to individual men, using this poetical licence, though they profess that the gods are very different in character from the demons, and far

exalted above them by their celestial abode and wealth of beatitude. This, I say, is the poets' fiction, to say that these are gods who are not gods and that, under the names of gods, they fight among themselves about the men whom they love or hate with keen partisan feeling. Apuleius says that this is not far from the truth, since, though they are wrongfully called by the names of the gods, they are described in their own proper character as demons. To this category, he says, belongs the Minerva of Homer, "who interposed in the ranks of the Greeks to restrain Achilles." For that this was Minerva he supposes to be poetical fiction; for he thinks that Minerva is a goddess, and he places her among the gods whom he believes to be all good and blessed in the sublime ethereal region, remote from intercourse with men. But that there was a demon favourable to the Greeks and adverse to the Trojans, as another, whom the same poet mentions under the name of Venus or Mars (gods exalted above earthly affairs in their heavenly habitations), was the Trojans' ally and the foe of the Greeks, and that these demons fought for those they loved against those they hated—in all this he owned that the poets stated something very like the truth. For they made these statements about beings to whom he ascribes the same violent and tempestuous passions as disturb men, and who are therefore capable of loves and hatreds not justly formed, but formed in a party spirit, as the spectators in races or hunts take fancies and prejudices. It seems to have been the great fear of this Platonist that the poetical fictions should be believed of the gods, and not of the demons who bore their names.

CHAP. 8. *How Apuleius defines the gods who dwell in heaven, the demons who occupy the air, and men who inhabit earth*

The definition which Apuleius gives of demons, and in which he of course includes all demons, is that they are in nature animals, in soul subject to passion, in mind reasonable, in body aerial, in duration eternal. Now in these five qualities he has named absolutely nothing which is proper to good men and not also to bad. For when Apuleius had spoken of the celestials first, and had then extended his description so as to include an account of those who dwell far below on the earth, that, after describing the two extremes of rational being, he might proceed to speak of the intermediate demons, he says, "Men, therefore, who are endowed with the faculty of reason and speech, whose soul is immortal and their members mortal, who have weak and anxious spirits, dull and corruptible bodies, dissimilar characters, similar ignorance, who are obstinate in their audacity and persistent in their hope, whose labour is vain, and whose fortune is ever on the wane, their race immortal, themselves perishing, each generation replenished with creatures whose life is swift and their wisdom slow, their death sudden and their life a wail—these are the men who dwell on the earth." In recounting so many qualities which belong to the large proportion of men, did he forget that which is the property of the few when he speaks of their wisdom being slow? If this had been omitted, this his description of the human race, so carefully elaborated, would have been defective. And when he commended the excellence of the gods, he affirmed that they excelled in that very blessedness to which he thinks men must attain by wisdom. And therefore, if he had wished us to believe that some of the demons are good, he should have inserted in his description something by which we might see that they have, in common with the gods, some share of blessedness, or, in common with men, some wisdom. But, as it is, he has mentioned no good quality by which the good may be distinguished from the bad. For although he refrained from giving a full account of their wickedness, through fear of offending, not themselves but their worshippers, for whom he was writing, yet he sufficiently indicated to discerning readers what opinion he had of them; for only in the one article of the eternity of their bodies does he assimilate them to the gods, all of whom, he asserts, are good and blessed, and absolutely free from what he himself calls the stormy passions of the demons; and as to the soul, he quite plainly affirms that they resemble men and not the gods, and that this resemblance lies not in the possession of wisdom, which even men can attain to, but in the perturbation of passions which sway the foolish and wicked, but is so ruled by the good and wise that they prefer not to admit rather than to conquer it. For if he had wished it to be understood that the demons resembled the gods in the eternity not of their bodies but of their souls, he would certainly have admitted men to share in this privilege, because, as a Platonist, he of course must hold that the human soul is eternal. Accordingly, when describing this race of living beings, he said that their souls were immortal, their members mortal. And, consequently, if men have not eternity in common with the gods because they have mortal bodies, demons have eternity in

common with the gods because their bodies are immortal.

CHAP. 9. *Whether the intercession of the demons can secure for men the friendship of the celestial gods*

How, then, can men hope for a favourable introduction to the friendship of the gods by such mediators as these, who are, like men, defective in that which is the better part of every living creature, viz., the soul, and who resemble the gods only in the body, which is the inferior part? For a living creature or animal consists of soul and body, and of these two parts the soul is undoubtedly the better; even though vicious and weak, it is obviously better than even the soundest and strongest body, for the greater excellence of its nature is not reduced to the level of the body even by the pollution of vice, as gold, even when tarnished, is more precious than the purest silver or lead. And yet these mediators, by whose interposition things human and divine are to be harmonized, have an eternal body in common with the gods and a vicious soul in common with men—as if the religion by which these demons are to unite gods and men were a bodily, and not a spiritual matter. What wickedness, then, or punishment has suspended these false and deceitful mediators, as it were head downwards, so that their inferior part, their body, is linked to the gods above, and their superior part, the soul, bound to men beneath; united to the celestial gods by the part that serves, and miserable, together with the inhabitants of earth, by the part that rules? For the body is the servant, as Sallust says: "We use the soul to rule, the body to obey"; adding, "the one we have in common with the gods, the other with the brutes." For he was here speaking of men; and they have, like the brutes, a mortal body. These demons, whom our philosophic friends have provided for us as mediators with the gods, may indeed say of the soul and body, the one we have in common with the gods, the other with men; but, as I said, they are as it were suspended and bound head downwards, having the slave, the body, in common with the gods, the master, the soul, in common with miserable men—their inferior part exalted, their superior part depressed. And therefore, if any one supposes that, because they are not subject, like terrestrial animals, to the separation of soul and body by death, they therefore resemble the gods in their eternity, their body must not be considered a chariot of an eternal triumph, but rather the chain of an eternal punishment.

CHAP. 10. *That, according to Plotinus, men, whose body is mortal, are less wretched than demons, whose body is eternal*

Plotinus, whose memory is quite recent, enjoys the reputation of having understood Plato better than any other of his disciples. In speaking of human souls, he says, "The Father in compassion made their bonds mortal";[1] that is to say, he considered it due to the Father's mercy that men, having a mortal body, should not be forever confined in the misery of this life. But of this mercy the demons have been judged unworthy, and they have received, in conjunction with a soul subject to passions, a body not mortal like man's, but eternal. For they should have been happier than men if they had, like men, had a mortal body, and, like the gods, a blessed soul. And they should have been equal to men, if in conjunction with a miserable soul they had at least received, like men, a mortal body, so that death might have freed them from trouble, if, at least, they should have attained some degree of piety. But, as it is, they are not only no happier than men, having, like them, a miserable soul, they are also more wretched, being eternally bound to the body; for he does not leave us to infer that by some progress in wisdom and piety they can become gods, but expressly says that they are demons forever.

CHAP. 11. *Of the opinion of the Platonists, that the souls of men become demons when disembodied*

He[2] says, indeed, that the souls of men are demons, and that men become *Lares* if they are good, *Lemures* or *Larvæ* if they are bad, and *Manes* if it is uncertain whether they deserve well or ill. Who does not see at a glance that this is a mere whirlpool sucking men to moral destruction? For, however wicked men have been, if they suppose they shall become Larvæ or divine Manes, they will become the worse the more love they have for inflicting injury; for, as the Larvæ are hurtful demons made out of wicked men, these men must suppose that after death they will be invoked with sacrifices and divine honours that they may inflict injuries. But this question we must not pursue. He also states that the blessed are called in Greek εὐδαίμονες, because they are good souls, that is to say, good demons, confirming his opinion that the souls of men are demons.

[1] *Enneads*, IV. 3. 12.   [2] Apuleius, not Plotinus.

CHAP. 12. *Of the three opposite qualities by which the Platonists distinguish between the nature of men and that of demons*

But at present we are speaking of those beings whom he described as being properly intermediate between gods and men, in nature animals, in mind rational, in soul subject to passion, in body aerial, in duration eternal. When he had distinguished the gods, whom he placed in the highest heaven, from men, whom he placed on earth, not only by position but also by the unequal dignity of their natures, he concluded in these words: "You have here two kinds of animals: the gods, widely distinguished from men by sublimity of abode, perpetuity of life, perfection of nature; for their habitations are separated by so wide an interval that there can be no intimate communication between them, and while the vitality of the one is eternal and indefeasible, that of the others is fading and precarious, and while the spirits of the gods are exalted in bliss, those of men are sunk in miseries." Here I find three opposite qualities ascribed to the extremes of being, the highest and lowest. For, after mentioning the three qualities for which we are to admire the gods, he repeated, though in other words, the same three as a foil to the defects of man. The three qualities are, "sublimity of abode, perpetuity of life, perfection of nature." These he again mentioned so as to bring out their contrasts in man's condition. As he had mentioned "sublimity of abode," he says, "Their habitations are separated by so wide an interval"; as he had mentioned "perpetuity of life," he says, that "while divine life is eternal and indefeasible, human life is fading and precarious"; and as he had mentioned "perfection of nature," he says, that "while the spirits of the gods are exalted in bliss, those of men are sunk in miseries." These three things, then, he predicates of the gods, exaltation, eternity, blessedness; and of man he predicates the opposite, lowliness of habitation, mortality, misery.

CHAP. 13. *How the demons can mediate between gods and men if they have nothing in common with both, being neither blessed like the gods, nor miserable like men*

If, now, we endeavour to find between these opposites the mean occupied by the demons, there can be no question as to their local position; for, between the highest and lowest place, there is a place which is rightly considered and called the middle place. The other two qualities remain, and to them we must give greater care, that we may see whether they are altogether foreign to the demons, or how they are so bestowed upon them without infringing upon their mediate position. We may dismiss the idea that they are foreign to them. For we cannot say that the demons, being rational animals, are neither blessed nor wretched, as we say of the beasts and plants, which are void of feeling and reason, or as we say of the middle place, that it is neither the highest nor the lowest. The demons, being rational, must be either miserable or blessed. And, in like manner, we cannot say that they are neither mortal nor immortal; for all living things either live eternally or end life in death. Our author, besides, stated that the demons are eternal. What remains for us to suppose, then, but that these mediate beings are assimilated to the gods in one of the two remaining qualities, and to men in the other? For if they received both from above, or both from beneath, they should no longer be mediate, but either rise to the gods above, or sink to men beneath. Therefore, as it has been demonstrated that they must possess these two qualities, they will hold their middle place if they receive one from each party. Consequently, as they cannot receive their eternity from beneath, because it is not there to receive, they must get it from above; and accordingly they have no choice but to complete their mediate position by accepting misery from men.

According to the Platonists, then, the gods, who occupy the highest place, enjoy eternal blessedness, or blessed eternity; men, who occupy the lowest, a mortal misery, or a miserable mortality; and the demons, who occupy the mean, a miserable eternity, or an eternal misery. As to those five things which Apuleius included in his definition of demons, he did not show, as he promised, that the demons are mediate. For three of them, that their nature is animal, their mind rational, their soul subject to passions, he said that they have in common with men; one thing, their eternity, in common with the gods; and one proper to themselves, their aerial body. How, then, are they intermediate, when they have three things in common with the lowest, and only one in common with the highest? Who does not see that the intermediate position is abandoned in proportion as they tend to, and are depressed towards, the lowest extreme? But perhaps we are to accept them as intermediate because of their one property of an aerial body, as the two extremes have each their proper body, the gods an ethereal, men a terrestrial body, and because two of the qualities they possess in common with man they possess also in common with the gods, namely, their animal nature and rational mind. For Apuleius himself, in speaking of gods and men, said, "You have two animal natures." And Platonists are wont to ascribe a rational mind to the gods. Two qualities remain, their liability to passion, and their eternity—the first of which they have in common with men, the second with the gods; so that they are neither wafted to the highest nor depressed to the lowest extreme, but perfectly poised in their intermediate position. But then, this is the very circumstance which constitutes the eternal misery, or miserable eternity, of the demons. For he who says that their soul is subject to passions would also have said that they are miserable, had he not blushed for their worshippers. Moreover, as the world is governed, not by fortuitous haphazard, but, as the Platonists themselves avow, by the providence of the supreme God, the misery of the demons would not be eternal unless their wickedness were great.

If, then, the blessed are rightly styled *eudemons,* the demons intermediate between gods and men are not eudemons. What, then, is the local position of those good demons, who, above men but beneath the gods, afford assistance to the former, minister to the latter? For if they are good and eternal, they are doubtless blessed. But eternal blessedness destroys their intermediate character, giving them a close resemblance to the gods and widely separating them from men. And therefore the Platonists will in vain strive to show how the good demons, if they are both immortal and blessed, can justly be said to hold a middle place between the gods, who are immortal and blessed, and men, who are mortal and miserable. For if they have both immortality and blessedness in common with the gods, and neither of these in common with men, who are both miserable and mortal, are they not rather remote from men and united with the gods, than intermediate between them? They would be intermediate if they held one of their qualities in common with the one party and the other with the other, as man is a kind of mean between angels and beasts—the beast being an irrational and mortal animal, the angel a rational and immortal one, while man, inferior to the angel and superior to the beast, and having in common with the one mortality, and with the other reason, is a rational and mortal animal. So, when we seek for an intermediate between the blessed immortals and miserable mortals, we should find a being which is either mortal and blessed, or immortal and miserable.

CHAP. 14. *Whether men, though mortal, can enjoy true blessedness*

It is a great question among men, whether man can be mortal and blessed. Some, taking the humbler view of his condition, have denied that he is capable of blessedness so long as he continues in this mortal life; others, again, have spurned this idea, and have been bold enough to maintain that, even though mortal, men may be blessed by attaining wisdom. But if this be the case, why are not these wise men constituted mediators between miserable mortals and the blessed immortals, since they have blessedness in common with the latter, and mortality in common with the former? Certainly, if they are blessed, they envy no one (for what more miserable than envy?), but seek with all their might to help miserable mortals on to blessedness, so that after death they may become immortal and be associated with the blessed and immortal angels.

CHAP. 15. *Of the man Christ Jesus, the mediator between God and men*

But if, as is much more probable and credible, it must needs be that all men, so long as they are mortal, are also miserable, we must seek an intermediate who is not only man, but also God, that, by the interposition of His blessed mortality, He may bring men out of their mortal misery to a blessed immortality. In this intermediate two things are requisite, that He become mortal and that He do not continue mortal. He did become mortal, not rendering the divinity of the Word infirm, but assuming the infirmity of flesh. Neither did He continue mortal in the flesh, but raised it from the dead; for it is the very fruit of His mediation that those, for the sake of whose redemption He became the Mediator, should not abide eternally in bodily death. Wherefore it became the Mediator between us and God to have both a transient mortality and a permanent blessedness, that by that which is transient He might be assimilated to mortals, and might translate them from mortality to that which is permanent. Good angels, therefore, cannot mediate between miserable mortals and blessed immortals, for they themselves also are both blessed and immortal; but evil angels can mediate, because they are immortal like the one party, miserable like the other. To these is opposed the good Mediator, Who, in opposition to their immortality and misery, has chosen to be mortal for a time and has been able to continue blessed in eternity. It

is thus He has destroyed, by the humility of His death and the benignity of His blessedness, those proud immortals and hurtful wretches, and has prevented them from seducing to misery by their boast of immortality those men whose hearts He has cleansed by faith and whom He has thus freed from their impure dominion.

Man, then, mortal and miserable, and far removed from the immortal and the blessed, what medium shall he choose by which he may be united to immortality and blessedness? The immortality of the demons, which might have some charm for man, is miserable; the mortality of Christ, which might offend man, exists no longer. In the one there is the fear of an eternal misery; in the other, death, which could not be eternal, can no longer be feared, and blessedness, which is eternal, must be loved. For the immortal and miserable mediator interposes himself to prevent us from passing to a blessed immortality, because that which hinders such a passage, namely, misery, continues in him; but the mortal and blessed Mediator interposed Himself, in order that, having passed through mortality, He might of mortals make immortals (showing His power to do this in His own resurrection), and from being miserable to raise them to the blessed company from the number of whom He had Himself never departed. There is, then, a wicked mediator, who separates friends, and a good Mediator, who reconciles enemies. And those who separate are numerous, because the multitude of the blessed are blessed only by their participation in the one God; of which participation the evil angels being deprived, they are wretched, and interpose to hinder rather than to help to this blessedness, and by their very number prevent us from reaching that one beatific good, to obtain which we need not many but one Mediator, the uncreated Word of God, by Whom all things were made, and in partaking of Whom we are blessed. I do not say that He is Mediator because He is the Word, for as the Word He is supremely blessed and supremely immortal, and therefore far from miserable mortals; but He is Mediator as He is man, for by His humanity He shows us that, in order to obtain that blessed and beatific good, we need not seek other mediators to lead us through the successive steps of this attainment, but that the blessed and beatific God, having Himself become a partaker of our humanity, has afforded us ready access to the participation of His divinity. For, in delivering us from our mortality and misery, He does not lead us to the immortal and blessed angels, so that we should become immortal and blessed by participating in their nature, but He leads us straight to that Trinity, by participating in which the angels themselves are blessed. Therefore, when He chose to be in the form of a servant and lower than the angels, that He might be our Mediator, He remained higher than the angels, in the form of God— Himself at once the way of life on earth and life itself in heaven.

CHAP. 16. *Whether it is reasonable in the Platonists to determine that the celestial gods decline contact with earthly things and intercourse with men, who therefore require the intercession of the demons*

That opinion, which the same Platonist avers that Plato uttered, is not true, "that no god holds intercourse with men." And this, he says, is the chief evidence of their exaltation, that they are never contaminated by contact with men. He admits, therefore, that the demons are contaminated; and it follows that they cannot cleanse those by whom they are themselves contaminated, and thus all alike become impure, the demons by associating with men, and men by worshipping the demons. Or, if they say that the demons are not contaminated by associating and dealing with men, then they are better than the gods, for the gods, were they to do so, would be contaminated. For this, we are told, is the glory of the gods, that they are so highly exalted that no human intercourse can sully them. He affirms, indeed, that the supreme God, the Creator of all things, Whom we call the true God, is spoken of by Plato as the only God Whom the poverty of human speech fails even passably to describe; and that even the wise, when their mental energy is as far as possible delivered from the trammels of connexion with the body, have only such gleams of insight into His nature as may be compared to a flash of lightning illuminating the darkness. If, then, this supreme God, Who is truly exalted above all things, does nevertheless visit the minds of the wise, when emancipated from the body, with an intelligible and ineffable presence, though this be only occasional, and as it were a swift flash of light athwart the darkness, why are the other gods so sublimely removed from all contact with men, as if they would be polluted by it? as if it were not a sufficient refutation of this to lift up our eyes to those heavenly bodies which give the earth its needful light. If the stars, though they, by his account, are visible gods, are not contaminated when we look at them, neither are the demons contaminated when men see them

quite closely. But perhaps it is the human voice, and not the eye, which pollutes the gods; and therefore the demons are appointed to mediate and carry men's utterances to the gods, who keep themselves remote through fear of pollution? What am I to say of the other senses? For by smell neither the demons, who are present, nor the gods, though they were present and inhaling the exhalations of living men, would be polluted if they are not contaminated with the effluvia of the carcasses offered in sacrifice. As for taste, they are pressed by no necessity of repairing bodily decay, so as to be reduced to ask food from men. And touch is in their own power. For while it may seem that contact is so called, because the sense of touch is specially concerned in it, yet the gods, if so minded, might mingle with men, so as to see and be seen, hear and be heard; and where is the need of touching? For men would not dare to desire this, if they were favoured with the sight or conversation of gods or good demons; and if through excessive curiosity they should desire it, how could they accomplish their wish without the consent of the god or demon, when they cannot touch so much as a sparrow unless it be caged?

There is, then, nothing to hinder the gods from mingling in a bodily form with men, from seeing and being seen, from speaking and hearing. And if the demons do thus mix with men, as I said, and are not polluted, while the gods, were they to do so, should be polluted, then the demons are less liable to pollution than the gods. And if even the demons are contaminated, how can they help men to attain blessedness after death, if, so far from being able to cleanse them and present them clean to the unpolluted gods, these mediators are themselves polluted? And if they cannot confer this benefit on men, what good can their friendly mediation do? Or shall its result be, not that men find entrance to the gods, but that men and demons abide together in a state of pollution, and consequently of exclusion from blessedness? Unless, perhaps, some one may say that, like sponges or things of that sort, the demons themselves, in the process of cleansing their friends, become themselves the filthier in proportion as the others become clean. But if this is the solution, then the gods, who shun contact or intercourse with men for fear of pollution, mix with demons who are far more polluted. Or perhaps the gods, who cannot cleanse men without polluting themselves, can without pollution cleanse the demons who have been contaminated by human contact? Who can believe such follies, unless the demons have practised their deceit upon him? If seeing and being seen is contamination, and if the gods, whom Apuleius himself calls visible, "the brilliant lights of the world,"[1] and the other stars, are seen by men, are we to believe that the demons, who cannot be seen unless they please, are safer from contamination? Or if it is only the seeing and not the being seen which contaminates, then they must deny that these gods of theirs, these brilliant lights of the world, see men when their rays beam upon the earth. Their rays are not contaminated by lighting on all manner of pollution, and are we to suppose that the gods would be contaminated if they mixed with men, and even if contact were needed in order to assist them? For there is contact between the earth and the sun's or moon's rays, and yet this does not pollute the light.

CHAP. 17. *That to obtain the blessed life, which consists in partaking of the supreme good, man needs such mediation as is furnished not by a demon, but by Christ alone*

I am considerably surprised that such learned men, men who pronounce all material and sensible things to be altogether inferior to those that are spiritual and intelligible, should mention bodily contact in connection with the blessed life. Is that sentiment of Plotinus forgotten? —"We must fly to our beloved fatherland. There is the Father, there our all. What fleet or flight shall convey us thither? Our way is, to become like God." If, then, one is nearer to God the liker he is to Him, there is no other distance from God than unlikeness to Him. And the soul of man is unlike that incorporeal and unchangeable and eternal essence, in proportion as it craves things temporal and mutable. And as the things beneath, which are mortal and impure, cannot hold intercourse with the immortal purity which is above, a mediator is indeed needed to remove this difficulty; but not a mediator who resembles the highest order of being by possessing an immortal body, and the lowest by having a diseased soul, which makes him rather grudge that we be healed than help our cure. We need a Mediator Who, being united to us here below by the mortality of His body, should at the same time be able to afford us truly divine help in cleansing and liberating us by means of the immortal righteousness of His spirit, whereby He remained heavenly even while here upon earth. Far be it from the incontaminable God to fear pollution from the man[2] He assumed, or from the men among whom He lived in the form of a man. For, though His incarnation showed us nothing else, these two wholesome facts were enough, that true divinity cannot be polluted by flesh, and that demons are not to be considered better than ourselves because they have not flesh. This, then, as Scripture says, is the "Mediator between God and man, the man Christ Jesus,"[3] of Whose divinity, whereby He is equal to the Father, and humanity, whereby He has become like us, this is not the place to speak as fully as I could.

CHAP. 18. *That the deceitful demons, while promising to conduct men to God by their intercession, mean to turn them from the path of truth*

As to the demons, these false and deceitful mediators, who, though their uncleanness of spirit frequently reveals their misery and malignity, yet, by virtue of the levity of their aerial bodies and the nature of the places they inhabit, do contrive to turn us aside and hinder our spiritual progress; they do not help us towards God, but rather prevent us from reaching Him. Since even in the bodily way, which is erroneous and misleading, and in which righteousness does not walk—for we must rise to God not by bodily ascent, but by incorporeal or spiritual conformity to Him—in this bodily way, I say, which the friends of the demons arrange according to the weight of the various elements, the aerial demons being set between the ethereal gods and earthy men, they imagine the gods to have this privilege, that by this local interval they are preserved from the pollution of human contact. Thus they believe that the demons are contaminated by men rather than men cleansed by the demons, and that the gods themselves should be polluted unless their local superiority preserved them. Who is so wretched a creature as to expect purification by a way in which men are contaminating, demons contaminated, and gods contaminable? Who would not rather choose that way whereby we escape the contamination of the demons, and are cleansed from pollution by the incontaminable God, so as to be associated with the uncontaminated angels?

CHAP. 19. *That even among their own worshippers the name "demon" has never a good signification*

But as some of these demonolators, as I may call them, and among them Labeo, allege that those whom they call demons are by others called angels, I must, if I would not seem to dis-

[1] Virgil, *Georgics*, BK. I. 5.   [2] Or, *humanity*.   [3] Tim. 2. 5.

pute merely about words, say something about the good angels. The Platonists do not deny their existence, but prefer to call them good demons. But we, following Scripture, according to which we are Christians, have learned that some of the angels are good, some bad, but never have we read in Scripture of good demons; but wherever this or any cognate term occurs, it is applied only to wicked spirits. And this usage has become so universal that, even among those who are called pagans and who maintain that demons as well as gods should be worshipped, there is scarcely a man, no matter how well read and learned, who would dare to say by way of praise to his slave, "You have a demon," or who could doubt that the man to whom he said this would consider it a curse. Why, then, are we to subject ourselves to the necessity of explaining away what we have said when we have given offence by using the word demon, with which every one, or almost every one, connects a bad meaning, while we can so easily evade this necessity by using the word angel?

CHAP. 20. *Of the kind of knowledge which puffs up the demons*

However, the very origin of the name suggests something worthy of consideration, if we compare it with the divine books. They are called demons from a Greek word meaning knowledge.[1] Now the apostle, speaking with the Holy Spirit, says, "Knowledge puffeth up, but charity buildeth up."[2] And this can only be understood as meaning that without charity knowledge does no good, but inflates a man or magnifies him with an empty windiness. The demons, then, have knowledge without charity, and are thereby so inflated or proud that they crave those divine honours and religious services which they know to be due to the true God, and still, as far as they can, exact these from all over whom they have influence. Against this pride of the demons, under which the human race was held subject as its merited punishment, there was exerted the mighty influence of the humility of God, Who appeared in the form of a servant; but men, resembling the demons in pride, but not in knowledge, and being puffed up with uncleanness, failed to recognize Him.

CHAP. 21. *To what extent the Lord was pleased to make Himself known to the demons*

The devils themselves knew this manifestation of God so well that they said to the Lord,

though clothed with the infirmity of flesh, "What have we to do with Thee, Jesus of Nazareth? Art Thou come to destroy us before the time?"[3] From these words, it is clear that they had great knowledge, and no charity. They feared His power to punish, and did not love His righteousness. He made known to them so much as He pleased, and He was pleased to make known so much as was needful. But He made Himself known not as to the holy angels, who know Him as the Word of God, and rejoice in His eternity, which they partake, but as was requisite to strike with terror the beings from whose tyranny He was going to free those who were predestined to His kingdom and the glory of it, eternally true and truly eternal. He made Himself known, therefore, to the demons, not by that which is life eternal and the unchangeable light which illumines the pious, whose souls are cleansed by the faith that is in Him, but by some temporal effects of His power and evidences of His mysterious presence, which were more easily discerned by the angelic senses even of wicked spirits than by human infirmity. But when He judged it advisable gradually to suppress these signs and to retire into deeper obscurity, the prince of the demons doubted whether He were the Christ and endeavoured to ascertain this by tempting Him, in so far as He permitted Himself to be tempted, that He might adapt the manhood He wore to be an example for our imitation. But after that temptation, when, as Scripture says, He was ministered to[4] by the angels who are good and holy, and therefore objects of terror to the impure spirits, He revealed more and more distinctly to the demons how great He was, so that, even though the infirmity of His flesh might seem contemptible, none dared to resist His authority.

CHAP. 22. *The difference between the knowledge of the holy angels and that of the demons*

The good angels, therefore, hold cheap all that knowledge of material and transitory things which the demons are so proud of possessing— not that they are ignorant of these things, but because the love of God, whereby they are sanctified, is very dear to them, and because, in comparison of that not merely immaterial but also unchangeable and ineffable beauty, with the holy love of which they are inflamed, they despise all things which are beneath it and all that is not it, that they may with every good thing that is in them enjoy that good which is the source of their goodness. And therefore they

---

[1]δαίμων = δαήμων, knowing; so Plato, *Cratylus*, 398.
[2]I Cor. 8. 1.
[3]Mark 1. 24.   [4]Matt. 4. 3–11.

have a more certain knowledge even of those temporal and mutable things, because they contemplate their principles and causes in the word of God, by which the world was made—those causes by which one thing is approved, another rejected, and all arranged. But the demons do not behold in the wisdom of God these eternal, and, as it were, cardinal causes of things temporal, but only foresee a larger part of the future than men do, by reason of their greater acquaintance with the signs which are hidden from us. Sometimes, too, it is their own intentions they predict. And, finally, the demons are frequently, the angels never, deceived. For it is one thing, by the aid of things temporal and changeable, to conjecture the changes that may occur in time, and to modify such things by one's own will and faculty—and this to a certain extent permitted to the demons—it is another thing to foresee the changes of times in the eternal and immutable laws of God, which live in His wisdom, and to know the will of God, the most infallible and powerful of all causes, by participating in His spirit; and this is granted to the holy angels by a just discretion. And thus they are not only eternal, but blessed. And the good wherein they are blessed is God, by Whom they were created. For without end they enjoy the contemplation and participation of Him.

CHAP. 23. *That the name of gods is falsely given to the gods of the Gentiles, though Scripture applies it both to the holy angels and just men*

If the Platonists prefer to call these angels gods rather than demons, and to reckon them with those whom Plato, their founder and master, maintains were created by the supreme God,[1] they are welcome to do so, for I will not spend strength in fighting about words. For if they say that these beings are immortal, and yet created by the supreme God, blessed but by cleaving to their Creator and not by their own power, they say what we say, whatever name they call these beings by. And that this is the opinion either of all or the best of the Platonists can be ascertained by their writings. And regarding the name itself, if they see fit to call such blessed and immortal creatures gods, this need not give rise to any serious discussion between us, since in our own Scriptures we read, "The God of gods, the Lord hath spoken";[2] and again, "Confess to the God of gods";[3] and again, "He is a great King above all gods."[4] And where it is said, "He is to be feared above all gods,"

the reason is forthwith added, for it follows, "for all the gods of the nations are idols, but the Lord made the heavens."[5] He said, "above all gods," but added, "of the nations"; that is to say, above all those whom the nations count gods, in other words, demons. By them He is to be feared with that terror in which they cried to the Lord, "Hast Thou come to destroy us?" But where it is said, "the God of gods," it cannot be understood as the god of the demons; and far be it from us to say that "great King above all gods" means "great King above all demons." But the same Scripture also calls men who belong to God's people "gods": "I have said, Ye are gods, and all of you children of the Most High."[6] Accordingly, when God is styled God of gods, this may be understood of these gods; and so, too, when He is styled a great King above all gods.

Nevertheless, some one may say, if men are called gods because they belong to God's people, whom He addresses by means of men and angels, are not the immortals, who already enjoy that felicity which men seek to attain by worshipping God, much more worthy of the title? And what shall we reply to this, if not that it is not without reason that in holy Scripture men are more expressly styled gods than those immortal and blessed spirits to whom we hope to be equal in the resurrection, because there was a fear that the weakness of unbelief, being overcome with the excellence of these beings, might presume to constitute some of them a god? In the case of men this was a result that need not be guarded against. Besides, it was right that the men belonging to God's people should be more expressly called gods, to assure and certify them that He who is called God of gods is their God; because, although those immortal and blessed spirits who dwell in the heavens are called gods, yet they are not called gods of gods, that is to say, gods of the men who constitute God's people, and to whom it is said, "I have said, Ye are gods, and all of you the children of the Most High." Hence the saying of the apostle, "Though there be that are called gods, whether in heaven or in earth, as there be gods many and lords many, but to us there is but one God, the Father, of Whom are all things, and we in Him; and one Lord Jesus Christ, by Whom are all things, and we by Him."[7]

We need not, therefore, laboriously contend about the name, since the reality is so obvious as to admit of no shadow of doubt. That which we say, that the angels who are sent to announce

[1]*Timæus.* [2]Ps. 50. 1. [3]Ps. 136. 2. [4]Ps. 95. 3. [5]Ps. 96. 5, 6. [6]Ps. 82. 6. [7]I Cor. 8. 5, 6.

the will of God to men belong to the order of blessed immortals, does not satisfy the Platonists, because they believe that this ministry is discharged, not by those whom they call gods, in other words, not by blessed immortals, but by demons, whom they dare not affirm to be blessed, but only immortal, or if they do rank them among the blessed immortals, yet only as good demons, and not as gods who dwell in the heaven of heavens remote from all human contact. But, though it may seem mere wrangling about a name, yet the name of demon is so detestable that we cannot bear in any sense to apply it to the holy angels. Now, therefore, let us close this book in the assurance that, whatever we call these immortal and blessed spirits, who yet are only creatures, they do not act as mediators to introduce to everlasting felicity miserable mortals, from whom they are severed by a twofold distinction. And those others who are mediators, in so far as they have immortality in

common with their superiors and misery in common with their inferiors (for they are justly miserable in punishment of their wickedness), cannot bestow upon us, but rather grudge that we should possess, the blessedness from which they themselves are excluded. And so the friends of the demons have nothing considerable to allege why we should rather worship them as our helpers than avoid them as traitors to our interests. As for those spirits who are good, and who are therefore not only immortal but also blessed, and to whom they suppose we should give the title of gods, and offer worship and sacrifices for the sake of inheriting a future life, we shall, by God's help, endeavour in the following book to show that these spirits, call them by what name, and ascribe to them what nature you will, desire that religious worship be paid to God alone, by Whom they were created, and by Whose communications of Himself to them they are blessed.

BOOK X

ARGUMENT. IN THIS BOOK AUGUSTINE TEACHES THAT THE GOOD ANGELS WISH GOD ALONE, WHOM THEY THEMSELVES SERVE, TO RECEIVE THAT DIVINE HONOUR WHICH IS RENDERED BY SACRIFICE, AND WHICH IS CALLED *LATREIA.* HE THEN GOES ON TO DISPUTE AGAINST PORPHYRY ABOUT THE PRINCIPLE AND WAY OF THE SOUL'S CLEANSING AND DELIVERANCE.

CHAP. I. *That the Platonists themselves have determined that God alone can confer happiness either on angels or men, but that it yet remains a question whether those spirits whom they direct us to worship, that we may obtain happiness, wish sacrifice to be offered to themselves, or to the one God only*

IT is the decided opinion of all who use their brains, that all men desire to be happy. But who are happy, or how they become so, these are questions about which the weakness of human understanding stirs endless and angry controversies, in which philosophers have wasted their strength and expended their leisure. To adduce and discuss their various opinions would be tedious and is unnecessary. The reader may remember what we said in the eighth book, while making a selection of the philosophers with whom we might discuss the question regarding the future life of happiness, whether we can reach it by paying divine honours to the one true God, the Creator of all gods, or by worshipping many gods, and he will not expect us to repeat here the same argument, especially as, even if he has for-

gotten it, he may refresh his memory by reperusal. For we made selection of the Platonists, justly esteemed the noblest of the philosophers, because they had the wit to perceive that the human soul, immortal and rational, or intellectual, as it is, cannot be happy except by partaking of the light of that God by Whom both itself and the world were made; and also that the happy life which all men desire cannot be reached by any who does not cleave with a pure and holy love to that one supreme good, the unchangeable God. But as even these philosophers, whether accommodating to the folly and ignorance of the people, or, as the apostle says, "becoming vain in their imaginations,"[1] supposed or allowed others to suppose that many gods should be worshipped, so that some of them considered that divine honour by worship and sacrifice should be rendered even to the demons (an error I have already exploded), we must now, by God's help, ascertain what is thought about our religious worship and piety by those immortal and blessed spirits, who dwell in the heavenly places among dominations, principali-

[1]Rom. I. 21.

ties, powers, whom the Platonists call gods, and some either good demons, or, like us, angels—that is to say, to put it more plainly, whether the angels desire us to offer sacrifice and worship, and to consecrate our possessions and ourselves, to them or only to God, theirs and ours.

For this is the worship which is due to the Divinity, or, to speak more accurately, to the Deity; and, to express this worship in a single word as there does not occur to me any Latin term sufficiently exact, I shall avail myself, whenever necessary, of a Greek word. Λατρεία, whenever it occurs in Scripture, is rendered by the word *service*. But that service which is due to men, and in reference to which the apostle writes that servants must be subject to their own masters,[1] is usually designated by another word in Greek,[2] whereas the service which is paid to God alone by worship, is always, or almost always, called λατρεία in the usage of those who wrote from the divine oracles. This cannot so well be called simply *cultus*, for in that case it would not seem to be due exclusively to God; for the same word is applied to the respect we pay either to the memory or the living presence of men. From it, too, we derive the words agriculture, colonist, and others. And the heathen call their gods *cœlicolœ*, not because they worship heaven, but because they dwell in it, and as it were colonize it—not in the sense in which we call those colonists who are attached to their native soil to cultivate it under the rule of the owners, but in the sense in which the great master of the Latin language says, "There was an ancient city inhabited by Tyrian colonists."[3] He called them colonists, not because they cultivated the soil, but because they inhabited the city. So, too, cities that have hived off from larger cities are called colonies. Consequently, while it is quite true that, using the word in a special sense, "cult" can be rendered to none but God, yet, as the word is applied to other things besides, the cult due to God cannot in Latin be expressed by this word alone.

The word "religion" might seem to express more definitely the worship due to God alone, and therefore Latin translators have used this word to represent Θρησκεία; yet, as not only the uneducated, but also the best instructed, use the word religion to express human ties, and relationships, and affinities, it would inevitably introduce ambiguity to use this word in discussing the worship of God, unable as we are to say that religion is nothing else than the worship of God,

without contradicting the common usage which applies this word to the observance of social relationships. "Piety," again, or, as the Greeks say, εὐσέβεια, is commonly understood as the proper designation of the worship of God. Yet this word also is used of dutifulness to parents. The common people, too, use it of works of charity, which, I suppose, arises from the circumstance that God enjoins the performance of such works, and declares that He is pleased with them instead of, or in preference to, sacrifices. From this usage it has also come to pass that God Himself is called pious,[4] in which sense the Greeks never use εὐσέβειν, though εὐσέβεια is applied to works of charity by their common people also. In some passages of Scripture, therefore, they have sought to preserve the distinction by using not εὐσέβεια, the more general word, but Θεοσέβεια, which literally denotes the worship of God. We, on the other hand, cannot express either of these ideas by one word. This worship, then, which in Greek is called λατρεία, and in Latin *servitus*, but the service due to God only; this worship, which in Greek is called Θρησκεία, and in Latin *religio*, but the religion by which we are bound to God only; this worship, which they call Θεοσέβεια, but which we cannot express in one word, but call it the worship of God—this, we say, belongs only to that God Who is the true God, and Who makes His worshippers gods.[5] And therefore, whoever these immortal and blessed inhabitants of heaven be, if they do not love us and wish us to be blessed, then we ought not to worship them; and if they do love us and desire our happiness, they cannot wish us to be made happy by any other means than they themselves have enjoyed—for how could they wish our blessedness to flow from one source, theirs from another?

CHAP. 2. *The opinion of Plotinus the Platonist regarding enlightenment from above*

But with these more estimable philosophers we have no dispute in this matter. For they perceived, and in various forms abundantly expressed in their writings, that these spirits have the same source of happiness as ourselves—a certain intelligible light, which is their God, and is different from themselves, and illumines them that they may be penetrated with light and enjoy perfect happiness in the participation of God. Plotinus, commenting on Plato, repeatedly and strongly asserts that not even the soul which they believe to be the soul of the world

[1]Eph. 6. 5.   [2]Namely, δουλεία.
[3]Virgil, *Æneid*, BK. I. 12.

[4]II Chron 30. 9; Eccl. 11. 13; Judith, 7. 20.   [5]Ps. 82. 6.

derives its blessedness from any other source than we do, viz., from that Light which is distinct from it and created it, and by whose intelligible illumination it enjoys light in things intelligible. He also compares those spiritual things to the vast and conspicuous heavenly bodies, as if God were the sun, and the soul the moon; for they suppose that the moon derives its light from the sun. That great Platonist, therefore, says that the rational soul, or rather the intellectual soul—in which class he comprehends the souls of the blessed immortals who inhabit heaven—has no nature superior to it save God, the Creator of the world and the soul itself, and that these heavenly spirits derive their blessed life, and the light of truth, from the same source as ourselves, agreeing with the gospel where we read, "There was a man sent from God whose name was John; the same came for a witness to bear witness of that Light, that through Him all might believe. He was not that Light, but that he might bear witness of the Light. That was the true Light which lighteth every man that cometh into the world";[1] a distinction which sufficiently proves that the rational or intellectual soul such as John had cannot be its own light, but needs to receive illumination from another, the true Light. This John himself avows when he delivers his witness: "We have all received of His fullness."[2]

CHAP. 3. *That the Platonists, though knowing something of the Creator of the universe, have misunderstood the true worship of God, by giving divine honour to angels, good or bad*

This being so, if the Platonists, or those who think with them, knowing God, glorified Him as God and gave thanks, if they did not become vain in their own thoughts, if they did not originate or yield to the popular errors, they would certainly acknowledge that neither could the blessed immortals retain, nor we miserable mortals reach, a happy condition without worshipping the one God of gods, who is both theirs and ours. To Him we owe the service which is called in Greek λατρεια, whether we render it outwardly or inwardly; for we are all His temple, each of us severally and all of us together, because He condescends to inhabit each individually and the whole harmonious body, being no greater in all than in each, since He is neither expanded nor divided. Our heart when it rises to Him is His altar; the priest who intercedes for us is His Only-begotten; we sacrifice to Him bleeding victims when we contend for His truth

[1]John, i. 6–9. [2]John, i. 16.

even unto blood; to Him we offer the sweetest incense when we come before Him burning with holy and pious love; to Him we devote and surrender ourselves and His gifts in us; to Him, by solemn feasts and on appointed days, we consecrate the memory of His benefits, lest through the lapse of time ungrateful oblivion should steal upon us; to Him we offer on the altar of our heart the sacrifice of humility and praise, kindled by the fire of burning love. It is that we may see Him, so far as He can be seen; it is that we may cleave to Him that we are cleansed from all stain of sins and evil passions and are consecrated in His name. For He is the fountain of our happiness, He the end of all our desires. Being attached to Him, or rather let me say, re-attached—for we had detached ourselves and lost hold of Him—being, I say, re-attached to Him,[3] we tend towards Him by love, that we may rest in Him, and find our blessedness by attaining that end. For our good, about which philosophers have so keenly contended, is nothing else than to be united to God. It is, if I may say so, by spiritually embracing Him that the intellectual soul is filled and impregnated with true virtues. We are enjoined to love this good with all our heart, with all our soul, with all our strength. To this good we ought to be led by those who love us, and to lead those we love. Thus are fulfilled those two commandments on which hang all the law and the prophets: "Thou shalt love the Lord thy God with all thy heart, and with all thy mind, and with all thy soul"; and "Thou shalt love thy neighbour as thyself."[4] For, that man might be intelligent in his self-love, there was appointed for him an end to which he might refer all his actions, that he might be blessed. For he who loves himself wishes nothing else than this. And the end set before him is "to draw near to God."[5] And so, when one who has this intelligent self-love is commanded to love his neighbour as himself, what else is enjoined than that he shall do all in his power to commend to him the love of God? This is the worship of God, this is true religion, this right piety, this the service due to God only. If any immortal power, then, no matter with what virtue endowed, loves us as himself, he must desire that we find our happiness by submitting ourselves to Him, in submission to whom he himself finds happiness. If he does not worship God, he is wretched, because deprived of God; if he worships God, he cannot wish to be worshipped

[3]Augustine here remarks, in a clause that cannot be given in English, that the word *religio* is derived from *religere*.
[4]Matt. 22. 37–40. [5]Ps. 73. 28.

in God's stead. On the contrary, these higher powers acquiesce heartily in the divine sentence in which it is written, "He that sacrificeth unto any god, save unto the Lord only, he shall be utterly destroyed."[1]

CHAP. 4. *That sacrifice is due to the true God only*

But, putting aside for the present the other religious services with which God is worshipped, certainly no man would dare to say that sacrifice is due to any but God. Many parts, indeed, of divine worship are unduly used in showing honour to men, whether through an excessive humility or pernicious flattery; yet, while this is done, those persons who are thus worshipped and venerated, or even adored, are reckoned no more than human; and whoever thought of sacrificing save to one whom he knew, supposed, or feigned to be a god? And how ancient a part of God's worship sacrifice is those two brothers, Cain and Abel, sufficiently show, of whom God rejected the elder's sacrifice and looked favourably on the younger's.

CHAP. 5. *Of the sacrifices which God does not require, but wished to be observed for the exhibition of those things which he does require*

And who is so foolish as to suppose that the things offered to God are needed by Him for some uses of His own? Divine Scripture in many places explodes this idea. Not to be wearisome, suffice it to quote this brief saying from a psalm: "I have said to the Lord, Thou art my God: for Thou needest not my goodness."[2] We must believe, then, that God has no need, not only of cattle, or any other earthly and material thing, but even of man's righteousness, and that whatever right worship is paid to God profits not Him but man. For no man would say he did a benefit to a fountain by drinking, or to the light by seeing. And the fact that the ancient church offered animal sacrifices, which the people of God nowadays read of without imitating, proves nothing else than this, that those sacrifices signified the things which we do for the purpose of drawing near to God, and inducing our neighbour to do the same. A sacrifice, therefore, is the visible sacrament or sacred sign of an invisible sacrifice. Hence that penitent in the psalm, or it may be the Psalmist himself, entreating God to be merciful to his sins, says, "If Thou desiredst sacrifice, I would give it: Thou delightest not in whole burnt-offerings. The sacrifice of God is a broken heart: a heart contrite and humble God will not despise."[3] Observe how, in the very words in which he is expressing God's refusal of sacrifice, he shows that God requires sacrifice. He does not desire the sacrifice of a slaughtered beast, but He desires the sacrifice of a contrite heart. Thus, that sacrifice which he says God does not wish is the symbol of the sacrifice which God does wish. God does not wish sacrifices in the sense in which foolish people think He wishes them, viz., to gratify His own pleasure. For if He had not wished that the sacrifices He requires, as, e.g., a heart contrite and humbled by penitent sorrow, should be symbolized by those sacrifices which He was thought to desire because pleasant to Himself, the old law would never have enjoined their presentation; and they were destined to be merged when the fit opportunity arrived, in order that men might not suppose that the sacrifices themselves, rather than the things symbolized by them, were pleasing to God or acceptable in us. Hence, in another passage from another psalm, he says, "If I were hungry, I would not tell thee; for the world is mine and the fullness thereof. Will I eat the flesh of bulls, or drink the blood of goats?"[4] as if He should say, Supposing such things were necessary to me, I would never ask thee for what I have in my own hand. Then he goes on to mention what these signify: "Offer unto God the sacrifice of praise, and pay thy vows unto the Most High. And call upon me in the day of trouble: I will deliver thee, and thou shalt glorify me."[5] So in another prophet: "Wherewith shall I come before the Lord, and bow myself before the High God? Shall I come before Him with burnt-offerings, with calves of a year old? Will the Lord be pleased with thousands of rams, or with ten thousands of rivers of oil? Shall I give my first-born for my transgression, the fruit of my body for the sin of my soul? Hath He showed thee, O man, what is good; and what doth the Lord require of thee, but to do justly, and to love mercy, and to walk humbly with thy God?"[6] In the words of this prophet, these two things are distinguished and set forth with sufficient explicitness, that God does not require these sacrifices for their own sakes and that He does require the sacrifices which they symbolize. In the epistle entitled "To the Hebrews" it is said, "To do good and to communicate, forget not: for with such sacrifices God is well pleased."[7] And so, when it is written, "I desire mercy rather than sacrifice,"[8] nothing else is meant than that one sacrifice is preferred to an-

---

[1]Ex. 22. 20.   [2]Ps. 16. 2.

[3]Ps. 51. 16, 17.   [4]Ps. 50. 12, 13.   [5]Ps. 50. 14, 15.
[6]Micah, 6. 6-8.   [7]Heb. 13. 16.   [8]Hos. 6. 6.

other; for that which in common speech is called sacrifice is only the symbol of the true sacrifice. Now mercy is the true sacrifice, and therefore it is said, as I have just quoted, "with such sacrifices God is well pleased." All the divine ordinances, therefore, which we read concerning the sacrifices in the service of the tabernacle or the temple, we are to refer to the love of God and our neighbour. For "on these two commandments," as it is written, "hang all the law and the prophets."[1]

Chap. 6. Of the true and perfect sacrifice

Thus a true sacrifice is every work which is done that we may be united to God in holy fellowship, and which has a reference to that supreme good and end in which alone we can be truly blessed. And therefore even the mercy we show to men, if it is not shown for God's sake, is not a sacrifice. For, though made or offered by man, sacrifice is a divine thing, as those who called it sacrifice[2] meant to indicate. Thus man himself, consecrated in the name of God and vowed to God, is a sacrifice in so far as he dies to the world that he may live to God. For this is a part of that mercy which each man shows to himself; as it is written, "Have mercy on thy soul by pleasing God."[3] Our body, too, is a sacrifice when we chasten it by temperance, if we do so as we ought, for God's sake, that we may not yield our members instruments of unrighteousness unto sin, but instruments of righteousness unto God.[4] Exhorting to this sacrifice, the apostle says, "I beseech you, therefore, brethren, by the mercy of God, that ye present your bodies a living sacrifice, holy, acceptable to God, which is your reasonable service."[5] If, then, the body, which, being inferior, the soul uses as a servant or instrument, is a sacrifice when it is used rightly and with reference to God, how much more does the soul itself become a sacrifice when it offers itself to God, in order that, being inflamed by the fire of His love, it may receive of His beauty and become pleasing to Him, losing the shape of earthly desire and being remoulded in the image of permanent loveliness? And this, indeed, the apostle subjoins, saying, "And be not conformed to this world; but be ye transformed in the renewing of your mind, that ye may prove what is that good, and acceptable, and perfect will of God."[6] Since, therefore, true sacrifices are works of mercy to ourselves or others, done with a reference to God,

and since works of mercy have no other object than the relief of distress or the conferring of happiness, and since there is no happiness apart from that good of which it is said, "It is good for me to be very near to God,"[7] it follows that the whole redeemed city, that is to say, the congregation or community of the saints, is offered to God as our sacrifice through the great High Priest, who offered Himself to God in His passion for us, that we might be members of this glorious head, according to the form of a servant. For it was this form He offered, in this He was offered, because it is according to it He is Mediator, in this He is our Priest, in this the Sacrifice. Accordingly, when the apostle had exhorted us to present our bodies a living sacrifice, holy, acceptable to God, our reasonable service, and not to be conformed to the world, but to be transformed in the renewing of our mind, that we might prove what is that good, and acceptable, and perfect will of God, that is to say, the true sacrifice of ourselves, he says, "For I say, through the grace of God which is given unto me, to every man that is among you, not to think of himself more highly than he ought to think, but to think soberly, according as God hath dealt to every man the measure of faith. For, as we have many members in one body, and all members have not the same office, so we, being many, are one body in Christ, and every one members one of another, having gifts differing according to the grace that is given to us."[8] This is the sacrifice of Christians: we, being many, are one body in Christ. And this also is the sacrifice which the Church continually celebrates in the sacrament of the altar, known to the faithful, in which she teaches that she herself is offered in the offering she makes to God.

Chap. 7. Of the love of the holy angels, which prompts them to desire that we worship the one true God and not themselves

It is very right that these blessed and immortal spirits, who inhabit celestial dwellings and rejoice in the communications of their Creator's fullness, firm in His eternity, assured in His truth, holy by His grace, since they compassionately and tenderly regard us miserable mortals, and wish us to become immortal and happy, do not desire us to sacrifice to themselves, but to Him whose sacrifice they know themselves to be in common with us. For we and they together are the one city of God, to which it is said in the psalm, "Glorious things are spoken of thee, O city of God";[9] the human part sojourning here

---

[1]Matt. 22. 40. [2]Literally, a sacred action.
[3]Ecclus. 30. 24. [4]Rom. 6. 13.
[5]Rom. 12. 1. [6]Rom. 12. 2.

[7]Ps. 73. 28. [8]Rom. 12. 3-6. [9]Ps. 87. 3.

below, the angelic aiding from above. For from that heavenly city, in which God's will is the intelligible and unchangeable law, from that heavenly council-chamber—for they sit in counsel regarding us—that holy Scripture, descended to us by the ministry of angels, in which it is written, "He that sacrificeth unto any god, save unto the Lord only, he shall be utterly destroyed"[1]—this Scripture, this law, these precepts, have been confirmed by such miracles, that it is sufficiently evident to whom these immortal and blessed spirits, who desire us to be like themselves, wish us to sacrifice.

CHAP. 8. *Of the miracles which God has condescended to adhibit, through the ministry of angels, to his promises for the confirmation of the faith of the godly*

I should seem tedious were I to recount all the ancient miracles, which were wrought in attestation of God's promises which He made to Abraham thousands of years ago, that in his seed all the nations of the earth should be blessed.[2] For who can but marvel that Abraham's barren wife should have given birth to a son at an age when not even a prolific woman could bear children; or, again, that when Abraham sacrificed, a flame from heaven should have run between the divided parts;[3] or that the angels in human form, whom he had hospitably entertained and who had renewed God's promise of offspring, should also have predicted the destruction of Sodom by fire from heaven;[4] and that his nephew Lot should have been rescued from Sodom by the angels as the fire was just descending, while his wife, who looked back as she went, and was immediately turned into salt, stood as a sacred beacon warning us that no one who is being saved should long for what he is leaving? How striking also were the wonders done by Moses to rescue God's people from the yoke of slavery in Egypt, when the magi of the Pharaoh, that is, the king of Egypt, who tyrannized over this people, were suffered to do some wonderful things that they might be vanquished all the more signally! They did these things by the magical arts and incantations to which the evil spirits or demons are addicted; while Moses, having as much greater power as he had right on his side, and having the aid of angels, easily conquered them in the name of the Lord Who made heaven and earth. And, in fact, the magicians failed at the third plague; whereas Moses, dealing out the miracles delegated to

him, brought ten plagues upon the land, so that the hard hearts of Pharaoh and the Egyptians yielded, and the people were let go. But, quickly repenting, and essaying to overtake the departing Hebrews, who had crossed the sea on dry ground, they were covered and overwhelmed in the returning waters. What shall I say of those frequent and stupendous exhibitions of divine power, while the people were conducted through the wilderness?—of the waters which could not be drunk, but lost their bitterness, and quenched the thirsty, when at God's command a piece of wood was cast into them? of the manna that descended from heaven to appease their hunger, and which begat worms and putrefied when any one collected more than the appointed quantity, and yet, though double was gathered on the day before the Sabbath (it not being lawful to gather it on that day), remained fresh? of the birds which filled the camp, and turned appetite into satiety when they longed for flesh, which it seemed impossible to supply to so vast a population? of the enemies who met them, and opposed their passage with arms, and were defeated without the loss of a single Hebrew, when Moses prayed with his hands extended in the form of a cross? of the seditious persons who arose among God's people, and separated themselves from the divinely-ordered community, and were swallowed up alive by the earth, a visible token of an invisible punishment? of the rock struck with the rod, and pouring out waters more than enough for all the host? of the deadly serpents' bites, sent in just punishment of sin, but healed by looking at the lifted brazen serpent, so that not only were the tormented people healed, but a symbol of the crucifixion of death set before them in this destruction of death by death? It was this serpent which was preserved in memory of this event, and was afterwards worshipped by the mistaken people as an idol, and was destroyed by the pious and God-fearing king Hezekiah, much to his credit.

CHAP. 9. *Of the illicit arts connected with demonolatry, and of which the Platonist Porphyry adopts some, and discards others*

These miracles, and many others of the same nature, which it were tedious to mention, were wrought for the purpose of commending the worship of the one true God, and prohibiting the worship of a multitude of false gods. Moreover, they were wrought by simple faith and godly confidence, not by the incantations and charms composed under the influence of a criminal tampering with the unseen world, of an art

[1]Ex. 22. 20.   [2]Gen. 18. 18.
[3]Gen. 15. 17.   [4]Gen. 18.

which they call either magic, or by the more abominable title necromancy, or the more honourable designation theurgy; for they wish to discriminate between those whom the people call magicians, who practise necromancy, and are addicted to illicit arts and condemned, and those others who seem to them to be worthy of praise for their practice of theurgy—the truth, however, being that both classes are the slaves of the deceitful rites of the demons whom they invoke under the names of angels.

For even Porphyry promises some kind of purgation of the soul by the help of theurgy, though he does so with some hesitation and shame, and denies that this art can secure to any one a return to God; so that you can detect his opinion vacillating between the profession of philosophy and an art which he feels to be presumptuous and sacrilegious. For at one time he warns us to avoid it as deceitful, and prohibited by law, and dangerous to those who practise it; then again, as if in deference to its advocates, he declares it useful for cleansing one part of the soul, not, indeed, the intellectual part, by which the truth of things intelligible, which have no sensible images, is recognized, but the spiritual part, which takes cognizance of the images of things material. This part, he says, is prepared and fitted for intercourse with spirits and angels, and for the vision of the gods, by the help of certain theurgic consecrations, or, as they call them, mysteries. He acknowledges, however, that these theurgic mysteries impart to the intellectual soul no such purity as fits it to see its God, and recognize the things that truly exist. And from this acknowledgment we may infer what kind of gods these are, and what kind of vision of them is imparted by theurgic consecrations, if by it one cannot see the things which truly exist. He says, further, that the rational, or, as he prefers calling it, the intellectual soul, can pass into the heavens without the spiritual part being cleansed by theurgic art, and that this art cannot so purify the spiritual part as to give it entrance to immortality and eternity. And therefore, although he distinguishes angels from demons, asserting that the habitation of the latter is in the air, while the former dwell in the ether and empyrean, and although he advises us to cultivate the friendship of some demon, who may be able after our death to assist us, and elevate us at least a little above the earth—for he owns that it is by another way we must reach the heavenly society of the angels—he at the same time distinctly warns us to avoid the society of demons, saying that the soul, expiating its sin after death, execrates the worship of demons by whom it was entangled. And of theurgy itself, though he recommends it as reconciling angels and demons, he cannot deny that it treats with powers which either themselves envy the soul its purity, or serve the arts of those who do envy it. He complains of this through the mouth of some Chaldæan or other: "A good man in Chaldæa complains," he says, "that his most strenuous efforts to cleanse his soul were frustrated, because another man, who had influence in these matters, and who envied him purity, had prayed to the powers, and bound them by his conjuring not to listen to his request. Therefore," adds Porphyry, "what the one man bound, the other could not loose." And from this he concludes that theurgy is a craft which accomplishes not only good but evil among gods and men; and that the gods also have passions and are perturbed and agitated by the emotions which Apuleius attributed to demons and men, but from which he preserved the gods by that sublimity of residence, which, in common with Plato, he accorded to them.

CHAP. 10. *Concerning theurgy, which promises a delusive purification of the soul by the invocation of demons*

But here we have another and a much more learned Platonist than Apuleius, Porphyry, to wit, asserting that, by I know not what theurgy, even the gods themselves are subjected to passions and perturbations; for by adjurations they were so bound and terrified that they could not confer purity of soul, were so terrified by him who imposed on them a wicked command, that they could not by the same theurgy be freed from that terror, and fulfill the righteous behest of him who prayed to them; or do the good he sought. Who does not see that all these things are fictions of deceiving demons, unless he be a wretched slave of theirs and an alien from the grace of the true Liberator? For if the Chaldæan had been dealing with good gods, certainly a well-disposed man, who sought to purify his own soul, would have had more influence with them than an evil-disposed man seeking to hinder him. Or, if the gods were just and considered the man unworthy of the purification he sought, at all events they should not have been terrified by an envious person, nor hindered, as Porphyry avows, by the fear of a stronger deity, but should have simply denied the boon on their own free judgment. And it is surprising that that well-disposed Chaldæan, who desired to purify his soul by theurgical rites, found no superior deity who could either terrify the frightened gods still more, and force them to confer the boon, or compose their fears, and so enable them to do good without compulsion, even supposing that the good theurgist had no rites by which he himself might purge away the taint of fear from the gods whom he invoked for the purification of his own soul. And why is it that there is a god who has power to terrify the inferior gods, and none who has power to free them from fear? Is there found a god who listens to the envious man and frightens the gods from doing good? and is there not found a god who listens to the well-disposed man and removes the fear of the gods that they may do him good? O excellent theurgy! O admirable purification of the soul!—a theurgy in which the violence of an impure envy has more influence than the entreaty of purity and holiness. Rather let us abominate and avoid the deceit of such wicked spirits, and listen to sound doctrine. As to those who perform these filthy cleansings by sacrilegious rites and see in their initiated state (as he further tells us, though we may question this vision) certain wonderfully lovely appearances of angels or gods, this is what the apostle refers to when he speaks of "Satan transforming himself into an angel of light."[1] For these are the delusive appearances of that spirit who longs to entangle wretched souls in the deceptive worship of many and false gods, and to turn them aside from the true worship of the true God, by Whom alone they are cleansed and healed, and who, as was said of Proteus, "turns himself into all shapes,"[2] equally hurtful, whether he assaults us as an enemy, or assumes the disguise of a friend.

CHAP. 11. *Of Porphyry's epistle to Anebo, in which he asks for information about the differences among demons*

It was a better tone which Porphyry adopted in his letter to Anebo the Egyptian, in which, assuming the character of an inquirer consulting him, he unmasks and explodes these sacrilegious arts. In that letter, indeed, he repudiates all demons, whom he maintains to be so foolish as to be attracted by the sacrificial vapours, and therefore residing not in the ether, but in the air beneath the moon and indeed in the moon itself. Yet he has not the boldness to attribute to all the demons all the deceptions and malicious and foolish practices which justly move his indignation. For, though he acknowledges that as a race demons are foolish, he so far accommodates himself to popular ideas as to call some of them

benignant demons. He expresses surprise that sacrifices not only incline the gods, but also compel and force them to do what men wish; and he is at a loss to understand how the sun and moon, and other visible celestial bodies—for bodies he does not doubt that they are—are considered gods, if the gods are distinguished from the demons by their incorporeality; also, if they are gods, how some are called beneficent and others hurtful, and how they, being corporeal, are numbered with the gods, who are incorporeal. He inquires further, and still as one in doubt, whether diviners and wonderworkers are men of unusually powerful souls, or whether the power to do these things is communicated by spirits from without. He inclines to the latter opinion, on the ground that it is by the use of stones and herbs that they lay spells on people, and open closed doors, and do similar wonders. And on this account, he says, some suppose that there is a race of beings whose property it is to listen to men— a race deceitful, full of contrivances, capable of assuming all forms, simulating gods, demons, and dead men—and that it is this race which bring about all these things which have the appearance of good or evil, but that what is really good they never help us in, and are indeed unacquainted with, for they make wickedness easy, but throw obstacles in the path of those who eagerly follow virtue; and that they are filled with pride and rashness, delight in sacrificial odours, are taken with flattery. These and the other characteristics of this race of deceitful and malicious spirits, who come into the souls of men and delude their senses, both in sleep and waking, he describes not as things of which he is himself convinced, but only with so much suspicion and doubt as to cause him to speak of them as commonly received opinions. We should sympathize with this great philosopher in the difficulty he experienced in acquainting himself with and confidently assailing the whole fraternity of devils, which any Christian old woman would unhesitatingly describe and most unreservedly detest. Perhaps, however, he shrank from offending Anebo, to whom he was writing, himself the most eminent patron of these mysteries, or the others who marvelled at these magical feats as divine works, and closely allied to the worship of the gods.

However, he pursues this subject, and, still in the character of an inquirer, mentions some things which no sober judgment could attribute to any but malicious and deceitful powers. He asks why, after the better class of spirits have been invoked, the worse should be commanded

---

[1] II Cor. 11. 14.   [2] Virgil, *Georgics*, BK. IV. 411.

to perform the wicked desires of men; why they do not hear a man who has just left a woman's embrace, while they themselves make no scruple of tempting men to incest and adultery; why their priests are commanded to abstain from animal food for fear of being polluted by the corporeal exhalations, while they themselves are attracted by the fumes of sacrifices and other exhalations; why the initiated are forbidden to touch a dead body, while their mysteries are celebrated almost entirely by means of dead bodies; why it is that a man addicted to any vice should utter threats, not to a demon or to the soul of a dead man, but to the sun and moon, or some of the heavenly bodies, which he intimidates by imaginary terrors, that he may wring from them a real boon—for he threatens that he will demolish the sky, and such like impossibilities—that those gods, being alarmed, like silly children, with imaginary and absurd threats, may do what they are ordered. Porphyry further relates that a man, Chæremon, profoundly versed in these sacred or rather sacrilegious mysteries, had written that the famous Egyptian mysteries of Isis and her husband Osiris had very great influence with the gods to compel them to do what they were ordered, when he who used the spells threatened to divulge or do away with these mysteries, and cried with a threatening voice that he would scatter the members of Osiris if they neglected his orders. Not without reason is Porphyry surprised that a man should utter such wild and empty threats against the gods—not against gods of no account, but against the heavenly gods, and those that shine with sidereal light—and that these threats should be effectual to constrain them with resistless power, and alarm them so that they fulfill his wishes. Not without reason does he, in the character of an inquirer into the reasons of these surprising things, give it to be understood that they are done by that race of spirits which he previously described as if quoting other people's opinions—spirits who deceive not, as he said, by nature, but by their own corruption, and who simulate gods and dead men, but not, as he said, demons, for demons they really are. As to his idea that by means of herbs, and stones, and animals, and certain incantations, and noises, and drawings, sometimes fanciful, and sometimes copied from the motions of the heavenly bodies, men create upon earth powers capable of bringing about various results, all that is only the mystification which these demons practise on those who are subject to them, for the sake of furnishing themselves with mer-

riment at the expense of their dupes. Either, then, Porphyry was sincere in his doubts and inquiries, and mentioned these things to demonstrate and put beyond question that they were the work, not of powers which aid us in obtaining life, but of deceitful demons; or, to take a more favourable view of the philosopher, he adopted this method with the Egyptian who was wedded to these errors and was proud of them, that he might not offend him by assuming the attitude of a teacher, nor discompose his mind by the altercation of a professed assailant, but, by assuming the character of an inquirer, and the humble attitude of one who was anxious to learn, might turn his attention to these matters, and show how worthy they are to be despised and relinquished. Towards the conclusion of his letter, he requests Anebo to inform him what the Egyptian wisdom indicates as the way to blessedness. But as to those who hold intercourse with the gods, and pester them only for the sake of finding a runaway slave, or acquiring property, or making a bargain of a marriage, or such things, he declares that their pretensions to wisdom are vain. He adds that these same gods, even granting that on other points their utterances were true, were yet so ill-advised and unsatisfactory in their disclosures about blessedness that they cannot be either gods or good demons, but are either that spirit who is called the deceiver, or mere fictions of the imagination.

CHAP. 12. *Of the miracles wrought by the true God through the ministry of the holy angels*

Since by means of these arts wonders are done which quite surpass human power, what choice have we but to believe that these predictions and operations, which seem to be miraculous and divine and which at the same time form no part of the worship of the one God, in adherence to whom, as the Platonists themselves abundantly testify, all blessedness consists, are the pastime of wicked spirits, who thus seek to seduce and hinder the truly godly? On the other hand, we cannot but believe that all miracles, whether wrought by angels or by other means, so long as they are so done as to commend the worship and religion of the one God in Whom alone is blessedness, are wrought by those who love us in a true and godly sort, or through their means, God Himself working in them. For we cannot listen to those who maintain that the invisible God works no visible miracles; for even they believe that He made the world, which surely they will not deny to be visible. Whatever marvel happens in this world, it is certainly less marvellous than this whole world itself—I mean the sky and earth and all that is in them—and these God certainly made. But, as the Creator Himself is hidden and incomprehensible to man, so also is the manner of creation. Although, therefore, the standing miracle of this visible world is little thought of, because always before us, yet, when we arouse ourselves to contemplate it, it is a greater miracle than the rarest and most unheard-of marvels. For man himself is a greater miracle than any miracle done through his instrumentality. Therefore God, Who made the visible heaven and earth, does not disdain to work visible miracles in heaven or earth, that He may thereby awaken the soul which is immersed in things visible to worship Himself, the Invisible. But the place and time of these miracles are dependent on His unchangeable will, in which things future are ordered as if already they were accomplished. For He moves things temporal without Himself moving in time. He does not in one way know things that are to be, and, in another, things that have been; neither does He listen to those who pray otherwise than as He sees those that will pray. For, even when His angels hear us, it is He Himself who hears us in them, as in His true temple not made with hands, as in those men who are His saints; and His answers, though accomplished in time, have been arranged by His eternal appointment.

CHAP. 13. *Of the invisible God, who has often made Himself visible, not as He really is, but as the beholders could bear the sight*

Neither need we be surprised that God, invisible as He is, should often have appeared visibly to the patriarchs. For as the sound which communicates the thought conceived in the silence of the mind is not the thought itself, so the form by which God, invisible in His own nature, became visible, was not God Himself. Nevertheless it is He Himself who was seen under that form, as that thought itself is heard in the sound of the voice; and the patriarchs recognized that, though the bodily form was not God, they saw the invisible God. For, though Moses conversed with God, yet he said, "If I have found grace in Thy sight, show me Thyself, that I may see and know Thee."[1] And as it was fit that the law, which was given, not to one man or a few enlightened men, but to the whole of a populous nation, should be accompanied by awe-inspiring signs, great marvels were wrought, by the ministry of angels, before the people on the mount where the law was being given to them through one man, while the multitude beheld the awful appearances. For the people of Israel believed Moses, not as the Lacedæmonians believed their Lycurgus, because he had received from Jupiter or Apollo the laws he gave them. For when the law which enjoined the worship of one God was given to the people, marvellous signs and earthquakes, such as the divine wisdom judged sufficient, were brought about in the sight of all, that they might know that it was the Creator who could thus use creation to promulgate His law.

CHAP. 14. *That the one God is to be worshipped not only for the sake of eternal blessings, but also in connexion with temporal prosperity, because all things are regulated by his providence*

The education of the human race, represented by the people of God, has advanced, like that of an individual, through certain epochs, or, as it were, ages, so that it might gradually rise from earthly to heavenly things, and from the visible to the invisible. This object was kept so clearly in view that, even in the period when temporal rewards were promised, the one God was presented as the object of worship, that men might not acknowledge any other than the true Creator and Lord of the spirit, even in connexion with the earthly blessings of this transitory life. For he who denies that all things, which either angels or men can give us, are in the hand of the one Almighty, is a madman. The Platonist Plotinus discourses concerning providence and, from the beauty of flowers and foliage, proves that from the supreme God, whose beauty is unseen and ineffable, providence reaches down even to these earthly things here below; and he argues that all these frail and perishing things could not have so exquisite and elaborate a beauty were they not fashioned by Him Whose unseen and unchangeable beauty continually pervades all things.[2] This is proved also by the Lord Jesus, where He says, "Consider the lilies, how they grow; they toil not, neither do they spin. And yet I say unto you that Solomon in all his glory was not arrayed like one of these. But if God so clothe the grass of the field, which to-day is and to-morrow is cast into the oven, how much more shall He clothe you, O ye of little faith!"[3] It was best, therefore, that the soul of man, which was still weakly desiring earthly things, should be accustomed to seek from God alone even these petty temporal boons

[1]Ex. 33. 13.   [2]*Enneads*, III. 2. 13.   [3]Matt. 6. 28-30.

and the earthly necessaries of this transitory life, which are contemptible in comparison with eternal blessings, in order that the desire even of these things might not draw it aside from the worship of Him, to Whom we come by despising and forsaking such things.

CHAP. 15. *Of the ministry of the holy angels, by which they fulfill the providence of God*

And so it has pleased Divine Providence, as I have said and as we read in the Acts of the Apostles,[1] that the law enjoining the worship of one God should be given by the disposition of angels. But among them the person of God Himself visibly appeared, not, indeed, in His proper substance, which ever remains invisible to mortal eyes, but by the infallible signs furnished by creation in obedience to its Creator. He made use, too, of the words of human speech, uttering them syllable by syllable successively, though in His own nature He speaks not in a bodily but in a spiritual way; not to sense, but to the mind; not in words that occupy time, but, if I may so say, eternally, neither beginning to speak nor coming to an end. And what He says is accurately heard, not by the bodily but by the mental ear of His ministers and messengers, who are immortally blessed in the enjoyment of His unchangeable truth; and the directions which they in some ineffable way receive, they execute without delay or difficulty in the sensible and visible world. And this law was given in conformity with the age of the world, and contained at the first earthly promises, as I have said, which, however, symbolized eternal ones; and these eternal blessings few understood, though many took a part in the celebration of their visible signs. Nevertheless, with one consent both the words and the visible rites of that law enjoin the worship of one God—not one of a crowd of gods, but Him Who made heaven and earth, and every soul and every spirit which is other than Himself. He created; all else was created; and, both for being and well-being, all things need Him Who created them.

CHAP. 16. *Whether those angels who demand that we pay them divine honour, or those who teach us to render holy service, not to themselves, but to God, are to be trusted about the way to life eternal*

What angels, then, are we to believe in this matter of blessed and eternal life?—those who wish to be worshipped with religious rites and observances, and require that men sacrifice to

them; or those who say that all this worship is due to one God, the Creator, and teach us to render it with true piety to Him, by the vision of Whom they are themselves already blessed, and in Whom they promise that we shall be so? For that vision of God is the beauty of a vision so great and is so infinitely desirable that Plotinus does not hesitate to say that he who enjoys all other blessings in abundance and has not this is supremely miserable.[2] Since, therefore, miracles are wrought by some angels to induce us to worship this God, by others, to induce us to worship themselves; and since the former forbid us to worship these, while the latter dare not forbid us to worship God, which are we to listen to? Let the Platonists reply, or any philosophers, or the theurgists, or rather, *periurgists*[3]—for this name is good enough for those who practise such arts. In short, let all men answer—if, at least, there survives in them any spark of that natural perception which, as rational beings, they possess when created—let them, I say, tell us whether we should sacrifice to the gods or angels who order us to sacrifice to them, or to that One to Whom we are ordered to sacrifice by those who forbid us to worship either themselves or these others. If neither the one party nor the other had wrought miracles, but had merely uttered commands, the one to sacrifice to themselves, the other forbidding that, and ordering us to sacrifice to God, a godly mind would have been at no loss to discern which command proceeded from proud arrogance, and which from true religion. I will say more. If miracles had been wrought only by those who demand sacrifice for themselves, while those who forbade this, and enjoined sacrificing to the one God only, thought fit entirely to forego the use of visible miracles, the authority of the latter was to be preferred by all who would use, not their eyes only, but their reason. But since God, for the sake of commending to us the oracles of His truth, has, by means of these immortal messengers, who proclaim His majesty and not their own pride, wrought miracles of surpassing grandeur, certainty, and distinctness, in order that the weak among the godly might not be drawn away to false religion by those who require us to sacrifice to them and endeavour to convince us by stupendous appeals to our senses, who is so utterly unreasonable as not to choose and follow the truth, when he finds that it is heralded by even more striking evidences than falsehood?

As for those miracles which history ascribes

---

[1] Acts, 7. 53.

[2] *Enneads*, 1. 6. 7.   [3] Meaning, *officious meddlers*.

to the gods of the heathen—I do not refer to those prodigies which at intervals happen from some unknown physical causes, and which are arranged and appointed by Divine Providence, such as monstrous births, and unusual meteorological phenomena, whether startling only, or also injurious, and which are said to be brought about and removed by communication with demons, and by their most deceitful craft—but I refer to these prodigies which manifestly enough are wrought by their power and force, as, that the household gods which Æneas carried from Troy in his flight moved from place to place; that Tarquin cut a whetstone with a razor; that the Epidaurian serpent attached himself as a companion to Æsculapius on his voyage to Rome; that the ship in which the image of the Phrygian mother stood, and which could not be moved by a host of men and oxen, was moved by one weak woman, who attached her girdle to the vessel and drew it, as proof of her chastity; that a vestal, whose virginity was questioned, removed the suspicion by carrying from the Tiber a sieve full of water without any of it dropping: these, then, and the like, are by no means to be compared for greatness and virtue to those which, we read, were wrought among God's people. How much less can we compare those marvels, which even the laws of heathen nations prohibit and punish—I mean the magical and theurgic marvels, of which the great part are merely illusions practised upon the senses, as the drawing down of the moon, "that," as Lucan says, "it may shed a stronger influence on the plants"? And if some of these do seem to equal those which are wrought by the godly, the end for which they are wrought distinguishes the two, and shows that ours are incomparably the more excellent. For those miracles commend the worship of a plurality of gods, who deserve worship the less the more they demand it; but these of ours commend the worship of the one God, Who, both by the testimony of His own Scriptures and by the eventual abolition of sacrifices, proves that He needs no such offerings. If, therefore, any angels demand sacrifice for themselves, we must prefer those who demand it not for themselves, but for God, the Creator of all, whom they serve. For thus they prove how sincerely they love us, since they wish by sacrifice to subject us, not to themselves, but to Him by the contemplation of Whom they themselves are blessed, and to bring us to Him from Whom they themselves have never strayed. If, on the other hand, any angels wish us to sacrifice, not to one, but to many, not, indeed,

to themselves, but to the gods whose angels they are, we must in this case also prefer those who are the angels of the one God of gods, and who so bid us to worship Him as to preclude our worshipping any other. But, further, if it be the case, as their pride and deceitfulness rather indicate, that they are neither good angels nor the angels of good gods, but wicked demons, who wish sacrifice to be paid, not to the one only and supreme God, but to themselves, what better protection against them can we choose than that of the one God Whom the good angels serve, the angels who bid us sacrifice, not to themselves, but to Him Whose sacrifice we ourselves ought to be?

CHAP. 17. *Concerning the ark of the covenant, and the miraculous signs whereby God authenticated the law and the promise*

On this account it was that the law of God, given by the disposition of angels, and which commanded that the one God of gods alone receive sacred worship, to the exclusion of all others, was deposited in the ark, called the ark of the testimony. By this name it is sufficiently indicated, not that God, Who was worshipped by all those rites, was shut up and enclosed in that place, though His responses emanated from it along with signs appreciable by the senses, but that His will was declared from that throne. The law itself, too, was engraven on tables of stone, and, as I have said, deposited in the ark, which the priests carried with due reverence during the sojourn in the wilderness, along with the tabernacle, which was in like manner called the tabernacle of the testimony; and there was then an accompanying sign, which appeared as a cloud by day and as a fire by night; when the cloud moved, the camp was shifted, and where it stood the camp was pitched. Besides these signs and the voices which proceeded from the place where the ark was, there were other miraculous testimonies to the law. For when the ark was carried across Jordan, on the entrance to the land of promise, the upper part of the river stopped in its course, and the lower part flowed on, so as to present both to the ark and the people dry ground to pass over. Then, when it was carried seven times round the first hostile and polytheistic city they came to, its walls suddenly fell down, though assaulted by no hand, struck by no battering-ram. Afterwards, too, when they were now resident in the land of promise, and the ark had, in punishment of their sin, been taken by their enemies, its captors triumphantly placed it in the temple of their favourite god and left it shut up there, but, on opening the temple next day, they found the image they used to pray to fallen to the ground and shamefully shattered. Then, being themselves alarmed by portents, and still more shamefully punished, they restored the ark of the testimony to the people from whom they had taken it. And what was the manner of its restoration? They placed it on a wagon, and yoked to it cows from which they had taken the calves, and let them choose their own course, expecting that in this way the divine will would be indicated; and the cows, without any man driving or directing them, steadily pursued the way to the Hebrews, without regarding the lowing of their calves, and thus restored the ark to its worshippers. To God these and such like wonders are small, but they are mighty to terrify and give wholesome instruction to men. For if philosophers, and especially the Platonists, are with justice esteemed wiser than other men, as I have just been mentioning, because they taught that even these earthly and insignificant things are ruled by Divine Providence, inferring this from the numberless beauties which are observable not only in the bodies of animals, but even in plants and grasses, how much more plainly do these things attest the presence of divinity which happen at the time predicted, and in which that religion is commended which forbids the offering of sacrifice to any celestial, terrestrial, or infernal being, and commands it to be offered to God only, Who alone blesses us by His love for us, and by our love to Him, and Who, by arranging the appointed times of those sacrifices, and by predicting that they were to pass into a better sacrifice by a better Priest, testified that He has no appetite for these sacrifices, but through them indicated others of more substantial blessing—and all this not that He himself may be glorified by these honours, but that we may be stirred up to worship and cleave to Him, being inflamed by His love, which is our advantage rather than His?

CHAP. 18. *Against those who deny that the books of the Church are to be believed about the miracles whereby the people of God were educated*

Will some one say that these miracles are false, that they never happened, and that the records of them are lies? Whoever says so, and asserts that in such matters no records whatever can be credited, may also say that there are no gods who care for human affairs. For they have induced men to worship them only by means of miraculous works, which the heathen histories testify, and by which the gods have made a display of their own power rather than done any real service. This is the reason why we have not undertaken in this work, of which we are now writing the tenth book, to refute those who either deny that there is any divine power, or contend that it does not interfere with human affairs, but those who prefer their own good to our God, the Founder of the holy and most glorious city, not knowing that He is also the invisible and unchangeable Founder of this visible and changing world and the truest bestower of the blessed life which resides not in things created but in Himself. For thus speaks His most trustworthy prophet: "It is good for me to be united to God."[1] Among philosophers it is a question, what is that end and good to the attainment of which all our duties are to have a relation? The Psalmist did not say, "It is good for me to have great wealth, or to wear imperial insignia, purple, sceptre, and diadem"; or, as some even of the philosophers have not blushed to say, "It is good for me to enjoy sensual pleasure"; or, as the better men among them seemed to say, "My good is my spiritual strength"; but, "It is good for me to be united to God." This he had learned from Him Whom the holy angels, with the accompanying witness of miracles, presented as the sole object of worship. And hence he himself became the sacrifice of God, Whose spiritual love inflamed him and into Whose ineffable and incorporeal embrace he yearned to cast himself. Moreover, if the worshippers of many gods (whatever kind of gods they fancy their own to be) believe that the miracles recorded in their civil histories, or in the books of magic, or of the more respectable theurgy, were wrought by these gods, what reason have they for refusing to believe the miracles recorded in those writings, to which we owe a credence as much greater as He is greater to Whom alone these writings teach us to sacrifice?

CHAP. 19. *On the reasonableness of offering, as the true religion teaches, a visible sacrifice to the one true and invisible God*

As to those who think that these visible sacrifices are suitably offered to other gods, but that invisible sacrifices, the graces of purity of mind and holiness of will, should be offered, as greater and better, to the invisible God, Himself greater and better than all others, they must be oblivious that these visible sacrifices are signs of the invisible, as the words we utter are the

[1]Ps. 73. 28.

signs of things. And therefore, as in prayer or praise we direct intelligible words to Him to Whom in our heart we offer the very feelings we are expressing, so we are to understand that in sacrifice we offer visible sacrifice only to Him to Whom in our heart we ought to present ourselves an invisible sacrifice. It is then that the angels, and all those superior powers who are mighty by their goodness and piety, regard us with pleasure, and rejoice with us and assist us to the utmost of their power. But if we offer such worship to them, they decline it; and when on any mission to men they become visible to the senses, they positively forbid it. Examples of this occur in holy writ. Some fancied they should, by adoration or sacrifice, pay the same honour to angels as is due to God, and were prevented from doing so by the angels themselves and ordered to render it to Him to Whom alone they know it to be due. And the holy angels have in this been imitated by holy men of God. For Paul and Barnabas, when they had wrought a miracle of healing in Lycaonia, were thought to be gods, and the Lycaonians desired to sacrifice to them, and they humbly and piously declined this honour, and announced to them the God in Whom they should believe. And those deceitful and proud spirits, who exact worship do so simply because they know it to be due to the true God. For that which they take pleasure in is not, as Porphyry says and some fancy, the smell of the victims, but divine honours. They have, in fact, plenty of odours on all hands, and, if they wished more, they could provide them for themselves. But the spirits who arrogate to themselves divinity are delighted not with the smoke of carcasses, but with the suppliant spirit which they deceive and hold in subjection, and hinder from drawing near to God, preventing him from offering himself in sacrifice to God by inducing him to sacrifice to others.

CHAP. 20. *Of the supreme and true sacrifice which was effected by the Mediator between God and men*

And hence that true Mediator, in so far as, by assuming the form of a servant, He became the Mediator between God and men, the man Christ Jesus, though in the form of God He received sacrifice together with the Father, with whom He is one God, yet in the form of a servant He chose rather to be than to receive a sacrifice, that not even by this instance any one might have occasion to suppose that sacrifice should be rendered to any creature. Thus He is both the Priest who offers and the Sacrifice offered. And

He designed that there should be a daily sign of this in the sacrifice of the Church, which, being His body, learns to offer herself through Him. Of this true Sacrifice the ancient sacrifices of the saints were the various and numerous signs; and it was thus variously figured, just as one thing is signified by a variety of words, that there may be less weariness when we speak of it much. To this supreme and true sacrifice all false sacrifices have given place.

CHAP. 21. *Of the power delegated to demons for the trial and glorification of the saints, who conquer not by propitiating the spirits of the air, but by abiding in God*

The power delegated to the demons at certain appointed and well-adjusted seasons, that they may give expression to their hostility to the city of God by stirring up against it the men who are under their influence, and may not only receive sacrifice from those who willingly offer it, but may also extort it from the unwilling by violent persecution; this power is found to be not merely harmless, but even useful to the Church, completing as it does the number of martyrs, whom the city of God esteems as all the more illustrious and honoured citizens, because they have striven even to blood against the sin of impiety. If the ordinary language of the Church allowed it, we might more elegantly call these men our heroes. For this name is said to be derived from Juno, who in Greek is called *Herè*, and hence, according to the Greek myths, one of her sons was called Heros. And these fables mystically signified that Juno was mistress of the air, which they suppose to be inhabited by the demons and the heroes, understanding by heroes the souls of the well-deserving dead. But for a quite opposite reason would we call our martyrs heroes—supposing, as I said, that the usage of ecclesiastical language would admit of it—not because they lived along with the demons in the air, but because they conquered these demons or powers of the air, and among them Juno herself, be she what she may, not unsuitably represented, as she commonly is by the poets, as hostile to virtue and jealous of men of mark aspiring to the heavens. Virgil, however, unhappily gives way, and yields to her; for, though he represents her as saying, "*I am conquered by Æneas*,"[1] Helenus gives Æneas himself this religious advice:

> *Pay vows to Juno: overbear*
> *Her queenly soul with gift and prayer.*[2]

In conformity with this opinion, Porphyry—ex-

[1] *Æneid*, BK. VII. 310. [2] *Ibid.*, BK. III. 438, 439.

pressing, however, not so much his own views as other people's—says that a good god or genius cannot come to a man unless the evil genius has been first of all propitiated, implying that the evil deities had greater power than the good; for, until they have been appeased and give place, the good can give no assistance; and if the evil deities oppose, the good can give no help; whereas the evil can do injury without the good being able to prevent them. This is not the way of the true and truly holy religion; not thus do our martyrs conquer Juno, that is to say, the powers of the air, who envy the virtues of the pious. Our heroes, if we could so call them, overcome Herè, not by suppliant gifts, but by divine virtues. As Scipio, who conquered Africa by his valour, is more suitably styled Africanus than if he had appeased his enemies by gifts and so won their mercy.

Chap. 22. *Whence the saints derive power against demons and true purification of heart*

It is by true piety that men of God cast out the hostile power of the air which opposes godliness; it is by exorcising it, not by propitiating it; and they overcome all the temptations of the adversary by praying, not to him, but to their own God against him. For the devil cannot conquer or subdue any but those who are in league with sin; and therefore he is conquered in the name of Him Who assumed humanity and that without sin, that Himself being both Priest and Sacrifice, He might bring about the remission of sins, that is to say, might bring it about through the Mediator between God and men, the man Christ Jesus, by Whom we are reconciled to God, the cleansing from sin being accomplished. For men are separated from God only by sins, from which we are in this life cleansed not by our own virtue, but by the divine compassion; through His indulgence, not through our own power. For, whatever virtue we call our own is itself bestowed upon us by His goodness. And we might attribute too much to ourselves while in the flesh, unless we lived in the receipt of pardon until we laid it down. This is the reason why there has been vouchsafed to us, through the Mediator, this grace, that we who are polluted by sinful flesh should be cleansed by the likeness of sinful flesh. By this grace of God, wherein He has shown His great compassion toward us, we are both governed by faith in this life and, after this life, are led onwards to the fullest perfection by the vision of immutable truth.

Chap. 23. *Of the principles which, according to the Platonists, regulate the purification of the soul*

Even Porphyry asserts that it was revealed by divine oracles that we are not purified by any sacrifices to sun or moon, meaning it to be inferred that we are not purified by sacrificing to any gods. For what mysteries can purify, if those of the sun and moon, which are esteemed the chief of the celestial gods, do not purify? He says, too, in the same place, that "principles" can purify, lest it should be supposed, from his saying that sacrificing to the sun and moon cannot purify, that sacrificing to some other of the host of gods might do so. And what he as a Platonist means by "principles," we know. For he speaks of God the Father and God the Son, whom he calls (writing in Greek) the intellect or mind of the Father;[1] but of the Holy Spirit he says either nothing, or nothing plainly, for I do not understand what other he speaks of as holding the middle place between these two. For if, like Plotinus in his discussion regarding the three principal substances,[2] he wished us to understand by this third the soul of nature, he would certainly not have given it the middle place between these two, that is, between the Father and the Son. For Plotinus places the soul of nature after the intellect of the Father, while Porphyry, making it the mean, does not place it after, but between the others. No doubt he spoke according to his light, or as he thought expedient; but we assert that the Holy Spirit is the Spirit not of the Father only, nor of the Son only, but of both. For philosophers speak as they have a mind to and in the most difficult matters do not scruple to offend religious ears; but we are bound to speak according to a certain rule, lest freedom of speech beget impiety of opinion about the matters themselves of which we speak.

Chap. 24. *Of the one only true principle which alone purifies and renews human nature*

Accordingly, when we speak of God, we do not affirm two or three principles, no more than we are at liberty to affirm two or three gods; although, speaking of each, of the Father, or of the Son, or of the Holy Ghost, we confess that each is God: and yet we do not say, as the Sabellian heretics say, that the Father is the same as the Son, and the Holy Spirit the same as the Father and the Son; but we say that the Father is the Father of the Son, and the Son the Son of the Father, and that the Holy Spirit of the

[1]See below, Chap. 28.   [2]*Enneads*, v. 1.

Father and the Son is neither the Father nor the Son. It was therefore truly said that man is cleansed only by a Principle, although the Platonists erred in speaking in the plural of *principles*. But Porphyry, being under the dominion of these envious powers, whose influence he was at once ashamed of and afraid to throw off, refused to recognize that Christ is the Principle by whose incarnation we are purified. Indeed he despised Him, because of the flesh itself which He assumed, that He might offer a sacrifice for our purification—a great mystery, unintelligible to Porphyry's pride, which that true and benignant Redeemer brought low by His humility, manifesting Himself to mortals by the mortality which He assumed, and which the malignant and deceitful mediators are proud of wanting, promising, as the boon of immortals, a deceptive assistance to wretched men. Thus the good and true Mediator showed that it is sin which is evil, and not the substance or nature of flesh; for this, together with the human soul, could without sin be both assumed and retained, and laid down in death, and changed to something better by resurrection. He showed also that death itself, although the punishment of sin, was submitted to by Him for our sakes without sin and must not be evaded by sin on our part, but rather, if opportunity serves, be borne for righteousness' sake. For he was able to expiate sins by dying, because He both died and not for sin of His own. But He has not been recognized by Porphyry as the Principle, otherwise he would have recognized Him as the Purifier. The Principle is neither the flesh nor the human soul in Christ, but the Word by which all things were made. The flesh, therefore, does not by its own virtue purify, but by virtue of the Word by which it was assumed, when "the Word became flesh and dwelt among us."[1] For speaking mystically of eating His flesh, when those who did not understand Him were offended and went away, saying, "This is an hard saying, who can hear it?" He answered to the rest who remained, "It is the Spirit that quickeneth; the flesh profiteth nothing."[2] The Principle, therefore, having assumed a human soul and flesh, cleanses the soul and flesh of believers. Therefore, when the Jews asked Him who He was, He answered that He was the *Principle*.[3] And this we carnal and feeble men, liable to sin and involved in the darkness of ignorance, could not possibly understand, unless we were cleansed and healed by Him, both by means of what we were and of what we were not. For we were men, but we were not righteous; whereas in His incarnation there was a human nature, but it was righteous and not sinful. This is the mediation whereby a hand is stretched to the lapsed and fallen; this is the seed "ordained by angels," by whose ministry the law also was given enjoining the worship of one God, and promising that this Mediator should come.

CHAP. 25. *That all the saints, both under the law and before it, were justified by faith in the mystery of Christ's incarnation*

It was by faith in this mystery, and godliness of life, that purification was attainable even by the saints of old, whether before the law was given to the Hebrews (for God and the angels were even then present as instructors), or in the periods under the law, although the promises of spiritual things, being presented in figure, seemed to be carnal, and hence the name of Old Testament. For it was then the prophets lived, by whom, as by angels, the same promise was announced; and among them was he whose grand and divine sentiment regarding the end and supreme good of man I have just now quoted, "It is good for me to cleave to God."[4] In this psalm the distinction between the Old and New Testaments is distinctly announced. For the Psalmist says that, when he saw that the carnal and earthly promises were abundantly enjoyed by the ungodly, his feet were almost gone, his steps had well-nigh slipped; and that it seemed to him as if he had served God in vain, when he saw that those who despised God increased in that prosperity which he looked for at God's hand. He says, too, that, in investigating this matter with the desire of understanding why it was so, he had laboured in vain, until he went into the sanctuary of God and understood the end of those whom he had erroneously considered happy. Then he understood that they were cast down by that very thing, as he says, which they had made their boast, and that they had been consumed and perished for their iniquities; and that that whole fabric of temporal prosperity had become as a dream when one awaketh, and suddenly finds himself destitute of all the joys he had imaged in sleep. And, as in this earth or earthly city they seemed to themselves to be great, he says, "O Lord, in Thy city Thou wilt reduce their image to nothing." He also shows how beneficial it had been for him to seek even earthly blessings only from the one true God, in Whose

[1]John, i. 14. [2]John, 6. 60-64.
[3]John, 8. 25; or "the beginning," following a different reading from ours. [4]Ps. 73. 28.

power are all things, for he says, "As a beast was I before Thee, and I am always with Thee." "As a beast," he says, meaning that he was stupid. For I ought to have sought from Thee such things as the ungodly could not enjoy as well as I, and not those things which I saw them enjoying in abundance, and hence concluded I was serving Thee in vain, because they who declined to serve Thee had what I had not. Nevertheless, "I am always with Thee," because even in my desire for such things I did not pray to other gods. And consequently he goes on, "Thou hast holden me by my right hand, and by Thy counsel Thou hast guided me, and with glory hast taken me up"; as if all earthly advantages were left-hand blessings, though, when he saw them enjoyed by the wicked, his feet had almost gone. "For what," he says, "have I in heaven, and what have I desired from Thee upon earth?" He blames himself, and is justly displeased with himself; because, though he had in heaven so vast a possession (as he afterwards understood), he yet sought from his God on earth a transitory and fleeting happiness—a happiness of mire, we may say. "My heart and my flesh," he says, "fail, O God of my heart." Happy failure, from things below to things above! And hence in another psalm He says, "My soul longeth, yea, even faileth, for the courts of the Lord."[1] Yet, though he had said of both his heart and his flesh that they were failing, he did not say, "O God of my heart and my flesh," but, "O God of my heart"; for by the heart the flesh is made clean. Therefore, says the Lord, "Cleanse that which is within, and the outside shall be clean also."[2] He then says that God Himself—not anything received from Him, but Himself—is his portion. "The God of my heart, and my portion for ever." Among the various objects of human choice, God alone satisfied him. "For, lo," he says, "they that are far from Thee shall perish: Thou destroyest all them that go a-whoring from Thee"—that is, who prostitute themselves to many gods. And then follows the verse for which all the rest of the psalm seems to prepare: "It is good for me to cleave to God"—not to go far off; not to go a-whoring with a multitude of gods. And then shall this union with God be perfected, when all that is to be redeemed in us has been redeemed. But for the present we must, as he goes on to say, "place our hope in God." "For that which is seen," says the apostle, "is not hope. For what a man sees, why does he yet hope for? But if we hope for that we see not, then do

we with patience wait for it."[3] Being, then, for the present established in this hope, let us do what the Psalmist further indicates, and become in our measure angels or messengers of God, declaring His will, and praising His glory and His grace. For when he had said, "To place my hope in God," he goes on, "that I may declare all Thy praises in the gates of the daughter of Zion." This is the most glorious city of God; this is the city which knows and worships one God: she is celebrated by the holy angels, who invite us to their society, and desire us to become fellow-citizens with them in this city; for they do not wish us to worship them as our gods, but to join them in worshipping their God and ours; nor to sacrifice to them, but, together with them, to become a sacrifice to God. Accordingly, whoever will lay aside malignant obstinacy and consider these things shall be assured that all these blessed and immortal spirits, who do not envy us (for if they envied they were not blessed), but rather love us and desire us to be as blessed as themselves, look on us with greater pleasure and give us greater assistance, when we join them in worshipping one God, Father, Son, and Holy Ghost, than if we were to offer to themselves sacrifice and worship.

CHAP. 26. *Of Porphyry's weakness in wavering between the confession of the true God and the worship of demons*

I know not how it is so, but it seems to me that Porphyry blushed for his friends the theurgists; for he knew all that I have adduced, but did not frankly condemn polytheistic worship. He said, in fact, that there are some angels who visit earth and reveal divine truth to theurgists, and others who publish on earth the things that belong to the Father, His height and depth. Can we believe, then, that the angels whose office it is to declare the will of the Father wish us to be subject to any but Him Whose will they declare? And hence, even this Platonist himself judiciously observes that we should rather imitate than invoke them. We ought not, then, to fear that we may offend these immortal and happy subjects of the one God by not sacrificing to them; for this they know to be due only to the one true God, in allegiance to Whom they themselves find their blessedness, and therefore they will not have it given to them, either in figure or in the reality, which the mysteries of sacrifice symbolized. Such arrogance belongs to proud and wretched demons, whose

---

[1] Ps. 84. 2.   [2] Matt. 23. 26.   [3] Rom. 8. 24, 25.

disposition is diametrically opposite to the piety of those who are subject to God, and whose blessedness consists in attachment to Him. And, that we also may attain to this bliss, they aid us, as is fit, with sincere kindliness, and usurp over us no dominion, but declare to us Him under Whose rule we are then fellow-subjects. Why, then, O philosopher, do you still fear to speak freely against the powers which are inimical both to true virtue and to the gifts of the true God? Already you have discriminated between the angels who proclaim God's will and those who visit theurgists, drawn down by I know not what art. Why do you still ascribe to these latter the honour of declaring divine truth? If they do not declare the will of the Father, what divine revelations can they make? Are not these the evil spirits who were bound over by the incantations of an envious man,[1] that they should not grant purity of soul to another and could not, as you say, be set free from these bonds by a good man anxious for purity, and recover power over their own actions? Do you still doubt whether these are wicked demons; or do you, perhaps, feign ignorance, that you may not give offence to the theurgists, who have allured you by their secret rites, and have taught you, as a mighty boon, these insane and pernicious devilries? Do you dare to elevate above the air, and even to heaven, these envious powers, or pests, let me rather call them, less worthy of the name of sovereign than of slave, as you yourself own; and are you not ashamed to place them even among your sidereal gods and so put a slight upon the stars themselves?

CHAP. 27. *Of the impiety of Porphyry, which is worse than even the mistake of Apuleius*

How much more tolerable and accordant with human feeling is the error of your Platonist co-sectary Apuleius! for he attributed the diseases and storms of human passions only to the demons who occupy a grade beneath the moon and makes even this avowal as by constraint regarding gods whom he honours; but the superior and celestial gods, who inhabit the ethereal regions, whether visible, as the sun, moon, and other luminaries, whose brilliancy makes them conspicuous, or invisible, but believed in by him, he does his utmost to remove beyond the slightest stain of these perturbations. It is not, then, from Plato, but from your Chaldæan teachers you have learned to elevate human vices to the ethereal and empyreal regions of the world and

to the celestial firmament, in order that your theurgists might be able to obtain from your gods divine revelations; and yet you make yourself superior to these divine revelations by your intellectual life, which dispenses with these theurgic purifications as not needed by a philosopher. But, by way of rewarding your teachers, you recommend these arts to other men, who, not being philosophers, may be persuaded to use what you acknowledge to be useless to yourself, who are capable of higher things; so that those who cannot avail themselves of the virtue of philosophy, which is too arduous for the multitude, may, at your instigation, betake themselves to theurgists by whom they may be purified, not, indeed, in the intellectual, but in the spiritual part of the soul. Now, as the persons who are unfit for philosophy form incomparably the majority of mankind, more may be compelled to consult these secret and illicit teachers of yours than frequent the Platonic schools. For these most impure demons, pretending to be ethereal gods, whose herald and messenger you have become, have promised that those who are purified by theurgy in the spiritual part of their soul shall not indeed return to the Father, but shall dwell among the ethereal gods above the aerial regions. But such fancies are not listened to by the multitudes of men whom Christ came to set free from the tyranny of demons. For in Him they have the most gracious cleansing, in which mind, spirit, and body alike participate. For, in order that He might heal the whole man from the plague of sin, He took without sin the whole human nature. Would that you had known Him, and would that you had committed yourself for healing to Him rather than to your own frail and infirm human virtue, or to pernicious and curious arts! He would not have deceived you; for Him your own oracles, on your own showing, acknowledged holy and immortal. It is of Him, too, that the most famous poet speaks, poetically indeed, since he applies it to the person of another, yet truly, if you refer it to Christ, saying, "Under thine auspices, if any traces of our crimes remain, they shall be obliterated, and earth freed from its perpetual fear."[2] By which he indicates that, by reason of the infirmity which attaches to this life, the greatest progress in virtue and righteousness leaves room for the existence, if not of crimes, yet of the traces of crimes, which are obliterated only by that Saviour of whom this verse speaks. For that he did not say this at the prompting of his own

---

[1]See above, Chap. 9.

[2]Virgil, *Eclogues*, BK. IV. 13, 14.

fancy, Virgil tells us in almost the last verse of that 4th Eclogue, when he says, "The last age predicted by the Cumæan sibyl has now arrived"; whence it plainly appears that this had been dictated by the Cumæan sibyl. But those theurgists, or rather demons, who assume the appearance and form of gods, pollute rather than purify the human spirit by false appearances and the delusive mockery of unsubstantial forms. How can those whose own spirit is unclean cleanse the spirit of man? Were they not unclean, they would not be bound by the incantations of an envious man and would neither be afraid nor grudge to bestow that hollow boon which they promise. But it is sufficient for our purpose that you acknowledge that the intellectual soul, that is, our mind, cannot be justified by theurgy; and that even the spiritual or inferior part of our soul cannot by this act be made eternal and immortal, though you maintain that it can be purified by it. Christ, however, promises life eternal; and therefore to Him the world flocks, greatly to your indignation, greatly also to your astonishment and confusion. What avails your forced avowal that theurgy leads men astray, and deceives vast numbers by its ignorant and foolish teaching, and that it is the most manifest mistake to have recourse by prayer and sacrifice to angels and principalities, when at the same time, to save yourself from the charge of spending labour in vain on such arts, you direct men to the theurgists, that by their means men, who do not live by the rule of the intellectual soul, may have their spiritual soul purified?

CHAP. 28. *How it is that Porphyry has been so blind as not to recognize the true wisdom—Christ*

You drive men, therefore, into the most palpable error. And yet you are not ashamed of doing so much harm, though you call yourself a lover of virtue and wisdom. Had you been true and faithful in this profession, you would have recognized Christ, the virtue of God and the wisdom of God, and would not, in the pride of vain science, have revolted from His wholesome humility. Nevertheless you acknowledge that the spiritual part of the soul can be purified by the virtue of chastity without the aid of those theurgic arts and mysteries which you wasted your time in learning. You even say, sometimes, that these mysteries do not raise the soul after death, so that, after the termination of this life, they seem to be of no service even to the part you call spiritual; and yet you recur on every

opportunity to these arts, for no other purpose, so far as I see, than to appear an accomplished theurgist, and gratify those who are curious in illicit arts, or else to inspire others with the same curiosity. But we give you all praise for saying that this art is to be feared, both on account of the legal enactments against it and by reason of the danger involved in the very practice of it. And would that in this, at least, you were listened to by its wretched votaries, that they might be withdrawn from entire absorption in it, or might even be preserved from tampering with it at all! You say, indeed, that ignorance, and the numberless vices resulting from it, cannot be removed by any mysteries, but only by the πατρικὸς νοῦς, that is, the Father's mind or intellect conscious of the Father's will. But that Christ is this mind you do not believe; for Him you despise on account of the body He took of a woman and the shame of the cross; for your lofty wisdom spurns such low and contemptible things and soars to more exalted regions. But He fulfils what the holy prophets truly predicted regarding Him: "I will destroy the wisdom of the wise, and bring to nought the prudence of the prudent."[1] For He does not destroy and bring to nought His own gift in them, but what they arrogate to themselves and do not hold of Him. And hence the apostle, having quoted this testimony from the prophet, adds, "Where is the wise? where is the scribe? where is the disputer of this world? Hath not God made foolish the wisdom of this world? For after that, in the wisdom of God, the world by wisdom knew not God, it pleased God by the foolishness of preaching to save them that believe. For the Jews require a sign, and the Greeks seek after wisdom; but we preach Christ crucified, unto the Jews a stumbling-block and unto the Greeks foolishness; but unto them which are called, both Jews and Greeks, Christ the power of God and the wisdom of God. Because the foolishness of God is wiser than men; and the weakness of God is stronger than men."[2] This is despised as a weak and foolish thing by those who are wise and strong in themselves; yet this is the grace which heals the weak, who do not proudly boast a blessedness of their own, but rather humbly acknowledge their real misery.

CHAP. 29. *Of the incarnation of our Lord Jesus Christ, which the Platonists in their impiety blush to acknowledge*

You proclaim the Father and His Son, whom you call the Father's intellect or mind, and be-

[1] Isa. 29. 14.   [2] I Cor. 1. 19-25.

tween these a third, by whom we suppose you mean the Holy Spirit, and in your own fashion you call these three Gods. In this, though your expressions are inaccurate, you do in some sort, and as through a veil, see what we should strive towards; but the incarnation of the unchangeable Son of God, whereby we are saved and are enabled to reach the things we believe, or in part understand, this is what you refuse to recognize. You see in a fashion, although at a distance, although with filmy eye, the country in which we should abide; but the way to it you know not. Yet you believe in grace, for you say it is granted to few to reach God by virtue of intelligence. For you do not say, "Few have thought fit or have wished," but, "It has been granted to few" —distinctly acknowledging God's grace, not man's sufficiency. You also use this word more expressly, when, in accordance with the opinion of Plato, you make no doubt that in this life a man cannot by any means attain to perfect wisdom, but that whatever is lacking is in the future life made up to those who live intellectually, by God's providence and grace. Oh, had you but recognized the grace of God in Jesus Christ our Lord, and that very incarnation of His, wherein He assumed a human soul and body, you might have seemed the brightest example of grace![1] But what am I doing? I know it is useless to speak to a dead man—useless, at least, so far as regards you, but perhaps not in vain for those who esteem you highly, and love you on account of their love of wisdom or curiosity about those arts which you ought not to have learned; and these persons I address in your name. The grace of God could not have been more graciously commended to us than thus, that the only Son of God, remaining unchangeable in Himself, should assume humanity, and should give us the hope of His love, by means of the mediation of a human nature, through which we, from the condition of men, might come to Him who was so far off—the immortal from the mortal; the unchangeable from the changeable; the just from the unjust; the blessed from the wretched. And, as He had given us a natural instinct to desire blessedness and immortality, He Himself continuing to be blessed, but assuming mortality, by enduring what we fear, taught us to despise it, that what we long for He might bestow upon us.

But in order to your acquiescence in this truth, it is lowliness that is requisite, and to this it is extremely difficult to bend you. For what is

[1]According to another reading: "You might have seen it to be," etc.

there incredible, especially to men like you, accustomed to speculation, which might have predisposed you to believe in this—what is there incredible, I say, in the assertion that God assumed a human soul and body? You yourselves ascribe such excellence to the intellectual soul, which is, after all, the human soul, that you maintain that it can become consubstantial with that intelligence of the Father Whom you believe in as the Son of God. What incredible thing is it, then, if some one soul be assumed by Him in an ineffable and unique manner for the salvation of many? Moreover, our nature itself testifies that a man is incomplete unless a body be united with the soul. This certainly would be more incredible, were it not of all things the most common; for we should more easily believe in a union between spirit and spirit, or, to use your own terminology, between the incorporeal and the incorporeal, even though the one were human, the other divine, the one changeable and the other unchangeable, than in a union between the corporeal and the incorporeal. But perhaps it is the unprecedented birth of a body from a virgin that staggers you? But, so far from this being a difficulty, it ought rather to assist you to receive our religion, that a miraculous person was born miraculously. Or, do you find a difficulty in the fact that, after His body had been given up to death, and had been changed into a higher kind of body by resurrection, and was now no longer mortal but incorruptible, He carried it up into heavenly places? Perhaps you refuse to believe this, because you remember that Porphyry, in these very books from which I have cited so much, and which treat of the return of the soul, so frequently teaches that a body of every kind is to be escaped from, in order that the soul may dwell in blessedness with God. But here, in place of following Porphyry, you ought rather to have corrected him, especially since you agree with him in believing such incredible things about the soul of this visible world and huge material frame. For, as scholars of Plato, you hold that the world is an animal, and a very happy animal, which you wish to be also everlasting. How, then, is it never to be loosed from a body and yet never lose its happiness, if, in order to the happiness of the soul, the body must be left behind? The sun, too, and the other stars, you not only acknowledge to be bodies, in which you have the cordial assent of all seeing men, but also, in obedience to what you reckon a profounder insight, you declare that they are very blessed animals, and eternal, together with their bodies. Why is it, then, that when the Christian faith is pressed upon you, you forget, or pretend to ignore, what you habitually discuss or teach? Why is it that you refuse to be Christians, on the ground that you hold opinions which, in fact, you yourselves demolish? Is it not because Christ came in lowliness and ye are proud? The precise nature of the resurrection bodies of the saints may sometimes occasion discussion among those who are best read in the Christian Scriptures; yet there is not among us the smallest doubt that they shall be everlasting and of a nature exemplified in the instance of Christ's risen body. But whatever be their nature, since we maintain that they shall be absolutely incorruptible and immortal and shall offer no hindrance to the soul's contemplation, by which it is fixed in God, and as you say that among the celestials the bodies of the eternally blessed are eternal, why do you maintain that, in order to blessedness, every body must be escaped from? Why do you thus seek such a plausible reason for escaping from the Christian faith, if not because, as I again say, Christ is humble and ye proud? Are ye ashamed to be corrected? This is the vice of the proud. It is, forsooth, a degradation for learned men to pass from the school of Plato to the discipleship of Christ, who by His Spirit taught a fisherman to think and to say, "In the beginning was the Word, and the Word was with God, and the Word was God. The same was in the beginning with God. All things were made by Him; and without Him was not anything made that was made. In Him was life; and the life was the light of men. And the light shineth in darkness; and the darkness comprehended it not."[1] The old saint Simplicianus, afterwards bishop of Milan, used to tell me that a certain Platonist was in the habit of saying that this opening passage of the holy gospel, entitled, "According to John," should be written in letters of gold, and hung up in all churches in the most conspicuous place. But the proud scorn to take God for their Master, because "the Word was made flesh and dwelt among us."[2] So that, with these miserable creatures, it is not enough that they are sick, but they boast of their sickness, and are ashamed of the medicine which could heal them. And, doing so, they secure not elevation, but a more disastrous fall.

CHAP. 30. *Porphyry's emendations and modifications of Platonism*

If it is considered unseemly to emend anything which Plato has touched, why did Porphyry himself make emendations, and these not

[1]John, I. 1–5.   [2]John, I. 14.

a few? for it is very certain that Plato wrote that the souls of men return after death to the bodies of beasts. Plotinus also, Porphyry's teacher, held this opinion; yet Porphyry justly rejected it. He was of opinion that human souls return indeed into human bodies, but not into the bodies they had left, but other new bodies. He shrank from the other opinion, lest a woman who had returned into a mule might possibly carry her own son on her back. He did not shrink, however, from a theory which admitted the possibility of a mother coming back into a girl and marrying her own son. How much more honourable a creed is that which was taught by the holy and truthful angels, uttered by the prophets who were moved by God's Spirit, preached by Him Who was foretold as the coming Saviour by His forerunning heralds, and by the apostles whom He sent forth and who filled the whole world with the gospel—how much more honourable, I say, is the belief that souls return once for all to their own bodies, than that they return again and again to divers bodies? Nevertheless Porphyry, as I have said, did considerably improve upon this opinion, in so far, at least, as he maintained that human souls could transmigrate only into human bodies, and made no scruple about demolishing the bestial prisons into which Plato had wished to cast them. He says, too, that God put the soul into the world that it might recognize the evils of matter, and return to the Father, and be for ever emancipated from the polluting contact of matter. And although here is some inappropriate thinking (for the soul is rather given to the body that it may do good; for it would not learn evil unless it did it), yet he corrects the opinion of other Platonists, and that on a point of no small importance, inasmuch as he avows that the soul, which is purged from all evil and received to the Father's presence, shall never again suffer the ills of this life. By this opinion he quite subverted the favourite Platonic dogma, that as dead men are made out of living ones, so living men are made out of dead ones; and he exploded the idea which Virgil seems to have adopted from Plato, that the purified souls which have been sent into the Elysian fields (the poetic name for the joys of the blessed) are summoned to the river Lethe, that is, to the oblivion of the past,

That earthward they may pass once more,
Remembering not the things before,
And with a blind propension yearn
To fleshly bodies to return.[3]

[3]*Æneid*, BK. VI. 750, 751.

This found no favour with Porphyry, and very justly; for it is indeed foolish to believe that souls should desire to return from that life, which cannot be very blessed unless by the assurance of its permanence, and to come back into this life, and to the pollution of corruptible bodies, as if the result of perfect purification were only to make defilement desirable. For if perfect purification effects the oblivion of all evils, and the oblivion of evils creates a desire for a body in which the soul may again be entangled with evils, then the supreme felicity will be the cause of infelicity, and the perfection of wisdom the cause of foolishness, and the purest cleansing the cause of defilement. And, however long the blessedness of the soul last, it cannot be founded on truth, if, in order to be blessed, it must be deceived. For it cannot be blessed unless it be free from fear. But, to be free from fear, it must be under the false impression that it shall be always blessed—the *false* impression, for it is destined to be also at some time miserable. How, then, shall the soul rejoice in truth, whose joy is founded on falsehood? Porphyry saw this and therefore said that the purified soul returns to the Father, that it may never more be entangled in the polluting contact with evil. The opinion, therefore, of some Platonists, that there is a necessary revolution carrying souls away and bringing them round again to the same things, is false. But, were it true, what were the advantage of knowing it? Would the Platonists presume to allege their superiority to us, because we were in this life ignorant of what they themselves were doomed to be ignorant of when perfected in purity and wisdom in another and better life, and which they must be ignorant of if they are to be blessed? If it were most absurd and foolish to say so, then certainly we must prefer Porphyry's opinion to the idea of a circulation of souls through constantly alternating happiness and misery. And if this is just, here is a Platonist emending Plato, here is a man who saw what Plato did not see and who did not shrink from correcting so illustrious a master, but preferred truth to Plato.

CHAP. 31. *Against the arguments on which the Platonists ground their assertion that the human soul is co-eternal with God*

Why, then, do we not rather believe the divinity in those matters, which human talent cannot fathom? Why do we not credit the assertion of divinity, that the soul is not co-eternal with God, but is created, and once was not? For the Platonists seemed to themselves to allege an adequate reason for their rejection of this doctrine, when they affirmed that nothing could be everlasting which had not always existed. Plato, however, in writing concerning the world and the gods in it, whom the Supreme made, most expressly states that they had a beginning and yet would have no end, but, by the sovereign will of the Creator, would endure eternally. But, by way of interpreting this, the Platonists have discovered that he meant a beginning, not of time, but of cause. "For as if a foot," they say, "had been always from eternity in dust, there would always have been a print underneath it; and yet no one would doubt that this print was made by the pressure of the foot, nor that, though the one was made by the other, neither was prior to the other; so," they say, "the world and the gods created in it have always been, their Creator always existing, and yet they were made." If, then, the soul has always existed, are we to say that its wretchedness has always existed? For if there is something in it which was not from eternity, but began in time, why is it impossible that the soul itself, though not previously existing, should begin to be in time? Its blessedness, too, which, as he owns, is to be more stable, and indeed endless, after the soul's experience of evils, —this undoubtedly has a beginning in time, and yet is to be always, though previously it had no existence. This whole argumentation, therefore, to establish that nothing can be endless except that which has had no beginning, falls to the ground. For here we find the blessedness of the soul, which has a beginning and yet has no end. And, therefore, let the incapacity of man give place to the authority of God; and let us take our belief regarding the true religion from the ever-blessed spirits, who do not seek for themselves that honour which they know to be due to their God and ours, and who do not command us to sacrifice save only to Him, Whose sacrifice, as I have often said already, and must often say again, we and they ought together to be, offered through that Priest Who offered Himself to death a sacrifice for us, in that human nature which He assumed, and according to which He desired to be our Priest.

CHAP. 32. *Of the universal way of the soul's deliverance, which Porphyry did not find because he did not rightly seek it, and which the grace of Christ has alone thrown open*

This is the religion which possesses the universal way for delivering the soul; for, except by this way, none can be delivered. This is a kind of royal way, which alone leads to a kingdom which does not totter like all temporal dignities, but stands firm on eternal foundations. And when Porphyry says, towards the end of the first book *De Regressu Animæ*, that no system of doctrine which furnishes the universal way for delivering the soul has as yet been received, either from the truest philosophy, or from the ideas and practices of the Indians, or from the reasoning[1] of the Chaldæans, or from any source whatever, and that no historical reading had made him acquainted with that way, he manifestly acknowledges that there is such a way, but that as yet he was not acquainted with it. Nothing of all that he had so laboriously learned concerning the deliverance of the soul, nothing of all that he seemed to others, if not to himself, to know and believe, satisfied him. For he perceived that there was still wanting a commanding authority which it might be right to follow in a matter of such importance. And when he says that he had not learned from any truest philosophy a system which possessed the universal way of the soul's deliverance, he shows plainly enough, as it seems to me, either that the philosophy of which he was a disciple was not the truest, or that it did not comprehend such a way. And how can that be the truest philosophy which does not possess this way? For what else is the universal way of the soul's deliverance than that by which all souls universally are delivered and without which, therefore, no soul is delivered? And when he says, in addition, "or from the ideas and practices of the Indians, or from the reasoning of the Chaldæans, or from any source whatever," he declares in the most unequivocal language that this universal way of the soul's deliverance was not embraced in what he had learned either from the Indians or the Chaldæans; and yet he could not forbear stating that it was from the Chaldæans he had derived these divine oracles of which he makes such frequent mention. What, therefore, does he mean by this universal way of the soul's deliverance, which had not yet been made known by any truest philosophy, or by the doctrinal systems of those nations which were considered to have great insight in things divine, because they indulged more freely in a curious and fanciful science and worship of angels? What is this universal way of which he acknowledges his ignorance, if not a way which does not belong to one nation as its special property, but is common to all and divinely bestowed? Porphyry, a man of no mediocre abilities, does not question

that such a way exists; for he believes that Divine Providence could not have left men destitute of this universal way of delivering the soul. For he does not say that this way does not exist, but that this great boon and assistance has not yet been discovered and has not come to his knowledge. And no wonder; for Porphyry lived in an age when this universal way of the soul's deliverance—in other words, the Christian religion—was exposed to the persecutions of idolaters and demon-worshippers, and earthly rulers,[2] that the number of martyrs or witnesses for the truth might be completed and consecrated, and that by them proof might be given that we must endure all bodily sufferings in the cause of the holy faith, and for the commendation of the truth. Porphyry, being a witness of these persecutions, concluded that this way was destined to a speedy extinction and that it, therefore, was not the universal way of the soul's deliverance, and did not see that the very thing that thus moved him and deterred him from becoming a Christian contributed to the confirmation and more effectual commendation of our religion.

This, then, is the universal way of the soul's deliverance, the way that is granted by the divine compassion to the nations universally. And no nation to which the knowledge of it has already come, or may hereafter come, ought to demand, "Why so soon?" or, "Why so late?"— for the design of Him Who sends it is impenetrable by human capacity. This was felt by Porphyry when he confined himself to saying that this gift of God was not yet received and had not yet come to his knowledge. For though this was so, he did not on that account pronounce that the way itself had no existence. This, I say, is the universal way for the deliverance of believers, concerning which the faithful Abraham received the divine assurance, "In thy seed shall all nations be blessed."[3] He, indeed, was by birth a Chaldæan; but, that he might receive these great promises, and that there might be propagated from him a seed "disposed by angels in the hand of a Mediator,"[4] in whom this universal way, thrown open to all nations for the deliverance of the soul, might be found, he was ordered to leave his country, and kindred, and father's house. Then was he himself, first of all, delivered from the Chaldæan superstitions, and by his obedience worshipped the one true God, Whose promises he faithfully trusted. This is the universal way, of which it is said in holy

[1] *Inductio.*

[2] Namely, under Diocletian and Maximian.
[3] Gen. 22. 18.   [4] Gal. 3. 19.

prophecy, "God be merciful unto us, and bless us, and cause His face to shine upon us; that Thy way may be known upon earth, Thy saving health among all nations."[1] And hence, when our Saviour, so long after, had taken flesh of the seed of Abraham, He says of Himself, "I am the way, the truth, and the life."[2] This is the universal way, of which so long before it had been predicted, "And it shall come to pass in the last days, that the mountain of the Lord's house shall be established in the top of the mountains, and shall be exalted above the hills; and all nations shall flow unto it. And many people shall go and say, Come ye, and let us go up to the mountain of the Lord, to the house of the God of Jacob; and He will teach us of His ways, and we will walk in His paths: for out of Sion shall go forth the law, and the word of the Lord from Jerusalem."[3] This way, therefore, is not the property of one, but of all nations. The law and the word of the Lord did not remain in Zion and Jerusalem, but issued thence to be universally diffused. And therefore the Mediator Himself, after His resurrection, says to His alarmed disciples, "These are the words which I spake unto you while I was yet with you, that all things must be fulfilled which were written in the law of Moses, and in the prophets, and in the Psalms, concerning Me. Then opened He their understandings that they might understand the Scriptures, and said unto them, Thus it is written, and thus it behoved Christ to suffer, and to rise from the dead the third day: and that repentance and remission of sins should be preached in His name among all nations, beginning at Jerusalem."[4] This is the universal way of the soul's deliverance, which the holy angels and the holy prophets formerly disclosed where they could among the few men who found the grace of God, and especially in the Hebrew nation, whose commonwealth was, as it were, consecrated to prefigure and fore-announce the city of God which was to be gathered from all nations, by their tabernacle, and temple, and priesthood, and sacrifices. In some explicit statements and in many obscure foreshadowings, this way was declared; but latterly came the Mediator Himself in the flesh, and His blessed apostles, revealing how the grace of the New Testament more openly explained what had been obscurely hinted to preceding generations, in conformity with the relation of the ages of the human race, and as it pleased God in His wisdom to appoint, who

also bore them witness with signs and miracles, some of which I have cited above. For not only were there visions of angels and words heard from those heavenly ministrants, but also men of God, armed with the word of simple piety, cast out unclean spirits from the bodies and senses of men and healed deformities and sicknesses; the wild beasts of earth and sea, the birds of air, inanimate things, the elements, the stars, obeyed their divine commands; the powers of hell gave way before them, the dead were restored to life. I say nothing of the miracles peculiar and proper to the Saviour's own person, especially the nativity and the resurrection; in the one of which He wrought only the mystery of a virgin maternity, while in the other He furnished an instance of the resurrection which all shall at last experience. This way purifies the whole man and prepares the mortal in all his parts for immortality. For, to prevent us from seeking for one purgation for the part which Porphyry calls intellectual, and another for the part he calls spiritual, and another for the body itself, our most mighty and truthful Purifier and Saviour assumed the whole human nature. Except by this way, which has been present among men both during the period of the promises and of the proclamation of their fulfillment, no man has been delivered, no man is delivered, no man shall be delivered.

As to Porphyry's statement that the universal way of the soul's deliverance had not yet come to his knowledge by any acquaintance he had with history, I would ask, what more remarkable history can be found than that which has taken possession of the whole world by its authoritative voice? or what more trustworthy than that which narrates past events, and predicts the future with equal clearness, and in the unfulfilled predictions of which we are constrained to believe by those that are already fulfilled? For neither Porphyry nor any Platonists can despise divination and prediction, even of things that pertain to this life and earthly matters, though they justly despise ordinary soothsaying and the divination that is connected with magical arts. They deny that these are the predictions of great men, or are to be considered important, and they are right; for they are founded, either on the foresight of subsidiary causes, as to a professional eye much of the course of a disease is foreseen by certain premonitory symptoms, or the unclean demons predict what they have resolved to do, that they may thus work upon the thoughts and desires of the wicked with an appearance of authority, and

[1] Ps. 67. 1.2.   [2] John, 14. 6.
[3] Isa. 2. 2. 3.   [4] Luke, 24. 44-47.

incline human frailty to imitate their impure actions. It is not such things that the saints who walk in the universal way care to predict as important, although, for the purpose of commending the faith, they knew and often predicted even such things as could not be detected by human observation, nor be readily verified by experience. But there were other truly important and divine events which they predicted, in so far as it was given them to know the will of God. For the incarnation of Christ, and all those important marvels that were accomplished in Him, and done in His name; the repentance of men and the conversion of their wills to God; the remission of sins, the grace of righteousness, the faith of the pious, and the multitudes in all parts of the world who believe in the true divinity; the overthrow of idolatry and demon worship, and the testing of the faithful by trials; the purification of those who persevered, and their deliverance from all evil; the day of judgment, the resurrection of the dead, the eternal damnation of the community of the ungodly, and the eternal kingdom of the most glorious city of God, ever-blessed in the enjoyment of the vision of God—these things were predicted and promised in the Scriptures of this way; and of these we see so many fulfilled, that we justly and pi-

ously trust that the rest will also come to pass. As for those who do not believe and consequently do not understand that this is the way which leads straight to the vision of God and to eternal fellowship with Him, according to the true predictions and statements of the Holy Scriptures, they may storm at our position, but they cannot storm it.

And therefore, in these ten books, though not meeting, I dare say, the expectation of some, yet I have, as the true God and Lord has vouchsafed to aid me, satisfied the desire of certain persons, by refuting the objections of the ungodly, who prefer their own gods to the Founder of the holy city, about which we undertook to speak. Of these ten books, the first five were directed against those who think we should worship the gods for the sake of the blessings of this life, and the second five against those who think we should worship them for the sake of the life which is to be after death. And now, in fulfilment of the promise I made in the first book, I shall go on to say, as God shall aid me, what I think needs to be said regarding the origin, history, and deserved ends of the two cities, which, as already remarked, are in this world commingled and implicated with one another.

. . . .

BOOK XI

ARGUMENT. HERE BEGINS THE SECOND PART[1] OF THIS WORK, WHICH TREATS OF THE ORIGIN, HISTORY, AND DESTINIES OF THE TWO CITIES, THE EARTHLY AND THE HEAVENLY. IN THE FIRST PLACE, AUGUSTINE SHOWS IN THIS BOOK HOW THE TWO CITIES WERE FORMED ORIGINALLY, BY THE SEPARATION OF THE GOOD AND BAD ANGELS; AND TAKES OCCASION TO TREAT OF THE CREATION OF THE WORLD, AS IT IS DESCRIBED IN HOLY SCRIPTURE IN THE BEGINNING OF THE BOOK OF GENESIS.

CHAP. I. *Of this part of the work, wherein we begin to explain the origin and end of the two cities*

THE city of God we speak of is the same to which testimony is borne by that Scripture, which excels all the writings of all nations by its divine authority, and has brought under its influence all kinds of minds, and this not by a casual intellectual movement, but obviously by an express providential arrangement. For there it is written, "Glorious things are spoken of thee, O city of God."[2] And in another psalm we read, "Great is the Lord, and greatly to be praised in the city of our God, in the mountain of His holi-

ness, increasing the joy of the whole earth."[3] And, a little after, in the same psalm, "As we have heard, so have we seen in the city of the Lord of hosts, in the city of our God. God has established it for ever." And in another, "There is a river the streams whereof shall make glad the city of our God, the holy place of the tabernacles of the Most High. God is in the midst of her, she shall not be moved."[4] From these and similar testimonies, all of which it were tedious to cite, we have learned that there is a city of God, and its Founder has inspired us with a love which makes us covet its citizenship. To this Founder of the holy city the citizens of the earthly city prefer their own gods, not knowing that He is the God of gods, not of false, i.e., of

---

[1]Written in the year 416 or 417.
[2]Ps. 87. 3.

[3]Ps. 47. 1. [4]Ps. 46. 4.

impious and proud gods, who, being deprived of His unchangeable and freely communicated light, and so reduced to a kind of poverty-stricken power, eagerly grasp at their own private privileges, and seek divine honours from their deluded subjects; but of the pious and holy gods, who are better pleased to submit themselves to one than to subject many to themselves, and who would rather worship God than be worshipped as God. But to the enemies of this city we have replied in the ten preceding books, according to our ability and the help afforded by our Lord and King. Now, recognizing what is expected of me, and not unmindful of my promise, and relying, too, on the same succour, I will endeavour to treat of the origin, and progress, and deserved destinies of the two cities (the earthly and the heavenly, to wit), which, as we said, are in this present world commingled, and as it were entangled together. And, first, I will explain how the foundations of these two cities were originally laid, in the difference that arose among the angels.

Chap. 2. Of the knowledge of God, to which no man can attain save through the Mediator between god and men, the man Christ Jesus

It is a great and very rare thing for a man, after he has contemplated the whole creation, corporeal and incorporeal, and has discerned its mutability, to pass beyond it, and, by the continued soaring of his mind, to attain to the unchangeable substance of God, and, in that height of contemplation, to learn from God Himself that none but He has made all that is not of the divine essence. For God speaks with a man not by means of some audible creature dinning in his ears, so that atmospheric vibrations connect Him that makes with him that hears the sound, nor even by means of a spiritual being with the semblance of a body, such as we see in dreams or similar states; for even in this case He speaks as if to the ears of the body, because it is by means of the semblance of a body He speaks, and with the appearance of a real interval of space—for visions are exact representations of bodily objects. Not by these, then, does God speak, but by the truth itself, if any one is prepared to hear with the mind rather than with the body. For He speaks to that part of man which is better than all else that is in him and than which God Himself alone is better. For since man is most properly understood (or, if that cannot be, then, at least, *believed*) to be made in God's image, no doubt it is that part of him by which he rises above those lower parts he has in common with the beasts, which brings him nearer to the Supreme. But since the mind itself, though naturally capable of reason and intelligence, is disabled by besotting and inveterate vices not merely from delighting and abiding in, but even from tolerating His unchangeable light, until it has been gradually healed, and renewed, and made capable of such felicity, it had, in the first place, to be impregnated with faith, and so purified. And that in this faith it might advance the more confidently towards the truth, the truth itself, God, God's Son, assuming humanity without destroying His divinity, established and founded this faith, that there might be a way for man to man's God through a God-man. For this is the Mediator between God and men, the man Christ Jesus. For it is as man that He is the Mediator and the Way. Since, if the way lieth between him who goes and the place whither he goes, there is hope of his reaching it; but if there be no way, or if he know not where it is, what boots it to know whither he should go? Now the only way that is infallibly secured against all mistakes, is when the very same person is at once God and man, God our end, man our way.[1]

Chap. 3. Of the authority of the canonical Scriptures composed by the Divine Spirit

This Mediator, having spoken what He judged sufficient first by the prophets, then by His own lips, and afterwards by the apostles, has besides produced the Scripture which is called canonical, which has paramount authority, and to which we yield assent in all matters of which we ought not to be ignorant, and yet cannot know of ourselves. For if we attain the knowledge of present objects by the testimony of our own senses,[2] whether internal or external, then, regarding objects remote from our own senses, we need others to bring their testimony, since we cannot know them by our own, and we credit the persons to whom the objects have been or are sensibly present. Accordingly, as in the case of visible objects which we have not seen, we trust those who have (and likewise with all sensible objects), so in the case of things which are perceived[3] by the mind and spirit, i.e., which are remote from our interior sense, it behoves us to trust those who have seen them set in that incorporeal light, or abidingly contemplate them.

[1] *Quo itur Deus, qua itur homo.*
[2] A clause is here inserted to give the etymology of *præsentia* from *præ sensibus.*
[3] Another derivation, *sententia* from *sensus,* the inward perception of the mind.

CHAP. 4. *That the world is neither without beginning, nor yet created by a new decree of God, by which He afterwards willed what He had not before willed*

Of all visible things, the world is the greatest; of all invisible, the greatest is God. But, that the world is, we see; that God is, we believe. That God made the world, we can believe from no one more safely than from God Himself. But where have we heard Him? Nowhere more distinctly than in the Holy Scriptures, where His prophet said, "In the beginning God created the heavens and the earth."[1] Was the prophet present when God made the heavens and the earth? No; but the wisdom of God, by whom all things were made, was there,[2] and wisdom insinuates itself into holy souls, and makes them the friends of God and His prophets, and noiselessly informs them of His works. They are taught also by the angels of God, who always behold the face of the Father,[3] and announce His will to whom it befits. Of these prophets was he who said and wrote, "In the beginning God created the heavens and the earth." And so fit a witness was he of God, that the same Spirit of God, who revealed these things to him, enabled him also so long before to predict that our faith also would be forthcoming.

But why did God choose then to create the heavens and earth which up to that time He had not made?[4] If they who put this question wish to make out that the world is eternal and without beginning, and that consequently it has not been made by God, they are strangely deceived and rave in the incurable madness of impiety. For, though the voices of the prophets were silent, the world itself, by its well-ordered changes and movements and by the fair appearance of all visible things, bears a testimony of its own, both that it has been created and also that it could not have been created save by God, whose greatness and beauty are unutterable and invisible. As for those[5] who own, indeed, that it was made by God, and yet ascribe to it not a temporal but only a creational beginning, so that in some scarcely intelligible way the world should always have existed a created world, they make an assertion which seems to them to defend God from the charge of arbitrary hastiness or of suddenly conceiving the idea of creating the world as a quite new idea, or of casually changing His

will, though He be unchangeable. But I do not see how this supposition of theirs can stand in other respects, and chiefly in respect of the soul; for if they contend that it is co-eternal with God, they will be quite at a loss to explain whence there has accrued to it new misery, which through a previous eternity had not existed. For if they said that its happiness and misery ceaselessly alternate, they must say, further, that this alternation will continue for ever; whence will result this absurdity, that, though the soul is called blessed, it is not so in this, that it foresees its own misery and disgrace. And yet, if it does not foresee it and supposes that it will be neither disgraced nor wretched, but always blessed, then it is blessed because it is deceived; and a more foolish statement one cannot make. But if their idea is that the soul's misery has alternated with its bliss during the ages of the past eternity, but that now, when once the soul has been set free, it will return henceforth no more to misery, they are nevertheless of opinion that it has never been truly blessed before, but begins at last to enjoy a new and uncertain happiness; that is to say, they must acknowledge that some new thing, and that an important and signal thing, happens to the soul which never in a whole past eternity happened it before. And if they deny that God's eternal purpose included this new experience of the soul, they deny that He is the Author of its blessedness, which is unspeakable impiety. If, on the other hand, they say that the future blessedness of the soul is the result of a new decree of God, how will they show that God is not chargeable with that mutability which displeases them? Further, if they acknowledge that it was created in time, but will never perish in time—that it has, like number, a beginning but no end—and that, therefore, having once made trial of misery and been delivered from it, it will never again return thereto, they will certainly admit that this takes place without any violation of the immutable counsel of God. Let them, then, in like manner believe regarding the world that it too could be made in time, and yet that God, in making it, did not alter His eternal design.

CHAP. 5. *That we ought not to seek to comprehend the infinite ages of time before the world, nor the infinite realms of space*

Next, we must see what reply can be made to those who agree that God is the Creator of the world, but have difficulties about the time of its creation, and what reply, also, they can make to

[1]Gen. I. I.   [2]Prov. 8. 27.   [3]Matt. 18. 10.
[4]See Augustine, *Confessions*, BK. XI. 12, 14.
[5]The Neo-Platonists.

difficulties we might raise about the place of its creation. For, as they demand why the world was created then and no sooner, we may ask why it was created just here where it is, and not elsewhere. For if they imagine infinite spaces of time before the world, during which God could not have been idle, in like manner they may conceive outside the world infinite realms of space, in which, if any one says that the Omnipotent cannot hold His hand from working, will it not follow that they must adopt Epicurus' dream of innumerable worlds? with this difference only, that he asserts that they are formed and destroyed by the fortuitous movements of atoms, while they will hold that they are made by God's hand, if they maintain that, throughout the boundless immensity of space, stretching interminably in every direction round the world, God cannot rest, and that the worlds which they suppose Him to make cannot be destroyed. For here the question is with those who, with ourselves, believe that God is spiritual, and the Creator of all existences but Himself. As for others, it is a condescension to dispute with them on a religious question, for they have acquired a reputation only among men who pay divine honours to a number of gods, and have become conspicuous among the other philosophers for no other reason than that, though they are still far from the truth, they are near it in comparison with the rest. While these, then, neither confine in any place, nor limit, nor distribute the divine substance, but, as is worthy of God, own it to be wholly though spiritually present everywhere, will they perchance say that this substance is absent from such immense spaces outside the world, and is occupied in one only (and that a very little one compared with the infinity beyond), the one, namely, in which is the world? I think they will not proceed to this absurdity. Since they maintain that there is but one world, of vast material bulk, indeed, yet finite, and in its own determinate position, and that this was made by the working of God, let them give the same account of God's resting in the infinite times before the world as they give of His resting in the infinite spaces outside of it. And as it does not follow that God set the world in the very spot it occupies and no other by accident rather than by divine reason, although no human reason can comprehend why it was so set, and though there was no merit in the spot chosen to give it the precedence of infinite others, so neither does it follow that we should suppose that God was guided by chance when He created the world in that and no earlier time, although previous times had been running by during an infinite past, and though there was no difference by which one time could be chosen in preference to another. But if they say that the thoughts of men are idle when they conceive infinite places, since there is no place beside the world, we reply that, by the same showing, it is vain to conceive of the past times of God's rest, since there is no time before the world.

CHAP. 6. *That the world and time had both one beginning, and the one did not anticipate the other*

For if eternity and time are rightly distinguished by this, that time does not exist without some movement and transition, while in eternity there is no change, who does not see that there could have been no time had not some creature been made, which by some motion could give birth to change—the various parts of which motion and change, as they cannot be simultaneous, succeed one another—and thus, in these shorter or longer intervals of duration, time would begin? Since then, God, in Whose eternity is no change at all, is the Creator and Ordainer of time, I do not see how He can be said to have created the world after spaces of time had elapsed, unless it be said that prior to the world there was some creature by whose movement time could pass. And if the sacred and infallible Scriptures say that in the beginning God created the heavens and the earth, in order that it may be understood that He had made nothing previously—for if He had made anything before the rest, this thing would rather be said to have been made "in the beginning"—then assuredly the world was made, not in time, but simultaneously with time. For that which is made in time is made both after and before some time—after that which is past, before that which is future. But none could then be past, for there was no creature by whose movements its duration could be measured. But simultaneously with time the world was made, if in the world's creation change and motion were created, as seems evident from the order of the first six or seven days. For in these days the morning and evening are counted, until, on the sixth day, all things which God then made were finished, and on the seventh the rest of God was mysteriously and sublimely signalized. What kind of days these were it is extremely difficult, or perhaps impossible for us to conceive, and how much more to say!

CHAP. 7. *Of the nature of the first days, which are said to have had morning and evening, before there was a sun*

We see, indeed, that our ordinary days have no evening but by the setting, and no morning but by the rising, of the sun; but the first three days of all were passed without sun, since it is reported to have been made on the fourth day. And first of all, indeed, light was made by the word of God, and God, we read, separated it from the darkness, and called the light Day, and the darkness Night; but what kind of light that was, and by what periodic movement it made evening and morning, is beyond the reach of our senses; neither can we understand how it was and yet must unhesitatingly believe it. For either it was some material light, whether proceeding from the upper parts of the world, far removed from our sight, or from the spot where the sun was afterwards kindled; or under the name of light the holy city was signified, composed of holy angels and blessed spirits, the city of which the apostle says, "Jerusalem which is above is our eternal mother in heaven";[1] and in another place, "For ye are all the children of the light, and the children of the day; we are not of the night, nor of darkness."[2] Yet in some respects we may appropriately speak of a morning and evening of this day also. For the knowledge of the creature is, in comparison of the knowledge of the Creator, but a twilight; and so it dawns and breaks into morning when the creature is drawn to the praise and love of the Creator; and night never falls when the Creator is not forsaken through love of the creature. In fine, Scripture, when it would recount those days in order, never mentions the word night. It never says, "Night was," but "The evening and the morning were the first day." So of the second and the rest. And, indeed, the knowledge of created things contemplated by themselves is, so to speak, more colorless than when they are seen in the wisdom of God, as in the art by which they were made. Therefore evening is a more suitable figure than night; and yet, as I said, morning returns when the creature returns to the praise and love of the Creator. When it does so in the knowledge of itself, that is the first day; when in the knowledge of the firmament, which is the name given to the sky between the waters above and those beneath, that is the second day; when in the knowledge of the earth, and the sea, and all things that grow out of the earth, that is the third day; when in the knowledge of the greater

[1]Gal. 4. 26.   [2]I Thess. 5. 5.

and less luminaries, and all the stars, that is the fourth day; when in the knowledge of all animals that swim in the waters and that fly in the air, that is the fifth day; when in the knowledge of all animals that live on the earth, and of man himself, that is the sixth day.

CHAP. 8. *What we are to understand of God's resting on the seventh day, after the six days' work*

When it is said that God rested on the seventh day from all His works, and hallowed it, we are not to conceive of this in a childish fashion, as if work were a toil to God, who "spake and it was done"—spake by the spiritual and eternal, not audible and transitory word. But God's rest signifies the rest of those who rest in God, as the joy of a house means the joy of those in the house who rejoice, though not the house, but something else, causes the joy. How much more intelligible is such phraseology, then, if the house itself, by its own beauty, makes the inhabitants joyful! For in this case we not only call it joyful by that figure of speech in which the thing containing is used for the thing contained (as when we say, "The theatres applaud," "The meadows low," meaning that the men in the one applaud, and the oxen in the other low), but also by that figure in which the cause is spoken of as if it were the effect, as when a letter is said to be joyful, because it makes its readers so. Most appropriately, therefore, the sacred narrative states that God rested, meaning thereby that those rest who are in Him and whom He makes to rest. And this the prophetic narrative promises also to the men to whom it speaks, and for whom it was written, that they themselves, after those good works which God does in and by them, if they have managed by faith to get near to God in this life, shall enjoy in Him eternal rest. This was pre-figured to the ancient people of God by the rest enjoined in their sabbath law, of which, in its own place, I shall speak more at large.

CHAP. 9. *What the Scriptures teach us to believe concerning the creation of the angels*

At present, since I have undertaken to treat of the origin of the holy city, and first of the holy angels, who constitute a large part of this city, and indeed the more blessed part, since they have never been expatriated, I will give myself to the task of explaining, by God's help, and as far as seems suitable, the Scriptures which relate to this point. Where Scripture speaks of the world's creation, it is not plainly said whether or when the angels were created; but if mention of them is made, it is implicitly under the name of "heaven," when it is said, "In the beginning God created the heavens and the earth," or perhaps rather under the name of "light," of which presently. But that they were wholly omitted, I am unable to believe, because it is written that God on the seventh day rested from all His works which He made; and this very book itself begins, "In the beginning God created the heavens and the earth," so that before heaven and earth God seems to have made nothing. Since, therefore, He began with the heavens and the earth—and the earth itself, as Scripture adds, was at first invisible and formless, light not being as yet made, and darkness covering the face of the deep (that is to say, covering an undefined chaos of earth and sea, for where light is not, darkness must needs be) —and then when all things, which are recorded to have been completed in six days, were created and arranged, how should the angels be omitted, as if they were not among the works of God, from which on the seventh day He rested? Yet, though the fact that the angels are the work of God is not omitted here, it is indeed not explicitly mentioned; but elsewhere Holy Scripture asserts it in the clearest manner. For in the "Song of the Three Children in the Furnace" it was said, "O all ye works of the Lord, bless ye the Lord";[1] and among these works mentioned afterwards in detail, the angels are named. And in the psalm it is said, "Praise ye the Lord from the heavens, praise Him in the heights. Praise ye Him, all His angels; praise ye Him, all His hosts. Praise ye Him, sun and moon; praise him, all ye stars of light. Praise Him, ye heaven of heavens; and ye waters that be above the heavens. Let them praise the name of the Lord; for He commanded, and they were created."[2] Here the angels are most expressly and by divine authority said to have been made by God, for of them among the other heavenly things it is said, "He commanded, and they were created." Who, then, will be bold enough to suggest that the angels were made after the six days' creation? If any one is so foolish, his folly is disposed of by a scripture of like authority, where God says, "When the stars were made, the angels praised me with a loud voice."[3] The angels therefore existed before the stars; and the stars were made the fourth day. Shall we then say that they were made the third day? Far from it; for we know what was made that day. The earth was separated from the water, and each element took its own distinct form, and the earth produced all that grows on it. On the second day, then? Not even on this; for on it the firmament was made between the waters above and beneath, and was called "Heaven," in which firmament the stars were made on the fourth day. There is no question, then, that if the angels are included in the works of God during these six days, they are that light which was called "Day," and whose unity Scripture signalizes by calling that day not the "first day," but "one day." For the second day, the third, and the rest are not other days; but the same "one" day is repeated to complete the number six or seven, so that there should be knowledge both of God's works and of His rest. For when God said, "Let there be light, and there was light," if we are justified in understanding in this light the creation of the angels, then certainly they were created partakers of the eternal light which is the unchangeable Wisdom of God, by which all things were made, and whom we call the only-begotten Son of God; so that they, being illumined by the Light that created them, might themselves become light and be called "Day," in participation of that unchangeable Light and Day which is the Word of God, by whom both themselves and all else were made. "The true Light, which lighteth every man that cometh into the world"[4]—this Light lighteth also every pure angel, that he may be light not in himself, but in God; from whom if an angel turn away, he becomes impure, as are all those who are called unclean spirits, and are no longer light in the Lord, but darkness in themselves, being deprived of the participation of Light eternal. For evil has no positive nature; but the loss of good has received the name "evil."

CHAP. 10. *Of the simple and unchangeable Trinity, Father, Son, and Holy Ghost, one God, in Whom substance and quality are identical*

There is, accordingly, a good which is alone simple and therefore alone unchangeable, and this is God. By this Good have all others been created, but not simple, and therefore not unchangeable. "Created," I say—that is, made, not begotten. For that which is begotten of the simple Good is simple as itself, and the same as itself. These two we call the Father and the Son; and both together with the Holy Spirit are one God; and to this Spirit the epithet Holy is in Scripture, as it were, appropriated. And He is another than the Father and the Son, for He is neither the Father nor the Son. I say "another,"

---

[1]Verse 35.   [2]Ps. 148. 1–5.   [3]Job, 38. 7.   [4]John, 1. 9.

not "another thing," because He is equally with them the simple Good, unchangeable and co-eternal. And this Trinity is one God; and none the less simple because a Trinity. For we do not say that the nature of the good is simple, because the Father alone possesses it, or the Son alone, or the Holy Ghost alone; nor do we say, with the Sabellian heretics, that it is only nominally a Trinity, and has no real distinction of persons; but we say it is simple, because it is what it has, with the exception of the relation of the persons to one another. For, in regard to this relation, it is true that the Father has a Son and yet is not Himself the Son; and the Son has a Father and is not Himself the Father. But, as regards Himself, irrespective of relation to the other, each is what He has; thus, He is in Himself living, for He has life, and is Himself the Life which He has.

It is for this reason, then, that the nature of the Trinity is called simple, because it has not anything which it can lose, and because it is not one thing and its contents another, as a cup and the liquor, or a body and its colour, or the air and the light or heat of it, or a mind and its wisdom. For none of these is what it has: the cup is not liquor, nor the body colour, nor the air light and heat, nor the mind wisdom. And hence they can be deprived of what they have and can be turned or changed into other qualities and states, so that the cup may be emptied of the liquid of which it is full, the body be discoloured, the air darken, the mind grow silly. The incorruptible body which is promised to the saints in the resurrection cannot, indeed, lose its quality of incorruption, but the bodily substance and the quality of incorruption are not the same thing. For the quality of incorruption resides entire in each several part, not greater in one and less in another; for no part is more incorruptible than another. The body, indeed, is itself greater in whole than in part; and one part of it is larger, another smaller, yet is not the larger more incorruptible than the smaller. The body, then, which is not in each of its parts a whole body, is one thing; incorruptibility, which is throughout complete, is another thing; for every part of the incorruptible body, however unequal to the rest otherwise, is equally incorrupt. For the hand, e.g., is not more incorrupt than the finger because it is larger than the finger; so, though finger and hand are unequal, their incorruptibility is equal. Thus, although incorruptibility is inseparable from an incorruptible body, yet the substance of the body is one thing, the quality of incorruption another. And therefore the body

is not what it has. The soul itself, too, though it be always wise (as it will be eternally when it is redeemed), will be so by participating in the unchangeable wisdom, which it is not; for though the air be never robbed of the light that is shed abroad in it, it is not on that account the same thing as the light. I do not mean that the soul is air, as has been supposed by some who could not conceive a spiritual nature; but, with much dissimilarity, the two things have a kind of likeness, which makes it suitable to say that the immaterial soul is illumined with the immaterial light of the simple wisdom of God, as the material air is irradiated with material light, and that, as the air, when deprived of this light, grows dark (for material darkness is nothing else than air wanting light), so the soul, deprived of the light of wisdom, grows dark.

According to this, then, those things which are essentially and truly divine are called simple, because in them quality and substance are identical, and because they are divine, or wise, or blessed in themselves, and without extraneous supplement. In Holy Scripture, it is true, the Spirit of wisdom is called "manifold"[1] because it contains many things in it; but what it contains it also is, and it being one is all these things. For neither are there many wisdoms, but one, in which are untold and infinite treasures of things intellectual, wherein are all invisible and unchangeable reasons of things visible and changeable which were created by it. For God made nothing unwittingly; not even a human workman can be said to do so. But if He knew all that He made, He made only those things which He had known. Whence flows a very striking but true conclusion, that this world could not be known to us unless it existed, but could not have existed unless it had been known to God.

CHAP. 11. *Whether the angels that fell partook of the blessedness which the holy angels have always enjoyed from the time of their creation*

And since these things are so, those spirits whom we call angels were never at any time or in any way darkness, but, as soon as they were made, were made light; yet they were not so created in order that they might exist and live in any way whatever, but were enlightened that they might live wisely and blessedly. Some of them, having turned away from this light, have not won this wise and blessed life, which is certainly eternal, and accompanied with the sure confidence of its eternity; but they have still the life of reason, though darkened with folly, and

[1]Wisd. 7. 22.

this they cannot lose even if they would. But who can determine to what extent they were partakers of that wisdom before they fell? And how shall we say that they participated in it equally with those who through it are truly and fully blessed, resting in a true certainty of eternal felicity? For if they had equally participated in this true knowledge, then the evil angels would have remained eternally blessed equally with the good, because they were equally expectant of it. For, though a life be never so long, it cannot be truly called eternal if it is destined to have an end; for it is called life inasmuch as it is lived, but eternal because it has no end. Wherefore, although everything eternal is not therefore blessed (for hell-fire is eternal), yet if no life can be truly and perfectly blessed except it be eternal, the life of these angels was not blessed, for it was doomed to end, and therefore not eternal, whether they knew it or not. In the one case fear, in the other ignorance, prevented them from being blessed. And even if their ignorance was not so great as to breed in them a wholly false expectation, but left them wavering in uncertainty whether their good would be eternal or would some time terminate, this very doubt concerning so grand a destiny was incompatible with the plenitude of blessedness which we believe the holy angels enjoyed. For we do not so narrow and restrict the application of the term "blessedness" as to apply it to God only, though doubtless He is so truly blessed that greater blessedness cannot be; and, in comparison of His blessedness, what is that of the angels, though, according to their capacity, they be perfectly blessed?

CHAP. 12. *A comparison of the blessedness of the righteous, who have not yet received the divine reward, with that of our first parents in Paradise*

And the angels are not the only members of the rational and intellectual creation whom we call blessed. For who will take upon him to deny that those first men in Paradise were blessed previously to sin, although they were uncertain how long their blessedness was to last and whether it would be eternal (and eternal it would have been had they not sinned)—who, I say, will do so, seeing that even now we not unbecomingly call those blessed whom we see leading a righteous and holy life, in hope of immortality, who have no harrowing remorse of conscience, but obtain readily divine remission of the sins of their present infirmity? These, though they are certain that they shall be rewarded if they persevere, are not certain that they will persevere. For what man can know that he will persevere to the end in the exercise and increase of grace, unless he has been certified by some revelation from Him Who, in His just and secret judgment, while He deceives none, informs few regarding this matter? Accordingly, so far as present comfort goes, the first man in Paradise was more blessed than any just man in this insecure state; but as regards the hope of future good, every man who not merely supposes, but certainly knows that he shall eternally enjoy the most high God in the company of angels, and beyond the reach of ill—this man, no matter what bodily torments afflict him, is more blessed than was he who, even in that great felicity of Paradise, was uncertain of his fate.

CHAP. 13. *Whether all the angels were so created in one common state of felicity, that those who fell were not aware that they would fall, and that those who stood received assurance of their own perseverance after the ruin of the fallen*

From all this, it will readily occur to any one that the blessedness which an intelligent being desires as its legitimate object results from a combination of these two things, namely, that it uninterruptedly enjoy the unchangeable good, which is God; and that it be delivered from all dubiety, and know certainly that it shall eternally abide in the same enjoyment. That it is so with the angels of light we piously believe; but that the fallen angels, who by their own default lost that light, did not enjoy this blessedness even before they sinned, reason bids us conclude. Yet if their life was of any duration before they fell, we must allow them a blessedness of some kind, though not that which is accompanied with foresight. Or, if it seems hard to believe that, when the angels were created, some were created in ignorance either of their perseverance or their fall, while others were most certainly assured of the eternity of their felicity —if it is hard to believe that they were not all from the beginning on an equal footing, until these who are now evil did of their own will fall away from the light of goodness, certainly it is much harder to believe that the holy angels are now uncertain of their eternal blessedness and do not know regarding themselves as much as we have been able to gather regarding them from the Holy Scriptures. For what Catholic Christian does not know that no new devil will ever arise among the good angels, as he knows that this present devil will never again return into the fellowship of the good? For the truth in the gospel promises to the saints and the faithful that they will be equal to the angels of God; and it is also promised them that they will "go away into life eternal."[1] But if we are certain that we shall never lapse from eternal felicity, while they are not certain, then we shall not be their equals, but their superiors. But as the truth never deceives, and as we shall be their equals, they must be certain of their blessedness. And because the evil angels could not be certain of that, since their blessedness was destined to come to an end, it follows either that the angels were unequal, or that, if equal, the good angels were assured of the eternity of their blessedness after the perdition of the others; unless, possibly, some one may say that the words of the Lord about the devil, "He was a murderer from the beginning, and abode not in the truth,"[2] are to be understood as if he was not only a murderer from the beginning of the human race, when man, whom he could kill by his deceit, was made, but also that he did not abide in the truth from the time of his own creation and was accordingly never blessed with the holy angels, but refused to submit to his Creator, and proudly exulted as if in a private lordship of his own and was thus deceived and deceiving. For the dominion of the Almighty cannot be eluded; and he who will not piously submit himself to things as they are, proudly feigns, and mocks himself with a state of things that does not exist; so that what the blessed Apostle John says thus becomes intelligible: "The devil sinneth from the beginning"[3] —that is, from the time he was created he refused righteousness, which none but a will piously subject to God can enjoy. Whoever adopts this opinion at least disagrees with those heretics, the Manichees, and with any other pestilential sect that may suppose that the devil has derived from some adverse evil principle a nature proper to himself. These persons are so befooled by error, that, although they acknowledge with ourselves the authority of the gospels, they do not notice that the Lord did not say, "The devil was naturally a stranger to the truth," but "The devil abode not in the truth," by which He meant us to understand that he had fallen from the truth, in which, if he had abode, he would have become a partaker of it, and have remained in blessedness along with the holy angels.

[1]Matt. 25. 46.
[2]John, 8. 44.
[3]I John, 3. 8.

CHAP. 14. *An explanation of what is said of the devil, that he did not abide in the truth, because the truth was not in him*

Moreover, as if we had been inquiring why the devil did not abide in the truth, our Lord subjoins the reason, saying, "because the truth is not in him." Now, it would be in him had he abode in it. But the phraseology is unusual. For, as the words stand, "He abode not in the truth, because the truth is not in him," it seems as if the truth's not being in him were the cause of his not abiding in it; whereas his not abiding in the truth is rather the cause of its not being in him. The same form of speech is found in the psalm: "I have called upon Thee, for Thou hast heard me, O God,"[4] where we should expect it to be said, "Thou hast heard me, O God, for I have called upon Thee." But when he had said, "I have called," then, as if some one were seeking proof of this, he demonstrates the effectual earnestness of his prayer by the effect of God's hearing it; as if he had said, "The proof that I have prayed is that Thou hast heard me."

CHAP. 15. *How we are to understand the words, "The devil sinneth from the beginning"*

As for what John says about the devil, "The devil sinneth from the beginning,"[5] they[6] who suppose it is meant hereby that the devil was made with a sinful nature, misunderstand it; for if sin be natural, it is not sin at all. And how do they answer the prophetic proofs—either what Isaiah says when he represents the devil under the person of the king of Babylon, "How art thou fallen, O Lucifer, son of the morning!"[7] or what Ezekiel says, "Thou hast been in Eden, the garden of God; every precious stone was thy covering,"[8] where it is meant that he was some time without sin; for a little after it is still more explicitly said, "Thou wast perfect in thy ways"? And if these passages cannot well be otherwise interpreted, we must understand by this one also, "He abode not in the truth," that he was once in the truth, but did not remain in it. And from this passage, "The devil sinneth from the beginning," it is not to be supposed that he sinned from the beginning of his created existence, but from the beginning of his sin, when by his pride he had once commenced to sin. There is a passage, too, in the Book of Job, of which the devil is the subject: "This is the beginning of the creation of God, which He

[4]Ps. 17. 6.   [5]I John, 3. 8.   [6]The Manichæans.
[7]Isa. 14. 12.   [8]Ezek. 28. 13.

made to be a sport to His angels,"[1] which agrees with the psalm, where it is said, "There is that dragon which Thou hast made to be a sport therein."[2] But these passages are not to lead us to suppose that the devil was originally created to be the sport of the angels, but that he was doomed to this punishment after his sin. His beginning, then, is the handiwork of God; for there is no nature, even among the least, and lowest, and last of the beasts, which was not the work of Him from Whom has proceeded all measure, all form, all order, without which nothing can be planned or conceived. How much more, then, is this angelic nature, which surpasses in dignity all else that He has made, the handiwork of the Most High!

CHAP. 16. *Of the ranks and differences of the creatures, estimated by their utility, or according to the natural gradations of being*

For among those beings which exist, and which are not of God the Creator's essence, those which have life are ranked above those which have none; those that have the power of generation, or even of desiring, above those which want this faculty. And, among things that have life, the sentient are higher than those which have no sensation, as animals are ranked above trees. And, among the sentient, the intelligent are above those that have not intelligence —men, e.g., above cattle. And, among the intelligent, the immortal, such as the angels, above the mortal, such as men. These are the gradations according to the order of nature; but according to the utility each man finds in a thing, there are various standards of value, so that it comes to pass that we prefer some things that have no sensation to some sentient beings. And so strong is this preference, that, had we the power, we would abolish the latter from nature altogether, whether in ignorance of the place they hold in nature, or, though, we know it, sacrificing them to our own convenience. Who, e.g., would not rather have bread in his house than mice, gold than fleas? But there is little to wonder at in this, seeing that even when valued by men themselves (whose nature is certainly of the highest dignity), more is often given for a horse than for a slave, for a jewel than for a maid. Thus the reason of one contemplating nature prompts very different judgments from those dictated by the necessity of the needy, or the desire of the voluptuous; for the former considers what value a thing in itself has in the scale of crea-

tion, while necessity considers how it meets its need; reason looks for what the mental light will judge to be true, while pleasure looks for what pleasantly titilates the bodily sense. But of such consequence in rational natures is the weight, so to speak, of will and of love, that though in the order of nature angels rank above men, yet, by the scale of justice, good men are of greater value than bad angels.

CHAP. 17. *That the flaw of wickedness is not nature, but contrary to nature, and has its origin, not in the Creator, but in the will*

It is with reference to the nature, then, and not to the wickedness of the devil, that we are to understand these words, "This is the beginning of God's handiwork";[3] for, without doubt, wickedness can be a flaw or vice only where the nature previously was not vitiated. Vice, too, is so contrary to nature, that it cannot but damage it. And therefore departure from God would be no vice, unless in a nature whose property it was to abide with God. So that even the wicked will is a strong proof of the goodness of the nature. But God, as He is the supremely good Creator of good natures, so is He of evil wills the most just Ruler; so that, while they make an ill use of good natures, He makes a good use even of evil wills. Accordingly, He caused the devil (good by God's creation, wicked by his own will) to be cast down from his high position and to become the mockery of His angels—that is, He caused his temptations to benefit those whom he wishes to injure by them. And because God, when He created him, was certainly not ignorant of his future malignity, and foresaw the good which He Himself would bring out of his evil, therefore says the psalm, "This leviathan whom Thou hast made to be a sport therein,"[4] that we may see that, even while God in His goodness created him good, He yet had already foreseen and arranged how He would make use of him when he became wicked.

CHAP. 18. *Of the beauty of the universe, which becomes, by God's ordinance, more brilliant by the opposition of contraries*

For God would never have created any, I do not say angel, but even man, whose future wickedness He foreknew, unless He had equally known to what uses in behalf of the good He could turn him, thus embellishing the course of the ages, as it were an exquisite poem set off with antitheses. For what are called antitheses

---

[1]Job, 40. 14. (LXX).   [2]Ps. 104. 26.

[3]Job, 40. 14 (LXX).   [4]Ps. 104. 26.

are among the most elegant of the ornaments of speech. They might be called in Latin "opposi- tions," or, to speak more accurately, "contra- positions"; but this word is not in common use among us, though the Latin, and indeed the lan- guages of all nations, avail themselves of the same ornaments of style. In the Second Epistle to the Corinthians the Apostle Paul also makes a graceful use of antithesis, in that place where he says, "By the armour of righteousness on the right hand and on the left, by honour and dis- honour, by evil report and good report: as de- ceivers, and yet true; as unknown, and yet well known; as dying, and, behold, we live; as chas- tened, and not killed; as sorrowful, yet always rejoicing; as poor, yet making many rich; as having nothing, and yet possessing all things."[1] As, then, these oppositions of contraries lend beauty to the language, so the beauty of the course of this world is achieved by the opposi- tion of contraries, arranged, as it were, by an eloquence not of words, but of things. This is quite plainly stated in the Book of Ecclesiasti- cus, in this way: "Good is set against evil, and life against death: so is the sinner against the godly. So look upon all the works of the Most High, and these are two and two, one against another."[2]

CHAP. 19. *What, seemingly, we are to under- stand by the words, "God divided the light from the darkness"*

Accordingly, though the obscurity of the di- vine word has certainly this advantage, that it causes many opinions about the truth to be started and discussed, each reader seeing some fresh meaning in it, yet, whatever is said to be meant by an obscure passage should be either confirmed by the testimony of obvious facts, or should be asserted in other and less ambiguous texts. This obscurity is beneficial, whether the sense of the author is at last reached after the discussion of many other interpretations, or whether, though that sense remain concealed, other truths are brought out by the discussion of the obscurity. To me it does not seem incongru- ous with the working of God, if we understand that the angels were created when that first light was made and that a separation was made be- tween the holy and the unclean angels, when, as is said, "God divided the light from the dark- ness; and God called the light Day, and the darkness He called Night." For He alone could make this discrimination, who was able also be- fore they fell, to foreknow that they would fall,

and that, being deprived of the light of truth, they would abide in the darkness of pride. For, so far as regards the day and night, with which we are familiar, He commanded those lumina- ries of heaven that are obvious to our senses to divide between the light and the darkness. "Let there be," He says, "lights in the firmament of the heaven, to divide the day from the night"; and shortly after He says, "And God made two great lights; the greater light to rule the day, and the lesser light to rule the night: the stars also. And God set them in the firmament of the heaven, to give light upon the earth, and to rule over the day and over the night, and to divide the light from the darkness."[3] But between that light, which is the holy company of the angels spiritually radiant with the illumination of the truth, and that opposing darkness, which is the noisome foulness of the spiritual condition of those angels who are turned away from the light of righteousness, only He Himself could divide, from whom their wickedness (not of nature, but of will), while yet it was future, could not be hidden or uncertain.

CHAP. 20. *Of the words which follow the separa- tion of light and darkness, "and God saw the light that it was good"*

Then, we must not pass from this passage of Scripture without noticing that when God said, "Let there be light, and there was light," it was immediately added, "And God saw the light that it was good." No such expression followed the statement that He separated the light from the darkness, and called the light Day and the dark- ness Night, lest the seal of His approval might seem to be set on such darkness, as well as on the light. For when the darkness was not subject of disapprobation, as when it was divided by the heavenly bodies from this light which our eyes discern, the statement that God saw that it was good is inserted, not before, but after the divi- sion is recorded. "And God set them," so runs the passage, "in the firmament of the heaven, to give light upon the earth, and to rule over the day and over the night, and to divide the light from the darkness: and God saw that it was good." For He approved of both, because both were sinless. But where God said, "Let there be light, and there was light; and God saw the light that it was good"; and the narrative goes on, "and God divided the light from the darkness! and God called the light Day, and the darkness He called Night," there was not in this place subjoined the statement, "And God saw that it

1 II Cor. 6. 7–10.   2 Ecclus. 33. 15.   3 Gen. 1. 14–18.

was good," lest both should be designated good, while one of them was evil, not by nature, but by its own fault. And therefore, in this case, the light alone received the approbation of the Creator, while the angelic darkness, though it had been ordained, was yet not approved.

CHAP. 21. *Of God's eternal and unchangeable knowledge and will, whereby all he has made pleased him in the eternal design as well as in the actual results*

For what else is to be understood by that invariable refrain, "And God saw that it was good," than the approval of the work in its design, which is the wisdom of God? For certainly God did not in the actual achievement of the work first learn that it was good, but, on the contrary, nothing would have been made had it not been first known by Him. While, therefore, He sees that that is good which, had He not seen it before it was made, would never have been made, it is plain that He is not discovering, but teaching that it is good. Plato, indeed, was bold enough to say that, when the universe was completed, God was, as it were, elated with joy.[1] And Plato was not so foolish as to mean by this that God was rendered more blessed by the novelty of His creation; but he wished thus to indicate that the work now completed met with its Maker's approval, as it had while yet in design. It is not as if the knowledge of God were of various kinds, knowing in different ways things which as yet are not, things which are, and things which have been. For not in our fashion does He look forward to what is future, nor at what is present, nor back upon what is past; but in a manner quite different and far and profoundly remote from our way of thinking. For He does not pass from this to that by transition of thought, but beholds all things with absolute unchangeableness; so that of those things which emerge in time, the future, indeed, are not yet, and the present are now, and the past no longer are; but all of these are by Him comprehended in His stable and eternal presence. Neither does He see in one fashion by the eye, in another by the mind, for He is not composed of mind and body; nor does His present knowledge differ from that which it ever was or shall be, for those variations of time, past, present, and future, though they alter our knowledge, do not affect His, "with whom is no variableness, neither shadow of turning."[2] Neither is there any growth from thought to thought in the conceptions of

Him in Whose spiritual vision all things which He knows are at once embraced. For as without any movement that time can measure, He Himself moves all temporal things, so He knows all times with a knowledge that time cannot measure. And therefore He saw that what He had made was good, when He saw that it was good to make it. And when He saw it made, He had not on that account a twofold nor any way increased knowledge of it; as if He had less knowledge before He made what He saw. For certainly He would not be the perfect worker He is, unless His knowledge were so perfect as to receive no addition from His finished works. Wherefore, if the only object had been to inform us who made the light, it had been enough to say, "God made the light"; and if further information regarding the means by which it was made had been intended, it would have sufficed to say, "And God said, Let there be light, and there was light," that we might know not only that God had made the world, but also that He had made it by the word. But because it was right that three leading truths regarding the creature be intimated to us, viz., who made it, by what means, and why, it is written, "God said, Let there be light, and there was light. And God saw the light that it was good." If, then, we ask who made it, it was "God." If, by what means, He said "Let it be," and it was. If we ask, why He made it, "it was good." Neither is there any author more excellent than God, nor any skill more efficacious than the word of God, nor any cause better than that good might be created by the good God. This also Plato has assigned as the most sufficient reason for the creation of the world, that good works might be made by a good God;[3] whether he read this passage, or, perhaps, was informed of these things by those who had read them, or, by his quick-sighted genius, penetrated to things spiritual and invisible through the things that are created, or was instructed regarding them by those who had discerned them.

CHAP. 22. *Of those who do not approve of certain things which are a part of this good creation of a good Creator, and who think that there is some natural evil*

This cause, however, of a good creation, namely, the goodness of God—this cause, I say, so just and fit, which, when piously and carefully weighed, terminates all the controversies of those who inquire into the origin of the world, has not been recognized by some heretics,[4] be-

---

[1] *Timæus*, 37.
[2] Jas. I. 17.
[3] *Timæus*, 29.
[4] The Manichæans.

cause there are, forsooth, many things, such as fire, frost, wild beasts, and so forth, which do not suit but injure this thin-blooded and frail mortality of our flesh, which is at present under just punishment. They do not consider how admirable these things are in their own places, how excellent in their own natures, how beautifully adjusted to the rest of creation, and how much grace they contribute to the universe by their own contributions as to a commonwealth; and how serviceable they are even to ourselves, if we use them with a knowledge of their fit adaptations—so that even poisons, which are destructive when used injudiciously, become wholesome and medicinal when used in conformity with their qualities and design; just as, on the other hand, those things which give us pleasure, such as food, drink, and the light of the sun, are found to be hurtful when immoderately or unseasonably used. And thus divine providence admonishes us not foolishly to vituperate things, but to investigate their utility with care; and, where our mental capacity or infirmity is at fault, to believe that there is a utility, though hidden, as we have experienced that there were other things which we all but failed to discover. For this concealment of the use of things is itself either an exercise of our humility or a levelling of our pride; for no nature at all is evil, and this is a name for nothing but the want of good. But from things earthly to things heavenly, from the visible to the invisible, there are some things better than others; and for this purpose are they unequal, in order that they might all exist. Now God is in such sort a great worker in great things, that He is not less in little things—for these little things are to be measured not by their own greatness (which does not exist), but by the wisdom of their Designer; as, in the visible appearance of a man, if one eyebrow be shaved off, how nearly nothing is taken from the body, but how much from the beauty!—for that is not constituted by bulk, but by the proportion and arrangement of the members. But we do not greatly wonder that persons, who suppose that some evil nature has been generated and propagated by a kind of opposing principle proper to it, refuse to admit that the cause of the creation was this, that the good God produced a good creation. For they believe that He was driven to this enterprise of creation by the urgent necessity of repulsing the evil that warred against Him, and that He mixed His good nature with the evil for the sake of restraining and conquering it; and that this nature of His, being thus shamefully polluted and most cruelly oppressed

and held captive, He labours to cleanse and deliver it, and with all His pains does not wholly succeed; but such part of it as could not be cleansed from that defilement is to serve as a prison and chain of the conquered and incarcerated enemy. The Manichæans would not drivel, or rather, rave in such a style as this, if they believed the nature of God to be, as it is, unchangeable and absolutely incorruptible, and subject to no injury; and if, moreover, they held in Christian sobriety that the soul which has shown itself capable of being altered for the worse by its own will, and of being corrupted by sin, and so, of being deprived of the light of eternal truth—that this soul, I say, is not a part of God, nor of the same nature as God, but is created by Him, and is far different from its Creator.

CHAP. 23. *Of the error in which the doctrine of Origen is involved*

But it is much more surprising that some even of those who, with ourselves, believe that there is one only source of all things, and that no nature which is not divine can exist unless originated by that Creator, have yet refused to accept with a good and simple faith this so good and simple a reason of the world's creation, that a good God made it good; and that the things created, being different from God, were inferior to Him, and yet were good, being created by none other than He. But they say that souls, though not, indeed, parts of God, but created by Him, sinned by abandoning God; that, in proportion to their various sins, they merited different degrees of debasement from heaven to earth, and diverse bodies as prison-houses; and that this is the world, and this the cause of its creation, not the production of good things, but the restraining of evil. Origen is justly blamed for holding this opinion. For in the books which he entitles περὶ αρχῶν, that is, *Of Origins,* this is his sentiment, this his utterance. And I cannot sufficiently express my astonishment that a man so erudite and well versed in ecclesiastical literature should not have observed, in the first place, how opposed this is to the meaning of this authoritative Scripture, which, in recounting all the works of God, regularly adds, "And God saw that it was good"; and, when all were completed, inserts the words, "And God saw everything that He had made, and, behold, it was very good."[1] Was it not obviously meant to be understood that there was no other cause of the world's creation than that good creatures should be made by a good God? In this creation,

[1]Gen. i. 31.

had no one sinned, the world would have been filled and beautified with natures good without exception; and though there is sin, all things are not therefore full of sin, for the great majority of the heavenly inhabitants preserve their nature's integrity. And the sinful will, though it violated the order of its own nature, did not on that account escape the laws of God, who justly orders all things for good. For as the beauty of a picture is increased by well-managed shadows, so, to the eye that has skill to discern it, the universe is beautified even by sinners, though, considered by themselves, their deformity is a sad blemish.

In the second place, Origen, and all who think with him, ought to have seen that if it were the true opinion that the world was created in order that souls might, for their sins, be accommodated with bodies in which they should be shut up as in houses of correction, the more venial sinners receiving lighter and more ethereal bodies, while the grosser and graver sinners received bodies more crass and grovelling, then it would follow that the devils, who are deepest in wickedness, ought, rather than even wicked men, to have earthly bodies, since these are the grossest and least ethereal of all. But in point of fact, that we might see that the deserts of souls are not to be estimated by the qualities of bodies, the wickedest devil possesses an ethereal body, while man, wicked, it is true, but with a wickedness small and venial in comparison with his, received even before his sin a body of clay. And what more foolish assertion can be advanced than that God, by this sun of ours, did not design to benefit the material creation, or lend lustre to its loveliness, and therefore created one single sun for this single world, but that it so happened that one soul only had so sinned as to deserve to be enclosed in such a body as it is? On this principle, if it had chanced that not one, but two, yea, or ten, or a hundred had sinned similarly, and with a like degree of guilt, then this world would have one hundred suns. And that such is not the case is due not to the considerate foresight of the Creator, contriving the safety and beauty of things material, but rather to the fact that so fine a quality of sinning was hit upon by only one soul, so that it alone has merited such a body. Manifestly persons holding such opinions should aim at confining, not souls of which they know not what they say, but themselves, lest they fall, and deservedly, far indeed from the truth. And as to these three answers which I formerly recommended when in the case of any creature the questions are put,

"Who made it?" "By what means?" "Why?" that it should be replied, "God," "By the Word," "Because it was good"—as to these three answers, it is very questionable whether the Trinity itself is thus mystically indicated, that is, the Father, the Son, and the Holy Ghost, or whether there is some good reason for this acceptation in this passage of Scripture,—this, I say, is questionable, and one can't be expected to explain everything in one volume.

CHAP. 24. *Of the divine Trinity, and the indications of its presence scattered everywhere among its works*

We believe, we maintain, we faithfully preach, that the Father begat the Word, that is, Wisdom, by which all things were made, the only-begotten Son, one as the Father is one, eternal as the Father is eternal, and, equally with the Father, supremely good; and that the Holy Spirit is the Spirit alike of Father and of Son, and is Himself consubstantial and co-eternal with both; and that this whole is a Trinity by reason of the individuality[1] of the persons, and one God by reason of the indivisible divine substance, as also one Almighty by reason of the indivisible omnipotence; yet so that, when we inquire regarding each singly, it is said that each is God and Almighty; and, when we speak of all together, it is said that there are not three Gods, nor three Almighties, but one God Almighty; so great is the indivisible unity of these Three, which requires that it be so stated. But, whether the Holy Spirit of the Father and of the Son, who are both good, can be with propriety called the goodness of both, because He is common to both, I do not presume to determine hastily. Nevertheless, I would have less hesitation in saying that He is the holiness of both, not as if He were a divine attribute merely, but Himself also the divine substance, and the third person in the Trinity. I am the rather emboldened to make this statement, because, though the Father is a spirit, and the Son a spirit, and the Father holy, and the Son holy, yet the third person is distinctively called the Holy Spirit, as if He were the substantial holiness consubstantial with the other two. But if the divine goodness is nothing else than the divine holiness, then certainly it is a reasonable studiousness and not presumptuous intrusion to inquire whether the same Trinity be not hinted at in an enigmatical mode of speech, by which our inquiry is stimulated, when it is written who made each creature, and by what means, and

[1]*Proprietas.*

why. For it is the Father of the Word who said, "Let there be." And that which was made when He spoke was certainly made by means of the Word. And by the words, "God saw that it was good," it is sufficiently intimated that God made what was made not from any necessity, nor for the sake of supplying any want, but solely from His own goodness, i.e., because it was good. And this is stated after the creation had taken place, that there might be no doubt that the thing made satisfied the goodness on account of which it was made. And if we are right in understanding that this goodness is the Holy Spirit, then the whole Trinity is revealed to us in the creation. In this, too, is the origin, the enlightenment, the blessedness of the holy city which is above among the holy angels. For if we inquire whence it is, God created it; or whence its wisdom, God illumined it; or whence its blessedness, God is its bliss. It has its form by subsisting in Him; its enlightenment by contemplating Him; its joy by abiding in Him. It is; it sees; it loves. In God's eternity is its life; in God's truth its light; in God's goodness its joy.

Chap. 25. *Of the division of philosophy into three parts*

As far as one can judge, it is for the same reason that philosophers have aimed at a threefold division of science, or rather, were enabled to see that there was a threefold division (for they did not invent, but only discovered it), of which one part is called physical, another logical, the third ethical. The Latin equivalents of these names are now naturalized in the writings of many authors, so that these divisions are called natural, rational, and moral, on which I have touched slightly in the eighth book. Not that I would conclude that these philosophers, in this threefold division, had any thought of a trinity in God, although Plato is said to have been the first to discover and promulgate this distribution, and he saw that God alone could be the author of nature, the bestower of intelligence, and the kindler of love by which life becomes good and blessed. But certain it is that, though philosophers disagree regarding the nature of things, and the mode of investigating truth, and of the good to which all our actions ought to tend, yet in these three great general questions all their intellectual energy is spent. And though there be a confusing diversity of opinion, every man striving to establish his own opinion in regard to each of these questions, yet no one of them all doubts that nature has some cause, sci-

ence some method, life some end and aim. Then, again, there are three things which every artificer must possess if he is to effect anything—nature, education, practice. Nature is to be judged by capacity, education by knowledge, practice by its fruit. I am aware that, properly speaking, fruit is what one enjoys, use [practice] what one uses. And this seems to be the difference between them, that we are said to *enjoy* that which in itself and irrespective of other ends delights us; to *use* that which we seek for the sake of some end beyond. For which reason the things of time are to be used rather than enjoyed, that we may deserve to enjoy things eternal; and not as those perverse creatures who would fain enjoy money and use God—not spending money for God's sake, but worshipping God for money's sake. However, in common parlance, we both use fruits and enjoy uses. For we correctly speak of the "fruits of the field," which certainly we all use in the present life. And it was in accordance with this usage that I said that there were three things to be observed in a man, nature, education, practice. From these the philosophers have elaborated, as I said, the threefold division of that science by which a blessed life is attained: the natural having respect to nature, the rational to education, the moral to practice. If, then, we were ourselves the authors of our nature, we should have generated knowledge in ourselves, and should not require to reach it by education, i.e., by learning it from others. Our love, too, proceeding from ourselves and returning to us, would suffice to make our life blessed, and would stand in need of no extraneous enjoyment. But now, since our nature has God as its requisite author, it is certain that we must have Him for our teacher that we may be wise; Him, too, to dispense to us spiritual sweetness that we may be blessed.

Chap. 26. *Of the image of the supreme Trinity, which we find in some sort in human nature even in its present state*

And we indeed recognize in ourselves the image of God, that is, of the supreme Trinity, an image which, though it be not equal to God, or rather, though it be very far removed from Him—being neither co-eternal, nor, to say all in a word, consubstantial with Him—is yet nearer to Him in nature than any other of His works and is destined to be yet restored, that it may bear a still closer resemblance. For we are, and know that we are, and delight in our being, and our knowledge of it. Moreover, in these three things no true-seeming illusion disturbs us; for we do not come into contact with these by some bodily sense, as we perceive the things outside of us—colours, e.g., by seeing, sounds by hearing, smells by smelling, tastes by tasting, hard and soft objects by touching—of all which sensible objects it is the images resembling them but not themselves which we perceive in the mind and hold in the memory, and which excite us to desire the objects. But, without any delusive representation of images or phantasms, I am most certain that I am and that I know and delight in this. In respect of these truths, I am not at all afraid of the arguments of the Academicians, who say, "What if you are deceived?" For if I am deceived, I am. For he who is not, cannot be deceived; and if I am deceived, by this same token I am. And since I am if I am deceived, how am I deceived in believing that I am? for it is certain that I am if I am deceived. Since, therefore, I, the person deceived, should be, even if I were deceived, certainly I am not deceived in this knowledge that I am. And, consequently, neither am I deceived in knowing that I know. For, as I know that I am, so I know this also, that I know. And when I love these two things, I add to them a certain third thing, namely, my love, which is of equal moment. For neither am I deceived in this, that I love, since in those things which I love I am not deceived; though even if these were false, it would still be true that I *loved* false things. For how could I justly be blamed and prohibited from loving false things, if it were false that I loved them? But, since they are true and real, who doubts that when they are loved, the love of them is itself true and real? Further, as there is no one who does not wish to be happy, so there is no one who does not wish to be. For how can he be happy, if he is nothing?

Chap. 27. *Of existence, and knowledge of it, and the love of both*

And truly the very fact of existing is by some natural spell so pleasant, that even the wretched are, for no other reason, unwilling to perish; and, when they feel that they are wretched, wish not that they themselves be annihilated, but that their misery be so. Take even those who, both in their own esteem and in point of fact, are utterly wretched and who are reckoned so, not only by wise men an account of their folly, but by those who count themselves blessed, and who think them wretched because they are poor and destitute—if any one should give these men

an immortality, in which their misery should be deathless, and should offer the alternative that if they shrank from existing eternally in the same misery they might be annihilated and exist nowhere at all, nor in any condition, on the instant they would joyfully, nay exultantly, make election to exist always, even in such a condition, rather than not exist at all. The well-known feeling of such men witnesses to this. For when we see that they fear to die, and will rather live in such misfortune than end it by death, is it not obvious enough how nature shrinks from annihilation? And, accordingly, when they know that they must die, they seek, as a great boon, that this mercy be shown them, that they may a little longer live in the same misery, and delay to end it by death. And so they indubitably prove with what glad alacrity they would accept immortality, even though it secured to them endless destruction. What! do not even all irrational animals, to whom such calculations are unknown, from the huge dragons down to the least worms, all testify that they wish to exist, and therefore shun death by every movement in their power? Nay, the very plants and shrubs, which have no such life as enables them to shun destruction by movements we can see, do not they all seek in their own fashion to conserve their existence, by rooting themselves more and more deeply in the earth, that so they may draw nourishment and throw out healthy branches towards the sky? In fine, even the lifeless bodies, which want not only sensation but seminal life, yet either seek the upper air or sink deep, or are balanced in an intermediate position, so that they may protect their existence in that situation where they can exist in most accordance with their nature.

And how much human nature loves the knowledge of its existence, and how it shrinks from being deceived, will be sufficiently understood from this fact, that every man prefers to grieve in a sane mind, rather than to be glad in madness. And this grand and wonderful instinct belongs to men alone of all animals; for, though some of them have keener eyesight than ourselves for this world's light, they cannot attain to that spiritual light with which our mind is somehow irradiated, so that we can form right judgments of all things. For our power to judge is proportioned to our acceptance of this light. Nevertheless, the irrational animals, though they have not knowledge, have certainly something resembling knowledge; whereas the other material things are said to be sensible, not because they have senses, but because they are the objects of our senses. Yet among plants, their nourishment and generation have some resemblance to sensible life. However, both these and all material things have their causes hidden in their nature; but their outward forms, which lend beauty to this visible structure of the world, are perceived by our senses, so that they seem to wish to compensate for their own want of knowledge by providing us with knowledge. But we perceive them by our bodily senses in such a way that we do not judge of them by these senses. For we have another and far superior sense, belonging to the inner man, by which we perceive what things are just, and what unjust—just by means of an intelligible idea, unjust by the want of it. This sense is aided in its functions neither by the eyesight, nor by the orifice of the ear, nor by the air-holes of the nostrils, nor by the palate's taste, nor by any bodily touch. By it I am assured both that I am and that I know this; and these two I love and in the same manner I am assured that I love them.

CHAP. 28. *Whether we ought to love the love itself with which we love our existence and our knowledge of it, that so we may more nearly resemble the image of the divine Trinity*

We have said as much as the scope of this work demands regarding these two things, to wit, our existence, and our knowledge of it, and how much they are loved by us, and how there is found even in the lower creatures a kind of likeness of these things, and yet with a difference. We have yet to speak of the love wherewith they are loved, to determine whether this love itself is loved. And doubtless it is; and this is the proof. Because in men who are justly loved, it is rather love itself that is loved; for he is not justly called a good man who knows what is good, but who loves it. Is it not then obvious that we love in ourselves the very love wherewith we love whatever good we love? For there is also a love wherewith we love that which we ought not to love; and this love is hated by him who loves that wherewith he loves what ought to be loved. For it is quite possible for both to exist in one man. And this co-existence is good for a man, to the end that this love which conduces to our living well may grow, and the other, which leads us to evil may decrease, until our whole life be perfectly healed and transmuted into good. For if we were beasts, we should love the fleshly and sensual life, and this would be our sufficient good; and when it was well with us in respect of it, we should seek nothing be-

yond. In like manner, if we were trees, we could not, indeed, in the strict sense of the word, love anything; nevertheless we should seem, as it were, to long for that by which we might become more abundantly and luxuriantly fruitful. If we were stones, or waves, or wind, or flame, or anything of that kind, we should want, indeed, both sensation and life, yet should possess a kind of attraction towards our own proper position and natural order. For the specific gravity of bodies is, as it were, their love, whether they are carried downwards by their weight, or upwards by their levity. For the body is borne by its gravity, as the spirit by love, whithersoever it is borne.[1] But we are men, created in the image of our Creator, Whose eternity is true, and Whose truth is eternal, Whose love is eternal and true, and Who Himself is the eternal, true, and adorable Trinity, without confusion, without separation; and, therefore, while, as we run over all the works which He has established, we may detect, as it were, His footprints, now more and now less distinct even in those things that are beneath us, since they could not so much as exist, or be bodied forth in any shape, or follow and observe any law, had they not been made by Him Who supremely is, and is supremely good and supremely wise; yet in ourselves beholding His image, let us, like that younger son of the gospel, come to ourselves, and arise and return to Him from Whom by our sin we had departed. There our being will have no death, our knowledge no error, our love no mishap. But now, though we are assured of our possession of these three things, not on the testimony of others, but by our own consciousness of their presence and because we see them with our own most truthful interior vision, yet, as we cannot of ourselves know how long they are to continue, and whether they shall never cease to be, and what issue their good or bad use will lead to, we seek for others who can acquaint us of these things, if we have not already found them. Of the trustworthiness of these witnesses, there will, not now, but subsequently, be an opportunity of speaking. But in this book let us go on as we have begun, with God's help, to speak of the city of God, not in its state of pilgrimage and mortality, but as it exists ever immortal in the heavens—that is, let us speak of the holy angels who maintain their allegiance to God, who never were, nor ever shall be, apostate, between whom and those who forsook light eternal and became darkness, God, as we have already said, made at the first a separation.

[1] Compare the *Confessions*, BK. XIII. 10.

CHAP. 29. *Of the knowledge by which the holy angels know God in His essence, and by which they see the causes of His works in the art of the worker, before they see them in the works of the artist*

Those holy angels come to the knowledge of God not by audible words, but by the presence to their souls of immutable truth, i.e., of the only-begotten Word of God; and they know this Word Himself, and the Father, and their Holy Spirit, and that this Trinity is indivisible, and that the three persons of it are one substance, and that there are not three Gods but one God; and this they so know, that it is better understood by them than we are by ourselves. Thus, too, they know the creature also, not in itself, but by this better way, in the wisdom of God, as if in the art by which it was created; and, consequently, they know themselves better in God than in themselves, though they have also this latter knowledge. For they were created, and are different from their Creator. In Him, therefore, they have, as it were, a noonday knowledge; in themselves, a twilight knowledge, according to our former explanations.[1] For there is a great difference between knowing a thing in the design in conformity to which it was made, and knowing it in itself—e.g., the straightness of lines and correctness of figures is known in one way when mentally conceived, in another when described on paper; and justice is known in one way in the unchangeable truth, in another in the spirit of a just man. So is it with all other things—as, the firmament between the water above and below, which was called the heaven; the gathering of the waters beneath, and the laying bare of the dry land, and the production of plants and trees; the creation of sun, moon, and stars; and of the animals out of the waters, fowls, and fish, and monsters of the deep; and of everything that walks or creeps on the earth, and of man himself, who excels all that is on the earth—all these things are known in one way by the angels in the Word of God, in which they see the eternally abiding causes and reasons according to which they were made, and in another way in themselves: in the former, with a clearer knowledge; in the latter, with a knowledge dimmer, and rather of the bare works than of the design. Yet, when these works are referred to the praise and adoration of the Creator Himself, it is as if morning dawned in the minds of those who contemplate them.

[1] Chap. 7.

CHAP. 30. *Of the perfection of the number six, which is the first of the numbers which is composed of its aliquot parts*

These works are recorded to have been completed in six days (the same day being six times repeated), because six is a perfect number—not because God required a protracted time, as if He could not at once create all things, which then should mark the course of time by the movements proper to them, but because the perfection of the works was signified by the number six. For the number six is the first which is made up of its own[2] parts, i.e., of its sixth, third, and half, which are respectively one, two, and three, and which make a total of six. In this way of looking at a number, those are said to be its parts which exactly divide it, as a half, a third, a fourth, or a fraction with any denominator—e.g., four is a part of nine, but not therefore an aliquot part; but one is, for it is the ninth part; and three is, for it is the third. Yet these two parts, the ninth and the third, or one and three, are far from making its whole sum of nine. So again, in the number ten, four is a part, yet does not divide it; but one is an aliquot part, for it is a tenth; so it has a fifth, which is two; and a half, which is five. But these three parts, a tenth, a fifth, and a half, or one, two, and five, added together, do not make ten, but eight. Of the number twelve, again, the parts added together exceed the whole; for it has a twelfth, that is, one; a sixth, or two; a fourth, which is three; a third, which is four; and a half, which is six. But one, two, three, four, and six make up, not twelve, but more, viz., sixteen. So much I have thought fit to state for the sake of illustrating the perfection of the number six, which is, as I said, the first which is exactly made up of its own parts added together; and in this number of days God finished His work. And, therefore, we must not despise the science of numbers, which, in many passages of holy Scripture, is found to be of eminent service to the careful interpreter. Neither has it been without reason numbered among God's praises, "Thou hast ordered all things in number, and measure, and weight."[3]

CHAP. 31. *Of the seventh day, in which completeness and repose are celebrated*

But, on the seventh day (i.e., the same day repeated seven times, which number is also a perfect one, though for another reason), the rest of God is set forth, and then, too, we first hear

[2] Or aliquot parts.   [3] Wisd. 11. 20.

of its being hallowed. So that God did not wish to hallow this day by His works, but by His rest, which has no evening, for it is not a creature; so that, being known in one way in the Word of God, and in another in itself, it should make a twofold knowledge, daylight and dusk (day and evening). Much more might be said about the perfection of the number seven, but this book is already too long, and I fear lest I should seem to catch at an opportunity of airing my little smattering of science more childishly than profitably. I must speak, therefore, in moderation and with dignity, lest, in too keenly following "number," I be accused of forgetting "weight" and "measure." Suffice it here to say, that three is the first whole number that is odd, four the first that is even, and of these two, seven is composed. On this account it is often put for all numbers together, as, "A just man falleth seven times, and riseth up again,"[1]—that is, let him fall never so often, he will not perish (and this was meant to be understood not of sins, but of afflictions conducing to lowliness). Again, "Seven times a day will I praise Thee,"[2] which elsewhere is expressed thus, "I will bless the Lord *at all times*."[3] And many such instances are found in the divine authorities, in which the number seven is, as I said, commonly used to express the whole, or the completeness of anything. And so the Holy Spirit, of whom the Lord says, "He will teach you all truth,"[4] is signified by this number.[5] In it is the rest of God, the rest His people find in Him. For rest is in the whole, i.e., in perfect completeness, while in the part there is labour. And thus we labour as long as we know in part; "but when that which is perfect is come, then that which is in part shall be done away."[6] It is even with toil we search into the Scriptures themselves. But the holy angels, towards whose society and assembly we sigh while in this our toilsome pilgrimage, as they already abide in their eternal home, so do they enjoy perfect facility of knowledge and felicity of rest. It is without difficulty that they help us; for their spiritual movements, pure and free, cost them no effort.

CHAP. 32. *Of the opinion that the angels were created before the world*

But if some one oppose our opinion, and say that the holy angels are not referred to when it is said, "Let there be light, and there was light";

if he suppose or teach that some material light, then first created, was meant, and that the angels were created, not only before the firmament dividing the waters and named "the heaven," but also before the time signified in the words, "In the beginning God created the heaven and the earth"; if he allege that this phrase, "In the beginning," does not mean that nothing was made before (for the angels were), but that God made all things by His Wisdom or Word, Who is named in Scripture "the Beginning," as He Himself, in the gospel, replied to the Jews when they asked Him who He was, that He was the Beginning;[7] I will not contest the point, chiefly because it gives me the liveliest satisfaction to find the Trinity celebrated in the very beginning of the book of Genesis. For having said "In the Beginning God created the heaven and the earth," meaning that the Father made them in the Son (as the psalm testifies where it says, "How manifold are Thy works, O Lord! in Wisdom hast Thou made them all"[8]), a little afterwards mention is fitly made of the Holy Spirit also. For, when it had been told us what kind of earth God created at first, or what the mass or matter was which God, under the name of "heaven and earth," had provided for the construction of the world, as is told in the additional words, "And the earth was without form, and void; and darkness was upon the face of the deep," then, for the sake of completing the mention of the Trinity, it is immediately added, "And the Spirit of God moved upon the face of the waters." Let each one, then, take it as he pleases; for it is so profound a passage, that it may well suggest, for the exercise of the reader's tact, many opinions, and none of them widely departing from the rule of faith. At the same time, let none doubt that the holy angels in their heavenly abodes are, though not, indeed, co-eternal with God, yet secure and certain of eternal and true felicity. To their company the Lord teaches that His little ones belong; and not only says, "They shall be equal to the angels of God,"[9] but shows, too, what blessed contemplation the angels themselves enjoy, saying, "Take heed that ye despise not one of these little ones; for I say unto you, that in heaven their angels do always behold the face of my Father which is in heaven."[10]

---

[7] John 8. 25; see p. 313. He might rather have referred to Rev. 3. 14.

[8] Ps. 104. 24.

[9] Matt. 22. 30.

[10] Matt. 18. 10.

[1] Prov. 24. 16.   [2] Ps. 119. 164.   [3] Ps. 34. 1.
[4] John 16. 13.   [5] Isa. 11. 2.
[6] I Cor. 13. 10.

CHAP. 33. *Of the two different and dissimilar communities of angels, which are not inappropriately signified by the names light and darkness*

That certain angels sinned, and were thrust down to the lowest parts of this world, where they are, as it were, incarcerated till their final damnation in the day of judgment, the Apostle Peter very plainly declares, when he says that "God spared not the angels that sinned, but cast them down to hell, and delivered them into chains of darkness to be reserved into judgment."[1] Who, then, can doubt that God, either in foreknowledge or in act, separated between these and the rest? And who will dispute that the rest are justly called "light"? For even we who are yet living by faith, hoping only and not yet enjoying equality with them, are already called "light" by the apostle: "For ye were sometimes darkness, but now are ye light in the Lord."[2] But as for these apostate angels, all who understand or believe them to be worse than unbelieving men are well aware that they are called "darkness." Wherefore, though light and darkness are to be taken in their literal signification in these passages of Genesis in which it is said, "God said, Let there be light, and there was light," and "God divided the light from the darkness," yet, for our part, we understand these two societies of angels—the one enjoying God, the other swelling with pride; the one to whom it is said, "Praise ye Him, all His angels,"[3] the other whose prince says, "All these things will I give Thee if Thou wilt fall down and worship me";[4] the one blazing with the holy love of God, the other reeking with the unclean lust of self-advancement. And since, as it is written, "God resisteth the proud, but giveth grace unto the humble,"[5] we may say, the one dwelling in the heaven of heavens, the other cast thence, and raging through the lower regions of the air; the one tranquil in the brightness of piety, the other tempest-tossed with beclouding desires; the one, at God's pleasure, tenderly succouring, justly avenging—the other, set on by its own pride, boiling with the lust of subduing and hurting; the one the minister of God's goodness to the utmost of their good pleasure, the other held in by God's power from doing the harm it would; the former laughing at the latter when it does good unwillingly by its persecutions, the latter envying the former when it gathers in its pilgrims. These two angelic communities, then, dissimilar and contrary to one another, the one both by nature good and by will upright, the other also good by nature but by will depraved, as they are exhibited in other and more explicit passages of holy writ, so I think they are spoken of in this book of Genesis under the names of "light" and "darkness"; and even if the author perhaps had a different meaning, yet our discussion of the obscure language has not been wasted time; for, though we have been unable to discover his meaning, yet we have adhered to the rule of faith, which is sufficiently ascertained by the faithful from other passages of equal authority. For, though it is the material works of God which are here spoken of, they have certainly a resemblance to the spiritual, so that Paul can say, "Ye are all the children of light, and the children of the day: we are not of the night, nor of darkness."[6] If, on the other hand, the author of Genesis saw in the words what we see, then our discussion reaches this more satisfactory conclusion, that the man of God, so eminently and divinely wise, or rather, that the Spirit of God who by him recorded God's works which were finished on the sixth day, may be supposed not to have omitted all mention of the angels whether he included them in the words "in the beginning," because He made them first, or, which seems most likely, because He made them in the only-begotten Word. And, under these names heaven and earth, the whole creation is signified, either as divided into spiritual and material, which seems the more likely, or into the two great parts of the world in which all created things are contained, so that, first of all, the creation is presented in sum, and then its parts are enumerated according to the mystic number of the days.

CHAP. 34. *Of the idea that the angels were meant where the separation of the waters by the firmament is spoken of, and of that other idea that the waters were not created*

Some,[7] however, have supposed that the angelic hosts are somehow referred to under the name of waters, and that this is what is meant by "Let there be a firmament in the midst of the waters":[8] that the waters above should be understood of the angels, and those below either of the visible waters, or of the multitude of bad angels, or of the nations of men. If this be so, then it does not here appear when the angels were created, but when they were separated. Though there have not been wanting men fool-

[1]II Peter 2. 4.   [2]Eph. 5. 8.   [3]Ps. 148. 2.
[4]Matt. 4. 9.   [5]Jas. 4. 6.
[6]I Thess. 5. 5.
[7]See Augustine's *Confessions*, BK. XIII. 47.   [8]Gen. 1. 6.

ish and wicked enough[1] to deny that the waters were made by God, because it is nowhere written, "God said, Let there be waters." With equal folly they might say the same of the earth, for nowhere do we read, "God said, Let the earth be." But, say they, it is written, "In the beginning God created the heaven and the earth." Yes, and there the water is meant, for both are included in one word. For "the sea is His," as the psalm says, "and He made it; and His hands formed the dry land."[2] But those who would understand the angels by the waters above the skies have a difficulty about the specific gravity of the elements, and fear that the waters, owing to their fluidity and weight, could not be set in the upper parts of the world. So that, if they were to construct a man upon their own principles, they would not put in his head any moist humours, or "phlegm" as the Greeks call it, and which acts the part of water among the elements

[1] Namely, the Audians and Sampsæans, insignificant heretical sects. [2] Ps. 95. 5.

of our body. But, in God's handiwork, the head is the seat of the phlegm, and surely most fitly; and yet, according to their supposition, so absurdly that if we were not aware of the fact, and were informed by this same record that God had put a moist and cold and therefore heavy humour in the uppermost part of man's body, these world-weighers would refuse belief. And if they were confronted with the authority of Scripture, they would maintain that something else must be meant by the words. But, were we to investigate and discover all the details which are written in this divine book regarding the creation of the world, we should have much to say, and should widely digress from the proposed aim of this work. Since, then, we have now said what seemed needful regarding these two diverse and contrary communities of angels, in which the origin of the two human communities (of which we intend to speak anon) is also found, let us at once bring this book also to a conclusion.

BOOK XII

ARGUMENT. AUGUSTINE FIRST INSTITUTES TWO INQUIRIES REGARDING THE ANGELS; NAMELY, WHENCE IS THERE IN SOME A GOOD, AND IN OTHERS AN EVIL WILL? AND, WHAT IS THE REASON OF THE BLESSEDNESS OF THE GOOD, AND THE MISERY OF THE EVIL? AFTERWARDS HE TREATS OF THE CREATION OF MAN, AND TEACHES THAT HE IS NOT FROM ETERNITY, BUT WAS CREATED, AND BY NONE OTHER THAN GOD.

CHAP. I. *That the nature of the angels, both good and bad, is one and the same*

IT has already, in the preceding book, been shown how the two cities originated among the angels. Before I speak of the creation of man and show how the cities took their rise, so far as regards the race of rational mortals, I see that I must first, so far as I can, adduce what may demonstrate that it is not incongruous and unsuitable to speak of a society composed of angels and men together; so that there are not four cities or societies—two, namely, of angels, and as many of men—but rather two in all, one composed of the good, the other of the wicked, angels or men indifferently.

That the contrary propensities in good and bad angels have arisen, not from a difference in their nature and origin, since God, the good Author and Creator of all essences, created them both, but from a difference in their wills and desires, it is impossible to doubt. While some steadfastly continued in that which was the common good of all, namely, in God Himself,

and in His eternity, truth, and love; others, being enamoured rather of their own power, as if they could be their own good, lapsed to this private good of their own, from that higher and beatific good which was common to all, and, bartering the lofty dignity of eternity for the inflation of pride, the most assured verity for the slyness of vanity, uniting love for factious partisanship, they became proud, deceived, envious. The cause, therefore, of the blessedness of the good is adherence to God. And so the cause of the others' misery will be found in the contrary, that is, in their not adhering to God. Wherefore, if when the question is asked, why are the former blessed, it is rightly answered, because they adhere to God; and when it is asked, why are the latter miserable, it is rightly answered, because they do not adhere to God—then there is no other good for the rational or intellectual creature save God only. Thus, though it is not every creature that can be blessed (for beasts, trees, stones, and things of that kind have not this capacity), yet that creature which has the capacity cannot be blessed of itself, since it is created out of nothing, but only by Him by whom it has been created. For it is blessed by the possession of that whose loss makes it miserable. He, then, who is blessed not in another, but in himself, cannot be miserable, because he cannot lose himself.

Accordingly we say that there is no unchangeable good but the one, true, blessed God; that the things which He made are indeed good because from Him, yet mutable because made not out of Him, but out of nothing. Although, therefore, they are not the supreme good, for God is a greater good, yet those mutable things which can adhere to the immutable good, and so be blessed, are very good; for so completely is He their good, that without Him they cannot but be wretched. And the other created things in the universe are not better on this account, that they cannot be miserable. For no one would say that the other members of the body are superior to the eyes, because they cannot be blind. But as the sentient nature, even when it feels pain, is superior to the stony, which can feel none, so the rational nature, even when wretched, is more excellent than that which lacks reason or feeling, and can therefore experience no misery. And since this is so, then in this nature which has been created so excellent that though it be mutable itself it can yet secure its blessedness by adhering to the immutable good, the supreme God; and since it is not satisfied unless it be perfectly blessed, and cannot be thus blessed save in God—in this nature, I say, not to adhere to God is manifestly a fault.[1] Now every fault injures the nature, and is consequently contrary to the nature. The creature, therefore, which cleaves to God, differs from those who do not, not by nature, but by fault; and yet by this very fault the nature itself is proved to be very noble and admirable. For that nature is certainly praised, the fault of which is justly blamed. For we justly blame the fault because it mars the praiseworthy nature. As, then, when we say that blindness is a defect of the eyes, we prove that sight belongs to the nature of the eyes; and when we say that deafness is a defect of the ears, hearing is thereby proved to belong to their nature; so, when we say that it is a fault of the angelic creature that it does not cleave to God, we hereby most plainly declare that it pertained to its nature to cleave to God. And who can worthily conceive or express how great a glory that is, to cleave to God, so as to live to Him, to draw wisdom from Him, to delight in Him, and

to enjoy this so great good, without death, error, or grief? And thus, since every vice is an injury of the nature, that very vice of the wicked angels, their departure from God, is sufficient proof that God created their nature so good, that it is an injury to it not to be with God.

CHAP. 2. *That there is no entity contrary to the divine, because nonentity seems to be that which is wholly opposite to Him Who supremely and always is*

This may be enough to prevent any one from supposing, when we speak of the apostate angels, that they could have another nature, derived, as it were, from some different origin and not from God. From the great impiety of this error we shall disentangle ourselves the more readily and easily, the more distinctly we understand that which God spoke by the angel when He sent Moses to the children of Israel: "I am that I am."[2] For since God is the supreme existence, that is to say, supremely is, and is therefore unchangeable, the things that He made He empowered to be, but not to be supremely like Himself. To some He communicated a more ample, to others a more limited existence, and thus arranged the natures of beings in ranks. For as from *sapere* comes *sapientia*, so from *esse* comes *essentia*—a new word indeed, which the old Latin writers did not use, but which is naturalized in our day, that our language may not want an equivalent for the Greek οὐσία. For this is expressed word for word by *essentia*. Consequently, to that nature which supremely is, and which created all else that exists, no nature is contrary save that which does not exist. For nonentity is the contrary of that which is. And thus there is no being contrary to God, the Supreme Being, and Author of all beings whatsoever.

CHAP. 3. *That the enemies of God are so, not by nature, but by will, which, as it injures them, injures a good nature; for if vice does not injure, it is not vice*

In Scripture they are called God's enemies who oppose His rule, not by nature, but by vice; having no power to hurt Him, but only themselves. For they are His enemies, not through their power to hurt, but by their will to oppose Him. For God is unchangeable, and wholly proof against injury. Therefore the vice which makes those who are called His enemies resist Him, is an evil not to God, but to themselves. And to them it is an evil, solely because it cor-

---

[1] *Vitium*: perhaps "fault" most nearly embraces all the uses of this word.

[2] Ex. 3. 14.

rupts the good of their nature. It is not nature, therefore, but vice, which is contrary to God. For that which is evil is contrary to the good. And who will deny that God is the supreme good? Vice, therefore, is contrary to God, as evil to good. Further, the nature it vitiates is a good, and therefore to this good also it is contrary. But while it is contrary to God only as evil to good, it is contrary to the nature it vitiates, both as evil and as hurtful. For to God no evils are hurtful; but only to natures mutable and corruptible, though, by the testimony of the vices themselves, originally good. For were they not good, vices could not hurt them. For how do they hurt them but by depriving them of integrity, beauty, welfare, virtue, and, in short, whatever natural good vice is wont to diminish or destroy? But if there be no good to take away, then no injury can be done, and consequently there can be no vice. For it is impossible that there should be a harmless vice. Whence we gather, that though vice cannot injure the unchangeable good, it can injure nothing but good; because it does not exist where it does not injure. This, then, may be thus formulated: Vice cannot be in the highest good, and cannot be but in some good. Things solely good, therefore, can in some circumstances exist; things solely evil, never; for even those natures which are vitiated by an evil will, so far indeed as they are vitiated, are evil, but in so far as they are natures they are good. And when a vitiated nature is punished, besides the good it has in being a nature, it has this also, that it is not unpunished.[1] For this is just, and certainly everything just is a good. For no one is punished for natural, but for voluntary vices. For even the vice which by the force of habit and long continuance has become a second nature, had its origin in the will. For at present we are speaking of the vices of the nature, which has a mental capacity for that enlightenment which discriminates between what is just and what is unjust.

CHAP. 4. *Of the nature of irrational and lifeless creatures, which in their own kind and order do not mar the beauty of the universe*

But it is ridiculous to condemn the faults of beasts and trees, and other such mortal and mutable things as are void of intelligence, sensation, or life, even though these faults should destroy their corruptible nature; for these creatures received, at their Creator's will, an existence fitting them, by passing away and giving place to others, to secure that lowest form of

[1]Compare Plato, *Gorgias.*

beauty, the beauty of seasons, which in its own place is a requisite part of this world. For things earthly were neither to be made equal to things heavenly, nor were they, though inferior, to be quite omitted from the universe. Since, then, in those situations where such things are appropriate, some perish to make way for others that are born in their room, and the less succumb to the greater, and the things that are overcome are transformed into the quality of those that have the mastery, this is the appointed order of things transitory. Of this order the beauty does not strike us, because by our mortal frailty we are so involved in a part of it that we cannot perceive the whole, in which these fragments that offend us are harmonized with the most accurate fitness and beauty. And therefore, where we are not so well able to perceive the wisdom of the Creator, we are very properly enjoined to believe it, lest in the vanity of human rashness we presume to find any fault with the work of so great an Artificer. At the same time, if we attentively consider even these faults of earthly things, which are neither voluntary nor penal, they seem to illustrate the excellence of the natures themselves, which are all originated and created by God; for it is that which pleases us in this nature which we are displeased to see removed by the fault—unless even the natures themselves displease men, as often happens when they become hurtful to them, and then men estimate them not by their nature, but by their utility, as in the case of those animals whose swarms scourged the pride of the Egyptians. But in this way of estimating, they may find fault with the sun itself; for certain criminals or debtors are sentenced by the judges to be set in the sun. Therefore it is not with respect to our convenience or discomfort, but with respect to their own nature that the creatures are glorifying to their Artificer. Thus even the nature of the eternal fire, penal though it be to the condemned sinners, is most assuredly worthy of praise. For what is more beautiful than fire flaming, blazing, and shining? What more useful than fire for warming, restoring, cooking, though nothing is more destructive than fire burning and consuming? The same thing, then, when applied in one way, is destructive, but when applied suitably, is most beneficial. For who can find words to tell its uses throughout the whole world? We must not listen, then, to those who praise the light of fire but find fault with its heat, judging it not by its nature, but by their convenience or discomfort. For they wish to see, but not to be burnt. But they forget that this very light which is so pleasant to them, disagrees with and hurts weak eyes; and in that heat which is disagreeable to them, some animals find the most suitable conditions of a healthy life.

CHAP. 5. *That in all natures, of every kind and rank, God is glorified*

All natures, then, inasmuch as they are, and have therefore a rank and species of their own, and a kind of internal harmony, are certainly good. And when they are in the places assigned to them by the order of their nature, they preserve such being as they have received. And those things which have not received everlasting being are altered for better or for worse, so as to suit the wants and motions of those things to which the Creator's law has made them subservient; and thus they tend in the divine providence to that end which is embraced in the general scheme of the government of the universe. So that, though the corruption of transitory and perishable things brings them to utter destruction, it does not prevent their producing that which was designed to be their result. And this being so, God, who supremely is, and who therefore created every being which has not supreme existence (for that which was made of nothing could not be equal to Him, and indeed could not be at all had He not made it), is not to be found fault with on account of the creature's faults, but is to be praised in view of the natures He has made.

CHAP. 6. *What the cause of the blessedness of the good angels is, and what the cause of the misery of the wicked*

Thus the true cause of the blessedness of the good angels is found to be this, that they cleave to Him who supremely is. And if we ask the cause of the misery of the bad, it occurs to us, and not unreasonably, that they are miserable because they have forsaken Him who supremely is and have turned to themselves who have no such essence. And this vice, what else is it called than pride? For "pride is the beginning of sin."[1] They were unwilling, then, to preserve their strength for God; and as adherence to God was the condition of their enjoying an ampler being, they diminished it by preferring themselves to Him. This was the first defect, and the first impoverishment, and the first flaw of their nature, which was created, not indeed supremely existent, but finding its blessedness in the enjoy-

[1] Eccles. 10. 13.

ment of the Supreme Being; whilst by abandoning Him it should become, not indeed no nature at all, but a nature with a less ample existence and therefore wretched.

If the further question be asked, What was the efficient cause of their evil will? there is none. For what is it which makes the will bad, when it is the will itself which makes the action bad? And consequently the bad will is the cause of the bad action, but nothing is the efficient cause of the bad will. For if anything is the cause, this thing either has or has not a will. If it has, the will is either good or bad. If good, who is so left to himself as to say that a good will makes a will bad? For in this case a good will would be the cause of sin; a most absurd supposition. On the other hand, if this hypothetical thing has a bad will, I wish to know what made it so; and that we may not go on forever, I ask at once, what made the *first* evil will bad? For that is not the first which was itself corrupted by an evil will, but that is the first which was made evil by no other will. For if it were preceded by that which made it evil, that will was first which made the other evil. But if it is replied, "Nothing made it evil; it always was evil," I ask if it has been existing in some nature. For if not, then it did not exist at all; and if it did exist in some nature, then it vitiated and corrupted it, and injured it, and consequently deprived it of good. And therefore the evil will could not exist in an evil nature, but in a nature at once good and mutable, which this vice could injure. For if it did no injury, it was no vice; and consequently the will in which it was could not be called evil. But if it did injury, it did it by taking away or diminishing good. And therefore there could not be from eternity, as was suggested, an evil will in that thing in which there had been previously a natural good, which the evil will was able to diminish by corrupting it. If, then, it was not from eternity, who, I ask, made it? The only thing that can be suggested in reply is that something which itself had no will, made the will evil. I ask, then, whether this thing was superior, inferior, or equal to it? If superior, then it is better. How, then, has it no will, and not rather a good will? The same reasoning applies if it was equal; for so long as two things have equally a good will, the one cannot produce in the other an evil will. Then remains the supposition that that which corrupted the will of the angelic nature which first sinned was itself an inferior thing without a will. But that thing, be it of the lowest and most earthly kind, is certainly itself good, since it is a nature and being, with a form and rank of its own in its own kind and order. How, then, can a good thing be the efficient cause of an evil will? How, I say, can good be the cause of evil? For when the will abandons what is above itself, and turns to what is lower, it becomes evil—not because that is evil to which it turns, but because the turning itself is wicked. Therefore it is not an inferior thing which has made the will evil, but it is itself which has become so by wickedly and inordinately desiring an inferior thing. For if two men, alike in physical and moral constitution, see the same corporal beauty, and one of them is excited by the sight to desire an illicit enjoyment while the other steadfastly maintains a modest restraint of his will, what do we suppose brings it about that there is an evil will in the one and not in the other? What produces it in the man in whom it exists? Not the bodily beauty, for that was presented equally to the gaze of both and yet did not produce in both an evil will. Did the flesh of the one cause the desire as he looked? But why did not the flesh of the other? Or was it the disposition? But why not the disposition of both? For we are supposing that both were of a like temperament of body and soul. Must we, then, say that the one was tempted by a secret suggestion of the evil spirit? As if it was not by his own will that he consented to this suggestion and to any inducement whatever! This consent, then, this evil will which he presented to the evil suasive influence—what was the cause of it, we ask? For, not to delay on such a difficulty as this, if both are tempted equally and one yields and consents to the temptation while the other remains unmoved by it, what other account can we give of the matter than this, that the one is willing, the other unwilling, to fall away from chastity? And what causes this but their own wills, in cases at least such as we are supposing, where the temperament is identical? The same beauty was equally obvious to the eyes of both; the same secret temptation pressed on both with equal violence. However minutely we examine the case, therefore, we can discern nothing which caused the will of the one to be evil. For if we say that the man himself made his will evil, what was the man himself before his will was evil but a good nature created by God, the unchangeable good? Here are two men who, before the temptation, were alike in body and soul, and of whom one yielded to the tempter who persuaded him, while the other could not be persuaded to desire that lovely body which was equally before the eyes of both. Shall we say of the successfully tempted man that he corrupted

his own will, since he was certainly good before his will became bad? Then, why did he do so? Was it because his will was a nature, or because it was made of nothing? We shall find that the latter is the case. For if a nature is the cause of an evil will, what else can we say than that evil arises from good or that good is the cause of evil? And how can it come to pass that a nature, good though mutable, should produce any evil —that is to say, should make the will itself wicked?

Chap. 7. *That we ought not to expect to find any efficient cause of the evil will*

Let no one, therefore, look for an efficient cause of the evil will; for it is not efficient, but deficient, as the will itself is not an effecting of something, but a defect. For defection from that which supremely is to that which has less of being, this is to begin to have an evil will. Now, to seek to discover the causes of these defections— causes, as I have said, not efficient, but deficient —is as if some one sought to see darkness, or hear silence. Yet both of these are known by us, and the former by means only of the eye, the latter only by the ear; but not by their positive actuality,[1] but by their want of it. Let no one, then seek to know from me what I know that I do not know; unless he perhaps wishes to learn to be ignorant of that of which all we know is, that it cannot be known. For those things which are known not by their actuality, but by their want of it, are known, if our expression may be allowed and understood, by not knowing them, that by knowing them they may be not known. For when the eyesight surveys objects that strike the sense, it nowhere sees darkness but where it begins not to see. And so no other sense but the ear can perceive silence, and yet it is only perceived by not hearing. Thus, too, our mind perceives intelligible forms by understanding them; but when they are deficient, it knows them by not knowing them; for "who can understand defects?"[2]

Chap. 8. *Of the misdirected love whereby the will fell away from the immutable to the mutable good*

This I do know, that the nature of God can never, nowhere, nowise be defective, and that natures made of nothing can. These latter, however, the more being they have and the more good they do (for then they do something positive), the more they have efficient causes; but in so far as they are defective in being, and con-

[1] *Specie.* [2] Ps. 19. 12.

sequently do evil (for then what is their work but vanity?), they have deficient causes. And I know likewise, that the will could not become evil, were it unwilling to become so; and therefore its failings are justly punished, being not necessary, but voluntary. For its defections are not to evil things, but are themselves evil; that is to say, are not towards things that are naturally and in themselves evil, but the defection of the will is evil, because it is contrary to the order of nature, and an abandonment of that which has supreme being for that which has less. For avarice is not a fault inherent in gold, but in the man who inordinately loves gold, to the detriment of justice, which ought to be held in incomparably higher regard than gold. Neither is luxury the fault of lovely and charming objects, but of the heart that inordinately loves sensual pleasures, to the neglect of temperance, which attaches us to objects more lovely in their spirituality, and more delectable by their incorruptibility. Nor yet is boasting the fault of human praise, but of the soul that is inordinately fond of the applause of men, and that makes light of the voice of conscience. Pride, too, is not the fault of him who delegates power, nor of power itself, but of the soul that is inordinately enamoured of its own power, and despises the more just dominion of a higher authority. Consequently he who inordinately loves the good which any nature possesses, even though he obtain it, himself becomes evil in the good, and wretched because deprived of a greater good.

CHAP. 9. *Whether the angels, besides receiving from God their nature, received from Him also their good will by the Holy Spirit imbuing them with love*

There is, then, no natural efficient cause, or, if I may be allowed the expression, no essential cause, of the evil will, since itself is the origin of evil in mutable spirits, by which the good of their nature is diminished and corrupted; and the will is made evil by nothing else than defection from God—a defection of which the cause, too, is certainly deficient. But as to the good will, if we should say that there is no efficient cause of it, we must beware of giving currency to the opinion that the good will of the good angels is not created, but is co-eternal with God. For if they themselves are created, how can we say that their good will was eternal? But if created, was it created along with themselves, or did they exist for a time without it? If along with themselves, then doubtless it was created by Him Who created them, and, as soon as ever

they were created, they attached themselves to Him Who created them, with the love He created in them. And they are separated from the society of the rest, because they have continued in the same good will; while the others have fallen away to another will, which is an evil one, by the very fact of its being a falling away from the good; from which, we may add, they would not have fallen away had they been unwilling to do so. But if the good angels existed for a time without a good will, and produced it in themselves without God's interference, then it follows that they made themselves better than He made them. Away with such a thought! For without a good will, what were they but evil? Or if they were not evil, because they had not an evil will any more than a good one (for they had not fallen away from that which as yet they had not begun to enjoy), certainly they were not the same, not so good, as when they came to have a good will. Or if they could not make themselves better than they were made by Him Who is surpassed by none in His work, then certainly, without His helpful operation, they could not come to possess that good will which made them better. And though their good will effected that they did not turn to themselves, who had a more stinted existence, but to Him Who supremely is, and that, being united to Him, their own being was enlarged, and they lived a wise and blessed life by His communications to them, what does this prove but that the will, however good it might be, would have continued helplessly only to desire Him, had not He Who had made their nature out of nothing, and yet capable of enjoying Him, first stimulated it to desire Him and then filled it with Himself, and so made it better?

Besides, this too has to be inquired into, whether, if the good angels made their own will good, they did so with or without will? If without, then it was not their doing. If with, was the will good or bad? If bad, how could a bad will give birth to a good one? If good, then already they had a good will. And who made this will, which already they had, but He Who created them with a good will, or with that chaste love by which they cleaved to Him, in one and the same act creating their nature, and endowing it with grace? And thus we are driven to believe that the holy angels never existed without a good will or the love of God. But the angels who, though created good, are yet evil now, became so by their own will. And this will was not made evil by their good nature, unless by its voluntary defection from good; for good is not the cause of evil, but a defection from good is. These angels, therefore either received less of the grace of the divine love than those who persevered in the same; or if both were created equally good, then, while the one fell by their evil will, the others were more abundantly assisted, and attained to that pitch of blessedness at which they became certain they should never fall from it—as we have already shown in the preceding book.[1] We must therefore acknowledge, with the praise due to the Creator, that not only of holy men, but also of the holy angels, it can be said that "the love of God is shed abroad in their hearts by the Holy Ghost, which is given unto them."[2] And that not only of men, but primarily and principally of angels it is true, as it is written, "It is good to draw near to God."[3] And those who have this good in common, have, both with Him to Whom they draw near and with one another, a holy fellowship, and form one city of God—His living sacrifice and His living temple. And I see that, as I have now spoken of the rise of this city among the angels, it is time to speak of the origin of that part of it which is hereafter to be united to the immortal angels, and which at present is being gathered from among mortal men, and is either sojourning on earth, or, in the persons of those who have passed through death, is resting in the secret receptacles and abodes of disembodied spirits. For from one man, whom God created as the first, the whole human race descended, according to the faith of Holy Scripture, which deservedly is of wonderful authority among all nations throughout the world; since, among its other true statements, it predicted, by its divine foresight, that all nations would give credit to it.

CHAP. 10. *Of the falseness of the history which allots many thousand years to the world's past*

Let us, then, omit the conjectures of men who know not what they say, when they speak of the nature and origin of the human race. For some hold the same opinion regarding men that they hold regarding the world itself, that they have always been. Thus Apuleius says when he is describing our race, "Individually they are mortal, but collectively, and as a race, they are immortal." And when they are asked, how, if the human race has always been, they vindicate the truth of their history, which narrates who were the inventors, and what they invented, and who first instituted the liberal studies and the other arts, and who first inhabited this or that region, and this or that island? they reply[4] that most,

if not all lands, were so desolated at intervals by fire and flood, that men were greatly reduced in numbers, and from these, again, the population was restored to its former numbers, and that thus there was at intervals a new beginning made, and though those things which had been interrupted and checked by the severe devastations were only renewed, yet they seemed to be originated then; but that man could not exist at all save as produced by man. But they say what they think, not what they know.

They are deceived, too, by those highly mendacious documents which profess to give the history of many thousand years, though, reckoning by the sacred writings, we find that not 6000 years have yet passed.[5] And, not to spend many words in exposing the baselessness of these documents, in which so many thousands of years are accounted for, nor in proving that their authorities are totally inadequate, let me cite only that letter which Alexander the Great wrote to his mother Olympias,[6] giving her the narrative he had from an Egyptian priest, which he had extracted from their sacred archives, and which gave an account of kingdoms mentioned also by the Greek historians. In this letter of Alexander's a term of upwards of 5000 years is assigned to the kingdom of Assyria; while in the Greek history only 1300 years are reckoned from the reign of Bel himself, whom both Greek and Egyptian agree in counting the first king of Assyria. Then to the empire of the Persians and Macedonians this Egyptian assigned more than 8000 years, counting to the time of Alexander, to whom he was speaking; while among the Greeks, 485 years are assigned to the Macedonians down to the death of Alexander, and to the Persians 233 years, reckoning to the termination of his conquests. Thus these give a much smaller number of years than the Egyptians; and indeed, though multiplied three times, the Greek chronology would still be shorter. For the Egyptians are said to have formerly reckoned only four months to their year; so that one year, according to the fuller and truer computation now in use among them as well as among ourselves, would comprehend three of their old years. But not even thus, as I said, does the Greek history correspond with the Egyptian in its chronology. And therefore the former must receive the greater credit, because it does not

---

[1]Chap. 13.   [2]Rom. 5. 5.   [3]Ps. 73. 28.
[4]See Plato, *Timæus*.

[5]Augustine here follows the chronology of Eusebius, who reckons 5611 years from the Creation to the taking of Rome by the Goths, adopting the Septuagint version of the Patriarchal ages.
[6]See above, BK. VIII. 5.

exceed the true account of the duration of the world as it is given by our documents, which are truly sacred. Further, if this letter of Alexander, which has become so famous, differs widely in this matter of chronology from the probable credible account, how much less can we believe these documents which, though full of fabulous and fictitious antiquities, they would fain oppose to the authority of our well-known and divine books, which predicted that the whole world would believe them, and which the whole world accordingly has believed; which proved, too, that it had truly narrated past events by its prediction of future events, which have so exactly come to pass!

CHAP. 11. *Of those who suppose that this world indeed is not eternal, but that either there are numberless worlds, or that one and the same world is perpetually resolved into its elements, and renewed at the conclusion of fixed cycles*

There are some, again, who, though they do not suppose that this world is eternal, are of opinion either that this is not the only world, but that there are numberless worlds, or that indeed it is the only one, but that it dies, and is born again at fixed intervals, and this times without number; but they must acknowledge that the human race existed before there were other men to beget them. For they cannot suppose that, if the whole world perish, some men would be left alive in the world, as they might survive in floods and conflagrations, which those other speculators suppose to be partial, and from which they can therefore reasonably argue that a few men survived whose posterity would renew the population; but as they believe that the world itself is renewed out of its own material, so they must believe that out of its elements the human race was produced, and then that the progeny of mortals sprang like that of other animals from their parents.

CHAP. 12. *How these persons are to be answered, who find fault with the creation of man on the score of its recent date*

As to those who are always asking why man was not created during these countless ages of the infinitely extended past, and came into being so lately that, according to Scripture, less than 6000 years have elapsed since He began to be, I would reply to them regarding the creation of man, just as I replied regarding the origin of the world to those who will not believe that it is not eternal, but had a beginning, which even Plato

himself most plainly declares, though some think his statement was not consistent with his real opinion.[1] If it offends them that the time that has elapsed since the creation of man is so short, and his years so few according to our authorities, let them take this into consideration, that nothing that has a limit is long, and that all the ages of time being finite, are very little, or indeed nothing at all, when compared to the interminable eternity. Consequently, if there had elapsed since the creation of man, I do not say five or six, but even sixty or six hundred thousand years, or sixty times as many, or six hundred or six hundred thousand times as many, or this sum multiplied until it could no longer be expressed in numbers, the same question could still be put, "Why was he not made before?" For the past and boundless eternity during which God abstained from creating man is so great that, compare it with what vast and untold number of ages you please, so long as there is a definite conclusion of this term of time, it is not even as if you compared the minutest drop of water with the ocean that everywhere flows around the globe. For of these two, one indeed is very small, the other incomparably vast, yet both are finite; but that space of time which starts from some beginning, and is limited by some termination, be it of what extent it may, if you compare it with that which has no beginning, I know not whether to say we should count it the very minutest thing, or nothing at all. For, take this limited time, and deduct from the end of it, one by one, the briefest moments (as you might take day by day from a man's life, beginning at the day in which he now lives, back to that of his birth), and though the number of moments you must subtract in this backward movement be so great that no word can express it, yet this subtraction will sometime carry you to the beginning. But if you take away from a time which has no beginning, I do not say brief moments one by one, nor yet hours, or days, or months, or years even in quantities, but terms of years so vast that they cannot be named by the most skillful arithmeticians—take away terms of years as vast as that which we have supposed to be gradually consumed by the deduction of moments—and take them away not once and again repeatedly, but always, and what do you effect, what do you make by your deduction, since you never reach the beginning, which has no existence? Wherefore, that which we now demand after five thousand odd years, our

[1] The Alexandrian Neo-Platonists endeavoured in this way to escape from the obvious meaning of the *Timæus*.

descendants might with like curiosity demand after six hundred thousand years, supposing these dying generations of men continue so long to decay and be renewed, and supposing posterity continues as weak and ignorant as ourselves. The same question might have been asked by those who have lived before us and while man was even newer upon earth. The first man himself in short might the day after or the very day of his creation have asked why he was created no sooner. And no matter at what earlier or later period he had been created, this controversy about the commencement of this world's history would have had precisely the same difficulties as it has now.

CHAP. 13. *Of the revolution of the ages, which some philosophers believe will bring all things round again, after a certain fixed cycle, to the same order and form as at first*

This controversy some philosophers have seen no other approved means of solving than by introducing cycles of time, in which there should be a constant renewal and repetition of the order of nature;[1] and they have therefore asserted that these cycles will ceaselessly recur, one passing away and another coming, though they are not agreed as to whether one permanent world shall pass through all these cycles, or whether the world shall at fixed intervals die out and be renewed so as to exhibit a recurrence of the same phenomena—the things which have been and those which are to be coinciding. And from this fantastic vicissitude they exempt not even the immortal soul that has attained wisdom, consigning it to a ceaseless transmigration between delusive blessedness and real misery. For how can that be truly called blessed which has no assurance of being so eternally, and is either in ignorance of the truth, and blind to the misery that is approaching, or, knowing it, is in misery and fear? Or if it passes to bliss, and leaves miseries forever, then there happens in time a new thing which time shall not end. Why not, then, the world also? Why may not man, too, be a similar thing? So that, by following the straight path of sound doctrine, we escape, I know not what circuitous paths, discovered by deceiving and deceived sages.

Some, too, in advocating these recurring cycles that restore all things to their original cite in favour of their supposition what Solomon says in the book of Ecclesiastes: "What is that which hath been? It is that which shall be. And what is that which is done? It is that which shall be done: and there is no new thing under the sun. Who can speak and say, See, this is new? It hath been already of old time, which was before us."[2] This he said either of those things of which he had just been speaking—the succession of generations, the orbit of the sun, the course of rivers—or else of all kinds of creatures that are born and die. For men were before us, are with us, and shall be after us; and so all living things and all plants. Even monstrous and irregular productions, though differing from one another, and though some are reported as solitary instances, yet resemble one another generally, in so far as they are miraculous and monstrous, and, in this sense, have been, and shall be, and are no new and recent things under the sun. However, some would understand these words as meaning that in the predestination of God all things have already existed, and that thus there is no new thing under the sun. At all events, far be it from any true believer to suppose that by these words of Solomon those cycles are meant, in which, according to those philosophers, the same periods and events of time are repeated; as if, for example, the philosopher Plato, having taught in the school at Athens which is called the Academy, so, numberless ages before, at long but certain intervals, this same Plato and the same school, and the same disciples existed, and so also are to be repeated during the countless cycles that are yet to be— far be it, I say, from us to believe this. For once Christ died for our sins; and, rising from the dead, He dieth no more. "Death hath no more dominion over Him";[3] and we ourselves after the resurrection shall be "ever with the Lord,"[4] to whom we now say, as the sacred Psalmist dictates, "Thou shalt keep us, O Lord, Thou shalt preserve us from this generation."[5] And that too which follows, is, I think, appropriate enough: "The wicked walk *in a circle*"; not because their life is to recur by means of these circles, which these philosophers imagine, but because the path in which their false doctrine now runs is circuitous.

CHAP. 14. *Of the creation of the human race in time, and how this was effected without any new design or change of purpose on God's part*

What wonder is it if, entangled in these circles, they find neither entrance nor egress? For they know not how the human race, and this

---

[1] M. Aurelius says (II. 14): "All things from eternity are of like forms, and come round in a circle." *Ibid.*, IX. 28.

[2] Eccles. I. 9, 10.   [3] Rom. 6. 9.   [4] I Thess. 4. 16.
[5] Ps. 12. 7.

mortal condition of ours, took its origin, nor how it will be brought to an end, since they cannot penetrate the inscrutable wisdom of God. For, though Himself eternal and without beginning, yet He caused time to have a beginning; and man, whom He had not previously made He made in time, not from a new and sudden resolution, but by His unchangeable and eternal design. Who can search out the unsearchable depth of this purpose, who can scrutinize the inscrutable wisdom, wherewith God, without change of will, created man, who had never before been, and gave him an existence in time, and increased the human race from one individual? For the Psalmist himself, when he had first said, "Thou shalt keep us, O Lord, Thou shalt preserve us from this generation for ever," and had then rebuked those whose foolish and impious doctrine preserves for the soul no eternal deliverance and blessedness, adds immediately, "The wicked walk in a circle." Then, as if it were said to him, "What then do you believe, feel, know? Are we to believe that it suddenly occurred to God to create man, whom He had never before made in a past eternity—God, to whom nothing new can occur, and in Whom is no changeableness?" the Psalmist goes on to reply, as if addressing God Himself, "According to the depth of Thy wisdom Thou hast multiplied the children of men." Let men, he seems to say, fancy what they please, let them conjecture and dispute as seems good to them, but Thou hast multiplied the children of men according to the depth of Thy wisdom, which no man can comprehend. For this is a depth indeed, that God always has been, and that man, whom He had never made before, He willed to make in time, and this without changing His design and will.

CHAP. 15. *Whether we are to believe that God, as he has always been sovereign Lord, has always had creatures over whom He exercised his sovereignty; and in what sense we can say that the creature has always been, and yet cannot say it is co-eternal*

For my own part, indeed, as I dare not say that there ever was a time when the Lord God was not Lord, so I ought not to doubt that man had no existence before time, and was first created in time. But when I consider what God could be the Lord of, if there was not always some creature, I shrink from making any assertion, remembering my own insignificance and that it is written, "What man is he that can know the counsel of God? or who can think what the will of the Lord is? For the thoughts

of mortal men are timid, and our devices are but uncertain. For the corruptible body presseth down the soul, and the earthly tabernacle weigheth down the mind that museth upon many things."[1] Many things certainly do I muse upon in this earthly tabernacle, because the one thing which is true among the many, or beyond the many, I cannot find. If, then, among these many thoughts, I say that there have always been creatures for Him to be Lord of, Who is always and ever has been Lord, but that these creatures have not always been the same, but succeeded one another (for we would not seem to say that any is co-eternal with the Creator, an assertion condemned equally by faith and sound reason), I must take care lest I fall into the absurd and ignorant error of maintaining that by these successions and changes mortal creatures have always existed, whereas the immortal creatures had not begun to exist until the date of our own world, when the angels were created; if at least the angels are intended by that light which was first made, or, rather, by that heaven of which it is said, "In the beginning God created the heavens and the earth."[2] The angels, at least, did not exist before they were created; for if we say that they have always existed, we shall seem to make them co-eternal with the Creator. Again, if I say that the angels were not created in time, but existed before all times, as those over whom God, Who has ever been Sovereign, exercised His sovereignty, then I shall be asked whether, if they were created before all time, they, being creatures, could possibly always exist. It may perhaps be replied, "Why not *always*, since that which is in all time may very properly be said to be 'always'?" Now so true is it that these angels have existed in all time that even before time was they were created; if at least time began with the heavens, and the angels existed before the heavens. And if time was even before the heavenly bodies, not indeed marked by hours, days, months, and years—for these measures of time's periods which are commonly and properly called times, did manifestly begin with the motion of the heavenly bodies, and so God said, when He appointed them, "Let them be for signs, and for seasons, and for days, and for years"[3]—if, I say, time was before these heavenly bodies by some changing movement, whose parts succeeded one another and could not exist simultaneously, and if there was some such movement among the angels which necessitated the existence of time, and that they from their very creation should be subject to these temporal

[1]Wisd. 9. 13-15.   [2]Gen. 1. 1.   [3]Gen. 1. 14.

changes, then they have existed in all time, for time came into being along with them. And who will say that what was in all time, was not always.

But if I make such a reply, it will be said to me, "How, then, are they not co-eternal with the Creator, if He and they always have been? How even can they be said to have been created, if we are to understand that they have always existed?" What shall we reply to this? Shall we say that both statements are true? that they always have been, since they have been in all time, they being created along with time, or time along with them, and yet that also they were created? For, similarly, we will not deny that time itself was created, though no one doubts that time has been in all time; for if it has not been in all time, then there was a time when there was no time. But the most foolish person could not make such an assertion. For we can reasonably say there was a time when Rome was not; there was a time when Jerusalem was not; there was a time when Abraham was not; there was a time when man was not, and so on: in fine, if the world was not made at the commencement of time, but after some time had elapsed, we can say there was a time when the world was not. But to say there was a time when time was not, is as absurd as to say there was a man when there was no man; or, this world was when this world was not. For if we are not referring to the same object, the form of expression may be used, as, there was another man when this man was not. Thus we can reasonably say there was another time when this time was not; but not the merest simpleton could say there was a time when there was no time. As, then, we say that time was created, though we also say that it always has been, since in all time time has been, so it does not follow that if the angels have always been, they were therefore not created. For we say that they have always been, because they have been in all time; and we say they have been in all time, because time itself could no wise be without them. For where there is no creature whose changing movements admit of succession, there cannot be time at all. And consequently, even if they have always existed, they were created; neither, if they have always existed, are they therefore co-eternal with the Creator. For He has always existed in unchangeable eternity; while they were created, and are said to have been always, because they have been in all time, time being impossible without the creature. But time passing away by its changefulness, cannot

be co-eternal with changeless eternity. And consequently, though the immortality of the angels does not pass in time, does not become past as if now it were not, nor has a future as if it were not yet, still their movements, which are the basis of time, do pass from future to past; and therefore they cannot be co-eternal with the Creator, in whose movement we cannot say that there has been that which now is not, or shall be that which is not yet. Wherefore, if God always has been Lord, He has always had creatures under His dominion—creatures, however, not begotten of Him, but created by Him out of nothing; nor co-eternal with Him, for He was before them though at no time without them, because He preceded them, not by the lapse of time, but by His abiding eternity. But if I make this reply to those who demand how He was always Creator, always Lord, if there were not always a subject creation; or how this was created, and not rather co-eternal with its Creator, if it always was, I fear I may be accused of recklessly affirming what I know not, instead of teaching what I know. I return, therefore, to that which our Creator has seen fit that we should know; and those things which He has allowed the abler men to know in this life, or has reserved to be known in the next by the perfected saints, I acknowledge to be beyond my capacity. But I have thought it right to discuss these matters without making positive assertions, that they who read may be warned to abstain from hazardous questions, and may not deem themselves fit for everything. Let them rather endeavour to obey the wholesome injunction of the apostle, when he says, "For I say, through the grace given unto me, to every man that is among you, not to think of himself more highly than he ought to think; but to think soberly, according as God hath dealt to every man the measure of faith."[1] For if an infant receive nourishment suited to its strength, it becomes capable, as it grows, of taking more; but if its strength and capacity be overtaxed, it dwines away in place of growing.

CHAP. 16. *How we are to understand God's promise of life eternal, which was uttered before the "eternal times"*

I own that I do not know what ages passed before the human race was created, yet I have no doubt that no created thing is co-eternal with the Creator. But even the apostle speaks of time as eternal, and this with reference, not to the future, but, which is more surprising, to the

[1] Rom. 12. 3.

past. For he says, "In hope of eternal life, which God that cannot lie promised before the eternal times, but hath in due times manifested His word."[1] You see he says that in the past there have been eternal times, which, however, were not co-eternal with God. And since God before these eternal times not only existed, but also, "promised" life eternal, which He manifested in its own times (that is to say, in due times), what else is this than His word? For this is life eternal. But then, how did He promise; for the promise was made to men, and yet they had no existence before eternal times? Does this not mean that, in His own eternity and in His co-eternal word, that which was to be in its own time was already predestined and fixed?

CHAP. 17. *What defence is made by sound faith regarding God's unchangeable counsel and will, against the reasonings of those who hold that the works of God are eternally repeated in revolving cycles that restore all things as they were*

Of this, too, I have no doubt, that before the first man was created, there never had been a man at all, neither this same man himself recurring by I know not what cycles, and having made I know not how many revolutions, nor any other of similar nature. From this belief I am not frightened by philosophical arguments, among which that is reckoned the most acute which is founded on the assertion that the infinite cannot be comprehended by any mode of knowledge. Consequently, they argue, God has in his own mind finite conceptions of all finite things which He makes. Now it cannot be supposed that His goodness was ever idle; for if it were, there should be ascribed to Him an awakening to activity in time, from a past eternity of inactivity, as if He repented of an idleness that had no beginning, and proceeded, therefore, to make a beginning of work. This being the case, they say it must be that the same things are always repeated, and that as they pass, so they are destined always to return, whether amidst all these changes the world remains the same—the world which has always been, and yet was created—or that the world in these revolutions is perpetually dying out and being renewed; otherwise, if we point to a time when the works of God were begun, it would be believed that He considered His past eternal leisure to be inert and indolent, and therefore condemned and altered it as displeasing to Himself. Now if God is

supposed to have been indeed always making temporal things, but different from one another, and one after the other, so, that He thus came at last to make man, whom He had never made before, then it may seem that He made man not with knowledge (for they suppose no knowledge can comprehend the infinite succession of creatures), but at the dictate of the hour, as it struck Him at the moment, with a sudden and accidental change of mind. On the other hand, say they, if those cycles be admitted, and if we suppose that the same temporal things are repeated, while the world either remains identical through all these rotations, or else dies away and is renewed, then there is ascribed to God neither the slothful ease of a past eternity, nor a rash and unforeseen creation. And if the same things be not thus repeated in cycles, then they cannot by any science or prescience be comprehended in their endless diversity. Even though reason could not refute, faith would smile at these argumentations, with which the godless endeavour to turn our simple piety from the right way that we may walk with them "in a circle." But by the help of the Lord our God, even reason, and that readily enough, shatters these revolving circles which conjecture frames. For that which specially leads these men astray to prefer their own circles to the straight path of truth is that they measure by their own human, changeable, and narrow intellect the divine mind, which is absolutely unchangeable, infinitely capacious, and without succession of thought, counting all things without number. So that saying of the apostle comes true of them, for, "comparing themselves with themselves, they do not understand."[2] For because they do, in virtue of a new purpose, whatever new thing has occurred to them to be done (their minds being changeable), they conclude it is so with God; and thus compare, not God—for they cannot conceive God, but think of one like themselves when they think of Him—not God, but themselves, and not with Him, but with themselves. For our part, we dare not believe that God is affected in one way when He works, in another when He rests. Indeed, to say that He is affected at all, is an abuse of language, since it implies that there comes to be something in His nature which was not there before. For he who is affected is acted upon, and whatever is acted upon is changeable. His leisure, therefore, is no laziness, indolence, inactivity; as in His work is no labour, effort, industry. He can act while He reposes, and repose

---

[1] Titus, 1. 2, 3. Augustine here follows the version of Jerome, and not the Vulgate.

[2] II Cor. 10. 12. Here Augustine follows the Greek, and not the Vulgate.

while He acts. He can begin a new work with (not a new, but) an eternal design; and what He has not made before, He does not now begin to make because He repents of His former repose. But when one speaks of His former repose and subsequent operation (and I know not how men can understand these things), this "former" and "subsequent" are applied only to the things created, which formerly did not exist and subsequently came into existence. But in God the former purpose is not altered and obliterated by the subsequent and different purpose, but by one and the same eternal and unchangeable will He effected regarding the things He created, both that formerly, so long as they were not, they should not be, and that subsequently, when they began to be, they should come into existence. And thus, perhaps, He would show, in a very striking way, to those who have eyes for such things, how independent He is of what He makes, and how it is of His own gratuitous goodness He creates, since from eternity He dwelt without creatures in no less perfect a blessedness.

CHAP. 18. *Against those who assert that things that are infinite cannot be comprehended by the knowledge of God*

As for their other assertion, that God's knowledge cannot comprehend things infinite, it only remains for them to affirm, in order that they may sound the depths of their impiety, that God does not know all numbers. For it is very certain that they are infinite; since, no matter of what number you suppose an end to be made, this number can be, I will not say, increased by the addition of one more, but however great it be, and however vast be the multitude of which it is the rational and scientific expression, it can still be not only doubled, but even multiplied. Moreover, each number is so defined by its own properties, that no two numbers are equal. They are therefore both unequal and different from one another; and while they are simply finite, collectively they are infinite. Does God, therefore, not know numbers on account of this infinity; and does His knowledge extend only to a certain height in numbers, while of the rest He is ignorant? Who is so left to himself as to say so? Yet they can hardly pretend to put numbers out of the question, or maintain that they have nothing to do with the knowledge of God; for Plato,[1] their great authority, represents God as framing the world on numerical principles: and in our books also it is said to God, "Thou hast ordered

all things in number, and measure, and weight."[2] The prophet also says, "Who bringeth out their host by number."[3] And the Saviour says in the Gospel, "The very hairs of your head are all numbered."[4] Far be it, then, from us to doubt that all number is known to Him "whose understanding," according to the Psalmist, "is infinite."[5] The infinity of number, though there be no numbering of infinite numbers, is yet not incomprehensible by Him whose understanding is infinite. And thus, if everything which is comprehended is defined or made finite by the comprehension of him who knows it, then all infinity is in some ineffable way made finite to God, for it is comprehensible by His knowledge. Wherefore, if the infinity of numbers cannot be infinite to the knowledge of God, by which it is comprehended, what are we poor creatures that we should presume to fix limits to His knowledge and say that unless the same temporal thing be repeated by the same periodic revolutions, God cannot either foreknow His creatures that He may make them, or know them when He has made them? God, whose knowledge is simply manifold, and uniform in its variety, comprehends all incomprehensibles with so incomprehensible a comprehension that, though He willed always to make His later works novel and unlike what went before them, He could not produce them without order and foresight, nor conceive them suddenly, but by His eternal foreknowledge.

CHAP. 19. *Of worlds without end, or ages of ages*

I do not presume to determine whether God does so, and whether these times which are called "ages of ages" are joined together in a continuous series, and succeed one another with a regulated diversity, and leave exempt from their vicissitudes only those who are freed from their misery, and abide without end in a blessed immortality; or whether these are called "ages of ages," that we may understand that the ages remain unchangeable in God's unwavering wisdom, and are the efficient causes, as it were, of those ages which are being spent in time. Possibly "ages" is used for "age," so that nothing else is meant by "ages of ages" than by "age of age," as nothing else is meant by "heavens of heavens" than by "heaven of heaven." For God called the firmament, above which are the waters, "Heaven," and yet the psalm says, "Let the waters that are above the *heavens* praise the name of the Lord."[6] Which of these two mean-

[1] In the *Timæus*.

[2] Wisd. 11. 20.   [3] Isa. 40. 26.   [4] Matt. 10. 30.
[5] Ps. 147. 5.   [6] Ps. 148. 4.

ings we are to attach to "ages of ages," or wheth-er there is not some other and better meaning still, is a very profound question; and the sub-ject we are at present handling presents no ob-stacle to our meanwhile deferring the discussion of it, whether we may be able to determine any-thing about it, or may only be made more cau-tious by its further treatment, so as to be de-terred from making any rash affirmations in a matter of such obscurity. For at present we are disputing the opinion that affirms the existence of those periodic revolutions by which the same things are always recurring at intervals of time. Now, whichever of these suppositions regarding the "ages of ages" be the true one, it avails nothing for the substantiating of those cycles; for whether the ages of ages be not a repetition of the same world, but different worlds succeed-ing one another in a regulated connection, the ransomed souls abiding in well-assured bliss without any recurrence of misery, or whether the ages of ages be the eternal causes which rule what shall be and is in time, it equally follows that those cycles which bring round the same things have no existence; and nothing more thoroughly explodes them than the fact of the eternal life of the saints.

CHAP. 20. *Of the impiety of those who assert that the souls which enjoy true and perfect blessedness, must yet again and again in these periodic revolutions return to labour and mis-ery*

What pious ears could bear to hear that after a life spent in so many and severe distresses (if, indeed, that should be called a life at all which is rather a death, so utter that the love of this present death makes us fear that death which delivers us from it), that after evils so disas-trous and miseries of all kinds have at length been expiated and finished by the help of true re-ligion and wisdom, and when we have thus at-tained to the vision of God, and have entered in-to bliss by the contemplation of spiritual light and participation in His unchangeable immor-tality, which we burn to attain—that we must at some time lose all this, and that they who do lose it are cast down from that eternity, truth, and felicity to infernal mortality and shameful foolishness, and are involved in accursed woes, in which God is lost, truth held in detestation, and happiness sought in iniquitous impurities? and that this will happen endlessly again and again, recurring at fixed intervals, and in regu-larly returning periods? and that this everlast-ing and ceaseless revolution of definite cycles,

which remove and restore true misery and de-ceitful bliss in turn, is contrived in order that God may be able to know His own works, since on the one hand He cannot rest from creating and on the other, cannot know the infinite num-ber of His creatures, if He always makes crea-tures? Who, I say, can listen to such things? Who can accept or suffer them to be spoken? Were they true, it were not only more prudent to keep silence regarding them, but even (to ex-press myself as best I can) it were the part of wisdom not to know them. For if in the future world we shall not remember these things and by this oblivion be blessed, why should we now increase our misery, already burdensome enough, by the knowledge of them? If, on the other hand, the knowledge of them will be forced up-on us hereafter, now at least let us remain in ig-norance, that in the present expectation we may enjoy a blessedness which the future reality is not to bestow; since in this life we are expecting to obtain life everlasting, but in the world to come are to discover it to be blessed, but not everlasting.

And if they maintain that no one can attain to the blessedness of the world to come, unless in this life he has been indoctrinated in those cycles in which bliss and misery relieve one another, how do they avow that the more a man loves God, the more readily he attains to blessedness —they who teach what paralyzes love itself? For who would not be more remiss and luke-warm in his love for a person whom he thinks he shall be forced to abandon, and whose truth and wisdom he shall come to hate; and this, too, aft-er he has quite attained to the utmost and most blissful knowledge of Him that he is capable of? Can any one be faithful in his love, even to a hu-man friend, if he knows that he is destined to become his enemy? God forbid that there be any truth in an opinion which threatens us with a real misery that is never to end, but is often and endlessly to be interrupted by intervals of fallacious happiness. For what happiness can be more fallacious and false than that in whose blaze of truth we yet remain ignorant that we shall be miserable, or in whose most secure cita-del we yet fear that we shall be so? For if, on the one hand, we are to be ignorant of coming calamity, then our present misery is not so short-sighted for it is assured of coming bliss. If, on the other hand, the disaster that threatens is not concealed from us in the world to come, then the time of misery which is to be at last ex-changed for a state of blessedness, is spent by the soul more happily than its time of happiness, which is to end in a return to misery. And thus our expectation of unhappiness is happy, but of happiness unhappy. And therefore, as we here suffer present ills, and hereafter fear ills that are imminent, it were truer to say that we shall always be miserable than that we can some time be happy.

But these things are declared to be false by the loud testimony of religion and truth; for religion truthfully promises a true blessedness, of which we shall be eternally assured, and which cannot be interrupted by any disaster. Let us therefore keep to the straight path, which is Christ, and, with Him as our Guide and Saviour, let us turn away in heart and mind from the unreal and futile cycles of the godless. Porphyry, Platonist though he was, abjured the opinion of his school that in these cycles souls are ceaselessly passing away and returning, either being struck with the extravagance of the idea, or sobered by his knowledge of Christianity. As I mentioned in the tenth book,[1] he preferred saying that the soul, as it had been sent into the world that it might know evil and be purged and delivered from it, was never again exposed to such an experience after it had once returned to the Father. And if he abjured the tenets of his school, how much more ought we Christians to abominate and avoid an opinion so unfounded and hostile to our faith? But having disposed of these cycles and escaped out of them, no necessity compels us to suppose that the human race had no beginning in time, on the ground that there is nothing new in nature which, by I know not what cycles, has not at some previous period existed, and is not hereafter to exist again. For if the soul, once delivered, as it never was before, is never to return to misery, then there happens in its experience something which never happened before; and this, indeed, something of the greatest consequence, to wit, the secure entrance into eternal felicity. And if in an immortal nature there can occur a novelty, which never has been, nor ever shall be, reproduced by any cycle, why is it disputed that the same may occur in mortal natures? If they maintain that blessedness is no new experience to the soul, but only a return to that state in which it has been eternally, then at least its deliverance from misery is something new, since, by their own showing, the misery from which it is delivered is itself, too, a new experience. And if this new experience fell out by accident, and was not embraced in the order of things appointed by Divine Providence, then

[1]Chap. 30.

where are those determinate and measured cycles in which no new thing happens, but all things are reproduced as they were before? If, however, this new experience was embraced in that providential order of nature (whether the soul was exposed to the evil of this world for the sake of discipline, or fell into it by sin), then it is possible for new things to happen which never happened before and which yet are not extraneous to the order of nature. And if the soul is able by its own imprudence to create for itself a new misery, which was not unforeseen by the Divine Providence, but was provided for in the order of nature along with the deliverance from it, how can we, even with all the rashness of human vanity, presume to deny that God can create new things—new to the world, but not to Him—which He never before created, but yet foresaw from all eternity? If they say that it is indeed true that ransomed souls return no more to misery, but that even so no new thing happens, since there always have been, now are, and ever shall be, a succession of ransomed souls, they must at least grant that in this case there are new souls to whom the misery and the deliverance from it are new. For if they maintain that those souls out of which new men are daily being made (from whose bodies, if they have lived wisely, they are so delivered that they never return to misery) are not new, but have existed from eternity, they must logically admit that they are infinite. For however great a finite number of souls there were, that would not have sufficed to make perpetually new men from eternity—men whose souls were to be eternally freed from this mortal state, and never afterwards to return to it. And our philosophers will find it hard to explain how there is an infinite number of souls in an order of nature which they require shall be finite, that it may be known by God.

And now that we have exploded these cycles which were supposed to bring back the soul at fixed periods to the same miseries, what can seem more in accordance with godly reason than to believe that it is possible for God both to create new things never before created, and in doing so, to preserve His will unaltered? But whether the number of eternally redeemed souls can be continually increased or not, let the philosophers themselves decide, who are so subtle in determining where infinity cannot be admitted. For our own part, our reasoning holds in either case. For if the number of souls can be indefinitely increased, what reason is there to deny that what had never before been created, could be created? since the number of ransomed souls never existed before, and has yet not only been once made, but will never cease to be anew coming into being. If, on the other hand, it be more suitable that the number of eternally ransomed souls be definite, and that this number will never be increased, yet this number, whatever it be, did assuredly never exist before, and it cannot increase, and reach the amount it signifies, without having some beginning; and this beginning never before existed. That this beginning, therefore, might be, the first man was created.

CHAP. 21. *That there was created at first but one individual, and that the human race was created in him*

Now that we have solved, as well as we could, this very difficult question about the eternal God creating new things, without any novelty of will, it is easy to see how much better it is that God was pleased to produce the human race from the one individual whom He created, than if He had originated it in several men. For as to the other animals, He created some solitary, and naturally seeking lonely places—as the eagles, kites, lions, wolves, and such like; others gregarious, which herd together, and prefer to live in company—as pigeons, starlings, stags, and little fallow deer, and the like: but neither class did He cause to be propagated from individuals, but called into being several at once. Man, on the other hand, whose nature was to be a mean between the angelic and bestial, He created in such sort that if he remained in subjection to His Creator as his rightful Lord, and piously kept His Commandments, he should pass into the company of the angels, and obtain, without the intervention of death,[1] a blessed and endless immortality; but if he offended the Lord his God by a proud and disobedient use of his free will, he should become subject to death, and live as the beasts do—the slave of appetite and doomed to eternal punishment after death. And therefore God created only one single man, not, certainly, that he might be a solitary, bereft of all society, but that by this means the unity of society and the bond of concord might be more effectually commended to him, men being bound together not only by similarity of nature, but by family affection. And indeed He did not even create the woman that was to be given him as his wife, as he created the man, but created her out of the man, that the whole human race might derive from one man.

[1] This is levelled against the Pelagians.

CHAP. 22. *That God foreknew that the first man would sin, and that he at the same time foresaw how large a multitude of godly persons would by His grace be translated to the fellowship of the angels*

And God was not ignorant that man would sin, and that, being himself made subject now to death, he would propagate men doomed to die, and that these mortals would run to such enormities in sin that even the beasts devoid of rational will, and who were created in numbers from the waters and the earth, would live more securely and peaceably with their own kind than men, who had been propagated from one individual for the very purpose of commending concord. For not even lions or dragons have ever waged with their kind such wars as men have waged with one another. But God foresaw also that by His grace a people would be called to adoption, and that they, being justified by the remission of their sins, would be united by the Holy Ghost to the holy angels in eternal peace, the last enemy, death, being destroyed; and He knew that this people would derive profit from the consideration that God had caused all men to be derived from one, for the sake of showing how highly He prizes unity in a multitude.

CHAP. 23. *Of the nature of the human soul created in the image of God*

God, then, made man in His own image. For He created for him a soul endowed with reason and intelligence, so that he might excel all the creatures of earth, air, and sea, which were not so gifted. And when He had formed the man out of the dust of the earth, and had willed that his soul should be such as I have said—whether He had already made it, and now by breathing imparted it to man, or rather made it by breathing, so that that breath which God made by breathing (for what else is "to breathe" than to make breath?) is the soul—He made also a wife for him, to aid him in the work of generating his kind, and her He formed of a bone taken out of the man's side, working in a divine manner. For we are not to conceive of this work in a carnal fashion, as if God wrought as we commonly see artisans, who use their hands and material furnished to them that by their artistic skill they may fashion some material object. God's hand is God's power; and He, working invisibly, effects visible results. But this seems fabulous rather than true to men, who measure by customary and everyday works the power and wisdom of God, whereby He understands and produces without seeds even seeds themselves; and because they cannot understand the things which at the beginning were created, they are sceptical regarding them—as if the very things which they do know about human propagation, conceptions and births, would seem less incredible if told to those who had no experience of them; though these very things, too, are attributed by many rather to physical and natural causes than to the work of the divine mind.

CHAP. 24. *Whether the angels can be said to be the creators of any, even the least creature*

But in this book we have nothing to do with those who do not believe that the divine mind made or cares for this world. As for those who believe their own Plato, that all mortal animals—among whom man holds the pre-eminent place, and is near to the gods themselves—were created not by that most high God Who made the world, but by other lesser gods created by the Supreme, and exercising a delegated power under His control—if only those persons be delivered from the superstition which prompts them to seek a plausible reason for paying divine honours and sacrificing to these gods as their creators, they will easily be disentangled also from this their error. For it is blasphemy to believe or to say (even before it can be understood) that any other than God is creator of any nature, be it never so small and mortal. And as for the angels, whom those Platonists prefer to call gods, although they do, so far as they are permitted and commissioned, aid in the production of the things around us, yet not on that account are we to call them creators, any more than we call gardeners the creators of fruits and trees.

CHAP. 25. *That God alone is the Creator of every kind of creature, whatever its nature or form*

For whereas there is one form which is given from without to every bodily substance—such as the form which is constructed by potters and smiths, and that class of artists who paint and fashion forms like the body of animals—but another and internal form which is not itself constructed, but, as the efficient cause, produces not only the natural bodily forms, but even the life itself of the living creatures, and which proceeds from the secret and hidden choice of an intelligent and living nature—let that first-mentioned form be attributed to every artificer, but this latter to one only, God, the Creator and Originator Who made the world itself and the angels, without the help of world or angels. For the same divine and, so to speak, creative energy, which cannot be made, but makes, and which gave to the earth and sky their roundness—this same divine, effective, and creative energy gave their roundness to the eye and to the apple; and the other natural objects which we anywhere see, received also their form, not from without, but from the secret and profound might of the Creator, Who said, "Do not I fill heaven and earth?"[1] and Whose wisdom it is that "reacheth from one end to another mightily; and sweetly doth she order all things."[2] Wherefore I know not what kind of aid the angels, themselves created first, afforded to the Creator in making other things. I cannot ascribe to them what perhaps they cannot do, neither ought I to deny them such faculty as they have. But, by their leave, I attribute the creating and originating work which gave being to all natures to God, to Whom they themselves thankfully ascribe their existence. We do not call gardeners the creators of their fruits, for we read, "Neither is he that planteth anything, neither he that watereth, but God that giveth the increase."[3] Nay, not even the earth itself do we call a creator, though she seems to be the prolific mother of all things which she aids in germinating and bursting forth from the seed, and which she keeps rooted in her own breast; for we likewise read, "God giveth it a body, as it hath pleased Him, and to every seed his own body."[4] We ought not even to call a woman the creatress of her own offspring; for He rather is its creator Who said to His servant, "Before I formed thee in the womb, I knew thee."[5] And although the various mental emotions of a pregnant woman do produce in the fruit of her womb similar qualities—as Jacob with his peeled wands caused piebald sheep to be produced—yet the mother as little creates her offspring as she created herself. Whatever bodily or seminal causes, then, may be used for the production of things, either by the co-operation of angels, men, or the lower animals, or by sexual generation; and whatever power the desires and mental emotions of the mother have to produce in the tender and plastic fœtus corresponding lineaments and colours; yet the natures themselves, which are thus variously affected, are the production of none but the most high God. It is His occult power which pervades all things, and is present in all without being contaminated, which gives being to all that is, and modifies and limits its existence; so that without

[1]Jer. 23. 24. [2]Wisd. 8. 1. [3]I Cor. 3. 7.
[4]I Cor. 15. 38. [5]Jer. 1. 5.

Him it would not be thus, or thus, nor would have any being at all. If, then, in regard to that outward form which the workman's hand imposes on his work, we do not say that Rome and Alexandria were built by masons and architects, but by the kings by whose will, plan, and resources they were built, so that the one has Romulus, the other Alexander, for its founder; with how much greater reason ought we to say that God alone is the Author of all natures, since He neither uses for His work any material which was not made by Him, nor any workmen who were not also made by Him, and since, if He were, so to speak, to withdraw from created things His creative power, they would straightway relapse into the nothingness in which they were before they were created? "Before," I mean, in respect of eternity, not of time. For what other creator could there be of time, than He who created those things whose movements make time?[1]

CHAP. 26. *Of that opinion of the Platonists, that the angels were themselves indeed created by God, but that afterwards they created man's body*

It is obvious, that in attributing the creation of the other animals to those inferior gods who were made by the Supreme, he meant it to be understood that the immortal part was taken from God Himself, and that these minor creators added the mortal part; that is to say, he meant them to be considered the creators of our bodies, but not of our souls. But since Porphyry maintains that if the soul is to be purified, all entanglement with a body must be escaped from; and at the same time agrees with Plato and the Platonists in thinking that those who have not spent a temperate and honourable life return to mortal bodies as their punishment (to bodies of brutes in Plato's opinion, to human bodies in Porphyry's); it follows that those whom they would have us worship as our parents and authors, that they may plausibly call them gods, are, after all, but the forgers of our fetters and chains—not our creators, but our jailers and turnkeys, who lock us up in the most bitter and melancholy house of correction. Let the Platonists, then, either cease menacing us with our bodies as the punishment of our souls, or preaching that we are to worship as gods those whose work upon us they exhort us by all means in our power to avoid and escape from. But, indeed, both opinions are quite false. It is false that souls return again to this life to be punished;

and it is false that there is any other creator of anything in heaven or earth, then He Who made the heaven and the earth. For if we live in a body only to expiate our sins, how says Plato in another place, that the world could not have been the most beautiful and good, had it not been filled with all kinds of creatures, mortal and immortal?[2] But if our creation even as mortals be a divine benefit, how is it a punishment to be restored to a body, that is, to a divine benefit? And if God, as Plato continually maintains, embraced in His eternal intelligence the ideas both of the universe and of all the animals, how, then, should He not with His own hand make them all? Could He be unwilling to be the constructor of works, the idea and plan of which called for His ineffable and ineffably to be praised intelligence?

CHAP. 27. *That the whole plentitude of the human race was embraced in the first man, and that God there saw the portion of it which was to be honoured and rewarded, and that which was to be condemned and punished*

With good cause, therefore, does the true religion recognize and proclaim that the same God who created the universal cosmos, created also all the animals, souls as well as bodies. Among the terrestrial animals man was made by Him in His own image, and, for the reason I have given, was made one individual, though he was not left solitary. For there is nothing so social by nature, so unsocial by its corruption, as this race. And human nature has nothing more appropriate, either for the prevention of discord, or for the healing of it, where it exists, than the remembrance of that first parent of us all, whom God was pleased to create alone, that all men might be derived from one, and that they might thus be admonished to preserve unity among their whole multitude. But from the fact that the woman was made for him from his side, it was plainly meant that we should learn how dear the bond between man and wife should be. These works of God do certainly seem extraordinary, because they are the first works. They who do not believe them, ought not to believe any prodigies; for these would not be called prodigies did they not happen out of the ordinary course of nature. But, is it possible that anything should happen in vain, however hidden be its cause, in so grand a government of divine providence? One of the sacred Psalmists says, "Come, behold the works of the Lord, what prodigies He hath wrought in the earth."[3] Why God made woman

[1]See BK. XI, chap. 5.

[2]See *Timæus*, 41.   [3]Ps. 46. 8.

out of man's side, and what this first prodigy prefigured, I shall, with God's help, tell in another place. But at present, since this book must be concluded, let us merely say that in this first man, who was created in the beginning, there was laid the foundation, not indeed evidently, but in God's foreknowledge, of these two cities or societies, so far as regards the human race. For from that man all men were to be derived—

some of them to be associated with the good angels in their reward, others with the wicked in punishment; all being ordered by the secret yet just judgment of God. For since it is written, "All the paths of the Lord are mercy and truth,"[1] neither can His grace be unjust, nor His justice cruel.

[1]Ps. 25. 10.

BOOK XIII

ARGUMENT. IN THIS BOOK IT IS TAUGHT THAT DEATH IS PENAL, AND HAD ITS ORIGIN IN ADAM'S SIN

CHAP. 1. *Of the fall of the first man, through which mortality has been contracted*

HAVING disposed of the very difficult questions concerning the origin of our world and the beginning of the human race, the natural order requires that we now discuss the fall of the first man (we may say of the first men), and of the origin and propagation of human death. For God had not made man like the angels, in such a condition that, even though they had sinned, they could none the more die. He had so made them, that if they discharged the obligations of obedience, an angelic immortality and a blessed eternity might ensue, without the intervention of death; but if they disobeyed, death should be visited on them with just sentence—which, too, has been spoken of in the preceding book.

CHAP. 2. *Of that death which can affect an immortal soul, and of that to which the body is subject*

But I see I must speak a little more carefully of the nature of death. For although the human soul is truly affirmed to be immortal, yet it also has a certain death of its own. For it is therefore called immortal, because, in a sense, it does not cease to live and to feel; while the body is called mortal, because it can be forsaken of all life, and cannot by itself live at all. The death, then, of the soul takes place when God forsakes it, as the death of the body when the soul forsakes it. Therefore the death of both—that is, of the whole man—occurs when the soul, forsaken by God, forsakes the body. For, in this case, neither is God the life of the soul, nor the soul the life of the body. And this death of the whole man is followed by that which, on the authority of the divine oracles, we call the second

death. This the Saviour referred to when He said, "Fear Him which is able to destroy both soul and body in hell."[2] And since this does not happen before the soul is so joined to its body that they cannot be separated at all, it may be matter of wonder how the body can be said to be killed by that death in which it is not forsaken by the soul, but, being animated and rendered sensitive by it, is tormented. For in that penal and everlasting punishment, of which in its own place we are to speak more at large, the soul is justly said to die, because it does not live in connection with God; but how can we say that the body is dead, seeing that it lives by the soul? For it could not otherwise feel the bodily torments which are to follow the resurrection. Is it because life of every kind is good, and pain an evil, that we decline to say that that body lives, in which the soul is the cause, not of life, but of pain? The soul, then, lives by God when it lives well, for it cannot live well unless by God working in it what is good; and the body lives by the soul when the soul lives in the body, whether itself be living by God or no. For the wicked man's life in the body is a life not of the soul, but of the body, which even dead souls—that is, souls forsaken of God—can confer upon bodies, how little soever of their own proper life, by which they are immortal, they retain. But in the last damnation, though man does not cease to feel, yet because this feeling of his is neither sweet with pleasure nor wholesome with repose, but painfully penal, it is not without reason called death rather than life. And it is called the second death because it follows the first, which sunders the two cohering essences, whether these be God and the soul, or the soul and the body. Of the first and bodily death, then, we may say that to the good it is good, and evil to

[2]Matt. 10. 28.

the evil. But, doubtless, the second, as it happens to none of the good, so it can be good for none.

CHAP. 3. *Whether death, which by the sin of our first parents has passed upon all men, is the punishment of sin, even to the good*

But a question not to be shirked arises: Whether in very truth death, which separates soul and body, is good to the good? For if it be, how has it come to pass that such a thing should be the punishment of sin? For the first men would not have suffered death had they not sinned. How, then, can that be good to the good, which could not have happened except to the evil? Then, again, if it could only happen to the evil, to the good it ought not to be good, but non-existent. For why should there be any punishment where there is nothing to punish? Wherefore we must say that the first men were indeed so created that if they had not sinned, they would not have experienced any kind of death; but that, having become sinners, they were so punished with death that whatsoever sprang from their stock should also be punished with the same death. For nothing else could be born of them than that which they themselves had been. Their nature was deteriorated in proportion to the greatness of the condemnation of their sin, so that what existed as punishment in those who first sinned, became a natural consequence in their children. For man is not produced by man, as he was from the dust. For dust was the material out of which man was made: man is the parent by whom man is begotten. Wherefore earth and flesh are not the same thing, though flesh be made of earth. But as man the parent is, such is man the offspring. In the first man, therefore, there existed the whole human nature, which was to be transmitted by the woman to posterity, when that conjugal union received the divine sentence of its own condemnation; and what man was made, not when created, but when he sinned and was punished, this he propagated, so far as the origin of sin and death are concerned. For neither by sin nor its punishment was he himself reduced to that infantine and helpless infirmity of body and mind which we see in children. For God ordained that infants should begin the world as the young of beasts begin it, since their parents had fallen to the level of the beasts in the fashion of their life and of their death; as it is written, "Man when he was in honour understood not; he became like the beasts that have no understanding."[1] Nay more, infants, we see,

[1]Ps. 49. 12.

are even feebler in the use and movement of their limbs, and more infirm to choose and refuse, than the most tender offspring of other animals; as if the force that dwells in human nature were destined to surpass all other living things so much the more eminently, as its energy has been longer restrained, and the time of its exercise delayed, just as an arrow flies the higher the further back it has been drawn. To this infantine imbecility the first man did not fall by his lawless presumption and just sentence; but human nature was in his person vitiated and altered to such an extent that he suffered in his members the warring of disobedient lust, and became subject to the necessity of dying. And what he himself had become by sin and punishment, such he generated those whom he begot; that is to say, subject to sin and death. And if infants are delivered from this bondage of sin by the Redeemer's grace, they can suffer only this death which separates soul and body; but being redeemed from the obligation of sin, they do not pass to that second endless and penal death.

CHAP. 4. *Why death, the punishment of sin, is not withheld from those who by the grace of regeneration are absolved from sin*

If, moreover, any one is solicitous about this point, how, if death be the very punishment of sin, they whose guilt is cancelled by grace do yet suffer death, this difficulty has already been handled and solved in our other work which we have written on the baptism of infants. There it was said that the parting of soul and body was left, though its connection with sin was removed, for this reason, that if the immortality of the body followed immediately upon the sacrament of regeneration, faith itself would be thereby enervated. For faith is then only faith when it waits in hope for what is not yet seen in substance. And by the vigour and conflict of faith, at least in times past, was the fear of death overcome. Specially was this conspicuous in the holy martyrs, who could have had no victory, no glory, to whom there could not even have been any conflict, if, after the laver of regeneration, saints could not suffer bodily death. Who would not, then, in company with the infants presented for baptism, run to the grace of Christ, that so he might not be dismissed from the body? And thus faith would not be tested with an unseen reward; and so would not even be faith, seeking and receiving an immediate recompense of its works. But now, by the greater and more admirable grace of the Saviour, the punishment of sin is turned to the service of righteousness. For then it was proclaimed to man, "If thou sinnest, thou shalt die"; now it is said to the martyr, "Die, that thou sin not." Then it was said, "If ye transgress the commandments, ye shall die"; now it is said, "If ye decline death, ye transgress the commandment." That which was formerly set as an object of terror, that men might not sin, is now to be undergone if we would not sin. Thus, by the unutterable mercy of God, even the very punishment of wickedness has become the armour of virtue, and the penalty of the sinner becomes the reward of the righteous. For then death was incurred by sinning, now righteousness is fulfilled by dying. In the case of the holy martyrs it is so; for to them the persecutor proposes the alternative, apostasy or death. For the righteous prefer by believing to suffer what the first transgressors suffered by not believing. For unless they had sinned, they would not have died; but the martyrs sin if they do not die. The one died because they sinned, the others do not sin because they die. By the guilt of the first, punishment was incurred; by the punishment of the second, guilt is prevented. Not that death, which was before an evil, has become something good, but only that God has granted to faith this grace, that death, which is the admitted opposite to life, should become the instrument by which life is reached.

CHAP. 5. *As the wicked make an ill use of the law, which is good, so the good make a good use of death, which is an ill*

The apostle, wishing to show how hurtful a thing sin is, when grace does not aid us, has not hesitated to say that the strength of sin is that very law by which sin is prohibited. "The sting of death is sin, and the strength of sin is the law."[1] Most certainly true; for prohibition increases the desire of illicit action, if righteousness is not so loved that the desire of sin is conquered by that love. But unless divine grace aid us, we cannot love nor delight in true righteousness. But lest the law should be thought to be an evil, since it is called the strength of sin, the apostle, when treating a similar question in another place, says, "The law indeed is holy, and the commandment holy, and just, and good. Was then that which is holy made death unto me? God forbid. But sin, that it might appear sin, working death in me by that which is good; that sin by the commandment might become exceeding sinful."[2] *Exceeding*, he says, because

[1] I Cor. 15. 56. [2] Rom. 7. 12, 13.

the transgression is more heinous when through the increasing lust of sin the law itself also is despised. Why have we thought it worth while to mention this? For this reason, because, as the law is not an evil when it increases the lust of those who sin, so neither is death a good thing when it increases the glory of those who suffer it, since either the former is abandoned wickedly, and makes transgressors, or the latter is embraced for the truth's sake, and makes martyrs. And thus the law is indeed good, because it is prohibition of sin, and death is evil because it is the wages of sin; but as wicked men make an evil use not only of evil, but also of good things, so the righteous make a good use not only of good, but also of evil things. Whence it comes to pass that the wicked make an ill use of the law, though the law is good; and that the good die well, though death is an evil.

CHAP. 6. *Of the evil of death in general, considered as the separation of soul and body*

Wherefore, as regards bodily death, that is, the separation of the soul from the body, it is good unto none while it is being endured by those whom we say are in the article of death. For the very violence with which body and soul are wrenched asunder, which in the living had been conjoined and closely intertwined, brings with it a harsh experience, jarring horridly on nature so long as it continues, till there comes a total loss of sensation, which arose from the very interpenetration of spirit and flesh. And all this anguish is sometimes forestalled by one stroke of the body or sudden flitting of the soul, the swiftness of which prevents it from being felt. But whatever that may be in the dying which with violently painful sensation robs of all sensation, yet, when it is piously and faithfully borne, it increases the merit of patience, but does not make the name of punishment inapplicable. Death, proceeding by ordinary generation from the first man, is the punishment of all who are born of him, yet, if it be endured for righteousness' sake, it becomes the glory of those who are born again; and though death be the award of sin, it sometimes secures that nothing be awarded to sin.

CHAP. 7. *Of the death which the unbaptized suffer for the confession of Christ*

For whatever unbaptized[3] persons die confessing Christ, this confession is of the same efficacy for the remission of sins as if they were washed in the sacred font of baptism. For He

[3] Literally, "unregenerate."

who said, "Except a man be born of water and of the Spirit, he cannot enter into the kingdom of God,"[1] made also an exception in their favour, in that other sentence where He no less absolutely said, "Whosoever shall confess me before men, him will I confess also before my Father which is in heaven";[2] and in another place, "Whosoever will lose his life for my sake, shall find it."[3] And this explains the verse, "Precious in the sight of the Lord is the death of His saints."[4] For what is more precious than a death by which a man's sins are all forgiven, and his merits increased an hundredfold? For those who have been baptized when they could no longer escape death, and have departed this life with all their sins blotted out, have not equal merit with those who did not defer death, though it was in their power to do so, but preferred to end their life by confessing Christ, rather than by denying Him to secure an opportunity of baptism. And even had they denied Him under pressure of the fear of death, this too would have been forgiven them in that baptism, in which was remitted even the enormous wickedness of those who had slain Christ. But how abundant in these men must have been the grace of the Spirit, Who breathes where He listeth, seeing that they so dearly loved Christ as to be unable to deny Him even in so sore an emergency, and with so sure a hope of pardon! Precious, therefore, is the death of the saints, to whom the grace of Christ has been applied with such gracious effects, that they do not hesitate to meet death themselves, if so be they might meet Him. And precious is it also, because it has proved that what was originally ordained for the punishment of the sinner, has been used for the production of a richer harvest of righteousness. But not on this account should we look upon death as a good thing, for it is diverted to such useful purposes, not by any virtue of its own, but by the divine interference. Death was originally proposed as an object of dread, that sin might not be committed; now it must be undergone that sin may not be committed, or, if committed, be remitted, and the award of righteousness bestowed on him whose victory has earned it.

CHAP. 8. *That the saints, by suffering the first death for the truth's sake, are freed from the second*

For if we look at the matter a little more carefully, we shall see that even when a man dies

faithfully and laudably for the truth's sake, it is still death he is avoiding. For he submits to some part of death, for the very purpose of avoiding the whole, and the second and eternal death over and above. He submits to the separation of soul and body, lest the soul be separated both from God and from the body, and so the whole first death be completed, and the second death receive him everlastingly. Wherefore death is indeed, as I said, good to none while it is being actually suffered, and while it is subduing the dying to its power; but it is meritoriously endured for the sake of retaining or winning what *is* good. And regarding what happens after death, it is no absurdity to say that death is good to the good, and evil to the evil. For the disembodied spirits of the just are at rest; but those of the wicked suffer punishment till their bodies rise again—those of the just to life everlasting, and of the others to death eternal, which is called the second death.

CHAP. 9. *Whether we should say that the moment of death, in which sensation ceases, occurs in the experience of the dying or in that of the dead*

The point of time in which the souls of the good and evil are separated from the body, are we to say it is after death, or in death rather? If it is after death, then it is not death which is good or evil, since death is done with and past, but it is the life which the soul has now entered on. Death was an evil when it was present, that is to say, when it was being suffered by the dying; for to them it brought with it a severe and grievous experience, which the good make a good use of. But when death is past, how can that which no longer is be either good or evil? Still further, if we examine the matter more closely, we shall see that even that sore and grievous pain which the dying experience is not death itself. For so long as they have any sensation, they are certainly still alive; and, if still alive, must rather be said to be in a state previous to death than in death. For when death actually comes, it robs us of all bodily sensation, which, while death is only approaching is painful. And thus it is difficult to explain how we speak of those who are not yet dead, but are agonized in their last and mortal extremity, as being in the article of death. Yet what else can we call them than dying persons? for when death which was imminent shall have actually come, we can no longer call them dying but dead. No one, therefore, is dying unless living; since even he who is in the last extremity of life,

[1]John, 3. 5.   [2]Matt. 10. 32.   [3]Matt. 16. 25.
[4]Ps. 116. 15.

and, as we say, giving up the ghost, yet lives. The same person is therefore at once dying and living, but drawing near to death, departing from life; yet in life, because his spirit yet abides in the body; not yet in death, because not yet has his spirit forsaken the body. But if, when it has forsaken it, the man is not even then in death, but after death, who shall say when he is in death? On the one hand, no one can be called dying, if a man cannot be dying and living at the same time; and as long as the soul is in the body, we cannot deny that he is living. On the other hand, if the man who is approaching death be rather called dying, I know not who is living.

CHAP. 10. *Of the life of mortals, which is rather to be called death than life*

For no sooner do we begin to live in this dying body, than we begin to move ceaselessly towards death. For in the whole course of this life (if life we must call it) its mutability tends towards death. Certainly there is no one who is not nearer it this year than last year, and to-morrow than to-day, and to-day than yesterday, and a short while hence than now, and now than a short while ago. For whatever time we live is deducted from our whole term of life, and that which remains is daily becoming less and less; so that our whole life is nothing but a race towards death, in which no one is allowed to stand still for a little space, or to go somewhat more slowly, but all are driven forwards with an impartial movement, and with equal rapidity. For he whose life is short spends a day no more swiftly than he whose life is longer. But while the equal moments are impartially snatched from both, the one has a nearer and the other a more remote goal to reach with this their equal speed. It is one thing to make a longer journey, and another to walk more slowly. He, therefore, who spends longer time on his way to death does not proceed at a more leisurely pace, but goes over more ground. Further, if every man begins to die, that is, is in death, as soon as death has begun to show itself in him (by taking away life, to wit; for when life is all taken away, the man will be then not in death, but after death), then he begins to die so soon as he begins to live. For what else is going on in all his days, hours, and moments, until this slow-working death is fully consummated? And then comes the time *after death,* instead of that in which life was being withdrawn, and which we called being *in death.* Man, then, is never in life from the moment he

dwells in this dying rather than living body, if, at least, he cannot be in life and death at once. Or rather, shall we say, he is in both?—in life, namely, which he lives till all is consumed; but in death also, which he dies as his life is consumed? For if he is not in life, what is it which is consumed till all be gone? And if he is not in death, what is this consumption itself? For when the whole of life has been consumed, the expression "after death" would be meaningless, had that consumption not been death. And if, when it has all been consumed, a man is not in death but after death, when is he in death, unless when life is being consumed away?

CHAP. 11. *Whether one can both be living and dead at the same time*

But if it is absurd to say that a man is in death before he reaches death (for to what is his course running as he passes through life, if already he is in death?), and if it outrage common usage to speak of a man being at once alive and dead, as much as it does so to speak of him as at once asleep and awake, it remains to be asked when a man is dying? For, before death comes, he is not dying but living; and when death has come, he is not dying but dead. The one is before, the other after death. When, then, is he in death so that we can say he is dying? For as there are three times, before death, in death, after death, so there are three states corresponding, living, dying, dead. And it is very hard to define when a man is in death or dying, when he is neither living, which is before death, nor dead, which is after death, but dying, which is in death. For so long as the soul is in the body, especially if consciousness remain, the man certainly lives; for body and soul constitute the man. And thus, before death, he cannot be said to be in death, but when, on the other hand, the soul has departed, and all bodily sensation is extinct, death is past, and the man is dead. Between these two states the dying condition finds no place; for if a man yet lives, death has not arrived; if he has ceased to live, death is past. Never, then, is he dying, that is, comprehended in the state of death. So also in the passing of time—you try to lay your finger on the present and cannot find it, because the present occupies no space, but is only the transition of time from the future to the past. Must we then conclude that there is thus no death of the body at all? For if there is, where is it, since it is in no one, and no one can be in it? Since, indeed, if there is yet life, death is not yet; for this state is before death, not in death: and if life has already ceased, death is not present; for this state is after death, not in death. On the other hand, if there is no death before or after, what do we mean when we say "after death," or "before death"? This is a foolish way of speaking if there is no death. And would that we had lived so well in Paradise that in very truth there were now no death! But not only does it now exist, but so grievous a thing is it, that no skill is sufficient either to explain or to escape it.

Let us, then, speak in the customary way—no man ought to speak otherwise—and let us call the time before death comes, "before death"; as it is written, "Praise no man before his death."[1] And when it has happened, let us say that "after death" this or that took place. And of the present time let us speak as best we can, as when we say, "He, when dying, made his will, and left this or that to such and such persons"—though, of course, he could not do so unless he were living, and did this rather before death than in death. And let us use the same phraseology as Scripture uses; for it makes no scruple of saying that the dead are not after but in death. So that verse, "For in death there is no remembrance of thee."[2] For until the resurrection men are justly said to be in death; as every one is said to be in sleep till he awakes. However, though we can say of persons in sleep that they are sleeping, we cannot speak in this way of the dead, and say they are dying. For, so far as regards the death of the body, of which we are now speaking, one cannot say that those who are already separated from their bodies continue dying. But this, you see, is just what I was saying—that no words can explain how either the dying are said to live, or how the dead are said, even after death, to be in death. For how can they be after death if they be in death, especially when we do not even call them dying, as we call those in sleep, sleeping; and those in languor, languishing; and those in grief, grieving; and those in life, living? And yet the dead, until they rise again, are said to be in death, but cannot be called dying.

And therefore I think it has not unsuitably nor inappropriately come to pass, though not by the intention of man, yet perhaps with divine purpose, that this Latin word *moritur* cannot be declined by the grammarians according to the rule followed by similar words. For *oritur* gives the form *ortus est* for the perfect; and all similar verbs form this tense from their perfect participles. But if we ask the perfect of *moritur*,

we get the regular answer *mortuus est*, with a double *u*. For thus *mortuus* is pronounced, like *fatuus, arduus, conspicuus*, and similar words, which are not perfect participles but adjectives, and are declined without regard to tense. But *mortuus*, though in form an adjective, is used as perfect participle, as if that were to be declined which cannot be declined; and thus it has suitably come to pass that, as the thing itself cannot in point of fact be declined, so neither can the word significant of the act be declined. Yet, by the aid of our Redeemer's grace, we may manage at least to decline the second. For that is more grievous still, and, indeed, of all evils the worst, since it consists not in the separation of soul and body, but in the uniting of both in death eternal. And there, in striking contrast to our present conditions, men will not be before or after death, but always in death; and thus never living, never dead, but endlessly dying. And never can a man be more disastrously in death than when death itself shall be deathless.

CHAP. 12. *What death God intended, when He threatened our first parents with death if they should disobey His commandment*

When, therefore, it is asked what death it was with which God threatened our first parents if they should transgress the commandment they had received from Him and should fail to preserve their obedience—whether it was the death of soul, or of body, or of the whole man, or that which is called second death—we must answer, "It is all." For the first consists of two; the second is the complete death, which consists of all. For, as the whole earth consists of many lands, and the Church universal of many churches, so death universal consists of all deaths. The first consists of two, one of the body, and another of the soul. So that the first death is a death of the whole man, since the soul without God and without the body suffers punishment for a time; but the second is when the soul, without God but with the body, suffers punishment everlasting. When, therefore, God said to that first man whom he had placed in Paradise, referring to the forbidden fruit, "In the day that thou eatest thereof thou shalt surely die,"[3] that threatening included not only the first part of the first death, by which the soul is deprived of God; nor only the subsequent part of the first death, by which the body is deprived of the soul; nor only the whole first death itself, by which the soul is

[1]Ecclus. 11. 28.   [2]Ps. 6. 5.   [3]Gen. 2. 17.

punished in separation from God and from the body; but it includes whatever of death there is, even to that final death which is called second, and to which none is subsequent.

CHAP. 13. *What was the first punishment of the transgression of our first parents?*

For, as soon as our first parents had transgressed the commandment, divine grace forsook them, and they were confounded at their own wickedness; and therefore they took fig-leaves (which were possibly the first that came to hand in their troubled state of mind), and covered their shame; for though their members remained the same, they had shame now where they had none before. They experienced a new motion of their flesh, which had become disobedient to them, in strict retribution of their own disobedience to God. For the soul, revelling in its own liberty and scorning to serve God, was itself deprived of the command it had formerly maintained over the body. And because it had willfully deserted its superior Lord, it no longer held its own inferior servant; neither could it hold the flesh subject, as it would always have been able to do had it remained itself subject to God. Then began the flesh to lust against the Spirit,[1] in which strife we are born, deriving from the first transgression a seed of death, and bearing in our members, and in our vitiated nature, the contest or even victory of the flesh.

CHAP. 14. *In what state man was made by God, and into what estate he fell by the choice of his own will*

For God, the author of natures, not of vices, created man upright; but man, being of his own will corrupted and justly condemned, begot corrupted and condemned children. For we all were in that one man, since we all were that one man, who fell into sin by the woman who was made from him before the sin. For not yet was the particular form created and distributed to us, in which we as individuals were to live, but already the seminal nature was there from which we were to be propagated; and this being vitiated by sin, and bound by the chain of death, and justly condemned, man could not be born of man in any other state. And thus, from the bad use of free will, there originated the whole train of evil, which, with its concatenation of miseries, convoys the human race from its depraved origin, as from a corrupt root, on to the destruction of the second death, which has no end, those only being excepted who are freed by the grace of God.

CHAP. 15. *That Adam in his sin forsook God ere God forsook him, and that his falling away from God was the first death of the soul*

It may perhaps be supposed that because God said, "Ye shall die the death,"[2] and not "deaths," we should understand only that death which occurs when the soul is deserted by God, Who is its life; for it was not deserted by God, and so deserted Him, but deserted Him, and so was deserted by Him. For its own will was the originator of its evil, as God was the originator of its motions towards good, both in making it when it was not and in remaking it when it had fallen and perished. But though we suppose that God meant only this death, and that the words, "In the day ye eat of it ye shall die the death," should be understood as meaning, "In the day ye desert me in disobedience, I will desert you in justice," yet assuredly in this death the other deaths also were threatened, which were its inevitable consequence. For in the first stirring of the disobedient motion which was felt in the flesh of the disobedient soul, and which caused our first parents to cover their shame, one death indeed is experienced, that, namely, which occurs when God forsakes the soul. (This was intimated by the words He uttered, when the man, stupefied by fear, had hid himself, "Adam, where art thou?"[3]—words which He used not in ignorance or inquiry, but warning him to consider where he was, since God was not with him.) But when the soul itself forsook the body, corrupted and decayed with age, the other death was experienced of which God had spoken in pronouncing man's sentence, "Earth thou art, and unto earth shalt thou return."[4] And of these two deaths that first death of the whole man is composed. And this first death is finally followed by the second, unless man be freed by grace. For the body would not return to the earth from which it was made, save only by the death proper to itself, which occurs when it is forsaken of the soul, its life. And therefore it is agreed among all Christians who truthfully hold the Catholic faith that we are subject to the death of the body, not by the law of nature, by which God ordained no death for man, but by His righteous infliction on account of sin; for God, taking vengeance on sin, said to the man, in whom we all then were, "Dust thou art, and unto dust shalt thou return."

[1] Gal. 5. 17.

[2] Gen. 2. 17. [3] Gen. 3. 9. [4] Gen. 3. 19.

CHAP. 16. *Concerning the philosophers who think that the separation of soul and body is not penal, though Plato represents the Supreme Deity as promising to the inferior gods that they shall never be dismissed from their bodies*

But the philosophers against whom we are defending the city of God, that is, His Church, seem to themselves to have good cause to deride us, because we say that the separation of the soul from the body is to be held as part of man's punishment. For they suppose that the blessedness of the soul then only is complete, when it is quite denuded of the body, and returns to God a pure and simple, and, as it were, naked soul. On this point, if I should find nothing in their own literature to refute this opinion, I should be forced laboriously to demonstrate that it is not the body, but the corruptibility of the body, which is a burden to the soul. Hence that sentence of Scripture we quoted in a foregoing book, "For the corruptible body presseth down the soul."[1] The word corruptible is added to show that the soul is burdened, not by any body whatsoever, but by the body such as it has become in consequence of sin. And even though the word had not been added, we could understand nothing else. But when Plato most expressly declares that the gods who are made by the Supreme have immortal bodies, and when he introduces their Maker himself, promising them as a great boon that they should abide in their bodies eternally, and never by any death be loosed from them, why do these adversaries of ours, for the sake of troubling the Christian faith, feign to be ignorant of what they quite well know, and even prefer to contradict themselves rather than lose an opportunity of contradicting us? Here are Plato's words, as Cicero has translated them,[2] in which he introduces the Supreme addressing the gods He had made, and saying, "Ye who are sprung from a divine stock, consider of what works I am the parent and author. These (your bodies) are indestructible so long as I will it; although all that is composed can be destroyed. But it is wicked to dissolve what reason has compacted. But, seeing that ye have been born, ye cannot indeed be immortal and indestructible; yet ye shall by no means be destroyed, nor shall any fates consign you to death, and prove superior to my will, which is a stronger assurance of your perpetuity than those bodies to which ye were joined when ye were born." Plato, you see, says that the gods

are both mortal by the connection of the body and soul, and yet are rendered immortal by the will and decree of their Maker. If, therefore, it is a punishment to the soul to be connected with any body whatever, why does God address them as if they were afraid of death, that is, of the separation of soul and body? Why does He seek to reassure them by promising them immortality, not in virtue of their nature, which is composite and not simple, but by virtue of His invincible will, whereby He can effect that neither things born die, nor things compounded be dissolved, but preserved eternally?

Whether this opinion of Plato's about the stars is true or not, is another question. For we cannot at once grant to him that these luminous bodies or globes, which by day and night shine on the earth with the light of their bodily substance, have also intellectual and blessed souls which animate each its own body, as he confidently affirms of the universe itself, as if it were one huge animal, in which all other animals were contained.[3] But this, as I said, is another question, which we have not undertaken to discuss at present. This much only I deemed right to bring forward, in opposition to those who so pride themselves on being, or on being called Platonists, that they blush to be Christians, and who cannot brook to be called by a name which the common people also bear, lest they vulgarize the philosophers' coterie, which is proud in proportion to its exclusiveness. These men, seeking a weak point in the Christian doctrine, select for attack the eternity of the body, as if it were a contradiction to contend for the blessedness of the soul, and to wish it to be always resident in the body, bound, as it were, in a lamentable chain; and this although Plato, their own founder and master, affirms that it was granted by the Supreme as a boon to the gods He had made, that they should not die, that is, should not be separated from the bodies with which He had connected them.

CHAP. 17. *Against those who affirm that earthly bodies cannot be made incorruptible and eternal*

These same philosophers further contend that terrestrial bodies cannot be eternal, though they make no doubt that the whole earth, which is itself the central member of their god—not, indeed, of the greatest, but yet of a great god, that is, of this whole world—is eternal. Since, then, the Supreme made for them another god, that is, this world, superior to the other gods beneath

---

[1]Wisd. 9. 15.   [2]Part of the *Timæus*.   [3]See Plato, *Timæus*, 34, 39.

Him; and since they suppose that this god is an animal, having, as they affirm, a rational or intellectual soul enclosed in the huge mass of its body, and having, as the fitly situated and adjusted members of its body, the four elements, whose union they wish to be indissoluble and eternal, lest perchance this great god of theirs might some day perish; what reason is there that the earth, which is the central member in the body of a greater creature, should be eternal, and the bodies of other terrestrial creatures should not possibly be eternal if God should so will it? But earth, say they, must return to earth, out of which the terrestrial bodies of the animals have been taken. For this, they say, is the reason of the necessity of their death and dissolution, and this the manner of their restoration to the solid and eternal earth whence they came. But if any one says the same thing of fire, holding that the bodies which are derived from it to make celestial beings must be restored to the universal fire, does not the immortality which Plato represents these gods as receiving from the Supreme evanesce in the heat of this dispute? Or does this not happen with those celestials because God, whose will, as Plato says, overpowers all powers, has willed it should not be so? What, then, hinders God from ordaining the same of terrestrial bodies? And since, indeed, Plato acknowledges that God can prevent things that are born from dying, and things that are joined from being sundered, and things that are composed from being dissolved, and can ordain that the souls once allotted to their bodies should never abandon them, but enjoy along with them immortality and everlasting bliss, why may He not also effect that terrestrial bodies die not? Is God powerless to do everything that is special to the Christian's creed, but powerful to effect everything the Platonists desire? The philosophers, forsooth, have been admitted to a knowledge of the divine purposes and power which has been denied to the prophets! The truth is, that the Spirit of God taught His prophets so much of His will as He thought fit to reveal, but the philosophers, in their efforts to discover it, were deceived by human conjecture.

But they should not have been so led astray, I will not say by their ignorance, but by their obstinacy, as to contradict themselves so frequently; for they maintain, with all their vaunted might, that in order to the happiness of the soul, it must abandon not only its earthly body, but every kind of body. And yet they hold that the gods, whose souls are most blessed, are bound to everlasting bodies, the celestials to fiery bodies, and the soul of Jove himself (or this world, as they would have us believe) to all the physical elements which compose this entire mass reaching from earth to heaven. For this soul Plato believes to be extended and diffused by musical numbers, from the middle of the inside of the earth, which geometricians call the centre, outwards through all its parts to the utmost heights and extremities of the heavens; so that this world is a very great and blessed immortal animal, whose soul has both the perfect blessedness of wisdom, and never leaves its own body, and whose body has life everlasting from the soul, and by no means clogs or hinders it, though itself be not a simple body, but compacted of so many and so huge materials. Since, therefore, they allow so much to their own conjectures, why do they refuse to believe that by the divine will and power immortality can be conferred on earthly bodies, in which the souls would be neither oppressed with the burden of them, nor separated from them by any death, but live eternally and blessedly? Do they not assert that their own gods so live in bodies of fire, and that Jove himself, their king, so lives in the physical elements? If, in order to its blessedness, the soul must quit every kind of body, let their gods flit from the starry spheres, and Jupiter from earth to sky; or, if they cannot do so, let them be pronounced miserable. But neither alternative will these men adopt. For, on the one hand, they dare not ascribe to their own gods a departure from the body, lest they should seem to worship mortals; on the other hand, they dare not deny their happiness, lest they should acknowledge wretches as gods. Therefore, to obtain blessedness, we need not quit every kind of body, but only the corruptible, cumbersome, painful, dying—not such bodies as the goodness of God contrived for the first man, but such only as man's sin entailed.

CHAP. 18. *Of earthly bodies, which the philosophers affirm cannot be in heavenly places, because whatever is of earth is by its natural weight attracted to earth*

But it is necessary, they say, that the natural weight of earthly bodies either keeps them on earth or draws them to it; and therefore they cannot be in heaven. Our first parents were indeed on earth, in a well-wooded and fruitful spot, which has been named Paradise. But let our adversaries a little more carefully consider this subject of earthly weight, because it has important bearings, both on the ascension of the body of Christ, and also on the resurrection body of the saints. If human skill can by some contrivance fabricate vessels that float, out of metals which sink as soon as they are placed on the water, how much more credible is it that God, by some occult mode of operation, should even more certainly effect that these earthy masses be emancipated from the downward pressure of their weight? This cannot be impossible to that God by whose almighty will, according to Plato, neither things born perish, nor things composed dissolve, especially since it is much more wonderful that spiritual and bodily essences be conjoined than that bodies be adjusted to other material substances. Can we not also easily believe that souls, being made perfectly blessed, should be endowed with the power of moving their earthly but incorruptible bodies as they please, with almost spontaneous movement, and of placing them where they please with the readiest action? If the angels transport whatever terrestrial creatures they please from any place they please, and convey them whither they please, is it to be believed that they cannot do so without toil and the feeling of burden? Why, then, may we not believe that the spirits of the saints, made perfect and blessed by divine grace, can carry their own bodies where they please, and set them where they will? For, though we have been accustomed to notice, in bearing weights, that the larger the quantity the greater the weight of earthly bodies is, and that the greater the weight the more burdensome it is, yet the soul carries the members of its own flesh with less difficulty when they are massive with health, than in sickness when they are wasted. And though the hale and strong man feels heavier to other men carrying him than the lank and sickly, yet the man himself moves and carries his own body with less feeling of burden when he has the greater bulk of vigorous health, than when his frame is reduced to a minimum by hunger or disease. Of such consequence, in estimating the weight of earthly bodies, even while yet corruptible and mortal, is the consideration not of dead weight, but of the healthy equilibrium of the parts. And what words can tell the difference between what we now call health and future immortality? Let not the philosophers, then, think to upset our faith with arguments from the weight of bodies; for I do not care to inquire why they cannot believe an earthly body can be in heaven, while the whole earth is suspended on nothing. For perhaps the world keeps its central place by the same law that attracts to its centre all heavy bodies. But

this I say, if the lesser gods, to whom Plato committed the creation of man and the other terrestrial creatures, were able, as he affirms, to withdraw from the fire its quality of burning, while they left it that of lighting, so that it should shine through the eyes; and if to the Supreme God Plato also concedes the power of preserving from death things that have been born, and of preserving from dissolution things that are composed of parts so different as body and spirit; are we to hesitate to concede to this same God the power to operate on the flesh of him whom He has endowed with immortality, so as to withdraw its corruption but leave its nature, remove its burdensome weight but retain its seemly form and members? But concerning our belief in the resurrection of the dead, and concerning their immortal bodies, we shall speak more at large, God willing, in the end of this work.

CHAP. 19. *Against the opinion of those who do not believe that the primitive men would have been immortal if they had not sinned*

At present let us go on, as we have begun, to give some explanation regarding the bodies of our first parents. I say then, that, except as the just consequence of sin, they would not have been subjected even to this death, which is good to the good—this death, which is not exclusively known and believed in by a few, but is known to all, by which soul and body are separated, and by which the body of an animal which was but now visibly living is now visibly dead. For though there can be no manner of doubt that the souls of the just and holy dead live in peaceful rest, yet so much better would it be for them to be alive in healthy, well-conditioned bodies, that even those who hold the tenet that it is most blessed to be quit of every kind of body, condemn this opinion in spite of themselves. For no one will dare to set wise men, whether yet to die or already dead—in other words, whether already quit of the body, or shortly to be so—above the immortal gods, to whom the Supreme, in Plato, promises as a munificent gift life indissoluble, or in eternal union with their bodies. But this same Plato thinks that nothing better can happen to men than that they pass through life piously and justly, and, being separated from their bodies, be received into the bosom of the gods, who never abandon theirs; "that, oblivious of the past, they may revisit the upper air, and conceive the longing to return again to the body."[1] Virgil is applauded for borrowing

[1] Virgil, *Æneid*, BK. VI. 750, 751.

this from the Platonic system. Assuredly Plato thinks that the souls of mortals cannot always be in their bodies, but must necessarily be dismissed by death; and, on the other hand, he thinks that without bodies they cannot endure for ever, but with ceaseless alteration pass from life to death, and from death to life. This difference, however, he sets between wise men and the rest, that they are carried after death to the stars, that each man may repose for a while in a star suitable for him, and may thence return to the labours and miseries of mortals when he has become oblivious of his former misery and possessed with the desire of being embodied. Those, again, who have lived foolishly transmigrate into bodies fit for them, whether human or bestial. Thus he has appointed even the good and wise souls to a very hard lot indeed, since they do not receive such bodies as they might always and even immortally inhabit, but such only as they can neither permanently retain nor enjoy eternal purity without. Of this notion of Plato's, we have in a former book already said[1] that Porphyry was ashamed in the light of these Christian times, so that he not only emancipated human souls from a destiny in the bodies of beasts, but also contended for the liberation of the souls of the wise from all bodily ties, so that, escaping from all flesh, they might, as bare and blessed souls, dwell with the Father time without end. And that he might not seem to be outbid by Christ's promise of life everlasting to His saints, he also established purified souls in endless felicity, without return to their former woes; but, that he might contradict Christ, he denies the resurrection of incorruptible bodies and maintains that these souls will live eternally, not only without earthly bodies, but without any bodies at all. And yet, whatever he meant by this teaching, he at least did not teach that these souls should offer no religious observance to the gods who dwelt in bodies. And why did he not, unless because he did not believe that the souls, even though separate from the body, were superior to those gods? Wherefore, if these philosophers will not dare (as I think they will not) to set human souls above the gods who are most blessed, and yet are tied eternally to their bodies, why do they find that absurd which the Christian faith preaches, namely, that our first parents were so created that, if they had not sinned, they would not have been dismissed from their bodies by any death, but would have been endowed with immortality as the reward of their obedience, and would have lived eternally with

[1]BK. X, chap. 30.

their bodies; and further, that the saints will in the resurrection inhabit those very bodies in which they have here toiled, but in such sort that neither shall any corruption or unwieldiness be suffered to attach to their flesh, nor any grief or trouble to cloud their felicity?

CHAP. 20. *That the flesh now resting in peace shall be raised to a perfection not enjoyed by the flesh of our first parents*

Thus the souls of departed saints are not affected by the death which dismisses them from their bodies, because their flesh rests in hope, no matter what indignities it receives after sensation is gone. For they do not desire that their bodies be forgotten, as Plato thinks fit, but rather, because they remember what has been promised by Him Who deceives no man, and Who gave them security for the safe keeping even of the hairs of their head, they with a longing patience wait in hope of the resurrection of their bodies, in which they have suffered many hardships, and are now to suffer never again. For if they did not "hate their own flesh" when it, with its native infirmity, opposed their will and had to be constrained by the spiritual law, how much more shall they love it when it shall even itself have become spiritual! For as, when the spirit serves the flesh, it is fitly called carnal, so, when the flesh serves the spirit, it will justly be called spiritual. Not that it is converted into spirit, as some fancy from the words, "It is sown in corruption, it is raised in incorruption,"[2] but because it is subject to the spirit with a perfect and marvellous readiness of obedience, and responds in all things to the will that has entered on immortality—all reluctance, all corruption, and all slowness being removed. For the body will not only be better than it was here in its best estate of health, but it will surpass the bodies of our first parents ere they sinned. For, though they were not to die unless they should sin, yet they used food as men do now, their bodies not being as yet spiritual, but animal only. And though they decayed not with years, nor drew nearer to death—a condition secured to them in God's marvellous grace by the tree of life, which grew along with the forbidden tree in the midst of Paradise—yet they took other nourishment, though not of that one tree, which was interdicted not because it was itself bad, but for the sake of commending a pure and simple obedience, which is the great virtue of the rational creature set under the Creator as his Lord. For, though no evil thing was touched, yet if a thing

[2]I Cor. 15. 42.

forbidden was touched, the very disobedience was sin. They were, then, nourished by other fruit, which they took that their animal bodies might not suffer the discomfort of hunger or thirst; but they tasted the tree of life, that death might not steal upon them from any quarter, and that they might not, spent with age, decay. Other fruits were, so to speak, their nourishment, but this their sacrament. So that the tree of life would seem to have been in the terrestrial Paradise what the wisdom of God is in the spiritual, of which it is written, "She is a tree of life to them that lay hold upon her."[1]

CHAP. 21. *Of Paradise, that it can be understood in a spiritual sense without sacrificing the historic truth of the narrative regarding the real place*

On this account some allegorize all that concerns Paradise itself, where the first men, the parents of the human race, are, according to the truth of holy Scripture, recorded to have been; and they understand all its trees and fruit-bearing plants as virtues and habits of life, as if they had no existence in the external world, but were only so spoken of or related for the sake of spiritual meanings. As if there could not be a real terrestrial Paradise! As if there never existed these two women, Sarah and Hagar, nor the two sons who were born to Abraham, the one of the bond woman, the other of the free, because the apostle says that in them the two covenants were prefigured; or as if water never flowed from the rock when Moses struck it, because therein Christ can be seen in a figure, as the same apostle says, "Now that rock was Christ!"[2] No one, then, denies that Paradise may signify the life of the blessed; its four rivers, the four virtues, prudence, fortitude, temperance, and justice; its trees, all useful knowledge; its fruits, the customs of the godly; its tree of life, wisdom herself, the mother of all good; and the tree of the knowledge of good and evil, the experience of a broken commandment. The punishment which God appointed was in itself, a just, and therefore a good thing; but man's experience of it is not good.

These things can also and more profitably be understood of the Church, so that they become prophetic foreshadowings of things to come. Thus Paradise is the Church, as it is called in the Canticles;[3] the four rivers of Paradise are the four gospels; the fruit-trees the saints, and the fruit their works; the tree of life is the holy of holies, Christ; the tree of the knowledge of good and evil, the will's free choice. For if man despise the will of God, he can only destroy himself; and so he learns the difference between consecrating himself to the common good and revelling in his own. For he who loves himself is abandoned to himself, in order that, being overwhelmed with fears and sorrows, he may cry, if there be yet soul in him to feel his ills, in the words of the psalm, "My soul is cast down within me,"[4] and when chastened, may say, "Because of his strength I will wait upon Thee."[5] These and similar allegorical interpretations may be suitably put upon Paradise without giving offence to any one, while yet we believe the strict truth of the history, confirmed by its circumstantial narrative of facts.

CHAP. 22. *That the bodies of the saints shall after the resurrection be spiritual, and yet flesh shall not be changed into spirit*

The bodies of the righteous, then, such as they shall be in the resurrection, shall need neither any fruit to preserve them from dying of disease or the wasting decay of old age, nor any other physical nourishment to allay the cravings of hunger or of thirst; for they shall be invested with so sure and every way inviolable an immortality, that they shall not eat save when they choose, nor be under the necessity of eating, while they enjoy the power of doing so. For so also was it with the angels who presented themselves to the eye and touch of men, not because they could do no otherwise, but because they were able and desirous to suit themselves to men by a kind of manhood ministry. For neither are we to suppose, when men receive them as guests, that the angels eat only in appearance, though to any who did not know them to be angels they might seem to eat from the same necessity as ourselves. So these words spoken in the Book of Tobit, "You saw me eat, but you saw it but in vision";[6] that is, you thought I took food as you do for the sake of refreshing my body. But if in the case of the angels another opinion seems more capable of defence, certainly our faith leaves no room to doubt regarding our Lord Himself, that even after His resurrection, and when now in spiritual but yet real flesh, He ate and drank with His disciples; for not the power, but the need, of eating and drinking is taken from these bodies. And so they will be spiritual, not because they shall cease to be bodies, but because they shall subsist by the quickening spirit.

[1] Prov. 3. 18. [2] I Cor. 10. 4.
[3] Song of Sol. 4. 13.

[4] Ps. 43. 6. [5] Ps. 59. 9. [6] Tobit, 12. 19.

CHAP. 23. *What we are to understand by the animal and spiritual body; or of those who die in Adam, and of those who are made alive in Christ*

For as those bodies of ours, that have a living soul, though not as yet a quickening spirit, are called soul-informed bodies, and yet are not souls but bodies, so also those bodies are called spiritual—yet God forbid we should therefore suppose them to be spirits and not bodies—which, being quickened by the Spirit, have the substance, but not the unwieldiness and corruption of flesh. Man will then be not earthly but heavenly—not because the body will not be that very body which was made of earth, but because by its heavenly endowment it will be a fit inhabitant of heaven, and this not by losing its nature, but by changing its quality. The first man, of the earth earthy, was made a living soul, not a quickening spirit—which rank was reserved for him as the reward of obedience. And therefore his body, which required meat and drink to satisfy hunger and thirst, and which had no absolute and indestructible immortality, but by means of the tree of life warded off the necessity of dying, and was thus maintained in the flower of youth—this body, I say, was doubtless not spiritual, but animal; and yet it would not have died but that it provoked God's threatened vengeance by offending. And though sustenance was not denied him even outside Paradise, yet, being forbidden the tree of life, he was delivered over to the wasting of time, at least in respect of that life which, had he not sinned, he might have retained perpetually in Paradise, though only in an animal body, till such time as it became spiritual in acknowledgment of his obedience.

Wherefore, although we understand that this manifest death, which consists in the separation of soul and body, was also signified by God when He said, "In the day thou eatest thereof thou shalt surely die,"[1] it ought not on that account to seem absurd that they were not dismissed from the body on that very day on which they took the forbidden and death-bringing fruit. For certainly on that very day their nature was altered for the worse and vitiated, and by their most just banishment from the tree of life they were involved in the necessity even of bodily death, in which necessity we are born. And therefore the apostle does not say, "The body indeed is doomed to die on account of sin," but he says, "The body indeed is dead because of

[1]Gen. 2. 17.

sin." Then he adds, "But if the Spirit of Him that raised up Jesus from the dead dwell in you, He that raised up Christ from the dead shall also quicken your mortal bodies by His Spirit that dwelleth in you."[2] Then accordingly shall the body become a quickening spirit which is now a living soul; and yet the apostle calls it "dead," because already it lies under the necessity of dying. But in Paradise it was so made a living soul, though not a quickening spirit, that it could not properly be called dead, for, save through the commission of sin, it could not come under the power of death. Now, since God by the words, "Adam, where art thou?" pointed to the death of the soul, which results when He abandons it, and since in the words, "Earth thou art, and unto earth shalt thou return,"[3] He signified the death of the body, which results when the soul departs from it, we are led, therefore, to believe that He said nothing of the second death, wishing it to be kept hidden, and reserving it for the New Testament dispensation, in which it is most plainly revealed. And this He did in order that, first of all, it might be evident that this first death, which is common to all, was the result of that sin which in one man became common to all. But the second death is not common to all, those being excepted who were "called according to His purpose. For whom He did foreknow, He also did predestinate to be conformed to the image of His Son, that He might be the first-born among many brethren."[4] Those the grace of God has, by a Mediator, delivered from the second death.

Thus the apostle states that the first man was made in an animal body. For, wishing to distinguish the animal body which now is from the spiritual, which is to be in the resurrection, he says, "It is sown in corruption, it is raised in incorruption: it is sown in dishonour, it is raised in glory: it is sown in weakness, it is raised in power: it is sown a natural body, it is raised a spiritual body." Then, to prove this, he goes on, "There is a natural body, and there is a spiritual body." And to show what the animated body is, he says, "Thus it was written, The first man Adam was made a living soul, the last Adam was made a quickening spirit."[5] He wished thus to show what the animated body is, though Scripture did not say of the first man Adam, when his soul was created by the breath of God, "Man was made in an animated body," but "Man was made a living soul."[6] By these words, therefore, "The first man was made a liv-

[2]Rom. 8. 10, 11.   [3]Gen. 3. 19.   [4]Rom. 8. 28, 29.
[5]I Cor. 15. 42–45.   [6]Gen. 2. 7.

ing soul," the apostle wishes man's animated body to be understood. But how he wishes the spiritual body to be understood he shows when he adds, "But the last Adam was made a quickening spirit," plainly referring to Christ, who has so risen from the dead that He cannot die any more. He then goes on to say, "But that was not first which is spiritual, but that which is natural; and afterward that which is spiritual." And here he much more clearly asserts that he referred to the animal body when he said that the first man was made a living soul, and to the spiritual when he said that the last man was made a quickening spirit. The animal body is the first, being such as the first Adam had, and which would not have died had he not sinned, being such also as we now have, its nature being changed and vitiated by sin to the extent of bringing us under the necessity of death, and being such as even Christ condescended first of all to assume, not indeed of necessity, but of choice; but afterwards comes the spiritual body, which already is worn by anticipation by Christ as our head, and will be worn by His members in the resurrection of the dead.

Then the apostle subjoins a notable difference between these two men, saying, "The first man is of the earth, earthy; the second man is the Lord from heaven. As is the earthy, such are they also that are earthy, and as is the heavenly, such are they also that are heavenly. And as we have borne the image of the earthy, we shall also bear the image of the heavenly."[1] So he elsewhere says, "As many of you as have been baptized into Christ have put on Christ";[2] but in very deed this shall be accomplished when that which is animal in us by our birth shall have become spiritual in our resurrection. For, to use his words again, "We are saved by hope."[3] Now we bear the image of the earthly man by the propagation of sin and death, which pass on us by ordinary generation; but we bear the image of the heavenly by the grace of pardon and life eternal, which regeneration confers upon us through the Mediator of God and men, the Man Christ Jesus. And He is the heavenly Man of Paul's passage, because He came from heaven to be clothed with a body of earthly mortality, that He might clothe it with heavenly immortality. And he calls others heavenly, because by grace they become His members, that, together with them, He may become one Christ, as head and body. In the same epistle he puts this yet more clearly: "Since by man came death, by Man came also the resurrection of the dead. For

as in Adam all die, even so in Christ shall all be made alive";[4] that is to say, in a spiritual body which shall be made a quickening spirit. Not that all who die in Adam shall be members of Christ—for the great majority shall be punished in eternal death—but he uses the word "all" in both clauses, because, as no one dies in an animal body except in Adam, so no one is quickened a spiritual body save in Christ. We are not, then, by any means to suppose that we shall in the resurrection have such a body as the first man had before he sinned, nor that the words, "As is the earthy such are they also that are earthy," are to be understood of that which was brought about by sin; for we are not to think that Adam had a spiritual body before he fell, and that, in punishment of his sin, it was changed into an animal body. If this be thought, small heed has been given to the words of so great a teacher, who says, "There is a natural body, there is also a spiritual body; as it is written, The first man Adam was made a living soul." Was it after sin he was made so? or was not this primal condition of man from which the blessed apostle selects his testimony to show what the animal body is?

CHAP 24. *How we must understand that breathing of God by which "the first man was made a living soul," and that also by which the Lord conveyed His spirit to His disciples when He said, "receive ye the Holy Ghost"*

Some have hastily supposed from the words, "God breathed into Adam's nostrils the breath of life, and man became a living soul,"[5] that a soul was not then first given to man, but that the soul already given was quickened by the Holy Ghost. They are encouraged in this supposition by the fact that the Lord Jesus after His resurrection breathed on His disciples and said, "Receive ye the Holy Spirit."[6] From this they suppose that the same thing was effected in either case, as if the evangelist had gone on to say, "And they became living souls." But if he had made this addition, we should only understand that the Spirit is in some way the life of souls; and that without Him reasonable souls must be accounted dead, though their bodies seem to live before our eyes. But that this was not what happened when man was created, the very words of the narrative sufficiently show: "And God made man dust of the earth"; which some have thought to render more clearly by the words, "And God formed man of the clay of

[1] I Cor. 15. 47–49.   [2] Gal. 3. 27.   [3] Rom. 8. 24.   [4] I Cor. 15. 21, 22.   [5] Gen. 2. 7.   [6] John. 20. 22.

the earth." For it had before been said that "there went up a mist from the earth, and watered the whole face of the ground,"[1] in order that the reference to clay, formed of this moisture and dust, might be understood. For on this verse there immediately follows the announcement, "And God created man dust of the earth"; so those Greek manuscripts have it from which this passage has been translated into Latin. But whether one prefers to read *"created"* or *"formed,"* where the Greek reads ἔπλασεν, is of little importance; yet *"formed"* is the better rendering. But those who preferred "created" thought they thus avoided the ambiguity arising from the fact, that in the Latin language the usage obtains that those are said to form a thing who frame some feigned and fictitious thing. This man, then, who was created of the dust of the earth, or of the moistened dust or clay— this "dust of the earth" (that I may use the express words of Scripture) was made, as the apostle teaches, an animated body when he received a soul. This man, he says, "was made a living soul"; that is, this fashioned dust was made a living soul.

They say, "Already he had a soul, else he would not be called a man; for man is not a body alone, nor a soul alone, but a being composed of both." This, indeed, is true, that the soul is not the whole man, but the better part of man; the body not the whole, but the inferior part of man; and that then, when both are joined, they receive the name of man—which, however, they do not severally lose even when we speak of them singly. For who is prohibited from saying, in colloquial usage, "That man is dead, and is now at rest or in torment," though this can be spoken only of the soul; or "He is buried in such and such a place," though this refers only to the body? Will they say that Scripture follows no such usage? On the contrary, it so thoroughly adopts it, that even while a man is alive, and body and soul are united, it calls each of them singly by the name *"man,"* speaking of the soul as the "inward man," and of the body as the "outward man,"[2] as if there were two men, though both together are indeed but one. But we must understand in what sense man is said to be in the image of God, and is yet dust, and to return to the dust. The former is spoken of the rational soul, which God by His breathing, or, to speak more appropriately, by His inspiration, conveyed to man, that is, to his body; but the latter refers to his body, which God formed of the dust, and to which a soul was given, that it might become a living body, that is, that man might become a living soul.

Wherefore, when our Lord breathed on His disciples and said, "Receive ye the Holy Ghost," He certainly wished it to be understood that the Holy Ghost was not only the Spirit of the Father, but of the only begotten Son Himself. For the same Spirit is, indeed, the Spirit of the Father and of the Son, making with them the Trinity of Father, Son, and Spirit, not a creature, but the Creator. For neither was that material breath which proceeded from the mouth of His flesh the very substance and nature of the Holy Spirit, but rather the intimation, as I said, that the Holy Spirit was common to the Father and to the Son; for they have not each a separate Spirit, but both one and the same. Now this Spirit is always spoken of in sacred Scripture by the Greek word πνεῦμα, as the Lord, too, named Him in the place cited when He gave Him to His disciples, and intimated the gift by the breathing of His lips; and there does not occur to me any place in the whole Scriptures where He is otherwise named. But in this passage where it is said, "And the Lord formed man dust of the earth, and breathed, or inspired, into his face the breath of life"; the Greek has not πνεῦμα, the usual word for the Holy Spirit, but πνοή, a word more frequently used of the creature than of the Creator; and for this reason some Latin interpreters have preferred to render it by "breath" rather than "spirit." For this word occurs also in the Greek in Isa. 57. 16, where God says, "I have made all breath," meaning, doubtless, all souls. Accordingly, this word πνοη is sometimes rendered "breath," sometimes "spirit," sometimes "inspiration," sometimes "aspiration," sometimes "soul," even when it is used of God. Πνεῦμα, on the other hand, is uniformly rendered "spirit," whether of man, of whom the apostle says, "For what man knoweth the things of a man, save the spirit of man which is in him?"[3] or of beast, as in the book of Solomon, "Who knoweth the spirit of man that goeth upward, and the spirit of the beast that goeth downward to the earth?"[4] or of that physical spirit which is called wind, for so the Psalmist calls it: "Fire and hail; snow and vapours; stormy wind";[5] or of the uncreated Creator Spirit, of whom the Lord said in the gospel, "Receive ye the Holy Ghost," indicating the gift by the breathing of His mouth;

[1]Gen. 2. 6.   [2]II Cor. 4. 16.   [3]I Cor. 2. 11.   [4]Eccles. 3. 21.   [5]Ps. 148. 8.

and when He says, "Go ye and baptize all nations in the name of the Father, of the Son, and of the Holy Ghost,"[1] words which very expressly and excellently commend the Trinity; and where it is said, "God is a Spirit";[2] and in very many other places of the sacred writings. In all these quotations from Scripture we do not find in the Greek the word πνοή used, but πνεῦμα, and in the Latin, not *flatus*, but *spiritus*. Wherefore, referring again to that place where it is written, "He inspired," or to speak more properly, "breathed into his face the breath of life," even though the Greek had not used πνοη (as it has) but πνεῦμα, it would not on that account necessarily follow that the Creator Spirit, who in the Trinity is distinctively called the Holy Ghost, was meant, since, as has been said, it is plain that πνεῦμα is used not only of the Creator, but also of the creature.

But, say they, when the Scripture used the word "spirit,"[3] it would not have added "of life" unless it meant us to understand the Holy Spirit; nor, when it said, "Man became a soul," would it also have inserted the word "living" unless that life of the soul were signified which is imparted to it from above by the gift of God. For, seeing that the soul by itself has a proper life of its own, what need, they ask, was there of adding living, save only to show that the life which is given it by the Holy Spirit was meant? What is this but to fight strenuously for their own conjectures, while they carelessly neglect the teaching of Scripture? Without troubling themselves much, they might have found in a preceding page of this very book of Genesis the words, "Let the earth bring forth the living soul,"[4] when all the terrestrial animals were created. Then at a slight interval, but still in the same book, was it impossible for them to notice this verse, "All in whose nostrils was the breath of life, of all that was in the dry land, died," by which it was signified that all the animals which lived on the earth had perished in the deluge? If, then, we find that Scripture is accustomed to speak both of the "living soul" and the "spirit of life" even in reference to beasts; and if in this place, where it is said, "All things which have the spirit of life," the word πνοη, not πνεῦμα, is used; why may we not say, What need was there to add "living," since the soul cannot exist without being alive? or, What need to add "of life" after the word spirit? But we understand that Scripture used these expressions in its or-

dinary style so long as it speaks of animals, that is, animated bodies, in which the soul serves as the residence of sensation; but when man is spoken of, we forget the ordinary and established usage of Scripture, whereby it signifies that man received a rational soul, which was not produced out of the waters and the earth like the other living creatures, but was created by the breath of God. Yet this creation was so ordered that the human soul should live in an animal body, like those other animals of which the Scripture said, "Let the earth produce every living soul," and regarding which it again says that in them is the breath of life, where the word πνοη and not πνεῦμα is used in the Greek, and where certainly not the Holy Spirit, but their spirit, is signified under that name.

But, again, they object that breath is understood to have been emitted from the mouth of God; and if we believe that is the soul, we must consequently acknowledge it to be of the same substance, and equal to that wisdom, which says, "I come out of the mouth of the Most High."[5] Wisdom, indeed, does not say it was breathed out of the mouth of God, but proceeded out of it. But as we are able, when we breathe, to make a breath, not of our own human nature, but of the surrounding air, which we inhale and exhale as we draw our breath and breathe again, so almighty God was able to make breath, not of His own nature, nor of the creature beneath Him, but even of nothing; and this breath, when He communicated it to man's body, He is most appropriately said to have breathed or inspired—the Immaterial breathing it also immaterial, but the Immutable not also the immutable; for it was created, He uncreated. Yet that these persons who are forward to quote Scripture, and yet know not the usages of its language, may know that not only what is equal and consubstantial with God is said to proceed out of His mouth, let them hear or read what God says: "So then because thou art lukewarm, and neither cold nor hot, I will spue thee out of my mouth."[6]

There is no ground, then, for our objecting, when the apostle so expressly distinguishes the animal body from the spiritual—that is to say, the body in which we now are from that in which we are to be. He says, "It is sown a natural body, it is raised a spiritual body. There is a natural body, and there is a spiritual body. And so it is written, 'The first man Adam was made a living soul; the last Adam was made a

[1]Matt. 28. 19.   [2]John, 4. 24.   [3]"Breath," Eng. ver.
[4]Gen. 1. 24.   [5]Ecclus. 24. 3.   [6]Rev. 3. 16.

quickening spirit.' Howbeit that was not first which is spiritual, but that which is natural; and afterward that which is spiritual. The first man is of the earth, earthy; the second man is the Lord from heaven. As is the earthy, such are they also that are earthy; and as is the heavenly, such are they also that are heavenly. And as we have borne the image of the earthy, we shall also bear the image of the heavenly."[1] Of all which words of his we have previously spoken. The animal body, accordingly, in which the apostle says that the first man Adam was made, was not so made that it could not die at all, but so that it should not die unless he should have sinned. That body, indeed, which shall be made spiritual and immortal by the quickening Spirit shall not be able to die at all; as the soul has been created immortal, and therefore, although by sin it may be said to die and does lose a certain life of its own, namely, the Spirit of God, by whom it was enabled to live wisely and blessedly, yet it does not cease living a kind of life, though a miserable, because it is immortal by creation. So, too, the rebellious angels, though by sinning they did in a sense die, because they forsook God, the Fountain of life, which while they drank they were able to live wisely and well, yet they could not so die as to utterly cease living and feeling, for they are im-

[1] I Cor. 15. 44-49.

mortals by creation. And so, after the final judgment, they shall be hurled into the second death, and not even there be deprived of life or of sensation, but shall suffer torment. But those men who have been embraced by God's grace, and are become the fellow-citizens of the holy angels who have continued in bliss, shall never more either sin or die, being endued with spiritual bodies; yet, being clothed with immortality, such as the angels enjoy, of which they cannot be divested even by sinning, the nature of their flesh shall continue the same, but all carnal corruption and unwieldiness shall be removed.

There remains a question which must be discussed, and, by the help of the Lord God of truth, solved: If the motion of concupiscence in the unruly members of our first parents arose out of their sin, and only when the divine grace deserted them; and if it was on that occasion that their eyes were opened to see, or, more exactly, notice their nakedness, and that they covered their shame because the shameless motion of their members was not subject to their will—how, then, would they have begotten children had they remained sinless as they were created? But as this book must be concluded, and so large a question cannot be summarily disposed of, we may relegate it to the following book, in which it will be more conveniently treated.

BOOK XIV

ARGUMENT. AUGUSTINE AGAIN TREATS OF THE SIN OF THE FIRST MAN, AND TEACHES THAT IT IS THE CAUSE OF THE CARNAL LIFE AND VICIOUS AFFECTIONS OF MAN. ESPECIALLY HE PROVES THAT THE SHAME WHICH ACCOMPANIES LUST IS THE JUST PUNISHMENT OF THAT DISOBEDIENCE, AND INQUIRES HOW MAN, IF HE HAD NOT SINNED, WOULD HAVE BEEN ABLE WITHOUT LUST TO PROPAGATE HIS KIND.

CHAP. I. *That the disobedience of the first man would have plunged all men into the endless misery of the second death, had not the grace of God rescued many*

WE have already stated in the preceding books that God, desiring not only that the human race might be able by their similarity of nature to associate with one another, but also that they might be bound together in harmony and peace by the ties of relationship, was pleased to derive all men from one individual, and created man with such a nature that the members of the race should not have died, had not the two first (of whom the one was created out of nothing, and

the other out of him) merited this by their disobedience; for by them so great a sin was committed that by it the human nature was altered for the worse, and was transmitted also to their posterity, liable to sin and subject to death. And the kingdom of death so reigned over men that the deserved penalty of sin would have hurled all headlong even into the second death, of which there is no end, had not the undeserved grace of God saved some therefrom. And thus it has come to pass that though there are very many and great nations all over the earth, whose rites and customs, speech, arms, and dress, are distinguished by marked differences, yet there are no more than two kinds of human society, which we may justly call two cities, according to the language of our Scriptures. The one consists of those who wish to live after the flesh, the other of those who wish to live after the spirit; and when they severally achieve what they wish, they live in peace, each after their kind.

CHAP. 2. *Of carnal life, which is to be understood not only of living in bodily indulgence, but also of living in the vices of the inner man*

First, we must see what it is to live after the flesh, and what to live after the spirit. For any one who either does not recollect, or does not sufficiently weigh, the language of sacred Scripture, may, on first hearing what we have said, suppose that the Epicurean philosophers live after the flesh, because they place man's highest good in bodily pleasure; and that those others do so who have been of opinion that in some form or other bodily good is man's supreme good; and that the mass of men do so who, without dogmatizing or philosophizing on the subject, are so prone to lust that they cannot delight in any pleasure save such as they receive from bodily sensations: and he may suppose that the Stoics, who place the supreme good of men in the soul, live after the spirit; for what is man's soul, if not spirit? But in the sense of the divine Scripture both are proved to live after the flesh. For by flesh it means not only the body of a terrestrial and mortal animal, as when it says, "All flesh is not the same flesh, but there is one kind of flesh of men, another flesh of beasts, another of fishes, another of birds,"[1] but it uses this word in many other significations; and among these various usages, a frequent one is to use flesh for man himself, the nature of man taking the part for the whole, as in the words, "By the deeds of the law there shall no flesh be justified";[2] for what does he mean here by "no flesh" but "no man?" And this, indeed, he shortly after says more plainly: "No man shall be justified by the law";[3] and in the Epistle to the Galatians, "Knowing that man is not justified by the works of the law." And so we understand the words, "And the Word was made flesh";[4] that is, man, which some not accepting in its right sense, have supposed that Christ had not a human soul.[5] For as the whole is used for the part in the words of Mary Magdalene in the Gospel, "That have taken away my Lord, and I know not where they have laid Him,"[6] by which she meant only the flesh of Christ, which she supposed had been taken from the tomb where it had been buried, so the part is used for the whole, flesh being named, while man is referred to, as in the quotations above cited.

Since, then, Scripture uses the word flesh in many ways, which there is not time to collect and investigate, if we are to ascertain what it is to live after the flesh (which is certainly evil, though the nature of flesh is not itself evil), we must carefully examine that passage of the epistle which the Apostle Paul wrote to the Galatians, in which he says, "Now the works of the flesh are manifest, which are these: adultery, fornication, uncleanness, lasciviousness, idolatry, witchcraft, hatred, variance, emulations, wrath, strife, seditions, heresies, envyings, murders, drunkenness, revellings, and such like; of the which I tell you before, as I have also told you in time past, that they which do such things shall not inherit the kingdom of God."[7] This whole passage of the apostolic epistle being considered, so far as it bears on the matter in hand, will be sufficient to answer the question, what it is to live after the flesh. For among the works of the flesh which he said were manifest, and which he cited for condemnation, we find not only those which concern the pleasure of the flesh, as fornications, uncleanness, lasciviousness, drunkenness, revellings, but also those which, though they be remote from fleshly pleasure, reveal the vices of the soul. For who does not see that idolatries, witchcrafts, hatreds, variance, emulations, wrath, strife, heresies, envyings, are vices rather of the soul than of the flesh? For it is quite possible for a man to abstain from fleshly pleasures for the sake of idolatry or some heretical error; and yet, even when he does so, he is proved by this apostolic authority to be living after the flesh; and in abstaining from fleshly pleasure, he is proved to be practising damnable works of the flesh. Who that has enmity has it not in his soul? or who would say to his enemy, or to the man he thinks his enemy, "You have a bad flesh towards me," and not rather, "You have a bad spirit towards me"? In fine, if any one heard of what I may call "carnalities," he would not fail to attribute them to the carnal part of man; so no one doubts that "animosities" belong to the soul of man. Why then does the doctor of the Gentiles in faith and verity call all these and similar things works of the flesh, unless because, by that mode of speech whereby the part is used for the whole, he means us to understand by the word flesh the man himself?

---

[1] I Cor. 15. 39.   [2] Rom. 3. 20.   [3] Gal. 3. 11.
[4] John, 1. 14.   [5] The Apollinarians.   [6] John, 20. 13.
[7] Gal. 5. 19–21.

CHAP. 3. *That the sin is caused not by the flesh, but by the soul, and that the corruption contracted from sin is not sin but sin's punishment*

But if any one says that the flesh is the cause of all vices and ill conduct, inasmuch as the soul lives wickedly only because it is moved by the flesh, it is certain he has not carefully considered the whole nature of man. For "the corruptible body, indeed, weigheth down the soul."[1] Whence, too, the apostle, speaking of this corruptible body, of which he had shortly before said, "though our outward man perish,"[2] says, "We know that if our earthly house of this tabernacle were dissolved, we have a building of God, an house not made with hands, eternal in the heavens. For in this we groan, earnestly desiring to be clothed upon with our house which is from heaven: if so be that being clothed we shall not be found naked. For we that are in this tabernacle do groan, being burdened: not for that we would be unclothed, but clothed upon, that mortality might be swallowed up in life."[3] We are then burdened with this corruptible body; but knowing that the cause of this burdensomeness is not the nature and substance of the body, but its corruption, we do not desire to be deprived of the body, but to be clothed with its immortality. For then, also, there will be a body, but it shall no longer be a burden, being no longer corruptible. At present, then, "the corruptible body presseth down the soul, and the earthly tabernacle weigheth down the mind that museth upon many things," nevertheless they are in error who suppose that all the evils of the soul proceed from the body.

Virgil, indeed, seems to express the sentiments of Plato in the beautiful lines, where he says:

> A fiery strength inspires their lives,
> An essence that from heaven derives,
> Though clogged in part by limbs of clay
> And the dull "vesture of decay";[4]

but though he goes on to mention the four most common mental emotions—desire, fear, joy, sorrow—with the intention of showing that the body is the origin of all sins and vices, saying:

> Hence wild desires and grovelling fears,
> And human laughter, human tears,
> Immured in dungeon-seeming night,
> They look abroad, yet see no light,[5]

yet we believe quite otherwise. For the corruption of the body, which weighs down the soul, is not the cause but the punishment of the first sin; and it was not the corruptible flesh that made the soul sinful, but the sinful soul that made the flesh corruptible. And though from this corruption of the flesh there arise certain incitements to vice, and indeed vicious desires, yet we must not attribute to the flesh all the vices of a wicked life, in case we thereby clear the devil of all these, for he has no flesh. For though we cannot call the devil a fornicator or drunkard, or ascribe to him any sensual indulgence (though he is the secret instigator and prompter of those who sin in these ways), yet he is exceedingly proud and envious. And this viciousness has so possessed him, that on account of it he is reserved in chains of darkness to everlasting punishment. Now these vices, which have dominion over the devil, the apostle attributes to the flesh, which certainly the devil has not. For he says "hatred, variance, emulations, strife, envying" are the works of the flesh; and of all these evils pride is the origin and head, and it rules in the devil though he has no flesh. For who shows more hatred to the saints? who is more at variance with them? who more envious, bitter, and jealous? And since he exhibits all these works, though he has no flesh, how are they works of the flesh, unless because they are the works of man, who is, as I said, spoken of under the name of flesh? For it is not by having flesh, which the devil has not, but by living according to himself—that is, according to man— that man became like the devil. For the devil too, wished to live according to himself when he did not abide in the truth; so that when he lied, this was not of God, but of himself, who is not only a liar, but the father of lies, he being the first who lied, and the originator of lying as of sin.

CHAP. 4. *What it is to live according to man, and what to live according to God*

When, therefore, man lives according to man, not according to God, he is like the devil. Because not even an angel might live according to an angel, but only according to God, if he was to abide in the truth, and speak God's truth and not his own lie. And of man, too, the same apostle says in another place, "If the truth of God hath more abounded through my lie";[6] "my lie," he said, and "God's truth." When, then, a man lives according to the truth, he lives not according to himself, but according to God; for He was God who said, "I am the truth."[7] When, therefore, man lives according to himself—that

---

[1] Wisd. 9. 15.   [2] II Cor. 4. 16.   [3] II Cor. 5. 1-4.
[4] *Æneid*, BK. VI. 730-32.   [5] *Ibid.*, 733, 734.
[6] Rom. 3. 7.   [7] John, 14. 6.

is, according to man, not according to God—assuredly he lives according to a lie; not that man himself is a lie, for God is his author and creator, Who is certainly not the author and creator of a lie, but because man was made upright, that he might not live according to himself, but according to Him that made him—in other words, that he might do His will and not his own; and not to live as he was made to live, that is a lie. For he certainly desires to be blessed even by not living so that he may be blessed. And what is a lie if this desire be not? Wherefore it is not without meaning said that all sin is a lie. For no sin is committed save by that desire or will by which we desire that it be well with us, and shrink from it being ill with us. That, therefore, is a lie which we do in order that it may be well with us, but which makes us more miserable than we were. And why is this, but because the source of man's happiness lies only in God, Whom he abandons when he sins, and not in himself, by living according to whom he sins?

In enunciating this proposition of ours, then, that because some live according to the flesh and others according to the spirit, there have arisen two diverse and conflicting cities, we might equally well have said, "because some live according to man, others according to God." For Paul says very plainly to the Corinthians, "For whereas there is among you envying and strife, are ye not carnal, and walk according to man?"[1] So that to walk according to man and to be carnal are the same; for by *flesh*, that is, by a part of man, man is meant. For before he said that those same persons were animal whom afterwards he calls carnal, saying, "For what man knoweth the things of a man, save the spirit of man which is in him? even so the things of God knoweth no man, but the Spirit of God. Now we have received not the spirit of this world, but the Spirit which is of God; that we might know the things which are freely given to us of God. Which things also we speak, not in the words which man's wisdom teacheth, but which the Holy Ghost teacheth; comparing spiritual things with spiritual. But the animal man perceiveth not the things of the Spirit of God; for they are foolishness unto him."[2] It is to men of this kind, then, that is, to animal men, he shortly after says, "And I, brethren, could not speak unto you as unto spiritual, but as unto carnal."[3] And this is to be interpreted by the same usage, a part being taken for the whole. For both the soul and the flesh, the component parts of man, can be used to signify the whole man; and so the

animal man and the carnal man are not two different things, but one and the same thing, viz., man living according to man. In the same way it is nothing else than men that are meant either in the words, "By the deeds of the law there shall no *flesh* be justified";[4] or in the words, "Seventy-five *souls* went down into Egypt with Jacob."[5] In the one passage, "no flesh" signifies "no man"; and in the other, by "seventy-five souls" seventy-five men are meant. And the expression, "not in words which man's wisdom teacheth," might equally be "not in words which fleshly wisdom teacheth"; and the expression, "ye walk according to man," might be "according to the flesh." And this is still more apparent in the words which followed: "For while one saith, I am of Paul, and another, I am of Apollos, are ye not men?" The same thing which he had before expressed by "ye are animal," "ye are carnal," he now expresses by "ye are men"; that is, ye live according to man, not according to God, for if you lived according to Him, you should be gods.

CHAP. 5. *That the opinion of the Platonists regarding the nature of body and soul is not so censurable as that of the Manichæans, but that even it is objectionable, because it ascribes the origin of vices to the nature of the flesh*

There is no need, therefore, that in our sins and vices we accuse the nature of the flesh to the injury of the Creator, for in its own kind and degree the flesh is good; but to desert the Creator good, and live according to the created good, is not good, whether a man choose to live according to the flesh, or according to the soul, or according to the whole human nature, which is composed of flesh and soul, and which is therefore spoken of either by the name flesh alone, or by the name soul alone. For he who extols the nature of the soul as the chief good, and condemns the nature of the flesh as if it were evil, assuredly is fleshly both in his love of the soul and hatred of the flesh; for these his feelings arise from human fancy, not from divine truth. The Platonists, indeed, are not so foolish as, with the Manichæans, to detest our present bodies as an evil nature; for they attribute all the elements of which this visible and tangible world is compacted, with all their qualities, to God their Creator. Nevertheless, from the death-infected members and earthly construction of the body they believe the soul is so affected that there are thus originated in it the diseases of

[1] I Cor. 3. 3.   [2] I Cor. 2. 11–14.   [3] I Cor. 3. 1.   [4] Rom. 3. 20.   [5] Gen. 46. 27.

desires, and fears, and joy, and sorrow, under which four perturbations, as Cicero calls them, or passions, as most prefer to name them with the Greeks, is included the whole viciousness of human life. But if this be so, how is it that Æneas in Virgil, when he had heard from his father in Hades that the souls should return to bodies, expresses surprise at this declaration, and exclaims:

> O father! and can thought conceive
> That happy souls this realm would leave,
>   And seek the upper sky,
> With sluggish clay to reunite?
> This direful longing for the light,
> Whence comes it, say, and why?[1]

This direful longing, then, does it still exist even in that boasted purity of the disembodied spirits, and does it still proceed from the death-infected members and earthly limbs? Does he not assert that, when they begin to long to return to the body, they have already been delivered from all these so-called pestilences of the body? From which we gather that, were this endlessly alternating purification and defilement of departing and returning souls as true as it is most certainly false, yet it could not be averred that all culpable and vicious motions of the soul originate in the earthly body; for, on their own showing, "this direful longing," to use the words of their noble exponent, is so extraneous to the body, that it moves the soul that is purged of all bodily taint, and is existing apart from any body whatever, and moves it, moreover, to be embodied again. So that even they themselves acknowledge that the soul is not only moved to desire, fear, joy, sorrow, by the flesh, but that it can also be agitated with these emotions at its own instance.

CHAP. 6. *Of the character of the human will which makes the affections of the soul right or wrong*

But the character of the human will is of moment; because, if it is wrong, these motions of the soul will be wrong, but if it is right, they will be not merely blameless, but even praiseworthy. For the will is in them all; yea, none of them is anything else than will. For what are desire and joy but a volition of consent to the things we wish? And what are fear and sadness but a volition of aversion from the things which we do not wish? But when consent takes the form of seeking to possess the things we wish, this is called desire; and when consent takes the form of enjoying the things we wish, this is called joy.

In like manner, when we turn with aversion from that which we do not wish to happen, this volition is termed fear; and when we turn away from that which has happened against our will, this act of will is called sorrow. And generally in respect of all that we seek or shun, as a man's will is attracted or repelled, so it is changed and turned into these different affections. Wherefore the man who lives according to God, and not according to man, ought to be a lover of good, and therefore a hater of evil. And since no one is evil by nature, but whoever is evil is evil by vice, he who lives according to God ought to cherish towards evil men a perfect hatred, so that he shall neither hate the man because of his vice, nor love the vice because of the man, but hate the vice and love the man. For the vice being cursed, all that ought to be loved, and nothing that ought to be hated, will remain.

CHAP. 7. *That the words love and regard* (amor *and* dilectio) *are in Scripture used indifferently of good and evil affection*

He who resolves to love God, and to love his neighbour as himself, not according to man but according to God, is on account of this love said to be of a good will; and this is in Scripture more commonly called charity, but it is also, even in the same books, called love. For the apostle says that the man to be elected as a ruler of the people must be a lover of good.[2] And when the Lord Himself had asked Peter, "Hast thou a regard for me (*diligis*) more than these?" Peter replied, "Lord, Thou knowest that I love (*amo*) Thee." And again a second time the Lord asked not whether Peter loved (*amaret*) Him, but whether he had a regard (*diligeret*) for Him, and he again answered, "Lord, Thou knowest that I love (*amo*) Thee." But on the third interrogation the Lord Himself no longer says, "Hast thou a regard (*diligis*) for me," but "Lovest thou (*amas*) me?" And then the evangelist adds, "Peter was grieved because He said unto him the third time, Lovest thou (*amas*) me?" though the Lord had not said three times but only once, "Lovest thou (*amas*) me?" and twice *"Diligis me?"* from which we gather that, even when the Lord said *"diligis,"* He used an equivalent for *"amas."* Peter, too, throughout used one word for the one thing, and the third time also replied, "Lord, Thou knowest all things, Thou knowest that I love (*amo*) Thee."[3]

I have judged it right to mention this, because some are of opinion that charity or regard

[1] *Æneid*, BK. VI. 719-21.

[2] Tit. 1. 8, according to Greek and Vulgate.
[3] John, 21. 15-17.

(*dilectio*) is one thing, love (*amor*) another. They say that *dilectio* is used of a good affection, *amor* of an evil love. But it is very certain that even secular literature knows no such distinction. However, it is for the philosophers to determine whether and how they differ, though their own writings sufficiently testify that they make great account of love (*amor*) placed on good objects and even on God Himself. But we wished to show that the Scriptures of our religion, whose authority we prefer to all writings whatsoever, make no distinction between *amor, dilectio*, and *caritas;* and we have already shown that *amor* is used in a good connection. And if any one fancy that *amor* is no doubt used both of good and bad loves, but that *dilectio* is reserved for the good only, let him remember what the psalm says, "He that loveth (*diligit*) iniquity hateth his own soul";[1] and the words of the Apostle John, "If any man love (*diligere*) the world, the love (*dilectio*) of the Father is not in him."[2] Here you have in one passage *dilectio* used both in a good and a bad sense. And if any one demands an instance of *amor* being used in a bad sense (for we have already shown its use in a good sense), let him read the words, "For men shall be lovers (*amantes*) of their own selves, lovers (*amatores*) of money."[3]

The right will is, therefore, well-directed love, and the wrong will is ill-directed love. Love, then, yearning to have what is loved, is desire; and having and enjoying it, is joy; fleeing what is opposed to it, it is fear; and feeling what is opposed to it, when it has befallen it, it is sadness. Now these motions are evil if the love is evil; good if the love is good. What we assert let us prove from Scripture. The apostle "desires to depart, and to be with Christ."[4] And, "My soul desired to long for Thy judgments";[5] or if it is more appropriate to say, "My soul longed to desire Thy judgments." And, "The desire of wisdom bringeth to a kingdom."[6] Yet there has always obtained the usage of understanding desire and concupiscence in a bad sense if the object be not defined. But joy is used in a good sense: "Be glad in the Lord, and rejoice, ye righteous."[7] And, "Thou hast put gladness in my heart."[8] And, "Thou wilt fill me with joy with Thy countenance."[9] Fear is used in a good sense by the apostle when he says, "Work out your salvation with fear and trembling."[10] And, "Be not high-minded, but fear."[11] And, "I fear,

lest by any means, as the serpent beguiled Eve through his subtlety, so your minds should be corrupted from the simplicity that is in Christ."[12] But with respect to sadness, which Cicero prefers to call sickness (*ægritudo*), and Virgil pain (*dolor*) (as he says, "*Dolent gaudentque*"[13]), but which I prefer to call sorrow, because sickness and pain are more commonly used to express bodily suffering—with respect to this emotion, I say, the question whether it can be used in a good sense is more difficult.

CHAP. 8. *Of the three perturbations, which the Stoics admitted in the soul of the wise man to the exclusion of grief or sadness, which the manly mind ought not to experience*

Those emotions which the Greeks call εὐπαθείαι, and which Cicero calls *constantiæ*, the Stoics would restrict to three; and, instead of three "perturbations" in the soul of the wise man, they substituted severally, in place of desire, will; in place of joy, contentment; and for fear, caution; and as to sickness or pain, which we, to avoid ambiguity, preferred to call sorrow, they denied that it could exist in the mind of a wise man. Will, they say, seeks the good, for this the wise man does. Contentment has its object in good that is possessed, and this the wise man continually possesses. Caution avoids evil, and this the wise man ought to avoid. But sorrow arises from evil that has already happened; and as they suppose that no evil can happen to the wise man, there can be no representative of sorrow in his mind. According to them, therefore, none but the wise man wills, is contented, uses caution; and that the fool can do no more than desire, rejoice, fear, be sad. The former three affections Cicero calls *constantiæ*, the last four *perturbationes*. Many, however, call these last *passiones;* and, as I have said, the Greeks call the former εὐπαθείαι, and the latter πάθη. And when I made a careful examination of Scripture to find whether this terminology was sanctioned by it, I came upon this saying of the prophet: "There is no contentment to the wicked, saith the Lord";[14] as if the wicked might more properly rejoice than be contented regarding evils, for contentment is the property of the good and godly. I found also that verse in the Gospel: "Whatsoever ye would that men should do unto you, do ye even so unto them";[15] which seems to imply that evil or shameful things may be the object of desire, but not of will. Indeed, some interpreters have added "good things," to

[1]Ps. 11. 5.   [2]I John, 2. 15.   [3]II Tim. 3. 2.
[4]Phil. 1. 23.   [5]Ps. 119. 20.   [6]Wisd. 6. 20.
[7]Ps. 32. 11.   [8]Ps. 4. 7.   [9]Ps. 16. 11.
[10]Phil. 2. 12.   [11]Rom. 11. 20.

[12]II Cor. 11. 3.   [13]*Æneid*, BK. VI. 733.
[14]Isa. 57. 21.   [15]Matt. 7. 12.

make the expression more in conformity with customary usage, and have given this meaning, "Whatsoever good deeds that ye would that men should do unto you." For they thought that this would prevent any one from wishing other men to provide him with unseemly, not to say shameful gratifications—luxurious banquets, for example—on the supposition that if he returned the like to them he would be fulfilling this precept. In the Greek Gospel, however, from which the Latin is translated, "good" does not occur, but only, "All things whatsoever ye would that men should do unto you, do ye even so unto them," and, as I believe, because "good" is already included in the word "would"; for He does not say "desire."

Yet though we may sometimes avail ourselves of these precise proprieties of language, we are not to be always bridled by them; and when we read those writers against whose authority it is unlawful to reclaim, we must accept the meanings above mentioned in passages where a right sense can be educed by no other interpretation, as in those instances we adduced partly from the prophet, partly from the Gospel. For who does not know that the wicked exult with joy? Yet "there is no *contentment* for the wicked, saith the Lord." And how so, unless because contentment, when the word is used in its proper and distinctive significance, means something different from joy? In like manner, who would deny that it were wrong to enjoin upon men that whatever they desire others to do to them they should themselves do to others, lest they should mutually please one another by shameful and illicit pleasure? And yet the precept, "Whatsoever ye *would* that men should do unto you, do ye even so to them," is very wholesome and just. And how is this, unless because the will is in this place used strictly, and signifies that will which cannot have evil for its object? But ordinary phraseology would not have allowed the saying, "Be unwilling to make any manner of lie,"[1] had there not been also an evil will, whose wickedness separates it from that which the angels celebrated, "Peace on earth, of good will to men."[2] For "good" is superfluous if there is no other kind of will but good will. And why should the apostle have mentioned it among the praises of charity as a great thing, that "it rejoices not in iniquity," unless because wickedness does so rejoice? For even with secular writers these words are used indifferently. For Cicero, that most fertile of orators, says, "I desire, conscript fathers, to be merciful." And who

would be so pedantic as to say that he should have said "I will" rather than "I desire," because the word is used in a good connection? Again, in Terence, the profligate youth, burning with wild lust, says, "I will nothing else than Philumena." That this "will" was lust is sufficiently indicated by the answer of his old servant which is there introduced: "How much better were it to try and banish that love from your heart, than to speak so as uselessly to inflame your passion still more!" And that contentment was used by secular writers in a bad sense, that verse of Virgil testifies, in which he most succinctly comprehends these four perturbations—

Hence they fear and desire, grieve and are content.[3]
The same author had also used the expression, "the evil contentments of the mind."[4] So that good and bad men alike will, are cautious and contented; or, to say the same thing in other words, good and bad men alike desire, fear, rejoice, but the former in a good, the latter in a bad fashion, according as the will is right or wrong. Sorrow itself, too, which the Stoics would not allow to be represented in the mind of the wise man, is used in a good sense, and especially in our writings. For the apostle praises the Corinthians because they had a godly sorrow. But possibly some one may say that the apostle congratulated them because they were penitently sorry, and that such sorrow can exist only in those who have sinned. For these are his words: "For I perceive that the same epistle hath made you sorry, though it were but for a season. Now I rejoice, not that ye were made sorry, but that ye sorrowed to repentance; for ye were made sorry after a godly manner, that ye might receive damage by us in nothing. For godly sorrow worketh repentance to salvation not to be repented of, but the sorrow of the world worketh death. For, behold, this selfsame thing that ye sorrowed after a godly sort, what carefulness it wrought in you!"[5] Consequently the Stoics may defend themselves by replying, that sorrow is indeed useful for repentance of sin, but that this can have no place in the mind of the wise man, inasmuch as no sin attaches to him of which he could sorrowfully repent, nor any other evil the endurance or experience of which could make him sorrowful. For they say that Alcibiades (if my memory does not deceive me), who believed himself happy, shed tears when Socrates argued with him, and demon-

---

[1] Ecclus. 7. 13.   [2] Luke, 2. 14.

[3] *Æneid*, BK. VI. 733.   [4] *Æneid*, BK. V. 278.
[5] II Cor. 7. 8–11.

strated that he was miserable because he was foolish. In his case, therefore, folly was the cause of this useful and desirable sorrow, wherewith a man mourns that he is what he ought not to be. But the Stoics maintain not that the fool, but that the wise man, cannot be sorrowful.

CHAP. 9. *Of the perturbations of the soul which appear as right affections in the life of the righteous*

But so far as regards this question of mental perturbations, we have answered these philosophers in the ninth book[1] of this work, showing that it is rather a verbal than a real dispute, and that they seek contention rather than truth. Among ourselves, according to the sacred Scriptures and sound doctrine, the citizens of the holy city of God, who live according to God in the pilgrimage of this life, both fear and desire, and grieve and rejoice. And because their love is rightly placed, all these affections of theirs are right. They fear eternal punishment, they desire eternal life; they grieve because they themselves groan within themselves, waiting for the adoption, the redemption of their body;[2] they rejoice in hope, because there "shall be brought to pass the saying that is written, Death is swallowed up in victory."[3] In like manner they fear to sin, they desire to persevere; they grieve in sin, they rejoice in good works. They fear to sin, because they hear that "because iniquity shall abound, the love of many shall wax cold."[4] They desire to persevere, because they hear that it is written, "He that endureth to the end shall be saved."[5] They grieve for sin, hearing that "If we say that we have no sin, we deceive ourselves, and the truth is not in us."[6] They rejoice in good works, because they hear that "the Lord loveth a cheerful giver."[7] In like manner, according as they are strong or weak, they fear or desire to be tempted, grieve or rejoice in temptation. They fear to be tempted, because they hear the injunction, "If a man be overtaken in a fault, ye which are spiritual restore such an one in the spirit of meekness; considering thyself, lest thou also be tempted."[8] They desire to be tempted, because they hear one of the heroes of the city of God saying, "Examine me, O Lord, and tempt me: try my reins and my heart."[9] They grieve in temptations, because they see Peter weeping;[10] they rejoice in tempta-

tions, because they hear James saying, "My brethren, count it all joy when ye fall into divers temptations."[11]

And not only on their own account do they experience these emotions, but also on account of those whose deliverance they desire and whose perdition they fear, and whose loss or salvation affects them with grief or with joy. For if we who have come into the Church from among the Gentiles may suitably instance that noble and mighty hero who glories in his infirmities, the teacher (*doctor*) of the nations in faith and truth, who also laboured more than all his fellow-apostles, and instructed the tribes of God's people by his epistles, which edified not only those of his own time, but all those who were to be gathered in—that hero, I say, and athlete of Christ, instructed by Him, anointed of His Spirit, crucified with Him, glorious in Him, lawfully maintaining a great conflict on the theatre of this world, and being made a spectacle to angels and men,[12] and pressing onwards for the prize of his high calling[13]—very joyfully do we with the eyes of faith behold him rejoicing with them that rejoice, and weeping with them that weep;[14] though hampered by fightings without and fears within;[15] desiring to depart and to be with Christ;[16] longing to see the Romans, that he might have some fruit among them as among other Gentiles;[17] being jealous over the Corinthians, and fearing in that jealousy lest their minds should be corrupted from the chastity that is in Christ;[18] having great heaviness and continual sorrow of heart for the Israelites,[19] because they, being ignorant of God's righteousness, and going about to establish their own righteousness, have not submitted themselves unto the righteousness of God;[20] and expressing not only his sorrow, but bitter lamentation over some who had formally sinned and had not repented of their uncleanness and fornications.[21]

If these emotions and affections, arising as they do from the love of what is good and from a holy charity, are to be called vices, then let us allow these emotions which are truly vices to pass under the name of virtues. But since these affections, when they are exercised in a becoming way, follow the guidance of right reason, who will dare to say that they are diseases or vicious passions? Wherefore even the Lord Himself, when He condescended to lead a hu-

---

[1]Chaps. 4, 5.   [2]Rom. 8. 23.   [3] ICor. 15. 54.
[4]Matt. 24. 12.   [5]Matt. 10. 22.   [6]I John, 1. 8.
[7]II Cor. 9. 7.   [8]Gal. 6. 1.   [9]Ps. 26. 2.
[10]Matt. 26. 75.

[11]Jas. 1. 2.   [12]I Cor. 4. 9.   [13]Phil. 3. 14.
[14]Rom. 12. 15.   [15]II Cor. 7. 5.   [16]Phil. 1. 23.
[17]Rom. 1. 11–13.   [18]II Cor. 11. 1–3.   [19]Rom. 9. 2.
[20]Rom. 10. 3.   [21]II Cor. 12. 21.

man life in the form of a slave, had no sin whatever, and yet exercised these emotions where
He judged they should be exercised. For as there
was in Him a true human body and a true human soul, so was there also a true human emotion. When, therefore, we read in the Gospel
that the hardheartedness of the Jews moved
Him to sorrowful indignation,[1] that He said,
"I am glad for your sakes, to the intent ye may
believe,"[2] that when about to raise Lazarus He
even shed tears,[3] that He earnestly desired to
eat the passover with His disciples,[4] that as His
passion drew near His soul was sorrowful,[5]
these emotions are certainly not falsely ascribed
to Him. But as He became man when it pleased
Him, so, in the grace of His definite purpose,
when it pleased Him He experienced those emotions in His human soul.

But we must further make the admission, that
even when these affections are well regulated,
and according to God's will, they are peculiar to
this life, not to that future life we look for, and
that often we yield to them against our will.
And thus sometimes we weep in spite of ourselves, being carried beyond ourselves, not indeed by culpable desire, but by praiseworthy
charity. In us, therefore, these affections arise
from human infirmity; but it was not so with
the Lord Jesus, for even His infirmity was the
consequence of His power. But so long as we
wear the infirmity of this life, we are rather
worse men than better if we have none of these
emotions at all. For the apostle vituperated and
abominated some who, as he said, were "without
natural affection."[6] The sacred Psalmist also
found fault with those of whom he said, "I
looked for some to lament with me, and there
was none."[7] For to be quite free from pain while
we are in this place of misery is only purchased,
as one of this world's *literati* perceived and remarked, at the price of blunted sensibilities both
of mind and body. And therefore that which
the Greeks call ἀπάθεια, and what the Latins
would call, if their language would allow them,
"impassibilitas," if it be taken to mean an im-
passibility of spirit and not of body, or, in other
words, a freedom from those emotions which
are contrary to reason and disturb the mind,
then it is obviously a good and most desirable
quality, but it is not one which is attainable in
this life. For the words of the apostle are the
confession, not of the common herd, but of the
eminently pious, just, and holy men: "If we say

we have no sin, we deceive ourselves, and the
truth is not in us."[8] When there shall be no sin
in a man, then there shall be this ἀπάθεια,
At present it is enough if we live without crime;
and he who thinks he lives without sin puts
aside not sin, but pardon. And if that is to be
called apathy, where the mind is the subject of
no emotion, then who would not consider this
insensibility to be worse than all vices? It may,
indeed, reasonably be maintained that the perfect blessedness we hope for shall be free from
all sting of fear or sadness; but who that is not
quite lost to truth would say that neither love
nor joy shall be experienced there? But if by
apathy a condition be meant in which no fear
terrifies nor any pain annoys, we must in this
life renounce such a state if we would live according to God's will, but may hope to enjoy it
in that blessedness which is promised as our
eternal condition.

For that fear of which the Apostle John says,
"There is no fear in love; but perfect love casteth out fear, because fear hath torment. He that
feareth is not made perfect in love";[9] that fear
is not of the same kind as the Apostle Paul felt
lest the Corinthians should be seduced by the
subtlety of the serpent; for love is susceptible
of this fear, yea, love alone is capable of it. But
the fear which is not in love is of that kind of
which Paul himself says, "For ye have not received the spirit of bondage again to fear."[10] But
as for that "clean fear which endureth for
ever,"[11] if it is to exist in the world to come (and
how else can it be said to endure for ever?), it is
not a fear deterring us from evil which may happen, but preserving us in the good which cannot
be lost. For where the love of acquired good is
unchangeable, there certainly the fear that
avoids evil is, if I may say so, free from anxiety.
For under the name of "clean fear" David signifies that will by which we shall necessarily
shrink from sin, and guard against it, not with
the anxiety of weakness, which fears that we
may strongly sin, but with the tranquillity of
perfect love. Or if no kind of fear at all shall
exist in that most imperturbable security of perpetual and blissful delights, then the expression,
"The fear of the Lord is clean, enduring for
ever," must be taken in the same sense as that
other, "The patience of the poor shall not perish
for ever."[12] For patience, which is necessary only
where ills are to be borne, shall not be eternal,
but that which patience leads us to will be eternal. So perhaps this "clean fear" is said to en-

---

[1]Mark, 3. 5. [2]John, 11. 15. [3]John, 11. 35.
[4]Luke, 22. 15. [5]Matt. 26. 38. [6]Rom. 1. 31.
[7]Ps. 69. 20.

[8]I John, 1. 8. [9]I John, 4. 18. [10]Rom. 8. 15.
[11]Ps. 19. 9. [12]Ps. 9. 18.

dure for ever, because that to which fear leads shall endure.

And since this is so—since we must live a good life in order to attain to a blessed life—a good life has all these affections right, a bad life has them wrong. But in the blessed life eternal there will be love and joy, not only right, but also assured; but fear and grief there will be none. Whence it already appears in some sort what manner of persons the citizens of the city of God must be in this their pilgrimage, who live after the spirit, not after the flesh—that is to say, according to God, not according to man—and what manner of persons they shall be also in that immortality whither they are journeying. And the city or society of the wicked, who live not according to God, but according to man, and who accept the doctrines of men or devils in the worship of a false and contempt of the true divinity, is shaken with those wicked emotions as by diseases and disturbances. And if there be some of its citizens who seem to restrain and, as it were, temper those passions, they are so elated with ungodly pride, that their disease is as much greater as their pain is less. And if some, with a vanity monstrous in proportion to its rarity, have become enamoured of themselves because they can be stimulated and excited by no emotion, moved or bent by no affection, such persons rather lose all humanity than obtain true tranquillity. For a thing is not necessarily right because it is inflexible, nor healthy because it is insensible.

CHAP. 10. *Whether it is to be believed that our first parents in Paradise, before they sinned, were free from all perturbation*

But it is a fair question, whether our first parent or first parents (for there was a marriage of two), before they sinned, experienced in their animal body such emotions as we shall not experience in the spiritual body when sin has been purged and finally abolished. For if they did, then how were they blessed in that boasted place of bliss, Paradise? For who that is affected by fear or grief can be called absolutely blessed? And what could those persons fear or suffer in such affluence of blessings, where neither death nor ill-health was feared, and where nothing was wanting which a good will could desire, and nothing present which could interrupt man's mental or bodily enjoyment? Their love to God was unclouded, and their mutual affection was that of faithful and sincere marriage; and from this love flowed a wonderful delight, because they always enjoyed what was loved. Their

avoidance of sin was tranquil; and, so long as it was maintained, no other ill at all could invade them and bring sorrow. Or did they perhaps desire to touch and eat the forbidden fruit, yet feared to die; and thus both fear and desire already, even in that blissful place, preyed upon those first of mankind? Away with the thought that such could be the case where there was no sin! And, indeed, this is already sin, to desire those things which the law of God forbids and to abstain from them through fear of punishment, not through love of righteousness. Away, I say, with the thought, that before there was any sin, there should already have been committed regarding that fruit the very sin which our Lord warns us against regarding a woman: "Whosoever looketh on a woman to lust after her, hath committed adultery with her already in his heart."[1] As happy, then, as were these our first parents, who were agitated by no mental perturbations, and annoyed by no bodily discomforts, so happy should the whole human race have been, had they not introduced that evil which they have transmitted to their posterity, and had none of their descendants committed iniquity worthy of damnation; but this original blessedness continuing until, in virtue of that benediction which said, "Increase and multiply,"[2] the number of the predestined saints should have been completed, there would then have been bestowed that higher felicity which is enjoyed by the most blessed angels—a blessedness in which there should have been a secure assurance that no one would sin, and no one die; and so should the saints have lived, after no taste of labour, pain, or death, as now they shall live in the resurrection, after they have endured all these things.

CHAP. 11. *Of the fall of the first man, in whom nature was created good, and can be restored only by its Author*

But because God foresaw all things, and was therefore not ignorant that man also would fall, we ought to consider this holy city in connection with what God foresaw and ordained, and not according to our own ideas, which do not embrace God's ordination. For man, by his sin, could not disturb the divine counsel, nor compel God to change what He had decreed; for God's foreknowledge had anticipated both—that is to say, both how evil the man whom He had created good should become, and what good He Himself should even thus derive from him. For though God is said to change His determinations

[1]Matt. 5. 28.   [2]Gen. 1. 28.

(so that in a tropical sense the Holy Scripture says even that God repented[1]), this is said with reference to man's expectation, or the order of natural causes, and not with reference to that which the Almighty had foreknown that He would do. Accordingly God, as it is written, made man upright,[2] and consequently with a good will. For if he had not had a good will, he could not have been upright. The good will, then, is the work of God; for God created him with it. But the first evil will, which preceded all man's evil acts, was rather a kind of falling away from the work of God to its own works than any positive work. And therefore the acts resulting were evil, not having God, but the will itself for their end; so that the will or the man himself, so far as his will is bad, was as it were the evil tree bringing forth evil fruit. Moreover, the bad will, though it be not in harmony with, but opposed to nature, inasmuch as it is a vice or blemish, yet it is true of it as of all vice, that it cannot exist except in a nature, and only in a nature created out of nothing, and not in that which the Creator has begotten of Himself, as He begot the Word, by Whom all things were made. For though God formed man of the dust of the earth, yet the earth itself, and every earthly material, is absolutely created out of nothing; and man's soul, too, God created out of nothing, and joined to the body, when He made man. But evils are so thoroughly overcome by good that, though they are permitted to exist for the sake of demonstrating how the most righteous foresight of God can make a good use even of them, yet good can exist without evil, as in the true and supreme God Himself, and as in every invisible and visible celestial creature that exists above this murky atmosphere; but evil cannot exist without good, because the natures in which evil exists, in so far as they are natures, are good. And evil is removed, not by removing any nature, or part of a nature, which had been introduced by the evil, but by healing and correcting that which had been vitiated and depraved. The will, therefore, is then truly free, when it is not the slave of vices and sins. Such was it given us by God; and this being lost by its own fault, can only be restored by Him Who was able at first to give it. And therefore the truth says, "If the Son shall make you free, ye shall be free indeed";[3] which is equivalent to saying, "If the Son shall save you, ye shall be saved indeed." For He is our Liberator, inasmuch as He is our Saviour.

Man then lived with God for his rule in a paradise at once physical and spiritual. For neither was it a paradise only physical for the advantage of the body, and not also spiritual for the advantage of the mind; nor was it only spiritual to afford enjoyment to man by his internal sensations, and not also physical to afford him enjoyment through his external senses. But obviously it was both for both ends. But after that proud and therefore envious angel (of whose fall I have said as much as I was able in the eleventh and twelfth books of this work, as well as that of his fellows, who, from being God's angels, became his angels), preferring to rule with a kind of pomp of empire rather than to be another's subject, fell from the spiritual Paradise, and essaying to insinuate his persuasive guile into the mind of man, whose unfallen condition provoked him to envy now that himself was fallen, he chose the serpent as his mouthpiece in that bodily Paradise in which it and all the other earthly animals were living with those two human beings, the man and his wife, subject to them, and harmless; and he chose the serpent because, being slippery, and moving in tortuous windings, it was suitable for his purpose. And this animal being subdued to his wicked ends by the presence and superior force of his angelic nature, he abused as his instrument, and first tried his deceit upon the woman, making his assault upon the weaker part of that human alliance, that he might gradually gain the whole, and not supposing that the man would readily give ear to him, or be deceived, but that he might yield to the error of the woman. For as Aaron was not induced to agree with the people when they blindly wished him to make an idol, and yet yielded to constraint; and as it is not credible that Solomon was so blind as to suppose that idols should be worshipped, but was drawn over to such sacrilege by the blandishments of women; so we cannot believe that Adam was deceived, and supposed the devil's word to be truth, and therefore transgressed God's law, but that he by the drawings of kindred yielded to the woman, the husband to the wife, the one human being to the only other human being. For not without significance did the apostle say, "And Adam was not deceived, but the woman being deceived was in the transgression";[4] but he speaks thus, because the woman accepted as true what the serpent told her, but the man could not bear to be severed from his only companion, even though this involved a partnership in sin. He was not on this account

[1]Gen. 6. 6; and I Sam. 15. 11.
[2]Eccles. 7. 29.   [3]I John, 8. 36.   [4]I Tim. 2. 14.

less culpable, but sinned with his eyes open. And so the apostle does not say, "He did not sin," but "He was not deceived." For he shows that he sinned when he says, "By one man sin entered into the world,"[1] and immediately after more distinctly, "In the likeness of Adam's transgression." But he meant that those are deceived who do not judge that which they do to be sin; but he knew. Otherwise how were it true "Adam was not deceived"? But having as yet no experience of the divine severity, he was possibly deceived in so far as he thought his sin venial. And consequently he was not deceived as the woman was deceived, but he was deceived as to the judgment which would be passed on his apology: "The woman whom thou gavest to be with me, she gave me, and I did eat."[2] What need of saying more? Although they were not both deceived by credulity, yet both were entangled in the snares of the devil, and taken by sin.

CHAP. 12. *Of the nature of man's first sin*

If any one finds a difficulty in understanding why other sins do not alter human nature as it was altered by the transgression of those first human beings, so that on account of it this nature is subject to the great corruption we feel and see, and to death, and is distracted and tossed with so many furious and contending emotions, and is certainly far different from what it was before sin, even though it were then lodged in an animal body—if, I say, any one is moved by this, he ought not to think that that sin was a small and light one because it was committed about food, and that not bad nor noxious, except because it was forbidden; for in that spot of singular felicity God could not have created and planted any evil thing. But by the precept He gave, God commanded obedience, which is, in a sort, the mother and guardian of all the virtues in the reasonable creature, which was so created that submission is advantageous to it, while the fulfillment of its own will in preference to the Creator's is destruction. And as this commandment enjoining abstinence from one kind of food in the midst of great abundance of other kinds was so easy to keep—so light a burden to the memory—and, above all, found no resistance to its observance in lust, which only afterwards sprung up as the penal consequence of sin, the iniquity of violating it was all the greater in proportion to the ease with which it might have been kept.

[1]Rom. 5. 12.
[2]Gen. 3. 12.

CHAP. 13. *That in Adam's sin an evil will preceded the evil act*

Our first parents fell into open disobedience because already they were secretly corrupted; for the evil act had never been done had not an evil will preceded it. And what is the origin of our evil will but pride? For "pride is the beginning of sin."[3] And what is pride but the craving for undue exaltation? And this is undue exaltation, when the soul abandons Him to whom it ought to cleave as its end, and becomes a kind of end to itself. This happens when it becomes its own satisfaction. And it does so when it falls away from that unchangeable good which ought to satisfy it more than itself. This falling away is spontaneous; for if the will had remained steadfast in the love of that higher and changeless good by which it was illumined to intelligence and kindled into love, it would not have turned away to find satisfaction in itself and so become frigid and benighted; the woman would not have believed the serpent spoke the truth, nor would the man have preferred the request of his wife to the command of God, nor have supposed that it was a venial transgression to cleave to the partner of his life even in a partnership of sin. The wicked deed, then—that is to say, the transgression of eating the forbidden fruit—was committed by persons who were already wicked. That "evil fruit"[4] could be brought forth only by "a corrupt tree." But that the tree was evil was not the result of nature; for certainly it could become so only by the vice of the will, and vice is contrary to nature. Now, nature could not have been depraved by vice had it not been made out of nothing. Consequently, that it is a nature, this is because it is made by God; but that it falls away from Him, this is because it is made out of nothing. But man did not so fall away as to become absolutely nothing; but being turned towards himself, his being became more contracted than it was when he clave to Him Who supremely is. Accordingly, to exist in himself, that is, to be his own satisfaction after abandoning God, is not quite to become a nonentity, but to approximate to that. And therefore the holy Scriptures designate the proud by another name, "self-pleasers." For it is good to have the heart lifted up, yet not to one's self, for this is proud, but to the Lord, for this is obedient, and can be the act only of the humble. There is, therefore, something in humility which, strangely enough, exalts the heart, and something in pride which

[3]Ecclus. 10. 13.   [4]Matt. 7. 18.

debases it. This seems, indeed, to be contradictory, that loftiness should debase and lowliness exalt. But pious humility enables us to submit to what is above us; and nothing is more exalted above us than God; and therefore humility, by making us subject to God, exalts us. But pride, being a defect of nature, by the very act of refusing subjection and revolting from Him who is supreme, falls to a low condition; and then comes to pass what is written: "Thou castedst them down when they lifted up themselves."[1] For he does not say, "when they had been lifted up," as if first they were exalted, and then afterwards cast down; but "when they lifted up themselves" even then they were cast down—that is to say, the very lifting up was already a fall. And therefore it is that humility is specially recommended to the city of God as it sojourns in this world, and is specially exhibited in the city of God, and in the person of Christ its King; while the contrary vice of pride, according to the testimony of the sacred writings, specially rules his adversary the devil. And certainly this is the great difference which distinguishes the two cities of which we speak, the one being the society of the godly men, the other of the ungodly, each associated with the angels that adhere to their party, and the one guided and fashioned by love of self, the other by love of God.

The devil, then, would not have ensnared man in the open and manifest sin of doing what God had forbidden, had man not already begun to live for himself. It was this that made him listen with pleasure to the words, "Ye shall be as gods,"[2] which they would much more readily have accomplished by obediently adhering to their supreme and true end than by proudly living to themselves. For created gods are gods not by virtue of what is in themselves, but by a participation of the true God. By craving to be more, man becomes less; and by aspiring to be self-sufficing, he fell away from Him Who truly suffices him. Accordingly, this wicked desire which prompts man to please himself as if he were himself light, and which thus turns him away from that light by which, had he followed it, he would himself have become light; this wicked desire, I say, already secretly existed in him, and the open sin was but its consequence. For that is true which is written, "Pride goeth before destruction, and before honour is humility";[3] that is to say, secret ruin precedes open ruin, while the former is not counted ruin. For who counts exaltation ruin, though no sooner is

the Highest forsaken than a fall is begun? But who does not recognize it as ruin, when there occurs an evident and indubitable transgression of the commandment? And consequently, God's prohibition had reference to such an act as, when committed, could not be defended on any pretence of doing what was righteous. And I make bold to say that it is useful for the proud to fall into an open and indisputable transgression, and so displease themselves, as already, by pleasing themselves, they had fallen. For Peter was in a healthier condition when he wept and was dissatisfied with himself, than when he boldly presumed and satisfied himself. And this is averred by the sacred Psalmist when he says, "Fill their faces with shame, that they may seek Thy name, O Lord";[4] that is, that they who have pleased themselves in seeking their own glory may be pleased and satisfied with Thee in seeking Thy glory.

CHAP. 14. *Of the pride in the sin, which was worse than the sin itself*

But it is a worse and more damnable pride which casts about for the shelter of an excuse even in manifest sins, as these our first parents did, of whom the woman said, "The serpent beguiled me, and I did eat"; and the man said, "The woman whom Thou gavest to be with me, she gave me of the tree, and I did eat."[5] Here there is no word of begging pardon, no word of entreaty for healing. For though they do not, like Cain, deny that they have perpetrated the deed, yet their pride seeks to refer its wickedness to another—the woman's pride to the serpent, the man's to the woman. But where there is a plain transgression of a divine commandment, this is rather to accuse than to excuse oneself. For the fact that the woman sinned on the serpent's persuasion, and the man at the woman's offer, did not make the transgression less, as if there were any one whom we ought rather to believe or yield to than God.

CHAP. 15. *Of the justice of the punishment with which our first parents were visited for their disobedience*

Therefore, because the sin was a despising of the authority of God—who had created man; who had made him in His own image; who had set him above the other animals; who had placed him in Paradise; who had enriched him with abundance of every kind and of safety; who had laid upon him neither many, nor great, nor difficult commandments, but, in order to

---

[1] Ps. 73. 18.   [2] Gen. 3. 5.   [3] Prov. 18. 12.   [4] Ps. 83. 16.   [5] Gen. 3. 12, 13.

make a wholesome obedience easy to him, had given him a single very brief and very light precept by which He reminded that creature whose service was to be free that He was Lord—it was just that condemnation followed, and condemnation such that man, who by keeping the commandments should have been spiritual even in his flesh, became fleshly even in his spirit; and as in his pride he had sought to be his own satisfaction, God in His justice abandoned him to himself, not to live in the absolute independence he affected, but instead of the liberty he desired, to live dissatisfied with himself in a hard and miserable bondage to him to whom by sinning he had yielded himself, doomed in spite of himself to die in body as he had willingly become dead in spirit, condemned even to eternal death (had not the grace of God delivered him) because he had forsaken eternal life. Whoever thinks such punishment either excessive or unjust shows his inability to measure the great iniquity of sinning where sin might so easily have been avoided. For as Abraham's obedience is with justice pronounced to be great, because the thing commanded, to kill his son, was very difficult, so in Paradise the disobedience was the greater, because the difficulty of that which was commanded was imperceptible. And as the obedience of the second Man was the more laudable because He became obedient even "unto death,"[1] so the disobedience of the first man was the more detestable because he became disobedient even unto death. For where the penalty annexed to disobedience is great, and the thing commanded by the Creator is easy, who can sufficiently estimate how great a wickedness it is, in a matter so easy, not to obey the authority of so great a power, even when that power deters with so terrible a penalty?

In short, to say all in a word, what but disobedience was the punishment of disobedience in that sin? For what else is man's misery but his own disobedience to himself, so that in consequence of his not being willing to do what he could do, he now wills to do what he cannot? For though he could not do all things in Paradise before he sinned, yet he wished to do only what he could do, and therefore he could do all things he wished. But now, as we recognize in his offspring, and as divine Scripture testifies, "Man is like to vanity."[2] For who can count how many things he wishes which he cannot do, so long as he is disobedient to himself, that is, so long as his mind and his flesh do not obey his will? For in spite of himself his mind is both fre-

quently disturbed, and his flesh suffers, and grows old, and dies; and in spite of ourselves we suffer whatever else we suffer, and which we would not suffer if our nature absolutely and in all its parts obeyed our will. But is it not the infirmities of the flesh which hamper it in its service? Yet what does it matter *how* its service is hampered, so long as the fact remains, that by the just retribution of the sovereign God Whom we refused to be subject to and serve, our flesh, which was subjected to us, now torments us by insubordination, although our disobedience brought trouble on ourselves, not upon God? For He is not in need of our service as we of our body's; and therefere what we did was no punishment to Him, but what we receive is so to us. And the pains which are called bodily are pains of the soul in and from the body. For what pain or desire can the flesh feel by itself and without the soul? But when the flesh is said to desire or to suffer, it is meant, as we have explained, that the man does so, or some part of the soul which is affected by the sensation of the flesh, whether a harsh sensation causing pain, or gentle, causing pleasure. But pain in the flesh is only a discomfort of the soul arising from the flesh, and a kind of shrinking from its suffering, as the pair of the soul which is called *sadness* is a shrinking from those things which have happened to us in spite of ourselves. But sadness is frequently preceded by fear, which is itself in the soul, not in the flesh; while bodily pain is not preceded by any kind of fear of the flesh, which can be felt in the flesh before the pain. But pleasure is preceded by a certain appetite which is felt in the flesh like a craving, as hunger and thirst and that generative appetite which is most commonly identified with the name *lust,* though this is the generic word for all desires. For anger itself was defined by the ancients as nothing else than the lust of revenge;[3] although sometimes a man is angry even at inanimate objects which cannot feel his vengeance, as when one breaks a pen, or crushes a quill that writes badly. Yet even this, though less reasonable, is in its way a lust of revenge, and is, so to speak, a mysterious kind of shadow of retribution, that they who do evil should suffer evil. There is therefore a lust for revenge, which is called *anger;* there is a lust of money, which goes by the name of *avarice;* there is a lust of conquering, no matter by what means, which is called *opinionativeness;* there is a lust of applause, which is named *boasting.* There are many and various lusts, of which some have names of their own, while others

<hr>

[1] Phil. 2. 8.   [2] Ps. 144. 4.

[3] So Aristotle.

have not. For who could readily give a name to the lust of ruling, which yet has a powerful influence in the soul of tyrants, as civil wars bear witness?

CHAP. 16. *Of the evil of lust—a word which, though applicable to many vices, is specially appropriated to sexual uncleanness*

Although, therefore, lust may have many objects, yet when no object is specified, the word lust usually suggests to the mind the lustful excitement of the organs of generation. And this lust not only takes possession of the whole body and outward members, but also makes itself felt within and moves the whole man with a passion in which mental emotion is mingled with bodily appetite, so that the pleasure which results is the greatest of all bodily pleasures. So possessing indeed is this pleasure that, at the moment of time in which it is consummated, all mental activity is suspended. What friend of wisdom and holy joys, who, being married, but knowing, as the apostle says, "how to possess his vessel in santification and honour, not in the disease of desire, as the Gentiles who know not God,"[1] would not prefer, if this were possible, to beget children without this lust, so that in this function of begetting offspring the members created for this purpose should not be stimulated by the heat of lust, but should be actuated by his volition, in the same way as his other members serve him for their respective ends? But even those who delight in this pleasure are not moved to it at their own will, whether they confine themselves to lawful or transgress to unlawful pleasures; but sometimes this lust importunes them in spite of themselves, and sometimes fails them when they desire to feel it, so that though lust rages in the mind, it stirs not in the body. Thus, strangely enough, this emotion not only fails to obey the legitimate desire to beget offspring, but also refuses to serve lascivious lust; and though it often opposes its whole combined energy to the soul that resists it, sometimes also it is divided against itself, and while it moves the soul, leaves the body unmoved.

CHAP. 17. *Of the nakedness of our first parents, which they saw after their base and shameful sin*

Justly is shame very specially connected with this lust; justly, too, these members themselves, being moved and restrained not at our will, but by a certain independent autocracy, so to speak, are called "shameful." Their condition was different before sin. For as it is written, "They were naked and were not ashamed";[2] not that their nakedness was unknown to them, but because nakedness was not yet shameful, because not yet did lust move those members without the will's consent; not yet did the flesh by its disobedience testify against the disobedience of man. For they were not created blind, as the unenlightened vulgar fancy;[3] for Adam saw the animals to whom he gave names, and of Eve we read, "The woman saw that the tree was good for food, and that it was pleasant to the eyes."[4] Their eyes, therefore, were open, but were not open to this, that is to say, were not observant so as to recognize what was conferred upon them by the garment of grace, for they had no consciousness of their members warring against their will. But when they were stripped of this grace, that their disobedience might be punished by fit retribution, there began in the movement of their bodily members a shameless novelty which made nakedness indecent: it at once made them observant and made them ashamed. And therefore, after they violated God's command by open transgression, it is written: "And the eyes of them both were opened, and they knew that they were naked; and they sewed fig leaves together, and made themselves aprons."[5] "The eyes of them both were opened," not to see, for already they saw, but to discern between the good they had lost and the evil into which they had fallen. And therefore also the tree itself which they were forbidden to touch was called the tree of the knowledge of good and evil from this circumstance, that if they ate of it it would impart to them this knowledge. For the discomfort of sickness reveals the pleasure of health. "They knew," therefore, "that they were naked"—naked of that grace which prevented them from being ashamed of bodily nakedness while the law of sin offered no resistance to their mind. And thus they obtained a knowledge which they would have lived in blissful ignorance of, had they, in trustful obedience to God, declined to commit that offence which involved them in the experience of the hurtful effects of unfaithfulness and disobedience. And therefore, being ashamed of the disobedience of their own flesh, which witnessed to their disobedience while it punished it, "they sewed fig leaves together, and made themselves aprons," that is, cinctures for their privy parts; for some

[1] I Thess. 4. 4.

[2] Gen. 2. 25.
[3] An error which arose from the words, "The eyes of them both were opened," Gen. 3. 7.
[4] Gen. 3. 6.   [5] Gen. 3. 7.

interpreters have rendered the word by *succinctoria*. *Campestria* is, indeed, a Latin word, but it is used of the drawers or aprons used for a similar purpose by the young men who stripped for exercise in the *campus;* hence those who were so girt were commonly called *campestrati.* Shame modestly covered that which lust disobediently moved in opposition to the will, which was thus punished for its own disobedience. Consequently all nations, being propagated from that one stock, have so strong an instinct to cover the shameful parts that some barbarians do not uncover them even in the bath, but wash with their drawers on. In the dark solitudes of India also, though some philosophers go naked, and are therefore called gymnosophists, yet they make an exception in the case of these members, and cover them.

CHAP. 18. *Of the shame which attends all sexual intercourse*

Lust requires for its consummation darkness and secrecy; and this not only when unlawful intercourse is desired, but even such fornication as the earthly city has legalized. Where there is no fear of punishment, these permitted pleasures still shrink from the public eye. Even where provision is made for this lust, secrecy also is provided; and while lust found it easy to remove the prohibitions of law, shamelessness found it impossible to lay aside the veil of retirement. For even shameless men call this shameful; and though they love the pleasure, dare not display it. What! does not even conjugal intercourse, sanctioned as it is by law for the propagation of children, legitimate and honourable though it be, does it not seek retirement from every eye? Before the bridegroom fondles his bride, does he not exclude the attendants, and even the paranymphs, and such friends as the closest ties have admitted to the bridal chamber? The greatest master of Roman eloquence says that all right actions wish to be set in the light, i.e., desire to be known. This right action, however, has such a desire to be known that yet it blushes to be seen. Who does not know what passes between husband and wife that children may be born? Is it not for this purpose that wives are married with such ceremony? And yet, when this well-understood act is gone about for the procreation of children, not even the children themselves, who may already have been born to them, are suffered to be witnesses. This right action seeks the light, in so far as it seeks to be known, but yet dreads being seen. And why so, if not because that

which is by nature fitting and decent is so done as to be accompanied with a shame-begetting penalty of sin?

CHAP. 19. *That it is now necessary, as it was not before man sinned, to bridle anger and lust by the restraining influence of wisdom*

Hence it is that even the philosophers who have approximated to the truth have avowed that anger and lust are vicious mental emotions, because, even when exercised towards objects which wisdom does not prohibit, they are moved in an ungoverned and inordinate manner, and consequently need the regulation of mind and reason. And they assert that this third part of the mind is posted as it were in a kind of citadel, to give rule to these other parts, so that, while it rules and they serve, man's righteousness is preserved without a breach.[1] These parts, then, which they acknowledge to be vicious even in a wise and temperate man, so that the mind, by its composing and restraining influence, must bridle and recall them from those objects towards which they are unlawfully moved, and give them access to those which the law of wisdom sanctions—that anger, e.g., may be allowed for the enforcement of a just authority, and lust for the duty of propagating offspring—these parts, I say, were not vicious in Paradise before sin, for they were never moved in opposition to a holy will towards any object from which it was necessary that they should be withheld by the restraining bridle of reason. For though now they are moved in this way and are regulated by a bridling and restraining power, which those who live temperately, justly, and godly, exercise, sometimes with ease, and sometimes with greater difficulty, this is not the sound health of nature, but the weakness which results from sin. And how is it that shame does not hide the acts and words dictated by anger or other emotions, as it covers the motions of lust, unless because the members of the body which we employ for accomplishing them are moved, not by the emotions themselves, but by the authority of the consenting will? For he who in his anger rails at or even strikes some one, could not do so were not his tongue and hand moved by the authority of the will, as also they are moved when there is no anger. But the organs of generation are so subjected to the rule of lust, that they have no motion but what it communicates. It is this we are ashamed of; it is this which blushingly hides from the eyes of onlookers. And rather will a man endure a crowd of witnesses when he is un-

[1] See Plato, *Republic*, BK. IV.

justly venting his anger on some one, than the eye of one man when he innocently copulates with his wife.

Chap. 20. Of the foolish beastliness of the Cynics

It is this which those Canine or Cynic[1] philosophers have overlooked, when they have, in violation of the modest instincts of men, boastfully proclaimed their unclean and shameless opinion, worthy indeed of dogs, viz., that as the matrimonial act is legitimate, no one should be ashamed to perform it openly, in the street or in any public place. Instinctive shame has overborne this wild fancy. For though it is related that Diogenes once dared to put his opinion in practice, under the impression that his sect would be all the more famous if his egregious shamelessness were deeply graven in the memory of mankind, yet this example was not afterwards followed. Shame had more influence with them, to make them blush before men, than error to make them affect a resemblance to dogs. And possibly, even in the case of Diogenes, and those who did imitate him, there was but an appearance and pretence of copulation, and not the reality. Even at this day there are still Cynic philosophers to be seen; for these are Cynics who are not content with being clad in the *pallium,* but also carry a club; yet no one of them dares to do this that we speak of. If they did, they would be spat upon, not to say stoned, by the mob. Human nature, then, is without doubt ashamed of this lust; and justly so, for the insubordination of these members, and their defiance of the will, are the clear testimony of the punishment of man's first sin. And it was fitting that this should appear specially in those parts by which is generated that nature which has been altered for the worse by that first and great sin—that sin from whose evil connection no one can escape, unless God's grace expiate in him individually that which was perpetrated to the destruction of all in common, when all were in one man, and which was avenged by God's justice.

Chap. 21. That man's transgression did not annul the blessing of fecundity pronounced upon man before he sinned, but infected it with the disease of lust

Far be it, then, from us to suppose that our first parents in Paradise felt that lust which caused them afterwards to blush and hide their

nakedness, or that by its means they should have fulfilled the benediction of God, "Increase and multiply and replenish the earth";[2] for it was after sin that lust began. It was after sin that our nature, having lost the power it had over the whole body, but not having lost all shame, perceived, noticed, blushed at, and covered it. But that blessing upon marriage, which encouraged them to increase and multiply and replenish the earth, though it continued even after they had sinned, was yet given before they sinned, in order that the procreation of children might be recognized as part of the glory of marriage, and not of the punishment of sin. But now, men being ignorant of the blessedness of Paradise, suppose that children could not have been begotten there in any other way than they know them to be begotten now, i.e., by lust, at which even honourable marriage blushes; some not simply rejecting, but sceptically deriding the divine Scriptures, in which we read that our first parents, after they sinned, were ashamed of their nakedness, and covered it; while others, though they accept and honour Scripture, yet conceive that this expression, "Increase and multiply," refers not to carnal fecundity, because a similar expression is used of the soul in the words, "Thou wilt multiply me with strength in my soul";[3] and so, too, in the words which follow in Genesis, "And replenish the earth, and subdue it," they understand by the earth the body which the soul fills with its presence, and which it rules over when it is multiplied in strength. And they hold that children could no more then than now be begotten without lust, which, after sin, was kindled, observed, blushed for, and covered; and even that children would not have been born in Paradise, but only outside of it, as in fact it turned out. For it was after they were expelled from it that they came together to beget children, and begot them.

Chap. 22. Of the conjugal union as it was originally instituted and blessed by God

But we, for our part, have no manner of doubt that to increase and multiply and replenish the earth in virtue of the blessing of God, is a gift of marriage as God instituted it from the beginning before man sinned, when He created them male and female—in other words, two sexes manifestly distinct. And it was this work of God on which His blessing was pronounced. For no sooner had Scripture said, "Male and female created He them,"[4] than it immediately

---

[1]The one word being the Latin form, the other the Greek, of the same adjective.

[2]Gen. I. 28. [3]Ps. 138. 3. [4]Gen. I. 27, 28.

continues, "And God blessed them, and God said unto them, Increase, and multiply, and replenish the earth, and subdue it," etc. And though all these things may not unsuitably be interpreted in a spiritual sense, yet "male and female" cannot be understood of two things in one man, as if there were in him one thing which rules, another which is ruled; but it is quite clear that they were created male and female, with bodies of different sexes, for the very purpose of begetting offspring, and so increasing, multiplying, and replenishing the earth; and it is great folly to oppose so plain a fact. It was not of the spirit which commands and the body which obeys, nor of the rational soul which rules and the irrational desire which is ruled, nor of the contemplative virtue which is supreme and the active which is subject, nor of the understanding of the mind and the sense of the body, but plainly of the matrimonial union by which the sexes are mutually bound together, that our Lord, when asked whether it were lawful for any cause to put away one's wife (for on account of the hardness of the hearts of the Israelites Moses permitted a bill of divorcement to be given), answered and said, "Have ye not read that He which made them at the beginning made them male and female, and said, For this cause shall a man leave father and mother, and shall cleave to his wife, and they twain shall be one flesh? Wherefore they are no more twain, but one flesh. What, therefore, God hath joined together, let not man put asunder."[1] It is certain, then, that from the first men were created, as we see and know them to be now, of two sexes, male and female, and that they are called one, either on account of the matrimonial union, or on account of the origin of the woman, who was created from the side of the man. And it is by this original example, which God Himself instituted, that the apostle admonishes all husbands to love their own wives in particular.[2]

CHAP. 23. *Whether generation should have taken place even in Paradise had man not sinned, or whether there should have been any contention there between chastity and lust*

But he who says that there should have been neither copulation nor generation but for sin, virtually says that man's sin was necessary to complete the number of the saints. For if these two by not sinning should have continued to live alone, because, as is supposed, they could not have begotten children had they not sinned, then certainly sin was necessary in order that there might be not only two but many righteous men. And if this cannot be maintained without absurdity, we must rather believe that the number of the saints fit to complete this most blessed city would have been as great though no one had sinned, as it is now that the grace of God gathers its citizens out of the multitude of sinners, so long as the children of this world generate and are generated.[3]

And therefore that marriage, worthy of the happiness of Paradise, should have had desirable fruit without the shame of lust, had there been no sin. But how that could be, there is now no example to teach us. Nevertheless, it ought not to seem incredible that one member might serve the will without lust then, since so many serve it now. Do we now move our feet and hands when we will to do the things we would by means of these members? do we meet with no resistance in them, but perceive that they are ready servants of the will, both in our own case and in that of others, and especially of artisans employed in mechanical operations, by which the weakness and clumsiness of nature become, through industrious exercise, wonderfully dexterous? and shall we not believe that, like as all those members obediently serve the will, so also should the members have discharged the function of generation, though lust, the award of disobedience, had been awanting? Did not Cicero in discussing the difference of governments in his *De Republica*, adopt a simile from human nature, and say that we command our bodily members as children, they are so obedient; but that the vicious parts of the soul must be treated as slaves, and be coerced with a more stringent authority? And no doubt, in the order of nature, the soul is more excellent than the body; and yet the soul commands the body more easily than itself. Nevertheless this lust, of which we at present speak, is the more shameful on this account, because the soul is therein neither master of itself, so as not to lust at all, nor of the body, so as to keep the members under the control of the will; for if they were thus ruled, there should be no shame. But now the soul is ashamed that the body, which by nature is inferior and subject to it, should resist its authority. For in the resistance experienced by the soul in the other emotions there is less shame, because the resistance is from itself, and thus, when it is conquered by itself, itself is the conqueror, although the conquest is inordinate and vicious, because accomplished by those parts of

[1]Matt. 19. 4, 5.   [2]Eph. 5. 25.   [3]Luke, 20. 34.

the soul which ought to be subject to reason, yet, being accomplished by its own parts and energies, the conquest is, as I say, its own. For when the soul conquers itself to a due subordination, so that its unreasonable motions are controlled by reason, while it again is subject to God, this is a conquest virtuous and praiseworthy. Yet there is less shame when the soul is resisted by its own vicious parts than when its will and order are resisted by the body, which is distinct from and inferior to it, and dependent on it for life itself.

But so long as the will retains under its authority the other members, without which the members excited by lust to resist the will cannot accomplish what they seek, chastity is preserved, and the delight of sin foregone. And certainly, had not culpable disobedience been visited with penal disobedience, the marriage of Paradise should have been ignorant of this struggle and rebellion, this quarrel between will and lust, that the will may be satisfied and lust restrained, but those members, like all the rest, should have obeyed the will. The field of generation[1] should have been sown by the organ created for this purpose, as the earth is sown by the hand. And whereas now, as we essay to investigate this subject more exactly, modesty hinders us and compels us to ask pardon of chaste ears, there would have been no cause to do so, but we could have discoursed freely, and without fear of seeming obscene, upon all those points which occur to one who meditates on the subject. There would not have been even words which could be called obscene, but all that might be said of these members would have been as pure as what is said of the other parts of the body. Whoever, then, comes to the perusal of these pages with unchaste mind, let him blame his disposition, not his nature; let him brand the actings of his own impurity, not the words which necessity forces us to use, and for which every pure and pious reader or hearer will very readily pardon me, while I expose the folly of that scepticism which argues solely on the ground of its own experience, and has no faith in anything beyond. He who is not scandalized at the apostle's censure of the horrible wickedness of the women who "changed the natural use into that which is against nature,"[2] will read all this without being shocked, especially as we are not, like Paul, citing and censuring a damnable uncleanness, but are explaining, so far as we can, human generation, while with Paul we avoid all obscenity of language.

[1]See Virgil, *Georgics*, BK. III. 136. [2]Rom. I. 26.

CHAP. 24. *That if men had remained innocent and obedient in Paradise, the generative organs should have been in subjection to the will as the other members are*

The man, then, would have sown the seed, and the woman received it, as need required, the generative organs being moved by the will, not excited by lust. For we move at will not only those members which are furnished with joints of solid bone, as the hands, feet, and fingers, but we move also at will those which are composed of slack and soft nerves: we can put them in motion, or stretch them out, or bend and twist them, or contract and stiffen them, as we do with the muscles of the mouth and face. The lungs, which are the very tenderest of the viscera except the brain, and are therefore carefully sheltered in the cavity of the chest, yet for all purposes of inhaling and exhaling the breath, and of uttering and modulating the voice, are obedient to the will when we breathe, exhale, speak, shout, or sing, just as the bellows obey the smith or the organist. I will not press the fact that some animals have a natural power to move a single spot of the skin with which their whole body is covered, if they have felt on it anything they wish to drive off—a power so great, that by this shivering tremor of the skin they can not only shake off flies that have settled on them, but even spears that have fixed in their flesh. Man, it is true, has not this power; but is this any reason for supposing that God could not give it to such creatures as He wished to possess it? And therefore man himself also might very well have enjoyed absolute power over his members had he not forfeited it by his disobedience; for it was not difficult for God to form him so that what is now moved in his body only by lust should have been moved only at will.

We know, too, that some men are differently constituted from others, and have some rare and remarkable faculty of doing with their body what other men can by no effort do, and, indeed, scarcely believe when they hear of others doing. There are persons who can move their ears, either one at a time, or both together. There are some who, without moving the head, can bring the hair down upon the forehead, and move the whole scalp backwards and forwards at pleasure. Some, by lightly pressing their stomach, bring up an incredible quantity and variety of things they have swallowed, and produce whatever they please, quite whole, as if out of a bag. Some so accurately mimic the voices of birds and beasts and other men, that, unless they are seen, the difference cannot be told. Some have such command of their bowels, that they can break wind continuously at pleasure, so as to produce the effect of singing. I myself have known a man who was accustomed to sweat whenever he wished. It is well known that some weep when they please, and shed a flood of tears. But far more incredible is that which some of our brethren saw quite recently. There was a presbyter called Restitutus, in the parish of the Calamensian[1] Church, who, as often as he pleased (and he was asked to do this by those who desired to witness so remarkable a phenomenon), on some one imitating the wailings of mourners, became so insensible, and lay in a state so like death, that not only had he no feeling when they pinched and pricked him, but even when fire was applied to him, and he was burned by it, he had no sense of pain except afterwards from the wound. And that his body remained motionless, not by reason of his self-command, but because he was insensible, was proved by the fact that he breathed no more than a dead man; and yet he said that, when any one spoke with more than ordinary distinctness, he heard the voice, but as if it were a long way off. Seeing, then, that even in this mortal and miserable life the body serves some men by many remarkable movements and moods beyond the ordinary course of nature, what reason is there for doubting that, before man was involved by his sin in this weak and corruptible condition, his members might have served his will for the propagation of offspring without lust? Man has been given over to himself because he abandoned God, while he sought to be self-satisfying; and disobeying God, he could not obey even himself. Hence it is that he is involved in the obvious misery of being unable to live as he wishes. For if he lived as he wished, he would think himself blessed; but he could not be so if he lived wickedly.

CHAP 25. *Of true blessedness, which this present life cannot enjoy*

However, if we look at this a little more closely, we see that no one lives as he wishes but the blessed, and that no one is blessed but the righteous. But even the righteous himself does not live as he wishes, until he has arrived where he cannot die, be deceived, or injured, and until he is assured that this shall be his eternal condition. For this nature demands; and nature is not fully and perfectly blessed till it attains

what it seeks. But what man is at present able to live as he wishes, when it is not in his power so much as to live? He wishes to live, he is compelled to die. How, then, does he live as he wishes who does not live as long as he wishes? or if he wishes to die, how can he live as he wishes, since he does not wish even to live? Or if he wishes to die, not because he dislikes life, but that after death he may live better, still he is not yet living as he wishes, but only has the prospect of so living when, through death, he reaches that which he wishes. But admit that he lives as he wishes, because he has done violence to himself, and forced himself not to wish what he cannot obtain, and to wish only what he can (as Terence has it, "Since you cannot do what you will, will what you can"), is he therefore blessed because he is patiently wretched? For a blessed life is possessed only by the man who loves it. If it is loved and possessed, it must necessarily be more ardently loved than all besides; for whatever else is loved must be loved for the sake of the blessed life. And if it is loved as it deserves to be—and the man is not blessed who does not love the blessed life as it deserves— then he who so loves it cannot but wish it to be eternal. Therefore it shall then only be blessed when it is eternal.

CHAP. 26. *That we are to believe that in Paradise our first parents begat offspring without blushing*

In Paradise, then, man lived as he desired so long as he desired what God had commanded. He lived in the enjoyment of God, and was good by God's goodness; he lived without any want, and had it in his power so to live eternally. He had food that he might not hunger, drink that he might not thirst, the tree of life that old age might not waste him. There was in his body no corruption, nor seed of corruption, which could produce in him any unpleasant sensation. He feared no inward disease, no outward accident. Soundest health blessed his body, absolute tranquillity his soul. As in Paradise there was no excessive heat or cold, so its inhabitants were exempt from the vicissitudes of fear and desire. No sadness of any kind was there, nor any foolish joy; true gladness ceaselessly flowed from the presence of God, who was loved "out of a pure heart, and a good conscience, and faith unfeigned."[2] The honest love of husband and wife made a sure harmony between them. Body and spirit worked harmoniously together, and the commandment was kept without labour. No lan-

---

[1] The position of Calama is described by Augustine as between Constantine and Hippo, but nearer Hippo.

[2] I Tim. i. 5.

guor made their leisure wearisome; no sleepiness interrupted their desire to labour. Men and women dwelling happily in this well-ordered world, did not beget their offspring in the weakness of passionate desire, for the sexual appetite, like all others, stirred but at the bidding of the will. And husband and wife embraced in the marital act, not goaded on by the heat and prickings of voluptuous desires, but rather in peace of soul and with integrity of body. Nor does it follow that what experience cannot prove must be rejected, for at that time those privy parts were not moved by the turbulence of lust, but acted in accordance with nature as the need arose. Hence, as now we know, a virgin is not physically changed by the menstrual flow, so in those days the wife could receive into the womb her husband's seed without rupture of the hymen; for indeed, the semen could flow in through the same ducts that bear out the menstrual discharge. And as the womb opens up to give birth, not when a woman cries in pain, but when in the course of nature her time has come, so the sexes should be joined together to beget and bring forth not out of lust, but in accordance with the right desires of the will. We speak of things which are now shameful, and although we try, as well as we are able, to conceive them as they were before they became shameful, yet necessity compels us rather to limit our discussion to the bounds set by modesty than to extend it as our moderate faculty of discourse might suggest. For since that which I have been speaking of was not experienced even by those who might have experienced it—I mean our first parents (for sin and its merited banishment from Paradise anticipated this passionless generation on their part)—when sexual intercourse is spoken of now, it suggests to men's thoughts not such a placid obedience to the will as is conceivable in our first parents, but such violent acting of lust as they themselves have experienced. And therefore modesty shuts my mouth, although my mind conceives the matter clearly. But Almighty God, the supreme and supremely good Creator of all natures, who aids and rewards good wills, while He abandons and condemns the bad, and rules both, was not destitute of a plan by which He might people His city with the fixed number of citizens which His wisdom had foreordained even out of the condemned human race, discriminating them not now by merits, since the whole mass was condemned as if in a vitiated root, but by grace, and showing, not only in the case of the redeemed, but also in those who were not delivered, how much grace He has bestowed upon them. For every one acknowledges that he has been rescued from evil, not by deserved, but by gratuitous goodness, when he is singled out from the company of those with whom he might justly have borne a common punishment, and is allowed to go scathless. Why, then, should God not have created those whom He foresaw would sin, since He was able to show in and by them both what their guilt merited, and what His grace bestowed, and since, under His creating and disposing hand, even the perverse disorder of the wicked could not pervert the right order of things?

CHAP. 27. *Of the angels and men who sinned, and that their wickedness did not disturb the order of God's providence*

The sins of men and angels do nothing to impede the "great works of the Lord which accomplish His will."[1] For He Who by His providence and omnipotence distributes to every one his own portion, is able to make good use not only of the good, but also of the wicked. And thus making a good use of the wicked angel, who, in punishment of his first wicked volition, was doomed to an obduracy that prevents him now from willing any good, why should not God have permitted him to tempt the first man, who had been created upright, that is to say, with a good will? For he had been so constituted that if he looked to God for help, man's goodness should defeat the angel's wickedness; but if by proud self-pleasing he abandoned God, his Creator and Sustainer, he should be conquered. If his will remained upright, through leaning on God's help, he should be rewarded; if it became wicked, by forsaking God, he should be punished. But even this trusting in God's help could not itself be accomplished without God's help, although man had it in his own power to relinquish the benefits of divine grace by pleasing himself. For as it is not in our power to live in this world without sustaining ourselves by food, while it is in our power to refuse this nourishment and cease to live, as those do who kill themselves, so it was not in man's power, even in Paradise, to live as he ought without God's help; but it was in his power to live wickedly, though thus he should cut short his happiness, and incur very just punishment. Since, then, God was not ignorant that man would fall, why should He not have suffered him to be tempted by an angel who hated and envied him? It was not, indeed, that He was unaware that he should

[1] Ps. iii. 2.

be conquered, but because He foresaw that by the man's seed, aided by divine grace, this same devil himself should be conquered, to the greater glory of the saints. All was brought about in such a manner, that neither did any future event escape God's foreknowledge, nor did His foreknowledge compel any one to sin, and so as to demonstrate in the experience of the intelligent creation, human and angelic, how great a difference there is between the private presumption of the creature and the Creator's protection. For who will dare to believe or say that it was not in God's power to prevent both angels and men from sinning? But God preferred to leave this in their power, and thus to show both what evil could be wrought by their pride, and what good by His grace.

CHAP. 28. *Of the nature of the two cities, the earthly and the heavenly*

Accordingly, two cities have been formed by two loves: the earthly by the love of self, even to the contempt of God: the heavenly by the love of God, even to the contempt of self. The former, in a word, glories in itself, the latter in the Lord. For the one seeks glory from men; but the greatest glory of the other is God, the witness of conscience. The one lifts up its head in its own glory; the other says to its God, "Thou art my glory, and the lifter up of mine head."[1]

[1]Ps. 3. 3.

In the one, the princes and the nations it subdues are ruled by the love of ruling; in the other, the princes and the subjects serve one another in love, the latter obeying, while the former take thought for all. The one delights in its own strength, represented in the persons of its rulers; the other says to its God, "I will love Thee, O Lord, my strength."[2] And therefore the wise men of the one city, living according to man, have sought for profit to their own bodies or souls, or both, and those who have known God "glorified Him not as God, neither were thankful, but became vain in their imaginations, and their foolish heart was darkened; professing themselves to be wise"—that is, glorying in their own wisdom, and being possessed by pride —"they became fools, and changed the glory of the incorruptible God into an image made like to corruptible man, and to birds, and four-footed beasts, and creeping things." For they were either leaders or followers of the people in adoring images, "and worshipped and served the creature more than the Creator, who is blessed for ever."[3] But in the other city there is no human wisdom, but only godliness, which offers due worship to the true God, and looks for its reward in the society of the saints, of holy angels as well as holy men, "that God may be all in all."[4]

[2]Ps. 18. 1.   [3]Rom. 1. 21–25.
[4]I Cor. 15. 28.

BOOK XV

ARGUMENT. HAVING TREATED IN THE FOUR PRECEDING BOOKS OF THE ORIGIN OF THE TWO CITIES, THE EARTHLY AND THE HEAVENLY, AUGUSTINE EXPLAINS THEIR GROWTH AND PROGRESS IN THE FOUR BOOKS WHICH FOLLOW; AND, IN ORDER TO DO SO, HE EXPLAINS THE CHIEF PASSAGES OF THE SACRED HISTORY WHICH BEAR UPON THIS SUBJECT. IN THIS FIFTEENTH BOOK HE OPENS THIS PART OF HIS WORK BY EXPLAINING THE EVENTS RECORDED IN GENESIS FROM THE TIME OF CAIN AND ABEL TO THE DELUGE.

CHAP. 1. *Of the two lines of the human race which from first to last divide it*

OF the bliss of Paradise, of Paradise itself, and of the life of our first parents there, and of their sin and punishment, many have thought much, spoken much, written much. We ourselves, too, have spoken of these things in the foregoing books, and have written either what we read in the Holy Scriptures, or what we could reasonably deduce from them. And were we to enter into a more detailed investigation of these matters, an endless number of endless questions

would arise, which would involve us in a larger work than the present occasion admits. We cannot be expected to find room for replying to every question that may be started by unoccupied and captious men, who are ever more ready to ask questions than capable of understanding the answer. Yet I trust we have already done justice to these great and difficult questions regarding the beginning of the world, or of the soul, or of the human race itself. This race we have distributed into two parts, the one consisting of those who live according to man, the other of those who live according to God. And these we also mystically call the two cities, or the two communities of men, of which the one is predestined to reign eternally with God, and the other to suffer eternal punishment with the devil. This, however, is their end, and of it we are to speak afterwards. At present, as we have said enough about their origin, whether among the angels, whose numbers we know not, or in the two first human beings, it seems suitable to attempt an account of their career, from the time when our two first parents began to propagate the race until all human generation shall cease. For this whole time or world-age, in which the dying give place and those who are born succeed, is the career of these two cities concerning which we treat.

Of these two first parents of the human race, then, Cain was the first-born, and he belonged to the city of men; after him was born Abel, who belonged to the city of God. For as in the individual the truth of the apostle's statement is discerned, "that is not first which is spiritual, but that which is natural and afterward that which is spiritual,"[1] whence it comes to pass that each man, being derived from a condemned stock, is first of all born of Adam evil and carnal, and becomes good and spiritual only afterwards, when he is grafted into Christ by regeneration: so was it in the human race as a whole. When these two cities began to run their course by a series of deaths and births, the citizen of this world was the first-born, and after him the stranger in this world, the citizen of the city of God, predestinated by grace, elected by grace, by grace a stranger below, and by grace a citizen above. By grace—for so far as regards himself he is sprung from the same mass, all of which is condemned in its origin: but God, like a potter (for this comparison is introduced by the apostle judiciously, and not without thought), of the same lump made one vessel to honour, another to dishonour.[2] But first the vessel to dishonour was made, and after it another to honour. For in each individual, as I have already said, there is first of all that which is reprobate, that from which we must begin, but in which we need not necessarily remain; afterwards is that which is well-approved, to which we may by advancing attain, and in which, when we have reached it, we may abide. Not, indeed, that every wicked man shall be good, but that no one will be good who was not first of all wicked; but the sooner any one becomes a good man, the more speedily does he receive this title, and abolish the old name in the new. Accordingly, it is recorded of

Cain that he built a city,[3] but Abel, being a sojourner, built none. For the city of the saints is above, although here below it begets citizens, in whom it sojourns till the time of its reign arrives, when it shall gather together all in the day of the resurrection; and then shall the promised kingdom be given to them, in which they shall reign with their Prince, the King of the ages, time without end.

CHAP. 2. *Of the children of the flesh and the children of the promise*

There was indeed on earth, so long as it was needed, a symbol and foreshadowing image of this city, which served the purpose of reminding men that such a city was to be, rather than of making it present; and this image was itself called the Holy City, as a symbol of the future city, though not itself the reality. Of this city which served as an image, and of that free city it typified, Paul writes to the Galatians in these terms: "Tell me, ye that desire to be under the law, do ye not hear the law? For it is written, that Abraham had two sons, the one by a bond maid, the other by a free woman. But he who was of the bond woman was born after the flesh, but he of the free woman was by promise. Which things are an allegory: for these are the two covenants; the one from the Mount Sinai, which gendereth to bondage, which is Agar. For this Agar is Mount Sinai in Arabia, and answereth to Jerusalem which now is, and is in bondage with her children. But Jerusalem which is above is free, which is the mother of us all. For it is written, Rejoice, thou barren that bearest not; break forth and cry, thou that travailest not for the desolate hath many more children than she which hath an husband. Now we, brethren, as Isaac was, are the children of promise. But as then he that was born after the flesh persecuted him that was born after the Spirit, even so it is now. Nevertheless, what saith the Scripture? Cast out the bond woman and her son: for the son of the bond woman shall not be heir with the son of the free woman. And we, brethren, are not children of the bond women, but of the free, in the liberty wherewith Christ hath made us free."[4] This interpretation of the passage, handed down to us with apostolic authority, shows how we ought to understand the Scriptures of the two covenants—the old and the new. One portion of the earthly city became an image of the heavenly city, not having a significance of its own, but signifying another city, and therefore serving, or "being in bondage." For it was

[1] I Cor. 15. 46.   [2] Rom. 9. 21.   [3] Gen. 4. 17.   [4] Gal. 4. 21-31.

founded not for its own sake, but to prefigure another city; and this shadow of a city was also itself foreshadowed by another preceding figure. For Sarah's handmaid Agar and her son were an image of this image. And as the shadows were to pass away when the full light came, Sarah, the free woman who prefigured the free city (which again was also prefigured in another way by that shadow of a city Jerusalem), therefore said, "Cast out the bond woman and her son; for the son of the bond woman shall not be heir with my son Isaac," or, as the apostle says, "with the son of the free woman." In the earthly city, then, we find two things—its own obvious presence, and its symbolic presentation of the heavenly city. Now citizens are begotten to the earthly city by nature vitiated by sin, but to the heavenly city by grace freeing nature from sin; whence the former are called "vessels of wrath," the latter "vessels of mercy." [1] And this was typified in the two sons of Abraham—Ishmael, the son of Agar the handmaid, being born according to the flesh, while Isaac was born of the free woman Sarah, according to the promise. Both, indeed, were of Abraham's seed; but the one was begotten by natural law, the other was given by gracious promise. In the one birth, human action is revealed; in the other, a divine kindness comes to light.

Chap. 3. *That Sarah's barrenness was made productive by God's grace*

Sarah, in fact, was barren; and, despairing of offspring, and being resolved that she would have at least through her handmaid that blessing she saw she could not in her own person procure, she gave her handmaid to her husband, to whom she herself had been unable to bear children. From him she required this conjugal duty, exercising her own right in another's womb. And thus Ishmael was born according to the common law of human generation, by sexual intercourse. Therefore it is said that he was born "according to the flesh"—not because such births are not the gifts of God, nor His handiwork, whose creative wisdom "reaches," as it is written, "from one end to another mightily, and sweetly doth she order all things," [2] but because, in a case in which the gift of God, which was not due to men and was the gratuitous largess of grace, was to be conspicuous, it was requisite that a son be given in a way which no effort of nature could compass. Nature denies children to persons of the age which Abraham and Sarah had now reached; besides that, in Sarah's case,

[1] Rom. 9. 22, 23.   [2] Wisd. 8. 1.

she was barren even in her prime. This nature, so constituted that offspring could not be looked for, symbolized the nature of the human race vitiated by sin and by just consequence condemned, which deserves no future felicity. Fitly, therefore, does Isaac, the child of promise, typify the children of grace, the citizens of the free city, who dwell together, in everlasting peace, in which self-love and self-will have no place, but a ministering love that rejoices in the common joy of all, of many hearts makes one, that is to say, secures a perfect concord.

Chap. 4. *Of the conflict and peace of the earthly city*

But the earthly city, which shall not be everlasting (for it will no longer be a city when it has been committed to the extreme penalty), has its good in this world and rejoices in it with such joy as such things can afford. But as this is not a good which can discharge its devotees of all distresses, this city is often divided against itself by litigations, wars, quarrels, and such victories as are either life-destroying or short-lived. For each part of it that arms against another part of it seeks to triumph over the nations through itself in bondage to vice. If, when it has conquered, it is inflated with pride, its victory is life-destroying; but if it turns its thoughts upon the common casualties of our mortal condition, and is rather anxious concerning the disasters that may befall it than elated with the successes already achieved, this victory, though of a higher kind, is still only short-lived; for it cannot abidingly rule over those whom it has victoriously subjugated. But the things which this city desires cannot justly be said to be evil, for it is itself, in its own kind, better than all other human good. For it desires earthly peace for the sake of enjoying earthly goods, and it makes war in order to attain to this peace; since, if it has conquered, and there remains no one to resist it, it enjoys a peace which it had not while there were opposing parties who contested for the enjoyment of those things which were too small to satisfy both. This peace is purchased by toilsome wars; it is obtained by what they style a glorious victory. Now, when victory remains with the party which had the juster cause, who hesitates to congratulate the victor, and style it a desirable peace? These things, then, are good things, and without doubt the gifts of God. But if they neglect the better things of the heavenly city, which are secured by eternal victory and peace never-ending, and so inordinately covet these present good things that they believe them to be the only desirable things, or love them better than those things which are believed to be better—if this be so, then it is necessary that misery follow and ever increase.

Chap. 5. *Of the fratricidal act of the founder of the earthly city, and the corresponding crime of the founder of Rome*

Thus the founder of the earthly city was a fratricide. Overcome with envy, he slew his own brother, a citizen of the eternal city, and a sojourner on earth. So that we cannot be surprised that this first specimen, or, as the Greeks say, archetype of crime, should, long afterwards, find a corresponding crime at the foundation of that city which was destined to reign over so many nations, and be the head of this earthly city of which we speak. For of that city also, as one of their poets has mentioned, "the first walls were stained with a brother's blood," or, as Roman history records, Remus was slain by his brother Romulus. And thus there is no difference between the foundation of this city and of the earthly city, unless it be that Romulus and Remus were both citizens of the earthly city. Both desired to have the glory of founding the Roman republic, but both could not have as much glory as if one only claimed it; for he who wished to have the glory of ruling would certainly rule less if his power were shared by a living consort. In order, therefore, that the whole glory might be enjoyed by one, his consort was removed; and by this crime the empire was made larger indeed, but inferior, while otherwise it would have been less, but better. Now these brothers, Cain and Abel, were not both animated by the same earthly desires, nor did the murderer envy the other because he feared that, by both ruling, his own dominion would be curtailed—for Abel was not solicitous to rule in that city which his brother built—he was moved by that diabolical, envious hatred with which the evil regard the good, for no other reason than because they are good while themselves are evil. For the possession of goodness is by no means diminished by being shared with a partner either permanent or temporarily assumed; on the contrary, the possession of goodness is increased in proportion to the concord and charity of each of those who share it. In short, he who is unwilling to share this possession cannot have it; and he who is most willing to admit others to a share of it will have the greatest abundance to himself. The quarrel, then, between Romulus and Remus shows how the earthly city is divided against itself; that which fell out between Cain and Abel illustrated the hatred that subsists between the two cities, that of God and that of men. The wicked war with the wicked; the good also war with the wicked. But with the good, good men, or at least perfectly good men, cannot war; though, while only going on towards perfection, they war to this extent, that every good man resists others in those points in which he resists himself. And in each individual "the flesh lusteth against the spirit, and the spirit against the flesh."[1] This spiritual lusting, therefore, can be at war with the carnal lust of another man; or carnal lust may be at war with the spiritual desires of another, in some such way as good and wicked men are at war; or, still more certainly, the carnal lusts of two men, good but not yet perfect, contend together, just as the wicked contend with the wicked, until the health of those who are under the treatment of grace attains final victory.

Chap. 6. *Of the weaknesses which even the citizens of the city of God suffer during this earthly pilgrimage in punishment of sin, and of which they are healed by God's care*

This sickliness—that is to say, that disobedience of which we spoke in the fourteenth book —is the punishment of the first disobedience. It is therefore not nature, but vice; and therefore it is said to the good who are growing in grace, and living in this pilgrimage by faith, "Bear ye one another's burdens, and so fulfill the law of Christ."[2] In like manner it is said elsewhere, "Warn them that are unruly, comfort the feebleminded, support the weak, be patient toward all men. See that none render evil for evil unto any man."[3] And in another place, "If a man be overtaken in a fault, ye which are spiritual restore such an one in the spirit of meekness; considering thyself, lest thou also be tempted."[4] And elsewhere, "Let not the sun go down upon your wrath."[5] And in the Gospel, "If thy brother shall trespass against thee, go and tell him his fault between thee and him alone."[6] So too of sins which may create scandal the apostle says, "Them that sin rebuke before all, that others also may fear."[7] For this purpose, and that we may keep that peace without which no man can see the Lord,[8] many precepts are given which carefully inculcate mutual forgiveness; among which we may number that terrible word in which the servant is ordered to pay his formerly remitted debt of ten thousand talents, because

[1]Gal. 5. 17. [2]Gal. 6. 2. [3]I Thess. 5. 14, 15.
[4]Gal. 6. 1. [5]Eph. 4. 26. [6]Matt. 18. 15.
[7]I Tim. 5. 20. [8]Heb. 12. 14.

he did not remit to his fellow-servant his debt of two hundred pence. To which parable the Lord Jesus added the words, "So likewise shall my heavenly Father do also unto you, if ye from your hearts forgive not every one his brother."[1] It is thus the citizens of the city of God are healed while still they sojourn in this earth and sigh for the peace of their heavenly country. The Holy Spirit, too, works within, that the medicine externally applied may have some good result. Otherwise, even though God Himself make use of the creatures that are subject to Him, and in some human form address our human senses, whether we receive those impressions in sleep or in some external appearance, still, if He does not by His own inward grace sway and act upon the mind, no preaching of the truth is of any avail. But this God does, distinguishing between the vessels of wrath and the vessels of mercy, by His own very secret but very just providence. When He Himself aids the soul in His own hidden and wonderful ways, and the sin which dwells in our members, and is, as the apostle teaches, rather the punishment of sin, does not reign in our mortal body to obey the lusts of it, and when we no longer yield our members as instruments of unrighteousness,[2] then the soul is converted from its own evil and selfish desires, and, God possessing it, it possesses itself in peace even in this life, and afterwards, with perfected health and endowed with immortality, will reign without sin in peace everlasting.

CHAP. 7. *Of the cause of Cain's crime and his obstinacy, which not even the word of God could subdue*

But though God made use of this very mode of address which we have been endeavouring to explain, and spoke to Cain in that form by which He was wont to accommodate Himself to our first parents and converse with them as a companion, what good influence had it on Cain? Did he not fulfill his wicked intention of killing his brother even after he was warned by God's voice? For when God had made a distinction between their sacrifices, neglecting Cain's, regarding Abel's, which was doubtless intimated by some visible sign to that effect; and when God had done so because the works of the one were evil but those of his brother good, Cain was very wroth, and his countenance fell. For thus it is written: "And the Lord said unto Cain, Why are thou wroth, and why is thy countenance

fallen? If thou offerest rightly, but dost not rightly distinguish, hast thou not sinned? Fret not thyself, for unto thee shall be his turning, and thou shalt rule over him."[3] In this admonition administered by God to Cain, that clause indeed, "If thou offerest rightly, but dost not rightly distinguish, hast thou not sinned?" is obscure, inasmuch as it is not apparent for what reason or purpose it was spoken, and many meanings have been put upon it, as each one who discusses it attempts to interpret it according to the rule of faith. The truth is, that a sacrifice is "rightly offered" when it is offered to the true God to Whom alone we must sacrifice. And it is "not rightly distinguished" when we do not rightly distinguish the places or seasons or materials of the offering, or the person offering, or the person to whom it is presented, or those to whom it is distributed for food after the oblation. Distinguishing[4] is here used for discriminating—whether when an offering is made in a place where it ought not or of a material which ought to be offered not there but elsewhere; or when an offering is made at a wrong time, or of a material suitable not then but at some other time; or when that is offered which in no place nor any time ought to be offered; or when a man keeps to himself choicer specimens of the same kind than he offers to God; or when he or any other who may not lawfully partake profanely eats of the oblation. In which of these particulars Cain displeased God, it is difficult to determine. But the Apostle John, speaking of these brothers, says, "Not as Cain, who was of that wicked one, and slew his brother. And wherefore slew he him? Because his own works were evil, and his brother's righteous."[5] He thus gives us to understand that God did not respect his offering because it was not rightly "distinguished" in this, that he gave to God something of his own but kept himself to himself. For this all do who follow not God's will but their own, who live not with an upright but a crooked heart, and yet offer to God such gifts as they suppose will procure from Him that He aid them not by healing but by gratifying their evil passions. And this is the characteristic of the earthly city, that it worships God or gods who may aid it in reigning victoriously and peacefully on earth not through love of doing good, but through lust of rule. The good use the world that they may enjoy God; the wicked, on the contrary, that they may enjoy the world would fain use God—those of them, at least, who have at-

[1] Matt. 18. 35.   [2] Rom. 6. 12, 13.

[3] Gen. 4. 6, 7.   [4] Literally, "division."
[5] I John, 3. 12.

tained to the belief that He is and takes an interest in human affairs. For they who have not yet attained even to this belief are still at a much lower level. Cain, then, when he saw that God had respect to his brother's sacrifice, but not to his own, should have humbly chosen his good brother as his example, and not proudly counted him his rival. But he was wroth, and his countenance fell. This angry regret for another person's goodness, even his brother's, was charged upon him by God as a great sin. And He accused him of it in the interrogation, "Why are thou wroth, and why is thy countenance fallen?" For God saw that he envied his brother, and of this He accused him. For to men, from whom the heart of their fellow is hid, it might be doubtful and quite uncertain whether that sadness bewailed his own wickedness by which, as he had learned, he had displeased God, or his brother's goodness, which had pleased God, and won His favourable regard to his sacrifice. But God, in giving the reason why He refused to accept Cain's offering and why Cain should rather have been displeased at himself than at his brother, shows him that though he was unjust in "not rightly distinguishing," that is, not rightly living and being unworthy to have his offering received, he was more unjust by far in hating his just brother without a cause.

Yet He does not dismiss him without counsel, holy, just, and good. "Fret not thyself," He says, "for unto thee shall be his turning, and thou shalt rule over him." Over his brother, does He mean? Most certainly not. Over what, then, but sin? For He had said, "Thou hast sinned," and then He added, "Fret not thyself, for to thee shall be its turning, and thou shalt rule over it." And the "turning" of sin to the man can be understood of his conviction that the guilt of sin can be laid at no other man's door but his own. For this is the health-giving medicine of penitence and the fit plea for pardon; so that, when it is said, "To thee its turning," we must not supply "shall be," but we must read, "To thee let its turning be," understanding it as a command, not as a prediction. For then shall a man rule over his sin when he does not prefer it to himself and defend it, but subjects it by repentance; otherwise he that becomes protector of it shall surely become its prisoner. But if we understand this sin to be that carnal concupiscence of which the apostle says, "The flesh lusteth against the spirit,"[1] among the fruits of which lust he names envy, by which assuredly Cain was stung and excited to destroy his brother, then we may

[1]Gal. 5. 17.

properly supply the words "shall be," and read, "To thee shall be its turning, and thou shalt rule over it." For when the carnal part which the apostle calls sin, in that place where he says, "It is not I who do it, but sin that dwelleth in me,"[2] that part which the philosophers also call vicious, and which ought not to lead the mind, but which the mind ought to rule and restrain by reason from illicit motions; when, then, this part has been moved to perpetrate any wickedness, if it be curbed and if it obey the word of the apostle, "Yield not your members instruments of unrighteousness unto sin,"[3] it is turned towards the mind and subdued and conquered by it, so that reason rules over it as a subject. It was this which God enjoined on him who was kindled with the fire of envy against his brother, so that he sought to put out of the way him whom he should have set as an example. "Fret not thyself," or compose thyself, He says: withhold thy hand from crime; let not sin reign in your mortal body to fulfill it in the lusts thereof, nor yield your members instruments of unrighteousness unto sin. "For to thee shall be its turning," so long as you do not encourage it by giving the rein, but bridle it by quenching its fire. "And thou shalt rule over it"; for when it is not allowed any external actings, it yields itself to the rule of the governing mind and righteous will, and ceases from even internal motions. There is something similar said in the same divine book of the woman, when God questioned and judged them after their sin, and pronounced sentence on them all—the devil in the form of the serpent, the woman and her husband in their own persons. For when He had said to her, "I will greatly multiply thy sorrow and thy conception; in sorrow shalt thou bring forth children," then He added, "and thy turning shall be to thy husband, and he shall rule over thee."[4] What is said to Cain about his sin, or about the vicious concupiscence of his flesh, is here said of the woman who had sinned; and we are to understand that the husband is to rule his wife as the soul rules the flesh. And therefore, says the apostle, "He that loveth his wife, loveth himself; for no man ever yet hated his own flesh."[5] This flesh, then, is to be healed, because it belongs to ourselves: is not to be abandoned to destruction as if it were alien to our nature. But Cain received that counsel of God in the spirit of one who did not wish to amend. In fact, the vice of envy grew stronger in him; and, having

[2]Rom. 7. 17.　　[3]Rom. 6. 13.
[4]Gen. 3. 16.
[5]Eph. 5. 28, 29.

entrapped his brother, he slew him. Such was the founder of the earthly city. He was also a figure of the Jews who slew Christ the Shepherd of the flock of men, prefigured by Abel the shepherd of sheep: but as this is an allegorical and prophetical matter, I forbear to explain it now; besides, I remember that I have made some remarks upon it in writing against Faustus the Manichæan.

CHAP. 8. *What Cain's reason was for building a city so early in the history of the human race*

At present it is the history which I aim at defending, that Scripture may not be reckoned incredible when it relates that one man built a city at a time in which there seem to have been but four men upon earth, or rather indeed but three, after one brother slew the other—to wit, the first man the father of all, and Cain himself, and his son Enoch, by whose name the city was itself called. But they who are moved by this consideration forget to take into account that the writer of the sacred history does not necessarily mention all the men who might be alive at that time, but those only whom the scope of his work required him to name. The design of that writer (who in this matter was the instrument of the Holy Ghost) was to descend to Abraham through the successions of ascertained generations propagated from one man, and then to pass from Abraham's seed to the people of God, in whom, separated as they were from other nations, was prefigured and predicted all that relates to the city whose reign is eternal, and to its king and founder Christ, which things were foreseen in the Spirit as destined to come; yet neither is this object so effected as that nothing is said of the other society of men which we call the earthly city, but mention is made of it so far as seemed needful to enhance the glory of the heavenly city by contrast to its opposite. Accordingly, when the divine Scripture, in mentioning the number of years which those men lived, concludes its account of each man of whom it speaks, with the words, "And he begat sons and daughters, and all his days were so and so, and he died," are we to understand that, because it does not name those sons and daughters, therefore, during that long term of years over which one lifetime extended in those early days, there might not have been born very many men, by whose united numbers not one but several cities might have been built? But it suited the purpose of God, by whose inspiration these histories were composed, to arrange and distinguish from the first these two societies in their several generations—that on the one side the generations of men, that is to say, of those who live according to man, and on the other side the generations of the sons of God, that is to say, of men living according to God, might be traced down together and yet apart from one another as far as the deluge, at which point their dissociation and association are exhibited: their dissociation, inasmuch as the generations of both lines are recorded in separate tables, the one line descending from the fratricide Cain, the other from Seth, who had been born to Adam instead of him whom his brother slew; their association, inasmuch as the good so deteriorated that the whole race became of such a character that it was swept away by the deluge, with the exception of one just man, whose name was Noah, and his wife and three sons and three daughters-in-law, which eight persons were alone deemed worthy to escape from that desolating visitation which destroyed all men.

Therefore, although it is written, "And Cain knew his wife, and she conceived and bare Enoch, and he builded a city and called the name of the city after the name of his son Enoch,"[1] it does not follow that we are to believe this to have been his first-born; for we cannot suppose that this is proved by the expression "he knew his wife," as if then for the first time he had had intercourse with her. For in the case of Adam, the father of all, this expression is used not only when Cain, who seems to have been his first-born, was conceived, but also afterwards the same Scripture says, "Adam knew Eve his wife, and she conceived, and bare a son, and called his name Seth."[2] Whence it is obvious that Scripture employs this expression neither always when a birth is recorded nor then only when the birth of a first-born is mentioned. Neither is it necessary to suppose that Enoch was Cain's first-born because he named his city after him. For it is quite possible that though he had other sons, yet for some reason the father loved him more than the rest. Judah was not the first-born, though he gives his name to Judæa and the Jews. But even though Enoch was the first-born of the city's founder, that is no reason for supposing that the father named the city after him as soon as he was born; for at that time he, being but a solitary man, could not have founded a civic community, which is nothing else than a multitude of men bound together by

[1] Gen. 4. 17.
[2] Gen. 4. 25.

some associating tie. But when his family increased to such numbers that he had quite a population, then it became possible to him both to build a city, and give it, when founded, the name of his son. For so long was the life of those antediluvians, that he who lived the shortest time of those whose years are mentioned in Scripture attained to the age of 753 years.[1] And though no one attained the age of a thousand years, several exceeded the age of nine hundred. Who then can doubt that during the lifetime of one man the human race might be so multiplied that there would be a population to build and occupy not one but several cities? And this might very readily be conjectured from the fact that from one man, Abraham, in not much more than four hundred years, the numbers of the Hebrew race so increased that in the exodus of that people from Egypt there are recorded to have been six hundred thousand men capable of bearing arms,[2] and this over and above the Idumæans, who, though not numbered with Israel's descendants, were yet sprung from his brother, also a grandson of Abraham; and over and above the other nations which were of the same stock of Abraham, though not through Sarah— that is, his descendants by Hagar and Keturah, the Ishmaelites, Midianites, etc.

CHAP. 9. *Of the long life and greater stature of the antediluvians*

Wherefore no one who considerately weighs facts will doubt that Cain might have built a city, and that a large one, when it is observed how prolonged were the lives of men, unless perhaps some sceptic take exception to this very length of years which our authors ascribe to the antediluvians and deny that this is credible. And so, too, they do not believe that the size of men's bodies was larger then than now, though the most esteemed of their own poets, Virgil, asserts the same, when he speaks of that huge stone which had been fixed as a landmark, and which a strong man of those ancient times snatched up as he fought, and ran, and hurled, and cast it:

> *Scarce twelve strong men of later mould*
> *That weight could on their necks uphold,*[3]

thus declaring his opinion that the earth then produced mightier men. And if in the more recent times, how much more in the ages before the world-renowned deluge? But the large size of the primitive human body is often proved to the incredulous by the exposure of sepulchres, either through the wear of time or the violence of torrents or some accident, and in which bones of incredible size have been found or have rolled out. I myself, along with some others, saw on the shore at Utica a man's molar tooth of such a size, that if it were cut down into teeth such as we have, a hundred, I fancy, could have been made out of it. But that, I believe, belonged to some giant. For though the bodies of ordinary men were then larger than ours, the giants surpassed all in stature. And neither in our own age nor any other have there been altogether wanting instances of gigantic stature, though they may be few. The younger Pliny, a most learned man, maintains that the older the world becomes, the smaller will be the bodies of men. And he mentions that Homer in his poems often lamented the same decline; and this he does not laugh at as a poetical figment, but in his character of a recorder of natural wonders accepts it as historically true. But, as I said, the bones which are from time to time discovered prove the size of the bodies of the ancients,[4] and will do so to future ages, for they are slow to decay. But the length of an antediluvian's life cannot now be proved by any such monumental evidence. But we are not on this account to withhold our faith from the sacred history, whose statements of past fact we are the more inexcusable in discrediting, as we see the accuracy of its prediction of what was future. And even that same Pliny tells us that there is still a nation in which men live 200 years. If, then, in places unknown to us, men are believed to have a length of days which is quite beyond our own experience, why should we not believe the same of times distant from our own? Or are we to believe that in other places there is what is not here, while we do not believe that in other times there has been anything but what is now?

CHAP. 10. *Of the different computation of the ages of the antediluvians, given by the Hebrew manuscripts and by our own*

Wherefore, although there is a discrepancy for which I cannot account between our manuscripts and the Hebrew,[5] in the very number of

---

[1] Lamech, according to the Septuagint.
[2] Ex. 12. 37.
[3] *Æneid*, BK. XII. 899, 900. Compare the *Iliad*, BK. V. 302.

[4] See the account given by Herodotus (BK. I. 67) of the discovery of the bones of Orestes, which, as the story goes, gave a stature of seven cubits.
[5] Our own MSS., of which Augustine here speaks, were the Latin versions of the Septuagint used by the Church before Jerome's was received; the "Hebrew MSS." were the versions made from the Hebrew text. Compare *On Christian Doctrine*, BK. II. ch. 15, ff.

years assigned to the antediluvians, yet the discrepancy is not so great that they do not agree about their longevity. For the very first man, Adam, before he begot his son Seth, is in our manuscripts found to have lived 230 years, but in the Hebrew mss. 130. But after he begot Seth, our copies read that he lived 700 years, while the Hebrew give 800. And thus, when the two periods are taken together, the sum agrees. And so throughout the succeeding generations, the period before the father begets a son is always made shorter by 100 years in the Hebrew, but the period after his son is begotten is longer by 100 years in the Hebrew than in our copies. And thus, taking the two periods together, the result is the same in both. And in the sixth generation there is no discrepancy at all. In the seventh, however, of which Enoch is the representative, who is recorded to have been translated without death because he pleased God, there is the same discrepancy as in the first five generations, 100 years more being ascribed to him by our mss. before he begat a son. But still the result agrees; for according to both documents he lived before he was translated 365 years. In the eighth generation the discrepancy is less than in the others, and of a different kind. For Methuselah, whom Enoch begat, lived, before he begat his successor, not 100 years less, but 100 years more, according to the Hebrew reading; and in our mss. again these years are added to the period after he begat his son; so that in this case also the sum total is the same. And it is only in the ninth generation, that is, in the age of Lamech, Methuselah's son and Noah's father, that there is a discrepancy in the sum total; and even in this case it is slight. For the Hebrew mss. represent him as living twenty-four years more than ours assign to him. For before he begat his son, who was called Noah, six years fewer are given to him by the Hebrew mss. than by ours; but after he begat this son, they give him thirty years more than ours; so that, deducting the former six, there remains, as we said, a surplus of twenty-four.

CHAP. 11. Of Methuselah's age, which seems to extend fourteen years beyond the deluge

From this discrepancy between the Hebrew books and our own arises the well-known question as to the age of Methuselah; for it is computed that he lived for fourteen years after the deluge, though Scripture relates that of all who were then upon the earth only the eight souls in the ark escaped destruction by the flood, and of these Methuselah was not one. For, according to our books, Methuselah, before he begat the son whom he called Lamech, lived 167 years; then Lamech himself, before his son Noah was born, lived 188 years, which together make 355 years. Add to these the age of Noah at the date of the deluge, 600 years, and this gives a total of 955 from the birth of Methuselah to the year of the flood. Now all the years of the life of Methuselah are computed to be 969; for when he had lived 167 years, and had begotten his son Lamech, he then lived after this 802 years, which makes a total, as we said, of 969 years. From this, if we deduct 955 years from the birth of Methuselah to the flood, there remains fourteen years, which he is supposed to have lived after the flood. And therefore some suppose that, though he was not on earth (in which it is agreed that every living thing which could not naturally live in water perished), he was for a time with his father, who had been translated, and that he lived there till the flood had passed away. This hypothesis they adopt, that they may not cast a slight on the trustworthiness of versions which the Church has received into a position of high authority, and because they believe that the Jewish mss. rather than our own are in error. For they do not admit that this is a mistake of the translators, but maintain that there is a falsified statement in the original, from which, through the Greek, the Scripture has been translated into our own tongue. They say that it is not credible that the seventy translators, who simultaneously and unanimously produced one rendering, could have erred, or, in a case in which no interest of theirs was involved, could have falsified their translation; but that the Jews, envying us our translation of their Law and Prophets, have made alterations in their texts so as to undermine the authority of ours. This opinion or suspicion let each man adopt according to his own judgment. Certain it is that Methuselah did not survive the flood, but died in the very year it occurred, if the numbers given in the Hebrew mss. are true. My own opinion regarding the seventy translators I will, with God's help, state more carefully in its own place, when I have come down (following the order which this work requires) to that period in which their translation was executed.[1] For the present question, it is enough that, according to our versions, the men of that age had lives so long as to make it quite possible that, during the lifetime of the first-born of the two sole parents then on earth, the human race multiplied sufficiently to form a community.

[1] See below, BK. XVIII. chaps. 42–44.

CHAP. 12. *Of the opinion of those who do not believe that in these primitive times men lived so long as is stated*

For they are by no means to be listened to who suppose that in those times years were differently reckoned, and were so short that one of our years may be supposed to be equal to ten of theirs. So that they say, when we read or hear that some man lived 900 years, we should understand ninety, ten of those years making but one of ours, and ten of ours equalling 100 of theirs. Consequently, as they suppose, Adam was twenty-three years of age when he begat Seth, and Seth himself was twenty years and six months old when his son Enos was born, though the Scripture calls these months 205 years. For, on the hypothesis of those whose opinion we are explaining, it was customary to divide one such year as we have into ten parts, and to call each part a year. And each of these parts was composed of six days squared; because God finished His works in six days, that He might rest the seventh. Of this I disputed according to my ability in the eleventh book.[1] Now six squared, or six times six, gives thirty-six days; and this multiplied by ten amounts to 360 days, or twelve lunar months. As for the five remaining days which are needed to complete the solar year, and for the fourth part of a day, which requires that into every fourth or leap-year a day be added, the ancients added such days as the Romans used to call "intercalary," in order to complete the number of the years. So that Enos, Seth's son, was nineteen years old when his son Cainan was born, though Scripture calls these years 190. And so through all the generations in which the ages of the antediluvians are given, we find in our versions that almost no one begat a son at the age of 100 or under, or even at the age of 120 or thereabouts; but the youngest fathers are recorded to have been 160 years old and upwards. And the reason of this, they say, is that no one can beget children when he is ten years old, the age spoken of by those men as 100, but that sixteen is the age of puberty, and competent now to propagate offspring; and this is the age called by them 160. And that it may not be thought incredible that in these days the year was differently computed from our own, they adduce what is recorded by several writers of history, that the Egyptians had a year of four months, the Acarnanians of six, and the Lavinians of thirteen months. The younger Pliny, after mentioning that some writers reported that one man had

[1] Chap. 8.

lived 152 years, another ten more, others 200, others 300, that some had even reached 500 and 600, and a few 800 years of age, gave it as his opinion that all this must be ascribed to mistaken computation. For some, he says, make summer and winter each a year; others make each season a year, like the Arcadians, whose years, he says, were of three months. He added, too, that the Egyptians, of whose little years of four months we have spoken already, sometimes terminated their year at the wane of each moon; so that with them there are produced lifetimes of 1000 years.

By these plausible arguments certain persons, with no desire to weaken the credit of this sacred history, but rather to facilitate belief in it by removing the difficulty of such incredible longevity, have been themselves persuaded, and think they act wisely in persuading others, that in these days the year was so brief that ten of their years equal but one of ours, while ten of ours equal 100 of theirs. But there is the plainest evidence to show that this is quite false. Before producing this evidence, however, it seems right to mention a conjecture which is yet more plausible. From the Hebrew manuscripts we could at once refute this confident statement; for in them Adam is found to have lived not 230 but 130 years before he begat his third son. If, then, this mean thirteen years by our ordinary computation, then he must have begotten his first son when he was only twelve or thereabouts. Who can at this age beget children according to the ordinary and familiar course of nature? But not to mention him, since it is possible he may have been able to beget his like as soon as he was created—for it is not credible that he was created so little as our infants are— not to mention him, his son was not 205 years old when he begat Enos, as our versions have it, but 105, and consequently, according to this idea, was not eleven years old. But what shall I say of his son Cainan, who, though by our version 170 years old, was by the Hebrew text seventy when he begat Mahalaleel? If seventy years in those times meant only seven of our years, what man of seven years old begets children?

CHAP. 13. *Whether, in computing years, we ought to follow the Hebrew or the Septuagint*

But if I say this, I shall presently be answered, "It is one of the Jews' lies." This, however, we have disposed of above, showing that it cannot be that men of so just a reputation as the seventy translators should have falsified their version. However, if I ask them which of the two is more credible, that the Jewish nation, scattered far and wide, could have unanimously conspired to forge this lie, and so, through envying others the authority of their Scriptures, have deprived themselves of their verity; or that seventy men, who were also themselves Jews, shut up in one place (for Ptolemy king of Egypt had got them together for this work), should have envied foreign nations that same truth, and by common consent inserted these errors: who does not see which can be more naturally and readily believed? But far be it from any prudent man to believe either that the Jews, however malicious and wrong-headed, could have tampered with so many and so widely-dispersed manuscripts; or that those renowned seventy individuals had any common purpose to grudge the truth to the nations. One must therefore more plausibly maintain, that when first their labours began to be transcribed from the copy in Ptolemy's library, some such misstatement might find its way into the first copy made, and from it might be disseminated far and wide; and that this might arise from no fraud, but from a mere copyist's error. This is a sufficiently plausible account of the difficulty regarding Methuselah's life, and of that other case in which there is a difference in the total of twenty-four years. But in those cases in which there is a methodical resemblance in the falsification, so that uniformly the one version allots to the period before a son and successor is born 100 years more than the other, and to the period subsequent 100 years less, and *vice versa,* so that the totals may agree —and this holds true of the first, second, third, fourth, fifth, and seventh generations—in these cases error seems to have, if we may say so, a certain kind of constancy, and savours not of accident, but of design.

Accordingly, that diversity of numbers which distinguishes the Hebrew from the Greek and Latin copies of Scripture, and which consists of a uniform addition and deduction of 100 years in each lifetime for several consecutive generations, is to be attributed neither to the malice of the Jews nor to men so diligent and prudent as the seventy translators, but to the error of the copyist who was first allowed to transcribe the manuscript from the library of the above mentioned king. For even now, in cases where numbers contribute nothing to the easier comprehension or more satisfactory knowledge of anything, they are both carelessly transcribed, and still more carelessly emended. For who will trouble himself to learn how many thousand men the several tribes of Israel contained? He sees no resulting benefit of such knowledge. Or how many men are there who are aware of the vast advantage that lies hid in this knowledge? But in this case, in which during so many consecutive generations 100 years are added in one manuscript where they are not reckoned in the other, and then, after the birth of the son and successor, the years which were wanting are added, it is obvious that the copyist who contrived this arrangement designed to insinuate that the antediluvians lived an excessive number of years only because each year was excessively brief, and that he tried to draw the attention to this fact by his statement of their age of puberty at which they became able to beget children. For, lest the incredulous might stumble at the difficulty of so long a lifetime, he insinuated that 100 of their years equalled but ten of ours; and this insinuation he conveyed by adding 100 years whenever he found the age below 160 years or thereabouts, deducting these years again from the period after the son's birth, that the total might harmonize. By this means he intended to ascribe the generation of offspring to a fit age, without diminishing the total sum of years ascribed to the lifetime of the individuals. And the very fact that in the sixth generation he departed from this uniform practice, inclines us all the rather to believe that when the circumstance we have referred to required his alterations, he made them; seeing that when this circumstance did not exist, he made no alteration. For in the same generation he found in the Hebrew mss. that Jared lived before he begat Enoch 162 years, which, according to the short year computation, is sixteen years and somewhat less than two months, an age capable of procreation; and therefore it was not necessary to add 100 short years, and so make the age twenty-six years of the usual length; and of course it was not necessary to deduct, after the son's birth, years which he had not added before it. And thus it comes to pass that in this instance there is no variation between the two manuscripts.

This is corroborated still further by the fact that in the eighth generation, while the Hebrew books assign 182[1] years to Methuselah before Lamech's birth, ours assign to him twenty less, though usually 100 years are added to this period; then, after Lamech's birth, the twenty years are restored, so as to equalize the total in

---

[1]One hundred and eighty-seven is the number given in the Hebrew, and one hundred and sixty-seven in the Septuagint.

the two books. For if his design was that these 170 years be understood as seventeen, so as to suit the age of puberty, as there was no need for him adding anything, so there was none for his subtracting anything; for in this case he found an age fit for the generation of children, for the sake of which he was in the habit of adding those 100 years in cases where he did not find the age already sufficient. This difference of twenty years we might, indeed, have supposed had happened accidentally, had he not taken care to restore them afterwards as he had deducted them from the period before, so that there might be no deficiency in the total. Or are we perhaps to suppose that there was the still more astute design of concealing the deliberate and uniform addition of 100 years to the first period and their deduction from the subsequent period; did he design to conceal this by doing something similar, that is to say, adding and deducting, not indeed a century, but some years, even in a case in which there was no need for his doing so? But whatever may be thought of this, whether it be believed that he did so or not, whether, in fine, it be so or not, I would have no manner of doubt that when any diversity is found in the books, since both cannot be true to fact, we do well to believe in preference that language out of which the translation was made into another by translators. For there are three Greek MSS., one Latin, and one Syriac, which agree with one another, and in all of these Methuselah is said to have died six years before the deluge.

CHAP. 14. *That the years in those ancient times were of the same length as our own*

Let us now see how it can be plainly made out that in the enormously protracted lives of those men the years were not so short that ten of their years were equal to only one of ours, but were of as great length as our own, which are measured by the course of the sun. It is proved by this, that Scripture states that the flood occurred in the six hundredth year of Noah's life. But why in the same place is it also written, "The waters of the flood were upon the earth in the six hundredth year of Noah's life, in the second month, the twenty-seventh day of the month,"[1] if that very brief year (of which it took ten to make one of ours) consisted of thirty-six days? For so scant a year, if the ancient usage dignified it with the name of year, either has not months, or this month must be three days, so that it may have twelve of them.

How then was it here said, "In the six hundredth year, the second month, the twenty-seventh day of the month," unless the months then were of the same length as the months now? For how else could it be said that the flood began on the twenty-seventh day of the second month? Then afterwards, at the end of the flood, it is thus written: "And the ark rested in the seventh month, on the twenty-seventh day of the month, on the mountains of Ararat. And the waters decreased continually until the eleventh month: on the first day of the month were the tops of the mountains seen."[2] But if the months were such as we have, then so were the years. And certainly months of three days each could not have a twenty-seventh day. Or if every measure of time was diminished in proportion, and a thirtieth part of three days was then called a day, then that great deluge, which is recorded to have lasted forty days and forty nights, was really over in less than four of our days. Who can away with such foolishness and absurdity? Far be this error from us—an error which seeks to build up our faith in the divine Scriptures on false conjecture only to demolish our faith at another point. It is plain that the day then was what it now is, a space of four-and-twenty hours, determined by the lapse of day and night; the month then equal to the month now, which is defined by the rise and completion of one moon; the year then equal to the year now, which is completed by twelve lunar months, with the addition of five days and a fourth to adjust it with the course of the sun. It was a year of this length which was reckoned the six hundredth of Noah's life, and in the second month, the twenty-seventh day of the month, the flood began—a flood which, as is recorded, was caused by heavy rains continuing for forty days, which days had not only two hours and a little more, but four-and-twenty hours completing a night and a day. And consequently those antediluvians lived more than 900 years, which were years as long as those which afterwards Abraham lived 175 of, and after him his son Isaac 180, and his son Jacob nearly 150, and some time after, Moses 120, and men now seventy or eighty, or not much longer, of which years it is said, "their strength is labour and sorrow."[3]

But that discrepancy of numbers which is found to exist between our own and the Hebrew text does not touch the longevity of the ancients; and if there is any diversity so great that both versions cannot be true, we must take our

---

[1]Gen. 7. 10, 11, (in our version the seventeenth day).   [2]Gen. 8. 4, 5.   [3]Ps. 90. 10.

ideas of the real facts from that text out of which our own version has been translated. However, though any one who pleases has it in his power to correct this version, yet it is not unimportant to observe that no one has presumed to emend the Septuagint from the Hebrew text in the many places where they seem to disagree. For this difference has not been reckoned a falsification; and for my own part I am persuaded it ought not to be reckoned so. But where the difference is not a mere copyist's error, and where the sense is agreeable to truth and illustrative of truth, we must believe that the divine Spirit prompted them to give a varying version, not in their function of translators, but in the liberty of prophesying. And therefore we find that the apostles justly sanction the Septuagint, by quoting it as well as the Hebrew when they adduce proofs from the Scriptures. But as I have promised to treat this subject more carefully, if God help me, in a more fitting place, I will now go on with the matter in hand. For there can be no doubt that, the lives of men being so long, the first-born of the first man could have built a city—a city, however, which was earthly, and not that which is called the city of God, to describe which we have taken in hand this great work.

CHAP. 15. *Whether it is credible that the men of the primitive age abstained from sexual intercourse until that date at which it is recorded that they begat children*

Some one, then, will say, "Is it to be believed that a man who intended to beget children, and had no intention of continence, abstained from sexual intercourse a hundred years and more, or even, according to the Hebrew version, only a little less, say eighty, seventy, or sixty years; or, if he did not abstain, was unable to beget offspring?" This question admits of two solutions. For either puberty was so much later as the whole life was longer, or, which seems to me more likely, it is not the first-born sons that are here mentioned, but those whose names were required to fill up the series until Noah was reached, from whom again we see that the succession is continued to Abraham, and after him down to that point of time until which it was needful to mark by pedigree the course of the most glorious city, which sojourns as a stranger in this world, and seeks the heavenly country. That which is undeniable is that Cain was the first who was born of man and woman. For had he not been the first who was added by birth to the two unborn persons, Adam could not have

said what he is recorded to have said, "I have gotten a man by the Lord."[1] He was followed by Abel, whom the elder brother slew, and who was the first to show, by a kind of foreshadowing of the sojourning city of God, what iniquitous persecutions that city would suffer at the hands of wicked and, at it were, earth-born men, who love their earthly origin, and delight in the earthly happiness of the earthly city. But how old Adam was when he begat these sons does not appear. After this the generations diverge, the one branch deriving from Cain, the other from him whom Adam begot in the room of Abel slain by his brother, and whom he called Seth, saying, as it is written, "For God hath raised me up another seed for Abel whom Cain slew."[2] These two series of generations accordingly, the one of Cain, the other of Seth, represent the two cities in their distinctive ranks, the one the heavenly city, which sojourns on earth, the other the earthly, which gapes after earthly joys, and grovels in them as if they were the only joys. But though eight generations, including Adam, are registered before the flood, no man of Cain's line has his age recorded at which the son who succeeded him was begotten. For the Spirit of God refused to mark the times before the flood in the generations of the earthly city, but preferred to do so in the heavenly line, as if it were more worthy of being remembered. Further, when Seth was born, the age of his father is mentioned; but already he had begotten other sons and who will presume to say that Cain and Abel were the only ones previously begotten? For it does not follow that they alone had been begotten of Adam, because they alone were named in order to continue the series of generations which it was desirable to mention. For though the names of all the rest are buried in silence, yet it is said that Adam begot sons and daughters; and who that cares to be free from the charge of temerity will dare to say how many his offspring numbered? It was possible enough that Adam was divinely prompted to say, after Seth was born, "For God hath raised up to me another seed for Abel," because that son was to be capable of representing Abel's holiness, not because he was born first after him in point of time. Then because it is written, "And Seth lived 205 years," or, according to the Hebrew reading, "105 years, and begat Enos,"[3] who but a rash man could affirm that this was his first-born? Will any man do so to excite our wonder, and cause us to inquire how for so many years he remained free from sexual intercourse,

[1]Gen. 4. 1.   [2]Gen. 4. 25.   [3]Gen. 5. 6.

though without any purpose of continuing so, or how, if he did not abstain, he yet had no children? Will any man do so when it is written of him, "And he begat sons and daughters, and all the days of Seth were 912 years, and he died"?[1] And similarly regarding those whose years are afterwards mentioned, it is not disguised that they begat sons and daughters.

Consequently it does not at all appear whether he who is named as the son was himself the first begotten. Nay, since it is incredible that those fathers were either so long in attaining puberty, or could not get wives, or could not impregnate them, it is also incredible that those sons were their first-born. But as the writer of the sacred history designed to descend by well-marked intervals through a series of generations to the birth and life of Noah, in whose time the flood occurred, he mentioned not those sons who were first begotten, but those by whom the succession was handed down.

Let me make this clearer by here inserting an example, in regard to which no one can have any doubt that what I am asserting is true. The evangelist Matthew, where he designs to commit to our memories the generation of the Lord's flesh by a series of parents, beginning from Abraham and intending to reach David, says, "Abraham begat Isaac";[2] why did he not say Ishmael, whom he first begat? Then "Isaac begat Jacob"; why did he not say Esau, who was the first-born? Simply because these sons would not have helped him to reach David. Then follows, "And Jacob begat Judah and his brethren": was Judah the first begotten? "Judah," he says, "begat Pharez and Zara"; yet neither were these twins the first-born of Judah, but before them he had begotten three other sons. And so in the order of the generations he retained those by whom he might reach David, so as to proceed onwards to the end he had in view. And from this we may understand that the antediluvians who are mentioned were not the first-born, but those through whom the order of the succeeding generations might be carried on to the patriarch Noah. We need not, therefore, weary ourselves with discussing the needless and obscure question as to their lateness of reaching puberty.

CHAP. 16. *Of marriage between blood-relations, in regard to which the present law could not bind the men of the earliest ages*

As, therefore, the human race, subsequently to the first marriage of the man who was made of dust, and his wife who was made out of his

[1]Gen. 5. 8.   [2]Matt. 1.

side, required the union of males and females in order that it might multiply, and as there were no human beings except those who had been born of these two, men took their sisters for wives—an act which was as certainly dictated by necessity in these ancient days as afterwards it was condemned by the prohibitions of religion. For it is very reasonable and just that men, among whom concord is honourable and useful, should be bound together by various relationships; and that one man should not himself sustain many relationships, but that the various relationships should be distributed among several, and should thus serve to bind together the greatest number in the same social interests. "Father" and "father-in-law" are the names of two relationships. When, therefore, a man has one person for his father, another for his father-in-law, friendship extends itself to a larger number. But Adam in his single person was obliged to hold both relations to his sons and daughters, for brothers and sisters were united in marriage. So too Eve his wife was both mother and mother-in-law to her children of both sexes; while, had there been two women, one the mother, the other the mother-in-law, the family affection would have had a wider field. Then the sister herself by becoming a wife sustained in her single person two relationships, which, had they been distributed among individuals, one being sister, and another being wife, the family tie would have embraced a greater number of persons. But there was then no material for effecting this, since there were no human beings but the brothers and sisters born of those two first parents. Therefore, when an abundant population made it possible, men ought to choose for wives women who were not already their sisters; for not only would there then be no necessity for marrying sisters, but, were it done, it would be most abominable. For if the grandchildren of the first pair, being now able to choose their cousins for wives, married their sisters, then it would no longer be only two but three relationships that were held by one man, while each of these relationships ought to have been held by a separate individual, so as to bind together by family affection a larger number. For one man would in that case be both father, and father-in-law, and uncle to his own children (brother and sister now man and wife); and his wife would be mother, aunt, and mother-in-law to them; and they themselves would be not only brother and sister, and man and wife, but cousins also, being the children of brother and sister. Now, all these relationships, which combined three men into one, would have embraced nine persons had each relationship been held by one individual, so that a man had one person for his sister, another his wife, another his cousin, another his father, another his uncle, another his father-in-law, another his mother, another his aunt, another his mother-in-law; and thus the social bond would not have been tightened to bind a few, but loosened to embrace a larger number of relations.

And we see that, since the human race has increased and multiplied, this is so strictly observed even among the profane worshippers of many and false gods, that though their laws perversely allow a brother to marry his sister,[1] yet custom, with a finer morality, prefers to forego this licence; and though it was quite allowable in the earliest ages of the human race to marry one's sister, it is now abhorred as a thing which no circumstances could justify. For custom has very great power either to attract or to shock human feeling. And in this matter, while it restrains concupiscence within due bounds, the man who neglects and disobeys it is justly branded as abominable. For if it is iniquitous to plough beyond our own boundaries through the greed of gain, is it not much more iniquitous to transgress the recognized boundaries of morals through sexual lust? And with regard to marriage in the next degree of consanguinity, marriage between cousins, we have observed that in our own time the customary morality has prevented this from being frequent, though the law allows it. It was not prohibited by divine law, nor as yet had human law prohibited it; nevertheless, though legitimate, people shrank from it, because it lay so close to what was illegitimate, and in marrying a cousin seemed almost to marry a sister—for cousins are so closely related that they are called brothers and sisters[2] and are almost really so. But the ancient fathers, fearing that near relationship might gradually in the course of generations diverge, and become distant relationship, or cease to be relationship at all, religiously endeavoured to limit it by the bond of marriage before it became distant, and thus, as it were, to call it back when it was escaping them. And on this account, even when the world was full of people, though they did not choose wives from among their sisters or half-sisters, yet they preferred them to be of the same stock as themselves. But who doubts that

the modern prohibition of the marriage even of cousins is the more seemly regulation—not merely on account of the reason we have been urging, the multiplying of relationships, so that one person might not absorb two, which might be distributed to two persons, and so increase the number of people bound together as a family, but also because there is in human nature I know not what natural and praiseworthy shamefacedness which restrains us from desiring that connexion which, though for propagation, is yet lustful, and which even conjugal modesty blushes over, with any one to whom consanguinity bids us render respect?

The sexual intercourse of man and woman, then, is in the case of mortals a kind of seed-bed of the city; but while the earthly city needs for its population only generation, the heavenly needs also regeneration to rid it of the taint of generation. Whether before the deluge there was any bodily or visible sign of regeneration, such as was afterwards enjoined upon Abraham when he was circumcised, or what kind of sign it was, the sacred history does not inform us. But it does inform us that even these earliest of mankind sacrificed to God, as appeared also in the case of the two first brothers; Noah, too, is said to have offered sacrifices to God when he had come forth from the ark after the deluge. And concerning this subject we have already said in the foregoing books that the devils arrogate to themselves divinity, and require sacrifice that they may be esteemed gods, and delight in these honours on no other account than this, because they know that true sacrifice is due to the true God.

CHAP. 17. *Of the two fathers and leaders who sprang from one progenitor*

Since, then, Adam was the father of both lines—the father, that is to say, both of the line which belonged to the earthly, and of that which belonged to the heavenly city—when Abel was slain, and by his death exhibited a marvellous mystery, there were henceforth two lines proceeding from two fathers, Cain and Seth, and in those sons of theirs, whom it behoved to register, the tokens of these two cities began to appear more distinctly. For Cain begat Enoch, in whose name he built a city, an earthly one, which was not from home in this world, but rested satisfied with its temporal peace and happiness. Cain, too, means "possession"; wherefore at his birth either his father or mother said, "I have gotten a man through God." Then Enoch means "dedication"; for the earthly city is dedi-

---

[1] This was allowed by the Egyptians and Athenians, never by the Romans.

[2] In Hebrew, Greek, and Latin, though not uniformly, nor in Latin commonly.

cated in this world in which it is built, for in this world it finds the end towards which it aims and aspires. Further, Seth signifies "resurrection," and Enos his son signifies "man," not as Adam, which also signifies man, but is used in Hebrew indifferently for man and woman, as it is written, "Male and female created He them, and blessed them, and called their name Adam,"[1] leaving no room to doubt that though the woman was distinctively called Eve, yet the name Adam, meaning man, was common to both. But Enos means man in so restricted a sense that Hebrew linguists tell us it cannot be applied to woman: it is the equivalent of the "child of the resurrection," when they neither marry nor are given in marriage.[2] For there shall be no generation in that place to which regeneration shall have brought us. Wherefore I think it not immaterial to observe that in those generations which are propagated from him who is called Seth, although daughters as well as sons are said to have been begotten, no woman is expressly registered by name; but in those which sprang from Cain at the very termination to which the line runs, the last person named as begotten is a woman. For we read, "Methusael begat Lamech. And Lamech took unto him two wives: the name of the one was Adah, and the name of the other Zillah. And Adah bare Jabal: he was the father of the shepherds that dwell in tents. And his brother's name was Jubal: he was the father of all such as handle the harp and organ. And Zillah, she also bare Tubal-cain, an instructor of every artificer in brass and iron: and the sister of Tubal-cain was Naamah."[3] Here terminate all the generations of Cain, being eight in number, including Adam—to wit, seven from Adam to Lamech, who married two wives, and whose children, among whom a woman also is named, form the eighth generation. Whereby it is elegantly signified that the earthly city shall to its termination have carnal generations proceeding from the intercourse of males and females. And therefore the wives themselves of the man who is the last named father of Cain's line, are registered in their own names—a practice nowhere followed before the deluge save in Eve's case. Now as Cain, signifying possession, the founder of the earthly city, and his son Enoch, meaning dedication, in whose name it was founded, indicate that this city is earthly both in its beginning and in its end—a city in which nothing more is hoped for than can be seen in this world —so Seth, meaning resurrection, and being the father of generations registered apart from the others, we must consider what this sacred history says of his son.

CHAP. 18. *The significance of Abel, Seth, and Enos to Christ and his body the Church*

"And to Seth," it is said, "there was born a son, and he called his name Enos: he hoped to call on the name of the Lord God."[4] Here we have a loud testimony to the truth. Man, then, the son of the resurrection, lives in hope: he lives in hope as long as the city of God, which is begotten by faith in the resurrection, sojourns in this world. For in these two men, Abel, signifying "grief," and his brother Seth, signifying "resurrection," the death of Christ and His life from the dead are prefigured. And by faith in these is begotten in this world the city of God, that is to say, the man who has hoped to call on the name of the Lord. "For by hope," says the apostle, "we are saved: but hope that is seen is not hope: for what a man seeth, why doth he yet hope for? But if we hope for that we see not, then do we with patience wait for it."[5] Who can avoid referring this to a profound mystery? For did not Abel hope to call upon the name of the Lord God when his sacrifice is mentioned in Scripture as having been accepted by God? Did not Seth himself hope to call on the name of the Lord God, of whom it was said, "For God hath appointed me another seed instead of Abel"? Why then is this which is found to be common to all the godly specially attributed to Enos, unless because it was fit that in him, who is mentioned as the first-born of the father of those generations which were separated to the better part of the heavenly city, there should be a type of the man, or society of men, who live not according to man in contentment with earthly felicity, but according to God in hope of everlasting felicity? And it was not said, "He hoped in the Lord God," nor "He called on the name of the Lord God," but "He hoped to call on the name of the Lord God." And what does this "hoped to call" mean, unless it is a prophecy that a people should arise who, according to the election of grace, would call on the name of the Lord God? It is this which has been said by another prophet, and which the apostle interprets of the people who belong to the grace of God: "And it shall be that whosoever shall call upon the name of the Lord shall be saved."[6] For these two expressions, "And he called his name Enos, which means man," and "He hoped to call on the name of the Lord God," are sufficient proof that man ought not to rest his hopes in himself;

---

[1]Gen. 5. 2.   [2]Luke, 20. 35, 36.   [3]Gen. 4. 18–22.   [4]Gen. 4. 26.   [5]Rom. 8. 24, 25.   [6]Rom. 10. 13.

as it is elsewhere written, "Cursed is the man that trusteth in man."[1] Consequently no one ought to trust in himself that he shall become a citizen of that other city which is not dedicated in the name of Cain's son in this present time, that is to say, in the fleeting course of this mortal world, but in the immortality of perpetual blessedness.

CHAP. 19. *The significance of Enoch's translation*

For that line also of which Seth is the father has the name "Dedication" in the seventh generation from Adam, counting Adam. For the seventh from him is Enoch, that is, Dedication. But this is that man who was translated because he pleased God, and who held in the order of the generations a remarkable place, being the seventh from Adam, a number signalized by the consecration of the Sabbath. But, counting from the diverging point of the two lines, or from Seth, he was the sixth. Now it was on the sixth day God made man, and consummated His works. But the translation of Enoch prefigured our deferred dedication; for though it is indeed already accomplished in Christ our Head, Who so rose again that He shall die no more, and Who was Himself also translated, yet there remains another dedication of the whole house, of which Christ Himself is the foundation, and this dedication is deferred till the end, when all shall rise again to die no more. And whether it is the house of God, or the temple of God, or the city of God, that is said to be dedicated, it is all the same, and equally in accordance with the usage of the Latin language. For Virgil himself calls the city of widest empire "the house of Assaracus,"[2] meaning the Romans, who were descended through the Trojans from Assaracus. He also calls them the house of Æneas, because Rome was built by those Trojans who had come to Italy under Æneas.[3] For that poet imitated the sacred writings, in which the Hebrew nation, though so numerous, is called the house of Jacob.

CHAP. 20. *How it is that Cain's line terminates in the eighth generation, while Noah, though descended from the same father, Adam, is found to be the tenth from him*

Some one will say, "If the writer of this history intended, in enumerating the generations from Adam through his son Seth, to descend through them to Noah, in whose time the deluge occurred, and from him again to trace the connected generations down to Abraham, with whom Matthew begins the pedigree of Christ the eternal King of the city of God, what did he intend by enumerating the generations from Cain, and to what terminus did he mean to trace them?" We reply, "To the deluge, by which the whole stock of the earthly city was destroyed, but repaired by the sons of Noah." For the earthly city and community of men who live after the flesh will never fail until the end of this world, of which our Lord says, "The children of this world generate, and are generated."[4] But the city of God, which sojourns in this world, is conducted by regeneration to the world to come, of which the children neither generate nor are generated. In this world generation is common to both cities; though even now the city of God has many thousand citizens who abstain from the act of generation; yet the other city also has some citizens who imitate these, though erroneously. For to that city belong also those who have erred from the faith, and introduced divers heresies; for they live according to man, not according to God. And the Indian gymnosophists, who are said to philosophize in the solitudes of India in a state of nudity, are its citizens; and they abstain from marriage. For continence is not a good thing, except when it is practised in the faith of the highest good, that is, God. Yet no one is found to have practised it before the deluge; for indeed even Enoch himself, the seventh from Adam, who is said to have been translated without dying, begat sons and daughters before he was translated, and among these was Methuselah, by whom the succession of the recorded generations is maintained.

Why, then, is so small a number of Cain's generations registered, if it was proper to trace them to the deluge, and if there was no such delay of the date of puberty as to preclude the hope of offspring for a hundred or more years? For if the author of this book had not in view some one to whom he might rigidly trace the series of generations, as he designed in those which sprang from Seth's seed to descend to Noah, and thence to start again by a rigid order, what need was there of omitting the first-born sons for the sake of descending to Lamech, in whose sons that line terminates—that is to say, in the eighth generation from Adam, or the seventh from Cain—as if from this point he had wished to pass on to another series, by which he might reach either the Israelitish people, among whom the earthly Jerusalem presented a prophetic figure of the heavenly city, or to Jesus

[1] Jer. 17. 5.　[2] *Æneid*, BK. I. 288.　[3] *Ibid.*, BK. III. 97.　[4] Luke, 20. 34.

Christ, "according to the flesh, who is over all, God blessed for ever,"[1] the Maker and Ruler of the heavenly city? What, I say, was the need of this, seeing that the whole of Cain's posterity were destroyed in the deluge? From this it is manifest that they are the first-born sons who are registered in this genealogy. Why, then, are there so few of them? Their numbers in the period before the deluge must have been greater, if the date of puberty bore no proportion to their longevity, and they had children before they were a hundred years old. For supposing they were on an average thirty years old when they began to beget children, then, as there are eight generations, including Adam and Lamech's children, 8 times 30 gives 240 years; did they then produce no more children in all the rest of the time before the deluge? With what intention, then, did he who wrote this record make no mention of subsequent generations? For from Adam to the deluge there are reckoned, according to our copies of Scripture, 2262 years, and according to the Hebrew text, 1656 years. Supposing, then, the smaller number to be the true one, and subtracting from 1656 years 240, is it credible that during the remaining 1400 and odd years until the deluge the posterity of Cain begat no children?

But let any one who is moved by this call to mind that when I discussed the question, how it is credible that those primitive men could abstain for so many years from begetting children, two modes of solution were found—either a puberty late in proportion to their longevity, or that the sons registered in the genealogies were not the first-born, but those through whom the author of the book intended to reach the point aimed at, as he intended to reach Noah by the generations of Seth. So that, if in the generations of Cain there occurs no one whom the writer could make it his object to reach by omitting the first-born and inserting those who would serve such a purpose, then we must have recourse to the supposition of late puberty, and say that only at some age beyond a hundred years they became capable of begetting children, so that the order of the generations ran through the first-born, and filled up even the whole period before the deluge, long though it was. It is, however, possible that, for some more secret reason which escapes me, this city, which we say is earthly, is exhibited in all its generations down to Lamech and his sons, and that then the writer withholds from recording the rest which may have existed before the deluge.

[1] Rom. 9. 5.

And without supposing so late a puberty in these men, there might be another reason for tracing the generations by sons who were not first-born, viz., that the same city which Cain built, and named after his son Enoch, may have had a widely extended dominion and many kings, not reigning simultaneously, but successively, the reigning king begetting always his successor. Cain himself would be the first of these kings; his son Enoch, in whose name the city in which he reigned was built, would be the second; the third Irad, whom Enoch begat; the fourth Mehujael, whom Irad begat; the fifth Methusael, whom Mehujael begat; the sixth Lamech, whom Methusael begat, and who is the seventh from Adam through Cain. But it was not necessary that the first-born should succeed their fathers in the kingdom, but those would succeed who were recommended by the possession of some virtue useful to the earthly city, or who were chosen by lot, or the son who was best liked by his father would succeed by a kind of hereditary right to the throne. And the deluge may have happened during the lifetime and reign of Lamech, and may have destroyed him along with all other men, save those who were in the ark. For we cannot be surprised that, during so long a period from Adam to the deluge, and with the ages of individuals varying as they did, there should not be an equal number of generations in both lines, but seven in Cain's, and ten in Seth's; for as I have already said, Lamech is the seventh from Adam, Noah the tenth; and in Lamech's case not one son only is registered, as in the former instances, but more, because it was uncertain which of them would have succeeded when he died, if there had intervened any time to reign between his death and the deluge.

But in whatever manner the generations of Cain's line are traced downwards, whether it be by firstborn sons or by the heirs to the throne, it seems to me that I must by no means omit to notice that, when Lamech had been set down as the seventh from Adam, there were named, in addition, as many of his children as made up this number to eleven, which is the number signifying sin; for three sons and one daughter are added. The wives of Lamech have another signification, different from that which I am now pressing. For at present I am speaking of the children, and not of those by whom the children were begotten. Since, then, the law is symbolized by the number ten—whence that memorable Decalogue—there is no doubt that the number eleven, which goes beyond ten, symbolizes the transgression of the law, and consequently sin. For this reason, eleven veils of goat's skin were ordered to be hung in the tabernacle of the testimony, which served in the wanderings of God's people as an ambulatory temple. And in that haircloth there was a reminder of sins, because the goats were to be set on the left hand of the Judge; and therefore, when we confess our sins, we prostrate ourselves in haircloth, as if we were saying what is written in the psalm, "My sin is ever before me."[1] The progeny of Adam, then, by Cain the murderer, is completed in the number eleven, which symbolizes sin; and this number itself is made up by a woman, as it was by the same sex that beginning was made of sin by which we all die. And it was committed that the pleasure of the flesh, which resists the spirit, might follow; and so Naamah, the daughter of Lamech, means "pleasure." But from Adam to Noah, in the line of Seth, there are ten generations. And to Noah three sons are added, of whom, while one fell into sin, two were blessed by their father; so that, if you deduct the reprobate and add the gracious sons to the number, you get twelve—a number signalized in the case of the patriarchs and of the apostles, and made up of the parts of the number seven multiplied into one another—for three times four, or four times three, give twelve. These things being so, I see that I must consider and mention how these two lines, which by their separate genealogies depict the two cities, one of earth-born, the other of regenerated persons, became afterwards so mixed and confused, that the whole human race, with the exception of eight persons, deserved to perish in the deluge.

CHAP. 21. *Why it is that, as soon as Cain's son Enoch has been named, the genealogy is forthwith continued as far as the deluge, while after the mention of Enos, Seth's son, the narrative returns again to the creation of man*

We must first see why, in the enumeration of Cain's posterity, after Enoch, in whose name the city was built, has been first of all mentioned, the rest are at once enumerated down to that terminus of which I have spoken, and at which that race and the whole line was destroyed in the deluge; while, after Enos the son of Seth, has been mentioned, the rest are not at once named down to the deluge, but a clause is inserted to the following effect: "This is the book of the generations of Adam. In the day that God created man, in the likeness of God made He him; male and female created He them; and blessed them, and called their name Adam, in the day

[1] Ps. 51. 3.

when they were created."[2] This seems to me to be inserted for this purpose, that here again the reckoning of the times may start from Adam himself—a purpose which the writer had not in view in speaking of the earthly city, as if God mentioned it, but did not take account of its duration. But why does he return to this recapitulation after mentioning the son of Seth, the man who hoped to call on the name of the Lord God, unless because it was fit thus to present these two cities, the one beginning with a murderer and ending in a murderer (for Lamech, too, acknowledges to his two wives that he had committed murder), the other built up by him who hoped to call upon the name of the Lord God? For the highest and complete terrestrial duty of the city of God, which is a stranger in this world, is that which was exemplified in the individual who was begotten by him who typified the resurrection of the murdered Abel. That one man is the unity of the whole heavenly city, not yet indeed complete, but to be completed, as this prophetic figure foreshows. The son of Cain, therefore, that is, the son of possession (and of what but an earthly possession?), may have a name in the earthly city which was built in his name. It is of such the Psalmist says, "They call their lands after their own names."[3] Wherefore they incur what is written in another psalm: "Thou, O Lord, in Thy city wilt despise their image."[4] But as for the son of Seth, the son of the resurrection, let him hope to call on the name of the Lord God. For he prefigures that society of men which says, "But I am like a green olive-tree in the house of God: I have trusted in the mercy of God."[5] But let him not seek the empty honours of a famous name upon earth, for "Blessed is the man that maketh the name of the Lord his trust, and respecteth not vanities nor lying follies."[6] After having presented the two cities, the one founded in the material good of this world, the other in hope in God, but both starting from a common gate opened in Adam into this mortal state, and both running on and running out to their proper and merited ends, Scripture begins to reckon the times, and in this reckoning includes other generations, making a recapitulation from Adam, out of whose condemned seed, as out of one mass handed over to merited damnation, God made some vessels of wrath to dishonour and others vessels of mercy to honour; in punishment rendering to the former what is due, in grace giving to the latter what is not due: in or-

[2] Gen. 5. 1.   [3] Ps. 49. 11.   [4] Ps. 73. 20.
[5] Ps. 52. 8.   [6] Ps. 40. 4.

der that by the very comparison of itself with the vessels of wrath, the heavenly city, which sojourns on earth, may learn not to put confidence in the liberty of its own will, but may hope to call on the name of the Lord God. For will, being a nature which was made good by the good God, but mutable by the immutable, because it was made out of nothing, can both decline from good to do evil, which takes place when it freely chooses, and can also escape the evil and do good, which takes place only by divine assistance.

CHAP. 22. *Of the fall of the sons of God who were captivated by the daughters of men, whereby all, with the exception of eight persons, deservedly perished in the deluge*

When the human race, in the exercise of this freedom of will, increased and advanced, there arose a mixture and confusion of the two cities by their participation in a common iniquity. And this calamity, as well as the first, was occasioned by woman, though not in the same way; for these women were not themselves betrayed, neither did they persuade the men to sin, but having belonged to the earthly city and society of the earthly, they had been of corrupt manners from the first, and were loved for their bodily beauty by the sons of God, or the citizens of the other city which sojourns in this world. Beauty is indeed a good gift of God; but that the good may not think it a great good, God dispenses it even to the wicked. And thus, when the good that is great and proper to the good was abandoned by the sons of God, they fell to a paltry good which is not peculiar to the good, but common to the good and the evil; and when they were captivated by the daughters of men, they adopted the manners of the earthly to win them as their brides, and forsook the godly ways they had followed in their own holy society. And thus beauty, which is indeed God's handiwork, but only a temporal, carnal, and lower kind of good, is not fitly loved in preference to God, the eternal, spiritual, and unchangeable good. When the miser prefers his gold to justice, it is through no fault of the gold, but of the man; and so with every created thing. For though it be good, it may be loved with an evil as well as with a good love: it is loved rightly when it is loved ordinately; evilly, when inordinately, It is this which some one has briefly said in these verses in praise of the Creator:[1] "These are Thine, they are good, because Thou

art good Who didst create them. There is in them nothing of ours, unless the sin we commit when we forget the order of things, and instead of Thee love that which Thou hast made."

But if the Creator is truly loved, that is, if He Himself is loved and not another thing in His stead, He cannot be evilly loved; for love itself is to be ordinately loved, because we do well to love that which, when we love it, makes us live well and virtuously. So that it seems to me that it is a brief but true definition of virtue to say, it is the order of love; and on this account, in the Canticles, the bride of Christ, the city of God, sings, "Order love within me."[2] It was the order of this love, then, this charity or attachment, which the sons of God disturbed when they forsook God, and were enamoured of the daughters of men.[3] And by these two names (sons of God and daughters of men) the two cities are sufficiently distinguished. For though the former were by nature children of men, they had come into possession of another name by grace. For in the same Scripture in which the sons of God are said to have loved the daughters of men, they are also called angels of God; whence many suppose that they were not men but angels.

CHAP. 23. *Whether we are to believe that angels, who are of a spiritual substance, fell in love with the beauty of women, and sought them in marriage, and that from this connection giants were born*

In the third book of this work (chap. 5) we made a passing reference to this question, but did not decide whether angels, inasmuch as they are spirits, could have bodily intercourse with women. For it is written, "Who maketh His angels spirits,"[4] that is, "He makes those who are by nature spirits His angels by appointing them to the duty of bearing His messages." For the Greek word ἄγγελος, which in Latin appears as *"angelus,"* means a messenger. But whether the Psalmist speaks of their bodies when he adds, "and His ministers a flaming fire," or means that God's ministers ought to blaze with love as with a spiritual fire, is doubtful. However, the same trustworthy Scripture testifies that angels have appeared to men in such bodies as could not only be seen, but also touched. There is, too, a very general rumour, which many have verified by their own experience, or which trustworthy persons who have heard the experi-

---

[1] Or, according to another reading: "Which I briefly said in these verses in praise of a taper."

[2] Song of Sol. 2. 4.
[3] See *On Christian Doctrine*, BK. I. ch. 27.
[4] Ps. 104. 4.

ence of others corroborate, that sylvans and fauns, who are commonly called *"incubi,"* had often made wicked assaults upon women, and satisfied their lust upon them; and that certain devils, called Duses by the Gauls, are constantly attempting and effecting this impurity is so generally affirmed, that it were impudent to deny it. From these assertions, indeed, I dare not determine whether there be some spirits embodied in an aerial substance (for this element, even when agitated by a fan, is sensibly felt by the body), and who are capable of lust and of mingling sensibly with women; but certainly I could by no means believe that God's holy angels could at that time have so fallen, nor can I think that it is of them the Apostle Peter said, "For if God spared not the angels that sinned, but cast them down to hell, and delivered them into chains of darkness, to be reserved unto judgment."[1] I think he rather speaks of those who first apostatized from God, along with their chief the devil, who enviously deceived the first man under the form of a serpent. But the same holy Scripture affords the most ample testimony that even godly men have been called angels; for of John it is written: "Behold, I send my messenger (angel) before Thy face, who shall prepare Thy way."[2] And the prophet Malachi, by a peculiar grace specially communicated to him, was called an angel.[3]

But some are moved by the fact that we have read that the fruit of the connexion between those who are called angels of God and the women they loved were not men like our own breed, but giants; just as if there were not born even in our own time (as I have mentioned above) men of much greater size than the ordinary stature. Was there not at Rome a few years ago, when the destruction of the city now accomplished by the Goths was drawing near, a woman, with her father and mother, who by her gigantic size over-topped all others? Surprising crowds from all quarters came to see her, and that which struck them most was the circumstance that neither of her parents were quite up to the tallest ordinary stature. Giants therefore might well be born, even before the sons of God, who are also called angels of God, formed a connexion with the daughters of men, or of those living according to men, that is to say, before the sons of Seth formed a connexion with the daughters of Cain. For thus speaks even the canonical Scripture itself in the book in which we read of this; its words are: "And it came to pass, when men began to multiply on the face of the earth, and

daughters were born unto them, that the sons of God saw the daughters of men that they were fair [good]; and they took them wives of all which they chose. And the Lord God said, My Spirit shall not always strive with man, for that he also is flesh: yet his days shall be an hundred and twenty years. There were giants in the earth in those days; and also after that, when the sons of God came in unto the daughters of men, and they bare children to them, the same became the giants, men of renown."[4] These words of the divine book sufficiently indicate that already there were giants in the earth in those days, in which the sons of God took wives of the children of men, when they loved them because they were good, that is, fair. For it is the custom of this Scripture to call those who are beautiful in appearance "good." But after this connexion had been formed, then too were giants born. For the words are: "There were giants in the earth in those days, *and also after that,* when the sons of God came in unto the daughters of men." Therefore there were giants both before, "in those days," and "also after that." And the words, "They bare children to them," show plainly enough that before the sons of God fell in this fashion they begat children to God, not to themselves—that is to say, not moved by the lust of sexual intercourse, but discharging the duty of propagation, intending to produce not a family to gratify their own pride, but citizens to people the city of God; and to these they as God's angels would bear the message, that they should place their hope in God, like him who was born of Seth, the son of resurrection, and who hoped to call on the name of the Lord God, in which hope they and their offspring would be co-heirs of eternal blessings, and brethren in the family of which God is the Father.

But that those angels were not angels in the sense of not being men, as some suppose, Scripture itself decides, which unambiguously declares that they were men. For when it had first been stated that "the angels of God saw the daughters of men that they were fair, and they took them wives of all which they chose," it was immediately added, "And the Lord God said, My Spirit shall not always strive with these men, for that they also are flesh." For by the Spirit of God they had been made angels of God and sons of God; but declining towards lower things, they are called "men," a name of nature, not of grace; and they are called "flesh," as deserters of the Spirit, and by their desertion deserted. The Septuagint indeed calls them both

[1] II Pet. 2. 4.   [2] Mark, I. 2.   [3] Mal. 2. 7.   [4] Gen. 6. I. 4.

angels of God and sons of God, though all the copies do not show this, some having only the name "sons of God." And Aquila, whom the Jews prefer to the other interpreters, has translated neither "angels of God" nor "sons of God," but "sons of gods." But both are correct. For they were both sons of God, and thus brothers of their own fathers, who were children of the same God; and they were sons of gods, because begotten by gods, together with whom they themselves also were gods, according to that expression of the psalm: "I have said, Ye are gods, and all of you are children of the Most High."[1] For the Septuagint translators are justly believed to have received the Spirit of prophecy; so that, if they made any alterations under His authority, and did not adhere to a strict translation, we could not doubt that this was divinely dictated. However, the Hebrew word may be said to be ambiguous, and to be susceptible of either translation, "sons of God," or "sons of gods."

Let us omit, then, the fables of those scriptures which are called apocryphal, because their obscure origin was unknown to the fathers from whom the authority of the true Scriptures has been transmitted to us by a most certain and well-ascertained succession. For though there is some truth in these apocryphal writings, yet they contain so many false statements that they have no canonical authority. We cannot deny that Enoch, the seventh from Adam, left some divine writings, for this is asserted by the Apostle Jude in his canonical epistle. But it is not without reason that these writings have no place in that canon of Scripture which was preserved in the temple of the Hebrew people by the diligence of successive priests; for their antiquity brought them under suspicion, and it was impossible to ascertain whether these were his genuine writings, and they were not brought forward as genuine by the persons who were found to have carefully preserved the canonical books by a successive transmission. So that the writings which are produced under his name, and which contain these fables about the giants, saying that their fathers were not men, are properly judged by prudent men to be not genuine; just as many writings are produced by heretics under the names both of other prophets, and, more recently, under the names of the apostles, all of which, after careful examination, have been set apart from canonical authority under the title of Apocrypha. There is therefore no doubt that, according to the Hebrew and Christian canon-

ical Scriptures, there were many giants before the deluge, and that these were citizens of the earthly society of men, and that the sons of God, who were according to the flesh the sons of Seth, sunk into this community when they forsook righteousness. Nor need we wonder that giants should be born even from these. For all of their children were not giants; but there were more then than in the remaining periods since the deluge. And it pleased the Creator to produce them, that it might thus be demonstrated that neither beauty, nor yet size and strength, are of much moment to the wise man, whose blessedness lies in spiritual and immortal blessings, in far better and more enduring gifts, in the good things that are the peculiar property of the good and are not shared by good and bad alike. It is this which another prophet confirms when he says, "These were the giants, famous from the beginning, that were of so great stature, and so expert in war. Those did not the Lord choose, neither gave He the way of knowledge unto them; but they were destroyed because they had no wisdom, and perished through their own foolishness."[2]

CHAP. 24. *How we are to understand this which the Lord said to those who were to perish in the flood: "their days shall be 120 years"*

But that which God said, "Their days shall be an hundred and twenty years," is not to be understood as a prediction that henceforth men should not live longer than 120 years—for even after the deluge we find that they lived more than 500 years—but we are to understand that God said this when Noah had nearly completed his fifth century, that is, had lived 480 years, which Scripture, as it frequently uses the name of the whole of the largest part, calls 500 years. Now the deluge came in the 600th year of Noah's life, the second month; and thus 120 years were predicted as being the remaining span of those who were doomed, which years being spent, they should be destroyed by the deluge. And it is not unreasonably believed that the deluge came as it did, because already there were not found upon earth any who were not worthy of sharing a death so manifestly judicial—not that a good man, who must die some time, would be a jot the worse of such a death after it was past. Nevertheless there died in the deluge none of those mentioned in the sacred Scripture as descended from Seth. But here is the divine account of the cause of the deluge: "The Lord God saw that the wickedness of man was great

---

[1] Ps. 82. 6.

[2] Baruch, 3. 26–28.

in the earth, and that every imagination of the thoughts of his heart was only evil continually. And it repented the Lord that He had made man on the earth, and it grieved Him at His heart. And the Lord said, I will destroy man, whom I have created, from the face of the earth; both man and beast, and the creeping thing, and the fowls of the air: for I am angry that I have made them."[1]

CHAP. 25. *Of the anger of God, which does not inflame His mind, nor disturb His unchangeable tranquillity*

The anger of God is not a disturbing emotion of His mind, but a judgment by which punishment is inflicted upon sin. His thought and reconsideration also are the unchangeable reason which changes things; for He does not, like man, repent of anything He has done, because in all matters His decision is as inflexible as His prescience is certain. But if Scripture were not to use such expressions as the above, it would not familiarly insinuate itself into the minds of all classes of men, whom it seeks access to for their good, that it may alarm the proud, arouse the careless, exercise the inquisitive, and satisfy the intelligent; and this it could not do, did it not first stoop, and in a manner descend, to them where they lie. But its denouncing death on all the animals of earth and air is a declaration of the vastness of the disaster that was approaching: not that it threatens destruction to the irrational animals as if they too had incurred it by sin.

CHAP. 26. *That the ark which Noah was ordered to make figures in every respect Christ and the Church*

Moreover, inasmuch as God commanded Noah, a just man, and, as the truthful Scripture says, a man perfect in his generation—not indeed with the perfection of the citizens of the city of God in that immortal condition in which they equal the angels, but in so far as they can be perfect in their sojourn in this world—inasmuch as God commanded him, I say, to make an ark, in which he might be rescued from the destruction of the flood, along with his family, i.e., his wife, sons, and daughters-in-law, and along with the animals who, in obedience to God's command, came to him into the ark: this is certainly a figure of the city of God sojourning in this world; that is to say, of the Church, which is rescued by the wood on which hung the Mediator of God and men, the man Christ Jesus.[2]

For even its very dimensions, in length, breadth, and height, represent the human body in which He came, as it had been foretold. For the length of the human body, from the crown of the head to the sole of the foot, is six times its breadth from side to side, and ten times its depth or thickness, measuring from back to front: that is to say, if you measure a man as he lies on his back or on his face, he is six times as long from head to foot as he is broad from side to side, and ten times as long as he is high from the ground. And therefore the ark was made 300 cubits in length, 50 in breadth, and 30 in height. And its having a door made in the side of it certainly signified the wound which was made when the side of the Crucified was pierced with the spear; for by this those who come to Him enter; for thence flowed the sacraments by which those who believe are initiated. And the fact that it was ordered to be made of squared timbers, signifies the immoveable steadiness of the life of the saints; for however you turn a cube, it still stands. And the other peculiarities of the ark's construction are signs of features of the church.

But we have not now time to pursue this subject; and, indeed, we have already dwelt upon it in the work we wrote against Faustus the Manichean, who denies that there is anything prophesied of Christ in the Hebrew books. It may be that one man's exposition excels another's, and that ours is not the best; but all that is said must be referred to this city of God we speak of, which sojourns in this wicked world as in a deluge, at least if the expositor would not widely miss the meaning of the author. For example, the interpretation I have given in the work against Faustus, of the words, "with lower, second, and third stories shalt thou make it," is that, because the church is gathered out of all nations, it is said to have two stories, to represent the two kinds of men—the circumcision, to wit, and the uncircumcision, or, as the apostle otherwise calls them, Jews and Gentiles; and to have three stories, because all the nations were replenished from the three sons of Noah. Now any one may object to this interpretation, and may give another which harmonizes with the rule of faith. For as the ark was to have rooms not only on the lower, but also on the upper stories, which were called "third stories," that there might be a habitable space on the third floor from the basement, some one may interpret these to mean the three graces commended by the apostle—faith, hope, and charity. Or

[1]Gen. 6. 5–7.　　　　　[2]I Tim. 2. 5.

even more suitably they may be supposed to represent those three harvests in the gospel, thirty-fold, sixty-fold, an hundred-fold—chaste marriage dwelling in the ground floor, chaste widowhood in the upper, and chaste virginity in the top story. Or any better interpretation may be given, so long as the reference to this city is maintained. And the same statement I would make of all the remaining particulars in this passage which require exposition, viz., that although different explanations are given, yet they must all agree with the one harmonious Catholic faith.

CHAP. 27. *Of the ark and the deluge, and that we cannot agree with those who receive the bare history, but reject the allegorical interpretation, nor with those who maintain the figurative and not the historical meaning*

Yet no one ought to suppose either that these things were written for no purpose, or that we should study only the historical truth, apart from any allegorical meanings; or, on the contrary, that they are only allegories, and that there were no such facts at all, or that, whether it be so or no, there is here no prophecy of the Church. For what right-minded man will contend that books so religiously preserved during thousands of years, and transmitted by so orderly a succession, were written without an object, or that only the bare historical facts are to be considered when we read them? For, not to mention other instances, if the number of the animals entailed the construction of an ark of great size, where was the necessity of sending into it two unclean and seven clean animals of each species, when both could have been preserved in equal numbers? Or could not God, Who ordered them to be preserved in order to replenish the race, restore them in the same way He had created them?

But they who contend that these things never happened, but are only figures setting forth other things, in the first place suppose that there could not be a flood so great that the water should rise fifteen cubits above the highest mountains, because it is said that clouds cannot rise above the top of Mount Olympus, because it reaches the sky where there is none of that thicker atmosphere in which winds, clouds, and rains have their origin. They do not reflect that the densest element of all, earth, can exist there; or perhaps they deny that the top of the mountain is earth. Why, then, do these measurers and weighers of the elements contend that earth can be raised to those aerial altitudes, and

that water cannot, while they admit that water is lighter, and liker to ascend than earth? What reason do they adduce why earth, the heavier and lower element, has for so many ages scaled to the tranquil ether, while water, the lighter, and more likely to ascend, is not suffered to do the same even for a brief space of time?

They say, too, that the area of that ark could not contain so many kinds of animals of both sexes, two of the unclean and seven of the clean. But they seem to me to reckon only one area of 300 cubits long and 50 broad, and not to remember that there was another similar in the story above, and yet another as large in the story above that again; and that there was consequently an area of 900 cubits by 150. And if we accept what Origen has with some appropriateness suggested, that Moses the man of God, being, as it is written, "learned in all the wisdom of the Egyptians,"[1] who delighted in geomtry, may have meant geometrical cubits, of which they say that one is equal to six of our cubits, then who does not see what a capacity these dimensions give to the ark? For as to their objection that an ark of such size could not be built, it is a very silly calumny; for they are aware that huge cities have been built, and they should remember that the ark was an hundred years in building. Or, perhaps, though stone can adhere to stone when cemented with nothing but lime, so that a wall of several miles may be constructed, yet plank cannot be riveted to plank by mortices, bolts, nails, and pitch-glue, so as to construct an ark which was not made with curved ribs but straight timbers, which was not to be launched by its builders, but to be lifted by the natural pressure of the water when **it** reached it, and which was to be preserved from shipwreck as it floated about rather by divine oversight than by human skill.

As to another customary inquiry of the scrupulous about the very minute creatures, not only such as mice and lizards, but also locusts, beetles, flies, fleas, and so forth, whether there were not in the ark a larger number of them than was determined by God in His command, those persons who are moved by this difficulty are to be reminded that the words "every creeping thing of the earth" only indicate that it was not needful to preserve in the ark the animals that can live in the water, whether the fishes that live submerged in it, or the sea-birds that swim on its surface. Then, when it is said "male and female," no doubt reference is made to the repairing of the races, and consequently there

[1]Acts, 7. 22.

was no need for those creatures being in the ark which are born without the union of the sexes from inanimate things, or from their corruption; or if they were in the ark, they might be there as they commonly are in houses, not in any determinate numbers; or if it was necessary that there should be a definite number of all those animals that cannot naturally live in the water, that so the most sacred mystery which was being enacted might be bodied forth and perfectly figured in actual realities, still this was not the care of Noah or his sons, but of God. For Noah did not catch the animals and put them into the ark, but gave them entrance as they came seeking it. For this is the force of the words, "They shall come unto thee"[1]—not, that is to say, by man's effort, but by God's will. But certainly we are not required to believe that those which have no sex also came; for it is expressly and definitely said, "They shall be male and female."[1] For there are some animals which are born out of corruption, but yet afterwards they themselves copulate and produce offspring, as flies; but others, which have no sex, like bees. Then, as to those animals which have sex, but without ability to propagate their kind, like mules and she-mules, it is probable that they were not in the ark, but that it was counted sufficient to preserve their parents, to wit, the horse and the ass; and this applies to all hybrids. Yet, if it was necessary for the completeness of the mystery, they were there; for even this species has "male and female."

Another question is commonly raised regarding the food of the carnivorous animals—whether, without transgressing the command which fixed the number to be preserved, there were necessarily others included in the ark for their sustenance; or, as is more probable, there might be some food which was not flesh, and which yet

[1]Gen. 6. 19, 20.

suited all. For we know how many animals whose food is flesh eat also vegetable products and fruits, especially figs and chestnuts. What wonder is it, therefore, if that wise and just man was instructed by God what would suit each, so that without flesh he prepared and stored provision fit for every species? And what is there which hunger would not make animals eat? Or what could not be made sweet and wholesome by God, Who, with a divine facility, might have enabled them to do without food at all, had it not been requisite to the completeness of so great a mystery that they should be fed? But none but a contentious man can suppose that there was no prefiguring of the Church in so manifold and circumstantial a detail. For the nations have already so filled the Church, and are comprehended in the framework of its unity, the clean and unclean together, until the appointed end, that this one very manifest fulfillment leaves no doubt how we should interpret even those others which are somewhat more obscure, and which cannot so readily be discerned. And since this is so, if not even the most audacious will presume to assert that these things were written without a purpose, or that though the events really happened they mean nothing, or that they did not really happen, but are only allegory, or that at all events they are far from having any figurative reference to the Church; if it has been made out that, on the other hand, we must rather believe that there was a wise purpose in their being committed to memory and to writing, and that they did happen, and have a significance, and that this significance has a prophetic reference to the Church, then this book, having served this purpose, may now be closed, that we may go on to trace in the history subsequent to the deluge the courses of the two cities—the earthly, that lives according to men, and the heavenly that lives according to God.

BOOK XVI

ARGUMENT. In the former part of this book, from the first to the twelfth chapter, the progress of the two cities, the earthly and the heavenly, from Noah to Abraham, is exhibited from Holy Scripture: in the latter part, the progress of the heavenly alone, from Abraham to the kings of Israel, is the subject.

Chap. 1. *Whether, after the deluge, from Noah to Abraham, any families can be found who lived according to God*

It is difficult to discover from Scripture, whether, after the deluge, traces of the holy city are continuous, or are so interrupted by intervening seasons of godlessness that not a single worshipper of the one true God was found among men; because from Noah, who, with his wife, three sons, and as many daughters-in-law, achieved deliverance in the ark from the destruction of the deluge, down to Abraham, we do not find in the canonical books that the piety of any one is celebrated by express divine testimony, unless it be in the case of Noah, who commends with a prophetic benediction his two sons Shem and Japheth, while he beheld and foresaw what was long afterwards to happen. It was also by this prophetic spirit that, when his middle son—that is, the son who was younger than the first and older than the last born—had sinned against him, he cursed him not in his own person, but in his son's (his own grandson's), in the words, "Cursed be the lad Canaan; a servant shall he be unto his brethren."[1] Now Canaan was born of Ham, who, so far from covering his sleeping father's nakedness, had divulged it. For the same reason also he subjoins the blessing on his two other sons, the oldest and youngest, saying, "Blessed be the Lord God of Shem; and Canaan shall be his servant. God shall gladden Japheth, and he shall dwell in the houses of Shem."[2] And so, too, the planting of the vine by Noah, and his intoxication by its fruit, and his nakedness while he slept, and the other things done at that time, and recorded, are all of them pregnant with prophetic meanings and veiled in mysteries.

Chap. 2. *What was prophetically prefigured in the sons of Noah*

The things which then were hidden are now sufficiently revealed by the actual events which have followed. For who can carefully and intelligently consider these things without recognizing them accomplished in Christ? Shem, of whom Christ was born in the flesh, means "named." And what is of greater name than Christ, the fragrance of Whose name is now everywhere perceived, so that even prophecy sings of it beforehand, comparing it in the Song of Songs[3] to ointment poured forth? Is it not also in the houses of Christ, that is, in the churches, that the "enlargement" of the nations dwells? For Japheth means "enlargement." And Ham (i.e., hot), who was the middle son of Noah, and, as it were, separated himself from both, and remained between them, neither belonging to the first-fruits of Israel nor to the fullness of the Gentiles, what does he signify but the tribe of heretics, hot with the spirit, not of patience, but of impatience, with which the breasts of heretics are wont to blaze, and with which they disturb the peace of the saints? But even the heretics yield an advantage to those that make proficiency, according to the apostle's saying, "There must also be heresies, that they which are approved may be made manifest among you."[4] Whence, too, it is elsewhere said, "The son that receives instruction will be wise, and he uses the foolish as his servant."[5] For while the hot restlessness of heretics stirs questions about many articles of the Catholic faith, the necessity of defending them forces us both to investigate them more accurately, to understand them more clearly, and to proclaim them more earnestly; and the question mooted by an adversary becomes the occasion of instruction. However, not only those who are openly separated from the Church, but also all who glory in the Christian name, and at the same time lead abandoned lives, may without absurdity seem to be figured by Noah's middle son: for the passion of Christ, which was signified by that man's nakedness, is at once proclaimed by their profession, and dishonoured by their wicked conduct. Of such, therefore, it has been said, "By their fruits ye shall know them."[6] And therefore was Ham cursed in his son, he being, as it were, his fruit. So, too, this son of his, Canaan,

[1] Gen. 9. 25.   [2] Gen. 9. 26, 27.
[3] Song of Sol. 1. 3.   [4] I Cor. 11. 19.
[5] Prov. 10. 5 in Septuagint.   [6] Matt. 7. 20.

is fitly interpreted "their movement," which is nothing else than their work. But Shem and Japheth, that is to say, the circumcision and uncircumcision, or, as the apostle otherwise calls them, the Jews and Greeks, but called and justified, having somehow discovered the nakedness of their father (which signifies the Saviour's passion), took a garment and laid it upon their backs, and entered backwards and covered their father's nakedness, without their seeing what their reverence hid. For we both honour the passion of Christ as accomplished for us, and we hate the crime of the Jews who crucified Him. The garment signifies the sacrament, their backs the memory of things past: for the Church celebrates the passion of Christ as already accomplished, and no longer to be looked forward to, now that Japheth already dwells in the habitations of Shem, and their wicked brother between them.

But the wicked brother is, in the person of his son (i.e., his work), the boy, or slave, of his good brothers, when good men make a skilful use of bad men, either for the exercise of their patience or for their advancement in wisdom. For the apostle testifies that there are some who preach Christ from no pure motives; "but," says he, "whether in pretence or in truth, Christ is preached; and I therein do rejoice, yea, and will rejoice."[1] For it is Christ Himself Who planted the vine of which the prophet says, "The vine of the Lord of hosts is the house of Israel";[2] and He drinks of its wine, whether we thus understand that cup of which He says, "Can ye drink of the cup that I shall drink of?"[3] and, "Father, if it be possible, let this cup pass from me,"[4] by which He obviously means His passion. Or, as wine is the fruit of the vine, we may prefer to understand that from this vine, that is to say, from the race of Israel, He has assumed flesh and blood that He might suffer; "and he was drunken," that is, He suffered; "and was naked," that is, His weakness appeared in His suffering, as the apostle says, "though He was crucified through weakness."[5] Wherefore the same apostle says, "The weakness of God is stronger than men; and the foolishness of God is wiser than men."[6] And when to the expression "he was naked" Scripture adds "in his house," it elegantly intimates that Jesus was to suffer the cross and death at the hands of His own household, His own kith and kin, the Jews. This passion of Christ is only externally and verbally professed by the reprobate, for what they profess they do not understand. But the elect hold in the inner man this so great mystery, and honour inwardly in the heart this weakness and foolishness of God. And of this there is a figure in Ham going out to proclaim his father's nakedness; while Shem and Japheth, to cover or honour it, went in, that is to say, did it inwardly.

These secrets of divine Scripture we investigate as well as we can. All will not accept our interpretation with equal confidence, but all hold it certain that these things were neither done nor recorded without some foreshadowing of future events, and that they are to be referred only to Christ and His Church, which is the city of God, proclaimed from the very beginning of human history by figures which we now see everywhere accomplished. From the blessing of the two sons of Noah, and the cursing of the middle son, down to Abraham, or for more than a thousand years, there is, as I have said, no mention of any righteous persons who worshipped God. I do not therefore conclude that there were none; but it had been tedious to mention every one, and would have displayed historical accuracy rather than prophetic foresight. The object of the writer of these sacred books, or rather of the Spirit of God in him, is not only to record the past, but to depict the future, so far as it regards the city of God; for whatever is said of those who are not its citizens, is given either for her instruction, or as a foil to enhance her glory. Yet we are not to suppose that all that is recorded has some signification; but those things which have no signification of their own are interwoven for the sake of the things which are significant. It is only the ploughshare that cleaves the soil; but to effect this, other parts of the plough are requisite. It is only the strings in harps and other musical instruments which produce melodious sounds; but that they may do so, there are other parts of the instrument which are not indeed struck by those who sing, but are connected with the strings which are struck, and produce musical notes. So in this prophetic history some things are narrated which have no significance, but are, as it were, the framework to which the significant things are attached.

CHAP. 3. *Of the generations of the three sons of Noah*

We must therefore introduce into this work an explanation of the generations of the three sons of Noah, in so far as that may illustrate the progress in time of the two cities. Scripture first mentions that of the youngest son, who is called

---

[1]Phil. 1. 18. [2]Isa. 5. 7. [3]Matt. 20. 22.
[4]Matt. 26. 39. [5]II Cor. 13. 4. [6]I Cor. 1. 25.

Japheth: he had eight sons,[1] and by two of these sons seven grandchildren, three by one son, four by the other; in all, fifteen descendants. Ham, Noah's middle son, had four sons, and by one of them five grandsons, and by one of these two great-grandsons; in all, eleven. After enumerating these, Scripture returns to the first of the sons, and says, "Cush begat Nimrod; he began to be a giant on the earth. He was a giant hunter against the Lord God: wherefore they say, As Nimrod the giant hunter against the Lord. And the beginning of his kingdom was Babylon, Erech, Accad, and Calneh, in the land of Shinar. Out of that land went forth Assur, and built Nineveh, and the city Rehoboth, and Calah, and Resen between Nineveh and Calah: this was a great city." Now this Cush, father of the giant Nimrod, is the first-named among the sons of Ham, to whom five sons and two grandsons are ascribed. But he either begat this giant after his grandsons were born, or, which is more credible, Scripture speaks of him separately on account of his eminence; for mention is also made of his kingdom, which began with that magnificent city Babylon, and the other places, whether cities or districts, mentioned along with it. But what is recorded of the land of Shinar which belonged to Nimrod's kingdom, to wit, that Assur went forth from it and built Nineveh and the other cities mentioned with it, happened long after; but he takes occasion to speak of it here on account of the grandeur of the Assyrian kingdom, which was wonderfully extended by Ninus son of Belus, and founder of the great city Nineveh, which was named after him, Nineveh, from Ninus. But Assur, father of the Assyrian, was not one of the sons of Ham, Noah's middle son, but is found among the sons of Shem, his eldest son. Whence it appears that among Shem's offspring there arose men who afterwards took possession of that giant's kingdom and, advancing from it, founded other cities, the first of which was called Nineveh, from Ninus. From him Scripture returns to Ham's other son, Mizraim; and his sons are enumerated, not as seven individuals, but as seven nations. And from the sixth, as if from the sixth son, the race called the Philistines are said to have sprung; so that there are in all eight. Then it returns again to Canaan, in whose person Ham was cursed; and his eleven sons are named. Then the territories they occupied, and some of the cities, are named. And thus, if we count sons and grandsons, there are thirty-one of Ham's descendants registered.

It remains to mention the sons of Shem, Noah's eldest son; for to him this genealogical narrative gradually ascends from the youngest. But in the commencement of the record of Shem's sons there is an obscurity which calls for explanation, since it is closely connected with the object of our investigation. For we read, "Unto Shem also, the father of all the children of Heber, the brother of Japheth the elder, were children born."[2] This is the order of the words: And to Shem was born Heber, even to himself, that is, to Shem himself was born Heber, and Shem is the father of all his children. We are intended to understand that Shem is the patriarch of all his posterity who were to be mentioned, whether sons, grandsons, great-grandsons, or descendants at any remove. For Shem did not beget Heber, who was indeed in the fifth generation from him. For Shem begat, among other sons, Arphaxad; Arphaxad begat Cainan, Cainan begat Salah, Salah begat Heber. And it was with good reason that he was named first among Shem's offspring, taking precedence even of his sons, though only a grandchild of the fifth generation; for from him, as tradition says, the Hebrews derived their name, though the other etymology which derives the name from Abraham (as if *Abrahews*) may possibly be correct. But there can be little doubt that the former is the right etymology, and that they were called after Heber, *Heberews,* and then, dropping a letter, Hebrews; and so was their language called Hebrew, which was spoken by none but the people of Israel among whom was the city of God, mysteriously prefigured in all the people and truly present in the saints. Six of Shem's sons then are first named, then four grandsons born to one of these sons; then it mentions another son of Shem, who begat a grandson; and his son, again, or Shem's great-grandson, was Heber. And Heber begat two sons, and called the one Peleg, which means "dividing"; and Scripture subjoins the reason of this name, saying, "for in his days was the earth divided." What this means will afterwards appear. Heber's other son begat twelve sons; consequently all Shem's descendants are twenty-seven. The total number of the progeny of the three sons of Noah is seventy-three, fifteen by Japheth, thirty-one by Ham, twenty-seven by Shem. Then Scripture adds, "These are the sons of Shem, after their families, after their

---

[1]Augustine here follows the Greek version, which introduces the name Elisa among the sons of Japheth, though not found in the Hebrew. It is not found in the Complutensian Greek translation, nor in the MSS. used by Jerome.

[2]Gen. 10. 21.

tongues, in their lands, after their nations." And so of the whole number: "These are the families of the sons of Noah after their generations, in their nations; and by these were the isles of the nations dispersed through the earth after the flood." From which we gather that the seventy-three (or rather, as I shall presently show, seventy-two) were not individuals, but nations. For in a former passage, when the sons of Japheth were enumerated, it is said in conclusion, "By these were the isles of the nations divided in their lands, every one after his language, in their tribes, and in their nations."

But nations are expressly mentioned among the sons of Ham, as I showed above. "Mizraim begat those who are called Ludim"; and so also of the other seven nations. And after enumerating all of them, it concludes, "These are the sons of Ham, in their families, according to their languages, in their territories, and in their nations." The reason, then, why the children of several of them are not mentioned is that they belonged by birth to other nations, and did not themselves become nations. Why else is it, that though eight sons are reckoned to Japheth, the sons of only two of these are mentioned; and though four are reckoned to Ham, only three are spoken of as having sons; and though six are reckoned to Shem, the descendants of only two of these are traced? Did the rest remain childless? We cannot suppose so; but they did not produce nations so great as to warrant their being mentioned, but were absorbed in the nations to which they belonged by birth.

CHAP. 4 *Of the diversity of languages, and of the founding of Babylon*

But though these nations are said to have been dispersed according to their languages, yet the narrator recurs to that time when all had but one language, and explains how it came to pass that a diversity of languages was introduced. "The whole earth," he says, "was of one lip, and all had one speech. And it came to pass, as they journeyed from the east, that they found a plain in the land of Shinar, and dwelt there. And they said one to another, Come, and let us make bricks, and burn them thoroughly. And they had bricks for stone, and slime for mortar. And they said, Come, and let us build for ourselves a city, and a tower whose top shall reach the sky; and let us make us a name, before we be scattered abroad on the face of all the earth. And the Lord came down to see the city and the tower, which the children of men builded. And the Lord God

said, Behold, the people is one, and they have all one language; and this they begin to do: and now nothing will be restrained from them, which they have imagined to do. Come, and let us go down, and confound there their language, that they may not understand one another's speech. And God scattered them thence on the face of all the earth: and they left off to build the city and the tower. Therefore the name of it is called Confusion; because the Lord did there confound the language of all the earth: and the Lord God scattered them thence on the face of all the earth." [1] This city, which was called Confusion, is the same as Babylon, whose wonderful construction Gentile history also notices. For Babylon means Confusion. Whence we conclude that the giant Nimrod was its founder, as had been hinted a little before, where Scripture, in speaking of him, says that the beginning of his kingdom was Babylon, that is, Babylon had a supremacy over the other cities as the metropolis and royal residence; although it did not rise to the grand dimensions designed by its proud and impious founder. The plan was to make it so high that it should reach the sky, whether this was meant of one tower which they intended to build higher than the others, or of all the towers, which might be signified by the singular number, as we speak of "the soldier," meaning the army, and of the frog or the locust, when we refer to the whole multitude of frogs and locusts in the plagues with which Moses smote the Egyptians.[2] But what did these vain and presumptuous men intend? How did they expect to raise this lofty mass against God, when they had built it above all the mountains and the clouds of the earth's atmosphere? What injury could any spiritual or material elevation do to God? The safe and true way to heaven is made by humility, which lifts up the heart to the Lord, not against Him; as this giant is said to have been a "hunter *against* the Lord." This has been misunderstood by some through the ambiguity of the Greek word, and they have translated it, not "against the Lord," but "before the Lord"; for ἐναντίον means both "before" and "against." In the Psalm this word is rendered, "Let us weep *before* the Lord our Maker."[3] The same word occurs in the book of Job, where it is written, "Thou hast broken into fury *against* the Lord."[4] And so this giant is to be recognized as a "hunter *against* the Lord." And what is meant by the term "hunter" but deceiver, oppressor, and destroyer of the animals of the earth? He and his

[1] Gen. 11. 1-9.   [2] Ex. 10.   [3] Ps. 95. 6.   [4] Job, 15. 13.

people therefore, erected this tower against the Lord, and so gave expression to their impious pride; and justly was their wicked intention punished by God, even though it was unsuccessful. But what was the nature of the punishment? As the tongue is the instrument of domination, in it pride was punished; so that man, who would not understand God when He issued His commands, should be misunderstood when he himself gave orders. Thus was that conspiracy disbanded, for each man retired from those he could not understand, and associated with those whose speech was intelligible; and the nations were divided according to their languages, and scattered over the earth as seemed good to God, who accomplished this in ways hidden from and incomprehensible to us.

CHAP. 5. *Of God's coming down to confound the languages of the builders of the city*

We read, "The Lord came down to see the city and the tower which the sons of men built": it was not the sons of God, but that society which lived in a merely human way, and which we call the earthly city. God, who is always wholly everywhere, does not move locally; but He is said to descend when He does anything in the earth out of the usual course, which, as it were, makes His presence felt. And in the same way, He does not by "seeing" learn some new thing, for He cannot ever be ignorant of anything; but He is said to see and recognize, in time, that which He causes others to see and recognize. And therefore that city was not previously being seen as God made it be seen when He showed how offensive it was to Him. We might, indeed, interpret God's descending to the city of the descent of His angels in whom He dwells; so that the following words, "And the Lord God said, Behold, they are all one race and of one language," and also what follows, "Come, and let us go down and confound their speech," are a recapitulation, explaining how the previously intimated "descent of the Lord" was accomplished. For if He had already gone down, why does He say, "Come, and let us go down and confound?"—words which seem to be addressed to the angels, and to intimate that He who was in the angels descended in their descent. And the words most appropriately are, not, "Go ye down and confound," but, "Let us confound their speech"; showing that He so works by His servants, that they are themselves also fellow-labourers with God, as the apostle says, "For we are fellow-labourers with God." [1]

[1] I Cor. 3. 9.

CHAP. 6. *What we are to understand by God's speaking to the angels*

We might have supposed that the words uttered at the creation of man, "Let us," and not "Let me," "make man," were addressed to the angels, had He not added "in our image"; but as we cannot believe that man was made in the image of angels, or that the image of God is the same as that of angels, it is proper to refer this expression to the plurality of the Trinity. And yet this Trinity, being one God, even after saying "Let *us* make," goes on to say, "And God made man in His image," [2] and not "Gods made," or "in their image." And were there any difficulty in applying to the angels the words, "Come, and let us go down and confound their speech," we might refer the plural to the Trinity, as if the Father were addressing the Son and the Holy Spirit; but it rather belongs to the angels to approach God by holy movements, that is, by pious thoughts, and thereby to avail themselves of the unchangeable truth which rules in the court of heaven as their eternal law. For they are not themselves the truth; but partaking in the creative truth, they are moved towards it as the fountain of life, that what they have not in themselves they may obtain in it. And this movement of theirs is steady, for they never go back from what they have reached. And to these angels God does not speak, as we speak to one another, or to God, or to angels, or as the angels speak to us, or as God speaks to us through them: He speaks to them in an ineffable manner of His own, and that which He says is conveyed to us in a manner suited to our capacity. For the speaking of God antecedent and superior to all His works, is the immutable reason of His work: it has no noisy and passing sound, but an energy eternally abiding and producing results in time. Thus He speaks to the holy angels; but to us, who are far off, He speaks otherwise. When, however, we hear with the inner ear some part of the speech of God, we approximate to the angels. But in this work I need not labour to give an account of the ways in which God speaks. For either the unchangeable Truth speaks directly to the mind of the rational creature in some indescribable way, or speaks through the changeable creature, either presenting spiritual images to our spirit, or bodily voices to our bodily sense.

The words, "Nothing will be restrained from them which they have imagined to do." [3] are as-

[2] Gen. 1. 26.   [3] Gen. 11. 6.

suredly not meant as an affirmation, but as an interrogation, such as is used by persons threatening, as e.g., when Dido exclaims,

They will not take arms and pursue?[1]

We are to understand the words as if it had been said, "Shall nothing be restrained from them which they have imagined to do?"[2] From these three men, therefore, the three sons of Noah we mean, 73, or rather, as the catalogue will show, 72 nations and as many languages were dispersed over the earth, and as they increased filled even the islands. But the nations multiplied much more than the languages. For even in Africa we know several barbarous nations which have but one language; and who can doubt that, as the human race increased, men contrived to pass to the islands in ships?

CHAP. 7. *Whether even the remotest islands received their fauna from the animals which were preserved, through the deluge, in the ark*

There is a question raised about all those kinds of beasts which are not domesticated, nor are produced like frogs from the earth, but are propagated by male and female parents, such as wolves and animals of that kind; and it is asked how they could be found in the islands after the deluge, in which all the animals not in the ark perished, unless the breed was restored from those which were preserved in pairs in the ark. It might, indeed, be said that they crossed to the islands by swimming, but this could only be true of those very near the mainland; whereas there are some so distant that we fancy no animal could swim to them. But if men caught them and took them across with themselves, and thus propagated these breeds in their new abodes, this would not imply an incredible fondness for the chase. At the same time, it cannot be denied that by the intervention of angels they might be transferred by God's order or permission. If, however, they were produced out of the earth as at their first creation, when God said, "Let the earth bring forth the living creature,"[3] this makes it more evident that all kinds of animals were preserved in the ark, not so much for the sake of renewing the stock, as of prefiguring the various nations which were to be saved in the Church; this, I saw, is more evident, if the earth brought forth many animals in islands to which they could not cross over.

CHAP. 8. *Whether certain monstrous races of men are derived from the stock of Adam or Noah's sons*

It is also asked whether we are to believe that certain monstrous races of men, spoken of in secular history, have sprung from Noah's sons, or rather, I should say, from that one man from whom they themselves were descended. For it is reported that some have one eye in the middle of the forehead; some, feet turned backwards from the heel; some, a double sex, the right breast like a man, the left like a woman, and that they alternately beget and bring forth: others are said to have no mouth, and to breathe only through the nostrils; others are but a cubit high, and are therefore called by the Greeks "Pigmies":[4] they say that in some places the women conceive in their fifth year, and do not live beyond their eighth. So, too, they tell of a race who have two feet but only one leg, and are of marvellous swiftness, though they do not bend the knee: they are called *Skiopodes,* because in the hot weather they lie down on their backs and shade themselves with their feet. Others are said to have no head, and their eyes in their shoulders; and other human or quasi-human races are depicted in mosaic in the harbour esplanade of Carthage, on the faith of histories of rarities. What shall I say of the Cynocephali, whose dog-like head and barking proclaim them beasts rather than men? But we are not bound to believe all we hear of these monstrosities. But whoever is anywhere born a man, that is, a rational, mortal animal, no matter what unusual appearance he presents in colour, movement, sound, nor how peculiar he is in some power, part, or quality of his nature, no Christian can doubt that he springs from that one protoplast. We can distinguish the common human nature from that which is peculiar and therefore wonderful.

The same account which is given of monstrous births in individual cases can be given of monstrous races. For God, the Creator of all, knows where and when each thing ought to be, or to have been created, because He sees the similarities and diversities which can contribute to the beauty of the whole. But he who cannot see the whole is offended by the deformity of the part, because he is blind to that which balances it, and to which it belongs. We know that men are born with more than four fingers on their hands or toes on their feet: this is a smaller matter; but far from us be the folly of supposing

---

[1] Virgil, *Æneid,* BK. IV. 592.
[2] Here Augustine remarks on the addition of the particle *ne* to the word *non,* which he has made to bring out the sense.　　[3] Gen. I. 24.
[4] From πυγμή, a cubit.

that the Creator mistook the number of a man's fingers, though we cannot account for the difference. And so in cases where the divergence from the rule is greater. He Whose works no man justly finds fault with, knows what He has done. At Hippo-Diarrhytus there is a man whose hands are crescent-shaped, and have only two fingers each, and his feet similarly formed. If there were a race like him, it would be added to the history of the curious and wonderful. Shall we therefore deny that this man is descended from that one man who was first created? As for the Androgyni, or Hermaphrodites, as they are called, though they are rare, yet from time to time there appear persons of sex so doubtful, that it remains uncertain from which sex they take their name; though it is customary to give them a masculine name, as the more worthy. For no one ever called them Hermaphroditesses. Some years ago, quite within my own memory, a man was born in the East, double in his upper, but single in his lower half—having two heads, two chests, four hands, but one body and two feet like an ordinary man; and he lived so long that many had an opportunity of seeing him. But who could enumerate all the human births that have differed widely from their ascertained parents? As, therefore, no one will deny that these are all descended from that one man, so all the races which are reported to have diverged in bodily appearance from the usual course which nature generally or almost universally preserves, if they are embraced in that definition of man as rational and mortal animals, unquestionably trace their pedigree to that one first father of all. We are supposing these stories about various races who differ from one another and from us to be true; but possibly they are not: for if we were not aware that apes, and monkeys, and sphinxes are not men, but beasts, those historians would possibly describe them as races of men, and flaunt with impunity their false and vainglorious discoveries. But supposing they are men of whom these marvels are recorded, what if God has seen fit to create some races in this way, that we might not suppose that the monstrous births which appear among ourselves are the failures of that wisdom whereby He fashions the human nature, as we speak of the failure of a less perfect workman? Accordingly, it ought not to seem absurd to us, that as in individual races there are monstrous births, so in the whole race there are monstrous races. Wherefore, to conclude this question cautiously and guardedly, either these things which have been told of some races have no existence at all; or if they do exist, they are not human races; or if they are human, they are descended from Adam.

CHAP. 9. *Whether we are to believe in the Antipodes*

But as to the fable that there are Antipodes, that is to say, men on the opposite side of the earth, where the sun rises when it sets to us, men who walk with their feet opposite ours, that is on no ground credible. And, indeed, it is not affirmed that this has been learned by historical knowledge, but by scientific conjecture, on the ground that the earth is suspended within the concavity of the sky, and that it has as much room on the one side of it as on the other: hence they say that the part which is beneath must also be inhabited. But they do not remark that, although it be supposed or scientifically demonstrated that the world is of a round and spherical form, yet it does not follow that the other side of the earth is bare of water; nor even, though it be bare, does it immediately follow that it is peopled. For Scripture, which proves the truth of its historical statements by the accomplishment of its prophecies, gives no false information; and it is too absurd to say that some men might have taken ship and traversed the whole wide ocean, and crossed from this side of the world to the other, and that thus even the inhabitants of that distant region are descended from that one first man. Wherefore let us seek if we can find the city of God that sojourns on earth among those human races who are catalogued as having been divided into seventy-two nations and as many languages. For it continued down to the deluge and the ark, and is proved to have existed still among the sons of Noah by their blessings, and chiefly in the eldest son Shem; for Japheth received this blessing, that he should dwell in the tents of Shem.

CHAP. 10. *Of the genealogy of Shem, in whose line the city of God is preserved till the time of Abraham*

It is necessary, therefore, to preserve the series of generations descending from Shem, for the sake of exhibiting the city of God after the flood; as before the flood it was exhibited in the series of generations descending from Seth. And therefore does divine Scripture, after exhibiting the earthly city as Babylon or "Confusion," revert to the patriarch Shem, and recapitulate the generations from him to Abraham, specifying besides, the year in which each father begat the son that belonged to this line, and how long he lived. And unquestionably it is this which fulfills the promise I made, that it should appear why it is said of the sons of Heber, "The name of the one was Peleg, for in his days the earth was divided." [1] For what can we understand by the division of the earth, if not the diversity of languages? And, therefore, omitting the other sons of Shem, who are not concerned in this matter, Scripture gives the genealogy of those by whom the line runs on to Abraham, as before the flood those are given who carried on the line to Noah from Seth. Accordingly this series of generations begins thus: "These are the generations of Shem: Shem was an hundred years old, and begat Arphaxad two years after the flood. And Shem lived after he begat Arphaxad five hundred years, and begat sons and daughters." In like manner it registers the rest, naming the year of his life in which each begat the son who belonged to that line which extends to Abraham. It specifies, too, how many years he lived thereafter, begetting sons and daughters, that we may not childishly suppose that the men named were the only men, but may understand how the population increased, and how regions and kingdoms so vast could be populated by the descendants of Shem; especially the kingdom of Assyria, from which Ninus subdued the surrounding nations, reigning with brilliant prosperity, and bequeathing to his descendants a vast but thoroughly consolidated empire, which held together for many centuries.

But, to avoid needless prolixity, we shall mention not the number of years each member of this series lived, but only the year of his life in which he begat his heir, that we may thus reckon the number of years from the flood to Abraham, and may at the same time leave room to touch briefly and cursorily upon some other matters necessary to our argument. In the second year, then, after the flood, Shem when he was a hundred years old begat Arphaxad; Arphaxad when he was 135 years old begat Cainan; Cainan when he was 130 years begat Salah. Salah himself, too, was the same age when he begat Heber. Heber lived 134 years, and begat Peleg, in whose days the earth was divided. Peleg himself lived 130 years, and begat Reu; and Reu lived 132 years, and begat Serug; Serug 130, and begat Nahor; and Nahor 79, and begat Terah; and Terah 70, and begat Abram, whose name God afterwards changed into *Abraham*. There are thus from the flood to Abraham 1072 years, according to the Vulgate or Septuagint versions. In the Hebrew copies far fewer years

are given; and for this either no reason or a not very credible one is given.

When, therefore, we look for the city of God in these seventy-two nations, we cannot affirm that while they had but one lip, that is, one language, the human race had departed from the worship of the true God, and that genuine godliness had survived only in those generations which descend from Shem through Arphaxad and reach to Abraham; but from the time when they proudly built a tower to heaven, a symbol of godless exaltation, the city or society of the wicked becomes apparent. Whether it was only disguised before, or non-existent; whether both cities remained after the flood—the godly in the two sons of Noah who were blessed, and in their posterity, and the ungodly in the cursed son and his descendants, from whom sprang that mighty hunter against the Lord—is not easily determined. For possibly—and certainly this is more credible—there were despisers of God among the descendants of the two sons, even before Babylon was founded, and worshippers of God among the descendants of Ham. Certainly neither race was ever obliterated from earth. For in both the Psalms in which it is said, "They are all gone aside, they are altogether become filthy; there is none that doeth good, no, not one," we read further, "Have all the workers of iniquity no knowledge? who eat up my people as they eat bread, and call not upon the Lord." [2] There was then a people of God even at that time. And therefore the words, "There is none that doeth good, no, not one," were said of the sons of men, not of the sons of God. For it had been previously said, "God looked down from heaven upon the sons of men, to see if any understood and sought after God"; and then follow the words which demonstrate that all the sons of men, that is, all who belong to the city which lives according to man, not according to God, are reprobate.

CHAP. 11. *That the original language in use among men was that which was afterwards called Hebrew, from Heber, in whose family it was preserved when the confusion of tongues occurred*

Wherefore, as the fact of all using one language did not secure the absence of sin-infected men from the race—for even before the deluge there was one language, and yet all but the single family of just Noah were found worthy of destruction by the flood—so when the nations, by a prouder godlessness, earned the punishment of the dispersion and the confusion of

[1] Gen. 10. 25.

[2] Ps. 14. 3, 4; Ps. 53. 3, 4.

tongues, and the city of the godless was called Confusion or Babylon, there was still the house of Heber in which the primitive language of the race survived. And therefore, as I have already mentioned, when an enumeration is made of the sons of Shem, who each founded a nation, Heber is first mentioned, although he was of the fifth generation from Shem. And because, when the other races were divided by their own peculiar languages, his family preserved that language which is not unreasonably believed to have been the common language of the race, it was on this account thenceforth named *Hebrew*. For it then became necessary to distinguish this language from the rest by a proper name; though, while there was only one, it had no other name than the language of man, or human speech, it alone being spoken by the whole human race. Some one will say: "If the earth was divided by languages in the days of Peleg, Heber's son, that language, which was formerly common to all, should rather have been called after Peleg." But we are to understand that Heber himself gave to his son this name Peleg, which means Division; because he was born when the earth was divided, that is, at the very time of the division, and that this is the meaning of the words, "In his days the earth was divided."[1] For unless Heber had been still alive when the languages were multiplied, the language which was preserved in his house would not have been called after him. We are induced to believe that this was the primitive and common language, because the multiplication and change of languages was introduced as a punishment, and it is fit to ascribe to the people of God an immunity from this punishment. Nor is it without significance that this is the language which Abraham retained, and that he could not transmit it to all his descendants, but only to those of Jacob's line, who distinctively and eminently constituted God's people, and received His covenants, and were Christ's progenitors according to the flesh. In the same way, Heber himself did not transmit that language to all his posterity, but only to the line from which Abraham sprang. And thus, although it is not expressly stated, that when the wicked were building Babylon there was a godly seed remaining, this indistinctness is intended to stimulate research rather than to elude it. For when we see that originally there was one common language, and that Heber is mentioned before all Shem's sons, though he belonged to the fifth generation from him, and that the language

[1]Gen. 10. 25.

which the patriarchs and prophets used, not only in their conversation, but in the authoritative language of Scripture, is called Hebrew, when we are asked where that primitive and common language was preserved after the confusion of tongues, certainly, as there can be no doubt that those among whom it was preserved were exempt from the punishment it embodied, what other suggestion can we make, than that it survived in the family of him whose name it took, and that this is no small proof of the righteousness of this family that the punishment with which the other families were visited did not fall upon it?

But yet another question is mooted: How did Heber and his son Peleg each found a nation, if they had but one language? For no doubt the Hebrew nation propagated from Heber through Abraham, and becoming through him a great people, is one nation. How, then, are all the sons of the three branches of Noah's family enumerated as founding a nation each, if Heber and Peleg did not so? It is very probable that the giant Nimrod founded also his nation, and that Scripture has named him separately on account of the extraordinary dimensions of his empire and of his body, so that the number of seventy-two nations remains. But Peleg was mentioned, not because he founded a nation (for his race and language are Hebrew), but on account of the critical time at which he was born, all the earth being then divided. Nor ought we to be surprised that the giant Nimrod lived to the time in which Babylon was founded and the confusion of tongues occurred, and the consequent division of the earth. For though Heber was in the sixth generation from Noah, and Nimrod in the fourth, it does not follow that they could not be alive at the same time. For when the generations are few, they live longer and are born later; but when they are many, they live a shorter time, and come into the world earlier. We are to understand that, when the earth was divided, the descendants of Noah who are registered as founders of nations were not only already born, but were of an age to have immense families, worthy to be called tribes or nations. And therefore we must by no means suppose that they were born in the order in which they were set down; otherwise, how could the twelve sons of Joktan, another son of Heber's, and brother of Peleg, have already founded nations, if Joktan was born, as he is registered, after his brother Peleg, since the earth was divided at Peleg's birth? We are therefore to understand that, though Peleg is named first, he was born long after Joktan, whose twelve sons had already families so large as to admit of their being divided by different languages. There is nothing extraordinary in the last born being first named: of the sons of Noah, the descendants of Japheth are first named; then the sons of Ham, who was the second son; and last the sons of Shem, who was the first and oldest. Of these nations the names have partly survived, so that at this day we can see from whom they have sprung, as the Assyrians from Assur, the Hebrews from Heber, but partly have been altered in the lapse of time, so that the most learned men, by profound research in ancient records, have scarcely been able to discover the origin, I do not say of all, but of some of these nations. There is, for example, nothing in the name Egyptians to show that they are descended from Misraim, Ham's son, nor in the name Ethiopians to show a connection with Cush, though such is said to be the origin of these nations. And if we take a general survey of the names, we shall find that more have been changed than have remained the same.

CHAP. 12. *Of the era in Abraham's life from which a new period in the holy succession begins*

Let us now survey the progress of the city of God from the era of the patriarch Abraham, from whose time it begins to be more conspicuous, and the divine promises which are now fulfilled in Christ are more fully revealed. We learn, then, from the intimations of holy Scripture, that Abraham was born in the country of the Chaldeans, a land belonging to the Assyrian empire. Now, even at that time impious superstitions were rife with the Chaldeans, as with other nations. The family of Terah, to which Abraham belonged, was the only one in which the worship of the true God survived, and the only one, we may suppose, in which the Hebrew language was preserved; although Joshua the son of Nun tells us that even this family served other gods in Mesopotamia.[1] The other descendants of Heber gradually became absorbed in other races and other languages. And thus, as the single family of Noah was preserved through the deluge of water to renew the human race, so, in the deluge of superstition that flooded the whole world, there remained but the one family of Terah in which the seed of God's city was preserved. And as, when Scripture has enumer-

ated the generations prior to Noah, with their ages, and explained the cause of the flood before God began to speak to Noah about the building of the ark, it is said, "These are the generations of Noah"; so also now, after enumerating the generations from Shem, Noah's son, down to Abraham, it then signalizes an era by saying, "These are the generations of Terah: Terah begat Abram, Nahor, and Haran; and Haran begat Lot. And Haran died before his father Terah in the land of his nativity, in Ur of the Chaldees. And Abram and Nahor took them wives: the name of Abram's wife was Sarai; and the name of Nahor's wife Milcah, the daughter of Haran, the father of Milcah, and the father of Iscah."[2] This Iscah is supposed to be the same as Sarah, Abraham's wife.

CHAP. 13. *Why, in the account of Terah's emigration, on his forsaking the Chaldeans and passing over into Mesopotamia, no mention is made of his son Nahor*

Next it is related how Terah with his family left the region of the Chaldeans and came into Mesopotamia, and dwelt in Haran. But nothing is said about one of his sons called Nahor, as if he had not taken him along with him. For the narrative runs thus: "And Terah took Abram his son, and Lot the son of Haran, his son's son, and Sarah his daughter-in-law, his son Abram's wife, and led them forth out of the region of the Chaldeans to go into the land of Canaan; and he came into Haran, and dwelt there."[3] Nahor and Milcah his wife are nowhere named here. But afterwards, when Abraham sent his servant to take a wife for his son Isaac, we find it thus written: "And the servant took ten camels of the camels of his lord, and of all the goods of his lord, with him; and arose, and went into Mesopotamia, into the city of Nahor."[4] This and other testimonies of this sacred history show that Nahor, Abraham's brother, had also left the region of the Chaldeans, and fixed his abode in Mesopotamia, where Abraham dwelt with his father. Why, then, did the Scripture not mention him, when Terah with his family went forth out of the Chaldean nation and dwelt in Haran, since it mentions that he took with him not only Abraham his son, but also Sarah his daughter-in-law, and Lot his grandson? The only reason we can think of is that perhaps he had lapsed from the piety of his father and brother, and adhered to the superstition of the Chaldeans, and had afterwards emigrated

[1]Josh. 24. 2.   [2]Gen. 11. 27–29.   [3]Gen. 11. 31.   [4]Gen. 24. 10.

thence, either through penitence, or because he was persecuted as a suspected person. For in the book called Judith, when Holofernes, the enemy of the Israelites, inquired what kind of nation that might be, and whether war should be made against them, Achior, the leader of the Ammonites, answered him thus: "Let our lord now hear a word from the mouth of thy servant, and I will declare unto thee the truth concerning the people which dwelleth near thee in this hill country, and there shall no lie come out of the mouth of thy servant. For this people is descended from the Chaldeans, and they dwelt heretofore in Mesopotamia, because they would not follow the gods of their fathers, which were glorious in the land of the Chaldeans, but went out of the way of their ancestors, and adored the God of heaven, whom they knew; and they cast them out from the face of their gods, and they fled into Mesopotamia, and dwelt there many days. And their God said to them that they should depart from their habitation, and go into the land of Canaan; and they dwelt,"[1] etc., as Achior the Ammonite narrates. Whence it is manifest that the house of Terah had suffered persecution from the Chaldeans for the true piety with which they worshipped the one and true God.

Chap. 14. Of the years of Terah, who completed his lifetime in Haran

On Terah's death in Mesopotamia, where he is said to have lived 205 years, the promises of God made to Abraham now begin to be pointed out; for thus it is written: "And the days of Terah in Haran were two hundred and five years, and he died in Haran."[2] This is not to be taken as if he had spent all his days there, but that he there completed the days of his life, which were two hundred and five years: otherwise it would not be known how many years Terah lived, since it is not said in what year of his life he came into Haran; and it is absurd to suppose that, in this series of generations, where it is carefully recorded how many years each one lived, his age was the only one not put on record. For although some whom the same Scripture mentions have not their age recorded, they are not in this series, in which the reckoning of time is continuously indicated by the death of the parents and the succession of the children. For this series, which is given in order from Adam to Noah, and from him down to Abraham, contains no one without the number of the years of his life.

Chap. 15. Of the time of the migration of Abraham, when, according to the commandment of God, he went out from Haran

When, after the record of the death of Terah, the father of Abraham, we next read, "And the Lord said to Abram, Get thee out of thy country, and from thy kindred, and from thy father's house,"[3] etc, it is not to be supposed, because this follows in the order of the narrative, that it also followed in the chronological order of events. For if it were so, there would be an insoluble difficulty. For after these words of God which were spoken to Abraham, the Scripture says: "And Abram departed, as the Lord had spoken unto him; and Lot went with him. Now Abraham was seventy-five years old when he departed out of Haran."[4] How can this be true if he departed from Haran after his father's death? For when Terah was seventy years old, as is intimated above, he begat Abraham; and if to this number we add the seventy-five years which Abraham reckoned when he went out of Haran, we get 145 years. Therefore that was the number of the years of Terah, when Abraham departed out of that city of Mesopotamia; for he had reached the seventy-fifth year of his life, and thus his father, who begat him in the seventieth year of his life, had reached, as was said, his 145th. Therefore he did not depart thence after his father's death, that is, after the 205 years his father lived; but the year of his departure from that place, seeing it was his seventy-fifth, is inferred beyond a doubt to have been the 145th of his father, who begat him in his seventieth year. And thus it is to be understood that the Scripture, according to its custom, has gone back to the time which had already been passed by the narrative; just as above, when it had mentioned the grandsons of Noah, it said that they were in their nations and tongues; and yet afterwards, as if this also had followed in order of time, it says, "And the whole earth was of one lip, and one speech for all."[5] How, then, could they be said to be in their own nations and according to their own tongues, if there was one for all; except because the narrative goes back to gather up what it had passed over? Here, too, in the same way, after saying, "And the days of Terah in Haran were 205 years, and Terah died in Haran," the Scripture, going back to what had been passed over in order to complete what had been begun about Terah, says, "And the Lord said to Abram, Get thee out of thy country,"[6] etc. After which words of God it is added,

[1]Judith, 5. 5–9.   [2]Gen. 11. 32.   [3]Gen. 12. 1.   [4]Gen. 12. 4.   [5]Gen. 11. 1.   [6]Gen. 12. 1.

"And Abram departed, as the Lord spake unto him; and Lot went with him. But Abram was seventy-five years old when he departed out of Haran." Therefore it was done when his father was in the 145th year of his age; for it was then the seventy-fifth of his own. But this question is also solved in another way, that the seventy-five years of Abraham when he departed out of Haran are reckoned from the year in which he was delivered from the fire of the Chaldeans, not from that of his birth, as if he were rather to be held as having been born then.

Now the blessed Stephen, in narrating these things in the Acts of the Apostles, says: "The God of glory appeared unto our father Abraham, when he was in Mesopotamia, before he dwelt in Charran, and said unto him, Get thee out of thy country, and from thy kindred, and from thy father's house, and come into the land which I will show thee."[1] According to these words of Stephen, God spoke to Abraham, not after the death of his father, who certainly died in Haran, where his son also dwelt with him, but before he dwelt in that city, although he was already in Mesopotamia. Therefore he had already departed from the Chaldeans. So that when Stephen adds, "Then Abraham went out of the land of the Chaldeans, and dwelt in Charran,"[2] this does not point out what took place after God spoke to him (for it was not after these words of God that he went out of the land of the Chaldeans, since he says that God spoke to him in Mesopotamia), but the word *"then"* which he uses refers to that whole period from his going out of the land of the Chaldeans and dwelling in Haran. Likewise in what follows, "And thenceforth, when his father was dead, he settled him in this land, wherein ye now dwell, and your fathers," he does not say, "after his father was dead he went out from Haran"; but thenceforth he settled him here, after his father was dead. It is to be understood, therefore, that God had spoken to Abraham when he was in Mesopotamia, before he dwelt in Haran; but that he came to Haran with his father, keeping in mind the precept of God, and that he went out thence in his own seventy-fifth year, which was his father's 145th. But he says that his settlement in the land of Canaan, not his going forth from Haran, took place after his father's death; because his father was already dead when he purchased the land, and personally entered on possession of it. But when, on his having already settled in Mesopotamia, that is, already gone out of the land of the Chaldeans,

God says, "Get thee out of thy country, and from thy kindred, and from thy father's house,"[3] this means, not that he should cast out his body from thence, for he had already done that, but that he should tear away his soul. For he had not gone out from thence in mind, if he was held by the hope and desire of returning—a hope and desire which was to be cut off by God's command and help, and by his own obedience. It would indeed be no incredible supposition that afterwards, when Nahor followed his father, Abraham then fulfilled the precept of the Lord, that he should depart out of Haran with Sarah his wife and Lot his brother's son.

CHAP. 16. *Of the order and nature of the promises of God which were made to Abraham*

God's promises made to Abraham are now to be considered; for in these the oracles of our God,[4] that is, of the true God, began to appear more openly concerning the godly people, whom prophetic authority foretold. The first of these reads thus: "And the Lord said unto Abram, Get thee out of thy country, and from thy kindred, and from thy father's house, and go into a land that I will show thee: and I will make of thee a great nation, and I will bless thee, and magnify thy name; and thou shalt be blessed: and I will bless them that bless thee, and curse them that curse thee: and in thee shall all tribes of the earth be blessed."[5] Now it is to be observed that two things are promised to Abraham, the one, that his seed should possess the land of Canaan, which is intimated when it is said, "Go into a land that I will show thee, and I will make of thee a great nation"; but the other far more excellent, not about the carnal but the spiritual seed, through which he is the father, not of the one Israelite nation, but of all nations who follow the footprints of his faith, which was first promised in these words, "And in thee shall all tribes of the earth be blessed." Eusebius thought this promise was made in Abraham's seventy-fifth year, as if soon after it was made Abraham had departed out of Haran; because the Scripture cannot be contradicted, in which we read, "Abram was seventy and five years old when he departed out of Haran." But if this promise was made in that year, then of course Abraham was staying in Haran with his father; for he could not depart thence unless he had first dwelt there. Does this, then, contradict what Stephen says, "The God of glory appeared

[1]Acts, 7. 2, 3.   [2]Acts, 7. 4.

[3]Gen. 12. 1.
[4]Variant reading: "of our Lord Jesus Christ."
[5]Gen. 12. 1–3.

to our father Abraham, when he was in Mesopotamia, before he dwelt in Charran"?[1] But it is to be understood that the whole took place in the same year—both the promise of God before Abraham dwelt in Haran, and his dwelling in Haran, and his departure thence—not only because Eusebius in the *Chronicles* reckons from the year of this promise, and shows that after 430 years the exodus from Egypt took place, when the law was given, but because the Apostle Paul also mentions it.

CHAP. 17. *Of the three most famous kingdoms of the nations, of which one, that is the Assyrian, was already very eminent when Abraham was born*

During the same period there were three famous kingdoms of the nations, in which the city of the earth-born, that is, the society of men living according to man under the domination of the fallen angels, chiefly flourished, namely, the three kingdoms of Sicyon, Egypt, and Assyria. Of these, Assyria was much the most powerful and sublime; for that king Ninus, son of Belus, had subdued the people of all Asia except India. By Asia I now mean not that part which is one province of this greater Asia, but what is called Universal Asia, which some set down as the half, but most as the third part of the whole world— the three being Asia, Europe, and Africa, thereby making an unequal division. For the part called Asia stretches from the south through the east even to the north; Europe from the north even to the west; and Africa from the west even to the south. Thus we see that two, Europe and Africa, contain one half of the world, and Asia alone the other half. And these two parts are made by the circumstance, that there enters between them from the ocean all the Mediterranean water, which makes this great sea of ours. So that, if you divide the world into two parts, the east and the west, Asia will be in the one, and Europe and Africa in the other. So that of the three kingdoms then famous, one, namely Sicyon, was not under the Assyrians, because it was in Europe; but as for Egypt, how could it fail to be subject to the empire which ruled all Asia with the single exception of India? In Assyria, therefore, the dominion of the impious city had the pre-eminence. Its head was Babylon—an earth-born city, most fitly named, for it means confusion. There Ninus reigned after the death of his father Belus, who first had reigned there sixty-five years. His son Ninus, who, on his father's death, succeeded to the kingdom, reigned

fifty-two years, and had been king forty-three years when Abraham was born, which was about the 1200th year before Rome was founded, as it were another Babylon in the west.

CHAP. 18. *Of the repeated address of God to Abraham, in which he promised the land of Canaan to him and to his seed*

Abraham, then, having departed out of Haran in the seventy-fifth year of his own age, and in the hundred and forty-fifth of his father's, went with Lot, his brother's son, and Sarah his wife, into the land of Canaan, and came even to Sichem, where again he received the divine oracle, of which it is thus written: "And the Lord appeared unto Abram, and said unto him, Unto thy seed will I give this land."[2] Nothing is promised here about that seed in which he is made the father of all nations, but only about that by which he is the father of the one Israelite nation; for by this seed that land was possessed.

CHAP. 19. *Of the divine preservation of Sarah's chastity in Egypt, when Abraham had called her not his wife but his sister*

Having built an altar there, and called upon God, Abraham proceeded thence and dwelt in the desert, and was compelled by pressure of famine to go on into Egypt. There he called his wife his sister, and told no lie. For she was this also, because she was near of blood; just as Lot, on account of the same nearness, being his brother's son, is called his brother. Now he did not deny that she was his wife, but held his peace about it, committing to God the defence of his wife's chastity, and providing as a man against human wiles; because if he had not provided against the danger as much as he could, he would have been tempting God rather than trusting in Him. We have said enough about this matter against the calumnies of Faustus the Manichæan. At last what Abraham had expected the Lord to do took place. For Pharaoh, king of Egypt, who had taken her to him as his wife, restored her to her husband on being severely plagued. And far be it from us to believe that she was defiled by lying with another; because it is much more credible that, by these great afflictions, Pharaoh was not permitted to do this.

CHAP. 20. *Of the parting of Lot and Abraham, which they agreed to without breach of charity*

On Abraham's return out of Egypt to the place he had left, Lot, his brother's son, depart-

---

[1] Acts, 7. 2.   [2] Gen. 12. 7.

ed from him into the land of Sodom, without breach of charity. For they had grown rich, and began to have many herdmen of cattle, and when these strove together, they avoided in this way the pugnacious discord of their families. Indeed, as human affairs go, this cause might even have given rise to some strife between themselves. Consequently these are the words of Abraham to Lot, when taking precaution against this evil, "Let there be no strife between me and thee, and between my herdmen and thy herdmen; for we be brethren. Behold, is not the whole land before thee? Separate thyself from me: if thou wilt go to the left hand, I will go to the right; or if thou wilt go to the right hand, I will go to the left."[1] From this, perhaps, has arisen a pacific custom among men, that when there is any partition of earthly things, the greater should make the division, the less the choice.

Chap. 21. Of the third promise of God, by which He assured the land of Canaan to Abraham and his seed in perpetuity

Now, when Abraham and Lot had separated, and dwelt apart, owing to the necessity of supporting their families, and not to vile discord, and Abraham was in the land of Canaan, but Lot in Sodom, the Lord said to Abraham in a third oracle, "Lift up thine eyes, and look from the place where thou now art, to the north, and to Africa, and to the east, and to the sea; for all the land which thou seest, to thee will I give it, and to thy seed for ever. And I will make thy seed as the dust of the earth: if any one can number the dust of the earth, thy seed shall also be numbered. Arise, and walk through the land, in the length of it, and in the breadth of it; for unto thee will I give it."[2] It does not clearly appear whether in this promise that also is contained by which he is made the father of all nations. For the clause, "And I will make thy seed as the dust of the earth," may seem to refer to this, being spoken by that figure the Greeks call hyperbole, which indeed is figurative, not literal. But no person of understanding can doubt in what manner the Scripture uses this and other figures. For that figure (that is, way of speaking) is used when what is said is far larger than what is meant by it; for who does not see how incomparably larger the number of the dust must be than that of all men can be from Adam himself down to the end of the world? How much greater, then, must it be than the seed of Abraham— not only that pertaining to the nation of Israel,

but also that which is and shall be according to the imitation of faith in all nations of the whole wide world! For that seed is indeed very small in comparison with the multitude of the wicked, although even those few of themselves make an innumerable multitude, which by a hyperbole is compared to the dust of the earth. Truly that multitude which was promised to Abraham is not innumerable to God, although to man; but to God not even the dust of the earth is so. Further, the promise here made may be understood not only of the nation of Israel, but of the whole seed of Abraham, which may be fitly compared to the dust for multitude, because regarding it also there is the promise[3] of many children, not according to the flesh, but according to the spirit. But we have therefore said that this does not clearly appear, because the multitude even of that one nation, which was born according to the flesh of Abraham through his grandson Jacob, has increased so much as to fill almost all parts of the world. Consequently, even it might by hyperbole be compared to the dust for multitude, because even it alone is innumerable by man. Certainly no one questions that only that land is meant which is called Canaan. But that saying, "To thee will I give it, and to thy seed for ever," may move some, if by "for ever" they understand "to eternity." But if in this passage they take "for ever" thus, as we firmly hold it means, that the beginning of the world to come is to be ordered from the end of the present, there is still no difficulty, because, although the Israelites are expelled from Jerusalem, they still remain in other cities in the land of Canaan, and shall remain even to the end; and when that whole land is inhabited by Christians, they also are the very seed of Abraham.

Chap. 22. Of Abraham's overcoming the enemies of Sodom, when he delivered Lot from captivity and was blessed by Melchizedek the priest

Having received this oracle of promise, Abraham migrated, and remained in another place of the same land, that is, beside the oak of Mamre, which was Hebron. Then on the invasion of Sodom, when five kings carried on war against four, and Lot was taken captive with the conquered Sodomites, Abraham delivered him from the enemy, leading with him to battle three hundred and eighteen of his home-born servants, and won the victory for the kings of Sodom, but would take nothing of the spoils when offered by the king for whom he had won them. He was

---

[1] Gen. 13. 8, 9.   [2] Gen. 13. 14–17.

[3] Variant reading: "the express promise."

then openly blessed by Melchizedek, who was priest of God Most High, about whom many and great things are written in the epistle which is inscribed to the Hebrews, which most say is by the Apostle Paul, though some deny this. For then first appeared the sacrifice which is now offered to God by Christians in the whole wide world, and that is fulfilled which long after the event was said by the prophet to Christ, Who was yet to come in the flesh, "Thou art a priest for ever after the order of Melchizedek"[1]—that is to say, not after the order of Aaron, for that order was to be taken away when the things shone forth which were intimated beforehand by these shadows.

CHAP. 23. *Of the word of the Lord to Abraham, by which it was promised to him that his posterity should be multiplied according to the multitude of the stars; on believing which he was declared justified while yet in uncircumcision*

The word of the Lord came to Abraham in a vision also. For when God promised him protection and exceeding great reward, he, being solicitous about posterity, said that a certain Eliezer of Damascus, born in his house, would be his heir. Immediately he was promised an heir, not that house-born servant, but one who was to come forth of Abraham himself; and again a seed innumerable, not as the dust of the earth, but as the stars of heaven—which rather seems to me a promise of a posterity exalted in celestial felicity. For, so far as multitude is concerned, what are the stars of heaven to the dust of the earth, unless one should say the comparison is like inasmuch as the stars also cannot be numbered? For it is not to be believed that all of them can be seen. For the more keenly one observes them, the more does he see. So that it is to be supposed some remain concealed from the keenest observers, to say nothing of those stars which are said to rise and set in another part of the world most remote from us. Finally, the authority of this book condemns those like Aratus or Eudoxus, or any others who boast that they have found out and written down the complete number of the stars. Here, indeed, is set down that sentence which the apostle quotes in order to commend the grace of God, "Abraham believed God, and it was counted to him for righteousness";[2] lest the circumcision should glory, and be unwilling to receive the uncircumcised nations to the faith of Christ. For at the

time when he believed, and his faith was counted to him for righteousness, Abraham had not yet been circumcised.

CHAP. 24. *Of the meaning of the sacrifice Abraham was commanded to offer when he supplicated to be taught about those things he had believed*

In the same vision, God in speaking to him also says, "I am God that brought thee out of the region of the Chaldees, to give thee this land to inherit it."[3] And when Abram asked whereby he might know that he should inherit it, God said to him, "Take me an heifer of three years old, and a she-goat of three years old, and a ram of three years old, and a turtle-dove, and a pigeon. And he took unto him all these, and divided them in the midst, and laid each piece one against another; but the birds divided he not. And the fowls came down," as it is written, "on the carcasses, and Abram sat down by them. But about the going down of the sun, great fear fell upon Abram; and, lo, an horror of great darkness fell upon him. And He said unto Abram, Know of a surety that thy seed shall be a stranger in a land not theirs, and they shall reduce them to servitude and shall afflict them four hundred years: but the nation whom they shall serve will I judge; and afterward shall they come out hither with great substance. And thou shalt go to thy fathers in peace; kept in a good old age. But in the fourth generation they shall come hither again: for the iniquity of the Amorites is not yet full. And when the sun was setting, there was a flame, and a smoking furnace, and lamps of fire, that passed through between those pieces. In that day the Lord made a covenant with Abram, saying, Unto thy seed will I give this land, from the river of Egypt unto the great river Euphrates: the Kenites, and the Kenizzites, and the Kadmonites, and the Hittites, and the Perizzites, and the Rephaims, and the Amorites, and the Canaanites, and the Hivites, and the Girgashites, and the Jebusites."[4]

All these things were said and done in a vision from God; but it would take long, and would exceed the scope of this work, to treat of them exactly in detail. It is enough that we should know that, after it was said, Abram believed in God, and it was counted to him for righteousness he did not fail in faith in saying, "Lord God, whereby shall I know that I shall inherit it?" for the inheritance of that land was promised to him. Now he does not say, "How shall I know," as if

[1]Ps. 110. 4.   [2]Rom. 4. 3; Gen. 15. 6.   [3]Gen. 15. 7.   [4]Gen. 15. 9–21.

he did not yet believe; but he says, "Whereby shall I know," meaning that some sign might be given by which he might know the manner of those things which he had believed, just as it is not for lack of faith the Virgin Mary says, "How shall this be, seeing I know not a man?"[1] for she inquired as to the way in which that should take place which she was certain would come to pass. And when she asked this, she was told, "The Holy Ghost shall come upon thee, and the power of the Highest shall overshadow thee."[2] Here also, in fine, a symbol was given, consisting of three animals, a heifer, a she-goat, and a ram, and two birds, a turtle-dove and pigeon, that he might know that the things which he had not doubted should come to pass were to happen in accordance with this symbol. Whether, therefore, the heifer was a sign that the people should be put under the law, the she-goat that the same people was to become sinful, the ram that they should reign (and these animals are said to be of three years old for this reason, that there are three remarkable divisions of time, from Adam to Noah, and from him to Abraham, and from him to David, who, on the rejection of Saul, was first established by the will of the Lord in the kingdom of the Israelite nation: in this third division, which extends from Abraham to David, that people grew up as if passing through the third age of life), or whether they had some other more suitable meaning, still I have no doubt whatever that spiritual things were prefigured by them as well as by the turtle-dove and pigeon. And it is said, "But the birds divided he not," because carnal men are divided among themselves, but the spiritual not at all, whether they seclude themselves from the busy conversation of men, like the turtle-dove, or dwell among them, like the pigeon; for both birds are simple and harmless, signifying that even in the Israelite people, to which that land was to be given, there would be individuals who were children of the promise and heirs of the kingdom that is to remain in eternal felicity. But the fowls coming down on the divided carcasses represent nothing good, but the spirits of this air, seeking some food for themselves in the division of carnal men. But that Abraham sat down with them, signifies that even amid these divisions of the carnal, true believers shall persevere to the end. And that about the going down of the sun great fear fell upon Abraham and a horror of great darkness, signifies

that about the end of this world believers shall be in great perturbation and tribulation, of which the Lord said in the Gospel, "For then shall be great tribulation, such as was not from the beginning."[3]

But what is said to Abraham, "Know of a surety that thy seed shall be a stranger in a land not theirs, and they shall reduce them to servitude, and shall afflict them 400 years," is most clearly a prophecy about the people of Israel which was to be in servitude in Egypt. Not that this people was to be in that servitude under the oppressive Egyptians for 400 years, but it is foretold that this should take place in the course of those 400 years. For as it is written of Terah the father of Abraham, "And the days of Terah in Haran were 205 years"[4] not because they were all spent there, but because they were completed there, so it is said here also, "And they shall reduce them to servitude, and shall afflict them 400 years," for this reason, because that number was completed, not because it was all spent in that affliction. The years are said to be 400 in round numbers, although they were a little more—whether you reckon from this time, when these things were promised to Abraham, or from the birth of Isaac, as the seed of Abraham, of which these things are predicted. For, as we have already said above, from the seventy-fifth year of Abraham, when the first promise was made to him, down to the exodus of Israel from Egypt, there are reckoned 430 years, which the apostle thus mentions: "And this I say, that the covenant confirmed by God, the law, which was made 430 years after, cannot disannul, that it should make the promise of none effect."[5] So then these 430 years might be called 400, because they are not much more, especially since part even of that number had already gone by when these things were shown and said to Abraham in vision, or when Isaac was born in his father's 100th year, twenty-five years after the first promise, when of these 430 years there now remained 405, which God was pleased to call 400. No one will doubt that the other things which follow in the prophetic words of God pertain to the people of Israel.

When it is added, "And when the sun was now setting there was a flame, and lo, a smoking furnace, and lamps of fire, which passed through between those pieces," this signifies that at the end of the world the carnal shall be judged by fire. For just as the affliction of the city of God, such as never was before, which is expected to

[1]Luke, I. 34.
[2]Luke, I. 35.
[3]Matt. 24. 21.   [4]Gen. 11. 32.   [5]Gal. 3. 17.

take place under Anti-christ, was signified by Abraham's horror of great darkness about the going down of the sun, that is, when the end of the world draws nigh—so at the going down of the sun, that is, at the very end of the world, there is signified by that fire the day of judgment, which separates the carnal who are to be saved by fire from those who are to be condemned in the fire. And then the covenant made with Abraham particularly sets forth the land of Canaan, and names eleven tribes in it from the river of Egypt even to the great river Euphrates. It is not then from the great river of Egypt, that is, the Nile, but from a small one which separates Egypt from Palestine, where the city of Rhinocorura is.

CHAP. 25. *Of Sarah's handmaid, Hagar, whom she herself wished to be Abraham's concubine*

And here follow the times of Abraham's sons, the one by Hagar the bond maid, the other by Sarah the free woman, about whom we have already spoken in the previous book. As regards this transaction, Abraham is in no way to be branded as guilty concerning this concubine, for he used her for the begetting of progeny, not for the gratification of lust; and not to insult, but rather to obey his wife, who supposed it would be a solace of her barrenness if she could make use of the fruitful womb of her handmaid to supply the defect of her own nature, and by that law of which the apostle says, "Likewise also the husband hath not power of his own body, but the wife," [1] could, as a wife, make use of him for childbearing by another, when she could not do so in her own person. Here there is no wanton lust, no filthy lewdness. The handmaid is delivered to the husband by the wife for the sake of progeny, and is received by the husband for the sake of progeny, each seeking, not guilty excess, but natural fruit. And when the pregnant bond woman despised her barren mistress, and Sarah, with womanly jealousy, rather laid the blame of this on her husband, even then Abraham showed that he was not a slavish lover, but a free begetter of children, and that in using Hagar he had guarded the chastity of Sarah his wife, and had gratified her will and not his own —had received her without seeking, had gone in to her without being attached, had impregnated without loving her—for he says, "Behold thy maid is in thy hands: do to her as it pleaseth thee"; [2] a man able to use women as a man should—his wife temperately, his handmaid compliantly, neither intemperately!

CHAP. 26. *Of God's attestation to Abraham, by which He assures him, when now old, of a son by the barren Sarah, and appoints him the father of the nations, and seals his faith in the promise by the sacrament of circumcision*

After these things Ishmael was born of Hagar; and Abraham might think that in him was fulfilled what God had promised him, saying, when he wished to adopt his home-born servant, "This shall not be thine heir; but he that shall come forth of thee, he shall be thine heir." [3] Therefore, lest he should think that what was promised was fulfilled in the handmaid's son, "when Abram was ninety years old and nine, God appeared to him, and said unto him, I am God; be well-pleasing in my sight, and be without complaint, and I will make my covenant between me and thee, and will fill thee exceedingly." [4]

Here there are more distinct promises about the calling of the nations in Isaac, that is, in the son of the promise, by which grace is signified, and not nature; for the son is promised from an old man and a barren old woman. For although God effects even the natural course of procreation, yet where the agency of God is manifest, through the decay or failure of nature, grace is more plainly discerned. And because this was to be brought about, not by generation, but by regeneration, circumcision was enjoined now, when a son was promised of Sarah. And by ordering all, not only sons, but also home-born and purchased servants to be circumcised, he testifies that this grace pertains to all. For what else does circumcision signify than a nature renewed on the putting off of the old? And what else does the eighth day mean than Christ, Who rose again when the week was completed, that is, after the Sabbath? The very names of the parents are changed: all things proclaim newness, and the new covenant is shadowed forth in the old. For what does the term old covenant imply but the concealing of the new? And what does the term new covenant imply but the revealing of the old? The laughter of Abraham is the exultation of one who rejoices, not the scornful laughter of one who mistrusts. And those words of his in his heart, "Shall a son be born to me that am an hundred years old? and shall Sarah, that is ninety years old, bear?" are not the words of doubt, but of wonder. And when it is said, "And I will give to thee, and to thy seed after thee, the land in which thou art a stranger, all the land of Canaan, for an everlast-

---

[1] I Cor. 7. 4. [2] Gen. 16. 6. [3] Gen. 15. 4. [4] Gen. 17. 1–22.

ing possession," if it troubles any one whether this is to be held as fulfilled, or whether its fulfilment may still be looked for, since no kind of earthly possession can be everlasting for any nation whatever, let him know that the word translated "everlasting" by our writers is what the Greeks term αἰώνιον, which is derived from αἰών, the Greek for *sæculum,* an age. But the Latins have not ventured to translate this by *secular,* lest they should change the meaning into something widely different. For many things are called secular which so happen in this world as to pass away even in a short time; but what is termed αἰώνιον either has no end, or lasts to the very end of this world.

CHAP. 27. *Of the male, who was to lose his soul if he was not circumcised on the eighth day, because he had broken God's covenant*

When it is said, "The male who is not circumcised in the flesh of his foreskin, that soul shall be cut off from his people, because he hath broken my covenant,"[1] some may be troubled how that ought to be understood, since it can be no fault of the infant whose life it is said must perish; nor has the covenant of God been broken by him, but by his parents, who have not taken care to circumcise him. But even the infants, not personally in their own life, but according to the common origin of the human race, have all broken God's covenant in that one in whom all have sinned.[2] Now there are many things called God's covenants besides those two great ones, the old and the new, which any one who pleases may read and know. For the first covenant, which was made with the first man, is just this: "In the day ye eat thereof, ye shall surely die."[3] Whence it is written in the book called Ecclesiasticus, "All flesh waxeth old as doth a garment. For the covenant from the beginning is, Thou shalt die the death."[4] Now, as the law was more plainly given afterward, and the apostle says, "Where no law is, there is no prevarication,"[5] on what supposition is what is said in the psalm true, "I accounted all the sinners of the earth prevaricators,"[6] except that all who are held liable for any sin are accused of dealing deceitfully (prevaricating) with some law? If on this account, then, even the infants are, according to the true belief, born in sin, not actual but original, so that we confess they have need of grace for the remission of sins, certainly it

must be acknowledged that in the same sense in which they are sinners they are also prevaricators of that law which was given in Paradise, according to the truth of both scriptures, "I accounted all the sinners of the earth prevaricators," and "Where no law is, there is no prevarication." And thus, because circumcision was the sign of regeneration, and the infant, on account of the original sin by which God's covenant was first broken, was not undeservedly to lose his generation unless delivered by regeneration, these divine words are to be understood as if it had been said, "Whoever is not born again, that soul shall perish from his people, because he hath broken my covenant, since he also has sinned in Adam with all others." For had He said, "Because he hath broken this my covenant," He would have compelled us to understand by it only this of circumcision; but since He has not expressly said what covenant the infant has broken, we are free to understand Him as speaking of that covenant of which the breach can be ascribed to an infant. Yet if any one contends that it is said of nothing else than circumcision, that in it the infant has broken the covenant of God because he is not circumcised, he must seek some method of explanation by which it may be understood without absurdity (such as this) that he has broken the covenant, because it has been broken in him although not by him. Yet in this case also it is to be observed that the soul of the infant, being guilty of no sin of neglect against itself, would perish unjustly, unless original sin rendered it obnoxious to punishment.

CHAP. 28. *Of the change of name in Abraham and Sarah, who received the gift of fecundity when they were incapable of regeneration owing to the barrenness of one, and the old age of both*

Now when a promise so great and clear was made to Abraham, in which it was so plainly said to him, "I have made thee a father of many nations, and I will increase thee exceedingly, and I will make nations of thee, and kings shall go forth of thee. And I will give thee a son of Sarah; and I will bless him, and he shall become nations, and kings of nations shall be of him"[7]— a promise which we now see fulfilled in Christ— from that time forward this couple are not called in Scripture, as formerly, Abram and Sarai, but Abraham and Sarah, as we have called them from the first, for every one does so now. The reason why the name of Abraham was

---

[1]Gen. 17. 14.   [2]Rom. 5. 12, 19.   [3]Gen. 2. 17.
[4]Ecclus. 15. 17.   [5]Rom. 4. 15.
[6]Ps. 119. 119. Augustine and the Vulgate follow the Septuagint.

[7]Gen. 17. 5, 6, 16.

changed is given: "For," He says, "I have made thee a father of many nations." This, then, is to be understood to be the meaning of *Abraham;* but *Abram,* as he was formerly called, means "exalted father." The reason of the change of Sarah's name is not given; but as those say who have written interpretations of the Hebrew names contained in these books, Sarah means "my princess," and Sarai "strength." Whence it is written in the Epistle to the Hebrews, "Through faith also Sarah herself received strength to conceive seed." [1] For both were old, as the Scripture testifies; but she was also barren, and had ceased to menstruate, so that she could no longer bear children even if she had not been barren. Further, if a woman is advanced in years, yet still retains the custom of women, she can bear children to a young man, but not to an old man, although that same old man can beget, but only of a young woman; as after Sarah's death Abraham could of Keturah, because he met with her in her lively age. This, then, is what the apostle mentions as wonderful, saying, besides, that Abraham's body was now dead; [2] because at that age he was no longer able to beget children of any woman who retained now only a small part of her natural vigour. Of course we must understand that his body was dead only to some purposes, not to all; for if it was so to all, it would no longer be the aged body of a living man, but the corpse of a dead one. Although that question, how Abraham begot children of Keturah, is usually solved in this way, that the gift of begetting which he received from the Lord, remained even after the death of his wife, yet I think that solution of the question which I have followed is preferable, because, although in our days an old man of a hundred years can beget children of no woman, it was not so then, when men still lived so long that a hundred years did not yet bring on them the decrepitude of old age.

CHAP. 29. *Of the three men or angels, in whom the Lord is related to have appeared to Abraham at the oak of Mamre*

God appeared again to Abraham at the oak of Mamre in three men, who it is not to be doubted were angels, although some think that one of them was Christ and assert that He was visible before He put on flesh. Now it belongs to the divine power, and invisible, incorporeal, and incommutable nature, without changing itself at all, to appear even to mortal men, not by what it is, but by what is subject to it. And what is not

subject to it? Yet if they try to establish that one of these three was Christ by the fact that, although he saw three, he addressed the Lord in the singular, as it is written, "And, lo, three men stood by him: and, when he saw them, he ran to meet them from the tent-door, and worshipped toward the ground, and said, Lord, if I have found favour before thee," [3] etc.; why do they not advert to this also, that when two of them came to destroy the Sodomites, while Abraham still spoke to one, calling him Lord, and interceding that he would not destroy the righteous along with the wicked in Sodom, Lot received these two in such a way that he too in his conversation with them addressed the Lord in the singular? For after saying to them in the plural, "Behold, my lords, turn aside into your servant's house," [4] etc., yet it is afterwards said, "And the angels laid hold upon his hand, and the hand of his wife, and the hands of his two daughters, because the Lord was merciful unto him. And it came to pass, whenever they had led him forth abroad, that they said, Save thy life; look not behind thee, neither stay thou in all this region: save thyself in the mountain, lest thou be caught. And Lot said unto them, I pray thee, Lord, since thy servant hath found grace in thy sight," [5] etc. And then after these words the Lord also answered him in the singular, although He was in two angels, saying, "See, I have accepted thy face," [6] etc. This makes it much more credible that both Abraham in the three men and Lot in the two recognized the Lord, addressing Him in the singular number, even when they were addressing men; for they received them as they did for no other reason than that they might minister human refection to them as men who needed it. Yet there was about them something so excellent that those who showed them hospitality as men could not doubt that God was in them as He was wont to be in the prophets, and therefore sometimes addressed them in the plural and sometimes God in them in the singular. But that they were angels the Scripture testifies, not only in this book of Genesis, in which these transactions are related, but also in the Epistle to the Hebrews, where in praising hospitality it is said, "For thereby some have entertained angels unawares." [7] By these three men, then, when a son Isaac was again promised to Abraham by Sarah, such a divine oracle was also given that it was said, "Abraham shall become a great and numerous nation, and all the nations of the earth shall

[1] Heb. 11. 11.   [2] Heb. 11. 12.

[3] Gen. 18. 2, 3.   [4] Gen. 19. 2.   [5] Gen. 19. 16–19.
[6] Gen. 19. 21.   [7] Heb. 13. 2.

be blessed in him." [1] And here these two things are promised with the utmost brevity and fullness—the nation of Israel according to the flesh, and all nations according to faith.

CHAP. 30. *Of Lot's deliverance from Sodom, and its consumption by fire from heaven; and of Abimelech, whose lust could not harm Sarah's chastity*

After this promise Lot was delivered out of Sodom, and a fiery rain from heaven turned into ashes that whole region of the impious city, where custom had made sodomy as prevalent as laws have elsewhere made other kinds of wickedness. But this punishment of theirs was a specimen of the divine judgment to come. For what is meant by the angels forbidding those who were delivered to look back, but that we are not to look back in heart to the old life which, being regenerated through grace, we have put off, if we think to escape the last judgment? Lot's wife, indeed, when she looked back, remained, and, being turned into salt, furnished to believing men a condiment by which to savour somewhat the warning to be drawn from that example. Then Abraham did again at Gerar, with Abimelech the king of that city, what he had done in Egypt about his wife, and received her back untouched in the same way. On this occasion, when the king rebuked Abraham for not saying she was his wife, and calling her his sister, he explained what he had been afraid of, and added this further, "And yet indeed she is my sister by the father's side, but not by the mother's";[2] for she was Abraham's sister by his own father, and so near of kin. But her beauty was so great, that even at that advanced age she could be fallen in love with.

CHAP. 31. *Of Isaac, who was born according to the promise, whose name was given on account of the laughter of both parents*

After these things a son was born to Abraham, according to God's promise, of Sarah, and was called Isaac, which means *laughter*. For his father had laughed when he was promised to him, in wondering delight, and his mother, when he was again promised by those three men, had laughed, doubting for joy; yet she was blamed by the angel because that laugher, although it was for joy, yet was not full of faith. Afterwards she was confirmed in faith by the same angel. From this, then, the boy got his name. For when Isaac was born and called by that name, Sarah showed that her laughter was not that of scorn-

ful reproach, but that of joyful praise; for she said, "God hath made me to laugh, so that every one who hears will laugh with me." [3] Then in a little while the bond maid was cast out of the house with her son; and, according to the apostle, these two women signify the old and new covenants—Sarah representing that of the Jerusalem which is above, that is, the city of God.[4]

CHAP. 32. *Of Abraham's obedience and faith, which were proved by the offering up of his son in sacrifice and of Sarah's death*

Among other things, of which it would take too long time to mention the whole, Abraham was tempted about the offering up of his well-beloved son Isaac, to prove his pious obedience, and so make it known to the world, not to God. Now every temptation is not blame-worthy; it may even be praise-worthy, because it furnishes probation. And, for the most part, the human mind cannot attain to self-knowledge otherwise than by making trial of its powers through temptation, by some kind of experimental and not merely verbal self-interrogation; when, if it has acknowledged the gift of God, it is pious and is consolidated by steadfast grace and not puffed up by vain boasting. Of course Abraham could never believe that God delighted in human sacrifices; yet when the divine commandment thundered, it was to be obeyed, not disputed. Yet Abraham is worthy of praise, because he all along believed that his son, on being offered up, would rise again; for God had said to him, when he was unwilling to fulfill his wife's pleasure by casting out the bond maid and her son, "In Isaac shall thy seed be called." No doubt He then goes on to say, "And as for the son of this bond woman, I will make him a great nation, because he is thy seed." [5] How then is it said, "In Isaac shall thy seed be called," when God calls Ishmael also his seed? The apostle, in explaining this, says, "In Isaac shall thy seed be called, that is, they which are the children of the flesh, these are not the children of God: but the children of the promise are counted for the seed." [6] In order, then, that the children of the promise may be the seed of Abraham, they are called in Isaac, that is, are gathered together in Christ by the call of grace. Therefore the father, holding fast from the first the promise which behoved to be fulfilled through this son whom God had ordered him to slay, did not doubt that he whom he once thought it hopeless he should ever receive would

[1] Gen. 18. 18.   [2] Gen. 20. 12.

[3] Gen. 21. 6.   [4] Gal. 4. 24-26.   [5] Gen. 21. 12, 13.
[6] Rom. 9. 7, 8.

be restored to him when he had offered him up. It is in this way the passage in the Epistle to the Hebrews is also to be understood and explained. "By faith," he says, "Abraham overcame, when tempted about Isaac: and he who had received the promise offered up his only son, to whom it was said, In Isaac shall thy seed be called: thinking that God was able to raise him up, even from the dead"; therefore he has added, "from whence also he received him in a similitude."[1] In Whose similitude but His of Whom the apostle says, "He that spared not His own Son, but delivered Him up for us all"?[2] And on this account Isaac also himself carried to the place of sacrifice the wood on which he was to be offered up, just as the Lord Himself carried His own cross. Finally, since Isaac was not to be slain, after his father was forbidden to smite him, who was that ram by the offering of which that sacrifice was completed with typical blood? For when Abraham saw him, he was caught by the horns in a thicket. What, then, did he represent but Jesus, Who, before He was offered up, was crowned with thorns by the Jews?

But let us rather hear the divine words spoken through the angel. For the Scripture says, "And Abraham stretched forth his hand to take the knife, that he might slay his son. And the Angel of the Lord called unto him from heaven, and said, Abraham. And he said, Here am I. And he said, Lay not thine hand upon the lad, neither do thou anything unto him: for now I know that thou fearest God, and hast not spared thy beloved son for my sake."[3] It is said, "Now I know," that is, "Now I have made to be known"; for God was not previously ignorant of this. Then, having offered up that ram instead of Isaac his son, "Abraham," as we read, "called the name of that place The Lord seeth: as they say this day, In the mount the Lord hath appeared."[4] As it is said, "Now I know," for "Now I have made to be known," so here, "The Lord sees," for "The Lord hath appeared," that is, made Himself to be seen. "And the Angel of the Lord called unto Abraham from heaven the second time, saying, By myself have I sworn, saith the Lord; because thou hast done this thing, and hast not spared thy beloved son for my sake; that in blessing I will bless thee, and in multiplying I will multiply thy seed as the stars of heaven, and as the sand which is upon the seashore; and thy seed shall possess by inheritance the cities of the adversaries: and in thy seed shall all the nations of the earth be

blessed; because thou hast obeyed my voice."[5] In this manner is that promise concerning the calling of the nations in the seed of Abraham confirmed even by the oath of God, after that burnt-offering which typified Christ. For He had often promised, but never sworn. And what is the oath of God, the true and faithful, but a confirmation of the promise, and a certain reproof to the unbelieving?

After these things Sarah died, in the 127th year of her life, and the 137th of her husband; for he was ten years older than she, as he himself says, when a son is promised to him by her: "Shall a son be born to me that am an hundred years old? and shall Sarah, that is ninety years old, bear?"[6] Then Abraham bought a field, in which he buried his wife. And then, according to Stephen's account, he was settled in that land, entering then on actual possession of it—that is, after the death of his father, who is inferred to have died two years before.

CHAP. 33. *Of Rebecca, the grand-daughter of Nahor, whom Isaac took to wife*

Isaac married Rebecca, the grand-daughter of Nahor, his father's brother, when he was forty years old, that is, in the 140th year of his father's life, three years after his mother's death. Now when a servant was sent to Mesopotamia by his father to fetch her, and when Abraham said to that servant, "Put thy hand under my thigh, and I will make thee swear by the Lord, the God of heaven, and the Lord of the earth, that thou shalt not take a wife unto my son Isaac of the daughters of the Canaanites,"[7] what else was pointed out by this, but that the Lord, the God of heaven, and the Lord of the earth, was to come in the flesh which was to be derived from that thigh? Are these small tokens of the foretold truth which we see fulfilled in Christ?

CHAP. 34. *What is meant by Abraham's marrying Keturah after Sarah's death*

What did Abraham mean by marrying Keturah after Sarah's death? Far be it from us to suspect him of incontinence, especially when he had reached such an age and such sanctity of faith. Or was he still seeking to beget children, though he held fast, with most approved faith, the promise of God that his children should be multiplied out of Isaac as the stars of heaven and the dust of the earth? And yet, if Hagar and Ishmael, as the apostle teaches us, signified the carnal people of the old covenant, why may not

---

[1]Heb. 11. 17–19.   [2]Rom. 8. 32.
[3]Gen. 22. 10–12.   [4]Gen. 22. 14.
[5]Gen. 22. 15–18.   [6]Gen. 17. 17.   [7]Gen. 24. 2, 3.

Keturah and her sons also signify the carnal people who think they belong to the new covenant? For both are called both the wives and the concubines of Abraham; but Sarah is never called a concubine (but only a wife). For when Hagar is given to Abraham, it is written. "And Sarai, Abram's wife, took Hagar the Egyptian, her handmaid, after Abraham had dwelt ten years in the land of Canaan, and gave her to her husband Abram to be his wife." [1] And of Keturah, whom he took after Sarah's departure, we read, "Then again Abraham took a wife, whose name was Keturah." [2] Lo! both are called wives, yet both are found to have been concubines; for the Scripture afterward says, "And Abraham gave his whole estate unto Isaac his son. But unto the sons of his concubines Abraham gave gifts, and sent them away from his son Isaac (while he yet lived), eastward, unto the east country." [3] Therefore the sons of the concubines, that is, the heretics and the carnal Jews, have some gifts, but do not attain the promised kingdom; "For they which are the children of the flesh, these are not the children of God: but the children of the promise are counted for the seed, of whom it was said, In Isaac shall thy seed be called." [4] For I do not see why Keturah, who was married after the wife's death, should be called a concubine, except on account of this mystery. But if any one is unwilling to put such meanings on these things, he need not calumniate Abraham. For what if even this was provided against the heretics who were to be the opponents of second marriages, so that it might be shown that it was no sin in the case of the father of many nations himself, when, after his wife's death, he married again? And Abraham died when he was 175 years old, so that he left his son Isaac seventy-five years old, having begotten him when 100 years old.

CHAP. 35. *What was indicated by the divine answer about the twins still shut up in the womb of Rebecca their mother*

Let us now see how the times of the city of God run on from this point among Abraham's descendants. In the time from the first year of Isaac's life to the seventieth, when his sons were born, the only memorable thing is that when he prayed God that his wife, who was barren, might bear, and the Lord granted what he sought, and she conceived, the twins leapt while still enclosed in her womb. And when she was troubled by this struggle, and inquired of the Lord, she received this answer: "Two nations are in thy womb, and two manner of people shall be separated from thy bowels; and the one people shall overcome the other people, and the elder shall serve the younger." [5] The Apostle Paul would have us understand this as a great instance of grace;[6] for the children being not yet born, neither having done any good or evil, the younger is chosen without any good desert, and the elder is rejected, when beyond doubt, as regards original sin, both were alike, and, as regards actual sin, neither had any. But the plan of the work on hand does not permit me to speak more fully of this matter now, and I have said much about it in other works. Only that saying, "The elder shall serve the younger," is understood by our writers, almost without exception, to mean that the elder people, the Jews, shall serve the younger people, the Christians. And truly, although this might seem to be fulfilled in the Idumean nation, which was born of the elder (who had two names, being called both Esau and Edom, whence the name Idumeans), because it was afterwards to be overcome by the people which sprang from the younger, that is, by the Israelites, and was to become subject to them; yet it is more suitable to believe that, when it was said, "The one people shall overcome the other people, and the elder shall serve the younger," that prophecy meant some greater thing; and what is that except what is evidently fulfilled in the Jews and Christians?

CHAP. 36. *Of the oracle and blessing which Isaac received, just as his father did, being beloved for his sake*

Isaac also received such an oracle as his father had often received. Of this oracle it is thus written: "And there was a famine over the land, beside the first famine that was in the days of Abraham. And Isaac went unto Abimelech king of the Philistines unto Gerar. And the Lord appeared unto him, and said, Go not down into Egypt; but dwell in the land which I shall tell thee of. And abide in this land, and I will be with thee, and will bless thee: unto thee and unto thy seed I will give all this land; and I will establish mine oath, which I sware unto Abraham thy father: and I will multiply thy seed as the stars of heaven, and will give unto thy seed all this land: and in thy seed shall all the nations of the earth be blessed; because that Abraham thy father obeyed my voice, and kept my precepts, my commandments, my righteousness, and my laws." [7] This patriarch neither had another wife,

[1]Gen. 16. 3.   [2]Gen. 25. 1.   [3]Gen. 25. 5. 6.
[4]Rom. 9. 7, 8.
[5]Gen. 25. 23.   [6]Rom. 9. 10-13.   [7]Gen. 26. 1-5.

nor any concubine, but was content with the twin-children begotten by one act of generation. He also was afraid, when he lived among strangers, of being brought into danger owing to the beauty of his wife, and did like his father in calling her his sister, and not telling that she was his wife; for she was his near blood-relation by the father's and mother's side. She also remained untouched by the strangers, when it was known she was his wife. Yet we ought not to prefer him to his father because he knew no woman besides his one wife. For beyond doubt the merits of his father's faith and obedience were greater, inasmuch as God says it is for his sake He does Isaac good: "In thy seed," He says, "shall all the nations of the earth be blessed, because that Abraham thy father obeyed my voice, and kept my precepts, my commandments, my statutes, and my laws." And again in another oracle He says, "I am the God of Abraham thy father: fear not, for I am with thee, and will bless thee, and multiply thy seed for my servant Abraham's sake."[1] So that we must understand how chastely Abraham acted, because imprudent men, who seek some support for their own wickedness in the Holy Scriptures, think he acted through lust. We may also learn this, not to compare men by single good things, but to consider everything in each; for it may happen that one man has something in his life and character in which he excels another, and it may be far more excellent than that in which the other excels him. And thus, according to sound and true judgment, while continence is preferable to marriage, yet a believing married man is better than a continent unbeliever; for the unbeliever is not only less praiseworthy, but is even highly detestable. We must conclude, then, that both are good; yet so as to hold that the married man who is most faithful and most obedient is certainly better than the continent man whose faith and obedience are less. But if equal in other things, who would hesitate to prefer the continent man to the married?

CHAP. 37. *Of the things mystically prefigured in Esau and Jacob*

Isaac's two sons, Esau and Jacob, grew up together. The primacy of the elder was transferred to the younger by a bargain and agreement between them, when the elder immoderately lusted after the lentils the younger had prepared for food, and for that price sold his birthright to him, confirming it with an oath. We learn from this that a person is to be blamed, not for the

kind of food he eats, but for immoderate greed. Isaac grew old, and old age deprived him of his eyesight. He wished to bless the elder son, and instead of the elder, who was hairy, unwittingly blessed the younger, who put himself under his father's hands, having covered himself with kidskins, as if bearing the sins of others. Lest we should think this guile of Jacob's was fraudulent guile, instead of seeking in it the mystery of a great thing, the Scripture has predicted in the words just before, "Esau was a cunning hunter, a man of the field; and Jacob was a simple man, dwelling at home."[2] Some of our writers have interpreted this, "without guile." But whether the Greek ἄπλαστος means *without guile* or *simple,* or rather *without feigning*, in the receiving of that blessing what is the guile of the man without guile? What is the guile of the simple, what the fiction of the man who does not lie, but a profound mystery of the truth? But what is the blessing itself? "See," he says, "the smell of my son is as the smell of a full field which the Lord hath blessed: therefore God give thee of the dew of heaven, and of the fruitfulness of the earth, and plenty of corn and wine: let nations serve thee, and princes adore thee: and be lord of thy brethren, and let thy father's sons adore thee: cursed be he that curseth thee, and blessed be he that blesseth thee."[3] The blessing of Jacob is therefore a proclamation of Christ to all nations. It is this which has come to pass, and is now being fulfilled. Isaac is the law and the prophecy: even by the mouth of the Jews Christ is blessed by prophecy as by one who knows not, because it is itself not understood. The world like a field is filled with the odour of Christ's name: His is the blessing of the dew of heaven, that is, of the showers of divine words; and of the fruitfulness of the earth, that is, of the gathering together of the peoples: His is the plenty of corn and wine, that is, the multitude that gathers bread and wine in the sacrament of His body and blood. Him the nations serve, Him princes adore. He is the Lord of His brethren, because His people rules over the Jews. Him His Father's sons adore, that is, the sons of Abraham according to faith; for He Himself is the son of Abraham according to the flesh. He is cursed that curseth Him, and he that blesseth Him is blessed. Christ, I say, Who is ours is blessed, that is, truly spoken of out of the mouths of the Jews, when, although erring, they yet sing the law and the prophets, and think they are blessing another for whom they erringly hope. So, when the elder son claims the prom-

[1] Gen. 26. 24.

[2] Gen. 25. 27. [3] Gen. 27. 27–29.

ised blessing, Isaac is greatly afraid, and wonders when he knows that he has blessed one instead of the other, and demands who he is; yet he does not complain that he has been deceived, yea, when the great mystery is revealed to him, in his secret heart he at once eschews anger, and confirms the blessing. "Who then," he says, "hath hunted me venison, and brought it me, and I have eaten of all before thou camest, and have blessed him, and he shall be blessed?" [1] Who would not rather have expected the curse of an angry man here, if these things had been done in an earthly manner, and not by inspiration from above? O things done, yet done prophetically; on the earth, yet celestially; by men, yet divinely! If everything that is fertile of so great mysteries should be examined carefully, many volumes would be filled; but the moderate compass fixed for this work compels us to hasten to other things.

CHAP. 38. *Of Jacob's mission to Mesopotamia to get a wife, and of the vision which he saw in a dream by the way, and of his getting four women when he sought one wife*

Jacob was sent by his parents to Mesopotamia that he might take a wife there. These were his father's words on sending him: "Thou shalt not take a wife of the daughters of the Canaanites. Arise fly to Mesopotamia, to the house of Bethuel, thy mother's father, and take thee a wife from thence of the daughters of Laban thy mother's brother. And my God bless thee, and increase thee, and multiply thee; and thou shalt be an assembly of peoples; and give to thee the blessing of Abraham thy father, and to thy seed after thee; that thou mayest inherit the land wherein thou dwellest, which God gave unto Abraham." [2] Now we understand here that the seed of Jacob is separated from Isaac's other seed which came through Esau. For when it is said, "In Isaac shall thy seed be called," [3] by this seed is meant solely the city of God; so that from it is separated Abraham's other seed, which was in the son of the bond woman, and which was to be in the sons of Keturah. But until now it had been uncertain regarding Isaac's twin-sons whether that blessing belonged to both or only to one of them; and if to one, which of them it was. This is now declared when Jacob is prophetically blessed by his father, and it is said to him, "And thou shalt be an assembly of peoples, and God give to thee the blessing of Abraham thy father."

When Jacob was going to Mesopotamia, he received in a dream an oracle, of which it is thus written: "And Jacob went out from the well of the oath,[4] and went to Haran. And he came to a place, and slept there, for the sun was set; and he took of the stones of the place, and put them at his head, and slept in that place, and dreamed. And behold a ladder set up on the earth, and the top of it reached to heaven; and the angels of God ascended and descended by it. And the Lord stood above it, and said, I am the God of Abraham thy father, and the God of Isaac; fear not: the land whereon thou sleepest, to thee will I give it, and to thy seed; and thy seed shall be as the dust of the earth; and it shall be spread abroad to the sea, and to Africa, and to the north, and to the east: and all the tribes of the earth shall be blessed in thee and in thy seed. And, behold, I am with thee, to keep thee in all thy way wherever thou goest, and I will bring thee back into this land; for I will not leave thee, until I have done all which I have spoken to thee of. And Jacob awoke out of his sleep, and said, Surely the Lord is in this place, and I knew it not. And he was afraid, and said, How dreadful is this place! this is none other but the house of God, and this is the gate of heaven. And Jacob arose, and took the stone that he had put under his head there, and set it up for a memorial, and poured oil upon the top of it. And Jacob called the name of that place the house of God." [5] This is prophetic. For Jacob did not pour oil on the stone in an idolatrous way, as if making it a god; neither did he adore that stone, or sacrifice to it. But since the name of Christ comes from the chrism or anointing, something pertaining to the great mystery was certainly represented in this. And the Saviour Himself is understood to bring this latter to remembrance in the Gospel, when He says of Nathanael, "Behold an Israelite indeed, in whom is no guile!" [6] because Israel who saw this vision is no other than Jacob. And in the same place He says, "Verily, verily, I say unto you, Ye shall see heaven open, and the angels of God ascending and descending upon the Son of man."

Jacob went on to Mesopotamia to take a wife from thence. And the divine Scripture points out how, without unlawfully desiring any of them, he came to have four women, of whom he begat twelve sons and one daughter; for he had come to take only one. But when one was falsely given him in place of the other, he did not send her away after unwittingly using her in the night, lest he should seem to have put her to shame; but as at that time, in order to multiply

[1]Gen. 27. 33.   [2]Gen. 28. 1-4.   [3]Gen. 21. 12.   [4]Beer-sheba.   [5]Gen. 28. 10-19.   [6]John. 1. 47, 51.

posterity, no law forbade a plurality of wives, he took her also to whom alone he had promised marriage. As she was barren, she gave her handmaid to her husband that she might have children by her; and her elder sister did the same thing in imitation of her, although she had borne, because she desired to multiply progeny. We do not read that Jacob sought any but one, or that he used many, except for the purpose of begetting offspring, saving conjugal rights; and he would not have done this, had not his wives, who had legitimate power over their own husband's body, urged him to do it. So he begat twelve sons and one daughter by four women. Then he entered into Egypt by his son Joseph, who was sold by his brethren for envy, and carried there, and who was there exalted.

CHAP. 39. *The reason why Jacob was also called Israel*

As I said a little ago, Jacob was also called Israel, the name which was most prevalent among the people descended from him. Now this name was given him by the angel who wrestled with him on the way back from Mesopotamia, and who was most evidently a type of Christ. For when Jacob overcame him, doubtless with his own consent, that the mystery might be represented, it signified Christ's passion, in which the Jews are seen overcoming Him. And yet he besought a blessing from the very angel he had overcome; and so the imposition of this name was the blessing. For Israel means *seeing God*,[1] which will at last be the reward of all the saints. The angel also touched him on the breadth of the thigh when he was overcoming him, and in that way made him lame. So that Jacob was at one and the same time blessed and lame: blessed in those among that people who believed in Christ, and lame in the unbelieving. For the breadth of the thigh is the multitude of the family. For there are many of that race of whom it was prophetically said beforehand, "And they have halted in their paths."[2]

CHAP. 40. *How it is said that Jacob went into Egypt with seventy-five souls, when most of those who are mentioned were born at a later period*

Seventy-five men are reported to have entered Egypt along with Jacob, counting him with his children. In this number only two women

are mentioned, one a daughter, the other a grand-daughter. But when the thing is carefully considered, it does not appear that Jacob's offspring was so numerous on the day or year when he entered Egypt. There are also included among them the great-grandchildren of Joseph, who could not possibly be born already. For Jacob was then 130 years old, and his son Joseph thirty-nine; and as it is plain that he took a wife when he was thirty or more, how could he in nine years have great-grandchildren by the children whom he had by that wife? Now since, Ephraim and Manasseh, the sons of Joseph, could not even have children, for Jacob found them boys under nine years old when he entered Egypt, in what way are not only their sons but their grandsons reckoned among those seventy-five who then entered Egypt with Jacob? For there is reckoned there Machir the son of Manasseh, grandson of Joseph, and Machir's son, that is, Gilead, grandson of Manasseh, great-grandson of Joseph; there, too, is he whom Ephraim, Joseph's other son, begot, that is, Shuthelah, grandson of Joseph, and Shuthelah's son Ezer, grandson of Ephraim, and great-grandson of Joseph, who could not possibly be in existence when Jacob came into Egypt, and there found his grandsons, the sons of Joseph, their grandsires, still boys under nine years of age.[3] But doubtless, when the Scripture mentions Jacob's entrance into Egypt with seventy-five souls, it does not mean one day, or one year, but that whole time as long as Joseph lived, who was the cause of his entrance. For the same Scripture speaks thus of Joseph: "And Joseph dwelt in Egypt, he and his brethren, and all his father's house: and Joseph lived 110 years, and saw Ephraim's children of the third generation."[4] That is, his great-grandson, the third from Ephraim; for the third generation means son, grandson, great-grandson. Then it is added, "The children also of Machir, the son of Manasseh, were born upon Joseph's knees."[5] And this is that grandson of Manasseh, and great-grandson of Joseph. But the plural number is employed according to scriptural usage; for the one daughter of Jacob is spoken of as daughters, just as in the usage of the Latin tongue *liberi* is used in the plural for children even when there is only one. Now, when Joseph's own happiness is proclaimed, because he could see his great-

---

[1]Gen. 32. 28: Israel=a prince of God; ver. 30: Peniel =the face of God.   [2]Ps. 18. 45.

[3]Augustine here follows the Septuagint, which at Gen. 46. 20 adds these names to those of Manasseh and Ephraim, and at ver. 27 gives the whole number as seventy-five.   [4]Gen. 50. 22, 23.   [5]Gen. 50. 23.

grandchildren, it is by no means to be thought they already existed in the thirty-ninth year of their great-grandsire Joseph, when his father Jacob came to him in Egypt. But those who diligently look into these things will the less easily be mistaken, because it is written, "These are the names of the sons of Israel who entered into Egypt along with Jacob their father." [1] For this means that the seventy-five are reckoned along with him, not that they were all with him when he entered Egypt; for, as I have said, the whole period during which Joseph, who occasioned his entrance, lived, is held to be the time of that entrance.

CHAP. 41. *Of the blessing which Jacob promised in Judah his son*

If, on account of the Christian people in whom the city of God sojourns in the earth, we look for the flesh of Christ in the seed of Abraham, setting aside the sons of the concubines, we have Isaac; if in the seed of Isaac, setting aside Esau, who is also Edom, we have Jacob, who also is Israel; if in the seed of Israel himself, setting aside the rest, we have Judah, because Christ sprang of the tribe of Judah. Let us hear, then, how Israel, when dying in Egypt, in blessing his sons, prophetically blessed Judah. He says: "Judah, thy brethren shall praise thee: thy hands shall be on the back of thine enemies; thy father's children shall adore thee. Judah is a lion's whelp: from the sprouting, my son, thou art gone up: lying down, thou hast slept as a lion, and as a lion's whelp; who shall awake him? A prince shall not be lacking out of Judah, and a leader from his thighs, until the things come that are laid up for him; and He shall be the expectation of the nations. Binding his foal unto the vine, and his ass's foal to the choice vine; he shall wash his robe in wine, and his clothes in the blood of the grape: his eyes are red with wine, and his teeth are whiter than milk." [2] I have expounded these words in disputing against Faustus the Manichæan; and I think it is enough to make the truth of this prophecy shine, to remark that the death of Christ is predicted by the word about his lying down, and not the necessity, but the voluntary character of His death, in the title of lion. That power He Himself proclaims in the Gospel, saying, "I have the power of laying down my life, and I have the power of taking it again. No man taketh it from me; but I lay it down of myself, and take it again." [3] So the lion roared, so He

fulfilled what He said. For to this power what is added about the resurrection refers, "Who shall awake him?" This means that no man but Himself has raised Him, who also said of His own body, "Destroy this temple, and in three days I will raise it up." [4] And the very nature of His death, that is, the height of the cross, is understood by the single word, "Thou are gone up." The evangelist explains what is added, "Lying down, thou hast slept," when he says, "He bowed His head, and gave up the ghost." [5] Or at least His burial is to be understood, in which He lay down sleeping, and whence no man raised Him, as the prophets did some, and as He Himself did others; but He Himself rose up as if from sleep. As for His robe which He washes in wine, that is, cleanses from sin in His own blood, of which blood those who are baptized know the mystery, so that he adds, "And his clothes in the blood of the grape," what is it but the Church? "And his eyes are red with wine," [these are] His spiritual people drunken with His cup, of which the psalm sings, "And thy cup that makes drunken, how excellent it is!" "And his teeth are whiter than milk" [6]—that is, the nutritive words which, according to the apostle, the babes drink, being as yet unfit for solid food.[7] And it is He in whom the promises of Judah were laid up, so that until they come, princes, that is, the kings of Israel, shall never be lacking out of Judah. "And He is the expectation of the nations." This is too plain to need exposition.

CHAP. 42. *Of the sons of Joseph, whom Jacob blessed, prophetically changing his hands*

Now, as Isaac's two sons, Esau and Jacob, furnished a type of the two people, the Jews and the Christians (although as pertains to carnal descent it was not the Jews but the Idumeans who came of the seed of Esau, nor the Christian nations but rather the Jews who came of Jacob's; for the type holds only as regards the saying, "The elder shall serve the younger" [8]), so the same thing happened in Joseph's two sons; for the elder was a type of the Jews, and the younger of the Christians. For when Jacob was blessing them, and laid his right hand on the younger, who was at his left, and his left hand on the elder, who was at his right, this seemed wrong to their father, and he admonished his father by trying to correct his mistake and show him which was the elder. But he would not

[1]Gen. 46. 8.   [2]Gen. 49. 8-12.   [3]John. 10. 18.   [4]John, 2. 19.   [5]John, 19. 30.   [6]Gen. 49. 12.   [7]I Pet. 2. 2; I Cor. 3. 2.   [8]Gen. 25. 23.

change his hands, but said, "I know, my son, I know. He also shall become a people, and he also shall be exalted; but his younger brother shall be greater than he, and his seed shall become a multitude of nations." [1] And these two promises show the same thing. For that one is to become "a people"; this one "a multitude of nations." And what can be more evident than that these two promises comprehend the people of Israel, and the whole world of Abraham's seed, the one according to the flesh, the other according to faith?

CHAP. 43. *Of the times of Moses and Joshua the son of Nun, of the judges, and thereafter of the kings, of whom Saul was the first, but David is to be regarded as the chief, both by the oath and by merit*

Jacob being dead, and Joseph also, during the remaining 144 years until they went out of the land of Egypt, that nation increased to an incredible degree, even although wasted by so great persecutions that at one time the male children were murdered at their birth, because the wondering Egyptians were terrified at the too great increase of that people. Then Moses, being stealthily kept from the murderers of the infants, was brought to the royal house, God preparing to do great things by him, and was nursed and adopted by the daughter of Pharaoh (that was the name of all the kings of Egypt), and became so great a man that he—yea, rather God, Who had promised this to Abraham, by him —drew that nation, so wonderfully multiplied, out of the yoke of hardest and most grievous servitude it had borne there. At first, indeed, he fled thence (we are told he fled into the land of Midian), because, in defending an Israelite, he had slain an Egyptian, and was afraid. Afterward, being divinely commissioned in the power of the Spirit of God, he overcame the magi of Pharaoh who resisted him. Then, when the Egyptians would not let God's people go, ten memorable plagues were brought by Him upon them—the water turned into blood, the frogs and lice, the flies, the death of the cattle, the boils, the hail, the locusts, the darkness, the death of the first-born. At last the Egyptians were destroyed in the Red Sea while pursuing the Israelites, whom they had let go when at length they were broken by so many great plagues. The divided sea made a way for the Israelites who were departing, but, returning on itself, it overwhelmed their pursuers with its waves. Then for forty years the people of God

[1] Gen. 48. 19.

went through the desert, under the leadership of Moses, when the tabernacle of testimony was dedicated, in which God was worshipped by sacrifices prophetic of things to come, and that was after the law had been very terribly given in the mount, for its divinity was most plainly attested by wonderful signs and voices. This took place soon after the exodus from Egypt, when the people had entered the desert, on the fiftieth day after the passover was celebrated by the offering up of a lamb, which is so completely a type of Christ, foretelling that through His sacrificial passion He should go from this world to the Father (for *pascha* in the Hebrew tongue means *transit*), that when the new covenant was revealed, after Christ our passover was offered up, the Holy Spirit came from heaven on the fiftieth day; and He is called in the gospel the Finger of God, because He recalls to our remembrance the things done before by way of types, and because the tables of that law are said to have been written by the finger of God.

On the death of Moses, Joshua the son of Nun ruled the people, and led them into the land of promise, and divided it among them. By these two wonderful leaders wars were also carried on most prosperously and wonderfully, God calling to witness that they had got these victories not so much on account of the merit of the Hebrew people as on account of the sins of the nations they subdued. After these leaders there were judges, when the people were settled in the land of promise, so that, in the meantime, the first promise made to Abraham began to be fulfilled about the one nation, that is, the Hebrew, and about the land of Canaan; but not as yet the promise about all nations, and the whole wide world, for that was to be fulfilled, not by the observances of the old law, but by the advent of Christ in the flesh, and by the faith of the gospel. And it was to prefigure this that it was not Moses, who received the law for the people on Mount Sinai, that led the people into the land of promise, but Joshua, whose name also was changed at God's command, so that he was called Jesus. But in the times of the judges prosperity alternated with adversity in war, according as the sins of the people and the mercy of God were displayed.

We come next to the times of the kings. The first who reigned was Saul; and when he was rejected and laid low in battle, and his offspring rejected so that no kings should arise out of it, David succeeded to the kingdom, whose son Christ is chiefly called. He was made a kind of starting-point and beginning of the advanced youth of God's people, who had passed a kind of age of puberty from Abraham to this David. And it is not in vain that the evangelist Matthew records the generations in such a way as to sum up this first period from Abraham to David in fourteen generations. For from the age of puberty man begins to be capable of generation; therefore he starts the list of generations from Abraham, who also was made the father of many nations when he got his name changed. So that previously this family of God's people was in its childhood, from Noah to Abraham; and for that reason the first language was then learned, that is, the Hebrew. For man begins to speak in childhood, the age succeeding infancy, which is so termed because then he cannot speak.[1] And that first age is quite drowned in oblivion, just as the first age of the human race was blotted out by the flood; for who is there that can remember his infancy? Wherefore in this progress of the city of God, as the previous book contained that first age, so this one ought to contain the second and third ages, in which third age, as was shown by the heifer of three years old, the she-goat of three years old, and the ram of three years old, the yoke of the law was imposed, and there appeared abundance of sins, and the beginning of the earthly kingdom arose, in which there were not lacking spiritual men, of whom the turtledove and pigeon represented the mystery.

[1]*Infans*, from *in*, not, and *fari*, to speak.

BOOK XVII

ARGUMENT. IN THIS BOOK THE HISTORY OF THE CITY OF GOD IS TRACED DURING THE PERIOD OF THE KINGS AND PROPHETS FROM SAMUEL TO DAVID, EVEN TO CHRIST; AND THE PROPHECIES WHICH ARE RECORDED IN THE BOOKS OF KINGS, PSALMS, AND THOSE OF SOLOMON, ARE INTERPRETED OF CHRIST AND THE CHURCH.

CHAP. 1. *Of the prophetic age*

BY the favour of God we have treated distinctly of His promises made to Abraham, that both the nation of Israel according to the flesh, and all nations according to faith, should be his seed, and the City of God, proceeding according to the order of time, will point out how they were fulfilled. Having therefore in the previous book come down to the reign of David, we shall now treat of what remains, so far as may seem sufficient for the object of this work, beginning at the same reign. Now, from the time when holy Samuel began to prophesy, and ever onward until the people of Israel was led captive into Babylonia, and until, according to the prophecy of holy Jeremiah, on Israel's return thence after seventy years, the house of God was built anew, this whole period is the prophetic age. For although both the patriarch Noah himself, in whose days the whole earth was destroyed by the flood, and others before and after him down to this time when there began to be kings over the people of God, may not undeservedly be styled prophets, on account of certain things pertaining to the city of God and the kingdom of heaven, which they either predicted or in any way signified should come to pass, and especially since we read that some of them, as Abraham and Moses, were expressly so styled, yet those are most and chiefly called the days of the prophets from the time when Samuel began to prophesy, who at God's command first anointed Saul to be king, and, on his rejection, David himself, whom others of his issue should succeed as long as it was fitting they should do so. If, therefore, I wished to rehearse all that the prophets have predicted concerning Christ, while the city of God, with its members dying and being born in constant succession, ran its course through those times, this work would extend beyond all bounds. First, because the Scripture itself, even when, in treating in order of the kings and of their deeds and the events of their reigns, it seems to be occupied in narrating as with historical diligence the affairs transacted, will be found, if the things handled by it are considered with the aid of the Spirit of God, either more, or certainly not less, intent on foretelling things to come than on relating things past. And who that thinks even a little about it does not know how laborious and prolix a work it would be, and how many volumes it would require to search this out by thorough investigation and demonstrate it by argument? And then, because of that which without dispute pertains to prophecy, there are so many things concerning Christ and the kingdom of heaven, which is the city of God, that to explain these a larger discussion would be necessary than the due proportion of this work admits of. Therefore I shall, if I can, so limit myself, that in carrying through this work, I may, with God's help, neither say what is superfluous nor omit what is necessary.

CHAP. 2. *At what time the promise of God was fulfilled concerning the land of Canaan, which even carnal Israel got in possession*

In the preceding book we said, that in the promise of God to Abraham two things were promised from the beginning, the one, namely, that his seed should possess the land of Canaan, which was intimated when it was said, "Go into a land that I will show thee, and I will make of thee a great nation";[1] but the other far more excellent, concerning not the carnal but the spiritual seed, by which he is the father, not of the one nation of Israel, but of all nations who follow the footsteps of his faith, which began to be promised in these words, "And in thee shall all families of the earth be blessed."[2] And thereafter we showed by yet many other proofs that these two things were promised. Therefore the seed of Abraham, that is, the people of Israel according to the flesh, already was in the land of promise; and there, not only by holding and possessing the cities of the enemies, but also by having kings, had already begun to reign, the promises of God concerning that people being already in great part fulfilled: not only those that were made to those three fathers, Abraham, Isaac, and Jacob, and whatever others were made in their times, but those also that were made through Moses himself, by whom the same people was set free from servitude in Egypt and by whom all bygone things were revealed in his times, when he led the people through the wilderness. But neither by the illustrious leader Jesus the son of Nun, who led that people into the land of promise, and, after driving out the nations, divided it among the twelve tribes according to God's command, and died; nor after him, in the whole time of the judges, was the promise of God concerning the land of Canaan fulfilled, that it should extend from some river of Egypt even to the great river Euphrates; nor yet was it still prophesied as to come, but its fulfillment was expected. And it was fulfilled through David, and Solomon his son, whose kingdom was extended over the whole promised space; for they subdued all those nations, and made them tributary. And thus, under those kings, the seed of Abraham was established in the land of promise according to the flesh, that is, in the land of Canaan, so that nothing yet remained to the complete fulfillment of that earthly promise of

God, except that, so far as pertains to temporal prosperity, the Hebrew nation should remain in the same land by the succession of posterity in an unshaken state even to the end of this mortal age, if it obeyed the laws of the Lord its God. But since God knew it would not do this, He used His temporal punishments also for training His few faithful ones in it and for giving needful warning to those who should afterwards be in all nations, in whom the other promise, revealed in the New Testament, was about to be fulfilled through the incarnation of Christ.

CHAP. 3. *Of the three-fold meaning of the prophecies, which are to be referred now to the earthly, now to the heavenly Jerusalem, and now again to both*

Wherefore just as that divine oracle to Abraham, Isaac, and Jacob, and all the other prophetic signs or sayings which are given in the earlier sacred writings, so also the other prophecies from this time of the kings pertain partly to the nation of Abraham's flesh and partly to that seed of his in which all nations are blessed as fellow-heirs of Christ by the New Testament, to the possessing of eternal life and the kingdom of the heavens. Therefore they pertain partly to the bond maid who gendereth to bondage, that is, the earthly Jerusalem, which is in bondage with her children; but partly to the free city of God, that is, the true Jerusalem eternal in the heavens, whose children are all those that live according to God in the earth: but there are some things among them which are understood to pertain to both—to the bond maid properly, to the free woman figuratively.[3]

Therefore prophetic utterances of three kinds are to be found; forasmuch as there are some relating to the earthly Jerusalem, some to the heavenly, and some to both. I think it proper to prove what I say by examples. The prophet Nathan was sent to convict king David of heinous sin, and predict to him what future evils should be consequent on it. Who can question that this and the like pertain to the terrestrial city, whether publicly, that is, for the safety or help of the people, or privately, when there are given forth for each one's private good divine utterances whereby something of the future may be known for the use of temporal life? But where we read, "Behold, the days come, saith the Lord, that I will make for the house of Israel, and for the house of Judah, a new testament: not according to the testament that I settled for their fathers in the day when I laid hold of their hand

[1]Gen. 12. 1, 2.　[2]Gen. 12. 3.　[3]Gal. 4. 22–31.

to lead them out of the land of Egypt; because they continued not in my testament, and I regarded them not, saith the Lord. For this is the testament that I will make for the house of Israel: after those days, saith the Lord, I will give my laws in their mind, and will write them upon their hearts, and I will see to them; and I will be to them a God, and they shall be to me a people";[1] without doubt this is prophesied to the Jerusalem above, whose reward is God Himself, and whose chief and entire good it is to have Him, and to be His. But this pertains to both, that the city of God is called Jerusalem, and that it is prophesied the house of God shall be in it; and this prophecy seems to be fulfilled when king Solomon builds that most noble temple. For these things both happened in the earthly Jerusalem, as history shows, and were types of the heavenly Jerusalem. And this kind of prophecy, as it were compacted and commingled of both the others in the ancient canonical books, containing historical narratives, is of very great significance, and has exercised and exercises greatly the wits of those who search holy writ. For example, what we read of historically as predicted and fulfilled in the seed of Abraham according to the flesh, we must also inquire the allegorical meaning of, as it is to be fulfilled in the seed of Abraham according to faith. And so much is this the case that some have thought there is nothing in these books either foretold and effected, or effected although not foretold, that does not insinuate something else which is to be referred by figurative signification to the city of God on high, and to her children who are pilgrims in this life. But if this be so, then the utterances of the prophets, or rather the whole of those Scriptures that are reckoned under the title of the Old Testament, will be not of three, but of two different kinds. For there will be nothing there which pertains to the terrestrial Jerusalem only, if whatever is there said and fulfilled of or concerning her signifies something which also refers by allegorical prefiguration to the celestial Jerusalem; but there will be only two kinds, one that pertains to the free Jerusalem, the other to both. But just as, I think, they err greatly who are of opinion that none of the records of affairs in that kind of writings mean anything more than that they so happened, so I think those very daring who contend that the whole gist of their contents lies in allegorical significations. Therefore I have said they are three-fold, not two-fold. Yet, in holding this opinion, I do not blame those who may be able

[1]Heb. 8. 8–10.

to draw out of everything there a spiritual meaning, only saving, first of all, the historical truth. For the rest, what believer can doubt that those things are spoken vainly which are such that, whether said to have been done or to be yet to come, they do not beseem either human or divine affairs? Who would not recall these to spiritual understanding if he could, or confess that they should be recalled by him who is able?

CHAP. 4. *About the prefigured change of the Israelitic kingdom and priesthood, and about the things Hannah the mother of Samuel prophesied, personating the Church*

Therefore the advance of the city of God, where it reached the times of the kings, yielded a figure, when, on the rejection of Saul, David first obtained the kingdom on such a footing that thenceforth his descendants should reign in the earthly Jerusalem in continual succession; for the course of affairs signified and foretold what is not to be passed by in silence, concerning the change of things to come, what belongs to both Testaments, the Old and the New— where the priesthood and kingdom are changed by one who is a priest, and at the same time a king, new and everlasting, even Christ Jesus. For both the substitution in the ministry of God, on Eli's rejection as priest, of Samuel, who executed at once the office of priest and judge, and the establishment of David in the kingdom, when Saul was rejected, typified this of which I speak. And Hannah herself, the mother of Samuel, who formerly was barren, and afterwards was gladdened with fertility, does not seem to prophesy anything else, when she exultingly pours forth her thanksgiving to the Lord, on yielding up to God the same boy she had borne and weaned with the same piety with which she had vowed him. For she says, "My heart is made strong in the Lord, and my horn is exalted in my God; my mouth is enlarged over mine enemies; I am made glad in Thy salvation. Because there is none holy as the Lord; and none is righteous as our God: there is none holy save Thee. Do not glory so proudly, and do not speak lofty things, neither let vaunting talk come out of your mouth; for a God of knowledge is the Lord, and a God preparing His curious designs. The bow of the mighty hath He made weak, and the weak are girded with strength. They that were full of bread are diminished; and the hungry have passed beyond the earth: for the barren hath borne seven; and she that hath many children is waxed feeble. The Lord killeth and maketh alive: He bringeth down to hell, and bringeth up again. The Lord maketh poor and maketh rich: He bringeth low and lifteth up. He raiseth up the poor out of the dust, and lifteth up the beggar from the dunghill, that He may set him among the mighty of [His] people, and maketh them inherit the throne of glory; giving the vow to him that voweth, and He hath blessed the years of the just: for man is not mighty in strength. The Lord shall make His adversary weak: the Lord is holy. Let not the prudent glory in his prudence; and let not the mighty glory in his might; and let not the rich glory in his riches: but let him that glorieth glory in this, to understand and know the Lord, and to do judgment and justice in the midst of the earth. The Lord hath ascended into the heavens, and hath thundered: He shall judge the ends of the earth, for He is righteous: and He giveth strength to our kings, and shall exalt the horn of His Christ." [1]

Do you say that these are the words of a single weak woman giving thanks for the birth of a son? Can the mind of men be so much averse to the light of truth as not to perceive that the sayings this woman pours forth exceed her measure? Moreover, he who is suitably interested in these things which have already begun to be fulfilled even in this earthly pilgrimage also, does he not apply his mind, and perceive, and acknowledge, that through this woman—whose very name, which is Hannah, means *His grace*—the very Christian religion, the very city of God, whose king and founder is Christ, in fine, the very grace of God, hath thus spoken by the prophetic Spirit, whereby the proud are cut off so that they fall, and the humble are filled so that they rise, which that hymn chiefly celebrates? Unless perchance any one will say that this woman prophesied nothing, but only lauded God with exulting praise on account of the son whom she had obtained in answer to prayer. What then does she mean when she says, "The bow of the mighty hath He made weak, and the weak are girded with strength; they that were full of bread are diminished, and the hungry have gone beyond the earth; for the barren hath borne seven, and she that hath many children is waxed feeble"? Had she herself borne seven, although she had been barren? She had only one when she said that; neither did she bear seven afterwards, nor six, with whom Samuel himself might be the seventh, but three males and two females. And then, when as yet no one was king over that people, whence, if she did not prophesy, did she

[1] I Sam. 2. 1-10.

say what she puts at the end, "He giveth strength to our kings, and shall exalt the horn of His Christ"?

Therefore let the Church of Christ, the city of the great King,[2] full of grace, prolific of offspring, let her say what the prophecy uttered about her so long before by the mouth of this pious mother confesses, "My heart is made strong in the Lord, and my horn is exalted in my God." Her heart is truly made strong, and her horn is truly exalted, because not in herself, but in the Lord her God. "My mouth is enlarged over mine enemies"; because even in pressing straits the word of God is not bound, not even in preachers who are bound.[3] "I am made glad," she says, "in Thy salvation." This is Christ Jesus Himself, whom old Simeon, as we read in the Gospel, embracing as a little one, yet recognizing as great, said, "Lord, now lettest Thou Thy servant depart in peace, for mine eyes have seen Thy salvation." [4] Therefore may the Church say, "I am made glad in Thy salvation. For there is none holy as the Lord, and none is righteous as our God"; as holy and sanctifying, just and justifying.[5] "There is none holy beside Thee"; because no one becomes so except by reason of Thee. And then it follows, "Do not glory so proudly, and do not speak lofty things, neither let vaunting talk come out of your mouth. For a God of knowledge is the Lord." He knows you even when no one knows; for "he who thinketh himself to be something when he is nothing deceiveth himself." [6] These things are said to the adversaries of the city of God who belong to Babylon, who presume in their own strength, and glory in themselves, not in the Lord; of whom are also the carnal Israelites, the earth-born inhabitants of the earthly Jerusalem, who, as saith the apostle, "being ignorant of the righteousness of God," [7] that is, which God, Who alone is just, and the justifier, gives to man, "and wishing to establish their own," that is, which is as it were procured by their own selves, not bestowed by Him, "are not subject to the righteousness of God," just because they are proud, and think they are able to please God with their own, not with that which is of God, who is the God of knowledge, and therefore also takes the oversight of consciences, there beholding the thoughts of men that they are vain,[8] if they are of men, and are not from Him. "And preparing," she says, "His curious designs."

[2] Ps. 48. 2. [3] II Tim. 2. 9; Eph. 6. 20.
[4] Luke, 2. 25-30. [5] Rom. 3. 26? [6] Gal. 6. 3.
[7] Rom. 10. 3. [8] Ps. 94. 11; I Cor. 3. 20.

What curious designs do we think these are, save that the proud must fall, and the humble rise? These curious designs she recounts, saying, "The bow of the mighty is made weak, and the weak are girded with strength." The bow is made weak, that is, the intention of those who think themselves so powerful, that without the gift and help of God they are able by human sufficiency to fulfill the divine commandments; and those are girded with strength whose inward cry is, "Have mercy upon me, O Lord, for I am weak."[1]

"They that were full of bread," she says, "are diminished, and the hungry have gone beyond the earth." Who are to be understood as full of bread except those same who were as if mighty, that is, the Israelites, to whom were committed the oracles of God?[2] But among that people the children of the bond maid were diminished—by which word *minus*, although it is Latin, the idea is well expressed that from being greater they were made less—because, even in the very bread, that is, the divine oracles, which the Israelites alone of all nations have received, they savour earthly things. But the nations to whom that law was not given, after they have come through the New Testament to these oracles, by thirsting much have gone beyond the earth, because in them they have savoured not earthly, but heavenly things. And the reason why this is done is as it were sought; "for the barren," she says, "hath borne seven, and she that hath many children is waxed feeble." Here all that had been prophesied hath shone forth to those who understood the number seven, which signifies the perfection of the universal Church. For which reason also the Apostle John writes to the seven churches,[3] showing in that way that he writes to the totality of the one Church; and in the Proverbs of Solomon it is said aforetime, prefiguring this, "Wisdom hath builded her house, she hath strengthened her seven pillars."[4] For the city of God was barren in all nations before that child arose whom we see. We also see that the temporal Jerusalem, who had many children, is now waxed feeble. Because, whoever in her were sons of the free woman were her strength; but now, forasmuch as the letter is there, and not the spirit, having lost her strength, she is waxed feeble.

"The Lord killeth and maketh alive": He has killed her who had many children, and made this barren one alive, so that she has borne seven. Although it may be more suitably understood that

He has made those same alive whom He has killed. For she, as it were, repeats that by adding, "He bringeth down to hell, and bringeth up." To whom truly the apostle says, "If ye be dead with Christ, seek those things which are above, where Christ sitteth on the right hand of God."[5] Therefore they are killed by the Lord in a salutary way, so that he adds, "Savour things which are above, not things on the earth"; so that these are they who, hungering, have passed beyond the earth. "For ye are dead," he says: behold how God savingly kills! Then there follows, "And your life is hid with Christ in God": behold how God makes the same alive! But does He bring them down to hell and bring them up again? It is without controversy among believers that we best see both parts of this work fulfilled in Him, to wit our Head, with whom the apostle has said our life is hid in God. "For when He spared not His own Son, but delivered Him up for us all,"[6] in that way, certainly, He has killed Him. And forasmuch as He raised Him up again from the dead, He has made Him alive again. And since His voice is acknowledged in the prophecy, "Thou wilt not leave my soul in hell,"[7] He has brought Him down to hell and brought Him up again. By this poverty of His we are made rich;[8] for "the Lord maketh poor and maketh rich." But that we may know what this is, let us hear what follows: "He bringeth low and lifteth up"; and truly He humbles the proud and exalts the humble. Which we also read elsewhere, "God resisteth the proud, but giveth grace to the humble."[9] This is the burden of the entire song of this woman whose name is interpreted *His grace.*

Farther, what is added, "He raiseth up the poor from the earth," I understand of none better than of Him Who, as was said a little ago, "was made poor for us, when He was rich, that by His poverty we might be made rich." For He raised Him from the earth so quickly that His flesh did not see corruption. Nor shall I divert from Him what is added, "And raiseth up the poor from the dunghill." For indeed he who is the poor man is also the beggar. But by the dunghill from which he is lifted up we are with the greatest reason to understand the persecuting Jews, of whom the apostle says, when telling that when he belonged to them he persecuted the Church, "What things were gain to me, those I counted loss for Christ; and I have

[1]Ps. 6. 2.   [2]Rom. 3. 2.   [3]Rev. 1. 4.   [4]Prov. 9. 1.

[5]Col. 3. 1–3.   [6]Rom. 8. 32.
[7]Ps. 16. 10; Acts, 2. 27, 31.   [8]II Cor. 8. 9.
[9]Jas. 4. 6; I Pet. 5. 5.

counted them not only loss, but even dung, that I might win Christ." [1] Therefore that poor one is raised up from the earth above all the rich, and that beggar is lifted up from that dunghill above all the wealthy, "that he may sit among the mighty of the people," to whom He says, "Ye shall sit upon twelve thrones," [2] "and to make them inherit the throne of glory." For these mighty ones had said, "Lo, we have forsaken all and followed Thee." They had most mightily vowed this vow.

But whence do they receive this, except from Him of whom it is here immediately said, "Giving the vow to him that voweth"? Otherwise they would be of those mighty ones whose bow is weakened. "Giving," she saith, "the vow to him that voweth." For no one could vow anything acceptable to God, unless he received from Him that which he might vow. There follows, "And He hath blessed the years of the just," to wit, that he may live for ever with Him to whom it is said, "And Thy years shall have no end." For there the years abide; but here they pass away, yea, they perish; for before they come they are not, and when they shall have come they shall not be, because they bring their own end with them. Now of these two, that is, "giving the vow to him that voweth," and "He hath blessed the years of the just," the one is what we do, the other what we receive. But this other is not received from God, the liberal giver, until He, the helper, Himself has enabled us for the former; "for man is not mighty in strength." "The Lord shall make his adversary weak," to wit, him who envies the man that vows, and resists him, lest he should fulfil what he has vowed. Owing to the ambiguity of the Greek, it may also be understood "his own adversary." For when God has begun to possess us, immediately he who had been our adversary becomes His, and is conquered by us; but not by our own strength, "for man is not mighty in strength." Therefore "the Lord shall make His own adversary weak, the Lord is holy," that he may be conquered by the saints, whom the Lord, the Holy of holies, hath made saints. For this reason, "let not the prudent glory in his prudence, and let not the mighty glory in his might, and let not the rich glory in his riches; but let him that glorieth glory in this—to understand and know the Lord, and to do judgment and justice in the midst of the earth." He in no small measure understands and knows the Lord who understands and knows that even this, that he can understand and know the Lord, is given to him

by the Lord. "For what hast thou," saith the apostle, "that thou hast not received? But if thou hast received it, why dost thou glory as if thou hadst not received it?" [3] That is, as if thou hadst of thine own self whereof thou mightest glory. Now, he does judgment and justice who lives aright. But he lives aright who yields obedience to God when He commands. "The end of the commandment," that is, to which the commandment has reference, "is charity out of a pure heart, and a good conscience, and faith unfeigned." Moreover, this "charity," as the Apostle John testifies, "is of God." [4] Therefore to do justice and judgment is of God. But what is "in the midst of the earth"? For ought those who dwell in the ends of the earth not to do judgment and justice? Who would say so? Why, then, is it added, "in the midst of the earth"? For if this had not been added, and it had only been said, "To do judgment and justice," this commandment would rather have pertained to both kinds of men—both those dwelling inland and those on the sea-coast. But lest any one should think that, after the end of the life led in this body, there remains a time for doing judgment and justice which he has not done while he was in the flesh, and that the divine judgment can thus be escaped, "in the midst of the earth" appears to me to be said of the time when every one lives in the body; for in this life every one carries about his own earth, which, on a man's dying, the common earth takes back, to be surely returned to him on his rising again. Therefore "in the midst of the earth," that is, while our soul is shut up in this earthly body, judgment and justice are to be done, which shall be profitable for us hereafter, when "every one shall receive according to that he hath done in the body, whether good or bad." [5] For when the apostle there says "in the body," he means in the time he has lived in the body. Yet if any one blaspheme with malicious mind and impious thought, without any member of his body being employed in it, he shall not therefore be guiltless because he has not done it with bodily motion, for he will have done it in that time which he has spent in the body. In the same way we may suitably understand what we read in the psalm, "But God, our King before the worlds, hath wrought salvation in the midst of the earth"; [6] so that the Lord Jesus may be understood to be our God Who is before the worlds, because by Him the worlds were made, working our salvation in the midst of the earth, for the

[1] Phil. 3. 7, 8.   [2] Matt. 19. 27, 28.

[3] I Cor. 4. 7.   [4] I John, 4. 7.   [5] II Cor. 5. 10.
[6] Ps. 74. 12.

Word was made flesh and dwelt in an earthly body.

Then after Hannah has prophesied in these words, that he who glorieth ought to glory not in himself at all, but in the Lord, she says, on account of the retribution which is to come on the day of judgment, "The Lord hath ascended into the heavens, and hath thundered: He shall judge the ends of the earth, for He is righteous." Throughout she holds to the order of the creed of Christians: "For the Lord Christ has ascended into heaven, and is to come thence to judge the quick and dead."[1] For, as saith the apostle, "Who hath ascended but He Who hath also descended into the lower parts of the earth? He that descended is the same also that ascended up above all heavens, that He might fill all things."[2] Therefore He hath thundered through His clouds, which He hath filled with His Holy Spirit when He ascended up. Concerning which the bond maid Jerusalem—that is, the unfruitful vineyard—is threatened in Isaiah the prophet that they shall rain no showers upon her. But "He shall judge the ends of the earth" is spoken as if it had been said, "even the extremes of the earth." For it does not mean that He shall not judge the other parts of the earth, who, without doubt, shall judge all men. But it is better to understand by the extremes of the earth the extremes of man, since those things shall not be judged which, in the middle time, are changed for the better or the worse, but the ending in which he shall be found who is judged. For which reason it is said, "He that shall persevere even unto the end, the same shall be saved."[3] He, therefore, who perseveringly does judgment and justice in the midst of the earth shall not be condemned when the extremes of the earth shall be judged. "And giveth," she saith, "strength to our kings," that He may not condemn them in judging. He giveth them strength whereby as kings they rule the flesh, and conquer the world in Him who hath poured out His blood for them. "And shall exalt the horn of His Christ." How shall Christ exalt the horn of His Christ? For He of Whom it was said above, "The Lord hath ascended into the heavens," meaning the Lord Christ, Himself, as it is said here, "shall exalt the horn of His Christ." Who, therefore, is the Christ of His Christ? Does it mean that He shall exalt the horn of each one of His believing people, as she says in the beginning of this hymn, "Mine horn is exalted in my God"? For we can rightly call all those christs who are anointed with His chrism, forasmuch as the whole body with its head is one Christ.[4] These things hath Hannah, the mother of Samuel, the holy and much-praised man, prophesied, in which, indeed, the change of the ancient priesthood was then figured and is now fulfilled, since she that had many children is waxed feeble, that the barren who hath borne seven might have the new priesthood in Christ.

CHAP. 5. *Of those things which a man of God spake by the Spirit to Eli the priest, signifying that the priesthood which had been appointed according to Aaron was to be taken away*

But this is said more plainly by a man of God sent to Eli the priest himself, whose name indeed is not mentioned, but whose office and ministry show him to have been indubitably a prophet. For it is thus written: "And there came a man of God unto Eli, and said, Thus saith the Lord, I plainly revealed myself unto thy father's house, when they were in the land of Egypt slaves in Pharaoh's house; and I chose thy father's house out of all the sceptres of Israel to fill the office of priest for me, to go up to my altar, to burn incense and wear the ephod; and I gave thy father's house for food all the offerings made by fire of the children of Israel. Wherefore then hast thou looked at mine incense and at mine offerings with an impudent eye, and hast glorified thy sons above me, to bless the first fruits of every sacrifice in Israel before me? Therefore thus saith the Lord God of Israel, I said thy house and thy father's house should walk before me for ever: but now the Lord saith, Be it far from me; for them that honour me will I honour, and he that despiseth me shall be despised. Behold, the days come, that I will cut off thy seed, and the seed of thy father's house, and thou shalt never have an old man in my house. And I will cut off the man of thine from mine altar, so that his eyes shall be consumed, and his heart shall melt away; and every one of thy house that is left shall fall by the sword of men. And this shall be a sign unto thee that shall come upon these thy two sons, Hophni and Phinehas; in one day they shall die both of them. And I will raise me up a faithful priest, that shall do according to all that is in mine heart and in my soul; and I will build him a sure house, and he shall walk before my Christ for ever. And it shall come to pass that he who is left in thine house shall come to worship him with a piece of money, saying, Put me into one part of thy priesthood, that I may eat bread."[5]

[1]Acts, 10. 42.   [2]Eph. 4. 9, 10.   [3]Matt. 24. 13.

[4]I Cor. 12. 12.   [5]I Sam. 2. 27-36.

We cannot say that this prophecy, in which the change of the ancient priesthood is foretold with so great plainness, was fulfilled in Samuel; for although Samuel was not of another tribe than that which had been appointed by God to serve at the altar, yet he was not of the sons of Aaron, whose offspring was set apart that the priests might be taken out of it. And thus by that transaction also the same change which should come to pass through Christ Jesus is shadowed forth, and the prophecy itself in deed, not in word, belonged to the Old Testament properly, but figuratively to the New, signifying by the fact just what was said by the word to Eli the priest through the prophet. For there were afterwards priests of Aaron's race, such as Zadok and Abiathar during David's reign, and others in succession, before the time came when those things which were predicted so long before about the changing of the priesthood behoved to be fulfilled by Christ. But who that now views these things with a believing eye does not see that they are fulfilled? Since, indeed, no tabernacle, no temple, no altar, no sacrifice, and therefore no priest either, has remained to the Jews, to whom it was commanded in the law of God that he should be ordained of the seed of Aaron; which is also mentioned here by the prophet, when he says, "Thus saith the Lord God of Israel, I said thy house and thy father's house shall walk before me for ever: but now the Lord saith, That be far from me: for them that honour me will I honour, and he that despiseth me shall be despised." For that in naming his father's house he does not mean that of his immediate father, but that of Aaron, who first was appointed priest, to be succeeded by others descended from him, is shown by the preceding words, when he says, "I was revealed unto thy father's house, when they were in the land of Egypt slaves in Pharaoh's house; and I chose thy father's house out of all the sceptres of Israel to fill the office of priest for me." Which of the fathers in that Egyptian slavery, but Aaron, was his father, who, when they were set free, was chosen to the priesthood? It was of his lineage, therefore, he has said in this passage it should come to pass that they should no longer be priests; which already we see fulfilled. If faith be watchful, the things are before us: they are discerned, they are grasped, and are forced on the eyes of the unwilling, so that they are seen: "Behold the days come," he says, "that I will cut off thy seed, and the seed of thy father's house, and thou shalt never have an old man in mine house. And I will cut off the man of thine from mine altar, so that his eyes shall be consumed and his heart shall melt away." Behold the days which were foretold have already come. There is no priest after the order of Aaron; and whoever is a man of his lineage, when he sees the sacrifice of the Christians prevailing over the whole world, but that great honour taken away from himself, his eyes fail and his soul melts away consumed with grief.

But what follows belongs properly to the house of Eli, to whom these things were said: "And every one of thine house that is left shall fall by the sword of men. And this shall be a sign unto thee that shall come upon these thy two sons, Hophni and Phinehas; in one day they shall die both of them." This, therefore, is made a sign of the change of the priesthood from this man's house, by which it is signified that the priesthood of Aaron's house is to be changed. For the death of this man's sons signified the death not of the men, but of the priesthood itself of the sons of Aaron. But what follows pertains to that Priest whom Samuel typified by succeeding this one. Therefore the things which follow are said of Christ Jesus, the true Priest of the New Testament: "And I will raise me up a faithful Priest that shall do according to all that is in mine heart and in my soul; and I will build Him a sure house." The same is the eternal Jerusalem above. "And He shall walk," saith He, "before my Christ always." "He shall walk" means "he shall be conversant with," just as He had said before of Aaron's house, "I said that thine house and thy father's house shall walk before me for ever." But what He says, "He shall walk before my Christ," is to be understood entirely of the house itself, not of the priest, who is Christ Himself, the Mediator and Saviour. His house, therefore, shall walk before Him. "Shall walk" may also be understood to mean from death to life, all the time this mortality passes through, even to the end of this world. But where God says, "Who will do all that is in mine heart and in my soul," we must not think that God has a soul, for He is the Author of souls; but this is said of God tropically, not properly, just as He is said to have hands and feet, and other corporal members. And, lest it should be supposed from such language that man in the form of this flesh is made in the image of God, wings also are ascribed to Him, which man has not at all; and it is said to God, "Hide me under the shadow of Thy wings,"[1]

[1] Ps. 17. 8.

that men may understand that such things are said of that ineffable nature not in proper but in figurative words.

But what is added, "And it shall come to pass that he who is left in thine house shall come to worship him," is not said properly of the house of this Eli, but of that Aaron, the men of which remained even to the advent of Jesus Christ, of which race there are not wanting men even to this present. For of that house of Eli it had already been said above, "And every one of thine house that is left shall fall by the sword of men." How, therefore, could it be truly said here, "And it shall come to pass that every one that is left shall come to worship him," if that is true that no one shall escape the avenging sword, unless he would have it understood of those who belong to the race of that whole priesthood after the order of Aaron? Therefore, if it is of these the predestinated remnant, about whom another prophet has said, "The remnant shall be saved";[1] whence the apostle also says, "Even so then at this time also the remnant according to the election of grace is saved";[2] since it is easily understood to be of such a remnant that it is said, "He that is left in thine house," assuredly he believes in Christ; just as in the time of the apostle very many of that nation believed; nor are there now wanting those, although very few, who yet believe, and in them is fulfilled what this man of God has here immediately added, "He shall come to worship him with a piece of money"; to worship whom, if not that Chief Priest, Who is also God? For in that priesthood after the order of Aaron men did not come to the temple or altar of God for the purpose of worshipping the priest. But what is that he says, "With a piece of money," if not the short word of faith, about which the apostle quotes the saying, "A consummating and shortening word will the Lord make upon the earth"?[3] But that money is put for the word the psalm is a witness, where it is sung, "The words of the Lord are pure words, money tried with the fire."[4]

What then does he say who comes to worship the priest of God, even the Priest Who is God? "Put me into one part of Thy priesthood, to eat bread." I do not wish to be set in the honour of my fathers, which is none; put me in a part of Thy priesthood. For "I have chosen to be mean in Thine house";[5] I desire to be a member, no matter what, or how small, of Thy priesthood. By the priesthood he here means the people itself, of which He is the Priest Who is the Mediator between God and men, the man Christ Jesus.[6] This people the Apostle Peter calls "a holy people, a royal priesthood."[7] But some have translated, "Of Thy sacrifice," not "Of Thy priesthood," which no less signifies the same Christian people. Whence the Apostle Paul says, "We being many are one bread, one body."[8] What, therefore, he has added, to "eat bread," also elegantly expresses the very kind of sacrifice of which the Priest Himself says, "The bread which I will give is my flesh for the life of the world."[9] The same is the sacrifice not after the order of Aaron, but after the order of Melchizedek:[10] let him that readeth understand.[11] Therefore this short and salutarily humble confession, in which it is said, "Put me in a part of Thy priesthood, to eat bread," is itself the piece of money, for it is both brief, and it is the Word of God who dwells in the heart of one who believes. For because He had said above, that He had given for food to Aaron's house the sacrificial victims of the Old Testament, where He says, "I have given thy father's house for food all things which are offered by fire of the children of Israel," which indeed were the sacrifices of the Jews; therefore here He has said, "To eat bread," which is in the New Testament the sacrifice of the Christians.

CHAP. 6. *Of the Jewish priesthood and kingdom, which, although promised to be established for ever, did not continue; so that other things are to be understood to which eternity is assured.*

While, therefore, these things now shine forth as clearly as they were loftily foretold, still some one may not vainly be moved to ask, How can we be confident that all things are to come to pass which are predicted in these books as about to come, if this very thing which is there divinely spoken, "Thine house and thy father's house shall walk before me for ever," could not have effect? For we see that priesthood has been changed; and there can be no hope that what was promised to that house may some time be fulfilled, because that which succeeds on its being rejected and changed is rather predicted as eternal. He who says this does not yet understand, or does not recollect, that this very priesthood after the order of Aaron was appointed as the shadow of a future eternal priesthood; and therefore, when eternity is promised to it, it is not promised to the mere shadow and figure, but

[1]Isa. 10. 21.   [2]Rom. 11. 5.   [3]Isa. 38. 22; Rom. 9. 28.
[4]Ps. 12. 6.   [5]Ps. 84. 10.   [6]I Tim. 2. 5.   [7]I Pet. 2. 9.   [8]I Cor. 10. 17.
[9]John, 6. 51.   [10]Heb. 7. 11, 27.   [11]Matt. 24. 15.

to what is shadowed forth and prefigured by it. But lest it should be thought the shadow itself was to remain, therefore its mutation also behoved to be foretold.

In this way, too, the kingdom of Saul himself, who certainly was reprobated and rejected, was the shadow of a kingdom yet to come which should remain to eternity. For, indeed, the oil with which he was anointed, and from that chrism he is called Christ, is to be taken in a mystical sense, and is to be understood as a great mystery; which David himself venerated so much in him, that he trembled with smitten heart when, being hid in a dark cave, which Saul also entered when pressed by the necessity of nature, he had come secretly behind him and cut off a small piece of his robe, that he might be able to prove him he had spared him when he could have killed him, and might thus remove from his mind the suspicion through which he had vehemently persecuted the holy David, thinking him his enemy. Therefore he was much afraid lest he should be accused of violating so great a mystery in Saul, because he had thus meddled even his clothes. For thus it is written: "And David's heart smote him because he had taken away the skirt of his cloak."[1] But to the men with him, who advised him to destroy Saul thus delivered up into his hands, he saith, "The Lord forbid that I should do this thing to my lord, the Lord's christ, to lay my hand upon him, because he is the Lord's christ." Therefore he showed so great reverence to this shadow of what was to come, not for its own sake, but for the sake of what it prefigured. Whence also that which Samuel says to Saul, "Since thou hast not kept my commandment which the Lord commanded thee, whereas now the Lord would have prepared thy kingdom over Israel for ever, yet now thy kingdom shall not continue for thee; and the Lord will seek Him a man after His own heart, and the Lord will command him to be prince over His people, because thou hast not kept that which the Lord commanded thee,"[2] is not to be taken as if God had settled that Saul himself should reign for ever, and, afterwards, on his sinning, would not keep this promise; nor was He ignorant that he would sin, but He had established his kingdom that it might be a figure of the eternal kingdom. Therefore he added, "Yet now thy kingdom shall not continue *for thee.*" Therefore what it signified has stood and shall stand; but it shall not stand for this man, because he himself was not to reign for ever, nor his offspring; so that at least that word "for

ever" might seem to be fulfilled through his posterity one to another. "And the Lord," he saith, "will seek Him a man," meaning either David or the Mediator of the New Testament,[3] who was figured in the chrism with which David also and his offspring was anointed. But it is not as if He knew not where he was that God thus seeks Him a man, but, speaking through a man, He speaks as a man, and in this sense seeks us. For not only to God the Father, but also to His Only-begotten, who came to seek what was lost,[4] we had been known already even so far as to be chosen in Him before the foundation of the world.[5] "He will seek Him" therefore means, "He will have His own" (just as if He had said, Whom He already has known to be His own He will show to others to be His friend). Whence in Latin this word (*quærit*) receives a preposition and becomes *acquirit* (acquires), the meaning of which is plain enough; although even without the addition of the preposition *quærere* is understood as *acquirere*, whence gains are called *quæstus.*

CHAP. 7. *Of the disruption of the kingdom of Israel, by which the perpetual division of the spiritual from the carnal Israel was prefigured*

Again Saul sinned through disobedience, and again Samuel says to him in the word of the Lord, "Because thou hast despised the word of the Lord, the Lord hath despised thee, that thou mayest not be king over Israel."[6] And again for the same sin, when Saul confessed it, and prayed for pardon, and besought Samuel to return with him to appease the Lord, he said, "I will not return with thee: for thou hast despised the word of the Lord, and the Lord will despise thee that thou mayest not be king over Israel. And Samuel turned his face to go away, and Saul laid hold upon the skirt of his mantle, and rent it. And Samuel said unto him, The Lord hath rent the kingdom from Israel out of thine hand this day, and will give it to thy neighbour, who is good above thee, and will divide Israel in twain. And He will not be changed, neither will He repent: for He is not as a man, that He should repent; who threatens and does not persist."[7] He to whom it is said, "The Lord will despise thee that thou mayest not be king over Israel," and "The Lord hath rent the kingdom from Israel out of thine hand this day," reigned forty years over Israel—that is, just as long a time as David himself—yet heard this in the first period of his reign that we may understand it was said because none of his race was to reign, and that we

[1] I Sam. 24. 5, 6.   [2] I Sam. 13. 13, 14.   [3] Heb. 9. 15.   [4] Luke, 19. 10.   [5] Eph. 1. 4.   [6] I Sam. 15. 23.   [7] I Sam. 15. 26–29.

may look to the race of David, whence also is sprung, according to the flesh,[1] the Mediator between God and men, the man Christ Jesus.[2]

But the Scripture has not what is read in most Latin copies, "The Lord hath rent the kingdom of Israel out of thine hand this day," but just as we have set it down it is found in the Greek copies, "The Lord hath rent the kingdom from Israel out of thine hand"; that the words "out of thine hand" may be understood to mean "from Israel." Therefore, this man figuratively represented the people of Israel, which was to lose the kingdom, Christ Jesus our Lord being about to reign, not carnally, but spiritually. And when it is said of Him, "And will give it to thy neighbour," that is to be referred to the fleshly kinship, for Christ, according to the flesh, was of Israel, whence also Saul sprang. But what is added, "Good above thee," may indeed be understood, "Better than thee," and indeed some have thus translated it; but it is better taken thus, "Good above thee," as meaning that because He is good, therefore He must be above thee, according to that other prophetic saying, "Till I put all Thine enemies under Thy feet."[3] And among them is Israel, from whom, as His persecutor, Christ took away the kingdom; although the Israel in whom there was no guile may have been there too, a sort of grain, as it were, of that chaff. For certainly thence came the apostles, thence so many martyrs, of whom Stephen is the first, thence so many churches, which the Apostle Paul names, magnifying God in their conversion.

Of which thing I do not doubt what follows is to be understood, "And will divide Israel in twain," to wit, into Israel pertaining to the bond woman and Israel pertaining to the free. For these two kinds were at first together, as Abraham still clave to the bond woman, until the barren, made fruitful by the grace of God, cried, "Cast out the bond woman and her son."[4] We know, indeed, that on account of the sin of Solomon, in the reign of his son Rehoboam, Israel was divided in two, and continued so, the separate parts having their own kings, until that whole nation was overthrown with a great destruction, and carried away by the Chaldeans. But what was this to Saul, when, if any such thing was threatened, it would be threatened against David himself, whose son Solomon was? Finally, the Hebrew nation is not now divided internally, but is dispersed through the earth indiscriminately in the fellowship of the same error. But that division with which God threatened the kingdom and people in the person of Saul, who represented them, is shown to be eternal and unchangeable by this which is added, "And He will not be changed, neither will He repent: for He is not as a man, that He should repent; who threatens and does not persist"; that is, a man threatens and does not persist, but not God, who does not repent like man. For when we read that He repents, a change of circumstance is meant, flowing from the divine immutable foreknowledge. Therefore, when God is said not to repent, it is to be understood that He does not change.

We see that this sentence concerning this division of the people of Israel, divinely uttered in these words, has been altogether irremediable and quite perpetual. For whoever have turned, or are turning, or shall turn thence to Christ, it has been according to the foreknowledge of God, not according to the one and the same nature of the human race. Certainly none of the Israelites, who, cleaving to Christ, have continued in Him, shall ever be among those Israelites who persist in being His enemies even to the end of this life, but shall for ever remain in the separation which is here foretold. For the Old Testament, from the Mount Sinai, which gendereth to bondage,[5] profiteth nothing, unless because it bears witness to the New Testament. Otherwise, however long Moses is read, the veil is put over their heart; but when any one shall turn thence to Christ, the veil shall be taken away.[6] For the very desire of those who turn is changed from the old to the new, so that each no longer desires to obtain carnal but spiritual felicity. Wherefore that great prophet Samuel himself, before he had anointed Saul, when he had cried to the Lord for Israel, and He had heard him, and when he had offered a whole burnt-offering, as the aliens were coming to battle against the people of God, and the Lord thundered above them and they were confused, and fell before Israel and were overcome; he took one stone and set it up between the old and new Massephat, and called its name Ebenezer, which means *the stone of the helper,* and said, "Hitherto hath the Lord helped us."[7] Massephat is interpreted *desire.* That stone of the helper is the mediation of the Saviour, by which we go from the old Massephat to the new—that is, from the desire with which carnal happiness was expected in the carnal kingdom to the desire with which the truest spiritual happiness is expected in the kingdom of heaven; and since nothing is better than that, the Lord helpeth us hitherto.

[1]Rom. 1. 3.   [2]I Tim. 2. 5.   [3]Ps. 110. 1.   [4]Gen. 21. 10.   [5]Gal. 4. 25.   [6]II Cor. 3. 15, 16.   [7]I Sam. 7. 9-12.

CHAP. 8. *Of the promises made to David in his son, which are in no wise fulfilled in Solomon, but most fully in Christ*

And now I see I must show what, pertaining to the matter I treat of, God promised to David himself, who succeeded Saul in the kingdom, whose change prefigured that final change on account of which all things were divinely spoken, all things were committed to writing. When many things had gone prosperously with king David, he thought to make a house for God, even that temple of most excellent renown which was afterwards built by king Solomon his son. While he was thinking of this, the word of the Lord came to Nathan the prophet, which he brought to the king, in which, after God had said that a house should not be built unto Him by David himself, and that in all that long time He had never commanded any of His people to build Him a house of cedar, he says, "And now thus shalt thou say unto my servant David, Thus saith God Almighty, I took thee from the sheep-cote that thou mightest be for a ruler over my people in Israel: and I was with thee withersoever thou wentest, and have cut off all thine enemies from before thy face, and have made thee a name, according to the name of the great ones who are over the earth. And I will appoint a place for my people Israel, and will plant him, and he shall dwell apart, and shall be troubled no more; and the son of wickedness shall not humble him any more, as from the beginning, from the days when I appointed judges over my people Israel. And I will give thee rest from all thine enemies, and the Lord will tell thee, because thou shalt build an house for Him. And it shall come to pass when thy days be fulfilled, and thou shalt sleep with thy fathers, that I will raise up thy seed after thee, which shall proceed out of thy bowels, and I will prepare his kingdom. He shall build me an house for my name; and I will order his throne even to eternity. I will be his Father, and he shall be my son. And if he commit iniquity, I will chasten him with the rod of men, and with the stripes of the sons of men: but my mercy I will not take away from him, as I took it away from those whom I put away from before my face. And his house shall be faithful, and his kingdom even for evermore before me, and his throne shall be set up even for evermore."[1]

He who thinks this grand promise was fulfilled in Solomon greatly errs; for he attends to the saying, "He shall build me an house," but

he does not attend to the saying, "His house shall be faithful, and his kingdom for evermore before me." Let him therefore attend and behold the house of Solomon full of strange women worshipping false gods, and the king himself, aforetime wise, seduced by them, and cast down into the same idolatry: and let him not dare to think that God either promised this falsely, or was unable to foreknow that Solomon and his house would become what they did. But we ought not to be in doubt here, or to see the fulfilment of these things save in Christ our Lord, Who was made of the seed of David according to the flesh,[2] lest we should vainly and uselessly look for some other here, like the carnal Jews. For even they understand this much, that the son whom they read of in that place as promised to David was not Solomon; so that, with wonderful blindness to Him Who was promised and is now declared with so great manifestation, they say they hope for another. Indeed, even in Solomon there appeared some image of the future event, in that he built the temple, and had peace according to his name (for Solomon means *pacific*), and in the beginning of his reign was wonderfully praiseworthy; but while, as a shadow of Him that should come, he foreshowed Christ our Lord, he did not also in his own person resemble Him. Whence some things concerning him are so written as if they were prophesied of himself, while the Holy Scripture, prophesying even by events, somehow delineates in him the figure of things to come. For, besides the books of divine history, in which his reign is narrated, the 72d Psalm also is inscribed in the title with his name, in which so many things are said which cannot at all apply to him, but which apply to the Lord Christ with such evident fitness as makes it quite apparent that in the one the figure is in some way shadowed forth, but in the other the truth itself is presented. For it is known within what bounds the kingdom of Solomon was enclosed; and yet in that psalm, not to speak of other things, we read, "He shall have dominion from sea even to sea, and from the river to the ends of the earth,"[3] which we see fulfilled in Christ. Truly he took the beginning of His reigning from the river where John baptized; for, when pointed out by him, He began to be acknowledged by the disciples, who called Him not only Master, but also Lord.

Nor was it for any other reason that, while his father David was still living, Solomon began to reign, which happened to none other of their kings, except that from this also it might be clearly apparent that it was not himself this prophecy spoken to his father signified beforehand, saying, "And it shall come to pass when thy days be fulfilled, and thou shalt sleep with thy fathers, that I will raise up thy seed which shall proceed out of thy bowels, and I will prepare His kingdom." How, therefore, shall it be thought on account of what follows, "He shall build me an house," that this Solomon is prophesied, and not rather be understood on account of what precedes, "When thy days be fulfilled, and thou shalt sleep with thy fathers, I will raise up thy seed after thee," that another pacific One is promised, who is foretold as about to be raised up, not before David's death, as he was, but after it? For however long the interval of time might be before Jesus Christ came, beyond doubt it was after the death of king David, to whom He was so promised, that He behoved to come, who should build an house of God, not of wood and stone, but of men, such as we rejoice He does build. For to this house, that is, to believers, the apostle saith, "The temple of God is holy, which temple ye are." [1]

CHAP. 9. *How like the prophecy about Christ in the 89th psalm is to the things promised in Nathan's prophecy in the books of Samuel*

Wherefore also in the 89th Psalm, of which the title is, "An instruction for himself by Ethan the Israelite," mention is made of the promises God made to king David, and some things are there added similar to those found in the Book of Samuel, such as this, "I have sworn to David my servant that I will prepare his seed for ever." [2] And again, "Then thou spakest in vision to thy sons, and saidst, I have laid help upon the mighty One, and have exalted the chosen One out of my people. I have found David my servant, and with my holy oil I have anointed him. For mine hand shall help him, and mine arm shall strengthen him. The enemy shall not prevail against him, and the son of iniquity shall harm him no more. And I will beat down his foes from before his face, and those that hate him will I put to flight. And my truth and my mercy shall be with him, and in my name shall his horn be exalted. I will set his hand also in the sea, and his right hand in the rivers. He shall cry unto me, Thou art my Father, my God, and the undertaker of my salvation. Also I will make him my first-born, high among the kings of the earth. My mercy will I keep for him for evermore, and my covenant shall be faithful (sure)

with him. His seed also will I set for ever and ever, and his throne as the days of heaven." [3] Which words, when rightly understood, are all understood to be about the Lord Jesus Christ, under the name of David, on account of the form of a servant, which the same Mediator assumed [4] from the virgin of the seed of David. [5] For immediately something is said about the sins of his children, such as is set down in the Book of Samuel, and is more readily taken as if of Solomon. For there, that is, in the Book of Samuel, he says, "And if he commit iniquity I will chasten him with the rod of men, and with the stripes of the sons of men; but my mercy will I not take away from him," [6] meaning by stripes the strokes of correction. Hence that saying, "Touch ye not my christs." [7] For what else is that than, Do not harm them? But in the psalm, when speaking as if of David, He says something of the same kind there too. "If his children," saith He, "forsake my law, and walk not in my judgments; if they profane my righteousnesses, and keep not my commandments; I will visit their iniquities with the rod, and their faults with stripes: but my mercy I will not make void from him." [8] He did not say "from them," although He spoke of his children, not of Himself; but he said "from him," which means the same thing if rightly understood. For of Christ Himself, Who is the head of the Church, there could not be found any sins which required to be divinely restrained by human correction, mercy being still continued; but they are found in His body and members, which is His people. Therefore in the Book of Samuel it is said, "iniquity of Him," but in the psalm, "of His children," that we may understand that what is said of His body is in some way said of Himself. Wherefore also, when Saul persecuted His body, that is, His believing people, He Himself saith from heaven, "Saul, Saul, why persecutest thou me?" [9] Then in the following words of the psalm He says, "Neither will I hurt in my truth, nor profane my covenant, and the things that proceed from my lips I will not disallow. Once have I sworn by my holiness, if I lie unto David" [10]— that is, I will in no wise lie unto David; for Scripture is wont to speak thus. But what that is in which He will not lie, He adds, saying, "His seed shall endure for ever, and his throne as the sun before me, and as the moon perfected for ever, and a faithful witness in heaven." [11]

---

[1]I Cor. 3. 17.   [2]Ps. 89. 3, 4.

[3]Ps. 89. 19-29.   [4]Phil. 2. 7.
[5]Matt. 1. 1, 18; Luke, 1. 27.   [6]II Sam. 7. 14, 15.
[7]Ps. 105. 15.   [8]Ps. 89. 30-33.   [9]Acts, 9. 4.
[10]Ps. 89. 34, 35.   [11]Ps. 89. 36, 37.

CHAP. 10. *How different the acts in the kingdom of the earthly Jerusalem are from those which God had promised, so that the truth of the promise should be understood to pertain to the glory of the other king and kingdom*

That it might not be supposed that a promise so strongly expressed and confirmed was fulfilled in Solomon, as if he hoped for, yet did not find it, he says, "But Thou hast cast off, and hast brought to nothing, O Lord."[1] This truly was done concerning the kingdom of Solomon among his posterity, even to the overthrow of the earthly Jerusalem itself, which was the seat of the kingdom, and especially the destruction of the very temple which had been built by Solomon. But lest on this account God should be thought to have done contrary to His promise, immediately he adds, "Thou hast delayed Thy Christ."[2] Therefore he is not Solomon, nor yet David himself, if the Christ of the Lord is delayed. For while all the kings are called His christs, who were consecrated with that mystical chrism, not only from king David downwards, but even from that Saul who first was anointed king of that same people, David himself indeed calling him the Lord's christ, yet there was one true Christ, whose figure they bore by the prophetic unction, who, according to the opinion of men, who thought he was to be understood as come in David or in Solomon, was long delayed, but who, according as God had disposed, was to come in His own time. The following part of this psalm goes on to say what in the meantime, while He was delayed, was to become of the kingdom of the earthly Jerusalem, where it was hoped He would certainly reign: "Thou hast overthrown the covenant of Thy servant; Thou hast profaned in the earth his sanctuary. Thou hast broken down all his walls; Thou hast put his strong-holds in fear. All that pass by the way spoil him; he is made a reproach to his neighbours. Thou hast set up the right hand of his enemies; Thou hast made all his enemies to rejoice. Thou hast turned aside the help of his sword, and hast not helped him in war. Thou hast destroyed him from cleansing; Thou hast dashed down his seat to the ground. Thou hast shortened the days of his seat; Thou hast poured confusion over him."[3] All these things came upon Jerusalem the bondwoman, in which some also reigned who were children of the free woman, holding that kingdom in temporary stewardship, but holding the kingdom of the heavenly Jerusalem, whose children they were,

in true faith, and hoping in the true Christ. But how these things came upon that kingdom, the history of its affairs points out if it is read.

CHAP. 11. *Of the substance of the people of God, which through His assumption of flesh is in Christ, Who alone had power to deliver His own soul from hell*

But after having prophesied these things, the prophet betakes him to praying to God; yet even the very prayer is prophecy: "How long, Lord, dost Thou turn away in the end?"[4] "Thy face" is understood, as it is elsewhere said, "How long dost Thou turn away Thy face from me?"[5] For therefore some copies have here not "dost," but "wilt Thou turn away"; although it could be understood, "Thou turnest away Thy mercy, which Thou didst promise to David." But when he says, "in the end," what does it mean, except even to the end? By which end is to be understood the last time, when even that nation is to believe in Christ Jesus, before which end what He has just sorrowfully bewailed must come to pass. On account of which it is also added here, "Thy wrath shall burn like fire. Remember what is my substance."[6] This cannot be better understood than of Jesus Himself, the substance of His people, of whose nature His flesh is. "For not in vain," he says, "hast Thou made all the sons of men."[7] For unless the one Son of man had been the substance of Israel, through which Son of man many sons of men should be set free, all the sons of men would have been made wholly in vain. But now, indeed, all mankind through the fall of the first man has fallen from the truth into vanity; for which reason another psalm says, "Man is like to vanity: his days pass away as a shadow";[8] yet God has not made all the sons of men in vain, because He frees many from vanity through the Mediator Jesus, and those whom He did not foreknow as to be delivered, He made not wholly in vain in the most beautiful and most just ordination of the whole rational creation, for the use of those who were to be delivered, and for the comparison of the two cities by mutual contrast. Thereafter it follows, "Who is the man that shall live, and shall not see death? shall he snatch his soul from the hand of hell?"[9] Who is this but that substance of Israel out of the seed of David, Christ Jesus, of Whom the apostle says, that "rising from the dead He now dieth not, and death shall no more have dominion over Him"?[10]

[1]Ps. 89. 38.   [2]*Ibid.*   [3]Ps. 89. 39–45.
[4]Ps. 89. 46.   [5]Ps. 13. 1.   [6]Ps. 89. 46, 47.
[7]Ps. 89. 47.   [8]Ps. 144. 4.   [9]Ps. 89. 48.
[10]Rom. 6. 9.

For He shall so live and not see death that yet He shall have been dead; but shall have delivered His soul from the hand of hell, whither He had descended in order to loose some from the chains of hell; but He hath delivered it by that power of which He says in the Gospel, "I have the power of laying down my life, and I have the power of taking it again."[1]

CHAP. 12. *To whose person the entreaty for the promises is to be understood to belong, when he says in the psalm, "Where are thine ancient compassions, Lord?" etc.*

But the rest of this psalm runs thus: "Where are Thine ancient compassions, Lord, which Thou swarest unto David in Thy truth? Remember, Lord, the reproach of Thy servants, which I have borne in my bosom of many nations; wherewith Thine enemies have reproached, O Lord, wherewith they have reproached the change of Thy Christ."[2] Now it may with very good reason be asked whether this is spoken in the person of those Israelites who desired that the promise made to David might be fulfilled to them; or rather of the Christians, who are Israelites not after the flesh but after the Spirit.[3] This certainly was spoken or written in the time of Ethan, from whose name this psalm gets its title, and that was the same as the time of David's reign; and therefore it would not have been said, "Where are Thine ancient compassions, Lord, which Thou hast sworn unto David in Thy truth?" unless the prophet had assumed the person of those who should come long afterwards, to whom that time when these things were promised to David was ancient. But it may be understood thus, that many nations, when they persecuted the Christians, reproached them with the passion of Christ, which Scripture calls His change, because by dying He is made immortal. The change of Christ, according to this passage, may also be understood to be reproached by the Israelites, because, when they hoped He would be theirs, He was made the Saviour of the nations; and many nations who have believed in Him by the New Testament now reproach them who remain in the Old with this: so that it is said, "Remember, Lord, the reproach of Thy servants"; because through the Lord's not forgetting, but rather pitying them, even they after this reproach are to believe. But what I have put first seems to me the most suitable meaning. For to the enemies of Christ who are reproached with

this, that Christ hath left them, turning to the Gentiles,[4] this speech is incongruously assigned, "Remember, Lord, the reproach of Thy servants," for such Jews are not to be styled the servants of God; but these words fit those who, if they suffered great humiliations through persecution for the name of Christ, could call to mind that an exalted kingdom had been promised to the seed of David, and in desire of it, could say not despairingly, but as asking, seeking, knocking,[5] "Where are Thine ancient compassions, Lord, which Thou swarest unto David in Thy truth? Remember, Lord, the reproach of Thy servants, that I have borne in my bosom of many nations"; that is, have patiently endured in my inward parts. "That Thine enemies have reproached, O Lord, wherewith they have reproached the change of Thy Christ," not thinking it a change, but a consumption.[6] But what does "Remember, Lord," mean, but that Thou wouldst have compassion, and wouldst for my patiently borne humiliation reward me with the excellency which Thou swarest unto David in Thy truth? But if we assign these words to the Jews, those servants of God who, on the conquest of the earthly Jerusalem, before Jesus Christ was born after the manner of men, were led into captivity, could say such things, understanding the change of Christ, because indeed through Him was to be surely expected, not an earthly and carnal felicity such as appeared during the few years of king Solomon, but a heavenly and spiritual felicity; and when the nations, then ignorant of this through unbelief, exulted over and insulted the people of God for being captives, what else was this than ignorantly to reproach with the change of Christ those who understand the change of Christ? And therefore what follows when this psalm is concluded, "Let the blessing of the Lord be for evermore, amen, amen," is suitable enough for the whole people of God belonging to the heavenly Jerusalem, whether for those things that lay hid in the Old Testament before the New was revealed, or for those that, being now revealed in the New Testament, are manifestly discerned to belong to Christ. For the blessing of the Lord in the seed of David does not belong to any particular time, such as appeared in the days of Solomon, but is for evermore to be hoped for, in which most certain hope it is said, "Amen, amen"; for this repetition of the word is the confirmation of that hope. Therefore, David, understanding this, says in the second Book of Kings, in the passage

[1]John, 10. 18.   [2]Ps. 89. 49–51.   [3]Rom. 3. 28, 29.
[4]Acts, 13. 46.   [5]Matt. 7. 7, 8.
[6]Another reading: "consummation."

from which we digressed to this psalm,[1] "Thou hast spoken also for Thy servant's house for a great while to come."[2] Therefore also a little after he says, "Now begin, and bless the house of Thy servant for evermore," etc., because the son was then about to be born from whom his posterity should be continued to Christ, through whom his house should be eternal, and should also be the house of God. For it is called the house of David on account of David's race; but the selfsame is called the house of God on account of the temple of God, made of men, not of stones, where shall dwell for evermore the people with and in their God, and God with and in His people, so that God may fill His people, and the people be filled with their God, while God shall be all in all, Himself their reward in peace Who is their strength in war. Therefore, when it is said in the words of Nathan, "And the Lord will tell thee what an house thou shalt build for Him,"[3] it is afterwards said in the words of David, "For Thou, Lord Almighty, God of Israel, hast opened the ear of Thy servant, saying, I will build thee an house."[4] For this house is built both by us through living well, and by God through helping us to live well; for "except the Lord build the house, they labour in vain that build it."[5] And when the final dedication of this house shall take place, then what God here says by Nathan shall be fulfilled, "And I will appoint a place for my people Israel, and will plant him, and he shall dwell apart, and shall be troubled no more; and the son of iniquity shall not humble him any more, as from the beginning, from the days when I appointed judges over my people Israel."[6]

CHAP. 13. *Whether the truth of this promised peace can be ascribed to those times passed away under Solomon*

Whoever hopes for this so great good in this world and in this earth, his wisdom is but folly. Can any one think it was fulfilled in the peace of Solomon's reign? Scripture certainly commends that peace with excellent praise as a shadow of that which is to come. But this opinion is to be vigilantly opposed, since after it is said, "And the son of iniquity shall not humble him any more," it is immediately added, "as from the beginning, from the days in which I appointed judges over my people Israel."[7] For the judges were appointed over that people from the time when they received the land of promise, before

kings had begun to be there. And certainly the son of iniquity, that is, the foreign enemy, humbled him through periods of time in which we read that peace alternated with wars; and in that period longer times of peace are found than Solomon had, who reigned forty years. For under that judge who is called Ehud there were eighty years of peace.[8] Be it far from us, therefore, that we should believe the times of Solomon are predicted in this promise, much less indeed those of any other king whatever. For none other of them reigned in such great peace as he; nor did that nation ever at all hold that kingdom so as to have no anxiety lest it should be subdued by enemies: for in the very great mutability of human affairs such great security is never given to any people, that it should not dread invasions hostile to this life. Therefore the place of this promised peaceful and secure habitation is eternal, and of right belongs eternally to Jerusalem the free mother, where the genuine people of Israel shall be: for this name is interpreted *Seeing God;* in the desire of which reward a pious life is to be led through faith in this miserable pilgrimage.[9]

CHAP. 14. *Of David's concern in the writing of the Psalms*

In the progress of the city of God through the ages, therefore, David first reigned in the earthly Jerusalem as a shadow of that which was to come. Now David was a man skilled in songs, who dearly loved musical harmony, not with a vulgar delight, but with a believing disposition, and by it served his God, who is the true God, by the mystical representation of a great thing. For the rational and well-ordered concord of diverse sounds in harmonious variety suggests the compact unity of the well-ordered city. Then almost all his prophecy is in psalms, of which a hundred and fifty are contained in what we call the Book of Psalms, of which some will have it those only were made by David which are inscribed with his name. But there are also some who think none of them were made by him except those which are marked "Of David"; but those which have in the title "For David" have been made by others who assumed his person. Which opinion is refuted by the voice of the Saviour Himself in the Gospel, when He says that David himself by the Spirit said Christ was his Lord; for the 110th Psalm begins thus, "The Lord said unto my Lord, Sit Thou at my right

---

[1]See above, Chap. 8.   [2]II Sam. 7. 19.
[3]II Sam. 7. 8.   [4]II Sam. 7. 2.   [5]Ps. 127. 1.
[6]II Sam. 7. 10, 11.   [7]*Ibid.*

[8]Judg. 3. 30.
[9]Israel = a prince of God; Peniel = the face of God (Gen. 32. 28–30).

hand, until I make Thine enemies Thy foot-stool." [1] And truly that very psalm, like many more, has in the title, not "of David," but "for David." But those seem to me to hold the more credible opinion who ascribe to him the author-ship of all these hundred and fifty psalms and think that he prefixed to some of them the names even of other men, who prefigured some-thing pertinent to the matter, but chose to have no man's name in the titles of the rest, just as God inspired him in the management of this va-riety, which, although dark, is not meaningless. Neither ought it to move one not to believe this that the names of some prophets who lived long after the times of king David are read in the in-scriptions of certain psalms in that book, and that the things said there seem to be spoken as it were by them. Nor was the prophetic Spirit unable to reveal to king David, when he prophe-sied, even these names of future prophets, so that he might prophetically sing something which should suit their persons; just as it was revealed to a certain prophet that king Josiah should arise and reign after more than three hundred years, who predicted his future deeds also along with his name. [2]

CHAP. 15. *Whether all the things prophesied in the Psalms concerning Christ and his Church should be taken up in the text of this work*

And now I see it may be expected of me that I shall open up in this part of this book what David may have prophesied in the Psalms con-cerning the Lord Jesus Christ or His Church. But although I have already done so in one in-stance, I am prevented from doing as that ex-pectation seems to demand, rather by the abun-dance than the scarcity of matter. For the ne-cessity of shunning prolixity forbids my setting down all things; yet I fear lest if I select some I shall appear to many, who know these things, to have passed by the more necessary. Besides, the proof that is adduced ought to be supported by the context of the whole psalm, so that at least there may be nothing against it if everything does not support it; lest we should seem, after the fashion of the centos, to gather for the thing we wish, as it were, verses out of a grand poem, what shall be found to have been written not about it, but about some other and widely differ-ent thing. But ere this could be pointed out in each psalm, the whole of it must be expounded; and how great a work that would be, the vol-umes of others, as well as our own, in which we

have done it, show well enough. Let him then who will, or can, read these volumes, and he will find out how many and great things David, at once king and prophet, has prophesied concern-ing Christ and His Church, to wit, concerning the King and the city which He has built.

CHAP. 16. *Of the things pertaining to Christ and the Church, said either openly or tropically in the 45th Psalm*

For whatever direct and manifest prophetic utterances there may be about anything, it is necessary that those which are tropical should be mingled with them; which, chiefly on account of those of slower understanding, thrust upon the more learned the laborious task of clearing up and expounding them. Some of them, indeed, on the very first blush, as soon as they are spok-en, exhibit Christ and the Church, although some things in them that are less intelligible re-main to be expounded at leisure. We have an ex-ample of this in that same Book of Psalms: "My heart bubbled up a good matter: I utter my words to the king. My tongue is the pen of a scribe, writing swiftly. Thy form is beautiful be-yond the sons of men; grace is poured out in Thy lips: therefore God hath blessed Thee for evermore. Gird Thy sword about Thy thigh, O Most Mighty. With Thy goodliness and Thy beauty go forward, proceed prosperously, and reign, because of Thy truth, and meekness, and righteousness; and Thy right hand shall lead Thee forth wonderfully. Thy sharp arrows are most powerful: in the heart of the king's ene-mies. The people shall fall under Thee. Thy throne, O God, is for ever and ever: a rod of di-rection is the rod of Thy kingdom. Thou hast loved righteousness, and hast hated iniquity: therefore God, Thy God, hath anointed Thee with the oil of exultation above Thy fellows. Myrrh and drops, and cassia from Thy vest-ments, from the houses of ivory: out of which the daughters of kings have delighted Thee in Thine honour." [3] Who is there, no matter how slow, but must here recognize Christ whom we preach, and in whom we believe, if he hears that He is God, whose throne is for ever and ever, and that He is anointed by God, as God indeed anoints, not with a visible, but with a spiritual and intelligible chrism? For who is so untaught in this religion, or so deaf to its far and wide spread fame, as not to know that Christ is named from this chrism, that is, from this anointing? But when it is acknowledged that this King is Christ, let each one who is already

---

[1] Ps. 110. 1, quoted in Matt. 22. 44.
[2] I Kings, 13. 2; fulfilled II Kings, 23. 15–17.

[3] Ps. 45. 1–9.

subject to Him who reigns because of truth, meekness, and righteousness, inquire at his leisure into these other things that are here said tropically: how His form is beautiful beyond the sons of men, with a certain beauty that is the more to be loved and admired the less it is corporeal; and what His sword, arrows, and other things of that kind may be, which are set down, not properly, but tropically.

Then let him look upon His Church, joined to her so great Husband in spiritual marriage and divine love, of which it is said in these words whch follow, "The queen stood upon Thy right hand in gold-embroidered vestments, girded about with variety. Hearken, O daughter, and look, and incline thine ear; forget also thy people, and thy father's house. Because the King hath greatly desired thy beauty; for He is the Lord thy God. And the daughters of Tyre shall worship Him with gifts; the rich among the people shall entreat Thy face. The daughter of the King has all her glory within, in golden fringes, girded about with variety. The virgins shall be brought after her to the King: her neighbours shall be brought to Thee. They shall be brought with gladness and exultation: they shall be led into the temple of the King. Instead of thy fathers, sons shall be born to thee: thou shalt establish them as princes over all the earth. They shall be mindful of thy name in every generation and descent. Therefore shall the people acknowledge thee for evermore, even for ever and ever."[1] I do not think any one is so stupid as to believe that some poor woman is here praised and described, as the spouse, to wit, of Him to whom it is said, "Thy throne, O God, is for ever and ever: a rod of direction is the rod of Thy kingdom. Thou hast loved righteousness and hated iniquity: therefore God, Thy God, hath anointed Thee with the oil of exultation above Thy fellows";[2] that is, plainly, Christ above Christians. For these are His fellows, out of the unity and concord of whom in all nations that queen is formed, as it is said of her in another psalm, "The city of the great King."[3] The same is Sion spiritually, which name in Latin is interpreted *speculatio* (discovery); for she descries the great good of the world to come, because her attention is directed thither. In the same way she is also Jerusalem spiritually, of which we have already said many things. Her enemy is the city of the devil, Babylon, which is interpreted "confusion." Yet out of this Babylon this queen is in all nations set free by regeneration, and passes from the worst to the best King—that is,

from the devil to Christ. Wherefore it is said to her, "Forget thy people and thy father's house." Of this impious city those also are a portion who are Israelites only in the flesh and not by faith, enemies also of this great King Himself and of His queen. For Christ, having come to them, and been slain by them, has the more become the King of others, whom He did not see in the flesh. Whence our King Himself says through the prophecy of a certain psalm, "Thou wilt deliver me from the contradictions of the people; Thou wilt make me head of the nations. A people whom I have not known hath served me: in the hearing of the ear it hath obeyed me."[4] Therefore this people of the nations, which Christ did not know in His bodily presence, yet has believed in that Christ as announced to it; so that it might be said of it with good reason, "In the hearing of the ear it hath obeyed me," for "faith is by hearing."[5] This people, I say, added to those who are the true Israelites both by the flesh and by faith, is the city of God, which has brought forth Christ Himself according to the flesh, since He was in these Israelites only. For thence came the Virgin Mary, in whom Christ assumed flesh that He might be man. Of which city another psalm says, "Mother Sion, shall a man say, and the man is made in her, and the Highest Himself hath founded her."[6] Who is this Highest, save God? And thus Christ, who is God, before He became man through Mary in that city, Himself founded it by the patriarchs and prophets. As therefore was said by prophecy so long before to this queen, the city of God, what we already can see fulfilled, "Instead of thy fathers, sons are born to thee; thou shalt make them princes over all the earth";[7] so out of her sons truly are set up even her fathers through all the earth, when the people, coming together to her, confess to her with the confession of eternal praise for ever and ever. Beyond doubt, whatever interpretation is put on what is here expressed somewhat darkly in figurative language ought to be in agreement with these most manifest things.

CHAP. 17. *Of those things in the 110th Psalm which relate to the priesthood of Christ, and in the 22d to his passion*

Just as in that psalm also where Christ is most openly proclaimed as Priest, even as He is here as King, "The Lord said unto my Lord, Sit Thou at my right hand, until I make Thine enemies Thy footstool."[8] That Christ sits on the right

[1]Ps. 45. 9–17.　　[2]Ps. 45. 7.　　[3]Ps. 48. 2.

[4]Ps. 18. 43.　　[5]Rom. 10. 5.　　[6]Ps. 87. 5.
[7]Ps. 45. 16.　　[8]Ps. 110. 1.

hand of God the Father is believed, not seen; that His enemies also are put under His feet doth not yet appear; it is being done, it will appear at last: yea, this is now believed, afterward it shall be seen. But what follows, "The Lord will send forth the rod of Thy strength out of Sion, and rule Thou in the midst of Thine enemies,"[1] is so clear that to deny it would imply not merely unbelief and mistake, but downright impudence. And even enemies must certainly confess that out of Sion has been sent the law of Christ which we call the gospel and acknowledge as the rod of His strength. But that He rules in the midst of His enemies, these same enemies among whom He rules themselves bear witness, gnashing their teeth and consuming away, and having power to do nothing against Him. Then what he says a little after, "The Lord hath sworn and will not repent,"[2] by which words He intimates that what He adds is immutable, "Thou art a priest for ever after the order of Melchizedek,"[3] who is permitted to doubt of whom these things are said, seeing that now there is nowhere a priesthood and sacrifice after the order of Aaron, and everywhere men offer under Christ as the Priest, which Melchizedek showed when he blessed Abraham? Therefore to these manifest things are to be referred, when rightly understood, those things in the same psalm that are set down a little more obscurely, and we have already made known in our popular sermons how these things are to be rightly understood. So also in that where Christ utters through prophecy the humiliation of His passion, saying, "They pierced my hands and feet; they counted all my bones. Yea, they looked and stared at me."[4] By which words he certainly meant His body stretched out on the cross, with the hands and feet pierced and perforated by the striking through of the nails, and that He had in that way made Himself a spectacle to those who looked and stared. And he adds, "They parted my garments among them, and over my vesture they cast lots."[5] How this prophecy has been fulfilled the Gospel history narrates. Then, indeed, the other things also which are said there less openly are rightly understood when they agree with those which shine with so great clearness; especially because those things also which we do not believe as past, but survey as present, are beheld by the whole world, being now exhibited just as they are read of in this very psalm as predicted so long before. For it is there said a little after, "All the ends of

the earth shall remember, and turn unto the Lord, and all the kindreds of the nations shall worship before Him; for the kingdom is the Lord's, and He shall rule the nations."

CHAP. 18. *Of the 3d, 41st, 16th, and 68th Psalms, in which the death and resurrection of the Lord are prophesied*

About His resurrection also the oracles of the Psalms are by no means silent. For what else is it that is sung in His person in the 3d Psalm, "I laid me down and took a sleep, and I awaked, for the Lord shall sustain me"?[6] Is there perchance any one so stupid as to believe that the prophet chose to point it out to us as something great that He had slept and risen up, unless that sleep had been death, and that awaking the resurrection, which behoved to be thus prophesied concerning Christ? For in the 41st Psalm also it is shown much more clearly, where in the person of the Mediator, in the usual way, things are narrated as if past which were prophesied as yet to come, since these things which were yet to come were in the predestination and foreknowledge of God as if they were done, because they were certain. He says, "Mine enemies speak evil of me; When shall he die, and his name perish? And if he came in to see me, his heart spake vain things: he gathered iniquity to himself. He went out of doors, and uttered it all at once. Against me all mine enemies whisper together: against me do they devise evil. They have planned an unjust thing against me. Shall not he that sleeps also rise again?"[7] These words are certainly so set down here that he may be understood to say nothing else than if he said, "Shall not He that died recover life again?" The previous words clearly show that His enemies have meditated and planned His death, and that this was executed by him who came in to see, and went out to betray. But to whom does not Judas here occur, who, from being His disciple, became His betrayer? Therefore because they were about to do what they had plotted—that is, were about to kill Him—he, to show them that with useless malice they were about to kill Him Who should rise again, so adds this verse, as if he said, "What vain thing are you doing? What will be your crime will be my sleep." "Shall not He that sleeps also rise again?" And yet he indicates in the following verses that they should not commit so great an impiety with impunity, saying, "Yea, the man of my peace in whom I trusted, who ate my bread, hath enlarged the heel over me";[8] that is, hath trampled me under foot.

[1]Ps. 110. 2.   [2]Ps. 110. 4.   [3]*Ibid.*
[4]Ps. 22. 16, 17.   [5]Ps. 22. 18, 19.

[6]Ps. 3. 5.   [7]Ps. 41. 5–8.   [8]Ps. 41. 9.

"But Thou," he saith, "O Lord, be merciful unto me, and raise me up, that I may requite them."[1] Who can now deny this who sees the Jews, after the passion and resurrection of Christ, utterly rooted up from their abodes by warlike slaughter and destruction? For, being slain by them, He has risen again, and has requited them meanwhile by temporary discipline, save that for those who are not corrected He keeps it in store for the time when He shall judge the quick and the dead.[2] For the Lord Jesus Himself, in pointing out that very man to the apostles as His betrayer, quoted this very verse of this psalm and said it was fulfilled in Himself: "He that ate my bread enlarged the heel over me." But what he says, "In whom I trusted," does not suit the head but the body. For the Saviour Himself was not ignorant of him concerning whom He had already said before, "One of you is a devil."[3] But He is wont to assume the person of His members, and to ascribe to Himself what should be said of them, because the head and the body is one Christ;[4] whence that saying in the Gospel, "I was an hungered, and ye gave me to eat."[5] Expounding which He says, "Since ye did it to one of the least of mine, ye did it to me."[6] Therefore He said that He had trusted, because his disciples then had trusted concerning Judas; for he was numbered with the apostles.[7]

But the Jews do not expect that the Christ whom they expect will die; therefore they do not think ours to be Him Whom the law and the prophets announced, but feign to themselves I know not whom of their own, exempt from the suffering of death. Therefore, with wonderful emptiness and blindness, they contend that the words we have set down signify, not death and resurrection, but sleep and awaking again. But the 16th Psalm also cries to them, "Therefore my heart is jocund, and my tongue hath exulted; moreover, my flesh also shall rest in hope: for Thou wilt not leave my soul in hell; neither wilt Thou give Thine Holy One to see corruption."[8] Who but He that rose again the third day could say His flesh had rested in this hope; that His soul, not being left in hell, but speedily returning to it, should revive it, that it should not be corrupted as corpses are wont to be, which they can in no wise say of David the prophet and king? The 68th Psalm also cries out, "Our God is the God of salvation: even of the Lord the exit was by death."[9] What could be more openly said? For the God of salvation is the Lord Jesus, which is interpreted *Saviour,* or *Healing One.* For this reason this name was given, when it was said before He was born of the virgin: "Thou shalt bring forth a Son, and shalt call His name Jesus; for He shall save His people from their sins."[10] Because His blood was shed for the remission of their sins, it behoved Him to have no other exit from this life than death. Therefore, when it had been said, "Our God is the God of salvation," immediately it was added, "Even of the Lord the exit was by death," in order to show that we were to be saved by His dying. But that saying is marvellous, "Even of the Lord," as if it was said, Such is that life of mortals, that not even the Lord Himself could go out of it otherwise save through death.

CHAP. 19. *Of the 69th Psalm, in which the obstinate unbelief of the Jews is declared*

But when the Jews will not in the least yield to the testimonies of this prophecy, which are so manifest, and are also brought by events to so clear and certain a completion, certainly that is fulfilled in them which is written in that psalm which here follows. For when the things which pertain to His passion are prophetically spoken there also in the person of Christ, that is mentioned which is unfolded in the Gospel: "They gave me gall for my meat; and in my thirst they gave me vinegar for drink."[11] And as it were after such a feast and dainties in this way given to Himself, presently He brings in: "Let their table become a trap before them, and a retribution, and an offence: let their eyes be dimmed that they see not, and their back be always bowed down,"[12] etc. Which things are not spoken as wished for, but are predicted under the prophetic form of wishing. What wonder, then, if those whose eyes are dimmed that they see not do not see these manifest things? What wonder if those do not look up at heavenly things whose back is always bowed down that they may grovel among earthly things? For these words transferred from the body signify mental faults. Let these things which have been said about the Psalms, that is, about king David's prophecy, suffice, that we may keep within some bound. But let those readers excuse us who knew them all before; and let them not complain about those perhaps stronger proofs which they know or think I have passed by.

---

[1] Ps. 41. 10. [2] II Tim. 4. 1; II Pet. 4. 5.
[3] John, 6. 70. [4] I Cor. 12. 12. [5] Matt. 25. 35.
[6] Matt. 25. 40. [7] Acts, 1. 17. [8] Ps. 16. 9, 10.

[9] Ps. 68. 20. [10] Matt. 1. 21.
[11] Ps. 69. 21; Matt. 27. 34, 48. [12] Ps. 69. 22, 23.

CHAP. 20. *Of David's reign and merit; and of his son Solomon, and that prophecy relating to Christ which is found either in those books which are joined to those written by him, or in those which are indubitably his*

David therefore reigned in the earthly Jerusalem, a son of the heavenly Jerusalem, much praised by the divine testimony; for even his faults are overcome by great piety, through the most salutary humility of his repentance, that he is altogether one of those of whom he himself says, "Blessed are they whose iniquities are forgiven and whose sins are covered." [1] After him Solomon his son reigned over the same whole people, who, as was said before, began to reign while his father was still alive. This man, after good beginnings, made a bad end. For indeed "prosperity, which wears out the minds of the wise," hurt him more than that wisdom profited him, which even yet is and shall hereafter be renowned, and was then praised far and wide. He also is found to have prophesied in his books, of which three are received as of canonical authority, Proverbs, Ecclesiastes, and the Song of Songs. But it has been customary to ascribe to Solomon other two, of which one is called Wisdom, the other Ecclesiasticus, on account of some resemblance of style—but the more learned have no doubt that they are not his; yet of old the Church, especially the Western, received them into authority—in the one of which, called the Wisdom of Solomon, the passion of Christ is most openly prophesied. For indeed His impious murderers are quoted as saying, "Let us lie in wait for the righteous, for he is unpleasant to us, and contrary to our works; and he upbraideth us with our transgressions of the law, and objecteth to our disgrace the transgressions of our education. He professeth to have the knowledge of God, and he calleth himself the Son of God. He was made to reprove our thoughts. He is grievous for us even to behold; for his life is unlike other men's, and his ways are different. We are esteemed of him as counterfeits; and he abstaineth from our ways as from filthiness. He extols the latter end of the righteous; and glorieth that he hath God for his Father. Let us see, therefore, if his words be true; and let us try what shall happen to him, and we shall know what shall be the end of him. For if the righteous be the Son of God, He will undertake for him, and deliver him out of the hand of those that are against him. Let us put

him to the question with contumely and torture, that we may know his reverence, and prove his patience. Let us condemn him to the most shameful death; for by His own sayings He shall be respected. These things did they imagine, and were mistaken; for their own malice hath quite blinded them." [2] But in Ecclesiasticus the future faith of the nations is predicted in this manner: "Have mercy upon us, O God, Ruler of all, and send Thy fear upon all the nations: lift up Thine hand over the strange nations, and let them see Thy power. As Thou wast sanctified in us before them, so be Thou sanctified in them before us, and let them acknowledge Thee, according as we also have acknowledged Thee; for there is not a God beside Thee, O Lord." [3] We see this prophecy in the form of a wish and prayer fulfilled through Jesus Christ. But the things which are not written in the canon of the Jews cannot be quoted against their contradictions with so great validity.

But as regards those three books which it is evident are Solomon's and held canonical by the Jews, to show what of this kind may be found in them pertaining to Christ and the Church demands a laborious discussion, which, if now entered on, would lengthen this work unduly. Yet what we read in the Proverbs of impious men saying, "Let us unrighteously hide in the earth the righteous man; yea, let us swallow him up alive as hell, and let us take away his memory from the earth: let us seize his precious possession," [4] is not so obscure that it may not be understood, without laborious exposition, of Christ and His possession the Church. Indeed, the Gospel parable about the wicked husbandmen shows that our Lord Jesus Himself said something like it: "This is the heir; come, let us kill him, and the inheritance shall be ours." [5] In like manner also that passage in this same book, on which we have already touched [6] when we were speaking of the barren woman who hath borne seven, must soon after it was uttered have come to be understood of only Christ and the Church by those who knew that Christ was the Wisdom of God. "Wisdom hath builded her an house, and hath set up seven pillars; she hath sacrificed her victims, she hath mingled her wine in the bowl; she hath also furnished her table. She hath sent her servants summoning to the bowl with excellent proclamation, saying, Who is simple, let him turn aside to me. And to the void of sense she hath said, Come, eat of my bread, and drink of

[1] Ps. 32. 1.

[2] Wisd. 2. 12–21.   [3] Ecclus. 36. 1–5.
[4] Prov. 1. 11–13.   [5] Matt. 21. 38.   [6] Chap. 4.

the wine which I have mingled for you."[1] Here certainly we perceive that the Wisdom of God, that is, the Word co-eternal with the Father, hath builded Him an house, even a human body in the virgin womb, and hath subjoined the Church to it as members to a head, hath slain the martyrs as victims, hath furnished a table with wine and bread, where appears also the priesthood after the order of Melchizedek, and hath called the simple and the void of sense, because, as saith the apostle, "He hath chosen the weak things of this world that He might confound the things which are mighty."[2] Yet to these weak ones she saith what follows, "Forsake simplicity, that ye may live; and seek prudence, that ye may have life."[3] But to be made partakers of this table is itself to begin to have life. For when he says in another book, which is called Ecclesiastes, "There is no good for a man, except that he should eat and drink,"[4] what can he be more credibly understood to say than what belongs to the participation of this table which the Mediator of the New Testament Himself, the Priest after the order of Melchizedek, furnishes with His own body and blood? For that sacrifice has succeeded all the sacrifices of the Old Testament, which were slain as a shadow of that which was to come; wherefore also we recognize the voice in the 40th Psalm as that of the same Mediator speaking through prophesy, "Sacrifice and offering Thou didst not desire; but a body hast Thou perfected for me."[5] Because, instead of all these sacrifices and oblations, His body is offered, and is served up to the partakers of it. For that this Ecclesiastes, in this sentence about eating and drinking, which he often repeats and very much commends, does not savour the dainties of carnal pleasures, is made plain enough when he says, "It is better to go into the house of mourning than to go into the house of feasting."[6] And a little after he says, "The heart of the wise is in the house of mourning, and the heart of the simple in the house of feasting."[7] But I think that more worthy of quotation from this book which relates to both cities, the one of the devil, the other of Christ, and to their kings, the devil and Christ: "Woe to thee, O land," he says, "when thy king is a youth, and thy princes eat in the morning! Blessed art thou, O land, when thy king is the son of nobles, and thy princes eat in season, in fortitude, and not in confusion!"[8] He has called the devil a youth, because of the folly and pride,

and rashness and unruliness, and other vices which are wont to abound at that age; but Christ is the Son of nobles, that is, of the holy patriarchs, of those belonging to the free city, of whom He was begotten in the flesh. The princes of that and other cities are eaters in the morning, that is, before the suitable hour, because they do not expect the seasonable felicity, which is the true, in the world to come, desiring to be speedily made happy with the renown of this world; but the princes of the city of Christ patiently wait for the time of a blessedness that is not fallacious. This is expressed by the words, "in fortitude, and not in confusion," because hope does not deceive them; of which the apostle says, "But hope maketh not ashamed."[9] A psalm also saith, "For they that hope in Thee shall not be put to shame."[10] But now the Song of Songs is a certain spiritual pleasure of holy minds, in the marriage of that King and Queen-city, that is, Christ and the Church. But this pleasure is wrapped up in allegorical veils, that the Bridegroom may be more ardently desired, and more joyfully unveiled, and may appear; to whom it is said in this same song, "Equity hath delighted Thee";[11] and the bride who there hears, "Charity is in thy delights."[12] We pass over many things in silence, in our desire to finish this work.

CHAP. 21. *Of the kings after Solomon, both in Judah and Israel*

The other kings of the Hebrews after Solomon are scarcely found to have prophesied, through certain enigmatic words or actions of theirs, what may pertain to Christ and the Church, either in Judah or Israel; for so were the parts of that people styled, when, on account of Solomon's offence, from the time of Rehoboam his son, who succeeded him in the kingdom, it was divided by God as a punishment. The ten tribes, indeed, which Jeroboam the servant of Solomon received, being appointed the king in Samaria, were distinctively called Israel, although this had been the name of that whole people; but the two tribes, namely, of Judah and Benjamin, which for David's sake, lest the kingdom should be wholly wrenched from his race, remained subject to the city of Jerusalem, were called Judah, because that was the tribe whence David sprang. But Benjamin, the other tribe which, as was said, belonged to the same kingdom, was that whence Saul sprang before David. But these two tribes together, as

---

[1]Prov. 9. 1-5.　　[2]I Cor. 1. 27.　　[3]Prov. 9. 6.
[4]Eccles. 2. 24; 3. 13; 5. 18; 8. 15.　　[5]Ps. 40. 6.
[6]Eccles. 7. 2　　[7]Eccles. 7. 4.　　[8]Eccles. 10. 16, 17.

[9]Rom. 5. 5.　　[10]Ps. 69. 6.?　　[11]Song of Sol. 1. 4.
[12]Song of Sol. 7. 6.

was said, were called Judah, and were distinguished by this name from Israel, which was the distinctive title of the ten tribes under their own king. For the tribe of Levi, because it was the priestly one, bound to the servitude of God, not of the kings, was reckoned the thirteenth. For Joseph, one of the twelve sons of Israel, did not, like the others, form one tribe, but two, Ephraim and Manasseh. Yet the tribe of Levi also belonged more to the kingdom of Jerusalem, where was the temple of God Whom it served. On the division of the people, therefore, Rehoboam, son of Solomon, reigned in Jerusalem as the first king of Judah, and Jeroboam, servant of Solomon, in Samaria as king of Israel. And when Rehoboam wished as a tyrant to pursue that separated part with war, the people were prohibited from fighting with their brethren by God, who told them through a prophet that He had done this; whence it appeared that in this matter there had been no sin either of the king or people of Israel, but the accomplished will of God the avenger. When this was known, both parts settled down peaceably, for the division made was not religious but political.

CHAP. 22. *Of Jeroboam, who profaned the people put under him by the impiety of idolatry, amid which, however, God did not cease to inspire the prophets, and to guard many from the crime of idolatry*

But Jeroboam king of Israel, with perverse mind, not believing in God, whom he had proved true in promising and giving him the kingdom, was afraid lest, by coming to the temple of God which was in Jerusalem, where, according to the divine law, that whole nation was to come in order to sacrifice, the people should be seduced from him and return to David's line as the seed royal; and set up idolatry in his kingdom, and with horrible impiety beguiled the people, ensnaring them to the worship of idols with himself. Yet God did not altogether cease to reprove by the prophets, not only that king, but also his successors and imitators in his impiety, and the people too. For there the great and illustrious prophet Elijah and Elisha his disciple arose, who also did many wonderful works. Even there, when Elijah said, "O Lord, they have slain Thy prophets, and they have digged down Thine altars; and I am left alone, and they seek my life," it was answered that seven thousand men were there who had not bowed the knee to Baal.[1]

[1] I Kings, 19. 10, 14, 15.

CHAP. 23. *Of the varying condition of both the Hebrew kingdoms, until the people of both were at different times led into captivity, Judah being afterwards recalled into his kingdom, which finally passed into the power of the Romans*

So also in the kingdom of Judah pertaining to Jerusalem prophets were not lacking even in the times of succeeding kings, just as it pleased God to send them, either for the prediction of what was needful, or for correction of sin and instruction in righteousness;[2] for there, too, although far less than in Israel, kings arose who grievously offended God by their impieties, and, along with their people, who were like them, were smitten with moderate scourges. The no small merits of the pious kings there are praised indeed. But we read that in Israel the kings were, some more, others less, yet all wicked. Each part, therefore, as the divine providence either ordered or permitted, was both lifted up by prosperity and weighed down by adversity of various kinds; and it was afflicted not only by foreign, but also by civil wars with each other, in order that by certain existing causes the mercy or anger of God might be manifested; until, by His growing indignation, that whole nation was by the conquering Chaldeans not only overthrown in its abode, but also for the most part transported to the lands of the Assyrians—first, that part of the thirteen tribes called Israel, but afterwards Judah also, when Jerusalem and that most noble temple was cast down—in which lands it rested seventy years in captivity. Being after that time sent forth thence, they rebuilt the overthrown temple. And although very many stayed in the lands of the strangers, yet the kingdom no longer had two separate parts, with different kings over each, but in Jerusalem there was one prince over them; and at certain times, from every direction wherever they were, and from whatever place they could, they all came to the temple of God which was there. Yet not even then were they without foreign enemies and conquerors; yea, Christ found them tributaries of the Romans.

CHAP. 24. *Of the prophets, who either were the last among the Jews, or whom the Gospel history reports about the time of Christ's nativity*

But in that whole time after they returned from Babylon, after Malachi, Haggai, and Zechariah, who then prophesied, and Ezra, they

[2] II Tim. 3. 16.

had no prophets down to the time of the Saviour's advent except another Zechariah, the father of John, and Elisabeth his wife, when the nativity of Christ was already close at hand; and when He was already born, Simeon the aged, and Anna a widow, and now very old; and, last of all, John himself, who, being a young man, did not predict that Christ, now a young man, was to come, but by prophetic knowledge pointed Him out although unknown; for which reason the Lord Himself says, "The law and the prophets were until John." [1] But the prophesying of these five is made known to us in the gospel, where the virgin mother of our Lord herself is also found to have prophesied before John. But this prophecy of theirs the wicked Jews do not

[1] Matt. ii. 13.

receive; but those innumerable persons received it who from them believed the gospel. For then truly Israel was divided in two, by that division which was foretold by Samuel the prophet to king Saul as immutable. But even the reprobate Jews hold Malachi, Haggai, Zechariah, and Ezra as the last received into canonical authority. For there are also writings of these, as of others, who being but a very few in the great multitude of prophets, have written those books which have obtained canonical authority, of whose predictions it seems good to me to put in this work some which pertain to Christ and His Church; and this, by the Lord's help, shall be done more conveniently in the following book, that we may not further burden this one, which is already too long.

BOOK XVIII

ARGUMENT. AUGUSTINE TRACES THE PARALLEL COURSES OF THE EARTHLY AND HEAVENLY CITIES FROM THE TIME OF ABRAHAM TO THE END OF THE WORLD; AND ALLUDES TO THE ORACLES REGARDING CHRIST, BOTH THOSE UTTERED BY THE SIBYLS, AND THOSE OF THE SACRED PROPHETS WHO WROTE AFTER THE FOUNDATION OF ROME, HOSEA, AMOS, ISAIAH, MICAH, AND THEIR SUCCESSORS.

CHAP. 1. *Of those things down to the times of the Saviour which have been discussed in the seventeen books*

I PROMISED to write of the rise, progress, and appointed end of the two cities, one of which is God's, the other this world's, in which, so far as mankind is concerned, the former is now a stranger. But first of all I undertook, so far as His grace should enable me, to refute the enemies of the city of God, who prefer their gods to Christ its founder, and fiercely hate Christians with the most deadly malice. And this I have done in the first ten books. Then, as regards my three-fold promise which I have just mentioned, I have treated distinctly, in the four books which follow the tenth, of the rise of both cities. After that, I have proceeded from the first man down to the flood in one book, which is the fifteenth of this work; and from that again down to Abraham our work has followed both in chronological order. From the patriarch Abraham down to the time of the Israelite kings, at which we close our sixteenth book, and thence down to the advent of Christ Himself in the flesh, to which period the seventeenth book reaches, the City of God appears from my way of writing to have run its course alone; whereas it did not run its course alone in this age, for both

cities, in their course amid mankind, certainly experienced chequered times together just as from the beginning. But I did this in order that, first of all, from the time when the promises of God began to be more clear, down to the virgin birth of Him in Whom those things promised from the first were to be fulfilled, the course of that city which is God's might be made more distinctly apparent, without interpolation of foreign matter from the history of the other city, although down to the revelation of the new covenant it ran its course, not in light, but in shadow. Now, therefore, I think fit to do what I passed by, and show, so far as seems necessary, how that other city ran its course from the times of Abraham, so that attentive readers may compare the two.

CHAP. 2. *Of the kings and times of the earthly city which were synchronous with the times of the saints, reckoning from the rise of Abraham*

The society of mortals spread abroad through the earth everywhere, and in the most diverse places, although bound together by a certain fellowship of our common nature, is yet for the most part divided against itself, and the strongest oppress the others, because all follow after their own interests and lusts, while what is longed for either suffices for none, or not for all, because it is not the very thing. For the vanquished succumb to the victorious, preferring any sort of peace and safety to freedom itself; so that they who chose to die rather than be slaves have been greatly wondered at. For in almost all nations the very voice of nature somehow proclaims, that those who happen to be conquered should choose rather to be subject to their conquerors than to be killed by all kinds of warlike destruction. This does not take place without the providence of God, in whose power it lies that any one either subdues or is subdued in war; that some are endowed with kingdoms, others made subject to kings. Now, among the very many kingdoms of the earth into which, by earthly interests or lust, society is divided (which we call by the general name of the city of this world), we see that two, settled and kept distinct from each other both in time and place, have grown far more famous than the rest, first that of the Assyrians, then that of the Romans. First came the one then the other. The former arose in the east, and, immediately on its close, the latter in the west. I may speak of other kingdoms and other kings as appendages of these.

Ninus, then, who succeeded his father Belus, the first king of Assyria, was already the second king of that kingdom when Abraham was born in the land of the Chaldees. There was also at that time a very small kingdom of Sicyon, with which, as from an ancient date, that most universally learned man Marcus Varro begins, in writing of the Roman race. For from these kings of Sicyon he passes to the Athenians, from them to the Latins, and from these to the Romans. Yet very little is related about these kingdoms, before the foundation of Rome, in comparison with that of Assyria. For although even Sallust, the Roman historian, admits that the Athenians were very famous in Greece, yet he thinks they were greater in fame than in fact. For in speaking of them he says, "The deeds of the Athenians, as I think, were very great and magnificent, but yet somewhat less than reported by fame. But because writers of great genius arose among them, the deeds of the Athenians were celebrated throughout the world as very great. Thus the virtue of those who did them was held to be as great as men of transcendent genius could represent it to be by the power of laudatory words." This city also derived no small glory from literature and philosophy, the study of which chiefly flourished there. But as regards empire, none in the earliest times was greater than the Assyrian, or so widely extended. For when Ninus the son of Belus was king, he is reported to have subdued the whole of Asia, even to the boundaries of Libya, which as to number is called the third part, but as to size is found to be the half of the whole world. The Indians in the eastern regions were the only people over whom he did not reign; but after his death Semiramis his wife made war on them. Thus it came to pass that all the people and kings in those countries were subject to the kingdom and authority of the Assyrians and did whatever they were commanded. Now Abraham was born in that kingdom among the Chaldees, in the time of Ninus. But since Grecian affairs are much better known to us than Assyrian, and those who have diligently investigated the antiquity of the Roman nation's origin have followed the order of time through the Greeks to the Latins, and from them to the Romans, who themselves are Latins, we ought on this account, where it is needful, to mention the Assyrian kings, that it may appear how Babylon, like a first Rome, ran its course along with the city of God, which is a stranger in this world. But the things proper for insertion in this work in comparing the two cities, that is, the earthly and heavenly, ought to be taken mostly from the Greek and Latin kingdoms, where Rome herself is like a second Babylon.

At Abraham's birth, then, the second kings of Assyria and Sicyon respectively were Ninus and Europs, the first having been Belus and Ægialeus. But when God promised Abraham, on his departure from Babylonia, that he should become a great nation, and that in his seed all nations of the earth should be blessed, the Assyrians had their seventh king, the Sicyons their fifth; for the son of Ninus reigned among them after his mother Semiramis, who is said to have been put to death by him for attempting to defile him by incestuously lying with him. Some think that she founded Babylon, and indeed she may have founded it anew. But we have told, in the sixteenth book, when or by whom it was founded. Now the son of Ninus and Semiramis, who succeeded his mother in the kingdom, is also called Ninus by some, but by others Ninias, a patronymic word. Telexion then held the kingdom of the Sicyons. In his reign times were quiet and joyful to such a degree that after his death they worshipped him as a god by offering sacrifices and by celebrating games, which are said to have been first instituted on this occasion.

CHAP. 3. *What kings reigned in Assyria and Sicyon when, according to the promise, Isaac was born to Abraham in his hundredth year, and when the twins Esau and Jacob were born of Rebecca to Isaac in his sixtieth year*

In his times also, by the promise of God, Isaac, the son of Abraham, was born to his father when he was a hundred years old, of Sarah his wife, who, being barren and old, had already lost hope of issue. Aralius was then the fifth king of the Assyrians. To Isaac himself, in his sixtieth year, were born twin-sons, Esau and Jacob, whom Rebecca his wife bore to him, their grandfather Abraham, who died on completing a hundred and seventy years, being still alive and reckoning his hundred and sixtieth year.[1] At that time there reigned as the seventh kings— among the Assyrians, that more ancient Xerxes, who was also called Balæus; and among the Sicyons, Thuriachus, or, as some write his name, Thurimachus. The kingdom of Argos, in which Inachus reigned first, arose in the time of Abraham's grandchildren. And I must not omit what Varro relates, that the Sicyons were also wont to sacrifice at the tomb of their seventh king Thuriachus. In the reign of Armamitres in Assyria and Leucippus in Sicyon as the eighth kings, and of Inachus as the first in Argos, God spoke to Isaac, and promised the same two things to him as to his father—namely, the land of Canaan to his seed and the blessing of all nations in his seed. These same things were promised to his son, Abraham's grandson, who was at first called Jacob, afterwards Israel, when Belocus was the ninth king of Assyria, and Phoroneus, the son of Inachus, reigned as the second king of Argos, Leucippus still continuing king of Sicyon. In those times, under the Argive king Phoroneus, Greece was made more famous by the institution of certain laws and judges. On the death of Phoroneus, his younger brother Phegous built a temple at his tomb, in which he was worshipped as God, and oxen were sacrificed to him. I believe they thought him worthy of so great honour, because in his part of the kingdom (for their father had divided his territories between them, in which they reigned during his life) he had founded chapels for the worship of the gods, and had taught them to measure time by months and years and to that extent to keep count and reckoning of events. Men still uncultivated, admiring him for these novelties, either fancied he was, or resolved that he should be

[1]In the Hebrew text, Gen. 25. 7, a hundred and seventy-five years.

made, a god after his death. Io also is said to have been the daughter of Inachus, who was afterwards called Isis, when she was worshipped in Egypt as a great goddess; although others write that she came as a queen out of Ethiopia, and because she ruled extensively and justly, and instituted for her subjects letters and many useful things, such divine honour was given her there after she died that, if any one said she had been human, he was charged with a capital crime.

CHAP. 4. *Of the times of Jacob and his son Joseph*

In the reign of Balæus, the ninth king of Assyria, and Mesappus, the eighth of Sicyon, who is said by some to have been also called Cephisos (if indeed the same man had both names, and those who put the other name in their writings have not rather confounded him with another man), while Apis was third king of Argos, Isaac died, a hundred and eighty years old, and left his twin-sons a hundred and twenty years old. Jacob, the younger of these, belonged to the city of God about which we write (the elder being wholly rejected) and had twelve sons, one of whom, called Joseph, was sold by his brothers to merchants going down to Egypt, while his grandfather Isaac was still alive. But when he was thirty years of age, Joseph stood before Pharaoh, being exalted out of the humiliation he endured, because, in divinely interpreting the king's dreams, he foretold that there would be seven years of plenty, the very rich abundance of which would be consumed by seven other years of famine that should follow. On this account the king made him ruler over Egypt, liberating him from prison, into which he had been thrown for keeping his chastity intact; for he bravely preserved it from his mistress, who wickedly loved him, and told lies to his weakly credulous master, and did not consent to commit adultery with her, but fled from her, leaving his garment in her hands when she laid hold of him. In the second of the seven years of famine Jacob came down into Egypt to his son with all he had, being a hundred and thirty years old, as he himself said in answer to the king's question. Joseph was then thirty-nine, if we add seven years of plenty and two of famine to the thirty he reckoned when honoured by the king.

CHAP. 5. *Of Apis king of Argos, whom the Egyptians called Serapis, and worshipped with divine honours*

In these times Apis king of Argos crossed over into Egypt in ships and, on dying there, was made Serapis, the chief god of all the Egyptians. Now Varro gives this very ready reason why, after his death, he was called, not Apis, but Serapis. The ark in which he was placed when dead, which every one now calls a sarcophagus, was then called in Greek σορο’ς, and they began to worship him when buried in it before his temple was built; and from Soros and Apis he was called first Sorapis, and then Serapis, by changing a letter, as easily happens. It was decreed regarding him also, that whoever should say he had been a man should be capitally punished. And since in every temple where Isis and Serapis were worshipped there was also an image which, with finger pressed on the lips, seemed to warn men to keep silence, Varro thinks this signifies that it should be kept secret that they had been human. But that bull which, with wonderful folly, deluded Egypt nourished with abundant delicacies in honour of him, was not called Serapis, but Apis, because they worshipped him alive without a sarcophagus. On the death of that bull, when they sought and found a calf of the same colour—that is, similarly marked with certain white spots—they believed it was something miraculous, and divinely provided for them. Yet it was no great thing for the demons, in order to deceive them, to show to a cow when she was conceiving and pregnant the image of such a bull, which she alone could see, and by it attract the breeding passion of the mother, so that it might appear in a bodily shape in her young, just as Jacob so managed with the spotted rods that the sheep and goats were born spotted. For what men can do with real colours and substances, the demons can very easily do by showing unreal forms to breeding animals.

CHAP. 6. *Who were kings of Argos, and of Assyria, when Jacob died in Egypt*

Apis, then, who died in Egypt, was not the king of Egypt, but of Argos. He was succeeded by his son Argus, from whose name the land was called Argos and the people Argives, for under the earlier kings neither the place nor the nation as yet had this name. While he then reigned over Argos, and Eratus over Sicyon, and Balæus still remained king of Assyria, Jacob died in Egypt a hundred and forty-seven years old, after he had, when dying, blessed his sons and his grandsons by Joseph, and prophesied most plainly of Christ, saying in the blessing of Judah, "A prince shall not fail out of Judah, nor a leader from his thighs, until those things come which are laid up for him; and He is the expectation of the nations."[1] In the reign of Argus, Greece began to use fruits, and to have crops of corn in cultivated fields, the seed having been brought from other countries. Argus also began to be accounted a god after his death, and was honoured with a temple and sacrifices. This honour was conferred in his reign, before being given to him, on a private individual for being the first to yoke oxen in the plough. This was one Homogyrus, who was struck by lightning.

CHAP. 7. *Who were kings when Joseph died in Egypt*

In the reign of Mamitus, the twelfth king of Assyria, and Plemnæus, the eleventh of Sicyon, while Argus still reigned over the Argives, Joseph died in Egypt a hundred and ten years old. After his death, the people of God, increasing wonderfully, remained in Egypt a hundred and forty-five years, in tranquillity at first, until those who knew Joseph were dead. Afterward, through envy of their increase and the suspicion that they would at length gain their freedom, they were oppressed with persecutions and the labours of intolerable servitude, amid which, however, they still grew, being multiplied with God-given fertility. During this period the same kingdoms continued in Assyria and Greece.

CHAP. 8. *Who were kings when Moses was born, and what gods began to be worshipped then*

When Saphrus reigned as the fourteenth king of Assyria, and Orthopolis as the twelfth of Sicyon, and Criasus as the fifth of Argos, Moses was born in Egypt, by whom the people of God were liberated from the Egyptian slavery, in which they behoved to be thus tried that they might desire the help of their Creator. Some have thought that Prometheus lived during the reign of the kings now named. He is reported to have formed men out of clay, because he was esteemed the best teacher of wisdom; yet it does not appear what wise men there were in his days. His brother Atlas is said to have been a great astrologer; and this gave occasion for the fable that he held up the sky, although the vulgar opinion about his holding up the sky appears rather to have been suggested by a high mountain named after him. Indeed, from those times many other fabulous things began to be invented in Greece; yet, down to Cecrops king of Athens, in whose reign that city received its name, and in whose reign God brought His people out of Egypt by Moses, only a few dead heroes are reported to have been deified according to the

[1] Gen. 49. 10.

vain superstition of the Greeks. Among these were Melantomice, the wife of king Criasus, and Phorbas their son, who succeeded his father as sixth king of the Argives, and Iasus, son of Triopas, their seventh king, and their ninth king, Sthenelas, or Stheneleus, or Sthenelus—for his name is given differently by different authors. In those times also, Mercury, the grandson of Atlas by his daughter Maia, is said to have lived, according to the common report in books. He was famous for his skill in many arts, and taught them to men, for which they resolved to make him, and even believed that he deserved to be, a god after death. Hercules is said to have been later, yet belonging to the same period; although some, whom I think mistaken, assign him an earlier date than Mercury. But at whatever time they were born, it is agreed among grave historians, who have committed these ancient things to writing, that both were men, and that they merited divine honours from mortals because they conferred on them many benefits to make this life more pleasant to them. Minerva was far more ancient than these; for she is reported to have appeared in virgin age in the times of Ogyges at the lake called Triton, from which she is also styled Tritonia, the inventress truly of many works and the more readily believed to be a goddess because her origin was so little known. For what is sung about her having sprung from the head of Jupiter belongs to the region of poetry and fable, and not to that of history and real fact. And historical writers are not agreed when Ogyges flourished, in whose time also a great flood occurred—not that greatest one from which no man escaped except those who could get into the ark, for neither Greek nor Latin history knew of it, yet a greater flood than that which happened afterward in Deucalion's time. For Varro begins the book I have already mentioned at this date, and does not propose to himself, as the starting-point from which he may arrive at Roman affairs, anything more ancient than the flood of Ogyges, that is, which happened in the time of Ogyges. Now our writers of chronicles—first Eusebius, and afterwards Jerome, who entirely follow some earlier historians in this opinion—relate that the flood of Ogyges happened more than three hundred years after, during the reign of Phoroneus, the second king of Argos. But whenever he may have lived, Minerva was already worshipped as a goddess when Cecrops reigned in Athens, in whose reign the city itself is reported to have been rebuilt or founded.

CHAP. 9. *When the city of Athens was founded, and what reason Varro assigns for its name*

Athens certainly derived its name from Minerva, who in Greek is called Ἀθήνη, and Varro points out the following reason why it was so called. When an olive-tree suddenly appeared there, and water burst forth in another place, these prodigies moved the king to send to the Delphic Apollo to inquire what they meant and what he should do. He answered that the olive signified Minerva, the water Neptune, and that the citizens had it in their power to name their city as they chose, after either of these two gods whose signs these were. On receiving this oracle, Cecrops convoked all the citizens of either sex to give their vote, for it was then the custom in those parts for the women also to take part in public deliberations. When the multitude was consulted, the men gave their votes for Neptune, the women for Minerva; and as the women had a majority of one, Minerva conquered. Then Neptune, being enraged, laid waste the lands of the Athenians, by casting up the waves of the sea; for the demons have no difficulty in scattering any waters more widely. The same authority said that to appease his wrath the women should be visited by the Athenians with the three-fold punishment—that they should no longer have any vote; that none of their children should be named after their mothers; and that no one should call them Athenians. Thus that city, the mother and nurse of liberal doctrines, and of so many and so great philosophers, than whom Greece had nothing more famous and noble, by the mockery of demons about the strife of their gods, a male and female, and from the victory of the female one through the women, received the name of Athens; and, on being damaged by the vanquished god, was compelled to punish the very victory of the victress, fearing the waters of Neptune more than the arms of Minerva. For in the women who were thus punished, Minerva, who had conquered, was conquered too, and could not even help her voters so far that, although the right of voting was henceforth lost and the mothers could not give their names to the children, they might at least be allowed to be called Athenians, and to merit the name of that goddess whom they had made victorious over a male god by giving her their votes. What and how much could be said about this, if we had not to hasten to other things in our discourse, is obvious.

CHAP. 10. *What Varro reports about the term Areopagus, and about Deucalion's flood*

Marcus Varro, however, is not willing to credit lying fables against the gods, lest he should find something dishonouring to their majesty; and therefore he will not admit that the Areopagus, the place where the Apostle Paul disputed with the Athenians, got this name because Mars, who in Greek is called 'Άρης, when he was charged with the crime of homicide and was judged by twelve gods in that field, was acquitted by the sentence of six; because it was the custom, when the votes were equal, to acquit rather than condemn. Against this opinion, which is much most widely published, he tries, from the notices of obscure books, to support another reason for this name, lest the Athenians should be thought to have called it Areopagus from the words "Mars" and "field,"[1] as if it were the field of Mars, to the dishonour of the gods, forsooth, from whom he thinks lawsuits and judgments far removed. And he asserts that this which is said about Mars is not less false than what is said about the three goddesses, to wit, Juno, Minerva, and Venus, whose contest for the palm of beauty, before Paris as judge, in order to obtain the golden apple, is not only related, but is celebrated in songs and dances amid the applause of the theatres, in plays meant to please the gods who take pleasure in these crimes of their own whether real or fabled. Varro does not believe these things, because they are incompatible with the nature of the gods and of morality; and yet, in giving not a fabulous but a historic reason for the name of Athens, he inserts in his books the strife between Neptune and Minerva as to whose name should be given to that city, which was so great that, when they contended by the display of prodigies, even Apollo dared not judge between them when consulted; but, in order to end the strife of the gods, just as Jupiter sent the three goddesses we have named to Paris, so he sent them to men, when Minerva won by the vote, and yet was defeated by the punishment of her own voters, for she was unable to confer the title of Athenians on the women who were her friends, although she could impose it on the men who were her opponents. In these times, when Cranaos reigned at Athens as the successor of Cecrops, as Varro writes, but, according to our Eusebius and Jerome, while Cecrops himself still remained, the flood occurred which is called Deucalion's, because it

occurred chiefly in those parts of the earth in which he reigned. But this flood did not at all reach Egypt or its vicinity.

CHAP. 11. *When Moses led the people out of Egypt; and who were kings when his successor Joshua the son of Nun died*

Moses led the people out of Egypt in the last time of Cecrops king of Athens, when Ascatades reigned in Assyria, Marathus in Sicyon, Triopas in Argos; and having led forth the people, he gave them at Mount Sinai the law he received from God, which is called the Old Testament, because it has earthly promises, and because, through Jesus Christ, there was to be a New Testament, in which the kingdom of heaven should be promised. For the same order behoved to be observed in this as is observed in each man who prospers in God, according to the saying of the apostle, "That is not first which is spiritual, but that which is natural," since, as he says, and that truly, "The first man of the earth, is earthly; the second man, from heaven, is heavenly."[2] Now Moses ruled the people for forty years in the wilderness and died a hundred and twenty years old, after he had prophesied of Christ by the types of carnal observances in the tabernacle, priesthood, and sacrifices, and many other mystic ordinances. Joshua the son of Nun succeeded Moses, and settled in the land of promise the people he had brought in, having by divine authority conquered the people by whom it was formerly possessed. He also died, after ruling the people twenty-seven years after the death of Moses, when Amyntas reigned in Assyria as the eighteenth king, Coracos as the sixteenth in Sicyon, Danaos as the tenth in Argos, Erichthonius as the fourth in Athens.

CHAP. 12. *Of the rituals of false gods instituted by the kings of Greece in the period from Israel's exodus from Egypt down to the death of Joshua the son of Nun*

During this period, that is, from Israel's exodus from Egypt down to the death of Joshua the son of Nun, through whom that people received the land of promise, rituals were instituted to the false gods by the kings of Greece, which, by stated celebration, recalled the memory of the flood, and of men's deliverance from it, and of that troublous life they then led in migrating to and fro between the heights and the plains. For even the Luperci, when they ascend and descend the sacred path, are said to represent the

[1] 'Άρης and πάγος.

[2] I Cor. 15. 46, 47.

men who sought the mountain summits because of the inundation of water, and returned to the lowlands on its subsidence. In those times, Dionysus, who was also called Father Liber, and was esteemed a god after death, is said to have shown the vine to his host in Attica. Then the musical games were instituted for the Delphic Apollo, to appease his anger, through which they thought the regions of Greece were afflicted with barrenness, because they had not defended his temple which Danaos burnt when he invaded those lands; for they were warned by his oracle to institute these games. But king Ericthonius first instituted games to him in Attica, and not to him only, but also to Minerva, in which games the olive was given as the prize to the victors, because they relate that Minerva was the discoverer of that fruit, as Liber was of the grape. In those years Europa is alleged to have been carried off by Xanthus king of Crete (to whom we find some give another name), and to have borne him Rhadamanthus, Sarpedon, and Minos, who are more commonly reported to have been the sons of Jupiter by the same woman. Now those who worship such gods regard what we have said about Xanthus king of Crete as true history; but this about Jupiter, which the poets sing, the theatres applaud, and the people celebrate, as empty fable got up as a reason for games to appease the deities, even with the false ascription of crimes to them. In those times Hercules was held in honour in Tyre, but that was not the same one as he whom we spoke of above. In the more secret history there are said to have been several who were called Father Liber and Hercules. This Hercules, whose great deeds are reckoned as twelve (not including the slaughter of Antæus the African, because that affair pertains to another Hercules), is declared in their books to have burned himself on Mount Œta, because he was not able, by that strength with which he had subdued monsters, to endure the disease under which he languished. At that time the king, or rather tyrant Busiris, who is alleged to have been the son of Neptune by Libya the daughter of Epaphus, is said to have offered up his guests in sacrifice to the gods. Now it must not be believed that Neptune committed this adultery, lest the gods should be criminated; yet such things must be ascribed to them by the poets and in the theatres, that they may be pleased with them. Vulcan and Minerva are said to have been the parents of Ericthonius king of Athens, in whose last years Joshua the son of Nun is found to have died. But since they will

have it that Minerva is a virgin, they say that Vulcan, being disturbed in the struggle between them, poured out his seed into the earth, and on that account the man born of it received that name; for in the Greek language ἔρις is "strife," and χθών "earth," of which two words Ericthonius is a compound. Yet it must be admitted that the more learned disprove and disown such things concerning their gods, and declare that this fabulous belief originated in the fact that in the temple at Athens, which Vulcan and Minerva had in common, a boy who had been exposed was found wrapped up in the coils of a dragon, which signified that he would become great, and, as his parents were unknown, he was called the son of Vulcan and Minerva, because they had the temple in common. Yet that fable accounts for the origin of his name better than this history. But what does it matter to us? Let the one in books that speak the truth edify religious men, and the other in lying fables delight impure demons. Yet these religious men worship them as gods. Still, while they deny these things concerning them they cannot clear them of all crime, because at their demand they exhibit plays in which the very things they wisely deny are basely done, and the gods are appeased by these false and base things. Now, even although the play celebrates an unreal crime of the gods, yet to delight in the ascription of an unreal crime is a real one.

CHAP. 13. *What fables were invented at the time when judges began to rule the Hebrews*

After the death of Joshua the son of Nun, the people of God had judges, in whose times they were alternately humbled by afflictions on account of their sins and consoled by prosperity through the compassion of God. In those times were invented the fables about Triptolemus, who, at the command of Ceres, borne by winged snakes, bestowed corn on the needy lands in flying over them; about that beast the Minotaur, which was shut up in the Labyrinth, from which men who entered its inextricable mazes could find no exit; about the Centaurs, whose form was a compound of horse and man; about Cerberus, the three-headed dog of hell; about Phryxus and his sister Hellas, who fled, borne by a winged ram; about the Gorgon, whose hair was composed of serpents, and who turned those who looked on her into stone; about Bellerophon, who was carried by a winged horse called Pegasus; about Amphion, who charmed and attracted the stones by the sweetness of his harp;

about the artificer Dædalus and his son Icarus, who flew on wings they had fitted on; about Œdipus, who compelled a certain four-footed monster with a human face, called a sphynx, to destroy herself by casting herself headlong, having solved the riddle she was wont to propose as insoluble; about Antæus, who was the son of the earth, for which reason, on falling on the earth, he was wont to rise up stronger, whom Hercules slew; and perhaps there are others which I have forgotten. These fables, easily found in histories containing a true account of events, bring us down to the Trojan war, at which Marcus Varro has closed his second book about the race of the Roman people; and they are so skillfully invented by men as to involve no scandal to the gods. But whoever have pretended as to Jupiter's rape of Ganymede, a very beautiful boy, that king Tantalus committed the crime, and the fable ascribed it to Jupiter; or as to his impregnating Danäe as a golden shower, that it means that the woman's virtue was corrupted by gold: whether these things were really done or only fabled in those days, or were really done by others and falsely ascribed to Jupiter, it is impossible to tell how much wickedness must have been taken for granted in men's hearts that they should be thought able to listen to such lies with patience. And yet they willingly accepted them, when, indeed, the more devotedly they worshipped Jupiter, they ought the more severely to have punished those who durst say such things of him. But they not only were not angry at those who invented these things, but were afraid that the gods would be angry at them if they did not act such fictions even in the theatres. In those times Latona bore Apollo, not him of whose oracle we have spoken above as so often consulted, but him who is said, along with Hercules, to have fed the flocks of king Admetus; yet he was so believed to be a god, that very many, indeed almost all, have believed him to be the self-same Apollo. Then also Father Liber made war in India, and led in his army many women called Bacchæ, who were notable not so much for valour as for fury. Some, indeed, write that this Liber was both conquered and bound; and some that he was slain in Persia, even telling where he was buried; and yet in his name, as that of a god, the unclean demons have instituted the sacred, or rather the sacrilegious, Bacchanalia, of the outrageous vileness of which the senate, after many years, became so much ashamed as to prohibit them in the city of Rome. Men believed that in those times Perseus and his wife Andro-

meda were raised into heaven after their death, so that they were not ashamed or afraid to mark out their images by constellations and call them by their names.

CHAP. 14. *Of the theological poets*

During the same period of time arose the poets, who were also called *theologues,* because they made hymns about the gods; yet about such gods as, although great men, were yet but men, or the elements of this world which the true God made, or creatures who were ordained as principalities and powers according to the will of the Creator and their own merit. And if, among much that was vain and false, they sang anything of the one true God, yet, by worshipping Him along with others who are not gods, and showing them the service that is due to Him alone, they did not serve Him at all rightly; and even such poets as Orpheus, Musæus, and Linus, were unable to abstain from dishonouring their gods by fables. But yet these theologues worshipped the gods, and were not worshipped as gods, although the city of the ungodly is wont, I know not how, to set Orpheus over the sacred, or rather sacrilegious, rites of hell. The wife of king Athamas, who was called Ino, and her son Melicertes, perished by throwing themselves into the sea, and were, according to popular belief, reckoned among the gods, like other men of the same times, Castor and Pollux. The Greeks, indeed, called her who was the mother of Melicertes, Leucothea, the Latins, Matuta; but both thought her a goddess.

CHAP. 15. *Of the fall of the kingdom of Argos, when Picus the son of Saturn first received his father's kingdom of Laurentum*

During those times the kingdom of Argos came to an end, being transferred to Mycene, from which Agamemnon came, and the kingdom of Laurentum arose, of which Picus son of Saturn was the first king, when the woman Deborah judged the Hebrews; but it was the Spirit of God who used her as His agent, for she was also a prophetess, although her prophecy is so obscure that we could not demonstrate, without a long discussion, that it was uttered concerning Christ. Now the Laurentes already reigned in Italy, from whom the origin of the Roman people is quite evidently derived after the Greeks; yet the kingdom of Assyria still lasted, in which Lampares was the twenty-third king when Picus first began to reign at Laurentum. The worshippers of such gods may see what they are to think of Saturn the father of Picus, who deny that he was a man; of whom some also have written that he himself reigned in Italy before Picus his son; and Virgil in his well-known book says,

That race indocile, and through mountains high
Dispersed, he settled, and endowed with laws,
And named their country Latium, because
Latent within their coasts he dwelt secure.
Tradition says the golden ages pure
Began when he was king.[1]

But they regard these as poetic fancies, and assert that the father of Picus was Sterces rather, and relate that, being a most skillful husbandman, he discovered that the fields could be fertilized by the dung of animals, which is called *stercus* from his name. Some say he was called Stercutius. But for whatever reason they chose to call him Saturn, it is yet certain they made this Sterces or Stercutius a god for his merit in agriculture; and they likewise received into the number of these gods Picus his son, whom they affirm to have been a famous augur and warrior. Picus begot Faunus, the second king of Laurentum; and he too is, or was, a god with them. These divine honours they gave to dead men before the Trojan war.

CHAP. 16. *Of Diomede, who after the destruction of Troy was placed among the gods, while his companions are said to have been changed into birds*

Troy was overthrown, and its destruction was everywhere sung and made well known even to boys; for it was signally published and spread abroad, both by its own greatness and by writers of excellent style. And this was done in the reign of Latinus the son of Faunus, from whom the kingdom began to be called Latium instead of Laurentum. The victorious Greeks, on leaving Troy destroyed and returning to their own countries, were torn and crushed by divers and horrible calamities. Yet even from among them they increased the number of their gods for they made Diomede a god. They allege that his return home was prevented by a divinely imposed punishment, and they prove, not by fabulous and poetic falsehood, but by historic attestation, that his companions were turned into birds. Yet they think that, even although he was made a god, he could neither restore them to the human form by his own power, nor yet obtain it from Jupiter his king, as a favour granted to a new inhabitant of heaven. They also say that his tem-

ple is in the island of Diomedæa, not far from Mount Garganus in Apulia, and that these birds fly around about this temple, and worship in it with such wonderful obedience, that they fill their beaks with water and sprinkle it; and if Greeks, or those born of the Greek race, come there, they are not only still, but fly to meet them; but if they are foreigners, they fly up at their heads and wound them with such severe strokes as even to kill them. For they are said to be well enough armed for these combats with their hard and large beaks.

CHAP. 17. *What Varro says of the incredible transformations of men*

In support of this story, Varro relates others no less incredible about that most famous sorceress Circe, who changed the companions of Ulysses into beasts, and about the Arcadians, who, by lot, swam across a certain pool, and were turned into wolves there, and lived in the deserts of that region with wild beasts like themselves. But if they never fed on human flesh for nine years, they were restored to the human form on swimming back again through the same pool. Finally, he expressly names one Demænetus, who, on tasting a boy offered up in sacrifice by the Arcadians to their god Lycæus according to their custom, was changed into a wolf, and, being restored to his proper form in the tenth year, trained himself as a pugilist, and was victorious at the Olympic Games. And the same historian thinks that the epithet Lycæus was applied in Arcadia to Pan and Jupiter for no other reason than this metamorphosis of men into wolves, because it was thought it could not be wrought except by a divine power. For a wolf is called in Greek λυκὸς, from which the name Lycæus appears to be formed. He says also that the Roman Luperci were as it were sprung of the seed of these mysteries.

CHAP. 18. *What we should believe concerning the transformations which seem to happen to men through the art of demons*

Perhaps our readers expect us to say something about this so great delusion wrought by the demons; and what shall we say but that men must fly out of the midst of Babylon?[2] For this prophetic precept is to be understood spiritually in this sense, that by going forward in the living God, by the steps of faith, which worketh by love, we must flee out of the city of this world, which is altogether a society of ungodly angels

---

[1] *Æneid*, BK. VIII. 321.

[2] Isa. 48. 20.

and men. Yea, the greater we see the power of the demons to be in these depths, so much the more tenaciously must we cleave to the Mediator through whom we ascend from these lowest to the highest places. For if we should say these things are not to be credited, there are not wanting even now some who would affirm that they had either heard on the best authority, or even themselves experienced, something of that kind. Indeed we ourselves, when in Italy, heard such things about a certain region there, where landladies of inns, imbued with these wicked arts, were said to be in the habit of giving to such travellers as they chose, or could manage, something in a piece of cheese by which they were changed on the spot into beasts of burden, and carried whatever was necessary, and were restored to their own form when the work was done. Yet their mind did not become bestial, but remained rational and human, just as Apuleius, in the books he wrote with the title of *The Golden Ass,* has told, or feigned, that it happened to his own self that, on taking poison, he became an ass, while retaining his human mind.

These things are either false, or so extraordinary as to be with good reason disbelieved. But it is to be most firmly believed that Almighty God can do whatever He pleases, whether in punishing or favouring, and that the demons can accomplish nothing by their natural power (for their created being is itself angelic, although made malign by their own fault), except what He may permit, whose judgments are often hidden, but never unrighteous. And indeed the demons, if they really do such things as these on which this discussion turns, do not create real substances, but only change the appearance of things created by the true God so as to make them seem to be what they are not. I cannot therefore believe that even the body, much less the mind, can really be changed into bestial forms and lineaments by any reason, art, or power of the demons; but the phantasm of a man which even in thought or dreams goes through innumerable changes, may, when the man's senses are laid asleep or overpowered, be presented to the senses of others in a corporeal form, in some indescribable way unknown to me, so that men's bodies themselves may lie somewhere, alive, indeed, yet with their senses locked up much more heavily and firmly than by sleep, while that phantasm, as it were embodied in the shape of some animal, may appear to the senses of others and may even seem to the man himself to be changed, just as he may seem to

himself in sleep to be so changed, and to bear burdens; and these burdens, if they are real substances, are borne by the demons, that men may be deceived by beholding at the same time the real substance of the burdens and the simulated bodies of the beasts of burden. For a certain man called Præstantius used to tell that it had happened to his father in his own house that he took that poison in a piece of cheese, and lay in his bed as if sleeping, yet could by no means be aroused. But he said that after a few days he as it were woke up and related the things he had suffered as if they had been dreams, namely, that he had been made a sumpter horse, and, along with other beasts of burden, had carried provisions for the soldiers of what is called the Rhœtian Legion, because it was sent to Rhœtia. And all this was found to have taken place just as he told, yet it had seemed to him to be his own dream. And another man declared that in his own house at night, before he slept, he saw a certain philosopher, whom he knew very well, come to him and explain to him some things in the Platonic philosophy which he had previously declined to explain when asked. And when he had asked this philosopher why he did in his house what he had refused to do at home, he said, "I did not do it, but I dreamed I had done it." And thus what the one saw when sleeping was shown to the other when awake by a phantasmal image.

These things have not come to us from persons we might deem unworthy of credit, but from informants we could not suppose to be deceiving us. Therefore what men say and have committed to writing about the Arcadians being often changed into wolves by the Arcadian gods, or demons rather, and what is told in song about Circe transforming the companions of Ulysses,[1] if they were really done, may, in my opinion, have been done in the way I have said. As for Diomede's birds, since their race is alleged to have been perpetuated by constant propagation, I believe they were not made through the metamorphosis of men, but were slyly substituted for them on their removal, just as the hind was for Iphigenia, the daughter of king Agamemnon. For juggleries of this kind could not be difficult for the demons if permitted by the judgment of God; and since that virgin was afterwards found alive it is easy to see that a hind had been slyly substituted for her. But because the companions of Diomede were of a sudden nowhere to be seen, and afterwards

[1]Virgil, *Eclogues*, BK. VIII. 70.

could nowhere be found, being destroyed by bad avenging angels, they were believed to have been changed into those birds, which were secretly brought there from other places where such birds were, and suddenly substituted for them by fraud. But that they bring water in their beaks and sprinkle it on the temple of Diomede, and that they fawn on men of Greek race and persecute aliens, is no wonderful thing to be done by the inward influence of the demons, whose interest it is to persuade men that Diomede was made a god, and thus to beguile them into worshipping many false gods, to the great dishonour of the true God; and to serve dead men, who even in their lifetime did not truly live, with temples, altars, sacrifices, and priests, all which, when of the right kind, are due only to the one living and true God.

CHAP. 19. *That Æneas came into Italy when Abdon the judge ruled over the Hebrews*

After the capture and destruction of Troy, Æneas, with twenty ships laden with the Trojan relics, came into Italy, when Latinus reigned there, Menestheus in Athens, Polyphidos in Sicyon, and Tautanos in Assyria, and Abdon was judge of the Hebrews. On the death of Latinus, Æneas reigned three years, the same kings continuing in the above-named places, except that Pelasgus was now king in Sicyon, and Samson was judge of the Hebrews, who is thought to be Hercules, because of his wonderful strength. Now the Latins made Æneas one of their gods, because at his death he was nowhere to be found. The Sabines also placed among the gods their first king, Sancus, or Sanctus, as some call him. At that time Codrus king of Athens exposed himself incognito to be slain by the Peloponnesian foes of that city, and so was slain. In this way, they say, he delivered his country. For the Peloponnesians had received a response from the oracle that they should overcome the Athenians only on condition that they did not slay their king. Therefore he deceived them by appearing in a poor man's dress, and provoking them, by quarrelling, to murder him. Whence Virgil says, "Or the quarrels of Codrus." [1] And the Athenians worshipped this man as a god with sacrificial honours. The fourth king of the Latins was Silvius the son of Æneas, not by Creüsa, of whom Ascanius the third king was born, but by Lavinia the daughter of Latinus, and he is said to have been his posthumous child. Oneus was the twenty-ninth king of Assyria, Melanthus the sixteenth of the Athenians, and

Eli the priest was judge of the Hebrews; and the kingdom of Sicyon then came to an end, after lasting, it is said, for nine hundred and fifty-nine years.

CHAP. 20. *Of the succession of the line of kings among the Israelites after the times of the judges*

While these kings reigned in the places mentioned, the period of the judges being ended, the kingdom of Israel next began with king Saul, when Samuel the prophet lived. At that date those Latin kings began who were surnamed Silvii, having that surname, in addition to their proper name, from their predecessor, that son of Æneas who was called Silvius; just as, long afterward, the successors of Cæsar Augustus were surnamed Cæsars. Saul being rejected, so that none of his issue should reign, on his death David succeeded him in the kingdom, after he had reigned forty years. Then the Athenians ceased to have kings after the death of Codrus, and began to have a magistracy to rule the republic. After David, who also reigned forty years, his son Solomon was king of Israel, who built that most noble temple of God at Jerusalem. In his time Alba was built among the Latins, from which thereafter the kings began to be styled kings not of the Latins, but of the Albans, although in the same Latium. Solomon was succeeded by his son Rehoboam, under whom that people was divided into two kingdoms, and its separate parts began to have separate kings.

CHAP. 21. *Of the kings of Latium, the first and twelfth of whom, Æneas and Aventinus, were made gods*

After Æneas, whom they deified, Latium had eleven kings, none of whom was deified. But Aventinus, who was the twelfth after Æneas, having been laid low in war, and buried in that hill still called by his name, was added to the number of such gods as they made for themselves. Some, indeed, were unwilling to write that he was slain in battle, but said he was nowhere to be found, and that it was not from his name, but from the alighting of birds, that hill was called Aventinus. After this no god was made in Latium except Romulus the founder of Rome. But two kings are found between these two, the first of whom I shall describe in the Virgilian verse:

> *Next came that Procas,*
> *Glory of the Trojan race.* [2]

[1] *Ibid.*, BK. V. II.

[2] *Æneid*, BK. VI. 767.

That greatest of all kingdoms, the Assyrian, had its long duration brought to a close in his time, the time of Rome's birth drawing nigh. For the Assyrian empire was transferred to the Medes after nearly thirteen hundred and five years, if we include the reign of Belus, who begot Ninus and, content with a small kingdom, was the first king there. Now Procas reigned before Amulius. And Amulius had made his brother Numitor's daughter, Rhea by name, who was also called Ilia, a vestal virgin, who conceived twin sons by Mars, as they will have it, in that way honouring or excusing her adultery, adding as a proof that a she-wolf nursed the infants when exposed. For they think this kind of beast belongs to Mars, so that the she-wolf is believed to have given her teats to the infants, because she knew they were the sons of Mars her lord; although there are not wanting persons who say that when the crying babes lay exposed, they were first of all picked up by I know not what harlot, and sucked her breasts first (now harlots were called *lupæ*, she-wolves, from which their vile abodes are even yet called *lupanaria*), and that afterwards they came into the hands of the shepherd Faustulus, and were nursed by Acca his wife. Yet what wonder is it, if, to rebuke the king who had cruelly ordered them to be thrown into the water, God was pleased, after divinely delivering them from the water, to succour, by means of a wild beast giving milk, these infants by whom so great a city was to be founded? Amulius was succeeded in the Latian kingdom by his brother Numitor, the grandfather of Romulus; and Rome was founded in the first year of this Numitor, who from that time reigned along with his grandson Romulus.

CHAP. 22. *That Rome was founded when the Assyrian kingdom perished, at which time Hezekiah reigned in Judah*

To be brief, the city of Rome was founded, like another Babylon, and as it were the daughter of the former Babylon, by which God was pleased to conquer the whole world, and subdue it far and wide by bringing it into one fellowship of government and laws. For there were already powerful and brave peoples and nations trained to arms, who did not easily yield, and whose subjugation necessarily involved great danger and destruction as well as great and horrible labour. For when the Assyrian kingdom subdued almost all Asia, although this was done by fighting, yet the wars could not be very fierce or difficult, because the nations were as yet untrained to resist, and neither so many nor so great as afterward; forasmuch as, after that greatest and indeed universal flood, when only eight men escaped in Noah's ark, not much more than a thousand years had passed when Ninus subdued all Asia with the exception of India. But Rome did not with the same quickness and facility wholly subdue all those nations of the east and west which we see brought under the Roman empire, because, in its gradual increase, in whatever direction it was extended, it found them strong and warlike. At the time when Rome was founded, then, the people of Israel had been in the land of promise seven hundred and eighteen years. Of these years twenty-seven belong to Joshua the son of Nun, and after that three hundred and twenty-nine to the period of the judges. But from the time when the kings began to reign there, three hundred and sixty-two years had passed. And at that time there was a king in Judah called Ahaz, or, as others compute, Hezekiah his successor, the best and most pious king, who it is admitted reigned in the times of Romulus. And in that part of the Hebrew nation called Israel, Hosea had begun to reign.

CHAP. 23. *Of the Erythræan sibyl, who is known to have sung many things about Christ more plainly than the other sibyls*

Some say the Erythræan sibyl prophesied at this time. Now Varro declares there were many sibyls, and not merely one. This sibyl of Erythræ certainly wrote some things concerning Christ which are quite manifest, and we first read them in the Latin tongue in verses of bad Latin, and unrhythmical, through the unskillfulness, as we afterwards learned, of some interpreter unknown to me. For Flaccianus, a very famous man, who was also a proconsul, a man of most ready eloquence and much learning, when we were speaking about Christ, produced a Greek manuscript, saying that it was the prophecies of the Erythræan sibyl, in which he pointed out a certain passage which had the initial letters of the lines so arranged that these words could be read in them: Ἰησοῦς Χριστος Θεοῦ υἱὸς σωτήρ, which means, "Jesus Christ the Son of God, the Saviour." And these verses, of which the initial letters yield that meaning, contain what follows as translated by some one into Latin in good rhythm:

Ɪ   *Judgment shall moisten the earth with the sweat of its standard,*

Ħ   *Ever enduring, behold the King shall come through the ages,*

ꞹ   *Sent to be here in the flesh, and Judge at the last of the world.*

O   *O God, the believing and faithless alike shall behold Thee*

Ↄ   *Uplifted with saints, when at last the ages are ended.*

Μ   *Seated before Him are souls in the flesh for His judgment.*

Ж   *Hid in thick vapours, the while desolate lieth the earth.*

Ⴇ   *Rejected by men are the idols and long hidden treasures;*

ⴹ   *Earth is consumed by the fire, and it searcheth the ocean and heaven;*

Ⱶ   *Issuing forth, it destroyeth the terrible portals of hell.*

Μ   *Saints in their body and soul freedom and light shall inherit;*

Ⱶ   *Those who are guilty shall burn in fire and brimstone for ever.*

Ↄ   *Occult actions revealing, each one shall publish his secrets;*

Μ   *Secrets of every man's heart God shall reveal in the light.*

Φ   *Then shall be weeping and wailing, yea, and gnashing of teeth;*

ⴹ   *Eclipsed is the sun, and silenced the stars in their chorus.*

O   *Over and gone is the splendour of moonlight, melted the heaven.*

Ↄ   *Uplifted by Him are the valleys, and cast down the mountains.*

Ↄ   *Utterly gone among men are distinctions of lofty and lowly.*

Ⱶ   *Into the plains rush the hills, the skies and oceans are mingled.*

O   *Oh, what an end of all things! earth broken in pieces shall perish;*

Μ   *Swelling together at once shall the waters and flames flow in rivers.*

Μ   *Sounding the archangel's trumpet shall peal down from heaven,*

Ⴢ   *Over the wicked who groan in their guilt and their manifold sorrows.*

Ⱶ   *Trembling, the earth shall be opened, revealing chaos and hell.*

Η   *Every king before God shall stand in that day to be judged.*

Ⴇ   *Rivers of fire and brimstone shall fall from the heavens.*

In these Latin verses the meaning of the Greek is correctly given, although not in the exact order of the lines as connected with the initial letters; for in three of them, the fifth, eighteenth, and nineteenth, where the Greek letter Υ occurs, Latin words could not be found beginning with the corresponding letter and yielding a suitable meaning. So that, if we note down together the initial letters of all the lines in our Latin translation except those three in which we retain the letter Υ in the proper place, they will express in five Greek words this meaning, "Jesus Christ the Son of God, the Saviour." And the verses are twenty-seven, which is the cube of three. For three times three are nine; and nine itself, if tripled, so as to rise from the superficial square to the cube, comes to twenty-seven. But if you join the initial letters of these five Greek words, Ἰησοῦς Χριστος Θεοῦ υἱὸς σωτήρ, which mean, "Jesus Christ the Son of God, the Saviour," they will make the word ἰχδὺς, that is, "fish," in which word Christ is mystically understood, because He was able to live, that is, to exist, without sin in the abyss of this mortality as in the depth of waters.

But this sibyl, whether she is the Erythræan, or, as some rather believe, the Cumæan, in her whole poem, of which this is a very small portion, not only has nothing that can relate to the worship of the false or feigned gods, but rather speaks against them and their worshippers in such a way that we might even think she ought to be reckoned among those who belong to the city of God. Lactantius also inserted in his work the prophecies about Christ of a certain sibyl, he does not say which. But I have thought fit to combine in a single extract, which may seem long, what he has set down in many short quotations. She says, "Afterward He shall come into the injurious hands of the unbelieving, and they will give God buffets with profane hands, and with impure mouth will spit out envenomed spittle; but He will with simplicity yield His holy back to stripes. And He will hold His peace when struck with the fist, that no one may find out what word, or whence, He comes to speak to hell; and He shall be crowned with a crown of thorns. And they gave Him gall for meat, and vinegar for His thirst: they will spread this table of inhospitality. For thou thyself, being foolish, hast not understood thy God, deluding the minds of mortals, but hast both crowned Him with thorns and mingled for Him bitter gall. But the veil of the temple shall be rent; and at midday it shall be darker than night for three hours. And He shall die the death, taking sleep for three days; and then returning from hell, He first shall come to the light, the beginning of the resurrection being shown to the recalled." Lactantius made use of these sibylline testimonies introducing them bit by bit in the course of his discussion as the things he intended to prove seemed to require, and we have set them down in one connected series, uninterrupted by comment, only taking care to mark them by capitals, if only the transcribers do not neglect to preserve them hereafter. Some writers, indeed, say that the Erythræan sibyl was not in the time of Romulus, but of the Trojan war.

CHAP. 24. *That the seven sages flourished in the reign of Romulus, when the ten tribes which were called Israel were led into captivity by the Chaldeans, and Romulus, when dead, had divine honours conferred on him*

While Romulus reigned, Thales the Milesian is said to have lived, being one of the seven sages, who succeeded the theological poets, of whom Orpheus was the most renowned, and were called Σοφοί, that is, sages. During that time the ten tribes, which on the division of the people were called Israel, were conquered by the Chaldeans and led captive into their lands, while the two tribes which were called Judah, and had the seat of their kingdom in Jerusalem, remained in the land of Judea. As Romulus, when dead, could nowhere be found, the Romans, as is everywhere notorious, placed him among the gods—a thing which by that time had already ceased to be done, and which was not done afterwards till the time of the Cæsars, and then not through error, but in flattery; so that Cicero ascribes great praises to Romulus, because he merited such honours not in rude and unlearned times, when men were easily deceived, but in times already polished and learned, although the subtle and acute loquacity of the philosophers had not yet culminated. But although the later times did not deify dead men, still they did not cease to hold and worship as gods those deified of old; nay, by images, which the ancients never had, they even increased the allurements of vain and impious superstition, the unclean demons effecting this in their heart, and also deceiving them by lying oracles, so that even the fabulous crimes of the gods, which were not once imagined by a more polite age, were yet basely acted in the plays in honour of these same false deities. Numa reigned after Romulus; and although he had thought that Rome would be better defended the more gods there were, yet on his death he himself was not counted worthy of a place among them, as if it were supposed that he had so crowded heaven that a place could not be found for him there. They report that the Samian sibyl lived while he reigned at Rome, and when Manasseh began to reign over the Hebrews—an impious king, by whom the prophet Isaiah is said to have been slain.

CHAP. 25. *What philosophers were famous when Tarquinius Priscus reigned over the Romans, and Zedekiah over the Hebrews, when Jerusalem was taken and the temple overthrown*

When Zedekiah reigned over the Hebrews, and Tarquinius Priscus, the successor of Ancus Martius, over the Romans, the Jewish people was led captive into Babylon, Jerusalem and the temple built by Solomon being overthrown. For the prophets, in chiding them for their iniquity and impiety, predicted that these things should come to pass, especially Jeremiah, who even stated the number of years. Pittacus of Mitylene, another of the sages, is reported to have lived at that time. And Eusebius writes that, while the people of God were held captive in Babylon, the five other sages lived, who must be added to Thales, whom we mentioned above, and Pittacus, in order to make up the seven. These are Solon of Athens, Chilo of Lacedæmon, Periander of Corinth, Cleobulus of Lindus, and Bias of Priene. These flourished after the theological poets, and were called sages, because they excelled other men in a certain laudable line of life, and summed up some moral precepts in epigrammatic sayings. But they left posterity no literary monuments, except that Solon is alleged to have given certain laws to the Athenians, and Thales was a natural philosopher and left books of his doctrine in short proverbs. In that time of the Jewish captivity, Anaximander, Anaximenes, and Xenophanes, the natural philosophers, flourished. Pythagoras also lived then, and at this time the name philosopher was first used.

CHAP. 26. *That at the time when the captivity of the Jews was brought to an end, on the completion of seventy years, the Romans also were freed from kingly rule*

At this time, Cyrus king of Persia, who also ruled the Chaldeans and Assyrians, having somewhat relaxed the captivity of the Jews, made fifty thousand of them return in order to rebuild the temple. They only began the first foundations and built the altar; but, owing to hostile invasions, they were unable to go on, and the work was put off to the time of Darius. During the same time also those things were done which are written in the book of Judith, which, indeed, the Jews are said not to have received into the canon of the Scriptures. Under Darius king of Persia, then, on the completion of the seventy years predicted by Jeremiah the prophet, the captivity of the Jews was brought to an end, and they were restored to liberty. Tarquin then reigned as the seventh king of the Romans. On his expulsion, they also began to be free from the rule of their kings. Down to this time the people of Israel had prophets; but, although they were numerous, the canonical writings of only a few of them have been preserved among the Jews and among us. In closing the previous book, I promised to set down something in this one about them, and I shall now do so.

CHAP. 27. *Of the times of the prophets whose oracles are contained in books, and who sang many things about the call of the Gentiles at the time when the Roman kingdom began and the Assyrian came to an end*

In order that we may be able to consider these times, let us go back a little to earlier times. At the beginning of the book of the prophet Hosea, who is placed first of twelve, it is written, "The word of the Lord which came to Hosea in the days of Uzziah, Jotham, Ahaz, and Hezekiah, kings of Judah."[1] Amos also writes that he prophesied in the days of Uzziah, and adds the name of Jeroboam king of Israel, who lived at the same time.[2] Isaiah the son of Amos—either the above-named prophet, or, as is rather affirmed, another who was not a prophet, but was called by the same name—also puts at the head of his book these four kings named by Hosea, saying by way of preface that he prophesied in their days.[3] Micah also names the same times as those of his prophecy, after the days of Uzziah;[4] for he names the same three kings as Hosea named—Jotham, Ahaz, and Hezekiah. We find from their own writings that these men prophesied contemporaneously. To these are added Jonah in the reign of Uzziah, and Joel in that of Jotham, who succeeded Uzziah. But we can find the date of these two prophets in the chronicles,[5] not in their own writings, for they say nothing about it themselves. Now these days extend from Procas king of the Latins, or his predecessor Aventinus, down to Romulus king of the Romans, or even to the beginning of the reign of his successor Numa Pompilius. Hezekiah king of Judah certainly reigned till then. So that thus these fountains of prophecy, as I may call them, burst forth at once during those times when the Assyrian kingdom failed and the Roman began; so that, just as in the first period of the Assyrian kingdom Abraham arose, to whom the most dis-

tinct promises were made that all nations should be blessed in his seed, so at the beginning of the western Babylon, in the time of whose government Christ was to come in Whom these promises were to be fulfilled, the oracles of the prophets were given not only in spoken but in written words, for a testimony that so great a thing should come to pass. For although the people of Israel hardly ever lacked prophets from the time when they began to have kings, these were only for their own use, not for that of the nations. But when the more manifestly prophetic Scripture began to be formed, which was to benefit the nations too, it was fitting that it should begin when this city was founded which was to rule the nations.

CHAP. 28. *Of the things pertaining to the Gospel of Christ which Hosea and Amos prophesied*

The prophet Hosea speaks so very profoundly that it is laborious work to penetrate his meaning. But, according to promise, we must insert something from his book. He says, "And it shall come to pass that in the place where it was said unto them, Ye are not my people, there they shall be called the sons of the living God."[6] Even the apostles understood this as a prophetic testimony of the calling of the nations who did not formerly belong to God; and because this same people of the Gentiles is itself spiritually among the children of Abraham, and for that reason is rightly called Israel, therefore he goes on to say, "And the children of Judah and the children of Israel shall be gathered together in one, and shall appoint themselves one headship, and shall ascend from the earth."[7] We should but weaken the savour of this prophetic oracle if we set ourselves to expound it. Let the reader but call to mind that corner-stone and those two walls of partition, the one of the Jews, the other of the Gentiles,[8] and he will recognize them, the one under the term *sons of Judah,* the other as *sons of Israel,* supporting themselves by one and the same headship, and ascending from the earth. But that those carnal Israelites who are now unwilling to believe in Christ shall afterward believe, that is, their children shall (for they themselves, of course, shall go to their own place by dying), this same prophet testifies, saying, "For the children of Israel shall abide many days without a king, without a prince, without a sacrifice, without an altar, without a priesthood, without manifestations."[9] Who does not see that the Jews are now thus? But let us hear what

---

[1]Hos. 1. 1.   [2]Amos, 1. 1.
[3]Isa. 1. 1. Isaiah's father was Amoz, a different name.
[4]Mic. 1. 1.   [5]The chronicles of Eusebius and Jerome.

[6]Hos. 1. 10.   [7]Hos. 1. 11.   [8]Gal. 2. 14-20.
[9]Hos. 3. 4.

he adds: "And afterward shall the children of Israel return, and seek the Lord their God, and David their king, and shall be amazed at the Lord and at His goodness in the latter days."[1] Nothing is clearer than this prophecy, in which by David, as distinguished by the title of king, Christ is to be understood, "who is made," as the apostle says, "of the seed of David according to the flesh."[2] This prophet has also foretold the resurrection of Christ on the third day, as it behoved to be foretold, with prophetic loftiness, when he says, "He will heal us after two days, and in the third day we shall rise again."[3] In agreement with this the apostle says to us, "If ye be risen with Christ, seek those things which are above."[4] Amos also prophesies thus concerning such things: "Prepare thee, that thou mayst invoke thy God, O Israel; for lo, I am binding the thunder, and creating the spirit, and announcing to men their Christ."[5] And in another place he says, "In that day will I raise up the tabernacle of David that is fallen, and build up the breaches thereof: and I will raise up his ruins, and will build them up again as in the days of old: that the residue of men may inquire for me and all the nations upon whom my name is invoked, saith the Lord that doeth this."[6]

Chap. 29. What things are predicted by Isaiah concerning Christ and the Church

The prophecy of Isaiah is not in the book of the twelve prophets, who are called the minor from the brevity of their writings, as compared with those who are called the greater prophets because they published larger volumes. Isaiah belongs to the latter, yet I connect him with the two above named, because he prophesied at the same time. Isaiah, then, together with his rebukes of wickedness, precepts of righteousness, and predictions of evil, also prophesied much more than the rest about Christ and the Church, that is, about the King and that city which he founded; so that some say he should be called an evangelist rather than a prophet. But, in order to finish this work, I quote only one out of many in this place. Speaking in the person of the Father, he says, "Behold, my servant shall understand, and shall be exalted and glorified very much. As many shall be astonished at Thee."[7] This is about Christ.

But let us now hear what follows about the Church. He says, "Rejoice, O barren, thou that barest not; break forth and cry, thou that didst not travail with child: for many more are the children of the desolate than of her that has an husband."[8] But these must suffice; and some things in them ought to be expounded; yet I think those parts sufficient which are so plain that even enemies must be compelled against their will to understand them.

Chap. 30. What Micah, Jonah, and Joel prophesied in accordance with the New Testament

The prophet Micah, representing Christ under the figure of a great mountain, speaks thus: "It shall come to pass in the last days, that the manifested mountain of the Lord shall be prepared on the tops of the mountains, and it shall be exalted above the hills; and people shall hasten unto it. Many nations shall go, and shall say, Come, let us go up into the mountain of the Lord, and into the house of the God of Jacob; and He will show us His way, and we will go in His paths: for out of Zion shall proceed the law, and the word of the Lord out of Jerusalem. And He shall judge among many people, and rebuke strong nations afar off."[9] This prophet predicts the very place in which Christ was born, saying, "And thou, Bethlehem, of the house of Ephratah, art the least that can be reckoned among the thousands of Judah; out of thee shall come forth unto me a leader, to be the prince in Israel; and His going forth is from the beginning, even from the days of eternity. Therefore will He give them even until the time when she that travaileth shall bring forth; and the remnant of His brethren shall be converted to the sons of Israel. And He shall stand, and see, and feed His flock in the strength of the Lord, and in the dignity of the name of the Lord His God: for now shall He be magnified even to the utmost of the earth."[10]

The prophet Jonah, not so much by speech as by his own painful experience, prophesied Christ's death and resurrection much more clearly than if he had proclaimed them with his voice. For why was he taken into the whale's belly and restored on the third day, but that he might be a sign that Christ should return from the depths of hell on the third day?

I should be obliged to use many words in explaining all that Joel prophesies in order to make those that pertain to Christ and the Church. But there is one passage I must not pass by, which the apostles also quoted when the Holy Spirit came down from above on the assembled believers according to Christ's promise. He says, "And it shall come to pass after these

---

[1]Hos. 3. 5.   [2]Rom. 1. 3.   [3]Hos. 6. 2.
[4]Col. 3. 1.   [5]Amos, 4. 12, 13.
[6]Amos, 9. 11, 12; Acts, 15. 15–17.   [7]Isa. 52. 13; 53. 13.   [8]Isa. 54. 1–5.   [9]Mic. 4. 1–3.   [10]Mic. 5. 2–4.

things, that I will pour out my Spirit upon all flesh; and your sons and your daughters shall prophesy, and your old men shall dream, and your young men shall see visions: and even on my servants and mine handmaids in those days will I pour out my Spirit."[1]

CHAP. 31. *Of the predictions concerning the salvation of the world in Christ, in Obadiah, Nahum, and Habakkuk*

The date of three of the minor prophets, Obadiah, Nahum, and Habakkuk, is neither mentioned by themselves nor given in the chronicles of Eusebius and Jerome. For although they put Obadiah with Micah, yet when Micah prophesied does not appear from that part of their writings in which the dates are noted. And this, I think, has happened through their error in negligently copying the works of others. But we could not find the two others now mentioned in the copies of the chronicles which we have; yet because they are contained in the canon, we ought not to pass them by.

Obadiah, so far as his writings are concerned, the briefest of all the prophets, speaks against Idumea, that is, the nation of Esau, that reprobate elder of the twin sons of Isaac and grandsons of Abraham. Now if, by that form of speech in which a part is put for the whole, we take Idumea as put for the nations, we may understand of Christ what he says among other things, "But upon Mount Sion shall be safety, and there shall be a Holy One."[2] And a little after, at the end of the same prophecy, he says, "And those who are saved again shall come up out of Mount Sion, that they may defend Mount Esau, and it shall be a kingdom to the Lord."[3] It is quite evident this was fulfilled when those saved again out of Mount Sion—that is, the believers in Christ from Judea, of whom the apostles are chiefly to be acknowledged—went up to defend Mount Esau. How could they defend it except by making safe, through the preaching of the gospel, those who believed that they might be "delivered from the power of darkness and translated into the kingdom of God"?[4] This he expressed as an inference, adding, "And it shall be to the Lord a kingdom." For Mount Sion signifies Judea, where it is predicted there shall be safety and a Holy One, that is, Christ Jesus. But Mount Esau is Idumea, which signifies the Church of the Gentiles, which, as I have expounded, those saved again out of Sion have defended that it should be a kingdom to the

Lord. This was obscure before it took place; but what believer does not find it out now that it is done?

As for the prophet Nahum, through him God says, "I will exterminate the graven and the molten things: I will make thy burial. For lo, the feet of Him that bringeth good tidings and announceth peace are swift upon the mountains! O Judah, celebrate thy festival days, and perform thy vows; for now they shall not go on any more so as to become antiquated. It is completed, it is consumed, it is taken away. He ascendeth who breathes in thy face, delivering thee out of tribulation."[5] Let him that remembers the gospel call to mind who hath ascended from hell and breathed the Holy Spirit in the face of Judah, that is, of the Jewish disciples; for they belong to the New Testament, whose festival days are so spiritually renewed that they cannot become antiquated. Moreover, we already see the graven and molten things, that is, the idols of the false gods, exterminated through the gospel, and given up to oblivion as of the grave, and we know that this prophecy is fulfilled in this very thing.

Of what else than the advent of Christ, who was to come, is Habakkuk understood to say, "And the Lord answered me, and said, Write the vision openly on a tablet of boxwood, that he that readeth these things may understand. For the vision is yet for a time appointed, and it will arise in the end, and will not become void: if it tarry, wait for it; because it will surely come, and will not be delayed"?[6]

CHAP. 32. *Of the prophecy that is contained in the prayer and song of Habakkuk*

In his prayer, with a song, to whom but the Lord Christ does he say, "O Lord, I have heard Thy hearing, and was afraid: O Lord, I have considered Thy works, and was greatly afraid"?[7] What is this but the inexpressible admiration of the foreknown, new, and sudden salvation of men? "In the midst of two living creatures thou shalt be recognized." What is this but either between the two testaments, or between the two thieves, or between Moses and Elias talking with Him on the mount? "While the years draw nigh, Thou wilt be recognized; at the coming of the time Thou wilt be shown," does not even need exposition. "While my soul shall be troubled at Him, in wrath Thou wilt be mindful of mercy." What is this but that He puts Himself for the Jews, of whose nation He was, who were troubled with great anger and crucified Christ,

---

[1]Joel, 2. 28, 29. [2]Obad. 17. [3]Obad. 21.
[4]Col. 1. 13.

[5]Nah. 1. 14; 2. 1. [6]Hab. 2. 2, 3. [7]Hab. 3. 2.

when He, mindful of mercy, said, "Father, forgive them, for they know not what they do"? [1] "God shall come from Teman, and the Holy One from the shady and close mountain." [2] What is said here, "He shall come from Teman," some interpret "from the south," or "from the southwest," by which is signified the noonday, that is, the fervour of charity and the splendour of truth. "The shady and close mountain" might be understood in many ways, yet I prefer to take it as meaning the depth of the divine Scriptures, in which Christ is prophesied: for in the Scriptures there are many things shady and close which exercise the mind of the reader; and Christ comes thence when he who has understanding finds Him there. "His power covereth up the heavens, and the earth is full of His praise." What is this but what is also said in the psalm, "Be Thou exalted, O God, above the heavens; and Thy glory above all the earth"? [3] "His splendour shall be as the light." What is it but that the fame of Him shall illuminate believers? "Horns are in His hands." What is this but the trophy of the cross? "And He hath placed the firm charity of His strength" [4] needs no exposition. "Before His face shall go the word, and it shall go forth into the field after His feet." What is this but that He should both be announced before His coming hither and after His return hence? "He stood, and the earth was moved." What is this but that "He stood" for succour, "and the earth was moved" to believe? "He regarded, and the nations melted"; that is, He had compassion, and made the people penitent. "The mountains are broken with violence"; that is, through the power of those who work miracles the pride of the haughty is broken "The everlasting hills flowed down"; that is, they are humbled in time that they may be lifted up for eternity. "I saw His goings eternal for his labours"; that is, I beheld His labour of love not left without the reward of eternity. "The tents of Ethiopia shall be greatly afraid, and the tents of the land of Midian"; that is, even those nations which are not under the Roman authority, being suddenly terrified by the news of Thy wonderful works, shall become a Christian people. "Wert Thou angry at the rivers, O Lord? or was Thy fury against the rivers? or was Thy rage against the sea?" This is said because He does not now come to condemn the world, but that the world through Him might be saved. [5] "For Thou shalt mount upon Thy horses, and Thy riding shall be salvation"; that is, Thine evangelists shall carry

Thee, for they are guided by Thee, and Thy gospel is salvation to them that believe in Thee. "Bending, Thou wilt bend Thy bow against the sceptres, saith the Lord"; that is, Thou wilt threaten even the kings of the earth with Thy judgment. "The earth shall be cleft with rivers"; that is, by the sermons of those who preach Thee flowing in upon them, men's hearts shall be opened to make confession, to whom it is said, "Rend your hearts and not your garments." [6] What does "The people shall see Thee and grieve" mean, but that in mourning they shall be blessed? [7] What is "Scattering the waters in marching," but that by walking in those who everywhere proclaim Thee, Thou wilt scatter hither and thither the streams of Thy doctrine? What is "The abyss uttered its voice"? Is it not that the depth of the human heart expressed what it perceived? The words, "The depth of its phantasy," are an explanation of the previous verse, for the depth is the abyss; and "Uttered its voice" is to be understood before them, that is, as we have said, it expressed what it perceived. Now the phantasy is the vision, which it did not hold or conceal, but poured forth in confession. "The sun was raised up, and the moon stood still in her course"; that is, Christ ascended into heaven, and the Church was established under her King. "Thy darts shall go in the light"; that is, Thy words shall not be sent in secret, but openly. For He had said to His own disciples, "What I tell you in darkness, that speak ye in the light." [8] "By threatening thou shalt diminish the earth"; that is, by that threatening Thou shalt humble men. "And in fury Thou shalt cast down the nations"; for in punishing those who exalt themselves Thou dashest them one against another. "Thou wentest forth for the salvation of Thy people, that Thou mightest save Thy Christ; Thou hast sent death on the heads of the wicked." None of these words require exposition. "Thou hast lifted up the bonds, even to the neck." This may be understood even of the good bonds of wisdom, that the feet may be put into its fetters, and the neck into its collar. "Thou hast struck off in amazement of mind the bonds" must be understood for, "He lifts up the good and strikes off the bad," about which it is said to Him, "Thou hast broken asunder my bonds," [9] and that "in amazement of mind," that is, wonderfully. "The heads of the mighty shall be moved in it"; to wit, in that wonder. "They shall open their teeth like a poor man eating secretly." For some of

---

[1]Luke, 23. 34.   [2]Hab. 3. 3.   [3]Ps. 57. 5, 11.
[4]Hab. 3. 4.   [5]John, 3, 17.

[6]Joel, 2. 13.   [7]Matt. 5. 4.   [8]Matt. 10. 27.
[9]Ps. 116. 16.

the mighty among the Jews shall come to the Lord, admiring His works and words, and shall greedily eat the bread of His doctrine in secret for fear of the Jews, just as the Gospel has shown they did. "And Thou hast sent into the sea Thy horses, troubling many waters," which are nothing else than many people; for unless all were troubled, some would not be converted with fear, others pursued with fury. "I gave heed, and my belly trembled at the voice of the prayer of my lips; and trembling entered into my bones, and my habit of body was troubled under me." He gave heed to those things which he said and was himself terrified at his own prayer, which he had poured forth prophetically and in which he discerned things to come. For when many people are troubled, he saw the threatening tribulation of the Church, and at once acknowledged himself a member of it, and said, "I shall rest in the day of tribulation," as being one of those who are rejoicing in hope, patient in tribulation.[1] "That I may ascend," he says, "among the people of my pilgrimage," departing quite from the wicked people of his carnal kinship, who are not pilgrims in this earth, and do not seek the country above.[2] "Although the fig-tree," he says, "shall not blossom, neither shall fruit be in the vines; the labour of the olive shall lie, and the fields shall yield no meat; the sheep shall be cut off from the meat, and there shall be no oxen in the stalls." He sees that nation which was to slay Christ about to lose the abundance of spiritual supplies, which, in prophetic fashion, he has set forth by the figure of earthly plenty. And because that nation was to suffer such wrath of God, because, being ignorant of the righteousness of God, it wished to establish its own,[3] he immediately says, "Yet will I rejoice in the Lord; I will joy in God my salvation. The Lord God is my strength, and He will set my feet in completion; He will place me above the heights, that I may conquer in His song," to wit, in that song of which something similar is said in the psalm, "He set my feet upon a rock, and directed my goings, and put in my mouth a new song, a hymn to our God."[4] He therefore conquers in the song of the Lord, who takes pleasure in His praise, not in his own; that "He that glorieth, let him glory in the Lord."[5] But some copies have, "I will joy in God my Jesus," which seems to me better than the version of those who, wishing to put it in Latin, have not set down that very name which for us it is dearer and sweeter to name.

CHAP. 33. *What Jeremiah and Zephaniah have, by the prophetic spirit, spoken before concerning Christ and the calling of the nations*

Jeremiah, like Isaiah, is one of the greater prophets, not of the minor, like the others from whose writings I have just given extracts. He prophesied when Josiah reigned in Jerusalem, and Ancus Martius at Rome, when the captivity of the Jews was already at hand; and he continued to prophesy down to the fifth month of the captivity, as we find from his writings. Zephaniah, one of the minor prophets, is put along with him, because he himself says that he prophesied in the days of Josiah; but he does not say till when. Jeremiah thus prophesied not only in the times of Ancus Martius, but also in those of Tarquinius Priscus, whom the Romans had for their fifth king. For he had already begun to reign when that captivity took place. Jeremiah, in prophesying of Christ, says, "The breath of our mouth, the Lord Christ, was taken in our sins,"[6] thus briefly showing both that Christ is our Lord and that He suffered for us. Also in another place he says, "This is my God, and there shall none other be accounted of in comparison of Him; who hath found out all the way of prudence, and hath given it to Jacob His servant, and to Israel His beloved: afterwards He was seen on the earth, and conversed with men."[7] Some attribute this testimony not to Jeremiah, but to his secretary, who was called Baruch; but it is more commonly ascribed to Jeremiah. Again the same prophet says concerning Him, "Behold the days come, saith the Lord, that I will raise up unto David a righteous shoot, and a King shall reign and shall be wise, and shall do judgment and justice in the earth. In those days Judah shall be saved, and Israel shall dwell confidently: and this is the name which they shall call Him, Our righteous Lord."[8] And of the calling of the nations which was to come to pass, and which we now see fulfilled, he thus spoke: "O Lord my God, and my refuge in the day of evils, to Thee shall the nations come from the utmost end of the earth, saying, Truly our fathers have worshipped lying images, wherein there is no profit."[9] But that the Jews, by whom He behoved even to be slain, were not going to acknowledge Him, this prophet thus intimates: "Heavy is the heart through all; and He is a man, and who shall know Him?"[10] That passage also is his which I have quoted in the seventeenth book concerning the new testament, of

---

[1] Rom. 12. 12.   [2] Heb. 11. 13. 16.   [3] Rom. 10. 3.
[4] Ps. 40. 2, 3.   [5] Jer. 9. 23, 24, as in I Cor. 1. 31.
[6] Lam. 4. 20.   [7] Bar. 3. 35–37.   [8] Jer. 23. 5, 6.
[9] Jer. 16. 19.   [10] Jer. 17. 9.

which Christ is the Mediator. For Jeremiah himself says, "Behold, the days come, saith the Lord, that I will complete over the house of Jacob a new testament," and the rest, which may be read there.[1]

For the present I shall put down those predictions about Christ by the prophet Zephaniah, who prophesied with Jeremiah. "Wait ye upon me, saith the Lord, in the day of my resurrection, in the future; because it is my determination to assemble the nations, and gather together the kingdoms."[2] And again he says, "The Lord will be terrible upon them, and will exterminate all the gods of the earth; and they shall worship Him every man from his place, even all the isles of the nations."[3] And a little after he says, "Then will I turn to the people a tongue, and to His offspring, that they may call upon the name of the Lord, and serve Him under one yoke. From the borders of the rivers of Ethiopia shall they bring sacrifices unto me. In that day thou shalt not be confounded for all thy curious inventions, which thou hast done impiously against me: for then I will take away from thee the naughtiness of thy trespass; and thou shalt no more magnify thyself above thy holy mountain. And I will leave in thee a meek and humble people, and they who shall be left of Israel shall fear the name of the Lord."[4] These are the remnant of whom the apostle quotes that which is elsewhere prophesied: "Though the number of the children of Israel be as the sand of the sea, a remnant shall be saved."[5] These are the remnant of that nation who have believed in Christ.

CHAP. 34. *Of the prophecy of Daniel and Ezekiel, other two of the greater prophets*

Daniel and Ezekiel, other two of the greater prophets, also first prophesied in the very captivity of Babylon. Daniel even defined the time when Christ was to come and suffer by the exact date. It would take too long to show this by computation, and it has been done often by others before us. But of His power and glory he has thus spoken: "I saw in a night vision, and, behold, one like the Son of man was coming with the clouds of heaven, and He came even to the Ancient of days, and He was brought into His presence. And to Him there was given dominion, and honour, and a kingdom: and all people, tribes, and tongues shall serve Him. His power is an everlasting power, which shall not pass away, and His kingdom shall not be destroyed."[6]

Ezekiel also, speaking prophetically in the person of God the Father, thus foretells Christ, speaking of Him in the prophetic manner as David, because He assumed flesh of the seed of David, and on account of that form of a servant in which He was made man, He who is the Son of God is also called the servant of God. He says, "And I will set up over my sheep one Shepherd, who will feed them, even my servant David; and He shall feed them, and He shall be their shepherd. And I the Lord will be their God, and my servant David a prince in the midst of them; I the Lord have spoken."[7] And in another place he says, "And one King shall be over them all: and they shall no more be two nations, neither shall they be divided any more into two kingdoms; neither shall they defile themselves any more with their idols, and their abominations, and all their iniquities. And I will save them out of all their dwelling-places wherein they have sinned, and will cleanse them; and they shall be my people, and I will be their God. And my servant David shall be king over them, and there shall be one Shepherd for them all."[8]

CHAP. 35. *Of the prophecy of the three prophets, Haggai, Zechariah, and Malachi*

There remain three minor prophets, Haggai, Zechariah, and Malachi, who prophesied at the close of the captivity. Of these Haggai more openly prophesies of Christ and the Church thus briefly: "Thus saith the Lord of hosts, Yet one little while, and I will shake the heaven, and the earth, and the sea, and the dry land; and I will move all nations, and the desired of all nations shall come."[9] The fulfillment of this prophecy is in part already seen, and in part hoped for in the end. For He moved the heaven by the testimony of the angels and the stars, when Christ became incarnate. He moved the earth by the great miracle of His birth of the virgin. He moved the sea and the dry land, when Christ was proclaimed both in the isles and in the whole world. So we see all nations moved to the faith; and the fulfillment of what follows, "And the desired of all nations shall come," is looked for at His last coming. For ere men can desire and wait for Him, they must believe and love Him.

Zechariah says of Christ and the Church, "Rejoice greatly, O daughter of Sion; shout joyfully, O daughter of Jerusalem; behold, thy King shall come unto thee, just and the Saviour; Himself poor, and mounting an ass, and a colt the foal of an ass: and His dominion shall be

---

[1]Jer. 31. 31; see BK. XVII. 3.   [2]Zeph. 3. 8.
[3]Zeph. 2. 11.   [4]Zeph. 3. 9-12.
[5]Isa. 10. 22; Rom. 9. 27.   [6]Dan. 7. 13, 14.
[7]Ezek. 34. 23.   [8]Ezek. 37. 22-24.   [9]Hag. 2. 6.

from sea to sea, and from the river even to the ends of the earth."[1] How this was done, when the Lord Christ on His journey used a beast of burden of this kind, we read in the Gospel, where, also, as much of this prophecy is quoted as appears sufficient for the context. In another place, speaking in the Spirit of prophecy to Christ Himself of the remission of sins through His blood, he says, "Thou also, by the blood of Thy testament, hast sent forth Thy prisoners from the lake wherein is no water."[2] Different opinions may be held, consistently with right belief, as to what he meant by this lake. Yet it seems to me that no meaning suits better than that of the depth of human misery, which is, as it were, dry and barren, where there are no streams of righteousness, but only the mire of iniquity. For it is said of it in the Psalms, "And He led me forth out of the lake of misery, and from the miry clay."[3]

Malachi, foretelling the Church which we now behold propagated through Christ, says most openly to the Jews, in the person of God, "I have no pleasure in you, and I will not accept a gift at your hand. For from the rising even to the going down of the sun, my name is great among the nations; and in every place sacrifice shall be made, and a pure oblation shall be offered unto my name: for my name shall be great among the nations, saith the Lord."[4] Since we can already see this sacrifice offered to God in every place, from the rising of the sun to his going down, through Christ's priesthood after the order of Melchisedek, while the Jews, to whom it was said, "I have no pleasure in you, neither will I accept a gift at your hand," cannot deny that their sacrifice has ceased, why do they still look for another Christ, when they read this in the prophecy, and see it fulfilled, which could not be fulfilled except through Him? And a little after he says of Him, in the person of God, "My covenant was with Him of life and peace; and I gave to Him that He might fear me with fear, and be afraid before my name. The law of truth was in His mouth: directing in peace He hath walked with me, and hath turned many away from iniquity. For the Priest's lips shall keep knowledge and they shall seek the law at His mouth: for He is the Angel of the Lord Almighty."[5] Nor is it to be wondered at that Christ Jesus is called the Angel of the Almighty God. For just as He is called a servant on account of the form of a servant in which He came to men, so He is called an angel on account of the *evan-*

gel which He proclaimed to men. For if we interpret these Greek words, *evangel* is *good news,* and *angel* is *messenger.* Again he says of Him, "Behold I will send mine angel, and He will look out the way before my face: and the Lord, Whom ye seek, shall suddenly come into His temple, even the Angel of the testament, whom ye desire. Behold, He cometh, saith the Lord Almighty, and who shall abide the day of His entry, or who shall stand at His appearing?"[6] In this place he has foretold both the first and second advent of Christ: the first, to wit, of which he says, "And He shall come suddenly into His temple": that is, into His flesh, of which He said in the Gospel, "Destroy this temple, and in three days I will raise it up again."[7] And of the second advent he says, "Behold, He cometh, saith the Lord Almighty, and who shall abide the day of His entry, or who shall stand at His appearing?" But what he says, "The Lord whom ye seek, and the Angel of the testament whom ye desire," just means that even the Jews, according to the Scriptures which they read, shall seek and desire Christ. But many of them did not acknowledge that He Whom they sought and desired had come, being blinded in their hearts, which were preoccupied with their own merits. Now what he here calls the testament, either above, where he says, "My testament had been with Him," or here, where he has called Him the Angel of the testament, we ought, beyond a doubt, to take to be the New Testament, in which the things promised are eternal, and not the Old, in which they are only temporal. Yet many who are weak are troubled when they see the wicked abound in such temporal things, because they value them greatly, and serve the true God to be rewarded with them. On this account, to distinguish the eternal blessedness of the New Testament, which shall be given only to the good, from the earthly felicity of the Old, which for the most part is given to the bad as well, the same prophet says, "Ye have made your words burdensome to me: yet ye have said, In what have we spoken ill of Thee? Ye have said, Foolish is every one who serves God; and what profit is it that we have kept His observances, and that we have walked as suppliants before the face of the Lord Almighty? And now we call the aliens blessed, yea, all that do wicked things are built up again; yea, they are opposed to God and are saved. They that feared the Lord uttered these reproaches every one to his neighbour: and the Lord hearkened and heard; and He wrote a book of remembrance before Him, for

[1]Zech. 9. 9, 10. [2]Zech. 9. 11. [3]Ps. 40. 2.
[4]Mal. 1. 10, 11. [5]Mal. 2. 5-7.

[6]Mal. 3. 1, 2. [7]John, 2. 19.

them that fear the Lord and that revere His name."¹ By that book is meant the New Testament. Finally, let us hear what follows: "And they shall be an acquisition for me, saith the Lord Almighty, in the day which I make; and I will choose them as a man chooseth his son that serveth him. And ye shall return, and shall discern between the just and the unjust, and between him that serveth God and him that serveth Him not. For, behold, the day cometh burning as an oven, and it shall burn them up; and all the aliens and all that do wickedly shall be stubble: and the day that shall come will set them on fire, saith the Lord Almighty, and shall leave neither root nor branch. And unto you that fear my name shall the Sun of Righteousness arise, and health shall be in His wings; and ye shall go forth, and exult as calves let loose from bonds. And ye shall tread down the wicked, and they shall be ashes under your feet, in the day in which I shall do, saith the Lord Almighty."² This day is the day of judgment, of which, if God will, we shall speak more fully in its own place.

CHAP. 36. *About Esdras and the books of the Maccabees*

After these three prophets, Haggai, Zechariah, and Malachi, during the same period of the liberation of the people from the Babylonian servitude Esdras also wrote, who is historical rather than prophetical, as is also the book called Esther, which is found to relate, for the praise of God, events not far from those times; unless, perhaps, Esdras is to be understood as prophesying of Christ in that passage where, on a question having arisen among certain young men as to what is the strongest thing, when one had said kings, another wine, the third women, who for the most part rule kings, yet that same third youth demonstrated that the truth is victorious over all.³ For by consulting the Gospel we learn that Christ is the Truth. From this time, when the temple was rebuilt, down to the time of Aristobulus, the Jews had not kings but princes; and the reckoning of their dates is found, not in the Holy Scriptures which are called canonical, but in others, among which are also the books of the Maccabees. These are held as canonical, not by the Jews, but by the Church, on account of the extreme and wonderful sufferings of certain martyrs, who, before Christ had come in the flesh, contended for the law of God even unto death and endured most grievous and horrible evils.

¹Mal. 3. 13–16.   ²Mal. 3. 17; 4. 3.   ³I Esdras, 3, 4.

CHAP. 37. *That prophetic records are found which are more ancient than any fountain of the Gentile philosophy*

In the time of our prophets, then, whose writings had already come to the knowledge of almost all nations, the philosophers of the nations had not yet arisen—at least, not those who were called by that name, which originated with Pythagoras the Samian, who was becoming famous at the time when the Jewish captivity ended. Much more, then, are the other philosophers found to be later than the prophets. For even Socrates the Athenian, the master of all who were then most famous, holding the pre-eminence in that department that is called the moral or active, is found after Esdras in the chronicles. Plato also was born not much later, who far outwent the other disciples of Socrates. If, besides these, we take their predecessors, who had not yet been styled philosophers, to wit, the seven sages, and then the physicists, who succeeded Thales, and imitated his studious search into the nature of things, namely, Anaximander, Anaximenes, and Anaxagoras, and some others, before Pythagoras first professed himself a philosopher, even these did not precede the whole of our prophets in antiquity of time, since Thales, whom the others succeeded, is said to have flourished in the reign of Romulus, when the stream of prophecy burst forth from the fountains of Israel in those writings which spread over the whole world. So that only those theological poets, Orpheus, Linus, and Musæus, and, it may be, some others among the Greeks, are found earlier in date than the Hebrew prophets whose writings we hold as authoritative. But not even these preceded in time our true divine, Moses, who authentically preached the one true God, and whose writings are first in the authoritative canon; and therefore the Greeks, in whose tongue the literature of this age chiefly appears, have no ground for boasting of their wisdom, in which our religion, wherein is true wisdom, is not evidently more ancient at least, if not superior. Yet it must be confessed that before Moses there had already been, not indeed among the Greeks, but among barbarous nations, as in Egypt, some doctrine which might be called their wisdom, else it would not have been written in the holy books that Moses was learned in all the wisdom of the Egyptians,⁴ as he was, when, being born there, and adopted and nursed by Pharaoh's daughter, he was also liberally educated. Yet not even the wisdom of the Egyp-

⁴Acts, 7. 22.

tians could be antecedent in time to the wisdom of our prophets, because even Abraham was a prophet. And what wisdom could there be in Egypt before Isis had given them letters, whom they thought fit to worship as a goddess after her death? Now Isis is declared to have been the daughter of Inachus, who first began to reign in Argos when the grandsons of Abraham are known to have been already born.

CHAP. 38. *That the ecclesiastical canon has not admitted certain writings on account of their too great antiquity, lest through them false things should be inserted instead of true*

If I may recall far more ancient times, our patriarch Noah was certainly even before that great deluge, and I might not undeservedly call him a prophet, forasmuch as the ark he made, in which he escaped with his family, was itself a prophecy of our times.[1] What of Enoch, the seventh from Adam? Does not the canonical epistle of the Apostle Jude declare that he prophesied?[2] But the writings of these men could not be held as authoritative either among the Jews or us, on account of their too great antiquity, which made it seem needful to regard them with suspicion, lest false things should be set forth instead of true. For some writings which are said to be theirs are quoted by those who, according to their own humour, loosely believe what they please. But the purity of the canon has not admitted these writings, not because the authority of these men who pleased God is rejected, but because they are not believed to be theirs. Nor ought it to appear strange if writings for which so great antiquity is claimed are held in suspicion, seeing that in the very history of the kings of Judah and Israel containing their acts, which we believe to belong to the canonical Scripture, very many things are mentioned which are not explained there, but are said to be found in other books which the prophets wrote, the very names of these prophets being sometimes given, and yet they are not found in the canon which the people of God received. Now I confess the reason of this is hidden from me; only I think that even those men, to whom certainly the Holy Spirit revealed those things which ought to be held as of religious authority, might write some things as men by historical diligence, and others as prophets by divine inspiration; and these things were so distinct, that it was judged that the former should be ascribed to themselves, but the latter to God speaking through them: and so the one pertained to the abundance of

knowledge, the other to the authority of religion. In that authority the canon is guarded. So that, if any writings outside of it are now brought forward under the name of the ancient prophets, they cannot serve even as an aid to knowledge, because it is uncertain whether they are genuine; and on this account they are not trusted, especially those of them in which some things are found that are even contrary to the truth of the canonical books, so that it is quite apparent they do not belong to them.

CHAP. 39. *About the Hebrew written characters which that language always possessed*

Now we must not believe that Heber, from whose name the word Hebrew is derived, preserved and transmitted the Hebrew language to Abraham only as a spoken language, and that the Hebrew letters began with the giving of the law through Moses; but rather that this language, along with its letters, was preserved by that succession of fathers. Moses, indeed, appointed some among the people of God to teach letters, before they could know any letters of the divine law. The Scripture calls these men γραμματεισαγωγεῖς, who may be called in Latin *inductores* or *introductores* of letters, because they, as it were, introduce them into the hearts of the learners, or rather lead those whom they teach into them. Therefore no nation could vaunt itself over our patriarchs and prophets by any wicked vanity for the antiquity of its wisdom; since not even Egypt, which is wont falsely and vainly to glory in the antiquity of her doctrines, is found to have preceded in time the wisdom of our patriarchs in her own wisdom, such as it is. Neither will any one dare to say that they were most skillful in wonderful sciences before they knew letters, that is, before Isis came and taught them there. Besides, what, for the most part, was that memorable doctrine of theirs which was called wisdom but astronomy, and it may be some other sciences of that kind, which usually have more power to exercise men's wit than to enlighten their minds with true wisdom? As regards philosophy, which professes to teach men something which shall make them happy, studies of that kind flourished in those lands about the times of Mercury, whom they called Trismegistus, long before the sages and philosophers of Greece, but yet after Abraham, Isaac, Jacob, and Joseph, and even after Moses himself. At that time, indeed, when Moses was born, Atlas is found to have lived, that great astronomer, the brother of Prometheus, and maternal grandson of the elder Mer-

[1]Heb. 11. 7; I Pet. 3. 20, 21.   [2]Jude, 14.

cury, of whom that Mercury Trismegistus was the grandson.

CHAP. 40. *About the most mendacious vanity of the Egyptians, in which they ascribe to their science an antiquity of a hundred thousand years*

In vain, then, do some babble with most empty presumption, saying that Egypt has understood the reckoning of the stars for more than a hundred thousand years. For in what books have they collected that number who learned letters from Isis their mistress, not much more than two thousand years ago? Varro, who has declared this, is no small authority in history, and it does not disagree with the truth of the divine books. For as it is not yet six thousand years since the first man, who is called Adam, are not those to be ridiculed rather than refuted who try to persuade us of anything regarding a space of time so different from, and contrary to, the ascertained truth? For what historian of the past should we credit more than him who has also predicted things to come which we now see fulfilled? And the very disagreement of the historians among themselves furnishes a good reason why we ought rather to believe him who does not contradict the divine history which we hold. But, on the other hand, the citizens of the impious city, scattered everywhere through the earth, when they read the most learned writers, none of whom seems to be of contemptible authority, and find them disagreeing among themselves about affairs most remote from the memory of our age, cannot find out whom they ought to trust. But we, being sustained by divine authority in the history of our religion, have no doubt that whatever is opposed to it is most false, whatever may be the case regarding other things in secular books, which, whether true or false, yield nothing of moment to our living rightly and happily.

CHAP. 41. *About the discord of philosophic opinion, and the concord of the Scriptures that are held as canonical by the Church*

But let us omit further examination of history, and return to the philosophers from whom we digressed to these things. They seem to have laboured in their studies for no other end than to find out how to live in a way proper for laying hold of blessedness. Why, then, have the disciples dissented from their masters, and the fellow-disciples from one another, except because as men they have sought after these things by human sense and human reasonings? Now, although there might be among them a desire of glory, so that each wished to be thought wiser and more acute than another and in no way addicted to the judgment of others, but the inventor of his own dogma and opinion, yet I may grant that there were some, or even very many of them, whose love of truth severed them from their teachers or fellow-disciples, that they might strive for what they thought was the truth, whether it was so or not. But what can human misery do, or how or where can it reach forth, so as to attain blessedness, if divine authority does not lead it? Finally, let our authors, among whom the canon of the sacred books is fixed and bounded, be far from disagreeing in any respect. It is not without good reason, then, that not merely a few people prating in the schools and gymnasia in captious disputations, but so many and great people, both learned and unlearned, in countries and cities, have believed that God spoke to them or by them, i.e., the canonical writers, when they wrote these books. There ought, indeed, to be but few of them, lest on account of their multitude what ought to be religiously esteemed should grow cheap; and yet not so few that their agreement should not be wonderful. For among the multitude of philosophers, who in their works have left behind them the monuments of their dogmas, no one will easily find any who agree in all their opinions. But to show this is too long a task for this work.

But what author of any sect is so approved in this demon-worshipping city, that the rest who have differed from or opposed him in opinion have been disapproved? The Epicureans asserted that human affairs were not under the providence of the gods; and the Stoics, holding the opposite opinion, agreed that they were ruled and defended by favourable and tutelary gods. Yet were not both sects famous among the Athenians? I wonder, then, why Anaxagoras was accused of a crime for saying that the sun was a burning stone, and denying that it was a god at all; while in the same city Epicurus flourished gloriously and lived securely, although he not only did not believe that the sun or any star was a god, but contended that neither Jupiter nor any of the gods dwelt in the world at all, so that the prayers and supplications of men might reach them! Were not both Aristippus and Antisthenes there, two noble philosophers and both Socratic? yet they placed the chief end of life within bounds so diverse and contradictory that the first made the delight of the body the chief good, while the other asserted that man was made happy mainly by the virtue of the mind. The one also said that the wise man should flee from the republic; the other, that he should administer its affairs. Yet did not each gather disciples to follow his own sect? Indeed, in the conspicuous and well-known porch, in gymnasia, in gardens, in places public and private, they openly strove in bands each for his own opinion, some asserting there was one world, others innumerable worlds; some that this world had a beginning, others that it had not; some that it would perish, others that it would exist always; some that it was governed by the divine mind, others by chance and accident; some that souls are immortal, others that they are mortal—and of those who asserted their immortality, some said they transmigrated through beasts, others that it was by no means so; while of those who asserted their mortality, some said they perished immediately after the body, others that they survived either a little while or a longer time, but not always; some fixing supreme good in the body, some in the mind, some in both; others adding to the mind and body external good things; some thinking that the bodily senses ought to be trusted always, some not always, others never. Now what people, senate, power, or public dignity of the impious city has ever taken care to judge between all these and other well-nigh innumerable dissensions of the philosophers, approving and accepting some, and disapproving and rejecting others? Has it not held in its bosom at random, without any judgment, and confusedly, so many controversies of men at variance, not about fields, houses, or anything of a pecuniary nature, but about those things which make life either miserable or happy? Even if some true things were said in it, yet falsehoods were uttered with the same licence; so that such a city has not amiss received the title of the mystic Babylon. For Babylon means confusion, as we remember we have already explained. Nor does it matter to the devil, its king, how they wrangle among themselves in contradictory errors, since all alike deservedly belong to him on account of their great and varied impiety.

But that nation, that people, that city, that republic, these Israelites, to whom the oracles of God were entrusted, by no means confounded with similar licence false prophets with the true prophets; but, agreeing together, and differing in nothing, acknowledged and upheld the authentic authors of their sacred books. These were their philosophers, these were their sages, divines, prophets, and teachers of probity and piety. Whoever was wise and lived according to them was wise and lived not according to men, but according to God Who hath spoken by them. If sacrilege is forbidden there, God hath forbidden it. If it is said, "Honour thy father and thy mother,"[1] God hath commanded it. If it is said, "Thou shalt not commit adultery, Thou shalt not kill, Thou shalt not steal,"[2] and other similar commandments, not human lips but the divine oracles have enounced them. Whatever truth certain philosophers, amid their false opinions, were able to see, and strove by laborious discussions to persuade men of—such as that God had made this world, and Himself most providently governs it, or of the nobility of the virtues, of the love of country, of fidelity in friendship, of good works and everything pertaining to virtuous manners, although they knew not to what end and what rule all these things were to be referred—all these, by words prophetic, that is, divine, although spoken by men, were commended to the people in that city, and not inculcated by contention in arguments, so that he who should know them might be afraid of contemning, not the wit of men, but the oracle of God.

CHAP. 42. *By what dispensation of God's providence the Sacred Scriptures of the Old Testament were translated out of Hebrew into Greek, that they might be made known to all the nations*

One of the Ptolemies, kings of Egypt, desired to know and have these sacred books. For after Alexander of Macedon, who is also styled the Great, had by his most wonderful, but by no means enduring power, subdued the whole of Asia, yea, almost the whole world, partly by force of arms, partly by terror, and, among other kingdoms of the East, had entered and obtained Judea also, on his death his generals did not peaceably divide that most ample kingdom among them for a possession, but rather dissipated it, wasting all things by wars. Then Egypt began to have the Ptolemies as her kings. The first of them, the son of Lagus, carried many captive out of Judea into Egypt. But another Ptolemy, called Philadelphus, who succeeded him, permitted all whom he had brought under the yoke to return free; and, more than that, sent kingly gifts to the temple of God, and begged Eleazar, who was the high priest, to give

[1] Ex. 20. 12.
[2] Ex. 20. 13–15, the order as in Mark, 10. 19.

him the Scriptures, which he had heard by report were truly divine, and therefore greatly desired to have in that most noble library he had made. When the high priest had sent them to him in Hebrew, he afterwards demanded interpreters of him, and there were given him seventy-two, out of each of the twelve tribes six men, most learned in both languages, to wit, the Hebrew and Greek; and their translation is now by custom called the Septuagint. It is reported, indeed, that there was an agreement in their words so wonderful, stupendous, and plainly divine, that when they had sat at this work, each one apart (for so it pleased Ptolemy to test their fidelity), they differed from each other in no word which had the same meaning and force, or, in the order of the words; but, as if the translators had been one, so what all had translated was one, because in very deed the one Spirit had been in them all. And they received so wonderful a gift of God, in order that the authority of these Scriptures might be commended not as human but divine, as indeed it was, for the benefit of the nations who should at some time believe, as we now see them doing.

CHAP. 43. *Of the authority of the Septuagint translation, which, saving the honour of the Hebrew original, is to be preferred to all translations*

For while there were other interpreters who translated these sacred oracles out of the Hebrew tongue into Greek, as Aquila, Symmachus, and Theodotion, and also that translation which, as the name of the author is unknown, is quoted as the fifth edition, yet the Church has received this Septuagint translation just as if it were the only one; and it has been used by the Greek Christian people, most of whom are not aware that there is any other. From this translation there has also been made a translation in the Latin tongue, which the Latin churches use. Our times, however, have enjoyed the advantage of the presbyter Jerome, a man most learned, and skilled in all three languages, who translated these same Scriptures into the Latin speech, not from the Greek, but from the Hebrew. But although the Jews acknowledge this very learned labour of his to be faithful, while they contend that the Septuagint translators have erred in many places, still the churches of Christ judge that no one should be preferred to the authority of so many men, chosen for this very great work by Eleazar, who was then high priest; for even if there had not appeared in them one spirit, with-

out doubt divine, and the seventy learned men had, after the manner of men, compared together the words of their translation, that what pleased them all might stand, no single translator ought to be preferred to them; but since so great a sign of divinity has appeared in them, certainly, if any other translator, of their Scriptures from the Hebrew into any other tongue is faithful, in that case he agrees with these seventy translators, and if he is not found to agree with them, then we ought to believe that the prophetic gift is with them. For the same Spirit who was in the prophets when they spoke these things was also in the seventy men when they translated them, so that assuredly they could also say something else, just as if the prophet himself had said both, because it would be the same Spirit who said both; and could say the same thing differently, so that, although the words were not the same, yet the same meaning should shine forth to those of good understanding; and could omit or add something, so that even by this it might be shown that there was in that work not human bondage, which the translator owed to the words, but rather divine power, which filled and ruled the mind of the translator. Some, however, have thought that the Greek copies of the Septuagint version should be emended from the Hebrew copies; yet they did not dare to take away what the Hebrew lacked and the Septuagint had, but only added what was found in the Hebrew copies and was lacking in the Septuagint, and noted them by placing at the beginning of the verses certain marks in the form of stars which they call asterisks. And those things which the Hebrew copies have not, but the Septuagint have, they have in like manner marked at the beginning of the verses by horizontal spitshaped marks like those by which we denote ounces; and many copies having these marks are circulated even in Latin.[1] But we cannot, without inspecting both kinds of copies, find out those things which are neither omitted nor added, but expressed differently, whether they yield another meaning not in itself unsuitable, or can be shown to explain the same meaning in another way. If, then, as it behoves us, we behold nothing else in these Scriptures than what the Spirit of God has spoken through men, if anything is in the Hebrew copies and is not in the version of the Seventy, the Spirit of God did not choose to say it through them, but only through the prophets. But whatever is in the Septuagint and not in the Hebrew

[1] Variant reading, "both in Greek and Latin."

copies, the same Spirit chose rather to say through the latter, thus showing that both were prophets. For in that manner He spoke as He chose, some things through Isaiah, some through Jeremiah, some through several prophets, or else the same thing through this prophet and through that. Further, whatever is found in both editions, that one and the same Spirit willed to say through both, but so as that the former preceded in prophesying, and the latter followed in prophetically interpreting them; because, as the one Spirit of peace was in the former when they spoke true and concordant words, so the self-same one Spirit hath appeared in the latter, when, without mutual conference, they yet interpreted all things as if with one mouth.

CHAP. 44. *How the threat of the destruction of the Ninevites is to be understood, which in the Hebrew extends to forty days, while in the Septuagint it is contracted to three*

But some one may say, "How shall I know whether the prophet Jonah said to the Ninevites, 'Yet *three* days and Nineveh shall be overthrown,' or *forty* days?"[1] For who does not see that the prophet could not say both, when he was sent to terrify the city by the threat of imminent ruin? For if its destruction was to take place on the third day, it certainly could not be on the fortieth; but if on the fortieth, then certainly not on the third. If, then, I am asked which of these Jonah may have said, I rather think what is read in the Hebrew, "Yet forty days and Nineveh shall be overthrown." Yet the Seventy, interpreting long afterward, could say what was different and yet pertinent to the matter, and agree in the self-same meaning, although under a different signification. And this may admonish the reader not to despise the authority of either, but to raise himself above the history and search for those things which the history itself was written to set forth. These things, indeed, took place in the city of Nineveh, but they also signified something else too great to apply to that city; just as, when it happened that the prophet himself was three days in the whale's belly, it signified besides, that He Who is Lord of all the prophets should be three days in the depths of hell. Wherefore, if that city is rightly held as prophetically representing the Church of the Gentiles, to wit, as brought down by penitence, so as no longer to be what it had been, since this was done by Christ in the Church of the Gentiles, which Nineveh repre-

sented, Christ Himself was signified both by the forty and by the three days: by the forty, because He spent that number of days with His disciples after the resurrection, and then ascended into heaven, but by the three days, because He rose on the third day. So that, if the reader desires nothing else than to adhere to the history of events, he may be aroused from his sleep by the Septuagint interpreters, as well as the prophets, to search into the depth of the prophecy, as if they had said, "In the forty days seek Him in whom thou mayest also find the three days—the one thou wilt find in His ascension, the other in His resurrection." Because that which could be most suitably signified by both numbers, of which one is used by Jonah the prophet, the other by the prophecy of the Septuagint version, the one and self-same Spirit hath spoken. I dread prolixity, so that I must not demonstrate this by many instances in which the seventy interpreters may be thought to differ from the Hebrew, and yet, when well understood, are found to agree. For which reason I also, according to my capacity, following the footsteps of the apostles, who themselves have quoted prophetic testimonies from both, that is, from the Hebrew and the Septuagint, have thought that both should be used as authoritative, since both are one, and divine. But let us now follow out as we can what remains.

CHAP. 45. *That the Jews ceased to have prophets after the rebuilding of the temple, and from that time until the birth of Christ were afflicted with continual adversity, to prove that the building of another temple had been promised by prophetic voices*

The Jewish nation no doubt became worse after it ceased to have prophets, just at the very time when, on the rebuilding of the temple after the captivity in Babylon, it hoped to become better. For so, indeed, did that carnal people understand what was foretold by Haggai the prophet, saying, "The glory of this latter house shall be greater than that of the former."[2] Now, that this is said of the New Testament, he showed a little above, where he says, evidently promising Christ, "And I will move all nations, and the desired One shall come to all nations."[3] In this passage the Septuagint translators, giving another sense more suitable to the body than the Head, that is, to the Church than to Christ, have said by prophetic authority, "The things shall come that are chosen of the Lord from all

[1] Jon. 3. 4.   [2] Hag. 2. 9.   [3] Hag. 2. 7.

nations," that is, *men,* of whom Jesus saith in the Gospel, "Many are called, but few are chosen." [1] For by such chosen ones of the nations there is built, through the New Testament, with living stones, a house of God far more glorious than that temple was which was constructed by king Solomon, and rebuilt after the captivity. For this reason, then, that nation had no prophets from that time, but was afflicted with many plagues by kings of alien race, and by the Romans themselves, lest they should fancy that this prophecy of Haggai was fulfilled by that rebuilding of the temple.

For not long after, on the arrival of Alexander, it was subdued, when, although there was no pillaging, because they dared not resist him, and thus, being very easily subdued, received him peaceably, yet the glory of that house was not so great as it was when under the free power of their own kings. Alexander, indeed, offered up sacrifices in the temple of God, not as a convert to His worship in true piety, but thinking, with impious folly, that He was to be worshipped along with false gods. Then Ptolemy son of Lagus, whom I have already mentioned, after Alexander's death carried them captive into Egypt. His successor, Ptolemy Philadelphus, most benevolently dismissed them; and by him it was brought about, as I have narrated a little before, that we should have the Septuagint version of the Scriptures. Then they were crushed by the wars which are explained in the books of the Maccabees. Afterward they were taken captive by Ptolemy king of Alexandria, who was called Epiphanes. Then Antiochus king of Syria compelled them by many and most grievous evils to worship idols, and filled the temple itself with the sacrilegious superstitions of the Gentiles. Yet their most vigorous leader Judas, who is also called Maccabæus, after beating the generals of Antiochus, cleansed it from all that defilement of idolatry.

But not long after, one Alcimus, although an alien from the sacerdotal tribe, was, through ambition, made pontiff, which was an impious thing. After almost fifty years, during which they never had peace, although they prospered in some affairs, Aristobulus first assumed the diadem among them, and was made both king and pontiff. Before that, indeed, from the time of their return from the Babylonish captivity and the rebuilding of the temple, they had not kings, but generals or *principes.* Although a king himself may be called a prince, from his principality

in governing, and a leader, because he leads the army, but it does not follow that all who are princes and leaders may also be called kings, as that Aristobulus was. He was succeeded by Alexander, also both king and pontiff, who is reported to have reigned over them cruelly. After him his wife Alexandra was queen of the Jews, and from her time downwards more grievous evils pursued them; for this Alexandra's sons, Aristobulus and Hyrcanus, when contending with each other for the kingdom, called in the Roman forces against the nation of Israel. For Hyrcanus asked assistance from them against his brother. At that time Rome had already subdued Africa and Greece, and ruled extensively in other parts of the world also, and yet, as if unable to bear her own weight, had, in a manner, broken herself by her own size. For indeed she had come to grave domestic seditions, and from that to social wars, and by and by to civil wars, and had enfeebled and worn herself out so much, that the changed state of the republic, in which she should be governed by kings, was now imminent. Pompey then, a most illustrious prince of the Roman people, having entered Judea with an army, took the city, threw open the temple, not with the devotion of a suppliant, but with the authority of a conqueror, and went, not reverently, but profanely, into the holy of holies, where it was lawful for none but the pontiff to enter. Having established Hyrcanus in the pontificate, and set Antipater over the subjugated nation as guardian or procurator, as they were then called, he led Aristobulus with him bound. From that time the Jews also began to be Roman tributaries. Afterward Cassius plundered the very temple. Then after a few years it was their desert to have Herod, a king of foreign birth, in whose reign Christ was born. For the time had now come signified by the prophetic Spirit through the mouth of the patriarch Jacob, when he says, "There shall not be lacking a prince out of Judah, nor a teacher from his loins, until He shall come for Whom it is reserved; and He is the expectation of the nations." [2] There lacked not therefore a Jewish prince of the Jews until that Herod, who was the first king of a foreign race received by them. Therefore it was now the time when He should come for Whom that was reserved which is promised in the New Testament, that He should be the expectation of the nations. But it was not possible that the nations should expect He would come, as we see they did, to do judgment in the splendour of power, unless they should first believe in Him when He came to suffer judgment in the humility of patience.

CHAP. 46. *Of the birth of our Saviour, whereby the Word was made Flesh; and of the dispersion of the Jews among all nations, as had been prophesied*

While Herod, therefore, reigned in Judea, and Cæsar Augustus was emperor at Rome, the state of the republic being already changed, and the world being set at peace by him, Christ was born in Bethlehem of Judah, man manifest out of a human virgin, God hidden out of God the Father. For so had the prophet foretold: "Behold, a virgin shall conceive in the womb, and bring forth a Son, and they shall call His name Immanuel, which, being interpreted, is, God with us."[1] He did many miracles that He might commend God in Himself, some of which, even as many as seemed sufficient to proclaim Him, are contained in the evangelic Scripture. The first of these is that He was so wonderfully born, and the last that with His body raised up again from the dead He ascended into heaven. But the Jews who slew Him and would not believe in Him, because it behoved Him to die and rise again, were yet more miserably wasted by the Romans, and utterly rooted out from their kingdom, where aliens had already ruled over them, and were dispersed through the lands (so that indeed there is no place where they are not), and are thus by their own Scriptures a testimony to us that we have not forged the prophecies about Christ. And very many of them, considering this, even before His passion, but chiefly after His resurrection, believed on Him, of Whom it was predicted, "Though the number of the children of Israel be as the sand of the sea, the remnant shall be saved."[2] But the rest are blinded, of whom it was predicted, "Let their table be made before them a trap, and a retribution, and a stumbling-block. Let their eyes be darkened lest they see, and bow down their back alway."[3] Therefore, when they do not believe our Scriptures, their own, which they blindly read, are fulfilled in them, lest perchance any one should say that the Christians have forged these prophecies about Christ which are quoted under the name of the sibyl, or of others, if such there be, who do not belong to the Jewish people. For us, indeed, those suffice which are quoted from the

books of our enemies, to whom we make our acknowledgment, on account of this testimony which, in spite of themselves, they contribute by their possession of these books, while they themselves are dispersed among all nations, wherever the Church of Christ is spread abroad. For a prophecy about this thing was sent before in the Psalms, which they also read, where it is written, "My God, His mercy shall prevent me. My God hath shown me concerning mine enemies, that Thou shalt not slay them, lest they should at last forget Thy law: disperse them in Thy might."[4] Therefore God has shown the Church in her enemies the Jews the grace of His compassion, since, as saith the apostle, "their offence is the salvation of the Gentiles."[5] And therefore He has not slain them, that is, He has not let the knowledge that they are Jews be lost in them, although they have been conquered by the Romans, lest they should forget the law of God, and their testimony should be of no avail in this matter of which we treat. But it was not enough that he should say, "Slay them not, lest they should at last forget Thy law," unless he had also added, "Disperse them"; because if they had only been in their own land with that testimony of the Scriptures, and not everywhere, certainly the Church which is everywhere could not have had them as witnesses among all nations to the prophecies which were sent before concerning Christ.

CHAP. 47. *Whether before Christian times there were any outside of the Israelite race who belonged to the fellowship of the heavenly city*

Wherefore if we read of any foreigner—that is, one neither born of Israel nor received by that people into the canon of the sacred books—having prophesied something about Christ, if it has come or shall come to our knowledge, we can refer to it over and above; not that this is necessary, even if wanting, but because it is not incongruous to believe that even in other nations there may have been men to whom this mystery was revealed, and who were also impelled to proclaim it, whether they were partakers of the same grace or had no experience of it, but were taught by bad angels, who, as we know, even confessed the present Christ, Whom the Jews did not acknowledge. Nor do I think the Jews themselves dare contend that no one has belonged to God except the Israelites, since the increase of Israel began on the rejection of his elder brother. For in very deed there was no other people

---

[1] Isa. 7. 14, as in Matt. 1. 23.
[2] Isa. 10. 22, as in Rom. 9. 27, 28.
[3] Ps. 69. 22, 23; Rom. 11. 9, 10.

[4] Ps. 69. 10, 11.   [5] Rom. 11. 11.

who were specially called the people of God; but they cannot deny that there have been certain men even of other nations who belonged, not by earthly but heavenly fellowship, to the true Israelites, the citizens of the country that is above. Because, if they deny this, they can be most easily confuted by the case of the holy and wonderful man Job, who was neither a native nor a proselyte, that is, a stranger joining the people of Israel, but, being bred of the Idumean race, arose there and died there too, and who is so praised by the divine oracle that no man of his times is put on a level with him as regards justice and piety. And although we do not find his date in the chronicles, yet from his book, which for its merit the Israelites have received as of canonical authority, we gather that he was in the third generation after Israel. And I doubt not it was divinely provided, that from this one case we might know that among other nations also there might be men pertaining to the spiritual Jerusalem who have lived according to God and have pleased Him. And it is not to be supposed that this was granted to any one, unless the one Mediator between God and men, the Man Christ Jesus,[1] was divinely revealed to him; Who was pre-announced to the saints of old as yet to come in the flesh, even as He is announced to us as having come, that the self-same faith through Him may lead all to God who are predestinated to be the city of God, the house of God, and the temple of God. But whatever prophecies concerning the grace of God through Christ Jesus are quoted, they may be thought to have been forged by the Christians. So that there is nothing of more weight for confuting all sorts of aliens, if they contend about this matter, and for supporting our friends, if they are truly wise, than to quote those divine predictions about Christ which are written in the books of the Jews, who have been torn from their native abode and dispersed over the whole world in order to bear this testimony, so that the Church of Christ has everywhere increased.

CHAP. 48. *That Haggai's prophecy, in which he said that the glory of the house of God would be greater than that of the first had been, was really fulfilled, not in the rebuilding of the temple, but in the Church of Christ*

This house of God is more glorious than that first one[2] which was constructed of wood and stone, metals and other precious things. Therefore the prophecy of Haggai was not fulfilled in the rebuilding of that temple. For it can never be shown to have had so much glory after it was rebuilt as it had in the time of Solomon; yea, rather, the glory of that house is shown to have been diminished, first by the ceasing of prophecy, and then by the nation itself suffering so great calamities, even to the final destruction made by the Romans, as the things above-mentioned prove. But this house which pertains to the New Testament is just as much more glorious as the living stones, even believing, renewed men, of which it is constructed are better. But it was typified by the rebuilding of that temple for this reason, because the very renovation of that edifice typifies in the prophetic oracle another testament which is called the New. When, therefore, God said by the prophet just named, "And I will give peace in this place,"[3] He is to be understood Who is typified by that typical place; for since by that rebuilt place is typified the Church which was to be built by Christ, nothing else can be accepted as the meaning of the saying, "I will give peace in this place," except I will give peace in the place which that place signifies. For all typical things seem in some way to personate those whom they typify, as it is said by the apostle, "That Rock was Christ."[4] Therefore the glory of this New Testament house is greater than the glory of the Old Testament house; and it will show itself as greater when it shall be dedicated. For then "shall come the desired of all nations,"[5] as we read in the Hebrew. For before His advent He had not yet been desired by all nations. For they knew not Him Whom they ought to desire, in Whom they had not believed. Then, also, according to the Septuagint interpretation (for it also is a prophetic meaning), "shall come those who are elected of the Lord out of all nations." For then indeed there shall come only those who are elected, whereof the apostle saith, "According as He hath chosen us in Him before the foundation of the world."[6] For the Master Builder who said. "Many are called, but few are chosen,"[7] did not say this of those who, on being called, came in such a way as to be cast out from the feast, but would point out the house built up of the elect, which henceforth shall dread no ruin. Yet because the churches are also full of those who shall be separated by the winnowing as in the threshing-floor, the glory of this house is not so apparent now as it shall be when every one who is there shall be there always.

[1] I Tim. 2. 5.   [2] Hag. 2. 9.

[3] Hag. 2. 9.   [4] I Cor. 10. 4; Ex. 17. 6.
[5] Hag. 2. 7.   [6] Eph. 1. 4.   [7] Matt. 22. 11–14.

CHAP. 49. *Of the indiscriminate increase of the Church, wherein many reprobates are in this world mixed with the elect*

In this wicked world, in these evil days, when the Church measures her future loftiness by her present humility, and is exercised by goading fears, tormenting sorrows, disquieting labours, and dangerous temptations, when she soberly rejoices, rejoicing only in hope, there are many reprobates mingled with the good, and both are gathered together by the gospel as in a drag-net;[1] and in this world, as in a sea, both swim enclosed without distinction in the net, until it is brought ashore, when the wicked must be separated from the good, that in the good, as in His temple, God may be all in all. We acknowledge, indeed, that His word is now fulfilled who spake in the psalm, and said, "I have announced and spoken; they are multiplied above number."[2] This takes place now, since He has spoken, first by the mouth of His forerunner John, and afterward by His own mouth, saying, "Repent: for the kingdom of heaven is at hand."[3] He chose disciples, whom He also called apostles,[4] of lowly birth, unhonoured, and illiterate, so that whatever great thing they might be or do, He might be and do it in them. He had one among them whose wickedness He could use well in order to accomplish His appointed passion, and furnish His Church an example of bearing with the wicked. Having sown the Holy Gospel as much as that behoved to be done by His bodily presence, He suffered, died, and rose again, showing by His passion what we ought to suffer for the truth, and by His resurrection what we ought to hope for in adversity; saving always the mystery of the sacrament, by which His blood was shed for the remission of sins. He held converse on the earth forty days with His disciples, and in their sight ascended into heaven, and after ten days sent the promised Holy Spirit. It was given as the chief and most necessary sign of His coming on those who had believed, that every one of them spoke in the tongues of all nations; thus signifying that the unity of the Catholic Church would embrace all nations and would in like manner speak in all tongues.

CHAP. 50. *Of the preaching of the Gospel, which is made more famous and powerful by the sufferings of its preachers*

Then was fulfilled that prophecy, "Out of Sion shall go forth the law, and the word of the Lord out of Jerusalem";[5] and the prediction of the Lord Christ Himself, when, after the resurrection, "He opened the understanding" of His amazed disciples "that they might understand the Scriptures, and said unto them, that thus it is written, and thus it behoved Christ to suffer, and to rise from the dead the third day, and that repentance and remission of sins should be preached in His name among all nations, beginning at Jerusalem."[6] And again, when, in reply to their questioning about the day of His last coming, He said, "It is not for you to know the times or the seasons which the Father hath put in His own power; but ye shall receive the power of the Holy Ghost coming upon you, and ye shall be witnesses unto me both in Jerusalem, and in all Judea, and Samaria, and even unto the ends of the earth."[7] First of all, the Church spread herself abroad from Jerusalem; and when very many in Judea and Samaria had believed, she also went into other nations by those who announced the gospel, whom, as lights, He Himself had both prepared by His word and kindled by His Holy Spirit. For He had said to them, "Fear ye not them which kill the body, but are not able to kill the soul."[8] And that they might not be frozen with fear, they burned with the fire of charity. Finally, the gospel of Christ was preached in the whole world, not only by those who had seen and heard Him both before His passion and after His resurrection, but also after their death by their successors, amid the horrible persecutions, diverse torments and deaths of the martyrs, God also bearing them witness, both with signs and wonders, and divers miracles and gifts of the Holy Ghost,[9] that the people of the nations, believing in Him Who was crucified for their redemption, might venerate with Christian love the blood of the martyrs which they had poured forth with devilish fury, and the very kings by whose laws the Church had been laid waste might become profitably subject to that name they had cruelly striven to take away from the earth, and might begin to persecute the false gods for whose sake the worshippers of the true God had formerly been persecuted.

CHAP. 51. *That the Catholic faith may be confirmed even by the dissensions of the heretics*

But the devil, seeing the temples of the demons deserted, and the human race running to the name of the liberating Mediator, has moved the heretics under the Christian name to resist

---

[1]Matt. 8. 47–50. [2]Ps. 40. 5. [3]Matt. 3. 2; 4. 17.
[4]Luke, 6. 13.

[5]Isa. 2. 3. [6]Luke, 24. 45–47. [7]Acts, 1. 7, 8.
[8]Matt. 10. 28. [9]Heb. 2. 4.

the Christian doctrine, as if they could be kept in the city of God indifferently without any correction, just as the city of confusion indifferently held the philosophers who were of diverse and adverse opinions. Those, therefore, in the Church of Christ who savour anything morbid and depraved, and, on being corrected that they may savour what is wholesome and right, contumaciously resist, and will not amend their pestiferous and deadly dogmas, but persist in defending them, become heretics, and, going without, are to be reckoned as enemies who serve for her discipline. For even thus they profit by their wickedness those true Catholic members of Christ, since God makes a good use even of the wicked, and all things work together for good to them that love Him.[1] For all the enemies of the Church, whatever error blinds or malice depraves them, exercise her patience if they receive the power to afflict her corporally; and if they only oppose her by wicked thought, they exercise her wisdom: but at the same time, if these enemies are loved, they exercise her benevolence, or even her beneficence, whether she deals with them by persuasive doctrine or by terrible discipline. And thus the devil, the prince of the impious city, when he stirs up his own vessels against the city of God that sojourns in this world, is permitted to do her no harm. For without doubt the divine providence procures for her both consolation through prosperity, that she may not be broken by adversity, and trial through adversity, that she may not be corrupted by prosperity; and thus each is tempered by the other, as we recognize in the Psalms that voice which arises from no other cause, "According to the multitude of my griefs in my heart, Thy consolations have delighted my soul."[2] Hence also is that saying of the apostle, "Rejoicing in hope, patient in tribulation."[3]

For it is not to be thought that what the same teacher says can at any time fail, "Whoever will live piously in Christ shall suffer persecution."[4] Because even when those who are without do not rage, and thus there seems to be, and really is, tranquillity, which brings very much consolation, especially to the weak, yet there are not wanting, yea, there are many within who by their abandoned manners torment the hearts of those who live piously, since by them the Christian and Catholic name is blasphemed; and the dearer that name is to those who will live piously in Christ, the more do they grieve that through the wicked, who have a place within, it

comes to be less loved than pious minds desire. The heretics themselves also, since they are thought to have the Christian name and sacraments, Scriptures, and profession, cause great grief in the hearts of the pious, both because many who wish to be Christians are compelled by their dissensions to hesitate, and many evil-speakers also find in them matter for blaspheming the Christian name, because they too are at any rate *called* Christians. By these and similar depraved manners and errors of men, those who will live piously in Christ suffer persecution, even when no one molests or vexes their body; for they suffer this persecution, not in their bodies, but in their hearts. Whence is that word, "According to the multitude of my griefs in my heart"; for he does not say, in my body. Yet, on the other hand, none of them can perish, because the immutable divine promises are thought of. And because the apostle says, "The Lord knoweth them that are His;[5] for whom He did foreknow, He also predestinated to be conformed to the image of His Son,"[6] none of them can perish; therefore it follows in that psalm, "Thy consolations have delighted my soul."[7] But that grief which arises in the hearts of the pious, who are persecuted by the manners of bad or false Christians, is profitable to the sufferers, because it proceeds from the charity in which they do not wish them either to perish or to hinder the salvation of others. Finally, great consolations grow out of their chastisement, which imbue the souls of the pious with a fecundity as great as the pains with which they were troubled concerning their own perdition. Thus in this world, in these evil days, not only from the time of the bodily presence of Christ and His apostles, but even from that of Abel, whom first his wicked brother slew because he was righteous,[8] and thenceforth even to the end of this world, the Church has gone forward on pilgrimage amid the persecutions of the world and the consolations of God.

CHAP. 52. *Whether we should believe what some think, that, as the ten persecutions which are past have been fulfilled, there remains no other beyond the eleventh, which must happen in the very time of Antichrist*

I do not think, indeed, that what some have thought or may think is rashly said or believed, that until the time of Antichrist the Church of Christ is not to suffer any persecutions besides those she has already suffered—that is, *ten*—

---

[1]Rom. 8. 28.   [2]Ps. 94. 19.   [3]Rom. 12. 12.
[4]II Tim. 3. 12.

[5]II Tim. 2. 19.   [6]Rom. 8. 29.   [7]Ps. 94. 19.
[8]I John, 3. 12.

and that the eleventh and last shall be inflicted by Antichrist. They reckon as the first that made by Nero, the second by Domitian, the third by Trajan, the fourth by Antoninus, the fifth by Severus, the sixth by Maximin, the seventh by Decius, the eighth by Valerian, the ninth by Aurelian, the tenth by Diocletian and Maximian. For as there were ten plagues in Egypt before the people of God could begin to go out, they think this is to be referred to as showing that the last persecution by Antichrist must be like the eleventh plague, in which the Egyptians, while following the Hebrews with hostility, perished in the Red Sea when the people of God passed through on dry land. Yet I do not think persecutions were prophetically signified by what was done in Egypt, however nicely and ingeniously those who think so may seem to have compared the two in detail, not by the prophetic Spirit, but by the conjecture of the human mind, which sometimes hits the truth, and sometimes is deceived. But what can those who think this say of the persecution in which the Lord Himself was crucified? In which number will they put it? And if they think the reckoning is to be made exclusive of this one, as if those must be counted which pertain to the body, and not that in which the Head Himself was set upon and slain, what can they make of that one which, after Christ ascended into heaven, took place in Jerusalem, when the blessed Stephen was stoned; when James the brother of John was slaughtered with the sword; when the Apostle Peter was imprisoned to be killed, and was set free by the angel; when the brethren were driven away and scattered from Jerusalem; when Saul, who afterward became the Apostle Paul, wasted the Church; and when he himself, publishing the glad tidings of the faith he had persecuted, suffered such things as he had inflicted, either from the Jews or from other nations, where he most fervently preached Christ everywhere? Why, then, do they think fit to start with Nero, when the Church in her growth had reached the times of Nero amid the most cruel persecutions, about which it would be too long to say anything? But if they think that only the persecutions made by kings ought to be reckoned, it was king Herod who also made a most grievous one after the ascension of the Lord. And what account do they give of Julian, whom they do not number in the ten? Did not he persecute the Church, who forbade the Christians to teach or learn liberal letters? Under him the elder Valentinian, who was the third

emperor after him, stood forth as a confessor of the Christian faith, and was dismissed from his command in the army. I shall say nothing of what he did at Antioch, except to mention his being struck with wonder at the freedom and cheerfulness of one most faithful and steadfast young man, who, when many were seized to be tortured, was tortured during a whole day, and sang under the instrument of torture, until the emperor feared lest he should succumb under the continued cruelties and put him to shame at last, which made him dread and fear that he would be yet more dishonourably put to the blush by the rest. Lastly, within our own recollection, did not Valens the Arian, brother of the foresaid Valentinian, waste the Catholic Church by great persecution throughout the East? But how unreasonable it is not to consider that the Church, which bears fruit and grows through the whole world, may suffer persecution from kings in some nations even when she does not suffer it in others! Perhaps, however, it was not to be reckoned a persecution when the king of the Goths, in Gothia itself, persecuted the Christians with wonderful cruelty, when there were none but Catholics there, of whom very many were crowned with martyrdom, as we have heard from certain brethren who had been there at that time as boys, and unhesitatingly called to mind that they had seen these things? And what took place in Persia of late? Was not persecution so hot against the Christians (if even yet it is allayed) that some of the fugitives from it came even to Roman towns? When I think of these and the like things, it does not seem to me that the number of persecutions with which the Church is to be tried can be definitely stated. But, on the other hand, it is no less rash to affirm that there will be some persecutions by kings besides that last one, about which no Christian is in doubt. Therefore we leave this undecided, supporting or refuting neither side of this question, but only restraining men from the audacious presumption of affirming either of them.

CHAP. 53. *Of the hidden time of the final persecution*

Truly Jesus Himself shall extinguish by His presence that last persecution which is to be made by Antichrist. For so it is written, that "He shall slay him with the breath of His mouth, and empty him with the brightness of His presence."[1] It is customary to ask, "When

[1] Isa. 11. 4; II Thess. 1. 9.

shall that be?" But this is quite unreasonable. For had it been profitable for us to know this, by whom could it better have been told than by God Himself, the Master, when the disciples questioned Him? For they were not silent when with Him, but inquired of Him, saying, "Lord, wilt Thou at this time present the kingdom to Israel, or when?" [1] But He said, "It is not for you to know the times, which the Father hath put in His own power." When they got that answer, they had not at all questioned Him about the hour, or day, or year, but about the time. In vain, then, do we attempt to compute definitely the years that may remain to this world, when we may hear from the mouth of the Truth that it is not for us to know this. Yet some have said that four hundred, some five hundred, others a thousand years, may be completed from the ascension of the Lord up to His final coming. But to point out how each of them supports his own opinion would take too long, and is not necessary; for indeed they use human conjectures, and bring forward nothing certain from the authority of the canonical Scriptures. But on this subject He puts aside the figures of the calculators, and orders silence, Who says, "It is not for you to know the times, which the Father hath put in His own power."

But because this sentence is in the Gospel, it is no wonder that the worshippers of the many and false gods have been none the less restrained from feigning that by the responses of the demons, whom they worship as gods, it has been fixed how long the Christian religion is to last. For when they saw that it could not be consumed by so many and great persecutions, but rather drew from them wonderful enlargements, they invented I know not what Greek verses, as if poured forth by a divine oracle to some one consulting it, in which, indeed, they make Christ innocent of this, as it were, sacrilegious crime, but add that Peter by enchantments brought it about that the name of Christ should be worshipped for three hundred and sixty-five years, and, after the completion of that number of years, should at once take end. Oh the hearts of learned men! Oh, learned wits, meet to believe such things *about* Christ as you are not willing to believe *in* Christ, that His disciple Peter did not learn magic arts from Him, yet that, although He was innocent, His disciple was an enchanter, and chose that His name rather than his own should be worshipped through his magic arts, his great labours and perils, and at last even

[1] Acts, I. 6, 7.

the shedding of his blood! If Peter the enchanter made the world so love Christ, what did Christ the innocent do to make Peter so love Him? Let them answer themselves then, and, if they can, let them understand that the world, for the sake of eternal life, was made to love Christ by that same supernal grace which made Peter also love Christ for the sake of the eternal life to be received from Him, and that even to the extent of suffering temporal death for Him. And then, what kind of gods are these who are able to predict such things, yet are not able to avert them, succumbing in such a way to a single enchanter and wicked magician (who, as they say, having slain a yearling boy and torn him to pieces, buried him with nefarious rites) that they permitted the sect hostile to themselves to gain strength for so great a time, and to surmount the horrid cruelties of so many great persecutions, not by resisting but by suffering, and to procure the overthrow of their own images, temples, rituals, and oracles? Finally, what god was it—not ours, certainly, but one of their own—who was either enticed or compelled by so great wickedness to perform these things? For those verses say that Peter bound, not any demon, but a god to do these things. Such a god have they who have not Christ.

CHAP. 54. *Of the very foolish lie of the pagans, in feigning that the Christian religion was not to last beyond three hundred and sixty-five years*

I might collect these and many similar arguments, if that year had not already passed by which lying divination has promised, and deceived vanity has believed. But as a few years ago three hundred and sixty-five years were completed since the time when the worship of the name of Christ was established by His presence in the flesh, and by the apostles, what other proof need we seek to refute that falsehood? For, not to place the beginning of this period at the nativity of Christ, because as an infant and boy He had no disciples, yet, when He began to have them, beyond doubt the Christian doctrine and religion then became known through His bodily presence, that is, after He was baptized in the river Jordan by the ministry of John. For on this account that prophecy went before concerning Him: "He shall reign from sea even to sea, and from the river even to the ends of the earth." [2] But since, before He suffered and rose

[2] Ps. 72. 8.

from the dead, the faith had not yet been defined to all, but was defined in the resurrection of Christ (for so the Apostle Paul speaks to the Athenians, saying, "But now He announces to men that all everywhere should repent, because He hath appointed a day in which to judge the world in equity, by the Man in whom He hath defined the faith to all men, raising Him from the dead" [1]), it is better that, in settling this question, we should start from that point, especially because the Holy Spirit was then given, just as He behoved to be given after the resurrection of Christ in that city from which the second law, that is, the New Testament, ought to begin. For the first, which is called the Old Testament, was given from Mount Sinai through Moses. But concerning this which was to be given by Christ it was predicted, "Out of Sion shall go forth the law and the word of the Lord out of Jerusalem"; [2] whence He Himself said, that repentance in His name behoved to be preached among all nations, but yet beginning at Jerusalem. [3] There, therefore, the worship of this name took its rise, that Jesus should be believed in, Who died and rose again. There this faith blazed up with such noble beginnings, that several thousand men, being converted to the name of Christ with wonderful alacrity, sold their goods for distribution among the needy, thus, by a holy resolution and most ardent charity, coming to voluntary poverty, and prepared themselves, amid the Jews who raged and thirsted for their blood, to contend for the truth even to death, not with armed power, but with more powerful patience. If this was accomplished by no magic arts, why do they hesitate to believe that the other could be done throughout the whole world by the same divine power by which this was done? But supposing Peter wrought that enchantment so that so great a multitude of men at Jerusalem was thus kindled to worship the name of Christ, who had either seized and fastened Him to the cross, or reviled Him when fastened there, we must still inquire when the three hundred and sixty-five years must be completed, counting from that year. Now Christ died when the Gemini were consuls, on the eighth day before the kalends of April. He rose the third day, as the apostles have proved by the evidence of their own senses. Then forty days after, He ascended into heaven. Ten days after, that is, on the fiftieth after his resurrection, He sent the Holy Spirit; then three thousand men believed when the apostles preached Him. Then,

[1] Acts, 17. 30, 31.   [2] Isa. 2. 3.   [3] Luke, 24. 47.

therefore, arose the worship of that name, as we believe, and according to the real truth, by the efficacy of the Holy Spirit, but, as impious vanity has feigned or thought, by the magic arts of Peter. A little afterward, too, on a wonderful sign being wrought, when at Peter's own word a certain beggar, so lame from his mother's womb that he was carried by others and laid down at the gate of the temple, where he begged alms, was made whole in the name of Jesus Christ, and leaped up, five thousand men believed, and thenceforth the Church grew by sundry accessions of believers. Thus we gather the very day with which that year began, namely, that on which the Holy Spirit was sent, that is, during the ides of May. And, on counting the consuls, the three hundred and sixty-five years are found completed on the same ides in the consulate of Honorius and Eutychianus. Now, in the following year, in the consulate of Mallius Theodorus, when, according to that oracle of the demons or figment of men, there ought already to have been no Christian religion, it was not necessary to inquire, what perchance was done in other parts of the earth. But, as we know, in the most noted and eminent city, Carthage, in Africa, Gaudentius and Jovius, officers of the Emperor Honorius, on the fourteenth day before the kalends of April, overthrew the temples and broke the images of the false gods. And from that time to the present, during almost thirty years, who does not see how much the worship of the name of Christ has increased, especially after many of those became Christians who had been kept back from the faith by thinking that divination true, but saw when that same number of years was completed that it was empty and ridiculous? We, therefore, who are called and *are* Christians, do not believe in Peter, but in Him Whom Peter believed—being edified by Peter's sermons about Christ, not poisoned by his incantations; and not deceived by his enchantments, but aided by his good deeds. Christ Himself, who was Peter's Master in the doctrine which leads to eternal life, is our Master too.

But let us now at last finish this book, after thus far treating of, and showing as far as seemed sufficient, what is the mortal course of the two cities, the heavenly and the earthly, which are mingled together from the beginning down to the end. Of these, the earthly one has made to herself of whom she would, either from any other quarter, or even from among men, false gods whom she might serve by sacrifice;

but she which is heavenly and is a pilgrim on the earth does not make false gods, but is herself made by the true God of Whom she herself must be the true sacrifice. Yet both alike either enjoy temporal good things, or are afflicted with temporal evils, but with diverse faith, diverse hope, and diverse love, until they must be separated by the last judgment, and each must receive her own end, of which there is no end. About these ends of both we must next treat.

BOOK XIX

ARGUMENT. In this book the end of the two cities, the earthly and the heavenly, is discussed. Augustine reviews the opinions of the philosophers regarding the supreme good, and their vain efforts to make for themselves a happiness in this life; and, while he refutes these, he takes occasion to show what the peace and happiness belonging to the heavenly city, or the people of christ, are both now and hereafter.

CHAP. 1. *That Varro has made out that two hundred and eighty-eight different sects of philosophy might be formed by the various opinions regarding the supreme good*

As I see that I have still to discuss the fit destinies of the two cities, the earthly and the heavenly, I must first explain, so far as the limits of this work allow me, the reasonings by which men have attempted to make for themselves a happiness in this unhappy life, in order that it may be evident, not only from divine authority, but also from such reasons as can be adduced to unbelievers, how the empty dreams of the philosophers differ from the hope which God gives to us, and from the substantial fulfillment of it which He will give us as our blessedness. Philosophers have expressed a great variety of diverse opinions regarding the end of goods and of evils, and this question they have eagerly canvassed, that they might, if possible, discover what makes a man happy. For the end of our good is that for the sake of which other things are to be desired, while it is to be desired for its own sake; and the end of evil is that on account of which other things are to be shunned, while it is avoided on its own account. Thus, by the *end of good,* we at present mean, not that by which good is destroyed, so that it no longer exists, but that by which it is finished, so that it becomes complete; and by the *end of evil* we mean, not that which abolishes it, but that which completes its development. These two ends, therefore, are the supreme good and the supreme evil; and, as I have said, those who have in this vain life professed the study of wisdom have been at great pains to discover these ends, and to obtain the supreme good and avoid the supreme evil in this life. And although they erred in a variety of ways, yet natural insight has prevented them from wandering from the truth so far that they have not placed the supreme good and evil, some in the soul, some in the body, and some in both. From this tripartite distribution of the sects of philosophy, Marcus Varro, in his book *De Philosophia,* has drawn so large a variety of opinions, that, by a subtle and minute analysis of distinctions, he numbers without difficulty as many as 288 sects—not that these have actually existed, but sects which are possible.

To illustrate briefly what he means, I must begin with his own introductory statement in the above-mentioned book, that there are four things which men desire, as it were by nature without a master, without the help of any instruction, without industry or the art of living which is called virtue, and which is certainly learned: either pleasure, which is an agreeable stirring of the bodily sense; or repose, which excludes every bodily inconvenience; or both these, which Epicurus calls by the one name, pleasure; or the primary objects of nature, which comprehend the things already named and other things, either bodily, such as health, and safety, and integrity of the members, or spiritual, such as the greater and less mental gifts that are found in men. Now these four things—pleasure, repose, the two combined, and the primary objects of nature—exist in us in such sort that we must either desire virtue on their account, or them for the sake of virtue, or both for their own sake; and consequently there arise from this distinction twelve sects, for each is by this consideration tripled. I will illustrate this in one instance, and, having done so, it will not be difficult to understand the others. According, then, as bodily pleasure is subjected, preferred, or united to virtue, there are three sects. It is subjected to virtue when it is chosen as subservient to virtue. Thus it is a duty of virtue to live for one's country, and for its sake to beget children, neither of which can be done without bodily pleasure. For there is pleasure in eating and drinking, pleasure also in sexual intercourse. But when it is preferred to virtue, it is desired for its own sake, and virtue is chosen only for its sake, and to effect nothing else than the attainment or preservation of bodily pleasure. And this, indeed, is to make life hideous; for where virtue is the slave of pleasure it no longer deserves the name of virtue. Yet even this disgraceful distortion has found some philosophers to patronize and defend it. Then virtue is united to pleasure when neither is desired for the other's sake, but both for their own. And therefore, as pleasure, according as it is subjected, preferred, or united to virtue, makes three sects, so also do repose, pleasure and repose combined, and the prime natural blessings, make their three sects each. For as men's opinions vary, and these four things are sometimes subjected, sometimes preferred, and sometimes united to virtue, there are produced twelve sects. But this number again is doubled by the addition of one difference, viz., the social life; for whoever attaches himself to any of these sects does so either for his own sake alone, or for the sake of a companion, for whom he ought to wish what he desires for himself. And thus there will be twelve of those who think some one of these opinions should be held for their own sakes, and other twelve who decide that they ought to follow this or that philosophy not for their own sakes only, but also for the sake of others whose good they desire as their own. These twenty-four sects again are doubled, and become forty-eight by adding a difference taken from the New Academy. For each of these four and twenty sects can hold and defend their opinion as certain, as the Stoics defended the position that the supreme good of man consisted solely in virtue; or they can be held as probable, but not certain, as the New Academics did. There are, therefore, twenty-four who hold their philosophy as certain true, other twenty-four who hold their opinions as probable, but not certain. Again, as each person who attaches himself to any of these sects may adopt the mode of life either of the Cynics or of the other philosophers, this distinction will double the number, and so make ninety-six sects. Then, lastly, as each of these sects may be adhered to either by men who love a life of ease, as those who have through choice or necessity addicted themselves to study, or by men who love a busy life, as those who, while philosophizing, have been much occupied with state affairs and public business, or by men who choose a mixed life, in imitation of those who have apportioned their time partly to erudite leisure, partly to necessary business: by these differences the number of the sects is tripled, and becomes 288.

I have thus, as briefly and lucidly as I could, given in my own words the opinions which Varro expresses in his book. But how he refutes all the rest of these sects, and chooses one, the Old Academy, instituted by Plato, and continuing to Polemo, the fourth teacher of that school of philosophy which held that their system was certain; and how on this ground he distinguishes it from the New Academy, which began with Polemo's successor Arcesilaus, and held that all things are uncertain; and how he seeks to establish that the Old Academy was as free from error as from doubt—all this, I say, were too long to enter upon in detail, and yet I must not altogether pass it by in silence. Varro then rejects, as a first step, all those differences which have multiplied the number of sects; and the ground on which he does so is that they are not differences about the supreme good. He maintains that in philosophy a sect is created only by its having an opinion of its own different from other schools on the point of the ends-in-chief. For man has no other reason for philosophizing than that he may be happy; but that which makes him happy is itself the supreme good. In other words, the supreme good is the reason of philosophizing; and therefore that cannot be called a sect of philosophy which pursues no way of its own towards the supreme good. Thus, when it is asked whether a wise man will adopt the social life, and desire and be interested in the supreme good of his friend as in his own, or will, on the contrary, do all that he does merely for his own sake, there is no question here about the supreme good, but only about the propriety of associating or not associating a friend in its participation; whether the wise man will do this not for his own sake, but for the sake of his friend in whose good he delights as in his own. So, too, when it is asked whether all things about which philosophy is concerned are to be considered uncertain, as by the New Academy, or certain, as the other philosophers maintain, the question here is not what end should be pursued, but whether or not we are to believe in the substantial existence of that end; or, to put it more plainly, whether he who pursues the supreme good must maintain that it is a true good, or only that it appears to him to be true, though possibly it may be delusive—both pursuing one and the same good. The distinction, too, which is founded on the dress and manners of the Cynics, does not touch the question of the chief good, but only the question whether he who pursues that good which seems to himself true should live as do the Cynics. There were, in fact, men who, though they pursued different things as the supreme good, some choosing pleasure, others virtue, yet adopted that mode of life which gave the Cynics their name. Thus, whatever it is which distinguishes the Cynics from other philosophers, this has no bearing on the choice and pursuit of that good which constitutes happiness. For if it had any such bearing, then the same habits of life would necessitate the pursuit of the same chief good, and diverse habits would necessitate the pursuit of different ends.

CHAP. 2. *How Varro, by removing all the differences which do not form sects, but are merely secondary questions, reaches three definitions of the chief good, of which we must choose one*

The same may be said of those three kinds of life, the life of studious leisure and search after truth, the life of easy engagement in affairs, and the life in which both these are mingled. When it is asked, which of these should be adopted, this involves no controversy about the end of good, but inquires which of these three puts a man in the best position for finding and retaining the supreme good. For this good, as soon as a man finds it, makes him happy; but lettered leisure, or public business, or the alternation of these, do not necessarily constitute happiness. Many, in fact, find it possible to adopt one or other of these modes of life, and yet to miss what makes a man happy. The question, therefore, regarding the supreme good and the supreme evil, and which distinguishes sects of philosophy, is one; and these questions concerning the social life, the doubt of the Academy, the dress and food of the Cynics, the three modes of life—the active, the contemplative, and the mixed—these are different questions, into none of which the question of the chief good enters. And therefore, as Marcus Varro multiplied the sects to the number of 288 (or whatever larger number he chose) by introducing these four differences derived from the social life, the New Academy, the Cynics, and the threefold form of life, so, by removing these differences as having no bearing on the supreme good, and as therefore not constituting what can properly be called sects, he returns to those twelve schools which concern themselves with

inquiring what that good is which makes man happy, and he shows that one of these is true, the rest false. In other words, he dismisses the distinction founded on the threefold mode of life, and so decreases the whole number by two-thirds, reducing the sects to ninety-six. Then, putting aside the Cynic peculiarities, the number decreases by a half, to forty-eight. Taking away next the distinction occasioned by the hesitancy of the New Academy, the number is again halved, and reduced to twenty-four. Treating in a similar way the diversity introduced by the consideration of the social life, there are left but twelve, which this difference had doubled to twenty-four. Regarding these twelve, no reason can be assigned why they should not be called sects. For in them the sole inquiry is regarding the supreme good and the ultimate evil—that is to say, regarding the supreme good, for this being found, the opposite evil is thereby found. Now, to make these twelve sects, he multiplies by three these four things—pleasure, repose, pleasure and repose combined, and the primary objects of nature which Varro calls *primigenia*. For as these four things are sometimes subordinated to virtue, so that they seem to be desired not for their own sake, but for virtue's sake; sometimes preferred to it, so that virtue seems to be necessary not on its own account, but in order to attain these things; sometimes joined with it, so that both they and virtue are desired for their own sakes—we must multiply the four by three, and thus we get twelve sects. But from those four things Varro eliminates three—pleasure, repose, pleasure and repose combined—not because he thinks these are not worthy of the place assigned them, but because they are included in the primary objects of nature. And what need is there, at any rate, to make a three-fold division out of these two ends, pleasure and repose, taking them first severally and then conjunctly, since both they, and many other things besides, are comprehended in the primary objects of nature? Which of the three remaining sects must be chosen? This is the question that Varro dwells upon. For whether one of these three or some other be chosen, reason forbids that more than one be true. This we shall afterwards see; but meanwhile let us explain as briefly and distinctly as we can how Varro makes his selection from these three, that is, from the sects which severally hold that the primary objects of nature are to be desired for virtue's sake, that virtue is to be desired for their sake, and that virtue and these objects are to be desired each for their own sake.

CHAP. 3. *Which of the three leading opinions regarding the chief good should be preferred, according to Varro, who follows Antiochus and the Old Academy*

Which of these three is true and to be adopted he attempts to show in the following manner. As it is the supreme good, not of a tree, or of a beast, or of a god, but of man, that philosophy is in quest of, he thinks that, first of all, we must define man. He is of opinion that there are two parts in human nature, body and soul, and makes no doubt that of these two the soul is the better and by far the more worthy part. But whether the soul alone is the man, so that the body holds the same relation to it as a horse to the horseman, this he thinks has to be ascertained. The horseman is not a horse and a man, but only a man, yet he is called a horseman, because he is in some relation to the horse. Again, is the body alone the man, having a relation to the soul such as the cup has to the drink? For it is not the cup and the drink it contains which are called the cup, but the cup alone; yet it is so called because it is made to hold the drink. Or, lastly, is it neither the soul alone nor the body alone, but both together, which are man, the body and the soul being each a part, but the whole man being both together, as we call two horses yoked together a pair, of which pair the near and the off horse is each a part, but we do not call either of them, no matter how connected with the other, a pair, but only both together? Of these three alternatives, then, Varro chooses the third, that man is neither the body alone, nor the soul alone, but both together. And therefore the highest good, in which lies the happiness of man, is composed of goods of both kinds, both bodily and spiritual. And consequently he thinks that the primary objects of nature are to be sought for their own sake, and that virtue, which is the art of living, and can be communicated by instruction, is the most excellent of spiritual goods. This virtue, then, or art of regulating life, when it has received these primary objects of nature which existed independently of it, and prior to any instruction, seeks them all, and itself also, for its own sake; and it uses them, as it also uses itself, that from them all it may derive profit and enjoyment, greater or less, according as they are themselves greater or less; and while it takes pleasure in all of them, it despises the less that it may obtain or retain the greater when occasion demands. Now, of all goods, spiritual or bodily, there is none at all to compare with virtue. For virtue makes a good use both of itself and of all other goods in which lies man's happiness; and where it is absent, no matter how many good things a man has, they are not for his good, and consequently should not be called good things while they belong to one who makes them useless by using them badly. The life of man, then, is called happy when it enjoys virtue and these other spiritual and bodily good things without which virtue is impossible. It is called happier if it enjoys some or many other good things which are not essential to virtue; and happiest of all, if it lacks not one of the good things which pertain to the body and the soul. For life is not the same thing as virtue, since not every life, but a wisely regulated life, is virtue; and yet, while there can be life of some kind without virtue, there cannot be virtue without life. This I might apply to memory and reason, and such mental faculties; for these exist prior to instruction, and without them there cannot be any instruction, and consequently no virtue, since virtue is learned. But bodily advantages, such as swiftness of foot, beauty, or strength, are not essential to virtue, neither is virtue essential to them, and yet they are good things; and, according to our philosophers, even these advantages are desired by virtue for its own sake, and are used and enjoyed by it in a becoming manner.

They say that this happy life is also social, and loves the advantages of its friends as its own, and for their sake wishes for them what it desires for itself, whether these friends live in the same family, as a wife, children, domestics; or in the locality where one's home is, as the citizens of the same town; or in the world at large, as the nations bound in common human brotherhood; or in the universe itself, comprehended in the heavens and the earth, as those whom they call gods, and provide as friends for the wise man, and whom we more familiarly call angels. Moreover, they say that, regarding the supreme good and evil, there is no room for doubt, and that they therefore differ from the New Academy in this respect, and they are not concerned whether a philosopher pursues those ends which they think true in the Cynic dress and manner of life or in some other. And, lastly, in regard to the three modes of life, the contemplative, the active, and the composite, they declare in favour of the third. That these were the opinions and doctrines of the Old Academy, Varro asserts on the authority of Antiochus, Cicero's master and his own, though Cicero makes him out to have been more frequently in accordance with the Stoics than with the Old Academy. But of what importance is this to us, who ought to judge the matter on its own merits, rather than to understand accurately what different men have thought about it?

CHAP. 4. *What the Christians believe regarding the supreme good and evil, in opposition to the philosophers, who have maintained that the supreme good is in themselves*

If, then, we be asked what the city of God has to say upon these points, and, in the first place, what its opinion regarding the supreme good and evil is, it will reply that life eternal is the supreme good, death eternal the supreme evil, and that to obtain the one and escape the other we must live rightly. And thus it is written, "The just lives by faith," [1] for we do not as yet see our good, and must therefore live by faith; neither have we in ourselves power to live rightly, but can do so only if He Who has given us faith to believe in His help do help us when we believe and pray. As for those who have supposed that the sovereign good and evil are to be found in this life, and have placed it either in the soul or the body, or in both, or, to speak more explicitly, either in pleasure or in virtue, or in both; in repose or in virtue, or in both; in pleasure and repose, or in virtue, or in all combined; in the primary objects of nature, or in virtue, or in both—all these have, with a marvelous shallowness, sought to find their blessedness in this life and in themselves. Contempt has been poured upon such ideas by the Truth, saying by the prophet, "The Lord knoweth the thoughts of men" (or, as the Apostle Paul cites the passage, "The Lord knoweth the thoughts of the *wise*") "that they are vain." [2]

For what flood of eloquence can suffice to detail the miseries of this life? Cicero, in the *Consolation* on the death of his daughter, has spent all his ability in lamentation; but how inadequate was even his ability here? For when, where, how, in this life can these primary objects of nature be possessed so that they may not be assailed by unforeseen accidents? Is the body of the wise man exempt from any pain which may dispel pleasure, from any disquietude which may banish repose? The amputation or decay of the members of the body puts an end to its integrity, deformity blights its beauty, weakness its health, lassitude its vigour, sleepiness or sluggishness its activity—and which of these is it that may not assail the flesh of the wise man? Comely and fitting attitudes

and movements of the body are numbered among the prime natural blessings; but what if some sickness makes the members tremble? what if a man suffers from curvature of the spine to such an extent that his hands reach the ground, and he goes upon all-fours like a quadruped? Does not this destroy all beauty and grace in the body, whether at rest or in motion? What shall I say of the fundamental blessings of the soul, sense and intellect, of which the one is given for the perception, and the other for the comprehension of truth? But what kind of sense is it that remains when a man becomes deaf and blind? where are reason and intellect when disease makes a man delirious? We can scarcely, or not at all, refrain from tears, when we think of or see the actions and words of such frantic persons, and consider how different from and even opposed to their own sober judgment and ordinary conduct their present demeanour is. And what shall I say of those who suffer from demoniacal possession? Where is their own intelligence hidden and buried while the malignant spirit is using their body and soul according to his own will? And who is quite sure that no such thing can happen to the wise man in this life? Then, as to the perception of truth, what can we hope for even in this way while in the body, as we read in the true book of Wisdom, "The corruptible body weigheth down the soul, and the earthly tabernacle presseth down the mind that museth upon many things"?[3] And eagerness, or desire of action, if this is the right meaning to put upon the Greek ὁρμή, is also reckoned among the primary advantages of nature; and yet is it not this which produces those pitiable movements of the insane, and those actions which we shudder to see, when sense is deceived and reason deranged?

In fine, virtue itself, which is not among the primary objects of nature, but succeeds to them as the result of learning, though it holds the highest place among human good things, what is its occupation save to wage perpetual war with vices—not those that are outside of us, but within; not other men's, but our own—a war which is waged especially by that virtue which the Greeks call σωφροσύνη, and we temperance, and which bridles carnal lusts, and prevents them from winning the consent of the spirit to wicked deeds? For we must not fancy that there is no vice in us, when, as the apostle says, "The flesh lusteth against the spirit";[4] for to this vice there is a contrary virtue, when, as the same writer says, "The spirit lusteth against

---

[1]Hab. 2. 4.   [2]Ps. 94. 11, and I Cor. 3. 20.   [3]Wisd. 9. 15.   [4]Gal. 5. 17.

the flesh." "For these two," he says, "are contrary one to the other, so that you cannot do the things which you would." But what is it we wish to do when we seek to attain the supreme good, unless that the flesh should cease to lust against the spirit, and that there be no vice in us against which the spirit may lust? And as we cannot attain to this in the present life, however ardently we desire it, let us by God's help accomplish at least this, to preserve the soul from succumbing and yielding to the flesh that lusts against it, and to refuse our consent to the perpetration of sin. Far be it from us, then, to fancy that while we are still engaged in this intestine war, we have already found the happiness which we seek to reach by victory. And who is there so wise that he has no conflict at all to maintain against his vices?

What shall I say of that virtue which is called prudence? Is not all its vigilance spent in the discernment of good from evil things, so that no mistake may be admitted about what we should desire and what we should avoid? And thus it is itself a proof that we are in the midst of evils, or that evils are in us; for it teaches us that it is an evil to consent to sin, and a good to refuse this consent. And yet this evil, to which prudence teaches and temperance enables us not to consent, is removed from this life neither by prudence nor by temperance. And justice, whose office it is to render to every man his due, whereby there is in man himself a certain just order of nature, so that the soul is subjected to God, and the flesh to the soul, and consequently both soul and flesh to God—does not this virtue demonstrate that it is as yet rather labouring towards its end than resting in its finished work? For the soul is so much the less subjected to God as it is less occupied with the thought of God; and the flesh is so much the less subjected to the spirit as it lusts more vehemently against the spirit. So long, therefore, as we are beset by this weakness, this plague, this disease, how shall we dare to say that we are safe? and if not safe, then how can we be already enjoying our final beatitude? Then that virtue which goes by the name of fortitude is the plainest proof of the ills of life, for it is these ills which it is compelled to bear patiently. And this holds good, no matter though the ripest wisdom co-exists with it. And I am at a loss to understand how the Stoic philosophers can presume to say that these are no ills, though at the same time they allow the wise man to commit suicide and pass out of this life if they become so grievous that he cannot or ought not to endure them. But such is the stupid pride of these men who fancy that the supreme good can be found in this life, and that they can become happy by their own resources, that their wise man, or at least the man whom they fancifully depict as such, is always happy, even though he become blind, deaf, dumb, mutilated, racked with pains, or suffer any conceivable calamity such as may compel him to make away with himself; and they are not ashamed to call the life that is beset with these evils happy. O happy life, which seeks the aid of death to end it? If it is happy, let the wise man remain in it; but if these ills drive him out of it, in what sense is it happy? Or how can they say that these are not evils which conquer the virtue of fortitude, and force it not only to yield, but so to rave that it in one breath calls life happy and recommends it to be given up? For who is so blind as not to see that if it were happy it would not be fled from? And if they say we should flee from it on account of the infirmities that beset it, why then do they not lower their pride and acknowledge that it is miserable? Was it, I would ask, fortitude or weakness which prompted Cato to kill himself? for he would not have done so had he not been too weak to endure Cæsar's victory. Where, then, is his fortitude? It has yielded, it has succumbed, it has been so thoroughly overcome as to abandon, forsake, flee this happy life. Or was it no longer happy? Then it was miserable. How, then, were these not evils which made life miserable, and a thing to be escaped from?

And therefore those who admit that these are evils, as the Peripatetics do, and the Old Academy, the sect which Varro advocates, express a more intelligible doctrine; but theirs also is a surprising mistake, for they contend that this is a happy life which is beset by these evils, even though they be so great that he who endures them should commit suicide to escape them. "Pains and anguish of body," says Varro, "are evils, and so much the worse in proportion to their severity; and to escape them you must quit this life." What life, I pray? This life, he says, which is oppressed by such evils. Then it is happy in the midst of these very evils on account of which you say we must quit it? Or do you call it happy because you are at liberty to escape these evils by death? What, then, if by some secret judgment of God you were held fast and not permitted to die, nor suffered to live without these evils? In that case, at least you would say that such a life was miserable. It is soon relinquished, no doubt, but this does not make it not miserable; for were it eternal, you yourself would pronounce it miserable. Its brevity, therefore, does not clear it of misery; neither ought it to be called happiness because it is a brief misery. Certainly there is a mighty force in these evils which compel a man—according to them, even a wise man—to cease to be a man that he may escape them, though they say, and say truly, that it is as it were the first and strongest demand of nature that a man cherish himself, and naturally therefore avoid death, and should so stand his own friend as to wish and vehemently aim at continuing to exist as a living creature, and subsisting in this union of soul and body. There is a mighty force in these evils to overcome this natural instinct by which death is by every means and with all a man's efforts avoided, and to overcome it so completely that what was avoided is desired, sought after, and if it cannot in any other way be obtained, is inflicted by the man on himself. There is a mighty force in these evils which make fortitude a homicide—if, indeed, that is to be called fortitude which is so thoroughly overcome by these evils, that it not only cannot preserve by patience the man whom it undertook to govern and defend, but is itself obliged to kill him. The wise man, I admit, ought to bear death with patience, but when it is inflicted by another. If, then, as these men maintain, he is obliged to inflict it on himself, certainly it must be owned that the ills which compel him to this are not only evils, but intolerable evils. The life, then, which is either subject to accidents, or environed with evils so considerable and grievous, could never have been called happy, if the men who give it this name had condescended to yield to the truth, and to be conquered by valid arguments, when they inquired after the happy life, as they yield to unhappiness, and are overcome by overwhelming evils, when they put themselves to death, and if they had not fancied that the supreme good was to be found in this mortal life; for the very virtues of this life, which are certainly its best and most useful possessions, are all the more telling proofs of its miseries in proportion as they are helpful against the violence of its dangers, toils, and woes. For if these are true virtues—and such cannot exist save in those who have true piety—they do not profess to be able to deliver the men who possess them from all miseries; for true virtues tell no such lies, but they profess that by the hope of the future world this life, which is miserably involved in the many and great evils of this world, is happy as it is also safe. For if not yet safe, how could it be happy? And

therefore the Apostle Paul, speaking not of men without prudence, temperance, fortitude, and justice, but of those whose lives were regulated by true piety, and whose virtues were therefore true, says, "For we are saved by hope: now hope which is seen is not hope; for what a man seeth, why doth he yet hope for? But if we hope for that we see not, then do we with patience wait for it." [1] As, therefore, we are saved, so we are made happy by hope. And as we do not as yet possess a present, but look for a future salvation, so is it with our happiness, and this "with patience"; for we are encompassed with evils, which we ought patiently to endure, until we come to the ineffable enjoyment of unmixed good; for there shall be no longer anything to endure. Salvation, such as it shall be in the world to come, shall itself be our final happiness. And this happiness these philosophers refuse to believe in, because they do not see it, and attempt to fabricate for themselves a happiness in this life, based upon a virtue which is as deceitful as it is proud.

CHAP. 5. *Of the social life, which, though most desirable, is frequently disturbed by many distresses*

We give a much more unlimited approval to their idea that the life of the wise man must be social. For how could the city of God (concerning which we are already writing no less than the nineteenth book of this work) either take a beginning or be developed, or attain its proper destiny, if the life of the saints were not a social life? But who can enumerate all the great grievances with which human society abounds in the misery of this mortal state? Who can weigh them? Hear how one of their comic writers makes one of his characters express the common feelings of all men in this matter: "I am married; this is one misery. Children are born to me; they are additional cares." What shall I say of the miseries of love which Terence also recounts—"slights, suspicions, quarrels, war to-day, peace to-morrow?" Is not human life full of such things? Do they not often occur even in honourable friendships? On all hands we experience these slights, suspicions, quarrels, war, all of which are undoubted evils; while, on the other hand, peace is a doubtful good, because we do not know the heart of our friend, and though we did know it to-day, we should be as ignorant of what it might be to-morrow. Who ought to be, or who are more friendly than those who live in the same family? And yet who can rely

[1] Rom. 8. 24.

even upon this friendship, seeing that secret treachery has often broken it up, and produced enmity as bitter as the amity was sweet, or seemed sweet by the most perfect dissimulation? It is on this account that the words of Cicero so move the heart of every one, and provoke a sigh: "There are no snares more dangerous than those which lurk under the guise of duty or the name of relationship. For the man who is your declared foe you can easily baffle by precaution; but this hidden, intestine, and domestic danger not merely exists, but overwhelms you before you can foresee and examine it." It is also to this that allusion is made by the divine saying, "A man's foes are those of his own household"[1]—words which one cannot hear without pain; for though a man have sufficient fortitude to endure it with equanimity, and sufficient sagacity to baffle the malice of a pretended friend, yet if he himself is a good man, he cannot but be greatly pained at the discovery of the perfidy of wicked men, whether they have always been wicked and merely feigned goodness, or have fallen from a better to a malicious disposition. If, then, home, the natural refuge from the ills of life, is itself not safe, what shall we say of the city, which, as it is larger, is so much the more filled with lawsuits civil and criminal, and is never free from the fear, if sometimes from the actual outbreak, of disturbing and bloody insurrections and civil wars?

CHAP. 6. *Of the error of human judgments when the truth is hidden*

What shall I say of these judgments which men pronounce on men, and which are necessary in communities, whatever outward peace they enjoy? Melancholy and lamentable judgments they are, since the judges are men who cannot discern the consciences of those at their bar, and are therefore frequently compelled to put innocent witnesses to the torture to ascertain the truth regarding the crimes of other men. What shall I say of torture applied to the accused himself? He is tortured to discover whether he is guilty, so that, though innocent, he suffers most undoubted punishment for crime that is still doubtful, not because it is proved that he committed it, but because it is not ascertained that he did not commit it. Thus the ignorance of the judge frequently involves an innocent person in suffering. And what is still more unendurable—a thing, indeed, to be bewailed, and, if that were possible, watered

[1] Matt. 10. 36.

with fountains of tears—is this, that when the judge puts the accused to the question, that he may not unwittingly put an innocent man to death, the result of this lamentable ignorance is that this very person, whom he tortured that he might not condemn him if innocent, is condemned to death both tortured and innocent. For if he has chosen, in obedience to the philosophical instructions to the wise man, to quit this life rather than endure any longer such tortures, he declares that he has committed the crime which in fact he has not committed. And when he has been condemned and put to death, the judge is still in ignorance whether he has put to death an innocent or a guilty person, though he put the accused to the torture for the very purpose of saving himself from condemning the innocent; and consequently he has both tortured an innocent man to discover his innocence and has put him to death without discovering it. If such darkness shrouds social life, will a wise judge take his seat on the bench or no? Beyond question he will. For human society, which he thinks it a wickedness to abandon, constrains him and compels him to this duty. And he thinks it no wickedness that innocent witnesses are tortured regarding the crimes of which other men are accused; or that the accused are put to the torture, so that they are often overcome with anguish, and, though innocent, make false confessions regarding themselves, and are punished; or that, though they be not condemned to die, they often die during, or in consequence of, the torture; or that sometimes the accusers, who perhaps have been prompted by a desire to benefit society by bringing criminals to justice, are themselves condemned through the ignorance of the judge, because they are unable to prove the truth of their accusations though they are true, and because the witnesses lie, and the accused endures the torture without being moved to confession. These numerous and important evils he does not consider sins; for the wise judge does these things, not with any intention of doing harm, but because his ignorance compels him, and because human society claims him as a judge. But though we therefore acquit the judge of malice, we must none the less condemn human life as miserable. And if he is compelled to torture and punish the innocent because his office and his ignorance constrain him, is he a happy as well as guiltless man? Surely it were proof of more profound considerateness and finer feeling were he to recognize the misery of these necessities, and shrink from his own implication in that misery; and had he any piety about him, he would cry to God "From my necessities deliver Thou me."[1]

CHAP. 7. *Of the diversity of languages, by which the intercourse of men is prevented; and of the misery of wars, even of those called just*

After the state or city comes the world, the third circle of human society—the first being the house, and the second the city. And the world, as it is larger, so it is fuller of dangers, as the greater sea is the more dangerous. And here, in the first place, man is separated from man by the difference of languages. For if two men, each ignorant of the other's language, meet, and are not compelled to pass, but, on the contrary, to remain in company, dumb animals, though of different species, would more easily hold intercourse than they, human beings though they be. For their common nature is no help to friendliness when they are prevented by diversity of language from conveying their sentiments to one another; so that a man would more readily hold intercourse with his dog than with a foreigner. But the imperial city has endeavoured to impose on subject nations not only her yoke, but her language, as a bond of peace, so that interpreters, far from being scarce, are numberless. This is true; but how many great wars, how much slaughter and bloodshed, have provided this unity! And though these are past, the end of these miseries has not yet come. For though there have never been wanting, nor are yet wanting, hostile nations beyond the empire, against whom wars have been and are waged, yet, supposing there were no such nations, the very extent of the empire itself has produced wars of a more obnoxious description—social and civil wars—and with these the whole race has been agitated either by the actual conflict or the fear of a renewed outbreak. If I attempted to give an adequate description of these manifold disasters, these stern and lasting necessities, though I am quite unequal to the task, what limit could I set? But, say they, the wise man will wage just wars. As if he would not all the rather lament the necessity of just wars, if he remembers that he is a man; for if they were not just he would not wage them, and would therefore be delivered from all wars. For it is the wrongdoing of the opposing party which compels the wise man to wage just wars; and this wrong-doing, even though it gave rise to no war, would still be matter of grief to man be-

[1]Ps. 25. 17.

cause it is man's wrong-doing. Let every one, then, who thinks with pain on all these great evils, so horrible, so ruthless, acknowledge that this is misery. And if any one either endures or thinks of them without mental pain, this is a more miserable plight still, for he thinks himself happy because he has lost human feeling.

CHAP. 8. *That the friendship of good men cannot be securely rested in, so long as the dangers of this life force us to be anxious*

In our present wretched condition we frequently mistake a friend for an enemy, and an enemy for a friend. And if we escape this pitiable blindness, is not the unfeigned confidence and mutual love of true and good friends our one solace in human society, filled as it is with misunderstandings and calamities? And yet the more friends we have, and the more widely they are scattered, the more numerous are our fears that some portion of the vast masses of the disasters of life may light upon them. For we are not only anxious lest they suffer from famine, war, disease, captivity, or the inconceivable horrors of slavery, but we are also affected with the much more painful dread that their friendship may be changed into perfidy, malice, and injustice. And when these contingencies actually occur—as they do the more frequently the more friends we have and the more widely they are scattered—and when they come to our knowledge, who but the man who has experienced it can tell with what pangs the heart is torn? We would, in fact, prefer to hear that they were dead, although we could not without anguish hear of even this. For if their life has solaced us with the charms of friendship, can it be that their death should affect us with no sadness? He who will have none of this sadness must, if possible, have no friendly intercourse. Let him interdict or extinguish friendly affection; let him burst with ruthless insensibility the bonds of every human relationship; or let him contrive so to use them that no sweetness shall distil into his spirit. But if this is utterly impossible, how shall we contrive to feel no bitterness in the death of those whose life has been sweet to us? Hence arises that grief which affects the tender heart like a wound or a bruise and which is healed by the application of kindly consolation. For though the cure is affected all the more easily and rapidly the better condition the soul is in, we must not on this account suppose that there is nothing at all to heal. Although, then, our present life is afflicted, sometimes in a milder, sometimes in a more painful degree, by the death of those very dear to us, and especially of useful public men, yet we would prefer to hear that such men were dead rather than to hear or perceive that they had fallen from the faith, or from virtue—in other words, that they were spiritually dead. Of this vast material for misery the earth is full, and therefore it is written, "Is not human life upon earth a trial?"[1] And with the same reference the Lord says, "Woe to the world because of offenses!"[2] and again, "Because iniquity abounded, the love of many shall wax cold."[3] And hence we enjoy some gratification when our good friends die; for though their death leaves us in sorrow, we have the consolatory assurance that they are beyond the ills by which in this life even the best of men are broken down or corrupted, or are in danger of both results.

CHAP. 9. *Of the friendship of the holy angels, which men cannot be sure of in this life, owing to the deceit of the demons who hold in bondage the worshippers of a plurality of gods*

The philosophers who wished us to have the gods for our friends rank the friendship of the holy angels in the fourth circle of society, advancing now from the three circles of society on earth to the universe, and embracing heaven itself. And in this friendship we have indeed no fear that the angels will grieve us by their death or deterioration. But as we cannot mingle with them as familiarly as with men (which itself is one of the grievances of this life), and as Satan, as we read,[4] sometimes transforms himself into an angel of light, to tempt those whom it is necessary to discipline, or just to deceive, there is great need of God's mercy to preserve us from making friends of demons in disguise, while we fancy we have good angels for our friends; for the astuteness and deceitfulness of these wicked spirits is equalled by their hurtfulness. And is this not a great misery of human life, that we are involved in such ignorance as, but for God's mercy, makes us a prey to these demons? And it is very certain that the philosophers of the godless city, who have maintained that the gods were their friends, had fallen a prey to the malignant demons who rule that city, and whose eternal punishment is to be shared by it. For the nature of these beings is sufficiently evinced by the sacred or rather sacrilegious observances which form their worship, and by the filthy games in which their crimes are celebrated, and

which they themselves originated and exacted from their worshippers as a fit propitiation.

CHAP. 10. *The reward prepared for the saints after they have endured the trial of this life*

But not even the saints and faithful worshippers of the one true and most high God are safe from the manifold temptations and deceits of the demons. For in this abode of weakness, and in these wicked days, this state of anxiety has also its use, stimulating us to seek with keener longing for that security where peace is complete and unassailable. There we shall enjoy the gifts of nature, that is to say, all that God the Creator of all natures has bestowed upon ours —gifts not only good, but eternal, not only of the spirit, healed now by wisdom, but also of the body renewed by the resurrection. There the virtues shall no longer be struggling against any vice or evil, but shall enjoy the reward of victory, the eternal peace which no adversary shall disturb. This is the final blessedness, this the ultimate consummation, the unending end. Here, indeed, we are said to be blessed when we have such peace as can be enjoyed in a good life; but such blessedness is mere misery compared to that final felicity. When we mortals possess such peace as this mortal life can afford, virtue, if we are living rightly, makes a right use of the advantages of this peaceful condition; and when we have it not, virtue makes a good use even of the evils a man suffers. But this is true virtue, when it refers all the advantages it makes a good use of, and all that it does in making good use of good and evil things, and itself also, to that end in which we shall enjoy the best and greatest peace possible.

CHAP. 11. *Of the happiness of the eternal peace, which constitutes the end or true perfection of the saints*

And thus we may say of peace, as we have said of eternal life, that it is the end of our good; and the rather because the Psalmist says of the city of God, the subject of this laborious work, "Praise the Lord, O Jerusalem; praise thy God, O Zion: for He hath strengthened the bars of thy gates; He hath blessed thy children within thee; who hath made thy borders peace."[5] For when the bars of her gates shall be strengthened, none shall go in or come out from her; consequently we ought to understand the peace of her borders as that final peace we are wishing to declare. For even the mystical name of the city itself, that is, *Jerusalem*, means, as I

---

[1]Job, 7. 1.   [2]Matt. 17. 7.   [3]Matt. 24. 12.
[4]II Cor. 11. 14.

[5]Ps. 147. 12–14.

have already said, *Vision of Peace*. But as the word *peace* is employed in connection with things in this world in which certainly life eternal has no place, we have preferred to call the end or supreme good of this city *life eternal* rather than *peace*. Of this end the apostle says, "But now, being freed from sin, and become servants to God, ye have your fruit unto holiness, and the end life eternal."[1] But, on the other hand, as those who are not familiar with Scripture may suppose that the life of the wicked is eternal life, either because of the immortality of the soul, which some of the philosophers even have recognized, or because of the endless punishment of the wicked, which forms a part of our faith, and which seems impossible unless the wicked live for ever, it may therefore be advisable, in order that every one may readily understand what we mean, to say that the end or supreme good of this city is either peace in eternal life, or eternal life in peace. For peace is a good so great, that even in this earthly and mortal life there is no word we hear with such pleasure, nothing we desire with such zest, or find to be more thoroughly gratifying. So that if we dwell for a little longer on this subject, we shall not, in my opinion, be wearisome to our readers, who will attend both for the sake of understanding what is the end of this city of which we speak, and for the sake of the sweetness of peace which is dear to all.

CHAP. 12. *That even the fierceness of war and all the disquietude of men make towards this one end of peace, which every nature desires*

Whoever gives even moderate attention to human affairs and to our common nature, will recognize that if there is no man who does not wish to be joyful, neither is there any one who does not wish to have peace. For even they who make war desire nothing but victory—desire, that is to say, to attain to peace with glory. For what else is victory than the conquest of those who resist us? and when this is done there is peace. It is therefore with the desire for peace that wars are waged, even by those who take pleasure in exercising their warlike nature in command and battle. And hence it is obvious that peace is the end sought for by war. For every man seeks peace by waging war, but no man seeks war by making peace. For even they who intentionally interrupt the peace in which they are living have no hatred of peace, but only wish it changed into a peace that suits them better. They do not, therefore, wish to have no peace,

[1]Rom. 6. 22.

but only one more to their mind. And in the case of sedition, when men have separated themselves from the community, they yet do not effect what that they wish, unless they maintain some kind of peace with their fellow-conspirators. And therefore even robbers take care to maintain peace with their comrades, that they may with greater effect and greater safety invade the peace of other men. And if an individual happen to be of such unrivalled strength, and to be so jealous of partnership, that he trusts himself with no comrades, but makes his own plots, and commits depredations and murders on his own account, yet he maintains some shadow of peace with such persons as he is unable to kill, and from whom he wishes to conceal his deeds. In his own home, too, he makes it his aim to be at peace with his wife and children, and any other members of his household; for unquestionably their prompt obedience to his every look is a source of pleasure to him. And if this be not rendered, he is angry, he chides and punishes; and even by this storm he secures the calm peace of his own home, as occasion demands. For he sees that peace cannot be maintained unless all the members of the same domestic circle be subject to one head, such as he himself is in his own house. And therefore if a city or nation offered to submit itself to him, to serve him in the same style as he had made his household serve him, he would no longer lurk in a brigand's hiding-places, but lift his head in open day as a king, though the same coveteousness and wickedness should remain in him. And thus all men desire to have peace with their own circle whom they wish to govern as suits themselves. For even those whom they make war against they wish to make their own, and impose on them the laws of their own peace.

But let us suppose a man such as poetry and mythology speak of—a man so insociable and savage as to be called rather a semi-man than a man. Although, then, his kingdom was the solitude of a dreary cave, and he himself was so singularly bad-hearted that he was named Kα-κός, which is the Greek word for *bad;* though he had no wife to soothe him with endearing talk, no children to play with, no sons to do his bidding, no friend to enliven him with intercourse, not even his father Vulcan (though in one respect he was happier than his father, not having begotten a monster like himself); although he gave to no man, but took as he wished whatever he could, from whomsoever he could, when he could; yet in that solitary den, the floor of which, as Virgil[1] says, was always reeking with recent slaughter, there was nothing else than peace sought, a peace in which no one should molest him, or disquiet him with any assault or alarm. With his own body he desired to be at peace, and he was satisfied only in proportion as he had this peace. For he ruled his members, and they obeyed him; and for the sake of pacifying his mortal nature, which rebelled when it needed anything, and of allaying the sedition of hunger which threatened to banish the soul from the body, he made forays, slew, and devoured, but used the ferocity and savageness he displayed in these actions only for the preservation of his own life's peace. So that, had he been willing to make with other men the same peace which he made with himself in his own cave, he would neither have been called bad, nor a monster, nor a semi-man. Or if the appearance of his body and his vomiting smoky fires frightened men from having any dealings with him, perhaps his fierce ways arose not from a desire to do mischief, but from the necessity of finding a living. But he may have had no existence, or, at least, he was not such as the poets fancifully describe him, for they had to exalt Hercules, and did so at the expense of Cacus. It is better, then, to believe that such a man or semi-man never existed, and that this, in common with many other fancies of the poets, is mere fiction. For the most savage animals (and he is said to have been almost a wild beast) encompass their own species with a ring of protecting peace. They cohabit, beget, produce, suckle, and bring up their young, though very many of them are not gregarious, but solitary— not like sheep, deer, pigeons, starlings, bees, but such as lions, foxes, eagles, bats. For what tigress does not gently purr over her cubs, and lay aside her ferocity to fondle them? What kite, solitary as he is when circling over his prey, does not seek a mate, build a nest, hatch the eggs, bring up the young birds, and maintain with the mother of his family as peaceful a domestic alliance as he can? How much more powerfully do the laws of man's nature move him to hold fellowship and maintain peace with all men so far as in him lies, since even wicked men wage war to maintain the peace of their own circle, and wish that, if possible, all men belonged to them, that all men and things might serve but one head, and might, either through love or fear, yield themselves to peace with him! It is thus that pride in its perversity apes

[1] *Æneid*, BK. VIII. 195.

God. It abhors equality with other men under Him; but, instead of His rule, it seeks to impose a rule of its own upon its equals. It abhors, that is to say, the just peace of God, and loves its own unjust peace; but it cannot help loving peace of one kind or other. For there is no vice so clean contrary to nature that it obliterates even the faintest traces of nature.

He, then, who prefers what is right to what is wrong, and what is well-ordered to what is perverted, sees that the peace of unjust men is not worthy to be called peace in comparison with the peace of the just. And yet even what is perverted must of necessity be in harmony with, and in dependence on, and in some part of the order of things, for otherwise it would have no existence at all. Suppose a man hangs with his head downwards, this is certainly a perverted attitude of body and arrangement of its members; for that which nature requires to be above is beneath, and *vice versa*. This perversity disturbs the peace of the body, and is therefore painful. Nevertheless the spirit is at peace with its body, and labours for its preservation, and hence the suffering; but if it is banished from the body by its pains, then, so long as the bodily framework holds together, there is in the remains a kind of peace among the members, and hence the body remains suspended. And inasmuch as the earthly body tends towards the earth, and rests on the bond by which it is suspended, it tends thus to its natural peace, and the voice of its own weight demands a place for it to rest; and though now lifeless and without feeling, it does not fall from the peace that is natural to its place in creation, whether it already has it, or is tending towards it. For if you apply embalming preparations to prevent the bodily frame from mouldering and dissolving, a kind of peace still unites part to part, and keeps the whole body in a suitable place on the earth—in other words, in a place that is at peace with the body. If, on the other hand, the body receive no such care, but be left to the natural course, it is disturbed by exhalations that do not harmonize with one another, and that offend our senses; for it is this which is perceived in putrefaction until it is assimilated to the elements of the world, and particle by particle enters into peace with them. Yet throughout this process the laws of the most high Creator and Governor are strictly observed, for it is by Him the peace of the universe is administered. For although minute animals are produced from the carcass of a larger animal, all these little atoms, by the law of the same Creator, serve the animals they belong to in peace. And although the flesh of dead animals be eaten by others, no matter where it be carried, nor what it be brought into contact with, nor what it be converted and changed into, it still is ruled by the same laws which pervade all things for the conservation of every mortal race, and which bring things that fit one another into harmony.

CHAP. 13. *Of the universal peace which the law of nature preserves through all disturbances, and by which every one reaches his desert in a way regulated by the just judge*

The peace of the body then consists in the duly proportioned arrangement of its parts. The peace of the irrational soul is the harmonious repose of the appetites, and that of the rational soul the harmony of knowledge and action. The peace of body and soul is the well-ordered and harmonious life and health of the living creature. Peace between man and God is the well-ordered obedience of faith to eternal law. Peace between man and man is well-ordered concord. Domestic peace is the well-ordered concord between those of the family who rule and those who obey. Civil peace is a similar concord among the citizens. The peace of the celestial city is the perfectly ordered and harmonious enjoyment of God, and of one another in God. The peace of all things is the tranquillity of order. Order is the distribution which allots things equal and unequal, each to its own place. And hence, though the miserable, in so far as they are such, do certainly not enjoy peace, but are severed from that tranquillity of order in which there is no disturbance, nevertheless, inasmuch as they are deservedly and justly miserable, they are by their very misery connected with order. They are not, indeed, conjoined with the blessed, but they are disjoined from them by the law of order. And though they are disquieted, their circumstances are notwithstanding adjusted to them, and consequently they have some tranquillity of order, and therefore some peace. But they are wretched because, although not wholly miserable, they are not in that place where any mixture of misery is impossible. They would, however, be more wretched if they had not that peace which arises from being in harmony with the natural order of things. When they suffer, their peace is in so far disturbed; but their peace continues in so far as they do not suffer, and in so far as their nature continues to exist. As, then, there may be life without pain, while there cannot be pain without some kind of life, so there may be peace without war, but there cannot be war without some kind of peace, because war supposes the existence of some natures to wage it, and these natures cannot exist without peace of one kind or other.

And therefore there is a nature in which evil does not or even cannot exist; but there cannot be a nature in which there is no good. Hence not even the nature of the devil himself is evil, in so far as it is nature, but it was made evil by being perverted. Thus he did not abide in the truth,[1] but could not escape the judgment of the Truth; he did not abide in the tranquillity of order, but did not therefore escape the power of the Ordainer. The good imparted by God to his nature did not screen him from the justice of God by which order was preserved in his punishment; neither did God punish the good which He had created, but the evil which the devil had committed. God did not take back all He had imparted to his nature, but something He took and something He left, that there might remain enough to be sensible of the loss of what was taken. And this very sensibility to pain is evidence of the good which has been taken away and the good which has been left. For, were nothing good left, there could be no pain on account of the good which had been lost. For he who sins is still worse if he rejoices in his loss of righteousness. But he who is in pain, if he derives no benefit from it, mourns at least the loss of health. And as righteousness and health are both good things, and as the loss of any good thing is matter of grief, not of joy—if, at least, there is no compensation, as spiritual righteousness may compensate for the loss of bodily health—certainly it is more suitable for a wicked man to grieve in punishment than to rejoice in his fault. As, then, the joy of a sinner who has abandoned what is good is evidence of a bad will, so his grief for the good he has lost when he is punished is evidence of a good nature. For he who laments the peace his nature has lost is stirred to do so by some relics of peace which make his nature friendly to itself. And it is very just that in the final punishment the wicked and godless should in anguish bewail the loss of the natural advantages they enjoyed, and should perceive that they were most justly taken from them by that God whose benign liberality they had despised. God, then, the most wise Creator and most just Ordainer of all natures, who placed the human race upon earth as its great-

[1] John, 8. 44.

est ornament, imparted to men some good things adapted to this life, to wit, temporal peace, such as we can enjoy in this life from health and safety and human fellowship, and all things needful for the preservation and recovery of this peace, such as the objects which are accommodated to our outward senses, light, night, the air, and waters suitable for us, and everything the body requires to sustain, shelter, heal, or beautify it: and all under this most equitable condition, that every man who made a good use of these advantages suited to the peace of this mortal condition, should receive ampler and better blessings, namely, the peace of immortality, accompanied by glory and honour in an endless life made fit for the enjoyment of God and of one another in God; but that he who used the present blessings badly should both lose them and should not receive the others.

CHAP. 14. *Of the order and law which obtain in heaven and earth, whereby it comes to pass that human society is served by those who rule it*

The whole use, then, of things temporal has a reference to this result of earthly peace in the earthly community, while in the city of God it is connected with eternal peace. And therefore, if we were irrational animals, we should desire nothing beyond the proper arrangement of the parts of the body and the satisfaction of the appetites—nothing, therefore, but bodily comfort and abundance of pleasures, that the peace of the body might contribute to the peace of the soul. For if bodily peace be awanting, a bar is put to the peace even of the irrational soul, since it cannot obtain the gratification of its appetites. And these two together help out the mutual peace of soul and body, the peace of harmonious life and health. For as animals, by shunning pain, show that they love bodily peace, and, by pursuing pleasure to gratify their appetites, show that they love peace of soul, so their shrinking from death is a sufficient indication of their intense love of that peace which binds soul and body in close alliance. But, as man has a rational soul, he subordinates all this which he has in common with the beasts to the peace of his rational soul, that his intellect may have free play and may regulate his actions and that he may thus enjoy the well-ordered harmony of knowledge and action which constitutes, as we have said, the peace of the rational soul. And for this purpose he must desire to be neither molested by pain, nor disturbed by desire, nor extinguished by death, that he may arrive at some useful knowledge by which he may regulate his life and manners. But, owing to the liability of the human mind to fall into mistakes, this very pursuit of knowledge may be a snare to him unless he has a divine Master, whom he may obey without misgiving, and who may at the same time give him such help as to preserve his own freedom. And because, so long as he is in this mortal body, he is a stranger to God, he walks by faith, not by sight; and he therefore refers all peace, bodily or spiritual or both, to that peace which mortal man has with the immortal God, so that he exhibits the well-ordered obedience of faith to eternal law. But as this divine Master inculcates two precepts—the love of God and the love of our neighbour—and as in these precepts a man finds three things he has to love—God, himself, and his neighbour—and that he who loves God loves himself thereby, it follows that he must endeavour to get his neighbour to love God, since he is ordered to love his neighbour as himself. He ought to make this endeavour in behalf of his wife, his children, his household, all within his reach, even as he would wish his neighbour to do the same for him if he needed it; and consequently he will be at peace, or in well-ordered concord, with all men, as far as in him lies. And this is the order of this concord, that a man, in the first place, injure no one, and, in the second, do good to every one he can reach. Primarily, therefore, his own household are his care, for the law of nature and of society gives him readier access to them and greater opportunity of serving them. And hence the apostle says, "Now, if any provide not for his own, and specially for those of his own house, he hath denied the faith, and is worse than an infidel." [1] This is the origin of domestic peace, or the well-ordered concord of those in the family who rule and those who obey. For they who care for the rest rule—the husband the wife, the parents the children, the masters the servants; and they who are cared for obey—the women their husbands, the children their parents, the servants their masters. But in the family of the just man who lives by faith and is as yet a pilgrim journeying on to the celestial city, even those who rule serve those whom they seem to command; for they rule not from a love of power, but from a sense of the duty they owe to others—not because they are proud of authority, but because they love mercy.

[1] I Tim. 5. 8.

CHAP. 15. *Of the liberty proper to man's nature, and the servitude introduced by sin—a servitude in which the man whose will is wicked is the slave of his own lust, though he is free so far as regards other men*

This is prescribed by the order of nature: it is thus that God has created man. For "let them," He says, "have dominion over the fish of the sea, and over the fowl of the air, and over every creeping thing which creepeth on the earth." [1] He did not intend that His rational creature, who was made in His image, should have dominion over anything but the irrational creation—not man over man, but man over the beasts. And hence the righteous men in primitive times were made shepherds of cattle rather than kings of men, God intending thus to teach us what the relative position of the creatures is, and what the desert of sin; for it is with justice, we believe, that the condition of slavery is the result of sin. And this is why we do not find the word "slave" in any part of Scripture until righteous Noah branded the sin of his son with this name. It is a name, therefore, introduced by sin and not by nature. The origin of the Latin word for slave is supposed to be found in the circumstance that those who by the law of war were liable to be killed were sometimes preserved by their victors, and were hence called servants. And these circumstances could never have arisen save through sin. For even when we wage a just war, our adversaries must be sinning; and every victory, even though gained by wicked men, is a result of the first judgment of God, who humbles the vanquished either for the sake of removing or of punishing their sins. Witness that man of God, Daniel, who, when he was in captivity, confessed to God his own sins and the sins of his people, and declares with pious grief that these were the cause of the captivity. [2] The prime cause, then, of slavery is sin, which brings man under the dominion of his fellow—that which does not happen save by the judgment of God, with Whom is no unrighteousness, and Who knows how to award fit punishments to every variety of offence. But our Master in heaven says, "Every one who doeth sin is the servant of sin." [3] And thus there are many wicked masters who have religious men as their slaves, and who are yet themselves in bondage; "for of whom a man is overcome, of the same is he brought in bondage." [4] And beyond question it is a happier thing to be the slave of a man than of a lust; for even this very lust of ruling, to mention no others, lays waste men's hearts with the most ruthless dominion. Moreover, when men are subjected to one another in a peaceful order, the lowly position does as much good to the servant as the proud position does harm to the master. But by nature, as God first created us, no one is the slave either of man or of sin. This servitude is, however, penal, and is appointed by that law which enjoins the preservation of the natural order and forbids its disturbance; for if nothing had been done in violation of that law, there would have been nothing to restrain by penal servitude. And therefore the apostle admonishes slaves to be subject to their masters, and to serve them heartily and with good-will, so that, if they cannot be freed by their masters, they may themselves make their slavery in some sort free, by serving not in crafty fear, but in faithful love, until all unrighteousness pass away, and all principality and every human power be brought to nothing, and God be all in all.

CHAP. 16. *Of equitable rule*

And therefore, although our righteous fathers [5] had slaves, and administered their domestic affairs so as to distinguish between the condition of slaves and the heirship of sons in regard to the blessings of this life, yet in regard to the worship of God, in whom we hope for eternal blessings, they took an equally loving oversight of all the members of their household. And this is so much in accordance with the natural order, that the head of the household was called *paterfamilias;* and this name has been so generally accepted, that even those whose rule is unrighteous are glad to apply it to themselves. But those who are true fathers of their households desire and endeavour that all the members of their household, equally with their own children, should worship and win God, and should come to that heavenly home in which the duty of ruling men is no longer necessary, because the duty of caring for their everlasting happiness has also ceased; but, until they reach that home, masters ought to feel their position of authority a greater burden than servants their service. And if any member of the family interrupts the domestic peace by disobedience, he is corrected either by word or blow, or some kind of just and legitimate punishment, such as society permits, that he may himself be the better for it, and be readjusted to the family har-

[1] Gen. 1. 26.   [2] Dan. 9.   [3] John, 8. 34.   [4] II Pet. 2. 19.   [5] The patriarchs.

mony from which he had dislocated himself. For as it is not benevolent to give a man help at the expense of some greater benefit he might receive, so it is not innocent to spare a man at the risk of his falling into graver sin. To be innocent, we must not only do harm to no man, but also restrain him from sin or punish his sin, so that either the man himself who is punished may profit by his experience, or others be warned by his example. Since, then, the house ought to be the beginning or element of the city, and every beginning bears reference to some end of its own kind, and every element to the integrity of the whole of which it is an element, it follows plainly enough that domestic peace has a relation to civic peace—in other words, that the well-ordered concord of domestic obedience and domestic rule has a relation to the well-ordered concord of civic obedience and civic rule. And therefore it follows, further, that the father of the family ought to frame his domestic rule in accordance with the law of the city, so that the household may be in harmony with the civic order.

CHAP. 17. *What produces peace, and what discord, between the heavenly and earthly cities*

But the families which do not live by faith seek their peace in the earthly advantages of this life; while the families which live by faith look for those eternal blessings which are promised, and use as pilgrims such advantages of time and of earth as do not fascinate and divert them from God, but rather aid them to endure with greater ease, and to keep down the number of those burdens of the corruptible body which weigh upon the soul. Thus the things necessary for this mortal life are used by both kinds of men and families alike, but each has its own peculiar and widely different aim in using them. The earthly city, which does not live by faith, seeks an earthly peace, and the end it proposes, in the well-ordered concord of civic obedience and rule, is the combination of men's wills to attain the things which are helpful to this life. The heavenly city, or rather the part of it which sojourns on earth and lives by faith, makes use of this peace only because it must, until this mortal condition which necessitates it shall pass away. Consequently, so long as it lives like a captive and a stranger in the earthly city, though it has already received the promise of redemption, and the gift of the Spirit as the earnest of it, it makes no scruple to obey the laws of the earthly city, whereby the things necessary for the maintenance of this mortal life are ad-

ministered; and thus, as this life is common to both cities, so there is a harmony between them in regard to what belongs to it. But, as the earthly city has had some philosophers whose doctrine is condemned by the divine teaching, and who, being deceived either by their own conjectures or by demons, supposed that many gods must be invited to take an interest in human affairs, and assigned to each a separate function and a separate department—to one the body, to another the soul; and in the body itself, to one the head, to another the neck, and each of the other members to one of the gods; and in like manner, in the soul, to one god the natural capacity was assigned, to another education, to another anger, to another lust; and so the various affairs of life were assigned—cattle to one, corn to another, wine to another, oil to another, the woods to another, money to another, navigation to another, wars and victories to another, marriages to another, births and fecundity to another, and other things to other gods: and as the celestial city, on the other hand, knew that one God only was to be worshipped, and that to Him alone was due that service which the Greeks call λατρεία, and which can be given only to a god, it has come to pass that the two cities could not have common laws of religion, and that the heavenly city has been compelled in this matter to dissent, and to become obnoxious to those who think differently, and to stand the brunt of their anger and hatred and persecutions, except in so far as the minds of their enemies have been alarmed by the multitude of the Christians and quelled by the manifest protection of God accorded to them. This heavenly city, then, while it sojourns on earth, calls citizens out of all nations and gathers together a society of pilgrims of all languages, not scrupling about diversities in the manners, laws, and institutions whereby earthly peace is secured and maintained, but recognizing that, however various these are, they all tend to one and the same end of earthly peace. It therefore is so far from rescinding and abolishing these diversities, that it even preserves and adopts them, so long only as no hindrance to the worship of the one supreme and true God is thus introduced. Even the heavenly city, therefore, while in its state of pilgrimage, avails itself of the peace of earth, and, so far as it can without injuring faith and godliness, desires and maintains a common agreement among men regarding the acquisition of the necessaries of life, and makes this earthly peace bear upon the peace of heaven; for this alone can be truly called and esteemed the peace of the reasonable creatures, consisting as it does in the perfectly ordered and harmonious enjoyment of God and of one another in God. When we shall have reached that peace, this mortal life shall give place to one that is eternal, and our body shall be no more this animal body which by its corruption weighs down the soul, but a spiritual body feeling no want, and in all its members subjected to the will. In its pilgrim state the heavenly city possesses this peace by faith; and by this faith it lives righteously when it refers to the attainment of that peace every good action towards God and man; for the life of the city is a social life.

CHAP. 18. *How different the uncertainty of the New Academy is from the certainty of the Christian faith*

As regards the uncertainty about everything which Varro alleges to be the differentiating characteristic of the New Academy, the city of God thoroughly detests such doubt as madness. Regarding matters which it apprehends by the mind and reason it has most absolute certainty, although its knowledge is limited because of the corruptible body pressing down the mind, for, as the apostle says, "We know in part." [1] It believes also the evidence of the senses which the mind uses by aid of the body; for he is more wretchedly deceived who fancies he should never trust them. It believes also the Holy Scriptures, old and new, which we call canonical, and which are the source of the faith by which the just lives[2] and by which we walk without doubting whilst we are absent from the Lord.[3] So long as this faith remains inviolate and firm, we may without blame entertain doubts regarding some things which we have neither perceived by sense nor by reason, and which have not been revealed to us by the canonical Scriptures, nor come to our knowledge through witnesses whom it is absurd to disbelieve.

CHAP. 19. *Of the dress and habits of the Christian people*

It is a matter of no moment in the city of God whether he who adopts the faith that brings men to God adopts it in one dress and manner of life or another, so long only as he lives in conformity with the commandments of God. And hence, when philosophers themselves become Christians, they are compelled, indeed, to abandon their erroneous doctrines, but not their dress and mode of living, which are no obstacle

to religion. So that we make no account of that distinction of sects which Varro adduced in connection with the Cynic school, provided always nothing indecent or self-indulgent is retained. As to these three modes of life, the contemplative, the active, and the composite, although, so long as a man's faith is preserved, he may choose any of them without detriment to his eternal interests, yet he must never overlook the claims of truth and duty. No man has a right to lead such a life of contemplation as to forget in his own ease the service due to his neighbour; nor has any man a right to be so immersed in active life as to neglect the contemplation of God. The charm of leisure must not be indolent vacancy of mind, but the investigation or discovery of truth, that thus every man may make solid attainments without grudging that others do the same. And, in active life, it is not the honours or power of this life we should covet, since all things under the sun are vanity, but we should aim at using our position and influence, if these have been honourably attained, for the welfare of those who are under us, in the way we have already explained.[4] It is to this the apostle refers when he says, "He that desireth the episcopate desireth a good work."[5] He wished to show that the episcopate is the title of a work, not of an honour. It is a Greek word, and signifies that he who governs superintends or takes care of those whom he governs: for ἐπί means *over,* and σκοπεῖν, *to see;* therefore ἐπισκοπεῖν means *to oversee.* So that he who loves to govern rather than to do good is no bishop. Accordingly no one is prohibited from the search after truth, for in this leisure may most laudably be spent; but it is unseemly to covet the high position requisite for governing the people, even though that position be held and that government be administered in a seemly manner. And therefore holy leisure is longed for by the love of truth; but it is the necessity of love to undertake requisite business. If no one imposes this burden upon us, we are free to sift and contemplate truth; but if it be laid upon us, we are necessitated for love's sake to undertake it. And yet not even in this case are we obliged wholly to relinquish the sweets of contemplation; for were these to be withdrawn, the burden might prove more than we could bear.

CHAP. 20. *That the saints are in this life blessed in hope*

Since, then, the supreme good of the city of God is perfect and eternal peace, not such as

[1] I Cor. 13. 9.   [2] Hab. 2. 4.   [3] II Cor. 5. 6.   [4] Chap. 6.   [5] I Tim. 3. 1.

mortals pass into and out of by birth and death, but the peace of freedom from all evil, in which the immortals ever abide, who can deny that that future life is most blessed, or that, in comparison with it, this life which now we live is most wretched, be it filled with all blessings of body and soul and external things? And yet, if any man uses this life with a reference to that other which he ardently loves and confidently hopes for, he may well be called even now blessed, though not in reality so much as in hope. But the actual possession of the happiness of this life, without the hope of what is beyond, is but a false happiness and profound misery. For the true blessings of the soul are not now enjoyed; for that is no true wisdom which does not direct all its prudent observations, manly actions, virtuous self-restraint, and just arrangements, to that end in which God shall be all and all in a secure eternity and perfect peace.

CHAP. 21. *Whether there ever was a Roman republic answering to the definitions of Scipio in Cicero's dialogue*

This, then, is the place where I should fulfill the promise given in the second book of this work,[1] and explain, as briefly and clearly as possible that, if we are to accept the definitions laid down by Scipio in Cicero's *De Republica,* there never was a Roman republic; for he briefly defines a republic as the weal of the people. And if this definition be true, there never was a Roman republic, for the people's weal was never attained among the Romans. For the people, according to his definition, is an assemblage associated by a common acknowledgment of right and by a community of interests. And what he means by a common acknowledgment of right he explains at large, showing that a republic cannot be administered without justice. Where, therefore, there is no true justice there can be no right. For that which is done by right is justly done, and what is unjustly done cannot be done by right. For the unjust inventions of men are neither to be considered nor spoken of as rights; for even they themselves say that right is that which flows from the fountain of justice, and deny the definition which is commonly given by those who misconceive the matter, that right is that which is useful to the stronger party. Thus, where there is not true justice there can be no assemblage of men associated by a common acknowledgment of right, and therefore there can be no people, as defined by Scipio or Cicero;

[1]Chap. 21.

and if no people, then no weal of the people, but only of some promiscuous multitude unworthy of the name of people. Consequently, if the republic is the weal of the people, and there is no people if it be not associated by a common acknowledgment of right, and if there is no right where there is no justice, then most certainly it follows that there is no republic where there is no justice. Further, justice is that virtue which gives every one his due. Where, then, is the justice of man, when he deserts the true God and yields himself to impure demons? Is this to give every one his due? Or is he who keeps back a piece of ground from the purchaser, and gives it to a man who has no right to it, unjust, while he who keeps back himself from the God who made him, and serves wicked spirits, is just?

This same book, *De Republica,* advocates the cause of justice against injustice with great force and keenness. The pleading for injustice against justice was first heard, and it was asserted that without injustice a republic could neither increase nor even subsist, for it was laid down as an absolutely unassailable position that it is unjust for some men to rule and some to serve; and yet the imperial city to which the republic belongs cannot rule her provinces without having recourse to this injustice. It was replied in behalf of justice, that this ruling of the provinces is just, because servitude may be advantageous to the provincials, and is so when rightly administered—that is to say, when lawless men are prevented from doing harm. And further, as they became worse and worse so long as they were free, they will improve by subjection. To confirm this reasoning, there is added an eminent example drawn from nature: for "why," it is asked, "does God rule man, the soul the body, the reason the passions and other vicious parts of the soul?" This example leaves no doubt that, to some, servitude is useful; and, indeed, to serve God is useful to all. And it is when the soul serves God that it exercises a right control over the body; and in the soul itself the reason must be subject to God if it is to govern as it ought the passions and other vices. Hence, when a man does not serve God, what justice can we ascribe to him, since in this case his soul cannot exercise a just control over the body, nor his reason over his vices? And if there is no justice in such an individual, certainly there can be none in a community composed of such persons. Here, therefore, there is not that common acknowledgment of right which makes an assemblage of men a people whose affairs we call a republic. And why need I speak of the advantageousness, the common participation in which, according to the definition, makes a people? For although, if you choose to regard the matter attentively, you will see that there is nothing advantageous to those who live godlessly, as every one lives who does not serve God but demons, whose wickedness you may measure by their desire to receive the worship of men though they are most impure spirits, yet what I have said of the common acknowledgment of right is enough to demonstrate that, according to the above definition, there can be no people, and therefore no republic, where there is no justice. For if they assert that in their republic the Romans did not serve unclean spirits, but good and holy gods, must we therefore again reply to this evasion, though already we have said enough, and more than enough, to expose it? He must be an uncommonly stupid or a shamelessly contentious person, who has read through the foregoing books to this point, and can yet question whether the Romans served wicked and impure demons. But, not to speak of their character, it is written in the law of the true God, "He that sacrificeth unto any god save unto the Lord only, he shall be utterly destroyed."[1] He, therefore, Who uttered so menacing a commandment decreed that no worship should be given either to good or bad gods.

CHAP. 22. *Whether the God Whom the Christians serve is the true God to Whom alone sacrifice ought to be paid*

But it may be replied, "Who is this God, or what proof is there that He alone is worthy to receive sacrifice from the Romans?" One must be very blind to be still asking Who this God is. He is the God Whose prophets predicted the things we see accomplished. He is the God from Whom Abraham received the assurance, "In thy seed shall all nations be blessed."[2] That this was fulfilled in Christ, Who according to the flesh sprang from that seed, is recognized, whether they will or no, even by those who have continued to be the enemies of this name. He is the God Whose divine Spirit spake by the men whose predictions I cited in the preceding books, and which are fulfilled in the Church which has extended over all the world. This is the God whom Varro, the most learned of the Romans, supposed to be Jupiter, though he knows not what he says; yet I think it right to note the circumstance that a man of such learning was unable to suppose that this God had no existence or

[1]Ex. 22. 20.   [2]Gen. 22. 18.

was contemptible, but believed Him to be the same as the supreme God. In fine, He is the God whom Porphyry, the most learned of the philosophers, though the bitterest enemy of the Christians, confesses to be a great God, even according to the oracles of those whom he esteems gods.

CHAP. 23. *Porphyry's account of the responses given by the oracles of the gods concerning Christ*

For in his book called ἐκ λογίων φιλοσοφίας, in which he collects and comments upon the responses which he pretends were uttered by the gods concerning divine things, he says—I give his own words as they have been translated from the Greek: "To one who inquired what god he should propitiate in order to recall his wife from Christianity, Apollo replied in the following verses." Then the following words are given as those of Apollo: "You will probably find it easier to write lasting characters on the water, or lightly fly like a bird through the air, than to restore right feeling in your impious wife once she has polluted herself. Let her remain as she pleases in her foolish deception, and sing false laments to her dead God, who was condemned by right-minded judges, and perished ignominiously by a violent death." Then after these verses of Apollo (which we have given in a Latin version that does not preserve the metrical form), he goes on to say: "In these verses Apollo exposed the incurable corruption of the Christians, saying that the Jews, rather than the Christians, recognized God." See how he misrepresents Christ, giving the Jews the preference to the Christians in the recognition of God. This was his explanation of Apollo's verses, in which he says that Christ was put to death by right-minded or just judges—in other words, that He deserved to die. I leave the responsibility of this oracle regarding Christ on the lying interpreter of Apollo, or on this philosopher who believed it or possibly himself invented it; as to its agreement with Porphyry's opinions or with other oracles, we shall in a little have something to say. In this passage, however, he says that the Jews, as the interpreters of God, judged justly in pronouncing Christ to be worthy of the most shameful death. He should have listened, then, to this God of the Jews to whom he bears this testimony, when that God says, "He that sacrificeth to any other god save to the Lord alone shall be utterly destroyed." But let us come to still plainer expressions, and hear how great a God Porphyry thinks the God of the Jews is. Apollo, he says, when asked whether word, i.e., reason, or law is the better thing, replied in the following verses. Then he gives the verses of Apollo, from which I select the following as sufficient: "God, the Generator, and the King prior to all things, before Whom heaven and earth, and the sea, and the hidden places of hell tremble, and the deities themselves are afraid, for their law is the Father whom the holy Hebrews honour." In this oracle of his god Apollo, Porphyry avowed that the God of the Hebrews is so great that the deities themselves are afraid before Him. I am surprised, therefore, that when God said, "He that sacrificeth to other gods shall be utterly destroyed," Porphyry himself was not afraid lest he should be destroyed for sacrificing to other gods.

This philosopher, however, has also some good to say of Christ, oblivious, as it were, of that contumely of his of which we have just been speaking; or as if his gods spoke evil of Christ only while asleep, and recognized Him to be good, and gave Him His deserved praise, when they awoke. For, as if he were about to proclaim some marvellous thing passing belief, he says, "What we are going to say will certainly take some by surprise. For the gods have declared that Christ was very pious, and has become immortal, and that they cherish his memory: that the Christians, however, are polluted, contaminated, and involved in error. And many other such things," he says, "do the gods say against the Christians." Then he gives specimens of the accusations made, as he says, by the gods against them, and then goes on: "But to some who asked Hecate whether Christ were a God, she replied, You know the condition of the disembodied immortal soul, and that if it has been severed from wisdom it always errs. The soul you refer to is that of a man foremost in piety: they worship it because they mistake the truth." To this so-called oracular response he adds the following words of his own: "Of this very pious man, then, Hecate said that the soul, like the souls of other good men, was after death dowered with immortality, and that the Christians through ignorance worship it. And to those who ask why he was condemned to die, the oracle of the goddess replied, The body, indeed, is always exposed to torments, but the souls of the pious abide in heaven. And the soul you inquire about has been the fatal cause of error to other souls which were not fated to receive the gifts of the gods, and to have the knowledge of immortal Jove. Such souls are therefore hated by the

gods; for they who were fated not to receive the gifts of the gods, and not to know God, were fated to be involved in error by means of him you speak of. He himself, however, was good, and heaven has been opened to him as to other good men. You are not, then, to speak evil of him, but to pity the folly of men: and through him men's danger is imminent."

Who is so foolish as not to see that these oracles were either composed by a clever man with a strong animus against the Christians, or were uttered as responses by impure demons with a similar design—that is to say, in order that their praise of Christ may win credence for their vituperation of Christians; and that thus they may, if possible, close the way of eternal salvation, which is identical with Christianity? For they believe that they are by no means counterworking their own hurtful craft by promoting belief in Christ, so long as their calumniation of Christians is also accepted; for they thus secure that even the man who thinks well of Christ declines to become a Christian, and is therefore not delivered from their own rule by the Christ he praises. Besides, their praise of Christ is so contrived that whosoever believes in Him as thus represented will not be a true Christian but a Photinian heretic, recognizing only the humanity, and not also the divinity of Christ, and will thus be precluded from salvation and from deliverance out of the meshes of these devilish lies. For our part, we are no better pleased with Hecate's praises of Christ than with Apollo's calumniation of Him. Apollo says that Christ was put to death by right-minded judges, implying that He was unrighteous. Hecate says that He was a most pious man, but no more. The intention of both is the same, to prevent men from becoming Christians, because if this be secured, men shall never be rescued from their power. But it is incumbent on our philosopher, or rather on those who believe in these pretended oracles against the Christians, first of all, if they can, to bring Apollo and Hecate to the same mind regarding Christ, so that either both may condemn or both praise Him. And even if they succeeded in this, we for our part would not withstanding repudiate the testimony of demons, whether favourable or adverse to Christ. But when our adversaries find a god and goddess of their own at variance about Christ the one praising, the other vituperating Him, they can certainly give no credence, if they have any judgment, to mere men who blaspheme the Christians.

When Porphyry or Hecate praises Christ,

and adds that He gave Himself to the Christians as a fatal gift, that they might be involved in error, he exposes, as he thinks, the causes of this error. But before I cite his words to that purpose, I would ask, "If Christ did thus give Himself to the Christians to involve them in error, did He do so willingly, or against His will?" If willingly, how is He righteous? If against His will, how is He blessed? However, let us hear the causes of this error. "There are," he says, "in a certain place very small earthly spirits, subject to the power of evil demons. The wise men of the Hebrews, among whom was this Jesus, as you have heard from the oracles of Apollo cited above, turned religious persons from these very wicked demons and minor spirits, and taught them rather to worship the celestial gods, and especially to adore God the Father. This," he said, "the gods enjoin; and we have already shown how they admonish the soul to turn to God, and command it to worship Him. But the ignorant and the ungodly, who are not destined to receive favours from the gods, nor to know the immortal Jupiter, not listening to the gods and their messages, have turned away from all gods, and have not only refused to hate, but have venerated the prohibited demons. Professing to worship God, they refuse to do those things by which alone God is worshipped. For God, indeed, being the Father of all, is in need of nothing; but for us it is good to adore Him by means of justice, chastity, and other virtues, and thus to make life itself a prayer to Him, by inquiring into and imitating His nature. For inquiry," says he, "purifies and imitation deifies us, by moving us nearer to Him." He is right in so far as he proclaims God the Father, and the conduct by which we should worship Him. Of such precepts the prophetic books of the Hebrews are full, when they praise or blame the life of the saints. But in speaking of the Christians he is in error, and calumniates them as much as is desired by the demons whom he takes for gods, as if it were difficult for any man to recollect the disgraceful and shameful actions which used to be done in the theatres and temples to please the gods, and to compare with these things what is heard in our churches, and what is offered to the true God, and from this comparison to conclude where character is edified, and where it is ruined. But who but a diabolical spirit has told or suggested to this man so manifest and vain a lie, as that the Christians reverenced rather than hated the demons, whose worship the Hebrews prohibited? But that God, whom the Hebrew sages worshipped, forbids sacrifice to be offered even to the holy angels of heaven and divine powers, whom we, in this our pilgrimage, venerate and love as our most blessed fellow-citizens. For in the law which God gave to His Hebrew people He utters this menace, as in a voice of thunder: "He that sacrificeth unto any god, save unto the Lord only, he shall be utterly destroyed."[1] And that no one might suppose that this prohibition extends only to the very wicked demons and earthly spirits, whom this philosopher calls very small and inferior—for even these are in the Scripture called gods, not of the Hebrews, but of the nations, as the Septuagint translators have shown in the psalm where it is said, "For all the gods of the nations are demons"[2]—that no one might suppose, I say, that sacrifice to these demons was prohibited, but that sacrifice might be offered to all or some of the celestials, it was immediately added, "save unto the Lord alone."[3] The God of the Hebrews, then, to Whom this renowned philosopher bears this signal testimony, gave to His Hebrew people a law, composed in the Hebrew language, and not obscure and unknown, but published now in every nation, and in this law it is written, "He that sacrificeth unto any god, save unto the Lord alone, he shall be utterly destroyed." What need is there to seek further proofs in the law or the prophets of this same thing? *Seek*, we need not say, for the passages are neither few nor difficult to find; but what need to collect and apply to my argument the proofs which are thickly sown and obvious, and by which it appears clear as day that sacrifice may be paid to none but the supreme and true God? Here is one brief but decided, even menacing, and certainly true utterance of that God whom the wisest of our adversaries so highly extol. Let this be listened to, feared, fulfilled, that there may be no disobedient soul cut off. "He that sacrifices," He says, not because He needs anything, but because it behoves us to be His possession. Hence the Psalmist in the Hebrew Scriptures sings, "I have said to the Lord, Thou art my God, for Thou needest not my good."[4] For we ourselves, who are His own city, are His most noble and worthy sacrifice, and it is this mystery we celebrate in our sacrifices, which are well known to the faithful, as we have explained in the preceding books. For through the prophets the oracles

---

[1]Ex. 22. 20.   [2]Ps. 96. 5.

[3]Augustine here warns his readers against a possible misunderstanding of the Latin word for alone (*soli*), which might be rendered "the sun."

[4]Ps. 16. 2.

of God declared that the sacrifices which the Jews offered as a shadow of that which was to be would cease, and that the nations, from the rising to the setting of the sun, would offer one sacrifice. From these oracles, which we now see accomplished, we have made such selections as seemed suitable to our purpose in this work. And therefore, where there is not this righteousness whereby the one supreme God rules the obedient city according to His grace, so that it sacrifices to none but Him, and whereby, in all the citizens of this obedient city, the soul consequently rules the body and reason the vices in the rightful order, so that, as the individual just man, so also the community and people of the just, live by faith, which works by love, that love whereby man loves God as He ought to be loved, and his neighbour as himself—there, I say, there is not an assemblage associated by a common acknowledgement of right, and by a community of interests. But if there is not this, there is not a people, if our definition be true, and therefore there is no republic; for where there is no people there can be no republic.

CHAP. 24. *The definition which must be given of a people and a republic, in order to vindicate the assumption of these titles by the Romans and by other kingdoms*

But if we discard this definition of a people, and, assuming another, say that a people is an assemblage of reasonable beings bound together by a common agreement as to the objects of their love, then, in order to discover the character of any people, we have only to observe what they love. Yet whatever it loves, if only it is an assemblage of reasonable beings and not of beasts, and is bound together by an agreement as to the objects of love, it is reasonably called a people; and it will be a superior people in proportion as it is bound together by higher interests, inferior in proportion as it is bound together by lower. According to this definition of ours, the Roman people is a people, and its weal is without doubt a commonwealth or republic. But what its tastes were in its early and subsequent days, and how it declined into sanguinary seditions and then to social and civil wars, and so burst asunder or rotted off the bond of concord in which the health of a people consists, history shows, and in the preceding books I have related at large. And yet I would not on this account say either that it was not a people, or that its administration was not a republic, so long as there remains an assemblage

of reasonable beings bound together by a common agreement as to the objects of love. But what I say of this people and of this republic I must be understood to think and say of the Athenians or any Greek state, of the Egyptians, of the early Assyrian Babylon, and of every other nation, great or small, which had a public government. For, in general, the city of the ungodly, which did not obey the command of God that it should offer no sacrifice save to Him alone and which, therefore, could not give to the soul its proper command over the body, nor to the reason its just authority over the vices, is void of true justice.

CHAP. 25. *That where there is no true religion there are no true virtues*

For though the soul may seem to rule the body admirably, and the reason the vices, if the soul and reason do not themselves obey God, as God has commanded them to serve Him, they have no proper authority over the body and the vices. For what kind of mistress of the body and the vices can that mind be which is ignorant of the true God, and which, instead of being subject to His authority, is prostituted to the corrupting influences of the most vicious demons? It is for this reason that the virtues which it seems to itself to possess, and by which it restrains the body and the vices that it may obtain and keep what it desires, are rather vices than virtues so long as there is no reference to God in the matter. For although some suppose that virtues which have a reference only to themselves and are desired only on their own account, are yet true and genuine virtues, the fact is that even then they are inflated with pride and are therefore to be reckoned vices rather than virtues. For as that which gives life to the flesh is not derived from flesh, but is above it, so that which gives blessed life to man is not derived from man, but is something above him; and what I say of man is true of every celestial power and virtue whatsoever.

CHAP. 26. *Of the peace which is enjoyed by the people that are alienated from God, and the use made of it by the people of God in the time of its pilgrimage*

Wherefore, as the life of the flesh is the soul, so the blessed life of man is God, of whom the sacred writings of the Hebrews say, "Blessed is the people whose God is the Lord."[1] Miserable, therefore, is the people which is alienated from God. Yet even this people has a peace of its

[1]Ps. 144. 15.

own which is not to be lightly esteemed, though, indeed, it shall not in the end enjoy it, because it makes no good use of it before the end. But it is our interest that it enjoy this peace meanwhile in this life; for as long as the two cities are commingled, we also enjoy the peace of Babylon. For from Babylon the people of God is so freed that it meanwhile sojourns in its company. And therefore the apostle also admonished the Church to pray for kings and those in authority, assigning as the reason, "that we may live a quiet and tranquil life in all godliness and love."[1] And the prophet Jeremiah, when predicting the captivity that was to befall the ancient people of God, and giving them the divine command to go obediently to Babylonia, and thus serve their God, counselled them also to pray for Babylonia, saying, "In the peace thereof shall ye have peace"[2]—the temporal peace which the good and the wicked together enjoy.

CHAP. 27. *That the peace of those who serve God cannot in this mortal life be apprehended in its perfection*

But the peace which is peculiar to ourselves we enjoy now with God by faith, and shall hereafter enjoy eternally with Him by sight. But the peace which we enjoy in this life, whether common to all or peculiar to ourselves, is rather the solace of our misery than the positive enjoyment of felicity. Our very righteousness, too, though true in so far as it has respect to the true good, is yet in this life of such a kind that it consists rather in the remission of sins than in the perfecting of virtues. Witness the prayer of the whole city of God in its pilgrim state, for it cries to God by the mouth of all its members, "Forgive us our debts as we forgive our debtors."[3] And this prayer is efficacious not for those whose faith is "without works and dead,"[4] but for those whose faith "worketh by love."[5] For as reason, though subjected to God, is yet "pressed down by the corruptible body,"[6] so long as it is in this mortal condition, it has not perfect authority over vice, and therefore this prayer is needed by the righteous. For though it exercises authority, the vices do not submit without a struggle. For however well one maintains the conflict, and however thoroughly he has subdued these enemies, there steals in some evil thing, which, if it do not find ready expression in act, slips out by the lips, or insinuates

itself into the thought; and therefore his peace is not full so long as he is at war with his vices. For it is a doubtful conflict he wages with those that resist, and his victory over those that are defeated is not secure, but full of anxiety and effort. Amidst these temptations, therefore, of all which it has been summarily said in the divine oracles, "Is not human life upon earth a temptation?"[7] who but a proud man can presume that he so lives that he has no need to say to God, "Forgive us our debts"? And such a man is not great, but swollen and puffed up with vanity, and is justly resisted by Him who abundantly gives grace to the humble. Whence it is said, "God resisteth the proud, but giveth grace to the humble."[8] In this, then, consists the righteousness of a man, that he submit himself to God, his body to his soul, and his vices, even when they rebel, to his reason, which either defeats or at least resists them; and also that he beg from God grace to do his duty, and the pardon of his sins, and that he render to God thanks for all the blessings he receives. But, in that final peace to which all our righteousness has reference, and for the sake of which it is maintained, as our nature shall enjoy a sound immortality and incorruption, and shall have no more vices, and as we shall experience no resistance either from ourselves or from others, it will not be necessary that reason should rule vices which no longer exist, but God shall rule the man, and the soul shall rule the body, with a sweetness and facility suitable to the felicity of a life which is done with bondage. And this condition shall there be eternal, and we shall be assured of its eternity; and thus the peace of this blessedness and the blessedness of this peace shall be the supreme good.

CHAP. 28. *The end of the wicked*

But, on the other hand, they who do not belong to this city of God shall inherit eternal misery, which is also called the second death, because the soul shall then be separated from God its life, and therefore cannot be said to live, and the body shall be subjected to eternal pains. And consequently this second death shall be the more severe, because no death shall terminate it. But war being contrary to peace, as misery to happiness, and life to death, it is not without reason asked what kind of war can be found in the end of the wicked answering to the peace which is declared to be the end of the righteous? The person who puts this question has only to observe what it is in war that is hurtful and de-

---

[1] I Tim. 2. 2; variant reading: "purity."   [2] Jer. 29. 7.
[3] Matt. 6. 12.   [4] Jas. 2. 17.   [5] Gal. 5. 6.
[6] Wisd. 9. 15.

[7] Job, 7. 1.   [8] Jas. 4. 6; I Pet. 5. 5.

structive, and he shall see that it is nothing else than the mutual opposition and conflict of things. And can he conceive a more grievous and bitter war than that in which the will is so opposed to passion, and passion to the will, that their hostility can never be terminated by the victory of either, and in which the violence of pain so conflicts with the nature of the body that neither yields to the other? For in this life, when this conflict has arisen, either pain con-

quers and death expels the feeling of it, or nature conquers and health expels the pain. But in the world to come the pain continues that it may torment, and the nature endures that it may be sensible of it; and neither ceases to exist, lest punishment also should cease. Now, as it is through the last judgment that men pass to these ends, the good to the supreme good, the evil to the supreme evil, I will treat of this judgment in the following book.

BOOK XX

ARGUMENT. CONCERNING THE LAST JUDGMENT, AND THE DECLARATIONS REGARDING IT IN THE OLD AND NEW TESTAMENTS.

CHAP. I. *That although God is always judging, it is nevertheless reasonable to confine our attention in this book to his last judgment*

INTENDING to speak, in dependence on God's grace, of the day of His final judgment, and to affirm it against the ungodly and incredulous, we must first of all lay, as it were, in the foundation of the edifice the divine declarations. Those persons who do not believe such declarations do their best to oppose to them false and illusive sophisms of their own, either contending that what is adduced from Scripture has another meaning, or altogether denying that it is an utterance of God's. For I suppose no man who understands what is written, and believes it to be communicated by the supreme and true God through holy men, refuses to yield and consent to these declarations, whether he orally confesses his consent, or is from some evil influence ashamed or afraid to do so; or even, with an opinionativeness closely resembling madness, makes strenuous efforts to defend what he knows and believes to be false against what he knows and believes to be true.

That, therefore, which the whole Church of the true God holds and professes as its creed, that Christ shall come from heaven to judge quick and dead, this we call the last day, or last time, of the divine judgment. For we do not know how many days this judgment may occupy; but no one who reads the Scriptures, however negligently, need be told that in them "day" is customarily used for "time." And when we speak of the day of God's judgment, we add the word last or final for this reason, because even now God judges, and has judged from the beginning of human history, banishing from Paradise, and excluding from the tree of life, those

first men who perpetrated so great a sin. Yea, He was certainly exercising judgment also when He did not spare the angels who sinned, whose prince, overcome by envy, seduced men after being himself seduced. Neither is it without God's profound and just judgment that the life of demons and men, the one in the air, the other on earth, is filled with misery, calamities, and mistakes. And even though no one had sinned, it could only have been by the good and right judgment of God that the whole rational creation could have been maintained in eternal blessedness by a persevering adherence to its Lord. He judges, too, not only in the mass, condemning the race of devils and the race of men to be miserable on account of the original sin of these races, but He also judges the voluntary and personal acts of individuals. For even the devils pray that they may not be tormented,[1] which proves that without injustice they might either be spared or tormented according to their deserts. And men are punished by God for their sins often visibly, always secretly, either in this life or after death, although no man acts rightly save by the assistance of divine aid; and no man or devil acts unrighteously save by the permission of the divine and most just judgment. For, as the apostle says, "There is no unrighteousness with God";[2] and as he elsewhere says, "His judgments are inscrutable, and His ways past finding out." [3] In this book, then, I shall speak, as God permits, not of those first judgments, nor of these intervening judgments of God, but of the last judgment, when Christ is to come from heaven to judge the quick and the dead. For that day is properly called the day of judgment, because in it there shall be no room left for the ignorant questioning why this wick-

[1]Matt. 8. 29.   [2]Rom. 9. 14.   [3]Rom. 11. 33.

ed person is happy and that righteous man unhappy. In that day true and full happiness shall be the lot of none but the good, while deserved and supreme misery shall be the portion of the wicked, and of them only.

CHAP. 2. *That in the mingled web of human affairs God's judgment is present, though it cannot be discerned*

In this present time we learn to bear with equanimity the ills to which even good men are subject, and to hold cheap the blessings which even the wicked enjoy. And consequently, even in those conditions of life in which the justice of God is not apparent, His teaching is salutary. For we do not know by what judgment of God this good man is poor and that bad man rich; why he who, in our opinion, ought to suffer acutely for his abandoned life enjoys himself, while sorrow pursues him whose praiseworthy life leads us to suppose he should be happy; why the innocent man is dismissed from the bar not only unavenged, but even condemned, being either wronged by the iniquity of the judge, or overwhelmed by false evidence, while his guilty adversary, on the other hand, is not only discharged with impunity, but even has his claims admitted; why the ungodly enjoys good health, while the godly pines in sickness; why ruffians are of the soundest constitution, while they who could not hurt any one even with a word are from infancy afflicted with complicated disorders; why he who is useful to society is cut off by premature death, while those who, as it might seem, ought never to have been so much as born have lives of unusual length; why he who is full of crimes is crowned with honours, while the blameless man is buried in the darkness of neglect. But who can collect or enumerate all the contrasts of this kind? But if this anomalous state of things were uniform in this life, in which, as the sacred Psalmist says, "Man is like to vanity, his days as a shadow that passeth away"[1]—so uniform that none but wicked men won the transitory prosperity of earth, while only the good suffered its ills—this could be referred to the just and even benign judgment of God. We might suppose that they who were not destined to obtain those everlasting benefits which constitute human blessedness were either deluded by transitory blessings as the just reward of their wickedness, or were, in God's mercy, consoled by them, and that they who were not destined to suffer eternal torments were afflicted with temporal chastisement for

their sins, or were stimulated to greater attainment in virtue. But now, as it is, since we not only see good men involved in the ills of life, and bad men enjoying the good of it, which seems unjust, but also that evil often overtakes evil men, and good surprises the good, the rather on this account are God's judgments unsearchable, and His ways past finding out. Although, therefore, we do not know by what judgment these things are done or permitted to be done by God, with Whom is the highest virtue, the highest wisdom, the highest justice, no infirmity, no rashness, no unrighteousness, yet it is salutary for us to learn to hold cheap such things, be they good or evil, as attach indifferently to good men and bad, and to covet those good things which belong only to good men, and flee those evils which belong only to evil men. But when we shall have come to that judgment, the date of which is called peculiarly the day of judgment and sometimes the day of the Lord, we shall then recognize the justice of all God's judgments, not only of such as shall then be pronounced, but of all which take effect from the beginning, or may take effect before that time. And in that day we shall also recognize with what justice so many, or almost all, the just judgments of God in the present life defy the scrutiny of human sense or insight, though in this matter it is not concealed from pious minds that what is concealed is just.

CHAP. 3. *What Solomon, in the book of Ecclesiastes, says regarding the things which happen alike to good and wicked men*

Solomon, the wisest king of Israel, who reigned in Jerusalem, thus commences the book called Ecclesiastes, which the Jews number among their canonical Scriptures: "Vanity of vanities, said Ecclesiastes, vanity of vanities; all is vanity. What profit hath a man of all his labour which he hath taken under the sun?"[2] And after going on to enumerate, with this as his text, the calamities and delusions of this life, and the shifting nature of the present time, in which there is nothing substantial, nothing lasting, he bewails, among the other vanities that are under the sun, this also, that though wisdom excelleth folly as light excelleth darkness, and though the eyes of the wise man are in his head, while the fool walketh in darkness,[3] yet one event happeneth to them all, that is to say, in this life under the sun, unquestionably alluding to those evils which we see befall good and bad men alike. He says, further, that the good suf-

[1] Ps. 144. 4.

[2] Eccles. 1. 2, 3.   [3] Eccles. 2. 13, 14.

fer the ills of life as if they were evil doers, and the bad enjoy the good of life as if they were good. "There is a vanity which is done upon the earth; that there be just men unto whom it happeneth according to the work of the wicked: again, there be wicked men, to whom it happeneth according to the work of the righteous. I said, that this also is vanity." [1] This wisest man devoted this whole book to a full exposure of this vanity, evidently with no other object than that we might long for that life in which there is no vanity under the sun, but verity under Him Who made the sun. In this vanity, then, was it not by the just and righteous judgment of God that man, made like to vanity, was destined to pass away? But in these days of vanity it makes an important difference whether he resists or yields to the truth, and whether he is destitute of true piety or a partaker of it—important not so far as regards the acquirement of the blessings or the evasion of the calamities of this transitory and vain life, but in connection with the future judgment which shall make over to good men good things, and to bad men bad things, in permanent, inalienable possession. In fine, this wise man concludes this book of his by saying, "Fear God, and keep His commandments: for this is every man. For God shall bring every work into judgment, with every despised person, whether it be good, or whether it be evil." [2] What truer, terser, more salutary enouncement could be made? "Fear God," he says, "and keep His commandments: for this is every man." For whosoever has real existence, is this, is a keeper of God's commandments; and he who is not this, is nothing. For so long as he remains in the likeness of vanity, he is not renewed in the image of the truth. "For God shall bring into judgment every work"—that is, whatever man does in this life—"whether it be good or whether it be evil, with every despised person"—that is, with every man who here seems despicable and is therefore not considered; for God sees even him, and does not despise him nor pass him over in His judgment.

CHAP. 4. *That proofs of the last judgment will be adduced, first from the New Testament, and then from the Old*

The proofs, then, of this last judgment of God which I propose to adduce shall be drawn first from the New Testament, and then from the Old. For although the Old Testament is prior in point of time, the New has the precedence in intrinsic value; for the Old acts the part of

herald to the New. We shall therefore first cite passages from the New Testament, and confirm them by quotations from the Old Testament. The Old contains the law and the prophets, the New the gospel and the apostolic epistles. Now the apostle says "By the law is the knowledge of sin. But now the righteousness of God without the law is manifested, being witnessed by the law and the prophets; now the righteousness of God is by faith of Jesus Christ upon all them that believe." [3] This righteousness of God belongs to the New Testament, and evidence for it exists in the old books, that is to say, in the law and the prophets. I shall first, then, state the case, and then call the witnesses. This order Jesus Christ Himself directs us to observe, saying, "The scribe instructed in the kingdom of God is like a good householder, bringing out of his treasure things new and old." [4] He did not say "old and new," which He certainly would have said had He not wished to follow the order of merit rather than that of time.

CHAP. 5. *The passages in which the Saviour declares that there shall be a divine judgment in the end of the world*

The Saviour Himself, while reproving the cities in which He had done great works, but which had not believed, and while setting them in unfavourable comparison with foreign cities, says, "But I say unto you, It shall be more tolerable for Tyre and Sidon at the day of judgment than for you." [5] And a little after He says, "Verily, I say unto you, It shall be more tolerable for the land of Sodom in the day of judgment than for thee." [6] Here He most plainly predicts that a day of judgment is to come. And in another place He says, "The men of Nineveh shall rise in judgment with this generation, and shall condemn it: because they repented at the preaching of Jonas; and, behold, a greater than Jonas is here. The queen of the south shall rise up in the judgment with this generation, and shall condemn it: for she came from the uttermost parts of the earth to hear the words of Solomon; and behold, a greater than Solomon is here." [7] Two things we learn from this passage, that a judgment is to take place, and that it is to take place at the resurrection of the dead. For when He spoke of the Ninevites and the queen of the south, He certainly spoke of dead persons, and yet He said that they should rise up in the day of judgment. He did not say, "They shall condemn," as

[1] Eccles. 8. 14.   [2] Eccles. 12. 13, 14.

[3] Rom. 3. 20–22.   [4] Matt. 13. 52.   [5] Matt. 11. 22.
[6] Matt. 11. 24.   [7] Matt. 12. 41, 42.

if they themselves were to be the judges, but because, in comparison with them, the others shall be justly condemned.

Again, in another passage, in which He was speaking of the present intermingling and future separation of the good and bad—the separation which shall be made in the day of judgment—He adduced a comparison drawn from the sown wheat and the tares sown among them, and gave this explanation of it to His disciples: "He that soweth the good seed is the Son of man," etc.[1] Here, indeed, He did not name the judgment or the day of judgment, but indicated it much more clearly by describing the circumstances, and foretold that it should take place in the end of the world.

In like manner He says to His disciples, "Verily I say unto you, That ye which have followed me, in the regeneration, when the Son of man shall sit on the throne of His glory, ye also shall sit upon twelve thrones, judging the twelve tribes of Israel."[2] Here we learn that Jesus shall judge with His disciples. And therefore He said elsewhere to the Jews, "If I by Beelzebub cast out devils, by whom do your sons cast them out? Therefore they shall be your judges."[3] Neither ought we to suppose that only twelve men shall judge along with Him, though He says that they shall sit upon twelve thrones; for by the number twelve is signified the completeness of the multitude of those who shall judge. For the two parts of the number seven (which commonly symbolizes totality), that is to say four and three, multiplied into one another, give twelve. For four times three, or three times four, are twelve. There are other meanings, too, in this number twelve. Were not this the right interpretation of the twelve thrones, then since we read that Matthias was ordained an apostle in the room of Judas the traitor, the Apostle Paul, though he laboured more than them all,[4] should have no throne of judgment; but he unmistakeably considers himself to be included in the number of the judges when he says, "Know ye not that we shall judge angels?"[5] The same rule is to be observed in applying the number twelve to those who are to be judged. For though it was said, "judging the twelve tribes of Israel," the tribe of Levi, which is the thirteenth, shall not on this account be exempt from judgment, neither shall judgment be passed only on Israel and not on the other nations. And by the words "in the regeneration," He certainly meant the resurrection of the dead to be un-

derstood; for our flesh shall be regenerated by incorruption, as our soul is regenerated by faith.

Many passages I omit, because, though they seem to refer to the last judgment, yet on a closer examination they are found to be ambiguous, or to allude rather to some other event—whether to that coming of the Saviour which continually occurs in His Church, that is, in His members, in which He comes little by little, and piece by piece, since the whole Church is His Body, or to the destruction of the earthly Jerusalem. For when He speaks even of this, He often uses language which is applicable to the end of the world and that last and great day of judgment, so that these two events cannot be distinguished unless all the corresponding passages bearing on the subject in the three evangelists, Matthew, Mark, and Luke, are compared with one another—for some things are put more obscurely by one evangelist and more plainly by another—so that it becomes apparent what things are meant to be referred to one event. It is this which I have been at pains to do in a letter which I wrote to Hesychius of blessed memory, bishop of Salon, and entitled, "Of the End of the World."

I shall now cite from the Gospel according to Matthew the passage which speaks of the separation of the good from the wicked by the most efficacious and final judgment of Christ: "When the Son of man," he says, "shall come in His glory, . . . then shall He say also unto them on His left hand, Depart from me, ye cursed, into everlasting fire, prepared for the devil and his angels."[6] Then He in like manner recounts to the wicked the things they had not done, but which He had said those on the right hand had done. And when they ask when they had seen Him in need of these things, He replies that, inasmuch as they had not done it to the least of His brethren, they had not done it unto Him, and concludes His address in the words, "And these shall go away into everlasting punishment, but the righteous into life eternal." Moreover, the evangelist John most distinctly states that He had predicted that the judgment should be at the resurrection of the dead. For after saying, "The Father judgeth no man, but hath committed all judgment unto the Son; that all men should honour the Son, even as they honour the Father: he that honoureth not the Son, honoureth not the Father which hath sent Him"; He immediately adds, "Verily, verily, I say unto you, He that heareth my word and believeth on Him that sent me, hath everlasting life, and

[1]Matt. 13. 37-43.   [2]Matt. 19. 28.   [3]Matt. 12. 27.
[4]I Cor. 15. 10.   [5]I Cor. 6. 3.

[6]Matt. 25. 34-41.

shall not come into judgment; but is passed from death to life." [1] Here He said that believers on Him should not come into judgment. How, then, shall they be separated from the wicked by judgment, and be set at His right hand, unless judgment be in this passage used for condemnation? For into judgment, in this sense, they shall not come who hear His word, and believe on Him that sent Him.

CHAP. 6. *What is the first resurrection, and what the second*

After that He adds the words, "Verily, verily, I say unto you, The hour is coming, and now is, when the dead shall hear the voice of the Son of God; and they that hear shall live. For as the Father hath life in Himself; so hath He given to the Son to have life in Himself." [2] As yet He does not speak of the second resurrection, that is, the resurrection of the body, which shall be in the end, but of the first, which now is. It is for the sake of making this distinction that He says, "The hour is coming, and now is." Now this resurrection regards not the body, but the soul. For souls, too, have a death of their own in wickedness and sins, whereby they are the dead of whom the same lips say, "Suffer the dead to bury their dead" [3]—that is, let those who are dead in soul bury them that are dead in body. It is of these dead, then—the dead in ungodliness and wickedness—that He says, "The hour is coming, and now is, when the dead shall hear the voice of the Son of God; and they that hear shall live." "They that hear," that is, they who obey, believe, and persevere to the end. Here no difference is made between the good and the bad. For it is good for all men to hear His voice and live, by passing to the life of godliness from the death of ungodliness. Of this death the Apostle Paul says, "Therefore all are dead, and He died for all, that they which live should not henceforth live unto themselves, but unto Him which died for them and rose again." [4] Thus all, without one exception, were dead in sins, whether original or voluntary sins, sins of ignorance, or sins committed against knowledge; and for all the dead there died the one only person who lived, that is, Who had no sin whatever, in order that they who live by the remission of their sins should live, not to themselves, but to Him Who died for all, for our sins, and rose again for our justification, that we, believing in Him Who justifies the ungodly, and being justified from ungodliness or quickened

from death, may be able to attain to the first resurrection which now is. For in this first resurrection none have a part save those who shall be eternally blessed; but in the second, of which He goes on to speak, all, as we shall learn, have a part, both the blessed and the wretched. The one is the resurrection of mercy, the other of judgment. And therefore it is written in the psalm, "I will sing of mercy and of judgment: unto Thee, O Lord, will I sing." [5]

And of this judgment He went on to say, "And hath given Him authority to execute judgment also, because He is the Son of man." Here He shows that He will come to judge in that flesh in which He had come to be judged. For it is to show this He says, "because He is the Son of man." And then follow the words for our purpose: "Marvel not at this: for the hour is coming, in the which all that are in the graves shall hear His voice, and shall come forth; they that have done good, unto the resurrection of life; and they that have done evil, unto the resurrection of judgment." [6] This judgment He uses here in the same sense as a little before, when He says, "He that heareth my word, and believeth on Him that sent me, hath everlasting life, and shall not come into *judgment*, but is passed from death to life"; i.e., by having a part in the first resurrection, by which a transition from death to life is made in this present time, he shall not come into damnation, which He mentions by the name of judgment, as also in the place where He says, "but they that have done evil unto the resurrection of judgment," i.e., of damnation. He, therefore, who would not be damned in the second resurrection, let him rise in the first. For "the hour is coming, and now is, when the dead shall hear the voice of the Son of God; and they that hear shall live," i.e., shall not come into damnation, which is called the second death; into which death, after the second or bodily resurrection, they shall be hurled who do not rise in the first or spiritual resurrection. For "the hour is coming" (but here He does not say, "and now is," because it shall come in the end of the world in the last and greatest judgment of God) "when all that are in the graves shall hear His voice and shall come forth." He does not say, as in the first resurrection, "And they that hear shall live." For all shall not live, at least with such life as ought alone to be called life because it alone is blessed. For some kind of life they must have in order to hear, and come forth from the graves in their rising bodies. And why all shall not live He

[1] John, 5. 22–24. [2] John, 5. 25, 26. [3] Matt. 8. 22.
[4] II Cor. 5. 14, 15.

[5] Ps. 101. 1. [6] John, 5. 28, 29.

teaches in the words that follow: "They that have done good, to the resurrection of life"—these are they who shall live; "but they that have done evil, to the resurrection of judgment"—these are they who shall not live, for they shall die in the second death. They have done evil because their life has been evil; and their life has been evil because it has not been renewed in the first or spiritual resurrection which now is, or because they have not persevered to the end in their renewed life. As, then, there are two regenerations, of which I have already made mention—the one according to faith, and which takes place in the present life by means of baptism; the other according to the flesh, and which shall be accomplished in its incorruption and immortality by means of the great and final judgment—so are there also two resurrections—the one the first and spiritual resurrection, which has place in this life, and preserves us from coming into the second death; the other the second, which does not occur now, but in the end of the world, and which is of the body, not of the soul, and which by the last judgment shall dismiss some into the second death, others into that life which has no death.

CHAP. 7. *What is written in the revelation of John regarding the two resurrections, and the thousand years, and what may reasonably be held on these points*

The evangelist John has spoken of these two resurrections in the book which is called the Apocalypse, but in such a way that some Christians do not understand the first of the two, and so construe the passage into ridiculous fancies. For the Apostle John says in the foresaid book, "And I saw an angel come down from heaven. . . . Blessed and holy is he that hath part in the first resurrection: on such the second death hath no power; but they shall be priests of God and of Christ, and shall reign with Him a thousand years." [1] Those who, on the strength of this passage, have suspected that the first resurrection is future and bodily, have been moved, among other things, specially by the number of a thousand years, as if it were a fit thing that the saints should thus enjoy a kind of Sabbath-rest during that period, a holy leisure after the labours of the six thousand years since man was created, and was on account of his great sin dismissed from the blessedness of Paradise into the woes of this mortal life, so that thus, as it is written, "One day is with the Lord as a thousand years, and a thousand years as one day," [2] there

should follow on the completion of six thousand years, as of six days, a kind of seventh-day Sabbath in the succeeding thousand years; and that it is for this purpose the saints rise, viz., to celebrate this Sabbath. And this opinion would not be objectionable, if it were believed that the joys of the saints in that Sabbath shall be spiritual, and consequent on the presence of God; for I myself, too, once held this opinion. But, as they assert that those who then rise again shall enjoy the leisure of immoderate carnal banquets, furnished with an amount of meat and drink such as not only to shock the feeling of the temperate, but even to surpass the measure of credulity itself, such assertions can be believed only by the carnal. They who do believe them are called by the spiritual *Chiliasts,* which we may literally reproduce by the name *Millenarians.* [3] It were a tedious process to refute these opinions point by point: we prefer proceeding to show how that passage of Scripture should be understood.

The Lord Jesus Christ Himself says, "No man can enter into a strong man's house, and spoil his goods, except he first bind the strong man" [4]—meaning by the strong man the devil, because he had power to take captive the human race; and meaning by his goods which he was to take, those who had been held by the devil in divers sins and iniquities, but were to become believers in Himself. It was then for the binding of this strong one that the apostle saw in the Apocalypse "an angel coming down from heaven, having the key of the abyss, and a chain in his hand. And he laid hold," he says, "on the dragon, that old serpent, which is called the devil and Satan, and bound him a thousand years"—that is, bridled and restrained his power so that he could not seduce and gain possession of those who were to be freed. Now the thousand years may be understood in two ways, so far as occurs to me: either because these things happen in the sixth thousand of years or sixth millennium (the latter part of which is now passing), as if during the sixth day, which is to be followed by a Sabbath which has no evening, the endless rest of the saints, so that, speaking of a part under the name of the whole, he calls the last part of the millennium—the part, that is, which had yet to expire before the end of the world—a thousand years; or he used the thousand years as an equivalent for the whole duration of this world, employing the number of perfection to mark the fullness of

---

[1] Rev. 20. 1–6.   [2] II Pet. 3. 8.   [3] *Milliarii.*
[4] Mark 3. 27; *Vasa* for goods.

time. For a thousand is the cube of ten. For ten times ten makes a hundred, that is, the square on a plane superficies. But to give this superfices height, and make it a cube, the hundred is again multiplied by ten, which gives a thousand. Besides, if a hundred is sometimes used for totality, as when the Lord said by way of promise to him that left all and followed Him, "He shall receive in this world an hundredfold";[1] of which the apostle gives, as it were, an explanation when he says, "As having nothing, yet possessing all things"[2]—for even of old it had been said, "The whole world is the wealth of a believer"—with how much greater reason is a thousand put for totality since it is the cube, while the other is only the square? And for the same reason we cannot better interpret the words of the psalm, "He hath been mindful of His covenant for ever, the word which He commanded to a thousand generations,"[3] than by understanding it to mean "to all generations."

"And he cast him into the abyss"—i.e., cast the devil into the abyss. By the *abyss* is meant the countless multitude of the wicked whose hearts are unfathomably deep in malignity against the Church of God; not that the devil was not there before, but he is said to be cast in thither, because, when prevented from harming believers, he takes more complete possession of the ungodly. For that man is more abundantly possessed by the devil who is not only alienated from God, but also gratuitously hates those who serve God. "And shut him up, and set a seal upon him, that he should deceive the nations no more till the thousand years should be fulfilled." "Shut him up"—i.e., prohibited him from going out, from doing what was forbidden. And the addition of "set a seal upon him" seems to me to mean that it was designed to keep it a secret who belonged to the devil's party and who did not. For in this world this is a secret, for we cannot tell whether even the man who seems to stand shall fall, or whether he who seems to lie shall rise again. But by the chain and prison-house of this interdict the devil is prohibited and restrained from seducing those nations which belong to Christ, but which he formerly seduced or held in subjection. For before the foundation of the world God chose to rescue these from the power of darkness, and to translate them into the kingdom of the Son of His love, as the apostle says.[4] For what Christian is not aware that he seduces nations even now, and draws them with himself to eternal punishment,

but not those predestined to eternal life? And let no one be dismayed by the circumstance that the devil often seduces even those who have been regenerated in Christ, and begun to walk in God's way. For "the Lord knoweth them that are His,"[5] and of these the devil seduces none to eternal damnation. For it is as God, from Whom nothing is hid even of things future, that the Lord knows them; not as a man, who sees a man at the present time (if he can be said to see one whose heart he does not see), but does not see even himself so far as to be able to know what kind of person he is to be. The devil, then, is bound and shut up in the abyss that he may not seduce the nations from which the Church is gathered, and which he formerly seduced before the Church existed. For it is not said "that he should not seduce any man," but "that he should not seduce the nations"—meaning, no doubt, those among which the Church exists—"till the thousand years should be fulfilled"—i.e., either what remains of the sixth day which consists of a thousand years, or all the years which are to elapse till the end of the world.

The words, "that he should not seduce the nations till the thousand years should be fulfilled," are not to be understood as indicating that afterwards he is to seduce only those nations from which the predestined Church is composed, and from seducing whom he is restrained by that chain and imprisonment; but they are used in conformity with that usage frequently employed in Scripture and exemplified in the psalm, "So our eyes wait upon the Lord our God, until He have mercy upon us"[6]—not as if the eyes of His servants would no longer wait upon the Lord their God when He had mercy upon them. Or the order of the words is unquestionably this, "And he shut him up and set a seal upon him, till the thousand years should be fulfilled"; and the interposed clause, "that he should seduce the nations no more," is not to be understood in the connexion in which it stands, but separately, and as if added afterwards, so that the whole sentence might be read, "And He shut him up and set a seal upon him till the thousand years should be fulfilled, that he should seduce the nations no more"—i.e., he is shut up till the thousand years be fulfilled, on this account, that he may no more deceive the nations.

CHAP. 8. *Of the binding and loosing of the devil*

"After that," says John, "he must be loosed a little season." If the binding and shutting up

[1]Matt. 19. 29.   [2]II Cor. 6. 10.   [3]Ps. 105. 8.
[4]Col. 1. 13.   [5]II Tim. 2. 19.   [6]Ps. 123. 2.

of the devil means his being made unable to seduce the Church, must his loosing be the recovery of this ability? By no means. For the Church predestined and elected before the foundation of the world, the Church of which it is said, "The Lord knoweth them that are His," shall never be seduced by him. And yet there shall be a Church in this world even when the devil shall be loosed, as there has been since the beginning, and shall be always, the places of the dying being filled by new believers. For a little after John says that the devil, being loosed, shall draw the nations whom he has seduced in the whole world to make war against the Church, and that the number of these enemies shall be as the sand of the sea. "And they went up on the breadth of the earth, and compassed the camp of the saints about, and the beloved city: and fire came down from God out of heaven and devoured them. And the devil who seduced them was cast into the lake of fire and brimstone, where the beast and the false prophet are, and shall be tormented day and night for ever and ever."[1] This relates to the last judgment, but I have thought fit to mention it now, lest any one might suppose that in that short time during which the devil shall be loose there shall be no Church upon earth, whether because the devil finds no Church, or destroys it by manifold persecutions. The devil, then, is not bound during the whole time which this book embraces—that is, from the first coming of Christ to the end of the world, when He shall come the second time—not bound in this sense, that during this interval, which goes by the name of a thousand years, he shall not seduce the Church, for not even when loosed shall he seduce it. For certainly if his being bound means that he is not able or not permitted to seduce the Church, what can the loosing of him mean but his being able or permitted to do so? But God forbid that such should be the case! But the binding of the devil is his being prevented from the exercise of his whole power to seduce men, either by violently forcing or fraudulently deceiving them into taking part with him. If he were during so long a period permitted to assail the weakness of men, very many persons, such as God would not wish to expose to such temptation, would have their faith overthrown, or would be prevented from believing; and that this might not happen, he is bound.

But when the short time comes he shall be loosed. For he shall rage with the whole force of himself and his angels for three years and six

[1] Rev. 20. 9. 10.

months; and those with whom he makes war shall have power to withstand all his violence and stratagems. And if he were never loosed, his malicious power would be less patent, and less proof would be given of the steadfast fortitude of the holy city: it would, in short, be less manifest what good use the Almighty makes of his great evil. For the Almighty does not absolutely seclude the saints from his temptation, but shelters only their inner man, where faith resides, that by outward temptation they may grow in grace. And He binds him that he may not, in the free and eager exercise of his malice, hinder or destroy the faith of those countless weak persons, already believing or yet to believe, from whom the Church must be increased and completed; and he will in the end loose him, that the city of God may see how mighty an adversary it has conquered, to the great glory of its Redeemer, Helper, Deliverer. And what are we in comparison with those believers and saints who shall then exist, seeing that they shall be tested by the loosing of an enemy with whom we make war at the greatest peril even when he is bound? Although it is also certain that even in this intervening period there have been and are some soldiers of Christ so wise and strong, that if they were to be alive in this mortal condition at the time of his loosing, they would both most wisely guard against, and most patiently endure, all his snares and assaults.

Now the devil was thus bound not only when the Church began to be more and more widely extended among the nations beyond Judea, but is now and shall be bound till the end of the world, when he is to be loosed. Because even now men are, and doubtless to the end of the world shall be, converted to the faith from the unbelief in which he held them. And this strong one is bound in each instance in which he is spoiled of one of his goods; and the abyss in which he is shut up is not at an end when those die who were alive when first he was shut up in it, but these have been succeeded, and shall to the end of the world be succeeded, by others born after them with a like hate of the Christians, and in the depth of whose blind hearts he is continually shut up as in an abyss. But it is a question whether, during these three years and six months when he shall be loose, and raging with all his force, any one who has not previously believed shall attach himself to the faith. For how in that case would the words hold good, "Who entereth into the house of a strong one to spoil his goods, unless first he shall have bound the strong one?" Consequently this verse seems to compel us to believe that during that time, short as it is, no one will be added to the Christian community, but that the devil will make war with those who have previously become Christians, and that, though some of these may be conquered and desert to the devil, these do not belong to the predestinated number of the sons of God. For it is not without reason that John, the same apostle as wrote this Apocalypse, says in his epistle regarding certain persons, "They went out from us, but they were not of us; for if they had been of us, they would no doubt have remained with us."[1] But what shall become of the little ones? For it is beyond all belief that in these days there shall not be found some Christian children born, but not yet baptized, and that there shall not also be some born during that very period; and if there be such, we cannot believe that their parents shall not find some way of bringing them to the laver of regeneration. But if this shall be the case, how shall these goods be snatched from the devil when he is loose, since into his house no man enters to spoil his goods unless he has first bound him? On the contrary, we are rather to believe that in these days there shall be no lack either of those who fall away from, or of those who attach themselves to the Church; but there shall be such resoluteness, both in parents to seek baptism for their little ones, and in those who shall then first believe, that they shall conquer that strong one, even though unbound— that is, shall both vigilantly comprehend, and patiently bear up against him, though employing such wiles and putting forth such force as he never before used; and thus they shall be snatched from him even though unbound. And yet the verse of the Gospel will not be untrue, "Who entereth into the house of the strong one to spoil his goods, unless he shall first have bound the strong one?" For in accordance with this true saying that order is observed—the strong one first bound, and then his goods spoiled; for the Church is so increased by the weak and strong from all nations far and near, that by its most robust faith in things divinely predicted and accomplished, it shall be able to spoil the goods of even the unbound devil. For as we must own that, "when iniquity abounds, the love of many waxes cold,"[2] and that those who have not been written in the book of life shall in large numbers yield to the severe and unprecedented persecutions and stratagems of the devil now loosed, so we cannot but think that not only those whom that time shall find

sound in the faith, but also some who till then shall be without, shall become firm in the faith they have hitherto rejected and mighty to conquer the devil even though unbound, God's grace aiding them to understand the Scriptures, in which, among other things, there is foretold that very end which they themselves see to be arriving. And if this shall be so, his binding is to be spoken of as preceding, that there might follow a spoiling of him both bound and loosed; for it is of this it is said, "Who shall enter into the house of the strong one to spoil his goods, unless he shall first have bound the strong one?"

CHAP. 9. *What the reign of the saints with Christ for a thousand years is, and how it differs from the eternal kingdom*

But while the devil is bound, the saints reign with Christ during the same thousand years, understood in the same way, that is, of the time of His first coming. For, leaving out of account that kingdom concerning which He shall say in the end, "Come, ye blessed of my Father, take possession of the kingdom prepared for you,"[3] the Church could not now be called His kingdom or the kingdom of heaven unless His saints were even now reigning with Him, though in another and far different way; for to His saints He says, "Lo, I am with you always, even to the end of the world."[4] Certainly it is in this present time that the scribe well instructed in the kingdom of God, and of whom we have already spoken, brings forth from his treasure things new and old. And from the Church those reapers shall gather out the tares which He suffered to grow with the wheat till the harvest, as He explains in the words, "The harvest is the end of the world; and the reapers are the angels. As therefore the tares are gathered together and burned with fire, so shall it be in the end of the world. The Son of man shall send His angels, and they shall gather out of His kingdom all offenses."[5] Can He mean out of that kingdom in which are no offenses? Then it must be out of His present kingdom, the Church, that they are gathered. So He says, "He that breaketh one of the least of these commandments, and teacheth men so, shall be called least in the kingdom of heaven: but he that doeth and teacheth thus shall be called great in the kingdom of heaven."[6] He speaks of both as being in the kingdom of heaven, both the man who does not perform the commandments which He teaches—for *to break* means *not to keep, not to perform*—and the

[1] I John, 2. 19.　　[2] Matt. 24. 12.

[3] Matt. 25. 34　　[4] Matt. 28. 20.　　[5] Matt. 13. 39-41.
[6] Matt. 5. 19.

man who does and teaches as He did; but the one He calls least, the other great. And He immediately adds, "For I say unto you, that except your righteousness exceed that of the scribes and Pharisees"—that is, the righteousness of those who break what they teach; for of the scribes and Pharisees He elsewhere says, "For they say and do not" [1]—unless, therefore, your righteousness exceed theirs, that is, so that you do not break but rather do what you teach, "ye shall not enter the kingdom of heaven." [2] We must understand in one sense the kingdom of heaven in which exist together both he who breaks what he teaches and he who does it, the one being least, the other great, and in another sense the kingdom of heaven into which only he who does what he teaches shall enter. Consequently, where both classes exist, it is the Church as it now is, but where only the one shall exist, it is the Church as it is destined to be when no wicked person shall be in her. Therefore the Church even now is the kingdom of Christ, and the kingdom of heaven. Accordingly, even now His saints reign with Him, though otherwise than as they shall reign hereafter; and yet, though the tares grow in the Church along with the wheat, they do not reign with Him. For they reign with Him who do what the apostle says, "If ye be risen with Christ, mind the things which are above, where Christ sitteth at the right hand of God. Seek those things which are above, not the things which are on the earth." [3] Of such persons he also says that their conversation is in heaven.[4] In fine, they reign with Him who are so in His kingdom that they themselves are His kingdom. But in what sense are those the kingdom of Christ who, to say no more, though they are in it until all offenses are gathered out of it at the end of the world, yet seek their own things in it and not the things that are Christ's? [5]

It is then of this kingdom militant, in which conflict with the enemy is still maintained, and war carried on with warring lusts, or government laid upon them as they yield, until we come to that most peaceful kingdom in which we shall reign without an enemy, and it is of this first resurrection in the present life that the Apocalypse speaks in the words just quoted. For, after saying that the devil is bound a thousand years and is afterwards loosed for a short season, it goes on to give a sketch of what the Church does or of what is done in the Church in those days, in the words, "And I saw seats and them that sat upon them, and judgment was given." It is not to be supposed that this refers to the last judgment, but to the seats of the rulers and to the rulers themselves by whom the Church is now governed. And no better interpretation of judgment being given can be produced than that which we have in the words, "What ye bind on earth shall be bound in heaven; and what ye loose on earth shall be loosed in heaven." [6] Whence the apostle says, "What have I to do with judging them that are without? do not ye judge them that are within?" [7] "And the souls," says John, "of those who were slain for the testimony of Jesus and for the word of God"—understanding what he afterwards says "reigned with Christ a thousand years" [8]—that is, the souls of the martyrs not yet restored to their bodies. For the souls of the pious dead are not separated from the Church, which even now is the kingdom of Christ; otherwise there would be no remembrance made of them at the altar of God in the partaking of the body of Christ, nor would it do any good in danger to run to His baptism, that we might not pass from this life without it; nor to reconciliation, if by penitence or a bad conscience any one may be severed from His body. For why are these things practised, if not because the faithful, even though dead, are His members? Therefore, while these thousand years run on, their souls reign with Him, though not as yet in conjunction with their bodies. And therefore in another part of this same book we read, "Blessed are the dead who die in the Lord from henceforth: and now, saith the Spirit, that they may rest from their labours; for their works do follow them." [9] The Church, then, begins its reign with Christ now in the living and in the dead. For, as the apostle says, "Christ died that He might be Lord both of the living and of the dead." [10] But he mentioned the souls of the martyrs only, because they who have contended even to death for the truth, themselves principally reign after death; but, taking the part for the whole, we understand the words of all others who belong to the Church, which is the kingdom of Christ.

As to the words following, "And if any have not worshipped the beast nor his image, nor have received his inscription on their forehead, or on their hand," we must take them of both the living and the dead. And what this beast is, though it requires a more careful investigation, yet it is not inconsistent with the true faith to

[1]Matt. 23. 3.   [2]Matt. 5. 20.   [3]Col. 3. 1, 2.
[4]Phil. 3. 20.   [5]Phil. 2. 21.

[6]Matt. 18. 18.   [7]I Cor. 5. 12.   [8]Rev. 20. 4.
[9]Rev. 14. 13.   [10]Rom. 14. 9.

understand it of the ungodly city itself and the community of unbelievers set in opposition to the faithful people and the city of God. "His image" seems to me to mean his simulation, to wit, in those men who profess to believe, but live as unbelievers. For they pretend to be what they are not, and are called Christians, not from a true likeness, but from a deceitful image. For to this beast belong not only the avowed enemies of the name of Christ and His most glorious city, but also the tares which are to be gathered out of His kingdom, the Church, in the end of the world. And who are they who do not worship the beast and his image, if not those who do what the apostle says, "Be not yoked with unbelievers"?[1] For such do not worship, i.e., do not consent, are not subjected; neither do they receive the inscription, the brand of crime, on their forehead by their profession, on their hand by their practice. They, then, who are free from these pollutions, whether they still live in this mortal flesh, or are dead, reign with Christ even now, through this whole interval which is indicated by the thousand years, in a fashion suited to this time.

"The rest of them," he says, "did not live." For now is the hour when the dead shall hear the voice of the Son of God, and they that hear shall live; and the rest of them shall not live. The words added, "until the thousand years are finished," mean that they did not live in the time in which they ought to have lived by passing from death to life. And therefore, when the day of the bodily resurrection arrives, they shall come out of their graves, not to life, but to judgment, namely, to damnation, which is called the second death. For whosoever has not lived until the thousand years be finished, i.e., during this whole time in which the first resurrection is going on—whosoever has not heard the voice of the Son of God, and passed from death to life, that man shall certainly in the second resurrection, the resurrection of the flesh, pass with his flesh into the second death. For he goes on to say, "This is the first resurrection. Blessed and holy is he that hath part in the first resurrection," or who experiences it. Now he experiences it who not only revives from the death of sin, but continues in this renewed life. "In these the second death hath no power." Therefore it has power in the rest, of whom he said above, "The rest of them did not live until the thousand years were finished"; for in this whole intervening time called a thousand years, however lustily they lived in the body, they were

[1]II Cor. 6. 14.

not quickened to life out of that death in which their wickedness held them, so that by this revived life they should become partakers of the first resurrection, and so the second death should have no power over them.

CHAP. 10. *What is to be replied to those who think that resurrection pertains only to bodies and not to souls*

There are some who suppose that resurrection can be predicated only of the body, and therefore they contend that this first resurrection (of the Apocalypse) is a bodily resurrection. For, say they, "to rise again" can only be said of things that fall. Now, bodies fall in death.[2] There cannot, therefore, be a resurrection of souls, but of bodies. But what do they say to the apostle who speaks of a resurrection of souls? For certainly it was in the inner and not the outer man that those had risen again to whom he says, "If ye have risen with Christ, mind the things that are above."[3] The same sense he elsewhere conveyed in other words, saying, "That as Christ has risen from the dead by the glory of the Father, so we also may walk in newness of life."[4] So, too, "Awake thou that sleepest, and arise from the dead, and Christ shall give thee light."[5] As to what they say about nothing being able to rise again but what falls, whence they conclude that resurrection pertains to bodies only, and not to souls, because bodies fall, why do they make nothing of the words, "Ye that fear the Lord, wait for His mercy; and go not aside lest ye fall";[6] and "To his own Master he stands or falls";[7] and "He that thinketh he standeth, let him take heed lest he fall"?[8] For I fancy this fall that we are to take heed against is a fall of the soul, not of the body. If, then, rising again belongs to things that fall, and souls fall, it must be owned that souls also rise again. To the words, "In them the second death hath no power," are added the words, "but they shall be priests of God and Christ, and shall reign with Him a thousand years"; and this refers not to the bishops alone, and presbyters, who are now specially called priests in the Church; but as we call all believers Christians on account of the mystical chrism, so we call all priests because they are members of the one Priest. Of them the Apostle Peter says, "A holy people, a royal priesthood."[9] Certainly he implied, though in a passing and incidental way, that Christ is God, saying priests

[2]*Cadavera*, from *cadere*, "to fall."   [3]Col. 3. 1.
[4]Rom. 6. 4.   [5]Eph. 5. 14.   [6]Ecclus. 2. 7.
[7]Rom. 14. 4.   [8]I Cor. 10. 12.   [9]I Peter, 2. 9.

of God and Christ, that is, of the Father and the Son, though it was in His servant-form and as Son of man that Christ was made a Priest for ever after the order of Melchizedek. But this we have already explained more than once.

CHAP. 11. Of Gog and Magog, who are to be roused by the devil to persecute the Church, when he is loosed in the end of the world

"And when the thousand years are finished, Satan shall be loosed from his prison, and shall go out to seduce the nations which are in the four corners of the earth, Gog and Magog, and shall draw them to battle, whose number is as the sand of the sea." This, then, is his purpose in seducing them, to draw them to this battle. For even before this he was wont to use as many and various seductions as he could continue. And the words "he shall go out" mean, he shall burst forth from lurking hatred into open persecution. For this persecution, occurring while the final judgment is imminent, shall be the last which shall be endured by the holy Church throughout the world, the whole city of Christ being assailed by the whole city of the devil, as each exists on earth. For these nations which he names Gog and Magog are not to be understood of some barbarous nations in some part of the world, whether the Getæ and Massagetæ, as some conclude from the initial letters, or some other foreign nations not under the Roman government. For John marks that they are spread over the whole earth, when he says, "The nations which are in the four corners of the earth," and he added that these are Gog and Magog. The meaning of these names we find to be, Gog, a roof, Magog, from a roof—a house, as it were, and he who comes out of the house. They are therefore the nations in which we found that the devil was shut up as in an abyss, and the devil himself coming out from them and going forth, so that they are the roof, he from the roof. Or if we refer both words to the nations, not one to them and one to the devil, then they are both the roof, because in them the old enemy is at present shut up, and as it were roofed in; and they shall be from the roof when they break forth from concealed to open hatred. The words, "And they went up on the breadth of the earth, and encompassed the camp of the saints and the beloved city," do not mean that they have come, or shall come, to one place, as if the camp of the saints and the beloved city should be in some one place; for this camp is nothing else than the Church of Christ extending over the whole world. And consequently wherever the Church shall be—and it shall be in all nations, as is signified by "the breadth of the earth" —there also shall be the camp of the saints and the beloved city, and there it shall be encompassed by the savage persecution of all its enemies; for they too shall exist along with it in all nations—that is, it shall be straitened, and hard pressed, and shut up in the straits of tribulation, but shall not desert its military duty, which is signified by the world "camp."

CHAP. 12. Whether the fire that came down out of heaven and devoured them refers to the last punishment of the wicked

The words, "And fire came down out of heaven and devoured them," are not to be understood of the final punishment which shall be inflicted when it is said, "Depart from me, ye cursed, into everlasting fire";[1] for then they shall be cast into the fire, not fire come down out of heaven upon them. In this place "fire out of heaven" is well understood of the firmness of the saints, wherewith they refuse to yield obedience to those who rage against them. For the firmament is "heaven," by whose firmness these assailants shall be pained with blazing zeal, for they shall be impotent to draw away the saints to the party of Antichrist. This is the fire which shall devour them, and this is "from God"; for it is by God's grace the saints become unconquerable, and so torment their enemies. For as in a good sense it is said, "The zeal of Thine house hath consumed me," [2] so in a bad sense it is said, "Zeal hath possessed the uninstructed people, and now fire shall consume the enemies."[3] "And now," that is to say, not the fire of the last judgment. Or if by this fire coming down out of heaven and consuming them, John meant that blow wherewith Christ in His coming is to strike those persecutors of the Church whom He shall then find alive upon earth, when He shall kill Antichrist with the breath of His mouth, [4] then even this is not the last judgment of the wicked; but the last judgment is that which they shall suffer when the bodily resurrection has taken place.

CHAP. 13. Whether the time of the persecution of Antichrist should be reckoned in the thousand years

This last persecution by Antichrist shall last for three years and six months, as we have already said, and as is affirmed both in the Book of Revelation and by Daniel the prophet.

[1]Matt. 25. 41.　　[2]Ps. 69. 9.　　[3]Isa. 26. 11.
[4]II Thess. 2. 8.

Though this time is brief, yet not without reason is it questioned whether it is comprehended in the thousand years in which the devil is bound and the saints reign with Christ, or whether this little season should be added over and above to these years. For if we say that they are included in the thousand years, then the saints reign with Christ during a more protracted period than the devil is bound. For they shall reign with their King and Conqueror mightily even in that crowning persecution when the devil shall now be unbound and shall rage against them with all his might. How then does Scripture define both the binding of the devil and the reign of the saints by the same thousand years, if the binding of the devil ceases three years and six months before this reign of the saints with Christ? On the other hand, if we say that the brief space of this persecution is not to be reckoned as a part of the thousand years, but rather as an additional period, we shall indeed be able to interpret the words, "The priests of God and of Christ shall reign with Him a thousand years; and when the thousand years shall be finished, Satan shall be loosed out of his prison"; for thus they signify that the reign of the saints and the bondage of the devil shall cease simultaneously, so that the time of the persecution we speak of should be contemporaneous neither with the reign of the saints nor with the imprisonment of Satan, but should be reckoned over and above as a superadded portion of time. But then in this case we are forced to admit that the saints shall not reign with Christ during that persecution. But who can dare to say that His members shall not reign with Him at that very juncture when they shall most of all, and with the greatest fortitude, cleave to Him, and when the glory of resistance and the crown of martyrdom shall be more conspicuous in proportion to the hotness of the battle? Or if it is suggested that they may be said not to reign, because of the tribulations which they shall suffer, it will follow that all the saints who have formerly, during the thousand years, suffered tribulation, shall not be said to have reigned with Christ during the period of their tribulation, and consequently even those whose souls the author of this book says that he saw, and who were slain for the testimony of Jesus and the word of God, did not reign with Christ when they were suffering persecution, and they were not themselves the kingdom of Christ, though Christ was then pre-eminently possessing them. This is indeed perfectly absurd, and to be scouted. But assuredly the victorious souls of the glorious martyrs having overcome and finished all griefs and toils, and having laid down their mortal members, have reigned and do reign with Christ till the thousand years are finished, that they may afterwards reign with Him when they have received their immortal bodies. And therefore during these three years and a half the souls of those who were slain for His testimony, both those which formerly passed from the body and those which shall pass in that last persecution, shall reign with Him till the mortal world come to an end, and pass into that kingdom in which there shall be no death. And thus the reign of the saints with Christ shall last longer than the bonds and imprisonment of the devil, because they shall reign with their King the Son of God for these three years and a half during which the devil is no longer bound. It remains, therefore, that when we read that "the priests of God and of Christ shall reign with Him a thousand years; and when the thousand years are finished, the devil shall be loosed from his imprisonment," that we understand either that the thousand years of the reign of the saints does not terminate, though the imprisonment of the devil does—so that both parties have their thousand years, that is, their complete time, yet each with a different actual duration appropriate to itself, the kingdom of the saints being longer, the imprisonment of the devil shorter—or at least that, as three years and six months is a very short time, it is not reckoned as either deducted from the whole time of Satan's imprisonment, or as added to the whole duration of the reign of the saints, as we have shown above in the sixteenth book[1] regarding the round number of four hundred years, which were specified as four hundred, though actually somewhat more; and similar expressions are often found in the sacred writings, if one will mark them.

CHAP. 14. *Of the damnation of the devil and his adherents; and a sketch of the bodily resurrection of all the dead, and of the final retributive judgment.*

After this mention of the closing persecution, he summarily indicates all that the devil, and the city of which he is the prince, shall suffer in the last judgment. For he says, "And the devil who seduced them is cast into the lake of fire and brimstone, in which are the beast and the false prophet, and they shall be tormented day and night for ever and ever." We have already said that by the beast is well understood the wicked city. His false prophet is either Anti-

[1]Chap. 24.

christ or that image or figment of which we have spoken in the same place. After this he gives a brief narrative of the last judgment itself, which shall take place at the second or bodily resurrection of the dead, as it had been revealed to him: "I saw a throne great and white, and One sitting on it from Whose face the heaven and the earth fled away, and their place was not found." He does not say, "I saw a throne great and white, and One sitting on it, and from His face the heaven and the earth fled away," for it had not happened then, i.e., before the living and the dead were judged; but he says that he saw Him sitting on the throne from Whose face heaven and earth fled away, but afterwards. For when the judgment is finished, this heaven and earth shall cease to be, and there will be a new heaven and a new earth. For this world shall pass away by transmutation, not by absolute destruction. And therefore the apostle says, "For the figure of this world passeth away. I would have you be without anxiety." [1] The figure, therefore, passes away, not the nature. After John had said that he had seen One sitting on the throne from Whose face heaven and earth fled, though not till afterwards, he said, "And I saw the dead, great and small: and the books were opened; and another book was opened, which is the book of the life of each man: and the dead were judged out of those things which were written in the books, according to their deeds." He said that the books were opened, and a book; but he left us at a loss as to the nature of this book, "which is," he says, "the book of the life of each man." By those books, then, which he first mentioned, we are to understand the sacred books old and new, that out of them it might be shown what commandments God had enjoined; and that book of the life of each man is to show what commandments each man has done or omitted to do. If this book be materially considered, who can reckon its size or length, or the time it would take to read a book in which the whole life of every man is recorded? Shall there be present as many angels as men, and shall each man hear his life recited by the angel assigned to him? In that case there will be not one book containing all the lives, but a separate book for every life. But our passage requires us to think of one only. "And another book was opened," it says. We must therefore understand it of a certain divine power, by which it shall be brought about that every one shall recall to memory all his own works, whether good or evil, and shall mentally

survey them with a marvellous rapidity, so that this knowledge will either accuse or excuse conscience, and thus all and each shall be simultaneously judged. And this divine power is called a book, because in it we shall as it were read all that it causes us to remember. That he may show who the dead, small and great, are who are to be judged, he recurs to this which he had omitted or rather deferred, and says, "And the sea presented the dead which were in it; and death and hell gave up the dead which were in them." This of course took place before the dead were judged, yet it is mentioned after. And so, I say, he returns again to what he had omitted. But now he preserves the order of events, and for the sake of exhibiting it repeats in its own proper place what he had already said regarding the dead who were judged. For after he had said, "And the sea presented the dead which were in it, and death and hell gave up the dead which were in them," he immediately subjoined what he had already said, "and they were judged every man according to their works." For this is just what he had said before, "And the dead were judged according to their works."

CHAP. 15. *Who the dead are who are given up to judgment by the sea, and by death and hell*

But who are the dead which were in the sea, and which the sea presented? For we cannot suppose that those who die in the sea are not in hell, nor that their bodies are preserved in the sea; nor yet, which is still more absurd, that the sea retained the good, while hell received the bad. Who could believe this? But some very sensibly suppose that in this place the sea is put for this world. When John then wished to signify that those whom Christ should find still alive in the body were to be judged along with those who should rise again, he called them dead, both the good to whom it is said, "For ye are dead, and your life is hid with Christ in God," [2] and the wicked of whom it is said, "Let the dead bury their dead." [3] They may also be called dead, because they wear mortal bodies, as the apostle says, "The body indeed is dead because of sin; but the spirit is life because of righteousness"; [4] proving that in a living man in the body there is both a body which is dead, and a spirit which is life. Yet he did not say that the body was mortal, but dead, although immediately after he speaks in the more usual way of mortal bodies. These, then, are the dead which were in the sea, and which the sea presented, to wit, the men who were in this world, because they had not

[1] I Cor. 7. 31, 32.   [2] Col. 3. 3.   [3] Matt. 8. 22.   [4] Rom. 8. 10.

yet died, and whom the world presented for judgment. "And death and hell," he says, "gave up the dead which were in them." The sea *presented* them because they had merely to be found in the place where they were; but death and hell *gave them up* or *restored* them, because they called them back to life, which they had already quitted. And perhaps it was not without reason that neither *death* nor *hell* were judged sufficient alone, and both were mentioned— death to indicate the good, who have suffered only death and not hell; hell to indicate the wicked, who suffer also the punishment of hell. For if it does not seem absurd to believe that the ancient saints who believed in Christ and His then future coming, were kept in places far removed indeed from the torments of the wicked, but yet in hell, until Christ's blood and His descent into these places delivered them, certainly good Christians, redeemed by that precious price already paid, are quite unacquainted with hell while they wait for their restoration to the body, and the reception of their reward. After saying, "They were judged every man according to their works," he briefly added what the judgment was: "Death and hell were cast into the lake of fire"; by these names designating the devil and the whole company of his angels, for he is the author of death and the pains of hell. For this is what he had already, by anticipation, said in clearer language: "The devil who seduced them was cast into a lake of fire and brimstone." The obscure addition he had made in the words, "in which were also the beast and the false prophet," he here explains, "They who were not found written in the book of life were cast into the lake of fire." This book is not for reminding God, as if things might escape Him by forgetfulness, but it symbolizes His predestination of those to whom eternal life shall be given. For it is not that God is ignorant, and reads in the book to inform Himself, but rather His infallible prescience is the book of life in which they are written, that is to say, known beforehand.

CHAP. 16. *Of the new heaven and the new earth*

Having finished the prophecy of judgment, so far as the wicked are concerned, it remains that he speak also of the good. Having briefly explained the Lord's words, "These will go away into everlasting punishment," it remains that he explain the connected words, "but the righteous into life eternal."[1] "And I saw," he says, "a new heaven and a new earth: for the first heaven

[1] Matt. 25. 46.

and the first earth have passed away; and there is no more sea."[2] This will take place in the order which he has by anticipation declared in the words, "I saw One sitting on the throne, from Whose face heaven and earth fled." For as soon as those who are not written in the book of life have been judged and cast into eternal fire— the nature of which fire, or its position in the world or universe, I suppose is known to no man, unless perhaps the divine Spirit reveal it to some one—then shall the figure of this world pass away in a conflagration of universal fire, as once before the world was flooded with a deluge of universal water. And by this universal conflagration the qualities of the corruptible elements which suited our corruptible bodies shall utterly perish, and our substance shall receive such qualities as shall, by a wonderful transmutation, harmonize with our immortal bodies, so that, as the world itself is renewed to some better thing, it is fitly accommodated to men, themselves renewed in their flesh to some better thing. As for the statement, "And there shall be no more sea," I would not lightly say whether it is dried up with that excessive heat, or is itself also turned into some better thing. For we read that there shall be a new heaven and a new earth, but I do not remember to have anywhere read anything of a new sea, unless what I find in this same book, "As it were a sea of glass like crystal."[3] But he was not then speaking of this end of the world, neither does he seem to speak of a literal sea, but "as it were a sea." It is possible that, as prophetic diction delights in mingling figurative and real language, and thus in some sort veiling the sense, so the words "And there is no more sea" may be taken in the same sense as the previous phrase, "And the sea presented the dead which were in it." For then there shall be no more of this world, no more of the surgings and restlessness of human life, and it is this which is symbolized by the *sea*.

CHAP. 17. *Of the endless glory of the Church*

"And I saw," he says, "a great city, new Jerusalem, coming down from God out of heaven, prepared as a bride adorned for her husband. And I heard a great voice from the throne, saying, Behold, the tabernacle of God is with men, and He will dwell with them, and they shall be His people, and God Himself shall be with them. And God shall wipe away all tears from their eyes; and there shall be no more death, neither sorrow, nor crying, but neither shall there be any more pain: because the former things have

[2] Rev. 21. 1.   [3] Rev. 15. 2.

passed away. And He that sat upon the throne said, Behold, I make all things new."[1] This city is said to come down out of heaven, because the grace with which God formed it is of heaven. Wherefore He says to it by Isaiah, "I am the Lord that formed thee."[2] It is indeed descended from heaven from its commencement, since its citizens during the course of this world grow by the grace of God, which cometh down from above through the layer of regeneration in the Holy Ghost sent down from heaven. But by God's final judgment, which shall be administered by His Son Jesus Christ, there shall by God's grace be manifested a glory so pervading and so new, that no vestige of what is old shall remain; for even our bodies shall pass from their old corruption and mortality to new incorruption and immortality. For to refer this promise to the present time, in which the saints are reigning with their King a thousand years, seems to me excessively barefaced, when it is most distinctly said, "God shall wipe away all tears from their eyes; and there shall be no more death, neither sorrow, nor crying, but there shall be no more pain." And who is so absurd, and blinded by contentious opinionativeness, as to be audacious enough to affirm that, in the midst of the calamities of this mortal state, God's people, or even one single saint, does live, or has ever lived, or shall ever live, without tears or pain—the fact being that the holier a man is, and the fuller of holy desire, so much the more abundant is the tearfulness of his supplication? Are not these the utterances of a citizen of the heavenly Jerusalem: "My tears have been my meat day and night";[3] and "Every night shall I make my bed to swim; with my tears shall I water my couch";[4] and "My groaning is not hid from Thee";[5] and "My sorrow was renewed"?[6] Or are not those God's children who groan, being burdened, not that they wish to be unclothed, but clothed upon, that mortality may be swallowed up of life?[7] Do not they even who have the first-fruits of the Spirit groan within themselves, waiting for the adoption, the redemption of their body?[8] Was not the Apostle Paul himself a citizen of the heavenly Jerusalem, and was he not so all the more when he had heaviness and continual sorrow of heart for his Israelitish brethren?[9] But when shall there be no more death in that city, except when it shall be said, "O death, where is thy contention? O death, where is thy sting? The sting of

death is sin."[10] Obviously there shall be no sin when it can be said, "Where is"— But as for the present it is not some poor weak citizen of this city, but this same Apostle John himself who says, "If we say that we have no sin, we deceive ourselves, and the truth is not in us."[11] No doubt, though this book is called the Apocalypse, there are in it many obscure passages to exercise the mind of the reader, and there are few passages so plain as to assist us in the interpretation of the others, even though we take pains; and this difficulty is increased by the repetition of the same things, in forms so different, that the things referred to seem to be different, although in fact they are only differently stated. But in the words, "God shall wipe away all tears from their eyes; and there shall be no more death, neither sorrow, nor crying, but there shall be no more pain," there is so manifest a reference to the future world and the immortality and eternity of the saints—for only then and only there shall such a condition be realized—that if we think this obscure, we need not expect to find anything plain in any part of Scripture.

CHAP. 18. *What the Apostle Peter predicted regarding the last judgment*

Let us now see what the Apostle Peter predicted concerning this judgment. "There shall come," he says, "in the last days scoffers. . . . Nevertheless we, according to His promise, look for new heavens and a new earth, wherein dwelleth righteousness."[12] There is nothing said here about the resurrection of the dead, but enough certainly regarding the destruction of this world. And by his reference to the deluge he seems as it were to suggest to us how far we should believe the ruin of the world will extend in the end of the world. For he says that the world which then was perished, and not only the earth itself, but also the heavens, by which we understand the air, the place and room of which was occupied by the water. Therefore the whole, or almost the whole, of the gusty atmosphere (which he calls heaven, or rather the heavens, meaning the earth's atmosphere, and not the upper air in which sun, moon, and stars are set) was turned into moisture, and in this way perished together with the earth, whose former appearance had been destroyed by the deluge. "But the heavens and the earth which are now, by the same word are kept in store, reserved unto fire against the day of judgment and perdition of ungodly men." Therefore the heavens

[1]Rev. 21. 2-5.   [2]Isa. 45. 8.   [3]Ps. 42. 3.   [4]Ps. 6. 6.
[5]Ps. 38. 9.   [6]Ps. 39. 2.   [7]II Cor. 5. 4.   [8]Rom. 8. 23.
[9]Rom. 9. 2.

[10]I Cor. 15. 55.   [11]I John, 1. 8.   [12]II Pet. 3. 3-13.

and the earth, or the world which was preserved from the water to stand in place of that world which perished in the flood, is itself reserved to fire at last in the day of the judgment and perdition of ungodly men. He does not hesitate to affirm that in this great change men also shall perish: their nature, however, shall notwithstanding continue, though in eternal punishments. Some one will perhaps put the question, "If after judgment is pronounced the world itself is to burn, where shall the saints be during the conflagration, and before it is replaced by a new heavens and a new earth, since somewhere they must be, because they have material bodies?" We may reply that they shall be in the upper regions into which the flame of that conflagration shall not ascend, as neither did the water of the flood; for they shall have such bodies that they shall be wherever they wish. Moreover, when they have become immortal and incorruptible, they shall not greatly dread the blaze of that conflagration, as the corruptible and mortal bodies of the three men were able to live unhurt in the blazing furnace.

CHAP. 19. *What the Apostle Paul wrote to the Thessalonians about the manifestation of Antichrist, which shall precede the day of the Lord*

I see that I must omit many of the statements of the gospels and epistles about this last judgment, that this volume may not become unduly long; but I can on no account omit what the Apostle Paul says, in writing to the Thessalonians, "We beseech you, brethren, by the coming of our Lord Jesus Christ," etc.[1]

No one can doubt that he wrote this of Antichrist and of the day of judgment, which he here calls the day of the Lord, nor that he declared that this day should not come unless he first came who is called the apostate—apostate, to wit, from the Lord God. And if this may justly be said of all the ungodly, how much more of him? But it is uncertain in what temple he shall sit, whether in that ruin of the temple which was built by Solomon, or in the Church; for the apostle would not call the temple of any idol or demon the temple of God. And on this account some think that in this passage Antichrist means not the prince himself alone, but his whole body, that is, the mass of men who adhere to him, along with him their prince; and they also think that we should render the Greek more exactly were we to read, not "in the temple of God," but "for" or "as the temple of

God," as if he himself were the temple of God, the Church.[2] Then as for the words, "And now ye know what withholdeth," i.e., ye know what hindrance or cause of delay there is, "that he might be revealed in his own time"; they show that he was unwilling to make an explicit statement, because he said that they knew. And thus we who have not their knowledge wish and are not able even with pains to understand what the apostle referred to, especially as his meaning is made still more obscure by what he adds. For what does he mean by "For the mystery of iniquity doth already work: only he who now holdeth, let him hold until he be taken out of the way: and then shall the wicked be revealed"? I frankly confess I do not know what he means. I will nevertheless mention such conjectures as I have heard or read.

Some think that the Apostle Paul referred to the Roman empire, and that he was unwilling to use language more explicit, lest he should incur the calumnious charge of wishing ill to the empire which it was hoped would be eternal; so that in saying, "For the mystery of iniquity doth already work," he alluded to Nero, whose deeds already seemed to be as the deeds of Antichrist. And hence some suppose that he shall rise again and be Antichrist. Others, again, suppose that he is not even dead, but that he was concealed that he might be supposed to have been killed, and that he now lives in concealment in the vigour of that same age which he had reached when he was believed to have perished, and will live until he is revealed in his own time and restored to his kingdom. But I wonder that men can be so audacious in their conjectures. However, it is not absurd to believe that these words of the apostle, "Only he who now holdeth, let him hold until he be taken out of the way," refer to the Roman empire, as if it were said, "Only he who now reigneth, let him reign until he be taken out of the way." "And then shall the wicked be revealed": no one doubts that this means Antichrist. But others think that the words, "Ye know what withholdeth," and "The mystery of iniquity worketh," refer only to the wicked and the hypocrites who are in the Church, until they reach a number so great as to furnish Antichrist with a great people, and that this is the *mystery* of iniquity, because it seems hidden; also that the apostle is exhorting the faithful tenaciously to hold the faith they hold when he says, "Only he who now holdeth, let

[1] II Thess. 2. 1–11.

[2] Augustine adds the words: "*Sicut dicimus, Sedet in amicum, id est, velut amicus; vel si quid aliud isto locutionis genere dici solet.*"

him hold until he be taken out of the way," that is, until the mystery of iniquity which now is hidden departs from the Church. For they suppose that it is to this same mystery John alludes when in his epistle he says, "Little children, it is the last time: and as ye have heard that Antichrist shall come, even now are there many antichrists; whereby we know that it is the last time. They went out from us, but they were not of us; for if they had been of us, they would no doubt have continued with us." [1] As therefore there went out from the Church many heretics, whom John calls "many antichrists," at that time prior to the end, and which John calls "the last time," so in the end they shall go out who do not belong to Christ, but to that last Antichrist, and then he shall be revealed.

Thus various, then, are the conjectural explanations of the obscure words of the apostle. That which there is no doubt he said is this, that Christ will not come to judge quick and dead unless Antichrist, His adversary, first come to seduce those who are dead in soul; although their seduction is a result of God's secret judgment already passed. For, as it is said "his presence shall be after the working of Satan, with all power, and signs, and lying wonders, and with all seduction of unrighteousness in them that perish." For then shall Satan be loosed, and by means of that Antichrist shall work with all power in a lying though a wonderful manner. It is commonly questioned whether these works are called "signs and lying wonders" because he is to deceive men's senses by false appearances, or because the things he does, though they be true prodigies, shall be a lie to those who shall believe that such things could be done only by God, being ignorant of the devil's power, and especially of such unexampled power as he shall then for the first time put forth. For when he fell from heaven as fire, and at a stroke swept away from the holy Job his numerous household and his vast flocks, and then as a whirlwind rushed upon and smote the house and killed his children, these were not deceitful appearances, and yet they were the works of Satan to whom God had given this power. Why they are called signs and lying wonders, we shall then be more likely to know when the time itself arrives. But whatever be the reason of the name, they shall be such signs and wonders as shall seduce those who shall deserve to be seduced, "because they received not the love of the truth that they might be saved." Neither did the apostle scruple to go on to say, "For this cause God

[1] I John, 2. 18, 19.

shall send upon them the working of error that they should believe a lie." For God shall *send*, because God shall permit the devil to do these things, the permission being by His own just judgment, though the doing of them is in pursuance of the devil's unrighteous and malignant purpose, "that they all might be judged who believed not the truth, but had pleasure in unrighteousness." Therefore, being judged, they shall be seduced, and, being seduced, they shall be judged. But, being judged, they shall be seduced by those secretly just and justly secret judgments of God, with which He has never ceased to judge since the first sin of the rational creatures; and, being seduced, they shall be judged in that last and manifest judgment administered by Jesus Christ, who was Himself most unjustly judged and shall most justly judge.

CHAP. 20. *What the same apostle taught in the first Epistle to the Thessalonians regarding the resurrection of the dead*

But the apostle has said nothing here regarding the resurrection of the dead; but in his first Epistle to the Thessalonians he says, "We would not have you to be ignorant, brethren, concerning them which are asleep," etc. [2] These words of the apostle most distinctly proclaim the future resurrection of the dead, when the Lord Christ shall come to judge the quick and the dead.

But it is commonly asked whether those whom our Lord shall find alive upon earth, personated in this passage by the apostle and those who were alive with him, shall never die at all, or shall pass with incomprehensible swiftness through death to immortality in the very moment during which they shall be caught up along with those who rise again to meet the Lord in the air? For we cannot say that it is impossible that they should both die and revive again while they are carried aloft through the air. For the words, "And so shall we ever be with the Lord," are not to be understood as if he meant that we shall always remain in the air with the Lord; for He Himself shall not remain there, but shall only pass through it as He comes. For we shall go to meet Him as He comes, not where He remains; but "so shall we be with the Lord," that is, we shall be with Him possessed of immortal bodies wherever we shall be with Him. We seem compelled to take the words in this sense, and to suppose that those whom the Lord shall find alive upon earth shall in that brief space both suffer death and receive immortality; for this

[2] I Thess. 4. 13–16.

same apostle says, "In Christ shall all be made alive";[1] while, speaking of the same resurrection of the body, he elsewhere says, "That which thou sowest is not quickened, except it die."[2] How, then, shall those whom Christ shall find alive upon earth be made alive to immortality in Him if they die not, since on this very account it is said, "That which thou sowest is not quickened, except it die"? Or if we cannot properly speak of human bodies as sown, unless in so far as by dying they do in some sort return to the earth, as also the sentence pronounced by God against the sinning father of the human race runs, "Earth thou art, and unto earth shalt thou return,"[3] we must acknowledge that those whom Christ at His coming shall find still in the body are not included in these words of the apostle nor in those of Genesis; for, being caught up into the clouds, they are certainly not sown, neither going nor returning to the earth, whether they experience no death at all or die for a moment in the air.

But, on the other hand, there meets us the saying of the same apostle when he was speaking to the Corinthians about the resurrection of the body, "We shall all rise," or, as other MSS. read, "We shall all sleep."[4] Since, then, there can be no resurrection unless death has preceded, and since we can in this passage understand by sleep nothing else than death, how shall *all* either sleep or rise again if so many persons whom Christ shall find in the body shall neither sleep nor rise again? If, then, we believe that the saints who shall be found alive at Christ's coming, and shall be caught up to meet Him, shall in that same ascent pass from mortal to immortal bodies, we shall find no difficulty in the words of the apostle, either when he says, "That which thou sowest is not quickened, except it die," or when he says, "We shall all rise," or "all sleep," for not even the saints shall be quickened to immortality unless they first die, however briefly; and consequently they shall not be exempt from resurrection which is preceded by sleep, however brief. And why should it seem to us incredible that that multitude of bodies should be, as it were, sown in the air, and should in the air forthwith revive immortal and incorruptible, when we believe, on the testimony of the same apostle, that the resurrection shall take place in the twinkling of an eye, and that the dust of bodies long dead shall return with incomprehensible facility and swiftness to those members that are now to live endlessly?

Neither do we suppose that in the case of these saints the sentence, "Earth thou art, and unto earth shalt thou return," is null, though their bodies do not, on dying, fall to earth, but both die and rise again at once while caught up into the air. For "Thou shalt return to earth" means, "Thou shalt at death return to that which thou wert before life began. Thou shalt, when exanimate, be that which thou wert before thou wast animate." For it was into a face of earth that God breathed the breath of life when man was made a living soul; as if it were said, "Thou art earth with a soul, which thou wast not; thou shalt be earth without a soul, as thou wast." And this is what all bodies of the dead are before they rot; and what the bodies of those saints shall be if they die, no matter where they die, as soon as they shall give up that life which they are immediately to receive back again. In this way, then, they return or go to earth, inasmuch as from being living men they shall be earth, as that which becomes cinder is said to go to cinder; that which decays, to go to decay; and so of six hundred other things. But the manner in which this shall take place we can now only feebly conjecture, and shall understand it only when it comes to pass. For that there shall be a bodily resurrection of the dead when Christ comes to judge quick and dead, we must believe if we would be Christians. But if we are unable perfectly to comprehend the manner in which it shall take place, our faith is not on this account vain. Now, however, we ought, as we formerly promised, to show, as far as seems necessary, what the ancient prophetic books predicted concerning this final judgment of God; and I fancy no great time need be spent in discussing and explaining these predictions, if the reader has been careful to avail himself of the help we have already furnished.

CHAP. 21. *Utterances of the prophet Isaiah regarding the resurrection of the dead and the retributive judgment*

The prophet Isaiah says, "The dead shall rise again, and all who were in the graves shall rise again; and all who are in the earth shall rejoice: for the dew which is from Thee is their health, and the earth of the wicked shall fall."[5] All the former part of this passage relates to the resurrection of the blessed; but the words, "the earth of the wicked shall fall," is rightly understood as meaning that the bodies of the wicked shall fall into the ruin of damnation. And if we would more exactly and carefully scrutinize the words

[1] I Cor. 15. 22.   [2] I Cor. 15. 36.   [3] Gen. 3. 19.
[4] I Cor. 15. 51.

[5] Isa. 26. 19.

which refer to the resurrection of the good, we may refer to the first resurrection the words, "the dead shall rise again," and to the second the following words, "and all who were in the graves shall rise again." And if we ask what relates to those saints whom the Lord at His coming shall find alive upon earth, the following clause may suitably be referred to them; "All who are in the earth shall rejoice: for the dew which is from Thee is their health." By "health" in this place it is best to understand immortality. For that is the most perfect health which is not repaired by nourishment as by a daily remedy. In like manner the same prophet, affording hope to the good and terrifying the wicked regarding the day of judgment, says, "Thus saith the Lord, Behold, I will flow down upon them as a river of peace, and upon the glory of the Gentiles as a rushing torrent; their sons shall be carried on the shoulders, and shall be comforted on the knees. As one whom his mother comforteth, so shall I comfort you; and ye shall be comforted in Jerusalem. And ye shall see, and your heart shall rejoice, and your bones shall rise up like a herb; and the hand of the Lord shall be known by His worshippers, and He shall threaten the contumacious. For, behold, the Lord shall come as a fire, and as a whirlwind His chariots, to execute vengeance with indignation, and wasting with a flame of fire. For with fire of the Lord shall all the earth be judged, and all flesh with His sword: many shall be wounded by the Lord." [1] In His promise to the good he says that He will flow down as a river of peace, that is to say, in the greatest possible abundance of peace. With this peace we shall in the end be refreshed; but of this we have spoken abundantly in the preceding book. It is this river in which he says He shall flow down upon those to whom He promises so great happiness, that we may understand that in the region of that felicity, which is in heaven, all things are satisfied from this river. But because there shall thence flow, even upon earthly bodies, the peace of incorruption and immortality, therefore he says that He shall flow down as this river, that He may as it were pour Himself from things above to things beneath, and make men the equals of the angels. By "Jerusalem," too, we should understand not that which serves with her children, but that which, according to the apostle, is our free mother, eternal in the heavens.[2] In her we shall be comforted as we pass toilworn from earth's cares and calamities, and be taken up as her children on her knees

and shoulders. Inexperienced and new to such blandishments, we shall be received into unwonted bliss. There we shall see, and our heart shall rejoice. He does not say what we shall see; but what but God, that the promise in the Gospel may be fulfilled in us, "Blessed are the pure in heart, for they shall see God"? [3] What shall we see but all those things which now we see not, but believe in, and of which the idea we form, according to our feeble capacity, is incomparably less than the reality? "And ye shall see," he says, "and your heart shall rejoice." Here ye believe, there ye shall see.

But because he said, "Your heart shall rejoice," lest we should suppose that the blessings of that Jerusalem are only spiritual, he adds, "And your bones shall rise up like a herb," alluding to the resurrection of the body, and as it were supplying an omission he had made. For it will not take place when we have seen; but we shall see when it has taken place. For he had already spoken of the new heavens and the new earth, speaking repeatedly, and under many figures, of the things promised to the saints, and saying, "There shall be new heavens, and a new earth: and the former shall not be remembered nor come into mind; but they shall find in it gladness and exultation. Behold, I will make Jerusalem an exultation, and my people a joy. And I will exult in Jerusalem, and joy in my people; and the voice of weeping shall be no more heard in her";[4] and other promises, which some endeavour to refer to carnal enjoyment during the thousand years. For, in the manner of prophecy, figurative and literal expressions are mingled, so that a serious mind may, by useful and salutary effort, reach the spiritual sense; but carnal sluggishness, or the slowness of an uneducated and undisciplined mind, rests in the superficial letter, and thinks there is nothing beneath to be looked for. But let this be enough regarding the style of those prophetic expressions just quoted. And now, to return to their interpretation. When he had said, "And your bones shall rise up like a herb," in order to show that it was the resurrection of the good, though a bodily resurrection, to which he alluded, he added, "And the hand of the Lord shall be known by His worshippers." What is this but the hand of Him who distinguishes those who worship from those who despise Him? Regarding these the context immediately adds, "And He shall threaten the contumacious," or, as another translator has it, "the unbelieving." He shall not actually threaten then,

[1]Isa. 66. 12, 16.　　[2]Gal. 4. 26.　　[3]Matt. 5. 8.　　[4]Isa. 65. 17-19.

but the threats which are now uttered shall then be fulfilled in effect. "For behold," he says, "the Lord shall come as a fire, and as a whirlwind His chariots, to execute vengeance with indignation, and wasting with a flame of fire. For with fire of the Lord shall all the earth be judged, and all flesh with His sword: many shall be wounded by the Lord." By *fire, whirlwind, sword,* he means the judicial punishment of God. For he says that the Lord Himself shall come as a fire, to those, that is to say, to whom His coming shall be penal. By His *chariots* (for the word is plural) we suitably understand the ministration of angels. And when he says that all flesh and all the earth shall be judged with His fire and sword, we do not understand the spiritual and holy to be included, but the earthly and carnal, of whom it is said that they "mind earthly things,"[1] and "to be carnally minded is death,"[2] and whom the Lord calls simply flesh when He says, "My Spirit shall not always remain in these men, for they are flesh."[3] As to the words, "Many shall be wounded by the Lord," this wounding shall produce the second death. It is possible, indeed, to understand *fire, sword,* and *wound* in a good sense. For the Lord said that He wished to send fire on the earth.[4] And the cloven tongues appeared to them as fire when the Holy Spirit came.[5] And our Lord says, "I am not come to send peace on earth, but a sword."[6] And Scripture says that the word of God is a doubly sharp sword,[7] on account of the two edges, the two Testaments. And in the Song of Songs the holy Church says that she is wounded with love[8]—pierced, as it were, with the arrow of love. But here, where we read or hear that the Lord shall come to execute vengeance, it is obvious in what sense we are to understand these expressions.

After briefly mentioning those who shall be consumed in this judgment, speaking of the wicked and sinners under the figure of the meats forbidden by the old law, from which they had not abstained, he summarily recounts the grace of the New Testament, from the first coming of the Saviour to the last judgment, of which we now speak; and herewith he concludes his prophecy. For he relates that the Lord declares that He is coming to gather all nations, that they may come and witness His glory.[9] For, as the apostle says, "All have sinned and are in want of the glory of God."[10] And he says that

He will do wonders among them, at which they shall marvel and believe in Him; and that from them He will send forth those that are saved into various nations, and distant islands which have not heard His name nor seen His glory, and that they shall declare His glory among the nations, and shall *bring* the brethren of those to whom the prophet was speaking, i.e., shall bring to the faith under God the Father the brethren of the elect Israelites; and that they shall bring from all nations an offering to the Lord on beasts of burden and waggons (which are understood to mean the aids furnished by God in the shape of angelic or human ministry), to the holy city Jerusalem, which at present is scattered over the earth, in the faithful saints. For where divine aid is given, men believe, and where they believe, they come. And the Lord compared them, in a figure, to the children of Israel offering sacrifice to Him in His house with psalms, which is already everywhere done by the Church; and He promised that from among them He would choose for Himself priests and Levites, which also we see already accomplished. For we see that priests and Levites are now chosen, not from a certain family and blood, as was originally the rule in the priesthood according to the order of Aaron, but as befits the new testament, under which Christ is the High Priest after the order of Melchizedek, in consideration of the merit which is bestowed upon each man by divine grace. And these priests are not to be judged by their mere title, which is often borne by unworthy men, but by that holiness which is not common to good men and bad.

After having thus spoken of this mercy of God which is now experienced by the Church, and is very evident and familiar to us, he foretells also the ends to which men shall come when the last judgment has separated the good and the bad, saying by the prophet, or the prophet himself speaking for God, "For as the new heavens and the new earth shall remain before me, said the Lord, so shall your seed and your name remain, and there shall be to them month after month, and Sabbath after Sabbath. All flesh shall come to worship before me in Jerusalem, said the Lord. And they shall go out, and shall see the members of the men who have sinned against me: their worm shall not die, neither shall their fire be quenched; and they shall be for a spectacle to all flesh."[11] At this point the prophet closed his book, as at this point the world shall come to an end. Some, in-

[1]Phil. 3. 19.   [2]Rom. 8. 6.   [3]Gen. 6. 3.
[4]Luke, 12. 49.   [5]Acts, 2. 3.   [6]Matt. 10. 34.
[7]Heb. 4. 12.   [8]Song of Sol. 2. 5.   [9]Isa. 66. 18.
[10]Rom. 3. 23.

[11]Isa. 66. 22–24.

deed, have translated "carcasses" [1] instead of "members of the men," meaning by *carcasses* the manifest punishment of the body, although *carcass* is commonly used only of dead flesh, while the bodies here spoken of shall be animated, else they could not be sensible of any pain; but perhaps they may, without absurdity, be called carcasses, as being the bodies of those who are to fall into the second death. And for the same reason it is said, as I have already quoted, by this same prophet, "The earth of the wicked shall fall." [2] It is obvious that those translators who use a different word for *men* do not mean to include only males, for no one will say that the women who sinned shall not appear in that judgment; but the male sex, being the more worthy, and that from which the woman was derived, is intended to include both sexes. But that which is especially pertinent to our subject is this, that since the words "All flesh shall come," apply to the good, for the people of God shall be composed of every race of men —for all men shall not be present, since the greater part shall be in punishment—but, as I was saying, since *flesh* is used of the good, and *members* or *carcasses* of the bad, certainly it is thus put beyond a doubt that that judgment in which the good and the bad shall be allotted to their destinies shall take place after the resurrection of the body, our faith in which is thoroughly established by the use of these words.

CHAP. 22. *What is meant by the good going out to see the punishment of the wicked*

But in what way shall the good go out to see the punishment of the wicked? Are they to leave their happy abodes by a bodily movement, and proceed to the places of punishment, so as to witness the torments of the wicked in their bodily presence? Certainly not; but they shall go out by knowledge. For this expression, *go out*, signifies that those who shall be punished shall be without. And thus the Lord also calls these places "the outer darkness," [3] to which is opposed that entrance concerning which it is said to the good servant, "Enter into the joy of thy Lord," that it may not be supposed that the wicked can enter thither and be known, but rather that the good by their knowledge go out to them, because the good are to know that which is without. For those who shall be in torment shall not know what is going on within in

the joy of the Lord; but they who shall enter into that joy shall know what is going on outside in the outer darkness. Therefore it is said, "They shall go out," because they shall know what is done by those who are without. For if the prophets were able to know things that had not yet happened, by means of that indwelling of God in their minds, limited though it was, shall not the immortal saints know things that have already happened, when God shall be all in all? [4] The seed, then, and the name of the saints shall remain in that blessedness—the seed to wit, of which John says, "And his seed remaineth in him"; [5] and the name, of which it was said through Isaiah himself, "I will give them an everlasting name." [6] "And there shall be to them month after month, and Sabbath after Sabbath," as if it were said, Moon after moon, and rest upon rest, both of which they shall themselves be when they shall pass from the old shadows of time into the new lights of eternity. The worm that dieth not, and the fire that is not quenched, which constitute the punishment of the wicked, are differently interpreted by different people. For some refer both to the body, others refer both to the soul; while others again refer the fire literally to the body, and the worm figuratively to the soul, which seems the more credible idea. But the present is not the time to discuss this difference, for we have undertaken to occupy this book with the last judgment, in which the good and the bad are separated: their rewards and punishments we shall more carefully discuss elsewhere.

CHAP. 23. *What Daniel predicted regarding the persecution of Antichrist, the judgment of God, and the kingdom of the saints*

Daniel prophesies of the last judgment in such a way as to indicate that Antichrist shall first come, and to carry on his description to the eternal reign of the saints. For when in prophetic vision he had seen four beasts, signifying four kingdoms, and the fourth conquered by a certain king, who is recognized as Antichrist, and after this the eternal kingdom of the Son of Man, that is to say, of Christ, he says, "My spirit was terrified, I Daniel in the midst of my body, and the visions of my head troubled me," etc. [7] Some have interpreted these four kingdoms as signifying those of the Assyrians, Persians, Macedonians, and Romans. They who desire to understand the fitness of this interpretation may read Jerome's book on Daniel, which

---

[1] As the Vulgate: *cadavera vivorum*.
[2] Here Augustine inserts the remark, "Who does not see that *cadavera* (carcasses) are so called from *cadendo* (falling)?"   [3] Matt. 25. 30.

[4] I Cor. 15. 28.   [5] I John, 3. 9.   [6] Isa. 56. 5.
[7] Dan. 7. 15-28.

is written with a sufficiency of care and erudition. But he who reads this passage, even half asleep, cannot fail to see that the kingdom of Antichrist shall fiercely, though for a short time, assail the Church before the last judgment of God shall introduce the eternal reign of the saints. For it is patent from the context that the *time, times, and half a time,* means a year, and two years, and half a year, that is to say, three years and a half. Sometimes in Scripture the same thing is indicated by months. For though the word *times* seems to be used here in the Latin indefinitely, that is only because the Latins have no dual, as the Greeks have, and as the Hebrews also are said to have. *Times,* therefore, is used for two times. As for the ten kings, whom, as it seems, Antichrist is to find in the person of ten individuals when he comes, I own I am afraid we may be deceived in this, and that he may come unexpectedly while there are not ten kings living in the Roman world. For what if this number ten signifies the whole number of kings who are to precede his coming, as totality is frequently symbolized by a thousand, or a hundred, or seven, or other numbers, which it is not necessary to recount?

In another place the same Daniel says, "And there shall be a time of trouble, such as was not since there was born a nation upon earth until that time: and in that time all Thy people which shall be found written in the book shall be delivered. And many of them that sleep in the mound of earth shall arise, some to everlasting life, and some to shame and everlasting confusion. And they that be wise shall shine as the brightness of the firmament; and many of the just as the stars for ever." [1] This passage is very similar to the one we have quoted from the Gospel,[2] at least so far as regards the resurrection of dead bodies. For those who are there said to be "in the graves" are here spoken of as "sleeping in the mound of earth," or, as others translate, "in the dust of earth." There it is said, "They shall come forth"; so here, "They shall arise." There, "They that have done good, to the resurrection of life; and they that have done evil, to the resurrection of judgment"; here, "Some to everlasting life, and some to shame and everlasting confusion." Neither is it to be supposed a difference, though in place of the expression in the Gospel, "All who are in their graves," the prophet does not say "all," but "many of them that sleep in the mound of

earth." For *many* is sometimes used in Scripture for *all.* Thus it was said to Abraham, "I have set thee as the father of many nations," though in another place it was said to him, "In thy seed shall all nations be blessed." [3] Of such a resurrection it is said a little afterwards to the prophet himself, "And come thou and rest: for there is yet a day till the completion of the consummation; and thou shalt rest, and rise in thy lot in the end of the days." [4]

CHAP. 24. *Passages from the Psalms of David which predict the end of the world and the last judgment*

There are many allusions to the last judgment in the Psalms, but for the most part only casual and slight. I cannot, however, omit to mention what is said there in express terms of the end of this world: "In the beginning hast Thou laid the foundations of the earth, O Lord; and the heavens are the work of Thy hands. They shall perish, but Thou shalt endure; yea, all of them shall wax old like a garment; and as a vesture Thou shalt change them, and they shall be changed: but Thou art the same, and Thy years shall not fail." [5] Why is it that Porphyry, while he lauds the piety of the Hebrews in worshipping a God great and true, and terrible to the gods themselves, follows the oracles of these gods in accusing the Christians of extreme folly because they say that this world shall perish? For here we find it said in the sacred books of the Hebrews, to that God Whom this great philosopher acknowledges to be terrible even to the gods themselves, "The heavens are the work of Thy hands; they shall perish." When the heavens, the higher and more secure part of the world, perish, shall the world itself be preserved? If this idea is not relished by Jupiter, whose oracle is quoted by this philosopher as an unquestionable authority in rebuke of the credulity of the Christians, why does he not similarly rebuke the wisdom of the Hebrews as folly, seeing that the prediction is found in their most holy books? But if this Hebrew wisdom, with which Porphyry is so captivated that he extols it through the utterances of his own gods, proclaims that the heavens are to perish, how is he so infatuated as to detest the faith of the Christians partly, if not chiefly, on this account, that they believe the world is to perish?— though how the heavens are to perish if the world does not is not easy to see. And, indeed,

[1]Dan. 12. 1-3. [2]John, 5. 28. [3]Gen. 17. 5, and 22. 18. [4]Dan. 12. 13. [5]Ps. 102. 25-27.

in the sacred writings which are peculiar to ourselves, and not common to the Hebrews and us —I mean the evangelic and apostolic books— the following expressions are used: "The figure of this world passeth away";[1] "The world passeth away";[2] "Heaven and earth shall pass away"[3]—expressions which are, I fancy, somewhat milder than "They shall *perish*." In the Epistle of the Apostle Peter, too, where the world which then was is said to have perished, being overflowed with water, it is sufficiently obvious what part of the world is signified by the whole, and in what sense the word *perished* is to be taken, and what heavens were kept in store, reserved unto fire against the day of judgment and perdition of ungodly men.[4] And when he says a little afterwards, "The day of the Lord will come as a thief; in the which the heavens shall pass away with a great rush; and the elements shall melt with burning heat, and the earth and the works which are in it shall be burned up," and then adds, "Seeing, then, that all these things shall be dissolved, what manner of persons ought ye to be?"[5]—these heavens which are to perish may be understood to be the same which he said were kept in store reserved for fire; and the elements which are to be burned are those which are full of storm and disturbance in this lowest part of the world in which he said that these heavens were kept in store; for the higher heavens in whose firmament are set the stars are safe, and remain in their integrity. For even the expression of Scripture, that "the stars shall fall from heaven,"[6] not to mention that a different interpretation is much preferable, rather shows that the heavens themselves shall remain, if the stars are to fall from them. This expression, then, is either figurative, as is more credible, or this phenomenon will take place in this lowest heaven, like that mentioned by Virgil—

A meteor with a train of light
Athwart the sky gleamed dazzling bright,
Then in Idæan woods was lost.[7]

But the passage I have quoted from the psalm seems to except none of the heavens from the destiny of destruction; for he says, "The heavens are the works of Thy hands: they shall perish"; so that, as none of them are excepted from the category of God's works, none of them are excepted from destruction. For our opponents

will not condescend to defend the Hebrew piety, which has won the approbation of their gods, by the words of the Apostle Peter, whom they vehemently detest; nor will they argue that, as the apostle in his epistle understands a part when he speaks of the whole world perishing in the flood, though only the lowest part of it, and the corresponding heavens were destroyed, so in the psalm the whole is used for a part, and it is said "They shall perish," though only the lowest heavens are to perish. But since, as I said, they will not condescend to reason thus, lest they should seem to approve of Peter's meaning, or ascribe as much importance to the final conflagration as we ascribe to the deluge, whereas they contend that no waters or flames could destroy the whole human race, it only remains to them to maintain that their gods lauded the wisdom of the Hebrews because they had not read this psalm.

It is the last judgment of God which is referred to also in the 50th Psalm in the words, "God shall come manifestly, our God, and shall not keep silence: fire shall devour before Him, and it shall be very tempestuous round about Him. He shall call the heaven above, and the earth, to judge His people. Gather His saints together to Him; they who make a covenant with Him over sacrifices."[8] This we understand of our Lord Jesus Christ, Whom we look for from heaven to judge the quick and the dead. For He shall come manifestly to judge justly the just and the unjust, who before came hiddenly to be unjustly judged by the unjust. He, I say, shall come manifestly, and shall not keep silence, that is, shall make Himself known by His voice of judgment, who before, when he came hiddenly, was silent before His judge when He was led as a sheep to the slaughter, and, as a lamb before the shearer, opened not His mouth, as we read that it was prophesied of Him by Isaiah,[9] and as we see it fulfilled in the Gospel.[10] As for the *fire* and *tempest*, we have already said how these are to be interpreted when we were explaining a similar passage in Isaiah.[11] As to the expression, "He shall call the heaven above," as the saints and the righteous are rightly called *heaven*, no doubt this means what the apostle says, "We shall be caught up together with them in the clouds, to meet the Lord in the air."[12] For if we take the bare literal sense, how is it possible to call the heaven above, as if the heaven could be anywhere else than above? And the

---

[1]I Cor. 7. 31.   [2]I John, 2. 17.   [3]Matt. 24. 35.
[4]II Pet. 3. 6.   [5]II Pet. 3. 10, 11.   [6]Matt. 24. 29.
[7]*Æneid*, BK. II. 694.

[8]Ps. 50. 3–5.   [9]Isa. 53. 7.   [10]Matt. 26. 63.
[11]Chap. 21.   [12]I Thess. 4. 17.

following expression, "And the earth to judge His people," if we supply only the words, "He shall call," that is to say, "He shall call the earth also," and do not supply "above," seems to give us a meaning in accordance with sound doctrine, the heaven symbolizing those who will judge along with Christ, and the earth those who shall be judged; and thus the words, "He shall call the heaven above," would not mean, "He shall catch up into the air," but "He shall lift up to seats of judgment." Possibly, too, "He shall call the heaven," may mean, He shall call the angels in the high and lofty places, that He may descend with them to do judgment; and "He shall call the earth also" would then mean, He shall call the men on the earth to judgment. But if with the words "and the earth" we understand not only "He shall call," but also "above," so as to make the full sense be, "He shall call the heaven above, and He shall call the earth above," then I think it is best understood of the men who shall be caught up to meet Christ in the air, and that they are called *the heaven* with reference to their souls, and *the earth* with reference to their bodies. Then what is "to judge His people," but to separate by judgment the good from the bad, as the sheep from the goats? Then he turns to address the angels: "Gather His saints together unto Him." For certainly a matter so important must be accomplished by the ministry of angels. And if we ask who the saints are who are gathered unto Him by the angels, we are told, "They who make a covenant with Him over sacrifices." This is the whole life of the saints, to make a covenant with God over sacrifices. For "over sacrifices" either refers to works of mercy, which are preferable to sacrifices in the judgment of God, who says, "I desire mercy more than sacrifices," [1] or if "over sacrifices" means in sacrifices, then these very works of mercy are the sacrifices with which God is pleased, as I remember to have stated in the tenth book of this work; [2] and in these works the saints make a covenant with God, because they do them for the sake of the promises which are contained in His New Testament or covenant. And hence, when His saints have been gathered to Him and set at His right hand in the last judgment, Christ shall say, "Come, ye blessed of my Father, take possession of the kingdom prepared for you from the foundation of the world. For I was hungry, and ye gave me to eat," [3] and so on, mentioning the good works of the good, and

their eternal rewards assigned by the last sentence of the Judge.

CHAP. 25. *Of Malachi's prophecy, in which he speaks of the last judgment, and of a cleansing which some are to undergo by purifying punishments*

The prophet Malachi or Malachias, who is also called Angel, and is by some (for Jerome tells us that this is the opinion of the Hebrews) identified with Ezra the priest, others of whose writings have been received into the canon, predicts the last judgment, saying, "Behold, He cometh, saith the Lord Almighty; and who shall abide the day of His entrance? . . . for I am the Lord your God, and I change not." [4] From these words it more evidently appears that some shall in the last judgment suffer some kind of purgatorial punishments; for what else can be understood by the word, "Who shall abide the day of His entrance, or who shall be able to look upon Him? for He enters as a moulder's fire, and as the herb of fullers: and He shall sit fusing and purifying as if over gold and silver: and He shall purify the sons of Levi, and pour them out like gold and silver"? Similarly Isaiah says, "The Lord shall wash the filthiness of the sons and daughters of Zion, and shall cleanse away the blood from their midst, by the spirit of judgment and by the spirit of burning." [5] Unless perhaps we should say that they are cleansed from filthiness and in a manner clarified, when the wicked are separated from them by penal judgment, so that the elimination and damnation of the one party is the purgation of the others, because they shall henceforth live free from the contamination of such men. But when he says, "And he shall purify the sons of Levi, and pour them out like gold and silver, and they shall offer to the Lord sacrifices in righteousness; and the sacrifices of Judah and Jerusalem shall be pleasing to the Lord," he declares that those who shall be purified shall then please the Lord with sacrifices of righteousness, and consequently they themselves shall be purified from their own unrighteousness which made them displeasing to God. Now they themselves, when they have been purified, shall be sacrifices of complete and perfect righteousness; for what more acceptable offering can such persons make to God than themselves? But this question of purgatorial punishments we must defer to another time, to give it a more adequate treatment. By the sons of Levi and Judah and Jerusa-

---

[1] Hos. 6. 6.   [2] Chap. 6.   [3] Matt. 25. 34.

[4] Mal. 3. 1–6.   [5] Isa. 4. 4.

lem we ought to understand the Church herself, gathered not from the Hebrews only, but from other nations as well; nor such a Church as she now is, when "if we say that we have no sin, we deceive ourselves, and the truth is not in us," [1] but as she shall then be, purged by the last judgment as a threshing-floor by a winnowing wind, and those of her members who need it being cleansed by fire, so that there remains absolutely not one who offers sacrifice for his sins. For all who make such offerings are assuredly in their sins, for the remission of which they make offerings, that having made to God an acceptable offering, they may then be absolved.

CHAP. 26. *Of the sacrifices offered to God by the saints, which are to be pleasing to him, as in the primitive days and former years*

And it was with the design of showing that His city shall not then follow this custom, that God said that the sons of Levi should offer sacrifices in righteousness—not therefore in sin, and consequently not for sin. And hence we see how vainly the Jews promise themselves a return of the old times of sacrificing according to the law of the Old Testament, grounding on the words which follow, "And the sacrifice of Judah and Jerusalem shall be pleasing to the Lord, as in the primitive days, and as in former years." For in the times of the law they offered sacrifices not in righteousness but in sins, offering especially and primarily for sins, so much so that even the priest himself, whom we must suppose to have been their most righteous man, was accustomed to offer, according to God's commandments, first for his own sins, and then for the sins of the people. And therefore we must explain how we are to understand the words, "as in the primitive days, and as in former years"; for perhaps he alludes to the time in which our first parents were in Paradise. Then, indeed, intact and pure from all stain and blemish of sin, they offered themselves to God as the purest sacrifices. But since they were banished thence on account of their transgression, and human nature was condemned in them, with the exception of the one Mediator and those who have been baptized, and are as yet infants, "there is none clean from stain, not even the babe whose life has been but for a day upon the earth." [2] But if it be replied that those who offer in faith may be said to offer in righteousness, because the righteous lives by faith[3]—he deceives him-

self, however, if he says that he has no sin, and therefore he does not say so, because he lives by faith—will any man say this time of faith can be placed on an equal footing with that consummation when they who offer sacrifices in righteousness shall be purified by the fire of the last judgment? And consequently, since it must be believed that after such a cleansing the righteous shall retain no sin, assuredly that time, so far as regards its freedom from sin, can be compared to no other period, unless to that during which our first parents lived in Paradise in the most innocent happiness before their transgression. It is this period, then, which is properly understood when it is said, "as in the primitive days, and as in former years." For in Isaiah, too, after the new heavens and the new earth have been promised, among other elements in the blessedness of the saints which are there depicted by allegories and figures, from giving an adequate explanation of which I am prevented by a desire to avoid prolixity, it is said, "According to the days of the tree of life shall be the days of my people." [4] And who that has looked at Scripture does not know where God planted the tree of life, from whose fruit He excluded our first parents when their own iniquity ejected them from Paradise, and round which a terrible and fiery fence was set?

But if any one contends that those days of the tree of life mentioned by the prophet Isaiah are the present times of the Church of Christ, and that Christ Himself is prophetically called the Tree of Life, because He is Wisdom, and of wisdom Solomon says, "It is a tree of life to all who embrace it";[5] and if they maintain that our first parents did not pass *years* in Paradise, but were driven from it so soon that none of their children were begotten there, and that therefore that time cannot be alluded to in words which run, "as in the primitive days, and as in former years," I forbear entering on this question, lest by discussing everything I become prolix and leave the whole subject in uncertainty. For I see another meaning, which should keep us from believing that a restoration of the primitive days and former years of the legal sacrifices could have been promised to us by the prophet as a great boon. For the animals selected as victims under the old law were required to be immaculate, and free from all blemish whatever, and symbolized holy men free from all sin, the only instance of which character was found in Christ. As, therefore, after the judg-

---

[1] I John, 1. 8.   [2] Job, 14. 4.
[3] Rom. 1. 17.
[4] Isa. 65. 22.   [5] Prov. 3. 18.

ment those who are worthy of such purification shall be purified even by fire, and shall be rendered thoroughly sinless, and shall offer themselves to God in righteousness, and be indeed victims immaculate and free from all blemish whatever, they shall then certainly be, "as in the primitive days, and as in former years," when the purest victims were offered, the shadow of this future reality. For there shall then be in the body and soul of the saints the purity which was symbolized in the bodies of these victims.

Then, with reference to those who are worthy not of cleansing but of damnation, He says, "And I will draw near to you to judgment, and I will be a swift witness against evil-doers and against adulterers"; and after enumerating other damnable crimes, He adds, "For I am the Lord your God, and I am not changed." It is as if He said, "Though your fault has changed you for the worse, and my grace has changed you for the better, I am not changed." And he says that He Himself will be a witness, because in His judgment He needs no witnesses; and that He will be "swift," either because He is to come suddenly, and the judgment which seemed to lag shall be very swift by His unexpected arrival, or because He will convince the consciences of men directly and without any prolix harangue. "For," as it is written, "in the thoughts of the wicked His examination shall be conducted." [1] And the apostle says, "The thoughts accusing or else excusing, in the day in which God shall judge the hidden things of men, according to my gospel in Jesus Christ." [2] Thus, then, shall the Lord be a swift witness, when He shall suddenly bring back into the memory that which shall convince and punish the conscience.

CHAP. 27. *Of the separation of the good and the bad, which proclaim the discriminating influence of the last judgment*

The passage also which I formerly quoted for another purpose from this prophet refers to the last judgment, in which he says, "They shall be mine, saith the Lord Almighty, in the day in which I make up my gains," etc. [3] When this diversity between the rewards and punishments which distinguish the righteous from the wicked shall appear under that Sun of righteousness in the brightness of life eternal—a diversity which is not discerned under this sun which shines on the vanity of this life—there shall then be such a judgment as has never before been.

CHAP. 28. *That the law of Moses must be spiritually understood to preclude the damnable murmurs of a carnal interpretation*

In the succeeding words, "Remember the law of Moses my servant, which I commanded to him in Horeb for all Israel," [4] the prophet opportunely mentions precepts and statutes, after declaring the important distinction hereafter to be made between those who observe and those who despise the law. He intends also that they learn to interpret the law spiritually and find Christ in it, by whose judgment that separation between the good and the bad is to be made. For it is not without reason that the Lord Himself says to the Jews, "Had ye believed Moses, ye would have believed me; for he wrote of me." [5] For by receiving the law carnally without perceiving that its earthly promises were figures of things spiritual, they fell into such murmurings as audaciously to say, "It is vain to serve God; and what profit is it that we have kept His ordinance, and that we have walked suppliantly before the face of the Lord Almighty? And now we call aliens happy; yea, they that work wickedness are set up." [6] It was these words of theirs which in a manner compelled the prophet to announce the last judgment, in which the wicked shall not even in appearance be happy, but shall manifestly be most miserable; and in which the good shall be oppressed with not even a transitory wretchedness, but shall enjoy unsullied and eternal felicity. For he had previously cited some similar expressions of those who said, "Every one that doeth evil is good in the sight of the Lord, and such are pleasing to Him." [7] It was, I say, by understanding the law of Moses carnally that they had come to murmur thus against God. And hence, too, the writer of the 73d Psalm says that his feet were almost gone, his steps had well-nigh slipped, because he was envious of sinners while he considered their prosperity, so that he said among other things, "How doth God know, and is there knowledge in the Most High?" and again, "Have I sanctified my heart in vain, and washed my hands in innocency?" He goes on to say that his efforts to solve this most difficult problem, which arises when the good seem to be wretched and the wicked happy, were in vain until he went into the sanctuary of God and understood the last things. [8] For in the last judgment things shall not be so; but in the manifest felicity of the righteous and manifest misery of

[1]Wisd. 1. 9.   [2]Rom. 2. 15, 16.   [3]Mal. 3. 17; 4. 3.

[4]Mal. 4. 4.   [5]John, 5. 46.   [6]Mal. 3. 14, 15.
[7]Mal. 2. 17.   [8]Ps. 73.

the wicked quite another state of things shall appear.

CHAP. 29. *Of the coming of Elias before the Judgment, that the Jews may be converted to Christ by his preaching and explanation of Scripture*

After admonishing them to give heed to the law of Moses, as he foresaw that for a long time to come they would not understand it spiritually and rightly, he went on to say, "And, behold, I will send to you Elias the Tishbite before the great and signal day of the Lord come: and he shall turn the heart of the father to the son, and the heart of a man to his next of kin, lest I come and utterly smite the earth." [1] It is a familiar theme in the conversation and heart of the faithful, that in the last days before the judgment the Jews shall believe in the true Christ, that is, our Christ, by means of this great and admirable prophet Elias who shall expound the law to them. For not without reason do we hope that before the coming of our Judge and Saviour Elias shall come, because we have good reason to believe that he is now alive; for, as Scripture most distinctly informs us,[2] he was taken up from this life in a chariot of fire. When, therefore, he is come, he shall give a spiritual explanation of the law which the Jews at present understand carnally, and shall thus "turn the heart of the father to the son," that is, the heart of fathers to their children; for the Septuagint translators have frequently put the singular for the plural number. And the meaning is, that the sons, that is, the Jews, shall understand the law as the fathers, that is, the prophets, and among them Moses himself, understood it. For the heart of the fathers shall be turned to their children when the children understand the law as their fathers did; and the heart of the children shall be turned to their fathers when they have the same sentiments as the fathers. The Septuagint used the expression, "and the heart of a man to his next of kin," because fathers and children are eminently neighbours to one another. Another and a preferable sense can be found in the words of the Septuagint translators, who have translated Scripture with an eye to prophecy, the sense, viz., that Elias shall turn the heart of God the Father to the Son, not certainly as if he should bring about this love of the Father for the Son, but meaning that he should make it known, and that the Jews also, who had previously hated, should then love the Son who is our Christ. For so far as regards the Jews, God has His heart turned away from our Christ, this being their conception about God and Christ. But in their case the heart of God shall be turned to the Son when they themselves shall turn in heart, and learn the love of the Father towards the Son. The words following, "and the heart of a man to his next of kin"— that is, Elias shall also turn the heart of a man to his next of kin—how can we understand this better than as the heart of a man to the man Christ? For though in the form of God He is our God, yet, taking the form of a servant, He condescended to become also our next of kin. It is this, then, which Elias will do, "lest," he says, "I come and smite the earth utterly." For they who mind earthly things are the earth. Such are the carnal Jews until this day; and hence these murmurs of theirs against God, "The wicked are pleasing to Him," and "It is a vain thing to serve God." [3]

CHAP. 30. *That in the books of the Old Testament, where it is said that God shall judge the world, the person of Christ is not explicitly indicated, but it plainly appears from some passages in which the Lord God speaks that Christ is meant*

There are many other passages of Scripture bearing on the last judgment of God—so many, indeed, that to cite them all would swell this book to an unpardonable size. Suffice it to have proved that both Old and New Testament enounce the judgment. But in the Old it is not so definitely declared as in the New that the judgment shall be administered by Christ, that is, that Christ shall descend from heaven as the Judge; for when it is therein stated by the Lord God or His prophet that the Lord God shall come, we do not necessarily understand this of Christ. For both the Father, and the Son, and the Holy Ghost are the Lord God. We must not, however, leave this without proof. And therefore we must first show how Jesus Christ speaks in the prophetical books under the title of the Lord God, while yet there can be no doubt that it is Jesus Christ Who speaks; so that in other passages where this is not at once apparent, and where nevertheless it is said that the Lord God will come to that last judgment, we may understand that Jesus Christ is meant. There is a passage in the prophet Isaiah which illustrates what I mean. For God says by the prophet, "Hear me, Jacob and Israel, whom I call. I am the first, and I am for ever: and my hand has founded the earth, and my right hand has estab-

---

[1] Mal. 4. 5, 6. [2] II Kings, 2. 11. [3] Mal. 2. 17; 3. 14.

lished the heaven. I will call them, and they shall stand together, and be gathered, and hear. Who has declared to them these things? In love of thee I have done thy pleasure upon Babylon, that I might take away the seed of the Chaldeans. I have spoken, and I have called: I have brought him, and have made his way prosperous. Come ye near unto me, and hear this. I have not spoken in secret from the beginning; when they were made, there was I. And now the Lord God and His Spirit hath sent me." [1] It was Himself Who was speaking as the Lord God; and yet we should not have understood that it was Jesus Christ had He not added, "And now the Lord God and His Spirit hath sent me." For He said this with reference to the form of a servant, speaking of a future event as if it were past, as in the same prophet we read, "He was led as a sheep to the slaughter," [2] not "He shall be led"; but the past tense is used to express the future. And prophecy constantly speaks in this way.

There is also another passage in Zechariah which plainly declares that the Almighty sent the Almighty; and of what persons can this be understood but of God the Father and God the Son? For it is written, "Thus saith the Lord Almighty, After the glory hath He sent me unto the nations which spoiled you; for he that toucheth you toucheth the apple of His eye. Behold, I will bring mine hand upon them, and they shall be a spoil to their servants: and ye shall know that the Lord Almighty hath sent me." [3] Observe, the Lord Almighty saith that the Lord Almighty sent Him. Who can presume to understand these words of any other than Christ, who is speaking to the lost sheep of the house of Israel? For He says in the Gospel, "I am not sent save to the lost sheep of the house of Israel," [4] which He here compared to the pupil of God's eye, to signify the profoundest love. And to this class of sheep the apostles themselves belonged. But after the glory, to wit, of His resurrection—for before it happened the evangelist said that "Jesus was not yet glorified" [5]—He was sent unto the nations in the persons of His apostles; and thus the saying of the psalm was fulfilled, "Thou wilt deliver me from the contradictions of the people; Thou wilt set me as the head of the nations." [6] So that those who had spoiled the Israelites, and whom the Israelites had served when they were subdued by them, were not themselves to be spoiled in the same fashion, but were in their own persons

to become the spoil of the Israelites. For this had been promised to the apostles when the Lord said, "I will make you fishers of men." [7] And to one of them He says, "From henceforth thou shalt catch men." [8] They were then to become a spoil, but in a good sense, as those who are snatched from that strong one when he is bound by a stronger. [9]

In like manner the Lord, speaking by the same prophet, says, "And it shall come to pass in that day, that I will seek to destroy all the nations that come against Jerusalem. And I will pour upon the house of David, and upon the inhabitants of Jerusalem, the spirit of grace and mercy; and they shall look upon me because they have insulted me, and they shall mourn for Him as for one very dear, and shall be in bitterness as for an only-begotten." [10] To Whom but to God does it belong to destroy all the nations that are hostile to the holy city Jerusalem, which "come against it," that is, are opposed to it, or, as some translate, "come upon it," as if putting it down under them; or to pour out upon the house of David and the inhabitants of Jerusalem the spirit of grace and mercy? This belongs doubtless to God, and it is to God the prophet ascribes the words; and yet Christ shows that He is the God who does these so great and divine things, when He goes on to say, "And they shall look upon me because they have insulted me, and they shall mourn for Him as if for one very dear (or beloved), and shall be in bitterness for Him as for an only-begotten." For in that day the Jews—those of them, at least, who shall receive the spirit of grace and mercy—when they see Him coming in His majesty, and recognize that it is He Whom they, in the person of their parents, insulted when He came before in His humiliation, shall repent of insulting Him in His passion: and their parents themselves, who were the perpetrators of this huge impiety, shall see Him when they rise; but this will be only for their punishment, and not for their correction. It is not of them we are to understand the words, "And I will pour upon the house of David, and upon the inhabitants of Jerusalem, the spirit of grace and mercy, and they shall look upon me because they have insulted me"; but we are to understand the words of their descendants, who shall at that time believe through Elias. But as we say to the Jews, You killed Christ, although it was their parents who did so, so these persons shall grieve that they in some sort did what their progenitors

[1] Isa. 48. 12–16. [2] Isa. 53. 7. [3] Zech. 2. 8, 9.
[4] Matt. 15. 24. [5] John, 7. 39. [6] Ps. 18. 43.
[7] Matt. 4. 19. [8] Luke, 5. 10. [9] Matt. 12. 29.
[10] Zech. 12. 9, 10.

did. Although, therefore, those that receive the spirit of mercy and grace, and believe, shall not be condemned with their impious parents, yet they shall mourn as if they themselves had done what their parents did. Their grief shall arise not so much from guilt as from pious affection. Certainly the words which the Septuagint have translated, "They shall look upon me because they insulted me," stand in the Hebrew, "They shall look upon me whom they pierced." And by this word the crucifixion of Christ is certainly more plainly indicated. But the Septuagint translators preferred to allude to the insult which was involved in His whole passion. For in point of fact they insulted Him both when He was arrested and when He was bound, when He was judged, when He was mocked by the robe they put on Him and the homage they did on bended knee, when He was crowned with thorns and struck with a rod on the head, when He bore His cross, and when at last He hung upon the tree. And therefore we recognize more fully the Lord's passion when we do not confine ourselves to one interpretation, but combine both, and read both "insulted" and "pierced."

When, therefore, we read in the prophetical books that God is to come to do judgment at the last, from the mere mention of the judgment, and although there is nothing else to determine the meaning, we must gather that Christ is meant; for though the Father will judge, He will judge by the coming of the Son. For He Himself, by His own manifested presence, "judges no man, but has committed all judgment to the Son";[1] for as the Son was judged as a man, He shall also judge in human form. For it is none but He of whom God speaks by Isaiah under the name of Jacob and Israel, of whose seed Christ took a body, as it is written, "Jacob is my servant, I will uphold Him; Israel is mine elect, my Spirit has assumed Him; I have put my Spirit upon Him; He shall bring forth judgment to the Gentiles. He shall not cry, nor cease, neither shall His voice be heard without. A bruised reed shall He not break, and the smoking flax shall He not quench: but in truth shall He bring forth judgment. He shall shine and shall not be broken, until He sets judgment in the earth: and the nations shall hope in His name."[2] The Hebrew has not "Jacob" and "Israel"; but the Septuagint translators, wishing to show the significance of the expression "my servant," and that it refers to the form of a servant in which the Most High humbled Himself, inserted the name of that man from

whose stock He took the form of a servant. The Holy Spirit was given to Him, and was manifested, as the evangelist testifies, in the form of a dove.[3] He brought forth judgment to the Gentiles, because He predicted what was hidden from them. In His meekness He did not cry, nor did He cease to proclaim the truth. But His voice was not heard, nor is it heard, without, because He is not obeyed by those who are outside of His body. And the Jews themselves, who persecuted Him, He did not break, though as a bruised reed they had lost their integrity, and as smoking flax their light was quenched; for He spared them, having come to be judged and not yet to judge. He brought forth judgment in truth, declaring that they should be punished did they persist in their wickedness. His face shone on the Mount,[4] His fame in the world. He is not broken nor overcome, because neither in Himself nor in His Church has persecution prevailed to annihilate Him. And therefore that has not, and shall not, be brought about which His enemies said or say, "When shall He die, and His name perish?"[5] "until He set judgment in the earth." Behold, the hidden thing which we were seeking is discovered. For this is the last judgment, which He will set in the earth when He comes from heaven. And it is in Him, too, we already see the concluding expression of the prophecy fulfilled: "In His name shall the nations hope." And by this fulfilment, which no one can deny, men are encouraged to believe in that which is most impudently denied. For who could have hoped for that which even those who do not yet believe in Christ now see fulfilled among us, and which is so undeniable that they can but gnash their teeth and pine away? Who, I say, could have hoped that the nations would hope in the name of Christ, when He was arrested, bound, scourged, mocked, crucified, when even the disciples themselves had lost the hope which they had begun to have in Him? The hope which was then entertained scarcely by the one thief on the cross is now cherished by nations everywhere on the earth, who are marked with the sign of the cross on which He died that they may not die eternally.

That the last judgment, then, shall be administered by Jesus Christ in the manner predicted in the sacred writings is denied or doubted by no one, unless by those who, through some incredible animosity or blindness, decline to believe these writings, though already their truth is demonstrated to all the world. And at or in connection with that judgment the following

[1]John, 5. 22.   [2]Isa. 42. 1–4.   [3]John, 1. 32.   [4]Matt. 17. 1, 2.   [5]Ps. 41. 5.

events shall come to pass, as we have learned: Elias the Tishbite shall come; the Jews shall believe; Antichrist shall persecute; Christ shall judge; the dead shall rise; the good and the wicked shall be separated; the world shall be burned and renewed. All these things, we believe, shall come to pass; but how, or in what order, human understanding cannot perfectly teach us, but only the experience of the events themselves. My opinion, however, is, that they will happen in the order that I have related.

Two books yet remain to be written by me, in order to complete, by God's help, what I promised. One of these will explain the punishment of the wicked, the other the happiness of the righteous and in them I shall be at special pains to refute, by God's grace, the arguments by which some unhappy creatures seem to themselves to undermine the divine promises and threatenings, and to ridicule as empty words statements which are the most salutary nutriment of faith. But they who are instructed in divine things hold the truth and omnipotence of God to be the strongest arguments in favour of those things which, however incredible they seem to men, are yet contained in the Scriptures, whose truth has already in many ways been proved; for they are sure that God can in no wise lie and that He can do what is impossible to the unbelieving.

BOOK XXI

ARGUMENT. OF THE END RESERVED FOR THE CITY OF THE DEVIL, NAMELY, THE ETERNAL PUNISHMENT OF THE DAMNED; AND OF THE ARGUMENTS WHICH UNBELIEF BRINGS AGAINST IT.

CHAP. I. *Of the order of the discussion, which requires that we first speak of the eternal punishment of the lost in company with the devil, and then of the eternal happiness of the saints*

I PROPOSE, with such ability as God may grant me, to discuss in this book more thoroughly the nature of the punishment which shall be assigned to the devil and all his retainers, when the two cities, the one of God, the other of the devil, shall have reached their proper ends through Jesus Christ our Lord, the Judge of quick and dead. And I have adopted this order, and preferred to speak, first of the punishment of the devils, and afterwards of the blessedness of the saints, because the *body* partakes of either destiny; and it seems to be more incredible that bodies endure in everlasting torments than that they continue to exist without any pain in everlasting felicity. Consequently, when I shall have demonstrated that that punishment ought not to be incredible, this will materially aid me in proving that which is much more credible, viz., the immortality of the bodies of the saints which are delivered from all pain. Neither is this order out of harmony with the divine writings, in which sometimes, indeed, the blessedness of the good is placed first, as in the words, "They that have done good, unto the resurrection of life; and they that have done evil, unto the resurrection of judgment";[1] but sometimes also last, as, "The Son of man shall send forth His angels, and they shall gather out of His kingdom all things which offend, and shall cast them into a furnace of fire: there shall be wailing and gnashing of teeth. Then shall the righteous shine forth as the sun in the kingdom of His Father";[2] and that, "These shall go away into eternal punishment, but the righteous into life eternal."[3] And though we have not room to cite instances, any one who examines the prophets will find that they adopt now the one arrangement and now the other. My own reason for following the latter order I have given.

CHAP. 2. *Whether it is possible for bodies to last for ever in burning fire*

What, then, can I adduce to convince those who refuse to believe that human bodies, animated and living, can not only survive death, but also last in the torments of everlasting fires? They will not allow us to refer this simply to the power of the Almighty, but demand that we persuade them by some example. If, then, we reply to them, that there are animals which certainly are corruptible, because they are mortal, and which yet live in the midst of flames; and likewise, that in springs of water so hot that no one can put his hand in it with impunity a species of worm is found, which not only lives there, but cannot live elsewhere; they either refuse to believe these facts unless we can show them, or, if we are in circumstances to prove them by ocular demonstration or by adequate

[1] John, 5. 29.   [2] Matt. 13. 41–43.   [3] Matt. 25. 46.

testimony, they contend, with the same scepticism, that these facts are not examples of what we seek to prove, inasmuch as these animals do not live for ever, and besides, they live in that blaze of heat without pain, the element of fire being congenial to their nature, and causing it to thrive and not to suffer—just as if it were not more incredible that it should thrive than that it should suffer in such circumstances. It is strange that anything should suffer in fire and yet live, but stranger that it should live in fire and not suffer. If, then, the latter be believed, why not also the former?

CHAP. 3. *Whether bodily suffering necessarily terminates in the destruction of the flesh*

But, say they, there is no body which can suffer and cannot also die. How do we know this? For who can say with certainty that the devils do not suffer in their bodies, when they own that they are grievously tormented? And if it is replied that there is no earthly body—that is to say, no solid and perceptible body, or, in one word, no flesh—which can suffer and cannot die, is not this to tell us only what men have gathered from experience and their bodily senses? For they indeed have no acquaintance with any flesh but that which is mortal; and this is their whole argument, that what they have had no experience of they judge quite impossible. For we cannot call it reasoning to make pain a presumption of death, while, in fact, it is rather a sign of life. For though it be a question whether that which suffers can continue to live for ever, yet it is certain that everything which suffers pain does live, and that pain can exist only in a living subject. It is necessary, therefore, that he who is pained be living, not necessary that pain kill him; for every pain does not kill even those mortal bodies of ours which are destined to die. And that any pain kills them is caused by the circumstance that the soul is so connected with the body that it succumbs to great pain and withdraws; for the structure of our members and vital parts is so infirm that it cannot bear up against that violence which causes great or extreme agony. But in the life to come this connexion of soul and body is of such a kind, that as it is dissolved by no lapse of time, so neither is it burst asunder by any pain. And so, although it be true that in this world there is no flesh which can suffer pain and yet cannot die, yet in the world to come there shall be flesh such as now there is not, as there will also be death such as now there is not. For death will not be abolished, but will be eternal, since the soul will nei-

ther be able to enjoy God and live, nor to die and escape the pains of the body. The first death drives the soul from the body against her will: the second death holds the soul in the body against her will. The two have this in common, that the soul suffers against her will what her own body inflicts.

Our opponents, too, make much of this, that in this world there is no flesh which can suffer pain and cannot die; while they make nothing of the fact that there is something which is greater than the body. For the spirit, whose presence animates and rules the body, can both suffer pain and cannot die. Here then is something which, though it can feel pain, is immortal. And this capacity, which we now see in the spirit of all, shall be hereafter in the bodies of the damned. Moreover, if we attend to the matter a little more closely, we see that what is called bodily pain is rather to be referred to the soul. For it is the soul, not the body, which is pained, even when the pain originates with the body— the soul feeling pain at the point where the body is hurt. As then we speak of bodies feeling and living, though the feeling and life of the body are from the soul, so also we speak of bodies being pained, though no pain can be suffered by the body apart from the soul. The soul, then, is pained with the body in that part where something occurs to hurt it; and it is pained alone, though it be in the body, when some invisible cause distresses it, while the body is safe and sound. Even when not associated with the body it is pained; for certainly that rich man was suffering in hell when he cried, "I am tormented in this flame."[1] But as for the body, it suffers no pain when it is soulless; and even when animate it can suffer only by the soul's suffering. If, therefore, we might draw a just presumption from the existence of pain to that of death, and conclude that where pain can be felt death can occur, death would rather be the property of the soul, for to it pain more peculiarly belongs. But, seeing that that which suffers most cannot die, what ground is there for supposing that those bodies, because destined to suffer, are therefore, destined to die? The Platonists indeed maintained that these earthly bodies and dying members gave rise to the fears, desires, griefs, and joys of the soul. "Hence," says Virgil (i.e., from these earthly bodies and dying members),

> Hence wild desires and grovelling fears,
> And human laughter, human tears.[2]

But in the fourteenth book of this work[3] we have proved that, according to the Platonists'

[1] Luke, 16. 24. [2] *Æneid*, BK. VI. 733. [3] Chaps. 3, 5, 6.

own theory, souls, even when purged from all pollution of the body, are yet possessed by a monstrous desire to return again into their bodies. But where desire can exist, certainly pain also can exist; for desire frustrated, either by missing what it aims at or losing what it had attained, is turned into pain. And therefore, if the soul, which is either the only or the chief sufferer, has yet a kind of immortality of its own, it is inconsequent to say that because the bodies of the damned shall suffer pain, therefore they shall die. In fine, if the body causes the soul to suffer, why can the body not cause death as well as suffering, unless because it does not follow that what causes pain causes death as well? And why then is it incredible that these fires can cause pain but not death to those bodies we speak of, just as the bodies themselves cause pain, but not therefore death, to the souls? Pain is therefore no necessary presumption of death.

CHAP. 4. *Examples from nature proving that bodies may remain unconsumed and alive in fire*

If, therefore, the salamander lives in fire, as naturalists[1] have recorded, and if certain famous mountains of Sicily have been continually on fire from the remotest antiquity until now, and yet remain entire, these are sufficiently convincing examples that everything which burns is not consumed. As the soul, too, is a proof that not everything which can suffer pain can also die, why then do they yet demand that we produce real examples to prove that it is not incredible that the bodies of men condemned to everlasting punishment may retain their soul in the fire, may burn without being consumed, and may suffer without perishing? For suitable properties will be communicated to the substance of the flesh by Him who has endowed the things we see with so marvellous and diverse properties, that their very multitude prevents our wonder. For who but God the Creator of all things has given to the flesh of the peacock its antiseptic property? This property, when I first heard of it, seemed to me incredible; but it happened at Carthage that a bird of this kind was cooked and served up to me, and, taking a suitable slice of flesh from its breast, I ordered it to be kept, and when it had been kept as many days as make any other flesh stinking, it was produced and set before me, and emitted no offensive smell. And after it had been laid by for thirty

[1] Aristotle does not affirm it as a fact observed by himself, but as a popular tradition (*History of Animals*, BK. V. 19).

days and more, it was still in the same state; and a year after, the same still, except that it was a little more shrivelled and drier. Who gave to chaff such power to freeze that it preserves snow buried under it, and such power to warm that it ripens green fruit?

But who can explain the strange properties of fire itself, which blackens everything it burns, though itself bright; and which, though of the most beautiful colours, discolours almost all it touches and feeds upon, and turns blazing fuel into grimy cinders? Still this is not laid down as an absolutely uniform law; for, on the contrary, stones baked in glowing fire themselves also glow, and though the fire be rather of a red hue, and they white, yet white is congruous with light, and black with darkness. Thus, though the fire burns the wood in calcining the stones, these contrary effects do not result from the contrariety of the materials. For though wood and stone differ, they are not contraries, like black and white, the one of which colours is produced in the stones, while the other is produced in the wood by the same action of fire, which imparts its own brightness to the former, while it begrimes the latter, and which could have no effect on the one were it not fed by the other. Then what wonderful properties do we find in charcoal, which is so brittle that a light tap breaks it and a slight pressure pulverizes it, and yet is so strong that no moisture rots it, nor any time causes it to decay. So enduring is it, that it is customary in laying down landmarks to put charcoal underneath them, so that if, after the longest interval, any one raises an action, and pleads that there is no boundary stone, he may be convicted by the charcoal below. What then has enabled it to last so long without rotting, though buried in the damp earth in which wood rots, except this same fire which consumes all things?

Again, let us consider the wonders of lime; for besides growing white in fire, which makes other things black, and of which I have already said enough, it has also a mysterious property of conceiving fire within it. Itself cold to the touch, it yet has a hidden store of fire, which is not at once apparent to our senses, but which experience teaches us, lies as it were slumbering within it even while unseen. And it is for this reason called "quick lime," as if the fire were the invisible soul quickening the visible substance or body. But the marvellous thing is, that this fire is kindled when it is extinguished. For to disengage the hidden fire the lime is moistened or drenched with water, and then, though it be cold before, it becomes hot by that very application which cools what is hot. As if the fire were departing from the lime and breathing its last, it no longer lies hid, but appears; and then the lime lying in the coldness of death cannot be requickened, and what we before called "quick," we now call "slaked." What can be stranger than this? Yet there is a greater marvel still. For if you treat the lime, not with water, but with oil, which is as fuel to fire, no amount of oil will heat it. Now if this marvel had been told us of some Indian mineral which we had no opportunity of experimenting upon, we should either have forthwith pronounced it a falsehood, or certainly should have been greatly astonished. But things that daily present themselves to our own observation we despise, not because they are really less marvellous, but because they are common; so that even some products of India itself, remote as it is from ourselves, cease to excite our admiration as soon as we can admire them at our leisure.[1]

The diamond is a stone possessed by many among ourselves, especially by jewellers and lapidaries, and the stone is so hard that it can be wrought neither by iron nor fire, nor, they say, by anything at all except goat's blood. But do you suppose it is as much admired by those who own it and are familiar with its properties as by those to whom it is shown for the first time? Persons who have not seen it perhaps do not believe what is said of it, or if they do, they wonder as at a thing beyond their experience; and if they happen to see it, still they marvel because they are unused to it, but gradually familiar experience dulls their admiration. We know that the loadstone has a wonderful power of attracting iron. When I first saw it I was thunderstruck, for I saw an iron ring attracted and suspended by the stone; and then, as if it had communicated its own property to the iron it attracted, and had made it a substance like itself, this ring was put near another, and lifted it up; and as the first ring clung to the magnet, so did the second ring to the first. A third and a fourth were similarly added, so that there hung from the stone a kind of chain of rings, with their hoops connected, not interlinking, but attached together by their outer surface. Who would not be amazed at this virtue of the stone, subsisting as it does not only in itself, but transmitted through so many suspended rings, and binding them together by invisible links? Yet far more astonishing is what I heard about this stone from my brother in the episcopate, Severus

[1]See Lucretius, BK. II. 1025.

bishop of Milevis. He told me that Bathanarius, once count of Africa, when the bishop was dining with him, produced a magnet, and held it under a silver plate on which he placed a bit of iron; then as he moved his hand with the magnet underneath the plate, the iron upon the plate moved about accordingly. The intervening silver was not affected at all, but precisely as the magnet was moved backwards and forwards below it, no matter how quickly, so was the iron attracted above. I have related what I myself have witnessed; I have related what I was told by one whom I trust as I trust my own eyes. Let me further say what I have read about this magnet. When a diamond is laid near it, it does not lift iron; or if it has already lifted it, as soon as the diamond approaches, it drops it. These stones come from India. But if we cease to admire them because they are now familiar, how much less must they admire them who procure them very easily and send them to us? Perhaps they are held as cheap as we hold lime, which, because it is common, we think nothing of, though it has the strange property of burning when water, which is wont to quench fire, is poured on it, and of remaining cool when mixed with oil, which ordinarily feeds fire.

CHAP. 5. *That there are many things which reason cannot account for, and which are nevertheless true*

Nevertheless, when we declare the miracles which God has wrought, or will yet work, and which we cannot bring under the very eyes of men, sceptics keep demanding that we shall explain these marvels to reason. And because we cannot do so, inasmuch as they are above human comprehension, they suppose we are speaking falsely. These persons themselves, therefore, ought to account for all these marvels which we either can or do see. And if they perceive that this is impossible for man to do, they should acknowledge that it cannot be concluded that a thing has not been or shall not be because it cannot be reconciled to reason, since there are things now in existence of which the same is true. I will not, then, detail the multitude of marvels which are related in books, and which refer not to things that happened once and passed away, but that are permanent in certain places, where, if any one has the desire and opportunity, he may ascertain their truth; but a few only I recount. The following are some of the marvels men tell us:—The salt of Agrigentum in Sicily, when thrown into the fire, becomes fluid as if it were in water, but in the water it crackles as if it were in the fire. The Garamantæ have a fountain so cold by day that no one can drink it, so hot by night no one can touch it. In Epirus, too, there is a fountain which, like all others, quenches lighted torches, but, unlike all others, lights quenched torches. There is a stone found in Arcadia, and called asbestos, because once lit it cannot be put out. The wood of a certain kind of Egyptian fig-tree sinks in water, and does not float like other wood; and, stranger still, when it has been sunk to the bottom for some time, it rises again to the surface, though nature requires that when soaked in water it should be heavier than ever. Then there are the apples of Sodom, which grow indeed to an appearance of ripeness, but, when you touch them with hand or tooth, the peel cracks, and they crumble into dust and ashes. The Persian stone pyrites burns the hand when it is tightly held in it, and so gets its name from fire. In Persia, too, there is found another stone called selenite, because its interior brilliancy waxes and wanes with the moon. Then in Cappadocia the mares are impregnated by the wind, and their foals live only three years. Tilon, an Indian island, has this advantage over all other lands, that no tree which grows in it ever loses its foliage.

These and numberless other marvels recorded in the history, not of past events, but of permanent localities, I have no time to enlarge upon and diverge from my main object; but let those sceptics who refuse to credit the divine writings give me, if they can, a rational account of them. For their only ground of unbelief in the Scriptures is, that they contain incredible things, just such as I have been recounting. For, say they, reason cannot admit that flesh burn and remain unconsumed, suffer without dying. Mighty reasoners, indeed, who are competent to give the reason of all the marvels that exist! Let them then give us the reason of the few things we have cited, and which, if they did not know they existed, and were only assured by us they would at some future time occur, they would believe still less than that which they now refuse to credit on our word. For which of them would believe us if, instead of saying that the living bodies of men hereafter will be such as to endure everlasting pain and fire without ever dying, we were to say that in the world to come there will be salt which becomes liquid in fire as if it were in water, and crackles in water as if it were in fire; or that there will be a fountain whose water in the chill air of night is so hot that it cannot be touched, while in the heat

of day it is so cold that it cannot be drunk; or that there will be a stone which by its own heat burns the hand when tightly held, or a stone which cannot be extinguished if it has been lit in any part; or any of those wonders I have cited, while omitting numberless others? If we were to say that these things would be found in the world to come, and our sceptics were to reply, "If you wish us to believe these things, satisfy our reason about each of them," we should confess that we could not, because the frail comprehension of man cannot master these and such-like wonders of God's working; and that yet our reason was thoroughly convinced that the Almighty does nothing without reason, though the frail mind of man cannot explain the reason; and that while we are in many instances uncertain what He intends, yet that it is always most certain that nothing which He intends is impossible to Him; and that when He declares His mind, we believe Him Whom we cannot believe to be either powerless or false. Nevertheless these cavillers at faith and exactors of reason, how do they dispose of those things of which a reason cannot be given, and which yet exist, though in apparent contrariety to the nature of things? If we had announced that these things were to be, these sceptics would have demanded from us the reason of them, as they do in the case of those things which we are announcing as destined to be. And consequently, as these present marvels are not non-existent, though human reason and discourse are lost in such works of God, so those things we speak of are not impossible because inexplicable; for in this particular they are in the same predicament as the marvels of earth.

CHAP. 6. *That all marvels are not of nature's production, but that some are due to human ingenuity and others to diabolic contrivance*

At this point they will perhaps reply, "These things have no existence; we don't believe one of them; they are travellers' tales and fictitious romances"; and they may add what has the appearance of argument, and say, "If you believe such things as these, believe what is recorded in the same books, that there was or is a temple of Venus in which a candelabrum set in the open air holds a lamp, which burns so strongly that no storm or rain extinguishes it, and which is therefore called, like the stone mentioned above, the asbestos or inextinguishable lamp." They may say this with the intention of putting us into a dilemma: for if we say this is incredible, then we shall impugn the truth of the other recorded marvels; if, on the other hand, we admit that this is credible, we shall avouch the pagan deities. But, as I have already said in the eighteenth book of this work, we do not hold it necessary to believe all that profane history contains, since, as Varro says, even historians themselves disagree on so many points that one would think they intended and were at pains to do so; but we believe, if we are disposed, those things which are not contradicted by these books, which we do not hesitate to say we *are* bound to believe. But as to those permanent miracles of nature, whereby we wish to persuade the sceptical of the miracles of the world to come, those are quite sufficient for our purpose which we ourselves can observe, or of which it is not difficult to find trustworthy witnesses. Moreover, that temple of Venus, with its inextinguishable lamp, so far from hemming us into a corner, opens an advantageous field to our argument. For to this inextinguishable lamp we add a host of marvels wrought by men, or by magic—that is, by men under the influence of devils, or by the devils directly—for such marvels we cannot deny without impugning the truth of the sacred Scriptures we believe. That lamp, therefore, was either by some mechanical and human device fitted with asbestos, or it was arranged by magical art in order that the worshippers might be astonished, or some devil under the name of Venus so signally manifested himself that this prodigy both began and became permanent. Now devils are attracted to dwell in certain temples by means of the creatures (God's creatures, not theirs), who present to them what suits their various tastes. They are attracted not by food like animals, but, like spirits, by such symbols as suit their taste, various kinds of stones, woods, plants, animals, songs, rites. And that men may provide these attractions, the devils first of all cunningly seduce them, either by imbuing their hearts with a secret poison, or by revealing themselves under a friendly guise, and thus make a few of them their disciples, who become the instructors of the multitude. For unless they first instructed men, it were impossible to know what each of them desires, what they shrink from, by what name they should be invoked or constrained to be present. Hence the origin of magic and magicians. But, above all, they possess the hearts of men, and are chiefly proud of this possession when they transform themselves into angels of light. Very many things that occur, therefore, are their doing; and these deeds of theirs we ought all the more carefully to shun as we ac-

knowledge them to be very surprising. And yet these very deeds forward my present arguments. For if such marvels are wrought by unclean devils, how much mightier are the holy angels! and what can not that God do Who made the angels themselves capable of working miracles!

If, then, very many effects can be contrived by human art, of so surprising a kind that the uninitiated think them divine, as when, e.g., in a certain temple two magnets have been adjusted, one in the roof, another in the floor, so that an iron image is suspended in mid-air between them, one would suppose by the power of the divinity, were he ignorant of the magnets above and beneath; or, as in the case of that lamp of Venus which we already mentioned as being a skillful adaptation of asbestos; if, again, by the help of magicians, whom Scripture calls sorcerers and enchanters, the devils could gain such power that the noble poet Virgil should consider himself justified in describing a very powerful magician in these lines:

> *Her charms can cure what souls she please,*
> *Rob other hearts of healthful ease,*
> *Turn rivers backward to their source,*
> *And make the stars forget their course,*
>   *And call up ghosts from night:*
> *The ground shall bellow 'neath your feet:*
> *The mountain-ash shall quit its seat,*
>   *And travel down the height;*[1]

if this be so, how much more able is God to do those things which to sceptics are incredible, but to His power easy, since it is He Who has given to stones and all other things their virtue, and to men their skill to use them in wonderful ways; He Who has given to the angels a nature more mighty than that of all that lives on earth; He Whose power surpasses all marvels, and Whose wisdom in working, ordaining, and permitting is no less marvellous in its governance of all things than in its creation of all!

CHAP. 7. *That the ultimate reason for believing miracles is the omnipotence of the Creator*

Why, then, cannot God effect both that the bodies of the dead shall rise, and that the bodies of the damned shall be tormented in everlasting fire—God, Who made the world full of countless miracles in sky, earth, air, and waters, while itself is a miracle unquestionably greater and more admirable than all the marvels it is filled with? But those with whom or against whom we are arguing, who believe both that there is a God Who made the world, and that

[1] *Æneid*, BK. IV. 487–491.

there are gods created by Him who administer the world's laws as His viceregents—our adversaries, I say, who, so far from denying emphatically, assert that there are powers in the world which effect marvellous results (whether of their own accord, or because they are invoked by some rite or prayer, or in some magical way), when we lay before them the wonderful properties of other things which are neither rational animals nor rational spirits, but such material objects as those we have just cited, are in the habit of replying, "This is their natural property, their nature; these are the powers naturally belonging to them." Thus the whole reason why Agrigentine salt dissolves in fire and crackles in water is that this is its nature. Yet this seems rather contrary to nature, which has given not to fire but to water the power of melting salt, and the power of scorching it not to water but to fire. But this, they say, is the natural property of *this* salt, to show effects contrary to these. The same reason, therefore, is assigned to account for that Garamantian fountain, of which one and the same runlet is chill by day and boiling by night, so that in either extreme it cannot be touched. So also of that other fountain which, though it is cold to the touch, and though it, like other fountains, extinguishes a lighted torch, yet, unlike other fountains, and in a surprising manner, kindles an extinguished torch. So of the asbestos stone, which, though it has no heat of its own, yet when kindled by fire applied to it, cannot be extinguished. And so of the rest, which I am weary of reciting, and in which, though there seems to be an extraordinary property contrary to nature, yet no other reason is given for them than this, that this is their nature—a brief reason truly and, I own, a satisfactory reply. But since God is the author of all natures, how is it that our adversaries, when they refuse to believe what we affirm, on the ground that it is impossible, are unwilling to accept from us a better explanation than their own, viz., that this is the will of Almighty God —for certainly He is called Almighty only because He is mighty to do all He will—He Who was able to create so many marvels, not only unknown, but very well ascertained, as I have been showing, and which, were they not under our own observation, or reported by recent and credible witnesses, would certainly be pronounced impossible? For as for those marvels which have no other testimony than the writers in whose books we read them, and who wrote without being divinely instructed, and are therefore liable to human error, we cannot justly blame any one who declines to believe them.

For my own part, I do not wish all the marvels I have cited to be rashly accepted, for I do not myself believe them implicitly, save those which have either come under my own observation, or which any one can readily verify, such as the lime which is heated by water and cooled by oil; the magnet which by its mysterious and insensible suction attracts the iron, but has no affect on a straw; the peacock's flesh which triumphs over the corruption from which not the flesh of Plato is exempt; the chaff so chilling that it prevents snow from melting, so heating that it forces apples to ripen; the glowing fire, which, in accordance with its glowing appearance, whitens the stones it bakes, while, contrary to its glowing appearance, it begrimes most things it burns (just as dirty stains are made by oil, however pure it be, and as the lines drawn by white silver are black); the charcoal, too, which by the action of fire is so completely changed from its original, that a finely marked piece of wood becomes hideous, the tough becomes brittle, the decaying incorruptible. Some of these things I know in common with many other persons, some of them in common with all men; and there are many others which I have not room to insert in this book. But of those which I have cited, though I have not myself seen, but only read about them, I have been unable to find trustworthy witnesses from whom I could ascertain whether they are facts, except in the case of that fountain in which burning torches are extinguished and extinguished torches lit, and of the apples of Sodom, which are ripe to appearance, but are filled with dust. And indeed I have not met with any who said they had seen that fountain in Epirus, but with some who knew there was a similar fountain in Gaul not far from Grenoble. The fruit of the trees of Sodom, however, is not only spoken of in books worthy of credit, but so many persons say that they have seen it that I cannot doubt the fact. But the rest of the prodigies I receive without definitely affirming or denying them; and I have cited them because I read them in the authors of our adversaries, and that I might prove how many things many among themselves believe, because they are written in the works of their own literary men, though no rational explanation of them is given, and yet they scorn to believe us when we assert that Almighty God will do what is beyond their experience and observation; and this they do even though we assign a reason for His work. For what better and stronger reason for such things can be given than to say that the Almighty is able to bring them to pass, and will bring them to pass, having predicted them in those books in which many other marvels which have already come to pass were predicted? Those things which are regarded as impossible will be accomplished according to the word, and by the power of that God Who predicted and effected that the incredulous nations should believe incredible wonders.

CHAP. 8. *That it is not contrary to nature that, in an object whose nature is known, there should be discovered an alteration of the properties which have been known as its natural properties*

But if they reply that their reason for not believing us when we say that human bodies will always burn and yet never die, is that the nature of human bodies is known to be quite otherwise constituted; if they say that for this miracle we cannot give the reason which was valid in the case of those natural miracles, viz., that this is the natural property, the nature of the thing—for we know that this is not the nature of human flesh—we find our answer in the sacred writings, that even this human flesh was constituted in one fashion before there was sin—was constituted, in fact, so that it could not die—and in another fashion after sin, being made such as we see it in this miserable state of mortality, unable to retain enduring life. And so in the resurrection of the dead shall it be constituted differently from its present well-known condition. But as they do not believe these writings of ours, in which we read what nature man had in paradise, and how remote he was from the necessity of death—and indeed, if they did believe them, we should, of course, have little trouble in debating with them the future punishment of the damned—we must produce from the writings of their own most learned authorities some instances to show that it is possible for a thing to become different from what it was formerly known characteristically to be.

From the book of Marcus Varro, entitled, *Of the Race of the Roman People*, I cite word for word the following instance: "There occurred a remarkable celestial portent; for Castor records that, in the brilliant star Venus, called Vesperugo by Plautus, and the lovely Hesperus by Homer, there occurred so strange a prodigy, that it changed its colour, size, form, course, which never happened before nor since. Adrastus of Cyzicus, and Dion of Naples, famous mathematicians, said that this occurred in the reign of Ogyges." So great an author as Varro would

certainly not have called this a portent had it not seemed to be contrary to nature. For we say that all portents are contrary to nature; but they are not so. For how is that contrary to nature which happens by the will of God, since the will of so mighty a Creator is certainly the nature of each created thing? A portent, therefore, happens not contrary to nature, but contrary to what we know as nature. But who can number the multitude of portents recorded in profane histories? Let us then at present fix our attention on this one only which concerns the matter in hand. What is there so arranged by the Author of the nature of heaven and earth as the exactly ordered course of the stars? What is there established by laws so sure and inflexible? And yet, when it pleased Him Who with sovereignty and supreme power regulates all He has created, a star conspicuous among the rest by its size and splendour changed its colour, size, form, and, most wonderful of all, the order and law of its course! Certainly that phenomenon disturbed the canons of the astronomers, if there were any then, by which they tabulate, as by unerring computation, the past and future movements of the stars, so as to take upon them to affirm that this which happened to the morning star (Venus) never happened before nor since. But we read in the divine books that even the sun itself stood still when a holy man, Joshua the son of Nun, had begged this from God until victory should finish the battle he had begun; and that it even went back, that the promise of fifteen years added to the life of king Hezekiah might be sealed by this additional prodigy. But these miracles, which were vouchsafed to the merits of holy men, even when our adversaries believe them, they attribute to magical arts; so Virgil, in the lines I quoted above, ascribes to magic the power to

Turn rivers backward to their source,
And make the stars forget their course.

For in our sacred books we read that this also happened, that a river "turned backward," was stayed above while the lower part flowed on, when the people passed over under the above-mentioned leader, Joshua the son of Nun; and also when Elias the prophet crossed; and afterwards, when his disciple Elisha passed through it: and we have just mentioned how, in the case of king Hezekiah, the greatest of the "stars forgot its course." But what happened to Venus, according to Varro, was not said by him to have happened in answer to any man's prayer.

Let not the sceptics then benight themselves in this knowledge of the nature of things, as if divine power cannot bring to pass in an object anything else than what their own experience has shown them to be in its nature. Even the very things which are most commonly known as natural would not be less wonderful nor less effectual to excite surprise in all who beheld them, if men were not accustomed to admire nothing but what is rare. For who that thoughtfully observes the countless multitude of men, and their similarity of nature, can fail to remark with surprise and admiration the individuality of each man's appearance, suggesting to us, as it does, that unless men were like one another, they would not be distinguished from the rest of the animals; while unless, on the other hand, they were unlike, they could not be distinguished from one another, so that those whom we declare to be like, we also find to be unlike? And the unlikeness is the more wonderful consideration of the two; for a common nature seems rather to require similarity. And yet, because the very rarity of things is that which makes them wonderful, we are filled with much greater wonder when we are introduced to two men so like, that we either always or frequently mistake in endeavouring to distinguish between them.

But possibly, though Varro is a heathen historian, and a very learned one, they may disbelieve that what I have cited from him truly occurred; or they may say the example is invalid, because the star did not for any length of time continue to follow its new course, but returned to its ordinary orbit. There is, then, another phenomenon at present open to their observation, and which, in my opinion, ought to be sufficient to convince them that, though they have observed and ascertained some natural law, they ought not on that account to prescribe to God, as if He could not change and turn it into something very different from what they have observed. The land of Sodom was not always as it now is; but once it had the appearance of other lands, and enjoyed equal if not richer fertility; for, in the divine narrative, it was compared to the paradise of God. But after it was touched from heaven, as even pagan history testifies, and as is now witnessed by those who visit the spot, it became unnaturally and horribly sooty in appearance; and its apples, under a deceitful appearance of ripeness, contain ashes within. Here is a thing which was of one kind and is of another. You see how its nature was converted by the wonderful transmutation wrought by the Creator of all natures into so very disgusting a diversity—an alteration which after so long a time took place, and after so long a time still continues. As therefore it was not impossible to God to create such natures as He pleased, so it is not impossible to Him to change these natures of His own creation into whatever He pleases, and thus spread abroad a multitude of those marvels which are called monsters, portents, prodigies, phenomena, and which if I were minded to cite and record, what end would there be to this work? They say that they are called "monsters," because they *demonstrate* or signify something; "portents," because they *portend* something; and so forth. But let their diviners see how they are either deceived, or even when they do predict true things, it is because they are inspired by spirits, who are intent upon entangling the minds of men (worthy, indeed, of such a fate) in the meshes of a hurtful curiosity, or how they light now and then upon some truth, because they make so many predictions. Yet, for our part, these things which happen contrary to nature, and are said to be contrary to nature (as the apostle, speaking after the manner of men, says that to graft the wild olive into the good olive, and to partake of its fatness, is contrary to nature), and are called monsters, phenomena, portents, prodigies, ought to demonstrate, portend, predict that God will bring to pass what He has foretold regarding the bodies of men, no difficulty preventing Him, no law of nature prescribing to Him His limit. How He has foretold what He is to do, I think I have sufficiently shown in the preceding book, culling from the sacred Scriptures, both of the New and Old Testaments, not, indeed, all the passages that relate to this, but as many as I judged to suffice for this work.

CHAP. 9. *Of hell, and the nature of eternal punishments*

So then what God by His prophet has said of the everlasting punishment of the damned shall come to pass—shall without fail come to pass—"their worm shall not die, neither shall their fire be quenched."[1] In order to impress this upon us most forcibly, the Lord Jesus Himself, when ordering us to cut off our members, meaning thereby those persons whom a man loves as the most useful members of his body, says, "It is better for thee to enter into life maimed, than having two hands to go into hell, into the fire that never shall be quenched; where their worm dieth not, and their fire is not quenched." Similarly of the foot: "It is better for thee to enter halt into life, than having two feet to be cast

[1] Isa. 66. 24.

into hell, into the fire that never shall be quenched; where their worm dieth not, and the fire is not quenched." So, too, of the eye: "It is better for thee to enter into the kingdom of God with one eye, than having two eyes to be cast into hell fire; where their worm dieth not, and the fire is not quenched."[1] He did not shrink from using the same words three times over in one passage. And who is not terrified by this repetition, and by the threat of that punishment uttered so vehemently by the lips of the Lord Himself?

Now they who would refer both the fire and the worm to the spirit, and not to the body, affirm that the wicked, who are separated from the kingdom of God, shall be burned, as it were, by the anguish of a spirit repenting too late and fruitlessly; and they contend that fire is therefore not inappropriately used to express this burning torment, as when the apostle exclaims "Who is offended, and I burn not?"[2] The worm, too, they think, is to be similarly understood. For it is written, they say, "As the moth consumes the garment, and the worm the wood, so does grief consume the heart of a man."[3] But they who make no doubt that in that future punishment both body and soul shall suffer, affirm that the body shall be burned with fire, while the soul shall be, as it were, gnawed by a worm of anguish. Though this view is more reasonable—for it is absurd to suppose that either body or soul will escape pain in the future punishment—yet, for my own part, I find it easier to understand both as referring to the body than to suppose that neither does; and I think that Scripture is silent regarding the spiritual pain of the damned, because, though not expressed, it is necessarily understood that in a body thus tormented the soul also is tortured with a fruitless repentance. For we read in the ancient Scriptures, "The vengeance of the flesh of the ungodly is fire and worms."[4] It might have been more briefly said, "The vengeance of the ungodly." Why, then, was it said, "The flesh of the ungodly," unless because both the fire and the worm are to be the punishment of the flesh? Or if the object of the writer in saying, "The vengeance of the flesh," was to indicate that this shall be the punishment of those who live after the flesh (for this leads to the second death, as the apostle intimated when he said, "For if ye live after the flesh, ye shall die"[5]), let each one make his own choice, either assigning the fire to the body and the worm to the soul—the one

figuratively, the other really—or assigning both really to the body. For I have already sufficiently made out that animals can live in the fire, in burning without being consumed, in pain without dying, by a miracle of the most omnipotent Creator, to Whom no one can deny that this is possible, if he be not ignorant by Whom has been made all that is wonderful in all nature. For it is God Himself Who has wrought all these miracles, great and small, in this world which I have mentioned, and incomparably more which I have omitted, and Who has enclosed these marvels in this world, itself the greatest miracle of all. Let each man, then, choose which he will, whether he thinks that the worm is real and pertains to the body, or that spiritual things are meant by bodily representations, and that it belongs to the soul. But which of these is true will be more readily discovered by the facts themselves, when there shall be in the saints such knowledge as shall not require that their own experience teach them the nature of these punishments, but as shall, by its own fullness and perfection, suffice to instruct them in this matter. For "now we know in part, until that which is perfect is come";[6] only, this we believe about those future bodies, that they shall be such as shall certainly be pained by the fire.

CHAP. 10. *Whether the fire of hell, if it be material fire, can burn the wicked spirits, that is to say, devils, who are immaterial*

Here arises the question: If the fire is not to be immaterial, analogous to the pain of the soul, but material, burning by contact, so that bodies may be tormented in it, how can evil spirits be punished in it? For it is undoubtedly the same fire which is to serve for the punishment of men and of devils, according to the words of Christ: "Depart from me, ye cursed, into everlasting fire, prepared for the devil and his angels";[7] unless, perhaps, as learned men have thought, the devils have a kind of body made of that dense and humid air which we feel strikes us when the wind is blowing. And if this kind of substance could not be affected by fire, it could not burn when heated in the baths. For in order to burn, it is first burned, and affects other things as itself is affected. But if any one maintains that the devils have no bodies, this is not a matter either to be laboriously investigated, or to be debated with keenness. For why may we not assert that even immaterial spirits may, in some extraordinary way, yet really be pained by the punishment of material fire, if the spirits of

---

[1]Mark, 9. 43–48.   [2]II Cor. 11. 29.   [3]Isa. 51. 8.
[4]Ecclus. 7. 17.   [5]Rom. 8. 13.

[6]I Cor. 13. 9, 10.   [7]Matt. 25. 41.

men, which also are certainly immaterial, are both now contained in material members of the body and in the world to come shall be indissolubly united to their own bodies? Therefore, though the devils have no bodies, yet their spirits, that is, the devils themselves, shall be brought into thorough contact with the material fires, to be tormented by them; not that the fires themselves with which they are brought into contact shall be animated by their connection with these spirits, and become animals composed of body and spirit, but, as I said, this junction will be effected in a wonderful and ineffable way, so that they shall receive pain from the fires, but give no life to them. And, in truth, this other mode of union, by which bodies and spirits are bound together and become animals, is thoroughly marvellous and beyond the comprehension of man, though this it is which is man.

I would indeed say that these spirits will burn without any body of their own, as that rich man was burning in hell when he exclaimed, "I am tormented in this flame,"[1] were I not aware that it is aptly said in reply, that that flame was of the same nature as the eyes he raised and fixed on Lazarus, as the tongue on which he entreated that a little cooling water might be dropped, or as the finger of Lazarus, with which he asked that this might be done—all of which took place where souls exist without bodies. Thus, therefore, both that flame in which he burned and that drop he begged were immaterial and resembled the visions of sleepers or persons in an ecstasy, to whom immaterial objects appear in a bodily form. For the man himself who is in such a state, though it be in spirit only, not in body, yet sees himself so like to his own body that he cannot discern any difference whatever. But that hell, which also is called a lake of fire and brimstone,[2] will be material fire, and will torment the bodies of the damned, whether men or devils—the solid bodies of the one, aerial bodies of the others; or if only men have bodies as well as souls, yet the evil spirits, though without bodies, shall be so connected with the bodily fires as to receive pain without imparting life. One fire certainly shall be the lot of both, for thus the truth has declared.

CHAP. 11. *Whether it is just that the punishments of sins last longer than the sins themselves lasted*

Some, however, of those against whom we are defending the city of God, think it unjust

that any man be doomed to an eternal punishment for sins which, no matter how great they were, were perpetrated in a brief space of time; as if any law ever regulated the duration of the punishment by the duration of the offence punished! Cicero tells us that the laws recognize eight kinds of penalty—damages, imprisonment, scourging, reparation, disgrace, exile, death, slavery. Is there any one of these which may be compressed into a brevity proportioned to the rapid commission of the offence, so that no longer time may be spent in its punishment than in its perpetration, unless, perhaps, reparation? For this requires that the offender suffer what he did, as that clause of the law says, "Eye for eye, tooth for tooth."[3] For certainly it is possible for an offender to lose his eye by the severity of legal retaliation in as brief a time as he deprived another of his eye by the cruelty of his own lawlessness. But if scourging be a reasonable penalty for kissing another man's wife, is not the fault of an instant visited with long hours of atonement, and the momentary delight punished with lasting pain? What shall we say of imprisonment? Must the criminal be confined only for so long a time as he spent on the offence for which he is committed? or is not a penalty of many years' confinement imposed on the slave who has provoked his master with a word, or has struck him a blow that is quickly over? And as to damages, disgrace, exile, slavery, which are commonly inflicted so as to admit of no relaxation or pardon, do not these resemble eternal punishments in so far as this short life allows a resemblance? For they are not eternal only because the life in which they are endured is not eternal; and yet the crimes which are punished with these most protracted sufferings are perpetrated in a very brief space of time. Nor is there any one who would suppose that the pains of punishment should occupy as short a time as the offense; or that murder, adultery, sacrilege, or any other crime, should be measured, not by the enormity of the injury or wickedness, but by the length of time spent in its perpetration. Then as to the award of death for any great crime, do the laws reckon the punishment to consist in the brief moment in which death is inflicted, or in this, that the offender is eternally banished from the society of the living? And just as the punishment of the first death cuts men off from this present mortal city, so does the punishment of the second death cut men off from that future immortal city. For as the laws of this present city do not provide for

[1]Luke, 16. 24.   [2]Rev. 20. 10.   [3]Ex. 21. 24.

the executed criminal's return to it, so neither is he who is condemned to the second death recalled again to life everlasting. But if temporal sin is visited with eternal punishment, how, then, they say, is that true which your Christ says, "With the same measure that ye mete withal it shall be measured to you again"?[1] and they do not observe that "the same measure" refers, not to an equal space of time, but to the retribution of evil, or, in other words, to the law by which he who has done evil suffers evil. Besides, these words could be appropriately understood as referring to the matter of which our Lord was speaking when He used them, viz., judgments and condemnation. Thus, if he who unjustly judges and condemns is himself justly judged and condemned, he receives "with the same measure" though not the same thing as he gave. For judgment he gave, and judgment he receives, though the judgment he gave was unjust, the judgment he receives just.

CHAP. 12. *Of the greatness of the first transgression, on account of which eternal punishment is due to all who are not within the pale of the Saviour's grace*

But eternal punishment seems hard and unjust to human perceptions, because in the weakness of our mortal condition there is wanting that highest and purest wisdom by which it can be perceived how great a wickedness was committed in that first transgression. The more enjoyment man found in God, the greater was his wickedness in abandoning Him; and he who destroyed in himself a good which might have been eternal, became worthy of eternal evil. Hence the whole mass of the human race is condemned; for he who at first gave entrance to sin has been punished with all his posterity who were in him as in a root, so that no one is exempt from this just and due punishment, unless delivered by mercy and undeserved grace; and the human race is so apportioned that in some is displayed the efficacy of merciful grace, in the rest the efficacy of just retribution. For both could not be displayed in all; for if all had remained under the punishment of just condemnation, there would have been seen in no one the mercy of redeeming grace. And, on the other hand, if all had been transferred from darkness to light, the severity of retribution would have been manifested in none. But many more are left under punishment than are delivered from it, in order that it may thus be shown what was due to all. And had it been inflicted on all, no

one could justly have found fault with the justice of Him Who taketh vengeance; whereas, in the deliverance of so many from that just award, there is cause to render the most cordial thanks to the gratuitous bounty of Him Who delivers.

CHAP. 13. *Against the opinion of those who think that the punishments of the wicked after death are purgatorial*

The Platonists, indeed, while they maintain that no sins are unpunished, suppose that all punishment is administered for remedial purposes,[2] be it inflicted by human or divine law, in this life or after death; for a man may be scathless here, or, though punished, may yet not amend. Hence that passage of Virgil, where, when he had said of our earthly bodies and mortal members, that our souls derive—

> Hence wild desires and grovelling fears,
> And human laughter, human tears;
> Immured in dungeon-seeming night,
> They look abroad, yet see no light,

goes on to say:

> Nay, when at last the life has fled,
> And left the body cold and dead,
> Ee'n then there passes not away
> The painful heritage of clay;
> Full many a long-contracted stain
> Perforce must linger deep in grain.
> So penal sufferings they endure
> For ancient crime, to make them pure;
> Some hang aloft in open view,
> For winds to pierce them through and through,
> While others purge their guilt deep-dyed
> In burning fire or whelming tide.[3]

They who are of this opinion would have all punishments after death to be purgatorial; and as the elements of air, fire, and water are superior to earth, one or other of these may be the instrument of expiating and purging away the stain contracted by the contagion of earth. So Virgil hints at the air in the words, "Some hang aloft for winds to pierce"; at the water in "whelming tide"; and at fire in the expression "in burning fire." For our part, we recognize that even in this life some punishments are purgatorial—not, indeed, to those whose life is none the better, but rather the worse for them, but to those who are constrained by them to amend their life. All other punishments, whether temporal or eternal, inflicted as they are on every one by divine providence, are sent either on account of past sins, or of sins presently allowed in the life, or to exercise and reveal a man's graces. They may be inflicted by the in-

[1]Luke, 6. 38.

[2]See Plato, *Protagoras*, 324.   [3]*Æneid*, BK. VI. 733.

strumentality of bad men and angels as well as of the good. For even if any one suffers some hurt through another's wickedness or mistake, the man indeed sins whose ignorance or injustice does the harm; but God, Who by His just though hidden judgment permits it to be done, sins not. But temporary punishments are suffered by some in this life only, by others after death, by others both now and then; but all of them before that last and strictest judgment. But of those who suffer temporary punishments after death, all are not doomed to those everlasting pains which are to follow that judgment; for to some, as we have already said, what is not remitted in this world is remitted in the next, that is, they are not punished with the eternal punishment of the world to come.

CHAP. 14. *Of the temporary punishments of this life to which the human condition is subject*

Quite exceptional are those who are not punished in this life, but only afterwards. Yet that there have been some who have reached the decrepitude of age without experiencing even the slightest sickness, and who have had uninterrupted enjoyment of life, I know both from report and from my own observation. However, the very life we mortals lead is itself all punishment, for it is all temptation, as the Scriptures declare, where it is written, "Is not the life of man upon earth a temptation?"[1] For ignorance is itself no slight punishment, or want of culture, which it is with justice thought so necessary to escape, that boys are compelled, under pain of severe punishment, to learn trades or letters; and the learning to which they are driven by punishment is itself so much of a punishment to them, that they sometimes prefer the pain that drives them to the pain to which they are driven by it. And who would not shrink from the alternative and elect to die, if it were proposed to him either to suffer death or to be again an infant? Our infancy, indeed, introducing us to this life not with laughter but with tears, seems unconsciously to predict the ills we are to encounter. Zoroaster alone is said to have laughed when he was born, and that unnatural omen portended no good to him. For he is said to have been the inventor of magical arts, though indeed they were unable to secure to him even the poor felicity of this present life against the assaults of his enemies. For, himself king of the Bactrians, he was conquered by Ninus king of the Assyrians. In short, the words of Scripture, "An heavy yoke is upon the sons of Adam, from the day that they go out of their mother's womb till the day that they return to the mother of all things"[2]—these words so infallibly find fulfilment that even the little ones, who by the laver of regeneration have been freed from the bond of original sin in which alone they were held, yet suffer many ills, and in some instances are even exposed to the assaults of evil spirits. But let us not for a moment suppose that this suffering is prejudicial to their future happiness, even though it has so increased as to sever soul from body and to terminate their life in that early age.

CHAP. 15. *That everything which the grace of God does in the way of rescuing us from the inveterate evils in which we are sunk, pertains to the future world, in which all things are made new*

Nevertheless, in the "heavy yoke that is laid upon the sons of Adam, from the day that they go out of their mother's womb to the day that they return to the mother of all things," there is found an admirable though painful monitor teaching us to be sober-minded, and convincing us that this life has become penal in consequence of that outrageous wickedness which was perpetrated in Paradise, and that all to which the New Testament invites belongs to that future inheritance which awaits us in the world to come, and is offered for our acceptance, as the earnest that we may, in its own due time, obtain that of which it is the pledge. Now, therefore, let us walk in hope, and let us by the spirit mortify the deeds of the flesh, and so make progress from day to day. For "the Lord knoweth them that are His";[3] and "as many as are led by the Spirit of God, they are sons of God,"[4] but by grace, not by nature. For there is but one Son of God by nature, Who in His compassion became Son of man for our sakes, that we, by nature sons of men, might by grace become through Him sons of God. For He, abiding unchangeable, took upon Him our nature, that thereby He might take us to Himself; and, holding fast His own divinity, He became partaker of our infirmity, that we, being changed into some better thing, might, by participating in His righteousness and immortality, lose our own properties of sin and mortality, and preserve whatever good quality He had implanted in our nature, perfected now by sharing in the goodness

[1]Job, 7. 1.

[2]Ecclus. 40. 1.   [3]II Tim. 2. 19.   [4]Rom. 8. 14.

of His nature. For as by the sin of one man we have fallen into a misery so deplorable, so by the righteousness of one Man, Who also is God, shall we come to a blessedness inconceivably exalted. Nor ought any one to trust that he has passed from the one man to the other until he shall have reached that place where there is no temptation and have entered into the peace which he seeks in the many and various conflicts of this war, in which "the flesh lusteth against the spirit, and the spirit against the flesh." [1] Now, such a war as this would have had no existence, if human nature had, in the exercise of free will, continued steadfast in the uprightness in which it was created. But now in its misery it makes war upon itself, because in its blessedness it would not continue at peace with God; and this, though it be a miserable calamity, is better than the earlier stages of this life, which do not recognize that a war is to be maintained. For better is it to contend with vices than without conflict to be subdued by them. Better, I say, is war with the hope of peace everlasting than captivity without any thought of deliverance. We long, indeed, for the cessation of this war, and, kindled by the flame of divine love, we burn for entrance on that well-ordered peace in which whatever is inferior is for ever subordinated to what is above it. But if (which God forbid) there had been no hope of so blessed a consummation, we should still have preferred to endure the hardness of this conflict, rather than, by our non-resistance, to yield ourselves to the dominion of vice.

CHAP. 16. *The laws of grace, which extend to all the epochs of the life of the regenerate*

But such is God's mercy towards the vessels of mercy which He has prepared for glory that even the first age of man, that is, infancy, which submits without any resistance to the flesh, and the second age, which is called boyhood, and which has not yet understanding enough to undertake this warfare, and therefore yields to almost every vicious pleasure (because though this age has the power of speech, and may therefore seem to have passed infancy, the mind is still too weak to comprehend the commandment), yet if either of these ages has received the sacraments of the Mediator, then, although the present life be immediately brought to an end, the child, having been translated from the power of darkness to the kingdom of Christ, shall not only be saved from eternal punish-

Gal. 5. 17.

ments, but shall not even suffer purgatorial torments after death. For spiritual regeneration of itself suffices to prevent any evil consequences resulting after death from the connection with death which carnal generation forms. But when we reach that age which can now comprehend the commandment, and submit to the dominion of law, we must declare war upon vices and wage this war keenly, lest we be landed in damnable sins. And if vices have not gathered strength, by habitual victory they are more easily overcome and subdued; but if they have been used to conquer and rule, it is only with difficulty and labour they are mastered. And indeed this victory cannot be sincerely and truly gained but by delighting in true righteousness, and it is faith in Christ that gives this. For if the law be present with its command, and the Spirit be absent with His help, the presence of the prohibition serves only to increase the desire to sin, and adds the guilt of transgression. Sometimes, indeed, patent vices are overcome by other and hidden vices, which are reckoned virtues, though pride and a kind of ruinous self-sufficiency are their informing principles. Accordingly vices are then only to be considered overcome when they are conquered by the love of God, which God Himself alone gives, and which He gives only through the Mediator between God and men, the man Christ Jesus, Who became a partaker of our mortality that He might make us partakers of His divinity. But few indeed are they who are so happy as to have passed their youth without committing any damnable sins, either by dissolute or violent conduct, or by following some godless and unlawful opinions, but have subdued by their greatness of soul everything in them which could make them the slaves of carnal pleasures. The greater number having first become transgressors of the law that they have received, and having allowed vice to have the ascendency in them, then flee to grace for help, and so, by a penitence more bitter, and a struggle more violent than it would otherwise have been, they subdue the soul to God, and thus give it its lawful authority over the flesh, and become victors. Whoever, therefore, desires to escape eternal punishment, let him not only be baptized, but also justified in Christ, and so let him in truth pass from the devil to Christ. And let him not fancy that there are any purgatorial pains except before that final and dreadful judgment. We must not, however, deny that even the eternal fire will be proportioned to the deserts of the wicked, so that to some it will be more, and to others less painful, whether this result be accomplished by a variation in the temperature of the fire itself, graduated according to every one's merit, or whether it be that the heat remains the same, but that all do not feel it with equal intensity of torment.

Chap. 17. *Of those who fancy that no men shall be punished eternally*

I must now, I see, enter the lists of amicable controversy with those tender-hearted Christians who decline to believe that any, or that all of those whom the infallibly just Judge may pronounce worthy of the punishment of hell, shall suffer eternally, and who suppose that they shall be delivered after a fixed term of punishment, longer or shorter according to the amount of each man's sin. In respect of this matter, Origen was even more indulgent; for he believed that even the devil himself and his angels, after suffering those more severe and prolonged pains which their sins deserved, should be delivered from their torments, and associated with the holy angels. But the Church, not without reason, condemned him for this and other errors, especially for his theory of the ceaseless alternation of happiness and misery, and the interminable transitions from the one state to the other at fixed periods of ages; for in this theory he lost even the credit of being merciful, by allotting to the saints real miseries for the expiation of their sins, and false happiness, which brought them no true and secure joy, that is, no fearless assurance of eternal blessedness. Very different, however, is the error we speak of, which is dictated by the tenderness of these Christians who suppose that the sufferings of those who are condemned in the judgment will be temporary, while the blessedness of all who are sooner or later set free will be eternal. Which opinion, if it is good and true because it is merciful, will be so much the better and truer in proportion as it becomes more merciful. Let, then, this fountain of mercy be extended, and flow forth even to the lost angels, and let them also be set free, at least after as many and long ages as seem fit! Why does this stream of mercy flow to all the human race, and dry up as soon as it reaches the angelic? And yet they dare not extend their pity further, and propose the deliverance of the devil himself. Or if any one is bold enough to do so, he does indeed put to shame their charity, but is himself convicted of error that is more unsightly, and a wresting of God's truth that is more perverse, in proportion as his clemency of sentiment seems to be greater.

Chap. 18. *Of those who fancy that, on account of the saints' intercession, no man shall be damned in the last judgment*

There are others, again, with whose opinions I have become acquainted in conversation, who, though they seem to reverence the holy Scriptures, are yet of reprehensible life, and who accordingly, in their own interest, attribute to God a still greater compassion towards men. For they acknowledge that it is truly predicted in the divine word that the wicked and unbelieving are worthy of punishment, but they assert that, when the judgment comes, mercy will prevail. For, say they, God, having compassion on them, will give them up to the prayers and intercession of His saints. For if the saints used to pray for them when they suffered from their cruel hatred, how much more will they do so when they see them prostrate and humble suppliants? For we cannot, they say, believe that the saints shall lose their bowels of compassion when they have attained the most perfect and complete holiness; so that they who, when still sinners, prayed for their enemies, should now, when they are freed from sin, withhold from interceding for their suppliants. Or shall God refuse to listen to so many of His beloved children, when their holiness has purged their prayers of all hindrance to His answering them? And the passage of the psalm which is cited by those who admit that wicked men and infidels shall be punished for a long time, though in the end delivered from all sufferings, is claimed also by the persons we are now speaking of as making much more for them. The verse runs: "Shall God forget to be gracious? Shall He in anger shut up His tender mercies?" [1] His anger, they say, would condemn all that are unworthy of everlasting happiness to endless punishment. But if He suffer them to be punished for a long time, or even at all, must He not shut up His tender mercies, which the Psalmist implies He will not do? For he does not say, Shall He in anger shut up His tender mercies for a long period? but he implies that He will not shut them up at all.

And they deny that thus God's threat of judgment is proved to be false even though He condemn no man, any more than we can say that His threat to overthrow Nineveh was false, though the destruction which was absolutely predicted was not accomplished. For He did not say, "Nineveh shall be overthrown if they do not repent and amend their ways," but without any such condition He foretold that the city

[1] Ps. 77. 9.

should be overthrown. And this prediction, they maintain, was true because God predicted the punishment which they deserved, although He was not to inflict it. For though He spared them on their repentance, yet He was certainly aware that they would repent, and, notwithstanding, absolutely and definitely predicted that the city should be overthrown. This was true, they say, in the truth of severity, because they were worthy of it; but in respect of the compassion which checked His anger, so that He spared the suppliants from the punishment with which He had threatened the rebellious, it was not true. If, then, He spared those whom His own holy prophet was provoked at His sparing, how much more shall He spare those more wretched suppliants for whom all His saints shall intercede? And they suppose that this conjecture of theirs is not hinted at in Scripture, for the sake of stimulating many to reformation of life through fear of very protracted or eternal sufferings, and of stimulating others to pray for those who have not reformed. However, they think that the divine oracles are not altogether silent in this point; for they ask to what purpose is it said, "How great is Thy goodness which Thou hast hidden for them that fear Thee," [1] if it be not to teach us that the great and hidden sweetness of God's mercy is concealed in order that men may fear? To the same purpose they think the apostle said, "For God hath concluded all men in unbelief, that He may have mercy upon all," [2] signifying that no one should be condemned by God. And yet they who hold this opinion do not extend it to the acquittal or liberation of the devil and his angels. Their human tenderness is moved only towards men, and they plead chiefly their own cause, holding out false hopes of impunity to their own depraved lives by means of this quasi compassion of God to the whole race. Consequently they who promise this impunity even to the prince of the devils and his satellites make a still further exhibition of the mercy of God.

CHAP. 19. *Of those who promise impunity from all sins even to heretics, through virtue of their participation of the body of Christ*

So, too, there are others who promise this deliverance from eternal punishment, not, indeed, to all men, but only to those who have been washed in Christian baptism, and who become partakers of the body of Christ, no matter how they have lived, or what heresy or impiety they have fallen into. They ground this opinion on the

saying of Jesus, "This is the bread which cometh down from heaven, that if any man eat thereof, he shall not die. I am the living bread which came down from heaven. If a man eat of this bread, he shall live for ever." [3] Therefore, say they, it follows that these persons must be delivered from death eternal, and at one time or other be introduced to everlasting life.

CHAP. 20. *Of those who promise this indulgence not to all, but only to those who have been baptized as Catholics, though afterwards they have broken out into many crimes and heresies*

There are others still who make this promise not even to all who have received the sacraments of the baptism of Christ and of His body, but only to the Catholics, however badly they have lived. For these have eaten the body of Christ, not only sacramentally but really, being incorporated in His body, as the apostle says, "We, being many, are one bread, one body"; [4] so that, though they have afterwards lapsed into some heresy, or even into heathenism and idolatry, yet by virtue of this one thing, that they have received the baptism of Christ and eaten the body of Christ, in the body of Christ, that is to say, in the Catholic Church, they shall not die eternally, but at one time or other obtain eternal life; and all that wickedness of theirs shall not avail to make their punishment eternal, but only proportionately long and severe.

CHAP. 21. *Of those who assert that all Catholics who continue in the faith, even though by the depravity of their lives they have merited hell fire, shall be saved on account of the "foundations" of their faith*

There are some, too, who found upon the expression of Scripture, "He that endureth to the end shall be saved," [5] and who promise salvation only to those who continue in the Church Catholic; and though such persons have lived badly, yet, say they, they shall be saved as by fire through virtue of the foundation of which the apostle says, "For other foundation hath no man laid than that which is laid, which is Christ Jesus. Now if any man build upon this foundation gold, silver, precious stones, wood, hay, stubble; every man's work shall be made manifest: for the day of the Lord shall declare it, for it shall be revealed by fire; and each man's work shall be proved of what sort it is. If any man's work shall endure which he hath built thereupon, he shall receive a reward. But if any man's work shall be burned, he shall suffer loss: but he himself shall be saved; yet so as through fire."[1] They say, accordingly, that the Catholic Christian, no matter what his life be, has Christ as his foundation, while this foundation is not possessed by any heresy which is separated from the unity of His body. And therefore, through virtue of this foundation, even though the Catholic Christian by the inconsistency of his life has been as one building up wood, hay, stubble, upon it they believe that he shall be saved by fire, in other words, that he shall be delivered after tasting the pain of that fire to which the wicked shall be condemned at the last judgment.

CHAP. 22. *Of those who fancy that the sins which are intermingled with alms-deeds shall not be charged at the day of judgment*

I have also met with some who are of opinion that such only as neglect to cover their sins with alms-deeds shall be punished in everlasting fire; and they cite the words of the Apostle James, "He shall have judgment without mercy who hath shown no mercy."[2] Therefore, say they, he who has not amended his ways, but yet has intermingled his profligate and wicked actions with works of mercy, shall receive mercy in the judgment, so that he shall either quite escape condemnation, or shall be liberated from his doom after some time shorter or longer. They suppose that this was the reason why the Judge Himself of quick and dead declined to mention anything else than works of mercy done or omitted, when awarding to those on His right hand life eternal, and to those on His left everlasting punishment.[3] To the same purpose, they say, is the daily petition we make in the Lord's prayer, "Forgive us our debts, as we forgive our debtors."[4] For, no doubt, whoever pardons the person who has wronged him does a charitable action. And this has been so highly commended by the Lord Himself, that He says, "For if ye forgive men their trespasses, your heavenly Father will also forgive you: but if ye forgive not men their trespasses, neither will your Father forgive your trespasses."[5] And so it is to this kind of alms-deeds that the saying of the Apostle James refers, "He shall have judgment without mercy that hath shown no mercy." And our Lord, they say, made no distinction of great and small sins, but "Your Father will forgive your sins, if ye forgive men theirs." Consequently they conclude that, though a man has led an abandoned life up to the last day of it, yet whatsoever his sins have been, they are all remitted by virtue of this daily prayer, if only he has been mindful to attend to this one thing, that when they who have done him any injury ask his pardon, he forgive them from his heart.

When, by God's help, I have replied to all these errors, I shall conclude this (twenty-first) book.

CHAP. 23. *Against those who are of opinion that the punishment neither of the devil nor of wicked men shall be eternal*

First of all, it behoves us to inquire and to recognize why the Church has not been able to tolerate the idea that promises cleansing or indulgence to the devil even after the most severe and protracted punishment. For so many holy men, imbued with the spirit of the Old and New Testament, did not grudge to angels of any rank or character that they should enjoy the blessedness of the heavenly kingdom after being cleansed by suffering, but rather they perceived that they could not invalidate nor evacuate the divine sentence which the Lord predicted that He would pronounce in the judgment, saying, "Depart from me, ye cursed, into everlasting fire, prepared for the devil and his angels."[6] For here it is evident that the devil and his angels shall burn in everlasting fire. And there is also that declaration in the Apocalypse, "The devil their deceiver was cast into the lake of fire and brimstone, where also are the beast and the false prophet. And they shall be tormented day and night for ever."[7] In the former passage "everlasting" is used, in the latter "for ever"; and by these words Scripture is wont to mean nothing else than endless duration. And therefore no other reason, no reason more obvious and just, can be found for holding it as the fixed and immovable belief of the truest piety that the devil and his angels shall never return to the justice and life of the saints than that Scripture, which deceives no man, says that God spared them not, and that they were condemned beforehand by Him and cast into prisons of darkness in hell,[8] being reserved to the judgment of the last day, when eternal fire shall receive them, in which they shall be tormented world without end. And if this be so, how can it be believed that all men, or even some, shall be withdrawn from the endurance of punishment after some time has been spent in it? how can this be believed without enervating our faith in the eternal punishment of the devils? For if all or some of those to

---

[1] I Cor. 3. 11–15. [2] Jas. 2. 13. [3] Matt. 25. 33.
[4] Matt. 6. 12. [5] Matt. 6. 14, 15.

[6] Matt. 25. 41. [7] Rev. 20. 10. [8] II Pet. 2. 4.

whom it shall be said, "Depart from me, ye cursed, into everlasting fire, prepared for the devil and his angels," [1] are not to be always in that fire, then what reason is there for believing that the devil and his angels shall always be there? Or is perhaps the sentence of God, which is to be pronounced on wicked men and angels alike, to be true in the case of the angels, false in that of men? Plainly it will be so if the conjectures of men are to weigh more than the word of God. But because this is absurd, they who desire to be rid of eternal punishment ought to abstain from arguing against God, and rather, while yet there is opportunity, obey the divine commands. Then what a fond fancy is it to suppose that eternal punishment means long continued punishment, while eternal life means life without end, since Christ in the very same passage spoke of both in similar terms in one and the same sentence, "These shall go away into eternal punishment, but the righteous into life eternal!" [2] If both destinies are "eternal," then we must either understand both as long-continued but at last terminating, or both as endless. For they are correlative—on the one hand, punishment eternal, on the other hand, life eternal. And to say in one and the same sense, life eternal shall be endless, punishment eternal shall come to an end, is the height of absurdity. Wherefore, as the eternal life of the saints shall be endless, so too the eternal punishment of those who are doomed to it shall have no end.

CHAP. 24. *Against those who fancy that in the judgment of God all the accused will be spared in virtue of the prayers of the saints*

And this reasoning is equally conclusive against those who, in their own interest, but under the guise of a greater tenderness of spirit, attempt to invalidate the words of God, and who assert that these words are true, not because men shall suffer those things which are threatened by God, but because they deserve to suffer them. For God, they say, will yield them to the prayers of His saints, who will then the more earnestly pray for their enemies, as they shall be more perfect in holiness, and whose prayers will be the more efficacious and the more worthy of God's ear, because now purged from all sin whatsoever. Why, then, if in that perfected holiness their prayers be so pure and all-availing, will they not use them in behalf of the angels for whom eternal fire is prepared, that God may mitigate His sentence and alter it, and extricate

them from that fire? Or will there, perhaps, be some one hardy enough to affirm that even the holy angels will make common cause with holy men (then become the equals of God's angels) and will intercede for the guilty, both men and angels, that mercy may spare them the punishment which truth has pronounced them to deserve? But this has been asserted by no one sound in the faith, nor will be. Otherwise there is no reason why the Church should not even now pray for the devil and his angels, since God her Master has ordered her to pray for her enemies. The reason, then, which prevents the Church from now praying for the wicked angels, whom she knows to be her enemies, is the identical reason which shall prevent her, however perfected in holiness, from praying at the last judgment for those men who are to be punished in eternal fire. At present she prays for her enemies among men, because they have yet opportunity for fruitful repentance. For what does she especially beg for them but that "God would grant them repentance," as the apostle says, "that they may return to soberness out of the snare of the devil, by whom they are held captive according to his will"? [3] But if the Church were certified who those are, who, though they are still abiding in this life, are yet predestinated to go with the devil into eternal fire, then for them she could no more pray than for him. But since she has this certainty regarding no man, she prays for all her enemies who yet live in this world; and yet she is not heard in behalf of all. But she is heard in the case of those only who, though they oppose the Church, are yet predestinated to become her sons through her intercession. But if any retain an impenitent heart until death, and are not converted from enemies into sons, does the Church continue to pray for them, for the spirits, i.e., of such persons deceased? And why does she cease to pray for them, unless because the man who was not translated into Christ's kingdom while he was in the body, is now judged to be of Satan's following?

It is then, I say, the same reason which prevents the Church at any time from praying for the wicked angels, which prevents her from praying hereafter for those men who are to be punished in eternal fire; and this also is the reason why, though she prays even for the wicked so long as they live, she yet does not even in this world pray for the unbelieving and godless who are dead. For some of the dead, indeed, the prayer of the Church or of pious individuals is

---

[1] Matt. 25. 41.   [2] Matt. 25. 46.

[3] II Tim. 2. 25, 26.

heard; but it is for those who, having been regenerated in Christ, did not spend their life so wickedly that they can be judged unworthy of such compassion, nor so well that they can be considered to have no need of it. As also, after the resurrection, there will be some of the dead to whom, after they have endured the pains proper to the spirits of the dead, mercy shall be accorded, and acquittal from the punishment of the eternal fire. For were there not some whose sins, though not remitted in this life, shall be remitted in that which is to come, it could not be truly said, "They shall not be forgiven, neither in this world, neither in that which is to come."[1] But when the Judge of quick and dead has said, "Come, ye blessed of my Father, inherit the kingdom prepared for you from the foundation of the world," and to those on the other side, "Depart from me, ye cursed, into the eternal fire, which is prepared for the devil and his angels," and "These shall go away into eternal punishment, but the righteous into eternal life,"[2] it were excessively presumptuous to say that the punishment of any of those whom God has said shall go away into eternal punishment shall not be eternal, and so bring either despair or doubt upon the corresponding promise of life eternal.

Let no man then so understand the words of the Psalmist, "Shall God forget to be gracious? shall He shut up in His anger His tender mercies"[3] as if the sentence of God were true of good men, false of bad men, or true of good men and wicked angels, but false of bad men. For the Psalmist's words refer to the vessels of mercy and the children of the promise, of whom the prophet himself was one; for when he had said, "Shall God forget to be gracious? shall He shut up in His anger His tender mercies?" and then immediately subjoins, "And I said, Now I begin: this is the change wrought by the right hand of the Most High,"[4] he manifestly explained what he meant by the words, "Shall he shut up in His anger His tender mercies?" For God's anger is this mortal life, in which man is made like to vanity, and his days pass as a shadow.[5] Yet in this anger God does not forget to be gracious, causing His sun to shine and His rain to descend on the just and the unjust;[6] and thus He does not in His anger cut short His tender mercies, and especially in what the Psalmist speaks of in the words, "Now I begin: this change is from the right hand of the Most High"; for He changes for the better the vessels

of mercy, even while they are still in this most wretched life, which is God's anger, and even while His anger is manifesting itself in this miserable corruption; for "in His anger He does not shut up His tender mercies." And since the truth of this divine canticle is quite satisfied by this application of it, there is no need to give it a reference to that place in which those who do not belong to the city of God are punished in eternal fire. But if any persist in extending its application to the torments of the wicked, let them at least understand it so that the anger of God, which has threatened the wicked with eternal punishment, shall abide, but shall be mixed with mercy to the extent of alleviating the torments which might justly be inflicted; so that the wicked shall neither wholly escape, nor only for a time endure these threatened pains, but that they shall be less severe and more endurable than they deserve. Thus the anger of God shall continue, and at the same time He will not in this anger shut up His tender mercies. But even this hypothesis I am not to be supposed to affirm because I do not positively oppose it.

As for those who find an empty threat rather than a truth in such passages as these: "Depart from me, ye cursed, into everlasting fire"; and "These shall go away into eternal punishment";[7] and "They shall be tormented for ever and ever";[8] and "Their worm shall not die, and their fire shall not be quenched"[9]—such persons, I say, are most emphatically and abundantly refuted, not by me so much as by the divine Scripture itself. For the men of Nineveh repented in this life, and therefore their repentance was fruitful, inasmuch as they sowed in that field which the Lord meant to be sown in tears that it might afterwards be reaped in joy. And yet who will deny that God's prediction was fulfilled in their case, if at least he observes that God destroys sinners not only in anger but also in compassion? For sinners are destroyed in two ways—either, like the Sodomites, the men themselves are punished for their sins, or, like the Ninevites, the men's sins are destroyed by repentance. God's prediction, therefore, was fulfilled—the wicked Nineveh was overthrown, and a good Nineveh built up. For its walls and houses remained standing; the city was overthrown in its depraved manners. And thus, though the prophet was provoked that the destruction which the inhabitants dreaded, because of his prediction, did not take place, yet that which God's foreknowledge had predicted did take place, for He Who foretold the destruc-

---

[1]Matt. 12. 32.　　[2]Matt. 25. 34, 41, 46.　　[3]Ps. 77. 9.
[4]Ps. 77. 10.　　[5]Ps. 144. 4.　　[6]Matt. 5. 45.

[7]Matt. 25. 41, 46.　　[8]Rev. 20. 10.　　[9]Isa. 66. 24.

tion knew how it should be fulfilled in a less calamitous sense.

But that these perversely compassionate persons may see what is the purport of these words, "How great is the abundance of Thy sweetness, Lord, which Thou hast hidden for them that fear Thee,"[1] let them read what follows. "And Thou hast perfected it for them that hope in Thee." For what means, "Thou hast hidden it for them that fear Thee," "Thou hast perfected it for them that hope in Thee," unless this, that to those who through fear of punishment seek to establish their own righteousness by the law, the righteousness of God is not sweet, because they are ignorant of it? They have not tasted it. For they hope in themselves, not in Him; and therefore God's abundant sweetness is hidden from them. They fear God, indeed, but it is with that servile fear "which is not in love; for perfect love casteth out fear."[2] Therefore to them that hope in Him He perfecteth His sweetness, inspiring them with His own love, so that with a holy fear, which love does not cast out, but which endureth for ever, they may, when they glory, glory in the Lord. For the righteousness of God is Christ, "who is of God made unto us," as the apostle says, "wisdom, and righteousness, and sanctification, and redemption: as it is written, He that glorieth, let him glory in the Lord."[3] This righteousness of God, which is the gift of grace without merits, is not known by those who go about to establish their own righteousness, and are therefore not subject to the righteousness of God, which is Christ.[4] But it is in this righteousness that we find the great abundance of God's sweetness, of which the psalm says, "Taste and see how sweet the Lord is."[5] And this we rather taste than partake of to satiety in this our pilgrimage. We hunger and thirst for it now, that hereafter we may be satisfied with it when we see Him as He is, and that is fulfilled which is written, "I shall be satisfied when Thy glory shall be manifested."[6] It is thus that Christ perfects the great abundance of His sweetness to them that hope in Him. But if God conceals His sweetness from them that fear Him in the sense that these our objectors fancy, so that men's ignorance of His purpose of mercy towards the wicked may lead them to fear Him and live better, and so that there may be prayer made for those who are not living as they ought, how then does He perfect His sweetness to them that hope in Him, since, if their dreams be true, it is this very sweetness

which will prevent Him from punishing those who do not hope in Him? Let us then seek that sweetness of His, which He perfects to them that hope in Him, not that which He is supposed to perfect to those who despise and blaspheme Him; for in vain, after this life, does a man seek for what he has neglected to provide while in this life.

Then, as to that saying of the apostle, "For God hath concluded all in unbelief, that He may have mercy upon all,"[7] it does not mean that He will condemn no one but the foregoing context shows what is meant. The apostle composed the epistle for the Gentiles who were already believers; and when he was speaking to them of the Jews who were yet to believe, he says, "For as ye in times past believed not God, yet have now obtained mercy through their unbelief; even so have these also now not believed, that through your mercy they also may obtain mercy." Then he added the words in question with which these persons beguile themselves: "For God concluded all in unbelief, that He might have mercy upon all." All whom, if not all those of whom he was speaking, just as if he had said, "Both you and them"? God then concluded all those in unbelief, both Jews and Gentiles, whom He foreknew and predestinated to be conformed to the image of His Son, in order that they might be confounded by the bitterness of unbelief, and might repent and believingly turn to the sweetness of God's mercy, and might take up that exclamation of the psalm, "How great is the abundance of Thy sweetness, O Lord, which Thou hast hidden for them that fear Thee, but hast perfected to them that hope," not in themselves, but "in Thee." He has mercy, then, on all the vessels of mercy. And what means "all"? Both those of the Gentiles and those of the Jews whom He predestinated, called, justified, glorified: none of these will be condemned by Him; but we cannot say none of all men whatever.

CHAP. 25. *Whether those who received heretical baptism, and have afterwards fallen away to wickedness of life; or those who have received Catholic baptism, but have afterwards passed over to heresy and schism; or those who have remained in the Catholic Church in which they were baptized, but have continued to live immorally—may hope through the virtue of the sacraments for the remission of eternal punishment*

But let us now reply to those who promise deliverance from eternal fire, not to the devil and

---

[1]Ps. 31. 19.   [2]I John, 4. 18.   [3]I Cor. 1. 30, 31.
[4]Rom. 10. 3.   [5]Ps. 34. 8.   [6]Ps. 17. 15.   [7]Rom. 11. 32.

his angels (as neither do they of whom we have been speaking), nor even to all men whatever, but only to those who have been washed by the baptism of Christ, and have become partakers of His body and blood, no matter how they have lived, no matter what heresy or impiety they have fallen into. But they are contradicted by the apostle, where he says, "Now the works of the flesh are manifest, which are these; fornication, uncleanness, lasciviousness, idolatry, witchcraft, hatred, variances, emulations, wrath, strife, heresies, envyings, drunkenness, revellings, and the like: of the which I tell you before, as I have also told you in time past, for they which do such things shall not inherit the kingdom of God." [1] Certainly this sentence of the apostle is false, if such persons shall be delivered after any lapse of time, and shall then inherit the kingdom of God. But as it is not false, they shall certainly never inherit the kingdom of God. And if they shall never enter that kingdom, then they shall always be retained in eternal punishment; for there is no middle place where he may live unpunished who has not been admitted into that kingdom.

And therefore we may reasonably inquire how we are to understand these words of the Lord Jesus: "This is the bread which cometh down from heaven, that a man may eat thereof, and not die. I am the living bread which came down from heaven. If any man eat of this bread, he shall live for ever." [2] And those, indeed, whom we are now answering, are refuted in their interpretation of this passage by those whom we are shortly to answer, and who do not promise this deliverance to all who have received the sacraments of baptism and the Lord's body, but only to the Catholics, however wickedly they live; for these, say they, have eaten the Lord's body not only sacramentally, but really, being constituted members of His body, of which the apostle says, "We being many are one bread, one body." [3] He then who is in the unity of Christ's body (that is to say, in the Christian membership), of which body the faithful have been wont to receive the sacrament at the altar, that man is truly said to eat the body and drink the blood of Christ. And consequently heretics and schismatics being separate from the unity of this body, are able to receive the same sacrament, but with no profit to themselves—nay, rather to their own hurt, so that they are rather more severely judged than liberated after some time. For they are not in that bond of peace which is symbolized by that sacrament.

But again, even those who sufficiently understand that he who is not in the body of Christ cannot be said to eat the body of Christ, are in error when they promise liberation from the fire of eternal punishment to persons who fall away from the unity of that body into heresy, or even into heathenish superstition. For, in the first place, they ought to consider how intolerable it is, and how discordant with sound doctrine, to suppose that many, indeed, or almost all, who have forsaken the Church Catholic, and have originated impious heresies and become heresiarchs, should enjoy a destiny superior to those who never were Catholics, but have fallen into the snares of these others; that is to say, if the fact of their Catholic baptism and original reception of the sacrament of the body of Christ in the true body of Christ is sufficient to deliver these heresiarchs from eternal punishment. For certainly he who deserts the faith, and from a deserter becomes an assailant, is worse than he who has not deserted the faith he never held. And, in the second place, they are contradicted by the apostle, who, after enumerating the works of the flesh, says with reference to heresies, "They who do such things shall not inherit the kingdom of God."

And therefore neither ought such persons as lead an abandoned and damnable life to be confident of salvation, though they persevere to the end in the communion of the Church Catholic and comfort themselves with the words, "He that endureth to the end shall be saved." By the iniquity of their life they abandon that very righteousness of life which Christ is to them, whether it be by fornication, or by perpetrating in their body the other uncleannesses which the apostle would not so much as mention, or by a dissolute luxury, or by doing any one of those things of which he says, "They who do such things shall not inherit the kingdom of God." Consequently, they who do such things shall not exist anywhere but in eternal punishment, since they cannot be in the kingdom of God. For, while they continue in such things to the very end of life, they cannot be said to abide in Christ to the end; for to abide in Him is to abide in the faith of Christ. And this faith, according to the apostle's definition of it, "worketh by love." [4] And "love," as he elsewhere says, "worketh no evil." [5] Neither can these persons be said to eat the body of Christ, for they cannot even be reckoned among His members. For, not to mention other reasons, they cannot be at once the members of Christ and the members of a har-

[1] Gal. 5. 19–21.   [2] John, 6. 50, 51.   [3] I Cor. 10. 17.

[4] Gal. 5. 6.   [5] Rom. 13. 10.

lot. In fine, **He Himself**, when He says, "He that eateth my flesh and drinketh my blood, dwelleth in me, and I in him," [1] shows what it is in reality, and not sacramentally, to eat His body and drink His blood; for this is to dwell in Christ, that He also may dwell in us. So that it is as if He said, He that dwelleth not in me, and in whom I do not dwell, let him not say or think that he eateth my body or drinketh my blood. Accordingly, they who are not Christ's members do not dwell in Him. And they who make themselves members of a harlot, are not members of Christ unless they have penitently abandoned that evil, and have returned to this good to be reconciled to it.

CHAP. 26. *What it is to have Christ for a foundation, and who they are to whom salvation as by fire is promised*

But, say they, the Catholic Christians have Christ for a foundation, and they have not fallen away from union with Him, no matter how depraved a life they have built on this foundation, as wood, hay, stubble; and accordingly the well-directed faith by which Christ is their foundation will suffice to deliver them some time from the continuance of that fire, though it be with loss, since those things they have built on it shall be burned. Let the Apostle James summarily reply to them: "If any man say he has faith, and have not works, can faith save him?" [2] And who then is it, they ask, of whom the Apostle Paul says, "But he himself shall be saved, yet so as by fire"? [3] Let us join them in their inquiry; and one thing is very certain, that it is not he of whom James speaks, else we should make the two apostles contradict one another, if the one says, "Though a man's works be evil, his faith will save him as by fire," while the other says, "If he have not good works, can his faith save him?"

We shall then ascertain who it is who can be saved by fire, if we first discover what it is to have Christ for a foundation. And this we may very readily learn from the image itself. In a building the foundation is first. Whoever, then, has Christ in his heart, so that no earthly or temporal things—not even those that are legitimate and allowed—are preferred to Him, has Christ as a foundation. But if these things be preferred, then even though a man seem to have faith in Christ, yet Christ is not the foundation to that man; and much more if he, in contempt of wholesome precepts, seek forbidden gratifications, is he clearly convicted of putting Christ

not first but last, since he has despised Him as his ruler and has preferred to fulfil his own wicked lusts, in contempt of Christ's commands and allowances. Accordingly, if any Christian man loves a harlot and, attaching himself to her, becomes one body, he has not now Christ for a foundation. But if any one loves his own wife and loves her as Christ would have him love her, who can doubt that he has Christ for a foundation? But if he loves her in the world's fashion, carnally, as the disease of lust prompts him, and as the Gentiles love who know not God, even this the apostle, or rather Christ by the apostle, allows as a venial fault. And therefore even such a man may have Christ for a foundation. For so long as he does not prefer such an affection or pleasure to Christ, Christ is his foundation, though on it he builds wood, hay, stubble; and therefore he shall be saved as by fire. For the fire of affliction shall burn such luxurious pleasures and earthly loves, though they be not damnable, because enjoyed in lawful wedlock. And of this fire the fuel is bereavement, and all those calamities which consume these joys. Consequently the superstructure will be lost to him who has built it, for he shall not retain it, but shall be agonized by the loss of those things in the enjoyment of which he found pleasure. But by this fire he shall be saved through virtue of the foundation, because even if a persecutor demanded whether he would retain Christ or these things, he would prefer Christ. Would you hear, in the apostle's own words, who he is who builds on the foundation gold, silver, precious stones? "He that is unmarried," he says, "careth for the things that belong to the Lord, how he may please the Lord." [4] Would you hear who he is that buildeth wood, hay, stubble? "But he that is married careth for the things that are of the world, how he may please his wife." [5] "Every man's work shall be made manifest: for the day shall declare it"—the day, no doubt, of tribulation—"because," says he, "it shall be revealed by fire." [6] He calls tribulation fire, just as it is elsewhere said, "The furnace proves the vessels of the potter, and the trial of affliction righteous men." [7] And "The fire shall try every man's work of what sort it is. If any man's work abide"—for a man's care for the things of the Lord, how he may please the Lord, abides—"which he hath built thereupon, he shall receive a reward"—that is, he shall reap the fruit of his care. "But if any man's work

---

[1] John. 6. 56.   [2] Jas. 2. 14.   [3] I Cor. 3. 15.

[4] I Cor. 7. 32.   [5] I Cor. 7. 33.   [6] I Cor. 3. 13.
[7] Ecclus. 27. 5.

shall be burned, he shall suffer loss"—for what he loved he shall not retain—"but he himself shall be saved"—for no tribulation shall have moved him from that stable foundation—"yet so as by fire";[1] for that which he possessed with the sweetness of love he does not lose without the sharp sting of pain. Here, then, as seems to me, we have a fire which destroys neither, but enriches the one, brings loss to the other, proves both.

But if this passage is to interpret that fire of which the Lord shall say to those on His left hand, "Depart from me, ye cursed, into everlasting fire,"[2] so that among these we are to believe there are those who build on the foundation wood, hay, stubble, and that they, through virtue of the good foundation, shall after a time be liberated from the fire that is the award of their evil deserts, what then shall we think of those on the right hand, to whom it shall be said, "Come, ye blessed of my Father, inherit the kingdom prepared for you,"[3] unless that they are those who have built on the foundation gold, silver, precious stones? But if the fire of which our Lord speaks is the same as that of which the apostle says, "Yet so as by fire," then both—that is to say, both those on the right as well as those on the left —are to be cast into it. For that fire is to try both, since it is said, "For the day of the Lord shall declare it, because it shall be revealed by fire; and the fire shall try every man's work of what sort it is."[4] If, therefore, the fire shall try both, in order that if any man's work abide —i.e., if the superstructure be not consumed by the fire—he may receive a reward, and that if his work is burned he may suffer loss, certainly that fire is not the eternal fire itself. For into this latter fire only those on the left hand shall be cast, and that with final and everlasting doom; but that former fire proves those on the right hand. But some of them it so proves that it does not burn and consume the structure which is found to have been built by them on Christ as the foundation; while others of them it proves in another fashion, so as to burn what they have built up, and thus cause them to suffer loss, while they themselves are saved because they have retained Christ, who was laid as their sure foundation, and have loved Him above all. But if they are saved, then certainly they shall stand at the right hand, and shall with the rest hear the sentence, "Come, ye blessed of my Father, inherit the kingdom prepared for you"; and not at the left hand, where those shall be who shall not be saved, and shall therefore hear the doom, "Depart from me, ye cursed, into everlasting fire." For from that fire no man shall be saved, because they all shall go away into eternal punishment, where their worms shall not die, nor their fire be quenched, in which they shall be tormented day and night for ever.

But if it be said that in the interval of time between the death of this body and that last day of judgment and retribution which shall follow the resurrection, the bodies of the dead shall be exposed to a fire of such a nature that it shall not affect those who have not in this life indulged in such pleasures and pursuits as shall be consumed like wood, hay, stubble, but shall affect those others who have carried with them structures of that kind; if it be said that such worldliness, being venial, shall be consumed in the fire of tribulation either here only, or here and hereafter both, or here that it may not be hereafter—this I do not contradict, because possibly it is true. For perhaps even the death of the body is itself a part of this tribulation, for it results from the first transgression, so that the time which follows death takes its colour in each case from the nature of the man's building. The persecutions, too, which have crowned the martyrs, and which Christians of all kinds suffer, try both buildings like a fire, consuming some, along with the builders themselves, if Christ is not found in them as their foundation, while others they consume without the builders, because Christ is found in them, and they are saved, though with loss; and other buildings still they do not consume, because such materials as abide for ever are found in them. In the end of the world there shall be in the time of Antichrist tribulation such as has never before been. How many edifices there shall then be, of gold or of hay, built on the best foundation, Christ Jesus, which that fire shall prove, bringing joy to some, loss to others, but without destroying either sort, because of this stable foundation! But whosoever prefers, I do not say his wife, with whom he lives for carnal pleasure, but any of those relatives who afford no delight of such a kind, and whom it is right to love—whosoever prefers these to Christ, and loves them after a human and carnal fashion, has not Christ as a foundation, and will therefore not be saved by fire, nor in-

[1] I Cor. 3. 14, 15.   [2] Matt. 25. 41.   [3] Matt. 25. 34.
[4] I Cor. 3. 13.

deed at all; for he shall not possibly dwell with the Saviour, Who says very explicitly concerning this very matter, "He that loveth father or mother more than me is not worthy of me; and he that loveth son or daughter more than me is not worthy of me."[1] But he who loves his relations carnally, and yet so that he does not prefer them to Christ, but would rather want them than Christ if he were put to the proof, shall be saved by fire, because it is necessary that by the loss of these relations he suffer pain in proportion to his love. And he who loves father, mother, sons, daughters, according to Christ, so that he aids them in obtaining His kingdom and cleaving to Him, or loves them because they are members of Christ, God forbid that this love should be consumed as wood, hay, stubble, and not rather be reckoned a structure of gold, silver, precious stones. For how can a man love those more than Christ whom he loves only for Christ's sake?

CHAP. 27. *Against the belief of those who think that the sins which have been accompanied with almsgiving will do them no harm*

It remains to reply to those who maintain that those only shall burn in eternal fire who neglect alms-deeds proportioned to their sins, resting this opinion on the words of the Apostle James, "He shall have judgment without mercy that hath showed no mercy."[2] Therefore, they say, he that hath showed mercy, though he has not reformed his dissolute conduct, but has lived wickedly and iniquitously even while abounding in alms, shall have a merciful judgment, so that he shall either be not condemned at all, or shall be delivered from final judgment after a time. And for the same reason they suppose that Christ will discriminate between those on the right hand and those on the left, and will send the one party into His kingdom, the other into eternal punishment on the sole ground of their attention to or neglect of works of charity. Moreover, they endeavour to use the prayer which the Lord Himself taught as a proof and bulwark of their opinion, that daily sins which are never abandoned can be expiated through alms-deeds, no matter how offensive or of what sort they be. For, say they, as there is no day on which Christians ought not to use this prayer, so there is no sin of any kind which, though committed every day, is not remitted when we say, "Forgive us our debts," if we take care to

fulfill what follows, "as we forgive our debtors."[3] For, they go on to say, the Lord does not say, "If ye forgive men their trespasses, your heavenly Father will forgive you your little daily sins," but "will forgive you your sins." Therefore, be they of any kind or magnitude whatever, be they perpetrated daily and never abandoned or subdued in this life, they can be pardoned, they presume, through alms-deeds.

But they are right to inculcate the giving of alms proportioned to past sins; for if they said that any kind of alms could obtain the divine pardon of great sins committed daily and with habitual enormity, if they said that such sins could thus be daily remitted, they would see that their doctrine was absurd and ridiculous. For they would thus be driven to acknowledge that it were possible for a very wealthy man to buy absolution from murders, adulteries, and all manner of wickedness, by paying a daily alms of ten paltry coins. And if it be most absurd and insane to make such an acknowledgment, and if we still ask what are those fitting alms of which even the forerunner of Christ said, "Bring forth therefore fruits meet for repentance,"[4] undoubtedly it will be found that they are not such as are done by men who undermine their life by daily enormities even to the very end. For they suppose that by giving to the poor a small fraction of the wealth they acquire by extortion and spoliation they can propitiate Christ, so that they may with impunity commit the most damnable sins, in the persuasion that they have bought from Him a license to transgress, or rather do buy a daily indulgence. And if they for one crime have distributed all their goods to Christ's needy members, that could profit them nothing unless they desisted from all similar actions, and attained charity which worketh no evil. He therefore who does alms-deeds proportioned to his sins must first begin with himself. For it is not reasonable that a man who exercises charity towards his neighbour should not do so towards himself, since he hears the Lord saying, "Thou shalt love thy neighbour as thyself,"[5] and again, "Have compassion on thy soul, and please God."[6] He then who has not compassion on his own soul that he may please God, how can he be said to do alms-deeds proportioned to his sins? To the same purpose is that written, "He who is bad to himself, to whom can he be good?"[7] We ought therefore to do alms that we may be heard when

[1]Matt. 10. 37.   [2]Jas. 2. 13.

[3]Matt. 6. 12.   [4]Matt. 3. 8.   [5]Matt. 22. 39.
[6]Ecclus. 30. 24.   [7]Ecclus. 21. 1.

we pray that our past sins may be forgiven, not that while we continue in them we may think to provide ourselves with a licence for wickedness by alms-deeds.

The reason, therefore, of our predicting that He will impute to those on His right hand the alms-deed they have done, and charge those on His left with omitting the same, is that He may thus show the efficacy of charity for the deletion of past sins, not for impunity in their perpetual commission. And such persons, indeed, as decline to abandon their evil habits of life for a better course cannot be said to do charitable deeds. For this is the purport of the saying, "Inasmuch as ye did it not to one of the least of these, ye did it not to me." [1] He shows them that they do not perform charitable actions even when they think they are doing so. For if they gave bread to a hungering Christian because he is a Christian, assuredly they would not deny to themselves the bread of righteousness, that is, Christ Himself; for God considers not the person to whom the gift is made, but the spirit in which it is made. He therefore who loves Christ in a Christian extends alms to him in the same spirit in which he draws near to Christ, not in that spirit which would abandon Christ if it could do so with impunity. For in proportion as a man loves what Christ disapproves does he himself abandon Christ. For what does it profit a man that he is baptized, if he is not justified? Did not He Who said, "Except a man be born of water and of the Spirit, he shall not enter into the kingdom of God," [2] say also, "Except your righteousness shall exceed the righteousness of the scribes and Pharisees, ye shall not enter into the kingdom of heaven"? [3] Why do many through fear of the first saying run to baptism, while few through fear of the second seek to be justified? As therefore it is not to his brother a man says, "Thou fool," if when he says it he is indignant not at the brotherhood, but at the sin of the offender—for otherwise he were guilty of hell fire—so he who extends charity to a Christian does not extend it to a Christian if he does not love Christ in him. Now he does not love Christ who refuses to be justified in Him. Or, again, if a man has been guilty of this sin of calling his brother "Fool," unjustly reviling him without any desire to remove his sin, his alms-deeds go a small way towards expiating this fault, unless he adds to this the remedy of reconciliation which the same passage enjoins. For it is there said, "Therefore, if thou bring thy gift to the altar, and there rememberest that

thy brother hath aught against thee; leave there thy gift before the altar, and go thy way; first be reconciled to thy brother, and then come and offer thy gift." [4] Just so it is a small matter to do alms-deeds, no matter how great they be, for any sin, so long as the offender continues in the practice of sin.

Then as to the daily prayer which the Lord Himself taught, and which is therefore called the Lord's prayer, it obliterates indeed the sins of the day, when day by day we say, "Forgive us our debts," and when we not only say but act out that which follows, "as we forgive our debtors"; [5] but we utter this petition because sins have been committed, and not that they may be. For by it our Saviour designed to teach us that, however righteously we live in this life of infirmity and darkness, we still commit sins for the remission of which we ought to pray, while we must pardon those who sin against us that we ourselves also may be pardoned. The Lord then did not utter the words, "If ye forgive men their trespasses, your Father will also forgive you your trespasses," [6] in order that we might contract from this petition such confidence as should enable us to sin securely from day to day, either putting ourselves above the fear of human laws, or craftily deceiving men concerning our conduct, but in order that we might thus learn not to suppose that we are without sins, even though we should be free from crimes; as also God admonished the priests of the old law to this same effect regarding their sacrifices, which He commanded them to offer first for their own sins, and then for the sins of the people. For even the very words of so great a Master and Lord are to be intently considered. For He does not say, "If ye forgive men their sins, your Father will also forgive you your sins, no matter of what sort they be," but He says, "your sins"; for it was a daily prayer He was teaching, and it was certainly to disciples already justified He was speaking. What, then, does He mean by "your sins," but those sins from which not even you who are justified and sanctified can be free? While, then, those who seek occasion from this petition to indulge in habitual sin maintain that the Lord meant to include great sins, because He did not say, "He will forgive you your small sins," but "your sins," we, on the other hand, taking into account the character of the persons He was addressing, cannot see our way to interpret the expression "your sins" of anything but small sins, because such persons are no longer guilty of

[1] Matt. 25. 45. [2] John, 3. 5. [3] Matt. 5. 20. [4] Matt. 5. 23, 24. [5] Matt. 6. 12. [6] Matt. 6. 14.

great sins. Nevertheless not even great sins themselves—sins from which we must flee with a total reformation of life—are forgiven to those who pray, unless they observe the appended precept, "as ye also forgive your debtors." For if the very small sins which attach even to the life of the righteous be not remitted without that condition, how much further from obtaining indulgence shall those be who are involved in many great crimes, if, while they cease from perpetrating such enormities, they still inexorably refuse to remit any debt incurred to themselves, since the Lord says, "But if ye forgive not men their trespasses, neither will your Father forgive your trespasses"?[1] For this is the purport of the saying of the Apostle James also, "He shall have judgment without mercy that hath showed no mercy."[2] For we should remember that servant whose debt of ten thousand talents his lord cancelled, but afterwards ordered him to pay up, because the servant himself had no pity for his fellow-servant who owed him an hundred pence.[3] The words which the Apostle James subjoins, "And mercy rejoiceth against judgment,"[4] find their application among those who are the children of the promise and vessels of mercy. For even those righteous men, who have lived with such holiness that they receive into the eternal habitations others also who have won their friendship with the mammon of unrighteousness,[5] became such only through the merciful deliverance of Him Who justifies the ungodly, imputing to him a reward according to grace, not according to debt. For among this number is the apostle, who says, "I obtained mercy to be faithful."[6]

But it must be admitted, that those who are thus received into the eternal habitations are not of such a character that their own life would suffice to rescue them without the aid of the saints, and consequently in their case especially does mercy rejoice against judgment. And yet we are not on this account to suppose that every abandoned profligate, who has made no amendment of his life, is to be received into the eternal habitations if only he has assisted the saints with the mammon of unrighteousness—that is to say, with money or wealth which has been unjustly acquired, or, if rightfully acquired, is yet not the true riches, but only what iniquity counts riches, because it knows not the true riches in which those persons abound, who even receive others also into eternal habitations. There is then a certain kind of life, which is nei-

ther, on the one hand, so bad that those who adopt it are not helped towards the kingdom of heaven by any bountiful alms-giving by which they may relieve the wants of the saints, and make friends who could receive them into eternal habitations, nor, on the other hand, so good that it of itself suffices to win for them that great blessedness, if they do not obtain mercy through the merits of those whom they have made their friends. And I frequently wonder that even Virgil should give expression to this sentence of the Lord, in which He says, "Make to yourselves friends of the mammon of unrighteousness, that they may receive you into everlasting habitations";[7] and this very similar saying, "He that receiveth a prophet, in the name of a prophet, shall receive a prophet's reward; and he that receiveth a righteous man, in the name of a righteous man, shall receive a righteous man's reward."[8] For when that poet described the Elysian fields, in which they suppose that the souls of the blessed dwell, he placed there not only those who had been able by their own merit to reach that abode, but added,

> And they who grateful memory won
> By services to others done;[9]

that is, they who had served others, and thereby merited to be remembered by them. Just as if they used the expression so common in Christian lips, where some humble person commends himself to one of the saints, and says, "Remember me," and secures that he do so by deserving well at his hand. But what that kind of life we have been speaking of is, and what those sins are which prevent a man from winning the kingdom of God by himself, but yet permit him to avail himself of the merits of the saints, it is very difficult to ascertain, very perilous to define. For my own part, in spite of all investigation, I have been up to the present hour unable to discover this. And possibly it is hidden from us, lest we should become careless in avoiding such sins, and so cease to make progress. For if it were known what these sins are, which, though they continue, and be not abandoned for a higher life, do yet not prevent us from seeking and hoping for the intercession of the saints, human sloth would presumptuously wrap itself in these sins, and would take no steps to be disentangled from such wrappings by the deft energy of any virtue, but would only desire to be rescued by the merits of other people, whose friendship had been won by a bountiful use of

---

[1]Matt. 6. 15.   [2]Jas. 2. 13.   [3]Matt. 18. 23.
[4]Jas. 2. 13.   [5]Luke, 16. 9.   [6]I Cor. 7. 25.

[7]Luke, 16. 9.   [8]Matt. 10. 41.   [9]Æneid, BK. VI. 664.

the mammon of unrighteousness. But now that we are left in ignorance of the precise nature of that iniquity which is venial, even though it be persevered in, certainly we are both more vigilant in our prayers and efforts for progress, and more careful to secure with the mammon of unrighteousness friends for ourselves among the saints.

But this deliverance, which is effected by one's own prayers, or the intercession of holy men, secures that a man be not cast into eternal fire, but not that, when once he has been cast into it, he should after a time be rescued from it. For even those who fancy that what is said of the good ground bringing forth abundant fruit, some thirty, some sixty, some an hundred fold, is to be referred to the saints, so that in proportion to their merits some of them shall deliver thirty men, some sixty, some an hundred—even those who maintain this are yet commonly inclined to suppose that this deliverance will take place at, and not after the day of judgment.

Under this impression, some one who observed the unseemly folly with which men promise themselves impunity on the ground that all will be included in this method of deliverance, is reported to have very happily remarked, that we should rather endeavour to live so well that we shall be all found among the number of those who are to intercede for the liberation of others, lest these should be so few in number, that, after they have delivered one thirty, another sixty, another an hundred, there should still remain many who could not be delivered from punishment by their intercessions, and among them every one who has vainly and rashly promised himself the fruit of another's labour. But enough has been said in reply to those who acknowledge the authority of the same sacred Scriptures as ourselves, but who, by a mistaken interpretation of them, conceive of the future rather as they themselves wish than as the Scriptures teach. And having given this reply, I now, according to promise, close this book.

BOOK XXII

ARGUMENT. THIS BOOK TREATS OF THE END OF THE CITY OF GOD, THAT IS TO SAY, OF THE ETERNAL HAPPINESS OF THE SAINTS; THE FAITH OF THE RESURRECTION OF THE BODY IS ESTABLISHED AND EXPLAINED; AND THE WORK CONCLUDES BY SHOWING HOW THE SAINTS, CLOTHED IN IMMORTAL AND SPIRITUAL BODIES, SHALL BE EMPLOYED.

CHAP. I. *Of the creation of angels and men*

As we promised in the immediately preceding book, this, the last of the whole work, shall contain a discussion of the eternal blessedness of the city of God. This blessedness is named eternal, not because it shall endure for many ages, though at last it shall come to an end, but because, according to the words of the gospel, "of His kingdom there shall be no end."[1] Neither shall it enjoy the mere appearance of perpetuity which is maintained by the rise of fresh generations to occupy the place of those that have died out, as in an evergreen the same freshness seems to continue permanently, and the same appearance of dense foliage is preserved by the growth of fresh leaves in the room of those that have withered and fallen; but in that city all the citizens shall be immortal, men now for the first time enjoying what the holy angels have never lost. And this shall be accomplished by God, the most almighty Founder of the city. For He has promised it, and cannot lie, and has already performed many of His promises, and has done many unpromised kindnesses to those whom He now asks to believe that He will do this also.

For it is He Who in the beginning created the world full of all visible and intelligible beings, among which He created nothing better than those spirits whom He endowed with intelligence, and made capable of contemplating and enjoying Him, and united in our society, which we call the holy and heavenly city, and in which the material of their sustenance and blessedness is God Himself, as it were their common food and nourishment. It is He Who gave to this intellectual nature free-will of such a kind, that if he wished to forsake God, i.e., his blessedness, misery should forthwith result. It is He Who, when He foreknew that certain angels would in their pride desire to suffice for their own blessedness, and would forsake their great good, did not deprive them of this power, deeming it to be more befitting His power and goodness to bring good out of evil than to prevent the evil from coming into existence. And indeed evil had

[1] Luke, I. 33.

never been, had not the mutable nature—mutable, though good, and created by the most high God and immutable Good, Who created all things good—brought evil upon itself by sin. And this its sin is itself proof that its nature was originally good. For had it not been very good, though not equal to its Creator, the desertion of God as its light could not have been an evil to it. For as blindness is a vice of the eye, and this very fact indicates that the eye was created to see the light, and as, consequently, vice itself proves that the eye is more excellent than the other members, because it is capable of light (for on no other supposition would it be a vice of the eye to want light), so the nature which once enjoyed God teaches, even by its very vice, that it was created the best of all, since it is now miserable because it does not enjoy God. It is He Who with very just punishment doomed the angels who voluntarily fell to everlasting misery, and rewarded those who continued in their attachment to the supreme good with the assurance of endless stability as the meed of their fidelity. It is He Who made also man himself upright, with the same freedom of will—an earthly animal, indeed, but fit for heaven if he remained faithful to his Creator, but destined to the misery appropriate to such a nature if he forsook Him. It is He Who, when He foreknew that man would in his turn sin by abandoning God and breaking His law, did not deprive him of the power of free-will, because He at the same time foresaw what good He Himself would bring out of the evil, and how from this mortal race, deservedly and justly condemned, He would by His grace collect, as now He does, a people so numerous, that He thus fills up and repairs the blank made by the fallen angels, and that thus that beloved and heavenly city is not defrauded of the full number of its citizens, but perhaps may even rejoice in a still more overflowing population.

CHAP. 2. *Of the eternal and unchangeable will of God*

It is true that wicked men do many things contrary to God's will; but so great is His wisdom and power, that all things which seem adverse to His purpose do still tend towards those just and good ends and issues which He Himself has foreknown. And consequently, when God is said to change His will, as when, e.g., He becomes angry with those to whom He was gentle, it is rather they than He who are changed, and they find Him changed in so far as their experience of suffering at His hand is new, as the

sun is changed to injured eyes, and becomes as it were fierce from being mild, and hurtful from being delightful, though in itself it remains the same as it was. That also is called the will of God which He does in the hearts of those who obey His commandments; and of this the apostle says, "For it is God that worketh in you both to will." [1] As God's "righteousness" is used not only of the righteousness wherewith He Himself is righteous, but also of that which He produces in the man whom He justifies, so also that is called His law, which, though given by God, is rather the law of men. For certainly they were men to whom Jesus said, "It is written in your law," [2] though in another place we read, "The law of his God is in his heart." [3] According to this will which God works in men, He is said also to will what He Himself does not will, but causes His people to will; as He is said to know what He has caused those to know who were ignorant of it. For when the apostle says, "But now, after that ye have known God, or rather are known of God," [4] we cannot suppose that God there for the first time knew those who were foreknown by Him before the foundation of the world; but He is said to have known them then, because then He caused them to know. But I remember that I discussed these modes of expression in the preceding books. According to this will, then, by which we say that God wills what He causes to be willed by others, from whom the future is hidden, He wills many things which He does not perform.

Thus His saints, inspired by His holy will, desire many things which never happen. They pray, e.g., for certain individuals—they pray in a pious and holy manner—but what they request He does not perform, though He Himself by His own Holy Spirit has wrought in them this will to pray. And consequently, when the saints, in conformity with God's mind, will and pray that all men be saved, we can use this mode of expression: God wills and does not perform—meaning that He Who causes them to will these things Himself wills them. But if we speak of that will of His which is eternal as His foreknowledge, certainly He has already done all things in heaven and on earth that He has willed—not only past and present things, but even things still future. But before the arrival of that time in which He has willed the occurrence of what He foreknew and arranged before all time, we say, "It will happen when God wills." But if we are ignorant not only of the time in which it is to be, but even whether it

<hr/>

[1]Phil. 2. 13.   [2]John, 8. 17.   [3]Ps. 37. 31.   [4]Gal. 4. 9.

shall be at all, we say, "It will happen if God wills"—not because God will then have a new will which He had not before, but because that event, which from eternity has been prepared in His unchangeable will, shall then come to pass.

Chap. 3. *Of the promise of eternal blessedness to the saints, and everlasting punishment to the wicked*

Wherefore, not to mention many other instances besides, as we now see in Christ the fulfilment of that which God promised to Abraham when He said, "In thy seed shall all nations be blessed,"[1] so this also shall be fulfilled which He promised to the same race, when He said by the prophet, "They that are in their sepulchres shall rise again,"[2] and also, "There shall be a new heaven and a new earth: and the former shall not be mentioned, nor come into mind; but they shall find joy and rejoicing in it: for I will make Jerusalem a rejoicing, and my people a joy. And I will rejoice in Jerusalem, and joy in my people, and the voice of weeping shall be no more heard in her."[3] And by another prophet He uttered the same prediction: "At that time thy people shall be delivered, every one that shall be found written in the book. And many of them that sleep in the dust (or, as some interpret it, "in the mound") of the earth shall awake, some to everlasting life, and some to shame and everlasting contempt."[4] And in another place by the same prophet: "The saints of the Most High shall take the kingdom, and shall possess the kingdom for ever, even for ever and ever."[5] And a little after he says, "His kingdom is an everlasting kingdom."[6] Other prophecies referring to the same subject I have advanced in the twentieth book, and others still which I have not advanced are found written in the same Scriptures; and these predictions shall be fulfilled, as those also have been which unbelieving men supposed would be frustrate. For it is the same God who promised both, and predicted that both would come to pass—the God whom the pagan deities tremble before, as even Porphyry, the noblest of pagan philosophers, testifies.

Chap. 4. *Against the wise men of the world, who fancy that the earthly bodies of men cannot be transferred to a heavenly habitation*

But men who use their learning and intellectual ability to resist the force of that great authority which, in fulfilment of what was so long before predicted, has converted all races of men to faith and hope in its promises, seem to themselves to argue acutely against the resurrection of the body while they cite what Cicero mentions in the third book *De Republica*. For when he was asserting the apotheosis of Hercules and Romulus, he says: "Whose bodies were not taken up into heaven; for nature would not permit a body of earth to exist anywhere except upon earth." This, forsooth, is the profound reasoning of the wise men, whose thoughts God knows that they are vain. For if we were only souls, that is, spirits without any body, and if we dwelt in heaven and had no knowledge of earthly animals, and were told that we should be bound to earthly bodies by some wonderful bond of union, and should animate them, should we not much more vigorously refuse to believe this, and maintain that nature would not permit an incorporeal substance to be held by a corporeal bond? And yet the earth is full of living spirits, to which terrestrial bodies are bound, and with which they are in a wonderful way implicated. If, then, the same God who has created such beings wills this also, what is to hinder the earthly body from being raised to a heavenly body, since a spirit, which is more excellent than all bodies, and consequently than even a heavenly body, has been tied to an earthly body? If so small an earthly particle has been able to hold in union with itself something better than a heavenly body, so as to receive sensation and life, will heaven disdain to receive, or at least to retain, this sentient and living particle, which derives its life and sensation from a substance more excellent than any heavenly body? If this does not happen now, it is because the time is not yet come which has been determined by Him who has already done a much more marvellous thing than that which these men refuse to believe. For why do we not more intensely wonder that incorporeal souls, which are of higher rank than heavenly bodies, are bound to earthly bodies, rather than that bodies, although earthly, are exalted to an abode which, though heavenly, is yet corporeal, except because we have been accustomed to see this, and indeed are this, while we are not as yet that other marvel, nor have as yet ever seen it? Certainly, if we consult sober reason, the more wonderful of the two divine works is found to be to attach somehow corporeal things to incorporeal, and not to connect earthly things with heavenly, which, though diverse, are yet both of them corporeal.

[1]Gen. 22. 18.   [2]Isa. 26. 19.   [3]Isa. 65. 17–19.
[4]Dan. 12. 1, 2.   [5]Dan. 7. 18.   [6]Dan. 7. 27.

CHAP. 5. *Of the resurrection of the flesh, which some refuse to believe, though the world at large believes it*

But granting that this was once incredible, behold, now, the world has come to the belief that the earthly body of Christ was received up into heaven. Already both the learned and unlearned have believed in the resurrection of the flesh and its ascension to the heavenly places, while only a very few either of the educated or uneducated are still staggered by it. If this is a credible thing which is believed, then let those who do not believe see how stolid they are; and if it is incredible, then this also is an incredible thing, that what is incredible should have received such credit. Here then we have two incredibles—to wit, the resurrection of our body to eternity, and that the world should believe so incredible a thing; and both these incredibles the same God predicted should come to pass before either had as yet occurred. We see that already one of the two has come to pass, for the world has believed what was incredible; why should we despair that the remaining one shall also come to pass, and that this which the world believed, though it was incredible, shall itself occur? For already that which was equally incredible has come to pass, in the world's believing an incredible thing. Both were incredible: the one we see accomplished, the other we believe shall be; for both were predicted in those same Scriptures by means of which the world believed. And the very manner in which the world's faith was won is found to be even more incredible, if we consider it. Men uninstructed in any branch of a liberal education, without any of the refinement of heathen learning, unskilled in grammar, not armed with dialectic, not adorned with rhetoric, but plain fishermen, and very few in number—these were the men whom Christ sent with the nets of faith to the sea of this world, and thus took out of every race so many fishes, and even the philosophers themselves, wonderful as they are rare. Let us add, if you please, or because you ought to be pleased, this third incredible thing to the two former. And now we have three incredibles, all of which have yet come to pass. It is incredible that Jesus Christ should have risen in the flesh and ascended with flesh into heaven; it is incredible that the world should have believed so incredible a thing; it is incredible that a very few men, of mean birth and the lowest rank, and no education, should have been able so effectually to persuade the world, and even its learned

men, of so incredible a thing. Of these three incredibles, the parties with whom we are debating refuse to believe the first; they cannot refuse to see the second, which they are unable to account for if they do not believe the third. It is indubitable that the resurrection of Christ, and His ascension into heaven with the flesh in which He rose, is already preached and believed in the whole world. If it is not credible, how is it that it has already received credence in the whole world? If a number of noble, exalted, and learned men had said that they had witnessed it, and had been at pains to publish what they had witnessed, it were not wonderful that the world should have believed it, but it were very stubborn to refuse credence; but if, as is true, the world has believed a few obscure, inconsiderable, uneducated persons, who state and write that they witnessed it, is it not unreasonable that a handful of wrong-headed men should oppose themselves to the creed of the whole world, and refuse their belief? And if the world has put faith in a small number of men, of mean birth and the lowest rank, and no education, it is because the divinity of the thing itself appeared all the more manifestly in such contemptible witnesses. The eloquence, indeed, which lent persuasion to their message, consisted of wonderful works, not words. For they who had not seen Christ risen in the flesh, nor ascending into heaven with His risen body, believed those who related how they had seen these things, and who testified not only with words but wonderful signs. For men whom they knew to be acquainted with only one, or at most two languages, they marvelled to hear speaking in the tongues of all nations. They saw a man, lame from his mother's womb, after forty years stand up sound at their word in the name of Christ; that handkerchiefs taken from their bodies had virtue to heal the sick; that countless persons, sick of various diseases, were laid in a row in the road where they were to pass, that their shadow might fall on them as they walked, and that they forthwith received health; that many other stupendous miracles were wrought by them in the name of Christ; and, finally, that they even raised the dead. If it be admitted that these things occurred as they are related, then we have a multitude of incredible things to add to those three incredibles. That the one incredibility of the resurrection and ascension of Jesus Christ may be believed, we accumulate the testimonies of countless incredible miracles, but even so we do not bend the frightful obstinacy of these sceptics. But if they do not believe that these miracles were wrought by Christ's apostles to gain credence to their preaching of His resurrection and ascension, this one grand miracle suffices for us, that the whole world has believed without any miracles.

CHAP. 6. *That Rome made its founder Romulus a god because it loved him; but the Church loved Christ because it believed Him to be God*

Let us here recite the passage in which Tully expresses his astonishment that the apotheosis of Romulus should have been credited. I shall insert his words as they stand: "It is most worthy of remark in Romulus, that other men who are said to have become gods lived in less educated ages, when there was a greater propensity to the fabulous, and when the uninstructed were easily persuaded to believe anything. But the age of Romulus was barely six hundred years ago, and already literature and science had dispelled the errors that attach to an uncultured age." And a little after he says of the same Romulus words to this effect: "From this we may perceive that Homer had flourished long before Romulus, and that there was now so much learning in individuals, and so generally diffused an enlightenment, that scarcely any room was left for fable. For antiquity admitted fables, and sometimes even very clumsy ones; but this age was sufficiently enlightened to reject whatever had not the air of truth." Thus one of the most learned men, and certainly the most eloquent, M. Tullius Cicero, says that it is surprising that the divinity of Romulus was believed in, because the times were already so enlightened that they would not accept a fabulous fiction. But who believed that Romulus was a god except Rome, which was itself small and in its infancy? Then afterwards it was necessary that succeeding generations should preserve the tradition of their ancestors that, drinking in this superstition with their mother's milk, the state might grow and come to such power that it might dictate this belief, as from a point of vantage, to all the nations over whom its sway extended. And these nations, though they might not believe that Romulus was a god, at least said so, that they might not give offence to their sovereign state by refusing to give its founder that title which was given him by Rome, which had adopted this belief, not by a love of error, but an error of love. But though Christ is the founder of the heavenly and eternal city, yet it did not believe Him to be God because it was founded by Him, but rather it is founded by Him, in vir-

tue of its belief. Rome, after it had been built and dedicated, worshipped its founder in a temple as a god; but this Jerusalem laid Christ, its God, as its foundation, that the building and dedication might proceed. The former city loved its founder, and therefore believed him to be a god; the latter believed Christ to be God, and therefore loved Him. There was an antecedent cause for the love of the former city, and for its believing that even a false dignity attached to the object of its love; so there was an antecedent cause for the belief of the latter, and for its loving the true dignity which a proper faith, not a rash surmise, ascribed to its object. For, not to mention the multitude of very striking miracles which proved that Christ is God, there were also divine prophecies heralding Him, prophecies most worthy of belief, which being already accomplished, we have not, like the fathers, to wait for their verification. Of Romulus, on the other hand, and of his building Rome and reigning in it, we read or hear the narrative of what did take place, not prediction which beforehand said that such things should be. And so far as his reception among the gods is concerned, history only records that this was believed, and does not state it as a fact for no miraculous signs testified to the truth of this. For as to that wolf which is said to have nursed the twin-brothers, and which is considered a great marvel, how does this prove him to have been divine? For even supposing that this nurse was a real wolf and not a mere courtezan, yet she nursed both brothers, and Remus is not reckoned a god. Besides, what was there to hinder any one from asserting that Romulus or Hercules, or any such man, was a god? Or who would rather choose to die than profess belief in his divinity? And did a single nation worship Romulus among its gods, unless it were forced through fear of the Roman name? But who can number the multitudes who have chosen death in the most cruel shapes rather than deny the divinity of Christ? And thus the dread of some slight indignation, which it was supposed, perhaps groundlessly, might exist in the minds of the Romans, constrained some states who were subject to Rome to worship Romulus as a god; whereas the dread, not of a slight mental shock, but of severe and various punishments and of death itself, the most formidable of all, could not prevent an immense multitude of martyrs throughout the world from not merely worshipping but also confessing Christ as God. The city of Christ, which, although as yet a stranger upon earth, had countless hosts of citizens, did not make war upon its godless persecutors for the sake of temporal security, but preferred to win eternal salvation by abstaining from war. They were bound, imprisoned, beaten, tortured, burned, torn in pieces, massacred, and yet they multiplied. It was not given to them to fight for their eternal salvation except by despising their temporal salvation for their Saviour's sake.

I am aware that Cicero, in the third book of his *De Republica,* if I mistake not, argues that a first-rate power will not engage in war except either for honour or for safety. What he has to say about the question of safety, and what he means by safety, he explains in another place, saying, "Private persons frequently evade, by a speedy death, destitution, exile, bonds, the scourge, and the other pains which even the most insensible feel. But to states, death, which seems to emancipate individuals from all punishments, is itself a punishment; for a state should be so constituted as to be eternal. And thus death is not natural to a republic as to a man, to whom death is not only necessary, but often even desirable. But when a state is destroyed, obliterated, annihilated, it is as if (to compare great things with small) this whole world perished and collapsed." Cicero said this because he, with the Platonists, believed that the world would not perish. It is therefore agreed that, according to Cicero, a state should engage in war for the safety which preserves the state permanently in existence, though its citizens change; as the foliage of an olive or laurel, or any tree of this kind, is perennial, the old leaves being replaced by fresh ones. For death, as he says, is no punishment to individuals, but rather delivers them from all other punishments, but it is a punishment to the state. And therefore it is reasonably asked whether the Saguntines did right when they chose that their whole state should perish rather than that they should break faith with the Roman republic; for this deed of theirs is applauded by the citizens of the earthly republic. But I do not see how they could follow the advice of Cicero, who tells us that no war is to be undertaken save for safety or for honour; neither does he say which of these two is to be preferred, if a case should occur in which the one could not be preserved without the loss of the other. For manifestly, if the Saguntines chose safety, they must break faith; if they kept faith, they must reject safety; as also it fell out. But the safety of the city of God is such that it can be retained, or rather acquired, by faith and with faith; but if faith be abandoned, no one can attain it. It is this thought of a most steadfast and patient spirit that has made so many noble martyrs, while Romulus has not had, and could not have, so much as one to die for his divinity.

CHAP. 7. *That the world's belief in Christ is the result of divine power, not of human persuasion*

But it is thoroughly ridiculous to make mention of the false divinity of Romulus as any way comparable to that of Christ. Nevertheless, if Romulus lived about six hundred years before Cicero, in an age which already was so enlightened that it rejected all impossibilities, how much more, in an age which certainly was more enlightened, being six hundred years later, the age of Cicero himself, and of the emperors Augustus and Tiberius, would the human mind have refused to listen to or believe in the resurrection of Christ's body and its ascension into heaven, and have scouted it as an impossibility, had not the divinity of the truth itself, or the truth of the divinity, and corroborating miraculous signs, proved that it could happen and had happened? Through virtue of these testimonies, and notwithstanding the opposition and terror of so many cruel persecutions, the resurrection and immortality of the flesh, first in Christ, and subsequently in all in the new world, was believed, was intrepidly proclaimed, and was sown over the whole world, to be fertilized richly with the blood of the martyrs. For the predictions of the prophets that had preceded the events were read, they were corroborated by powerful signs, and the truth was seen to be not contradictory to reason, but only different from customary ideas, so that at length the world embraced the faith it had furiously persecuted.

CHAP. 8. *Of miracles which were wrought that the world might believe in Christ, and which have not ceased since the world believed*

Why, they say, are those miracles, which you affirm were wrought formerly, wrought no longer? I might, indeed, reply that miracles were necessary before the world believed, in order that it might believe. And whoever nowadays demands to see prodigies that he may believe, is himself a great prodigy, because he does not believe, though the whole world does. But they make these objections for the sole purpose of insinuating that even those former miracles were never wrought. How, then, is it that everywhere Christ is celebrated with such firm belief in His resurrection and ascension? How is it that in enlightened times, in which every impossibility is rejected, the world has, without any miracles, believed things marvellously incredible? Or will they say that these things were credible, and therefore were credited? Why then do they themselves not believe? Our argument, therefore, is a summary one—either incredible things which were not witnessed have caused the world to believe other incredible things which both occurred and were witnessed, or this matter was so credible that it needed no miracles in proof of it and therefore convicts these unbelievers of unpardonable scepticism. This I might say for the sake of refuting these most frivolous objectors. But we cannot deny that many miracles were wrought to confirm that one grand and health-giving miracle of Christ's ascension to heaven with the flesh in which He rose. For these most trustworthy books of ours contain in one narrative both the miracles that were wrought and the creed which they were wrought to confirm. The miracles were published that they might produce faith, and the faith which they produced brought them into greater prominence. For they are read in congregations that they may be believed, and yet they would not be so read unless they were believed. For even now miracles are wrought in the name of Christ, whether by His sacraments or by the prayers or relics of His saints; but they are not so brilliant and conspicuous as to cause them to be published with such glory as accompanied the former miracles. For the canon of the sacred writings, which behoved to be closed,[1] causes those to be everywhere recited, and to sink into the memory of all the congregations; but these modern miracles are scarcely known even to the whole population in the midst of which they are wrought, and at the best are confined to one spot. For frequently they are known only to a very few persons, while all the rest are ignorant of them, especially if the state is a large one; and when they are reported to other persons in other localities, there is no sufficient authority to give them prompt and unwavering credence, although they are reported to the faithful by the faithful.

The miracle which was wrought at Milan when I was there, and by which a blind man was restored to sight, could come to the knowledge of many; for not only is the city a large one, but also the Emperor was there at the time, and the occurrence was witnessed by an immense concourse of people that had gathered to the bodies of the martyrs Protasius and Gervasius, which had long lain concealed and un-

known, but were now made known to the bishop Ambrose in a dream, and discovered by him. By virtue of these remains the darkness of that blind man was scattered, and he saw the light of day.[2]

But who but a very small number are aware of the cure which was wrought upon Innocentius, ex-advocate of the deputy prefecture, a cure wrought at Carthage, in my presence and under my own eyes? For when I and my brother Alypius,[3] who were not yet clergymen,[4] though already servants of God, came from abroad, this man received us, and made us live with him, for he and all his household were devotedly pious. He was being treated by medical men for fistulæ, of which he had a large number intricately seated in the rectum. He had already undergone an operation, and the surgeons were using every means at their command for his relief. In that operation he had suffered long-continued and acute pain; yet, among the many folds of the gut, one had escaped the operators so entirely, that, though they ought to have laid it open with the knife, they never touched it. And thus, though all those that had been opened were cured, this one remained as it was, and frustrated all their labour. The patient, having his suspicions awakened by the delay thus occasioned, and fearing greatly a second operation, which another medical man—one of his own domestics—had told him he must undergo, though this man had not even been allowed to witness the first operation, and had been banished from the house, and with difficulty allowed to come back to his enraged master's presence—the patient, I say, broke out to the surgeons, saying, "Are you going to cut me again? Are you, after all, to fulfil the prediction of that man whom you would not allow even to be present?" The surgeons laughed at the unskilful doctor, and soothed their patient's fears with fair words and promises. So several days passed, and yet nothing they tried did him good. Still they persisted in promising that they would cure that fistula by drugs, without the knife. They called in also another old practitioner of great repute in that department, Ammonius (for he was still alive at that time); and he, after examining the part, promised the same result as themselves from their care and skill. On this great authority, the patient became confident, and, as if already well, vented his good spirits in facetious remarks at the expense of his domestic physician, who had predicted a second opera-

[1] Another reading has *diffamatum*, "published."

[2] See also *Confessions*, BK. IX. 16.
[3] See *Confessions, passim.*   [4] *Cleros.*

tion. To make a long story short, after a number of days had thus uselessly elapsed, the surgeons, wearied and confused, had at last to confess that he could only be cured by the knife. Agitated with excessive fear, he was terrified, and grew pale with dread; and when he collected himself and was able to speak, he ordered them to go away and never to return. Worn out with weeping, and driven by necessity, it occurred to him to call in an Alexandrian, who was at that time esteemed a wonderfully skilful operator, that he might perform the operation his rage would not suffer them to do. But when he had come, and examined with a professional eye the traces of their careful work, he acted the part of a good man, and persuaded his patient to allow those same hands the satisfaction of finishing his cure which had begun it with a skill that excited his admiration, adding that there was no doubt his only hope of a cure was by an operation, but that it was thoroughly inconsistent with his nature to win the credit of the cure by doing the little that remained to be done, and rob of their reward men whose consummate skill, care, and diligence he could not but admire when he saw the traces of their work. They were therefore again received to favour; and it was agreed that, in the presence of the Alexandrian, they should operate on the fistula, which, by the consent of all, could now only be cured by the knife. The operation was deferred till the following day. But when they had left, there arose in the house such a wailing, in sympathy with the excessive despondency of the master, that it seemed to us like the mourning at a funeral, and we could scarcely repress it. Holy men were in the habit of visiting him daily; Saturninus of blessed memory, at that time bishop of Uzali, and the presbyter Gelosus, and the deacons of the church of Carthage; and among these was the bishop Aurelius, who alone of them all survives—a man to be named by us with due reverence—and with him I have often spoken of this affair, as we conversed together about the wonderful works of God, and I have found that he distinctly remembers what I am now relating. When these persons visited him that evening according to their custom, he besought them, with pitiable tears, that they would do him the honour of being present next day at what he judged his funeral rather than his suffering. For such was the terror his former pains had produced, that he made no doubt he would die in the hands of the surgeons. They comforted him, and exhorted him to put his trust in God, and nerve his will like a man. Then we went to prayer; but while we, in the usual way, were kneeling and bending to the ground, he cast himself down, as if some one were hurling him violently to the earth, and began to pray; but in what a manner, with what earnestness and emotion, with what a flood of tears, with what groans and sobs, that shook his whole body, and almost prevented him speaking, who can describe! Whether the others prayed, and had not their attention wholly diverted by this conduct, I do not know. For myself, I could not pray at all. This only I briefly said in my heart: "O Lord, what prayers of Thy people dost Thou hear if Thou hearest not these?" For it seemed to me that nothing could be added to this prayer, unless he expired in praying. We rose from our knees, and, receiving the blessing of the bishop, departed, the patient beseeching his visitors to be present next morning, they exhorting him to keep up his heart. The dreaded day dawned. The servants of God were present, as they had promised to be; the surgeons arrived; all that the circumstances required was ready; the frightful instruments are produced; all look on in wonder and suspense. While those who have most influence with the patient are cheering his fainting spirit, his limbs are arranged on the couch so as to suit the hand of the operator; the knots of the bandages are untied; the part is bared; the surgeon examines it, and, with knife in hand, eagerly looks for the sinus that is to be cut. He searches for it with his eyes; he feels for it with his finger; he applies every kind of scrutiny: he finds a perfectly firm cicatrix! No words of mine can describe the joy, and praise, and thanksgiving to the merciful and almighty God which was poured from the lips of all, with tears of gladness. Let the scene be imagined rather than described!

In the same city of Carthage lived Innocentia, a very devout woman of the highest rank in the state. She had cancer in one of her breasts, a disease which, as physicians say, is incurable. Ordinarily, therefore, they either amputate, and so separate from the body the member on which the disease has seized, or, that the patient's life may be prolonged a little, though death is inevitable even if somewhat delayed, they abandon all remedies, following, as they say, the advice of Hippocrates. This the lady we speak of had been advised to by a skilful physician, who was intimate with her family; and she betook herself to God alone by prayer. On the approach of Easter, she was instructed in a dream to wait for the first woman that came out from the baptistery after being baptized, and to ask her to make the sign of Christ upon her sore. She did so, and was immediately cured. The physician who had advised her to apply no remedy if she wished to live a little longer, when he had examined her after this, and found that she who, on his former examination, was afflicted with that disease was now perfectly cured, eagerly asked her what remedy she had used, anxious, as we may well believe, to discover the drug which should defeat the decision of Hippocrates. But when she told him what had happened, he is said to have replied, with religious politeness, though with a contemptuous tone, and an expression which made her fear he would utter some blasphemy against Christ, "I thought you would make some great discovery to me." She, shuddering at his indifference, quickly replied, "What great thing was it for Christ to heal a cancer, who raised one who had been four days dead?" When, therefore, I had heard this, I was extremely indignant that so great a miracle, wrought in that well-known city, and on a person who was certainly not obscure, should not be divulged, and I considered that she should be spoken to, if not reprimanded on this score. And when she replied to me that she had not kept silence on the subject, I asked the women with whom she was best acquainted whether they had ever heard of this before. They told me they knew nothing of it. "See," I said, "what your not keeping silence amounts to, since not even those who are so familiar with you know of it." And as I had only briefly heard the story, I made her tell how the whole thing happened, from beginning to end, while the other women listened in great astonishment, and glorified God.

A gouty doctor of the same city, when he had given in his name for baptism, and had been prohibited the day before his baptism from being baptized that year by black woolly-haired boys who appeared to him in his dreams, and whom he understood to be devils, and when, though they trod on his feet, and inflicted the acutest pain he had ever yet experienced, he refused to obey them, but overcame them, and would not defer being washed in the laver of regeneration, was relieved in the very act of baptism, not only of the extraordinary pain he was tortured with, but also of the disease itself, so that, though he lived a long time afterwards, he never suffered from gout; and yet who knows of this miracle? We, however, do know it, and so, too, do the small number of brethren who were in the neighbourhood, and to whose ears it might come.

An old comedian of Curubis[1] was cured at baptism not only of paralysis, but also of hernia, and, being delivered from both afflictions, came up out of the font of regeneration as if he had had nothing wrong with his body. Who outside of Curubis knows of this, or who but a very few who might hear it elsewhere? But we, when we heard of it, made the man come to Carthage, by order of the holy bishop Aurelius, although we had already ascertained the fact on the information of persons whose word we could not doubt.

Hesperius, of a tribunitian family, and a neighbour of our own, has a farm called Zubedi in the Fussalian district;[2] and, finding that his family, his cattle, and his servants were suffering from the malice of evil spirits, he asked our presbyters, during my absence, that one of them would go with him and banish the spirits by his prayers. One went, offered there the sacrifice of the body of Christ, praying with all his might that that vexation might cease. It did cease forthwith, through God's mercy. Now he had received from a friend of his own some holy earth brought from Jerusalem, where Christ, having been buried, rose again the third day. This earth he had hung up in his bedroom to preserve himself from harm. But when his house was purged of that demoniacal invasion, he began to consider what should be done with the earth; for his reverence for it made him unwilling to have it any longer in his bedroom. It so happened that I and Maximinus bishop of Synita, and then my colleague, were in the neighbourhood. Hesperius asked us to visit him, and we did so. When he had related all the circumstances, he begged that the earth might be buried somewhere, and that the spot should be made a place of prayer where Christians might assemble for the worship of God. We made no objection: it was done as he desired. There was in that neighbourhood a young countryman who was paralytic, who, when he heard of this, begged his parents to take him without delay to that holy place. When he had been brought there, he prayed, and forthwith went away on his own feet perfectly cured.

There is a country-seat called Victoriana, less than thirty miles from Hippo-Regius. At it there is a monument to the Milanese martyrs, Protasius and Gervasius. Thither a young man was carried, who, when he was watering his horse one summer day at noon in a pool of a river, had been taken possession of by a devil. As he lay at

---

[1] A town near Carthage.
[2] Near Hippo.

the monument, near death, or even quite like a dead person, the lady of the manor, with her maids and religious attendants, entered the place for evening prayer and praise, as her custom was, and they began to sing hymns. At this sound the young man, as if electrified, was thoroughly aroused, and with frightful screaming seized the altar, and held it as if he did not dare or were not able to let it go, and as if he were fixed or tied to it; and the devil in him, with loud lamentation, besought that he might be spared, and confessed where and when and how he took possession of the youth. At last, declaring that he would go out of him, he named one by one the parts of his body which he threatened to mutilate as he went out and with these words he departed from the man. But his eye, falling out on his cheek, hung by a slender vein as by a root, and the whole of the pupil which had been black became white. When this was witnessed by those present (others too had now gathered to his cries, and had all joined in prayer for him), although they were delighted that he had recovered his sanity of mind, yet, on the other hand, they were grieved about his eye, and said he should seek medical advice. But his sister's husband, who had brought him there, said, "God, who has banished the devil, is able to restore his eye at the prayers of His saints." Therewith he replaced the eye that was fallen out and hanging, and bound it in its place with his handkerchief as well as he could, and advised him not to loose the bandage for seven days. When he did so, he found it quite healthy. Others also were cured there, but of them it were tedious to speak.

I know that a young woman of Hippo was immediately dispossessed of a devil, on anointing herself with oil, mixed with the tears of the presbyter who had been praying for her. I know also that a bishop once prayed for a demoniac young man whom he never saw, and that he was cured on the spot.

There was a fellow-townsman of ours at Hippo, Florentius, an old man, religious and poor, who supported himself as a tailor. Having lost his coat, and not having means to buy another, he prayed to the Twenty Martyrs, who have a very celebrated memorial shrine in our town, begging in a distinct voice that he might be clothed. Some scoffing young men, who happened to be present, heard him, and followed him with their sarcasm as he went away, as if he had asked the martyrs for fifty pence to buy a coat. But he, walking on in silence, saw on the shore a great fish, gasping as if just cast up, and

having secured it with the good-natured assistance of the youths, he sold it for curing to a cook of the name of Catosus, a good Christian man, telling him how he had come by it, and receiving for it three hundred pence, which he laid out in wool, that his wife might exercise her skill upon, and make into a coat for him. But, on cutting up the fish, the cook found a gold ring in its belly; and forthwith, moved with compassion, and influenced, too, by religious fear, gave it up to the man, saying, "See how the Twenty Martyrs have clothed you."

When the bishop Projectus was bringing the relics of the most glorious martyr Stephen to the waters of Tibilis, a great concourse of people came to meet him at the shrine. There a blind woman entreated that she might be led to the bishop who was carrying the relics. He gave her the flowers he was carrying. She took them, applied them to her eyes, and forthwith saw. Those who were present were astounded, while she, with every expression of joy, preceded them, pursuing her way without further need of a guide.

Lucillus bishop of Sinita, in the neighbourhood of the colonial town of Hippo, was carrying in procession some relics of the same martyr, which had been deposited in the castle of Sinita. A fistula under which he had long laboured, and which his private physician was watching an opportunity to cut, was suddenly cured by the mere carrying of that sacred fardel—at least, afterwards there was no trace of it in his body.

Eucharius, a Spanish priest, residing at Calama, was for a long time a sufferer from stone. By the relics of the same martyr, which the bishop Possidius brought him, he was cured. Afterwards the same priest, sinking under another disease, was lying dead, and already they were binding his hands. By the succour of the same martyr he was raised to life, the priest's cloak having been brought from the oratory and laid upon the corpse.

There was there an old nobleman named Martial, who had a great aversion to the Christian religion, but whose daughter was a Christian, while her husband had been baptized that same year. When he was ill, they besought him with tears and prayers to become a Christian, but he positively refused, and dismissed them from his presence in a storm of indignation. It occurred to the son-in-law to go to the oratory of St. Stephen, and there pray for him with all earnestness that God might give him a right mind, so that he should not delay believing in Christ. This he did with great groaning and tears and the burning fervour of sincere piety; then, as he left the place, he took some of the flowers that were lying there and, as it was already night, laid them by his father's head, who so slept. And lo! before dawn, he cries out for some one to run for the bishop; but he happened at that time to be with me at Hippo. So when he had heard that he was from home, he asked the presbyters to come. They came. To the joy and amazement of all, he declared that he believed, and he was baptized. As long as he remained in life, these words were ever on his lips: "Christ, receive my spirit," though he was not aware that these were the last words of the most blessed Stephen when he was stoned by the Jews. They were his last words also, for not long after he himself also gave up the ghost.

There, too, by the same martyr, two men, one a citizen, the other a stranger, were cured of gout; but while the citizen was absolutely cured, the stranger was only informed what he should apply when the pain returned; and when he followed this advice, the pain was at once relieved.

Audurus is the name of an estate, where there is a church that contains a memorial shrine of the martyr Stephen. It happened that, as a little boy was playing in the court, the oxen drawing a wagon went out of the track and crushed him with the wheel, so that immediately he seemed at his last gasp. His mother snatched him up, and laid him at the shrine, and not only did he revive, but also appeared uninjured.

A religious female, who lived at Caspalium, a neighbouring estate, when she was so ill as to be despaired of, had her dress brought to this shrine, but before it was brought back she was gone. However, her parents wrapped her corpse in the dress, and, her breath returning, she became quite well.

At Hippo a Syrian called Bassus was praying at the relics of the same martyr for his daughter, who was dangerously ill. He too had brought her dress with him to the shrine. But as he prayed, behold, his servants ran from the house to tell him she was dead. His friends, however, intercepted them, and forbade them to tell him, lest he should bewail her in public. And when he had returned to his house, which was already ringing with the lamentations of his family and had thrown on his daughter's body the dress he was carrying, she was restored to life.

There, too, the son of a man, Irenæus, one of our tax-gatherers, took ill and died. And while his body was lying lifeless, and the last rites were being prepared, amidst the weeping and mourning of all, one of the friends who were consoling the father suggested that the body should be anointed with the oil of the same martyr. It was done, and he revived.

Likewise Eleusinus, a man of tribunitian rank among us, laid his infant son, who had died, on the shrine of the martyr, which is in the suburb where he lived, and, after prayer, which he poured out there with many tears, he took up his child alive.

What am I to do? I am so pressed by the promise of finishing this work, that I cannot record all the miracles I know; and doubtless several of our adherents, when they read what I have narrated, will regret that I have omitted so many which they, as well as I, certainly know. Even now I beg these persons to excuse me, and to consider how long it would take me to relate all those miracles, which the necessity of finishing the work I have undertaken forces me to omit. For were I to be silent of all others, and to record exclusively the miracles of healing which were wrought in the district of Calama and of Hippo by means of this martyr—I mean the most glorious Stephen—they would fill many volumes; and yet all even of these could not be collected, but only those of which narratives have been written for public recital. For when I saw, in our own times, frequent signs of the presence of divine powers similar to those which had been given of old, I desired that narratives might be written, judging that the multitude should not remain ignorant of these things. It is not yet two years since these relics were first brought to Hippo-Regius, and though many of the miracles which have been wrought by it have not, as I have the most certain means of knowing, been recorded, those which have been published amount to almost seventy at the hour at which I write. But at Calama, where these relics have been for a longer time, and where more of the miracles were narrated for public information, there are incomparably more.

At Uzali, too, a colony near Utica, many signal miracles were, to my knowledge, wrought by the same martyr, whose relics had found a place there by direction of the bishop Evodius, long before we had them at Hippo. But there the custom of publishing narratives does not obtain, or, I should say, did not obtain, for possibly it may now have been begun. For, when I was there recently, a woman of rank, Petronia, had been miraculously cured of a serious illness of long standing, in which all medical appliances had failed, and, with the consent of the above-named bishop of the place, I exhorted her to publish an account of it that might be read to the people. She most promptly obeyed, and inserted in her narrative a circumstance which I cannot omit to mention, though I am compelled to hasten on to the subjects which this work requires me to treat. She said that she had been persuaded by a Jew to wear next her skin, under all her clothes, a hair girdle, and on this girdle a ring, which, instead of a gem, had a stone which had been found in the kidneys of an ox. Girt with this charm, she was making her way to the threshold of the holy martyr. But, after leaving Carthage, and when she had been lodging in her own demesne on the river Bagrada, and was now rising to continue her journey, she saw her ring lying before her feet. In great surprise she examined the hair girdle, and when she found it bound, as it had been, quite firmly with knots, she conjectured that the ring had been worn through and dropped off; but when she found that the ring was itself also perfectly whole, she presumed that by this great miracle she had received somehow a pledge of her cure, whereupon she untied the girdle, and cast it into the river, and the ring along with it. This is not credited by those who do not believe either that the Lord Jesus Christ came forth from His mother's womb without destroying her virginity and entered among His disciples when the doors were shut; but let them make strict inquiry into this miracle, and if they find it true, let them believe those others. The lady is of distinction, nobly born, married to a nobleman. She resides at Carthage. The city is distinguished, the person is distinguished, so that they who make inquiries cannot fail to find satisfaction. Certainly the martyr himself, by whose prayers she was healed, believed on the Son of her who remained a virgin; on Him Who came in among the disciples when the doors were shut, in fine—and to this tends all that we have been retailing—on Him Who ascended into heaven with the flesh in which He had risen; and it is because he laid down his life for this faith that such miracles were done by his means.

Even now, therefore, many miracles are wrought, the same God Who wrought those we read of still performing them, by whom He will and as He will; but they are not as well known, nor are they beaten into the memory, like gravel, by frequent reading, so that they cannot fall out of mind. For even where, as is now done among ourselves, care is taken that the pamphlets of those who receive benefit be read publicly, yet those who are present hear the narrative but once, and many are absent; and so it comes to pass that even those who are present forget in a few days what they heard, and scarcely one of them can be found who will tell what he heard to one who he knows was not present.

One miracle was wrought among ourselves, which, though no greater than those I have mentioned, was yet so signal and conspicuous, that I suppose there is no inhabitant of Hippo who did not either see or hear of it, none who could possibly forget it. There were seven brothers and three sisters of a noble family of the Cappadocian Cæsarea, who were cursed by their mother, a new-made widow, on account of some wrong they had done her, and which she bitterly resented, and who were visited with so severe a punishment from Heaven, that all of them were seized with a hideous shaking in all their limbs. Unable, while presenting this loathsome appearance, to endure the eyes of their fellow-citizens, they wandered over almost the whole Roman world, each following his own direction. Two of them came to Hippo, a brother and a sister, Paulus and Palladia, already known in many other places by the fame of their wretched lot. Now it was about fifteen days before Easter when they came, and they came daily to church, and specially to the relics of the most glorious Stephen, praying that God might now be appeased, and restore their former health. There, and wherever they went, they attracted the attention of everyone. Some who had seen them elsewhere, and knew the cause of their trembling, told others as occasion offered. Easter arrived, and on the Lord's day, in the morning, when there was now a large crowd present, and the young man was holding the bars of the holy place where the relics were, and praying, suddenly he fell down, and lay precisely as if asleep, but not trembling as he was wont to do even in sleep. All present were astonished. Some were alarmed, some were moved with pity; and while some were for lifting him up, others prevented them, and said they should rather wait and see what would result. And behold! he rose up, and trembled no more, for he was healed, and stood quite well, scanning those who were scanning him. Who then refrained himself from praising God? The whole church was filled with the voices of those who were shouting and congratulating him. Then they came running to me, where I was sitting ready to come into the church. One after another they throng in, the last comer telling me as news what the first had told me already; and while I rejoiced and inwardly gave God thanks, the young man himself also enters, with a number of others, falls at my knees, is raised up to receive my kiss. We go in to the congregation: the church was full, and ringing with the shouts of joy, "Thanks to God! Praised be God!" every one joining and shouting on all sides, "I have healed the people," and then with still louder voice shouting again. Silence being at last obtained, the customary lessons of the divine Scriptures were read. And when I came to my sermon, I made a few remarks suitable to the occasion and the happy and joyful feeling, not desiring them to listen to me, but rather to consider the eloquence of God in this divine work. The man dined with us, and gave us a careful account of his own, his mother's, and his family's calamity. Accordingly, on the following day, after delivering my sermon, I promised that next day I would read his narrative to the people. And when I did so, the third day after Easter Sunday, I made the brother and sister both stand on the steps of the raised place from which I used to speak; and while they stood there their pamphlet was read. The whole congregation, men and women alike, saw the one standing without any unnatural movement, the other trembling in all her limbs; so that those who had not before seen the man himself saw in his sister what the divine compassion had removed from him. In him they saw matter of congratulation, in her subject for prayer. Meanwhile, their pamphlet being finished, I instructed them to withdraw from the gaze of the people; and I had begun to discuss the whole matter somewhat more carefully, when lo! as I was proceeding, other voices are heard from the tomb of the martyr, shouting new congratulations. My audience turned round, and began to run to the tomb. The young woman, when she had come down from the steps where she had been standing, went to pray at the holy relics, and no sooner had she touched the bars than she, in the same way as her brother, collapsed, as if falling asleep, and rose up cured. While, then, we were asking what had happened, and what occasioned this noise of joy, they came into the basilica where we were, leading her from the martyr's tomb in perfect health. Then, indeed, such a shout of wonder rose from men and women together, that the exclamations and the tears seemed like never to come to an end. She was led to the place where she had a little before stood trembling. They now rejoiced that she was like her brother, as before they had mourned that she remained unlike him; and as they had not yet uttered their prayers in her behalf, they perceived that their intention of doing so had been speedily heard. They shouted

God's praises without words, but with such a noise that our ears could scarcely bear it. What was there in the hearts of these exultant people but the faith of Christ, for which Stephen had shed his blood?

CHAP. 9. *That all the miracles which are done by means of the martyrs in the name of Christ testify to that faith which the martyrs had in Christ*

To what do these miracles witness, but to this faith which preaches Christ risen in the flesh, and ascended with the same into heaven? For the martyrs themselves were martyrs, that is to say, witnesses of this faith, drawing upon themselves by their testimony the hatred of the world, and conquering the world not by resisting it, but by dying. For this faith they died, and can now ask these benefits from the Lord in Whose name they were slain. For this faith their marvellous constancy was exercised, so that in these miracles great power was manifested as the result. For if the resurrection of the flesh to eternal life had not taken place in Christ, and were not to be accomplished in His people, as predicted by Christ, or by the prophets who foretold that Christ was to come, why do the martyrs who were slain for this faith which proclaims the resurrection possess such power? For whether God Himself wrought these miracles by that wonderful manner of working by which, though Himself eternal, He produces effects in time; or whether He wrought them by servants, and if so, whether He made use of the spirits of martyrs as He uses men who are still in the body, or effects all these marvels by means of angels, over whom He exerts an invisible, immutable, incorporeal sway, so that what is said to be done by the martyrs is done not by their operation, but only by their prayer and request; or whether, finally, some things are done in one way, others in another, and so that man cannot at all comprehend them—nevertheless these miracles attest this faith which preaches the resurrection of the flesh to eternal life.

CHAP. 10. *That the martyrs who obtain many miracles in order that the true God may be worshipped, are worthy of much greater honour than the demons, who do some marvels that they themselves may be supposed to be God*

Here perhaps our adversaries will say that their gods also have done some wonderful things, if now they begin to compare their gods to our dead men. Or will they also say that they have gods taken from among dead men, such as Hercules, Romulus, and many others whom they fancy to have been received into the number of the gods? But our martyrs are not our gods; for we know that the martyrs and we have both but one God, and that the same. Nor yet are the miracles which they maintain to have been done by means of their temples at all comparable to those which are done by the tombs of our martyrs. If they seem similar, their gods have been defeated by our martyrs as Pharaoh's magi were by Moses. In reality, the demons wrought these marvels with the same impure pride with which they aspired to be the gods of the nations; but the martyrs do these wonders, or rather God does them while they pray and assist, in order that an impulse may be given to the faith by which we believe that they are not our gods, but have, together with ourselves, one God. In fine, they built temples to these gods of theirs, and set up altars, and ordained priests, and appointed sacrifices; but to our martyrs we build, not temples as if they were gods, but monuments as to dead men whose spirits live with God. Neither do we erect altars at these monuments that we may sacrifice to the martyrs, but to the one God of the martyrs and of ourselves; and in this sacrifice they are named in their own place and rank as men of God who conquered the world by confessing Him, but they are not invoked by the sacrificing priest. For it is to God, not to them, he sacrifices, though he sacrifices at their monument; for he is God's priest, not theirs. The sacrifice itself, too, is the body of Christ, which is not offered to them, because they themselves are this body. Which then can more readily be believed to work miracles? They who wish themselves to be reckoned gods by those on whom they work miracles, or those whose sole object in working any miracle is to induce faith in God, and in Christ also as God? They who wished to turn even their crimes into sacred rites, or those who are unwilling that even their own praises be consecrated and seek that everything for which they are justly praised be ascribed to the glory of Him in Whom they are praised? For in the Lord their souls are praised. Let us therefore believe those who both speak the truth and work wonders. For by speaking the truth they suffered, and so won the power of working wonders. And the leading truth they professed is that Christ rose from the dead, and first showed in His own flesh the immortality of the resurrection which He promised should be ours, either in the beginning of the world to come, or in the end of this world.

CHAP. 11. *Against the Platonists, who argue from the physical weight of the elements that an earthly body cannot inhabit heaven*

But against this great gift of God, these reasoners, "whose thoughts the Lord knows that they are vain"[1] bring arguments from the weights of the elements; for they have been taught by their master Plato that the two greatest elements of the world, and the furthest removed from one another, are coupled and united by the two intermediate, air and water. And consequently they say, since the earth is the first of the elements, beginning from the base of the series, the second the water above the earth, the third the air above the water, the fourth the heaven above the air, it follows that a body of earth cannot live in the heaven; for each element is poised by its own weight so as to preserve its own place and rank. Behold with what arguments human infirmity, possessed with vanity, contradicts the omnipotence of God! What, then, do so many earthly bodies do in the air, since the air is the third element from the earth? Unless perhaps He Who has granted to the earthly bodies of birds that they be carried through the air by the lightness of feathers and wings, has not been able to confer upon the bodies of men made immortal the power to abide in the highest heaven. The earthly animals, too, which cannot fly, among which are men, ought on these terms to live under the earth, as fishes, which are the animals of the water, live under the water. Why, then, can an animal of earth not live in the second element, that is, in water, while it can in the third? Why, though it belongs to the earth, is it forthwith suffocated if it is forced to live in the second element next above earth, while it lives in the third, and cannot live out of it? Is there a mistake here in the order of the elements, or is not the mistake rather in their reasonings, and not in the nature of things? I will not repeat what I said in the thirteenth book,[2] that many earthly bodies, though heavy like lead, receive from the workman's hand a form which enables them to swim in water; and yet it is denied that the omnipotent Worker can confer on the human body a property which shall enable it to pass into heaven and dwell there.

But against what I have formerly said they can find nothing to say, even though they introduce and make the most of this order of the elements in which they confide. For if the order be that the earth is first, the water second, the

[1] Ps. 94. 11   [2] Chap. 18.

air third, the heaven fourth, then the soul is above all. For Aristotle said that the soul was a fifth body, while Plato denied that it was a body at all. If it were a fifth body, then certainly it would be above the rest; and if it is not a body at all, so much the more does it rise above all. What, then, does it do in an earthly body? What does this soul, which is finer than all else, do in such a mass of matter as this? What does the lightest of substances do in this ponderosity? this swiftest substance in such sluggishness? Will not the body be raised to heaven by virtue of so excellent a nature as this? and if now earthly bodies can retain the souls below, shall not the souls be one day able to raise the earthly bodies above?

If we pass now to their miracles which they oppose to our martyrs as wrought by their gods, shall not even these be found to make for us, and help out our argument? For if any of the miracles of their gods are great, certainly that is a great one which Varro mentions of a vestal virgin, who, when she was endangered by a false accusation of unchastity, filled a sieve with water from the Tiber, and carried it to her judges without any part of it leaking. Who kept the weight of water in the sieve? Who prevented any drop from falling from it through so many open holes? They will answer, "Some god or some demon." If a god, is he greater than the God Who made the world? If a demon, is he mightier than an angel who serves the God by Whom the world was made? If, then, a lesser god, angel, or demon could so sustain the weight of this liquid element that the water might seem to have changed its nature, shall not Almighty God, Who Himself created all the elements, be able to eliminate from the earthly body its heaviness, so that the quickened body shall dwell in whatever element the quickening spirit pleases?

Then, again, since they give the air a middle place between the fire above and the water beneath, how is it that we often find it between water and water, and between the water and the earth? For what do they make of those watery clouds, between which and the seas air is constantly found intervening? I should like to know by what weight and order of the elements it comes to pass that very violent and stormy torrents are suspended in the clouds above the earth before they rush along upon the earth under the air. In fine, why is it that throughout the whole globe the air is between the highest heaven and the earth, if its place is between the sky and the water, as the place of the water is between the sky and the earth?

Finally, if the order of the elements is so disposed that, as Plato thinks, the two extremes, fire and earth, are united by the two means, air and water, and that the fire occupies the highest part of the sky, and the earth the lowest part, or as it were the foundation of the world, and that therefore earth cannot be in the heavens, how is fire in the earth? For, according to this reasoning, these two elements, earth and fire, ought to be so restricted to their own places, the highest and the lowest, that neither the lowest can rise to the place of the highest, nor the highest sink to that of the lowest. Thus, as they think that no particle of earth is or shall ever be in the sky so we ought to see no particle of fire on the earth. But the fact is that it exists to such an extent, not only on but even under the earth, that the tops of mountains vomit it forth; besides that we see it to exist on earth for human uses, and even to be produced from the earth, since it is kindled from wood and stones, which are without doubt earthly bodies. But that fire, they say, is tranquil, pure, harmless, eternal; but this fire is turbid, smoky, corruptible, and corrupting. But it does not corrupt the mountains and caverns of the earth in which it rages continually. But grant that the earthly fire is so unlike the other as to suit its earthly position, why then do they object to our believing that the nature of earthly bodies shall some day be made incorruptible and fit for the sky, even as now fire is corruptible and suited to the earth? They therefore adduce from their weights and order of the elements nothing from which they can prove that it is impossible for Almighty God to make our bodies such that they can dwell in the skies.

CHAP. 12. *Against the calumnies with which unbelievers throw ridicule upon the Christian faith in the resurrection of the flesh*

But their way is to feign a scrupulous anxiety in investigating this question, and to cast ridicule on our faith in the resurrection of the body, by asking, "Whether abortions shall rise?" And as the Lord says, "Verily I say unto you, not a hair of your head shall perish,"[1] shall all bodies have an equal stature and strength, or shall there be differences in size? For if there is to be equality, where shall those abortions, supposing that they rise again, get that bulk which they had not here? Or if they shall not rise be-

[1]Luke, 21. 18.

cause they were not born but cast out, they raise the same question about children who have died in childhood, asking us whence they get the stature which we see they had not here; for we will not say that those who have been not only born, but born again, shall not rise again. Then, further, they ask of what size these equal bodies shall be. For if all shall be as tall and large as were the tallest and largest in this world, they ask us how it is that not only children but many full-grown persons shall receive what they here did not possess, if each one is to receive what he had here. And if the saying of the apostle, that we are all to come to the "measure of the age of the fullness of Christ,"[1] or that other saying, "Whom He predestinated to be conformed to the image of His Son,"[2] is to be understood to mean that the stature and size of Christ's body shall be the measure of the bodies of all those who shall be in His kingdom, then, say they, the size and height of many must be diminished; and if so much of the bodily frame itself be lost, what becomes of the saying, "Not a hair of your head shall perish"? Besides, it might be asked regarding the hair itself, whether all that the barber has cut off shall be restored? And if it is to be restored, who would not shrink from such deformity? For as the same restoration will be made of what has been pared off the nails, much will be replaced on the body which a regard for its appearance had cut off. And where, then, will be its beauty, which assuredly ought to be much greater in that immortal condition than it could be in this corruptible state? On the other hand, if such things are not restored to the body, they must perish; how, then, they say, shall not a hair of the head perish? In like manner they reason about fatness and leanness; for if all are to be equal, then certainly there shall not be some fat, others lean. Some, therefore, shall gain, others lose something. Consequently there will not be a simple restoration of what formerly existed, but, on the one hand, an addition of what had no existence, and, on the other, a loss of what did before exist.

The difficulties, too, about the corruption and dissolution of dead bodies—that one is turned into dust, while another evaporates into the air; that some are devoured by beasts, some by fire, while some perish by shipwreck or by drowning in one shape or other, so that their bodies decay into liquid—these difficulties give them immoderate alarm, and they believe that all those dissolved elements cannot be gathered

[1] Eph. 4. 13.   [2] Rom. 8. 29.

again and reconstructed into a body. They also make eager use of all the deformities and blemishes which either accident or birth has produced, and accordingly, with horror and derision, cite monstrous births and ask if every deformity will be preserved in the resurrection. For if we say that no such thing shall be reproduced in the body of a man, they suppose that they confute us by citing the marks of the wounds which we assert were found in the risen body of the Lord Christ. But of all these the most difficult question is, into whose body that flesh shall return which has been eaten and assimilated by another man constrained by hunger to use it so; for it has been converted into the flesh of the man who used it as his nutriment, and it filled up those losses of flesh which famine had produced. For the sake, then, of ridiculing the resurrection, they ask, "Shall this return to the man whose flesh it first was, or to him whose flesh it afterwards became?" And thus, too, they seek to give promise to the human soul of alternations of true misery and false happiness, in accordance with Plato's theory; or, in accordance with Porphyry's, that, after many transmigrations into different bodies, it ends its miseries, and never more returns to them, not, however, by obtaining an immortal body, but by escaping from every kind of body.

CHAP. 13. *Whether abortions, if they are numbered among the dead, shall not also have a part in the resurrection*

To these objections, then, of our adversaries which I have thus detailed, I will now reply, trusting that God will mercifully assist my endeavours. That abortions, which, even supposing they were alive in the womb, did also die there, shall rise again, I make bold neither to affirm nor to deny, although I fail to see why, if they are not excluded from the number of the dead, they should not attain to the resurrection of the dead. For either all the dead shall not rise, and there will be to all eternity some souls without bodies though they once had them—only in their mother's womb, indeed; or, if all human souls shall receive again the bodies which they had wherever they lived, and which they left when they died, then I do not see how I can say that even those who died in their mother's womb shall have no resurrection. But whichever of these opinions any one may adopt concerning them, we must at least apply to them, if they rise again, all that we have to say of infants who have been born.

CHAP. 14. *Whether infants shall rise in that body which they would have had had they grown up*

What, then, are we to say of infants, if not that they will not rise in that diminutive body in which they died, but shall receive by the marvellous and rapid operation of God that body which time by a slower process would have given them? For in the Lord's words, where He says, "Not a hair of your head shall perish,"[1] it is asserted that nothing which was possessed shall be wanting; but it is not said that nothing which was not possessed shall be given. To the dead infant there was wanting the perfect stature of its body; for even the perfect infant lacks the perfection of bodily size, being capable of further growth. This perfect stature is, in a sense, so possessed by all that they are conceived and born with it—that is, they have it potentially, though not yet in actual bulk; just as all the members of the body are potentially in the seed, though, even after the child is born, some of them, the teeth for example, may be wanting. In this seminal principle of every substance, there seems to be, as it were, the beginning of everything which does not yet exist, or rather does not appear, but which in process of time will come into being, or rather into sight. In this, therefore, the child who is to be tall or short is already tall or short. And in the resurrection of the body, we need, for the same reason, fear no bodily loss; for though all should be of equal size, and reach gigantic proportions, lest the men who were largest here should lose anything of their bulk and it should perish, in contradiction to the words of Christ, Who said that not a hair of their head should perish, yet why should there lack the means by which that wonderful Worker should make such additions, seeing that He is the Creator, Who Himself created all things out of nothing?

CHAP. 15. *Whether the bodies of all the dead shall rise the same size as the Lord's body*

It is certain that Christ rose in the same bodily stature in which He died, and that it is wrong to say that, when the general resurrection shall have arrived, His body shall, for the sake of equalling the tallest, assume proportions which it had not when He appeared to the disciples in the figure with which they were familiar. But if we say that even the bodies of taller men are to be reduced to the size of the Lord's body, there

[1]Luke, 21. 18.

will be a great loss in many bodies, though He promised that not a hair of their head should perish. It remains, therefore, that we conclude that every man shall receive his own size which he had in youth, though he died an old man, or which he would have had, supposing he died before his prime. As for what the apostle said of the measure of the age of the fullness of Christ, we must either understand him to refer to something else, viz., to the fact that the measure of Christ will be completed when all the members among the Christian communities are added to the Head; or if we are to refer it to the resurrection of the body, the meaning is that all shall rise neither beyond nor under youth, but in that vigour and age to which we know that Christ had arrived. For even the world's wisest men have fixed the bloom of youth at about the age of thirty; and when this period has been passed, the man begins to decline towards the defective and duller period of old age. And therefore the apostle did not speak of the measure of the body, nor of the measure of the stature but of "the measure of the age of the fullness of Christ."

CHAP. 16. *What is meant by the conforming of the saints to the image of the Son of God*

Then, again, these words, "Predestinate to be conformed to the image of the Son of God,"[2] may be understood of the inner man. So in another place He says to us, "Be not conformed to this world, but be ye transformed in the renewing of your mind."[3] In so far, then, as we are transformed so as not to be conformed to the world, we are conformed to the Son of God. It may also be understood thus, that as He was conformed to us by assuming mortality, we shall be conformed to Him by immortality; and this indeed is connected with the resurrection of the body. But if we are also taught in these words what form our bodies shall rise in, as the measure we spoke of before, so also this conformity is to be understood not of size, but of age. Accordingly all shall rise in the stature they either had attained or would have attained had they lived to their prime, although it will be no great disadvantage even if the form of the body be infantine or aged, while no infirmity shall remain in the mind nor in the body itself. So that even if any one contends that every person will rise again in the same bodily form in which he died, we need not spend much labour in disputing with him.

[2]Rom. 8. 29.   [3]Rom. 12. 2.

CHAP. 17. *Whether the bodies of women shall retain their own sex in the resurrection*

From the words, "Till we all come to a perfect man, to the measure of the age of the fullness of Christ," [1] and from the words, "Conformed to the image of the Son of God," [2] some conclude that women shall not rise women, but that all shall be men, because God made man only of earth and woman of the man. For my part, they seem to be wiser who make no doubt that both sexes shall rise. For there shall be no lust, which is now the cause of confusion. For before they sinned, the man and the woman were naked and were not ashamed. From those bodies, then, vice shall be withdrawn, while nature shall be preserved. And the sex of woman is not a vice, but nature. It shall then indeed be superior to carnal intercourse and child-bearing; nevertheless the female members shall remain adapted not to the old uses, but to a new beauty, which, so far from provoking lust, now extinct, shall excite praise to the wisdom and clemency of God, who both made what was not and delivered from corruption what He made. For at the beginning of the human race the woman was made of a rib taken from the side of the man while he slept; for it seemed fit that even then Christ and His Church should be foreshadowed in this event. For that sleep of the man was the death of Christ, whose side, as He hung lifeless upon the cross, was pierced with a spear, and there flowed from it blood and water, and these we know to be the sacraments by which the Church is "built up." For Scripture used this very word, not saying "He formed" or "framed," but "built her up into a woman"; [3] whence also the apostle speaks of the *edification* of the body of Christ, [4] which is the Church. The woman, therefore, is a creature of God even as the man; but by her creation from man unity is commended; and the manner of her creation prefigured, as has been said, Christ and the Church. He, then, who created both sexes will restore both. Jesus Himself also, when asked by the Sadducees, who denied the resurrection, which of the seven brothers should have to wife the woman whom all in succession had taken to raise up seed to their brother, as the law enjoined, says, "Ye do err, not knowing the Scriptures nor the power of God." [5] And though it was a fit opportunity for His saying, "She about whom you make inquiries shall herself be a man, and not a woman," He said nothing of the kind; but "In the resurrection they neither marry nor are given in marriage, but are as the angels of God in heaven." [6] They shall be equal to the angels in immortality and happiness, not in flesh, nor in resurrection, which the angels did not need, because they could not die. The Lord then denied that there would be in the resurrection, not women, but marriages; and He uttered this denial in circumstances in which the question mooted would have been more easily and speedily solved by denying that the female sex would exist, if this had in truth been foreknown by Him. But, indeed, He even affirmed that the sex should exist by saying, "They shall not be given in marriage," which can only apply to females; "Neither shall they marry," which applies to males. There shall therefore be those who are in this world accustomed to marry and be given in marriage, only they shall there make no such marriages.

CHAP. 18. *Of the perfect man, that is, Christ; and of His body, that is, the Church, which is his fullness*

To understand what the apostle means when he says that we shall all come to a perfect man, we must consider the connection of the whole passage, which runs thus: "He that descended is the same also that ascended up far above all heavens, that He might fill all things. And He gave some, apostles; and some, prophets; and some, evangelists; and some, pastors and teachers; for the perfecting of the saints, for the work of the ministry, for the edifying of the body of Christ: till we all come to the unity of the faith and knowledge of the Son of God, to a perfect man, to the measure of the age of the fullness of Christ: that we henceforth be no more children, tossed and carried about with every wind of doctrine, by the sleight of men, and cunning craftiness, whereby they lie in wait to deceive; but, speaking the truth in love, may grow up in Him in all things, which is the Head, even Christ: from Whom the whole body fitly joined together and compacted by that which every joint supplieth, according to the effectual working in the measure of every part, maketh increase of the body, unto the edifying of itself in love." [7] Behold what the perfect man is—the head and the body, which is made up of all the members, which in their own time shall be perfected. But new additions are daily being made to this body while the Church is being built up,

[1]Eph. 4. 13.　　[2]Rom. 8. 29.　　[3]Gen. 2. 22.
[4]Eph. 4. 12.　　[5]Matt. 22. 29.

[6]Matt. 22. 30.　　[7]Eph. 4. 10–16.

to which it is said, "Ye are the body of Christ and His members";[1] and again, "For His body's sake," he says, "which is the Church";[2] and again, "We being many are one head, one body."[3] It is of the edification of this body that it is here, too, said, "For the perfecting of the saints, for the work of the ministry, for the edification of the body of Christ"; and then that passage of which we are now speaking is added, "Till we all come to the unity of the faith and knowledge of the Son of God, to a perfect man, to the measure of the age of the fullness of Christ," and so on. And he shows of what body we are to understand this to be the measure, when he says, "That we may grow up into Him in all things, which is the Head, even Christ: from Whom the whole body fitly joined together and compacted by that which every joint supplieth, according to the effectual working in the measure of every part." As, therefore, there is a measure of every part, so there is a measure of the fullness of the whole body which is made up of all its parts, and it is of this measure it is said, "To the measure of the age of the fullness of Christ." This fullness he spoke of also in the place where he says of Christ, "And gave Him to be the Head over all things to the Church, which is His body, the fullness of Him that filleth all in all."[4] But even if this should be referred to the form in which each one shall rise, what should hinder us from applying to the woman what is expressly said of the man, understanding both sexes to be included under the general term "man"? For certainly in the saying, "Blessed is he who feareth the Lord,"[5] women also who fear the Lord are included.

CHAP. 19. *That all bodily blemishes which mar human beauty in this life shall be removed in the resurrection, the natural substance of the body remaining, but the quality and quantity of it being altered so as to produce beauty*

What am I to say now about the hair and nails? Once it is understood that no part of the body shall so perish as to produce deformity in the body, it is at the same time understood that such things as would have produced a deformity by their excessive proportions shall be added to the total bulk of the body, not to parts in which the beauty of the proportion would thus be marred. Just as if, after making a vessel of clay, one wished to make it over again of the same clay, it would not be necessary that the same portion of the clay which had formed the handle should again form the new handle, or that what had formed the bottom should again do so, but only that the whole clay should go to make up the whole new vessel, and that no part of it should be left unused. Wherefore, if the hair that has been cropped and the nails that have been cut would cause a deformity were they to be restored to their places, they shall not be restored; and yet no one will lose these parts at the resurrection, for they shall be changed into the same flesh, their substance being so altered as to preserve the proportion of the various parts of the body. However, what our Lord said, "Not a hair of your head shall perish," might more suitably be interpreted of the number, and not of the length of the hairs, as He elsewhere says, "The hairs of your head are all numbered."[6] Nor would I say this because I suppose that any part naturally belonging to the body can perish, but that whatever deformity was in it and served to exhibit the penal condition in which we mortals are, should be restored in such a way that, while the substance is entirely preserved, the deformity shall perish. For if even a human workman, who has, for some reason, made a deformed statue, can recast it and make it very beautiful, and this without suffering any part of the substance, but only the deformity to be lost—if he can, for example, remove some unbecoming or disproportionate part, not by cutting off and separating this part from the whole, but by so breaking down and mixing up the whole as to get rid of the blemish without diminishing the quantity of his material—shall we not think as highly of the almighty Worker? Shall He not be able to remove and abolish all deformities of the human body, whether common ones or rare and monstrous, which, though in keeping with this miserable life, are yet not to be thought of in connection with that future blessedness; and shall He not be able so to remove them that, while the natural but unseemly blemishes are put an end to, the natural substance shall suffer no diminution?

And consequently overgrown and emaciated persons need not fear that they shall be in heaven of such a figure as they would not be even in this world if they could help it. For all bodily beauty consists in the proportion of the parts, together with a certain agreeableness of colour. Where there is no proportion, the eye is offended, either because there is something want-

---

[1] I Cor. 12. 27.　[2] Col. 1. 24.　[3] I Cor. 10. 17.
[4] Eph. 1. 22, 23.　[5] Ps. 112. 1.　[6] Luke, 12. 7.

ing, or too small, or too large. And thus there shall be no deformity resulting from want of proportion in that state in which all that is wrong is corrected, and all that is defective supplied from resources the Creator wots of, and all that is excessive removed without destroying the integrity of the substance. And as for the pleasant colour, how conspicuous shall it be where "the just shall shine forth as the sun in the kingdom of their Father!"[1] This brightness we must rather believe to have been concealed from the eyes of the disciples when Christ rose, than to have been awanting. For weak human eyesight could not bear it, and it was necessary that they should so look upon Him as to be able to recognize Him. For this purpose also He allowed them to touch the marks of His wounds, and also ate and drank—not because He needed nourishment, but because He could take it if He wished. Now, when an object, though present, is invisible to persons who see other things which are present, as we say that that brightness was present but invisible by those who saw other things, this is called in Greek ἀορασία; and our Latin translators, for want of a better word, have rendered this *cæcitas* (blindness) in the book of Genesis. This blindness the men of Sodom suffered when they sought the just Lot's gate and could not find it. But if it had been blindness, that is to say, if they could see nothing, then they would not have asked for the gate by which they might enter the house, but for guides who might lead them away.

But the love we bear to the blessed martyrs causes us, I know not how, to desire to see in the heavenly kingdom the marks of the wounds which they received for the name of Christ, and possibly we shall see them. For this will not be a deformity, but a mark of honour, and will add lustre to their appearance, and a spiritual, if not a bodily beauty. And yet we need not believe that they to whom it has been said, "Not a hair of your head shall perish," shall, in the resurrection, want such of their members as they have been deprived of in their martyrdom. But if it will be seemly in that new kingdom to have some marks of these wounds still visible in that immortal flesh, the places where they have been wounded or mutilated shall retain the scars without any of the members being lost. While, therefore, it is quite true that no blemishes which the body has sustained shall appear in the resurrection, yet we are not to reckon or name these marks of virtue blemishes.

[1]Matt. 13. 43.

CHAP. 20. *That, in the resurrection, the substance of our bodies, however disintegrated, shall be entirely reunited*

Far be it from us to fear that the omnipotence of the Creator cannot, for the resuscitation and reanimation of our bodies, recall all the portions which have been consumed by beasts or fire, or have been dissolved into dust or ashes, or have decomposed into water, or evaporated into the air. Far from us be the thought, that anything which escapes our observation in any most hidden recess of nature either evades the knowledge or transcends the power of the Creator of all things. Cicero, the great authority of our adversaries, wishing to define God as accurately as possible, says, "God is a mind free and independent, without materiality, perceiving and moving all things, and itself endowed with eternal movement." This he found in the systems of the greatest philosophers. Let me ask, then, in their own language, how anything can either lie hid from Him Who perceives all things, or irrevocably escape Him Who moves all things?

This leads me to reply to that question which seems the most difficult of all—"To whom, in the resurrection, will belong the flesh of a dead man which has become the flesh of a living man?" For if some one, famishing for want and pressed with hunger, use human flesh as food—an extremity not unknown, as both ancient history and the unhappy experience of our own days have taught us—can it be contended, with any show of reason, that all the flesh eaten has been evacuated, and that none of it has been assimilated to the substance of the eater though the very emaciation which existed before, and has now disappeared, sufficiently indicates what large deficiencies have been filled up with this food? But I have already made some remarks which will suffice for the solution of this difficulty also. For all the flesh which hunger has consumed finds its way into the air by evaporation, whence, as we have said, God Almighty can recall it. That flesh, therefore, shall be restored to the man in whom it first became human flesh. For it must be looked upon as borrowed by the other person, and, like a pecuniary loan, must be returned to the lender. His own flesh, however, which he lost by famine, shall be restored to him by Him Who can recover even what has evaporated. And though it had been absolutely annihilated, so that no part of its substance remained in any secret spot of nature, the Almighty could restore it by such means as He saw fit. For this sentence uttered by the Truth, "Not a hair of your head shall perish," forbids us to suppose that, though no hair of a man's head can perish, yet the large portions of his flesh eaten and consumed by the famishing can perish.

From all that we have thus considered, and discussed with such poor ability as we can command, we gather this conclusion, that in the resurrection of the flesh the body shall be of that size which it either had attained or should have attained in the flower of its youth, and shall enjoy the beauty that arises from preserving symmetry and proportion in all its members. And it is reasonable to suppose that, for the preservation of this beauty, any part of the body's substance, which, if placed in one spot, would produce a deformity, shall be distributed through the whole of it, so that neither any part, nor the symmetry of the whole, may be lost, but only the general stature of the body somewhat increased by the distribution in all the parts of that which, in one place, would have been unsightly. Or if it is contended that each will rise with the same stature as that of the body he died in, we shall not obstinately dispute this, provided only there be no deformity, no infirmity, no languor, no corruption—nothing of any kind which would ill become that kingdom in which the children of the resurrection and of the promise shall be equal to the angels of God, if not in body and age, at least in happiness.

CHAP. 21. *Of the new spiritual body into which the flesh of the saints shall be transformed*

Whatever, therefore, has been taken from the body, either during life or after death, shall be restored to it, and, in conjunction with what has remained in the grave, shall rise again, transformed from the oldness of the animal body into the newness of the spiritual body, and clothed in incorruption and immortality. But even though the body has been all quite ground to powder by some severe accident, or by the ruthlessness of enemies, and though it has been so diligently scattered to the winds, or into the water, that there is no trace of it left, yet it shall not be beyond the omnipotence of the Creator —no, not a hair of its head shall perish. The flesh shall then be spiritual, and subject to the spirit, but still flesh, not spirit, as the spirit itself, when subject to the flesh, was fleshly, but still spirit and not flesh. And of this we have experimental proof in the deformity of our penal condition. For those persons were carnal, not in a fleshly, but in a spiritual way, to whom the apostle said,

"I could not speak to you as unto spiritual, but as unto carnal."[1] And a man is in this life spiritual in such a way, that he is yet carnal with respect to his body, and sees another law in his members warring against the law of his mind; but even in his body he will be spiritual when the same flesh shall have had that resurrection of which these words speak, "It is sown an animal body, it shall rise a spiritual body."[2] But what this spiritual body shall be and how great its grace, I fear it were but rash to pronounce, seeing that we have as yet no experience of it. Nevertheless, since it is fit that the joyfulness of our hope should utter itself, and so show forth God's praise, and since it was from the profoundest sentiment of ardent and holy love that the Psalmist cried, "O Lord, I have loved the beauty of Thy house,"[3] we may, with God's help, speak of the gifts He lavishes on men, good and bad alike, in this most wretched life, and may do our best to conjecture the great glory of that state which we cannot worthily speak of, because we have not yet experienced it. For I say nothing of the time when God made man upright; I say nothing of the happy life of "the man and his wife" in the fruitful garden, since it was so short that none of their children experienced it: I speak only of this life which we know, and in which we now are, from the temptations of which we cannot escape so long as we are in it, no matter what progress we make, for it is all temptation, and I ask, Who can describe the tokens of God's goodness that are extended to the human race even in this life?

CHAP. 22. *Of the miseries and ills to which the human race is justly exposed through the first sin, and from which none can be delivered save by Christ's grace*

That the whole human race has been condemned in its first origin, this life itself, if life it is to be called, bears witness by the host of cruel ills with which it is filled. Is not this proved by the profound and dreadful ignorance which produces all the errors that enfold the children of Adam, and from which no man can be delivered without toil, pain, and fear? Is it not proved by his love of so many vain and hurtful things, which produces gnawing cares, disquiet, griefs, fears, wild joys, quarrels, lawsuits, wars, treasons, angers, hatreds, deceit, flattery, fraud, theft, robbery, perfidy, pride, ambition, envy, murders, parricides, cruelty, ferocity, wickedness, luxury, insolence, impudence, shamelessness, fornications, adulteries,

[1] I Cor. 3. 1.   [2] I Cor. 15. 44.   [3] Ps. 26. 8.

incests, and the numberless uncleannesses and unnatural acts of both sexes, which it is shameful so much as to mention; sacrileges, heresies, blasphemies, perjuries, oppression of the innocent, calumnies, plots, falsehoods, false witnessings, unrighteous judgments, violent deeds, plunderings, and whatever similar wickedness has found its way into the lives of men, though it cannot find its way into the conception of pure minds? These are indeed the crimes of wicked men, yet they spring from that root of error and misplaced love which is born with every son of Adam. For who is there that has not observed with what profound ignorance, manifesting itself even in infancy, and with what superfluity of foolish desires, beginning to appear in boyhood, man comes into this life, so that, were he left to live as he pleased, and to do whatever he pleased, he would plunge into all, or certainly into many of those crimes and iniquities which I mentioned, and could not mention?

But because God does not wholly desert those whom He condemns, nor shuts up in His anger His tender mercies, the human race is restrained by law and instruction, which keep guard against the ignorance that besets us, and oppose the assaults of vice, but are themselves full of labour and sorrow. For what mean those multifarious threats which are used to restrain the folly of children? What mean pedagogues, masters, the birch, the strap, the cane, the schooling which Scripture says must be given a child, "beating him on the sides lest he wax stubborn,"[1] and it be hardly possible or not possible at all to subdue him? Why all these punishments, save to overcome ignorance and bridle evil desires—these evils with which we come into the world? For why is it that we remember with difficulty, and without difficulty forget? learn with difficulty, and without difficulty remain ignorant? are diligent with difficulty, and without difficulty are indolent? Does not this show what vitiated nature inclines and tends to by its own weight, and what succour it needs if it is to be delivered? Inactivity, sloth, laziness, negligence, are vices which shun labour, since labour, though useful, is itself a punishment.

But, besides the punishments of childhood, without which there would be no learning of what the parents wish—and the parents rarely wish anything useful to be taught—who can describe, who can conceive the number and severity of the punishments which afflict the human race—pains which are not only the accom-

[1] Ecclus. 30. 12.

paniment of the wickedness of godless men, but are a part of the human condition and the common misery—what fear and what grief are caused by bereavement and mourning, by losses and condemnations, by fraud and falsehood, by false suspicions, and all the crimes and wicked deeds of other men? For at their hands we suffer robbery, captivity, chains, imprisonment, exile, torture, mutilation, loss of sight, the violation of chastity to satisfy the lust of the oppressor, and many other dreadful evils. What numberless casualties threaten our bodies from without—extremes of heat and cold, storms, floods, inundations, lightning, thunder, hail, earthquakes, houses falling; or from the stumbling, or shying, or vice of horses; from countless poisons in fruits, water, air, animals; from the painful or even deadly bites of wild animals; from the madness which a mad dog communicates, so that even the animal which of all others is most gentle and friendly to its own master, becomes an object of intenser fear than a lion or dragon, and the man whom it has by chance infected with his pestilential contagion becomes so rabid, that his parents, wife, children, dread him more than any wild beast! What disasters are suffered by those who travel by land or sea! What man can go out of his own house without being exposed on all hands to unforeseen accidents? Returning home sound in limb, he slips on his own doorstep, breaks his leg, and never recovers. What can seem safer than a man sitting in his chair? Eli the priest fell from his, and broke his neck. How many accidents do farmers, or rather all men, fear that the crops may suffer from the weather, or the soil, or the ravages of destructive animals? Commonly they feel safe when the crops are gathered and housed. Yet, to my certain knowledge, sudden floods have driven the labourers away and swept the barns clean of the finest harvest. Is innocence a sufficient protection against the various assaults of demons? That no man might think so, even baptized infants, who are certainly unsurpassed in innocence, are sometimes so tormented, that God, Who permits it, teaches us hereby to bewail the calamities of this life, and to desire the felicity of the life to come. As to bodily diseases, they are so numerous that they cannot all be contained even in medical books. And in very many, or almost all of them, the cures and remedies are themselves tortures, so that men are delivered from a pain that destroys by a cure that pains. Has not the madness of thirst driven men to drink human urine, and even their own? Has not hunger driven men to eat human flesh, and that the flesh not of bodies found dead, but of bodies slain for the purpose? Have not the fierce pangs of famine driven mothers to eat their own children, incredibly savage as it seems? In fine, sleep itself, which is justly called repose, how little of repose there sometimes is in it when disturbed with dreams and visions; and with what terror is the wretched mind overwhelmed by the appearances of things which are so presented, and which, as it were, so stand out before the senses, that we cannot distinguish them from realities! How wretchedly do false appearances distract men in certain diseases! With what astonishing variety of appearances are even healthy men sometimes deceived by evil spirits, who produce these delusions for the sake of perplexing the senses of their victims, if they cannot succeed in seducing them to their side!

From this hell upon earth there is no escape, save through the grace of the Saviour Christ, our God and Lord. The very name Jesus shows this, for it means Saviour; and He saves us especially from passing out of this life into a more wretched and eternal state, which is rather a death than a life. For in this life, though holy men and holy pursuits afford us great consolations, yet the blessings which men crave are not invariably bestowed upon them, lest religion should be cultivated for the sake of these temporal advantages, while it ought rather to be cultivated for the sake of that other life from which all evil is excluded. Therefore, also, does grace aid good men in the midst of present calamities, so that they are enabled to endure them with a constancy proportioned to their faith. The world's sages affirm that philosophy contributes something to this—that philosophy which, according to Cicero, the gods have bestowed in its purity only on a few men. They have never given, he says, nor can ever give, a greater gift to men. So that even those against whom we are disputing have been compelled to acknowledge, in some fashion, that the grace of God is necessary for the acquisition, not, indeed, of any philosophy, but of the true philosophy. And if the true philosophy—this sole support against the miseries of this life—has been given by Heaven only to a few, it sufficiently appears from this that the human race has been condemned to pay this penalty of wretchedness. And as, according to their acknowledgment, no greater gift has been bestowed by God, so it must be believed that it could be given only by that God whom they themselves recognize as greater than all the gods they worship.

CHAP. 23. *Of the miseries of this life which attach peculiarly to the toil of good men, irrespective of those which are common to the good and bad*

But, irrespective of the miseries which in this life are common to the good and bad, the righteous undergo labours peculiar to themselves, in so far as they make war upon their vices, and are involved in the temptations and perils of such a contest. For though sometimes more violent and at other times slacker, yet without intermission does the flesh lust against the spirit and the spirit against the flesh, so that we cannot do the things we would,[1] and extirpate all lust, but can only refuse consent to it, as God gives us ability, and so keep it under, vigilantly keeping watch lest a semblance of truth deceive us, lest a subtle discourse blind us, lest error involve us in darkness, lest we should take good for evil or evil for good, lest fear should hinder us from doing what we ought, or desire precipitate us into doing what we ought not, lest the sun go down upon our wrath, lest hatred provoke us to render evil for evil, lest unseemly or immoderate grief consume us, lest an ungrateful disposition make us slow to recognize benefits received, lest calumnies fret our conscience, lest rash suspicion on our part deceive us regarding a friend, or false suspicion of us on the part of others give us too much uneasiness, lest sin reign in our mortal body to obey its desires, lest our members be used as the instruments of unrighteousness, lest the eye follow lust, lest thirst for revenge carry us away, lest sight or thought dwell too long on some evil thing which gives us pleasure, lest wicked or indecent language be willingly listened to, lest we do what is pleasant but unlawful, and lest in this warfare, filled so abundantly with toil and peril, we either hope to secure victory by our own strength, or attribute it when secured to our own strength, and not to His grace of Whom the apostle says, "Thanks be unto God, Who giveth us the victory through our Lord Jesus Christ";[2] and in another place he says, "In all these things we are more than conquerors through Him that loved us."[3] But yet we are to know this, that however valorously we resist our vices, and however successful we are in overcoming them, yet as long as we are in this body we have always reason to say to God, "Forgive us our debts."[4] But in that kingdom where we shall dwell for ever, clothed in immortal bodies, we shall no longer have either

[1]Gal. 5. 17.   [2]I Cor. 15. 57.   [3]Rom. 8. 37.
[4]Matt. 6. 12.

conflicts or debts—as indeed we should not have had at any time or in any condition, had our nature continued upright as it was created. Consequently even this our conflict, in which we are exposed to peril, and from which we hope to be delivered by a final victory, belongs to the ills of this life, which is proved by the witness of so many grave evils to be a life under condemnation.

CHAP. 24. *Of the blessings with which the Creator has filled this life, obnoxious though it be to the curse*

But we must now contemplate the rich and countless blessings with which the goodness of God, Who cares for all He has created, has filled this very misery of the human race, which reflects His retributive justice. That first blessing which He pronounced before the fall, when He said, "Increase, and multiply, and replenish the earth," [1] He did not inhibit after man had sinned, but the fecundity originally bestowed remained in the condemned stock; and the vice of sin, which has involved us in the necessity of dying, has yet not deprived us of that wonderful power of seed, or rather of that still more marvellous power by which seed is produced, and which seems to be as it were inwrought and inwoven in the human body. But in this river, as I may call it, or torrent of the human race, both elements are carried along together—both the evil which is derived from him who begets, and the good which is bestowed by Him Who creates us. In the original evil there are two things, sin and punishment; in the original good, there are two other things, propagation and conformation. But of the evils, of which the one, sin, arose from our audacity, and the other, punishment, from God's judgment, we have already said as much as suits our present purpose. I mean now to speak of the blessings which God has conferred or still confers upon our nature, vitiated and condemned as it is. For in condemning it He did not withdraw all that He had given it, else it had been annihilated; neither did He, in penally subjecting it to the devil, remove it beyond His own power; for not even the devil himself is outside of God's government, since the devil's nature subsists only by the supreme Creator, Who gives being to all that in any form exists.

Of these two blessings, then, which we have said flow from God's goodness, as from a fountain, towards our nature, vitiated by sin and condemned to punishment, the one, propaga-

tion, was conferred by God's benediction when He made those first works, from which He rested on the seventh day. But the other, conformation, is conferred in that work of His wherein "He worketh hitherto." [2] For were He to withdraw His efficacious power from things, they should neither be able to go on and complete the periods assigned to their measured movements, nor should they even continue in possession of that nature they were created in. God, then, so created man that He gave him what we may call fertility, whereby he might propagate other men, giving them a congenital capacity to propagate their kind, but not imposing on them any necessity to do so. This capacity God withdraws at pleasure from individuals, making them barren; but from the whole race He has not withdrawn the blessing of propagation once conferred. But though not withdrawn on account of sin, this power of propagation is not what it would have been had there been no sin. For since "man placed in honour fell, he has become like the beasts," [3] and generates as they do, though the little spark of reason, which was the image of God in him, has not been quite quenched. But if conformation were not added to propagation, there would be no reproduction of one's kind. For even though there were no such thing as copulation, and God wished to fill the earth with human inhabitants, He might create all these as He created one without the help of human generation. And, indeed, even as it is, those who copulate can generate nothing save by the creative energy of God. As, therefore, in respect of that spiritual growth whereby a man is formed to piety and righteousness, the apostle says, "Neither is he that planteth anything, neither he that watereth, but God that giveth the increase," [4] so also it must be said that it is not he that generates that is anything, but God that giveth the essential form; that it is not the mother who carries and nurses the fruit of her womb that is anything, but God that giveth the increase. For He alone, by that energy wherewith "He worketh hitherto," causes the seed to develop, and to evolve from certain secret and invisible folds into the visible forms of beauty which we see. He alone, coupling and connecting in some wonderful fashion the spiritual and corporeal natures, the one to command, the other to obey, makes a living being. And this work of His is so great and wonderful that not only man, who is a rational animal, and consequently more excellent than all other animals of the earth, but even the most diminutive insect, cannot be considered attentively without astonishment and without praising the Creator.

It is He, then, Who has given to the human soul a mind, in which reason and understanding lie as it were asleep during infancy, and as if they were not, destined, however, to be awakened and exercised as years increase, so as to become capable of knowledge and of receiving instruction, fit to understand what is true and to love what is good. It is by this capacity the soul drinks in wisdom, and becomes endowed with those virtues by which, in prudence, fortitude, temperance, and righteousness, it makes war upon error and the other inborn vices, and conquers them by fixing its desires upon no other object than the supreme and unchangeable Good. And even though this be not uniformly the result, yet who can competently utter or even conceive the grandeur of this work of the Almighty, and the unspeakable boon He has conferred upon our rational nature, by giving us even the capacity of such attainment? For over and above those arts which are called virtues, and which teach us how we may spend our life well, and attain to endless happiness—arts which are given to the children of the promise and the kingdom by the sole grace of God which is in Christ—has not the genius of man invented and applied countless astonishing arts, partly the result of necessity, partly the result of exuberant invention, so that this vigour of mind, which is so active in the discovery not merely of superfluous but even of dangerous and destructive things, betokens an inexhaustible wealth in the nature which can invent, learn, or employ such arts? What wonderful—one might say stupefying—advances has human industry made in the arts of weaving and building, of agriculture and navigation! With what endless variety are designs in pottery, painting, and sculpture produced, and with what skill executed! What wonderful spectacles are exhibited in the theatres, which those who have not seen them cannot credit! How skillful the contrivances for catching, killing, or taming wild beasts! And for the injury of men, also, how many kinds of poisons, weapons, engines of destruction, have been invented, while for the preservation or restoration of health the appliances and remedies are infinite! To provoke appetite and please the palate, what a variety of seasonings have been concocted! To express and gain entrance for thoughts, what a multitude and variety of signs there are, among which speaking and writing hold the first place! what ornaments has eloquence at command to delight the mind! what

wealth of song is there to captivate the ear! how many musical instruments and strains of harmony have been devised! What skill has been attained in measures and numbers! with what sagacity have the movements and connections of the stars been discovered! Who could tell the thought that has been spent upon nature, even though, despairing of recounting it in detail, he endeavoured only to give a general view of it? In fine, even the defence of errors and misapprehensions, which has illustrated the genius of heretics and philosophers, cannot be sufficiently declared. For at present it is the nature of the human mind which adorns this mortal life which we are extolling, and not the faith and the way of truth which lead to immortality. And since this great nature has certainly been created by the true and supreme God, Who administers all things He has made with absolute power and justice, it could never have fallen into these miseries, nor have gone out of them to miseries eternal—saving only those who are redeemed—had not an exceeding great sin been found in the first man from whom the rest have sprung.

Moreover, even in the body, though it dies like that of the beasts, and is in many ways weaker than theirs, what goodness of God, what providence of the great Creator, is apparent! The organs of sense and the rest of the members, are not they so placed, the appearance, and form, and stature of the body as a whole, is it not so fashioned as to indicate that it was made for the service of a reasonable soul? Man has not been created stooping towards the earth, like the irrational animals; but his bodily form, erect and looking heavenwards, admonishes him to mind the things that are above. Then the marvellous nimbleness which has been given to the tongue and the hands, fitting them to speak, and write, and execute so many duties, and practise so many arts, does it not prove the excellence of the soul for which such an assistant was provided? And even apart from its adaptation to the work required of it, there is such a symmetry in its various parts, and so beautiful a proportion maintained that one is at a loss to decide whether, in creating the body, greater regard was paid to utility or to beauty. Assuredly no part of the body has been created for the sake of utility which does not also contribute something to its beauty. And this would be all the more apparent, if we knew more precisely how all its parts are connected and adapted to one another, and were not limited in our observations to what appears on the surface; for as to what is covered up and hidden from our view, the intricate web of veins and nerves, the vital parts of all that lies under the skin, no one can discover it. For although, with a cruel zeal for science, some medical men, who are called anatomists, have dissected the bodies of the dead, and sometimes even of sick persons who died under their knives, and have inhumanly pried into the secrets of the human body to learn the nature of the disease and its exact seat, and how it might be cured, yet those relations of which I speak, and which form the concord, or, as the Greeks call it, *harmony,* of the whole body outside and in, as of some instrument, no one has been able to discover, because no one has been audacious enough to seek for them. But if these could be known, then even the inward parts, which seem to have no beauty, would so delight us with their exquisite fitness as to afford a profounder satisfaction to the mind—and the eyes are but its ministers—than the obvious beauty which gratifies the eye. There are some things, too, which have such a place in the body, that they obviously serve no useful purpose, but are solely for beauty, as e.g., the teats on a man's breast, or the beard on his face; for that this is for ornament, and not for protection, is proved by the bare faces of women, who ought rather, as the weaker sex, to enjoy such a defence. If, therefore, of all those members which are exposed to our view, there is certainly not one in which beauty is sacrificed to utility, while there are some which serve no purpose but only beauty, I think it can readily be concluded that in the creation of the human body comeliness was more regarded than necessity. In truth, necessity is a transitory thing; and the time is coming when we shall enjoy one another's beauty without any lust—a condition which will specially redound to the praise of the Creator, who, as it is said in the psalm, has "put on praise and comeliness," [1]

How can I tell of the rest of creation, with all its beauty and utility, which the divine goodness has given to man to please his eye and serve his purposes, condemned though he is, and hurled into these labours and miseries? Shall I speak of the manifold and various loveliness of sky, and earth, and sea; of the plentiful supply and wonderful qualities of the light; of sun, moon, and stars; of the shade of trees; of the colours and perfume of flowers; of the multitude of birds, all differing in plumage and in song; of the variety of animals, of which the smallest in size are often the most wonderful—the works of ants and bees astonishing us more than the huge bodies of whales? Shall I speak of the sea, which itself is so grand a spectacle, when it arrays itself as it were in vestures of various colours, now running through every shade of green, and again becoming purple or blue? Is it not delightful to look at it in storm, and experience the soothing complacency which it inspires, by suggesting that we ourselves are not tossed and shipwrecked? [2] What shall I say of the numberless kinds of food to alleviate hunger, and the variety of seasonings to stimulate appetite which are scattered everywhere by nature, and for which we are not indebted to the art of cookery? How many natural appliances are there for preserving and restoring health! How grateful is the alternation of day and night! how pleasant the breezes that cool the air! how abundant the supply of clothing furnished us by trees and animals! Who can enumerate all the blessings we enjoy? If I were to attempt to detail and unfold only these few which I have indicated in the mass, such an enumeration would fill a volume. And all these are but the solace of the wretched and condemned, not the rewards of the blessed. What then shall these rewards be, if such be the blessings of a condemned state? What will He give to those whom He has predestined to life, Who has given such things even to those whom He has predestined to death? What blessings will He in the blessed life shower upon those for whom, even in this state of misery, He has been willing that His only-begotten Son should endure such sufferings even to death? Thus the apostle reasons concerning those who are predestined to that kingdom: "He that spared not His own Son, but delivered Him up for us all, how shall He not with Him also give us all things?" [3] When this promise is fulfilled, what shall we be? What blessings shall we receive in that kingdom, since already we have received as the pledge of them Christ's dying? In what condition shall the spirit of man be, when it has no longer any vice at all; when it neither yields to any, nor is in bondage to any, nor has to make war against any, but is perfected, and enjoys undisturbed peace with itself? Shall it not then know all things with certainty, and without any labour or error, when unhindered and joyfully it drinks the wisdom of God at the fountain-head? What shall the body be, when it is in every respect subject to the spirit, from which it shall draw a life so sufficient, as to stand in need of no other nutriment? For it shall no longer be

[1] Ps. 104. 1.

[2] He apparently has in view the celebrated passage in the opening of the second book of Lucretius.

[3] Rom. 8. 32.

animal, but spiritual, having indeed the substance of flesh, but without any fleshly corruption.

CHAP. 25. *Of the obstinacy of those individuals who impugn the resurrection of the body, though, as was predicted, the whole world believes it*

The foremost of the philosophers agree with us about the spiritual felicity enjoyed by the blessed in the life to come; it is only the resurrection of the flesh they call in question, and with all their might deny. But the mass of men, learned and unlearned, the world's wise men and its fools, have believed, and have left in meagre isolation the unbelievers, and have turned to Christ, Who in His own resurrection demonstrated the reality of that which seems to our adversaries absurd. For the world has believed this which God predicted, as it was also predicted that the world would believe—a prediction not due to the sorceries of Peter,[1] since it was uttered so long before. He Who has predicted these things, as I have already said, and am not ashamed to repeat, is the God before Whom all other divinities tremble, as Porphyry himself owns, and seeks to prove, by testimonies from the oracles of these gods, and goes so far as to call Him God the Father and King. Far be it from us to interpret these predictions as they do who have not believed, along with the whole world, in that which it was predicted the world would believe in. For why should we not rather understand them as the world does, whose belief was predicted, and leave that handful of unbelievers to their idle talk and obstinate and solitary infidelity? For if they maintain that they interpret them differently only to avoid charging Scripture with folly, and so doing an injury to that God to Whom they bear so notable a testimony, is it not a much greater injury they do Him when they say that His predictions must be understood otherwise than the world believed them, though He Himself praised, promised, accomplished this belief on the world's part? And why cannot He cause the body to rise again, and live for ever? or is it not to be believed that He will do this, because it is an undesirable thing, and unworthy of God? Of His omnipotence, which effects so many great miracles, we have already said enough. If they wish to know what the Almighty cannot do, I shall tell them He cannot lie. Let us therefore believe what He can do, by refusing to believe what He cannot do. Refusing to believe that He

[1]See BK. XVIII, chap. 53.

can lie, let them believe that He will do what He has promised to do; and let them believe it as the world has believed it, whose faith He predicted, whose faith He praised, whose faith He promised, whose faith He now points to. But how do they prove that the resurrection is an undesirable thing? There shall then be no corruption, which is the only evil thing about the body. I have already said enough about the order of the elements, and the other fanciful objections men raise; and in the thirteenth book I have, in my own judgment, sufficiently illustrated the facility of movement which the incorruptible body shall enjoy, judging from the ease and vigour we experience even now, when the body is in good health. Those who have either not read the former books, or wish to refresh their memory, may read them for themselves.

CHAP. 26. *That the opinion of Porphyry, that the soul, in order to be blessed, must be separated from every kind of body, is demolished by Plato, who says that the Supreme God promised the gods that they should never be ousted from their bodies*

But, say they, Porphyry tells us that the soul, in order to be blessed, must escape connexion with every kind of body. It does not avail, therefore, to say that the future body shall be incorruptible, if the soul cannot be blessed till delivered from every kind of body. But in the book above mentioned I have already sufficiently discussed this. This one thing only will I repeat—let Plato, their master, correct his writings, and say that their gods, in order to be blessed, must quit their bodies, or, in other words, die; for he said that they were shut up in celestial bodies, and that, nevertheless, the God Who made them promised them immortality—that is to say, an eternal tenure of these same bodies, such as was not provided for them naturally, but only by the further intervention of His will, that thus they might be assured of felicity. In this he obviously overturns their assertion that the resurrection of the body cannot be believed because it is impossible; for, according to him, when the uncreated God promised immortality to the created gods, He expressly said that He would do what was impossible. For Plato tells us that He said, "As ye have had a beginning, so you cannot be immortal and incorruptible; yet ye shall not decay, nor shall any fate destroy you or prove stronger than my will, which more effectually binds you to immortality than the bond of your nature keeps you from it." If they who hear these words have, we do not say understanding, but ears, they cannot doubt that Plato believed that God promised to the gods He had made that He would effect an impossibility. For He Who says, "Ye cannot be immortal, but by my will ye shall be immortal," what else does He say than this, "I shall make you what ye cannot be"? The body, therefore, shall be raised incorruptible, immortal, spiritual, by Him Who, according to Plato, has promised to do that which is impossible. Why then do they still exclaim that this which God has promised, which the world has believed on God's promise as was predicted, is an impossibility? For what we say is, that the God Who, even according to Plato, does impossible things, will do this. It is not, then, necessary to the blessedness of the soul that it be detached from a body of any kind whatever, but that it receive an incorruptible body. And in what incorruptible body will they more suitably rejoice than in that in which they groaned when it was corruptible? For thus they shall not feel that dire craving which Virgil, in imitation of Plato, has ascribed to them when he says that they wish to return again to their bodies.[1] They shall not, I say, feel this desire to return to their bodies, since they shall have those bodies to which a return was desired, and shall, indeed, be in such thorough possession of them that they shall never lose them even for the briefest moment, nor ever lay them down in death.

CHAP. 27. *Of the apparently conflicting opinions of Plato and Porphyry, which would have conducted them both to the truth if they could have yielded to one another*

Statements were made by Plato and Porphyry singly, which if they could have seen their way to hold in common, they might possibly have become Christians. Plato said that souls could not exist eternally without bodies; for it was on this account, he said, that the souls even of wise men must some time or other return to their bodies. Porphyry, again, said that the purified soul, when it has returned to the Father, shall never return to the ills of this world. Consequently, if Plato had communicated to Porphyry that which he saw to be true, that souls, though perfectly purified and belonging to the wise and righteous, must return to human bodies; and if Porphyry, again, had imparted to Plato the truth which he saw, that holy souls shall never return to the miseries of a corruptible body, so that they should not have each held only his own opinion, but should both have held

both truths, I think they would have seen that it follows that the souls return to their bodies, and also that these bodies shall be such as to afford them a blessed and immortal life. For, according to Plato, even holy souls shall return to the body; according to Porphyry, holy souls shall not return to the ills of this world. Let Porphyry then say with Plato, "They shall return to the body"; let Plato say with Porphyry, "They shall not return to their old misery": and they will agree that they return to bodies in which they shall suffer no more. And this is nothing else than what God has promised—that He will give eternal felicity to souls joined to their own bodies. For this, I presume, both of them would readily concede, that if the souls of the saints are to be reunited to bodies, it shall be to their own bodies, in which they have endured the miseries of this life, and in which, to escape these miseries, they served God with piety and fidelity.

CHAP. 28. *What Plato or Labeo, or even Varro, might have contributed to the true faith of the resurrection, if they had adopted one another's opinions into one scheme*

Some Christians, who have a liking for Plato on account of his magnificent style and the truths which he now and then uttered, say that he even held an opinion similar to our own regarding the resurrection of the dead. Cicero, however, alluding to this in his *Republic*, asserts that Plato meant it rather as a playful fancy than as a reality; for he introduces a man[2] who had come to life again, and gave a narrative of his experience in corroboration of the doctrines of Plato. Labeo, too, says that two men died on one day, and met at a cross-road, and that, being afterwards ordered to return to their bodies, they agreed to be friends for life, and were so till they died again. But the resurrection which these writers instance resembles that of those persons whom we have ourselves known to rise again, and who came back indeed to this life, but not so as never to die again. Marcus Varro, however, in his work *On the Origin of the Roman People,* records something more remarkable; I think his own words should be given. "Certain astrologers," he says, "have written that men are destined to a new birth, which the Greeks call *palingenesy.* This will take place after four hundred and forty years have elapsed; and then the same soul and the same body, which were formerly united in the person, shall again be reunited." This Varro, indeed, or those

[1] *Æneid,* BK. VI. 751.

[2] In the *Republic,* BK. X.

nameless astrologers—for he does not give us the names of the men whose statement he cites —have affirmed what is indeed not altogether true; for once the souls have returned to the bodies they wore, they shall never afterwards leave them. Yet what they say upsets and demolishes much of that idle talk of our adversaries about the impossibility of the resurrection. For those who have been or are of this opinion, have not thought it possible that bodies which have dissolved into air, or dust, or ashes, or water, or into the bodies of the beasts or even of the men that fed on them, should be restored again to that which they formerly were. And therefore, if Plato and Porphyry, or rather, if their disciples now living, agree with us that holy souls shall return to the body, as Plato says, and that, nevertheless, they shall not return to misery, as Porphyry maintains—if they accept the consequence of these two propositions which is taught by the Christian faith, that they shall receive bodies in which they may live eternally without suffering any misery—let them also adopt from Varro the opinion that they shall return to the same bodies as they were formerly in, and thus the whole question of the eternal resurrection of the body shall be resolved out of their own mouths.

CHAP. 29. *Of the beatific vision*

And now let us consider, with such ability as God may vouchsafe, how the saints shall be employed when they are clothed in immortal and spiritual bodies, and when the flesh shall live no longer in a fleshly but a spiritual fashion. And indeed, to tell the truth, I am at a loss to understand the nature of that employment, or, shall I rather say, repose and ease, for it has never come within the range of my bodily senses. And if I should speak of my mind or understanding, what is our understanding in comparison of its excellence? For then shall be that "peace of God which," as the apostle says, "passeth all understanding" [1]—that is to say, all human, and perhaps all angelic understanding, but certainly not the divine. That it passeth ours there is no doubt; but if it passeth that of the angels—and he who says *"all* understanding" seems to make no exception in their favour—then we must understand him to mean that neither we nor the angels can understand, as God understands, the peace which God Himself enjoys. Doubtless this passeth all understanding but His own. But as we shall one day be made to participate, according to our slender capacity, in His peace,

[1]Phil. 4. 7.

both in ourselves, and with our neighbour, and with God our chief good, in this respect the angels understand the peace of God in their own measure, and men too, though now far behind them, whatever spiritual advance they have made. For we must remember how great a man he was who said, "We know in part, and we prophesy in part, until that which is perfect is come"; [2] and "Now we see through a glass, darkly; but then face to face." [3] Such also is now the vision of the holy angels, who are also called our angels, because we, being rescued out of the power of darkness, and receiving the earnest of the Spirit, are translated into the kingdom of Christ, and already begin to belong to those angels with whom we shall enjoy that holy and most delightful city of God of which we have now written so much. Thus, then, the angels of God are our angels, as Christ is God's and also ours. They are God's, because they have not abandoned Him; they are ours, because we are their fellow-citizens. The Lord Jesus also said, "See that ye despise not one of these little ones: for I say unto you, That in heaven their angels do always see the face of my Father which is in heaven." [4] As, then, they see, so shall we also see; but not yet do we thus see. Wherefore the apostle uses the words cited a little ago, "Now we see through a glass, darkly; but then face to face." This vision is reserved as the reward of our faith; and of it the Apostle John also says, "When He shall appear, we shall be like Him, for we shall see Him as He is." [5] By "the face" of God we are to understand His manifestation, and not a part of the body similar to that which in our bodies we call by that name.

And so, when I am asked how the saints shall be employed in that spiritual body, I do not say what I see, but I say what I believe, according to that which I read in the psalm, "I believed, therefore have I spoken." [6] I say, then, they shall in the body see God; but whether they shall see Him by means of the body, as now we see the sun, moon, stars, sea, earth, and all that is in it, that is a difficult question. For it is hard to say that the saints shall then have such bodies that they shall not be able to shut and open their eyes as they please; while it is harder still to say that every one who shuts his eyes shall lose the vision of God. For if the prophet Elisha, though at a distance, saw his servant Gehazi, who thought that his wickedness would escape his master's observation and accepted gifts from Naaman the Syrian, whom the prophet had

[2]I Cor. 13. 9, 10.   [3]I Cor. 13. 12.   [4]Matt. 18. 10.
[5]I John, 3. 2.   [6]Ps. 116. 10.

cleansed from his foul leprosy, how much more shall the saints in the spiritual body see all things, not only though their eyes be shut, but though they themselves be at a great distance? For then shall be "that which is perfect," of which the apostle says, "We know in part, and we prophesy in part; but when that which is perfect is come, then that which is in part shall be done away." Then, that he may illustrate as well as possible, by a simile, how superior the future life is to the life now lived, not only by ordinary men, but even by the foremost of the saints, he says, "When I was a child, I understood as a child, I spake as a child, I thought as a child; but when I became a man, I put away childish things. Now we see through a glass, darkly; but then face to face: now I know in part; but then shall I know even as also I am known." [1] If, then, even in this life, in which the prophetic power of remarkable men is no more worthy to be compared to the vision of the future life than childhood is to manhood, Elisha, though distant from his servant, saw him accepting gifts, shall we say that when that which is perfect is come, and the corruptible body no longer oppresses the soul, but is incorruptible and offers no impediment to it, the saints shall need bodily eyes to see, though Elisha had no need of them to see his servant? For, following the Septuagint version, these are the prophet's words: "Did not my heart go with thee, when the man came out of his chariot to meet thee, and thou tookedst his gifts?" [2] Or, as the presbyter Jerome rendered it from the Hebrew, "Was not my heart present when the man turned from his chariot to meet thee?" The prophet said that he saw this with his heart, miraculously aided by God, as no one can doubt. But how much more abundantly shall the saints enjoy this gift when God shall be all in all? Nevertheless the bodily eyes also shall have their office and their place, and shall be used by the spirit through the spiritual body. For the prophet did not forego the use of his eyes for seeing what was before them, though he did not need them to see his absent servant, and though he could have seen these present objects in spirit, and with his eyes shut, as he saw things far distant in a place where he himself was not. Far be it, then, from us to say that in the life to come the saints shall not see God when their eyes are shut, since they shall always see Him with the spirit.

But the question arises, whether, when their eyes are open, they shall see Him with the bodily eye? If the eyes of the spiritual body have no more power than the eyes which we now possess, manifestly God cannot be seen with them. They must be of a very different power if they can look upon that incorporeal nature which is not contained in any place, but is all in every place. For though we say that God is in heaven and on earth, as He Himself says by the prophet, "I fill heaven and earth," [3] we do not mean that there is one part of God in heaven and another part on earth; but He is all in heaven and all on earth, not at alternate intervals of time, but both at once, as no bodily nature can be. The eye, then, shall have a vastly superior power—the power not of keen sight, such as is ascribed to serpents or eagles, for however keenly these animals see, they can discern nothing but bodily substances—but the power of seeing things incorporeal. Possibly it was this great power of vision which was temporarily communicated to the eyes of the holy Job while yet in this mortal body, when he says to God, "I have heard of Thee by the hearing of the ear; but now mine eye seeth Thee: wherefore I abhor myself, and melt away, and count myself dust and ashes"; [4] although there is no reason why we should not understand this of the eye of the heart, of which the apostle says, "Having the eyes of your heart illuminated." [5] But that God shall be seen with these eyes no Christian doubts who believingly accepts what our God and Master says, "Blessed are the pure in heart: for they shall see God." [6] But whether in the future life God shall also be seen with the bodily eye, this is now our question.

The expression of Scripture, "And all flesh shall see the salvation of God," [7] may without difficulty be understood as if it were said, "And every man shall see the Christ of God." And He certainly was seen in the body, and shall be seen in the body when He judges quick and dead. And that Christ is the salvation of God, many other passages of Scripture witness, but especially the words of the venerable Simeon, who, when he had received into his hands the infant Christ, said, "Now lettest Thou Thy servant depart in peace, according to Thy word: for mine eyes have seen Thy salvation." [8] As for the words of the above-mentioned Job, as they are found in the Hebrew manuscripts, "And in my flesh I shall see God," [9] no doubt they were a prophecy of the resurrection of the flesh; yet he does not say "by the flesh." And indeed, if he had said this, it would still be possible that

[1] I Cor. 13. 11, 12.   [2] II Kings, 5. 26.

[3] Jer. 23. 24.   [4] Job, 42. 5, 6.   [5] Eph. 1. 18.   [6] Matt. 5. 8.
[7] Luke, 3. 6   [8] Luke, 2. 29, 30.   [9] Job, 19. 26.

Christ was meant by "God"; for Christ shall be seen by the flesh in the flesh. But even understanding it of God, it is only equivalent to saying, I shall be in the flesh when I see God. Then the apostle's expression, "face to face," [1] does not oblige us to believe that we shall see God by the bodily face in which are the eyes of the body, for we shall see Him without intermission in spirit. And if the apostle had not referred to the face of the inner man, he would not have said, "But we, with unveiled face beholding as in a glass the glory of the Lord, are transformed into the same image, from glory to glory, as by the spirit of the Lord." [2] In the same sense we understand what the Psalmist sings, "Draw near unto Him, and be enlightened; and your faces shall not be ashamed." [3] For it is by faith we draw near to God, and faith is an act of the spirit, not of the body. But as we do not know what degree of perfection the spiritual body shall attain—for here we speak of a matter of which we have no experience, and upon which the authority of Scripture does not definitely pronounce—it is necessary that the words of the Book of Wisdom be illustrated in us: "The thoughts of mortal men are timid, and our forecastings uncertain." [4]

For if that reasoning of the philosophers, by which they attempt to make out that intelligible or mental objects are so seen by the mind, and sensible or bodily objects so seen by the body, that the former cannot be discerned by the mind through the body, nor the latter by the mind itself without the body—if this reasoning were trustworthy, then it would certainly follow that God could not be seen by the eye even of a spiritual body. But this reasoning is exploded both by true reason and by prophetic authority. For who is so little acquainted with the truth as to say that God has no cognizance of sensible objects? Has He therefore a body, the eyes of which give Him this knowledge? Moreover, what we have just been relating of the prophet Elisha, does this not sufficiently show that bodily things can be discerned by the spirit without the help of the body? For when that servant received the gifts, certainly this was a bodily or material transaction, yet the prophet saw it not by the body, but by the spirit. As, therefore, it is agreed that bodies are seen by the spirit, what if the power of the spiritual body shall be so great that spirit also is seen by the body? For God is a spirit. Besides, each man recognizes his own life—that life by which he now lives in the body, and which vivifies these earthly members and causes them to grow—by an interior sense, and not by his bodily eye; but the life of other men, though it is invisible, he sees with the bodily eye. For how do we distinguish between living and dead bodies, except by seeing at once both the body and the life which we cannot see save by the eye? But a life without a body we cannot see thus.

Wherefore it may very well be, and it is thoroughly credible, that we shall in the future world see the material forms of the new heavens and the new earth in such a way that we shall most distinctly recognize God everywhere present and governing all things, material as well as spiritual, and shall see Him, not as now we understand the invisible things of God, by the things which are made, [5] and see Him darkly, as in a mirror, and in part, and rather by faith than by bodily vision of material appearances, but by means of the bodies we shall wear and which we shall see wherever we turn our eyes. As we do not believe, but see that the living men around us who are exercising vital functions are alive, though we cannot see their life without their bodies, but see it most distinctly by means of their bodies, so, wherever we shall look with those spiritual eyes of our future bodies, we shall then, too, by means of bodily substances behold God, though a spirit, ruling all things. Either, therefore, the eyes shall possess some quality similar to that of the mind, by which they may be able to discern spiritual things, and among these God—a supposition for which it is difficult or even impossible to find any support in Scripture—or, which is more easy to comprehend, God will be so known by us, and shall be so much before us, that we shall see Him by the spirit in ourselves, in one another, in Himself, in the new heavens and the new earth, in every created thing which shall then exist; and also by the body we shall see Him in every body which the keen vision of the eye of the spiritual body shall reach. Our thoughts also shall be visible to all, for then shall be fulfilled the words of the apostle, "Judge nothing before the time, until the Lord come, who both will bring to light the hidden things of darkness, and will make manifest the thoughts of the heart, and then shall every one have praise of God." [6]

CHAP. 30. *Of the eternal felicity of the city of God, and of the perpetual Sabbath*

How great shall be that felicity, which shall be tainted with no evil, which shall lack no

[1] I Cor. 13. 12.   [2] II Cor. 3. 18.   [3] Ps. 34. 5.
[4] Wisd. 9. 14.

[5] Rom. 1. 20.   [6] I Cor. 4. 5.

good, and which shall afford leisure for the praises of God, Who shall be all in all! For I know not what other employment there can be where no lassitude shall slacken activity, nor any want stimulate to labour. I am admonished also by the sacred song, in which I read or hear the words, "Blessed are they that dwell in Thy house, O Lord; they will be still praising Thee."[1] All the members and organs of the incorruptible body, which now we see to be suited to various necessary uses, shall contribute to the praises of God; for in that life necessity shall have no place, but full, certain, secure, everlasting felicity. For all those parts[2] of the bodily harmony, which are distributed through the whole body, within and without, and of which I have just been saying that they at present elude our observation, shall then be discerned; and, along with the other great and marvellous discoveries which shall then kindle rational minds in praise of the great Artificer, there shall be the enjoyment of a beauty which appeals to the reason. What power of movement such bodies shall possess, I have not the audacity rashly to define, as I have not the ability to conceive. Nevertheless I will say that in any case, both in motion and at rest, they shall be, as in their appearance, seemly; for into that state nothing which is unseemly shall be admitted. One thing is certain, the body shall forthwith be wherever the spirit wills, and the spirit shall will nothing which is unbecoming either to the spirit or to the body. True honour shall be there, for it shall be denied to none who is worthy, nor yielded to any unworthy; neither shall any unworthy person so much as sue for it, for none but the worthy shall be there. True peace shall be there, where no one shall suffer opposition either from himself or any other. God Himself, Who is the Author of virtue, shall there be its reward; for, as there is nothing greater or better, He has promised Himself. What else was meant by His word through the prophet, "I will be your God, and ye shall be my people,"[3] than, "I shall be their satisfaction, I shall be all that men honourably desire"—life, and health, and nourishment, and plenty, and glory, and honour, and peace, and all good things? This, too, is the right interpretation of the saying of the apostle, "That God may be all in all." [4] He shall be the end of our desires who shall be seen without end, loved without cloy, praised without weariness. This outgoing of affection, this employment, shall certainly be, like eternal life itself, common to all.

But who can conceive, not to say describe, what degrees of honour and glory shall be awarded to the various degrees of merit? Yet it cannot be doubted that there shall be degrees. And in that blessed city there shall be this great blessing, that no inferior shall envy any superior, as now the archangels are not envied by the angels, because no one will wish to be what he has not received, though bound in strictest concord with him who has received; as in the body the finger does not seek to be the eye, though both members are harmoniously included in the complete structure of the body. And thus, along with his gift, greater or less, each shall receive this further gift of contentment to desire no more than he has.

Neither are we to suppose that, because sin shall have no power to delight them, free will must be withdrawn. It will, on the contrary, be all the more truly free, because set free from delight in sinning to take unfailing delight in not sinning. For the first freedom of will which man received when he was created upright consisted in an ability not to sin, but also in an ability to sin; whereas this last freedom of will shall be superior, inasmuch as it shall not be able to sin. This, indeed, shall not be a natural ability, but the gift of God. For it is one thing to be God, another thing to be a partaker of God. God by nature cannot sin, but the partaker of God receives this inability from God. And in this divine gift there was to be observed this gradation, that man should first receive a free will by which he was able not to sin, and at last a free will by which he was not able to sin—the former being adapted to the acquiring of merit, the latter to the enjoying of the reward. But the nature thus constituted, having sinned when it had the ability to do so, it is by a more abundant grace that it is delivered so as to reach that freedom in which it cannot sin. For as the first immortality which Adam lost by sinning consisted in his being able not to die, while the last shall consist in his not being able to die; so the first free will consisted in his being able not to sin, the last in his not being able to sin. And thus piety and justice shall be as indefeasible as happiness. For certainly by sinning we lost both piety and happiness; but when we lost happiness, we did not lose the love of it. Are we to say that God Himself is not free because He cannot sin? In that city, then, there shall be free will, one in all the citizens, and indivisible in each, delivered from all ill, filled with all good, enjoying indefeasibly the delights of eternal joys, oblivious of sins, oblivious of sufferings, and yet not so oblivious

[1]Ps. 84. 4.   [2]Numbers.   [3]Lev. 26. 12.   [4]I Cor. 15. 28.

of its deliverance as to be ungrateful to its Deliverer.

The soul, then, shall have an intellectual remembrance of its past ills; but, so far as regards sensible experience, they shall be quite forgotten. For a skillful physician knows, indeed, professionally almost all diseases; but experimentally he is ignorant of a great number which he himself has never suffered from. As, therefore, there are two ways of knowing evil things—one by mental insight, the other by sensible experience, for it is one thing to understand all vices by the wisdom of a cultivated mind, another to understand them by the foolishness of an abandoned life—so also there are two ways of forgetting evils. For a well-instructed and learned man forgets them one way, and he who has experimentally suffered from them forgets them another—the former by neglecting what he has learned, the latter by escaping what he has suffered. And in this latter way the saints shall forget their past ills, for they shall have so thoroughly escaped them all that they shall be quite blotted out of their experience. But their intellectual knowledge, which shall be great, shall keep them acquainted not only with their own past woes, but with the eternal sufferings of the lost. For if they were not to know that they had been miserable, how could they, as the Psalmist says, for ever sing the mercies of God? Certainly that city shall have no greater joy than the celebration of the grace of Christ, Who redeemed us by His blood. There shall be accomplished the words of the psalm, "Be still, and know that I am God." [1] There shall be the great Sabbath which has no evening, which God celebrated among His first works, as it is written, "And God rested on the seventh day from all His works which He had made. And God blessed the seventh day, and sanctified it; because that in it He had rested from all His work which God began to make." [2] For we shall ourselves be the seventh day, when we shall be filled and replenished with God's blessing and sanctification. There shall be still, and know that He is God; that He is that which we ourselves aspired to be when we fell away from Him, and listened to the voice of the seducer, "Ye shall be as gods," [3] and so abandoned God, Who would have made us as gods, not by deserting Him, but by participating in Him. For without Him what have we accomplished, save to perish in His anger? But when we are restored by Him and perfected with greater grace, we shall have eternal leisure to see that He is God, for we shall be full of Him when He shall be all in all. For even our good works, when they are understood to be rather His than ours, are imputed to us that we may enjoy this Sabbath rest. For if we attribute them to ourselves, they shall be servile; for it is said of the Sabbath, "Ye shall do no servile work in it." [4] Wherefore also it is said by Ezekiel the prophet, "And I gave them my Sabbaths to be a sign between me and them, that they might know that I am the Lord who sanctify them." [5] This knowledge shall be perfected when we shall be perfectly at rest, and shall perfectly know that He is God.

This Sabbath shall appear still more clearly if we count the ages as days, in accordance with the periods of time defined in Scripture, for that period will be found to be the seventh. The first age, as the first day, extends from Adam to the deluge; the second from the deluge to Abraham, equalling the first, not in length of time, but in the number of generations, there being ten in each. From Abraham to the advent of Christ there are, as the evangelist Matthew calculates, three periods, in each of which are fourteen generations—one period from Abraham to David, a second from David to the captivity, a third from the captivity to the birth of Christ in the flesh. There are thus five ages in all. The sixth is now passing, and cannot be measured by any number of generations, as it has been said, "It is not for you to know the times, which the Father hath put in His own power." [6] After this period God shall rest as on the seventh day, when He shall give us (who shall be the seventh day) rest in Himself. [7] But there is not now space to treat of these ages; suffice it to say that the seventh shall be our Sabbath, which shall be brought to a close, not by an evening, but by the Lord's day, as an eighth and eternal day, consecrated by the resurrection of Christ and prefiguring the eternal repose not only of the spirit, but also of the body. There we shall rest and see, see and love, love and praise. This is what shall be in the end without end. For what other end do we propose to ourselves than to attain to the kingdom of which there is no end?

I think I have now, by God's help, discharged my obligation in writing this large work. Let those who think I have said too little, or those who think I have said too much, forgive me; and let those who think I have said just enough join me in giving thanks to God. Amen.

[4] Deut. 5. 14.   [5] Ezek. 20. 12.   [6] Acts, i. 7.
[7] See BK. XX, Chaps. 6–10.

[1] Ps. 46. 10.   [2] Gen. 2. 2, 3.   [3] Gen. 3. 5.

CONTENTS: ON CHRISTIAN DOCTRINE

PREFACE *showing the utility of the treatise on Christian doctrine.* 621

BOOK I. *The author divides his work into two parts, one relating to the discovery, the other to the expression, of the true sense of Scripture. He shows that to discover the meaning we must attend both to things and to signs, as it is necessary to know what things we ought to teach to the Christian people, and also the signs of these things, that is, where the knowledge of these things is to be sought. In this first book he treats of things, which he divides into three classes— things to be enjoyed, things to be used, and things which use and enjoy. The only object which ought to be enjoyed is the triune God, Who is our highest good and our true happiness. We are prevented by our sins from enjoying God; and that our sins might be taken away, "The Word was made flesh," our Lord suffered, and died, and rose again, and ascended into heaven, taking to Himself as His bride the Church, in which we receive remission of our sins. And if our sins are remitted and our souls renewed by grace, we may await with hope the resurrection of the body to eternal glory; if not, we shall be raised to everlasting punishment. These matters relating to faith having been expounded, the author goes on to show that all objects, except God, are for use; for, though some of them may be loved, yet our love is not to rest in them, but to have reference to God. And we ourselves are not objects of enjoyment to God: he uses us, but for our own advantage. He then goes on to show that love—the love of God for his own sake and the love of our neighbour for God's sake—is the fulfillment and the end of all Scripture. After adding a few words about hope, he shows, in conclusion, that faith, hope, and love are graces essentially necessary for him who would understand and explain aright the Holy Scriptures.* 624

BOOK II. *Having completed his exposition of things, the author now proceeds to discuss the subject of signs. He first defines what a sign is, and shows that there are two classes of signs, the natural and the conventional. Of conventional signs (which are the only class here noticed), words are the most numerous and important, and are those with which the interpreter of Scripture is chiefly concerned. The difficulties and obscurities of Scripture spring chiefly from two sources, unknown and ambiguous signs. The present book deals only with unknown signs, the ambiguities of language being reserved for treatment in the next book. The difficulty arising from ignorance of signs is to be removed by learning the Greek and Hebrew languages, in which Scripture is written, by comparing the various translations, and by attending to the context. In the interpretation of figurative expressions, knowledge of things is as necessary as knowledge of words; and the various sciences and arts of the heathen, so far as they are true and useful, may be turned to account in removing our ignorance of signs, whether these be direct or figurative. Whilst exposing the folly and futility of many heathen superstitions and practices, the author points out how all that is sound and useful in their science and philosophy may be turned to a Christian use. And in conclusion, he shows the spirit in which it behoves us to address ourselves to the study and interpretation of the sacred books.* 636

BOOK III. *The author, having discussed in the preceding book the method of dealing with unknown signs, goes on in this third book to treat of ambiguous signs. Signs may be either direct or figurative. In the case of direct signs ambiguity may arise from the punctuation, the pronunciation, or the doubtful signification of the words, and is to be resolved by attention to the context, a comparison of translations, or a reference to the original tongue. In the case of figurative signs we need to guard against two mistakes: 1. the interpreting literal expressions figuratively; 2. the interpreting figurative expressions literally. The author lays down rules by which we may decide whether an expression is literal or figurative; the general rule being, that whatever can be shown to be in its literal sense inconsistent either with purity of life or correctness of doctrine must be taken figuratively. He then goes on to lay down rules for the interpretation of expressions which have been proved to be figurative; the general principle being, that no interpretation can be true which does not promote the love of God and the love of man. The author then proceeds to expound and illustrate the seven rules of Tichonius the Donatist, which he commends to the attention of the student of Holy Scripture.* 657

BOOK IV. *Passing to the second part of his work, that which treats of expression, the author pre-*

mises that it is no part of his intention to write a treatise on the laws of rhetoric. These can be learned elsewhere, and ought not to be neglected, being indeed specially necessary for the Christian teacher, whom it behoves to excel in eloquence and power of speech. After detailing with much care and minuteness the various qualities of an orator, he recommends the authors of the Holy Scriptures as the best models of eloquence, far excelling all others in the combination of eloquence with wisdom. He points out that perspicuity is the most essential quality of style, and ought to be cultivated with especial care by the teacher, as it is the main requisite for instruction, although other qualities are required for delighting and persuading the hearer. All these gifts are to be sought in earnest prayer from God, though we are not to forget to be zealous and diligent in study. He shows that there are three species of style—the subdued, the elegant, and the majestic; the first serving for instruction, the second for praise, and the third for exhortation: and of each of these he gives examples, selected both from Scripture and from early teachers of the Church, Cyprian and Ambrose. He shows that these various styles may be mingled, and when and for what purpose they are mingled; and that they all have the same end in view, to bring home the truth to the hearer, so that he may understand it, hear it with gladness, and practice it in his life. Finally, he exhorts the teacher himself, pointing out the dignity and responsibility of the office he holds, to lead a life in harmony with his own teaching, and to show a good example to all. 675

ON CHRISTIAN DOCTRINE

❖❖❖❖❖❖❖❖❖❖

PREFACE

Showing that to teach rules for the interpretation of Scripture is not a superfluous task

1. THERE are certain rules for the interpretation of Scripture which I think might with great advantage be taught to earnest students of the word, that they may profit not only from reading the works of others who have laid open the secrets of the sacred writings, but also from themselves opening such secrets to others. These rules I propose to teach to those who are able and willing to learn, if God our Lord do not withhold from me, while I write, the thoughts He is wont to vouchsafe to me in my meditations on this subject. But before I enter upon this undertaking, I think it well to meet the objections of those who are likely to take exception to the work, or who would do so, did I not conciliate them beforehand. And if, after all, men should still be found to make objections, yet at least they will not prevail with others (over whom they might have influence, did they not find them forearmed against their assaults), to turn them back from a useful study to the dull sloth of ignorance.

2. There are some, then, likely to object to this work of mine, because they have failed to understand the rules here laid down. Others, again, will think that I have spent my labour to no purpose, because, though they understand the rules, yet in their attempts to apply them and to interpret Scripture by them, they have failed to clear up the point they wish cleared up; and these, because they have received no assistance from this work themselves, will give it as their opinion that it can be of no use to anybody. There is a third class of objectors who either really do understand Scripture well, or think they do, and who, because they know (or imagine) that they have attained a certain power of interpreting the sacred books without reading any directions of the kind that I propose to lay down here, will cry out that such rules are not necessary for any one, but that everything rightly done towards clearing up the obscurities of Scripture could be better done by the unassisted grace of God.

3. To reply briefly to all these: To those who do not understand what is here set down, my answer is that I am not to be blamed for their want of understanding. It is just as if they were anxious to see the new or the old moon, or some very obscure star, and I should point it out with my finger: if they had not sight enough to see even my finger, they would surely have no right to fly into a passion with me on that account. As for those who, even though they know and understand my directions, fail to penetrate the meaning of obscure passages in Scripture, they may stand for those who, in the case I have imagined, are just able to see my finger, but cannot see the stars at which it is pointed. And so both these classes had better give up blaming me, and pray instead that God would grant them the sight of their eyes. For though I can move my finger to point out an object, it is out of my power to open men's eyes that they may see either the fact that I am pointing, or the object at which I point.

4. But now as to those who talk vauntingly of Divine Grace, and boast that they understand and can explain Scripture without the aid of such directions as those I now propose to lay down, and who think, therefore, that what I have undertaken to write is entirely superfluous. I would such persons could calm themselves so far as to remember that, however justly they may rejoice in God's great gift, yet it was from human teachers they themselves learnt to read. Now, they would hardly think it right that they should for that reason be held in contempt by the Egyptian monk Antony, a just and holy man, who, not being able to read himself, is said to have committed the Scriptures to memory through hear-

ing them read by others, and by dint of wise meditation to have arrived at a thorough understanding of them; or by that barbarian slave Christianus, of whom I have lately heard from very respectable and trustworthy witnesses, who, without any teaching from man, attained a full knowledge of the art of reading simply through prayer that it might be revealed to him; after three days' supplication obtaining his request that he might read through a book presented to him on the spot by the astonished bystanders.

5. But if any one thinks that these stories are false, I do not strongly insist on them. For, as I am dealing with Christians who profess to understand the Scriptures without any directions from man (and if the fact be so, they boast of a real advantage, and one of no ordinary kind), they must surely grant that every one of us learnt his own language by hearing it constantly from childhood, and that any other language we have learnt—Greek, or Hebrew, or any of the rest—we have learnt either in the same way, by hearing it spoken, or from a human teacher. Now, then, suppose we advise all our brethren not to teach their children any of these things, because on the outpouring of the Holy Spirit the apostles immediately began to speak the language of every race; and warn every one who has not had a like experience that he need not consider himself a Christian, or may at least doubt whether he has yet received the Holy Spirit? No, no; rather let us put away false pride and learn whatever can be learnt from man; and let him who teaches another communicate what he has himself received without arrogance and without jealousy. And do not let us tempt Him in Whom we have believed, lest, being ensnared by such wiles of the enemy and by our own perversity, we may even refuse to go to the churches to hear the gospel itself, or to read a book, or to listen to another reading or preaching, in the hope that we shall be carried up to the third heaven, "whether in the body or out of the body," as the apostle says,[1] and there hear unspeakable words, such as it is not lawful for man to utter, or see the Lord Jesus Christ and hear the gospel from His own lips rather than from those of men.

6. Let us beware of such dangerous temptations of pride, and let us rather consider the fact that the Apostle Paul himself, although stricken down and admonished by the voice of God from heaven, was yet sent to a man

to receive the sacraments and be admitted into the Church;[2] and that Cornelius the centurion, although an angel announced to him that his prayers were heard and his alms had in remembrance, was yet handed over to Peter for instruction, and not only received the sacraments from the apostle's hands, but was also instructed by him as to the proper objects of faith, hope, and love.[3] And without doubt it was *possible* to have done everything through the instrumentality of angels, but the condition of our race would have been much more degraded if God had not chosen to make use of men as the ministers of His word to their fellow-men. For how could that be true which is written, "The temple of God is holy, which temple ye are,"[4] if God gave forth no oracles from His human temple, but communicated everything that He wished to be taught to men by voices from heaven, or through the ministration of angels? Moreover, love itself, which binds men together in the bond of unity, would have no means of pouring soul into soul, and, as it were, mingling them one with another, if men never learnt anything from their fellow-men.

7. And we know that the eunuch who was reading Isaiah the prophet, and did not understand what he read, was not sent by the apostle to an angel, nor was it an angel who explained to him what he did not understand, nor was he inwardly illuminated by the grace of God without the interposition of man; on the contrary, at the suggestion of God, Philip, who *did* understand the prophet, came to him, and sat with him, and in human words, and with a human tongue, opened to him the Scriptures.[5] Did not God talk with Moses, and yet he, with great wisdom and entire absence of jealous pride, accepted the plan of his father-in-law, a man of an alien race, for ruling and administering the affairs of the great nation entrusted to him?[6] For Moses knew that a wise plan, in whatever mind it might originate, was to be ascribed not to the man who devised it, but to Him Who is the Truth, the unchangeable God.

8. In the last place, every one who boasts that he, through divine illumination, understands the obscurities of Scripture, though not instructed in any rules of interpretation, at the same time believes, and rightly believes, that this power is not his own, in the sense of originating with himself, but is the gift of God. For so he seeks God's glory, not his own. But reading and understanding, as he does, without

[1] II Cor. 12. 2–4.

[2] Acts, 9. 3.   [3] Acts, 10.   [4] I Cor. 3. 17.
[5] Acts, 8. 26.   [6] Ex. 18. 13.

the aid of any human interpreter, why does he himself undertake to interpret for others? Why does he not rather send them direct to God, that they too may learn by the inward teaching of the Spirit without the help of man? The truth is, he fears to incur the reproach: "Thou wicked and slothful servant, thou oughtest to have put my money to the exchangers."[1] Seeing, then, that these men teach others, either through speech or writing, what they understand, surely they cannot blame me if I likewise teach not only what they understand, but also the rules of interpretation they follow. For no one ought to consider anything as his own, except perhaps what is false. All truth is of Him who says, "I am the truth."[2] For what have we that we did not receive? and if we have received it, why do we glory, as if we had not received it?[3]

9. He who reads to an audience pronounces aloud the words he sees before him: he who teaches reading, does it that others may be able to read for themselves. Each, however, communicates to others what he has learnt him-

self. Just so, the man who explains to an audience the passages of Scripture he understands is like one who reads aloud the words before him. On the other hand, the man who lays down rules for interpretation is like one who teaches reading, that is, shows others how to read for themselves. So that, just as he who knows how to read is not dependent on some one else, when he finds a book, to tell him what is written in it, so the man who is in possession of the rules which I here attempt to lay down, if he meet with an obscure passage in the books which he reads, will not need an interpreter to lay open the secret to him, but, holding fast by certain rules, and following up certain indications, will arrive at the hidden sense without any error, or at least without falling into any gross absurdity. And so although it will sufficiently appear in the course of the work itself that no one can justly object to this undertaking of mine, which has no other object than to be of service, yet as it seemed convenient to reply at the outset to any one who might make preliminary objections, such is the start I have thought good to make on the road I am about to traverse in this book.

[1]Matt. 25. 26, 27.   [2]John, 14. 6.
[3]I Cor. 4. 7.

BOOK I

ARGUMENT. THE AUTHOR DIVIDES HIS WORK INTO TWO PARTS, ONE RELATING TO THE DISCOVERY, THE OTHER TO THE EXPRESSION, OF THE TRUE SENSE OF SCRIPTURE. HE SHOWS THAT TO DISCOVER THE MEANING WE MUST ATTEND BOTH TO THINGS AND TO SIGNS, AS IT IS NECESSARY TO KNOW WHAT THINGS WE OUGHT TO TEACH THE CHRISTIAN PEOPLE, AND ALSO THE SIGNS OF THESE THINGS, THAT IS, WHERE THE KNOWLEDGE OF THESE THINGS IS TO BE SOUGHT. IN THIS FIRST BOOK HE TREATS OF THINGS, WHICH HE DIVIDES INTO THREE CLASSES—THINGS TO BE ENJOYED, THINGS TO BE USED, AND THINGS WHICH USE AND ENJOY. THE ONLY OBJECT WHICH OUGHT TO BE ENJOYED IS THE TRIUNE GOD, WHO IS OUR HIGHEST GOOD AND OUR TRUE HAPPINESS. WE ARE PREVENTED BY OUR SINS FROM ENJOYING GOD; AND THAT OUR SINS MIGHT BE TAKEN AWAY, "THE WORD WAS MADE FLESH," OUR LORD SUFFERED, AND DIED, AND ROSE AGAIN, AND ASCENDED INTO HEAVEN, TAKING TO HIMSELF AS HIS BRIDE THE CHURCH, IN WHICH WE RECEIVE REMISSION OF OUR SINS. AND IF OUR SINS ARE REMITTED AND OUR SOULS RENEWED BY GRACE, WE MAY AWAIT WITH HOPE THE RESURRECTION OF THE BODY TO ETERNAL GLORY; IF NOT, WE SHALL BE RAISED TO EVERLASTING PUNISHMENT. THESE MATTERS RELATING TO FAITH HAVING BEEN EXPOUNDED, THE AUTHOR GOES ON TO SHOW THAT ALL OBJECTS, EXCEPT GOD, ARE FOR USE; FOR, THOUGH SOME OF THEM MAY BE LOVED, YET OUR LOVE IS NOT TO REST IN THEM, BUT TO HAVE REFERENCE TO GOD. AND WE OURSELVES ARE NOT OBJECTS OF ENJOYMENT TO GOD: HE USES US, BUT FOR OUR OWN ADVANTAGE. HE THEN GOES ON TO SHOW THAT LOVE—THE LOVE OF GOD FOR HIS OWN SAKE AND THE LOVE OF OUR NEIGHBOUR FOR GOD'S SAKE—IS THE FULFILLMENT AND THE END OF ALL SCRIPTURE. AFTER ADDING A FEW WORDS ABOUT HOPE, HE SHOWS, IN CONCLUSION, THAT FAITH, HOPE, AND LOVE ARE GRACES ESSENTIALLY NECESSARY FOR HIM WHO WOULD UNDERSTAND AND EXPLAIN ARIGHT THE HOLY SCRIPTURES.

CHAPTER 1

The interpretation of Scripture depends on the discovery and enunciation of the meaning, and is to be undertaken in dependence on God's aid

1. THERE are two things on which all interpretation of Scripture depends: the mode of ascertaining the proper meaning, and the mode of making known the meaning when it is ascertained. We shall treat first of the mode of ascertaining, next of the mode of making known, the meaning—a great and arduous undertaking, and one that, if difficult to carry out, it is, I fear, presumptuous to enter upon. And presumptuous it would undoubtedly be, if I were counting on my own strength; but since my hope of accomplishing the work rests on Him Who has already supplied me with many thoughts on this subject, I do not fear but that He will go on to supply what is yet wanting when once I have begun to use what He has already given. For a possession which is not diminished by being shared with others, if it is possessed and not shared, is not yet possessed as it ought to be possessed. The Lord saith,

"Whosoever hath, to him shall be given."[1] He will give, then, to those who have; that is to say, if they use freely and cheerfully what they have received, He will add to and perfect His gifts. The loaves in the miracle were only five and seven in number before the disciples began to divide them among the hungry people. But when once they began to distribute them, though the wants of so many thousands were satisfied, they filled baskets with the fragments that were left.[2] Now, just as that bread increased in the very act of breaking it, so those thoughts which the Lord has already vouchsafed to me with a view to undertaking this work will, as soon as I begin to impart them to others, be multiplied by His grace, so that, in this very work of distribution in which I have engaged, so far from incurring loss and poverty, I shall be made to rejoice in a marvellous increase of wealth.

CHAP. 2. *What a thing is, and what a sign*

2. All instruction is either about things or about signs; but things are learnt by means of

[1] Matt. 13. 12.
[2] Matt. 14. 17, etc.; 20. 34, etc.

signs. I now use the word "thing" in a strict sense to signify that which is never employed as a sign of anything else: for example, wood, stone, cattle, and other things of that kind. Not, however, the wood which we read Moses cast into the bitter waters to make them sweet,[1] nor the stone which Jacob used as a pillow,[2] nor the ram which Abraham offered up instead of his son;[3] for these, though they are things, are also signs of other things. There are signs of another kind, those which are never employed except as signs: for example, words. No one uses words except as signs of something else; and hence may be understood what I call signs: those things, to wit, which are used to indicate something else. Accordingly, every sign is also a thing; for what is not a thing is nothing at all. Every thing, however, is not also a sign. And so, in regard to this distinction between things and signs, I shall, when I speak of things, speak in such a way that even if some of them may be used as signs also, that will not interfere with the division of the subject according to which I am to discuss things first and signs afterwards. But we must carefully remember that what we have now to consider about things is what they are in themselves, not what other things they are signs of.

Chap. 3. *Some things are for use, some for enjoyment*

3. There are some things, then, which are to be enjoyed, others which are to be used, others still which enjoy and use. Those things which are objects of enjoyment make us happy. Those things which are objects of use assist, and (so to speak) support us in our efforts after happiness, so that we can attain the things that make us happy and rest in them. We ourselves, again, who enjoy and use these things, being placed among both kinds of objects, if we set ourselves to enjoy those which we ought to use, are hindered in our course, and sometimes even led away from it; so that, getting entangled in the love of lower gratifications, we lag behind in, or even altogether turn back from, the pursuit of the real and proper objects of enjoyment.

Chap. 4. *Difference of use and enjoyment*

4. For to enjoy a thing is to rest with satisfaction in it for its own sake. To use, on the other hand, is to employ whatever means are at one's disposal to obtain what one desires, if it is a proper object of desire; for an unlawful use ought rather to be called an abuse. Sup-

pose, then, we were wanderers in a strange country, and could not live happily away from our fatherland, and that we felt wretched in our wandering, and wishing to put an end to our misery, determined to return home. We find, however, that we must make use of some mode of conveyance, either by land or water, in order to reach that fatherland where our enjoyment is to commence. But the beauty of the country through which we pass, and the very pleasure of the motion, charm our hearts, and turning these things which we ought to use into objects of enjoyment, we become unwilling to hasten the end of our journey; and becoming engrossed in a factitious delight, our thoughts are diverted from that home whose delights would make us truly happy. Such is a picture of our condition in this life of mortality. We have wandered far from God; and if we wish to return to our Father's home, this world must be used, not enjoyed, that so the invisible things of God may be clearly seen, being understood by the things that are made[4]—that is, that by means of what is material and temporary we may lay hold upon that which is spiritual and eternal.

Chap. 5. *The Trinity the true object of enjoyment*

5. The true objects of enjoyment, then, are the Father and the Son and the Holy Spirit, Who are at the same time the Trinity, one Being, supreme above all, and common to all who enjoy Him, if He is an object, and not rather the cause of all objects, or indeed even if He is the cause of all. For it is not easy to find a name that will suitably express so great excellence, unless it is better to speak in this way: The Trinity, one God, of Whom are all things, through Whom are all things, in Whom are all things.[5] Thus the Father and the Son and the Holy Spirit, and each of these by Himself, is God, and at the same time they are all one God; and each of them by Himself is a complete substance, and yet they are all one substance. The Father is not the Son nor the Holy Spirit; the Son is not the Father nor the Holy Spirit; the Holy Spirit is not the Father nor the Son: but the Father is only Father, the Son is only Son, and the Holy Spirit is only Holy Spirit. To all three belong the same eternity, the same unchangeableness, the same majesty, the same power. In the Father is unity, in the Son equality, in the Holy Spirit the harmony of unity and equality; and these three attributes

---

[1] Ex. 15. 25.   [2] Gen. 28. 11.   [3] Gen. 22. 13.   [4] Rom. 1. 20.   [5] Rom. 11. 36.

are all one because of the Father, all equal because of the Son, and all harmonious because of the Holy Spirit.

CHAP. 6. *In what sense God is ineffable*

6. Have I spoken of God, or uttered His praise, in any worthy way? Nay, I feel that I have done nothing more than desire to speak; and if I have said anything, it is not what I desired to say. How do I know this, except from the fact that God is unspeakable? But what I have said, if it had been unspeakable, could not have been spoken. And so God is not even to be called "unspeakable," because to say even this is to speak of Him. Thus there arises a curious contradiction of words, because if the unspeakable is what cannot be spoken of, it is not unspeakable if it can be called unspeakable. And this opposition of words is rather to be avoided by silence than to be explained away by speech. And yet God, although nothing worthy of His greatness can be said of Him, has condescended to accept the worship of men's mouths, and has desired us through the medium of our own words to rejoice in His praise. For on this principle it is that He is called *Deus* (God). For the sound of those two syllables in itself conveys no true knowledge of His nature; but yet all who know the Latin tongue are led, when that sound reaches their ears, to think of a nature supreme in excellence and eternal in existence.

CHAP. 7. *What all men understand by the term God*

7. For when the one supreme God of gods is thought of, even by those who believe that there are other gods, and who call them by that name, and worship them as gods, their thought takes the form of an endeavour to reach the conception of a nature, than which nothing more excellent or more exalted exists. And since men are moved by different kinds of pleasures, partly by those which pertain to the bodily senses, partly by those which pertain to the intellect and soul, those of them who are in bondage to sense think that either the heavens, or what appears to be most brilliant in the heavens, or the universe itself, is God of gods: or if they try to get beyond the universe, they picture to themselves something of dazzling brightness, and think of it vaguely as infinite, or of the most beautiful form conceivable; or they represent it in the form of the human body, if they think that superior to all

others. Or if they think that there is no one God supreme above the rest, but that there are many or even innumerable gods of equal rank, still these too they conceive as possessed of shape and form, according to what each man thinks the pattern of excellence. Those, on the other hand, who endeavour by an effort of the intelligence to reach a conception of God, place Him above all visible and bodily natures, and even above all intelligent and spiritual natures that are subject to change. All, however, strive emulously to exalt the excellence of God: nor could any one be found to believe that any being to whom there exists a superior is God. And so all concur in believing that God is that which excels in dignity all other objects.

CHAP. 8. *God to be esteemed above all else, because he is unchangeable wisdom*

8. And since all who think about God think of Him as living, they only can form any conception of Him that is not absurd and unworthy who think of Him as life itself; and, whatever may be the bodily form that has suggested itself to them, recognize that it is by life it lives or does not live, and prefer what is living to what is dead; who understand that the living bodily form itself, however it may outshine all others in splendour, overtop them in size, and excel them in beauty, is quite a distinct thing from the life by which it is quickened; and who look upon the life as incomparably superior in dignity and worth to the mass which is quickened and animated by it. Then, when they go on to look into the nature of the life itself, if they find it mere nutritive life, without sensibility, such as that of plants, they consider it inferior to sentient life, such as that of cattle; and above this, again, they place intelligent life, such as that of men. And, perceiving that even this is subject to change, they are compelled to place above it, again, that unchangeable life, which is not at one time foolish, at another time wise, but on the contrary is wisdom itself. For a wise intelligence, that is, one that has attained to wisdom, was, previous to its attaining wisdom, unwise. But wisdom itself never was unwise, and never can become so. And if men never caught sight of this wisdom, they could never with entire confidence prefer a life which is unchangeably wise to one that is subject to change. This will be evident, if we consider that the very rule of truth by which they affirm the unchangeable life to be the more excellent,

is itself unchangeable: and they cannot find such a rule, except by going beyond their own nature; for they find nothing in themselves that is not subject to change.

CHAP. 9. *All acknowledge the superiority of unchangeable wisdom to that which is variable*

9. Now, no one is so egregiously silly as to ask, "How do you know that a life of unchangeable wisdom is preferable to one of change?" For that very truth about which he asks, how I know it? is unchangeably fixed in the minds of all men, and presented to their common contemplation. And the man who does not see it is like a blind man in the sun, whom it profits nothing that the splendour of its light, so clear and so near, is poured into his very eye-balls. The man, on the other hand, who sees, but shrinks from this truth, is weak in his mental vision from dwelling long among the shadows of the flesh. And thus men are driven back from their native land by the contrary blasts of evil habits, and pursue lower and less valuable objects in preference to that which they own to be more excellent and more worthy.

CHAP. 10. *To see God, the soul must be purified*

10. Wherefore, since it is our duty fully to enjoy the truth which lives unchangeably, and since the triune God takes counsel in this truth for the things which He has made, the soul must be purified that it may have power to perceive that light, and to rest in it when it is perceived. And let us look upon this purification as a kind of journey or voyage to our native land. For it is not by change of place that we can come nearer to Him Who is in every place, but by the cultivation of pure desires and virtuous habits.

CHAP. 11. *Wisdom becoming incarnate, a pattern to us of purification*

11. But of this we should have been wholly incapable, had not Wisdom condescended to adapt Himself to our weakness, and to show us a pattern of holy life in the form of our own humanity. Yet, since we when we come to Him do wisely, He when He came to us was considered by proud men to have done very foolishly. And since we when we come to Him become strong, He when He came to us was looked upon as weak. But "the foolishness of God is wiser than men; and the weakness of God is

stronger than men."[1] And thus, though Wisdom was Himself our home, He made Himself also the way by which we should reach our home.

CHAP. 12. *In what sense the wisdom of God came to us*

And though He is everywhere present to the inner eye when it is sound and clear, He condescended to make Himself manifest to the outward eye of those whose inward sight is weak and dim. "For after that, in the wisdom of God, the world by wisdom knew not God, it pleased God by the foolishness of preaching to save them that believe."[2]

12. Not then in the sense of traversing space, but because He appeared to mortal men in the form of mortal flesh, He is said to have come to us. For He came to a place where He had always been, seeing that "He was in the world, and the world was made by Him." But, because men, who in their eagerness to enjoy the creature instead of the Creator had grown into the likeness of this world, and are therefore most appropriately named "the world," did not recognize Him, therefore the evangelist says, "and the world knew Him not."[3] Thus, in the wisdom of God, the world by wisdom knew not God. Why then did He come, seeing that He was already here, except that it pleased God through the foolishness of preaching to save them that believe?

CHAP. 13. *The Word was made flesh*

In what way did He come but this, "The Word was made flesh, and dwelt among us"?[4] Just as when we speak, in order that what we have in our minds may enter through the ear into the mind of the hearer, the word which we have in our hearts becomes an outward sound and is called speech; and yet our thought does not lose itself in the sound, but remains complete in itself, and takes the form of speech without being modified in its own nature by the change: so the Divine Word, though suffering no change of nature, yet became flesh, that He might dwell among us.

CHAP. 14. *How the wisdom of God healed man*

13. Moreover, as the use of remedies is the way to health, so this remedy took up sinners to heal and restore them. And just as surgeons, when they bind up wounds, do it not in a slovenly way, but carefully, that there may be

[1] I Cor. 1. 25. [2] I Cor. 1. 21.
[3] John, 1. 10. [4] John, 1. 14.

a certain degree of neatness in the binding, in addition to its mere usefulness, so our medicine, Wisdom, was by His assumption of humanity adapted to our wounds, curing some of them by their opposites, some of them by their likes. And just as he who ministers to a bodily hurt in some cases applies contraries, as cold to hot, moist to dry, etc., and in other cases applies likes, as a round cloth to a round wound, or an oblong cloth to an oblong wound, and does not fit the same bandage to all limbs, but puts like to like; in the same way the Wisdom of God in healing man has applied Himself to his cure, being Himself healer and medicine both in one. Seeing, then, that man fell through pride, He restored him through humility. We were ensnared by the wisdom of the serpent: we are set free by the foolishness of God. Moreover, just as the former was called wisdom, but was in reality the folly of those who despised God, so the latter is called foolishness, but is true wisdom in those who overcome the devil. We used our immortality so badly as to incur the penalty of death: Christ used His mortality so well as to restore us to life. The disease was brought in through a woman's corrupted soul: the remedy came through a woman's virgin body. To the same class of opposite remedies it belongs, that our vices are cured by the example of His virtues. On the other hand, the following are, as it were, bandages made in the same shape as the limbs and wounds to which they are applied: He was born of a woman to deliver us who fell through a woman. He came as a man to save us who are men, as a mortal to save us who are mortals, by death to save us who were dead. And those who can follow out the matter more fully, who are not hurried on by the necessity of carrying out a set undertaking, will find many other points of instruction in considering the remedies, whether opposites or likes, employed in the medicine of Christianity.

CHAP. 15. *Faith is buttressed by the resurrection and ascension of Christ, and is stimulated by his coming to judgment*

14. The belief of the resurrection of our Lord from the dead, and of His ascension into heaven, has strengthened our faith by adding a great buttress of hope. For it clearly shows how freely He laid down His life for us when He had it in His power thus to take it up again. With what assurance, then, is the hope of believers animated, when they reflect how great He was Who suffered so great things for them

while they were still in unbelief! And when men look for Him to come from heaven as the judge of quick and dead, it strikes great terror into the careless, so that they betake themselves to diligent preparation, and learn by holy living to long for His approach, instead of quaking at it on account of their evil deeds. And what tongue can tell, or what imagination can conceive, the reward He will bestow at the last, when we consider that for our comfort in this earthly journey He has given us so freely of His Spirit that in the adversities of this life we may retain our confidence in, and love for, Him Whom as yet we see not; and that He has also given to each gifts suitable for the building up of His Church, that we may do what He points out as right to be done, not only without a murmur, but even with delight?

CHAP. 16. *Christ purges his Church by medicinal afflictions*

15. For the Church is His body, as the apostle's teaching shows us;[1] and it is even called His spouse.[2] His body, then, which has many members, and all performing different functions, He holds together in the bond of unity and love, which is its true health. Moreover He exercises it in the present time, and purges it with many wholesome afflictions, that, when He has transplanted it from this world to the eternal world, He may take it to Himself as His bride, without spot or wrinkle, or any such thing.

CHAP. 17. *Christ, by forgiving our sins, opened the way to our home*

16. Further, when we are on the way, and that not a way that lies through space, but through a change of affections, and one which the guilt of our past sins like a hedge of thorns barred against us, what could He, Who was willing to lay Himself down as the way by which we should return, do that would be still gracious and more merciful, except to forgive us all our sins, and by being crucified for us to remove the stern decrees that barred the door against our return?

CHAP. 18. *The keys given to the Church*

17. He has given, therefore, the keys to His Church, that whatsoever it should bind on earth might be bound in heaven, and whatsoever it should loose on earth might be loosed in heaven;[3] that is to say, that whosoever in the Church should not believe that his sins are remitted, they should not be remitted to him; but that

---

[1]Cf. Eph. 1. 23 with Rom. 12. 5.
[2]Rev. 19. 7; 21. 9.   [3]Cf. Matt. 16. 19 with 18. 18.

whosoever should believe, and should repent, and turn from his sins, should be saved by the same faith and repentance on the ground of which he is received into the bosom of the Church. For he who does not believe that his sins can be pardoned falls into despair, and becomes worse, as if no greater good remained for him than to be evil, when he has ceased to have faith in the results of his own repentance.

CHAP. 19. *Bodily and spiritual death and resurrection*

18. Furthermore, as there is a kind of death of the soul, which consists in the putting away of former habits and former ways of life, and which comes through repentance, so also the death of the body consists in the dissolution of the former principle of life. And just as the soul, after it has put away and destroyed by repentance its former habits, is created anew after a better pattern, so we must hope and believe that the body, after that death which we all owe as a debt contracted through sin, shall at the resurrection be changed into a better form; not that flesh and blood shall inherit the kingdom of God (for that is impossible), but that this corruptible shall put on incorruption, and this mortal shall put on immortality.[1] And thus the body, being the source of no uneasiness because it can feel no want, shall be animated by a spirit perfectly pure and happy, and shall enjoy unbroken peace.

CHAP. 20. *The resurrection to damnation*

19. Now he whose soul does not die to this world and begin here to be conformed to the truth, falls when the body dies into a more terrible death, and shall revive, not to change his earthly for a heavenly habitation, but to endure the penalty of his sin.

CHAP. 21. *Neither body nor soul extinguished at death*

And so faith clings to the assurance, and we must believe that it is so in fact, that neither the human soul nor the human body suffers complete extinction, but that the wicked rise again to endure inconceivable punishment, and the good to receive eternal life.

CHAP. 22. *God alone to be enjoyed*

20. Among all these things, then, those only are the true objects of enjoyment which we have spoken of as eternal and unchangeable. The rest are for use, that we may be able to arrive at the

[1] Cor. 15. 50–53.

full enjoyment of the former. We, however, who enjoy and use other things are things ourselves. For a great thing truly is man, made after the image and similitude of God, not as respects the mortal body in which he is clothed, but as respects the rational soul by which he is exalted in honour above the beasts. And so it becomes an important question, whether men ought to enjoy, or to use, themselves, or to do both. For we are commanded to love one another: but it is a question whether man is to be loved by man for his own sake, or for the sake of something else. If it is for his own sake, we enjoy him; if it is for the sake of something else, we use him. It seems to me, then, that he is to be loved for the sake of something else. For if a thing is to be loved for its own sake, then in the enjoyment of it consists a happy life, the hope of which at least, if not yet the reality, is our comfort in the present time. But a curse is pronounced on him who places his hope in man.[2]

21. Neither ought any one to have joy in himself, if you look at the matter clearly, because no one ought to love even himself for his own sake, but for the sake of Him Who is the true object of enjoyment. For a man is never in so good a state as when his whole life is a journey towards the unchangeable life, and his affections are entirely fixed upon that. If, however, he loves himself for his own sake, he does not look at himself in relation to God, but turns his mind in upon himself, and so is not occupied with anything that is unchangeable. And thus he does not enjoy himself at his best, because he is better when his mind is fully fixed upon, and his affections wrapped up in, the unchangeable good, than when he turns from that to enjoy even himself. Wherefore if you ought not to love even yourself for your own sake, but for His in Whom your love finds its most worthy object, no other man has a right to be angry if you love him too for God's sake. For this is the law of love that has been laid down by Divine authority: "Thou shalt love thy neighbour as thyself"; but, "Thou shalt love God with all thy heart, and with all thy soul, and with all thy mind":[3] so that you are to concentrate all your thoughts, your whole life, and your whole intelligence upon Him from Whom you derive all that you bring. For when He says, "With all thy heart, and with all thy soul, and with all thy mind," He means that no part of our life is to be unoccupied, and to afford room, as it were, for the wish to enjoy some other object, but that

[2] Jer. 17. 5.
[3] Matt. 22. 37–39. Cf. Lev. 19. 18; Deut. 6. 5.

whatever else may suggest itself to us as an object worthy of love is to be borne into the same channel in which the whole current of our affections flows. Whoever, then, loves his neighbour aright, ought to urge upon him that he too should love God with his whole heart, and soul, and mind. For in this way, loving his neighbour as himself, a man turns the whole current of his love both for himself and his neighbour into the channel of the love of God, which suffers no stream to be drawn off from itself by whose diversion its own volume would be diminished.

CHAP. 23. *Man needs no injunction to love himself and his own body*

22. Those things which are objects of use are not all, however, to be loved, but those only which are either united with us in a common relation to God, such as a man or an angel, or are so related to us as to need the goodness of God through our instrumentality, such as the body. For assuredly the martyrs did not love the wickedness of their persecutors, although they used it to attain the favour of God. As, then, there are four kinds of things that are to be loved—first, that which is above us; second, ourselves; third, that which is on a level with us; fourth, that which is beneath us—no precepts need be given about the second and fourth of these. For, however far a man may fall away from the truth, he still continues to love himself, and to love his own body. The soul which flies away from the unchangeable Light, the Ruler of all things, does so that it may rule over itself and over its own body; and so it cannot but love both itself and its own body.

23. Moreover, it thinks it has attained something very great if it is able to lord it over its companions, that is, other men. For it is inherent in the sinful soul to desire above all things, and to claim as due to itself, that which is properly due to God only. Now such love of itself is more correctly called hate. For it is not just that it should desire what is beneath it to be obedient to it while itself will not obey its own superior; and most justly has it been said, "He who loveth iniquity hateth his own soul." [1] And accordingly the soul becomes weak and endures much suffering about the mortal body. For, of course, it must love the body, and be grieved at its corruption; and the immortality and incorruptibility of the body spring out of the health of the soul. Now the health of the soul is to cling steadfastly to the better part, that is, to the unchangeable God. But when it aspires to lord it

[1]Ps. 10. 5 (Septuagint).

even over those who are by nature its equals—that is, its fellow-men—this is a reach of arrogance utterly intolerable.

CHAP. 24. *No man hates his own flesh, not even those who abuse it*

24. No man, then, hates himself. On this point, indeed, no question was ever raised by any sect. But neither does any man hate his own body. For the apostle says truly, "No man ever yet hated his own flesh." [2] And when some people say that they would rather be without a body altogether, they entirely deceive themselves. For it is not their body, but its corruptions and its heaviness, that they hate. And so it is not no body, but an uncorrupted and very light body, that they want. But they think a body of that kind would be no body at all, because they think such a thing as that must be a spirit. And as to the fact that they seem in some sort to scourge their bodies by abstinence and toil, those who do this in the right spirit do it not that they may get rid of their body, but that they may have it in subjection and ready for every needful work. For they strive by a kind of toilsome exercise of the body itself to root out those lusts that are hurtful to the body, that is, those habits and affections of the soul that lead to the enjoyment of unworthy objects. They are not destroying themselves; they are taking care of their health.

25. Those, on the other hand, who do this in a perverse spirit, make war upon their own body as if it were a natural enemy. And in this matter they are led astray by a mistaken interpretation of what they read: "The flesh lusteth against the spirit, and the spirit against the flesh, and these are contrary the one to the other." [3] For this is said of the carnal habit yet unsubdued, against which the spirit lusteth, not to destroy the body, but to eradicate the lust of the body—i.e., its evil habit—and thus to make it subject to the spirit, which is what the order of nature demands. For as, after the resurrection, the body, having become wholly subject to the spirit, will live in perfect peace to all eternity; even in this life we must make it an object to have the carnal habit changed for the better, so that its inordinate affections may not war against the soul. And until this shall take place, "the flesh lusteth against the spirit, and the spirit against the flesh"; the spirit struggling, not in hatred, but for the mastery, because it desires that what it loves should be subject to the higher principle; and the flesh struggling, not in hatred, but because of the bondage of habit which

[2]Eph. 5. 29.   [3]Gal. 5. 17.

it has derived from its parent stock, and which has grown in upon it by a law of nature till it has become inveterate. The spirit, then, in subduing the flesh, is working as it were to destroy the ill-founded peace of an evil habit, and to bring about the real peace which springs out of a good habit. Nevertheless, not even those who, led astray by false notions, hate their bodies would be prepared to sacrifice one eye, even supposing they could do so without suffering any pain, and that they had as much sight left in one as they formerly had in two, unless some object was to be attained which would overbalance the loss. This and other indications of the same kind are sufficient to show those who candidly seek the truth how well-founded is the statement of the apostle when he says, "No man ever yet hated his own flesh." He adds too, "but nourisheth and cherisheth it, even as the Lord the Church." [1]

CHAP. 25. *A man may love something more than his body, but does not therefore hate his body*

26. Man, therefore, ought to be taught the due measure of loving, that is, in what measure he may love himself so as to be of service to himself. For that he does love himself, and does desire to do good to himself, nobody but a fool would doubt. He is to be taught, too, in what measure to love his body, so as to care for it wisely and within due limits. For it is equally manifest that he loves his body also, and desires to keep it safe and sound. And yet a man may have something that he loves better than the safety and soundness of his body. For many have been found voluntarily to suffer both pains and amputations of some of their limbs that they might obtain other objects which they valued more highly. But no one is to be told not to desire the safety and health of his body because there is something he desires more. For the miser, though he loves money, buys bread for himself—that is, he gives away money that he is very fond of and desires to heap up—but it is because he values more highly the bodily health which the bread sustains. It is superfluous to argue longer on a point so very plain, but this is just what the error of wicked men often compels us to do.

CHAP. 26. *The command to love God and our neighbour includes a command to love ourselves*

27. Seeing, then, that there is no need of a command that every man should love himself and his own body—seeing, that is, that we love

[1]Eph. 5. 29.

ourselves, and what is beneath us but connected with us, through a law of nature which has never been violated, and which is common to us with the beasts (for even the beasts love themselves and their own bodies)—it only remained necessary to lay injunctions upon us in regard to God above us, and our neighbour beside us. "Thou shalt love," He says, "the Lord thy God with all thy heart, and with all thy soul, and with all thy mind; and thou shalt love thy neighbour as thyself. On these two commandments hang all the law and the prophets." [2] Thus the end of the commandment is love, and that twofold, the love of God and the love of our neighbour. Now, if you take yourself in your entirety—that is, soul and body together—and your neighbour in his entirety, soul and body together (for man is made up of soul and body), you will find that none of the classes of things that are to be loved is overlooked in these two commandments. For though, when the love of God comes first, and the measure of our love for Him is prescribed in such terms that it is evident all other things are to find their centre in Him, nothing seems to be said about our love for ourselves; yet when it is said, "Thou shalt love thy neighbour as thyself," it at once becomes evident that our love for ourselves has not been overlooked.

CHAP. 27. *The order of love*

28. Now he is a man of just and holy life who forms an unprejudiced estimate of things, and keeps his affections also under strict control, so that he neither loves what he ought not to love, nor fails to love what he ought to love, nor loves that more which ought to be loved less, nor loves that equally which ought to be loved either less or more, nor loves that less or more which ought to be loved equally. No sinner is to be loved as a sinner; and every man is to be loved as a man for God's sake; but God is to be loved for His own sake. And if God is to be loved more than any man, each man ought to love God more than himself. Likewise we ought to love another man better than our own body, because all things are to be loved in reference to God, and another man can have fellowship with us in the enjoyment of God, whereas our body cannot; for the body only lives through the soul, and it is by the soul that we enjoy God.

CHAP. 28. *How we are to decide whom to aid*

29. Further, all men are to be loved equally. But since you cannot do good to all, you are to

[2]Matt. 22. 37–40.

pay special regard to those who, by the accidents of time, or place, or circumstance, are brought into closer connection with you. For, suppose that you had a great deal of some commodity, and felt bound to give it away to somebody who had none, and that it could not be given to more than one person; if two persons presented themselves, neither of whom had either from need or relationship a greater claim upon you than the other, you could do nothing fairer than choose by lot to which you would give what could not be given to both. Just so among men: since you cannot consult for the good of them all, you must take the matter as decided for you by a sort of lot, according as each man happens for the time being to be more closely connected with you.

CHAP. 29. *We are to desire and endeavour that all men may love God*

30. Now of all who can with us enjoy God, we love partly those to whom we render services, partly those who render services to us, partly those who both help us in our need and in turn are helped by us, partly those upon whom we confer no advantage and from whom we look for none. We ought to desire, however, that they should all join with us in loving God, and all the assistance that we either give them or accept from them should tend to that one end. For in the theatres, dens of iniquity though they be, if a man is fond of a particular actor, and enjoys his art as a great or even as the very greatest good, he is fond of all who join with him in admiration of his favourite, not for their own sakes, but for the sake of him whom they admire in common; and the more fervent he is in his admiration, the more he works in every way he can to secure new admirers for him, and the more anxious he becomes to show him to others; and if he find any one comparatively indifferent, he does all he can to excite his interest by urging his favourite's merits: if, however, he meet with any one who opposes him, he is exceedingly displeased by such a man's contempt of his favourite, and strives in every way he can to remove it. Now, if this be so, what does it become us to do who live in the fellowship of the love of God, the enjoyment of whom is true happiness of life, to whom all who love Him owe both their own existence and the love they bear Him, concerning whom we have no fear that any one who comes to know Him will be disappointed in Him, and who desires our love, not for any gain to Himself, but that those who love Him may obtain an eternal reward, even Himself

Whom they love? And hence it is that we love even our enemies. For we do not fear them, seeing they cannot take away from us what we love; but we pity them rather, because the more they hate us the more are they separated from Him Whom we love. For if they would turn to Him, they must of necessity love Him as the supreme good, and love us too as partakers with them in so great a blessing.

CHAP. 30. *Whether angels are to be reckoned our neighbours*

31. There arises further in this connection a question about angels. For they are happy in the enjoyment of Him Whom we long to enjoy; and the more we enjoy Him in this life as through a glass darkly, the more easy do we find it to bear our pilgrimage, and the more eagerly do we long for its termination. But it is not irrational to ask whether in those two commandments is included the love of angels also. For that He who commanded us to love our neighbour made no exception, as far as men are concerned, is shown both by our Lord Himself in the Gospel, and by the Apostle Paul. For when the man to whom our Lord delivered those two commandments, and to whom He said that on these hang all the law and the prophets, asked Him, "And who is my neighbour?" He told him of a certain man who, going down from Jerusalem to Jericho, fell among thieves, and was severely wounded by them, and left naked and half dead.[1] And He showed him that nobody was neighbour to this man except him who took pity upon him and came forward to relieve and care for him. And the man who had asked the question admitted the truth of this when he was himself interrogated in turn. To whom our Lord says, "Go and do thou likewise"; teaching us that he is our neighbour whom it is our duty to help in his need, or whom it would be our duty to help if he were in need. Whence it follows, that he whose duty it would be in turn to help us is our neighbour. For the name "neighbour" is a relative one, and no one can be neighbour except to a neighbour. And, again, who does not see that no exception is made of any one as a person to whom the offices of mercy may be denied when our Lord extends the rule even to our enemies? "Love your enemies, do good to them that hate you."[2]

32. And so also the Apostle Paul teaches when he says: "For this, Thou shalt not commit adultery, Thou shalt not kill, Thou shalt not steal, Thou shalt not bear false witness, Thou shalt

[1] Luke, 10. 29, ff.   [2] Matt. 5. 44.

not covet; and if there be any other commandment, it is briefly comprehended in this saying, namely, Thou shalt love thy neighbour as thyself. Love worketh no ill to his neighbour." [1] Whoever then supposes that the apostle did not embrace every man in this precept, is compelled to admit, what is at once most absurd and most pernicious, that the apostle thought it no sin, if a man were not a Christian or were an enemy, to commit adultery with his wife, or to kill him, or to covet his goods. And as nobody but a fool would say this, it is clear that every man is to be considered our neighbour, because we are to work no ill to any man.

33. But now, if every one to whom we ought to show, or who ought to show to us, the offices of mercy is by right called a neighbour, it is manifest that the command to love our neighbour embraces the holy angels also, seeing that so great offices of mercy have been performed by them on our behalf, as may easily be shown by turning the attention to many passages of Holy Scripture. And on this ground even God Himself, our Lord, desired to be called our neighbour. For our Lord Jesus Christ points to Himself under the figure of the man who brought aid to him who was lying half dead on the road, wounded and abandoned by the robbers. And the Psalmist says in his prayer, "I behaved myself as though he had been my friend or brother." [2] But as the Divine nature is of higher excellence than, and far removed above, our nature, the command to love God is distinct from that to love our neighbour. For He shows us pity on account of His own goodness, but we show pity to one another on account of His; that is, He pities us that we may fully enjoy Himself; we pity one another that we may fully enjoy Him.

CHAP. 31. *God uses rather than enjoys us*

34. And on this ground, when we say that we enjoy only that which we love for its own sake, and that nothing is a true object of enjoyment except that which makes us happy, and that all other things are for use, there seems still to be something that requires explanation. For God loves us, and Holy Scripture frequently sets before us the love He has towards us. In what way then does He love us? As objects of use or as objects of enjoyment? If He enjoys us, He must be in need of good from us, and no sane man will say that; for all the good we enjoy is either Himself, or what comes from Himself. And no one can be ignorant or in doubt as to the

fact that the light stands in no need of the glitter of the things it has itself lit up. The Psalmist says most plainly, "I said to the Lord, Thou art my God, for Thou needest not my goodness." [3] He does not enjoy us then, but makes use of us. For if He neither enjoys nor uses us, I am at a loss to discover in what way He can love us.

CHAP. 32. *In what way God uses man*

35. But neither does He use after our fashion of using. For when we use objects, we do so with a view to the full enjoyment of the goodness of God. God, however, in His use of us, has reference to His own goodness. For it is because He is good we exist; and so far as we truly exist we are good. And, further, because He is also just, we cannot with impunity be evil; and so far as we are evil, so far is our existence less complete. Now He is the first and supreme existence, Who is altogether unchangeable, and Who could say in the fullest sense of the words, "I AM THAT I AM," and "Thou shalt say to them, I AM hath sent me unto you"; [4] so that all other things that exist, both owe their existence entirely to Him, and are good only so far as He has given it to them to be so. That use, then, which God is said to make of us has no reference to His own advantage, but to ours only; and, so far as He is concerned, has reference only to His goodness. When we take pity upon a man and care for him, it is for his advantage we do so; but somehow or other our own advantage follows by a sort of natural consequence, for God does not leave the mercy we show to him who needs it to go without reward. Now this is our highest reward, that we should fully enjoy Him, and that all who enjoy Him should enjoy one another in Him.

CHAP. 33. *In what way man should be enjoyed*

36. For if we find our happiness complete in one another, we stop short upon the road, and place our hope of happiness in man or angel. Now the proud man and the proud angel arrogate this to themselves, and are glad to have the hope of others fixed upon them. But, on the contrary, the holy man and the holy angel, even when we are weary and anxious to stay with them and rest in them, set themselves to recruit our energies with the provision which they have received of God for us or for themselves; and then urge us thus refreshed to go on our way towards Him, in the enjoyment of Whom we find our common happiness. For even the apostle exclaims, "Was Paul crucified for you? or were ye

---

[1]Rom. 13. 9, 10.   [2]Ps. 35. 14.   [3]Ps. 16. 2 (Septuagint).   [4]Ex. 3. 14.

baptized in the name of Paul?"[1] and again: "Neither is he that planteth anything, neither he that watereth; but God that giveth the increase."[2] And the angel admonisheth the man who is about to worship him, that he should rather worship Him Who is his Master, and under Whom he himself is a fellow-servant.[3]

37. But when you have joy of a man in God, it is God rather than man that you enjoy. For you enjoy Him by Whom you are made happy, and you rejoice to have come to Him in Whose presence you place your hope of joy. And accordingly, Paul says to Philemon, "Yea, brother, let me have joy of thee in the Lord."[4] For if he had not added "in the Lord," but had only said, "Let me have joy of thee," he would have implied that he fixed his hope of happiness upon him, although even in the immediate context to "enjoy" is used in the sense of to "use with delight." For when the thing that we love is near us, it is a matter of course that it should bring delight with it. And if you pass beyond this delight, and make it a means to that which you are permanently to rest in, you are using it, and it is an abuse of language to say that you enjoy it. But if you cling to it, and rest in it, finding your happiness complete in it, then you may be truly and properly said to enjoy it. And this we must never do except in the case of the Blessed Trinity, who is the Supreme and Unchangeable Good.

CHAP. 34. *Christ the first way to God*

38. And mark that even when He Who is Himself the Truth and the Word, by Whom all things were made, had been made flesh that He might dwell among us, the apostle yet says: "Yea, though we have known Christ after the flesh, yet now henceforth know we Him no more."[5] For Christ, desiring not only to give the possession to those who had completed the journey, but also to be Himself the way to those who were just setting out, determined to take a fleshly body. Whence also that expression, "The Lord created[6] me in the beginning of His way,"[7] that is, that those who wished to come might begin their journey in Him. The apostle, therefore, although still on the way, and following after God Who called him to the reward of His heavenly calling, yet forgetting those things which were behind, and pressing on towards those things which were before,[8] had already passed over the beginning of the way, and had

now no further need of it; yet by this way all must commence their journey who desire to attain to the truth, and to rest in eternal life. For He says: "I am the way, and the truth, and the life";[9] that is, by Me men come, to Me they come, in Me they rest. For when we come to Him, we come to the Father also, because through an equal an equal is known; and the Holy Spirit binds, and as it were seals us, so that we are able to rest permanently in the supreme and unchangeable Good. And hence we may learn how essential it is that nothing should detain us on the way, when not even our Lord Himself, so far as He has condescended to be our way, is willing to detain us, but wishes us rather to press on; and, instead of weakly clinging to temporal things, even though these have been put on and worn by Him for our salvation, to pass over them quickly, and to struggle to attain unto Himself, Who has freed our nature from the bondage of temporal things and has set it down at the right hand of His Father.

CHAP. 35. *The fulfilment and end of Scripture is the love of God and our neighbour*

39. Of all, then, that has been said since we entered upon the discussion about things, this is the sum: that we should clearly understand that the fulfilment and the end of the Law, and of all Holy Scripture, is the love of an object which is to be enjoyed, and the love of an object which can enjoy that other in fellowship with ourselves. For there is no need of a command that each man should love himself. The whole temporal dispensation for our salvation, therefore, was framed by the providence of God that we might know this truth and be able to act upon it; and we ought to use that dispensation, not with such love and delight as if it were a good to rest in, but with a transient feeling rather, such as we have towards the road, or carriages, or other things that are merely means. Perhaps some other comparison can be found that will more suitably express the idea that we are to love the things by which we are borne only for the sake of that towards which we are borne.

CHAP. 36. *That interpretation of Scripture which builds us up in love is not perniciously deceptive nor mendacious, even though it be faulty. The interpreter, however, should be corrected*

40. Whoever, then, thinks that he understands the Holy Scriptures, or any part of them, but

---

[1]I Cor. 1. 13. [2]I Cor. 3. 7. [3]Rev. 19. 10.
[4]Philem. 20. [5]II Cor. 5. 16. [7]Prov. 8. 22.
[6]Authorized Version: *possessed*. [8]Cf. Phil. 3. 13.
[9]John, 14. 6.

puts such an interpretation upon them as does not tend to build up this twofold love of God and our neighbour, does not yet understand them as he ought. If, on the other hand, a man draws a meaning from them that may be used for the building up of love, even though he does not happen upon the precise meaning which the author whom he reads intended to express in that place, his error is not pernicious, and he is wholly clear from the charge of deception. For there is involved in deception the intention to say what is false; and we find plenty of people who intend to deceive, but nobody who wishes to be deceived. Since, then, the man who knows practises deceit, and the ignorant man is practised upon, it is quite clear that in any particular case the man who is deceived is a better man than he who deceives, seeing that it is better to suffer than to commit injustice. Now every man who lies commits an injustice; and if any man thinks that a lie is ever useful, he must think that injustice is sometimes useful. For no liar keeps faith in the matter about which he lies. He wishes, of course, that the man to whom he lies should place confidence in him; and yet he betrays his confidence by lying to him. Now every man who breaks faith is unjust. Either, then, injustice is sometimes useful (which is impossible), or a lie is never useful.

41. Whoever takes another meaning out of Scripture than the writer intended, goes astray, but not through any falsehood in Scripture. Nevertheless, as I was going to say, if his mistaken interpretation tends to build up love, which is the end of the commandment, he goes astray in much the same way as a man who by mistake quits the high road, but yet reaches through the fields the same place to which the road leads. He is to be corrected, however, and to be shown how much better it is not to quit the straight road, lest, if he get into a habit of going astray, he may sometimes take cross roads, or even go in the wrong direction altogether.

CHAP. 37. *Dangers of mistaken interpretation*

For if he takes up rashly a meaning which the author whom he is reading did not intend, he often falls in with other statements which he cannot harmonize with this meaning. And if he admits that these statements are true and certain, then it follows that the meaning he had put upon the former passage cannot be the true one: and so it comes to pass, one can hardly tell how, that, out of love for his own opinion, he begins to feel more angry with Scripture than he is

with himself. And if he should once permit that evil to creep in, it will utterly destroy him. "For we walk by faith, not by sight." [1] Now faith will totter if the authority of Scripture begin to shake. And then, if faith totter, love itself will grow cold. For if a man has fallen from faith, he must necessarily also fall from love; for he cannot love what he does not believe to exist. But if he both believes and loves, then through good works, and through diligent attention to the precepts of morality, he comes to hope also that he shall attain the object of his love. And so these are the three things to which all knowledge and all prophecy are subservient: faith, hope, love.

CHAP. 38. *Love never faileth*

42. But sight shall displace faith; and hope shall be swallowed up in that perfect bliss to which we shall come: love, on the other hand, shall wax greater when these others fail. For if we love by faith that which as yet we see not, how much more shall we love it when we begin to see! And if we love by hope that which as yet we have not reached, how much more shall we love it when we reach it! For there is this great difference between things temporal and things eternal, that a temporal object is valued more before we possess it and begins to prove worthless the moment we attain it, because it does not satisfy the soul, which has its only true and sure resting-place in eternity: an eternal object, on the other hand, is loved with greater ardour when it is in possession than while it is still an object of desire, for no one in his longing for it can set a higher value on it than really belongs to it, so as to think it comparatively worthless when he finds it of less value than he thought; on the contrary, however high the value any man may set upon it when he is on his way to possess it, he will find it, when it comes into his possession, of higher value still.

CHAP. 39. *He who is mature in faith, hope and love, needs Scripture no longer*

43. And thus a man who is resting upon faith, hope and love, and who keeps a firm hold upon these, does not need the Scriptures except for the purpose of instructing others. Accordingly, many live without copies of the Scriptures, even in solitude, on the strength of these three graces. So that in their case, I think, the saying is already fulfilled: "Whether there be prophecies, they shall fail; whether there be tongues, they shall cease; whether there be knowledge, it shall

[1] II Cor. 5. 7.

vanish away." [1] Yet by means of these instruments (as they may be called), so great an edifice of faith and love has been built up in them, that, holding to what is perfect, they do not seek for what is only in part perfect—of course, I mean, so far as is possible in this life; for, in comparison with the future life, the life of no just and holy man is perfect here. Therefore the apostle says: "Now abideth faith, hope, charity, these three; but the greatest of these is charity";[2] because, when a man shall have reached the eternal world, while the other two graces will fail, love will remain greater and more assured.

CHAP. 40. *What manner of reader Scripture demands*

44. And, therefore, if a man fully understands that "the end of the commandment is charity, out of a pure heart, and of a good conscience, and of faith unfeigned," [3] and is bent upon making all his understanding of Scripture to bear

[1] I Cor. 13. 8.   [2] I Cor. 13. 13.   [3] I Tim. 1. 5.

upon these three graces, he may come to the interpretation of these books with an easy mind. For while the apostle says "love," he adds "out of a pure heart," to provide against anything being loved but that which is worthy of love. And he joins with this "a good conscience," in reference to hope; for, if a man has the burthen of a bad conscience, he despairs of ever reaching that which he believes in and loves. And in the third place he says: "and of faith unfeigned." For if our faith is free from all hypocrisy, then we both abstain from loving what is unworthy of our love, and by living uprightly we are able to indulge the hope that our hope shall not be in vain.

For these reasons I have been anxious to speak about the objects of faith, as far as I thought it necessary for my present purpose; for much has already been said on this subject in other volumes, either by others or by myself. And so let this be the end of the present book. In the next I shall discuss, as far as God shall give me light, the subject of signs.

BOOK II

ARGUMENT. HAVING COMPLETED HIS EXPOSITION OF THINGS, THE AUTHOR NOW PROCEEDS TO DISCUSS THE SUBJECT OF SIGNS. HE FIRST DEFINES WHAT A SIGN IS, AND SHOWS THAT THERE ARE TWO CLASSES OF SIGNS, THE NATURAL AND THE CONVENTIONAL. OF CONVENTIONAL SIGNS (WHICH ARE THE ONLY CLASS HERE NOTICED), WORDS ARE THE MOST NUMEROUS AND IMPORTANT, AND ARE THOSE WITH WHICH THE INTERPRETER OF SCRIPTURE IS CHIEFLY CONCERNED. THE DIFFICULTIES AND OBSCURITIES OF SCRIPTURE SPRING CHIEFLY FROM TWO SOURCES, UNKNOWN AND AMBIGUOUS SIGNS. THE PRESENT BOOK DEALS ONLY WITH UNKNOWN SIGNS, THE AMBIGUITIES OF LANGUAGE BEING RESERVED FOR TREATMENT IN THE NEXT BOOK. THE DIFFICULTY ARISING FROM IGNORANCE OF SIGNS IS TO BE REMOVED BY LEARNING THE GREEK AND HEBREW LANGUAGES, IN WHICH SCRIPTURE IS WRITTEN, BY COMPARING THE VARIOUS TRANSLATIONS, AND BY ATTENDING TO THE CONTEXT. IN THE INTERPRETATION OF FIGURATIVE EXPRESSIONS, KNOWLEDGE OF THINGS IS AS NECESSARY AS KNOWLEDGE OF WORDS; AND THE VARIOUS SCIENCES AND ARTS OF THE HEATHEN, SO FAR AS THEY ARE TRUE AND USEFUL, MAY BE TURNED TO ACCOUNT IN REMOVING OUR IGNORANCE OF SIGNS, WHETHER THESE BE DIRECT OR FIGURATIVE. WHILST EXPOSING THE FOLLY AND FUTILITY OF MANY HEATHEN SUPERSTITIONS AND PRACTICES, THE AUTHOR POINTS OUT HOW ALL THAT IS SOUND AND USEFUL IN THEIR SCIENCE AND PHILOSOPHY MAY BE TURNED TO A CHRISTIAN USE. AND IN CONCLUSION, HE SHOWS THE SPIRIT IN WHICH IT BEHOVES US TO ADDRESS OURSELVES TO THE STUDY AND INTERPRETATION OF THE SACRED BOOKS.

CHAP. 1. *Signs, their nature and variety*

1. As when I was writing about things, I introduced the subject with a warning against attending to anything but what they are in themselves,[4] even though they are signs of something else, so now, when I come in its turn to dis-

[4] See BK. I. ch. 2.

cuss the subject of signs, I lay down this direction, not to attend to what they are in themselves, but to the fact that they are signs, that is, to what they signify. For a sign is a thing which, over and above the impression it makes on the senses, causes something else to come into the mind as a consequence of itself: as when we see a footprint, we conclude that an animal whose footprint this is has passed by; and when we see smoke, we know that there is fire beneath; and when we hear the voice of a living man, we think of the feeling in his mind; and when the trumpet sounds, soldiers know that they are to advance or retreat, or do whatever else the state of the battle requires.

2. Now some signs are natural, others conventional. Natural signs are those which, apart from any intention or desire of using them as signs, do yet lead to the knowledge of something else, as, for example, smoke when it indicates fire. For it is not from any intention of making it a sign that it is so, but through attention to experience we come to know that fire is beneath, even when nothing but smoke can be seen. And the footprint of an animal passing by belongs to this class of signs. And the countenance of an angry or sorrowful man indicates the feeling in his mind, independently of his will: and in the same way every other emotion of the mind is betrayed by the tell-tale countenance, even though we do nothing with the intention of making it known. This class of signs, however, it is no part of my design to discuss at present. But as it comes under this division of the subject, I could not altogether pass it over. It will be enough to have noticed it thus far.

CHAP. 2. *Of the kind of signs we are now concerned with*

3. Conventional signs, on the other hand, are those which living beings mutually exchange for the purpose of showing, as well as they can, the feelings of their minds, or their perceptions, or their thoughts. Nor is there any reason for giving a sign except the desire of drawing forth and conveying into another's mind what the giver of the sign has in his own mind. We wish, then, to consider and discuss this class of signs so far as men are concerned with it, because even the signs which have been given us of God, and which are contained in the Holy Scriptures, were made known to us through men—those, namely, who wrote the Scriptures. The beasts, too, have certain signs among themselves by which they make known the desires in their mind. For when the poultry-cock has discovered food, he signals with his voice for the hen to run to him, and the dove by cooing calls his mate, or is called by her in turn; and many signs of the same kind are matters of common observation. Now whether these signs, like the expression or the cry of a man in grief, follow the movement of the mind instinctively and apart from any purpose, or whether they are really used with the purpose of signification, is another question, and does not pertain to the matter in hand. And this part of the subject I exclude from the scope of this work as not necessary to my present object.

CHAP. 3. *Among signs, words hold the chief place*

4. Of the signs, then, by which men communicate their thoughts to one another, some relate to the sense of sight, some to that of hearing, a very few to the other senses. For, when we nod, we give no sign except to the eyes of the man to whom we wish by this sign to impart our desire. And some convey a great deal by the motion of the hands: and actors by movements of all their limbs give certain signs to the initiated, and, so to speak, address their conversation to the eyes: and the military standards and flags convey through the eyes the will of the commanders. And all these signs are as it were a kind of visible words. The signs that address themselves to the ear are, as I have said, more numerous, and for the most part consist of words. For though the bugle and the flute and the lyre frequently give not only a sweet but a significant sound, yet all these signs are very few in number compared with words. For among men words have obtained far and away the chief place as a means of indicating the thoughts of the mind. Our Lord, it is true, gave a sign through the odour of the ointment which was poured out upon His feet;[1] and in the sacrament of His body and blood He signified His will through the sense of taste; and when by touching the hem of His garment the woman was made whole, the act was not wanting in significance.[2] But the countless multitude of the signs through which men express their thoughts consist of words. For I have been able to put into words all those signs, the various classes of which I have briefly touched upon, but I could by no effort express words in terms of those signs.

CHAP. 4. *Origin of writing*

5. But because words pass away as soon as they strike upon the air, and last no longer than their sound, men have by means of letters formed signs of words. Thus the sounds of the voice are made visible to the eye, not of course as sounds, but by means of certain signs. It has been found impossible, however, to make those signs common to all nations owing to the sin of discord among men, which springs from every

[1]John, 12. 3-7; Mark, 14. 8.   [2]Matt. 9. 20.

man trying to snatch the chief place for himself. And that celebrated tower which was built to reach to heaven was an indication of this arrogance of spirit; and the ungodly men concerned in it justly earned the punishment of having not their minds only, but their tongues besides, thrown into confusion and discordance.[1]

CHAP. 5. *Scripture translated into various languages*

6. And hence it happened that even Holy Scripture, which brings a remedy for the terrible diseases of the human will, being at first set forth in one language, by means of which it could at the fit season be disseminated through the whole world, was interpreted into various tongues and spread far and wide, and thus became known to the nations for their salvation. And in reading it, men seek nothing more than to find out the thought and will of those by whom it was written and through these to find out the will of God, in accordance with which they believe these men to have spoken.

CHAP. 6. *Use of the obscurities in Scripture which arise from its figurative language*

7. But hasty and careless readers are led astray by many and manifold obscurities and ambiguities, substituting one meaning for another; and in some places they cannot hit upon even a fair interpretation. Some of the expressions are so obscure as to shroud the meaning in the thickest darkness. And I do not doubt that all this was divinely arranged for the purpose of subduing pride by toil, and of preventing a feeling of satiety in the intellect, which generally holds in small esteem what is discovered without difficulty. For why is it, I ask, that if any one says that there are holy and just men whose life and conversation the Church of Christ uses as a means of redeeming those who come to it from all kinds of superstitions, and making them through their imitation of good men members of its own body; men who, as good and true servants of God, have come to the baptismal font laying down the burdens of the world, and who rising thence do, through the implanting of the Holy Spirit, yield the fruit of a twofold love, a love, that is, of God and their neighbour; how is it, I say, that if a man says this, he does not please his hearer so much as when he draws the same meaning from that passage in Canticles, where it is said of the Church, when it is being praised under the figure of a beautiful woman, "Thy teeth are like a

flock of sheep that are shorn, which came up from the washing, whereof every one bears twins, and none is barren among them"?[2] Does the hearer learn anything more than when he listens to the same thought expressed in the plainest language, without the help of this figure? And yet, I don't know why, I feel greater pleasure in contemplating holy men, when I view them as the teeth of the Church, tearing men away from their errors, and bringing them into the Church's body, with all their harshness softened down, just as if they had been torn off and masticated by the teeth. It is with the greatest pleasure, too, that I recognize them under the figure of sheep that have been shorn, laying down the burthens of the world like fleeces, and coming up from the washing, i.e., from baptism, and all bearing twins, i.e., the twin commandments of love, and none among them barren in that holy fruit.

8. But why I view them with greater delight under that aspect than if no such figure were drawn from the sacred books, though the fact would remain the same and the knowledge the same, is another question, and one very difficult to answer. Nobody, however, has any doubt about the facts, both that it is pleasanter in some cases to have knowledge communicated through figures, and that what is attended with difficulty in the seeking gives greater pleasure in the finding. For those who seek but do not find suffer from hunger. Those, again, who do not seek at all because they have what they require just beside them often grow languid from satiety. Now weakness from either of these causes is to be avoided. Accordingly the Holy Spirit has, with admirable wisdom and care for our welfare, so arranged the Holy Scriptures as by the plainer passages to satisfy our hunger, and by the more obscure to stimulate our appetite. For almost nothing is dug out of those obscure passages which may not be found set forth in the plainest language elsewhere.

CHAP. 7. *Steps to wisdom: first, fear; second, piety; third, knowledge; fourth, resolution; fifth, counsel; sixth, purification of heart; seventh, wisdom*

9. First of all, then, it is necessary that we should be led by the *fear of God* to seek the knowledge of His will, what He commands us to desire and what to avoid. Now this fear will of necessity excite in us the thought of our mortality and of the death that is before us, and crucify all the motions of pride as if our flesh

---

[1] Gen. II.

[2] Song of Sol. 4. 2.

were nailed to the tree. Next it is necessary to have our hearts subdued by *piety,* and not to run in the face of Holy Scripture, whether when understood it strikes at some of our sins, or, when not understood, we feel as if we could be wiser and give better commands ourselves. We must rather think and believe that whatever is there written, even though it be hidden, is better and truer than anything we could devise by our own wisdom.

10. After these two steps of fear and piety, we come to the third step, *knowledge,* of which I have now undertaken to treat. For in this every earnest student of the Holy Scriptures exercises himself, to find nothing else in them but that God is to be loved for His own sake, and our neighbour for God's sake; and that God is to be loved with all the heart, and with all the soul, and with all the mind, and one's neighbour as one's self—that is, in such a way that all our love for our neighbour, like all our love for ourselves, should have reference to God.[1] And on these two commandments I touched in the previous book when I was treating about things.[2] It is necessary, then, that each man should first of all find in the Scriptures that he, through being entangled in the love of this world—i.e., of temporal things—has been drawn far away from such a love for God and such a love for his neighbour as Scripture enjoins. Then that fear which leads him to think of the judgment of God, and that piety which gives him no option but to believe in and submit to the authority of Scripture, compel him to bewail his condition. For the knowledge of a good hope makes a man not boastful, but sorrowful. And in this frame of mind he implores with unremitting prayers the comfort of the Divine help that he may not be overwhelmed in despair, and so he gradually comes to the fourth step—that is, *strength* and *resolution*—in which he hungers and thirsts after righteousness. For in this frame of mind he extricates himself from every form of fatal joy in transitory things, and turning away from these, fixes his affection on things eternal, to wit, the unchangeable Trinity in unity.

11. And when, to the extent of his power, he has gazed upon this object shining from afar, and has felt that owing to the weakness of his sight he cannot endure that matchless light, then in the fifth step—that is, in the *counsel of compassion*—he cleanses his soul, which is violently agitated and disturbs him with base desires, from the filth it has contracted. And at this stage he exercises himself diligently in the

love of his neighbour; and when he has reached the point of loving his enemy, full of hopes and unbroken in strength, he mounts to the sixth step, in which he *purifies the eye itself which can see God,*[3] so far as God can be seen by those who as far as possible die to this world. For men see Him just so far as they die to this world; and so far as they live to it they see Him not. But yet, although that light may begin to appear clearer, and not only more tolerable, but even more delightful, still it is only through a glass darkly that we are said to see, because we walk by faith, not by sight, while we continue to wander as strangers in this world, even though our conversation be in heaven.[4] And at this stage, too, a man so purges the eye of his affections as not to place his neighbour before, or even in comparison with, the truth, and therefore not himself, because not him whom he loves as himself. Accordingly, that holy man will be so single and so pure in heart that he will not step aside from the truth, either for the sake of pleasing men or with a view to avoid any of the annoyances which beset this life. Such a son ascends to *wisdom,* which is the seventh and last step, and which he enjoys in peace and tranquillity. For the fear of God is the beginning of wisdom.[5] From that beginning, then, till we reach wisdom itself, our way is by the steps now described.

CHAP. 8. *The canonical books*

12. But let us now go back to consider the third step here mentioned, for it is about it that I have set myself to speak and reason as the Lord shall grant me wisdom. The most skillful interpreter of the sacred writings, then, will be he who in the first place has read them all and retained them in his knowledge, if not yet with full understanding, still with such knowledge as reading gives—those of them, at least, that are called *canonical.* For he will read the others with greater safety when built up in the belief of the truth, so that they will not take first possession of a weak mind, nor, cheating it with dangerous falsehoods and delusions, fill it with prejudices adverse to a sound understanding. Now, in regard to the canonical Scriptures, he must follow the judgment of the greater number of Catholic Churches; and among these, of course, a high place must be given to such as have been thought worthy to be the seat of an apostle and to receive epistles. Accordingly, among the canonical Scriptures he will judge according to

---

[3]Matt. 5. 8.   [4]I Cor. 13. 12; II Cor. 5. 7.
[5]Ps. 111. 10.

[1]Cf. Matt. 22. 37–40.   [2]See BK. I chap. 22.

the following standard: to prefer those that are received by all the Catholic Churches to those which some do not receive. Among those, again, which are not received by all, he will prefer such as have the sanction of the greater number and those of greater authority, to such as are held by the smaller number and those of less authority. If, however, he shall find that some books are held by the greater number of churches, and others by the churches of greater authority (though this is not a very likely thing to happen), I think that in such a case the authority on the two sides is to be looked upon as equal.

13. Now the whole canon of Scripture on which we say this judgment is to be exercised, is contained in the following books: Five books of Moses, that is, Genesis, Exodus, Leviticus, Numbers, Deuteronomy; one book of Joshua the son of Nun; one of Judges; one short book called Ruth, which seems rather to belong to the beginning of Kings; next, four books of Kings, and two of Chronicles—these last not following one another, but running parallel, so to speak, and going over the same ground. The books now mentioned are history, which contains a connected narrative of the times, and follows the order of the events. There are other books which seem to follow no regular order, and are connected neither with the order of the preceding books nor with one another, such as Job, and Tobias, and Esther, and Judith, and the two books of Maccabees, and the two of Ezra,[1] which last look more like a sequel to the continuous regular history which terminates with the books of Kings and Chronicles. Next are the Prophets, in which there is one book of the Psalms of David; and three books of Solomon, viz., Proverbs, Song of Songs, and Ecclesiastes. For two books, one called Wisdom and the other Ecclesiasticus, are ascribed to Solomon from a certain resemblance of style, but the most likely opinion is that they were written by Jesus the son of Sirach. Still they are to be reckoned among the prophetical books, since they have attained recognition as being authoritative. The remainder are the books which are strictly called the Prophets: twelve separate books of the prophets which are connected with one another, and having never been disjoined, are reckoned as one book; the names of these prophets are as follows: Hosea, Joel, Amos, Obadiah, Jonah, Micah, Nahum, Habakkuk, Zephaniah, Haggai, Zechariah, Malachi; then

[1]That is, Ezra and Nehemiah.

there are the four greater prophets Isaiah, Jeremiah, Daniel, Ezekiel. The authority of the Old Testament is contained within the limits of these forty-four books. That of the New Testament, again, is contained within the following: Four books of the Gospel, according to Matthew, according to Mark, according to Luke, according to John; fourteen epistles of the Apostle Paul—one to the Romans, two to the Corinthians, one to the Galatians, to the Ephesians, to the Philippians, two to the Thessalonians, one to the Colossians, two to Timothy, one to Titus, to Philemon, to the Hebrews; two of Peter; three of John; one of Jude; and one of James; one book of the Acts of the Apostles; and one of the Revelation of John.

CHAP. 9. *How we should proceed in studying Scripture*

14. In all these books those who fear God and are of a meek and pious disposition seek the will of God. And in pursuing this search the first rule to be observed is, as I said, to know these books, if not yet with the understanding, still to read them so as to commit them to memory, or at least so as not to remain wholly ignorant of them. Next, those matters that are plainly laid down in them, whether rules of life or rules of faith, are to be searched into more carefully and more diligently; and the more of these a man discovers, the more capacious does his understanding become. For among the things that are plainly laid down in Scripture are to be found all matters that concern faith and the manner of life—to wit, hope and love, of which I have spoken in the previous book. After this, when we have made ourselves to a certain extent familiar with the language of Scripture, we may proceed to open up and investigate the obscure passages, and in doing so draw examples from the plainer expressions to throw light upon the more obscure, and use the evidence of passages about which there is no doubt to remove all hesitation in regard to the doubtful passages. And in this matter memory counts for a great deal; but if the memory be defective, no rules can supply the want.

CHAP. 10. *Unknown or ambiguous signs prevent Scripture from being understood*

15. Now there are two causes which prevent what is written from being understood: its being veiled either under unknown, or under ambiguous signs. Signs are either proper or figurative. They are called proper when they are used to

point out the objects they were designed to point out, as we say *bos* when we mean an ox, because all men who with us use the Latin tongue call it by this name. Signs are figurative when the things themselves which we indicate by the proper names are used to signify something else, as we say *bos,* and understand by that syllable the ox, which is ordinarily called by that name; but then further by that ox understand a preacher of the gospel, as Scripture signifies, according to the apostle's explanation, when it says: "Thou shalt not muzzle the ox that treadeth out the corn." [1]

Chap. 11. *Knowledge of languages, especially of Greek and Hebrew, necessary to remove ignorance of signs*

16. The great remedy for ignorance of proper signs is knowledge of languages. And men who speak the Latin tongue, of whom are those I have undertaken to instruct, need two other languages for the knowledge of Scripture, Hebrew and Greek, that they may have recourse to the original texts if the endless diversity of the Latin translators throw them into doubt. Although, indeed, we often find Hebrew words untranslated in the books, as for example, *Amen, Halleluia, Racha, Hosanna,* and others of the same kind. Some of these, although they could have been translated, have been preserved in their original form on account of the more sacred authority that attaches to it, as for example, *Amen* and *Halleluia.* Some of them, again, are said to be untranslatable into another tongue, of which the other two I have mentioned are examples. For in some languages there are words that cannot be translated into the idiom of another language. And this happens chiefly in the case of interjections, which are words that express rather an emotion of the mind than any part of a thought we have in our mind. And the two given above are said to be of this kind, *Racha* expressing the cry of an angry man, *Hosanna* that of a joyful man. But the knowledge of these languages is necessary, not for the sake of a few words like these which it is very easy to mark and to ask about, but, as has been said, on account of the diversities among translators. For the translations of the Scriptures from Hebrew into Greek can be counted, but the Latin translators are out of all number. For in the early days of the faith every man who happened to get his hands upon a Greek manuscript, and who thought he had any knowledge, were it ever so little, of the two languages, ventured upon the work of translation.

Chap. 12. *A diversity of interpretations is useful. Errors arising from ambiguous words*

17. And this circumstance would assist rather than hinder the understanding of Scripture, if only readers were not careless. For the examination of a number of texts has often thrown light upon some of the more obscure passages; for example, in that passage of the prophet Isaiah,[2] one translator reads: "And do not despise the domestics of thy seed"; another reads: "And do not despise thine own flesh." Each of these in turn confirms the other. For the one is explained by the other; because "flesh" may be taken in its literal sense, so that a man may understand that he is admonished not to despise his own body; and "the domestics of thy seed" may be understood figuratively of Christians, because they are spiritually born of the same seed as ourselves, namely, the Word. When now the meaning of the two translators is compared, a more likely sense of the words suggests itself, viz., that the command is not to despise our kinsmen, because when one brings the expression "domestics of thy seed" into relation with "flesh," kinsmen most naturally occur to one's mind. Whence, I think, that expression of the apostle, when he says, "If by any means I may provoke to emulation them which are my flesh, and might save some of them";[3] that is, that through emulation of those who had believed, some of them might believe too. And he calls the Jews his "flesh," on account of the relationship of blood. Again, that passage from the same prophet Isaiah:[4] "If ye will not believe, ye shall not understand," another has translated: "If ye will not believe, ye shall not abide." Now which of these is the literal translation cannot be ascertained without reference to the text in the original tongue. And yet to those who read with knowledge, a great truth is to be found in each. For it is difficult for interpreters to differ so widely as not to touch at some point. Accordingly here, as understanding consists in sight, and is abiding, but faith feeds us as babes, upon milk, in the cradles of temporal things (for now we walk by faith, not by sight);[5] as, moreover, unless we walk by faith, we shall not attain to sight, which does not pass away, but abides, our understanding being purified by holding to the truth; for these reasons one says, "If ye will

[1] I Cor. 9. 9.

[2] Isa. 58. 7.   [3] Rom. 11. 14.   [4] Isa. 7. 9.
[5] II Cor. 5. 7.

not believe, ye shall not understand"; but the other, "If ye will not believe, ye shall not abide."

18. And very often a translator, to whom the meaning is not well known, is deceived by an ambiguity in the original language, and puts upon the passage a construction that is wholly alien to the sense of the writer. As for example, some texts read: "Their feet are *sharp* to shed blood";[1] for the word ὀξύς among the Greeks means both *sharp* and *swift*. And so he saw the true meaning who translated: "Their feet are swift to shed blood." The other, taking the wrong sense of an ambiguous word, fell into error. Now translations such as this are not obscure, but false; and there is a wide difference between the two things. For we must learn not to interpret, but to correct texts of this sort. For the same reason it is, that because the Greek word μόσχος means a calf, some have not understood that μοσχεύματα[2] are shoots of trees, and have translated the word "calves"; and this error has crept into so many texts, that you can hardly find it written in any other way. And yet the meaning is very clear; for it is made evident by the words that follow. For "the plantings of an adulterer will not take deep root," is a more suitable form of expression than the "calves"; because these walk upon the ground with their feet, and are not fixed in the earth by roots. In this passage, indeed, the rest of the context also justifies this translation.

CHAP. 13. *How faulty interpretations can be emended*

19. But since we do not clearly see what the actual thought is which the several translators endeavour to express, each according to his own ability and judgment, unless we examine it in the language which they translate; and since the translator, if he be not a very learned man, often departs from the meaning of his author, we must either endeavour to get a knowledge of those languages from which the Scriptures are translated into Latin, or we must get hold of the translations of those who keep rather close to the letter of the original, not because these are sufficient, but because we may use them to correct the freedom or the error of others, who in their translations have chosen to follow the sense quite as much as the words. For not only single words, but often whole phrases are translated, which could not be translated at all into the Latin idiom by any one who wished to hold by the usage of the ancients who spoke Latin. And though these sometimes do not interfere

with the understanding of the passage, yet they are offensive to those who feel greater delight in things when even the signs of those things are kept in their own purity. For what is called a solecism is nothing else than the putting of words together according to a different rule from that which those of our predecessors who spoke with any authority followed. For whether we say *inter homines* (among men) or *inter hominibus,* is of no consequence to a man who only wishes to know the facts. And in the same way, what is a *barbarism* but the pronouncing of a word in a different way from that in which those who spoke Latin before us pronounced it? For whether the word *ignoscere* (to pardon) should be pronounced with the third syllable long or short, is not a matter of much concern to the man who is beseeching God, in any way at all that he can get the words out, to pardon his sins. What then is purity of speech, except the preserving of the custom of language established by the authority of former speakers?

20. And men are easily offended in a matter of this kind, just in proportion as they are weak; and they are weak just in proportion as they wish to seem learned, not in the knowledge of things which tend to edification, but in that of signs, by which it is hard not to be puffed up,[3] seeing that the knowledge of things even would often set up our neck, if it were not held down by the yoke of our Master. For how does it prevent our understanding it to have the following passage thus expressed: *"Quæ est terra in qua isti insidunt super eam, si bona est an nequam; et quæ sunt civitates, in quibus ipsi inhabitant in ipsis"?*[4] And I am more disposed to think that this is simply the idiom of another language than that any deeper meaning is intended. Again, that phrase, which we cannot now take away from the lips of the people who sing it: *"Super ipsum autem floriet sanctificatio mea,"*[5] surely takes away nothing from the meaning. Yet a more learned man would prefer that this should be corrected, and that we should say, not *floriet,* but *florebit.* Nor does anything stand in the way of the correction being made, except the usage of the singers. Mistakes of this kind, then, if a man do not choose to avoid them altogether, it is easy to treat with indifference, as not interfering with a right understanding. But

[1] Rom. 3. 15.   [2] Wisd. 4. 3.

[3] Cf. I Cor. 8. 1.

[4] "And what the land is that they dwell in, whether it be good or bad; and what cities they be that they dwell in."—Num. 13. 19 (Authorized Version).

[5] "But upon himself shall my holiness flourish."—Ps. 132. 18 (see Septuagint). "But upon himself shall his crown flourish" (Authorized Version).

take, on the other hand, the saying of the apostle: *"Quod stultum est Dei, sapientius est hominibus, et quod infirmum est Dei, fortius est hominibus."* [1] If any one should retain in this passage the Greek idiom, and say, *"Quod stultum est Dei, sapientius est hominum et quod infirmum est Dei fortius est hominum,"* [2] a quick and careful reader would indeed by an effort attain to the true meaning, but still a man of slower intelligence either would not understand it at all, or would put an utterly false construction upon it. For not only is such a form of speech faulty in the Latin tongue, but it is ambiguous too, as if the meaning might be, that the folly of men or the weakness of men is wiser or stronger than that of God. But indeed even the expression *sapientius est hominibus* (stronger than men) is not free from ambiguity, even though it be free from solecism. For whether *hominibus* is put as the plural of the dative or as the plural of the ablative, does not appear, unless by reference to the meaning. It would be better then to say, *sapientius est quam homines,* and *fortius est quam homines.*

CHAP. 14. *How the meaning of unknown words and idioms is to be discovered*

21. About ambiguous signs, however, I shall speak afterwards. I am treating at present of unknown signs, of which, as far as the words are concerned, there are two kinds. For either a word or an idiom, of which the reader is ignorant, brings him to a stop. Now if these belong to foreign tongues, we must either make inquiry about them from men who speak those tongues, or if we have leisure we must learn the tongues ourselves, or we must consult and compare several translators. If, however, there are words or idioms in our own tongue that we are unacquainted with, we gradually come to know them through being accustomed to read or to hear them. There is nothing that it is better to commit to memory than those kinds of words and phrases whose meaning we do not know, so that where we happen to meet either with a more learned man of whom we can inquire, or with a passage that shows, either by the preceding or succeeding context, or by both, the force and significance of the phrase we are ignorant of, we can easily by the help of our memory turn our attention to the matter and learn all about it. So great, however, is the force of custom, even in regard to learning, that those who have been in a sort of way nurtured and brought up on the study of Holy Scripture are surprised at other forms of speech, and think them less pure Latin than those which they have learnt from Scripture, but which are not to be found in Latin authors. In this matter, too, the great number of the translators proves a very great assistance, if they are examined and discussed with a careful comparison of their texts. Only all positive error must be removed. For those who are anxious to know the Scriptures ought in the first place to use their skill in the correction of the texts, so that the uncorrected ones should give way to the corrected, at least when they are copies of the same translation.

CHAP. 15. *Among versions a preference is given to the Septuagint and the Itala*

22. Now among translations themselves the Italian (*Itala*)[3] is to be preferred to the others, for it keeps closer to the words without prejudice to clearness of expression. And to correct the Latin we must use the Greek versions, among which the authority of the Septuagint is pre-eminent as far as the Old Testament is concerned; for it is reported through all the more learned churches that the seventy translators enjoyed so much of the presence and power of the Holy Spirit in their work of translation, that among that number of men there was but one voice. And if, as is reported, and as many not unworthy of confidence assert,[4] they were separated during the work of translation, each man being in a cell by himself, and yet nothing was found in the manuscript of any one of them that was not found in the same words and in the same order of words in all the rest, who dares put anything in comparison with an authority like this, not to speak of preferring anything to it? And even if they conferred together with the result that a unanimous agreement sprang out of the common labour and judgment of them all; even so, it would not be right or becoming for any one man, whatever his experience, to aspire to correct the unanimous opinion of many venerable and learned men. Wherefore, even if anything is found in the original Hebrew in a different form from that in which these men have expressed it, I think we must give way to the dispensation of Providence which used these men to bring it about, that books which the Jewish race were unwilling, either from religious scruple or from jealousy, to

---

[1] "Because the foolishness of God is wiser than men, and the weakness of God is stronger than men" (I Cor. 1. 25).

[2] "What is foolish of God is wiser of men, and what is weak of God is stronger of men."

[3] The *Vetus Latina*, commonly called the Vulgate.

[4] Cf. Augustine, *City of God*, BK. XVIII. 43.

make known to other nations, were, with the assistance of the power of King Ptolemy, made known so long beforehand to the nations which in the future were to believe in the Lord. And thus it is possible that they translated in such a way as the Holy Spirit, Who worked in them and had given them all one voice, thought most suitable for the Gentiles. But nevertheless, as I said above, a comparison of those translators also who have kept most closely to the words, is often not without value as a help to the clearing up of the meaning. The Latin texts, therefore, of the Old Testament are, as I was about to say, to be corrected if necessary by the authority of the Greek, and especially by that of those who, though they were seventy in number, are said to have translated as with one voice. As to the books of the New Testament, again, if any perplexity arises from the diversities of the Latin texts, we must of course yield to the Greek, especially those that are found in the churches of greater learning and research.

CHAP. 16. *The knowledge both of language and things is helpful for the understanding of figurative expressions*

23. In the case of figurative signs, again, if ignorance of any of them should chance to bring the reader to a stand-still, their meaning is to be traced partly by the knowledge of languages, partly by the knowledge of things. The pool of Siloam, for example, where the man whose eyes our Lord had anointed with clay made out of spittle was commanded to wash, has a figurative significance, and undoubtedly conveys a secret sense; but yet if the evangelist had not interpreted that name,[1] a meaning so important would lie unnoticed. And we cannot doubt that, in the same way, many Hebrew names which have not been interpreted by the writers of those books, would, if any one could interpret them, be of great value and service in solving the enigmas of Scripture. And a number of men skilled in that language have conferred no small benefit on posterity by explaining all these words without reference to their place in Scripture, and telling us what Adam means, what Eve, what Abraham, what Moses, and also the names of places, what Jerusalem signifies, or Sion, or Sinai, or Lebanon, or Jordan, and whatever other names in that language we are not acquainted with. And when these names have been investigated and explained, many figurative expressions in Scripture become clear.

[1] John, 9. 7.

24. Ignorance of things, too, renders figurative expressions obscure, as when we do not know the nature of the animals, or minerals, or plants, which are frequently referred to in Scripture by way of comparison. The fact so well known about the serpent, for example, that to protect its head it will present its whole body to its assailants—how much light it throws upon the meaning of our Lord's command that we should be wise as serpents;[2] that is to say, that for the sake of our head, which is Christ, we should willingly offer our body to the persecutors, lest the Christian faith should, as it were, be destroyed in us, if to save the body we deny our God! Or again, the statement that the serpent gets rid of its old skin by squeezing itself through a narrow hole, and thus acquires new strength—how appropriately it fits in with the direction to imitate the wisdom of the serpent, and to put off the old man, as the apostle says, that we may put on the new;[3] and to put it off, too, by coming through a narrow place, according to the saying of our Lord, "Enter ye in at the strait gate!"[4] As, then, knowledge of the nature of the serpent throws light upon many metaphors which Scripture is accustomed to draw from that animal, so ignorance of other animals, which are no less frequently mentioned by way of comparison, is a very great drawback to the reader. And so in regard to minerals and plants: knowledge of the carbuncle, for instance, which shines in the dark, throws light upon many of the dark places in books too, where it is used metaphorically; and ignorance of the beryl or the adamant often shuts the doors of knowledge. And the only reason why we find it easy to understand that perpetual peace is indicated by the olive branch which the dove brought with it when it returned to the ark,[5] is that we know both that the smooth touch of olive oil is not easily spoiled by a fluid of another kind, and that the tree itself is an evergreen. Many, again, by reason of their ignorance of hyssop, not knowing the virtue it has in cleansing the lungs, nor the power it is said to have of piercing rocks with its roots, although it is a small and insignificant plant, cannot make out why it is said, "Purge me with hyssop, and I shall be clean."[6]

25. Ignorance of numbers, too, prevents us from understanding things that are set down in Scripture in a figurative and mystical way. A candid mind, if I may so speak, cannot but be

[2] Matt. 10. 16.   [3] Eph. 4. 22.   [4] Matt. 7. 13.
[5] Gen. 8. 11.   [6] Ps. 51. 7.

anxious, for example, to ascertain what is meant by the fact that Moses and Elijah, and our Lord Himself, all fasted for forty days.[1] And except by knowledge of and reflection upon the number, the difficulty of explaining the figure involved in this action cannot be got over. For the number contains ten four times, indicating the knowledge of all things, and that knowledge interwoven with time. For both the diurnal and the annual revolutions are accomplished in periods numbering four each; the diurnal in the hours of the morning, the noontide, the evening, and the night; the annual in the spring, summer, autumn, and winter months. Now while we live in time, we must abstain and fast from all joy in time, for the sake of that eternity in which we wish to live; although by the passage of time we are taught this very lesson of despising time and seeking eternity. Further, the number ten signifies the knowledge of the Creator and the creature, for there is a trinity in the Creator; and the number seven indicates the creature, because of the life and the body. For the life consists of three parts, whence also God is to be loved with the whole heart, the whole soul, and the whole mind; and it is very clear that in the body there are four elements of which it is made up. In this number ten, therefore, when it is placed before us in connexion with time, that is, when it is taken four times, we are admonished to live unstained by, and not partaking of, any delight in time, that is, to fast for forty days. Of this we are admonished by the law personified in Moses, by prophecy personified in Elijah, and by our Lord Himself, Who, as if receiving the witness both of the law and the prophets, appeared on the mount between the other two, while His three disciples looked on in amazement. Next, we have to inquire in the same way, how out of the number forty springs the number fifty, which in our religion has no ordinary sacredness attached to it on account of the Pentecost, and how this number taken thrice on account of the three divisions of time, before the law, under the law, and under grace, or perhaps on account of the name of the Father, Son, and Holy Spirit, and the Trinity itself being added over and above, has reference to the mystery of the most Holy Church, and reaches to the number of the one hundred and fifty-three fishes which were taken after the resurrection of our Lord, when the nets were cast out on the right-hand side of the boat.[2] And in the same way, many other numbers and combinations of numbers are used in the sacred writings, to convey instruction under a figurative guise, and ignorance of numbers often shuts out the reader from this instruction.

26. Not a few things, too, are closed against us and obscured by ignorance of music. One man, for example, has not unskilfully explained some metaphors from the difference between the psaltery and the harp.[3] And it is a question which it is not out of place for learned men to discuss, whether there is any musical law that compels the psaltery of ten chords to have just so many strings; or whether, if there be no such law, the number itself is not on that very account the more to be considered as of sacred significance, either with reference to the ten commandments of the law (and if again any question is raised about that number, we can only refer it to the Creator and the creature), or with reference to the number ten itself as interpreted above. And the number of years the temple was in building, which is mentioned in the Gospel[4]—viz., forty-six—has a certain undefinable musical sound, and when referred to the structure of our Lord's body, in relation to which the temple was mentioned, compels many heretics to confess that our Lord put on, not a false, but a true and human body. And in several places in the Holy Scriptures we find both numbers and music mentioned with honour.

CHAP. 17. *Origin of the legend of the nine Muses*

27. For we must not listen to the falsities of heathen superstition, which represent the nine Muses as daughters of Jupiter and Mercury. Varro refutes these, and I doubt whether any one can be found among them more curious or more learned in such matters. He says that a certain state (I do not recollect the name) ordered from each of three artists a set of statues of the Muses, to be placed as an offering in the temple of Apollo, intending that whichever of the artists produced the most beautiful statues, they should select and purchase from him. It so happened that these artists executed their works with equal beauty, that all nine pleased the state, and that all were bought to be dedicated in the temple of Apollo; and he says that afterwards Hesiod the poet gave names to them all. It was not Jupiter, therefore, that begat the nine Muses, but three artists created three each. And the state had originally given the order for three, not because it had seen them in visions,

nor because they had presented themselves in that number to the eyes of any of the citizens, but because it was obvious to remark that all sound, which is the material of song, is by nature of three kinds. For it is either produced by the voice, as in the case of those who sing with the mouth without an instrument; or by blowing, as in the case of trumpets and flutes; or by striking, as in the case of harps and drums, and all other instruments that give their sound when struck.

Chap. 18. *No help is to be despised, even though it come from a profane source*

28. But whether the fact is as Varro has related, or is not so, still we ought not to give up music because of the superstition of the heathen, if we can derive anything from it that is of use for the understanding of Holy Scripture; nor does it follow that we must busy ourselves with their theatrical trumpery because we enter upon an investigation about harps and other instruments, that may help us to lay hold upon spiritual things. For we ought not to refuse to learn letters because they say that Mercury discovered them; nor because they have dedicated temples to Justice and Virtue, and prefer to worship in the form of stones things that ought to have their place in the heart, ought we on that account to forsake justice and virtue. Nay, but let every good and true Christian understand that wherever truth may be found, it belongs to his Master; and while he recognizes and acknowledges the truth, even in their religious literature, let him reject the figments of superstition, and let him grieve over and avoid men who, "when they knew God, glorified him not as God, neither were thankful; but became vain in their imaginations, and their foolish heart was darkened. Professing themselves to be wise, they became fools, and changed the glory of the uncorruptible God into an image made like to corruptible man, and to birds, and four-footed beasts, and creeping things." [1]

Chap. 19. *Two kinds of heathen knowledge*

29. But to explain more fully this whole topic (for it is one that cannot be omitted), there are two kinds of knowledge which are in vogue among the heathen. One is the knowledge of things instituted by men, the other of things which they have noted, either as transacted in the past or as instituted by God. The former kind, that which deals with human institutions, is partly superstitious, partly not.

[1] Rom. i. 21–23.

Chap. 20. *The superstitious nature of human institutions*

30. All the arrangements made by men for the making and worshipping of idols are superstitious, pertaining as they do either to the worship of what is created or of some part of it as God, or to consultations and arrangements about signs and leagues with devils, such, for example, as are employed in the magical arts, and which the poets are accustomed not so much to teach as to celebrate. And to this class belong, but with a bolder reach of deception, the books of the haruspices and augurs. In this class we must place also all amulets and cures which the medical art condemns, whether these consist in incantations, or in marks which they call *characters*, or in hanging or tying on or even dancing in a fashion certain articles, not with reference to the condition of the body, but to certain signs hidden or manifest; and these remedies they call by the less offensive name of *physica*, so as to appear not to be engaged in superstitious observances, but to be taking advantage of the forces of nature. Examples of these are the ear-rings on the top of each ear, or the rings of ostrich bone on the fingers, or telling you when you hiccup to hold your left thumb in your right hand.

31. To these we may add thousands of the most frivolous practices, that are to be observed if any part of the body should jump, or if, when friends are walking arm-in-arm, a stone, or a dog, or a boy, should come between them. And the kicking of a stone, as if it were a divider of friends, does less harm than to cuff an innocent boy if he happens to run between men who are walking side by side. But it is delightful that the boys are sometimes avenged by the dogs; for frequently men are so superstitious as to venture upon striking a dog who has run between them—not with impunity however, for instead of a superstitious remedy, the dog sometimes makes his assailant run in hot haste for a real surgeon. To this class, too, belong the following rules: To tread upon the threshold when you go out in front of the house; to go back to bed if any one should sneeze when you are putting on your slippers; to return home if you stumble when going to a place; when your clothes are eaten by mice, to be more frightened at the prospect of coming misfortune than grieved by your present loss. Whence that witty saying of Cato, who, when consulted by a man who told him that the mice had eaten his boots, replied, "That is not strange, but it would have been

very strange indeed if the boots had eaten the mice."

CHAP. 21. *Superstition of astrologers*

32. Nor can we exclude from this kind of superstition those who were called *genethliaci*, on account of their attention to birthdays, but are now commonly called *mathematici*. For these, too, although they may seek with pains for the true position of the stars at the time of our birth, and may sometimes even find it out, yet in so far as they attempt thence to predict our actions, or the consequences of our actions, grievously err, and sell inexperienced men into a miserable bondage. For when any freeman goes to an astrologer of this kind, he gives money that he may come away the slave either of Mars or of Venus, or rather, perhaps, of all the stars to which those who first fell into this error, and handed it on to posterity, have given the names either of beasts on account of their likeness to beasts, or of men with a view to confer honour on those men. And this is not to be wondered at, when we consider that even in times more recent and nearer our own, the Romans made an attempt to dedicate the star which we call Lucifer to the name and honour of Cæsar. And this would, perhaps, have been done, and the name handed down to distant ages, only that his ancestress Venus had given her name to this star before him, and could not by any law transfer to her heirs what she had never possessed, nor sought to possess, in life. For where a place was vacant, or not held in honour of any of the dead of former times, the usual proceeding in such cases was carried out. For example, we have changed the names of the months Quintilis and Sextilis to July and August, naming them in honour of the men Julius Cæsar and Augustus Cæsar; and from this instance any one who cares can easily see that the stars spoken of above formerly wandered in the heavens without the names they now bear. But as the men were dead whose memory people were either compelled by royal power or impelled by human folly to honour, they seemed to think that in putting their names upon the stars they were raising the dead men themselves to heaven. But whatever they may be called by men, still there are stars which God has made and set in order after His own pleasure, and they have a fixed movement, by which the seasons are distinguished and varied. And when any one is born, it is easy to observe the point at which this movement has arrived, by use of the rules discovered and laid down by those who

are rebuked by Holy Writ in these terms: "For if they were able to know so much that they could weigh the world, how did they not more easily find out the Lord thereof?" [1]

CHAP. 22. *The folly of observing the stars in order to predict the events of a life*

33. But to desire to predict the characters, the acts, and the fate of those who are born from such an observation, is a great delusion and great madness. And among those at least who have any sort of acquaintance with matters of this kind (which, indeed, are only fit to be unlearnt again), this superstition is refuted beyond the reach of doubt. For the observation is of the position of the stars, which they call constellations, at the time when the person was born about whom these wretched men are consulted by their still more wretched dupes. Now it may happen that, in the case of twins, one follows the other out of the womb so closely that there is no interval of time between them that can be apprehended and marked in the position of the constellations. Whence it necessarily follows that twins are in many cases born under the same stars, while they do not meet with equal fortune either in what they do or what they suffer, but often meet with fates so different that one of them has a most fortunate life, the other a most unfortunate. As, for example, we are told that Esau and Jacob were born twins, and in such close succession, that Jacob, who was born last, was found to have laid hold with his hand upon the heel of his brother, who preceded him.[2] Now, assuredly, the day and hour of the birth of these two could not be marked in any way that would not give both the same constellation. But what a difference there was between the characters, the actions, the labours, and the fortunes of these two, the Scriptures bear witness, which are now so widely spread as to be in the mouth of all nations.

34. Nor is it to the point to say that the very smallest and briefest moment of time that separates the birth of twins produces great effects in nature and in the extremely rapid motion of the heavenly bodies. For, although I may grant that it does produce the greatest effects, yet the astrologer cannot discover this in the constellations, and it is by looking into these that he professes to read the fates. If, then, he does not discover the difference when he examines the constellations, which must, of course, be the same whether he is consulted about Jacob or his brother, what does it profit him that there is a

[1]Wisd. 13. 9. [2]Gen. 25. 24.

difference in the heavens, which he rashly and carelessly brings into disrepute, when there is no difference in his chart, which he looks into anxiously but in vain? And so these notions also, which have their origin in certain signs of things being arbitrarily fixed upon by the presumption of men, are to be referred to the same class as if they were leagues and covenants with devils.

CHAP. 23. *Why we repudiate arts of divination*

35. For in this way it comes to pass that men who lust after evil things are, by a secret judgment of God, delivered over to be mocked and deceived, as the just reward of their evil desires. For they are deluded and imposed on by the false angels, to whom the lowest part of the world has been put in subjection by the law of God's providence, and in accordance with His most admirable arrangement of things. And the result of these delusions and deceptions is, that through these superstitious and baneful modes of divination, many things in the past and future are made known, and turn out just as they are foretold; and in the case of those who practise superstitious observances, many things turn out agreeably to their observances, and ensnared by these successes, they become more eagerly inquisitive, and involve themselves further and further in a labyrinth of most pernicious error. And to our advantage, the Word of God is not silent about this species of fornication of the soul; and it does not warn the soul against following such practices on the ground that those who profess them speak lies, but it says, "Even if what they tell you should come to pass, hearken not unto them."[1] For though the ghost of the dead Samuel foretold the truth to King Saul,[2] that does not make such sacrilegious observances as those by which his ghost was brought up the less detestable; and though the ventriloquist woman[3] in the Acts of the Apostles bore true testimony to the apostles of the Lord, the Apostle Paul did not spare the evil spirit on that account, but rebuked and cast it out, and so made the woman clean.[4]

36. All arts of this sort, therefore, are either nullities, or are part of a guilty superstition, springing out of a baleful fellowship between men and devils, and are to be utterly repudiated and avoided by the Christian as the covenants of a false and treacherous friendship. "Not as if the idol were anything," says the apostle; "but because the things which they sacrifice they sacrifice to devils and not to God; and I would not that ye should have fellowship with devils."[5] Now, what the apostle has said about idols and the sacrifices offered in their honour, that we ought to feel in regard to all fancied signs which lead either to the worship of idols, or to worshipping creation or its parts instead of God, or which are connected with attention to medicinal charms and other observances; for these are not appointed by God as the public means of promoting love towards God and our neighbour, but they waste the hearts of wretched men in private and selfish strivings after temporal things. Accordingly, in regard to all these branches of knowledge, we must fear and shun the fellowship of demons, who, with the Devil their prince, strive only to shut and bar the door against our return. As, then, from the stars which God created and ordained, men have drawn lying omens of their own fancy, so also from things that are born, or in any other way come into existence under the government of God's providence, if there chance only to be something unusual in the occurrence—as when a mule brings forth young, or an object is struck by lightning—men have frequently drawn omens by conjectures of their own, and have committed them to writing, as if they had drawn them by rule.

CHAP. 24. *The intercourse and agreement with demons which superstitious observances maintain*

37. And all these omens are of force just so far as has been arranged with the devils by that previous understanding in the mind which is, as it were, the common language, but they are all full of hurtful curiosity, torturing anxiety, and deadly slavery. For it was not because they had meaning that they were attended to, but it was by attending to and marking them that they came to have meaning. And so they are made different for different people, according to their serveral notions and prejudices. For those spirits which are bent upon deceiving, take care to provide for each person the same sort of omens as they see his own conjectures and preconceptions have already entangled him in. For, to take an illustration, the same figure of the letter X, which is made in the shape of a cross, means one thing among the Greeks and another among the Latins, not by nature, but by agreement and pre-arrangement as to its signification; and so, any one who knows both languages uses this letter in a different sense when writing to a Greek

[1]Cf. Deut. 13. 1–3.
[2]I Sam, 28; cf. Ecclus. 46. 20.
[3]See I Sam. 28. 7.   [4]Acts, 16. 16–18.
[5]I Cor. 10. 19, 20.

from that in which he uses it when writing to a Latin. And the same sound, *beta*, which is the name of a letter among the Greeks, is the name of a vegetable among the Latins; and when I say, *lege*, these two syllables mean one thing to a Greek and another to a Latin. Now, just as all these signs affect the mind according to the arrangements of the community in which each man lives, and affect different men's minds differently, because these arrangements are different; and as, further, men did not agree upon them as signs because they were already significant, but on the contrary they are now significant because men have agreed upon them; in the same way also, those signs by which the ruinous intercourse with devils is maintained have meaning just in proportion to each man's observations. And this appears quite plainly in the rites of the augurs; for they, both before they observe the omens and after they have completed their observations, take pains not to see the flight or hear the cries of birds, because these omens are of no significance apart from the previous arrangement in the mind of the observer.

CHAP. 25. *In human institutions which are not superstitious, there are some things superfluous and some convenient and necessary*

38. But when all these have been cut away and rooted out of the mind of the Christian, we must then look at human institutions which are not superstitious, that is, such as are not set up in association with devils, but by men in association with one another. For all arrangements that are in force among men, because they have agreed among themselves that they should be in force, are human institutions; and of these, some are matters of superfluity and luxury, some of convenience and necessity. For if those signs which the actors make in dancing were of force by nature, and not by the arrangement and agreement of men, the public crier would not in former times have announced to the people of Carthage, while the pantomime was dancing, what it was he meant to express—a thing still remembered by many old men from whom we have frequently heard it. And we may well believe this, because even now, if any one who is unaccustomed to such follies goes into the theatre, unless some one tells him what these movements mean, he will give his whole attention to them in vain. Yet all men aim at a certain degree of likeness in their choice of signs, that the signs may as far as possible be like the things they signify. But because one thing may resemble another in many ways, such signs are not always of the same significance among men, except when they have mutually agreed upon them.

39. But in regard to pictures and statues, and other works of this kind, which are intended as representations of things, nobody makes a mistake, especially if they are executed by skilled artists, but every one, as soon as he sees the likenesses, recognizes the things they are likenesses of. And this whole class are to be reckoned among the superfluous devices of men, unless when it is a matter of importance to inquire in regard to any of them, for what reason, where, when, and by whose authority it was made. Finally, the thousands of fables and fictions, in whose lies men take delight, are human devices, and nothing is to be considered more peculiarly man's own and derived from himself than anything that is false and lying. Among the convenient and necessary arrangements of men with men are to be reckoned whatever differences they choose to make in bodily dress and ornament for the purpose of distinguishing sex or rank; and the countless varieties of signs without which human intercourse either could not be carried on at all, or would be carried on at great inconvenience; and the arrangements as to weights and measures, and the stamping and weighing of coins, which are peculiar to each state and people, and other things of the same kind. Now these, if they were not devices of men, would not be different in different nations, and could not be changed among particular nations at the discretion of their respective sovereigns.

40. This whole class of human arrangements, which are of convenience for the necessary intercourse of life, the Christian is not by any means to neglect, but on the contrary should pay a sufficient degree of attention to them, and keep them in memory.

CHAP. 26. *What human contrivances we are to adopt, and what we are to avoid*

For certain institutions of men are in a sort of way representations and likenesses of natural objects. And of these, such as have relation to fellowship with devils must, as has been said, be utterly rejected and held in detestation; those, on the other hand, which relate to the mutual intercourse of men, are, so far as they are not matters of luxury and superfluity, to be adopted, especially the forms of the letters which are necessary for reading, and the various languages as far as is required—a matter I have spoken of above.[1] To this class also belong shorthand characters, those who are acquainted with which are called shorthand writers. All these are useful, and there is nothing unlawful in learning them, nor do they involve us in superstition, or enervate us by luxury, if they only occupy our minds so far as not to stand in the way of more important objects to which they ought to be subservient.

CHAP. 27. *Some departments of knowledge, not of mere human invention, aid us in interpreting Scripture*

41. But, coming to the next point, we are not to reckon among human institutions those things which men have handed down to us, not as arrangements of their own, but as the result of investigation into the occurrences of the past, and into the arrangements of God's providence. And of these, some pertain to the bodily senses, some to the intellect. Those which are reached by the bodily senses we either believe on testimony, or perceive when they are pointed out to us, or infer from experience.

CHAP. 28. *To what extent history is an aid*

42. Anything, then, that we learn from history about the chronology of past times assists us very much in understanding the Scriptures, even if it be learnt without the pale of the Church as a matter of childish instruction. For we frequently seek information about a variety of matters by use of the Olympiads, and the names of the consuls; and ignorance of the consulship in which our Lord was born, and that in which He suffered, has led some into the error of supposing that He was forty-six years of age when He suffered, that being the number of years He was told by the Jews the temple (which He took as a symbol of His body) was in building.[2] Now we know on the authority of the evangelist that He was about thirty years of age when He was baptized;[3] but the number of years He lived afterwards, although by putting His actions together we can make it out, yet that no shadow of doubt might arise from another source, can be ascertained more clearly and more certainly from a comparison of profane history with the gospel. It will still be evident, however, that it was not without a purpose it was said that the temple was forty and six years in building; so that, as this cannot be referred to our Lord's age, it may be referred to the more secret formation of the body which, for our sakes, the only-begotten Son of God, by Whom all things were made, condescended to put on.[4]

43. As to the utility of history, moreover, passing over the Greeks, what a great question our own Ambrose has set at rest! For, when the readers and admirers of Plato dared calumniously to assert that our Lord Jesus Christ learnt all those sayings of His, which they are compelled to admire and praise, from the books of Plato—because (they urged) it cannot be denied that Plato lived long before the coming of our Lord!—did not the illustrious bishop, when by his investigations into profane history he had discovered that Plato made a journey into Egypt at the time when Jeremiah the prophet was there, show that it is much more likely that Plato was through Jeremiah's means initiated into our literature, so as to be able to teach and write those views of his which are so justly praised? For not even Pythagoras himself, from whose successors these men assert Plato learnt theology, lived at a date prior to the books of that Hebrew race, among whom the worship of one God sprang up, and of whom as concerning the flesh our Lord came. And thus, when we reflect upon the dates, it becomes much more probable that those philosophers learnt whatever they said that was good and true from our literature, than that the Lord Jesus Christ learnt from the writings of Plato—a thing which it is the height of folly to believe.

44. And even when in the course of an historical narrative former institutions of men are described, the history itself is not to be reckoned among human institutions; because things that are past and gone and cannot be undone are to be reckoned as belonging to the course of time, of which God is the author and governor. For it is one thing to tell what has been done, another to show what ought to be done. History narrates what has been done, faithfully and with advantage; but the books of the haruspices, and all writings of the same kind, aim at teaching what ought to be done or observed, using the boldness of an adviser, not the fidelity of a narrator.

CHAP. 29. *To what extent natural science is an exegetical aid*

45. There is also a species of narrative resembling description, in which not a past but an existing state of things is made known to those who are ignorant of it. To this species belongs all that has been written about the situation of places, and the nature of animals, trees, herbs, stones, and other bodies. And of this species I

[1]See above Chap. 11.   [2]John, 2. 19.   [3]Luke, 3. 23.   [4]See above, Chap. 16.

have treated above, and have shown that this kind of knowledge is serviceable in solving the difficulties of Scripture, not that these objects are to be used conformably to certain signs as nostrums or the instruments of superstition; for that kind of knowledge I have already set aside as distinct from the lawful and free kind now spoken of. For it is one thing to say: "If you bruise down this herb and drink it, it will remove the pain from your stomach"; and another to say: "If you hang this herb round your neck, it will remove the pain from your stomach." In the former case the wholesome mixture is approved of, in the latter the superstitious charm is condemned; although indeed, where incantations and invocations and marks are not used, it is frequently doubtful whether the thing that is tied or fixed in any way to the body to cure it, acts by a natural virtue, in which case it may be freely used; or acts by a sort of charm, in which case it becomes the Christian to avoid it the more carefully, the more efficacious it may seem to be. But when the reason why a thing is of virtue does not appear, the intention with which it is used is of great importance, at least in healing or in tempering bodies, whether in medicine or in agriculture.

46. The knowledge of the stars, again, is not a matter of narration, but of description. Very few of these, however, are mentioned in Scripture. And as the course of the moon, which is regularly employed in reference to celebrating the anniversary of our Lord's passion, is known to most people, so the rising and setting and other movements of the rest of the heavenly bodies are thoroughly known to very few. And this knowledge, although in itself it involves no superstition, renders very little, indeed almost no assistance, in the interpretation of Holy Scripture, and by engaging the attention unprofitably is a hindrance rather; and as it is closely related to the very pernicious error of the diviners of the fates, it is more convenient and becoming to neglect it. It involves, moreover, in addition to a description of the present state of things, something like a narrative of the past also; because one may go back from the present position and motion of the stars, and trace by rule their past movements. It involves also regular anticipations of the future, not in the way of forebodings and omens, but by way of sure calculation; not with the design of drawing any information from them as to our own acts and fates, in the absurd fashion of the *genethliaci,* but only as to the motions of the heavenly bod-

ies themselves. For, as the man who computes the moon's age can tell, when he has found out her age to-day, what her age was any number of years ago, or what will be her age any number of years hence, in just the same way men who are skilled in such computations are accustomed to answer like questions about every one of the heavenly bodies. And I have stated what my views are about all this knowledge, so far as regards its utility.

CHAP. 30. *What the mechanical arts contribute to exegetics*

47. Further, as to the remaining arts, whether those by which something is made which, when the effort of the workman is over, remains as a result of his work, as, for example, a house, a bench, a dish, and other things of that kind; or those which, so to speak, assist God in His operations, as medicine, and agriculture, and navigation: or those whose sole result is an action, as dancing, and racing, and wrestling; in all these arts experience teaches us to infer the future from the past. For no man who is skilled in any of these arts moves his limbs in any operation without connecting the memory of the past with the expectation of the future. Now of these arts a very superficial and cursory knowledge is to be acquired, not with a view to practising them (unless some duty compel us, a matter on which I do not touch at present), but with a view to forming a judgment about them, that we may not be wholly ignorant of what Scripture means to convey when it employs figures of speech derived from these arts.

CHAP. 31. *Use of dialectics. Of fallacies*

48. There remain those branches of knowledge which pertain not to the bodily senses, but to the intellect, among which the science of reasoning and that of number are the chief. The science of reasoning is of very great service in searching into and unravelling all sorts of questions that come up in Scripture, only in the use of it we must guard against the love of wrangling and the childish vanity of entrapping an adversary. For there are many of what are called *sophisms,* inferences in reasoning that are false, and yet so close an imitation of the true, as to deceive not only dull people, but clever men too, when they are not on their guard. For example, one man lays before another with whom he is talking, the proposition, "What I am, you are not." The other assents, for the proposition is in part true, the one man being cunning and the other simple. Then the first speaker adds: "I

am a man"; and when the other has given his assent to this also, the first draws his conclusion: "Then you are not a man." Now of this sort of ensnaring arguments, Scripture, as I judge, expresses detestation in that place where it is said, "There is one that showeth wisdom in words, and is hated";[1] although, indeed, a style of speech which is not intended to entrap, but only aims at verbal ornamentation more than is consistent with seriousness of purpose, is also called sophistical.

49. There are also valid processes of reasoning which lead to false conclusions, by following out to its logical consequences the error of the man with whom one is arguing; and these conclusions are sometimes drawn by a good and learned man, with the object of making the person from whose error these consequences result, feel ashamed of them, and of thus leading him to give up his error, when he finds that if he wishes to retain his old opinion, he must of necessity also hold other opinions which he condemns. For example, the apostle did not draw true conclusions when he said, "Then is Christ not risen," and again, "Then is our preaching vain, and your faith is also vain";[2] and further on drew other inferences which are all utterly false; for Christ has risen, the preaching of those who declared this fact was not in vain, nor was their faith in vain who had believed it. But all these false inferences followed legitimately from the opinion of those who said that there is no resurrection of the dead. These inferences, then, being repudiated as false, it follows that since they would be true if the dead rise not, there will be a resurrection of the dead. As, then, valid conclusions may be drawn not only from true but from false propositions, the laws of valid reasoning may easily be learnt in the schools, outside the pale of the Church. But the truth of propositions must be inquired into in the sacred books of the Church.

CHAP. 32. *Valid logical sequence is not devised but only observed by man*

50. And yet the validity of logical sequences is not a thing devised by men, but is observed and noted by them that they may be able to learn and teach it; for it exists eternally in the reason of things, and has its origin with God. For as the man who narrates the order of events does not himself create that order; and as he who describes the situations of places, or the natures of animals, or roots, or minerals, does not describe arrangements of man; and as he

who points out the stars and their movements does not point out anything that he himself or any other man has ordained; in the same way, he who says, "When the consequent is false, the antecedent must also be false," says what is most true; but he does not himself make it so, he only points out that it is so. And it is upon this rule that the reasoning I have quoted from the Apostle Paul proceeds. For the antecedent is, "There is no resurrection of the dead"—the position taken up by those whose error the apostle wished to overthrow. Next, from this antecedent, the assertion, viz., that there is no resurrection of the dead, the necessary consequence is, "Then Christ is not risen." But this consequence is false, for Christ has risen; therefore the antecedent is also false. But the antecedent is that there is no resurrection of the dead. We conclude, therefore, that there is a resurrection of the dead. Now all this is briefly expressed thus: "If there is no resurrection of the dead, then is Christ not risen; but Christ is risen, therefore there is a resurrection of the dead." This rule, then, that when the consequent is removed, the antecedent must also be removed, is not made by man, but only pointed out by him. And this rule has reference to the validity of the reasoning, not to the truth of the statements.

CHAP. 33. *False inferences may be drawn from valid reasonings, and vice versa*

51. In this passage, however, where the argument is about the resurrection, both the law of the inference is valid, and the conclusion arrived at is true. But in the case of false conclusions, too, there is a validity of inference in some such way as the following. Let us suppose some man to have admitted: "If a snail is an animal, it has a voice." This being admitted, then, when it has been proved that the snail has no voice, it follows (since when the consequent is proved false, the antecedent is also false) that the snail is not an animal. Now this conclusion is false, but it is a true and valid inference from the false admission. Thus, the truth of a statement stands on its own merits; the validity of an inference depends on the statement or the admission of the man with whom one is arguing. And thus, as I said above, a false inference may be drawn by a valid process of reasoning, in order that he whose error we wish to correct may be sorry that he has admitted the antecedent, when he sees that its logical consequences are utterly untenable. And hence it is easy to understand that as the inferences may be valid

where the opinions are false, so the inferences may be unsound where the opinions are true. For example, suppose that a man propounds the statement, "If this man is just, he is good," and we admit its truth. Then he adds, "But he is not just"; and when we admit this too, he draws the conclusion, "Therefore he is not good." Now although every one of these statements may be true, still the principle of the inference is unsound. For it is not true that, as when the consequent is proved false the antecedent is also false, so when the antecedent is proved false the consequent is false. For the statement is true, "If he is an orator, he is a man." But if we add, "He is not an orator," the consequence does not follow, "He is not a man."

CHAP. 34. *It is one thing to know the laws of inference, another to know the truth of opinions*

52. Therefore it is one thing to know the laws of inference, and another to know the truth of opinions. In the former case we learn what is consequent, what is inconsequent, and what is incompatible. An example of a consequent is, "If he is an orator, he is a man"; of an inconsequent, "If he is a man, he is an orator"; of an incompatible, "If he is a man, he is a quadruped." In these instances we judge of the connexion. In regard to the truth of opinions, however, we must consider propositions as they stand by themselves, and not in their connexion with one another; but when propositions that we are not sure about are joined by a valid inference to propositions that are true and certain, they themselves, too, necessarily become certain. Now some, when they have ascertained the validity of the inference, plume themselves as if this involved also the truth of the propositions. Many, again, who hold the true opinions have an unfounded contempt for themselves, because they are ignorant of the laws of inference; whereas the man who knows that there is a resurrection of the dead is assuredly better than the man who only knows that it follows that if there is no resurrection of the dead, then is Christ not risen.

CHAP. 35. *The science of definition is not false, though it may be applied to falsities*

53. Again, the science of definition, of division, and of partition, although it is frequently applied to falsities, is not itself false, nor framed by man's device, but is evolved from the reason of things. For although poets have applied it to their fictions, and false philosophers, or

even heretics—that is, false Christians—to their erroneous doctrines, that is no reason why it should be false, for example, that neither in definition, nor in division, nor in partition, is anything to be included that does not pertain to the matter in hand, nor anything to be omitted that does. This is true, even though the things to be defined or divided are not true. For even falsehood itself is defined when we say that falsehood is the declaration of a state of things which is not as we declare it to be; and this definition is true, although falsehood itself cannot be true. We can also divide it, saying that there are two kinds of falsehood, one in regard to things that cannot be true at all, the other in regard to things that are not, though it is possible they might be, true. For example, the man who says that seven and three are eleven, says what cannot be true under any circumstances; but he who says that it rained on the kalends of January, although perhaps the fact is not so, says what possibly might have been. The definition and division, therefore, of what is false may be perfectly true, although what is false cannot, of course, itself be true.

CHAP. 36. *The rules of eloquence are true, though sometimes used to persuade men of what is false*

54. There are also certain rules for a more copious kind of argument, which is called *eloquence,* and these rules are not the less true that they can be used for persuading men of what is false; but as they can be used to enforce the truth as well, it is not the faculty itself that is to be blamed, but the perversity of those who put it to a bad use. Nor is it owing to an arrangement among men that the expression of affection conciliates the hearer, or that a narrative, when it is short and clear, is effective, and that variety arrests men's attention without wearying them. And it is the same with other directions of the same kind, which, whether the cause in which they are used be true or false, are themselves true just in so far as they are effective in producing knowledge or belief, or in moving men's minds to desire and aversion. And men rather found out that these things are so than arranged that they should be so.

CHAP. 37. *Use of rhetoric and dialectic*

55. This art, however, when it is learnt, is not to be used so much for ascertaining the meaning as for setting forth the meaning when it is ascertained. But the art previously spoken of, which deals with inferences, and definitions, and

divisions, is of the greatest assistance in the discovery of the meaning, provided only that men do not fall into the error of supposing that when they have learnt these things they have learnt the true secret of a happy life. Still, it sometimes happens that men find less difficulty in attaining the object for the sake of which these sciences are learnt, than in going through the very intricate and thorny discipline of such rules. It is just as if a man wishing to give rules for walking should warn you not to lift the hinder foot before you set down the front one, and then should describe minutely the way you ought to move the hinges of the joints and knees. For what he says is true, and one cannot walk in any other way; but men find it easier to walk by executing these movements than to attend to them while they are going through them, or to understand when they are told about them. Those, on the other hand, who cannot walk, care still less about such directions, as they cannot prove them by making trial of them. And in the same way a clever man often sees that an inference is unsound more quickly than he apprehends the rules for it. A dull man, on the other hand, does not see the unsoundness, but much less does he grasp the rules. And in regard to all these laws, we derive more pleasure from them as exhibitions of truth, than assistance in arguing or forming opinions, except perhaps that they put the intellect in better training. We must take care, however, that they do not at the same time make it more inclined to mischief or vanity—that is to say, that they do not give those who have learnt them an inclination to lead people astray by plausible speech and catching questions, or make them think that they have attained some great thing that gives them an advantage over the good and innocent.

CHAP. 38. *The science of numbers not created, but only discovered, by man*

56. Coming now to the science of numbers it is clear to the dullest apprehension that this was not created by man, but was discovered by investigation. For, though Virgil could at his own pleasure make the first syllable of *Italia* long, while the ancients pronounced it short, it is not in any man's power to determine at his pleasure that three times three are not nine, or do not make a square, or are not the triple of three, nor one and a half times the number six, or that it is not true that they are not the double of any number because odd numbers have no half. Whether, then, numbers are considered in themselves, or as applied to the laws of figures, or of sounds, or of other motions, they have fixed laws which were not made by man, but which the acuteness of ingenious men brought to light.

57. The man, however, who puts so high a value on these things as to be inclined to boast himself one of the learned, and who does not rather inquire after the source from which those things which he perceives to be true derive their truth, and from which those others which he perceives to be unchangeable also derive their truth and unchangeableness, and who, mounting up from bodily appearances to the mind of man, and finding that it too is changeable (for it is sometimes instructed, at other times uninstructed), although it holds a middle place between the unchangeable truth above it and the changeable things beneath it, does not strive to make all things redound to the praise and love of the one God from Whom he knows that all things have their being; the man, I say, who acts in this way may seem to be learned, but wise he cannot in any sense be deemed.

CHAP. 39. *To which of the above-mentioned studies attention should be given, and in what spirit*

58. Accordingly, I think that it is well to warn studious and able young men, who fear God and are seeking for happiness of life, not to venture heedlessly upon the pursuit of the branches of learning that are in vogue beyond the pale of the Church of Christ, as if these could secure for them the happiness they seek; but soberly and carefully to discriminate among them. And if they find any of those which have been instituted by men varying by reason of the varying pleasure of their founders, and unknown by reason of erroneous conjectures, especially if they involve entering into fellowship with devils by means of leagues and covenants about signs, let these be utterly rejected and held in detestation. Let the young men also withdraw their attention from such institutions of men as are unnecessary and luxurious. But for the sake of the necessities of this life we must not neglect the arrangements of men that enable us to carry on intercourse with those around us. I think, however, there is nothing useful in the other branches of learning that are found among the heathen, except information about objects, either past or present, that relate to the bodily senses, in which are included also the experiments and conclusions of the useful mechanical arts, except also the sciences of reasoning and of numbers. And in regard to all these we must hold by the maxim, "Not too much of anything"; espe-

cially in the case of those which, pertaining as they do to the senses, are subject to the relations of space and time.

59. What, then, some men have done in regard to all words and names found in Scripture, in the Hebrew, and Syriac, and Egyptian, and other tongues, taking up and interpreting separately such as were left in Scripture without interpretation; and what Eusebius has done in regard to the history of the past with a view to the questions arising in Scripture that require a knowledge of history for their solution; what, I say, these men have done in regard to matters of this kind, making it unnecessary for the Christian to spend his strength on many subjects for the sake of a few items of knowledge, the same, I think, might be done in regard to other matters, if any competent man were willing in a spirit of benevolence to undertake the labour for the advantage of his brethren. In this way he might arrange in their several classes, and give an account of the unknown places, and animals, and plants, and trees, and stones, and metals, and other species of things that are mentioned in Scripture, taking up these only, and committing his account to writing. This might also be done in relation to numbers, so that the theory of those numbers, and those only, which are mentioned in Holy Scripture, might be explained and written down. And it may happen that some or all of these things have been done already (as I have found that many things I had no notion of have been worked out and committed to writing by good and learned Christians), but are either lost amid the crowds of the careless, or are kept out of sight by the envious. And I am not sure whether the same thing can be done in regard to the theory of reasoning; but it seems to me it cannot, because this runs like a system of nerves through the whole structure of Scripture, and on that account is of more service to the reader in disentangling and explaining ambiguous passages, of which I shall speak hereafter, than in ascertaining the meaning of unknown signs, the topic I am now discussing.

CHAP. 40. *Whatever has been rightly said by the heathen, we must appropriate to our uses*

60. Moreover, if those who are called philosophers, and especially the Platonists, have said aught that is true and in harmony with our faith, we are not only not to shrink from it, but to claim it for our own use from those who have unlawful possession of it. For, as the Egyptians had not only the idols and heavy burdens which the people of Israel hated and fled from, but also vessels and ornaments of gold and silver, and garments, which the same people when going out of Egypt appropriated to themselves, designing them for a better use, not doing this on their own authority, but by the command of God, the Egyptians themselves, in their ignorance, providing them with things which they themselves were not making a good use of;[1] in the same way all branches of heathen learning have not only false and superstitious fancies and heavy burdens of unnecessary toil, which every one of us, when going out under the leadership of Christ from the fellowship of the heathen, ought to abhor and avoid; but they contain also liberal instruction which is better adapted to the use of the truth, and some most excellent precepts of morality; and some truths in regard even to the worship of the One God are found among them. Now these are, so to speak, their gold and silver, which they did not create themselves, but dug out of the mines of God's providence which are everywhere scattered abroad, and are perversely and unlawfully prostituting to the worship of devils. These, therefore, the Christian, when he separates himself in spirit from the miserable fellowship of these men, ought to take away from them, and to devote to their proper use in preaching the gospel. Their garments, also—that is, human institutions such as are adapted to that intercourse with men which is indispensable in this life—we must take and turn to a Christian use.

61. And what else have many good and faithful men among our brethren done? Do we not see with what a quantity of gold and silver and garments Cyprian, that most persuasive teacher and most blessed martyr, was loaded when he came out of Egypt? How much Lactantius brought with him? And Victorinus, and Optatus, and Hilary, not to speak of living men! How much Greeks out of number have borrowed! And prior to all these, that most faithful servant of God, Moses, had done the same thing; for of him it is written that he was learned in all the wisdom of the Egyptians.[2] And to none of all these would heathen superstition (especially in those times when, kicking against the yoke of Christ, it was persecuting the Christians) have ever furnished branches of knowledge it held useful, if it had suspected they were about to turn them to the use of worshipping the One God, and thereby overturning the vain worship of idols. But they gave their gold and their silver and their garments to the people of God

[1] Ex. 3. 21, 22; 12. 35, 36.   [2] Acts, 7. 22.

as they were going out of Egypt, not knowing how the things they gave would be turned to the service of Christ. For what was done at the time of the exodus was no doubt a type prefiguring what happens now. And this I say without prejudice to any other interpretation that may be as good, or better.

CHAP. 41. *What kind of spirit is required for the study of Holy Scripture*

62. But when the student of the Holy Scriptures, prepared in the way I have indicated, shall enter upon his investigations, let him constantly meditate upon that saying of the apostle's, "Knowledge puffeth up, but charity edifieth." [1] For so he will feel that, whatever may be the riches he brings with him out of Egypt, yet unless he has kept the passover, he cannot be safe. Now Christ is our passover sacrificed for us,[2] and there is nothing the sacrifice of Christ more clearly teaches us than the call which He himself addresses to those whom He sees toiling in Egypt under Pharaoh: "Come unto me, all ye that labour and are heavy laden, and I will give you rest. Take my yoke upon you, and learn of me; for I am meek and lowly in heart: and ye shall find rest unto your souls. For my yoke is easy, and my burden is light." [3] To whom is it light but to the meek and lowly in heart, whom knowledge doth not puff up, but charity edifieth? Let them remember, then, that those who celebrated the passover at that time in type and shadow, when they were ordered to mark their door-posts with the blood of the lamb, used hyssop to mark them with.[4] Now this is a meek and lowly herb, and yet nothing is stronger and more penetrating than its roots; that being rooted and grounded in love, we may be able to comprehend with all saints what is the breadth, and length, and depth, and height[5] —that is, to comprehend the cross of our Lord, the breadth of which is indicated by the transverse wood on which the hands are stretched, its length by the part from the ground up to the cross-bar on which the whole body from the head downwards is fixed, its height by the part from the cross-bar to the top on which the head lies, and its depth by the part which is hidden, being fixed in the earth. And by this sign of the cross all Christian action is symbolized, viz., to

do good works in Christ, to cling with constancy to Him, to hope for heaven, and not to desecrate the sacraments. And purified by this Christian action, we shall be able to know even "the love of Christ which passeth knowledge," Who is equal to the Father, by Whom all things, were made, "that we may be filled with all the fullness of God." [6] There is besides in hyssop a purgative virtue, that the breast may not be swollen with that knowledge which puffeth up, nor boast vainly of the riches brought out from Egypt. "Purge me with hyssop," the psalmist says,[7] "and I shall be clean; wash me, and I shall be whiter than snow. Make me to hear joy and gladness." Then he immediately adds, to show that it is purifying from pride that is indicated by hyssop, "that the bones which Thou hast broken may rejoice."

CHAP. 42. *Sacred Scripture compared with profane authors*

63. But just as poor as the store of gold and silver and garments which the people of Israel brought with them out of Egypt was in comparison with the riches which they afterwards attained at Jerusalem, and which reached their height in the reign of King Solomon, so poor is all the useful knowledge which is gathered from the books of the heathen when compared with the knowledge of Holy Scripture. For whatever man may have learnt from other sources, if it is hurtful, it is there condemned; if it is useful, it is therein contained. And while every man may find there all that he has learnt of useful elsewhere, he will find there in much greater abundance things that are to be found nowhere else, but can be learnt only in the wonderful sublimity and wonderful simplicity of the Scriptures.

When, then, the reader is possessed of the instruction here pointed out, so that unknown signs have ceased to be a hindrance to him; when he is meek and lowly of heart, subject to the easy yoke of Christ, and loaded with His light burden, rooted and grounded and built up in faith, so that knowledge cannot puff him up, let him then approach the consideration and discussion of ambiguous signs in Scripture. And about these I shall now, in a third book, endeavour to say what the Lord shall be pleased to vouchsafe.

[1] I Cor. 8. 1.   [2] I Cor. 5. 7.   [3] Matt. 11. 28–30.
[4] Ex. 12. 22.   [5] Eph. 3. 17, 18.

[6] Eph. 3. 19.   [7] Ps. 51. 7, 8.

BOOK III

ARGUMENT. THE AUTHOR, HAVING DISCUSSED IN THE PRECEDING BOOK THE METHOD OF DEALING WITH UNKNOWN SIGNS, GOES ON IN THIS THIRD BOOK TO TREAT OF AMBIGUOUS SIGNS. SUCH SIGNS MAY BE EITHER DIRECT OR FIGURATIVE. IN THE CASE OF DIRECT SIGNS AMBIGUITY MAY ARISE FROM THE PUNCTUATION, THE PRO-NUNCIATION, OR THE DOUBTFUL SIGNIFICATION OF THE WORDS, AND IS TO BE RE-SOLVED BY ATTENTION TO THE CONTEXT, A COMPARISON OF TRANSLATIONS, OR A REF-ERENCE TO THE ORIGINAL TONGUE. IN THE CASE OF FIGURATIVE SIGNS WE NEED TO GUARD AGAINST TWO MISTAKES:—1. THE INTERPRETING LITERAL EXPRESSIONS FIG-URATIVELY; 2. THE INTERPRETING FIGURATIVE EXPRESSIONS LITERALLY. THE AU-THOR LAYS DOWN RULES BY WHICH WE MAY DECIDE WHETHER AN EXPRESSION IS LIT-ERAL OR FIGURATIVE; THE GENERAL RULE BEING, THAT WHATEVER CAN BE SHOWN TO BE IN ITS LITERAL SENSE INCONSISTENT EITHER WITH PURITY OF LIFE OR COR-RECTNESS OF DOCTRINE MUST BE TAKEN FIGURATIVELY. HE THEN GOES ON TO LAY DOWN RULES FOR THE INTERPRETATION OF EXPRESSIONS WHICH HAVE BEEN PROVED TO BE FIGURATIVE; THE GENERAL PRINCIPLE BEING, THAT NO INTERPRETATION CAN BE TRUE WHICH DOES NOT PROMOTE THE LOVE OF GOD AND THE LOVE OF MAN. THE AUTHOR THEN PROCEEDS TO EXPOUND AND ILLUSTRATE THE SEVEN RULES OF TICHO-NIUS THE DONATIST, WHICH HE COMMENDS TO THE ATTENTION OF THE STUDENT OF HOLY SCRIPTURE.

CHAP. 1. *Summary of the foregoing books, and scope of that which follows*

1. THE man who fears God seeks diligently in Holy Scripture for a knowledge of His will. And when he has become meek through piety, so as to have no love of strife; when furnished also with a knowledge of languages, so as not to be stopped by unknown words and forms of speech, and with the knowledge of certain necessary objects, so as not to be ignorant of the force and nature of those which are used figuratively; and assisted, besides, by accuracy in the texts, which has been secured by skill and care in the matter of correction; when thus prepared, let him proceed to the examination and solution of the ambiguities of Scripture. And that he may not be led astray by ambiguous signs, so far as I can give him instruction (it may happen, how-ever, that either from the greatness of his in-tellect, or the greater clearness of the light he enjoys, he shall laugh at the methods I am go-ing to point out as childish), but yet, as I was going to say, so far as I can give instruction, let him who is in such a state of mind that he can be instructed by me know, that the ambiguity of Scripture lies either in proper words or in metaphorical, classes which I have already de-scribed in the second book.[1]

[1]See BK. II. Chap. 10.

CHAP. 2. *Rule for removing ambiguity by at-tending to punctuation*

2. But when proper words make Scripture ambiguous, we must see in the first place that there is nothing wrong in our punctuation or pronunciation. Accordingly, if, when attention is given to the passage, it shall appear to be un-certain in what way it ought to be punctuated or pronounced, let the reader consult the rule of faith which he has gathered from the plainer passages of Scripture, and from the authority of the Church, and of which I treated at sufficient length when I was speaking in the first book about things. But if both readings, or all of them (if there are more than two), give a mean-ing in harmony with the faith, it remains to consult the context, both what goes before and what comes after, to see which interpretation, out of many that offer themselves, it pronounces for and permits to be dovetailed into itself.

3. Now look at some examples. The hereti-cal pointing,[2] *"In principio erat verbum, et ver-bum erat apud Deum, et Deus erat,"*[3] so as to make the next sentence run, *"Verbum hoc erat in principio apud Deum,"*[4] arises out of unwill-

[2]John, I. 1, 2.
[3]In the beginning was the Word, and the Word was with God, and God was.
[4]This Word was in the beginning with God.

ingness to confess that the Word was God. But this must be rejected by the rule of faith, which, in reference to the equality of the Trinity, directs us to say: *"et Deus erat verbum,"* [1] and then to add: *"hoc erat in principio apud Deum."* [2]

4. But the following ambiguity of punctuation does not go against the faith in either way you take it, and therefore must be decided from the context. It is where the apostle says: "What I shall choose I wot not: for I am in a strait betwixt two, having a desire to depart, and to be with Christ, which is far better: nevertheless to abide in the flesh is more needful for you." [3] Now it is uncertain whether we should read, *"ex duobus concupiscentiam habens"* [having a desire for two things], or *"compellor autem ex duobus"* [I am in a strait betwixt two]; and so to add: *"concupiscentiam habens dissolvi, et esse cum Christo"* [having a desire to depart, and to be with Christ]. But since there follows *"multo enim magis optimum"* [for it is far better], it is evident that he says he has a desire for that which is better; so that, while he is in a strait betwixt two, yet he has a desire for one and sees a necessity for the other; a desire, viz., to be with Christ, and a necessity to remain in the flesh. Now this ambiguity is resolved by one word that follows, which is translated *enim* [for]; and the translators who have omitted this particle have preferred the interpretation which makes the apostle seem not only in a strait betwixt two, but also to have a desire for two. We must therefore punctuate the sentence thus: *"et quid eligam ignoro: compellor autem ex duobus"* [what I shall choose I wot not: for I am in a strait betwixt two]; and after this point follows: *"concupiscentiam habens dissolvi, et esse cum Christo"* [having a desire to depart, and to be with Christ]. And, as if he were asked why he has a desire for this in preference to the other, he adds: *"multo enim magis optimum"* [for it is far better]. Why, then, is he in a strait betwixt the two? Because there is a need for his remaining, which he adds in these terms: *"manere in carne necessarium propter vos"* [nevertheless to abide in the flesh is more needful for you].

5. Where, however, the ambiguity cannot be cleared up, either by the rule of faith or by the context, there is nothing to hinder us to point the sentence according to any method we choose of those that suggest themselves. As is the case

in that passage to the Corinthians: "Having therefore these promises, dearly beloved, let us cleanse ourselves from all filthiness of the flesh and spirit, perfecting holiness in the fear of God. Receive us; we have wronged no man." [4] It is doubtful whether we should read, *"mundemus nos ab omni coinquinatione carnis et spiritus"* [let us cleanse ourselves from all filthiness of the flesh and spirit], in accordance with the passage, "that she may be holy both in body and in spirit," [5] or, *"mundemus nos ab omni coinquinatione carnis"* [let us cleanse ourselves from all filthiness of the flesh], so as to make the next sentence, *"et spiritus perficientes sanctificationem in timore Dei capite nos"* [and perfecting holiness of spirit in the fear of God, receive us]. Such ambiguities of punctuation, therefore, are left to the reader's discretion.

CHAP. 3. *How pronunciation serves to remove ambiguity. Different kinds of interrogation*

6. And all the directions that I have given about ambiguous punctuations are to be observed likewise in the case of doubtful pronunciations. For these too, unless the fault lies in the carelessness of the reader, are corrected either by the rule of faith, or by a reference to the preceding or succeeding context; or if neither of these methods is applied with success, they will remain doubtful, but so that the reader will not be in fault in whatever way he may pronounce them. For example, if our faith that God will not bring any charges against His elect, and that Christ will not condemn His elect, did not stand in the way, this passage, "Who shall lay anything to the charge of God's elect?" might be pronounced in such a way as to make what follows an answer to this question, "God who justifieth," and to make a second question, "Who is he that condemneth?" with the answer, "Christ Jesus who died." [6] But as it would be the height of madness to believe this, the passage will be pronounced in such a way as to make the first part a question of inquiry[7] and the second a rhetorical interrogative.[8] Now the ancients said that the difference between an inquiry and an interrogative was this, that an inquiry admits of many answers, but to an interrogative the answer must be either "No" or "Yes." The passage will be pronounced, then, in such a way that after the inquiry, "Who shall lay anything to the charge of God's elect?" what follows will be put as an in-

---

[1] And the Word was God.
[2] The same was in the beginning with God.
[3] Phil. I. 22–24.

[4] II Cor. 7. 1, 2.   [5] I Cor. 7. 34.   [6] Rom. 8. 33, 34.
[7] *Percontatio.*   [8] *Interrogatio.*

terrogative: "Shall God who justifieth?"—the answer "No" being understood. And in the same way we shall have the inquiry, "Who is he that condemneth?" and the answer here again in the form of an interrogative, "Is it Christ Who died? yea, rather, Who is risen again? Who is even at the right hand of God? Who also maketh intercession for us?"—the answer "No" being understood to every one of these questions. On the other hand, in that passage where the apostle says, "What shall we say then? That the Gentiles which followed not after righteousness have attained to righteousness";[1] unless after the inquiry, "What shall we say then?" what follows were given as the answer to this question: "That the Gentiles, which followed not after righteousness, have attained to righteousness"; it would not be in harmony with the succeeding context. But with whatever tone of voice one may choose to pronounce that saying of Nathanael's, "Can any good thing come out of Nazareth?"[2]—whether with that of a man who gives an affirmative answer, so that "out of Nazareth" is the only part that belongs to the interrogation, or with that of a man who asks the whole question with doubt and hesitation— I do not see how a difference can be made. But neither sense is opposed to faith.

7. There is, again, an ambiguity arising out of the doubtful sound of syllables; and this of course has relation to pronunciation. For example, in the passage, "My bone [os meum] was not hid from Thee, which Thou didst make in secret,"[3] it is not clear to the reader whether he should take the word os as short or long. If he make it short, it is the singular of ossa [bones]; if he make it long, it is the singular of ora [mouths]. Now difficulties such as this are cleared up by looking into the original tongue, for in the Greek we find not στόμα [mouth], but ὀστέον [bone]. And for this reason the vulgar idiom is frequently more useful in conveying the sense than the pure speech of the educated. For I would rather have the barbarism, non est absconditum a te ossum meum,[4] than have the passage in better Latin, but the sense less clear. But sometimes when the sound of a syllable is doubtful, it is decided by a word near it belonging to the same sentence. As, for example, that saying of the apostle, "Of the which I tell you before [prædico], as I have also told you in time past [prædixi], that they which do such things shall not inherit the kingdom of God."[5] Now if he had only said, "Of the which

I tell you before [quæ prædico vobis]," and had not added, "as I have also told you in time past [sicut prædixi]," we could not know without going back to the original whether in the word prædico the middle syllable should be pronounced long or short. But as it is, it is clear that it should be pronounced long; for he does not say, sicut prædicavi, but sicut prædixi.

CHAP. 4. How ambiguities may be solved

8. And not only these, but also those ambiguities that do not relate either to punctuation or pronunciation, are to be examined in the same way. For example, that one in the Epistle to the Thessalonians: Propterea consolati sumus fratres in vobis.[6] Now it is doubtful whether fratres [brethren] is in the vocative or accusative case, and it is not contrary to faith to take it either way. But in the Greek language the two cases are not the same in form; and accordingly, when we look into the original, the case is shown to be vocative. Now if the translator had chosen to say, propterea consolationem habuimus fratres in vobis, he would have followed the words less literally, but there would have been less doubt about the meaning; or, indeed, if he had added nostri, hardly any one would have doubted that the vocative case was meant when he heard propterea consolati sumus fratres nostri in vobis. But this is a rather dangerous liberty to take. It has been taken, however, in that passage to the Corinthians, where the apostle says, "I protest by your rejoicing [per vestram gloriam] which I have in Christ Jesus our Lord, I die daily."[7] For one translator has it, per vestram juro gloriam, the form of adjuration appearing in the Greek without any ambiguity. It is therefore very rare and very difficult to find any ambiguity in the case of proper words, as far at least as Holy Scripture is concerned, which neither the context, showing the design of the writer, nor a comparison of translations, nor a reference to the original tongue, will suffice to explain.

CHAP. 5. It is a wretched slavery which takes the figurative expressions of Scripture in a literal sense

9. But the ambiguities of metaphorical words, about which I am next to speak, demand no ordinary care and diligence. In the first place, we must beware of taking a figurative expression literally. For the saying of the apostle applies in this case too: "The letter killeth, but the spirit

---

[1]Rom. 9. 30. [2]John, 1. 47. [3]Ps. 139. 16.
[4]My bone was not hid from Thee. [5]Gal. 5. 21.

[6]I Thess. 3. 7. "Therefore, brethren, we were comforted over you." [7]I Cor. 15. 31.

giveth life." [1] For when what is said figuratively is taken as if it were said literally, it is understood in a carnal manner. And nothing is more fittingly called the death of the soul than when that in it which raises it above the brutes, the intelligence namely, is put in subjection to the flesh by a blind adherence to the letter. For he who follows the letter takes figurative words as if they were proper, and does not carry out what is indicated by a proper word into its secondary signification; but, if he hears of the Sabbath, for example, thinks of nothing but the one day out of seven which recurs in constant succession; and when he hears of a sacrifice, does not carry his thoughts beyond the customary offerings of victims from the flock, and of the fruits of the earth. Now it is surely a miserable slavery of the soul to take signs for things, and to be unable to lift the eye of the mind above what is corporeal and created, that it may drink in eternal light.

CHAP. 6. *Utility of the bondage of the Jews*

10. This bondage, however, in the case of the Jewish people, differed widely from what it was in the case of the other nations; because, though the former were in bondage to temporal things, it was in such a way that in all these the One God was put before their minds. And although they paid attention to the signs of spiritual realities in place of the realities themselves, not knowing to what the signs referred, still they had this conviction rooted in their minds, that in subjecting themselves to such a bondage they were doing the pleasure of the one invisible God of all. And the apostle describes this bondage as being like to that of boys under the guidance of a schoolmaster.[2] And those who clung obstinately to such signs could not endure our Lord's neglect of them when the time for their revelation had come; and hence their leaders brought it as a charge against Him that He healed on the Sabbath, and the people, clinging to these signs as if they were realities, could not believe that one who refused to observe them in the way the Jews did was God, or came from God. But those who did believe, from among whom the first Church at Jerusalem was formed, showed clearly how great an advantage it had been to be so guided by the schoolmaster that signs, which had been for a season imposed on the obedient, fixed the thoughts of those who observed them on the worship of the One God Who made heaven and earth. These men, because they had been very near to spiritual things (for even in the temporal and carnal offerings and types, though they did not clearly apprehend their spiritual meaning, they had learnt to adore the One Eternal God), were filled with such a measure of the Holy Spirit that they sold all their goods, and laid their price at the apostles' feet to be distributed among the needy,[3] and consecrated themselves wholly to God as a new temple, of which the old temple they were serving was but the earthly type.

11. Now it is not recorded that any of the Gentile churches did this, because men who had for their gods idols made with hands had not been so near to spiritual things.

CHAP. 7. *The useless bondage of the Gentiles*

And if ever any of them endeavoured to make it out that their idols were only signs, yet still they used them in reference to the worship and adoration of the creature. What difference does it make to me, for instance, that the image of Neptune is not itself to be considered a god, but only as representing the wide ocean, and all the other waters besides that spring out of fountains? As it is described by a poet of theirs,[4] who says, if I recollect aright, "Thou, Father Neptune, whose hoary temples are wreathed with the resounding sea, whose beard is the mighty ocean flowing forth unceasingly, and whose hair is the winding rivers." This husk shakes its rattling stones within a sweet covering, and yet it is not food for men, but for swine. He who knows the gospel knows what I mean.[5] What profit is it to me, then, that the image of Neptune is used with a reference to this explanation of it, unless indeed the result be that I worship neither? For any statue you like to take is as much god to me as the wide ocean. I grant, however, that they who make gods of the works of man have sunk lower than they who make gods of the works of God. But the command is that we should love and serve the One God, who is the Maker of all those things, the images of which are worshipped by the heathen either as gods, or as signs and representations of gods. If, then, to take a sign which has been established for a useful end instead of the thing itself which it was designed to signify, is bondage to the flesh, how much more so is it to take signs intended to represent useless things for the things themselves! For even if you go back to the very things signified by such signs, and engage your mind in the worship of these, you will not be anything the more free from the burden and the livery of bondage to the flesh.

[1] II Cor. 3. 6. [2] Gal. 3. 24. [3] Acts, 4. 34, 35. [4] Claudian. [5] Luke, 15. 16.

Chap. 8. *The Jews liberated from their bondage in one way, the Gentiles in another*

12. Accordingly the liberty that comes by Christ took those whom it found under bondage to useful signs, and who were (so to speak) near to it, and, interpreting the signs to which they were in bondage, set them free by raising them to the realities of which these were signs. And out of such were formed the churches of the saints of Israel. Those, on the other hand, whom it found in bondage to useless signs, it not only freed from their slavery to such signs, but brought to nothing and cleared out of the way all these signs themselves, so that the Gentiles were turned from the corruption of a multitude of false gods, which Scripture frequently and justly speaks of as fornication, to the worship of the One God: not that they might now fall into bondage to signs of a useful kind, but rather that they might exercise their minds in the spiritual understanding of such.

Chap. 9. *Who is in bondage to signs, and who not*

13. Now he is in bondage to a sign who uses, or pays homage to, any significant object without knowing what it signifies: he, on the other hand, who either uses or honours a useful sign divinely appointed, whose force and significance he understands, does not honour the sign which is seen and temporal, but that to which all such signs refer. Now such a man is spiritual and free even at the time of his bondage, when it is not yet expedient to reveal to carnal minds those signs by subjection to which their carnality is to be overcome. To this class of spiritual persons belonged the patriarchs and the prophets, and all those among the people of Israel through whose instrumentality the Holy Spirit ministered unto us the aids and consolations of the Scriptures. But at the present time, after that the proof of our liberty has shone forth so clearly in the resurrection of our Lord, we are not oppressed with the heavy burden of attending even to those signs which we now understand, but our Lord Himself and apostolic practice have handed down to us a few rites in place of many, and these at once very easy to perform, most majestic in their significance, and most sacred in the observance; such, for example, as the sacrament of baptism, and the celebration of the body and blood of the Lord. And as soon as any one looks upon these observances he knows to what they refer, and so reveres them not in carnal bondage, but in spiritual freedom. Now,

as to follow the letter, and to take signs for the things that are signified by them, is a mark of weakness and bondage; so to interpret signs wrongly is the result of being misled by error. He, however, who does not understand what a sign signifies, but yet knows that it is a sign, is not in bondage. And it is better even to be in bondage to unknown but useful signs than, by interpreting them wrongly, to draw the neck from under the yoke of bondage only to insert it in the coils of error.

Chap. 10. *How we are to discern whether a phrase is figurative*

14. But in addition to the foregoing rule, which guards us against taking a metaphorical form of speech as if it were literal, we must also pay heed to that which tells us not to take a literal form of speech as if it were figurative. In the first place, then, we must show the way to find out whether a phrase is literal or figurative. And the way is certainly as follows: Whatever there is in the word of God that cannot, when taken literally, be referred either to purity of life or soundness of doctrine, you may set down as figurative. Purity of life has reference to the love of God and one's neighbour; soundness of doctrine to the knowledge of God and one's neighbour. Every man, moreover, has hope in his own conscience, so far as he perceives that he has attained to the love and knowledge of God and his neighbour. Now all these matters have been spoken of in the first book.

15. But as men are prone to estimate sins, not by reference to their inherent sinfulness, but rather by reference to their own customs, it frequently happens that a man will think nothing blameable except what the men of his own country and time are accustomed to condemn, and nothing worthy of praise or approval except what is sanctioned by the custom of his companions; and thus it comes to pass, that if Scripture either enjoins what is opposed to the customs of the hearers, or condemns what is not so opposed, and if at the same time the authority of the word has a hold upon their minds, they think that the expression is figurative. Now Scripture enjoins nothing except charity, and condemns nothing except lust, and in that way fashions the lives of men. In the same way, if an erroneous opinion has taken possession of the mind, men think that whatever Scripture asserts contrary to this must be figurative. Now Scripture asserts nothing but the Catholic faith, in regard to things past, future, and present. It is a narrative of the past, a prophecy of the future, and a

description of the present. But all these tend to nourish and strengthen charity, and to overcome and root out lust.

16. I mean by charity that affection of the mind which aims at the enjoyment of God for His own sake, and the enjoyment of one's self and one's neighbour in subordination to God; by lust I mean that affection of the mind which aims at enjoying one's self and one's neighbour, and other corporeal things, without reference to God. Again, what lust, when unsubdued, does towards corrupting one's own soul and body, is called *vice*; but what it does to injure another is called *crime*. And these are the two classes into which all sins may be divided. But the vices come first; for when these have exhausted the soul, and reduced it to a kind of poverty, it easily slides into crimes, in order to remove hindrances to, or to find assistance in, its vices. In the same way, what charity does with a view to one's own advantage is *prudence*; but what it does with a view to a neighbour's advantage is called *benevolence*. And here prudence comes first; because no one can confer an advantage on another which he does not himself possess. Now in proportion as the dominion of lust is pulled down, in the same proportion is that of charity built up.

CHAP. 11. *Rule for interpreting phrases which seem to ascribe severity to God and the saints*

17. Every severity, therefore, and apparent cruelty, either in word or deed, that is ascribed in Holy Scripture to God or His saints, avails to the pulling down of the dominion of lust. And if its meaning be clear, we are not to give it some secondary reference, as if it were spoken figuratively. Take, for example, that saying of the apostle: "But, after thy hardness and impenitent heart, treasurest up unto thyself wrath against the day of wrath and revelation of the righteous judgment of God; Who will render to every man according to his deeds: to them who, by patient continuance in well-doing, seek for glory, and honour, and immortality, eternal life; but unto them that are contentious, and do not obey the truth, but obey unrighteousness, indignation and wrath, tribulation and anguish, upon every soul of man that doeth evil, of the Jew first, and also of the Gentile." [1] But this is addressed to those who, being unwilling to subdue their lust, are themselves involved in the destruction of their lust. When, however, the dominion of lust is overturned in a man over whom

it had held sway, this plain expression is used: "They that are Christ's have crucified the flesh, with the affections and lusts." [2] Only that, even in these instances, some words are used figuratively, as for example, "the wrath of God" and "crucified." But these are not so numerous, nor placed in such a way as to obscure the sense, and make it allegorical or enigmatical, which is the kind of expresssion properly called *figurative*. But in the saying addressed to Jeremiah, "See, I have this day set thee over the nations, and over the kingdoms, to root out, and to pull down, and to destroy, and to throw down," [3] there is no doubt the whole of the language is figurative, and to be referred to the end I have spoken of.

CHAP. 12. *Rule for interpreting those sayings and actions which are ascribed to God and the saints, and which yet seem to the unskilful to be wicked*

18. Those things, again, whether only sayings or whether actual deeds, which appear to the inexperienced to be sinful, and which are ascribed to God, or to men whose holiness is put before us as an example, are wholly figurative, and the hidden kernel of meaning they contain is to be picked out as food for the nourishment of charity. Now, whoever uses transitory objects less freely than is the custom of those among whom he lives, is either temperate or superstitious; whoever, on the other hand, uses them so as to transgress the bounds of the custom of the good men about him, either has a further meaning in what he does, or is sinful. In all such matters it is not the use of the objects, but the lust of the user, that is to blame. Nobody in his sober senses would believe, for example, that when our Lord's feet were anointed by the woman with precious ointment, [4] it was for the same purpose for which luxurious and profligate men are accustomed to have theirs anointed in those banquets which we abhor. For the sweet odour means the good report which is earned by a life of good works; and the man who wins this, while following in the footsteps of Christ, anoints His feet (so to speak) with the most precious ointment. And so that which in the case of other persons is often a sin, becomes, when ascribed to God or a prophet, the sign of some great truth. Keeping company with a harlot, for example, is one thing when it is the result of abandoned manners, another thing when done in the course of his prophecy by the proph-

[1] Rom. 2. 5–9. [2] Gal. 5. 24. [3] Jer. 1. 10. [4] John, 12. 3.

et Hosea.[1] Because it is a shamefully wicked thing to strip the body naked at a banquet among the drunken and licentious, it does not follow that it is a sin to be naked in the baths.

19. We must, therefore, consider carefully what is suitable to times and places and persons, and not rashly charge men with sins. For it is possible that a wise man may use the daintiest food without any sin of epicurism or gluttony, while a fool will crave for the vilest food with a most disgusting eagerness of appetite. And any sane man would prefer eating fish after the manner of our Lord, to eating lentils after the manner of Esau, or barley after the manner of oxen. For there are several beasts that feed on commoner kinds of food, but it does not follow that they are more temperate than we are. For in all matters of this kind it is not the nature of the things we use, but our reason for using them, and our manner of seeking them, that make what we do either praiseworthy or blameable.

20. Now the saints of ancient times were, under the form of an earthly kingdom, foreshadowing and foretelling the kingdom of heaven. And on account of the necessity for a numerous offspring, the custom of one man having several wives was at that time blameless: and for the same reason it was not proper for one woman to have several husbands, because a woman does not in that way become more fruitful, but, on the contrary, it is base harlotry to seek either gain or offspring by promiscuous intercourse. In regard to matters of this sort, whatever the holy men of those times did without lust, Scripture passes over without blame, although they did things which could not be done at the present time, except through lust. And everything of this nature that is there narrated we are to take not only in its historical and literal, but also in its figurative and prophetical sense, and to interpret as bearing ultimately upon the end of love towards God or our neighbour, or both. For as it was disgraceful among the ancient Romans to wear tunics reaching to the heels, and furnished with sleeves, but now it is disgraceful for men honourably born not to wear tunics of that description: so we must take heed in regard to other things also, that lust do not mix with our use of them; for lust not only abuses to wicked ends the customs of those among whom we live, but frequently also transgressing the bounds of custom, betrays, in a disgraceful outbreak, its

[1]Hos. 1. 2.

own hideousness, which was concealed under the cover of prevailing fashions.

Chap. 13. *Same subject, continued*

21. Whatever, then, is in accordance with the habits of those with whom we are either compelled by necessity, or undertake as a matter of duty, to spend this life, is to be turned by good and great men to some prudent or benevolent end, either directly, as is our duty, or figuratively, as is allowable to prophets.

Chap. 14. *Error of those who think that there is no absolute right and wrong*

22. But when men unacquainted with other modes of life than their own meet with the record of such actions, unless they are restrained by authority, they look upon them as sins, and do not consider that their own customs either in regard to marriage, or feasts, or dress, or the other necessities and adornments of human life, appear sinful to the people of other nations and other times. And, distracted by this endless variety of customs, some who were half asleep (as I may say)—that is, who were neither sunk in the deep sleep of folly, nor were able to awake into the light of wisdom—have thought that there was no such thing as absolute right, but that every nation took its own custom for right; and that, since every nation has a different custom, and right must remain unchangeable, it becomes manifest that there is no such thing as right at all. Such men did not perceive, to take only one example, that the precept, "Whatsoever ye would that men should do to you, do ye even so to them," [2] cannot be altered by any diversity of national customs. And this precept, when it is referred to the love of God, destroys all vices; when to the love of one's neighbour, puts an end to all crimes. For no one is willing to defile his own dwelling; he ought not, therefore, to defile the dwelling of God, that is, himself. And no one wishes an injury to be done him by another; he himself, therefore, ought not to do injury to another.

Chap. 15. *Rule for interpreting figurative expressions*

23. The tyranny of lust being thus overthrown, charity reigns through its supremely just laws of love to God for His own sake, and love to one's self and one's neighbour for God's sake. Accordingly, in regard to figurative expressions, a rule such as the following will be

[2]Matt. 7. 12. Cf. Tobit, 4. 15.

observed, to carefully turn over in our minds and meditate upon what we read till an interpretation be found that tends to establish the reign of love. Now, if when taken literally it at once gives a meaning of this kind, the expression is not to be considered figurative.

CHAP. 16. *Rule for interpreting commands and prohibitions*

24. If the sentence is one of command, either forbidding a crime or vice, or enjoining an act of prudence or benevolence, it is not figurative. If, however, it seems to enjoin a crime or vice, or to forbid an act of prudence or benevolence, it is figurative. "Except ye eat the flesh of the Son of man," says Christ, "and drink His blood, ye have no life in you." [1] This seems to enjoin a crime or a vice; it is therefore a figure, enjoining that we should have a share in the sufferings of our Lord, and that we should retain a sweet and profitable memory of the fact that His flesh was wounded and crucified for us. Scripture says: "If thine enemy hunger, feed him; if he thirst, give him drink"; and this is beyond doubt a command to do a kindness. But in what follows, "for in so doing thou shalt heap coals of fire on his head," [2] one would think a deed of malevolence was enjoined. Do not doubt, then, that the expression is figurative; and, while it is possible to interpret it in two ways, one pointing to the doing of an injury, the other to a display of superiority, let charity on the contrary call you back to benevolence, and interpret the coals of fire as the burning groans of penitence by which a man's pride is cured who bewails that he has been the enemy of one who came to his assistance in distress. In the same way, when our Lord says, "He who loveth his life shall lose it," [3] we are not to think that He forbids the prudence with which it is a man's duty to care for his life, but that He says in a figurative sense, "Let him lose his life"—that is, let him destroy and lose that perverted and unnatural use which he now makes of his life, and through which his desires are fixed on temporal things so that he gives no heed to eternal. It is written: "Give to the godly man, and help not a sinner." [4] The latter clause of this sentence seems to forbid benevolence; for it says, "help not a sinner." Understand, therefore, that "sinner" is put figuratively for sin, so that it is his sin you are not to help.

[1] John, 6. 53.
[2] Rom. 12. 20; Prov. 25. 21, 22.
[3] John, 12. 25. Cf. Matt. 10. 39.
[4] Ecclus. 12. 4. Cf. Tobit, 4. 17.

CHAP. 17. *Some commands are given to all in common, others to particular classes*

25. Again, it often happens that a man who has attained, or thinks he has attained, to a higher grade of spiritual life, thinks that the commands given to those who are still in the lower grades are figurative; for example, if he has embraced a life of celibacy and made himself a eunuch for the kingdom of heaven's sake, he contends that the commands given in Scripture about loving and ruling a wife are not to be taken literally, but figuratively; and if he has determined to keep his virgin unmarried, he tries to put a figurative interpretation on the passage where it is said, "Marry thy daughter, and so shalt thou have performed a weighty matter." [5] Accordingly, another of our rules for understanding the Scriptures will be as follows—to recognize that some commands are given to all in common, others to particular classes of persons, that the medicine may act not only upon the state of health as a whole, but also upon the special weakness of each member. For that which cannot be raised to a higher state must be cared for in its own state.

CHAP. 18. *We must take into consideration the time at which anything was enjoyed or allowed*

26. We must also be on our guard against supposing that what in the Old Testament, making allowance for the condition of those times, is not a crime or a vice even if we take it literally and not figuratively, can be transferred to the present time as a habit of life. For no one will do this except lust has dominion over him, and endeavours to find support for itself in the very Scriptures which were intended to overthrow it. And the wretched man does not perceive that such matters are recorded with this useful design, that men of good hope may learn the salutary lesson, both that the custom they spurn can be turned to a good use, and that which they embrace can be used to condemnation, if the use of the former be accompanied with charity, and the use of the latter with lust.

27. For, if it was possible for one man to use many wives with chastity, it is possible for another to use one wife with lust. And I look with greater approval on the man who uses the fruitfulness of many wives for the sake of an ulterior object, than on the man who enjoys the body of one wife for its own sake. For in the former case the man aims at a useful object suited to the

[5] Ecclus. 7. 27.

circumstances of the times; in the latter case he gratifies a lust which is engrossed in temporal enjoyments. And those men to whom the apostle permitted as a matter of indulgence to have one wife, because of their incontinence,[1] were less near to God than those who, though they had each of them numerous wives, yet just as a wise man uses food and drink only for the sake of bodily health, used marriage only for the sake of offspring. And, accordingly, if these last had been still alive at the advent of our Lord, when the time not of casting stones away but of gathering them together had come,[2] they would have immediately made themselves eunuchs for the kingdom of heaven's sake. For there is no difficulty in abstaining unless when there is lust in enjoying. And assuredly those men of whom I speak knew that wantonness even in regard to wives is abuse and intemperance, as is proved by Tobit's prayer when he was married to his wife. For he says: "Blessed art Thou, O God of our fathers, and blessed is Thy holy and glorious name for ever; let the heavens bless Thee, and all Thy creatures. Thou madest Adam, and gavest him Eve his wife for an helper and stay. . . . And now, O Lord, Thou knowest that I take not this my sister for lust, but uprightly: therefore have pity on us, O Lord."[3]

CHAP. 19. *Wicked men judge others by themselves*

28. But those who, giving the rein to lust, either wander about steeping themselves in a multitude of debaucheries, or even in regard to one wife not only exceed the measure necessary for the procreation of children, but with the shameless licence of a sort of slavish freedom heap up the filth of a still more beastly excess, such men do not believe it possible that the men of ancient times used a number of wives with temperance, looking to nothing but the duty, necessary in the circumstances of the time, of propagating the race; and what they themselves, who are entangled in the meshes of lust, do not accomplish in the case of a single wife, they think utterly impossible in the case of a number of wives.

29. But these same men might say that it is not right even to honour and praise good and holy men, because they themselves when they are honoured and praised, swell with pride, becoming the more eager for the emptiest sort of distinction the more frequently and the more widely they are blown about on the tongue of flattery, and so become so light that a bī rumour, whether it appear prosperous or verse, will carry them into the whirlpool of viᴄ or dash them on the rocks of crime. Let them, then, learn how trying and difficult it is for themselves to escape either being caught by the bait of praise, or pierced by the stings of insult; but let them not measure others by their own standard.

CHAP. 20. *Consistency of good men in all outward circumstances*

Let them believe, on the contrary, that the apostles of our faith were neither puffed up when they were honoured by men, nor cast down when they were despised. And certainly neither sort of temptation was wanting to those great men. For they were both cried up by the loud praises of believers, and cried down by the slanderous reports of their persecutors. But the apostles used all these things, as occasion served, and were not corrupted; and in the same way the saints of old used their wives with reference to the necessities of their own times, and were not in bondage to lust as they are who refuse to believe these things.

30. For if they had been under the influence of any such passion, they could never have restrained themselves from implacable hatred towards their sons, by whom they knew that their wives and concubines were solicited and debauched.

CHAP. 21. *David not lustful, though he fell into adultery*

But when King David had suffered this injury at the hands of his impious and unnatural son, he not only bore with him in his mad passion, but mourned over him in his death. He certainly was not caught in the meshes of carnal jealousy, seeing that it was not his own injuries but the sins of his son that moved him. For it was on this account he had given orders that his son should not be slain if he were conquered in battle, that he might have a place of repentance after he was subdued; and when he was baffled in this design, he mourned over his son's death, not because of his own loss, but because he knew to what punishment so impious an adulterer and parricide had been hurried.[4] For prior to this, in the case of another son who had been guilty of no crime, though he was dreadfully afflicted for him while he was sick, yet he comforted himself after his death.[5]

31. And with what moderation and self-

---

[1] I Cor. 7. 1, 2, 9.   [2] Eccles. 3. 5.   [3] Tobit, 8. 5–7.   [4] Cf. II Sam. 16. 22; 18. 5; 19. 1.   [5] II Sam. 12. 19–23.

...en used their wives appears ...t when this same king, carried ...t of passion and by temporal ...taken unlawful possession of ...se husband also he ordered to ...le was accused of his crime by ...when he had come to show him his sin, set before him the parable of the poor man who had but one ewe-lamb, and whose neighbour, though he had many, yet when a guest came to him spared to take of his own flock, but set his poor neighbour's one lamb before his guest to eat. And David's anger being kindled against the man, he commanded that he should be put to death, and the lamb restored fourfold to the poor man; thus unwittingly condemning the sin he had wittingly committed.[1] And when he had been shown this, and God's punishment had been denounced against him, he wiped out his sin in deep penitence. But yet in this parable it was the adultery only that was indicated by the poor man's ewe-lamb; about the killing of the woman's husband—that is, about the murder of the poor man himself who had the one ewe-lamb—nothing is said in the parable, so that the sentence of condemnation is pronounced against the adultery alone. And hence we may understand with what temperance he possessed a number of wives when he was forced to punish himself for transgressing in regard to one woman. But in his case the immoderate desire did not take up its abode with him, but was only a passing guest. On this account the unlawful appetite is called even by the accusing prophet, a guest. For he did not say that he took the poor man's ewe-lamb to make a feast for his king, but for his guest. In the case of his son Solomon, however, this lust did not come and pass away like a guest, but reigned as a king. And about him Scripture is not silent, but accuses him of being a lover of strange women; for in the beginning of his reign he was inflamed with a desire for wisdom, but after he had attained it through spiritual love, he lost it through carnal lust.[2]

CHAP. 22. *Rule regarding passages of Scripture in which approval is expressed of actions which are now condemned by good men*

32. Therefore, although all, or nearly all, the transactions recorded in the Old Testament are to be taken not literally only, but figuratively as well, nevertheless even in the case of those which the reader has taken literally, and which,

though the authors of them are praised, are repugnant to the habits of the good men who since our Lord's advent are the custodians of the divine commands, let him refer the figure to its interpretation, but let him not transfer the act to his habits of life. For many things which were done as duties at that time cannot now be done except through lust.

CHAP. 23. *Rule regarding the narrative of sins of great men*

33. And when he reads of the sins of great men, although he may be able to see and to trace out in them a figure of things to come, let him yet put the literal fact to this use also, to teach him not to dare to vaunt himself in his own good deeds, and in comparison with his own righteousness, to despise others as sinners, when he sees in the case of men so eminent both the storms that are to be avoided and the shipwrecks that are to be wept over. For the sins of these men were recorded to this end, that men might everywhere and always tremble at that saying of the apostle: "Wherefore let him that thinketh he standeth take heed lest he fall."[3] For there is hardly a page of Scripture on which it is not clearly written that God resisteth the proud and giveth grace to the humble.[4]

CHAP. 24. *The character of the expressions used is above all to have weight*

34. The chief thing to be inquired into, therefore, in regard to any expression that we are trying to understand is, whether it is literal or figurative. For when it is ascertained to be figurative, it is easy, by an application of the laws of things which we discussed in the first book, to turn it in every way until we arrive at a true interpretation, especially when we bring to our aid experience strengthened by the exercise of piety. Now we find out whether an expression is literal or figurative by attending to the considerations indicated above.

CHAP. 25. *The same word does not always signify the same thing*

And when it is shown to be figurative, the words in which it is expressed will be found to be drawn either from like objects or from objects having some affinity.

35. But as there are many ways in which things show a likeness to each other, we are not to suppose there is any rule that what a thing signifies by similitude in one place it is to be taken to signify in all other places. For our Lord

---

[1] II Sam. 12. 1–6.
[2] II Chron. 1. 10–12; I Kings 11. 1–3.
[3] I Cor. 10. 12. [4] Cf. Jas. 4. 6 and I Pet. 5. 6.

used leaven both in a bad sense, as when He said, "Beware of the leaven of the Pharisees," [1] and in a good sense, as when He said, "The kingdom of heaven is like unto leaven, which a woman took and hid in three measures of meal, till the whole was leavened." [2]

36. Now the rule in regard to this variation has two forms. For things that signify now one thing and now another, signify either things that are contrary, or things that are only different. They signify contraries, for example, when they are used metaphorically at one time in a good sense, at another in a bad, as in the case of the leaven mentioned above. Another example of the same is that a lion stands for Christ in the place where it is said, "The lion of the tribe of Judah hath prevailed"; [3] and again, stands for the devil where it is written, "Your adversary the devil, as a roaring lion, walketh about seeking whom he may devour." [4] In the same way the serpent is used in a good sense, "Be wise as serpents"; [5] and again, in a bad sense, "The serpent beguiled Eve through his subtlety." [6] Bread is used in a good sense, "I am the living bread which came down from heaven"; [7] in a bad, "Bread eaten in secret is pleasant." [8] And so in a great many other cases. The examples I have adduced are indeed by no means doubtful in their signification, because only plain instances ought to be used as examples. There are passages, however, in regard to which it is uncertain in what sense they ought to be taken, as for example, "In the hand of the Lord there is a cup, and the wine is red: it is full of mixture." [9] Now it is uncertain whether this denotes the wrath of God, but not to the last extremity of punishment, that is, "to the very dregs"; or whether it denotes the grace of the Scriptures passing away from the Jews and coming to the Gentiles, because "He has put down one and set up another"—certain observances, however, which they understand in a carnal manner, still remaining among the Jews, for "the dregs hereof is not yet wrung out." The following is an example of the same object being taken, not in opposite, but only in different significations: water denotes people, as we read in the Apocalypse, [10] and also the Holy Spirit, as for example, "Out of his belly shall flow rivers of living water"; [11] and many other things besides water must be interpreted according to the place in which they are found.

37. And in the same way other objects are not single in their signification, but each one of them denotes not two only but sometimes even several different things, according to the connexion in which it is found.

CHAP. 26. *Obscure passages are to be interpreted by those which are clearer*

Now from the places where the sense in which they are used is more manifest we must gather the sense in which they are to be understood in obscure passages. For example, there is no better way of understanding the words addressed to God, "Take hold of shield and buckler and stand up for mine help," [12] than by referring to the passage where we read, "Thou, Lord, hast crowned us with Thy favour as with a shield." [13] And yet we are not so to understand it as that wherever we meet with a shield put to indicate a protection of any kind, we must take it as signifying nothing but the favour of God. For we hear also of the shield of faith, "wherewith," says the apostle, "ye shall be able to quench all the fiery darts of the wicked." [14] Nor ought we, on the other hand, in regard to spiritual armour of this kind to assign faith to the shield only; for we read in another place of the *breastplate* of faith: "putting on," says the apostle, "the breastplate of faith and love. [15]

CHAP. 27. *One passage susceptible of various interpretations*

38. When, again, not some one interpretation, but two or more interpretations are put upon the same words of Scripture, even though the meaning the writer intended remain undiscovered, there is no danger if it can be shown from other passages of Scripture that any of the interpretations put on the words is in harmony with the truth. And if a man in searching the Scriptures endeavours to get at the intention of the author through whom the Holy Spirit spake, whether he succeeds in this endeavour, or whether he draws a different meaning from the words, but one that is not opposed to sound doctrine, he is free from blame so long as he is supported by the testimony of some other passage of Scripture. For the author perhaps saw that this very meaning lay in the words which we are trying to interpret; and assuredly the Holy Spirit, who through him spake these words, foresaw that this interpretation would occur to the reader, nay, made provision that it should occur to him, seeing that it too is founded on truth. For what more liberal and more fruitful provi-

---

[1] Matt. 16. 6; Luke, 12. 1.   [2] Luke, 13. 21.
[3] Rev. 5. 5.   [4] I Pet. 5. 8.   [5] Matt. 10. 16.
[6] II Cor. 11. 3.   [7] John, 6. 51.   [8] Prov. 9. 17.
[9] Ps. 75. 8.   [10] Rev. 17. 15.   [11] John, 7. 38.

[12] Ps. 35. 2.   [13] Ps. 5. 12.   [14] Eph. 6. 16.   [15] I Thess. 5. 8.

sion could God have made in regard to the Sacred Scriptures than that the same words might be understood in several senses, all of which are sanctioned by the concurring testimony of other passages equally divine?

CHAP. 28. *It is safer to explain a doubtful passage by other passages of Scripture than by reason*

39. When, however, a meaning is evolved of such a kind that what is doubtful in it cannot be cleared up by indubitable evidence from Scripture, it remains for us to make it clear by the evidence of reason. But this is a dangerous practice. For it is far safer to walk by the light of Holy Scripture; so that when we wish to examine the passages that are obscured by metaphorical expressions, we may either obtain a meaning about which there is no controversy, or if a controversy arises, may settle it by the application of testimonies sought out in every portion of the same Scripture.

CHAP. 29. *The knowledge of tropes is necessary*

40. Moreover, I would have learned men to know that the authors of our Scriptures use all those forms of expression which grammarians call by the Greek name *tropes,* and use them more freely and in greater variety than people who are unacquainted with the Scriptures, and have learnt these figures of speech from other writings, can imagine or believe. Nevertheless those who know these tropes recognize them in Scripture, and are very much assisted by their knowledge of them in understanding Scripture. But this is not the place to teach them to the illiterate, lest it might seem that I was teaching grammar. I certainly advise, however, that they be learnt elsewhere, although indeed I have already given that advice above, in the second book—namely, where I treated of the necessary knowledge of languages. For the written characters from which grammar itself gets its name (the Greek name for letters being γράμματα) are the signs of sounds made by the articulate voice with which we speak. Now of some of these figures of speech we find in Scripture not only examples (which we have of them all), but the very names as well: for instance, *allegory, enigma,* and *parable.* However, nearly all these tropes which are said to be learnt as a matter of liberal education are found even in the ordinary speech of men who have learnt no grammar, but are content to use the vulgar idiom. For who does not say, "So may you flourish"? And this is the figure of speech called *metaphor.* Who

does not speak of a fish-pond in which there is no fish, which was not made for fish, and yet gets its name from fish? And this is the figure called *catachresis.*

41. It would be tedious to go over all the rest in this way; for the speech of the vulgar makes use of them all, even of those more curious figures which mean the very opposite of what they say, as for example, those called *irony* and *antiphrasis.* Now in irony we indicate by the tone of voice the meaning we desire to convey; as when we say to a man who is behaving badly, "You are doing well." But it is not by the tone of voice that we make an antiphrasis to indicate the opposite of what the words convey; but either the words in which it is expressed are used in the opposite of their etymological sense, as a grove is called *lucus* from its want of light; or it is customary to use a certain form of expression, although it puts *yes* for *no* by a law of contraries, as when we ask in a place for what is not there, and get the answer, "There is plenty"; or we add words that make it plain we mean the opposite of what we say, as in the expression, "Beware of him, for he is a good man." And what illiterate man is there that does not use such expressions, although he knows nothing at all about either the nature or the names of these figures of speech? And yet the knowledge of these is necessary for clearing up the difficulties of Scripture; because when the words taken literally give an absurd meaning, we ought forthwith to inquire whether they may not be used in this or that figurative sense which we are unacquainted with; and in this way many obscure passages have had light thrown upon them.

CHAP. 30. *The rules of Tichonius the Donatist examined*

42. One Tichonius, who, although a Donatist himself, has written most triumphantly against the Donatists (and herein showed himself of a most inconsistent disposition, that he was unwilling to give them up altogether), wrote a book which he called the *Book of Rules,* because in it he laid down seven rules, which are, as it were, keys to open the secrets of Scripture. And of these rules, the first relates to the Lord and His body, the second to the twofold division of the Lord's body, the third to the promises and the law, the fourth to *species* and *genus,* the fifth to times, the sixth to recapitulation, the seventh to the devil and his body. Now these rules, as expounded by their author, do indeed, when carefully considered, afford considerable assistance in penetrating the secrets of

the sacred writings; but still they do not explain all the difficult passages, for there are several other methods required, which are so far from being embraced in this number of seven, that the author himself explains many obscure passages without using any of his rules; finding, indeed, that there was no need for them, as there was no difficulty in the passage of the kind to which his rules apply. As, for example, he inquires what we are to understand in the Apocalypse by the seven angels of the churches to whom John is commanded to write; and after much and various reasoning, arrives at the conclusion that the angels are the churches themselves. And throughout this long and full discussion, although the matter inquired into is certainly very obscure, no use whatever is made of the rules. This is enough for an example, for it would be too tedious and troublesome to collect all the passages in the canonical Scriptures which present obscurities of such a kind as require none of these seven rules for their elucidation.

43. The author himself, however, when commending these rules, attributes so much value to them that it would appear as if, when they were thoroughly known and duly applied, we should be able to interpret all the obscure passages in the law—that is, in the sacred books. For he thus commences this very book: "Of all the things that occur to me, I consider none so necessary as to write a little book of rules, and, as it were, to make keys for, and put windows in, the secret places of the law. For there are certain mystical rules which hold the key to the secret recesses of the whole law, and render visible the treasures of truth that are to many invisible. And if this system of rules be received as I communicate it, without jealousy, what is shut shall be laid open, and what is obscure shall be elucidated, so that a man travelling through the vast forest of prophecy shall, if he follow these rules as pathways of light, be preserved from going astray." Now, if he had said, "There are certain mystical rules which hold the key to some of the secrets of the law," or even "which hold the key to the great secrets of the law," and not what he does say, "the secret recesses of the whole law"; and if he had not said "What is shut shall be laid open," but, "Many things that are shut shall be laid open," he would have said what was true, and he would not, by attributing more than is warranted by the facts to his very elaborate and useful work, have led the reader into false expectations. And I have thought it right to say thus much, in order both

that the book may be read by the studious (for it is of very great assistance in understanding Scripture), and that no more may be expected from it than it really contains. Certainly it must be read with caution, not only on account of the errors into which the author falls as a man, but chiefly on account of the heresies which he advances as a Donatist. And now I shall briefly indicate what these seven rules teach or advise.

CHAP. 31. *The first rule of Tichonius*

44. The first is about *the Lord and His body,* and it is this, that, knowing as we do that the head and the body—that is, Christ and His Church—are sometimes indicated to us under one person (for it is not in vain that it is said to believers, "Ye then are Abraham's seed," [1] when there is but one seed of Abraham, and that is Christ), we need not be in a difficulty when a transition is made from the head to the body or from the body to the head, and yet no change made in the person spoken of. For a single person is represented as saying, "He hath decked me as a bridegroom with ornaments, and adorned me as a bride with jewels"; [2] and yet it is, of course, a matter for interpretation which of these two refers to the head and which to the body, that is, which to Christ and which to the Church.

CHAP. 32. *The second rule of Tichonius*

45. The second rule is about *the twofold division of the body of the Lord;* but this indeed is not a suitable name, for that is really no part of the body of Christ which will not be with Him in eternity. We ought, therefore, to say that the rule is about the true and the mixed body of the Lord, or the true and the counterfeit, or some such name; because, not to speak of eternity, hypocrites cannot even now be said to be in Him, although they seem to be in His Church. And hence this rule might be designated thus: *Concerning the mixed Church.* Now this rule requires the reader to be on his guard when Scripture, although it has now come to address or speak of a different set of persons, seems to be addressing or speaking of the same persons as before, just as if both sets constituted one body in consequence of their being for the time united in a common participation of the sacraments. An example of this is that passage in the Song of Solomon, "I am black, but comely, as the tents of Kedar, as the curtains of Solomon." [3] For it is not said, I *was* black as the

[1]Gal. 3. 29.   [2]Isa. 61. 10 (Septuagint).
[3]Song of Sol. 1. 5.

tents of Kedar, but am *now* comely as the curtains of Solomon. The Church declares itself to be at present both; and this because the good fish and the bad are for the time mixed up in the one net.[1] For the tents of Kedar pertain to Ishmael, who "shall not be heir with the son of the free woman." [2] And in the same way, when God says of the good part of the Church, "I will bring the blind by a way that they knew not; I will lead them in paths that they have not known; I will make darkness light before them, and crooked things straight: these things will I do unto them, and not forsake them";[3] He immediately adds in regard to the other part, the bad that is mixed with the good, "They shall be turned back." Now these words refer to a set of persons altogether different from the former; but as the two sets are for the present united in one body, He speaks as if there were no change in the subject of the sentence. They will not, however, always be in one body; for one of them is that wicked servant of whom we are told in the Gospel, whose lord, when he comes, "shall cut him asunder and appoint him his portion with the hypocrites." [4]

CHAP. 33. *The third rule of Tichonius*

46. The third rule relates to the *promises and the law,* and may be designated in other terms as relating to the spirit and the letter, which is the name I made use of when writing a book on this subject. It may be also named, of grace and the law. This, however, seems to me to be a great question in itself, rather than a rule to be applied to the solution of other questions. It was the want of clear views on this question that originated, or at least greatly aggravated, the Pelagian heresy. And the efforts of Tichonius to clear up this point were good, but not complete. For, in discussing the question about faith and works, he said that works were given us by God as the reward of faith, but that faith itself was so far our own that it did not come to us from God; not keeping in mind the saying of the apostle: "Peace be to the brethren, and love with faith, from God the Father and the Lord Jesus Christ." [5] But he had not come into contact with this heresy, which has arisen in our time, and has given us much labour and trouble in defending against it the grace of God which is through our Lord Jesus Christ, and which (according to the saying of the apostle, "There must be also heresies among you, that they which are approved may be made manifest among you" [6])

has made us much more watchful and diligent to discover in Scripture what escaped Tichonius, who, having no enemy to guard against, was less attentive and anxious on this point, namely, that even faith itself is the gift of Him Who "hath dealth to every man the measure of faith." [7] Whence it is said to certain believers: "Unto you it is given, in the behalf of Christ, not only to believe on Him, but also to suffer for His sake." [8] Who, then, can doubt that each of these is the gift of God, when he learns from this passage, and believes, that each of them is given? There are many other testimonies besides which prove this. But I am not now treating of this doctrine. I have, however, dealt with it, one place or another, very frequently.

CHAP. 34. *The fourth rule of Tichonius*

47. The fourth rule of Tichonius is about *species and genus.* For so he calls it, intending that by species should be understood a part, by genus the whole of which that which he calls species is a part: as, for example, every single city is a part of the great society of nations: the city he calls a species, all nations constitute the genus. There is no necessity for here applying that subtlety of distinction which is in use among logicians, who discuss with great acuteness the difference between a part and a species. The rule is of course the same, if anything of the kind referred to is found in Scripture, not in regard to a single city, but in regard to a single province, or tribe, or kingdom. Not only, for example, about Jerusalem, or some of the cities of the Gentiles, such as Tyre or Babylon, are things said in Scripture whose significance oversteps the limits of the city, and which are more suitable when applied to all nations; but in regard to Judea also, and Egypt, and Assyria, or any other nation you choose to take which contains numerous cities, but still is not the whole world, but only a part of it, things are said which pass over the limits of that particular country, and apply more fitly to the whole of which this is a part; or, as our author terms it, to the genus of which this is a species. And hence these words have come to be commonly known, so that even uneducated people understand what is laid down specially, and what generally, in any given Imperial command. The same thing occurs in the case of men: things are said of Solomon, for example, the scope of which reaches far beyond him, and which are only properly understood when applied to Christ and His Church, of which Solomon is a part.[9]

[1]Matt. 13. 47, 48.   [2]Gal. 4. 30.   [3]Isa. 42. 16.
[4]Matt. 24. 50, 51.   [5]Eph. 6. 23.   [6]I Cor. 11. 19.
[7]Rom. 12. 3.   [8]Phil. 1. 29.   [9]II Sam. 7. 14-16.

48. Now the species is not always overstepped, for things are often said of such a kind as evidently apply to it also, or perhaps even to it exclusively. But when Scripture, having up to a certain point been speaking about the species, makes a transition at that point from the species to the genus, the reader must then be carefully on his guard against seeking in the species what he can find much better and more surely in the genus. Take, for example, what the prophet Ezekiel says: "When the house of Israel dwelt in their own land, they defiled it by their own way, and by their doings: their way was before me as the uncleanness of a removed woman. Wherefore I poured my fury upon them for the blood that they had shed upon the land, and for their idols wherewith they had polluted it: and I scattered them among the heathen, and they were dispersed through the countries: according to their way, and according to their doings, I judged them." [1] Now it is easy to understand that this applies to that house of Israel of which the apostle says, "Behold Israel after the flesh"; [2] because the people of Israel after the flesh did both perform and endure all that is here referred to. What immediately follows, too, may be understood as applying to the same people. But when the prophet begins to say, "And I will sanctify my great name, which was profaned among the heathen, which ye have profaned in the midst of them; and the heathen shall know that I am the Lord," [3] the reader ought now carefully to observe the way in which the species is overstepped and the genus taken in. For he goes on to say: "And I shall be sanctified in you before their eyes. For I will take you from among the heathen, and gather you out of all countries, and will bring you into your own land. Then will I sprinkle clean water upon you, and ye shall be clean: from all your filthiness, and from all your idols, will I cleanse you. A new heart also will I give you, and a new spirit will I put within you; and I will take away the stony heart out of your flesh and I will give you a heart of flesh. And I will put my Spirit within you, and cause you to walk in my statutes, and ye shall keep my commandments, and do them. And ye shall dwell in the land that I gave to your fathers; and ye shall be my people, and I will be your God. I will also save you from all your uncleannesses." [4] Now that this is a prophecy of the New Testament, to which pertain not only the remnant of that one nation of which it is elsewhere said, "For though the number of the

children of Israel be as the sand of the sea, yet a remnant of them shall be saved," [5] but also the other nations which were promised to their fathers and our fathers; and that there is here a promise of that washing of regeneration which, as we see, is now imparted to all nations, no one who looks into the matter can doubt. And that saying of the apostle, when he is commending the grace of the New Testament and its excellence in comparison with the Old, "Ye are our epistle . . . written not with ink, but with the Spirit of the living God; not in tables of stone, but in fleshy tables of the heart," [6] has an evident reference to this place where the prophet says, "A new heart also will I give you, and a new spirit will I put within you; and I will take away the stony heart out of your flesh, and I will give you an heart of flesh." [7] Now the heart of flesh from which the apostle's expression, "the fleshy tables of the heart," is drawn, the prophet intended to point out as distinguished from the stony heart by the possession of sentient life; and by sentient he understood intelligent life. And thus the spiritual Israel is made up, not of one nation, but of all the nations which were promised to the fathers in their seed, that is, in Christ.

49. This spiritual Israel, therefore, is distinguished from the carnal Israel which is of one nation, by newness of grace, not by nobility of descent, in feeling, not in race; but the prophet, in his depth of meaning, while speaking of the carnal Israel, passes on, without indicating the transition, to speak of the spiritual, and although now speaking of the latter, seems to be still speaking of the former; not that he grudges us the clear apprehension of Scripture, as if we were enemies, but that he deals with us as a physician, giving us a wholesome exercise for our spirit. And therefore we ought to take this saying, "And I will bring you into your own land," and what he says shortly afterwards, as if repeating himself, "And ye shall dwell in the land that I gave to your fathers," not literally, as if they referred to Israel after the flesh, but spiritually, as referring to the spiritual Israel. For the Church, without spot or wrinkle, gathered out of all nations, and destined to reign for ever with Christ, is itself the land of the blessed, the land of the living; and we are to understand that this was given to the fathers when it was promised to them in the sure and immutable purpose of God; for what the fathers believed would be given in its own time was to them, on account of the unchangeableness of

---

[1] Ezek. 36. 17-19. [2] I Cor. 10. 18. [3] Ezek. 36. 23.
[4] Ezek. 36. 23-29.

[5] Isa. 10. 22. [6] II Cor. 3. 2, 3. [7] Ezek. 38. 26.

the promise and purpose, the same as if it were already given; just as the apostle, writing to Timothy, speaks of the grace which is given to the saints: "Not according to our works, but according to His own purpose and grace, which was given us in Christ Jesus before the world began; but is now made manifest by the appearing of our Saviour." [1] He speaks of the grace as given at a time when those to whom it was to be given were not yet in existence; because he looks upon that as having been already done in the arrangement and purpose of God, which was to take place in its own time, and he himself speaks of it as now made manifest. It is possible, however, that these words may refer to the land of the age to come, when there will be a new heaven and a new earth, wherein the unrighteous shall be unable to dwell. And so it is truly said to the righteous, that the land itself is theirs, no part of which will belong to the unrighteous; because it is the same as if it were itself given, when it is firmly settled that it shall be given.

CHAP. 35. *The fifth rule of Tichonius*

50. The fifth rule Tichonius lays down is one he designates *of times*—a rule by which we can frequently discover or conjecture quantities of time which are not expressly mentioned in Scripture. And he says that this rule applies in two ways: either to the figure of speech called *synecdoche,* or to legitimate numbers. The figure synecdoche either puts the part for the whole, or the whole for the part. As, for example, in reference to the time when, in the presence of only three of His disciples, our Lord was transfigured on the mount, so that His face shone as the sun, and His raiment was white as snow, one evangelist says that this event occurred "after eight days," [2] while another says that it occurred "after six days." [3] Now both of these statements about the number of days cannot be true, unless we suppose that the writer who says "after eight days," counted the latter part of the day on which Christ uttered the prediction and the first part of the day on which he showed its fulfilment as two whole days; while the writer who says "after six days," counted only the whole unbroken days between these two. This figure of speech, which puts the part for the whole, explains also the great question about the resurrection of Christ. For unless to the latter part of the day on which He suffered we join the previous night, and count it as a whole day, and to the latter part of the night in which He arose we join the Lord's day which was just dawning, and count it also a whole day, we cannot make out the three days and three nights during which He foretold that He would be in the heart of the earth. [4]

51. In the next place, our author calls those numbers *legitimate* which Holy Scripture more highly favours, such as seven, or ten, or twelve, or any of the other numbers which the diligent reader of Scripture soon comes to know. Now numbers of this sort are often put for time universal; as, for example, "Seven times in the day do I praise Thee," means just the same as "His praise shall continually be in my mouth." [5] And their force is exactly the same, either when multiplied by ten, as seventy and seven hundred (whence the seventy years mentioned in Jeremiah may be taken in a spiritual sense for the whole time during which the Church is a sojourner among aliens); [6] or when multiplied into themselves, as ten into ten gives one hundred, and twelve into twelve gives one hundred and forty-four, which last number is used in the Apocalypse to signify the whole body of the saints. [7] Hence it appears that it is not merely questions about times that are to be settled by these numbers, but that their significance is of much wider application, and extends to many subjects. That number in the Apocalypse, for example, mentioned above, has not reference to times, but to men.

CHAP. 36. *The sixth rule of Tichonius*

52. The sixth rule Tichonius calls the *recapitulation,* which, with sufficient watchfulness, is discovered in difficult parts of Scripture. For certain occurrences are so related, that the narrative appears to be following the order of time, or the continuity of events, when it really goes back without mentioning it to previous occurrences, which had been passed over in their proper place. And we make mistakes if we do not understand this, from applying the rule here spoken of. For example, in the book of Genesis we read, "And the Lord God planted a garden eastward in Eden; and there He put the man whom He had formed. And out of the ground made the Lord God to grow every tree that is pleasant to the sight, and good for food." [8] Now here it seems to be indicated that the events last mentioned took place after God had formed man and put him in the garden; whereas the fact is, that the two events having been briefly

---

[1] II Tim. 1. 9, 10.   [2] Luke, 9. 28.
[3] Matt. 17. 1; Mark, 9. 2.

[4] Matt. 12. 40.   [5] Cf. Ps. 119. 164. with 34. 2.
[6] Jer. 25. 11.   [7] Rev. 7. 4.   [8] Gen. 2. 8, 9.

mentioned, viz., that God planted a garden, and there put the man whom He had formed, the narrative goes back, by way of recapitulation, to tell what had before been omitted, the way in which the garden was planted: that out of the ground God made to grow every tree that is pleasant to the sight, and good for food. Here there follows "The tree of life also was in the midst of the garden, and the tree of knowledge of good and evil." Next the river is mentioned which watered the garden, and which was parted into four heads, the sources of four streams; and all this has reference to the arrangements of the garden. And when this is finished, there is a repetition of the fact which had been already told, but which in the strict order of events came after all this: "And the Lord God took the man, and put him into the garden of Eden." [1] For it was after all these other things were done that man was put in the garden, as now appears from the order of the narrative itself: it was not after man was put there that the other things were done, as the previous statement might be thought to imply, did we not accurately mark and understand the recapitulation by which the narrative reverts to what had previously been passed over.

53. In the same book, again, when the generations of the sons of Noah are recounted, it is said: "These are the sons of Ham, after their families, after their tongues, in their countries, and in their nations." [2] And, again, when the sons of Shem are enumerated: "These are the sons of Shem, after their families, after their tongues, in their lands, after their nations." [3] And it is added in reference to them all: "These are the families of the sons of Noah, after their generations, in their nations; and by these were the nations divided in the earth after the flood. And the whole earth was of one language and of one speech." [4] Now the addition of this sentence, "And the whole earth was of one language and of one speech," seems to indicate that at the time when the nations were scattered over the earth they had all one language in common; but this is evidently inconsistent with the previous words, "after their families, after their tongues." For each family or nation could not be said to have its own language if all had one language in common. And so it is by way of recapitulation it is added, "And the whole earth was of one language and of one speech," the narrative here going back, without indicating the change, to tell how it was, that from

having one language in common, the nations were divided into a multitude of tongues. And, accordingly, we are forthwith told of the building of the tower, and of this punishment being there laid upon them as the judgment of God upon their arrogance; and it was after this that they were scattered over the earth according to their tongues.

54. This recapitulation is found in a still more obscure form; as, for example, our Lord says in the gospel: "The same day that Lot went out of Sodom it rained fire from heaven, and destroyed them all. Even thus shall it be in the day when the Son of man is revealed. In that day, he which shall be upon the house-top, and his stuff in the house, let him not come down to take it away; and he that is in the field, let him likewise not return back. Remember Lot's wife." [5] Is it when our Lord shall have been revealed that men are to give heed to these sayings, and not to look behind them, that is, not to long after the past life which they have renounced? Is not the present rather the time to give heed to them, that when the Lord shall have been revealed every man may receive his reward according to the things he has given heed to or despised? And yet because Scripture says, "In that day," the time of the revelation of the Lord will be thought the time for giving heed to these sayings, unless the reader be watchful and intelligent so as to understand the recapitulation, in which he will be assisted by that other passage of Scripture which even in the time of the apostles proclaimed: "Little children, it is the last time." [6] The very time then when the gospel is preached, up to the time that the Lord shall be revealed, is the day in which men ought to give heed to these sayings: for to the same day, which shall be brought to a close by a day of judgment, belongs that very revelation of the Lord here spoken of. [7]

CHAP. 37. *The seventh rule of Tichonius*

55. The seventh rule of Tichonius and the last, is about *the devil and his body.* For he is the head of the wicked, who are in a sense his body, and destined to go with him into the punishment of everlasting fire, just as Christ is the head of the Church, which is His body, destined to be with Him in His eternal kingdom and glory. Accordingly, as the first rule, which is called *of the Lord and His body,* directs us, when Scripture speaks of one and the same person, to take pains to understand which part of

[1]Gen. 2. 15.   [2]Gen. 10. 20.   [3]Gen. 10. 31.
[4]Gen. 10. 32; 11. 1.
[5]Luke, 17. 29–32.   [6]I John, 2. 18.   [7]Cf. Rom. 2. 5.

the statement applies to the head and which to the body; so this last rule shows us that statements are sometimes made about the devil, whose truth is not so evident in regard to himself as in regard to his body; and his body is made up not only of those who are manifestly out of the way, but of those also who, though they really belong to him, are for a time mixed up with the Church, until they depart from this life, or until the chaff is separated from the wheat at the last great winnowing. For example, what is said in Isaiah, "How he is fallen from heaven, Lucifer, son of the morning!" [1] and the other statements of the context which, under the figure of the king of Babylon, are made about the same person, are of course to be understood of the devil; and yet the statement which is made in the same place, "He is ground down on the earth, who sendeth to all nations,"[2] does not altogether fitly apply to the head himself. For, although the devil sends his angels to all nations, yet it is his body, not himself, that is ground down on the earth, except that he himself is in his body, which is beaten small like the dust which the wind blows from the face of the earth.

56. Now all these rules, except the one about the promises and the law, make one meaning to be understood where another is expressed, which is the peculiarity of figurative diction; and this kind of diction, it seems to me, is too widely spread to be comprehended in its full extent by any one. For, wherever one thing is said with the intention that another should be un-

derstood we have a figurative expression, even though the name of the trope is not to be found in the art of rhetoric. And when an expression of this sort occurs where it is customary to find it, there is no trouble in understanding it; when it occurs, however, where it is not customary, it costs labour to understand it, from some more, from some less, just as men have got more or less from God of the gifts of intellect, or as they have access to more or fewer external helps. And, as in the case of proper words which I discussed above, and in which things are to be understood just as they are expressed, so in the case of figurative words, in which one thing is expressed and another is to be understood, and which I have just finished speaking of as much as I thought enough, students of these venerable documents ought to be counselled not only to make themselves acquainted with the forms of expression ordinarily used in Scripture, to observe them carefully, and to remember them accurately, but also, what is especially and before all things necessary, to pray that they may understand them. For in these very books on the study of which they are intent, they read, "The Lord giveth wisdom: out of His mouth cometh knowledge and understanding";[3] and it is from Him they have received their very desire for knowledge, if it is wedded to piety. But about signs, so far as relates to words, I have now said enough. It remains to discuss, in the following book, so far as God has given me light, the means of communicating our thoughts to others.

[1]Isa. 14. 12 (Septuagint).   [2]Ibid.   [3]Prov. 2. 6.

BOOK IV

ARGUMENT. PASSING TO THE SECOND PART OF HIS WORK, THAT WHICH TREATS OF EXPRESSION, THE AUTHOR PREMISES THAT IT IS NO PART OF HIS INTENTION TO WRITE A TREATISE ON THE LAWS OF RHETORIC. THESE CAN BE LEARNED ELSEWHERE, AND OUGHT NOT TO BE NEGLECTED, BEING INDEED SPECIALLY NECESSARY FOR THE CHRISTIAN TEACHER, WHOM IT BEHOVES TO EXCEL IN ELOQUENCE AND POWER OF SPEECH. AFTER DETAILING WITH MUCH CARE AND MINUTENESS THE VARIOUS QUALITIES OF AN ORATOR, HE RECOMMENDS THE AUTHORS OF THE HOLY SCRIPTURES AS THE BEST MODELS OF ELOQUENCE, FAR EXCELLING ALL OTHERS IN THE COMBINATION OF ELOQUENCE WITH WISDOM. HE POINTS OUT THAT PERSPICUITY IS THE MOST ESSENTIAL QUALITY OF STYLE, AND OUGHT TO BE CULTIVATED WITH ESPECIAL CARE BY THE TEACHER, AS IT IS THE MAIN REQUISITE FOR INSTRUCTION, ALTHOUGH OTHER QUALITIES ARE REQUIRED FOR DELIGHTING AND PERSUADING THE HEARER. ALL THESE GIFTS ARE TO BE SOUGHT IN EARNEST PRAYER FROM GOD, THOUGH WE ARE NOT TO FORGET TO BE ZEALOUS AND DILIGENT IN STUDY. HE SHOWS THAT THERE ARE THREE SPECIES OF STYLE, THE SUBDUED, THE ELEGANT, AND THE MAJESTIC; THE FIRST SERVING FOR INSTRUCTION, THE SECOND FOR PRAISE, AND THE THIRD FOR EXHORTATION: AND OF EACH OF THESE HE GIVES EXAMPLES, SELECTED BOTH FROM SCRIPTURE AND FROM EARLY TEACHERS OF THE CHURCH, CYPRIAN AND AMBROSE. HE SHOWS THAT THESE VARIOUS STYLES MAY BE MINGLED, AND WHEN AND FOR WHAT PURPOSES THEY ARE MINGLED; AND THAT THEY ALL HAVE THE SAME END IN VIEW, TO BRING HOME THE TRUTH TO THE HEARER, SO THAT HE MAY UNDERSTAND IT, HEAR IT WITH GLADNESS, AND PRACTISE IT IN HIS LIFE. FINALLY, HE EXHORTS THE CHRISTIAN TEACHER HIMSELF, POINTING OUT THE DIGNITY AND RESPONSIBILITY OF THE OFFICE HE HOLDS, TO LEAD A LIFE IN HARMONY WITH HIS OWN TEACHING, AND TO SHOW A GOOD EXAMPLE TO ALL.

CHAP. 1. *This work not intended as a treatise on rhetoric*

1. THIS work of mine, which is entitled *On Christian Doctrine*, was at the commencement divided into two parts. For, after a preface, in which I answered by anticipation those who were likely to take exception to the work, I said, "There are two things on which all interpretation of Scripture depends: the mode of ascertaining the proper meaning, and the mode of making known the meaning when it is ascertained. I shall treat first of the mode of ascertaining, next of the mode of making known, the meaning." [1] As, then, I have already said a great deal about the mode of ascertaining the meaning, and have given three books to this one part of the subject, I shall only say a few things about the mode of making known the meaning, in order if possible to bring them all within the compass of one book, and so finish the whole work in four books.

2. In the first place, then, I wish by this preamble to put a stop to the expectations of readers who may think that I am about to lay down rules of rhetoric such as I have learnt, and

[1] BK. I, Chap. I.

taught too, in the secular schools, and to warn them that they need not look for any such from me. Not that I think such rules of no use, but that whatever use they have is to be learnt elsewhere; and if any good man should happen to have leisure for learning them, he is not to ask me to teach them either in this work or any other.

CHAP. 2. *It is lawful for a Christian teacher to use the art of rhetoric*

3. Now, the art of rhetoric being available for the enforcing either of truth or falsehood, who will dare to say that truth in the person of its defenders is to take its stand unarmed against falsehood? For example, that those who are trying to persuade men of what is false are to know how to introduce their subject, so as to put the hearer into a friendly, or attentive, or teachable frame of mind, while the defenders of the truth shall be ignorant of that art? That the former are to tell their falsehoods briefly, clearly, and plausibly, while the latter shall tell the truth in such a way that it is tedious to listen to, hard to understand, and, in fine, not easy to believe it? That the former are to oppose the truth and defend falsehood with sophistical arguments, while

the latter shall be unable either to defend what is true, or to refute what is false? That the former, while imbuing the minds of their hearers with erroneous opinions, are by their power of speech to awe, to melt, to enliven, and to rouse them, while the latter shall in defence of the truth be sluggish, and frigid, and somnolent? Who is such a fool as to think this wisdom? Since, then, the faculty of eloquence is available for both sides, and is of very great service in the enforcing either of wrong or right, why do not good men study to engage it on the side of truth, when bad men use it to obtain the triumph of wicked and worthless causes, and to further injustice and error?

CHAP. 3. *The proper age and the proper means for acquiring rhetorical skill*

4. But the theories and rules on this subject (to which, when you add a tongue thoroughly skilled by exercise and habit in the use of many words and many ornaments of speech, you have what is called *eloquence* or *oratory*) may be learnt apart from these writings of mine, if a suitable space of time be set aside for the purpose at a fit and proper age. But only by those who can learn them quickly; for the masters of Roman eloquence themselves did not shrink from saying that any one who cannot learn this art quickly can never thoroughly learn it at all. Whether this be true or not, why need we inquire? For even if this art can occasionally be in the end mastered by men of slower intellect, I do not think it of so much importance as to wish men who have arrived at mature age to spend time in learning it. It is enough that boys should give attention to it; and even of these, not all who are to be fitted for usefulness in the Church, but only those who are not yet engaged in any occupation of more urgent necessity, or which ought evidently to take precedence of it. For men of quick intellect and glowing temperament find it easier to become eloquent by reading and listening to eloquent speakers than by following rules for eloquence. And even outside the canon, which to our great advantage is fixed in a place of secure authority, there is no want of ecclesiastical writings, in reading which a man of ability will acquire a tinge of the eloquence with which they are written, even though he does not aim at this, but is solely intent on the matters treated of; especially, of course, if in addition he practise himself in writing, or dictating, and at last also in speaking, the opinions he has formed on grounds of piety and faith. If, however, such ability be wanting,

the rules of rhetoric are either not understood, or if, after great labour has been spent in enforcing them, they come to be in some small measure understood, they prove of no service. For even those who have learnt them, and who speak with fluency and elegance, cannot always think of them when they are speaking so as to speak in accordance with them, unless they are discussing the rules themselves. Indeed, I think there are scarcely any who can do both things—that is, speak well, and, in order to do this, think of the rules of speaking while they are speaking. For we must be careful that what we have got to say does not escape us whilst we are thinking about saying it according to the rules of art. Nevertheless, in the speeches of eloquent men, we find rules of eloquence carried out which the speakers did not think of as aids to eloquence at the time when they were speaking, whether they had ever learnt them, or whether they had never even met with them. For it is because they are eloquent that they exemplify these rules; it is not that they use them in order to be eloquent.

5. And, therefore, as infants cannot learn to speak except by learning words and phrases from those who do speak, why should not men become eloquent without being taught any art of speech, simply by reading and learning the speeches of eloquent men, and by imitating them as far as they can? And what do we find from the examples themselves to be the case in this respect? We know numbers who, without acquaintance with rhetorical rules, are more eloquent than many who have learnt these; but we know no one who is eloquent without having read and listened to the speeches and debates of eloquent men. For even the art of grammar, which teaches correctness of speech, need not be learnt by boys, if they have the advantage of growing up and living among men who speak correctly. For without knowing the names of any of the faults, they will, from being accustomed to correct speech, lay hold upon whatever is faulty in the speech of any one they listen to, and avoid it; just as citybred men, even when illiterate, seize upon the faults of rustics.

CHAP. 4. *The duty of the Christian teacher*

6. It is the duty, then, of the interpreter and teacher of Holy Scripture, the defender of the true faith and the opponent of error, both to teach what is right and to refute what is wrong, and in the performance of this task to conciliate the hostile, to rouse the careless, and to tell the ignorant both what is occurring at present and

what is probable in the future. But once that his hearers are friendly, attentive, and ready to learn, whether he has found them so, or has himself made them so, the remaining objects are to be carried out in whatever way the case requires. If the hearers need teaching, the matter treated of must be made fully known by means of narrative. On the other hand, to clear up points that are doubtful requires reasoning and the exhibition of proofs. If, however, the hearers require to be roused rather than instructed, in order that they may be diligent to do what they already know, and to bring their feelings into harmony with the truths they admit, greater vigour of speech is needed. Here entreaties and reproaches, exhortations and upbraidings, and all the other means of rousing the emotions, are necessary.

7. And all the methods I have mentioned are constantly used by nearly every one in cases where speech is the agency employed.

CHAP. 5. *Wisdom of more importance than eloquence to the Christian teacher*

But as some men employ these coarsely, inelegantly, and frigidly, while others use them with acuteness, elegance, and spirit, the work that I am speaking of ought to be undertaken by one who can argue and speak with wisdom, if not with eloquence, and with profit to his hearers, even though he profit them less than he would if he could speak with eloquence too. But we must beware of the man who abounds in eloquent nonsense, and so much the more if the hearer is pleased with what is not worth listening to, and thinks that because the speaker is eloquent what he says must be true. And this opinion is held even by those who think that the art of rhetoric should be taught: for they confess that "though wisdom without eloquence is of little service to states, yet eloquence without wisdom is frequently a positive injury, and is of service never." If, then, the men who teach the principles of eloquence have been forced by truth to confess this in the very books which treat of eloquence, though they were ignorant of the true, that is, the heavenly wisdom which comes down from the Father of Lights, how much more ought we to feel it who are the sons and the ministers of this higher wisdom! Now a man speaks with more or less wisdom just as he has made more or less progress in the knowledge of Scripture; I do not mean by reading them much and committing them to memory, but by understanding them aright and carefully searching into their meaning. For there are those who read and yet neglect them; they read to remember the words, but are careless about knowing the meaning. It is plain we must set far above these the men who are not so retentive of the words, but see with the eyes of the heart into the heart of Scripture. Better than either of these, however, is the man who, when he wishes, can repeat the words, and at the same time correctly apprehends their meaning.

8. Now it is especially necessary for the man who is bound to speak wisely, even though he cannot speak eloquently, to retain in memory the words of Scripture. For the more he discerns the poverty of his own speech, the more he ought to draw on the riches of Scripture, so that what he says in his own words he may prove by the words of Scripture; and he himself, though small and weak in his own words, may gain strength and power from the confirming testimony of great men. For his proof gives pleasure when he cannot please by his mode of speech. But if a man desire to speak not only with wisdom, but with eloquence also (and assuredly he will prove of greater service if he can do both), I would rather send him to read, and listen to, and exercise himself in imitating, eloquent men, than advise him to spend time with the teachers of rhetoric; especially if the men he reads and listens to are justly praised as having spoken, or as being accustomed to speak, not only with eloquence, but with wisdom also. For eloquent speakers are heard with pleasure; wise speakers with profit. And, therefore, Scripture does not say that the multitude of the eloquent, but "the multitude of the wise is the welfare of the world." [1] And as we must often swallow wholesome bitters, so we must always avoid unwholesome sweets. But what is better than wholesome sweetness or sweet wholesomeness? For the sweeter we try to make such things, the easier it is to make their wholesomeness serviceable. And so there are writers of the Church who have expounded the Holy Scriptures, not only with wisdom, but with eloquence as well; and there is not more time for the reading of these than is sufficient for those who are studious and at leisure to exhaust them.

CHAP. 6. *The sacred writers unite eloquence with wisdom*

9. Here, perhaps, some one inquires whether the authors whose divinely inspired writings constitute the canon, which carries with it a most wholesome authority, are to be considered wise only, or eloquent as well. A question which

[1] Wisd. 6. 24.

to me, and to those who think with me, is very easily settled. For where I understand these writers, it seems to me not only that nothing can be wiser, but also that nothing can be more eloquent. And I venture to affirm that all who truly understand what these writers say, perceive at the same time that it could not have been properly said in any other way. For as there is a kind of eloquence that is more becoming in youth, and a kind that is more becoming in old age, and nothing can be called eloquence if it be not suitable to the person of the speaker, so there is a kind of eloquence that is becoming in men who justly claim the highest authority, and who are evidently inspired of God. With this eloquence they spoke; no other would have been suitable for them; and this itself would be unsuitable in any other, for it is in keeping with their character, while it mounts as far above that of others (not from empty inflation, but from solid merit) as it seems to fall below them. Where, however, I do not understand these writers, though their eloquence is then less apparent, I have no doubt but that it is of the same kind as that I do understand. The very obscurity, too, of these divine and wholesome words was a necessary element in eloquence of a kind that was designed to profit our understandings, not only by the discovery of truth, but also by the exercise of their powers.

10. I could, however, if I had time, show those men who cry up their own form of language as superior to that of our authors (not because of its majesty, but because of its inflation), that all those powers and beauties of eloquence which they make their boast, are to be found in the sacred writings which God in His goodness has provided to mould our characters and to guide us from this world of wickedness to the blessed world above. But it is not the qualities which these writers have in common with the heathen orators and poets that give me such unspeakable delight in their eloquence; I am more struck with admiration at the way in which, by an eloquence peculiarly their own, they so use this eloquence of ours that it is not conspicuous either by its presence or its absence: for it did not become them either to condemn it or to make an ostentatious display of it; and if they had shunned it, they would have done the former; if they had made it prominent, they might have appeared to be doing the latter. And in those passages where the learned do note its presence, the matters spoken of are such that the words in which they are put seem not so much to be sought out

by the speaker as spontaneously to suggest themselves; as if wisdom were walking out of its house, that is, the breast of the wise man, and eloquence, like an inseparable attendant, followed it without being called for.

CHAP. 7. *Examples of true eloquence drawn from the epistles of Paul and the prophecies of Amos*

11. For who would not see what the apostle meant to say, and how wisely he has said it, in the following passage: "We glory in tribulations also: knowing that tribulation worketh patience; and patience, experience; and experience, hope: and hope maketh not ashamed; because the love of God is shed abroad in our hearts by the Holy Ghost which is given unto us"? [1] Now were any man unlearnedly learned (if I may use the expression) to contend that the apostle had here followed the rules of rhetoric, would not every Christian, learned or unlearned, laugh at him? And yet here we find the figure which is called in Greek κλίμαξ (climax), and by some in Latin *gradatio*, for they do not care to call it *scala* (a ladder), when the words and ideas have a connection of dependency the one upon the other, as we see here that patience arises out of tribulation, experience out of patience, and hope out of experience. Another ornament, too, is found here; for after certain statements finished in a single tone of voice, which we call clauses and sections (*membra et cæsa*), but the Greeks κῶλα and κόμματα, there follows a rounded sentence (*ambitus sive circuitus*) which the Greeks call περίοδος, the clauses of which are suspended on the voice of the speaker till the whole is completed by the last clause. For of the statements which precede the period, this is the first clause, "knowing that tribulation worketh patience"; the second, "and patience, experience"; the third, "and experience, hope." Then the period which is subjoined is completed in three clauses, of which the first is, "and hope maketh not ashamed"; the second, "because the love of God is shed abroad in our hearts"; the third, "by the Holy Ghost which is given unto us." But these and other matters of the same kind are taught in the art of elocution. As then I do not affirm that the apostle was guided by the rules of eloquence, so I do not deny that his wisdom naturally produced, and was accompanied by, eloquence.

12. In the Second Epistle to the Corinthians, again, he refutes certain false apostles who had gone out from the Jews, and had been trying to

[1] Rom. 5. 3–5.

injure his character; and being compelled to speak of himself, though he ascribes this as folly to himself, how wisely and how eloquently he speaks! But wisdom is his guide, eloquence his attendant; he follows the first, the second follows him, and yet he does not spurn it when it comes after him. "I say again," he says, "Let no man think me a fool: if otherwise, yet as a fool receive me, that I may boast myself a little. That which I speak, I speak it not after the Lord, but as it were foolishly, in this confidence of boasting. Seeing that many glory after the flesh, I will glory also. For ye suffer fools gladly, seeing ye yourselves are wise. For ye suffer, if a man bring you into bondage, if a man devour you, if a man take of you, if a man exalt himself, if a man smite you on the face. I speak as concerning reproach, as though we had been weak. Howbeit, whereinsoever any is bold (I speak foolishly), I am bold also. Are they Hebrews? so am I. Are they Israelites? so am I. Are they the seed of Abraham? so am I. Are they ministers of Christ? (I speak as a fool), I am more: in labours more abundant, in stripes above measure, in prisons more frequent, in deaths oft. Of the Jews five times received I forty stripes save one, thrice was I beaten with rods, once was I stoned, thrice I suffered shipwreck, a night and a day I have been in the deep; in journeyings often, in perils of waters, in perils of robbers, in perils by mine own countrymen, in perils by the heathen, in perils in the city, in perils in the wilderness, in perils in the sea, in perils among false brethren; in weariness and painfulness, in watchings often, in hunger and thirst, in fastings often, in cold and nakedness. Besides those things which are without, that which cometh upon me daily, the care of all the churches. Who is weak, and I am not weak? who is offended, and I burn not? If I must needs glory, I will glory of the things which concern my infirmities."[1] The thoughtful and attentive perceive how much wisdom there is in these words. And even a man sound asleep must notice what a stream of eloquence flows through them.

13. Further still, the educated man observes that those sections which the Greeks call κόμματα, and the clauses and periods of which I spoke a short time ago, being intermingled in the most beautiful variety, make up the whole form and features (so to speak) of that diction by which even the unlearned are delighted and affected. For, from the place where I commenced to quote, the passage consists of periods: the first the smallest possible, consisting of two members; for a period cannot have less than two members, though it may have more: "I say again, let no man think me a fool." The next has three members: "if otherwise, yet as a fool receive me, that I may boast myself a little." The third has four members: "That which I speak, I speak it not after the Lord, but as it were foolishly, in this confidence of boasting." The fourth has two: "Seeing that many glory after the flesh, I will glory also." And the fifth has two: "For ye suffer fools gladly, seeing ye yourselves are wise." The sixth again has two members: "for ye suffer, if a man bring you into bondage." Then follow three sections (cæsa): "if a man devour you, if a man take of you, if a man exalt himself." Next three clauses (membra): "if a man smite you on the face. I speak as concerning reproach, as though we had been weak." Then is subjoined a period of three members: "Howbeit, whereinsoever any is bold (I speak foolishly), I am bold also." After this, certain separate sections being put in the interrogatory form, separate sections are also given as answers, three to three: "Are they Hebrews? so am I. Are they Israelites? so am I. Are they the seed of Abraham? so am I." But a fourth section being put likewise in the interrogatory form, the answer is given not in another section (cæsum) but in a clause (membrum): "Are they the ministers of Christ? (I speak as a fool.) I am more." Then the next four sections are given continuously, the interrogatory form being most elegantly suppressed: "in labours more abundant, in stripes above measure, in prisons more frequent, in deaths oft." Next is interposed a short period; for, by a suspension of the voice, "of the Jews five times" is to be marked off as constituting one member, to which is joined the second, "received I forty stripes save one." Then he returns to sections, and three are set down: "Thrice was I beaten with rods, once was I stoned, thrice I suffered shipwreck." Next comes a clause: "a night and a day I have been in the deep." Next fourteen sections burst forth with a vehemence which is most appropriate: "In journeyings often, in perils of waters, in perils of robbers, in perils by mine own countrymen, in perils by the heathen, in perils in the city, in perils in the wilderness, in perils in the sea, in perils among false brethren, in weariness and painfulness, in watchings often, in hunger and thirst, in fastings often, in cold and nakedness." After this comes in a period of three members: "Besides those things which are without, that which cometh upon me

[1] II Cor. 11. 16–30.

daily, the care of all the churches." And to this he adds two clauses in a tone of inquiry: "Who is weak, and I am not weak? who is offended, and I burn not?" In fine, this whole passage, as if panting for breath, winds up with a period of two members: "If I must needs glory, I will glory of the things which concern mine infirmities." And I cannot sufficiently express how beautiful and delightful it is when after this outburst he rests himself, and gives the hearer rest, by interposing a slight narrative. For he goes on to say: "The God and Father of our Lord Jesus Christ, which is blessed for evermore, knoweth that I lie not." And then he tells, very briefly the danger he had been in, and the way he escaped it.

14. It would be tedious to pursue the matter further, or to point out the same facts in regard to other passages of Holy Scripture. Suppose I had taken the further trouble, at least in regard to the passages I have quoted from the apostle's writings, to point out figures of speech which are taught in the art of rhetoric? Is it not more likely that serious men would think I had gone too far, than that any of the studious would think I had done enough? All these things when taught by masters are reckoned of great value; great prices are paid for them, and the vendors puff them magniloquently. And I fear lest I too should smack of that puffery while thus descanting on matters of this kind. It was necessary, however, to reply to the ill-taught men who think our authors contemptible; not because they do not possess, but because they do not display, the eloquence which these men value so highly.

15. But perhaps some one is thinking that I have selected the Apostle Paul because he is our great orator. For when he says, "Though I be rude in speech, yet not in knowledge,"[1] he seems to speak as if granting so much to his detractors, not as confessing that he recognized its truth. If he had said, "I am indeed rude in speech, but not in knowledge," we could not in any way have put another meaning upon it. He did not hesitate plainly to assert his knowledge, because without it he could not have been the teacher of the Gentiles. And certainly if we bring forward anything of his as a model of eloquence, we take it from those epistles which even his very detractors, who thought his bodily presence weak and his speech contemptible, confessed to be weighty and powerful.[2]

I see, then, that I must say something about the eloquence of the prophets also, where many things are concealed under a metaphorical style, which the more completely they seem buried under figures of speech give the greater pleasure when brought to light. In this place, however, it is my duty to select a passage of such a kind that I shall not be compelled to explain the matter, but only to commend the style. And I shall do so, quoting principally from the book of that prophet who says that he was a shepherd or herdsman, and was called by God from that occupation, and sent to prophesy to the people of God.[3] I shall not, however, follow the Septuagint translators, who, being themselves under the guidance of the Holy Spirit in their translation, seem to have altered some passages with the view of directing the reader's attention more particularly to the investigation of the spiritual sense (and hence some passages are more obscure, because more figurative, in their translation); but I shall follow the translation made from the Hebrew into Latin by the presbyter Jerome, a man thoroughly acquainted with both tongues.

16. When, then, this rustic, or quondam rustic prophet, was denouncing the godless, the proud, the luxurious, and therefore the most neglectful of brotherly love, he called aloud, saying: "Woe to you who are at ease in Zion, and trust in the mountain of Samaria, who are heads and chiefs of the people, entering with pomp into the house of Israel! Pass ye unto Calneh, and see; and from thence go ye to Hamath the great; then go down to Gath of the Philistines, and to all the best kingdoms of these: is their border greater than your border? Ye that are set apart for the day of evil, and that come near to the seat of oppression; that lie upon beds of ivory, and stretch yourselves upon couches; that eat the lamb of the flock, and the calves out of the midst of the herd; that chant to the sound of the viol. They thought that they had instruments of music like David; drinking wine in bowls, and anointing themselves with the costliest ointment: and they were not grieved for the affliction of Joseph."[4] Suppose those men who, assuming to be themselves learned and eloquent, despise our prophets as untaught and unskilful of speech, had been obliged to deliver a message like this, and to men such as these, would they have chosen to express themselves in any respect differently—those of them, at least, who would have shrunk from raving like madmen?

17. For what is there that sober ears could wish changed in this speech? In the first place,

[1] II Cor. 11. 6. [2] II Cor. 10. 10. [3] Amos, 1. 1; 7. 14. [4] Amos, 6. 1-6.

the invective itself; with what vehemence it throws itself upon the drowsy senses to startle them into wakefulness: "Woe to you who are at ease in Zion, and trust in the mountains of Samaria, who are heads and chiefs of the people, entering with pomp into the house of Israel!" Next, that he may use the favours of God, Who has bestowed upon them ample territory, to show their ingratitude in trusting to the mountain of Samaria, where idols were worshipped: "Pass ye unto Calneh," he says, "and see; and from thence go ye to Hamath the great; then go down to Gath of the Philistines, and to all the best kingdoms of these: is their border greater than your border?" At the same time also that these things are spoken of, the style is adorned with names of places as with lamps, such as "Zion," "Samaria," "Calneh," "Hamath the great," and "Gath of the Philistines." Then the words joined to these places are most appropriately varied: "ye are at ease," "ye trust," "pass on," "go," "descend."

18. And then the future captivity under an oppressive king is announced as approaching, when it is added: "Ye that are set apart for the day of evil, and come near to the seat of oppression." Then are subjoined the evils of luxury: "ye that lie upon beds of ivory, and stretch yourselves upon couches; that eat the lamb from the flock, and the calves out of the midst of the herd." These six clauses form three periods of two members each. For he does not say: "Ye who are set apart for the day of evil, who come near to the seat of oppression, who sleep upon beds of ivory, who stretch yourselves upon couches, who eat the lamb from the flock, and calves out of the herd." If he had so expressed it, this would have had its beauty: six separate clauses running on, the same pronoun being repeated each time, and each clause finished by a single effort of the speaker's voice. But it is more beautiful as it is, the clauses being joined in pairs under the same pronoun, and forming three sentences, one referring to the prophecy of the captivity: "Ye that are set apart for the day of evil, and come near the seat of oppression"; the second to lasciviousness: "ye that lie upon beds of ivory, and stretch yourselves upon couches"; the third to gluttony: "who eat the lamb from the flock, and the calves out of the midst of the herd." So that it is at the discretion of the speaker whether he finish each clause separately and make six altogether, or whether he suspend his voice at the first, the third, and the fifth, and by joining the second to the first, the fourth to the third, and the sixth to the fifth,

make three most elegant periods of two members each: one describing the imminent catastrophe; another, the lascivious couch; and the third, the luxurious table.

19. Next he reproaches them with their luxury in seeking pleasure for the sense of hearing. And here, when he had said, "Ye who chant to the sound of the viol," seeing that wise men may practise music wisely, he, with wonderful skill of speech, checks the flow of his invective, and not now speaking to, but of, these men, and to show us that we must distinguish the music of the wise from the music of the voluptuary, he does not say, "Ye who chant to the sound of the viol, and think that ye have instruments of music like David"; but he first addresses to themselves what it is right the voluptuaries should hear, "Ye who chant to the sound of the viol"; and then, turning to others, he intimates that these men have not even skill in their art: "they thought that they had instruments of music like David; drinking wine in bowls, and anointing themselves with the costliest ointment." These three clauses are best pronounced when the voice is suspended on the first two members of the period, and comes to a pause on the third.

20. But now as to the sentence which follows all these: "and they were not grieved for the affliction of Joseph." Whether this be pronounced continuously as one clause, or whether with more elegance we hold the words, "and they were not grieved," suspended on the voice, and then add, "for the affliction of Joseph," so as to make a period of two members; in any case, it is a touch of marvellous beauty not to say, "and they were not grieved for the affliction of their brother"; but to put Joseph for brother, so as to indicate brothers in general by the proper name of him who stands out illustrious from among his brethren, both in regard to the injuries he suffered and the good return he made. And, indeed, I do not know whether this figure of speech, by which Joseph is put for brothers in general, is one of those laid down in that art which I learnt and used to teach. But how beautiful it is, and how it comes home to the intelligent reader, it is useless to tell any one who does not himself feel it.

21. And a number of other points bearing on the laws of eloquence could be found in this passage which I have chosen as an example. But an intelligent reader will not be so much instructed by carefully analysing it as kindled by reciting it with spirit. Nor was it composed by man's art and care, but it flowed forth in wis-

dom and eloquence from the Divine mind; wisdom not aiming at eloquence, yet eloquence not shrinking from wisdom. For if, as certain very eloquent and acute men have perceived and said, the rules which are laid down in the art of oratory could not have been observed, and noted, and reduced to system, if they had not first had their birth in the genius of orators, is it wonderful that they should be found in the messengers of Him Who is the author of all genius? Therefore let us acknowledge that the canonical writers are not only wise but eloquent also, with an eloquence suited to a character and position like theirs.

CHAP. 8. *The obscurity of the sacred writers, though compatible with eloquence, not to be imitated by Christian teachers*

22. But although I take some examples of eloquence from those writings of theirs which there is no difficulty in understanding, we are not by any means to suppose that it is our duty to imitate them in those passages where, with a view to exercise and train the minds of their readers, and to break in upon the satiety and stimulate the zeal of those who are willing to learn, and with a view also to throw a veil over the minds of the godless either that they may be converted to piety or shut out from a knowledge of the mysteries, from one or other of these reasons they have expressed themselves with a useful and wholesome obscurity. They have indeed expressed themselves in such a way that those who in after ages understood and explained them aright have in the Church of God obtained an esteem, not indeed equal to that with which they are themselves regarded, but coming next to it. The expositors of these writers, then, ought not to express themselves in the same way, as if putting forward their expositions as of the same authority; but they ought in all their deliverances to make it their first and chief aim to be understood, using as far as possible such clearness of speech that either he will be very dull who does not understand them, or that if what they say should not be very easily or quickly understood, the reason will lie not in their manner of expression, but in the difficulty and subtlety of the matter they are trying to explain.

CHAP. 9. *How, and with whom, difficult passages are to be discussed*

23. For there are some passages which are not understood in their proper force, or are understood with great difficulty, at whatever length, however clearly, or with whatever eloquence the speaker may expound them; and these should never be brought before the people at all, or only on rare occasions when there is some urgent reason. In books, however, which are written in such a style that, if understood, they, so to speak, draw their own readers, and if not understood, give no trouble to those who do not care to read them, and in private conversations we must not shrink from the duty of bringing the truth which we ourselves have reached within the comprehension of others, however difficult it may be to understand it and whatever labour in the way of argument it may cost us. Only two conditions are to be insisted upon, that our hearer or companion should have an earnest desire to learn the truth, and should have capacity of mind to receive it in whatever form it may be communicated, the teacher not being so anxious about the eloquence as about the clearness of his teaching.

CHAP. 10. *The necessity for perspicuity of style*

24. Now a strong desire for clearness sometimes leads to neglect of the more polished forms of speech, and indifference about what sounds well, compared with what clearly expresses and conveys the meaning intended. Whence a certain author, when dealing with speech of this kind, says that there is in it "a kind of careful negligence." Yet while taking away ornament, it does not bring in vulgarity of speech; though good teachers have, or ought to have, so great an anxiety about teaching that they will employ a word which cannot be made pure Latin without becoming obscure or ambiguous, but which when used according to the vulgar idiom is neither ambiguous nor obscure not in the way the learned, but rather in the way the unlearned employ it. For if our translators did not shrink from saying, *"Non congregabo conventicula eorum de sanguinibus,"*[1] because they felt that it was important for the sense to put a word here in the plural which in Latin is only used in the singular; why should a teacher of godliness who is addressing an unlearned audience shrink from using *ossum* instead of *os*, if he fear that the latter might be taken not as the singular of *ossa*, but as the singular of *ora*, seeing that African ears have no quick perception of the shortness or length of vowels? And what advantage is there in purity of speech which does not lead to understanding in the hearer, seeing that there is no use at all in speak-

[1] "I shall not assemble their assemblies of blood," Ps. 16. 4. (Vulgate)

ing, if they do not understand us for whose sake we speak? He, therefore, who teaches will avoid all words that do not teach; and if instead of them he can find words which are at once pure and intelligible, he will take these by preference; if, however, he cannot, either because there are no such words, or because they do not at the time occur to him, he will use words that are not quite pure, if only the substance of his thought be conveyed and apprehended in its integrity.

25. And this must be insisted on as necessary to our being understood, not only in conversations, whether with one person or with several, but much more in the case of a speech delivered in public: for in conversation any one has the power of asking a question; but when all are silent that one may be heard, and all faces are turned attentively upon him, it is neither customary nor decorous for a person to ask a question about what he does not understand; and on this account the speaker ought to be especially careful to give assistance to those who cannot ask it. Now a crowd anxious for instruction generally shows by its movements if it understands what is said; and until some indication of this sort be given, the subject discussed ought to be turned over and over, and put in every shape and form and variety of expression, a thing which cannot be done by men who are repeating words prepared beforehand and committed to memory. As soon, however, as the speaker has ascertained that what he says is understood, he ought either to bring his address to a close, or pass on to another point. For if a man gives pleasure when he throws light upon points on which people wish for instruction, he becomes wearisome when he dwells at length upon things that are already well known, especially when men's expectation was fixed on having the difficulties of the passage removed. For even things that are very well known are told for the sake of the pleasure they give, if the attention be directed not to the things themselves, but to the way in which they are told. Nay, even when the style itself is already well known, if it be pleasing to the hearers, it is almost a matter of indifference whether he who speaks be a speaker or a reader. For things that are gracefully written are often not only read with delight by those who are making their first acquaintance with them, but re-read with delight by those who have already made acquaintance with them, and have not yet forgotten them; nay, both these classes will derive pleasure even from hearing another man repeat them. And if a man

has forgotten anything, when he is reminded of it he is taught. But I am not now treating of the mode of giving pleasure. I am speaking of the mode in which men who desire to learn ought to be taught. And the best mode is that which secures that he who hears shall hear the truth, and that what he hears he shall understand. And when this point has been reached, no further labour need be spent on the truth itself, as if it required further explanation; but perhaps some trouble may be taken to enforce it so as to bring it home to the heart. If it appear right to do this, it ought to be done so moderately as not to lead to weariness and impatience.

CHAP. 11. *The Christian teacher must speak clearly, but not inelegantly*

26. For teaching, of course, true eloquence consists, not in making people like what they disliked, nor in making them do what they shrank from, but in making clear what was obscure; yet if this be done without grace of style, the benefit does not extend beyond the few eager students who are anxious to know whatever is to be learnt, however rude and unpolished the form in which it is put; and who, when they have succeeded in their object, find the plain truth pleasant food enough. And it is one of the distinctive features of good intellects not to love words, but the truth in words. For of what service is a golden key, if it cannot open what we want it to open? Or what objection is there to a wooden one if it can, seeing that to open what is shut is all we want? But as there is a certain analogy between learning and eating, the very food without which it is impossible to live must be flavoured to meet the tastes of the majority.

CHAP. 12. *The aim of the orator, according to Cicero, is to teach, to delight, and to move. Of these, teaching is the most essential*

27. Accordingly a great orator has truly said that "an eloquent man must speak so as to teach, to delight, and to persuade."[1] Then he adds: "To teach is a necessity, to delight is a beauty, to persuade is a triumph." Now of these three, the one first mentioned, the teaching, which is a matter of necessity, depends on what we say; the other two on the way we say it. He, then, who speaks with the purpose of teaching should not suppose that he has said what he has to say as long as he is not understood; for although what he has said be intelligible to himself, it is not said at all to the man who does not

[1]Cicero, *Orator*, 21.

understand it. If, however, he is understood, he has said his say, whatever may have been his manner of saying it. But if he wishes to delight or persuade his hearer as well, he will not accomplish that end by putting his thought in any shape no matter what, but for that purpose the style of speaking is a matter of importance. And as the hearer must be pleased in order to secure his attention, so he must be persuaded in order to move him to action. And as he is pleased if you speak with sweetness and elegance, so he is persuaded if he be drawn by your promises, and awed by your threats; if he reject what you condemn, and embrace what you commend; if he grieve when you heap up objects for grief, and rejoice when you point out an object for joy; if he pity those whom you present to him as objects of pity, and shrink from those whom you set before him as men to be feared and shunned. I need not go over all the other things that can be done by powerful eloquence to move the minds of the hearers, not telling them what they ought to do, but urging them to do what they already know ought to be done.

28. If, however, they do not yet know this, they must of course be instructed before they can be moved. And perhaps the mere knowledge of their duty will have such an effect that there will be no need to move them with greater strength of eloquence. Yet when this is needful, it ought to be done. And it is needful when people, knowing what they ought to do, do it not. Therefore, to teach is a necessity. For what men know, it is in their own hands either to do or not to do. But who would say that it is their duty to do what they do not know? On the same principle, to persuade is not a necessity: for it is not always called for; as, for example, when the hearer yields his assent to one who simply teaches or give pleasure. For this reason also to persuade is a triumph, because it is possible that a man may be taught and delighted, and yet not give his consent. And what will be the use of gaining the first two ends if we fail in the third? Neither is it a necessity to give pleasure; for when, in the course of an address, the truth is clearly pointed out (and this is the true function of teaching), it is not the fact, nor is it the intention, that the style of speech should make the truth pleasing, or that the style should of itself give pleasure; but the truth itself, when exhibited in its naked simplicity, gives pleasure, because it is the truth. And hence even falsities are frequently a source of pleasure when they are brought to light and exposed. It is not, of course, their falsity that gives pleasure; but as

it is true that they are false, the speech which shows this to be true gives pleasure.

CHAP. 13. *The hearer must be moved as well as instructed.*

29. But for the sake of those who are so fastidious that they do not care for truth unless it is put in the form of a pleasing discourse, no small place has been assigned in eloquence to the art of pleasing. And yet even this is not enough for those stubborn-minded men who both understand and are pleased with the teacher's discourse, without deriving any profit from it. For what does it profit a man that he both confesses the truth and praises the eloquence, if he does not yield his consent, when it is only for the sake of securing his consent that the speaker in urging the truth gives careful attention to what he says? If the truths taught are such that to believe or to know them is enough, to give one's assent implies nothing more than to confess that they are true. When, however, the truth taught is one that must be carried into practice, and that is taught for the very purpose of being practised, it is useless to be persuaded of the truth of what is said, it is useless to be pleased with the manner in which it is said, if it be not so learnt as to be practised. The eloquent divine, then, when he is urging a practical truth, must not only teach so as to give instruction, and please so as to keep up the attention, but he must also sway the mind so as to subdue the will. For if a man be not moved by the force of truth, though it is demonstrated to his own confession, and clothed in beauty of style, nothing remains but to subdue him by the power of eloquence.

CHAP. 14. *Beauty of diction to be in keeping with the matter*

30. And so much labour has been spent by men on the beauty of expression here spoken of that not only is it not our duty to do, but it is our duty to shun and abhor, many and heinous deeds of wickedness and baseness which wicked and base men have with great eloquence recommended, not with a view to gaining assent but merely for the sake of being read with pleasure. But may God avert from His Church what the prophet Jeremiah says of the synagogue of the Jews: "A wonderful and horrible thing is committed in the land: the prophets prophesy falsely, and the priests applaud them with their hands;[1] and my people love to have it so: and

[1] "And the priests bear rule by their means." (Authorized Version)

what will ye do in the end thereof?"[1] O eloquence, which is the more terrible from its purity, and the more crushing from its solidity! Assuredly it is "a hammer that breaketh the rock in pieces." For to this God Himself has by the same prophet compared His own word spoken through His holy prophets.[2] God forbid, then, God forbid that with us the priest should applaud the false prophet, and that God's people should love to have it so. God forbid, I say, that with us there should be such terrible madness! For what shall we do in the end thereof? And assuredly it is preferable, even though what is said should be less intelligible, less pleasing, and less persuasive, that truth be spoken, and that what is just, not what is iniquitous, be listened to with pleasure. But this, of course, cannot be, unless what is true and just expressed with elegance.

31. In a serious assembly, moreover, such as is spoken of when it is said, "I will praise Thee among much people,"[3] no pleasure is derived from that species of eloquence which indeed says nothing that is false, but which buries small and unimportant truths under a frothy mass of ornamental words, such as would not be graceful or dignified even if used to adorn great and fundamental truths. And something of this sort occurs in a letter of the blessed Cyprian, which, I think, came there by accident, or else was inserted designedly with this view, that posterity might see how the wholesome discipline of Christian teaching had cured him of that redundancy of language, and confined him to a more dignified and modest form of eloquence, such as we find in his subsequent letters, a style which is admired without effort, is sought after with eagerness, but is not attained without great difficulty. He says, then, in one place, "Let us seek this abode: the neighbouring solitudes afford a retreat where, whilst the spreading shoots of the vine trees, pendulous and intertwined, creep amongst the supporting reeds, the leafy covering has made a portico of vine." There is wonderful fluency and exuberance of language here; but it is too florid to be pleasing to serious minds. But people who are fond of this style are apt to think that men who do not use it, but employ a more chastened style, do so because they cannot attain the former, not because their judgment teaches them to avoid it. Wherefore this holy man shows both that he can speak in that style, for he has done so once, and that he does not choose, for he never uses it again.

CHAP. 15. *The Christian teacher should pray before preaching*

32. And so our Christian orator, while he says what is just, and holy, and good (and he ought never to say anything else), does all he can to be heard with intelligence, with pleasure, and with obedience; and he need not doubt that if he succeed in this object, and so far as he succeeds, he will succeed more by piety in prayer than by gifts of oratory; and so he ought to pray for himself and for those he is about to address, before he attempts to speak. And when the hour is come that he must speak, he ought, before he opens his mouth, to lift up his thirsty soul to God, to drink in what he is about to pour forth, and to be himself filled with what he is about to distribute. For, as in regard to every matter of faith and love there are many things that may be said and many ways of saying them, who knows what it is expedient at a given moment for us to say, or to be heard saying, except God Who knows the hearts of all? And who can make us say what we ought, and in the way we ought, except Him in Whose hand both we and our speeches are? Accordingly, he who is anxious both to know and to teach should learn all that is to be taught, and acquire such a faculty of speech as is suitable for a divine. But when the hour for speech arrives, let him reflect upon that saying of our Lord's, as better suited to the wants of a pious mind: "Take no thought how or what ye shall speak; for it shall be given you in that same hour what ye shall speak. For it is not ye that speak, but the Spirit of your Father which speaketh in you."[4] The Holy Spirit, then, speaks thus in those who for Christ's sake are delivered to the persecutors; why not also in those who deliver Christ's message to those who are willing to learn?

CHAP. 16. *Human directions not to be despised, though God makes the true teacher*

33. Now if any one says that we need not direct men how or what they should teach, since the Holy Spirit makes them teachers, he may as well say that we need not pray, since our Lord says, "Your Father knoweth what things ye have need of before ye ask Him";[5] or that the Apostle Paul should not have given directions to Timothy and Titus as to how or what they should teach others. And these three apostolic epistles ought to be constantly before the eyes of every one who has obtained the position of a teacher in the Church. In the First Epistle to

[1]Jer. 5. 30, 31 (Septuagint).
[2]Jer. 23. 29.   [3]Ps. 35. 18.

[4]Matt. 10. 19, 20.   [5]Matt. 6. 8.

Timothy do we not read: "These things command and teach"?[1] What these things are, has been told previously. Do we not read there: "Rebuke not an elder, but entreat him as a father"?[2] Is it not said in the Second Epistle: "Hold fast the form of sound words, which thou hast heard of me"?[3] And is he not there told: "Study to show thyself approved unto God, a workman that needeth not to be ashamed, rightly dividing the word of truth"?[4] And in the same place: "Preach the word; be instant in season, out of season; reprove, rebuke, exhort, with all long-suffering and doctrine."[5] And so in the Epistle to Titus, does he not say that a bishop ought to "hold fast the faithful word as he hath been taught, that he may be able by sound doctrine both to exhort and to convince the gainsayers"?[6] There, too, he says: "But speak thou the things which become sound doctrine: that the aged men be sober,"[7] and so on. And there, too: "These things speak, and exhort, and rebuke with all authority. Let no man despise thee. Put them in mind to be subject to principalities and powers,"[8] and so on. What then are we to think? Does the apostle in any way contradict himself, when, though he says that men are made teachers by the operation of the Holy Spirit, he yet himself gives them directions how and what they should teach? Or are we to understand, that though the duty of men to teach even the teachers does not cease when the Holy Spirit is given, yet that neither is he who planteth anything, nor he who watereth, but God Who giveth the increase?[9] Wherefore though holy men be our helpers, or even holy angels assist us, no one learns aright the things that pertain to life with God, until God makes him ready to learn from Himself, that God Who is thus addressed in the psalm: "Teach me to do Thy will; for Thou art my God."[10] And so the same apostle says to Timothy himself, speaking, of course, as teacher to disciple: "But continue thou in the things which thou hast learned, and hast been assured of, knowing of Whom thou hast learned them."[11] For as the medicines which men apply to the bodies of their fellowmen are of no avail except God gives them virtue (Who can heal without their aid, though they cannot without His), and yet they are applied; and if it be done from a sense of duty, it is esteemed a work of mercy or benevolence; so the aids of teaching, applied through the instru-

mentality of man, are of advantage to the soul only when God works to make them of advantage, Who could give the Gospel to man even without the help or agency of men.

Chap. 17. *Threefold division of the various styles of speech*

34. He then who, in speaking, aims at enforcing what is good, should not despise any of those three objects, either to teach, or to give pleasure, or to move, and should pray and strive, as we have said above, to be heard with intelligence, with pleasure, and with ready compliance. And when he does this with elegance and propriety, he may justly be called eloquent, even though he do not carry with him the assent of his hearer. For it is these three ends, viz., teaching, giving pleasure, and moving, that the great master of Roman eloquence himself seems to have intended that the following three directions should subserve: "He, then, shall be eloquent, who can say little things in a subdued style, moderate things in a temperate style, and great things in a majestic style": as if he had taken in also the three ends mentioned above, and had embraced the whole in one sentence thus: "He, then, shall be eloquent, who can say little things in a subdued style, in order to give instruction, moderate things in a temperate style, in order to give pleasure, and great things in a majestic style, in order to sway the mind."

Chap. 18. *The Christian orator is constantly dealing with great matters*

35. Now the author I have quoted could have exemplified these three directions, as laid down by himself, in regard to legal questions: he could not, however, have done so in regard to ecclesiastical questions—the only ones that an address such as I wish to give shape to is concerned with. For of legal questions those are called small which have reference to pecuniary transactions; those great where a matter relating to man's life or liberty comes up. Cases, again, which have to do with neither of these, and where the intention is not to get the hearer to do, or to pronounce judgment upon anything, but only to give him pleasure, occupy as it were a middle place between the former two, and are on that account called middling, or moderate. For moderate things get their name from *modus* (a measure); and it is an abuse, not a proper use of the word *moderate,* to put it for *little.* In questions like ours, however, where all things, and especially those addressed to the

[1]I Tim. 4. 11. [2]I Tim. 5. 1. [3]II Tim. 1. 13.
[4]II Tim. 2. 15. [5]II Tim. 4. 2. [6]Tit. 1. 9.
[7]Tit. 2. 1, 2. [8]Tit. 2. 15; 3. 1. [9]I Cor. 3. 7.
[10]Ps. 143. 10. [11]II Tim. 3. 14.

people from the place of authority, ought to have reference to men's salvation, and that not their temporal but their eternal salvation, and where also the thing to be guarded against is eternal ruin, everything that we say is important; so much so, that even what the preacher says about pecuniary matters, whether it have reference to loss or gain, whether the amount be great or small, should not seem unimportant. For justice is never unimportant, and justice ought assuredly to be observed, even in small affairs of money, as our Lord says: "He that is faithful in that which is least, is faithful also in much." [1] That which is least, then, is very little; but to be faithful in that which is least is great. For as the nature of the circle, viz., that all lines drawn from the centre to the circumference are equal, is the same in a great disk that it is in the smallest coin; so the greatness of justice is in no degree lessened, though the matters to which justice is applied be small.

36. And when the apostle spoke about trials in regard to secular affairs (and what were these but matters of money?), he says: "Dare any of you, having a matter against another, go to law before the unjust, and not before the saints? Do ye not know that the saints shall judge the world? and if the world shall be judged by you, are ye unworthy to judge the smallest matters? Know ye not that we shall judge angels? how much more things that pertain to this life? If, then, ye have judgments of things pertaining to this life, set them to judge who are least esteemed in the Church. I speak to your shame. Is it so, that there is not a wise man among you? no, not one that shall be able to judge between his brethren? But brother goeth to law with brother, and that before the unbelievers. Now therefore there is utterly a fault among you, because ye go to law one with another: why do ye not rather take wrong? why do ye not rather suffer yourselves to be defrauded? Nay, ye do wrong, and defraud, and that your brethren. Know ye not that the unrighteous shall not inherit the kingdom of God?" [2] Why is it that the apostle is so indignant, and that he thus accuses, and upbraids, and chides, and threatens? Why is it that the changes in his tone, so frequent and so abrupt, testify to the depth of his emotion? Why is it, in fine, that he speaks in a tone so exalted about matters so very trifling? Did secular matters deserve so much at his hands? God forbid. No; but all this is done for the sake of justice, charity, and piety, which in the judg-

ment of every sober mind are great, even when applied to matters the very least.

37. Of course, if we were giving men advice as to how they ought to conduct secular cases, either for themselves or for their connexions, before the Church courts, we would rightly advise them to conduct them quietly as matters of little moment. But we are treating of the manner of speech of the man who is to be a teacher of the truths which deliver us from eternal misery and bring us to eternal happiness; and wherever these truths are spoken of, whether in public or private, whether to one or many, whether to friends or enemies, whether in a continuous discourse or in conversation, whether in tracts, or in books, or in letters long or short, they are of great importance. Unless indeed we are prepared to say that, because a cup of cold water is a very trifling and common thing, the saying of our Lord, that he who gives a cup of cold water to one of His disciples shall in no wise lose his reward, [3] is very trivial and unimportant. Or that when a preacher takes this saying as his text, he should think his subject very unimportant, and therefore speak without either eloquence or power, but in a subdued and humble style. Is it not the case that when we happen to speak on this subject to the people, and the presence of God is with us, so that what we say is not altogether unworthy of the subject, a tongue of fire springs up out of that cold water which inflames even the cold hearts of men with a zeal for doing works of mercy in hope of an eternal reward?

CHAP. 19. *The Christian teacher must use different styles on different occasions*

38. And yet, while our teacher ought to speak of great matters, he ought not always to be speaking of them in a majestic tone, but in a subdued tone when he is teaching, temperately when he is giving praise or blame. When, however, something is to be done, and we are speaking to those who ought, but are not willing, to do it, then great matters must be spoken of with power, and in a manner calculated to sway the mind. And sometimes the same important matter is treated in all these ways at different times, quietly when it is being taught, temperately when its importance is being urged, and powerfully when we are forcing a mind that is averse to the truth to turn and embrace it. For is there anything greater than God Himself? Is nothing, then, to be learnt about Him? Or ought he who is teaching the Trinity in unity to speak of it

[1] Luke, 16. 10.
[2] I Cor. 6. 1–9.
[3] Matt. 10. 42.

otherwise than in the method of calm discussion, so that in regard to a subject which it is not easy to comprehend, we may understand as much as it is given us to understand? Are we in this case to seek out ornaments instead of proofs? Or is the hearer to be moved to do something instead of being instructed so that he may learn something? But when we come to praise God, either in Himself, or in His works, what a field for beauty and splendour of language opens up before man, who can task his powers to the utmost in praising Him Whom no one can adequately praise, though there is no one who does not praise Him in some measure! But if He be not worshipped, or if idols, whether they be demons or any created being whatever, be worshipped with Him or in preference to Him, then we ought to speak out with power and impressiveness, show how great a wickedness this is, and urge men to flee from it.

CHAP. 20. *Examples of the various styles drawn from Scripture*

39. But now to come to something more definite. We have an example of the calm, subdued style in the Apostle Paul, where he says: "Tell me, ye that desire to be under the law, do ye not hear the law? For it is written, that Abraham had two sons; the one by a bond maid, the other by a free woman. But he who was of the bond woman was born after the flesh; but he of the free woman was by promise. Which things are an allegory: for these are the two covenants; the one from the Mount Sinai, which gendereth to bondage, which is Hagar. For this Hagar is Mount Sinai in Arabia, and answereth to Jerusalem which now is, and is in bondage with her children. But Jerusalem which is above is free, which is the mother of us all";[1] and so on. And in the same way where he reasons thus: "Brethren, I speak after the manner of men: Though it be but a man's covenant, yet if it be confirmed, no man disannulleth, or addeth thereto. Now to Abraham and his seed were the promises made. He saith not, And to seeds, as of many; but as of one, And to thy seed, which is Christ. And this I say, that the covenant, that was confirmed before of God in Christ, the law, which was four hundred and thirty years after, cannot disannul, that it should make the promise of none effect. For if the inheritance be of the law, it is no more of promise: but God gave it to Abraham by promise."[2] And because it might possibly occur to the hearer to ask, "If there is no inheritance by the law, why then was the law

given?" he himself anticipates this objection and asks, "Wherefore then serveth the law?" And the answer is given: "It was added because of transgressions, till the seed should come to whom the promise was made; and it was ordained by angels in the hand of a mediator. Now a mediator is not a mediator of one; but God is one." And here an objection occurs which he himself has stated: "Is the law then against the promises of God?" He answers: "God forbid." And he also states the reason in these words: "For if there had been a law given which could have given life, verily righteousness should have been by the law. But the Scripture hath concluded all under sin, that the promise by faith of Jesus Christ might be given to them that believe."[3] It is part, then, of the duty of the teacher not only to interpret what is obscure and to unravel the difficulties of questions, but also, while doing this, to meet other questions which may chance to suggest themselves, lest these should cast doubt or discredit on what we say. If, however, the solution of these questions suggest itself as soon as the questions themselves arise, it is useless to disturb what we cannot remove. And besides, when out of one question other questions arise, and out of these again still others; if these be all discussed and solved, the reasoning is extended to such a length, that unless the memory be exceedingly powerful and active, the reasoner finds it impossible to return to the original question from which he set out. It is, however, exceedingly desirable that whatever occurs to the mind as an objection that might be urged should be stated and refuted, lest it turn up at a time when no one will be present to answer it, or lest, if it should occur to a man who is present but says nothing about it, it might never be thoroughly removed.

40. In the following words of the apostle we have the temperate style: "Rebuke not an elder, but entreat him as a father; and the younger men as brethren; the elder women as mothers, the younger as sisters."[4] And also in these: "I beseech you, therefore, brethren, by the mercies of God, that ye present your bodies a living sacrifice, holy, acceptable unto God, which is your reasonable service."[5] And almost the whole of this hortatory passage is in the temperate style of eloquence; and those parts of it are the most beautiful in which, as if paying what was due, things that belong to each other are gracefully brought together. For example: "Having then gifts, differing according to the grace that is given to us, whether prophecy, let us proph-

---

[1]Gal. 4. 21–26.   [2]Gal. 3. 15–18.   [3]Gal. 3. 19–22.   [4]I Tim. 5. 1, 2.   [5]Rom. 12. 1.

esy according to the proportion of faith; or ministry, let us wait on our ministering; or he that teacheth, on teaching; or he that exhorteth, on exhortation; he that giveth, let him do it with simplicity; he that ruleth, with diligence; he that showeth mercy, with cheerfulness. Let love be without dissimulation. Abhor that which is evil, cleave to that which is good. Be kindly affectioned one to another with brotherly love; in honour preferring one another; not slothful in business; fervent in spirit; serving the Lord; rejoicing in hope; patient in tribulation; continuing instant in prayer; distributing to the necessity of saints; given to hospitality. Bless them which persecute you: bless, and curse not. Rejoice with them that do rejoice, and weep with them that weep. Be of the same mind one toward another." [1] And how gracefully all this is brought to a close in a period of two members: "Mind not high things, but condescend to men of low estate!" And a little afterwards: "Render therefore to all their dues: tribute to whom tribute is due; custom to whom custom; fear to whom fear; honour to whom honour." [2] And these also, though expressed in single clauses, are terminated by a period of two members: "Owe no man anything, but to love one another." And a little farther on: "The night is far spent, the day is at hand: let us therefore cast off the works of darkness, and let us put on the armour of light. Let us walk honestly, as in the day; not in rioting and drunkenness, not in chambering and wantonness, not in strife and envying: but put ye on the Lord Jesus Christ, and make not provision for the flesh, to fulfill the lusts thereof." [3] Now if the passage were translated thus, *"et carnis providentiam ne in concupiscentiis feceritis,"* the ear would no doubt be gratified with a more harmonious ending; but our translator, with more strictness, preferred to retain even the order of the words. And how this sounds in the Greek language, in which the apostle spoke, those who are better skilled in that tongue may determine. My opinion, however, is that what has been translated to us in the same order of words does not run very harmoniously even in the original tongue.

41. And, indeed, I must confess that our authors are very defective in that grace of speech which consists in harmonious endings. Whether this be the fault of the translators, or whether, as I am more inclined to believe, the authors designedly avoided such ornaments, I dare not affirm; for I confess I do not know. This I know, however, that if any one who is skilled in

this species of harmony would take the closing sentences of these writers and arrange them according to the law of harmony (which he could very easily do by changing some words for words of equivalent meaning, or by retaining the words he finds and altering their arrangement), he will learn that these divinely inspired men are not defective in any of those points which he has been taught in the schools of the grammarians and rhetoricians to consider of importance; and he will find in them many kinds of speech of great beauty—beautiful even in our language, but especially beautiful in the original—none of which can be found in those writings of which they boast so much. But care must be taken that, while adding harmony, we take away none of the weight from these divine and authoritative utterances. Now our prophets were so far from being deficient in the musical training from which this harmony we speak of is most fully learnt that Jerome, a very learned man, describes even the metres employed by some of them, in the Hebrew language at least; though, in order to give an accurate rendering of the words, he has not preserved these in his translation. I, however (to speak of my own feeling, which is better known to me than it is to others, and than that of others is to me), while I do not in my own speech, however modestly I think it done, neglect these harmonious endings, am just as well pleased to find them in the sacred authors very rarely.

42. The majestic style of speech differs from the temperate style just spoken of, chiefly in that it is not so much decked out with verbal ornaments as exalted into vehemence by mental emotion. It uses, indeed, nearly all the ornaments that the other does; but if they do not happen to be at hand, it does not seek for them. For it is borne on by its own vehemence; and the force of the thought, not the desire for ornament, makes it seize upon any beauty of expression that comes in its way. It is enough for its object that warmth of feeling should suggest the fitting words; they need not be selected by careful elaboration of speech. If a brave man be armed with weapons adorned with gold and jewels, he works feats of valour with those arms in the heat of battle, not because they are costly, but because they are arms; and yet the same man does great execution, even when anger furnishes him with a weapon that he digs out of the ground. [4] The apostle in the following passage is urging that, for the sake of the ministry of the gospel, and sustained by the consolations

---

[1] Rom. 12. 6–16.   [2] Rom. 13. 7.   [3] Rom. 13. 12–14.   [4] Virgil, *Æneid*, BK. VII. 508.

of God's grace, we should bear with patience all the evils of this life. It is a great subject, and is treated with power, and the ornaments of speech are not wanting: "Behold," he says, "now is the accepted time; behold, now is the day of salvation. Giving no offence in anything, that the ministry be not blamed: but in all things approving ourselves as the ministers of God, in much patience, in afflictions, in necessities, in distresses, in strifes, in imprisonments, in tumults, in labours, in watchings, in fastings; by pureness, by knowledge, by long-suffering, by kindness, by the Holy Ghost, by love unfeigned, by the word of truth, by the power of God, by the armour of righteousness on the right hand and on the left, by honour and dishonour, by evil report and good report: as deceivers, and yet true; as unknown, and yet well known; as dying, and, behold, we live; as chastened, and not killed; as sorrowful, yet alway rejoicing; as poor, yet making many rich; as having nothing, and yet possessing all things." [1] See him still burning: "O ye Corinthians, our mouth is opened unto you, our heart is enlarged," and so on; it would be tedious to go through it all.

43. And in the same way, writing to the Romans, he urges that the persecutions of this world should be overcome by charity, in assured reliance on the help of God. And he treats this subject with both power and beauty: "We know," he says, "that all things work together for good to them that love God, to them who are the called according to His purpose. For whom He did foreknow, He also did predestinate to be conformed to the image of His Son, that He might be the first-born among many brethren. Moreover, whom He did predestinate, them He also called; and whom He called, them He also justified; and whom He justified, them He also glorified. What shall we then say to these things? If God be for us, who can be against us? He that spared not His own Son, but delivered Him up for us all, how shall He not with Him also freely give us all things? Who shall lay anything to the charge of God's elect? It is God that justifieth; who is he that condemneth? It is Christ that died, yea, rather, that is risen again, who is even at the right hand of God, who also maketh intercession for us. Who shall separate us from the love of Christ? shall tribulation, or distress, or persecution, or famine, or nakedness, or peril, or sword? (As it is written, For Thy sake we are killed all the day long; we are accounted as sheep for the slaughter.) Nay, in all these things we are more than conquerors, through Him that loved us. For I am persuaded, that neither death, nor life, nor angels, nor principalities, nor powers, nor things present, nor things to come, nor height, nor depth, nor any other creature, shall be able to separate us from the love of God, which is in Christ Jesus our Lord." [2]

44. Again, in writing to the Galatians, although the whole epistle is written in the subdued style, except at the end, where it rises into a temperate eloquence, yet he interposes one passage of so much feeling that, notwithstanding the absence of any ornaments such as appear in the passages just quoted, it cannot be called anything but powerful: "Ye observe days, and months, and times, and years. I am afraid of you, lest I have bestowed upon you labour in vain. Brethren, I beseech you, be as I am; for I am as ye are: ye have not injured me at all. Ye know how, through infirmity of the flesh, I preached the gospel unto you at the first. And my temptation which was in my flesh ye despised not, nor rejected; but received me as an angel of God, even as Christ Jesus. Where is then the blessedness ye spake of? for I bear you record, that, if it had been possible, ye would have plucked out your own eyes, and have given them to me. Am I therefore become your enemy, because I tell you the truth? They zealously affect you, but not well; yea, they would exclude you, that ye might affect them. But it is good to be zealously affected always in a good thing, and not only when I am present with you. My little children, of whom I travail in birth again until Christ be formed in you, I desire to be present with you now, and to change my voice; for I stand in doubt of you." [3] Is there anything here of contrasted words arranged antithetically, or of words rising gradually to a climax, or of sonorous clauses, and sections, and periods? Yet, notwithstanding, there is a glow of strong emotion that makes us feel the fervour of eloquence.

CHAP. 21. *Examples of the various styles, drawn from the teachers of the Church, especially Ambrose and Cyprian*

45. But these writings of the apostles, though clear, are yet profound, and are so written that one who is not content with a superficial acquaintance, but desires to know them thoroughly, must not only read and hear them, but must have an expositor. Let us, then, study these various modes of speech as they are exemplified in the writings of men who, by reading the Scrip-

[1] II Cor. 6. 2–10.   [2] Rom. 8. 28–39.   [3] Gal. 4. 10–20.

tures, have attained to the knowledge of divine and saving truth, and have ministered it to the Church. Cyprian of blessed memory writes in the subdued style in his treatise on the sacrament of the cup. In this book he resolves the question, whether the cup of the Lord ought to contain water only, or water mingled with wine. But we must quote a passage by way of illustration. After the customary introduction, he proceeds to the discussion of the point in question. "Observe," he says, "that we are instructed, in presenting the cup, to maintain the custom handed down to us from the Lord, and to do nothing that our Lord has not first done for us: so that the cup which is offered in remembrance of Him should be mixed with wine. For, as Christ says, 'I am the true vine,'[1] it follows that the blood of Christ is wine, not water; and the cup cannot appear to contain His blood by which we are redeemed and quickened, if the wine be absent; for by the wine is the blood of Christ typified, that blood which is foreshadowed and proclaimed in all the types and declarations of Scripture. For we find that in the book of Genesis this very circumstance in regard to the sacrament is foreshadowed, and our Lord's sufferings typically set forth, in the case of Noah, when he drank wine, and was drunken, and was uncovered within his tent, and his nakedness was exposed by his second son, and was carefully hidden by his elder and his younger sons.[2] It is not necessary to mention the other circumstances in detail, as it is only necessary to observe this point, that Noah, foreshadowing the future reality, drank, not water, but wine, and thus showed forth our Lord's passion. In the same way we see the sacrament of the Lord's supper prefigured in the case of Melchizedek the priest, according to the testimony of the Holy Scriptures, where it says: 'And Melchizedek king of Salem brought forth bread and wine: and he was the priest of the most high God. And he blessed Abraham.'[3] Now, that Melchizedek was a type of Christ, the Holy Spirit declares in the Psalms, where the Father addressing the Son says, "Thou art a priest for ever after the order of Melchizedek.'[4]" In this passage, and in all of the letter that follows, the subdued style is maintained, as the reader may easily satisfy himself.

46. St. Ambrose also, though dealing with a question of very great importance, the equality of the Holy Spirit with the Father and the Son, employs the subdued style, because the object he has in view demands, not beauty of diction, nor the swaying of the mind by the stir of emotion, but facts and proofs. Accordingly, in the introduction to his work, we find the following passage among others: "When Gideon was startled by the message he had heard from God, that, though thousands of the people failed, yet through one man God would deliver His people from their enemies, he brought forth a kid of the goats, and by direction of the angel laid it with unleavened cakes upon a rock, and poured the broth over it; and as soon as the angel of God touched it with the end of the staff that was in his hand, there rose up fire out of the rock and consumed the offering.[5] Now this sign seems to indicate that the rock was a type of the body of Christ, for it is written, 'They drank of that spiritual rock that followed them, and that rock was Christ';[6] this, of course, referring not to Christ's divine nature, but to His flesh, whose ever-flowing fountain of blood has ever satisfied the hearts of His thirsting people. And so it was at that time declared in a mystery that the Lord Jesus, when crucified, should abolish in His flesh the sins of the whole world, and not their guilty acts merely, but the evil lusts of their hearts. For the kid's flesh refers to the guilt of the outward act, the broth to the allurement of lust within, as it is written, 'And the mixed multitude that was among them fell a lusting; and the children of Israel also wept again and said, Who shall give us flesh to eat?'[7] When the angel, then, stretched out his staff and touched the rock, and fire rose out of it, this was a sign that our Lord's flesh, filled with the Spirit of God, should burn up all the sins of the human race. Whence also the Lord says, 'I am come to send fire on the earth.'[8]" And in the same style he pursues the subject, devoting himself chiefly to proving and enforcing his point.

47. An example of the *temperate* style is the celebrated encomium on virginity from Cyprian: "Now our discourse addresses itself to the virgins, who, as they are the objects of higher honour, are also the objects of greater care. These are the flowers on the tree of the Church, the glory and ornament of spiritual grace, the joy of honour and praise, a work unbroken and unblemished, the image of God answering to the holiness of the Lord, the brighter portion of the flock of Christ. The glorious fruitfulness of their mother the Church rejoices in them, and in them flourishes more abundantly; and in

---

[1]John, 15. 1.　　[2]Gen. 9. 20–24.　　[3]Gen. 14. 18, 19.
[4]Ps. 110. 4.

[5]Judges, 6. 14-21.　　[6]I Cor. 10. 4.　　[7]Num. 11. 4.
[8]Luke, 12. 49.

proportion as bright virginity adds to her numbers, in the same proportion does the mother's joy increase. And at another place in the end of the epistle, 'As we have borne,' he says, 'the image of the earthly, we shall also bear the image of the heavenly.'[1] Virginity bears this image, integrity bears it, holiness and truth bear it; they bear it who are mindful of the chastening of the Lord, who observe justice and piety, who are strong in faith, humble in fear, steadfast in the endurance of suffering, meek in the endurance of injury, ready to pity, of one mind and of one heart in brotherly peace. And every one of these things ought ye, holy virgins, to observe, to cherish, and fulfil, who having hearts at leisure for God and for Christ, and having chosen the greater and better part, lead and point the way to the Lord, to whom you have pledged your vows. Ye who are advanced in age, exercise control over the younger. Ye who are younger, wait upon the elders, and encourage your equals; stir up one another by mutual exhortations; provoke one another to glory by emulous examples of virtue; endure bravely, advance in spirituality, finish your course with joy; only be mindful of us when your virginity shall begin to reap its reward of honour."

48. Ambrose also uses the temperate and ornamented style when he is holding up before virgins who have made their profession a model for their imitation, and says: "She was a virgin not in body only, but also in mind; not mingling the purity of her affection with any dross of hypocrisy; serious in speech; prudent in disposition; sparing of words; delighting in study; not placing her confidence in uncertain riches, but in the prayer of the poor; diligent in labour; reverent in word; accustomed to look to God, not man, as the guide of her conscience; injuring no one, wishing well to all; dutiful to her elders, not envious of her equals; avoiding boastfulness, following reason, loving virtue. When did she wound her parents even by a look? When did she quarrel with her neighbours? When did she spurn the humble, laugh at the weak, or shun the indigent? She is accustomed to visit only those haunts of men that pity would not blush for, nor modesty pass by. There is nothing haughty in her eyes, nothing bold in her words, nothing wanton in her gestures: her bearing is not voluptuous, nor her gait too free, nor her voice petulant; so that her outward appearance is an image of her mind, and a picture of purity. For a good house ought to be known for such at the very threshold, and

[1] I Cor. 15. 49.

show at the very entrance that there is no dark recess within, as the light of a lamp set inside sheds its radiance on the outside. Why need I detail her sparingness in food, her superabundance in duty—the one falling beneath the demands of nature, the other rising above its powers? The latter has no intervals of intermission, the former doubles the days by fasting; and when the desire for refreshment does arise, it is satisfied with food such as will support life, but not minister to appetite." Now I have cited these latter passages as examples of the temperate style, because their purpose is not to induce those who have not yet devoted themselves to take the vows of virginity, but to show of what character those who have taken vows ought to be. To prevail on any one to take a step of such a nature and of so great importance, requires that the mind should be excited and set on fire by the majestic style. Cyprian the martyr, however, did not write about the duty of taking up the profession of virginity, but about the dress and deportment of virgins. Yet that great bishop urges them to their duty even in these respects by the power of a majestic eloquence.

49. But I shall select examples of the majestic style from their treatment of a subject which both of them have touched. Both have denounced the women who colour, or rather discolour, their faces with paint. And the first, in dealing with this topic, says: "Suppose a painter should depict in colours that rival nature's the features and form and complexion of some man, and that, when the portrait had been finished with consummate art, another painter should put his hand over it, as if to improve by his superior skill the painting already completed; surely the first artist would feel deeply insulted, and his indignation would be justly roused. Dost thou, then, think that thou wilt carry off with impunity so audacious an act of wickedness, such an insult to God the great artificer? For, granting that thou art not immodest in thy behaviour towards men, and that thou art not polluted in mind by these meretricious deceits, yet, in corrupting and violating what is God's, thou provest thyself worse than an adulteress. The fact that thou considerest thyself adorned and beautified by such arts is an impeachment of God's handiwork, and a violation of truth. Listen to the warning voice of the apostle: 'Purge out the old leaven, that ye may be a new lump, as ye are unleavened. For even Christ our passover is sacrificed for us: therefore let us keep the feast, not with old leaven, neither with the leaven of malice and wicked-

ness; but with the unleavened bread of sincerity and truth.'[1] Now can sincerity and truth continue to exist when what is sincere is polluted, and what is true is changed by meretricious colouring and the deceptions of quackery into a lie? Thy Lord says, 'Thou canst not make one hair white or black';[2] and dost thou wish to have greater power so as to bring to nought the words of thy Lord? With rash and sacrilegious hand thou wouldst fain change the colour of thy hair: I would that, with a prophetic look to the future, thou shouldst dye it the colour-of-flame." It would be too long to quote all that follows.

50. Ambrose again, inveighing against such practices, says: "Hence arise these incentives to vice, that women, in their fear that they may not prove attractive to men, paint their faces with carefully chosen colours, and then from stains on their features go on to stains on their chastity. What folly it is to change the features of nature into those of a painting, and from fear of incurring their husband's disapproval, to proclaim openly that they have incurred their own! For the woman who desires to alter her natural appearance pronounces condemnation on herself; and her eager endeavours to please another prove that she has first been displeasing to herself. And what testimony to thine ugliness can we find, O woman, that is more unquestionable than thine own, when thou art afraid to show thyself? If thou art comely why dost thou hide thy comeliness? If thou art plain, why dost thou lyingly pretend to be beautiful, when thou canst not enjoy the pleasure of the lie either in thine own consciousness or in that of another? For he loves another woman, thou desirest to please another man; and thou art angry if he love another, though he is taught adultery in thee. Thou art the evil promptress of thine own injury. For even the woman who has been the victim of a pander shrinks from acting the pander's part, and though she be vile, it is herself she sins against and not another. The crime of adultery is almost more tolerable than thine; for adultery tampers with modesty, but thou with nature." It is sufficiently clear, I think, that this eloquence calls passionately upon women to avoid tampering with their appearance by deceitful arts, and to cultivate modesty and fear. Accordingly, we notice that the style is neither subdued nor temperate, but majestic throughout. Now in these two authors whom I have selected as specimens of the rest, and in other ecclesiastical writers who both speak the truth and speak it well—speak it, that is, judiciously,

[1] I Cor. 5. 7, 8.   [2] Matt. 5. 36.

pointedly, and with beauty and power of expression—many examples may be found of the three styles of speech, scattered through their various writings and discourses; and the diligent student may by assiduous reading, intermingled with practice on his own part, become thoroughly imbued with them all.

CHAP. 22. *The necessity of variety in style*

51. But we are not to suppose that it is against rule to mingle these various styles: on the contrary, every variety of style should be introduced so far as is consistent with good taste. For when we keep monotonously to one style, we fail to retain the hearer's attention; but when we pass from one style to another, the discourse goes off more gracefully, even though it extend to greater length. Each separate style, again, has varieties of its own which prevent the hearer's attention from cooling or becoming languid. We can bear the subdued style, however, longer without variety than the majestic style. For the mental emotion which it is necessary to stir up in order to carry the hearer's feelings with us, when once it has been sufficiently excited, the higher the pitch to which it is raised, can be maintained the shorter time. And therefore we must be on our guard, lest, in striving to carry to a higher point the emotion we have excited, we rather lose what we have already gained. But after the interposition of matter that we have to treat in a quieter style, we can return with good effect to that which must be treated forcibly, thus making the tide of eloquence to ebb and flow like the sea. It follows from this, that the majestic style, if it is to be long continued, ought not to be unvaried, but should alternate at intervals with the other styles; the speech or writing as a whole, however, being referred to that style which is the prevailing one.

CHAP. 23. *How the various styles should be mingled*

52. Now it is a matter of importance to determine what style should be alternated with what other, and the places where it is necessary that any particular style should be used. In the majestic style, for instance, it is always, or almost always, desirable that the introduction should be temperate. And the speaker has it in his discretion to use the subdued style even where the majestic would be allowable, in order that the majestic when it is used may be the more majestic by comparison, and may as it were shine out with greater brilliance from the

dark background. Again, whatever may be the style of the speech or writing, when knotty questions turn up for solution, accuracy of distinction is required, and this naturally demands the subdued style. And accordingly this style must be used in alternation with the other two styles whenever questions of that sort turn up; just as we must use the temperate style, no matter what may be the general tone of the discourse, whenever praise or blame is to be given without any ulterior reference to the condemnation or acquittal of any one, or to obtaining the concurrence of any one in a course of action. In the majestic style, then, and in the quiet likewise, both the other two styles occasionally find place. The temperate style, on the other hand, not indeed always, but occasionally, needs the quiet style; for example, when, as I have said, a knotty question comes up to be settled, or when some points that are susceptible of ornament are left unadorned and expressed in the quiet style, in order to give greater effect to certain exuberances (as they may be called) of ornament. But the temperate style never needs the aid of the majestic; for its object is to gratify, never to excite, the mind.

CHAP. 24. *The effects produced by the majestic style*

53. If frequent and vehement applause follows a speaker, we are not to suppose on that account that he is speaking in the majestic style; for this effect is often produced both by the accurate distinctions of the quiet style, and by the beauties of the temperate. The majestic style, on the other hand, frequently silences the audience by its impressiveness, but calls forth their tears. For example, when at Cæsarea in Mauritania I was dissuading the people from that civil, or worse than civil, war which they called *Caterva* (for it was not fellow-citizens merely, but neighbours, brothers, fathers and sons even, who, divided into two factions and armed with stones, fought annually at a certain season of the year for several days continuously, every one killing whomsoever he could), I strove with all the vehemence of speech that I could command to root out and drive from their hearts and lives an evil so cruel and inveterate; it was not, however, when I heard their applause, but when I saw their tears, that I thought I had produced an effect. For the applause showed that they were instructed and delighted, but the tears that they were subdued. And when I saw their tears I was confident, even before the event proved it, that this horri-

ble and barbarous custom (which had been handed down to them from their fathers and their ancestors of generations long gone by and which like an enemy was besieging their hearts, or rather had complete possession of them) was overthrown; and immediately that my sermon was finished I called upon them with heart and voice to give praise and thanks to God. And, lo, with the blessing of Christ, it is now eight years or more since anything of the sort was attempted there. In many other cases besides I have observed that men show the effect made on them by the powerful eloquence of a wise man, not by clamorous applause so much as by groans, sometimes even by tears, finally by change of life.

54. The quiet style, too, has made a change in many; but it was to teach them what they were ignorant of, or to persuade them of what they thought incredible, not to make them do what they knew they ought to do but were unwilling to do. To break down hardness of this sort, speech needs to be vehement. Praise and censure, too, when they are eloquently expressed, even in the temperate style, produce such an effect on some, that they are not only pleased with the eloquence of the encomiums and censures, but are led to live so as themselves to deserve praise, and to avoid living so as to incur blame. But no one would say that all who are thus delighted change their habits in consequence, whereas all who are moved by the majestic style act accordingly, and all who are taught by the quiet style know or believe a truth which they were previously ignorant of.

CHAP. 25. *How the temperate style is to be used*

55. From all this we may conclude, that the end arrived at by the two styles last mentioned is the one which it is most essential for those who aspire to speak with wisdom and eloquence to secure. On the other hand, what the temperate style properly aims at, viz., to please by beauty of expression, is not in itself an adequate end; but when what we have to say is good and useful, and when the hearers are both acquainted with it and favourably disposed towards it, so that it is not necessary either to instruct or persuade them, beauty of style may have its influence in securing their prompter compliance, or in making them adhere to it more tenaciously. For as the function of all eloquence, whichever of these three forms it may assume, is to speak persuasively, and its object is to persuade, an eloquent man will speak persuasively, whatever style he may adopt; but unless he succeeds in

persuading, his eloquence has not secured its object. Now in the subdued style, he persuades his hearers that what he says is true; in the majestic style, he persuades them to do what they are aware they ought to do, but do not; in the temperate style, he persuades them that his speech is elegant and ornate. But what use is there in attaining such an object as this last? They may desire it who are vain of their eloquence and make a boast of panegyrics, and such-like performances, where the object is not to instruct the hearer, or to persuade him to any course of action, but merely to give him pleasure. We, however, ought to make that end subordinate to another, viz., the effecting by this style of eloquence what we aim at effecting when we use the majestic style. For we may by the use of this style persuade men to cultivate good habits and give up evil ones, if they are not so hardened as to need the vehement style; or if they have already begun a good course, we may induce them to pursue it more zealously, and to persevere in it with constancy. Accordingly, even in the temperate style we must use beauty of expression not for ostentation, but for wise ends; not contenting ourselves merely with pleasing the hearer, but rather seeking to aid him in the pursuit of the good end which we hold out before him.

CHAP. 26. *In every style the orator should aim at perspicuity, beauty, and persuasiveness*

56. Now in regard to the three conditions I laid down a little while ago[1] as necessary to be fulfilled by any one who wishes to speak with wisdom and eloquence, viz. perspicuity, beauty of style, and persuasive power, we are not to understand that these three qualities attach themselves respectively to the three several styles of speech, one to each, so that perspicuity is a merit peculiar to the subdued style, beauty to the temperate, and persuasive power to the majestic. On the contrary, all speech, whatever its style, ought constantly to aim at, and as far as possible to display, all these three merits. For we do not like even what we say in the subdued style to pall upon the hearer; and therefore we would be listened to, not with intelligence merely, but with pleasure as well. Again, why do we enforce what we teach by divine testimony, except that we wish to carry the hearer with us, that is, to compel his assent by calling in the assistance of Him of Whom it is said, "Thy testimonies are very sure"?[2] And when any one narrates a story, even in the subdued style, what

[1]Chaps. 15 and 17.　[2]Ps. 93. 5.

does he wish but to be believed? But who will listen to him if he do not arrest attention by some beauty of style? And if he be not intelligible, is it not plain that he can neither give pleasure nor enforce conviction? The subdued style, again, in its own naked simplicity, when it unravels questions of very great difficulty and throws an unexpected light upon them; when it worms out and brings to light some very acute observations from a quarter whence nothing was expected; when it seizes upon and exposes the falsity of an opposing opinion, which seemed at its first statement to be unassailable; especially when all this is accompanied by a natural, unsought grace of expression, and by a rhythm and balance of style which is not ostentatiously obtruded, but seems rather to be called forth by the nature of the subject: this style, so used, frequently calls forth applause so great that one can hardly believe it to be the subdued style. For the fact that it comes forth without either ornament or defence, and offers battle in its own naked simplicity, does not hinder it from crushing its adversary by weight of nerve and muscle, and overwhelming and destroying the falsehood that opposes it by the mere strength of its own right arm. How explain the frequent and vehement applause that waits upon men who speak thus, except by the pleasure that truth so irresistibly established, and so victoriously defended, naturally affords? Wherefore the Christian teacher and speaker ought, when he uses the subdued style, to endeavour not only to be clear and intelligible, but to give pleasure and to bring home conviction to the hearer.

57. Eloquence of the temperate style, also, must, in the case of the Christian orator, be neither altogether without ornament, nor unsuitably adorned, nor is it to make the giving of pleasure its sole aim, which is all it professes to accomplish in the hands of others; but in its encomiums and censures it should aim at inducing the hearer to strive after or hold more firmly by what it praises, and to avoid or renounce what it condemns. On the other hand, without perspicuity this style cannot give pleasure. And so the three qualities, perspicuity, beauty, and persuasiveness, are to be sought in this style also; beauty, of course, being its primary object.

58. Again, when it becomes necessary to stir and sway the hearer's mind by the majestic style (and this is always necessary when he admits that what you say is both true and agreeable, and yet is unwilling to act accordingly),

you must, of course, speak in the majestic style. But who can be moved if he does not understand what is said? and who will stay to listen if he receives no pleasure? Wherefore, in this style, too, when an obdurate heart is to be persuaded to obedience, you must speak so as to be both intelligible and pleasing, if you would be heard with a submissive mind.

Chap. 27. *The man whose life is in harmony with his teaching will teach with greater effect*

59. But whatever may be the majesty of the style, the life of the speaker will count for more in securing the hearer's compliance. The man who speaks wisely and eloquently, but lives wickedly, may, it is true, instruct many who are anxious to learn; though, as it is written, he "is unprofitable to himself." [1] Wherefore, also, the apostle says: "Whether in pretence or in truth Christ is preached." [2] Now Christ is the truth; yet we see that the truth can be preached, though not in truth—that is, what is right and true in itself may be preached by a man of perverse and deceitful mind. And thus it is that Jesus Christ is preached by those that seek their own, and not the things that are Jesus Christ's. But since true believers obey the voice, not of any man, but of the Lord Himself, Who says, "All therefore whatsoever they bid you observe, that observe and do: but do not ye after their works; for they say and do not"; [3] therefore it is that men who themselves lead unprofitable lives are heard with profit by others. For though they seek their own objects, they do not dare to teach their own doctrines, sitting as they do in the high places of ecclesiastical authority, which is established on sound doctrine. Wherefore our Lord Himself, before saying what I have just quoted about men of this stamp, made this observation: "The scribes and the Pharisees sit in Moses' seat." [4] The seat they occupied, then, which was not theirs but Moses', compelled them to say what was good, though they did what was evil. And so they followed their own course in their lives, but were prevented by the seat they occupied, which belonged to another, from preaching their own doctrines.

60. Now these men do good to many by preaching what they themselves do not perform; but they would do good to very many more if they lived as they preach. For there are numbers who seek an excuse for their own evil lives in comparing the teaching with the conduct of their instructors, and who say in their hearts, or even go a little further, and say with their lips: "Why do you not do yourself what you bid me do?" And thus they cease to listen with submission to a man who does not listen to himself, and in despising the preacher they learn to despise the word that is preached. Wherefore the apostle, writing to Timothy, after telling him, "Let no man despise thy youth," adds immediately the course by which he would avoid contempt: "but be thou an example of the believers, in word, in conversation, in charity, in spirit, in faith, in purity." [5]

Chap. 28. *Truth is more important than expression. What is meant by strife about words*

61. Such a teacher as is here described may, to secure compliance, speak not only quietly and temperately, but even vehemently, without any breach of modesty, because his life protects him against contempt. For while he pursues an upright life, he takes care to maintain a good reputation as well, providing things honest in the sight of God and men, [6] fearing God, and caring for men. In his very speech even he prefers to please by matter rather than by words; thinks that a thing is well said in proportion as it is true in fact, and that a teacher should govern his words, not let the words govern him. This is what the apostle says: "Not with wisdom of words, lest the cross of Christ should be made of none effect." [7] To the same effect also is what he says to Timothy: "Charging them before the Lord that they strive not about words to no profit, but to the subverting of the hearers." [8] Now this does not mean that, when adversaries oppose the truth, we are to say nothing in defence of the truth. For where, then, would be what he says when he is describing the sort of man a bishop ought to be: "that he may be able by sound doctrine both to exhort and convince the gainsayers"? [9] To strive about words is not to be careful about the way to overcome error by truth, but to be anxious that your mode of expression should be preferred to that of another. The man who does not strive about words, whether he speak quietly, temperately, or vehemently, uses words with no other purpose than to make the truth plain, pleasing, and effective; for not even love itself, which is the end of the commandment and the fulfilling of the law, [10] can be rightly exercised unless the objects of love are true and not false. For as a

---

[1] Ecclus. 37. 19.　[2] Phil. 1. 18.　[3] Matt. 23. 3.
[4] Matt. 23. 2.

[5] I Tim. 4. 12.　[6] II Cor. 8. 21.　[7] I Cor. 2. 17.
[8] II Tim. 2. 14.　[9] Tit. 1. 9.
[10] I Tim. 1. 5; Rom. 13. 10.

man with a comely body but an ill-conditioned mind is a more painful object than if his body too were deformed, so men who teach lies are the more pitiable if they happen to be eloquent in speech. To speak eloquently, then, and wisely as well, is just to express truths which it is expedient to teach in fit and proper words— words which in the subdued style are adequate, in the temperate, elegant, and in the majestic, forcible. But the man who cannot speak both eloquently and wisely should speak wisely without eloquence, rather than eloquently without wisdom.

CHAP. 29. *It is permissible for a preacher to deliver to the people what has been written by a more eloquent man than himself*

If, however, he cannot do even this, let his life be such as shall not only secure a reward for himself, but afford an example to others; and let his manner of living be an eloquent sermon in itself.

62. There are, indeed, some men who have a good delivery, but cannot compose anything to deliver. Now, if such men take what has been written with wisdom and eloquence by others, and commit it to memory, and deliver it to the people, they cannot be blamed, supposing them to do it without deception. For in this way many become preachers of the truth (which is certainly desirable), and yet not many teachers; for all deliver the discourse which one real teacher has composed, and there are no divisions among them. Nor are such men to be alarmed by the words of Jeremiah the prophet, through whom God denounces those who steal His words every one from his neighbour.[1] For those who steal take what does not belong to them, but the word of God belongs to all who obey it; and it is the man who speaks well, but lives badly, who really takes the words that belong to another. For the good things he says seem to be the result of his own thought, and yet they have nothing in common with his manner of life. And so God has said that they steal His words who would appear good by speaking God's words, but are in fact bad, as they follow their own ways. And if you look closely into the matter, it is not really themselves who say the good things they say. For how can they say in words what they deny in deeds? It is not for nothing that the apostle says of such men: "They profess that they know God, but in works they deny Him."[2] In one sense, then, they do say the things, and in another sense they do not

say them; for both these statements must be true, both being made by Him Who is the Truth. Speaking of such men, in one place He says, "Whatsoever they bid you observe, that observe and do; but do not ye after their works"; that is to say, what ye hear from their lips, that do; what ye see in their lives, that do ye not; "for they say and do not."[3] And so, though they do not, yet they say. But in another place, upbraiding such men, He says, "O generation of vipers, how can ye, being evil, speak good things?"[4] And from this it would appear that even what they say, when they say what is good, it is not themselves who say, for in will and in deed they deny what they say. Hence it happens that a wicked man who is eloquent may compose a discourse in which the truth is set forth to be delivered by a good man who is not eloquent; and when this takes place, the former draws from himself what does not belong to him, and the latter receives from another what really belongs to himself. But when true believers render this service to true believers, both parties speak what is their own, for God is theirs, to Whom belongs all that they say; and even those who could not compose what they say make it their own by composing their lives in harmony with it.

CHAP. 30. *The preacher should commence his discourse with prayer to God*

63. But whether a man is going to address the people or to dictate what others will deliver or read to the people, he ought to pray God to put into his mouth a suitable discourse. For if Queen Esther prayed, when she was about to speak to the king touching the temporal welfare of her race, that God would put fit words into her mouth,[5] how much more ought he to pray for the same blessing who labours in word and doctrine for the eternal welfare of men? Those, again, who are to deliver what others compose for them ought, before they receive their discourse, to pray for those who are preparing it; and when they have received it, they ought to pray both that they themselves may deliver it well, and that those to whom they address it may give ear; and when the discourse has a happy issue, they ought to render thanks to Him from Whom they know such blessings come, so that all the praise may be His "in whose hand are both we and our words."[6]

[3]Matt. 23. 3.
[4]Matt. 12. 34.
[5]Esth. 4. 16 (Septuagint).
[6]Wisd. 7. 16.

[1]Jer. 23. 30.   [2]Tit. 1. 16.

CHAP. 31. *Apology for the length of the work*

64. This book has extended to a greater length than I expected or desired. But the reader or hearer who finds pleasure in it will not think it long. He who thinks it long, but is anxious to know its contents, may read it in parts. He who does not care to be acquainted with it need not complain of its length. I, however, give thanks to God that with what little ability I possess I have in these four books striven to depict, not the sort of man I am myself (for my defects are very many), but the sort of man he ought to be who desires to labour in sound, that is, in Christian doctrine, not for his own instruction only, but for that of others also.